ENCYCLOPEDIA
OF
EUROPEAN CINEMA

ENCYCLOPEDIA
OF
EUROPEAN CINEMA

EDITED BY
GINETTE VINCENDEAU

Facts On File®

AN INFOBASE HOLDINGS COMPANY

Encyclopedia of European Cinema

Copyright © 1995 by the British Film Institute
First published in Great Britain by Cassell and the
British Film Institute

Facts On File, Inc.
11 Penn Plaza
New York, NY 10001

Library of Congress Cataloging-in-Publication Data

Vincendeau. Ginette, 1948–
    Encyclopedia of European cinema / edited by Ginette
    Vincendeau.
        p.   cm.
    ISBN 0–8160–3394–3 (hc). – ISBN 0–8160–3395–1 (pb)
    1. Motion pictures – Europe – Encyclopedias.
  PN1993.5.E8V56   1995
791.43'094 – dc20   95–34717

Jacket design by Ben Cracknell

Printed and bound in Great Britain by Redwood Books,
Trowbridge, Wiltshire

10 9 8 7 6 5 4 3 2 1

CONTENTS

ACKNOWLEDGMENTS

My thanks go first of all to the section editors and writers on the *Encyclopedia*, whose accumulated knowledge and skills made the book possible in the first place, and who all worked on it while holding other jobs and commitments. A special mention is due to Peter Evans, who commissioned, part-wrote and edited the Spanish material at extremely short notice; also, for their speedy writing of late commissions, to Chris Darke, Richard Dyer, Simon Horrocks, Carol Jenks, Anu Koivunen, Jonathan Munby, Augusto M. Seabra, Gian-Luca Sergi and Ulrike Sieglohr. For their painstaking checking work, I wish to acknowledge the help of Milica Budimir, Nicki Foster, Simon Horrocks, Guy Jowett, Petra Küppers, Jacqueline McGee, Richard Martin, Rachel Moseley, Matthew May, Valerie Orpen, Markku Salmi, Gian-Luca Sergi, Ulrike Sieglohr, Sissel Vik, David Wilson, Ania Witkowska. Guy Jowett also helped gather the statistics and bibliography. For their assistance with editing and research, I am grateful to Jim Cook, Kevin Dwyer, Csaba Farkas, Guy Jowett, Eeva Lennon, Teodora Nedialkova, Valerie Orpen and Paul Willemen, and to Gianna Cappello, Karen Pelha and Peter Graham for translations. I owe special thanks to the staff of the BFI Library, and especially David Sharp and Gillian Hartnoll, and to Sue Bobbermein, Ed Buscombe and Roma Gibson in BFI Publishing.

A work such as this inevitably relies on other sources: trade publications, data provided by embassies and film commissions, journals, filmographies, catalogues, dictionaries, monographs, etc. It is impossible to cite them all, though many appear in the bibliographical notes at the end of some entries and in the final bibliography, as well as with the statistics. May they all be thanked collectively here, including the BFI Library, as well as Annette Kuhn for permission to reproduce in altered form two entries from the *Women's Companion to International Film* (Virago, 1990).

Stills were provided by BFI Stills, Posters and Designs.

Last but not least, I am most grateful to my husband Simon Caulkin, for his heroic moral, practical and professional support.

Ginette Vincendeau
London, June 1995

CONTRIBUTORS

Indicated here are details about section editors and main writers (although the material in the *Encyclopedia* appears in alphabetical sequence, section editors were involved at the commissioning and pre-editing stage in order to draw on local and specialised expertise). Below is also a key to the writers' initials that appear at the end of each entry.

Editor
Ginette Vincendeau, Professor of Film Studies at the University of Warwick (UK). Co-editor of *French Film, Texts and Contexts*, *Popular European Cinema*, and *20 ans de théories féministes*, and co-author of *Jean Gabin, Anatomie d'un mythe*. Author of the forthcoming BFI Classic on *Pépé le Moko* and of *The Art of Spectacle: Popular French Cinema in the 1930s*.

Belgium
Belgian entries: Cathy Fowler, lecturer in film studies at the Southampton Institute of Education (UK), and Sandra Schillemans, lecturer in media studies at the Vrije Universiteit, Brussels (Belgium).

Central and Eastern Europe
Section editor: Nancy Wood, lecturer in media studies at the University of Sussex (UK), co-editor of *In Search of Central Europe* and former managing editor of *East European Reporter*; currently researching the role of memory in post-war European film and television.
– Czech/Slovak entries: Peter Hames, lecturer in film at Staffordshire University; author of *The Czechoslovak New Wave* (1985) and editor of *Dark Alchemy: The Films of Jan Svankmajer*.
– Polish entries: Ania Witkowska, a freelance film-maker of Polish origin, based in Manchester (UK).
– Romanian and Albanian entries: Matthew May, film researcher and programmer based in Brighton (UK).
– Bulgarian entries: Ron Holloway, a freelance author based in Berlin and author of numerous books and articles on Bulgarian cinema.
– (Former) Yugoslav entries: Stojan Pelko, researcher and lecturer on film theory at the University of Llubljana (Slovenia) and editor-in-chief of the Slovenian film journal *Ekran*.
– Hungarian entries: András Bálint Kovács, who teaches in the department of Aesthetics and Communication, ELTE University, Budapest, and is editor of the Hungarian monthly *Filmvilág* and author of *Les mondes d'Andrej Tarkovski*.

France
Section editor and author of French entries: Ginette Vincendeau (as above, under 'Editor').

Germany, Austria, The Netherlands and Switzerland
Section editor: Thomas Elsaesser, Professor of Film Studies at the University of Amsterdam, whose numerous publications include, as author, *New German Cinema*, and, as editor, *Early Cinema: Space Frame Narrative*.
– German and Austrian entries: Thomas Elsaesser, Michael Wedel (Frankfurt-based film researcher), and Joseph Garncarz (lecturer in film studies at the University of Cologne), with Andrea Lang, Franz Marksteiner, Isabella Reicher, Sonja Schachinger and Katja Uhlenbrok.
– Dutch entries: Karel Dibbets, who teaches film history at the University of Amsterdam and whose publications include *Sprekende films: de komst van de geluidsfilm in Nederland, 1928–1933* ('On the introduction of sound cinema in the Netherlands'), with Hans Beerekamp, Ansje van Beusekom, Bert Hogenkamp, Rob de Kam, Hans Kroon, Stan Lapinski, Ati Mul, Anke Noorman, Jorrit Roerdinkholder, Femke Woldring.
– Swiss entries: Roland Cosandey, researcher and writer in film based in Lausanne, and author of numerous publications on Swiss cinema, including *Julius Pinschewer: Cinquante ans de cinéma d'animation*, and Michael Wedel, with Claire Koenig.

Greece
Greek entries: Thodoros Natsinas, freelance film writer based in Thessaloniki, specialist in popular Greek cinema of the 1950s and 1960s. Contributes to several Greek film journals, including *Othoni* and *Parallaxis*. Other entries by Alinda Dimitriou, Notis Forsos, Nikos Kolovos, Alexandros Moumtzis, Thomas Nedelkos.

Italy
Section editors: Geoffrey Nowell-Smith, senior research fellow at the British Film Institute (London), author of *Visconti*, and editor of the forthcoming *The Oxford History of the Cinema*, and James Hay, Professor of Cinema Studies in the Department of Speech Communication at the University of Illinois at Urbana-Champaign (USA) and author of *Popular Film Culture in Fascist Italy: The Passing of the Rex*.
– Italian entries by Giuliana Bruno, Gianni Canova, Paolo D'Agostini, James Hay, Simon Horrocks, Millicent Marcus, Paolo Mereghetti, Morando Morandini, Geoffrey Nowell-Smith, Gian-Luca Sergi, Paolo Vecchi, and Gianni Volpi.

Denmark, Finland, Norway, Sweden
Section editor: Jukka Sihvonen, Professor of Cinema and Television Studies at the University of Turku (Finland) and author of several books in Finnish on film language and on television, and, in English, of *Exceeding the Limits, On the Poetics and Politics of Audiovisuality*.

– Finnish entries: Jukka Sihvonen, with Ari Honka-Hallila, Anu Koivunen, Kommo Laine, Hannu Salmi.

– Danish entries: Marguerite Engberg, who has recently retired from her post as Professor of Film History at the University of Copenhagen and is now a consultant and film restorer; she has published widely on Danish cinema.

– Swedish entries: Lars-Gustaf Andersson and Bo Florin, of the Department of Theatre and Cinema Studies at the University of Stockholm.

– Norwegian entries: Katherine Skretting, lecturer in film at the University of Trondheim, Norway.

Portugal

Portuguese entries: Augusto M. Seabra, film and music critic for the daily *O Público*, Lisbon, adviser to the European Script Fund, and author of several publications on Portuguese cinema, including, in Italian: *Portogallo: il nuovo cinema e oltre*.

Spain

Section editor: Peter Evans, Professor of Spanish in the Department of Hispanic Studies at Queen Mary and Westfield College, University of London, co-author of several books on Hollywood cinema, and author of *The Films of Luis Buñuel: Subjectivity and Desire* .

– Spanish entries: José Arroyo, Celestino Deleyto, María Delgado, Peter Evans, Robin Fiddian, John Hopewell, Barry Jordan, Dominic Keown, Richard Martin, Rikki Morgan, Stephen Roberts, Xon de Ros, Isabel Santaolalla, Paul Julian Smith, Nuria Toribio Triana.

(Former) Soviet Union

Section editor and author of Soviet/Russian entries: Richard Taylor, Professor of Politics and Russian Studies at the University of Wales, Swansea. General editor of Eisenstein's *Selected Works* and author and editor of numerous books on Russian and Soviet cinema, including *The Politics of Soviet Cinema 1917–1929*, *Inside the Film Factory* (with Ian Christie), and the forthcoming *A Cinema for the Millions: Socialist Realism and Soviet Cinema, 1928–38*.

– Other Soviet/Russian entries by Julian Graffy, Senior Lecturer in the Department of Russian Language and Literature at the School of Slavonic and East European Studies, University of London.

UK/Ireland

Section editor and author of the British entries: John Caughie, Professor of Film and Television Studies at the University of Glasgow. Editor of *Theories of Authorship* and author of *Cinema 2000: a Report on the Future of Public Cinema Exhibition in Britain* and *Television and Young People*.

– Irish entries by Kevin Rockett, lecturer in film at University College, Dublin, and co-author of *Cinema and Ireland*.

Pan-European entries

Pan-European entries by Chris Darke, freelance lecturer in film studies and writer for several film publications, including *Sight and Sound* and *Screen*; Richard Dyer, Professor of Film Studies at the University of Warwick; Simon Horrocks, lecturer in film at Cardiff University and programmer at Cardiff Chapter House cinema; and Ginette Vincendeau.

KEY TO CONTRIBUTORS

AD – Alinda Dimitriou
AHH – Ari Honka-Hallila
AK – Anu Koivunen
AL – Andrea Lang
AM – Alexandros Moumtzis
AMS – Augusto M. Seabra
AMu – Ati Mul
AN – Anke Noorman
AvB – Ansje van Beusekom
AW – Ania Witkowska
BF – Bo Florin
BH – Bert Hogenkamp
BJ – Barry Jordan
CDa – Chris Darke
CDe – Celestino Deleyto
CF – Cathy Fowler
CJ – Carol Jenks
CK – Claire Koenig
DK – Dominic Keown
FC – Farkas Csaba
FM – Franz Marksteiner
FW – Femke Woldring
GB – Giuliana Bruno
GC – Gianni Canova
GF – Goffredo Fofi
GLS – Gian-Luca Sergi
GM – Gaetana Marrone
GNS – Geoffrey Nowell-Smith
GV – Ginette Vincendeau
GVo – Gianni Volpi
HB – Hans Beerekamp
HK – Hans Kroon
HS – Hannu Salmi
IH – Ilona Halberstadt
IR – Isabella Reicher
IS – Isabel Santaolalla
JA – José Arroyo
JC – John Caughie
JG – Joseph Garncarz
JGf – Julian Graffy
JHa – James Hay
JHo – John Hopewell
JM – Jonathan Munby
JR – Jorrit Roerdinkholder
JS – Jukka Sihvonen
KAB – András Bálint Kovács

KD – Karel Dibbets
KL – Kimmo Laine
KP – Karen Pehla
KR – Kevin Rockett
KS – Katherine Skretting
KU – Katja Uhlenbrok
LGA – Lars-Gustaf Andersson
MD – María Delgado
ME – Marguerite Engberg
MM – Matthew May
MMa – Millicent Marcus
MMo – Morando Morandini
MW – Michael Wedel
NF – Notis Forsos
NK – Nikos Kolovos
NTT – Nuria Toribio Triana
PDA – Paolo D'Agostini
PH – Peter Hames
PJS – Paul Julian Smith
PM – Paolo Mereghetti
PV – Paolo Vecchi
PW – Paul Willemen
PWE – Peter W. Evans
RC – Roland Cosandey
RD – Richard Dyer
RdK – Rob de Kam
RF – Robin Fiddian
RH – Ron Holloway
RJM – Richard J. Martin
RM – Rikki Morgan
RT – Richard Taylor
RvdL – Robbert van der Lek
SG – Sabine Gottgetreu
SGHR – Stephen Roberts
SH – Simon Horrocks
SL – Stan Lapinski
SP – Stojan Pelko
SS – Sandra Schillemans
SSc – Sonja Schachinger
TE – Thomas Elsaesser
TN – Thodoros Natsinas
TNe – Thomas Nedelkos
US – Ulrike Sieglohr
WB – Warren Buckland
XR – Xon de Ros

INTRODUCTION

by Ginette Vincendeau

'If World War I enabled American cinema to ruin French cinema, World War II, together with the advent of television, enabled it to finance, that is to say ruin, all the cinemas of Europe.'

Jean-Luc Godard, *Histoires du cinéma*

In 1995, Godard's typically sweeping statement may seem to have come true. Even France, the most vigorous defender of the European 'cultural exception' in the 1993 GATT negotiations, and the only country in Europe still with a substantial film industry, is in trouble. *Jurassic Park*, *The Lion King* and *True Lies* (ironically a remake of a French film) have dominated European screens, and audiences continue to fall. While European films are confined to under 2.5 per cent of North American screens, Europe is America's largest export market, currently generating $4 billion a year, more than the US domestic market. The 'invasion' of US films (helped by massive advertising campaigns and generous tax breaks in the US) and the poor export performance of European films have been the subject of heated debate since the 1920s, escalating in the last decade, and finally coming to a head with GATT. In the most pessimistic vision, American 'cultural imperialism' is on the brink of eradicating European culture, from cinema to food and music. The threat to European cinema is not just from American films either: ubiquitous television, commercials, music videos and computer-generated images make the cinema *qua* cinema, if not obsolete, at least no longer a privileged player in the culture industries. And just at the point when the very nature of the cinematographic image is in doubt, Europe itself is in turmoil, with profound and largely negative implications for central and eastern European national cinemas, now that their production has been virtually wiped out, opening the door to an even bigger market for Hollywood.

The drama of a beleaguered European cinema seems all the more poignant in the year of the centenary of its birth. But rather than mourning, this anniversary is cause for celebration, reassessment and (re)discovery. This is the project of *The Encyclopedia of European Cinema*, which gathers together, for the first time in one volume, the achievements of the cinemas of Europe over the last hundred years. For although European cinema may have been economically weak, it has nevertheless always shown amazing resilience; as Pierre Sorlin put it, 'The wonder is that in Europe the cinematic institution did not collapse.'[1] And, while it may be relatively insignificant on the world market, it has gathered and maintained enormous cultural prestige and importance, far beyond its box-office results. Its film masterpieces are preserved by archives the world over, and its great film-makers justly celebrated in history books, cinema and television retrospectives and surveys such as the *Sight and Sound* 'ten best' lists (however debatable the actual choices). But we should not

forget the wider picture: European cinema also boasts popular stars and genres, as can be seen in the pages of this *Encyclopedia*, and while Hollywood has become synonymous with 'entertainment' (in Europe as elsewhere), European cinema has equally entertained its audiences with its own wonderful comedies, musicals and melodramas. In its 'high' and 'low' forms, it has been part of both the history and the collective memory of Europe, ever since its first film-makers projected its images on screen.

Pioneers

Edison's Kinetograph, perfected in 1891, was the world's first movie camera. His Kinetoscope, however, designed for the individual viewing of Kinetograph films, proved a blind alley. The pioneers of cinema as we know it (a strip of celluloid projected on to a screen to an audience) were Europeans. Max and Emil Skladanowsky showed their Bioscope in Berlin on 1 November 1895, and, more famously, the Lumière brothers demonstrated their Cinematograph in Paris on 28 December 1895. Despite Louis Lumière's notorious declaration that 'the cinema is an invention without a future', the Cinématographe became the prototype of, and gave its name to, the cinema. Before Hollywood was even officially a town (1903), *La Fée aux choux/The Cabbage Fairy* in France and *The Soldier's Courtship* in Britain (both 1896) could claim the title of the world's first fiction films. Meanwhile, the most extraordinary cinematic activity was taking place. Demonstrations of the Cinematograph swept the length and breadth of Europe, reaching London, Belgrade, St Petersburg and various cities in Hungary, Poland and Romania in 1896, followed by Spain, Greece, Belgium and Bulgaria in 1897 – fascinating both the old elites (royal families, from Greece to Scandinavia, proved fond of being filmed) and the illiterate masses, educating and entertaining in equal measure. Polish pioneers, such as Kazimierz Proszynski and his Pleograf, and British ones, including Birt Acres and R. W. Paul, were also at work. Paul's Animatograph was demonstrated in Portugal as early as 1896, while Skladanowsky's Bioscope was shown in Norway and Sweden. French entrepreneurs Charles Pathé and Léon Gaumont built empires throughout the world (including the US), while Oskar Messter, the first 'universal movie man', single-handedly started the German film industry. But except for Germany and its vertically integrated conglomerate Ufa, no European country survived World War I with a film *industry*. Hollywood in the process of industrialisation ended the era of the European artisan-entrepreneurs. The coming of sound, with the heavy investments it required (and although some of the finance came from Europe, especially the Netherlands), completed the process, despite the attempts, led by Germany, to raise a first pan-European defence against Hollywood, with the 'Film Europe' venture. It may comfort Europeans to know that most sound and colour systems were invented by Europeans, but it cut little ice in the world film market, since, with the exception of Germany (and its Tri-Ergon), these European inventors had neither the patents nor the means of commercialising them. Most European countries nevertheless managed to maintain production throughout the 1920s and 1930s, however disorganised or bankrupt. In fact, despite familiar complaints of 'crisis', in many cases the 1930s constituted a golden age of popular cinema, even if, in the case of Germany and the Soviet Union, this has been hidden, in the traditional histories, by the political agenda.

Besides film technology, Europe can also claim to have invented the kind of film culture which elevated the movies to the level of a self-conscious *art*. Before World War I, Boleslaw Matuszewski in Poland, Ricciotto Canudo (who coined the phrase 'the seventh art') in France, and Emilie Altenloh in Germany, had published analytical, poetic and/or reflexive texts on the cinema, followed by the French theoreticians of the 1920s in France, such as Louis Delluc and Jean Epstein. In the 1930s and 1940s came the pioneers of film history – Siegfried Kracauer and Lotte Eisner in Germany, Jean Mitry, Robert Brasillach, Maurice Bardèche and Georges Sadoul in France, Paul Rotha in Britain – and later still the first modern film theoreticians: Rudolf Arnheim, Béla Balázs and André Bazin.

From the mid-1910s there also appeared throughout Europe the 'first wave' (in Richard Abel's phrase[2]) of art and avant-garde film, initiating European cinema's 'noble' traditions: the *film d'art* or *autorenfilm* (literary adaptations, especially in France, Germany and Denmark), modernist and experimental film, *auteur* films, and realist cinema (both documentary and fictional). Film clubs appeared across Europe, and intellectuals (the Surrealists, the Futurists) took the cinema seriously; groups such as Les Amis du Septième Art in France, START and SAF in Poland, the journal *Close Up* in Switzerland, began an active reflection on the medium. After its popular fairground beginnings, European cinema was the first to become deliberately an art form.

European art cinema

The European high filmic tradition has its well-charted landmarks: Soviet montage, German expressionism, the British documentary movement, Poetic Realism, neo-realism, the Polish school, the French, British and Czech New Waves, the Yugoslav Black Films, the New Spanish Cinema, the New German Cinema; and its heroes (and, rarely, heroines): Sjöström, Lang, Eisenstein, Renoir, Rossellini, Bergman, Buñuel, Wajda, Fellini, Mészáros, Oliveira, Godard, Akerman, etc. 'European art cinema', as it has become – somewhat reductively – known, has undoubtedly, beyond its differences, common aesthetic features, especially in its postwar manifestations: a slower narrative and editing pace, a strong 'authorial voice', an investment in realism and ambiguity, the desire to provoke thought and sometimes shock, and a taste for unhappy endings, features which interestingly echo values identified by Antoine Compagnon as being especially 'European', in particular 'transgression, blasphemy, and plurality of meaning'.[3]

Culturally, partisans of European art cinema see it as the inheritor of high European culture. Its movements, genres and *auteurs* reflect older arts such as literature and painting;

its 'great themes' and personal visions, its political and philosophical commitments oppose Hollywood escapism; its artisanal base is heroically contrasted to the dream factory. Others more recently have seen it as a defensive marketing ploy, aided by state subsidies, designed to fight Hollywood's supremacy with the only weapons at its disposal. Both explanations contain some truth, but European art cinema is bound up with European identities in other ways too. Cinema in Europe has often been the direct tool of ideologies: in communist countries, in Nazi Germany, in Fascist Italy, in Popular Front France or Franco's Spain, film has been used for propaganda. Conversely, under totalitarian regimes it has also been – sometimes under the protection of irony and metaphor – the channel of political resistance, as the history of 'shelved' films across eastern Europe shows, while forms such as animation have flourished in these countries, some argue, as a way of bypassing censorship. In a less direct fashion, the mirror or window effect of realist film – from Storck's documentaries on Belgian mining villages to Rossellini's *Roma città aperta/Rome Open City*, or Frears' *My Beautiful Laundrette* – have promoted the landscapes, events, cultural artefacts and heroes of national histories. Since censorship in European countries has on the whole been more concerned with politics than sex, eroticism was also, until the 1970s porn boom, associated with an image of 'serious' Europeanness through art cinema, with the films of Antonioni, Makavejev, Buñuel, Bergman, Godard and others offering an image of 'sophisticated' European sexuality.

Paradoxically too, the subjective vision of individual *auteurs* has been part of national identity formation, providing a guarantee of authenticity and belonging and a personal 'refraction' of dominant national cultural concerns. As Claire Denis, director of *Chocolat*, recently put it, 'Cinema is [...] a very personal medium, and if European cinema is anything it is a reflection of subjective European experiences.'[4] European *auteurs* also play a crucial role in the livelihood of their national cinemas, securing funding and attracting critical attention in film journals and at film festivals. Equally, they play an important public relations role for the image of European cinema, especially since the 1960s. Some are synonymous with their whole country (Bergman, Oliveira), some have acted as its 'humanitarian conscience' (Wajda), or raised its international profile, either in a repudiation of previous generations (the French New Wave film-makers) or after a period of oblivion (the New German Cinema *auteurs*); others have played the 'enfant terrible' or 'artiste maudit' (Polanski, Akerman, Godard) or militated on behalf of particular groups (Brückner for women directors) or the whole of Europe (Beineix, Bertolucci and Tavernier during the GATT negotiations). Directors like Kieślowski and Wenders have almost ceased to be Polish or German, and become 'European': recently Wenders declared that working in the USA made him realise that it was 'a much nicer profession to be a European film-maker',[5] and Kieślowski's *Blue*, *White* and *Red* trilogy has been hailed for the way it 'pinpointed the mood of Europe in the 90s'.[6] This much celebrated public, and international, face of European film-making is not, however, all there is to European cinema. Other traditions have been just as important, and sometimes more important, in their own country, and yet have been less recognised.

Popular traditions

As audiences have known all along, but history books have been more reluctant to acknowledge, each European country has produced its own distinct entertainment films, with favourite genres, familiar narratives and cherished stars. The list is long: French comedies (from Max Linder to Louis de Funès and the recent *Les Visiteurs*), German and Soviet musicals of the 1930s, the Danish and Norwegian *Olsenbanden* series, the Finnish *Uuno Turhapuro* and Lumberjack films, Totò's films in Italy, the German revue films or 'doctors' films', the Swedish melodramas of the 1930s, the British *Carry On...* and James Bond series, the Yugoslav partisan films and the Romanian historical epics, Portuguese musical comedies, to name a few. The connections between popular films and national identity are both closer and harder to define than in the case of art cinema, because they form part of an uncharted, 'lowly' and diffuse collective memory. What is clear, however, is that cinema-going has been a very important social activity in Europe for most of the century and that indigenous films have often been preferred by audiences, or at least have been enjoyed as much as Hollywood films (here again, but for different reasons than for art cinema, box-office results are not the best guide to audiences' tastes). Now that film-going as an activity has dramatically declined, national television networks across Europe have taken up some of this social function, as well as performing the role of popular film archive by broadcasting genre classics and cult films in daytime or even 'film club' slots.

Popular European genres, however, with the exception of porn and the heritage film, have exported poorly, including to other European countries, because of their dependence on other indigenous art forms (music-hall revues and operettas, as in the German and French musicals of the 1930s and the Spanish *folklóricas*, sentimental novels, etc.) and the narrative patterns they dictate, and on stars who themselves are usually unknown outside their own countries (Louis de Funès, Urbanus, Vesa-Matti Loiri, Paula Wessely, and many others). They also depend on a knowledge of the national history and class systems which allow the spectator to decipher the most allusive or oblique readings,[7] and of course on language, the single most important obstacle to a pan-European film industry.

Can there be a pan-European cinema?

When sound came to Europe, many hoped it would usher in a new golden age, as national audiences would want to hear their own language. They did, but while they reacted violently against badly dubbed American films, solutions were quickly found, swelling the flow of American films on European screens. Today, when the industry itself is increasingly international and co-production deals – including with America – are the order of the day, language remains the main problem. What gives a national audience pleasure – hearing nuances of slang, dialects and class accents, as in the '*swanze*' humour of Gaston Schoukens' comedies, the '*verlan*' of *Beur* films, Gracie Fields' or Fernandel's accents, or the refinements of dialogue in adaptations of plays and novels – is also what limits the impact of its national film industry.

The multiplicity of tongues is itself indicative of the 'patchwork' or 'kaleidoscope' aspect of European cultures. It is ironic that Europe, so intent on its 'cultural exception' when faced with America in the GATT negotiations, based the European Union (as it is now called) on industry and commerce, rather than culture, turning to the latter almost as an afterthought: the Council of Europe was founded in 1949 and the European Community in 1957, but directives on the cinema only came into action in the mid-1980s. And while the European Union has since come up with legislation to help script development, and the production and distribution of films in Europe, there is no pan-European distribution system able to release a European film simultaneously across Europe, and take advantage of its large collective audience with the same 'muscle' as Hollywood. Equally, although there are stars who move across borders (Jeremy Irons, Hannah Schygulla, Gérard Depardieu, Juliette Binoche), there is no pan-European star system as such.[8] Where concerted policy is nonexistent or fails to unite, what chance is there of a European cinema as a coherent entity, except in terms of its difference from others (Hollywood, 'world cinema')?

Until recently, there were great institutional differences between the cinemas of Europe – between capitalist West and nationalised East, between 'free market' industries such as in Britain and highly subsidised ones such as in France. Less tangible differences also have an impact: when German directors went to France in the 1930s, they found working conditions almost as strange as they would later find them in Hollywood. Attempts at multi-language versions in the early 1930s failed partly because narratives were not amenable to duplication across European countries. More recently, some European co-production deals have come unstuck in trying to match, for example, director-oriented French practices with script-oriented British ones.[9] To make matters worse, deliberately European ventures tend to attract derision in Europe: witness the connotations of the prefix Euro, as in 'Euro-pudding', 'Euro-trash', Eurovision song contest or Eurodisney (though the glamorous new Eurostar trans-Channel train might change this). The failure of soaps such as *Riviera* and *Eldorado* and of films like *Aria* did not help. If, at an institutional level, Euro-ventures are not a success, can some common themes be found across the cinemas of Europe?

The two world wars, especially World War II and, in Chantal Akerman's words, 'the collective guilt in allowing the Nazis' slaughter of the Jews',[10] have provided the most widespread and haunting theme of European cinema, sporadically or systematically, in dramas, epics or comedies, in official versions or underground exposés. Yet World War II, its occupations and especially its resistance movements, did not become, as Pierre Sorlin notes,[11] the 'epic of modern Europe' and did not produce a strong genre such as the Western in America. This is not surprising, given the divisive nature of the World War II experience *within* each European country as well as between them. It nevertheless provides markers of 'Europeanness'. Beyond World War II, films throughout European cinema have delved into the common stock of a popular vision of history: the Bible and antiquity, for instance, have fed genres as diverse as serious historical dramas – especially in silent cinema – and the 'muscleman epic' Italian *peplum* of the 1950s. All European national cinemas have at one point or another produced costume dramas centred on traumatic focal points of their own history, but Europe as a whole also possesses a reservoir of mythical 'pan-European' heroes and anti-heroes, both historical – Joan of

Arc, Napoleon, Pasteur, Freud, Henry VIII, Jack the Ripper, Beethoven, Van Gogh, Hitler – and fictional – Dracula, Hamlet, Sherlock Holmes, Tartuffe, Tintin, Inspector Maigret, Astérix, Cyrano de Bergerac, Don Juan, Don Quixote and Sissi – together with semi-mythical lands such as Transylvania or purely fictional ones such as 'Ruritania', a reservoir which has been exploited by its own cinemas as well as by Hollywood. The critically derided heritage film of the last fifteen years has itself added a new set of 'mythical' places, including Provence, Edwardian London, and villages in southern Italy. But while at the more commercial end many films tend to turn nostalgically, in a nationalistic move, to their pre-industrial, agrarian past, echoing earlier genres such as the Norwegian rural melodrama and the German *Heimat* films, a few others have recently begun to tell the story of post-colonial Europe, of its migrations and 'minorities' – for instance the films of the French *Cinéma Beur*, Nordic films about the Lapps and Emir Kusturica's *Time of the Gypsies* (though it should not be forgotten that earlier films such as the Zurich dialect films of the 1930s and Polish Yiddish films already represented and catered for 'minorities').

European cinema is numerically depleted and under constant threat. Some miss the era of its 'great' classic directors, such as Renoir or Bergman, others the 'Age of the dream palace' when people could enjoy their own national cinema as well as Hollywood and others. However, in the last few years, all has not been gloomy. The French comedy *Les Visiteurs* broke all box-office records in France, and directors as diverse as Kieślowski, Muratova, Almodóvar, Denis, Holland and Kusturica have emerged or come to prominence. There is still life in European cinema and perhaps the more aggressive distribution policies advocated by film-makers such as Bernardo Bertolucci in the post-GATT period will succeed in showing the rest of the world that this is the case.

The Encyclopedia of European Cinema: aims and conventions

This book aims to bring together under one volume the breadth and variety of European cinema in a concise, accessible and informative form. Written entirely by specialists (see **Contributors**), it is meant equally for professionals – teachers, students – and for film enthusiasts. The desire to include a considerable amount of information in a manageable and affordable single volume dictated drastic choices. A general principle has been to privilege coverage, including of recent material, with a large number of short entries. The entries contain key factual points about a person, institution or critical concept, as well as areas of interest and debate, in other words not just what a person or institution did and when, but why are they interesting, famous or controversial.

The *Encyclopedia* does not claim to be exhaustive or 'impartial'; all entries express, to some extent, the opinion of their writers (who are identified by their initials – see under **Key to Contributors**). At the same time, it tries to be as inclusive and accurate as possible, given all the difficulties that such an enterprise presents. Extreme care has been taken to check all sources, in the hope of reducing errors to a minimum. All historical works have more or less hidden agendas and have to operate choices further to those dictated by constraints of space. Choices in the *Encyclopedia of European Cinema* have been made according to the following principles:

– the necessity to acknowledge the important figures and landmarks of European cinema, as sanctioned by reputable historians and by the expertise of the writers;
– the desire, at the same time, to redress the balance of established film history:

a) towards the cinema of 'small' countries (Belgium, Ireland, Switzerland, Greece, Portugal, Yugoslavia),
b) towards popular traditions (the entertainment cinema, the despised, supposedly mediocre, genres, and the stars and directors of popular cinema often unknown outside their own countries),
c) towards 'other voices': women, gays and lesbians, postcolonial communities – as John Caughie put it, 'the Europeans who are not included in the notion of Europeanness'[12] – see, for instance, the entries on **Isaac Julien**, **Ulrike Ottinger**, **Yiddish cinema in Poland**, *Cinéma Beur*, the Flemish comedies of **Jan Vanderheyden**, etc.

– as far as possible, the desire to provide a perspective from *within* the national cinemas. Most writers are nationals; when they are not, their expertise has made them intimately familiar with the cinema they are writing about;
– finally, the variety of contexts within which European cinemas operate means that critical agendas are not uniform. As a result, though an overall balance has been sought in the weight given to different types of personnel, institutions and critical concepts, there is not absolute parity between countries. For instance, as the star system is more developed in western Europe, the entries on those national cinemas tend to include more stars than those of central and eastern Europe, more dominated by directors. Equally, the exigencies of authoritarian regimes mean that the relationship between personnel and institutions tends to acquire more of an overtly political slant (at least until recently) in central and eastern Europe than in western Europe where, by contrast, concepts such as gender and race have recently come to the fore.

The *Encyclopedia of European Cinema* was prepared under separate, national and regional sections according to the section editors and contributors' specialism. However, entries are arranged in the final book in alphabetical sequence, under their main heading. When there is a possibility of confusion, or when initials or several forms are in common use, a cross-reference entry is used: e.g. **BFI: see BRITISH FILM INSTITUTE**. There are four major types of entries:

1. *National essays*, under the name of the country: **Germany**, **Poland**, **Spain**, etc. Countries whose status has recently changed are indicated under their most common form – e.g. **(Former) Soviet Union** (under 'S'), **(Former) Yugoslavia** (under 'Y'), **Czechoslovakia**. The different regions or countries now included in these (former) countries are indicated where relevant, e.g. '**Slovenian director**'. When 'browsing' rather than looking up a specific reference, readers are advised to read the national essay first. This gives an overview of the national cinema throughout its existence, and, through the referencing system (see below), signals important persons, institutions and concepts.

2. *Entries on personnel*: directors, actors, cinematographers, musicians, writers, even politicians (e.g. **Joseph Stalin**), are classified under their surname or most common name. This is followed by their date and place of birth and, as the case may be, death, as well as their real name, if relevant. The first words of the entry briefly characterise the person. To save space, the country in which a person was born and/or died is indicated next to their birth/death place only if situated outside this person's country, e.g.:

DALLE, Béatrice   Brest 1964

French actress ...

but

POLANSKI, Roman   Raymond Polanski; Paris, France 1933

Polish director ...

As a rule, biographical details such as marriage and children are indicated only if considered relevant to the work or achievements of the person – for instance, the fact that Claude Chabrol was married to Stéphane Audran is mentioned (under **Chabrol** and **Audran**) since they worked as a team for many years, while the fact that Stéphane Audran was previously married to Jean-Louis Trintignant is not.

3. *Critical entries*, ranging from well-established genres or movements such as **Poetic Realism** or **New German Cinema** to series such as the **Bond films** and *Olsenbanden/Olsen Gang* films, and critical and pan-European concepts, like **Lesbian and Gay Cinema in Europe** or **Avant-garde cinema in Europe**. In some cases, genres that are common to many European countries but have specific national manifestations are grouped under a single heading, with national subheadings: e.g. **Documentary**, **Comedy**, **Animation**; if specific national versions of the genre have acquired a separate identity under a particular name, this is dealt with under a separate entry: for instance, *Commedia all'italiana* and *comique troupier* have separate entries, but are cross-referenced under **Comedy**.

4. *Entries on institutions*, ranging from film schools (**VGIK**) and studios (**Balázs Béla Stúdió, BBS**) to production companies (**Ufa**), archives (**Cinémathèque Française**), and other institutions. Film festivals are included under a separate entry (**Film festivals**), with information on the festivals of each country, and cross-references to major festivals with a separate entry (e.g. **Cannes, Berlin, Venice**). There is also an entry on the various European film institutions brought into existence by the European Union (**The European Community [now European Union] and the Cinema**) and one on the **European Film Awards**.

Other conventions
– *Filmographies, film titles and film dates*. On first mention, films are indicated in the entry under their original title, followed by their British release title or an English translation of the meaning of the title, when necessary; thereafter only the original title is mentioned. A certain amount of flexibility has been used, in order not to burden the text unnecessarily while

making the meaning of the titles clear. For space reasons, filmographies are not necessarily exhaustive; it was felt more appropriate to make room for the text, while indicating major films. Three possible cases apply:
– all films, or all important films, are mentioned in the text, in which case no filmography follows;
– all other films made by the person (and not mentioned in the text) are added at the end. This is indicated by **Other films**, followed by the films in chronological order. If a complete filmography is provided, it is indicated by **Films**;
– other major films made by the person (and not mentioned in the text) are added at the end. This is indicated by **Other films include**, followed by the films in chronological order.

Whenever possible, the date indicated is that of the release of the film in its country of origin. All dates for each country have been checked against reliable sources (indicated under **Acknowledgments**) in order to achieve consistency, as far as is possible.

Cross-referencing
• Within entries: an asterisk at the end of a name denotes a separate entry – for instance, 'such films prefigured the French New Wave* ...'; 'great masters of European art cinema such as Federico Fellini* ...'.
• At the end of entries (or within the text) attention may be drawn to other related entries [> FRENCH NEW WAVE, BRITISH NEW WAVE].
• Between entries: different terminologies, or related persons, may be signalled: e.g. **BATCHELOR, Joy: see HALAS, John.**

Bibliography
• At the end of entries, a single short bibliographical reference may be indicated (under **Bib**) in an abbreviated form, to direct the reader to further reading.
• At the end of the Encyclopedia, a general bibliography contains full references to books on European cinema, as well as on each national cinema. Preference has been given to works in English, though authoritative works in other languages are included.

Statistics
• Statistical data on European film production and audiences are also provided.

Notes
1. Pierre Sorlin, *European Cinemas, European Societies, 1939–1990* (London: Routledge, 1991), p 2.
2. Richard Abel, *French Cinema: The First Wave, 1919–1929* (Princeton, NJ: Princeton University Press, 1985).
3. Antoine Compagnon, 'Mapping the European Mind', in Duncan Petrie (ed.), *Screening Europe: Image and Identity in Contemporary European Cinema* (London: BFI, 1992), pp. 106–13.
4. Claire Denis, in *Screening Europe*, p. 66.
5. NFT *Guardian* interview, London, 27 June 1994.

6. Tony Rayns, 'Glowing in the Dark', *Sight and Sound*, June 1994, p. 10.
7. See Jean-Pierre Jeancolas, 'The Inexportable: the case of French cinema and radio in the 1950s', in Richard Dyer and Ginette Vincendeau (eds.), *Popular European Cinema* (London: Routledge, 1992).
8. See Angus Finney, 'Falling Stars', *Sight and Sound*, May 1994, pp. 22–4.
9. See Sharon Strover, 'Institutional Adaptations to Trade: The Case of US–European Coproductions', paper delivered at the 'Turbulent Europe' Conference, London, NFT, July 1994.
10. Chantal Akerman, in *Screening Europe*, p. 67.
11. Pierre Sorlin, *European Cinemas, European Societies*, p. 79.
12. John Caughie, in *Screening Europe*, p. 58.

THE
ENCYCLOPEDIA

A

ABDRASHITOV, Vadim Yu.
Kharkov, Ukraine [USSR] 1945

Russian director. In 1974 Abdrashitov graduated from VGIK*, where he had studied in the workshop of Mikhail Romm* and Lev Kulidzhanov*. In constant collaboration with the scriptwriter Alexander Mindadze, he has made a series of films analysing the official institutions and the moral ambiguities of the late Soviet era. In *Slovo dlya zashchity/ Submission for the Defence* (1977), *Povorot/The Turning Point* (1978), *Okhota na lis/Fox Hunting* (1980) and *Ostanovilsya poezd/A Train Stopped* (1982), personal crisis forces the hitherto conformist protagonist into moral re-assessment. In the allegorical *Parad planet/Parade of the Planets* (1984) a group of army reservists enter a mysterious 'other' world. *Plyumbum, ili opasnaya igra/Plumbum, or A Dangerous Game* (1986) is another parable of the dangers of blind conformism, this time in a teenage boy. In *Sluga/The Servant* (1988), a conductor picks up a hitch-hiker and, as their roles are reversed, layers of Soviet corruption are revealed. In Abdrashitov and Mindadze's recent film *Armavir* (1991), a Soviet liner sinks and its passengers are forced to re-assess their lives. JGf

ABRIL, Victoria
Victoria Mérida Rojas; Madrid 1959

Spanish actress, the most ubiquitous and international of her generation. The first of her films to make an impact was Vicente Aranda's* *Cambio de sexo/Sex Change* (1977), in which she played a male-to-female transsexual. In the first decade of her career she made no less than thirty-one films, in Spain and abroad, notably in France. In the state-supported Spanish cinema of the 1980s she became a regular feature of any prestige production, adding intelligence and energy to sometimes dull literary adaptations. She also appeared in more commercial projects, where her talents were underused. But it was with Pedro Almodóvar* that she achieved inter-national fame. *¡Atame!/Tie Me Up! Tie Me Down!* (1989) is perhaps her quintessential role, combining sensuality with wit, sentimentality with autonomy. Even when bound to the bed and gagged with tape, she gives a more eloquent per-formance than her stolid aggressor Antonio Banderas*. At the moment when she finally asks to be tied up she subtly manages to suggest a woman strong enough to overcome the man who professes to dominate her. In *Tacones lejanos/High Heels* (1991), however, as the neurotic daughter who loves her negligent mother too well, she seems immobilised by Almodóvar's heavy-handed melodrama. Sold abroad on its graphic sex scenes, Aranda's *Amantes/Lovers* (1990) saw her

successfully make the transition to an older woman initiating a young man's sexual education. Finally invited to the US, she supported Jo Pesci as the kooky love interest in *Jimmy Hollywood* (1994). Rumoured to be the highest paid Spanish actress, and certainly the most exportable, Abril embodies a gravely elegant and intelligent sensuality, while her recent French films – such as Gérard Jugnot's *Casque bleu* (1994) and Josiane Balasko's* *Gazon maudit* (1995) – have also drawn on her talent for light comedy. PJS

Other Films Include: *La muchacha de las bragas de oro/The Girl with the Golden Panties* (1980); *La Lune dans le caniveau/The Moon in the Gutter* (1982, Fr.); *Río abajo/On the Line* (1984); *La colmena/The Beehive* (1982); *Tiempo de silencio/Time of Silence* (1986); *El Lute, camina o revienta/El Lute, Walk or Die* (1987); *A solas contigo/Alone Together* (1990); *Kika* (1993).

ABULADZE, Tengiz E.
Kutaisi, Georgia [USSR] 1924 – Tbilisi, Georgia 1994

Georgian director, who studied at the Rustaveli Theatrical Institute in Tbilisi (1943–6) and at VGIK*, in the workshop of Sergei Yutkevich*. In 1947, under the influence of *Ivan Groznyi/Ivan the Terrible*, he and a fellow student, Revaz Chkheidze, wrote to Sergei Eisenstein* asking for work: he told them to complete their studies first. Abuladze graduated in 1953 and returned to Tbilisi, where he joined the Gruziafilm studios. His first films were documentaries, co-directed in 1954 with Chkheidze. In 1955 they co-directed *Lurdzha Magdany/Magdana's Donkey*, which won the Best Short Film award at Cannes in 1956. Abuladze's later films include *Chuzhie deti/Other People's Children* (1958), set in contemporary Tbilisi; *Ya, babushka, Iliko i Illarion/I, Grandmother, Iliko and Illarion* (1963), a tragi-comedy set in a mountain village; and *Ozherel'e dlya moyei lyubimoi/A Necklace for my Beloved* (1973). But Abuladze's reputation rests on a trilogy of philosophical films concerned with ques-tions of good and evil, life and death. *Vedreba/The Prayer* (Russian title *Mol'ba*) (1968), based on the poems of Vazha Pshavela, is an epic tale of love, hatred and revenge, shot in black and white in the harsh Georgian landscape. *Natris Khe/The Wishing Tree* (Russian title *Drevo zhelaniya*) (1978) is set in a Georgian village before the Revolution and con-cerns the dreams and aspirations of a beautiful young girl and a man's search for the legendary tree that can make dreams come true. The third film of the trilogy, *Monanieba/ Repentance* (Russian title *Pokayanie*) (1984) is one of the most important films of the *perestroika* period. It tells the story of the death of an old man of power, Varlam Aravidze, and the refusal of a woman, Ketevan Barateli, to let his corpse rest in peace. At the woman's trial the evil past is revealed and confusion is sown among Aravidze's family, especially his son Abel (played by the same actor, Avtandil Makharadze) and his grandson. Varlam Aravidze is given the physical features of Hitler, Mussolini, Beria and Stalin to turn him into a composite dictator, and Abuladze uses anachronism (blending mediaeval knights and Rubik cubes) to point to the universality of his parable, but the film is also decked with the realities of the Soviet 1930s. *Monanieba* was written for Georgian television in 1981–82, and shot in late 1983 and early 1984. It was released in Tbilisi in October 1986, after support from Eduard Shevardnadze, then Soviet Foreign Minister, later President of Georgia. It was also the first film to benefit from the intervention of the Conflict Commission established by the Union of Cinematographers* after their Fifth Congress in May 1986. It was released in Moscow in January 1987, and then shown widely throughout the Soviet Union and the rest of the world. *Monanieba* is over-long and its stylistic confusion links it to the contradictory moods of the mid-1980s. But it is a brilliantly acted and sometimes deeply moving evocation of the seductions of power. JGf

ADJANI, Isabelle
Paris 1955

French actress. Though Adjani has starred in relatively few major films, her talent, glamour and tumultuous personality have made her a top French star since the late 1970s. She started very young in film (1969) and on stage, joining the Comédie Française in 1973. Claude Pinoteau's comedy *La Gifle/The Slap* (1974) and François Truffaut's* drama *L'Histoire d'Adèle H/The Story of Adèle H* (1975) were her first important films. Though she continued making comedies (Jean-Paul Rappeneau's* *Tout feu tout flamme*, 1981, Philomène Esposito's *Toxic Affair*, 1993), her dominant image is one of intensity, mystery and high drama, usually in *auteur* cinema. Her arresting beauty and assertiveness predisposed her for passionate and rebellious (often self-destructive) heroines, such as the daughter figures in Jean Becker's *L'Eté meurtrier/One Deadly Summer* and Claude Miller's *Mortelle Randonnée/Deadly Circuit* (both 1983). Adjani was the target of a right-wing smear campaign in 1986, after she took up anti-National Front positions by claiming her Algerian antecedents. She nevertheless successfully produced (and starred in) Bruno Nuytten's *Camille Claudel* (1988), her powerful performance earning her her third César*. While defining glamorous French femininity, Adjani, like Catherine Deneuve*, projects a Hollywood-type aura of stardom, playfully evoked in Luc Besson's* *Subway* (1985). Despite a three-year absence from the screen in the early 1990s and the failure of *Toxic Affair*, her place in the firmament of French stars is confirmed by her highly charged performance as the heroine of Patrice Chéreau's *La Reine Margot* (1994). GV

Other Films Include: *Le Locataire/The Tenant, Barocco* (1976); *Violette et François* (1977); *The Driver* (1978, US); *Nosferatu – Phantom der Nacht/Nosferatu the Vampyre* [Ger./

Fr.], *Les Soeurs Brontë/The Brontë Sisters* (1979); *Quartet* [UK/Fr.], *Possession* [Fr./Ger.] (1981); *Ishtar* (1987, US).

ADORF, Mario
Zurich 1930

Swiss-born actor whose imposing stature and clear-cut features lent themselves to a wide range of (stereo)types in national (German and Italian) and international productions. After a brief debut appearance in Joe May's* *08/15* (3 parts, 1955), Adorf's breakthrough came with his convincingly traumatised mass murderer in Robert Siodmak's* *Nachts, wenn der Teufel kam/The Devil Strikes at Night* (1957). Primarily typecast as a villain, he confirmed his talent for projecting inner conflict as the sensitive male in *Am Tag als der Regen kam/The Day the Rains Came* (1959). 'Rediscovered' in the 1970s, he became one of the New German Cinema's* most acclaimed actors in Volker Schlöndorff* and Margarethe von Trotta's* *Die verlorene Ehre der Katharina Blum/The Lost Honour of Katharina Blum* (1975), Schlöndorff's Oscar-winning *Die Blechtrommel/The Tin Drum* (1980) and R. W. Fassbinder's* *Lola* (1981). Adorf returned to one-dimensional villains in European co-productions, before settling for German television drama's favourite father figure. KU

Bib: Meinhold Zurhorst and Heiko R. Blum, *Mario Adorf: Seine Filme – Sein Leben* (1992).

Other Films Include: *Das Totenschiff* (1959); *Winnetou I* (1963); *Major Dundee* (1965, US); *Ganovenehre* (1966); *Fedora* (1978).

AGE, Agenore Incrocci
Brescia 1919
and
SCARPELLI, Furio
Rome 1919

Italian scriptwriters. The scriptwriting duo of Age and Scarpelli came together in the late 1940s, scoring a notable hit with their script for the comedy *Totò cerca casa/Totò Wants a Home* (1949) and other Totò* vehicles. They developed a more distinctive style of their own with the emergence of *Commedia all'italiana** in the late 1950s, writing scripts for Mario Monicelli* (*I soliti ignoti/Persons Unknown*, 1958; *La grande guerra/The Great War*, 1959) and other directors. Adept at mixing light comedy, social satire and occasional tragedy, they went on to write vehicles for the comic actor Alberto Sordi*, for the more theatrical Vittorio Gassman*, and for Marcello Mastroianni* (*I compagni/The Strikers*, 1963). Their biggest success came with Luigi Comencini's* epic tragi-comedy about the 1943 armistice *Tutti a casa/Everybody Go Home!* (1960), but they are probably most famous for their collaboration with director Ettore Scola*, beginning with *Dramma della gelosia/The Pizza Triangle* (1970), including *C'eravamo tanto amati/We All Loved Each Other So Much* (1974), and culminating with *La terrazza/The Terrace* (1979). *La terrazza* was their last important film together but Scarpelli returned to work with Scola on *Il viaggio del capitan Fracasso* (1990). PDA

AGIT-FILMS

Soviet short films, also known as 'agitki'. Produced during the Civil War of 1917–21, these films were simple in form and straightforward in content and dealt with topical matters of politics, production, health and hygiene. They were primarily intended for exhibition through the network of agit-trains touring the front lines and areas recently recaptured from the White forces.

Agit-films were a temporary solution to an emergency problem: they were a short cut to resolving communication difficulties between rulers and ruled and provided valuable experience in film-making – especially in montage* as a method of using scant resources economically – for a new generation of directors such as Lev Kuleshov* and Dziga Vertov*, who worked together on the 'October Revolution' agit-train. RT

AKERMAN, Chantal   Brussels 1950

Belgian director, born of émigré Polish Jewish parents. Akerman's early aspirations to be a writer were swiftly exchanged, on viewing Jean-Luc Godard's* *Pierrot le fou* (1965), for a career as a film-maker. After spending a year at the Brussels film school INSAS, Akerman travelled to Paris, then to New York after making her first short film, *Saute ma ville/Blow up My Town* (1968). Her films reflect these early years of displacement, yet despite their constant changes of form and location, evidence of a strong authorial personality remains.

Akerman's most (in)famous film, *Jeanne Dielman 23 Quai du Commerce 1080 Bruxelles* (1975), depicts roughly three days in the life of a housewife who is also a prostitute, played by Delphine Seyrig*. Rejecting both linear classical narrative and the conventional use of woman as a seductive presence, *Jeanne Dielman* offers instead a film which is shaped by Jeanne's own sense of ritual, time and space. *News from Home* (1976) extends this film's system of 'anti-seduction', replacing classical narrative's voyeuristic and fragmented gaze with an intimate and lingering look (the film consists of a series of long takes of New York with Akerman's voice-over reading letters written to her by her mother). In *Les Rendez-vous d'Anna* (1978), Aurore Clément plays a (semi-autobiographical?) Belgian film-maker who journeys from Cologne to Paris. This film won awards at festivals in Chicago and Paris. *Toute une nuit/All Night Long* (1982), a choreography around one hot night in Brussels, was followed by *Golden Eighties* (1986), a post-modern musical. The setting of this film in a shopping mall triggers an exploration of spectacle and performance, in which love becomes something to be bought and sold like a dress. Despite its charm and vitality, the film was not a success, and with her next film, *Histoires d'Amérique: Food, Family and Philosophy/American Stories* (1989), Akerman returned to a more intimate mode of production.

Akerman has moved from the avant-garde to art cinema, from feminist experiment to European *auteur* film, and from Brussels via New York to Paris, the setting of *Nuit et jour/Night and Day* (1991). Triply displaced as Belgian, Jewish and female, Akerman's cinema remains marginal, yet it should not be marginalised since its fundamental project is to challenge our preconceptions of what cinema can or should be. CF

Bib: Angela Martin, 'Chantal Akerman's Films, A Dossier', in Charlotte Brunsdon (ed.), *Films for Women* (London, 1986).

Other Films: *Je joue à être une femme mariée/Playing at Being Married* [short] (1971); *La Chambre/The Bedroom, Hotel Monterey* (1972); *Hanging out – Yonkers, Le 15/8* [co-dir. Samy Szlingerbaum] (1973); *Dis-moi/Tell Me* [short] (1980); *Les Années 80/The Eighties, Un Jour Pina a demandé/One Day Pina Asked* [doc] (1983); *L'Homme à la valise/The Man with the Suitcase* [TV], *J'ai faim, J'ai froid/I'm Hungry, I'm Cold* [short for *Paris vu par ... vingt ans après*], *A Family Business* [short for Channel 4] (1984); *Le Marteau/The Hammer* [short video], *Mallet Stevens* (1986); *Letters Home* [video], *Sloth* [short for *Seven Women, Seven Sins*] (1987); *Trois strophes sur le nom de Sacher* [short video] (1988); *Le Déménagement/Moving* [short for *Monologues*] (1992); *D'Est* [doc]; *Portrait d'une jeune fille de la fin des années 60, à Bruxelles* (1993).

ALBANIA

Until World War II, isolated and largely illiterate Albania possessed about twenty cinemas in the main towns, showing exclusively imported material. The only cinematic evidence of prewar Albania is in a few foreign newsreels and travelogues. The communist regime of Enver Hoxha (1944–85) nationalised the cinema in 1947, and immediately began using it for propaganda by making two newsreels with Soviet assistance. Moscow was largely responsible for the building of the Shqiperia e re/New Albania film studio in Tirana, and was virtually the only source of equipment and technical skills. Its construction, begun in 1952, allowed a steady production of newsreels, and documentaries such as *Rruga e lavdishme/The Glorious Road* (1952). Soviet director Sergei Yutkevich's* *Skanderbeg* (1954), about Albania's medieval national hero, was partly put together in the Albanian studio, and presented for political reasons as a Soviet-Albanian co-production. It helped confirm film as a mass medium, and by the mid-1950s there was an annual audience of 5 million for the hundred or so cinemas (from a population of c. 3 million), including mobile units for rural areas.

Until 1958, features were almost entirely from the Soviet Union and eastern Europe. The first Albanian feature, *Tana* (1958), directed by Kristaq Dhamo and starring Tinka Kurti, relied on the modest documentary tradition in its handling of the collectivisation of the countryside. Hysen Hakani's *Debatik/Communist Youth* (1961), on the resistance of children during the Italian occupation of 1938–43, set a pattern for storylines based on this period and subject. The break with Moscow in 1960, and growing political and cultural isolationism, made it necessary to increase domestic production. This was hampered by the loss of most foreign assistance, though there were enough Moscow-trained technicians and directors to begin to develop an autonomous film industry and provide some training at the Tirana Higher Institute of

Arts. Only one film a year was made until the late 1960s, but then production rose steadily to about twelve features annually in the early 1980s.

Hoxha's insistence on sticking to a Stalinist line of ideological struggle, and his refusal to follow Soviet revisionism, turned Albania into a bastion of Socialist Realist* film production. Every film was obliged to perform some political task, though in the special context of Albanian history. With slow television development, film had a key role, along with schools and various state institutions, in promulgating not merely the propaganda of class struggle but a 'socialist morality'. In particular this meant the central role of the 'positive hero' – the 'new man' educated by the Party. This pattern is firmly established in Dhimitër Anagnosti and Viktor Gjika's *Komisari i dritës/Commissar of the Light* (1966), in which a man returns to his home village after the liberation in 1944 to fight against the local priest and landowner, and a counter-revolutionary brigade, but whose greatest achievement is to set up the first school in the village and to inspire pupils. Anagnosti's other main films include *Cuca e maleve/The Mountain Girl* (1974), a ballet showing the strong influence of Chinese 'heroic' opera; *Lulëkuqet mbi mure/Red Poppies on Walls* (1976), starring Kadri Rashi and dynamically describing a children's rebellion against a fascist schoolmaster; the satirical comedy *Perralle nga e kaluara/A Tale from the Past* (1988); and *Kthimi i ushtisë së vdekur/Return of the Dead Army* (1989).

Ibrahim Mucaj and Kristaq Mitro portray collective heroism in *Dimeri i fundit/The Last Winter* (1976), where a group of village women put up resistance to occupation during World War II. Viktor Gjika achieves a subtler political approach with strong performances in *Rrugë të bardha/White Roads* (1974), where the 'new man' is a sympathetic contemporary figure struggling for love and against snowdrifts. Gjika's sensitivity for images, music and dramatic development can also be seen in *Gjeneral gramafoni/The General Gramophone* (1977), which shows the struggle to preserve Albanian folk music during the Italian occupation. *Yje mbi Drin/Stars above the Drin* (1977, dir. I. Zhabjaku) shows the final phase of almost complete ideological isolationism, the enemies now the Chinese 'revisionists' conspiring to destroy a hydro-electric plant. Kujtim Çashku and Piro Milkani's *Ballë për ballë/Face to Face* (1979), starring Sulejman Pitarka, has a conspiracy theme set around the departure of the Russians in 1960. With a significant annual production, a wider range of subjects could now be covered. In the record year of 1984, seven of the fourteen features dealt with contemporary subjects, while most of the rest were set in or around World War II. Productions included comedies, children's films and films based on ancient history and folklore. But as an Albanian delegate said at a Balkan film festival, whatever the subject matter every effort had to be made to omit 'sentimentality, physiological and moral anomalies, pornography, sadism, psychological and Freudian dimensions, naturalism and individualism'.

Cinema screens increased to 450 in 1975, and attendances reportedly reached 20 million, with a carefully chosen selection of heavily censored and selectively subtitled French, Italian and other European films. In 1978 a modernisation of the film studio began, but lack of access to the latest technology made it a limited project. The first colour feature, made with East German assistance, appeared in 1974. By the 1980s, most films were in colour and processing quality improved, though remaining relatively poor. Production of short documentaries increased to about thirty annually by the mid-1980s, mostly devoted to propaganda, scientific and educational subjects, and the activities of Hoxha. Occasional full-length documentaries, like *Kujtime te vegjëlisë/Memories of Childhood* (1985), were usually homages to Hoxha. Leading woman director Xhanfize Keko made a series of features about and for children, notably *Beni ecen vete/Beni's First Steps* (1978). Cartoon and puppet films were first made in the 1970s, and production reached about twelve films annually in the 1980s; worthy of note are *Zogu pushbardhe/The Fluffy White Chick* (1984–85), a popular children's series, and *Plumb ballit/Bullet in the Head* (1985), a grotesque satire on traitors. Television began in 1969, producing the only films shown at the biennial national film festival in Tirana. Most notable is Vladimir Prifti's *Udha e shkronjave/The Path of Letters* (1982), starring Sander Proci. Attempts to export Albanian films have been very limited, though a few foreign festival prizes were won by children's and documentary films. The national film archive contains 5,000 titles. The literary monthly *Nentori* and the weekly *Drita* publish film reviews and other film news.

The collapse of Hoxha's successor Ramiz Alia's regime (1990–92), and economic paralysis, reduced feature production to five films in 1990, and almost nothing since. Saimir Kumbaro's *Vdekja e kalit/Death of the Horse* (1992) is the major exception, an intense evocation of the fate of the individual under totalitarianism. The younger generation of talented film actors, as well as many others in the industry, are scattered outside Albania. Cinemas currently remain open, despite their difficulties in obtaining international releases (which are nonetheless often shown in pirated form on Albanian television), offering a mix of genres never before seen in Albania, including Greek soft-porn comedies and Japanese action films. The Minister of Culture in the post-1992 government is director Dhimitër Anagnosti, reflecting the important role of film personnel during and after the fall of the regime. The national film studio is seriously run down, and hopes for foreign investment have yet to be fulfilled. MM

ALBERS, Hans
Hamburg 1891 – Tutzing, Munich 1960

German actor, the most popular and best-paid male star of his generation. Originally a vaudeville dancer, singer and comedian, he played minor film roles as shady seducer or charming rake, rising to stardom in *Die Nacht gehört uns/The Night Belongs to Us* (1929) and *Der blaue Engel/The Blue Angel* (1930). Despite Goebbels' disapproval of him, Albers maintained his pre-eminence in movies ranging from costume comedies (*Münchhausen*, 1943) to Westerns (*Wasser für Canitoga/Water for Canitoga*, 1939), and detective stories (*Der Mann, der Sherlock Holmes war/The Man Who Was Sherlock Holmes*, 1937), playing daredevils with a mission (*Flüchtlinge/Refugees*, 1933) and melancholy heroes with broken dreams (*Große Freiheit Nr.7/Port of Freedom*, 1944; banned in Nazi Germany). Even with advancing age, Albers' light-hearted version of (Hanseatic) machismo was unremittingly cast in romantic narratives (*Auf der Reeperbahn nachts um halb eins/On the Reeperbahn at Half Past Midnight*, 1954, *Das Herz von St. Pauli/The Heart of St Pauli*, 1957), while his acting increasingly focused on his characteristically hoarse voice. Albers' uniquely enduring appeal as the archetypal blue-eyed, blond male sex symbol continues to resonate in the nation's popular culture. KU/TE

Other Films Include: *Asphalt* (1929); *Bomben auf Monte Carlo/Monte Carlo Madness* (1931); *F.P.1 antwortet nicht* (1932).

ALDO, G. R.
Aldo Rossano Graziati; Scorzè 1905 – Albara di Pianiga 1953

Italian cinematographer, who emigrated to Paris in 1923 where he became a photographer (from 1937 a set photographer) and acquired experience as a cinematographer, for instance on Marcel L'Herbier's* *Les Derniers jours de Pompei/The Last Days of Pompeii* (1947–50). Back in Italy he met Luchino Visconti* and was offered the role of director of photography on *La terra trema* (1947). He also worked with Augusto Genina* on *Cielo sulla palude/Heaven over the Marshes* (1949) and *Tre storie proibite/Three Forbidden Stories* (1952), and with Vittorio De Sica* on *Miracolo a Milano/Miracle in Milan* (1951), *Umberto D.* (1952), and *Stazione Termini/Indiscretion of an American Wife* (1953), during which his concern for the film as a whole rather than the beauty of Jennifer Jones angered producer David O. Selznick, who employed Oswald Morris for the close-ups of his wife. Aldo worked with Orson Welles on part of *Otello/Othello* (1951), and with directors such as Mario Soldati* (*La provinciale/The Wayward Wife*, 1953). Profoundly influenced by his stay in France, but at the same time loyal to a mythic vision of Caravaggio's and Venetian painting, Aldò – as he was called by everyone, with the stress on the last syllable – was both a traditionalist and a forerunner of self-conscious modern cinematography. His most immediate successor is Giuseppe Rotunno*, his colleague and friend from 1947. Aldo died in a car accident during the shooting of Visconti's *Senso* (1954), which Rotunno and Robert Krasker went on to complete. MMo

ALEKAN, Henri
Paris 1909

French cinematographer. After studying at the Paris Conservatoire des Arts et Métiers and the Institut d'Optique, and working as a puppeteer, Alekan was camera assistant on French films from 1929, including two – Marcel Carné's* *Drôle de drame* (1937) and *Quai des brumes* (1938) – with Eugen Schüfftan*, a great influence. Alekan's career took off with the resistance drama *La Bataille du rail/Battle of the Rails* (dir. René Clément*) and Jean Cocteau's* fairy tale *La Belle et la bête* (both 1946). He subsequently worked on numerous films with distinguished directors, including Yves Allégret*, Abel Gance*, Joseph Losey* and Jules Dassin*, but *La Bataille du rail* and *La Belle et la bête* epitomised his

mastery of black and white photography, his preferred medium: as he declared in 1993, 'I absolutely prefer black and white. [...] I believe film should transcend the banal world.' This was literally the case in Wim Wenders' *Der Himmel über Berlin/Wings of Desire* (1987, Ger./Fr.) in which he filmed angels. In his later career, Alekan worked on other Wenders films and with Raul Ruiz*; he appears as an actor in Wenders' *In weiter Ferne, so nah!/Far Away, So Close* (1993, Ger.). GV

Bib: Henri Alekan, *Des lumières et des ombres* (1984).

ALESSANDRINI, Goffredo
Cairo, Egypt 1904–78

Italian director. A prolific director of some of the most popular Italian films of the 1930s and early 1940s, Alessandrini worked in a variety of genres, including romantic comedy, melodrama and the biopic, but his fame was (and is) mostly tied to his war epics, which mythologised fascist colonialist initiatives. Many of his films were set in North Africa, the site of Italian occupation in the early twentieth century and the place where the director was reared and to which he frequently returned.

After working as a scriptwriter and assistant director for Alessandro Blasetti* at Cines*, Alessandrini directed his first feature-length film for Cines, *La segretaria privata/The Private Secretary* (1931), an Italian remake of a popular German film. After a stint working for MGM on Italian versions of Hollywood films, he returned to Italy to make *Seconda B* (1934), a quaint and nostalgic melodrama set in 1911 at a girls' school, which he co-scripted with Umberto Barbaro*. Alessandrini then directed *Don Bosco* (1935), a biopic commemorating the founder of the Salesian Catholic order in Italy. The film was funded by the Salesians and (unusually for the period) used mainly non-professional actors. Alessandrini's subsequent epics follow on from *Don Bosco* in the quasi-religious tone they give to the exploits of modern Italian crusaders. *Cavalleria* (1936) charted the rite of passage of a cavalryman played by the young Amedeo Nazzari*, who forgoes his horse for an aeroplane at the outbreak of World War I. In Alessandrini's next film, *Luciano Serra pilota/The Pilot Luciano Serra* (1938), the central character, also played by Nazzari, is a successful World War I pilot whose disillusionment with his country can only be assuaged through his return to the battlefields of North Africa, where he re-emerges as a protector of a 'new' Italy and the future of his soldier son. The quasi-sacred quests of the central characters in these two films are consonant with the more literally religious mission of Cardinal Messias to North Africa in Alessandrini's following film, *Abuna Messias* (1939), which attempts to demonstrate the cultural basis for ties between Ethiopia and Catholic Italy.

The popularity of the colonial war genre in Italy during the late 1930s led to Alessandrini being contracted in 1942 to direct another war epic, *Giarabub* (1942), again set in North Africa. *Giarabub*, made partly in the war zone (drawing Italian soldiers from the battlefront to play the opposing armies) and partly at Cinecittà*, is an ironic allegory of the relation between the cultural politics of film-making and the state politics of war. Alessandrini's other successful epics during the early 1940s include the biography of Caravaggio (*Caravaggio, il pittore maledetto/Caravaggio, The Cursed Painter*, 1941) and *Noi vivi – Addio, Kira!/We The Living* (1942), a long (in some versions, two-part) romantic melodrama set during the Russian revolution, based on a novel by Ayn Rand and starring Alida Valli* and Rossano Brazzi*. Alessandrini's career as a director was significantly limited after the war amid the emerging neo-realist* aesthetic. JHa

ALEXANDER, Peter   Peter Alexander Neumayer; Vienna 1926

Austrian actor with a solid career as a singer and stage comedian in radio shows from 1948 onwards. In the early 1950s Alexander played minor film roles before landing the lead part of a pop singer in *Verliebte Leute* (1954), a 'Viennese' comedy. After appearing in two German films with Caterina Valente – *Liebe, Tanz und 1000 Schlager* (1955) and *Bonjour Kathrin* (1955) – he became the undisputed star of the *Schlagerfilme* (musical) with a 'boy-next-door' image to which he added, in the 1960s, cabaret-type parody (*Kriminaltango*, 1960). After operetta adaptations (such as the Austrian-French co-production *Die lustige Witwe/La Veuve joyeuse*, 1962), comedy classics (*Schwejk's Flegeljahre*, 1964) and the popular 'Pauker' and 'Lümmel' series (for instance *Hurra, die Schule brennt*, 1969), Alexander has weathered well as a television host and popular stage actor. KU

Bib: Peter Lanz, *Peter Alexander, Ein Leben für die Musik* (1986).

Other Films Include: *Verlorene Melodie* (1952); *Wehe, wenn sie losgelassen* (1958); *Die Abenteuer des Grafen Bobby* (1961); *Die Fledermaus* (1962).

ALEXANDROV [ALEKSANDROV], Grigori V.   Grigori Mormonenko; Sverdlovsk [now Yekaterinburg], Russian Empire 1903 – Moscow 1983

Soviet director and scriptwriter, who began his career as a stage assistant at the Yekaterinburg Opera and first appeared on stage at the Proletkult Theatre in Moscow in 1921, the beginning of his creative association with Sergei Eisenstein*. Alexandrov moved with Eisenstein from theatre to cinema in 1924, helping with *Stachka/The Strike* (1925) as both actor and assistant director. He acted in and co-directed *Bronenosets Potëmkin/The Battleship Potemkin* (1926) and, with Eisenstein, scripted and directed both *Oktyabr'/October* (1928) and *Staroe i novoe/The Old and the New* (1929). He spent the years 1929–32 travelling with Eisenstein and Eduard Tisse* in Western Europe, the USA and Mexico, assisting on the unfinished project for *¡Que viva México!* (1930–32). Alexandrov returned to the USSR before his associates and made the film that was to found the Soviet genre of musical comedies, *Vesëlye rebyata/The Happy Guys*

(1934), starring his wife Lyubov Orlova*. His films reflected the ideological preoccupations of the age, but with their lavish choreography they were hugely popular with Soviet audiences. *Tsirk/The Circus*, with its anti-fascist message, followed in 1936, and *Volga-Volga*, with Igor Ilyinsky's* unforgettable parody of the bureaucrat Byvalov, in 1938. In the following decade Alexandrov made two more musical comedies, *Svetlyi put'/The Radiant Path* (1940), extolling the virtues of shock labour, and *Vesna/Springtime* (1947). In 1949 he made the war film *Vstrecha na El'be/Meeting on the Elbe*, and in 1952 the biographical *Kompozitor Glinka/The Composer Glinka*. His last film, *Lyubov' Orlova* (1983), was a study of his wife. In the 1950s Alexandrov taught at VGIK*. His films were influential in creating a Soviet popular cinema, combining the constraints of the political correctness associated with Socialist Realism* and a genuine feel for the emotions of mass audiences. RT

ALLÉGRET, Marc   Basel, Switzerland 1900 – Paris 1973

French director. The older brother of Yves Allégret*, Marc Allégret was a prolific and skilled mainstream director whose disparate work included documentaries (*Voyage au Congo*, 1927, with the writer André Gide, whose nephew, contrary to legend, he was *not*), comedy – adapted operettas (*Mam'zelle Nitouche*, 1931), a Fernandel* vehicle (*Pétrus*, 1947) – and melodrama (*Orage*, 1937). He also directed Marcel Pagnol's* *Fanny* (1932). Dominant themes emerge, however: an interest in youth often combined with artistic milieux is evident from *Zouzou* (1934, with Josephine Baker*) and *Entrée des artistes/The Curtain Rises* (1938, starring Louis Jouvet*) to *Les Parisiennes* (1962, with Catherine Deneuve* and the singer Johnny Halliday). Allégret also showed an interest in women characters, giving Micheline Presle*, for instance, one of her best parts in *Félicie Nanteuil* (1942, rel. 1945). He acquired a reputation as a 'discoverer' of stars, launching Simone Simon in *Lac aux dames* (1934) and Michèle Morgan* in *Gribouille/Heart of Paris* (1937). He spotted Brigitte Bardot's* potential from a magazine cover, later casting her as the star of *En effeuillant la marguerite/Please Mr Balzac* (1956). GV

ALLÉGRET, Yves   Asnières 1907 – Paris 1987

French director. Brother of Marc Allégret*, on some of whose films he worked as assistant in the 1930s. Yves Allégret was part of the generation who emerged during the German occupation. His main contribution to the history of French film is as one of the exponents of postwar French *noir* cinema with a small body of films made in the late 1940s. *Dédée d'Anvers* (1948), *Une si jolie petite plage/Riptide* (1949) and *Manèges/The Cheat* (1950) fixed the Allégret universe – a dystopian vision of postwar France which evoked prewar Poetic Realism* without the 'poetry', and in which Marcel Carné's* and Jacques Prévert's* romantic belief in fate had been replaced by an emphasis on the sordid; indeed Allégret was attacked by left-wing critics for his negative and backward-looking portrayal of the period. Nevertheless, the films were seductive, wonderful lighting effects moulding the chiselled features of Gérard Philipe* in *Une si jolie petite plage* and *Les Orgueilleux/The Proud Ones* (1953, from a script by Jean-Paul Sartre) and those of Simone Signoret* (then Allégret's wife) in *Dédée d'Anvers* and *Manèges*. The performances of the superb Signoret concealed the films' deep misogyny, which can be seen as part of a backlash following the (relative) prominence of women in wartime French cinema and society. Allégret and Signoret had a daughter, Catherine Allégret, who is also an actress. GV

Bib: Noël Burch and Geneviève Sellier, *Le Ciné-roman familial de la société traditionnelle* (1995).

ALLGEIER, Sepp   Freiburg 1895–1968

German cameraman, who cut his teeth on newsreels and expedition films for the Welt-Kinematograph company in 1918. A year later he became chief cameraman on Arnold Fanck's* mountain films [> HEIMATFILM]. His special skills included shooting atmospheric, static landscapes and photographing athletes, which won him not only a wide audience but high praise in the profession. Cameramen such as R. Angst, A. Benitz, K. Neubert and H. Schneeberger learned their trade from Allgeier, who also worked on British productions and was crucial to Leni Riefenstahl's* Nazi Party films. In the 1950s, the television network Südwestfunk employed Allgeier as chief director of photography. TE/SG

Other Films Include: *Der Berg des Schicksals* (1924), *Alpentragödie, Im Luxuszug* (1927); *Frau Sorge* (1928); *Das Tagebuch einer Verlorenen/Diary of a Lost Girl, Die weiße Hölle vom Piz Palü* (1929); *Baroud/Lost in Morocco* (1932, UK); *Der Sieg des Glaubens/Victory of Faith* (1933); *Triumph des Willens/Triumph of the Will, Escape Me Never* [UK], *Friesennot* (1935); *The Great Barrier* (1937, UK); *Der Feldzug in Polen* (1940); *Wetterleuchten um Barbara* (1941).

ALLGOOD, Sara   Dublin 1883 – Los Angeles, USA 1950

Irish actress. At a young age, Allgood became a successful actress at the Abbey Theatre, playing in J. M. Synge's 1904 play *Riders to the Sea*, and as Pegeen Mike in Synge's *The Playboy of the Western World* (1907). Other high points of her theatrical career included the Sean O'Casey plays *Juno and the Paycock* (1924), in which she played Juno to Barry Fitzgerald's* Paycock, and *The Plough and the Stars* (1926). Though she made one film, *Just Peggy*, while on tour in Australia in 1918, her first British feature was in Alfred Hitchcock's*, and Britain's, first film with synchronous sound, *Blackmail* (1929). The following year she played Juno in Hitchcock's version of O'Casey's play. She settled in Hollywood after receiving enthusiastic reviews for her performances while touring with the Abbey Theatre in America. Her career there, though, was not a success; she was offered only minor Irishwomen roles as cooks, landladies and other matronly figures. KR

Other Films Include: *That Hamilton Woman/Lady Hamilton, How Green Was My Valley* (1941); *The Lodger* (1944); *My Wild Irish Rose* (1947).

ALMEIDA, Acácio de   Soto 1938

Portuguese cinematographer, whose first important film was *O Cerco/The Roundup* (1969), directed by António da Cunha Telles*. Almeida elicited remarkable loyalty from the directors he worked with, including, apart from Telles, João César Monteiro*, António Reis* and Margarida Cordeiro*, António Campos* and Silva Melo. An established professional in his own right, he also worked as assistant to French cinematographer Henri Alekan* on Raul Ruiz's* *Território/Le Territoire/The Territory* (1981). Thus began a prolific cooperation with Ruiz, from *La Ville des pirates/City of Pirates* (1983) to *L'Île au trésor/Treasure Island* (1986–90). But the film that established Almeida's international reputation was Alain Tanner's* *Dans la ville blanche/In the White City* (1983). Almeida is equally at ease with the colours, filters and mirrors of Ruiz's baroque imagination as he is with documentary, putting his camera on the streets for, among other films, Jacques Rozier's *Maine-Océan* (1985) and Tanner's *Une Flamme dans mon coeur/A Flame in My Heart* (1987). He was able to 'paint' Lisbon with the white sunny light of *Dans la ville blanche* or the autumn melancholy of *La Dérive/Drifting* (1994, dir. Telles). He worked on Manoel de Oliveira's* *O Passado e o Presente/Past and Present* (1971) and, as co-cinematographer, on Paulo Rocha's* *A Ilha dos Amores/The Island of Loves* (1983). He also produced a number of films directed by Silva Melo. AMS

ALMENDROS, Nestor   Barcelona, Spain 1930 – New York 1992

French-based cinematographer of Spanish origin. One of the most renowned postwar cinematographers. After studying in Cuba, New York and Rome, and working on short films in Cuba (where he founded Havana's first film club), Almendros moved to Paris. He worked on a late New Wave* project, the collective *Paris vu par...* (1965), and became a regular collaborator with Eric Rohmer* and François Truffaut*. His impressive filmography includes Rohmer's *Le Genou de Claire/Claire's Knee* (1970) and *Pauline à la plage* (1982), and Truffaut's *L'Enfant sauvage/The Wild Child* (1970) and *Le Dernier métro/The Last Metro* (1980), for which Almendros received a César*. He also worked with Jean Eustache*, Marguerite Duras* and Vicente Aranda*, and in the US with Terrence Malick (*Days of Heaven*, 1978, which won him an Oscar), Alan Pakula (*Sophie's Choice*, 1982) and Martin Scorsese (*New York Stories*, ep. 'Life Lessons', 1989), among others. He directed documentaries in Cuba and the US and worked for French television. An advocate of realism, he excelled in using natural light, finding inspiration in painters and taking, as he put it, 'a "window" light from Vermeer, a "candle" light from De la Tour, a chiaroscuro from Rembrandt'. GV

Bib: Nestor Almendros, *A Man With a Camera* (1980).

ALMODÓVAR, Pedro
Pedro Almodóvar Caballero; Calzada de Calatrava, Mancha 1949

Spanish director, writer and producer, who began his career in the mid-1970s in Madrid where he was associated with the post-Franco *movida*, the lively cultural scene identified with the mayorship of Tierno Galván in the early 1980s. During this period he was involved in numerous experimental ventures, using Super-8 cameras and amateur actors. In 1979 he began making commercial films, earning national and international recognition and, in the case of *Mujeres al borde de un ataque de nervios/Women on the Verge of a Nervous Breakdown* (1988), breaking box-office records.

Almodóvar's first film to reach a wide audience was *Pepi, Luci, Bom y otras chicas del montón/Pepi, Luci, Bom and Other Girls in the Crowd* (1980). With its idiosyncratic punk-pop style and comic portrayal of the new post-dictatorship generation, this film was acclaimed as a cult classic by Spanish youth. It was followed by *Laberinto de pasiones/Labyrinth of Passions* (1982), which, like its predecessor, explored dissident sexualities. From 1983 Almodóvar's films tended towards melodrama, often characterised by a darkly comic tone, and an exploration of love and desire, avoiding the preoccupation with Spain's recent past so characteristic of the previous generation of film-makers. Background references to popular music, television commercials and other non-cinematic elements are contemporary and urban. Melodrama and comedy, from both the Hollywood and Spanish traditions, combine to form Almodóvar's distinctively kitschy, highly colourful, heterogeneous style: a simultaneous celebration and parody of *cinéma-vérité**, neo-realism*, thrillers, musicals and horror. Almodóvar's controversial attitudes towards sex, morality and political correctness, as well as the shocking explicitness of his films, have often met with disapproval. El Deseo, his production company, has given him unprecedented freedom, and is also responsible for the striking debut of Alex de La Iglesia's *Acción mutante/Mutant Action* (1993). Almodóvar's *Mujeres al borde de un ataque de nervios* was nominated for the Best Foreign Film Oscar and won over fifty awards worldwide. NTT

Bib: Paul Julian Smith, *Desire Unlimited: The Cinema of Pedro Almodóvar* (1994).

Other Films Include: *Folle ... Folle ... Fólleme, Tim/Fuck ... Fuck ... Fuck Me, Tim* (1978); *Entre tinieblas/Dark Habits* (1983); *¿Qué he hecho yo para merecer esto?/What Have I Done to Deserve This?* (1984); *Trayler para amantes de lo prohibido/Trailer for Lovers of the Forbidden* (1985); *Matador* (1986); *La ley del deseo/The Law of Desire* (1987); *¡Atame!/ Tie Me Up! Tie Me Down!* (1989); *Tacones lejanos/High Heels* (1991); *Kika* (1993).

ALMROTH, Greta
Stockholm 1888–1981

Swedish actress, who played in provincial theatre before going into film. She worked with Victor Sjöström* in films such as *Blodets röst/The Voice of the Blood* (1913) and *Havsgamar/The Sea Vultures* (1916), and with Mauritz Stiller* in *Lyckonålen/The Lucky Pin* (1916), among other films. Her greatest triumph was Sjöström's *Tösen från Stormyrtorpet/The Lass from Stormyrtorpet* (1917). She worked with Stiller again in *Sången om den eldröda blomman/The Song of the Scarlet Flower* (1919) and performed for Carl Theodor Dreyer* in *Prästänkan/The Parson's Widow* (1920), one of his Swedish films. Her screen persona was characterised by graceful 'naturalness', emphasised by her fresh looks and blonde hair. Although her career was short, she acted in over thirty films; she played few roles after quitting Svensk Filmindustri* in 1920. LGA/BF

ALTENLOH, Emilie
Vörde, Westphalia 1888 – Hamburg 1985

German theorist. Author of one of the earliest serious studies of the cinema, *Sociology of the Cinema*, which considers spectator preferences and attitudes in the context of an industrial city. Not least thanks to its emphasis on women as a significant part of the early cinema audience, Altenloh's work has become a classic. Though unprejudiced in her evaluation of the cinema, the author belonged to the conservative circles around the 'Kino reform movement'*, most clearly shown in an earlier article from 1913, 'Theater und Kino', in which she argued for cinema's superiority over theatre by inverting the typically reformist notion of art versus entertainment, making a plea for the latter since the cinema was better able to meet the leisure needs of ordinary people. In later years she applied herself to broader questions of social policy, and was a co-founder of the Freie Demokratische Partei (FDP) in 1945, for which she served as a member of the Bundestag between 1961 and 1965. MW

Bib: Sabine Hake, *The Cinema's Third Machine: Writing on Film in Germany 1907–1933* (1994).

ALWYN, William
Northampton 1905 – [?] 1985

British composer. As well as being Professor of Composition at the Royal Academy of Music with a number of symphonic works to his credit, Alwyn scored more British films than any other composer (he was also, incidentally, the second cousin of Gary Cooper). He began film composition as part of the British Documentary Movement* and worked particularly with Paul Rotha* and Humphrey Jennings*, for whom he scored *Fires Were Started* (1943). After the war, he composed scores for around eighty feature films, forming particular associations with Carol Reed* and with Frank Launder and Sidney Gilliat*. JC

AMBROSIO, Arturo   Turin 1869–1960

Italian producer. Ambrosio, the owner of a photographic equipment shop with technical and commercial connections with Pathé*, produced *La prima corsa automobilistica Susa-Moncenisio/The First Susa-Moncenisio Car Race* with Roberto Omegna in 1904, followed by a series of short (*c.* five-minute) documentaries. From these modest beginnings Ambrosio rose to worldwide recognition as the founding father of Italian cinema, with Turin as its capital. In 1907 he founded l'Anonima Ambrosio, a well-capitalised and rigorously organised company, with new large studios, new 'cinematographic' actors (Mary Tarlarini, Gigetta Morano, Alberto Collo), cameramen (G. Vitrotti) and scriptwriters (Arrigo Frusta), which produced popular adventure melodramas and comedies, as well as more ambitious films. Of particular interest are Luigi Maggi's *Spergiura!* (1909) with its real settings, Omegna's *Caccia al leopardo/The Leopard Hunt*, entirely shot in Africa; the early epic, *Gli ultimi giorni di Pompei/The Last Days of Pompeii* (1908) and Omegna's documentary *La vita delle farfalle/The Life of Butterflies* (1911), made in collaboration with the poet Guido Gozzano. In 1911–12, Ambrosio produced six dramas written by the poet Gabriele D'Annunzio. Contributing to the worldwide triumph of Italian historical cinema, he produced spectaculars such as Mario Caserini's unforgettable version of *Gli ultimi giorni di Pompei* (1913) and *I promessi sposi* (1913, dir. Ernesto Maria Pasquali). The company also had its regular comedian in 'Robinet' (Marcel Fabre). In 1916, Ambrosio produced the only film performance of stage *diva* Eleonora Duse [> DIVISMO], in Febo Mari's *Cenere*. Ambrosio's company entered a period of crisis after the war. He joined UCI (Unione Cinematografica Italiana, a trust created to fight off international competition), for whom he produced three films, including Gabriellino (the son of Gabriele) D'Annunzio's *La nave/The Ship* (1920). When UCI in turn went bust, he retired to his farm in the country, and returned to cinema only to manage Scalera Film from 1939 to 1943. GVo

AMELIO, Gianni   San Pietro Magisano 1945

Italian director. Graduating from assistant on low-budget films, Amelio quickly learnt to apply a personal touch to all sorts of genres, formats and commissions before reaching international recognition in the late 1980s. His talent first emerged in his television work at RAI*, beginning with *La fine del gioco/The End of the Game* (1970), and followed by the philosophical *La città del sole/City of the Sun* (1973, based on Tommaso Campanella's eponymous utopian treatise) and his free adapatations of Aldous Huxley (*Il piccolo Archimede/Young Archimedes*, 1979) and Anna Banfi (*I velieri/The Sailing Ships*, 1982). Often focusing on the world of the media and the ambiguity of his own role within it, he revealed an acute moral sense of social relations, mingling public and private themes, allied to an alert consciousness of film language. Notable are *Colpire al cuore/Straight to the Heart* (1982), the story of a father–son relationship caught in the poisonous climate of terrorism; *I ragazzi di via Panisperna/The Panisperna Street Boys* (1988), about the complex relationship between a teacher and his pupil; *Porte aperte/Open Doors* (1990), original both in its treatment of Leonardo Sciascia's novel and in Gian Maria Volonté's* central performance; and *Il ladro di bambini/Stolen Children* (1992), a journey from North to South by a policeman and two children, which is also a journey into the depths of Italy, open to many different readings. Most recently *Lamerica* (1994), the encounter of a 'son' without an identity and a 'father' without a present, against the background of the almost biblical exodus of the Albanians into Italy, confirms Amelio's status as one of the most important Italian directors of the present generation. GVo

Other Films Include: *La morte al lavoro/Death at Work* (1978, video); *Effetti speciali/Special Effects* (1978, video).

AMIDEI, Sergio   Trieste 1904 – Rome 1981

Italian scriptwriter. Initially a jack of all trades at the FERT studio in Turin, Amidei started to write scripts in 1938 with Pietro Micca. As an anti-fascist in a cinema ruled by dictatorship, he focused on technical proficiency by devising a sort of 'language for cinema'. He worked on genre films, such as the so-called 'Hungarian' comedies, and historical reconstructions for Mario Bonnard, Nunzio Malasomma, Carmine Gallone* and Carlo Lodovico Bragaglia, participating at all levels of production. Only in his work with Ferdinando Maria Poggioli did he manage to work more creatively. His talent achieved full expression in the postwar period. He was Roberto Rossellini's* regular scriptwriter from *Roma città aperta/Rome, Open City* (1945) to *Stromboli, terra di Dio/Stromboli* (1949). His name appears on the credits of films by Vittorio De Sica* (*Sciuscià/Shoeshine*, 1946), Luigi Zampa* (*Anni difficili/Difficult Years*, 1948; *Anni facili/Easy Years*, 1953), Renato Castellani* (*Sotto il sole di Roma*, 1948), Luciano Emmer (*Una domenica d'agosto/Sunday in August*, 1950), and Carlo Lizzani* (*Cronache di poveri amanti/Stories of Poor Lovers*, 1954). He was thus one of the protagonists (some critics claim an originator) of neo-realism* in all its forms, including *commedia all'italiana** – a genre for which, rightly or wrongly, the scriptwriters rather than the directors have tended to receive the credit. A versatile and pragmatic craftsman, he excelled in a kind of 'everyday epic poetry' inhabited by a wide variety of popular characters, his work ranging from moral reflection on society to criticism of manners. His position on society was, however, shot through with paradox – which, he maintained, 'captures reality more than documentation can' – and with irony which 'releases more truth than anger'. He continued collaborating with Rossellini (for instance, on *La paura/Fear*, 1954, and *Viva l'Italia*, 1961), and worked in comedy, contributing to a number of masterpieces of the genre such as *Un borghese piccolo piccolo/An Average Man* (1977, dir. Mario Monicelli*), and creating many other roles for Alberto Sordi*. *Il mondo nuovo/The New World* (1982), which came out after his death and which is dedicated to him, was the last of more than 150 films written by Amidei. GVo

AMMELROOY, Willeke van   Amsterdam 1944

Dutch actress, who appeared in over forty films in the 1970s and 1980s, mostly in leading roles. She was the first star to make a living from film work in the Netherlands. After graduating from the Academy of Dramatic Arts in Amsterdam, Ammelrooy made her screen debut in 1966 in Joris Ivens'* Dutch comeback film *Rotterdam Europoort*. Fame came with her performance as a *femme fatale* in Fons Rademakers'* *Mira* (1971), the first of many such roles. In the 1970s she appeared in films directed by Pim de la Parra and Wim Verstappen* for Scorpio Films, vehicles which offered little scope for her acting ability. The same was true of work in French soft porn films of the 1970s – such as the infamous *L'Arrière-train sifflera trois fois* (1974; the title is a pun on 'arrière-train' meaning 'posterior' and the French title of *High Noon*, *Le Train sifflera trois fois*). Better use of her acting talents was made by directors such as Harry Kümel* in *De komst van Joachim Stiller/The Return of Joachim Stiller* (1976), Frans Zwartjes in *It's Me* (1976), and Raul Ruiz* in *Le Toît de la baleine/On Top of the Whale* (1982). Since the 1980s she has directed short films and a feature, *De vlinder tilt de kat op/The Butterfly Lifts the Cat* (1994). KD

ANA BELÉN   María del Pilar Cuesta Acosta; Madrid 1950

Spanish actress, singer and director. She began her career as a child star* in *Zampo y yo/Zampo and I* (1965), at a time when the genre was on the wane. Subsequently she achieved fame as a singer on television, stage and film. Her dramatic television roles include the highly successful series *Fortunata y Jacinta*. In films she alternated between light parts – for instance *La corte de Faraón/Pharaoh's Court* (1985) and *Sé infiel y no mires con quién/Be Wanton and Tread No Shame* (1985) – and more dramatic ones, such as *La petición/The Engagement Party* (1976) and *Divinas palabras/Divine Words* (1987). Though not a voluptuous star, she is sensual, forceful and enormously popular. She has recently directed *Cómo ser mujer y no morir en el intento/How to Be a Woman and not Die in the Attempt* (1991), starring Carmen Maura*, and appeared in Vicente Aranda's* *Pasíon Turca/Turkish Passion* (1994) IS

ANDERSON, Lindsay   Bangalore, India 1923 – London 1994

British director and critic. Anderson's importance to British cinema was both as a director and as a critic and polemicist. As one of the editors of *Sequence** from 1947 to 1951, Anderson introduced the concept of the director as poet of the cinema, and when the Western was still a despised genre in British criticism, offered John Ford as a prime example. As a writer for *Sight and Sound**, the *New Statesman* and the *Observer* in the 1950s he argued for a socially engaged cinema and for the poetry of everyday life, and as one of the organisers of and contributors to Free Cinema* in 1956, he put his polemics into practice with a number of social documentaries which developed from the Humphrey Jennings* poetic tra-

dition rather than the sociological tradition of the John Grierson* school. (He received his only Oscar, for Best Short Subject, for *Thursday's Children*, 1953.) From 1956 Anderson was closely associated, as assistant director, with the theatre revolution which was going on at London's Royal Court Theatre under the banner of the 'angry young men' and directed his first production there in 1957.

Discussing his first feature, *This Sporting Life* (1963), one of the key films of the British New Wave*, Anderson rejected the notion of a representative social realism in favour of the poet's sense of the unique: 'We were not making a film about a "worker", but about an extraordinary (and therefore more deeply significant) man, and about an extraordinary relationship. We were not, in a word, making sociology.' This sets Anderson in opposition to the naturalistic 'kitchen sink' tag under which British social realism is often subsumed, an opposition which becomes even more apparent with the allegorical nature of the trilogy centred round the character Mick Travis (played by Malcolm McDowell*): *If....* (1968), which was awarded the Palme d'Or at Cannes, *O Lucky Man!* (1973), and *Britannia Hospital* (1982).

In a famous article written for *Sight and Sound* in 1956, 'Stand Up! Stand Up!', Anderson says, 'Fighting means commitment, means believing what you say, and saying what you believe. It will also mean being called sentimental, irresponsible, self-righteous and out of date by those who equate maturity with scepticism, art with amusement, and responsibility with romantic excess.' In his last years, Anderson seemed to have become irascible rather than angry – irritated by lack of recognition, lack of support, lack of a British film industry, by the need to make pop promos to support himself, by the British Film Institute*, and, particularly, by 'pernicious' film studies. JC

Bib: Jonathan Hacker and David Price, *Take 10: Contemporary British Film Directors* (1991).

Other Films Include: Documentaries – *Meet the Pioneers* (1948); *Idlers That Work* (1949); *Three Installations, Trunk Conveyor, Wakefield Express* (1952); *O Dreamland* (1953); *Green and Pleasant Land, Henry, The Children Upstairs, A Hundred Thousand Children, £20 a Ton, Energy First, Foot and Mouth* (1955); *Every Day Except Christmas* (1957); *Raz, dwa, trzy/The Singing Lesson* (1967, Poland); **Features –** *The White Bus* (1967); *In Celebration* (1976); *Chariots of Fire* [as actor] (1981); *The Whales of August* (1987, US); *Glory! Glory!* (TV/1988, Canada/US).

ANDERSSON, Bibi   Birgitta Andersson; Stockholm 1935

Swedish actress. Since the age of sixteen Andersson has been connected with the theatre, as an actress and later a director. She came to prominence in Ingmar Bergman's *Sommarnattens leende/Smiles of a Summer Night* (1955), the start of a long association with the director – embracing, among other films, *Det sjunde inseglet/The Seventh Seal* (1957), *Beröringen/The Touch* (1971), and *Scener ur ett äktenskap/Scenes from a Marriage* (1974) – an association which has dominated her image, if not her actual career. Her screen persona evolved from her double role in *Smultronstället/Wild Strawberries* (1957) as the vivacious, sexually 'free' blonde hitchhiker who triggers off the memories of Professor Borg (Victor Sjöström*) and as his childhood love, to the complex heroine of *Persona* (1966), in which the celebrated extreme close-ups of her face (along with those of Liv Ullmann*) personified 1960s angst. She has appeared in films by other Swedish directors, such as Gustaf Molander's* *Herr Arnes penningar/Mr Arne's Money* (1954), Vilgot Sjöman's* *Syskonbädd 1782/My Sister, My Love* (1966) and Mai Zetterling's* *Flickorna/The Girls* (1968), as well as in international productions such as Robert Altman's *Quintet* (1978, US) and Gabriel Axel's* *Babettes gæstebud/Babette's Feast* (1987). GV

ANDERSSON, Harriet   Stockholm 1932

Swedish actress. Like her blonde counterparts Bibi Andersson*, Ingrid Thulin* and Liv Ullmann*, the dark-haired Harriet Andersson stood for a while for a certain idea of 'Nordic' eroticism through her films with Ingmar Bergman*. An accomplished actress, also like them she started in the theatre and worked in Bergman's Malmö company. Bergman's *Sommaren med Monika/Summer with Monika* (1953), the story of a rebellious young woman which was written for her, brought her to international attention. Her long collaboration with Bergman, which also includes *Gycklarnas afton/Sawdust and Tinsel* (1953) and *Sommarnattens leende/Smiles of a Summer Night* (1955), extends to his later films such as *Viskningar och rop/Cries and Whispers* (1973), in which she harrowingly plays the sick heroine, and *Fanny och Alexander/Fanny and Alexander* (1982). She also acted in a number of films directed by Jörn Donner*, including *Att älska/To Love* (1964), for which she was awarded a best actress award at the Venice* film festival. The image of sensuality (for Robin Wood the 'keynote' of her screen personality) as well as rebellion still attaches to her, for instance in her part as the sympathetic teacher in *Høyere enn himmelen/Beyond the Sky* (1993, Nor.), directed by Berit Nesheim. GV

ANDERSSON, Roy   Gothenburg 1943

Swedish director. Andersson started in films as a cameraman and assistant director, notably for Bo Widerberg*. His first major feature was *En kärlekshistoria/A Swedish Love Story* (1970), a gentle evocation of teenage summer love which was an instant critical and popular success. Not so the follow-up, *Giliap* (1975), the desultory story of an eponymous drifter, set in a claustrophobic hotel, which (though it had been long in the making) failed to live up to its director's grand artistic designs. Since 1976 Andersson has been best known as Sweden's leading director of commercials, picking up several awards. *Giliap*, meanwhile, has been resurrected by *cinephiles* as a cult movie, giving hope for a renewal of Andersson's feature-film career. LGA/BF

ANDONOV, Metodi   Kališče 1932 – Sofia 1974

Bulgarian director. A master of the psychological drama, Andonov is primarily known as the director of the biggest box-office hit in Bulgarian film history. After graduating from the Sofia Academy of Dramatic Art (VITIS), he directed stage productions at the Satirical Theatre for a decade before making *Bjalata staja/The White Room* (1968), based on a novel by Bogomil Rainov. This uncompromising confrontation with dogmatism in the Stalinist period won him instant recognition at home and abroad. And it was, surprisingly, approved for release in the post-'thaw' period. Andonov next directed *Njama ništo po-hubavo ot lošoto vreme/There's Nothing Finer than Bad Weather* (1971), another detective story from a screenplay by Rainov, and then the box-office hit *Kozijat rog/The Goat Horn* (1972). Seen by more than three million people during its original release, it established writer-screenwriter Nikolai Haitov* as the country's leading movie storyteller. Andonov's last film, *Goljamata skuka/The Great Boredom* (1973), was another thriller scripted by Rainov. His premature death in 1974 at the age of 42 was a major loss to Bulgarian cinema. RH

ANDRESS, Ursula   Berne 1936

Swiss-born actress, who came to international prominence as a 'Bond girl' in the first – highly successful – Bond* film, *Dr. No* (1962). Andress started her career in Rome in the mid-1950s, where she made a number of 'quickie' Italian films and married the director John Derek in 1957, a source of much speculation in the gossip press of the time. Andress' athletic and voluptuous body, and a much-reproduced bikini, was a central feature of *Dr. No*. This was the era of statuesque international stars (Raquel Welch, Anita Ekberg) as well as the rise in beach tourism, and Andress merged the two trends into one icon. Though many other actresses followed in her footsteps as Bond girls, they never made quite such a mark. Andress herself remained more or less a one-movie star, none of her subsequent films – including Philippe de Broca's *Les Tribulations d'un Chinois en Chine/Up to His Ears* (1965), co-starring Jean-Paul Belmondo* – much furthering her career. MW/GV

Other European Films Include: *What's New Pussycat* (1964, US/Fr.); *Casino Royale* (1967, UK); *Soleil rouge/Red Sun* (1971, Fr./It./Sp.); *Clash of the Titans* (1981, UK).

ANDRIEN, Jean-Jacques   Verviers 1944

Belgian director, whose films are rooted in a documentary interest in the Belgian landscape. Aware of the man-made divisions of his country, Andrien turns to the land to suggest a sense of identity, truth and origin. In his first film, *Le Fils d'Amr est mort!/Amr's Son is Dead!* (1975, winner of the Grand Prix at Locarno), the main character journeys to southern Tunisia, seeking some clue to the death of a man with whom he stole, yet about whom he knew nothing. Andrien observes the life and customs of the Tunisian people with a documentary authenticity, while retaining a distanced, panoramic view.

The gold and grey hues of Tunisia are exchanged for the green of the 'Fourons' in *Le Grand paysage d'Alexis Droeven/The Wide Horizons of Alexis Droeven* (1981), which evokes the struggles of local farmers. The impressionistic quality of both these films is created by complex soundtracks, as well as a narrative system which cuts back and forth in time. *Australia* (1989) a Belgian/French/Swiss co-production starring Jeremy Irons* and Fanny Ardant, was Andrien's first love story, retaining nevertheless his early themes and pre-occupations. CF

ANGELOPOULOS, Thodoros   Athens 1935

Greek director, scriptwriter, critic and producer. Angelopoulos grew up in Athens in the climate of the Nazi occupation and civil war. He read law at the University of Athens, then studied at IDHEC* in Paris. Expelled from the latter because of disagreements with one of his professors, he found refuge with Jean Rouch* at the Musée de l'homme. He returned to Greece in 1964, and contributed to the film journal *Synchronos Kinimatografos**.

After a short, *Ekpombi/The Broadcast* (1968), Angelopoulos's first feature, *Anaparastassi/Reconstruction* – which won awards at the Thessaloniki* Film Festival (1970), the Prix Georges Sadoul* (1971), and for best foreign film at Hyères (1971) – was an essay on life in the lesser-known Greek countryside. It is generally agreed to have inaugurated the New Greek Cinema*. *Anaparastassi* was a quest for an individual critical and dialectical narrative voice. It was followed by the 'trilogy of history': *Meres tou 36/Days of 36* (1972), *O thiassos/The Travelling Players* (1975), and *I kinigi/ The Huntsmen* (1977), all dealing with the events and political debates of twenty years of turbulent Greek history covering the Metaxas dictatorship, the civil war and its aftermath. The films engage with the cruelty and terror, the fading hopes and deep scars left by that period, as well as the defeat of the Left and its impact on activists and the Greek people as a whole. They employ cinematic forms that productively exploit silence (*Meres tou 36*), rework stage traditions, popular drama and ancient tragedy (*O thiassos*), and give shape to the worst nightmares of the bourgeoisie (*I kinigi*). The trilogy established Angelopoulos as a director of international stature, garnering awards at festivals around the world.

Megalexandros (1980) is a complex, epic work, simultaneously accepting and questioning the grandeur of history. It is a requiem for the teachings and prophecies of historical change, and represents the peak of what may be called the director's dialectical materialist period. *Megalexandros* won the Golden Lion in Venice in 1980.

Taxidi sta Kithira/Voyage to Cythera (1984) begins the eloquent 'trilogy of silence'. History leads to exile, a continuous space of silent but insistent persecution. The old man in *Taxidi sta Kithira* arrives and departs, a passer-by even in his former home. He transports his history almost wordlessly from one place of exile to another, lost in time and space. The hero of *O melissokomos/The Beekeeper* (1986) loses even more, his body and his love. His journey is accomplished in biological, ideological and spiritual silence. *Topio stin omih-*

li/Landscape in the Mist (1988) is a study of aimlessness in a mute and poignant landscape. Two children set out to go somewhere, or nowhere, in Germany. When they reach what may be the end of their journey, they understand that in this nothingness and silence they can only build and speak: they must remake the world anew. In these three films, Angelopoulos achieved his definitive filmic style. Predominantly medium or long shots function autonomously, while at the same time being actively integrated in the films' textual system. Tracking and pan shots serve the same stylistic economy, contributing to a series of intertwined, parallel or enveloping sequences. 'Dead time' and fragmented narration are other characteristics of Angelopoulos's filmic *écriture*.

To meteoro vima tou pelargou/The Suspended Stride of the Stork (1991) begins (perhaps) a third trilogy, that of the 'new world' of humanity and brotherhood. What are borders? What do they divide? Why should people not move and communicate unhindered? These are the questions the director poses and tries to answer, without substantial modification to the style that has made his reputation as one of the most important European directors of our time. NK

Bib: Nikos Kolovos, *Thodoros Angelopoulos* (1990).

Other Films: *I istoria ton Forminx/The Forminx Story* (1965, unfinished); *Horio ena, katikos enas/One Village, One Inhabitant* [TV] (1981); *Athina, epistrofi stin Akropoli/Athens, Return to the Acropolis* [TV] (1983); *To vlemma tou Odissea/ Ulysses' Gaze* (1995).

ANIMAFILM

Romanian animation studio, established in 1964 in Bucharest. The earliest animation was in the 1920s, but regular production began in 1950 as part of the new Bucharest studio, with Matty Aslan, Constantin Popescu and his son Ion Popescu-Gopo*. Following the international success of Popescu-Gopo's 'little man with the flower' in 1956, a School of Animation was created, and eventually the specialist AnimaFilm studio. Other pioneers were Olimp Varasteanu, Nell Color, Florin Angelescu and inventive puppeteer Bob Calinescu. Annual production increased from fifteen films to over sixty in the 1980s. International awards in the 1970s, for technical creativity, were won by Isabella Petrasincu's *Parada fiurilor/The Figures' Parade* (1973) and Laurentiu Sirbu's *Puiul/The Chick* (1974). Since 1966 the important biennial Mamaia Animation Festival has shown the genre's best. Internationally successful science-fiction animation, and the 'little man with the flower' style, have continued to flourish. Techniques include cut-up paper, puppetry, pixilation and computerised drawing. Animation series, mostly for television, were developed from the mid-1970s. Zoltan Szilagyi won many prizes in the 1980s, the first for *Nodul Gordian/The Gordian Knot* (1980). From 1985 there has been more concentration on feature-length films, about two a year, and popular series. Since the 1989 revolution, AnimaFilm, dominating hard currency earnings from foreign sales, has been the only relatively viable part of the industry in Romania. Its break from the bureaucratic state monopoly and entry into joint ventures with Spanish-based Dale Multibrook (1991) have resulted in the importation of much-needed modern technology. MM

Bib: *Romanian Animation Films* (1966–84).

ANIMATION

Animation films have been made throughout Europe since the very early days of the cinema. Information will be found under national entries, as well as under individual film-maker's entries (e.g. Emile Cohl*), together with the texts below which focus on Belgium, Czechoslovakia, Denmark and Poland.

Belgium

For a country with a strong pictorial tradition, in terms of both painting and strip-cartoons, it seems appropriate that one of Belgium's most fruitful products has been the animation film, centring primarily on cartoon techniques. For many, the earliest cartoonist was the painter Madou, who, while Joseph Plateau* was discovering cinematography, was painting his characters directly on to revolving discs. From 1928 to 1930 Joseph Houssiau and his son produced several cartoons, including *Fantaisie Macabre* (1930) with Charles Conrad. Conrad also attempted the first colour cartoon, but never finished his work.

It was, ironically, in occupied Belgium in the 1940s that animation flourished for the first time: it needed limited resources, and American animated films were banned. Three studios were created, of which Boitsfort, owned by perhaps the first woman of Belgian animation, Claude Misonne, was one of the most successful. Misonne is remembered for two main achievements: her puppet/marionette films, which preceded the work of the Czech masters, and her feature-length film *Tintin et le crabe aux pinces d'or/Tintin and the Crab with the Golden Claws* (1946), which was the first to bring Hergé's now famous strip-cartoon to life. Unfortunately the pioneering efforts of all three studios were wiped out by the Gestapo, freak fires or bankruptcy.

The first Belgian feature-length cartoon, *Pinocchio dans l'espace/Pinocchio in Space* (1965), was directed by Ray Goossens, who in 1959 had become production manager at Belvision Studios (founded by Raymond Leblanc), one of Belgium's biggest animation outlets. It was Belvision who signed some of the first co-production agreements with French television, which led to serialisations of *Tintin* and *Les Schtroumpfs* (1961, by Peyo, successfully marketed in America as *The Smurfs*). The public release of feature-length cartoons of Asterix, also made by Belvision, confirmed the transition of Belgian animation from a selective art form to a commercially viable industry which successfully exported, especially to the US.

The 1960s marked a turning point in Belgian animation, with the introduction of state subsidies. Meanwhile the appearance of such figures as Eddy Ryssack, Jean Coignon and Belgium's most famous animator Raoul Servais* lifted Belgian animation out of its 'Disney phase' towards more original works. Proper training was instigated, with courses in Brussels and Ghent, producing a new generation of Belgian

animators. The conventional family audience for cartoons was challenged by Picha (Jean-Paul Walravens). His first film, *Tarzoon la honte de la Jungle/Tarzan Shame of the Jungle* (1975), introduced sex, violence and black comedy, to which he added political satire in *Le Big Bang* (1987).

To the auteurist vision of Raoul Servais should be added the name of Gerald Frydman, whose first film *Scarabus* (1971) won several prizes. Frydman's surrealist collages combine photo-animation with live action, using a black humour which recalls Magritte. Belgian animation won its first Oscar in 1987, for Nicole Van Goethem's short *Een Griekse Tragedie/Une tragédie grecque/A Greek Tragedy* (1985). CF

Czechoslovakia

Czechoslovak animation dates back to the 1920s but first attracted international attention when Karel Dodal's work was shown at the 1937 Paris Exhibition. His best known film was *Hra bublinek/The Bubble Game* (1936), a colour animation advertising Sapona soap, which featured abstract design and recalls Len Lye's* work for the GPO Film Unit. Dodal's assistant, Hermína Týrlová, made her debut as a puppet film-maker with *Ferda mravenec/Ferda and the Ants* (1942), beginning a long career in which she worked exclusively on children's films. Týrlová, and others working at the Baťa film studios at Zlín (later Gottwaldov, now Zlín again), were to provide the basis of the postwar development of Czech animation. It was, however, the nationalisation of the industry in August 1945 that laid the foundations for major developments. The leading figures were Jiří Trnka* and Karel Zeman*, both of whom made cartoon and puppet films, and carried off the main prizes for these categories at the first Cannes festival in 1946. Already well established before the Communist takeover of 1948, animation continued to flourish in the 1950s when mainstream cinema was subject to the restrictions of Socialist Realism*. The success of Trnka's *Císařův slavík/The Emperor's Nightingale* (1948) and *Staré pověsti české/Old Czech Legends* (1953), and of Zeman's *Cesta do pravěku/A Journey to Primeval Times* (1955) and *Vynález skázy/An Invention for Destruction* (1958), established Czech animated features as the principal alternative to the Disney tradition. While its public image was overshadowed by the Czech New Wave* in the 1960s, animation continued to make a striking impact, with Zeman making features through to the 1970s. Trnka's former assistants, Břetislav Pojar and Stanislav Látal, also established themselves in the area of puppet film. Among many other outstanding film-makers to emerge from the Czech studios were Jiří Brdečka, Václav Bedřich, Zdeněk Miler (best known for his delightful 'Mole' series) and the trio of Jaroslav Doubrava, Adolf Born and Miloš Macourek, who produced some of the most acute and acerbic short films of the 1980s. The pioneer of Slovak animation, Viktor Kubal, made the first two Slovak animated features, *Zbojník Jurko/Jurko the Outlaw* (1976) and *Krvavá paní/Bloody Lady* (1980).

The outstanding figure of the past twenty years has been Jan Švankmajer*, although official disapproval ensured only limited exhibition of his films in Czechoslovakia. His disturbing visions won acclaim at festivals from the late 1970s and his films have become a major international influence. A new generation of animators began to emerge in the 1980s, including Jiří Barta, Pavel Koutský and Igor Ševčík. Barta's work in puppet film has gained him an international following, especially with *Zaniklý svět rukavic/The Extinct World of Gloves* (1982), an elaborate satire on film genres, and his feature *Krysař/The Pied Piper* (1986), which uses carved walnut puppets. PH

Denmark

The first Danish animation film was *Meningen er god nok/The Intention is Good Enough*, made by the painter Sven Brasch (1886–1970) in 1919. Almost simultaneously, the actor, painter and cartoonist Robert Storm-Petersen shot his first nine-minute fiction animation from his own popular comic strip, *De tre smaa Mænd/The Three Little Men*. In the next few years 'Storm-P' made a series of short animation films, some of them for publicity purposes. His style was naive but charming; unfortunately his career was ended by technical problems. Others followed in his footsteps, however; one-minute commercials were made from the late 1920s, such as the 'Skibsted cartoons'. In 1943–44 Henning Dahl-Mikkelsen made two black-and-white films based on his comic strip 'Ferdinand'.

The first feature-length colour animation film was *Fyrtøjet/The Tinder Box* (1946), directed by Svend Methling from the Andersen fairy tale. The following year Jørgen Roos* and the painter Søren Melson collaborated on a so-called *ridsefilm* (scratch film) with images drawn directly on celluloid, entitled *Opus One*. Bent Barfod made his name with *Noget om Norden/Something about the Nordic Countries* (1956) and soon established an animation 'factory' where many budding film-makers learned the techniques. Other films by Barfod include *Ballet-Ballade* (1963) in black and white and, in colour, *Solen er rød/The Sun is Red* (1973). Jannik Hastrup began his career as an independent with *Jazzens Historie* (1959) and came to prominence with the twelve so-called 'Cirkeline films' from 1968 to 1970. With Flemming Quist Møller he shot *Concerto Erotica* (1964) and the 45-minute *Bennys badekar/Benny's Bathtub,* one of the best Danish colour animations. In the 1970s Hastrup made political animation films such as *Historiebogen/The History Book* (1972) and *Trællenes Oprør/The Revolt of the Thralls* (1979), and, in 1984, *Samson og Sally/The Song of the Whales* (the last two are features). Peter Madsen and Jeffrey J. Varab made a colour feature, *Valhalla* in 1980 (released in 1986), after a cartoon series based on popular legend. In 1993 Anders Sørensen and Hans Perk directed the two-part *Verdenshistorien/The History of the World*, aimed at children.

The puppet film is represented by the work of Jørgen Vestergaard. Most of his films were made for Danish television and most are based on Andersen's fairy tales. One of the best known is *Skyggen/The Shadow* (1975). ME

Poland

Poland boasts one of the great pioneers of animation, Władysław Starewicz*, whose work, made in Russia, Lithuania and France and using a mixture of model animation, live action and drawing, is bizarre, witty and inventive. In Poland itself animation work dates from the establishment of the Experimental Cartoon Film Studio in Katowice in 1947, which moved to Bielsko Biała in 1956.

Until the mid-1950s most Polish animation was geared to the children's market. With the political changes in 1956, animators such as Witold Giersz began to make the satirical, surreal and politically coded animated films associated with Eastern Europe. Giersz's *Mały Western/Little Western* (1960) and *Czerwone i Czarne/Red and Black* (1963) gained several international awards. In the late 1950s, Jan Lenica* and Walerian Borowczyk* worked together on several shorts, using collage and photo-montage techniques. Borowczyk later moved to live-action films but Lenica, known also for his poster designs, continued to animate. His *Labirynt/Labyrinth* (1963) is a post-modern vision of the Icarus myth set in an eerie city inhabited by monstrous beings.

In the late 1970s and 1980s the work of Jerzy Kucia from the Krakow unit and Zbigniew Rybczyński* from Se Ma For Studios was especially noted. The surreal films of Piotr Dumała, such as *Wolność Nogi/The Freedom of the Leg* (1990) and *Franz Kafka* (1991), have attracted international attention. Dumała works as an independent, financing his own films and studio by working for the expanding commercial market. With large and well-staffed animation studios, Poland, like other Eastern European countries, is increasingly used as a cheap production partner for Western animation productions. Although many studios are closing down with the advent of the free market, others are forming partnerships with larger, foreign companies. AW

ANKERSTJERNE, Johan   Randers 1886 – Copenhagen 1959

Danish cinematographer, who began his career as a watchmaker. After becoming a projectionist in 1907 he began shooting small reportage films. Hired by the expanding Nordisk Films* in 1911, Ankerstjerne soon became August Blom's* favourite cinematographer. He worked at Nordisk until 1915, when he left to work on *Hævnens Nat/The Night of Revenge* (1916), directed by Benjamin Christensen*. From 1917 to 1921 he was chief cameraman at Dansk Films , and in 1921 was again hired by Christensen to work on *Häxan/Witchcraft Through the Ages* (1922). He remained at Nordisk from 1923 to 1931 as chief technical adviser before leaving to start his own film developing laboratory, which he ran until his death.

Ankerstjerne was the most talented cinematographer of Danish silent cinema. The side-lighting for which these films are famous was largely his creation. His talent for exploiting the whole range of tones from black to white is seen in August Blom's* major film, *Atlantis* (1913). The chiaroscuro effects in *Häxan* are also remarkable. ME

Other Films Include: *Gar el Hama/A Dead Man's Child* (1911); *Bristet Lykke/A Paradise Lost* (1913); *Verdens Undergang/The End of the World* (1916); *Pigen fra Palls/The Girl from Whitley* (1917).

ANNABELLA   Suzanne Charpentier; Paris 1909

French actress. Annabella was the biggest female French star of the early and mid-1930s. She appeared in Abel Gance's* *Napoléon* (1927) and Jean Grémillon's* *Maldone* (1928), but her fame came from two René Clair* films, *Le Million* (1931)

and *Quatorze juillet* (1932). She starred in European productions made in Britain, Germany, Hungary (Paul Féjos' *Tavaszi zapor/Marie légende hongroise*, 1932) and Austria (Féjos' *Sonnenstrahl/Gardez le sourire*, 1933). In France, she was the star of popular comedies, such as *Paris-Méditerranée* (1931, co-starring her husband Jean Murat), and melodramas like Anatole Litvak's* *L'Equipage* (1935). She was one of the few French stars invited to Hollywood who actually made films there, in particular Allan Dwan's *Suez* (1938; she subsequently married her co-star, Tyrone Power) and Henry Hathaway's *13 Rue Madeleine* (1946). She appeared as an 'Arab' woman in Julien Duvivier's* *La Bandera* (1935) and as the doomed lover in Marcel Carné's* *Hôtel du Nord* (1938). Petite and delicately pretty, Annabella embodied shy and sentimental heroines, epitomising – especially in the Clair films – a romantic type close to the operatic *midinette*. Such a screen persona did not age well, and her career quickly declined after the war. GV

ANNAUD, Jean-Jacques   Juvisy-sur-Orge 1943

French director, one of the few truly international French film-makers. A graduate of IDHEC*, Annaud had a highly successful career in commercials before his first feature, *La Victoire en chantant/Black and White in Colour* (1976, Fr./Ger.), a sardonic view of colonialism, won an Oscar for Best Foreign Film in 1977. After *Coup de tête* (1979), he moved on to large budgets and spectacular *mise-en-scène*, with *La Guerre du feu/Quest for Fire* (1981, Fr./Canada), *Le Nom de la rose/Der Name der Rose/The Name of the Rose* (1986, based on Umberto Eco's novel) and *L'Ours/The Bear* (1988). *L'Amant/The Lover* (1991), from Marguerite Duras' novel aroused controversy for its 'betrayal' of Duras, its glossy orientalism and, not least, its use of the English language. It encapsulates the Annaud paradox: low critical esteem (Serge Daney called Annaud a 'post-film-maker'), but huge commercial success in France and abroad. GV

ANSORGE, Ernest   Lausanne 1925

Swiss director and co-founder of the Swiss Animated Film Group (1968). Ansorge studied mechanical engineering at the Lausanne Institute of Technology but in 1958 began to work on film, especially on animation films in collaboration with his wife Gisèle (1923–93), who co-wrote their scripts. In 1959 he produced a glossary on animation techniques, *Techniques du film d'animation,* and two short documentary portraits made with the Lausanne University Psychiatric Clinic film group: *Sonnenstern, le Moralunaire/Friedrich Schröder – Sonnenstern* (1964), and *Jessica N.* (1965). His international recognition came with three films which genuinely explored new territory in animation with their inventive use of black and white, and later colour: *Les Corbeaux/The Ravens* (1968), which evokes the hunting and hanging of a man who tries to live on the fringes of society; *Fantasmatic* (1969), an intriguing visualisation of male fantasies and obsessions from childhood to maturity; and *Alunissons/Off to the Moon* (1970), about a couple's three-minute trip to the moon. In his only feature film, *D'un jour à l'autre/From One Day to the Next*

(1973), an unhappy love story between a young Swiss researcher and a lackadaisical English hippie, Ansorge turned a rather conventional *amour fou* tale into an engaging meditation on cultural, national and sexual differences, exemplifying a degree of abstraction that marks most of his work. MW

Other Films Include: *Tempus* (1970); *Smile 1+2+3* (1975); *Anima* (1977); *Das Veilchen* (1982); *Les Enfants de laine* (1984); *Le Petit garçon qui vola la lune* (1989); *Sabbat* (1990); *Alchemia* (1991).

ANSTEY, Edgar   Watford 1907 – London 1987

British director/producer, who joined John Grierson's* documentary unit at the Empire Marketing Board in 1931. His most significant contribution was *Housing Problems* (1935), co-produced with Arthur Elton, and with Ruby Grierson, Grierson's sister, directing the to-camera interviews which gave the film its distinctive innovation. A similar approach was adopted in *Enough to Eat?* (1936), a documentary on malnutrition. Anstey was associated with the *March of Time* documentaries in New York and London from 1937 to 1939, and with propaganda documentaries during the war. He established the British Transport Film Unit in 1949, and used it as a documentary training unit until his retirement in 1974. JC

Bib: Elizabeth Sussex, 'Basil Wright and Edgar Anstey', *Sight and Sound* (Winter 1987/88).

ANTEL, Franz   François Legrand; Vienna 1913

Austrian director and producer. Antel started out in the 1930s as production supervisor at Wien-Film, working with directors such as E. W. Emo and Arthur Maria Rabenalt*. He directed his first feature, *Das singende Haus*, in 1948. From the 1950s onwards his films were hugely popular, among them classics such as *Hallo Dienstmann* (1952), starring Hans Moser* and Paul Hörbiger*, *Spionage* (1955), and the remake of Erik Charell's *Der Kongress tanzt/The Congress Dances* (1955). The decline of the Austrian film industry in the 1960s obliged Antel to work with German and Italian producers. He turned to recycling some of his own works, directing (very) light comedies and soft-porn movies, such as the *Wirtinnen* series (1967–73). A craftsman who sees his task as entertaining a mass audience, Antel has been criticised for making 'superficial' and overtly commercial films. But *Der Bockerer* (1981) revealed the other side of his populism: set in the period of the *Anschluss* (1938–45), the film is a telling portrait of the era, centred on a character who resists Nazism with a mixture of stubbornness, humour and sarcasm. IR

Bib: Franz Antel, *Großaufnahme. Mein verdrehtes, verliebtes Leben* (1988).

Other Films Include: *Der alte Sünder* (1951); *Lumpazivagabundus* (1956); *Liebesgrüße aus Tirol* (1964); *Außer Rand und Band am Wolfgangsee* (1971, Aust./Ger.); *Die lustigen Vier von der Tankstelle* (1972, Aust./Ger.); *Casanova u. Co./Treize femmes pour Casanova/Casanova e &* (1977, Aust./Ger./Fr./It.).

ANTOINE, André   Limoges 1858 – Le Pouliguen 1943

French director. A great pioneer of French theatre, founder of the Théâtre Libre in 1897, where he applied principles of literary naturalism. Signed on by SCAGL (Société cinématographique des auteurs et gens de lettres) in 1914, he directed *Les Frères corses/The Corsican Brothers* (based on Alexandre Dumas) in 1917, and directed nine films altogether, mostly adaptations of novels (Victor Hugo, Emile Zola) and plays. *L'Hirondelle et la mésange/The Swallow and the Bluetit*, from an original script, was shot in 1920–21 on a barge in Belgium and northern France. A disappointed SCAGL left it unfinished; it was rediscovered by the Cinémathèque française* in 1982 and re-released in 1983. Its use of locations, canal-side milieux and a blend of actors and non-professionals make it a key work in early realist French cinema. Between 1924 and 1940 Antoine was theatre and film critic for a number of publications, including *Le Journal* and *Comœdia*. GV

ANTONIONI, Michelangelo   Ferrara 1912

Italian director. Italy's foremost modernist *auteur*, Antonioni made a successful transition from postwar realism to an abstract, formalist style which embodied his characters' increasingly alienated and dehumanised world view.

Antonioni graduated from the University of Bologna with a degree in economics and business before becoming a film critic for the newspaper *Corriere Padano*. In l939 he moved to Rome, joined the editorial staff of the journal *Cinema*, and studied film-making at the Centro Sperimentale* for three months. After collaborating on the screenplay of Roberto Rossellini's* *Un pilota ritorna* (1942), he travelled to Paris to assist Marcel Carné* on *Les Visiteurs du soir* (1942). Upon his return, the agency LUCE* commissioned a documentary on the Po valley (*Gente del Po*, begun in 1943 but not completed until 1947 because of Fascist censorship and wartime interruptions). Antonioni's immediate postwar activities included critical writing, collaboration on screenplays (Giuseppe De Santis'* *Caccia tragica/Tragic Hunt*, 1947, Federico Fellini's* *Lo sceicco bianco/The White Sheik*, 1952) and the shooting of documentaries (*N.U./Nettezza urbana*, 1948, and *L'amorosa menzogna*, 1949). His first feature, *Cronaca di un amore/Story of a Love Affair* (1950), was a conventional story of adultery and intended murder, distinguished by Antonioni's attention to formal values. His next work, a film in three episodes entitled *I vinti/The Vanquished* (1952), incurred the wrath of government censors for its unflinching treatment of drug and crime problems among postwar youth in France, Italy and Britain. In *La signora senza camelie/The Lady Without Camelias* (1953) Antonioni criticised the Italian film industry for its exploitation of women, while Turin high society became his target in *Le amiche/The Girlfriends* (1955, based on Cesare Pavese). *Il grido/The Cry* (1957), his only film with working-class characters, followed its protagonist's desperate odyssey through the film-maker's native Po valley landscape.

Antonioni's *L'avventura*, along with Fellini's *La dolce vita* (both 1960), marked the birth of a new, anti-conventional film language and disjointed narrative structure homologous to the radically altered conditions of Italian life. *L'avventura* inaugurated Antonioni's exploration of the moral and emotional bankruptcy of the bourgeois condition, the difficulty (if not impossibility) of personal intimacy and the individual's increasing alienation from social and natural contexts. It was followed by *La notte/The Night* (1961), *L'eclisse/The Eclipse* (1962) and *Deserto rosso/The Red Desert* (1964). Through Monica Vitti's* intelligent performances in these films, Antonioni focused on the crisis of women in the midst of failed love relationships and non-sustaining social environments. Antonioni's use of *rosso* (red) in the title of *Deserto rosso*, his first colour film, called attention to his aggressive, non-naturalistic colour technique in representing industrialised Ravenna.

Blowup (1966, UK/It.) marked the beginning of Antonioni's international phase. From 1967 to 1982 he filmed outside Italy and his concerns became increasingly abstract and universal. Set in the fashionable London of the mid-1960s, *Blowup* reflected on the knowability and representability of 'the real'. *Zabriskie Point* (1969, US), shot in California, was his attempt to fathom American counter-culture and find a revolutionary film language to represent it. *Professione: Reporter/The Passenger* (1975), the story of a journalist (Jack Nicholson) who impulsively takes on someone else's identity only to learn that his new 'self' was a gun-runner caught in a death trap, raised questions of identity, destiny and the relationship of the mass media to lived experience. Returning to his roots as a documentarist in 1972, Antonioni shot *Chung-Kuo Cina*, a RAI*-sponsored film on China, critically acclaimed in the West but reviled by the Chinese authorities as subversive of official photographic etiquette. Experiments with visual effects and colour culminated in *Il mistero di Oberwald/The Oberwald Mystery* (1980), an adaptation of a Cocteau play starring Vitti and featuring the latest video and laser technology. Antonioni's most recent feature (to date) is *Identificazione di una donna/Identification of a Woman* (1982), a reworking of earlier concerns with bourgeois crisis and the impossible quest for intimacy. Plagued by ill-health, Antonioni was not able to complete several projects, but his career has received widespread recognition, including lifetime achievement awards at film festivals in Taormina (1981), Cannes (1982) and Venice (1983), and most recently an Oscar (1995). MMo

Bib: Sam Rohdie, *Antonioni* (1990).

Other Films: **Documentaries**: *Superstizione, Sette canne, un vestito* (1949); *La funivia del Faloria, La villa dei mostri* (1950); *Kumbha Mela* (1989); *Roma* (1990). **Features**: *Amore in città/Love in the City* (1953, ep., *Tentato suicidio*); *I tre volti/Three Times* (1965, ep. *Il provino*).

APARICIO, Rafaela   Rafaela Díaz Valiente; Marbella 1906

Spanish actress, who began in the theatre, in straight plays and musicals. She made over a hundred films, most of them for popular directors like Mariano Ozores* and Pedro Lazaga*. Her diminutive, roly-poly shape and shrill voice destined her for stereotypical maiden aunts and mothers-in-law.

Yet an element of eccentricity in her characteristically self-contained poses also attracted a number of *auteurs* who adapted the caricatural features of her persona. In this mode she is remembered, above all, for her roles in Victor Erice's* *El Sur/The South* (1983), Fernán Gómez's *La vida por delante/Life Ahead* (1958) and *El extraño viaje/Strange Journey* (1964), and Carlos Saura's* *Ana y los lobos/Ana and the Wolves* (1972) and *Mamá cumple cien años/Mum's a Hundred Years Old* (1979). In the Saura films her performance as the slightly demented mother of deranged, violent sons was used to symbolise the colonisation of Spain by the repressive mechanisms of Francoism. PWE

ARANDA, Vicente
Vicente Aranda Ezquerra;
Barcelona 1926

Spanish director, mainly identified with adaptations of novels by Juan Marsé, such as *Si te dicen que caí/If They Tell You I've Fallen* (1989) and *El amante bilingüe/The Bilingual Lover* (1993). Aranda began as a founder-member of the Barcelona School*. Under Franco, his films, for instance *Fata Morgana/Morgan le Fay* (1966), were codedly politicised, increasingly so after the collapse of the regime. In most of his work the memory traces of Francoism appear to endure. In *La muchacha de las bragas de oro/The Girl with the Golden Panties* (1980), for instance, a Falangist character accommodates himself to the new democratic realities, in the process becoming someone to whom others significantly grow reconciled. In *Tiempo de silencio/Time of Silence* (1986), Aranda's uncompromising treatment of social issues is inspired by Martín Santos's great novel about government failure, individual loss of responsiblity, and urban poverty. *El Lute, camina o revienta/El Lute, Walk or Die* (1987) and *El Lute II* (1988), based on the true story of a famous criminal, deal with ethnic minorities, avoiding the banalities of pre-democratic representations. Imanol Arias* as El Lute to a certain extent romanticises the role, but the exploration of the rougher edges of Spanish society pulls no punches. Aranda's films, often starring Victoria Abril*, are also characterised by a highly charged treatment of sexuality. For instance, in *Amantes/Lovers* (1990), Abril drives her young lover to steal from and murder his fiancée. *Amour fou* is also a feature of *El amante bilingüe*, where a pattern of doubles extends to questions about the meaning of nationalism – its ironised as well as its more serious sides – in modern-day Spain. PWE

Bib: José Luis Guarner and Peter Besas, *El inquietante cine de Vicente Aranda* (1985).

ARBEITERFILME

German film 'genre' (meaning 'Proletarian films'). In 1922 the distribution of Soviet proletarian films in Germany caused a demand among leftist intellectuals such as Béla Balázs* for an alternative to the dominant capitalist film ideology promoted by Ufa*. The successful German release of S. M. Eisenstein's* *Bronenosets Potëmkin/The Battleship Potemkin* in 1926 provided further ammunition. Between 1926 and 1931, the Prometheus Film company produced powerful fiction films with a revolutionary perspective, attracting substantial critical and popular acclaim; titles include *Eins + Eins = Drei* (Béla Balázs*, 1927), and two classics, *Mutter Krausens Fahrt ins Glück/Mother Krause's Journey to Happiness* (Piel Jutzi, 1929 [> STRASSENFILME]) and *Kuhle Wampe oder Wem gehört die Welt?/Kuhle Wampe* (Bertolt Brecht/Slatan Dudow, 1932), which demonstrate the class aspect of social conflicts through a critical use of documentary material and distancing intertitles. The cultural heritage of the proletarian film was taken up in the mid-1950s in the GDR, beginning with Dudow's *Stärker als die Nacht/Stronger than the Night* (1954). In the Federal Republic, some films by, among others, Rainer Werner Fassbinder*, Christian Ziewer* and Helke Sander* represented a reworking of the realist aesthetics of the *Arbeiterfilm* tradition in the context of television genres such as soap opera or semi-documentary. MW

Bib: Bruce Murray, *Film and the German Left in the Weimar Republic: From Caligari to Kuhle Wampe* (1981).

ARDMORE STUDIOS

Irish film studios. Ardmore (near Dublin, a three-stage studio), was established in 1958 with a mixture of private and state capital. Its initial policy of adapting Abbey Theatre plays as films quickly gave way to a policy of encouraging foreign producers to make films at the studios. Productions based there have included *Shake Hands With the Devil* (1959), *A Terrible Beauty* (1960) and *Excalibur* (1981; made during the time director John Boorman* was the studios' chairman). The use of state funding to subsidise Ardmore while under state ownership during 1975–82 was a major target in the campaign for an indigenous Irish cinema by independent film-makers, which led to the setting up of the Irish Film Board*. No state funds have been allocated to Ardmore since 1982. KR

ARGENTINA, Imperio
Magdalena Nile del Río;
Buenos Aires, Argentina 1906

Spanish actress and singer of Argentinian origins, one of the few popular stars of the prewar Spanish cinema. 'Petite Imperio' was popular throughout Spain and Latin America as a child performer before making a highly successful series of films with her first husband Florián Rey*, such as *La hermana San Sulpicio/Sister San Sulpicio* (1927 silent, 1934 sound), *Nobleza baturra/Aragonese Virtue* (1935), *Morena clara/Dark and Bright* (1936) and *La canción de Aixa/The Song of Aixa* (1939), as well as Paramount productions shot at the Paris Joinville Studios (such as Robert Florey's *L'Amour chante*, 1930). The evocative nostalgia of her most celebrated songs has been used to pertinent effect by José Luis Borau* in *Tata mía/Dear Nanny* (1986). MD

ARGENTO, Dario
Rome 1940

Italian director, son of producer Salvatore Argento and Brazilian photographer Elda Luxardo. After an abortive start

17

as a film critic for the Roman daily *Paese Sera*, Argento started working as a scriptwriter, collaborating with Bernardo Bertolucci* and director Sergio Leone* on the writing of *C'era una volta il West/Once Upon a Time in the West* (1968). His directorial debut came in 1970 with *L'uccello dalle piume di cristallo/The Gallery Murders*, a tense and realistic thriller which achieved unexpected public success. The subsequent *Il gatto a nove code/The Cat o' Nine Tails* (1971), *Quattro mosche di velluto grigio/Four Flies on Grey Velvet* (1971), *Le cinque giornate/Five Days* (1973) and *Profondo rosso/Deep Red* (1975) confirmed Argento's visionary talent and contributed to a revival of the Italian horror* B-movie tradition, marked by excess and violence. A turning point came with *Suspiria* (1977) in which the gradual eruption of horror and breakdown of narrative logic prepared the ground for the baroque fantasies and lurid neo-gothic delirium of *Inferno/Hell* (1979), *Tenebre/Unsane* (1982), *Phenomena/Creepers* (1985) and *Opera* (1987). Argento also worked as a producer for young Italian directors in the horror genre inspired by his example (Lamberto Bava, Michele Soavi) and helped his American friend George A. Romero, maker of *Zombi* (1978), with whom he directed *Due occhi diabolici/Two Diabolical Eyes* (1990), a two-part film based on tales by Edgar Allan Poe (Argento's part was called *Il gatto nero/The Black Cat*). With *Trauma* (1993), shot in the US with his daughter Asia in a starring role, he returned to the thriller atmosphere of his early films. The outcome, however, was largely disappointing and confirmed that bloodthirsty and irrational horror is indeed the only genre which really suits him. GC

ARIAS, Imanol   Manuel Arias Domínguez; Riaño, León 1956

Spanish actor, regarded as one of the genuine sex symbols of the contemporary Spanish cinema. Achieving critical success at Madrid's Centro Dramático Nacional in the 1970s, Arias went on to work extensively in cinema and television, receiving popular acclaim for his performances in such television series as *Anillos de oro/Golden Rings* (1983) and *Brigada central/Central Brigade* (1989), as well as critical respect for his collaborations with directors like Imanol Uribe*, Mario Camús*, Pedro Almodóvar*, and especially Vicente Aranda*, with whom he has made five films to date. Habitually cast in outsider roles, where he appears ill at ease within the constraints of Spanish machismo, Arias offered an alternative perspective on male identities in 1980s and 1990s Spanish cinema. As the Robin Hood-like renegade in Aranda's *El Lute, camina o revienta/El Lute, Walk or Die* (1987) and *El Lute II* (1988), Arias provided a complex interpretation of an elusive object of desire on whom the film's oppressed populace could project their fantasies and hopes for a free Spain. Although he has not achieved the international stature of his contemporary Antonio Banderas*, his swarthy classical looks have made him an attractive export, and his sensitive portrait of a tortured priest in Maria Luisa Bemberg's *Camila* (1983) generated Hollywood interest in his elusive, vulnerable yet always mesmeric persona. MD

ARLETTY   Léonie Bathiat; Courbevoie 1898 – Paris 1992

French actress. In the pantheon of film culture, Arletty has her place as the heroine of two wartime classics by Marcel Carné* and Jacques Prévert*: *Les Visiteurs du soir* (1942) and, especially, *Les Enfants du paradis* (1943–45), in which as Garance she achieves a rare combination of romantic beauty and humour. While her wit and accent locate her as unmistakably working-class and Parisian, her performance owed much to her early career in music hall and boulevard theatre. Her 1930s film career was mainly in comedy: in the popular classic *Hôtel du Nord* (1938), she and Louis Jouvet outclassed Annabella* and Jean-Pierre Aumont, the romantic leads. Similarly, in *Le Jour se lève* (1939), a classic of Poetic Realism*, she was more of a match for Jean Gabin* than the bland Jacqueline Laurent. Despite her spirited defence that 'my heart is French but my body is international', her career suffered badly because of her wartime liaison with a German officer, though she went on to make a few films, including Jacqueline Audry's* *Huis-clos* (1954) and the underrated *L'Air de Paris* (1954, dir. Marcel Carné). She also acted on stage until blindness forced her to retire in the 1960s.

If Arletty rarely got the top billing she deserved in her films, the impact of her performances, full of heart and wisecracks, ensured her place as one of the great populist stars of French cinema. GV

Bib: Arletty, *La Défense* (1971).

Other Films Include: *Pension Mimosas* (1934); *La Garçonne* (1936); *Les Perles de la couronne, Désiré* (1937); *Fric-Frac, Circonstances atténuantes* (1939); *Madame Sans-Gêne* (1941); *Le Grand jeu* (1954).

ARMIÑÁN, Jaime de   Jaime de Armiñán Oliver; Madrid 1927

Spanish director, a scriptwriter and director of television as well as feature films, whose work is concerned with the emotional and psychological effects of repression. Armiñán's most notable films are *El amor del Capitán Brando/The Love of Captain Brando* (1974) and *El nido/The Nest* (1980). One of the first films to explore the possibility of screen nudity under the cosmetic easing of censorship laws in the 1970s, and echoing the pre-transitional preoccupation with change, *El amor del Capitán Brando* comments on the intolerance of a rural Castilian community faced with a progressive schoolteacher who champions sexual education for her pupils. The process of maturation for the lovestruck pupil, Juan, points allegorically to the atmosphere of a nation poised at the end of dictatorship and the beginning of a period of transition to democracy. Oedipal undercurrents are even more obviously present in *El nido*, which explores the sinister effects of repression on a rebellious young girl. The film relates the tragic consequences of the girl's manipulation of a middle-aged man, shot dead by real bullets as he fires blanks at a policeman at the behest of his adolescent paramour. RM

Other Films Include: *Mi querida señorita/My Dearest Señorita* (1971); *Stico* (1984); *La hora bruja/The Witching Hour* (1985); *Mi general/General* (1987).

ARNHEIM, Rudolf   Berlin 1904

German film theorist. One of the most prominent exponents of the anti-realist tendency in film aesthetics, Arnheim saw film less as an optical-mechanical reproduction process than as an autonomous art form translating reality into significant forms (colour, shape, size, density, brightness), through which all human perception of natural phenomena takes place. While still a psychology student, he became a member of the editorial board of *Die Weltbühne* in the late 1920s, in which the seventy articles at the core of his 1932 *Film als Kunst* (in English: *Film*, 1933) first appeared, forming the basis of his theory of the cinema. In August 1933, after the book was banned by the Nazi authorities, Arnheim left Germany for Italy and eventually emigrated to the US. Though film was no longer at the centre of his interests, he frequently reaffirmed his belief in his earlier ideas. First at Harvard, then at Ann Arbor, he has remained a prolific writer on aesthetics (*Art and Visual Perception*, 1954; *Visual Thinking*, 1969; *The Power of the Center: A Study in Composition of the Visual Arts*, 1982). MW

Bib: Dudley Andrew, *The Major Film Theories: An Introduction* (1976).

ARNOLD, Malcolm   Northampton 1921

British composer, whose best-known work was on *The Bridge on the River Kwai* (1957), a score which won him an Academy Award. Arnold had previously scored *The Sound Barrier* (1952) and *Hobson's Choice* (1954) for David Lean*, varying the tempo with the 'St. Trinian's' films for Launder and Gilliat*. He has around fifty distinguished British films to his credit, and is the composer of a number of orchestral works, including incidental music for ballet and theatre. JC

ASHCROFT, (Dame) Peggy   Croydon 1907 – London 1991

British actress, who made her London stage debut in 1927, and was the leading theatrical dame for more than half a century. Unlike the triumvirate of theatrical knights – John Gielgud*, Laurence Olivier*, Ralph Richardson* – Ashcroft made very few films. She made her debut in *The Wandering Jew* (1933) and had a cameo role in Hitchcock's* *The 39 Steps* (1935), but during the 'golden years' of the 1940s and 1950s, when men were being men, she concentrated on her stage career. It was in the 1980s (and her seventies) that her strength as a supporting actress on screen became widely recognised, first on television and then in the cinema. Her Barbie in *The Jewel in the Crown* (Granada, 1984) was one of the understated delights of British acting, and her Oscar for Best Supporting Actress for *A Passage to India* (1985) was only

surprising because it was not clear who she was supporting. JC

Other Films Include: *Quiet Wedding* (1941); *The Nun's Story* (1958, US); *Secret Ceremony* (1968); *Sunday Bloody Sunday* (1971); *Der Fussgänger/The Pedestrian* (1974, Ger./Switz).

ASKOLDOV, Alexander   Moscow 1932

Russian director. Askoldov's parents were arrested in 1937 and his father shot. After studying in the Philological Faculty of Moscow University, Askoldov took courses in direction and scriptwriting in 1964–65. His only feature is *Komissar/ The Commissar* (1967), a film shelved until 1987. Work on the script, based on Vasili Grossman's 1934 short story 'In the Town of Berdichev', began in 1965, and *Komissar* was planned as one of a number of films that would look back at the revolutionary period in time for its fiftieth anniversary. But with its pregnant female commissar, the film could never be a conventional paean to the new era, and Askoldov's treatment, which stressed the joys and humanity of the Jewish family at the centre of the film, caused repeated interventions from censorship. After the victory of Israel in the 1967 Six Day War, the film's fate was sealed. Askoldov's intransigence over attempts to get him to alter his film led to the end of his film career and dismissal from the Communist Party. During the late 1970s and early 1980s he directed experimental musical theatre. The film was finally shown after Askoldov's intervention at a press conference during the 1987 Moscow Film Festival. With a remarkable central performance by Nonna Mordyukova, and stunning black and white photography that evokes Sergei Eisenstein* and Alexander Dovzhenko*, *Komissar* has at last achieved the recognition it merits. JGf

ASQUITH, Anthony   London 1902–68

British director. Son of Lord Herbert Asquith, the Liberal Prime Minister, and educated at Winchester and Balliol College, Oxford, 'Puffin' Asquith was a founder member of the London Film Society* in 1925, was wooed by John Grierson* for the documentary unit, and was president of the ACT, the leading film trade union, from 1937 until his death in 1968. His early films, *Shooting Stars* (dir. A. V. Bramble, 1928) and *A Cottage on Dartmoor* (1929), were compared favourably to Alfred Hitchcock's*. An actor's director, his films from the late 1930s adopt a highly literate approach to dialogue well suited to stage adaptations, and he is credited with the best adaptation of Shaw in *Pygmalion* (1938) and of Wilde in *The Importance of Being Earnest* (1952). He developed an association with the playwright Terence Rattigan, adapting such stage successes as *French Without Tears* (1939), *The Winslow Boy* (1948) and *The Browning Version* (1951), and using Rattigan's scripts for *The Way to the Stars* (1945) and *The Yellow Rolls-Royce* (1964). For Gainsborough*, somewhat surprisingly, he directed the costume melodrama *Fanny by Gaslight* (1944).

His *Times* obituary said of Asquith, 'He holds a minor but secure place among the world's best film directors.' 'The world' may be an exaggeration, but he holds an honourable place in British cinema. JC

Bib: J. R. Minney, *Puffin Asquith: A biography of the Hon. Anthony Asquith* (1973).

Other Films Include: *Tell England* (1931); *Moscow Nights* (1935); *Channel Incident* (1940); *Freedom Radio, Quiet Wedding, Cottage to Let* (1941); *Uncensored* (1942); *We Dive at Dawn, The Demi-Paradise* (1943); *While the Sun Shines* (1947); *The Woman in Question* (1950); *The Net* (1953); *The Young Lovers, Carrington V.C.* (1954); *Orders to Kill* (1958); *The Doctor's Dilemma* (1959); *The Millionairess* (1960); *The V.I.P.s* (1963).

ASTHER, Nils — Hellerup, Denmark 1897 – Stockholm 1981

Swedish actor. Asther trained as an actor in Denmark, where he was born. His first screen part in Sweden was in *Vingarne/The Wings*, directed by Mauritz Stiller* (1916), and he appeared in Victor Sjöström's* *Vem dömer?/Love's Crucible* (1922). He also worked in Denmark and Germany before leaving for Hollywood in 1927. In the US, Asther became a popular romantic star in the last years of the silent era, performing with Greta Garbo* in *Wild Orchids* and *The Single Standard* (both 1929). His foreign accent, however, limited his scope with the coming of sound, condemning him to play 'foreigners'. His greatest success was in Frank Capra's *The Bitter Tea of General Yen* (1933, US), after which he tended to be typecast in oriental roles in international productions, such as *Abdul the Damned* (1935, UK) and *Tea Leaves in the Wind* (1938, UK). In the 1960s he returned to Sweden, where he played small parts in crime films by Arne Mattsson. Altogether he made over seventy films, of which the last, *Gudrun* (1963), was made in Denmark. LGA/BF

ATTENBOROUGH, (Lord) Richard — Cambridge 1923

British actor, director and producer. Attenborough made his film debut in 1942 in *In Which We Serve*. Though the part was small it established him as the juvenile funk whose upper lip began to quiver when all around were stiffening theirs. An interesting coward in a cinema full of heroes, Attenborough was the alter ego of John Mills* – the same milieu, but lacking fibre and simple, working-class decency. In civilian clothes, his characters were delinquent before teenagers were invented, and his fresh young face brought a compelling and ambivalent menace to the 17-year-old psychotic, Pinky, in *Brighton Rock* (1947). In the late 1950s, he said, 'I decided for all intents and purposes to give up acting, to go into production and wait until this idiotic cherubic face had sunk sufficiently to allow me to do something else.' From 1959 he was involved in production with Bryan Forbes*, working behind the cameras of *The Angry Silence* (1960) as well as acting in it, receiving his first producer credit on *Whistle Down the Wind* (1961), and co-producing *The L-Shaped Room* (1962). He claims that he wanted to direct in order to make *Gandhi*

(1982), a project he nurtured for twenty years. His directorial debut, which he also produced, was *Oh! What a Lovely War* (1969), a screen adaptation of Joan Littlewood's dramatised documentary, where he persuaded a complete roll-call of British stars to give their services for a daily rate. As a director, particularly on *Gandhi* and *Cry Freedom* (1987), he has gone for the grand scale, the broad emotional wash and the high ethical tone rather than the intimate and ambivalent observation which makes his acting memorable, but at least in *Magic* (1978, US) the menace of the William Goldman script survives.

Attenborough has won British Academy Best Actor awards for *Guns at Batasi* and *Seance on a Wet Afternoon* (both 1964), Golden Globe awards for Best Supporting Actor in *The Sand Pebbles* (1966, US) and *Doctor Dolittle* (1967, US), and a host of awards, including the Oscar for Best Film, for *Gandhi*. Since the 1970s, he has been at the centre of the British cultural establishment, and has become one of the leading figures in the attempt to refloat British cinema. He was knighted in 1976 and received a life peerage in 1993. JC

Bib: Jonathan Hacker and David Price, *Take 10: Contemporary British Film Directors* (1991).

Other Films Include: As Actor – *A Matter of Life and Death* (1946); *London Belongs to Me* (1948); *Morning Departure* (1950); *The Magic Box* (1951); *The Ship that Died of Shame* (1955); *Private's Progress* (1956); *Brothers in Law, The Scamp* (1957); *Sea of Sand* (1958); *I'm All Right Jack, Jet Storm, The League of Gentlemen* (1960); *The Great Escape* (1963, US); *The Flight of the Phoenix* (1965, US); *A Severed Head, Loot* (1970); *10 Rillington Place* (1970); *Rosebud* [US], *Conduct Unbecoming* (1976); *Shatranj ke khilari/The Chess Players* (1978, India); *The Human Factor* (1980); *Jurassic Park* (1993, US). **As Director** – *Young Winston* (1972); *A Bridge Too Far* (1977); *A Chorus Line* (1985, US); *Chaplin* (1992).

AUDIARD, Michel — Paris 1920 – Dourdan 1985

French scriptwriter. A journalist, novelist and scriptwriter, Audiard's chief claim to fame derives from his work in a category peculiar to the French cinema: *dialoguiste* (dialogue writer). Like his illustrious predecessors Henri Jeanson* and Jacques Prévert*, Audiard mixed classic French and slang and delighted in derision and *bons mots*, though his dialogue was coarser (a sign of the times) and more shocking. Like theirs, his humour had an edge of bitterness ('the trouble with life is that you don't get out of it alive'). Audiard's witty, hard-hitting dialogue underpins much of the best popular French cinema from the late 1950s to the mid-1980s, notably in his collaborations with Jean Gabin*, for whom he wrote tailor-made dialogue for, among many other films, *Gas-oil* (1955), *Les Grandes familles* (1958), *Le Président* (1961), *Un singe en hiver/A Monkey in Winter* (1962) and *Mélodie en sous-sol/The Big Snatch* (1963) – actor and *dialoguiste* constituting the true *auteurs* of the films. He directed nine features between 1968 and 1974. His son Jacques Audiard is also a scriptwriter and has directed two features. GV

AUDRAN, Stéphane
Colette Dacheville; Versailles 1932

French actress. Audran is, with Jeanne Moreau* and Anna Karina*, a key actress of the French New Wave*, especially in the films of her then husband Claude Chabrol*. A woman of elegant beauty, she projected an image of the cool yet sensual bourgeoise; her talent was to inject emotion and humour into such characters. She is integral to the appeal of Chabrol's bourgeois dramas of the 1960s and 1970s, especially *Les Biches* (1968), *La Femme infidèle* (1969) and *Le Boucher* (1970), and of Luis Buñuel's* *Le Charme discret de la bourgeoisie/The Discreet Charm of the Bourgeoisie* (1972). After smaller roles, for instance in *Violette Nozière* (1978) and Bertrand Tavernier's* *Coup de torchon/Clean Slate* (1981), she revived her international fame in Gabriel Axel's* *Babettes Gæstebud/Babette's Feast* (1987, Den.). GV

AUDRY, Jacqueline
Orange 1908 – Poissy 1977

French director. Audry followed the classic route of continuity and assistantship to (among others) Jean Delannoy* and Max Ophuls* before directing her first short, *Les Chevaux du Vercors*, in 1943. Her well-made literary adaptations belong to the 1950s 'tradition of quality'*; not so her choice of subject matter, however. Adaptations from Colette* (*Gigi*, 1949, *Minne, l'ingénue libertine/Minne*, 1950, *Mitsou*, 1956) and Victor Marguerite (*La Garçonne*, 1957), and her portrayal of lesbian relationships in *Olivia/Pit of Loneliness* (1951), show her consistent interest in transgressive women. Even though their subversiveness is constrained by conventional narratives and the titillating potential of the subjects, Audry's women are never treated as perverse curiosities. Though several of her films were box-office successes, she suffered setbacks in her career; that she managed to make as many as eighteen features is remarkable. Apart from the celebrated *Olivia*, which has aroused feminist interest, her work is still in need of critical reappraisal. GV

Other Films: *Les Malheurs de Sophie* (1946); *Sombre dimanche* (1948); *La Caraque blonde, Huis-clos* (1954); *L'Ecole des cocottes, C'est la faute d'Adam* (1958); *Le Secret du chevalier d'Eon* (1960); *Les Petits Matins* (1962); *Cadavres en vacances* (1963); *Cours de bonheur conjugal* (1964, TV); *Fruits amers* (also *Soledad*, 1967); *Le Lys de mer* (1969); *Un Grand amour de Balzac* (1972, TV).

AUGUST, Bille
Brede 1948

Danish director, trained as a photographer in Stockholm. He later studied at the Danish Film School, qualifying as a cinematographer in 1971. After working for several years in this capacity in Sweden, August directed his first feature, *Honningmåne/In My Life*, in 1978, followed by two films about teenagers, *Zappa* (1983) and *Tro, Håb og Kærlighed/Twist and Shout* (1984). He has also worked for television since 1973. *Pelle Erobreren/Pelle the Conqueror* (1987) was August's major breakthrough, winning the Palme d'or at Cannes in 1988 and an Oscar for Best Foreign Film a year later. Since then he has directed a series for Swedish television, *Den Goda viljan/The Best Intentions* (1991, later released theatrically), based on a script by Ingmar Bergman*. August's new standing allowed him to make *Åndernes Hus/The House of the Spirits* (1993), based on Isabel Allende's novel, with an international cast including Meryl Streep, Glenn Close and Jeremy Irons*. ME

Other Films Include: *Verden er så stor, så stor/The World is so Very Big* [TV] (1980); *Busters verden/Buster's World* (1984).

AURENCHE, Jean
Pierrelatte 1904 – Bandol 1992

and

BOST, Pierre
Lasalle 1901 – Paris 1975

French scriptwriters. Aurenche worked in advertising in the early 1930s. He co-scripted films with Jean Anouilh, Marcel Achard and Henri Jeanson* as well as writing his own screenplays. Bost wrote plays and novels from the 1920s, adding film dialogues in the late 1930s. Aurenche and Bost met in 1943; their partnership as script/dialogue writers, starting with Claude Autant-Lara's* *Douce* (1943), lasted thirty years. 'Aurenche-et-Bost' films, typically directed by Autant-Lara, were the epitome of 'tradition of quality'* French cinema: carefully structured, studio-shot literary adaptations performed by bankable French stars. Notable examples among many are *Le Diable au corps/Devil in the Flesh* (1947), *L'Auberge rouge/The Red Inn* (1951), *Gervaise* (1956) and *La Traversée de Paris/A Pig Across Paris* (1956). François Truffaut* singled out Aurenche and Bost for special attention in his famous 1954 assault on the quality tradition, denouncing them as 'nothing but the Viollet-Leduc of adaptation' after the painstaking nineteenth-century restorer of gothic architecture. Aurenche and Bost's work is nonetheless testimony to the importance of the word in classic French cinema. Bertrand Tavernier* later reclaimed this heritage, inviting them to script *L'Horloger de Saint-Paul/The Watchmaker of Saint-Paul* (1973). Aurenche scripted other films by Tavernier, who also adapted a novella by Bost for *Un dimanche à la campagne/Sunday in the Country* (1983). GV

AUSTRIA

Film historians usually like to point out that Austria is not a film-producing nation, and – its cinema being no exception – that Austria's fate has been to be overshadowed by Germany, the powerful neighbour to the north. But there are at least three salient facts that complicate this apparently self-evident assessment. First, since the early 1960s Austria has developed a very distinctive cinematic voice – principally in the area of experimental and avant-garde cinema associated with Peter Kubelka*, Kurt Kren, Peter Weibel and Valie Export*, but since the mid-1970s also in the form of an *auteur* cinema of at least half a dozen internationally recognised directors, among them Franz Novotny*, Peter Patzak*, Niki List* and Michael Haneke*. Secondly, Austria has, almost since the beginnings of the cinema, nurtured an indigenous 'commercial' production sector. Associated with names like Luise Kolm, Count Sascha Kolowrat, Willi Forst*, Hans Moser* and Paula Wessely*, it may have been comparatively small (1,009 silent films between 1907 and 1930, with an average of 120 films a year during the peak years 1918–22; 197 sound films between 1930 and 1945, averaging twenty-four films a year during the peak years 1933–37). Nonetheless, this production amounted to a distinct cinematic tradition, boasting a special kind of continuity in its themes and genres over a lengthy period. Finally, there is the matter of 'colonisation'. In so far as Austria was perceived by distributors as a mere annexe to the German market, it may seem that much of Austrian cinema happened in Germany. But the inverse is equally true, for much of the most popular German cinema since the 1920s has come from directors and stars 'made in Austria' and the Austro-Hungarian empire. The Austrians may have been seeing 'German' films, but very many of them had Austrian personnel. The list is endless: Joe May*, Sándor (Alexander) Korda*, Mihály Kertész (Michael Curtiz), Fritz Lang*, G. W. Pabst*, Richard Oswald*, Karl Grune, Carl Mayer*, Ferenc Feher, Geza von Bolvary*, Geza von Cziffra*, Peter Lorre*, Marika Rökk*, Rudolf Forster*, Fritz Kortner*, Jenny Jugo*, Käthe von Nagy, to name a few. But the 'talent drain' from Budapest to Vienna, and from Vienna to Berlin, did not stop there. The impressively versatile German 'invasion' of Hollywood in the 1930s was made up of many who had originated from Austria: directors Otto Preminger, Billy Wilder, Fred Zinnemann, Walter Reisch; actors Oskar Homolka, Alexander von Granach, Bertold Viertel, Paul Henreid, Hedy Lamarr; musicians Max Steiner, Hugo Riesenfeld, Robert Stolz and many more. It is said that in the making of *Casablanca* no fewer than twenty Austro-Hungarians were involved.

Thus the distinctive voice of Austrian cinema until 1945 has to be sought along the creative axis Vienna-Berlin-Hollywood, with an additional twist, namely that both in Germany and in Hollywood these adventurers and émigrés significantly contributed to a mythical Vienna (of Austro-Hungarian decadence), made for export, and consisting of Vienna waltzes, Emperor Franz Josef court intrigues, the Prater amusement gardens, charming but penniless aristocrats, and the epitome of seductive naiveté, the '*Wiener Mädl*' (the 'Viennese girl'). This myth was serviced by Austrian stars and directors, but even more so – indicating its imaginary pull – by barely native directors such as Erich von Stroheim (whose parents emigrated in 1909) and Joseph von Sternberg (who left in 1914), and altogether non-natives such as Ernst Lubitsch* (from his Prince Nukki in *Die Austernprinzessin/The Oyster Princess* in 1919, to *The Smiling Lieutenant* in 1931), Max Ophuls* (*Liebelei*, 1933, *Letter from an Unknown Woman*, 1948) and Ludwig Berger* (*Ein Walzertraum/The Waltz Dream*, 1925).

1896–1918: Austria had its own generation of pioneers who, characteristically, excelled not so much in the technical field as in understanding the nature of popular entertainment, spanning curio-cabinets and vaudeville shows at one end of the social scale, and operetta and boulevard theatre at the other. However, it was the French Cinematograph that brought moving pictures to Vienna (first showing: 27 March 1896), thanks to Eugène Dupont, the Austrian representative of Lumière*. The close connection with France persisted for the first indigenous productions, by Louis Veltée, who in the summer of 1896 began showing films at his waxworks museum housed in the so-called 'City-panoptikum'. One of Veltée's daughters, Luise, married Anton Kolm, a photographer, and in 1908 the Kolms, together with an assistant, Jakob Fleck, and a relative, Claudius Veltée, inaugurated Austrian feature film production with *Von Stufe zu Stufe* (1908). The film, 600m long, was produced by Anton Kolm, scripted and edited by Heinz Hanus and Luise Kolm, with camerawork by Jakob Fleck and direction by Hanus, who also played the male lead, a raffish count who seduces and then abandons a young ingénue. Thus the first Austrian fiction film already set the pattern for one of the dominant genres, and the Wiener Kunstfilm-Industrie (a typical family firm, founded by the Kolms and Jakob Fleck) took the lead in Austrian documentary and feature film productions. It is notable that one of Austria's pioneers should be a woman, for Luise Kolm not only produced, scripted and edited, she also directed (*Der Unbekannte*, 1912).

Drawing on the ethnic diversity of its empire, and the mostly comic genres of popular performance arts, Austrian cinema in the 1910s derived its energy if not its identity from adaptations of fairground attractions, peasant farces and passion plays, while also pioneering *actualités*. Early Austrian cinema also produced an entrepreneur of genius, Count Alexander Kolowrat-Krakowsky, who in 1910 founded his first film company, which, in 1914, became Sascha-Film, Vienna. Until his death in 1927 the 'film count', as he was known, headed Austria's most important production company, not least by gambling on super-productions and attracting talent from the other arts. For just like France and Germany, Austria had its *film d'art** debate around the cinema's competition with the stage for middle-class audiences, which was won in 1913 when several noted Austrian authors began writing original screenplays: Arthur Schnitzler, Egon Friedell, Hugo von Hofmannsthal, Felix Dörmann. 1913 also saw the first example of another Austrian speciality, the operetta film as musical biography: *Johann Strauß an der schönen blauen Donau/Johann Strauss and the Blue Danube*. By 1915 Vienna had 150 movie theatres, while Sascha-Film stabilised its economic basis with newsreels and patriotic films, trying, after the war, to expand into the world market by following the examples of Italian and American epics and spectaculars.

1918–1933: The Hungarians Sándor (Alexander) Korda* and Mihély Kertész (Michael Curtiz) were the most active filmmakers after 1918. Korda made six films for Sascha-Film between 1919 and 1924 (among them *Samson und Delila*, 1922). Kertész made fifteen films between 1919 and 1926 (including international box-office hits such as *Das sechste Gebot/The Sixth Commandment*, 1923, and *Die Sklavenkönigin/The Queen of the Slaves*, 1924). Two other Austro-Hungarians destined for a career elsewhere, the Czech Gustav Ucicky* and the Hungarian Ferenc Feher, also worked successfully in Vienna during the 1920s. By the end of the silent era, however, the film industry had become heavily dependent on German distribution, with some German directors preferring (the lower production costs of) Vienna. Robert Wiene, for instance, made *Orlacs Hände/The Hands of Orlac* there in 1924.

In the transition to sound, Sascha-Film was bought out by the German Tobis. Austrian film production peaked in the early 1930s, for with sound films 'Austria' could become a distinctive cinematic and aural signifier, not least because of the pleasingly lilting Viennese accent, cultivated by armies of highly trained stage actors from the Burgtheater and the Theater an der Josephstadt. The result was the so-called 'Viennese film', a genre of erotic melodrama in operetta night-life settings, told in a tone of resigned irony, and most supremely embodied in the films of Willy Forst*, whose decorative opulence as a director was perfectly matched by his world-weary elegance as an actor (*Maskerade/Masquerade in Vienna*, 1934; *Bel Ami*, 1938; *Operette*, 1940). Austria excelled in musical biopics (such as *Leise flehen meine Lieder*, 1933), and cornered the market in other sub-genres of musical entertainment films, such as ice-skating revue films and especially operetta. On the one hand, well-known operas by the likes of Franz Léhar, Nikolaus Dostal, Robert Stolz and Emerich Kalman were adapted; on the other hand, attempts were made to give operetta a new life through film, with music specially composed for the cinema. The popularity of singers such as Richard Tauber, Jan Kiepura and Martha Eggert enlivened the genre. Others, whose range was not sufficient for musical theatre (such as Joseph Schmidt), found a perfect medium in sound film. Austrian productions of the 1930s and early 1940s were often quality investments, with stars like Paula Wessely* earning huge salaries, and Ernst Marischka* (and his brother Hubert) breathing life into costume and *Heimat** films, which were to retain their popularity well into the 1950s. While the Viennese element was crucial for the Nazi entertainment cinema, there is no Austrian cinema strictly speaking between 1938 and 1945, since after the 1938 *Anschluss* Austrian production companies were amalgamated into the Wien-Film company, at first majority-owned by Tobis, and in turn absorbed by the Ufa* holding company when Goebbels 'nationalised' the German film industry in 1941.

1945–1960: In its artistic personnel and generic identity, Austrian commercial cinema cannot be said to have experienced a 'zero hour', as did Germany, in 1945. Yet the country's administrative division into Allied zones, splitting Vienna's traditional film-making sites between them until 1955, may well have contributed to the decline of indigenous studios, increasingly hired out to foreign productions (from Carol Reed's* *The Third Man*, 1949, to Robert Wise's *The Sound of Music*, 1965). At the same time Austria continued to provide the stars and stories that Germany wanted: Nadja Tiller*, Oskar Werner*, Maria Schell*, Helmut Berger were all headed for careers outside Austria, and after creating with Magda and Romy Schneider* the ideal on-screen, off-screen mother-daughter pair, Marischka made an international superstar out of Romy Schneider with the hugely successful *Sissi* trilogy (1955–57), skilfully presenting every conceivable Austrian national cliché and thus mightily reviving the country's much-needed tourist industry.

Alongside this cinema for Euro-export, the first shoots of a new independent cinema emerged. Kurt Steinwendner's *Der Rabe/The Raven* (1951), Herbert Vesely's *Nicht mehr fliehen/* *Flee No More* (1955) and Edwin Zbonek's *Erschießungs-befehl/Execution Order* (1962) announced a formally and thematically more individual cinema, but what shaped the image of Austrian cinema in the 1960s came from an iconoclastic, non-narrative film avant-garde.

1965–1995: The famous Austrian experimental school emerged in total opposition to the commercial film industry. Partly because the movement's intellectual and artistic core had affinities with modern painting ('tachism'), Austrian literary and art school avant-gardes (Wiener Aktionismus), as well as links with the American 'expanded cinema', its radicalism was quite different from that of other European 'young' cinemas and New Waves* of the 1960s. Austrian experimental cinema divides into an abstract-formalist wing (most pronounced in the work of Peter Kubelka* and Ferry Radax) and a politically interventionist grouping around Kurt Kren, Günther Brus and Otto Muehl, who came out of the 'fluxus' movement and 'happening' aesthetics, scandalising the public with provocative, often pornographic and scatological body-centred action pieces. The common denominator was an angry antagonism to postwar Austrian society and the Austrian state apparatus, castigated as corrupt, hypocritical and mired in its fascist past. Altogether wittier and more playful, but no less bitingly satirical, were the films of Valie Export* (often made with her then partner Peter Weibel), whose features *Unsichtbare Gegner/Invisible Adversaries* (1978) and *Die Praxis der Liebe/The Practice of Love* (1984) have become classics of international women's cinema.

By the time some of the protagonists of Vienna actionism, rather than face prosecution and prison, had chosen to emigrate to Germany (where they called themselves 'Austrian government in exile'), another generation of film-makers had come to the fore, whose films were under the sign of a more latent violence. The 'New Austrian cinema' of Franz Novotny* and Peter Patzak* focused on their country's troubled relation to its fascist past as it reverberated in psychologically damaged individuals. Films depicted an urban underclass at odds with the values but also deprived of the benefits of the prosperous Austrian 'Second Republic' (Novotny's *Die Ausgesperrten/Locked Out*, 1982), or they went to the countryside, where the Alpine idylls of summer tourists and skiing instructors peel away to reveal still-lifes of brutalising everyday existence in the provinces, as traditional peasant structures make way for Mafia-like agri-business and political wheeler-dealing (Christian Berger's *Raffl*, 1984). Some combined the Nazi past with the provincial theme, such as Wolfram Paulus'* *Heidenlöcher* (1985). A key term of this cinema is '*abreagieren*' (giving vent to frustration), encompassing violence within the petit-bourgeois family, silent rages and sexual humiliations, a culture of resentment that leads to racism, xenophobia and anti-semitic aggression: phenomena which have marred official Austria's liberal self-image and are skilfully worked into the popular genre films of Patzak, such as *Kassbach* (1979). Where these concerns are more stylised and formally controlled, as in Michael Haneke's* work (*Der siebente Kontinent/The Seventh Continent*, 1989; *Benny's Video*, 1992), the films attain an intense, claustrophobic intimacy that has impressed festival juries and foreign audiences.

Austrian cinema in the 1990s exists, as in so many other European countries, thanks to a network of legal provisions and funding systems, including especially the Österreichisches Filmförderungsgesetz (ÖFG) (Austrian Film Funding Law), in force since 1981 and amended in 1987 and 1993, which regulates subsidies to Austrian films. While this funding authority is obliged to take into consideration a project's commercial potential as well as its artistic and cultural value, the Filmbeirat at the Ministry for Education and Arts promotes art and experimental films. In addition, the City Council of Vienna has had its own fund since 1976 to subsidise foreign productions using Vienna locations, personnel or service industries, and since 1981 the Film-Fernseh-Abkommen (Film and Television Agreement) defines the co-operation between Austria's national broadcasting company ORF and the Austrian Film Institute, thereby confirming ORF's role as the most important commissioner of Austrian films. While these measures relaunched national production in the 1980s and form the basis of the survival of an *auteur* cinema, commentators have voiced their doubts about this occasional oxygen boost. But television, the obvious alternative, is no less problematic to those believing in the cinema, so that the inevitable co-productions have had a mixed response, except for the so-called 'New *Heimatfilm*'* which has brought forth some remarkable television series, especially Austria's anticipation of Edgar Reitz's* *Heimat*, the family chronicle *Alpensaga* (1976–80), with camerawork by Xaver Schwarzenberger*, one of R. W. Fassbinder's* preferred cinematographers and a leading Austrian director. Whatever the balance will be between *auteur* cinema and television, one fact seems certain: the Austrian cinema is unlikely in the near future to be overshadowed by the German cinema, in comparison to which it appears vibrant and full of promise. TE

AUTANT-LARA, Claude

Claude Autant; Luzarches 1901

French director. Autant-Lara came from an artistic milieu and made his debut in the avant-garde of the 1920s, working in set and costume design, and as assistant to Marcel L'Herbier* and René Clair*. His early short, *Construire un feu* (1928, rel. 1930), was notable for its use of the Hypergonar, an early version of CinemaScope. From 1930 to 1932 Autant-Lara was in Hollywood, making French versions of American films. He directed his first feature, *Ciboulette* (scripted by Jacques Prévert*), in 1933 and worked on some films uncredited. His wartime costume dramas established him as a leading exponent of the 'tradition of quality'*. They were distinguished by a bleak vision of the French bourgeoisie, but also by complex and strong women characters (especially in *Douce*, 1943). The controversial *Le Diable au corps/Devil in the Flesh* (1947), seen as anti-clerical and anti-war, confirmed Autant-Lara's status and won many prizes. He continued alternating costume films with comedies such as *L'Auberge rouge/The Red Inn* (1951) and *La Jument verte/The Green Mare's Nest* (1959), earning much hostility from New Wave* critics. François Truffaut*, however, applauded *La Traversée de Paris/A Pig Across Paris* (1956), a war comedy starring Jean Gabin* and Bourvil*, admiring

both its ferocity and the precision of its *mise-en-scène*. Autant-Lara worked less successfully in the mainstream French cinema of the 1960s. In 1984 he published the first volume of his memoirs, remarkable for its vituperation, bitterness and extreme right-wing views. He remains, however, one of the most gifted and provocative film-makers of classical French cinema. GV

Other Films Include: *Le Mariage de Chiffon, Lettres d'amour* (1942); *Sylvie et le Fantôme* (1946); *Occupe-toi d'Amélie* (1949); *Le Blé en herbe/The Game of Love, Le Rouge et le noir/Scarlet and Black* (1954); *Marguerite de la nuit* (1956); *En cas de malheur/Love is My Profession* (1958); *Le Comte de Monte-Cristo* (1961); *Tu ne tueras point/Non uccidere/Thou Shalt Not Kill* (1963); *Le Journal d'une femme en blanc* (1965); *Le Franciscain de Bourges* (1968).

AVANCE SUR RECETTES (Advance on box-office receipts)

French funding system designed to promote *auteur* films and usually thought of (not entirely correctly) as a key element in the New Wave*. The *avance*, set up in 1960, complemented existing state support measures funded from box-office levies by putting in place more selective financing for the promotion of 'original', especially first, films. It was granted by a commission, nominated by the Minister of Culture, which made decisions predominantly on script submission. Its other novelty was that it did not entail repayment unless the film made money. The system has been criticised for its occasional support of 'commercial' film-makers (Yves Robert, Claude Lelouch*), while the likes of Eric Rohmer* often failed to qualify. The *avance* budget (over FF100m [c. £12m] in the early 1990s) is modest by French production standards, yet enviable relative to other European countries; it is only part of the substantial aid package available to film production every year. Altogether, over 1,000 films, often low-budget or 'difficult', have benefited from the *avance*, which as part of the increasingly complex financing system of the 1980s and 1990s remains a force in the promotion and survival of *auteur* cinema. GV

Bib: René Prédal, *Le Cinéma français depuis 1945* (1991).

AVANT-GARDE CINEMA IN EUROPE

From our present postmodern vantage point, the concept of the avant-garde might appear as simultaneously archaic and elitist, now that it is behind us historically and seemingly beyond us politically. Two factors recur: the relationship of film to the other arts, and of aesthetics to politics, with the term 'avant-garde' breaking into the following registers of aspiration – experimentation and abstraction, independence and opposition.

Soviet montage*, German expressionism*, French impressionism [> FRENCH AVANT-GARDE] and surrealism are traditionally considered the 'historical avant-gardes' of European cinema and the overlap of film with fine arts is characteristic of each of these founding moments. At its most militantly innovative and highly theorised in the work of Sergei Eisenstein* and Dziga Vertov*, Soviet montage was wrought from the combination of a modernist consciousness of the revolutionary moment – 1917, Bolshevism – and a fertile cross-pollination of film with Constructivist design, Futurist sound poetry [> FUTURISM] and Suprematist experimentation with form. In France, impressionism and surrealism lacked the political impetus of the Soviets, but endorsed cinema as the manifestation of the Wagnerian idea of the *Gesamtkunstwerk*, the means of synthesising all the arts in the new, unique art of film, termed by Ricciotto Canudo* 'the seventh art'.

The encounter between film and the fine arts has persistently characterised the abstract tendency of the European avant-garde. And while recent work in video-art can be seen as maintaining this tradition, it might equally be seen in the Structuralist/Materialist films of the 1970s. Malcolm Le Grice, one of the leading British exponents of such work, has identified abstract work as taking place as early as 1910–12 in the experiments of Bruno Corra and Arnaldo Ginna. Corra's theoretical text, *Abstract Cinema – Chromatic Music*, serves as an early indication of the enduring tendency in abstract film to seek aesthetic alliances with painting and music. This example predates the work of abstract animators Walther Ruttmann*, Viking Eggeling*, Hans Richter and Oskar Fischinger, often seen as inaugurating this aesthetic tendency. Richter gave perhaps the best summary of the abstract film position when he wrote: 'Problems in modern art lead directly into the film. The connection to theatre and literature was completely severed. Cubism, Expressionism, Dadaism, Abstract Art, Surrealism found not only their expression in film, but a new fulfilment on a new level.'

Two words serve to encapsulate the motivation of this first, historical phase of the European avant-garde: silence and 'specificity'. It is noticeable that this experimental phase ended with the coming of sound. While for the Soviet directors this can in part be attributed to Stalin's* cultural policies of the late 1920s and early 1930s, the termination was also informed by the anti-realist agendas common to all the avant-gardes, with sound representing a decisively realist 'supplement' to the image. The change in the mode of production from the artisanal/patronage-based one enjoyed by the avant-garde to the labour and capital intensive base demanded by the new sound cinema also had a part to play in the end of the silent avant-gardes. The search for cinematic 'specificity' was polemical and separatist on the one hand – against theatrical and narrative models – synthesising and hybridising on the other, with models from painting and music.

The notion of the avant-garde in film was constructed around the idea of its oppositional status vis-à-vis the established cinematic order both generally and specifically in European cinema. This tendency can be defined in terms either of opposition or of independence, the former being predicated along militant political lines, the latter a means of constructing an alternative space for independent production, distribution and exhibition. This taxonomy works usefully in respect of the works of the 1960s and 1970s that best illustrate the bifurcation of European avant-garde practice into what Peter Wollen christened in 1975 'the Two Avant-Gardes', one concerned with a politically oriented 'politics of form', the other with a formalist 'politics of perception'. The strand of European practice that came to be known as Counter-Cinema, while having its immediate origins in the political revolt of May 1968 in France, nevertheless took its conceptual and asthetic leads from a longer European tradition of radical, oppositional aesthetic practices, drawing on ideas from Brechtian dramaturgy – distancation, the *Verfremdungseffekt* – and lauding Vertov over Eisenstein in the 'second discovery' of Soviet cinema of the mid- to late 1960s. While Jean-Luc Godard* is most commonly associated with the counter-cinematic turning away from what he dubbed 'the Hollywood-Mosfilm' and towards a didactic cinema of '*films tableaux noirs*' (blackboard films), he was by no means alone in opting for this radical strategy. Chris Marker* in France, Rainer Werner Fassbinder* and Werner Schroeter* in Germany, Věra Chytilová* in Czechoslovakia and Dušan Makavejev* in Yugoslavia experimented with a Brechtian challenge to narrative transparency against the perceived stylistic – hence ideological – hegemony of Hollywood cinema.

The other more Formalist/Structuralist-Materialist strand of avant-garde film-making rooted itself in an opposition to conventional narrative that owed much to the abstract cinema of the 1920s, although it might be said that the master-text of both the Structuralist-Materialist and counter-cinematic movements of the 1960s and 1970s remains Vertov's remarkable *Chelovek s kinoapparatom/The Man with the Movie Camera* (1929). The Co-op movements of the 1970s, particularly the London Film-makers Co-op*, represented the pursuit of a radical, independent practice both aesthetically and institutionally. Film-makers such as Malcolm Le Grice and Peter Gidal participated in a cinema of minimal effects concerned with the material properties of film – grain, emulsion, flicker, qualities of light – and in the spectatorial experience, experimenting with duration and performance-art styled interventions during projection. This strand arguably had more in common with the North American and Canadian avant-garde of Brakhage, Sharits and Snow than with the militancy of European counter-cinema. Godard himself attempted, in *Tout va bien* (1972), a Brechtian cinema-with-stars (Jane Fonda and Yves Montand*), while other art cinema directors such as Yvonne Rainer and Chantal Akerman* employed avant-garde strategies to question the sexual politics of cinematic representation, notably in Akerman's *Jeanne Dielman 23 Quai du Commerce 1080 Bruxelles* (1975), with its experimentation with duration.

With the advent of video technologies in the mid-1960s one would have imagined a revival of the European avant-gardes. However, in the hands of Godard and Marker, video has been used as a means of thinking cinema and of expressing an analytic relationship with the image. Marker's *Sans soleil/Sunless* (1983) and Godard's *Scénario du film Passion* (1982) are most representative of this application of video, the Marker film also being an eloquent piece of mourning-work for the lost illusions of 1960s political radicalism and so-called 'guerrilla film-making', while fully and euphorically exploiting the possibilities of video. European video-art *per se* has yet to achieve the international visibility of North American and Canadian video-artists such as Bill Viola, Gary Hill and Nam June Paik. However, the avant-garde has been – and, in the example of video-art, remains – an international, exportable phenomenon that cuts across both national, cultural and artistic boundaries, addressing a wide set of disparate art/film constituencies, in contrast to European popular cinemas that remain more firmly embedded in specific national traditions and hence export less effectively. CDa

Bib: Peter Wollen, 'The Two Avant-Gardes', in *Readings and Writings: Semiotic Counter-Strategies* (1982).

AVATI, Pupi
Giuseppe Avati; Bologna 1938

Italian director. After spending his youth as an amateur jazz player, making a living in various jobs (including as knitwear salesman), Avati, at the age of thirty, finally discovered his ideal medium of self-expression: cinema. He made his debut with *Balsamus, l'uomo di Satana/Blood Relations* (1968), where he freely expressed his naive and provocative taste for the esoteric, the supernatural and black magic – a tendency he pursued throughout his career, especially in his films of the 1970s. A penchant for horror and impressive effects characterised *La casa dalle finestre che ridono/The House with the Laughing Windows* (1976), *Tutti defunti ... tranne i morti* (1977), the horror-style remake of *Zeder/Revenge of the Dead* (1983), and *Magnificat* (1993), a film imbued with ambiguous millenarian pessimism. The eclectic Avati moved between genres, stepping easily from farce and comedy (*La mazurka del barone, della santa e del fico fiorone*, 1974) into the musical (*Aiutami a sognare/Help Me Dream*, 1980; *Jazz Band*, 1978 [TV]; *Dancing Paradise*, 1981) and historical drama (*Noi tre/The Three of Us*, 1984, about Mozart's journey to Bologna). His most personal vein can be found in the nostalgic evocations of past provincial life (in particular his native Emilia Romagna) which occasionally slide into mawkishness. In all these films, however, Avati displayed a remarkable talent for choosing and directing young actors. *Una gita scolastica* (1983) and *Storia di ragazzi e ragazze* (1989) skilfully recreate the 1930s and 1940s with their old-fashioned prudery but also moral values which seem now to have disappeared. More ambiguous are the films shot in contemporary settings (*Impiegati*, 1985; *Festa di Laurea*, 1985; *Regalo di Natale*, 1986; *Fratelli e sorelle*, 1992), which, despite a certain introspective finesse, fail to probe sufficiently their petit-bourgeois milieux. PM

Other Films Include: *Thomas ... gli indemoniati/Thomas ... The Possessed* (1969); *Bordella* (1975); *Le strelle nel fosso* (1979); *Ultimo minuto* (1987); *Sposi* (1988); *Bix* (1990).

AXEL, Gabriel
Gabriel Mørch; Paris, France 1918

Danish director. Gabriel Axel lived in France until joining the Royal School of Acting in Copenhagen in 1935. From 1945 to 1950 he was back in France as an actor in Louis Jouvet's* theatre company. In the early 1950s Axel returned to Denmark and became the leading director of Danish television drama, starting with *Døden/Death* (1951), which, with its numerous close-ups and small cast, demonstrated his talent for the new medium. An adaptation of a well-known Danish novel, *En kvinde er overflødig/A Woman is Superfluous*, followed in 1956. Its success prompted Nordisk Films* to invite him to remake it as a film, with the same actress, the veteran Clara Pontoppidan*, in the lead. Subsequently, Axel directed a large number of films, mostly light comedies. An exception was his adaptation of an Icelandic saga, *Rauda Sikkjan/Den røde kappe/The Red Mantle,* in 1967; the Icelandic locations were well used, but the film was badly served by the acting. Now back in Paris, he scored a hit with a French television drama, *La Ronde de nuit/The Night Watch* (1977). The excellent French actor Michel Bouquet played the lead, as he did in another Axel-directed work, *Le Curé de Tours* (1979). Back in Denmark, he made *Babettes gæstebud/Babette's Feast* (1987, based on a story by Karen Blixen), which won him international prominence and an Oscar for the best foreign film in 1988, the first awarded to a Danish director. *Babettes gæstebud* is the story of a French woman's impact on a small community in the remote Jutland peninsula in the 1870s, where she delights and shocks the puritan locals with a sumptuous feast. Starring Stéphane Audran*, the film was a great success with art cinema audiences round the world and is a key example of the European heritage film*. Axel's next film was *Prince of Jutland* (1993). ME

AZCONA, Rafael
Rafael Azcona Fernández; Logroño 1926

Spanish scriptwriter, with a prolific and lengthy career in cinema, both scripting for and co-scripting with some of the most prominent directors of the 1960s, 1970s and 1980s. He started in the 1950s as a cartoonist for the satirical magazine *La Codorniz*. Two collaborations with Marco Ferreri* immediately established him as a scriptwriter of wit and panache, while *Peppermint frappé* (1967) marked the beginning of a successful six-film partnership with Carlos Saura*. Azcona's most productive working relationship, however, was with Luis García Berlanga*, with over twelve co-scripted projects to date: dark, humorous, acerbic indictments of the materialism of petit-bourgeois life. The 1980s and 1990s have seen Azcona script a range of commercially successful comedies, including the 1994 Oscar winner for Best Foreign Film, *Belle Epoque* (1992, dir. Fernando Trueba*). MD

B

BAAROVÁ, Lida
Prague [then Austria-Hungary] 1914

Czech actress. Lida Baarová made her film debut in Miroslav J. Krňanský's comedy *Kariéra Pavla Čamrdy/The Career of Pavel Čamrda* (1931), following this with two films opposite Vlasta Burian*. She was soon signed up by Ufa* and appeared in a number of German films, including the successful romantic comedy *Barcarole*, 1935. In Germany she became Joseph Goebbels' mistress, rejecting an offer from MGM in order to stay with him. When Hitler refused Goebbels' request to divorce his wife and marry Baarová, all her films were banned in Germany. Despite the scandal, she maintained her Czech career and reputedly became involved in anti-Nazi espionage. She was expelled from the Czech studios by the Nazis in 1941 and continued her career in Italy, making her final appearances in Federico Fellini's* *I Vitelloni* (1953) and the Spanish film *Rapsodia de sangre* (1957). Her best films, however, were those made in Czechoslovakia between 1937 and 1941, where she appeared in *Ohnivé léto/Fiery Summer* (1939), directed by Václav Krška and František Čáp*, and in four films for Otakar Vávra*, including *Panenství/Virginity* (1937) and *Dívka v modrém/The Girl in Blue* (1940). She retired to Austria, where she continued to act in the theatre, appearing on stage in R. W. Fassbinder's* *The Bitter Tears of Petra von Kant* in the 1970s. PH

Other Films Include: *Funebrák, Leliček ve službách Sherlocka Holmese/Leliček in the Service of Sherlock Holmes* (1932); **In Germany**: *Verräter/The Traitor* (1936); *Die Fledermaus, Patrioten* (1937); *Preussische Liebesgeschichte/ Prussian Love Story* (1938, released 1950); **In Czechoslovakia**: *Maskovaná milenka/The Masked Lover* (1940); *Turbina/The Turbine* (1941); **In Italy**: *La Fornarina* (1942).

BAGH, Peter Von
Helsinki 1943

Finnish film critic, writer and director, a key figure in Finnish film culture. Von Bagh founded *Filmihullu*, the largest-selling Finnish film magazine, which he still edits. He has worked in various positions at the Finnish Film Archive*, and has written and edited several books on Finnish and international cinema, among them *Elokuvan historia* ('History of Film', 1975). He is the curator of the Midnight Sun film festival and has directed a feature film, *Kreivi/The Gust* (1971), and dozens of television programmes on cinema and popular culture. A key reason for von Bagh's popularity is his ability to articulate passionate concern for films, especially classic Finnish films. Good examples are his television compilations, which vividly recreate a particular historical moment with film clips and interviews – for instance *1939* (1993). AH-H

BAJO ULLOA, Juanma
Vitoria 1968

Spanish director, who made his first short film when he was thirteen. Ten years later, thanks to financial support from his family and director Fernando Trueba*, he directed his first feature, *Alas de mariposa/Butterfly Wings* (1992), which was awarded a prize at the San Sebastián film festival. It traces the growing despair of a daughter despised and marginalised by a mother whose maternal feelings are finally released by the son she eventually gives birth to. The oppressive, threatening atmosphere of the child-centred narrative in *Alas de mariposa* is exacerbated in Bajo Ulloa's *La madre muerta/The Dead Mother* (1994), where the subjective shots and the intimacy of treatment which had softened the former film are replaced by unrestrained psychological torture and black-humoured cynicism. IS

BAKER, Josephine
St Louis, Missouri 1906 – Paris 1975

American-born performer who moved to France in 1925. Baker's beauty, allied to her astonishing 'dislocated' dancing in the *Revue nègre*, clad only in a string of bananas, made her the toast of European capitals. Although her 'exoticism' was fetishised, she found in France a relatively racist-free environment. She starred in music hall, had her own cabaret in Paris and launched a successful recording career with Vincent Scotto's song *J'ai deux amours* ('My country and Paris'). Her brief filmography is notable for *Zouzou* (Marc Allégret*, 1934, co-starring Jean Gabin*) and *Princesse Tam-Tam* (Edmond T. Gréville, 1935), musicals showcasing her performance and bearing ample witness to her impact on French culture. Her support for the Resistance and founding of a children's home (a financial catastrophe) turned her into a French folk heroine. She performed on stage to the very end of her life. GV

BAKER, (Sir) Stanley
Ferndale, Wales 1927 – Malaga, Spain 1976

British actor. Robert Murphy suggests that 'Stanley Baker is the key figure in 60s crime films, just as Jack Hawkins* had been in the 50s.' Where Hawkins is avuncular, honest and domesticated, Baker is tough, ambiguous and solitary. The contrast can be traced back to *The Cruel Sea* (1953), where Hawkins' concerned and caring Captain is opposed to Baker's car salesman become First Lieutenant, a sadistic bully who cowers before Hawkins' confident authority and is invalided out (of the war and the film) with a duodenal ulcer. As so often in British cinema, the distinction is played out around class, but Baker's characteristic persona also suggests a much more threatened masculinity which is later exploited in a series of films with Joseph Losey*: *Blind Date* (1959), *The Criminal* (1960), *Eva/Eve* (1962, Fr./It.) and *Accident* (1967).

Baker was knighted in 1976, a month before he died of cancer at the age of 49. JC

Other Films Include: *Obsession* (1949); *The Red Beret* (1953); *Helen of Troy* (1955, US); *Hell Drivers, Campbell's Kingdom* (1957); *Violent Playground* (1958); *Jet Storm* (1960); *The Guns of Navarone* (1961); *Zulu* (1963); *Robbery* (1967).

BAKY, Josef von
Bacska, Hungary 1902 – Munich 1966

Hungarian-born director working at Ufa* in the 1930s and 1940s, with a sure hand for navigating the propagandist ends to which his films could be put. In 1928 Baky became assistant director to Geza von Bolvary*. From 1936 he directed for Ufa, specialising in popular comedies (*Intermezzo*, 1936; *Menschen vom Variete/People from the Variety*, 1939) and women's pictures (*Die kleine und die große Liebe/Minor Love and the Real Thing*, 1938). The enormous success of *Annelie* (1941), a combination of both genres, prompted Goebbels to assign him to *Münchhausen* (1943), the hugely successful twenty-fifth anniversary Ufa colour production. However, Baky's 1944 *Via Mala*, an alpine story of patricide, was banned and not shown until after the war. In 1947 Baky founded Objektiv-Film which, among other films, produced *Der Ruf/The Last Illusion* (1949), starring Fritz Kortner* as an émigré academic returning to a professorial chair in Germany. Today counted among the few '*Trümmerfilme*' ('ruin films') which have retained their unsettling potential beyond their historical moment, it was not a commercial success, and Baky's company folded. Other more profitable films, across a range of genres, followed in the 1950s, before he retired in 1961. MW

Other Films Include: *Ihr erstes Erlebnis/Her First Experience* (1939); *Der Kleinstadtpoet/Small Town Poet* (1940); *Und über uns der Himmel/And the Sky Above Us* (1947); *Der träumende Mund/Dreaming Lips* (1953); *Tagebuch einer Verliebten/Diary of a Married Woman* (1953); *Hotel Adlon* (1955); *Robinson soll nicht sterben/The Girl and the Legend* (1957); *Die seltsame Gräfin/The Mysterious Countess* (1961).

BALASKO, Josiane
Paris 1951

French actress, director and scriptwriter. Known outside France for her part as the ostentatiously plain secretary in Bertrand Blier's* *Trop belle pour toi!* (1989), Balasko has been an important force in French comedy since her training in *café-théâtre* in the early 1970s [> COMEDY (FRANCE)]. Within this irreverent tradition, she has turned her plump physique and considerable wit to a type of comedy which, while not strictly feminist, consistently deflates the excesses of French machismo – sometimes as actress (Patrice Leconte's *Les Bronzés*, 1978), sometimes as scriptwriter (the successful *Les Hommes préfèrent les grosses/Men Prefer Fat Girls*, dir. Jean-Marie Poiré*, 1981). Balasko has written, starred in and directed several plays and films, such as *Les Keufs/Flatfoots* (1987). In *Gazon maudit* (1995; the title – literally 'cursed

lawn' – is a sexual joke), she turned a lesbian comedy into a family film and box-office hit. Together with Coline Serreau*, Balasko is one of the significant women film-makers in popular French cinema, and as such deserves more attention than she has had so far. GV

BALÁZS, Béla
Herbert Bauer; Szeged 1884 – Budapest 1949

Hungarian film theoretician, scriptwriter, poet and film critic. Balázs was one of the first important theorists of the cinema, proclaiming its independence as an art form. His first theoretical work, *Der sichtbare Mensch* (*The Visible Man*, 1924), is widely considered the foundation of silent film aesthetics. Here he emphasises the importance of the 'physiognomy of the visible world' as the basis of cinematic expression. In his other key theoretical work, *Der Geist des Films (The Spirit of the Film*, 1930), Balázs treats in a detailed manner the dynamics of montage, taking a position opposed to the intellectual montage theory of Sergei Eisenstein*. In this book he also begins to analyse sound film.

Balázs had to leave Hungary because of his participation in the 1919 communist revolution. He lived in Vienna and later in Berlin, working both as a scriptwriter and film critic. He wrote the scripts of more than two dozen films and also tried his hand at directing. The films made from his scripts were not significant for the most part, though two are worth mentioning: an expressionist film from 1926, *Die Abenteuer eines Zehnmarkscheines* (dir. Berthold Viertel), and *Das blaue Licht/The Blue Light* (1932) by Leni Riefenstahl*. Balázs wrote a number of poems, short stories and dramas, two of which were made world-famous by Hungarian composer Béla Bartók: *Fából faragott királyfi* (*The Wooden Prince*) and *A kékszakállú herceg vára* (*Bluebeard's Castle*). From the 1930s until the end of the war he lived in Moscow, teaching at the Academy of Film Art (VGIK*). He returned to Hungary in 1945, founded the Hungarian Film Research Institute (now the Hungarian Film Institute), taught at the Academy of Theatre and Film Arts and was guest lecturer at a number of film schools all over Europe. He died in 1949, right at the beginning of the communist dictatorship. Ironically, given his earlier communist allegiances, he was viewed by the communists as a 'bourgeois' theorist and author, which is why they began to marginalise him shortly before his death. KAB

Bib: Joseph Zsuffa, *Béla Balázs: the Man and the Artist* (1987).

BALÁZS BÉLA STÚDIÓ (BBS)

Hungarian film studio. BBS is a unique film studio of its kind. It was founded – informally in 1959, then officially in 1961 – as an experimental studio by the second postwar Hungarian generation of film directors to which István Szabó*, Zoltán Huszárik*, István Gaál, Pál Gábor, Sándor Sára*, Zsolt Kézdy-Kovács, Ferenc Kardos, Judit Elek, János Rózsa and others belonged. BBS has enjoyed a special status in the Hungarian state-owned and politically controlled film production sector. It was subsidised (by an annual sum equal to the budget of an average Hungarian feature film), and was run entirely by young film-makers, whose decisions did not need the approval of higher authorities. BBS had no obligation to release publicly the films it produced; hence, these films were free of both dependence on the market and political censorship. Such conditions allowed BBS to become an important centre for independent short, documentary and experimental film-making.

In the early 1970s, when a new generation took over the management, the studio became more involved politically, as evidenced by a new trend in social issues documentaries. More and more films were denied authorisation for public release, though the authorities could not stop a film being made. In 1976 a special section was created by director Gábor Bódy* for experimental and avant-garde cinema. The studio became increasingly open, allowing virtually anyone to make films if their proposal was accepted by the leadership. In the early 1980s it became a key centre of experimental and avant-garde art in Hungary, as painters, sculptors, musicians and writers tried their hand at film-making. In 1985 the studio was awarded a special prize, in Milan, for its activities. Since 1989 it has been a non-profit foundation. KAB

BALCON, (Sir) Michael
Birmingham 1896 – Sussex 1977

British producer. Less of a showman than Alexander Korda* or Herbert Wilcox* and less of a missionary than John Grierson*, Balcon is a key figure not only for the British film industry, but also for projecting an image of Britishness, and particularly of Englishness, in the years immediately after the war.

Balcon's career began in partnership with Victor Saville*, with whom he founded a distribution company, Victory Motion Pictures, in 1919. He produced his first film, *The Story of Oil*, a documentary directed by Saville, in 1921. In 1923, he produced Graham Cutts'* film *Woman to Woman*, and in 1924 Cutts and Balcon founded Gainsborough Pictures, from which came *The Rat* (1925) with Ivor Novello*, and Alfred Hitchcock's* *The Lodger* (1926). Balcon remained with the studio when it was taken over by Gaumont-British, and during the 1930s he produced some of the most successful films of the decade, including Saville's films with Jessie Matthews*, Robert Flaherty's* *Man of Aran* (1934), and Hitchcock's *The Man Who Knew Too Much* (1934) and *The 39 Steps* (1935). From 1936 until 1938 he was head of production for MGM-British, and in 1938 he took over from Basil Dean* as head of production at Ealing* Studios.

It was at Ealing that Balcon left his most distinctive mark on British cinema and on the representation of Britishness. The image which Balcon cultivated was of the 'team spirit', a self-regulating community like the ones they created in the films. Balcon, however, was the man in charge, and his values and tastes are written all over the output. 'By and large we were a group of liberal-minded, like-minded people,' he told John Ellis in 1975. 'We voted Labour for the first time after the war; that was our mild revolution.' When the studio was sold to the BBC in 1955, Balcon erected a plaque which read,

'Here during a quarter of a century were made many films projecting Britain and the British character.'

Balcon spent the rest of his career as an influential elder statesman, still at the heart of things. He served as chairman of Bryanston (the production company which became a significant force in the British New Wave*), a director of Border Television, and chairman of the British Film Institute Experimental Film Fund (subsequently the BFI Production Board) from its founding in 1951 until 1972. Of the three men who exerted the greatest influence on the shape of British cinema – Grierson, Korda and Balcon – all were producers, but only Balcon was English. JC

Bib: Michael Fleugel (ed.), *Michael Balcon: The Pursuit of British Cinema* (1984).

BALFOUR, Betty
London 1903 – Weybridge 1978

British actress. 'Betty Balfour,' says Anthony Slide, 'was without doubt the most popular and most adorable film star that this country has ever produced, or ever will produce.' In the 1920s, though other stars like Alma Taylor, Chrissie White or Stewart Rome had strong local followings, only Betty Balfour and Ivor Novello* ranked in the international popularity polls along with the stars of Hollywood. She was known as the 'British Mary Pickford' or as 'Britain's Queen of Happiness', her popularity based on her comic gamine charm and common touch rather than on her sexual allure. Prefiguring Gracie Fields*, her most popular creation, Squibs, was based on a music-hall sketch featuring her as a pert, Cockney flower girl. Under contract till 1925 to the Welsh-Pearson company and directed by George Pearson*, Balfour made no attempt to break into Hollywood, but like Novello she was able to export her talents to mainland Europe, working with Louis Mercanton on *La Petite bonne du palace* (1926, Fr.) and *Croquette* (1927, Fr.), and with Marcel L'Herbier* on *Le Diable au coeur* (1926, Fr.). Her popularity waned with the coming of sound, though she played a supporting role to Jessie Matthews* in *Evergreen* (1934) and appeared with John Mills* in *Forever England* (1935). JC

Bib: Anthony Slide, 'Britain's Queen of Happiness', *Silent Picture* 2 (Spring 1969).

Other Films Include (Directed by Pearson except where indicated): *Mary-Find-the-Gold*, *Squibs* (1921); *The Wee MacGregor's Sweetheart*, *Squibs Wins the Calcutta Sweep* (1922); *Squibs' Honeymoon*, *Squibs, MP, Love, Life and Laughter* (1923); *Reveille* (1924); *Satan's Sister* (1925); *The Sea Urchin* [Graham Cutts] (1926); *Paradise* [Denison Clift] (1928); *Die Regimentstochter* [Hans Behrendt] (Ger.); *Champagne* [Alfred Hitchcock] (1928); *Squibs* (1935); *29 Acacia Avenue* [Henry Cass] (1945).

BALLHAUS, Michael
Berlin 1935

German cinematographer. After training as a photographer, Ballhaus began working for television in 1959, but his feature film debut was *Mehrmals täglich/Several Times Daily* (1969). A superb craftsman, renowned for his fluid tracking shots and sensual interiors (perhaps a tribute to his relative Max Ophuls*), Ballhaus' crucial phase began in 1970, when he became Rainer Werner Fassbinder's* preferred cameraman, responsible for the sinuous energy animating so many of the director's claustrophobic sets. After working on fourteen Fassbinder films in total (until Xaver Schwarzenberger took over on *Berlin Alexanderplatz*, 1980), Ballhaus was cameraman for Peter Lilienthal and on some television documentaries. Thanks to Lilienthal's *Dear Mr Wonderful* (1980), shot in New York, he made contact with Martin Scorsese, the start of his American career. Since being granted American film union membership, Ballhaus has been much in demand, as cinematographer on films such as *Baby, It's You* (1982), *The Color of Money* (1986), *Bram Stoker's Dracula* (1992) and *The Age of Innocence* (1993). TE

BALLING, Erik
Nyborg 1924

Danish director, who began his career in 1946 as an assistant director at Nordisk Films*, where he has worked ever since. His first feature film was the comedy *Adam og Eva/Adam and Eve* (1953), and he subsequently directed many other comedies, among them the first Danish colour feature, *Kispus/Puss in the Corner* (1956). Balling became production head at Nordisk in 1954 and managing director in 1957. In the mid-1960s he made two lively parodies of secret agent movies: *Slå først, Frede/Strike First Freddie* (1965) and *Slap af, Frede/Relax, Freddie* (1966). Inspired by their success, in 1968 he launched a series of films depicting the adventures of the *Olsen Banden/Olsen Gang*, a band of inept petty crooks. The series eventually numbered thirteen films, the last made in 1981, and all were extraordinarily successful with Danish audiences; the rights were sold to Sweden and Norway, where the gang became, respectively, *Jönsson Liga* and *Olsenbanden**. During the same period Balling produced two television series – *Huset på Christianshavn/The House at Christianshavn* (1970–77, 84 episodes) and *Matador* (1978–81, 18 episodes) – inspired by British television models, the soap opera *Coronation Street* and the series *Upstairs Downstairs*. Balling's films are characterised by a witty, sometimes satirical style and an inventive use of *mise-en-scène*. ME

Other Films Include: *Qivitoq* (1956); *Midt om Natten/In the Middle of the Night* (1984).

BALS, Hubert
Utrecht 1937–88

Dutch film personality. Bals began his career in film exhibition and public relations, organised his first independent film festival, Cinemanifestatie, in Utrecht in 1966 (it ran for six years), and became the first director of the Rotterdam international film festival in 1972. He combined organisational skill with artistic instinct, creating new structures for film culture where old ones had failed. Apart from the Rotterdam festival, he was instrumental in creating a non-profit making cinema chain in the Netherlands and laid the foundations of an art-film distribution company. He travelled the world as a talent scout, eager to bring his discoveries to his festivals. He not only tracked down new talents, but also did his best to give independent film-makers an audience and distribution outlets. His assistant Kees Kasander* founded the Anglo-Dutch production company Allarts. After Bals' untimely death in 1988, the Hubert Bals Fund was created to support innovative film projects worldwide. KD

Bib: Reg ten Zijthoff, 'Huub Bals', *Nederlands Jaarboek Film 1987* (1987).

BANDERAS, Antonio
José Antonio Domínguez Banderas; Malaga 1960

Spanish actor. Despite distinguished work for such prestigious directors as Carlos Saura* (*Los zancos/Stilts*, 1984) and Vicente Aranda* (*Si te dicen que caí/If They Tell You I've Fallen*, 1989), Banderas is best known for his association with Pedro Almodóvar* since his screen debut in *Laberinto de pasiones/Labyrinth of Passions* (1982). The core of Banderas's persona in the 1980s is that of a naive young man burdened and slightly unbalanced by familial and religious repression (*Matador*, 1986), a great passion (for Muslim fundamentalism in *Laberinto de pasiones*, for the Republic in *Si te dicen que caí*, for Victoria Abril* in *¡Atame!/Tie Me Up! Tie Me Down!*, 1989), or both: *La ley del deseo/The Law of Desire* (1987). He has regularly played gay men – in *Laberinto*, *La ley* and *Philadelphia* (1993, US) without any loss of popularity. Banderas has appeared in comedy (*Mujeres al borde de un ataque de nervios/Women on the Verge of a Nervous Breakdown*, 1988) and drama (*La blanca paloma/The White Dove*, 1990) with equal ease. However, although his performance in the latter won him the prize for best actor at the Valladolid film festival, Banderas is more acclaimed for his charisma and sex appeal than for his acting. In the 1990s, his international popularity led to work in Italy (*Il ladro di bambini/Child Thief*, 1992) and Hollywood. However, his international career has carried a price, as his roles in American cinema – *The Mambo Kings* (1991), *Philadelphia* and *Interview with the Vampire* (1994) – tend to be pale carbon copies of his Spanish performances. JA

BARBARO, Umberto
Acireale 1902 – Rome 1959

Italian theoretician and scriptwriter. The erudite, self-taught Barbaro placed cinema at the centre of a multiplicity of interests and experiences. Also a novelist (*Luce fredda, L'isola del sole*), he founded a late futurist movement ('Immaginismo') [> FUTURISM], edited literary reviews, wrote comic plays and translated theoretical writings on film by Rudolf Arnheim*, Béla Balász* and Vsevolod Pudovkin* among others. In the early 1930s, at the height of the Fascist dictatorship, he acquainted himself with the works of Freud and Marx. Together with art historian Roberto Longhi he made the documentaries *Carpaccio* (1947) and *Caravaggio* (1948). He worked for Cecchi Gori's* Cines*, for which he directed a Walther Ruttmann*-style social documentary (*I cantieri dell'Adriatico*, 1933) and scripted Goffredo Alessandrini's* melodrama *Seconda B* (1934). Although an anti-Fascist, he was offered a teaching position at the new Centro Sperimentale* in 1935. A leading light of the Italian cultural changes of the late 1930s, he developed a notion of neo-realism* as synthesis of the 'national tradition' and elaborated a materialist aesthetic as well as an anti-idealist notion of 'collective creativity'. After the fall of Fascism, he worked at the Centro Sperimentale (1944–47) as special commissioner, and taught at the Polish film school in Łódź*. He combined all this with scriptwriting (for instance for Giuseppe De Santis'* *Caccia tragica/Tragic Hunt*, 1947) and directing (the unsuccessful *L'ultima nemica/The Last Enemy*, 1938). A journalist for *L'Unità* and *Vie Nuove*, his communist stance became increasingly rigid and his 'poetics of realism' turned into absolute, normative criteria. Some of his writings were collected posthumously by his students in *Il film e il risarcimento marxista dell'arte* (1960) and *Servitú e grandezza del cinema* (1962), which document thirty years of research on film, from the 1932 preface to Pudovkin's writings to an unfinished treatise on general aesthetics. GVo

BARCELONA SCHOOL

Spanish film group. The term describes a group of film-makers working in the late 1960s, based in Barcelona. The first film produced by the 'school' (a term the film-makers did not really accept) was Vicente Aranda's* second film, *Fata Morgana/Morgan Le Fay* (1966). Other directors covered by the term include Jorge Grau, Joaquín Jordá, Jacinto Esteva, Carlos Durán and Gonzalo Suárez*. The aims of the group were recorded by Jordá in the journal *Nuestro Cine/Our Cinema*. These can be summarised as a desire for self-financed production as well as a greater commitment than that shown by Madrid-based directors to experimentation in form and content. The movement was a response to both mainstream popular cinema and the more socially oriented Madrid-based directors. The group soon dispersed because of its minority appeal, and its impact on Spanish audiences was very limited. PWE
[> SPANISH REGIONAL CINEMA]

BARDÈCHE, Maurice and BRASILLACH, Robert

Dun-sur-Auron 1909

Perpignan 1909 – Fresnes 1945

French film historians. With their *Histoire du cinéma* (translated as *The History of Motion Pictures*), first published in 1935, revised in 1943 and reprinted many times since, Bardèche and Brasillach inaugurated the pioneering wave of French film historiography which also included Jean Mitry and Georges Sadoul*. Ideologically opposed to the communist Sadoul, Bardèche and Brasillach were overtly fascistic

and anti-semitic, not least in their opinions on film. They shared with Sadoul, however, an enthusiasm for silent cinema and *auteur* films and a distrust of popular entertainment. They were particularly hostile to the coming of sound, seeing it – like many then – as 'the agony of an art'. But they could rise above their political bias to recognise artistic value, for instance in Jean Renoir*. Brasillach was an intellectual and novelist (Bardèche, an academic, was his brother-in-law), and a literary and film critic for the royalist *L'Action française* and the fascist *Je suis partout*. He was executed for collaboration and 'intellectual crime'. Bardèche was imprisoned and deprived of his university chair but continued to write, notably on fascism. GV

BARDEM, Juan Antonio

Juan Antonio Bardem Muñoz; Madrid 1922

Spanish director, who, with Luis García Berlanga*, brought about a sea-change in Spanish cinema in the early 1950s; both were key figures in the 'Conversaciones de Salamanca' in May 1955. Reacting against the officially sanctioned comedies and historical films of the 1940s, and influenced partly by Italian neo-realism*, Bardem set out to create a cinema which dealt with the everyday realities of life under Franco and which can be referred to as 'Spanish neo-realism'*. After his early collaboration with Berlanga – with whom he co-directed *Esa pareja feliz/That Happy Couple* (1951) and co-scripted *¡Bienvenido, Mr Marshall!/Welcome Mr Marshall!* (1952) – Bardem made his masterpiece *Calle Mayor/Main Street* (1956), a devastatingly realistic portrayal of the claustrophobia and inertia of Spanish provincial life which, like his *Muerte de un ciclista/Death of a Cyclist* (1955), both uncovers the moral bankruptcy of 1950s Spain and encourages a sense of social and moral responsibility in the spectator. Such attitudes, however elliptically or allegorically conveyed, caused Bardem constant problems with censors throughout the 1950s and 60s. He was arrested several times and even imprisoned. After Franco's death, Bardem made more stridently political films reflecting his Communist beliefs, such as *El puente/The Long Weekend* (1976) and *Siete días de enero/Seven Days in January* (1978), both of which were commercial and critical flops. After spending some time working outside Spain, he made *Lorca, muerte de un poeta/Lorca, Death of a Poet* for Televisión Española in 1988. SGHR

BARDOT, Brigitte

Paris 1934

French actress. One of the very few French stars to achieve equivalent world fame, Bardot was propelled to stardom by *Et Dieu ... créa la femme/And God Created Woman* (1956), directed by her then husband Roger Vadim*. While the film has been hailed – somewhat exaggeratedly – as a precursor of the New Wave*, it launched 'BB', a former model, as the most potent female sexual myth in 1950s France and a valuable export commodity. Bardot's screen persona defined the sex-kitten, wedding 'natural' and unruly sexuality with childish attributes – slim but full-breasted, blonde with a girlish fringe, the pout and the giggle. After her spectacular breakthrough, she went on to star in many unremarkable vehicles, with a few intelligent exceptions: Henri-Georges Clouzot's* *La Vérité* (1960), a courtroom drama in which her sexuality itself is on trial, Louis Malle's* semi-biographical *Vie privée* (1962), and Jean-Luc Godard's* *Le Mépris/Contempt* (1963). She was idolised – her gingham dresses, hairstyle and pout were copied by millions of women, and she modelled for the effigy of the French Republic – but also viciously attacked and abused. The archetypal object of male fantasies, Bardot was also a rebel (on and off screen), delighting in her own body and sexuality: 'as much a hunter as she is a prey,' as Simone de Beauvoir put it. As a result she was box-office although she wasn't always popular. Unlike her contemporaries Marilyn Monroe and Diana Dors*, Bardot showed stamina and a shrewd business sense. She retired from acting in 1973 and is now a devoted campaigner for animal rights. GV

Bib: Simone de Beauvoir, *Brigitte Bardot and the Lolita Syndrome* (1960).

Other Films Include: *Le Trou normand/Crazy for Love* (1952); *Doctor at Sea* [UK], *Les Grandes manoeuvres, Helen of Troy* [US] (1955); *La Lumière d'en face/The Light Across the Street, Cette sacrée gamine/Mam'zelle Pigalle, La Mariée est trop belle/The Bride is Too Beautiful* (1956); *Une Parisienne* (1957); *Les Bijoutiers du clair de lune/The Night Heaven Fell, En cas de malheur/Love is My Profession* (1958); *La Femme et le pantin/A Woman Like Satan, Babette s'en va-t-en guerre/Babette Goes to War* (1959); *Les Amours célèbres* (1961); *Le Repos du guerrier/Warrior's Rest* (1962); *Une ravissante idiote/A Ravishing Idiot* (1964); *Viva Maria!* (1965); *Histoires extraordinaires/Spirits of the Dead, Shalako* [UK] (1968); *L'Ours et la poupée/The Bear and the Doll* (1970); *Boulevard du rhum/Rum Runner, Les Pétroleuses/The Legend of Frenchie King* (1971); *Don Juan 1973 ou si Don Juan était une femme/Don Juan or if Don Juan were a woman...* (1973).

BARKER, (Sir) William G. London 1867 – [?] 1951

British producer and director of the early silent cinema. A travelling salesman, whose early interest in cinema was as a cameraman on 'topicals', Barker became manager of the successful Warwick Trading Company in 1906 and formed his own company, Barker Motion Photography, in 1909, building the first studios at Ealing. For his first major success, *Henry VIII* (1911), he hired Sir Herbert Beerbohm Tree at a reputed fee of £1,000 for a day's shooting, and then boosted his rentals by announcing that he would publicly burn all circulation copies after a release of six weeks. Rachael Low compares him with Cecil Hepworth*, ascribing to Hepworth 'the greatness of dignity' and to Barker 'the greatness of the preposterous, the larger-than-life'. He retired from the cinema in 1916. JC

Bib: Rachael Low, *The History of British Film, 1906–1914* (1948).

Other Films Include: *The Fighting Parson* (1912); *The Tube of Death/The Anarchist's Doom, The Battle of Waterloo, Sixty Years a Queen, East Lynne, The Great Bullion Robbery, In the Hands of the London Crooks* (1913); *The Lights O' London* (1914); *Jane Shore* (1915).

BARNET, Boris V.   Moscow 1902 – Riga, Latvia [USSR] 1965

Soviet director, actor and scriptwriter. Barnet, who came from an English family, trained as a boxer in the army, then studied in Lev Kuleshov's* workshop and acted in the latter's *Neobychainye priklyucheniya Mistera Vesta v strane Bol'shevikov/The Extraordinary Adventures of Mr West in the Land of the Bolsheviks* (1924), and in Fyodor Otsep's* *Miss Mend* (1926), which he also co-scripted and co-directed, before directing a series of light-hearted comedies beginning with *Devushka s korobkoi/The Girl with a Hatbox* (1927) and *Dom na Trubnoi/The House on Trubnaya* (1928). His first sound film was *Okraina/The Outskirts* (1933), a study of the effects of the Revolution on a small provincial town and a comment on the relationship between the individual and history. In 1936 he made a comedy about a collective fish farm, *U samogo sinego morya/By the Bluest of Seas*. His three World War II films, including *Staryi naezdnik/The Old Jockey* (1940, released 1959), were banned. As a reaction perhaps, Barnet, usually a most unpolitical man, directed and acted in one of the earliest Cold War films, *Podvig razvedchika/The Exploits of a Scout* (1947), awarded a Stalin Prize in 1948. In his later films he returned to comedy, as in *Shchedroe leto/Bounteous Summer* (1950), *Liana* (1955), and his last film, *Polustanok/Whistle-Stop* (1963), which foreshadows the work of Vasili Shukshin*. He also made a number of film dramas dealing with the history of the revolutionary movement and socialist construction, such as *Stranitsy zhizni/Pages from a Life* (1948), *Poet/The Poet* (1956), *Borets i kloun/The Wrestler and the Clown* (1957), *Annushka* (1959, about the suffering endured by Soviet women during World War II) and *Alyonka* (1961). Barnet committed suicide while making *Sūtņu sazvērestība/The Ambassadors' Plot* in Riga. RT

BARRANCO, María   María de los Remedios Barranco García; 1961

Spanish actress. Lanky, Andalusian-accented supporting star who rose to prominence in Pedro Almodóvar's* *Mujeres al borde de un ataque de nervios/Women on the Verge of a Nervous Breakdown* (1988). Her role as Candela staked out her territory as the essence of gullible kind-heartedness, the woman too innocent or trusting to notice that her lover is a Shiite terrorist. The same aura of innocence and vulnerability surrounds her roles as the golden-hearted transvestite in *Las edades de Lulú/The Ages of Lulu* (1990, dir. Juan José Bigas Luna*) and as the whore in *El rey pasmado/The Stupefied King* (1991, dir. Imanol Uribe*). PWE

BARRANDOV FILM STUDIOS

The main studios in Czechoslovakia were designed by Max Urban, architect and film pioneer, and built in 1932–33. The studios stand on a small plateau to the west of Prague, named after Joachim Barrande, a French geologist. Planned as a centre for international production, in the 1930s Barrandov saw the filming of Julien Duvivier's* French-language version of *Le Golem/Golem* (1936) and multi-language versions of Victor Tourjansky's *Volga en flammes/Volha v plamenech/Volga in Flames* (1933) and Nicolas Farkas' *Port Arthur* (1936). However, the studios developed mainly as a centre for national production, catering for an increased domestic audience until they were expanded again during the Nazi occupation as an alternative centre for German production (G. W. Pabst* made *Paracelsus* there in 1942). After the war, along with the newly built Koliba Film Studios in Bratislava, Barrandov became a centre for the nationalised industry. The studios again showed interest in attracting foreign companies during the 1970s and 1980s, usually with politically correct subjects. Among the films made there were *Operation: Daybreak* (1975), *Yentl* (1983), *Amadeus* (1984), and *Rosa Luxemburg* (1986). Since 1989, facilities have been provided for films responding to the city's more obvious exotic attractions (for example, Steven Soderbergh's *Kafka* [1991], Ian Sellar's *Prague* [1991], George Sluizer's *Utz* [1992], Harold Pinter's adaptation of *The Trial* [1992]). In 1991 a controversial decision was made to cut back the large permanent staff at Barrandov, with the loss of many skills and trades and over 1,700 jobs. In 1993 a new holding company was established with an advisory board that included Miloš Forman*. PH

BARRAULT, Jean-Louis
Le Vésinet 1910 – Paris 1994

French actor, who made his mark primarily in the theatre. His performance in Marcel Carné's* *Les Enfants du paradis* (1943–45) alone ensured his place in film history. Barrault studied acting and mime. He met Madeleine Renaud* in 1936 and married her in 1940; they founded a long-lived stage company. Barrault's thin physique, feverish look and theatrical performance style destined him for romantic parts such as Berlioz in *La Symphonie fantastique* (1942) and the poet in Max Ophuls'* *La Ronde* (1950). He also played mannered cynics – the killers of *Drôle de drame* and *Le Puritain* (both 1937) – and the dual hero of Jean Renoir's* *Le Testament du Dr Cordelier* (1961). His triumph was Baptiste in *Les Enfants du paradis*, based on the mime Debureau, a character he suggested to Carné and Jacques Prévert*, thus also reviving popular interest in pantomime. His last important part was in Ettore Scola's* *La Nuit de Varennes* (1982). GV

BARROS, José Leitão de
Oporto 1896 – Lisbon 1967

Portuguese director. A journalist, painter, set designer and playwright, Barros became involved in cinema in 1918, but his career really began at the end of the silent era with three remarkable films. The first two were the documentary *Nazaré, Praia de Pescadores/The Fishermen of Nazaré* (1929), followed by a fiction film made in the same location, *Maria do Mar/Mary of the Sea* (1930); both films show clear Soviet influence. The third film is *Lisboa, Crónica Anedótica* (1930), a

blend of documentary and fiction with situations recreated on the streets of Lisbon by actors, and reminiscent of René Clair's* early work, especially *Entr'acte* (1924). Barros met Clair when he went to the Epinay studio near Paris to make the first Portuguese sound film, *A Severa* (1931). Adapted from a play by the academic author Júlio Dantas, *A Severa* deals with two archetypes of Portuguese mythology, the 'fado' singer marked by destiny and her macho lover. With the exception of *Maria Papoila* (1937), *A Varanda dos Rouxinois/The Balcony of the Nightingales* (1939) and *Ala-Arriba* (1942), in which he returned to a more realistic approach, Barros contented himself with conventional features, most of them biopics, until the resounding failure of *Vendaval Maravilhoso/The Magic Storm* (1949), a Brazilian co-production, persuaded him to retire. Barros was also a specialist in staging historical commemorations. He worked on the grandiose Exhibition of the Portuguese World in 1940, a propaganda event which was the subject of a full-length documentary by António Lopes Ribeiro*, the two men thus qualifying as the Leni Riefensthals* of the Salazar regime. AMS

Other Films Include: *Pupilas do Senhor Reitor* (1935); *Bocage* (1936); *Inês de Castro* (1944); *Camões* (1946).

BARRY, John
York 1933

British composer. Unlike the other distinguished names of British film music – William Alwyn*, Malcolm Arnold*, Walton, Vaughan Williams – Barry's roots were in popular music. He played in a military band during National Service, was a rock and roll trumpeter, worked with Johnny Dankworth and Jack Parnell, and had his own group, the John Barry Seven, in the 1960s. Best known for his work on the James Bond* films, most of which he scored, he is also responsible for such memorable scores as *Midnight Cowboy* (1969, US), *A Clockwork Orange* (1972) and *Body Heat* (1981, US). He received an Oscar for *Born Free* (1965), and a British Academy award for *The Lion in Winter* (1968). JC

BATALOV, Nikolai P.
Moscow 1899–1937

Soviet actor, who began his career on stage at the Moscow Art Theatre and first appeared in film as a Red Army soldier in Yakov Protazanov's* *Aelita* (1924). Subsequently he often played heroic workers, as in Vsevolod Pudovkin's* *Mat'/The Mother* (1926; as Pavel), Fyodor Otsep's* *Zemlya v plenu/Earth in Captivity* (1928), Nikolai Ekk's* *Putëvka v zhizn'/The Path to Life* (1931) and Lev Kuleshov's* *Gorizont* (1933). His acting was marked by depth and warmth of characterisation and he was always popular with Soviet audiences. RT

BATCHELOR, Joy
Watford 1914 – London 1991
and
HALAS, John
Budapest, Hungary 1912 – London 1995

British animators, forming Halas-Batchelor cartoons in 1940, who made many information and propaganda cartoons for the Ministry of Information during the war. Halas-Batchelor became the largest animation unit in postwar Britain, making shorts for information and educational uses and for entertainment. Their most successful film was the animated feature-length version of *Animal Farm* (1954), which took three years to make. Their only other feature-length film was a version of *Ruddigore* (1966). JC

Other Films Include: *Carnival in the Clothes Cupboard* (1941); *Dustbin Parade, Digging for Victory* (1942); *Jungle Warfare* (1943, also *Six Little Jungle Boys*); *A Modern Guide to Health* (1946); *The Owl and the Pussycat* (1953); *History of the Cinema* (1956); *Dam the Delta* (1960); *Automania 2000* (1963); *What is a Computer?* (1970).

BAUER, Branko   Dubrovnik, Croatia 1921

Croatian director and scriptwriter. What Hitchcock and Hawks were for the French *politique des auteurs**, Bauer was for the young film critics in 1970s Yugoslavia. By discovering him, they rediscovered the notion of *auteur* and genre: from teen adventures (*Sinji galeb/Blue Seagull*, 1953) to war psycho-thrillers (*Ne okreći se, sine/Don't Turn Back, Son*, 1956), Bauer knew how to play with emotions, and children. He would repeat this game twenty years later with a television series (and the movie) *Zimovanje u Jakobsfeldu/Wintering in Jakobsfeld* (1975), the story of a young boy finding shelter and work in a small Pannonic village during World War II. One of the most successful television series ever in former Yugoslavia, it turned the young actor Slavko Štimac into a national hero. As a film-maker with high social awareness, Bauer found an original way of putting a tough political message into a genre form and occasionally diluting it with a touch of humour. Back in 1957, he directed the highly acclaimed *Samo ljudi/Traces*, a melodramatic love story about a war invalid and a blind girl, full of half-hidden dark undertones. His most successful socially critical film was *Licem u lice/Face to Face* (1963), which demonstrated how the idea of socialist self-management could degenerate into local nepotism and corruption. SP

Other Films: *Milioni na otoku/Millions on the Island* (1954); *Tri Ane/The Three Annes* (1959); *Martin u oblacima/Martin in the Clouds* (1961); *Prekobrojna/Superfluous* (1962); *Nikoletina Bursać* (1964); *Doći i ostati/To Come and to Stay* (1965); *Četvrti suputnik/Fourth Companion* (1967); *Salaš u Malom Ritu* (1976); *Boško Buha* (1979).

BAUER, Yevgeni F.   Moscow 1865 – Crimea [Russian Empire] 1917

Russian director. After a brief career as a newspaper caricaturist, actor and stage designer for popular winter garden theatres, Bauer became, even more briefly, the leading figure in Russian pre-Revolutionary cinema. He began by designing the sets for *Trëkhsotletie tsarstvovaniya doma Romanovykh/ The Tercentenary of the Rule of the House of Romanov* (1913), and directed more than eighty films in the ensuing

four years. Heavily influenced by Russian literary Symbolism and the national version of *art nouveau* known as *style moderne*, Bauer's films were characterised by their sense of architecture and volume, their distinctively spacious sets, the sparing use of furniture and furnishings and subtle use of light and shade. He was the first to create a new sense of screen reality, as opposed to straightforward naturalism. Ivan Perestiani* remarked: 'Bauer had a gift for using light. His scenery was alive, mixing the monumental with the intimate. ... A beam of light in his hands was an artist's brush.' Bauer's best-known films dealt with the extremes of human experience, the borderlines between life, art and death, as in *Ditya bol'shogo goroda/A Child of the Big City* (1914), *Grëzy/ Daydreams* and *Posle smerti/After Death* (both 1915) and *Zhizn' za zhizn'/A Life for a Life* (1916). He produced, designed, scripted and photographed most of his films, which were very popular with Russian audiences. He made Vera Kholodnaya* a star and became, from 1913, the principal money-earner for Alexander Khanzhonkov's* studio, which paid him the largest salary in Russian cinema at the time and in which he became a principal shareholder. But he never achieved his ambition to become a screen actor: while practising in the Crimea to play the part of a lame artist, he fell and broke his leg, caught pneumonia and died. RT

BAUR, Harry   Henri Baur; Montrouge 1880 – Paris 1943

French actor. A prominent stage actor who became one of the most popular stars of the 1930s. After a few silent parts, Baur's film career proper started with the coming of sound, in Julien Duvivier's* *David Golder* (1930). He then embarked on a prolific screen career, including many films with Duvivier. A corpulent man with a resonant voice, his stagey performance style ranged from the hammy (as in Granowsky's *Tarass Boulba*, 1936, or Duvivier's *Un carnet de bal*, 1937) to the soberly moving, especially as Jean Valjean in Raymond Bernard's* *Les Misérables* (1933), as the judge in Pierre Chenal's* *Crime et châtiment/Crime and Punishment* (1935), and in Robert Siodmak's* *Mollenard* (1937).

Baur died horrifyingly after torture by the Gestapo (though, ironically, he had worked for the German firm Continental). GV

BAUTISTA, Aurora   Aurora Bautista Zumel; Valladolid 1925

Spanish actress. Contracted by Cifesa* following her discovery by Juan de Orduña*, she achieved stardom in *Locura de amor/Love Crazy* (1948). Other Cifesa successes include *Agustina de Aragón/Agustina of Aragon* (1950) and *Pequeñeces/Trifles* (1950). Though characterised by an occasionally excessive performance style, she had an aura of power and endurance which brought her success in less eroticised leading roles in films like *Teresa de Jesús* (1961) and *La tía Tula/Aunt Tula* (1964). Her deglamorisation in the latter added force to a narrative about a woman's edginess and unease about sex. PWE

BAVA, Mario
San Remo 1914 – Rome 1980

Italian director and cinematographer. A highly inventive photographer, Bava started his career as an assistant cameraman, graduating to cinematographer in the late 1930s and working for directors as diverse as Roberto Rossellini*, Steno, Mario Monicelli*, Dino Risi*, G. W. Pabst* and Federico Fellini*. Moving into direction, he became a master of ultra-low-budget special effects in the studio. His first full direction credit was on *La maschera del demonio/Mask of the Demon/Black Sunday* (1960), which launched the career of British-born actress Barbara Steele* as unquestioned star of the Italian horror film*. Though he ventured into other genres, such as the peplum* (*Ercole al centro della terra/Hercules in the Haunted World*, 1961), it was in the mainstream Italian horror film – for instance *La frusta e il corpo/Night is the Phantom* (1963) and *I tre volti della paura/Black Sabbath* (1963) – that his visual imagination and skill with lighting and decor were put to best effect. GF

BAXTER, John
Foots Cray, Kent 1896 – [?] 1975

British director and producer. A theatre manager and agent before he came to the cinema in the early 1930s, Baxter brought with him a love of music hall and a commitment to the victims of the Depression. The love of music hall was expressed in his work with Arthur Lucan* in two films featuring Old Mother Riley (a popular cross-dress 'dame'), *Old Mother Riley in Society* (1940) and *Old Mother Riley in Business* (1940), and in three films with Flanagan and Allen, *Theatre Royal* (1943), *Dreaming* (1944) and *Here Comes the Sun* (1945). His commitment to society's victims is expressed in a series of not particularly elegant but hard-hitting films in the 1930s and 1940s, beginning with his debut semi-documentary *Doss House* (1933). His best-known film, *Love on the Dole* (1941), adapted from Walter Greenwood's best-selling novel, presents a rather different image of life in the Northern slums than had been circulated by Gracie Fields*.

Described by Richard Dyer McCann as a 'poor man's Mick Balcon*', Baxter took up production after the war. He was instrumental in the establishment of the National Film Finance Corporation (NFFC) in 1948, and he became the Managing Director of Group 3, an attempt to establish a government-supported feature film unit, during its brief life from 1951 until 1957. JC

Bib: Geoff Brown and Tony Aldgate, *The Common Touch: the Films of John Baxter* (1989).

Other Films Include: *Say It With Flowers, Music Hall, Flood Tide* (1934); *A Real Bloke, The Small Man* (1935); *Men of Yesterday, Hearts of Humanity* (1936); *Song of the Road* (1937); *Crook's Tour* (1940); *The Common Touch* (1941); *Let the People Sing, We'll Smile Again* (1942); *The Shipbuilders, When We Are Married* (1943).

BAYE, Nathalie
[Judith Mesnil?] Mainneville 1948

French actress, trained in theatre and dance and launched in film by François Truffaut's* *La Nuit américaine/Day for Night* (1973), in which she plays the continuity person. With Miou-Miou*, Isabelle Huppert* and Isabelle Adjani*, Baye became one of the quartet of strong French actresses of the 1970s and 1980s. Truffaut's *La Chambre verte/The Green Room* (1978), Bertrand Tavernier's* *Une semaine de vacances* and Jean-Luc Godard's* *Sauve qui peut (la vie)/Slow Motion* (1980, Best Actress César*) established her screen persona. Capitalising on her discreet good looks, they revealed a vulnerable yet determined personality whose naturalistic performances are characterised by graceful gestures, a shy smile and occasional tearfulness. This image endures even in against-the-grain roles like the prostitute in Bob Swaim's *La Balance* (1982, Best Actress César) or the sensual heroine of *Le Retour de Martin Guerre/The Return of Martin Guerre* (1982).

Baye's brief marriage to pop star Johnny Halliday in the early 1980s was newsworthy, but her career declined somewhat in the latter part of the decade. She has, however, successfully reappeared in 'independent yet vulnerable' roles in Diane Kurys'* *La Baule-les-Pins/C'est la vie* (1989) and Nicole Garcia's *Un Week-end sur deux* (1990). She starred in *Mensonge/The Lie* (1993), one of the first French AIDS movies. GV

BAZIN, André
Angers 1918 – Bry-sur-Marne 1958

French film critic and theoretician. An eminent film critic and educator in France in the 1940s and 1950s (he taught at IDHEC* among other institutions), Bazin is the single most influential writer in film studies, 'as central a figure in film aesthetics as Freud is in psychology' (Andrew Sarris). Although he had predecessors – Louis Delluc*, Rudolf Arnheim*, Béla Balázs*, Paul Rotha* – Bazin's uniqueness was to combine rigorous film analysis, militant pedagogic vocation and popularising journalism (as film critic for *Le Parisien libéré*). His intellectual training was a blend of Catholicism, Catholic-inspired philosophy and socialist commitment. Working for *Travail et Culture*, he took the cinema to factories, trade union halls and the *ciné-clubs* which he did much to develop, tirelessly commenting and stimulating discussion; some of his best essays are the result of these activities, such as his celebrated analysis of *Le Jour se lève* (1939), published in 1947. Working during the war and the period of liberation, a time of unparalleled enthusiasm for the cinema, Bazin charted the main areas of film studies as we know them, effectively creating the discipline: authorship (a pioneering study of Orson Welles, a defence of Chaplin, writings on Jean Renoir* and new independent film-makers such as Jean-Pierre Melville* and Jacques Tati*, which led Bazin's disciples to develop the *politique des auteurs**), realism (sparked by his interest in documentary and neo-realism*), stars (Humphrey Bogart, Jean Gabin*), the notion of a 'classical' Hollywood cinema. His idea of cinema as a 'window on the world' and his defence of long takes and deep-focus cinematography against Soviet montage* are his best known (sometimes reductively) and most controversial views – even at the time, when Bazin was accused of 'formalism' by critics such as Georges Sadoul*. It is also the case that for all his openness to the social and historical world Bazin was oblivious of the male bias of his milieu and filmic interests. Bazin's theoretical work came under renewed attack in the 1970s, when his 'bourgeois' emphasis on *auteurs* and his belief in the integrity of visual space were out of step with new thinking inspired by psycho-analysis, semiology and Marxism. However, these critiques, initiated at *Cahiers du cinéma**, contained more than a hint of Oedipal rebellion; they could not have existed without the solid foundations that Bazin had laid down. Furthermore, as Dudley Andrew points out, some of the concerns of 1980s and 1990s film studies, such as the status of images, are indebted to his work on the 'ontology' of the image. By all accounts a captivating, generous personality, Bazin acted as mentor to the New Wave* and was an adoptive father to François Truffaut*, who characterised him as 'intelligence itself'. He died prematurely just before the release of Truffaut's first feature, *Les Quatre cents coups/The 400 Blows* (1959), which was dedicated to him. GV

Bib: Dudley Andrew, *André Bazin* (1978, reprinted 1990).

BBFC: see BRITISH BOARD OF FILM CENSORS

BEAUREGARD, Georges de
Edgar de Beauregard;
Marseilles 1920 – Paris 1984

French producer, who became a key player in the development of *auteur* cinema in France. Beauregard earned the so-briquet 'father of the New Wave*' for his work with Jean-Luc Godard*, especially their legendary collaboration on *A bout de souffle/Breathless* (1960). A former journalist, Beauregard had worked in French film export, especially to Spain, which had led him to produce two of Juan Antonio Bardem's* films. He introduced Godard to Raoul Coutard* and saw them through the difficult shoot of *A bout de souffle*. He produced many of Godard's subsequent films, as well as films by Jacques Demy*, Agnès Varda*, Jean-Pierre Melville*, Jacques Rivette* and Eric Rohmer*, among others. A cinema in Paris bears his name. GV

BECCE, Giuseppe
Lonigo, Italy 1877 –
Berlin 1973

Italian composer who worked in Germany, adapting existing musical compositions for Messter*-Film and other companies in 1913 (for instance *Richard Wagner* in which he starred as the composer), while simultaneously writing original accompanying music which he called '*Autorenillustrationen*' (author's illustrations). Becce decisively shaped the musical dramaturgy of German silent cinema and his *Kinothek*, an alternative to foreign music compilations, appeared in print from 1919. In the 1920s Becce became head of Ufa's* music division. His most notable compositions were incidental music for F. W. Murnau's* *Tartüff* (1926, use of leitmotif and quotations) and *Der letzte Mann/The Last Laugh* (1924, rhythm). He remained one of Germany's most productive film composers of the sound era. Famous from the later period are his soundtracks for Luis Trenker's* Berge in

Flammen/The Doomed Battalion (1931) and *Der Berg ruft/The Challenge* (1938), and Leni Riefenstahl's* *Das blaue Licht/The Blue Light* (1932). SG

BECKER, Jacques
Paris 1906–60

French director. The son of an Anglo-French upper middle-class family, Becker acted as assistant to Jean Renoir* in the 1930s. This was a key influence on his work and critical reputation, locating him within the realist-humanist tradition of French cinema.

A co-director of the communist propaganda film *La Vie est à nous* (1936) and a number of short films, Becker started making features in 1942 with the thriller *Dernier atout,* and *Goupi Mains-rouges/It Happened at the Inn* (1943), a sombre peasant saga. *Falbalas*, an elegant yet acid-tinged portrait of a fashion house, followed in 1945. Although lacking a clear social agenda, Becker's work can be seen, like Renoir's, as an ethnocentric panorama of his time: *Rendez-vous de juillet* (1949) is a study of the postwar generation; *Antoine et Antoinette* (1947), *Édouard et Caroline* (1951) and *Rue de l'Estrapade* (1953) are light comedies which gently interrogate their popular and bourgeois settings; as Becker put it, 'I am French, I work on Frenchmen, I look at Frenchmen, I am interested in Frenchmen.' At the same time, Becker's two greatest films were genre works. *Casque d'or/Golden Marie* (1952, with Simone Signoret*) is a romantic costume drama set in turn-of-the-century Paris; undercutting the ostentation of the genre with the sobriety of its performances, it provides a rare sympathetic portrait of female desire. *Touchez pas au grisbi/Honour Among Thieves* (1954), starring Jean Gabin*, defined the postwar *policier**, with its families of Parisian gangsters for whom loyalty and conviviality were as important as the heists. In the 1950s, Becker also made star vehicles such as *Montparnasse 19/Modigliani of Montparnasse* (1958, with Gérard Philipe*) and comedies, before the tense prison drama *Le Trou/The Night Watch* (1960), finished by his son Jean Becker (who as a director in his own right made *L'Été meurtrier/One Deadly Summer* with Isabelle Adjani* in 1982).

Underlying Becker's diversity were a vision of 'French-ness' in its quotidian dimension and the qualities of classical French cinema: 'professionalism, forthrightness, authenticity' (Dudley Andrew). GV

Other Films Include: *Ali Baba et les 40 voleurs/Ali Baba* (1954); *Les Aventures d'Arsène Lupin/The Adventures of Arsène Lupin* (1956).

BEINEIX, Jean-Jacques
Paris 1946

French director. Beineix's career is marked by spectacular successes – *Diva* (1981), *37°2 le matin/Betty Blue* (1986) – and equally spectacular commercial failures: *La Lune dans le caniveau/The Moon in the Gutter* (1983, Fr./It.), *Roselyne et les lions/Roselyne and the Lions* (1989), *IP5* (1992). An eclectic transatlantic training with directors ranging from Jerry Lewis to Claude Berri*, and extensive work in advertising (post-*Diva*), are regularly cited by critics to account for

Beineix's penchant for non-naturalistic colours, object fetishism and startling framings, and have led to accusations of 'style over substance', connecting him to the cinéma du look* and film-makers such as Luc Besson* and Leos Carax*.

Beineix has convincingly argued that advertising is the idiom of youth culture, but has rarely successfully 'spoken' to that youth culture, except in Diva, a cult film of the 1980s, and 37°2 le matin (thanks largely to the exuberant performance of Béatrice Dalle*). Despite a coherent aesthetic programme, Beineix has failed to win over critics in France, where he is rarely considered an auteur. Yet his work combines the baroque mise-en-scène and romantic streak characteristic of many European film-makers whose work he vigorously defended during the 1993 GATT negotiations. GV

BEK-NAZAROV, Amo Yerevan, Armenia [Russian Empire] 1892 – Moscow 1965

Armenian Soviet director, actor and scriptwriter. Bek-Nazarov began his career as a screen actor during World War I in the films of Evgeni Bauer*, Ivan Perestiani* and Vladimir Gardin*, and directed his first features in the Georgian studio in the 1920s. His best-known works were the silent Namus (1926), generally regarded as the first Armenian feature film, the historical drama Zore (1927) and the comedy Shor i Shorshor/Shor and Shorshor (1927). His career continued throughout the sound period and his Zangezur (1938) was awarded the Stalin Prize in 1941. After his death the Armenian film studio was named after him. RT

BELGIUM

Belgium is a small country – only slightly larger than Wales or Massachusetts – and yet it hosts Europe's largest variety of film festivals, has relatively the highest number of film schools, and one of the most extensive archives, in its Cinémathèque Royale*. Successful though it is at nurturing international film culture, Belgium has continually failed to propagate its own cinema, despite boasting, in Joseph Plateau*, one of the inventors of early cinema technology.

The home of Georges Simenon*, René Magritte, George Rémy (Hergé, the creator of Tintin), Pieter Paul Rubens and Jacques Brel*, as a country Belgium has often been the target of (undeserved) international contempt. Examples range from Charles Baudelaire, who criticised its capital city ('Strolling, something that nations with imagination love, is not possible in Brussels. There is nothing to see, and the streets are unusable.') to Billy Wilder, who described Belgium as 'the most unnecessary country'. Struggling to prove its worth, Belgian cinema has had to cope with problems both at home and abroad. The main barrier to creating a viable commercial cinema is Belgium's size, which makes it virtually impossible for a film to make a profit on the domestic market. This problem is compounded by the country's bilingualism, which divides Belgium between Francophone Wallonia and 'Flemish' Flanders (a small German community also exists in the eastern, Eupen-Malmedy area). If the cultural diversity which such divisions create has provided a perfect environment for small-scale, experimental film-making,

Belgian directors who aim for an exportable product are forced to seek wider appeal through 'European' stars, documentary and art cinema or co-productions (Marion Hänsel* is one successful example). Wallonia has also struggled against the appropriation and exile of many of its talented directors, actors and technicians to France. Examples include the director Jacques Feyder* and the scriptwriter Charles Spaak, the writer Georges Simenon, and Raoul J. Lévy, producer of Brigitte Bardot's* films among others (a more recent high-profile émigré is the Brussels-born Hollywood star Jean-Claude Van Damme).

The situation is even more complicated in what is often called the Flemish part of Belgium – more accurately the Dutch-speaking part, Flemish being dialects spoken only in the provinces of East and West Flanders. Here the struggle is against a variety of factors: the prestige and cultural power of the unilingual Netherlands, the deep divisions within Dutch-speaking Belgium stemming from the extensive and enthusiastic collaboration by 'Flemish' activists with the Nazis during World War II, the consistent political and economic domination of a Francophone élite, and the pervasive influence of a deeply conservative Catholic hierarchy. It is important to note the complexities attaching to the use of the label 'Flemish' when discussing Dutch-speaking Belgium. 'Flemish' connotes a commitment to the Catholic hierarchy (as opposed to the more liberal Protestantism of the Netherlands, from which Belgium obtained its independence in 1830) and a rejection of Francophone domination; it also mobilises the myth of late medieval glories to boost the political pedigree of Flemish wartime collaborators who have appropriated the term as a political slogan and label to designate an area over which they want to re-establish control. In Belgium, the language is 'Nederlands' ('Neerlandophone' in French), not 'Vlaams' (Flemish), a word avoided by those who refuse to offer legitimacy to the fascist roots of the 'Flemish' political parties and organisations. Both the 'Flemish' and Francophone cinemas, however, share the problems of a weak administrative structure, insufficient official aid and a shortage of original scripts.

Cinema came to Belgium via France: after the first screenings of the Lumière* brothers' films in Brussels and Louvain in 1897, Pathé* sent the Frenchman Alfred Machin to set up the first Belgian studio in the Karreveld neighbourhood of Brussels. The distribution of Machin's films by Pathé guaranteed them a place in cinemas from the Champs-Elysées to Broadway. Pathé's collapse served to stem the flow of Belgian product to international screens; however, in 1921 the Machelen studio was born, this time a wholly national project set up by Hippolyte de Kempener. Although Machelen's output was extremely varied, mixing patriotic documentaries with adaptations of popular Flemish literature, most of its money was made through foreign productions. Julien Duvivier's* Le Mariage de Mlle Beulemans (1927), filmed at Machelen using both French and Belgian actors, is one of the most famous examples, and stands as the first non-Belgian film to capture Brussels on screen.

The coming of sound divided the Belgian cinema linguistically in two, further marginalising the home market. With no national cinema established before World War I, by the end of the war Belgium had yet again been invaded, this time by American films. Perhaps in response to this 'invasion', the only sustained Belgian output was often adapted from Flemish or Francophone literature, and used regional dialects and a regular troupe of Belgian actors and actresses. At its worst, 'Flemish' cinema was characterised by an anecdotal treatment of its subject and a folkloric, traditional style most frequently adapted from Flemish literature. Meanwhile Francophone cinema often settled for a bourgeois imitation of commercial French cinema. At their best, however, the films of Gaston Schoukens* and Emile De Meyst (in Wallonia) and Jan Vanderheyden* and Edith Kiel (in Flanders) were to set a precedent for a popular Belgian cinema which extends to the present day. Thus Schoukens' use of the Bruxellois accent and 'zwanze' humour is present in the work of Benoît Lamy*, while Vanderheyden's 'Flemish' farce filters down to the recent cinematic success of the comedian Urbanus*.

At the same time as it was developing a popular heritage at home, Belgian cinema was making its mark internationally, through the experimental and documentary work of Henri Storck*, Charles Dekeukeleire* and André Cauvin. Both Storck and Dekeukeleire came to cinema via the cine-clubs of Antwerp (the first was founded in 1921). While Dekeukeleire is generally presumed to have made the first Belgian avant-garde film (Combat de boxe, 1927), and Cauvin is noted particularly for his ethnographic work on the Belgian Congo (Congo, 1944, nominated for an Oscar), it is to Storck that the promotion and development of cinema in Belgium can be credited. Along with critics such as Pierre Vermeylen and André Thirifays, Storck helped to create Belgium's Cinémathèque Royale* (1938) and its first international Film Festival (1947), while, in his films, studying many aspects of Flemish and Walloon culture, life and customs. Other exponents of Belgium's documentary traditions have been Gérard de Boe, Luc de Heusch* and Thierry Michel.

The introduction of state aid in the 1960s ('Flanders' in 1964, Wallonia in 1967) marked a turning point in Belgian cinema. Of equal importance was the appearance of a new generation of film-makers in both communities. In 1956 Meewen sterven in de haven/Les Mouettes meurent au port, based in Antwerp (not in Flanders), was the first Belgian film to be shown at Cannes, launching the careers of Eric De Kuyper*, Ivo Michiels and Roland Verhavert*. The success of this Antwerp thriller (a sort of On the Waterfront) was swiftly followed by André Delvaux's* debut De Man die zijn Haar Kort Liet Knippen/The Man Who Had His Hair Cut Short (1965) which, far from attempting to fit into the international commercial film circuit, gave full rein to subjective settings and atmospheres redolent of the 'Flemish' 'magic realism' pioneered by the novelist Johan Daisne, whose classic novel was adapted for the film. Following Delvaux's example, and with state aid more fully in place, the Belgian auteur cinema was born, with Chantal Akerman*, Jean-Jacques Andrien* and Raoul Servais* among its most successful figures.

Since the 1960s Belgian cinema has managed more skilfully to combine art with commerce. In 1962 the Musée du Cinéma was opened, which provided an outlet for non-commercial product. Aspiring film-makers could be trained at one of Belgium's several film schools (INSAS, IAD and RITICS) and make their first films with help from the workshops of CBA* (Centre Belge de l'Audiovisuel). For more commer-

cial productions, three choices of funding exist: state subsidy, television or co-production. State aid is granted by the respective (Francophone or 'Flemish') Ministry of Education and Culture. Production aid is given as an advance on receipts, similar to the French 'avance sur recettes'*. Co-production agreements are established by Foreign Affairs and Trade, while the Ministry of Economic Affairs grants aid for festivals and theatrical exploitation. Although subsidy can provide a third or even half of the budget of a film, the ministry's process is highly selective and can lead to constraints and delays.

Belgian television has always had a rather ambivalent attitude to Belgian cinema. While directors such as Paul Meyer* and Manu Bonmariage have managed to make a living since the 1960s through television work, the financial collaboration of Belgian television with the cinema did not really begin until the late 1980s. Belgium has two public channels, BRT and RTBF; two private European broadcasters, RTL and TV1; and Canal Belgium, a pay channel. RTBF chooses two or three projects a year to co-produce, with an annual investment of BF 10 million. Collaboration, then, is poor, and where it does occur, television tends to profit more. The third option for film-makers, co-production (typically with linguistic neighbours France or the Netherlands), is equally problematic. While co-production has the advantage of addressing two markets at once, it inevitably leads to compromise, and Belgium's size compared to its partner(s) means that it will often have a smaller input and its role may be reduced to co-financing with little artistic or technical involvement.

As in most of Europe, the Belgian market is dominated by American product. In 'Flanders' the greatest success (besides Flemish/Dutch productions) is for English-speaking films, which are shown subtitled in both Dutch and French. In Wallonia, not surprisingly, French titles are still popular, all non-Francophone films being dubbed. Cinema attendance has declined further since the introduction of Cable television in the 1970s. Multiplexes, in particular the 25-screen Kinepolis on the outskirts of Brussels (opened in 1990) and the even more massive one outside Antwerp (1994), have introduced new exhibition patterns which threaten the future of Belgium's art cinemas. Despite its many divisions and its history of invasion, appropriation and erasure, Belgium has much to offer in accounts of cinema past and present. While it shares European cinema's struggle against American domination, it has offered specific variations to this dominant model. Belgian cinema has made an important contribution to European cinema, from the 'magic realism' of such film-makers as André Delvaux to the 'fantastic' animation of Raoul Servais, Picha or Gerald Frydman; in the 1970s, Harry Kümel* was internationally successful with his idiosyncratic reworking of the horror genre. Historically, Belgian cinema's mark is strongest in documentary, the Film sur l'art* as well as the social/anthropological cinema of such film-makers as Storck – whose Borinage (1933, co-dir. Joris Ivens*) is a classic – or Dekeukeleire. Indigenous popular genres, with their fascination for the physically grotesque, endure; even if, like other European cinemas, Belgian cinema has been more successful in exporting its auteurs, from Akerman to Jaco Van Dormael*. CF

[> ANIMATION (BELGIUM), DOCUMENTARY (BELGIUM), FUGITIVE CINEMA, EUROPEAN CINEMA AND EMIGRATION]

BELLOCCHIO, Marco
Piacenza 1939

Italian director. Born to a well-off middle-class provincial family and educated at religious schools, Bellocchio enrolled at the Centro Sperimentale* in Rome, graduating in 1962 with a 55-minute film, *Ginepro fatto uomo*. In 1965, he made a sensational debut with *I pugni in tasca/Fists in the Pocket*. Autobiographical acrimony and expressive violence mingled in the young protagonist's abstract rages against family values, bigoted provincialism and normality, in a manner so radical and so remote from the humanism of neo-realism* that public and critics were violently split over it. In his later films Bellocchio coherently pursued a critique of institutions such as the family, the middle classes and reformist parties, Catholicism, the press, the army and psychiatric institutions: *La Cina è vicina/China is Near* (1967), *Nel nome del padre/In the Name of the Father* (1971), *Sbatti il mostro in prima pagina* (1972), *Marcia trionfale/Victory March* (1976), the pitiless *Salto nel vuoto/Leap into the Void* (1979) and the gentler *Gli occhi, la bocca/The Eyes, The Mouth* (1982). *Nessuno o tutti/Matti da slegare* (1974) was an outstanding investigative documentary on mental hospitals in two versions, shot with Silvano Agosti, Stefano Rulli and Sandro Petraglia, who were also co-directors of the five-part television programme *La macchina cinema* (1978). After two interesting literary adaptations – Chekhov's *Il gabbiano/The Seagull* (1977) and Pirandello's *Enrico IV/Henry IV* (1984) – Bellocchio's work entered a new and controversial phase in which he drew more explicitly on psychoanalysis (influenced by his own psychoanalyst, the unorthodox Massimo Fagioli): *Diavolo in corpo/Devil in the Flesh* (1986), which remains the best film on post-terrorism Italy, *La visione del Sabba* (1987) and *La condanna* (1991). MMo

BELMONDO, Jean-Paul
Neuilly-sur-Seine 1933

French actor and producer. Jean-Paul Belmondo will always be remembered for his embodiment of the emblematic anti-heroes of the New Wave* in Jean-Luc Godard's* *A bout de souffle/Breathless* (1960) and *Pierrot le fou* (1965), but he has also been a pillar of the French mainstream cinema for over two decades.

Belmondo's early success stemmed from stage-bred acting skills and unconventional looks: his engagingly lived-in face, dangling *gauloise* and casually insolent delivery memorably defined the persona of his early films, from Claude Sautet's* *Classe tous risques/The Big Risk* (1960) and the Godard films to Peter Brook and Marguerite Duras'* *Moderato Cantabile* (1960) and Jean-Pierre Melville's* *Léon Morin, prêtre* (1961). Like his rival Alain Delon*, Belmondo turned away from *auteur* cinema towards popular genres after the success of the swashbuckler *Cartouche* (1961) and especially *L'Homme de Rio/That Man from Rio* (1964). Also like Delon, Belmondo favoured stories of virile adventure and friendship, but laced with humour and famously undoubled stunts (if Delon emulated Clint Eastwood, Belmondo was in the James Bond* mode). 'Bébel' became one of the populist heroes of French cinema in a series of vehicles such as *Borsalino* (1970, with Delon), *Le Casse* (1971, Fr./It.), *Le Magnifique* (1973) and *L'As des as* (1982). But again like Delon, his popularity de-

clined in the late 1980s and his output slowed. Apart from producing his own as well as some *auteur* films (Alain Resnais'* *Stavisky...*, 1974, Claire Denis' *Chocolat*, 1988), he has triumphantly returned to the Parisian stage. He starred as Jean Valjean in Claude Lelouch's* 1995 version of *Les Misérables*. GV

Other Films Include: *Les Tricheurs, Charlotte et son Jules* [short] (1958); *A double tour/Web of Passion* (1959); *Une femme est une femme* (1961); *Un singe en hiver* (1962); *Le Doulos, L'Aîné des Ferchaux* (1963); *Cent mille dollars au soleil, Week-end à Zuydcoote/Weekend at Dunkirk* (1964); *Les Tribulations d'un Chinois en Chine/Up to His Ears* (1965); *Tendre voyou* (1966); *Le Voleur/The Thief of Paris* (1967); *Le Cerveau, La Sirène du Mississipi/Mississippi Mermaid* (1969); *Docteur Popaul* (1972); *Peur sur la ville/The Night Caller* (1975); *L'Alpagueur* (1976); *L'Animal* (1977); *Flic ou voyou* (1979); *Le Guignolo* (1980); *Le Professionnel* (1981); *Le Marginal* (1983); *Les Morfalous, Joyeuses Pâques* (1984); *Hold-up* (1985); *Le Solitaire* (1987); *L'Itinéraire d'un enfant gâté* (1988).

BENDTSEN, Henning
Copenhagen 1925

Danish cinematographer. Bendtsen trained as an advertising photographer before becoming a cameraman in 1946, working on short films. He has taught camerawork at the Danish Film School* and the Institute of Film at the University of Copenhagen. He was for a time manager of one of the few drive-in cinemas in Denmark. As cinematographer, Bendtsen has worked on *Paw* (1959), *Den røde kappe/The Red Mantle* (1967) and *Epidemic* (1987) among other films, but he is chiefly remembered for his work on two films directed by Carl Theodor Dreyer*, *Ordet/The Word* (1955) and *Gertrud* (1964). ME

BENE, Carmelo
Campi Salentina 1937

Italian actor and director. A restless personality, intolerant of any form of academicism, Bene made a name for himself as a leading exponent of theatrical reform. Plays staged by him include *Salomè, Faust* and *Hamlet*, based on reworked extracts taken from classics. In the cinema, he had a small part in Franco Indovina's *Lo scatenato* (1967), after which he was an excellent Creon in Pier Paolo Pasolini's* *Edipo re/Oedipus Rex* (1967). As a film director, he began by adapting his own novel *Nostra Signora dei Turchi/Our Lady of the Turks* (1968). This film, a dazzling baroque phantasmagoria about the landing of the Turks in Otranto, was awarded a special jury prize at the Venice festival. Bene's later films, *Capricci* (1969), *Don Giovanni* (1970) and *Salomè* (1972), confirmed his iconoclastic fury and experimental provocativeness with their gaudy colour schemes and abrupt changes in rhythm. With *Un Amleto di meno* (1973) Bene went further in experimentation, attempting to dissolve the image just as his plays had sought to dissolve words. He subsequently moved away from the cinema, concentrating on theatre and literature. Particularly well known in this context are his experiments with verse and sound during public readings of cantos from Dante's *Divine Comedy*. GC

BENIGNI, Roberto   Misericordia 1952

Italian actor and director, one of Italy's most popular comic actors of the 1980s and 1990s. Benigni's fourth film as director and actor, *Johnny Stecchino* (1991), a hilarious lighthearted comedy about the Mafia, broke all box-office records in Italy for either Italian or American films. He had already achieved similar, if less spectacular, success in 1984 with the boisterous *Non ci resta che piangere* (co-written, co-directed and co-acted with Massimo Troisi*) and in 1988 with *Il piccolo diavolo/The Little Devil*, the story of the catastrophic apprenticeship of a mischievous imp. Benigni's first experience as a director was with *Tu mi turbi* (1983), an unusual film composed of four monologues, first conceived as comic sketches; but he had already made a name for himself in 1975 with *Cioni Mario fu Gaspare di Giulia*, a monologue written with Giuseppe Bertolucci, Bernardo's brother, which toured experimental theatres throughout Italy and was eventually used as a source for *Berlinguer, ti voglio bene* (1977). With his transgressive and boorish sense of comedy, his mixture of rustic intelligence and surrealist whims, it was not long before Benigni started to make his mark in television with such programmes as *Onda libera* ('Free Wave', from *Televacca* – 'Cow TV' – a local network pretending to broadcast from a cowshed) and *L'altra domenica* ('The Other Sunday') where he created the figure of a bizarre but ultimately acute film critic. Benigni once defined himself as 'the product of a dispute between God and the PCI' (the former Italian communist party), which in fact continue to be two important sources of inspiration for his humour. He has also been described as 'a dung-heap Woody Allen'. In reality, he is an oddly aggressive and surrealistic genius, an 'innocently' malign spirit who subjugates the audience with the frenetic use of his body and voice. He has essentially remained faithful to these characteristics in his film performances, from 'low' comedies to dramatic films by *auteurs* such as Luigi Zampa* and Antonio Pietrangeli*, Bertolucci (*La luna*, 1979), Marco Ferreri* (*Chiedo asilo*, 1979) and Federico Fellini* (*La voce della luna/The Voice of the Moon*, 1990), as well as, in the US, Jim Jarmusch (*Down by Law*, 1985) and Blake Edwards (*The Son of the Pink Panther*, 1993). *Tuttobenigni* (1985), directed by Giuseppe Bertolucci, is an account of one of Benigni's theatre tours. MMo

BENOÎT-LÉVY, Jean – see EPSTEIN, Marie

BERGER, Ludwig   Mainz 1892 – Schlangenbad 1969

German director, who began as an opera and theatre director. Berger's first films, all adaptations from the stage and examples of the *Kammerspielfilm**, were made with producer Erich Pommer*, first for Decla-Bioscop*, then for Ufa*. Berger gained a considerable reputation in the fantasy genre with the Cinderella variation *Der verlorene Schuh/Cinderella*

in 1923, marked by an ironic lightness which contrasted with the nightmarish world of other German fantasy films of the period. In 1928 he went to Hollywood, where, among other projects, he collaborated with Mauritz Stiller* on *The Street of Sin* (1928) and completed the first musical in colour, *The Vagabond King* (1930). Back in Germany in 1932, he began shooting *Walzerkrieg/Court Waltzes*, which premiered in September 1933 without his name on the credits. In 1936 an offer from Rudi Meyer* took him to the Netherlands, where he made a film of Shaw's *Pygmalion* (1937). He then worked in France (*Trois valses/Three Waltzes*, 1938), in Britain (co-directing *The Thief of Bagdad*, 1940, with Tim Whelan and Michael Powell*) and again in the Netherlands, where he survived the German occupation under a false identity and directed *Ergens in Nederland/Somewhere in Holland* (1940), a pivotal film for the Dutch cinema. After one more film in France (*Ballerina/Poor Little Ballerina*, 1950), Berger started another career in Germany as a prolific scriptwriter for the cinema, radio and television. MW

Bib: Hans-Michael Bock and Wolfgang Jacobsen (eds.), *Ludwig Berger* (1992).

Other Films Include: *Die Meistersinger von Nürnberg/The Meistersingers, The Woman from Moscow* [US], *Sins of the Fathers* [US] (1928); *Das brennende Herz/The Burning Heart* (1929); *Playboy of Paris* (1930, US; Fr. version *Le Petit café*); *Early to Bed* (UK, 1932). **Television**: *Die Spieler* (1954); *Frau Mozart* (1954); *Undine* (1956); *Stresemann, Der Tod des Sokrates, Der Widerspenstigen Zähmung* (1957); *Was Ihr wollt, Viel Lärm um Nichts, Wie es Euch gefällt, Maß für Maß, Ein Sommernachtstraum* (1958); *Das Paradies und die Peri, Die Nacht in Zaandam* (1960); *Hermann und Dorothea* (1961); *Alpenkönig und Menschenfeind* (1962); *Ottiliens Tollheiten* (1964); *Samen von Kraut und Unkraut* (1967); *Odysseus auf Ogygia* (1968); *Demetrius* (1969).

BERGMAN, Hjalmar   Örebro 1883 – Berlin 1931

Swedish scriptwriter. Bergman was one of Sweden's most important and prolific twentieth-century playwrights, known particularly for his satire and his pointed, sometimes caricatured, character portraits. Quick to see the possibilities of the film medium, he was one of the first to write scripts directly for film. He worked primarily with Victor Sjöström*, including a short period in Hollywood. His most important screenplays for Sjöström are *Mästerman/A Lover in Pawn/Masterman* (1920) and *Vem dömer/Love's Crucible* (1922). LGA/BF

BERGMAN, Ingmar   Uppsala 1918

Swedish director, a towering figure in European art cinema*, whose career has throughout intertwined cinema and his other chosen medium, the theatre.

Starting out as a theatre director and manager, Bergman also wrote for both theatre and films. His earliest screen credits were for the script and assistant direction on Alf Sjöberg's* *Hets/Frenzy* (1944), followed two years later by his first film as director, *Kris/Crisis* (1946). Subsequent efforts such as *Det regnar på vår kärlek/It Rains on Our Love* (1946) and *Musik i mörker/Music in Darkness/Night is My Future* (1948) were influenced by American *film noir* and the pessimistic mood of the mid-1940s, while *Hamnstad/Port of Call* (1948) was a genuflection to neo-realism*. The first film over which Bergman had full artistic control was *Fängelse/Prison/The Devil's Wanton* (1949), an elegant blend of 1940s nightmare and urban irony. With cinematographer Gunnar Fischer* and a regular troupe of actors, mainly from the Malmö Municipal Theatre, Bergman embarked on an impressive series of films in the 1950s, starting with *Kvinnors väntan/Waiting Women* (1952) and the successful *Sommaren med Monika/Summer with Monika* (1953). His greatest achievements in this period, however, are generally considered to be *Gycklarnas afton/Sawdust and Tinsel* (1953), *Sommarnattens leende/Smiles of a Summer Night* (1955), *Det sjunde inseglet/The Seventh Seal* (1957) and *Smultronstället/Wild Strawberries* (1957), the last starring the great silent film director Victor Sjöström* in a powerful performance. During the 1960s Bergman's films took on more ascetic qualities. Films such as *Tystnaden/The Silence* (1963), *Persona* (1966) and *Vargtimmen/Hour of the Wolf* (1968) are intense psychological dramas which have their antecedents in the German *Kammerspielfilm*. Bergman also had considerable international success with the dreamlike but harrowing *Viskningar och rop/Cries and Whispers* (1973) and a series for television, also edited into a theatrical version, *Scener ur ett äktenskap/Scenes from a Marriage* (1974). From the 1950s to the early 1970s, Bergman's work represented the epitome of art cinema in its recourse to symbolic imagery – beautifully visualised (mostly in black and white) by Fischer and then Sven Nykvist* – and especially in its serious involvement with 'big' themes: death, religious faith, ethics and the modernist concerns with identity, anxiety and alienation.

While on the international scene they came to embody 'Swedish cinema', Bergman's films have had an uneasy relationship to their national context. Critics have variously claimed that they should rather be looked upon as part of European art cinema, or as utterly personal statements related only to his own background, or as the transcendental work of a 'genius'. Despite their world reputation, Bergman's films were not always positively received by critics in Sweden. Animosity peaked in 1962 when despite, or possibly because of, Bergman's increasing commercial success rival Swedish director Bo Widerberg* published a pamphlet attacking him for reinforcing national stereotypes and calling for a new and more socially conscious national cinema. By this time, however, Bergman's international status was unshakeable. Two films of the 1950s in particular were responsible for propelling him to the position of European *auteur*-in-chief – *Sommaren med Monika* and *Sommarnattens leende*. The first of these, re-released in Paris in 1957, inspired Jean-Luc Godard* to write his legendary eulogy in *Cahiers du cinéma* entitled 'Bergmanorama', in which he claimed that Bergman was both 'the most original film-maker of the European cinema' and stylistically a New Wave* director *avant la lettre*. If one dimension of Bergman's international profile was his influence on the emerging French New Wave, the other was the association of his films with an idea of 'e(u)roticism' [> SEXUALITY, EROTICISM AND PORNOGRAPHY IN EUROPEAN CINEMA]. This was particularly strong in the US; *Sommaren med Monika*, released there in 1954, suffered and profited in equal measure from the association, prints being confiscated in Los Angeles, distributors being arrested and imprisoned and a judge declaring that the film 'appeals to potential sex murderers'; *Sommarnattens leende* continued the prurience-driven marketing that underwrote much US art cinema exhibition; for its American release in 1957, the distribution material promoted the film as 'a Swedish smorgasbord of sex, sin and psychiatry ... for the grown-ups, please'. In *cinéphile* circles, François Truffaut* best summed up the impact of the eroticism of Bergman's cinema by having Antoine Doinel (Jean-Pierre Léaud*), the young hero of *Les Quatre cents coups* (1959), steal a publicity still of Harriet Andersson* in her *décolleté* sweater. Indeed Andersson, together with Bibi Andersson*, Ingrid Thulin* and Liv Ullmann*, was at the core of Bergman's remarkable ensemble of players (whose main male representatives are Max von Sydow* and Gunnar Björnstrand) who brought to world cinema a Nordic, cool yet physical sensuality, a more tormented version than that embodied by New Wave actresses such as Jeanne Moreau* and Anna Karina*. Long praised for the centrality and complexity of his women characters, Bergman came under a different type of criticism in the 1970s and 1980s, when feminists pointed out that, as so often in Western culture, these women were always, precisely, equated with the sexual and biological, leaving the men free to pursue their important metaphysical quests. The fact remains that Bergman's fascination with women, combined with the charisma of his actresses, makes him the most prominent 'woman's director' among European *auteurs*.

After a controversy with the Swedish tax authorities (later settled in his favour), Bergman left Sweden in the 1970s to work as director at the Residenztheater in Munich. He also made films, such as *Das Schlangenei/Ormens ägg/The Serpent's Egg* (1977, Ger./US), reminiscent in its expressionistic frenzy of his 1940s work. Most notable of his productions from this period, however, is *Höstsonaten/Herbstsonate/Autumn Sonata* (1978), starring Ingrid Bergman* and Liv Ullmann as a tense mother-daughter couple. With the great fresco *Fanny och Alexander/Fanny and Alexander* (1982), based on his own childhood memories, Bergman returned to Sweden where he also wrote scripts for other directors (Bille August* and Daniel Bergman), and went back to the theatre, directing at the Royal Swedish Theatre. A prolific writer, Bergman has produced two volumes of memoirs and a stage play about the Swedish silent film director Georg af Klercker*. Bedecked with awards, honorary degrees and a professorship from the Swedish government, Bergman is now certainly recognised in Sweden as occupying a unique place in the country's cultural life. LGA/BF/CD

Bib: Maaret Koskinen, *Ingmar Bergman* (1993); Birgitta Steene, *Ingmar Bergman: A Guide to References and Resources* (1982).

Other Films: *Skepp till Indialand/Ship to India* (1947); *Törst/Thirst* (1949); *Till glädjen/Towards Joy, Sånt händer inte här/This Can't Happen Here/High Tension* (1950); *Sommarlek/Summer Interlude* (1951); *En lektion i kärlek/A Lesson in Love* (1954); *Kvinnodröm/Journey into Autumn/Dreams*

(1955); *Nära livet/So Close to Life/Brink of Life, Ansiktet/The Face/The Magician* (1958); *Jungfrukällan/The Virgin Spring, Djävulens öga/The Devil's Eye* (1960); *Såsom i en spegel/Through a Glass Darkly* (1961); *Nattvardsgästerna/Winter Light* (1963); *För att inte tala om alla dessa kvinnor/Now About These Women/All These Women* (1964); *Stimulantia* (1967, ep. 'Daniel'); *Skammen/Shame* (1968); *Riten/The Rite/The Ritual* [TV]; *Fårödokument 1969/The Fårö Document* (1970); *Beröringen/The Touch* (1971); *Trollflöjten/The Magic Flute, Ansikte mot ansikte/Face to Face* (1975); *Fårödokument 1979/Fårö Document 1979* (1979); *Aus dem Leben der Marionetten/Ur marionetternas liv/From the Life of the Marionettes* (1980); *Efter repetitionen/After the Rehearsal* (1983, TV); *De två saliga* (1986, TV); *Dokument Fanny och Alexander/Document Fanny and Alexander* (1986); *Karins ansikte/Karin's Face* (1985, short).

BERGMAN, Ingrid   Stockholm 1915 – London 1982

Swedish actress, alongside Greta Garbo* Sweden's most famous export to Hollywood. In 1933 Bergman enrolled at the School of the Royal Dramatic Theatre in Stockholm and two years later made her screen debut in *Munkbrogreven/The Count of Munkbron* (1935), directed by Edvin Adolphson and Sigurd Wallén. She came to prominence in Gustaf Edgren's melodrama *Valborgsmässoafton/Walpurgis Night* (1935), in which she plays the 'ideal woman', the beautiful, gentle blonde who longs to be a wife and mother. She made six films with Gustaf Molander*, among them *Intermezzo* (1936), another melodrama in which she is a young pianist hopelessly in love with a famous violinist (Gösta Ekman*). It was on the strength of this film that David O. Selznick invited her to Hollywood, to star in a 1939 American version of the film (co-starring Leslie Howard*). By then she had solidified the basic elements of her screen persona, a combination of naturalness, romantic passion and distinction, her 'wholesome' beauty contrasted to Garbo's more distant glamour. In the 1940s Bergman bloomed into major stardom with films such as *Casablanca* (1942), *Gaslight* (1944) and *Notorious* (1946). Her career and reputation suffered in 1949 when she left Hollywood and her family for Roberto Rossellini* (for several years she was unable to work in American films). She starred in five features and an episode directed by Rossellini, including *Stromboli, terra di Dio/Stromboli* (1950) and *Viaggio in Italia/Journey to Italy* (1954), which failed at the box office but were praised by critics, especially in France. She also starred in Jean Renoir's* *Eléna et les hommes/Elena and Men/Paris Does Strange Things* (1956, Fr.), while regaining her status in Hollywood with *Anastasia* (1956, for which she was awarded her second Oscar). She continued her career, though at a slower rate, in international productions in the 1960s and 1970s. In 1978 she worked for the first and only time with her unrelated namesake Ingmar Bergman* in *Höstsonaten/Autumn Sonata*. One of her daughters with Rossellini, Isabella Rossellini, is a famous model as well as a film and television actress. BF

Other Films Include: *Swedenhielms/The Family Swedenhielms* (1935); *Dollar, En kvinnas ansikte/A Woman's Face*

(1938); *For Whom the Bell Tolls* (1943, US); *Spellbound, The Bells of St. Mary's* (1945, US); *Joan of Arc* (1948, US); *Under Capricorn* (1949, US); *Europa '51* (1952, It.); *Siamo donne/We the Women* (1953, It.; ep. 'Ingrid Bergman'); *Giovanna d'Arco al rogo/Joan of Arc at the Stake* [It.], *La paura/Fear* (1954, It.); *Indiscreet* (1958, US); *Murder on the Orient Express* (1974, UK).

BERGNER, Elisabeth   Drohobycz, Galicia, Poland (now Russia) 1897 – London 1986

German actress, who worked in repertory under Max Reinhardt* between 1923 and 1933. Mostly directed by Paul Czinner* (her husband from 1933), she began her film career with a number of *Kammerspielfilme* for which her tomboyish femininity with its erotic understatement was perfectly suited, her androgynous persona stretching to cross-dressing (*Der Geiger von Florenz/Impetuous Youth/The Violinist of Florence*, 1926; *Dona Juana*, 1927). Just as she was to gain major star status with her performances in *Ariane* (1931) and *Der träumende Mund* (1932; she also starred in the English version, *Dreaming Lips*, 1932), she was forced to leave Nazi Germany for Britain (1933). There, she continued to play leads in films directed by Czinner, receiving an Academy Award for her performance in *Escape Me Never* (1935), before once more devoting herself to the theatre. MW

Bib: Helga Belach (ed.), *Elisabeth Bergner* (1983).

Other Films Include: *Catherine the Great* (1934, UK); *As You Like It* (1936, UK); *Paris Calling* (1941, US); *Die glücklichen Jahre der Thorwalds/The Happy Years of the Thorwald Family* (1962; dir. Wolfgang Staudte*); *Der Osterspaziergang* (1984).

BERLANGA, Luis García – see GARCÍA BERLANGA, Luis

BERLIN

German film festival. Founded in 1951 by Alfred Bauer (its director until 1976), the Berlin International Film Festival (*Berliner Filmfestspiele*, or *Berlinale*) is Germany's most important festival, and also one of the three major festivals in Europe (along with Cannes* and Venice*). In the *Wettbewerb* (international competition) for the Golden Bear award, films are assessed by a jury of international celebrities. Affiliated to the Berlinale since 1971 but independently organised and administered by the Freunde der deutschen Kinemathek ('Friends of the German Cinematheque'), the Internationales Forum des Jungen Films ('International Forum of Young Cinema') puts an emphasis on independent and innovative film-making (features, documentaries, experimental films) from all over the world. MW

BERNA, Emil   Zurich 1907

Swiss cinematographer. After collaborating on Ufa's* famous 'Kulturfilm' documentary, *Wege zu Kraft und Schönheit/*

Ways to Health and Beauty (1925, co-dir. W. Prager and N. Kaufmann), and heading the animation department of Corona Kunstfilm Zurich, Berna was hired by Lazar Wechsler* at Praesens-Film in 1927, where he became Switzerland's leading cinematographer from the late 1930s to the 1960s, thanks to his compellingly sober and unpretentious early camerawork on his own documentaries and films by Eduard Tisse*, Walther Ruttmann* and Hans Richter, among others. As chief cameraman of the nation's most prosperous film company, Berna deployed his talents with exceptional continuity in over forty national and international productions by leading directors such as Fred Zinnemann (*The Search/Die Gezeichneten* 1947), Leopold Lindtberg*, Franz Schnyder* and Kurt Früh*. In 1964 Berna moved to Central-Film. He retired shortly afterwards. MW

BERNARD, Raymond   Paris 1891–1977

French director, son of playwright Tristan Bernard. Bernard's acting debut was in *Jeanne Doré* with Sarah Bernhardt (play 1913, film 1915). He joined his father at Gaumont*, where both worked with Jacques Feyder*, and started directing in 1917. After *Le Petit café* (1919) with Max Linder*, and other mainstream films, Bernard achieved prominence in historical dramas, starting with *Le Miracle des loups/The Miracle of the Wolves* (1924), a spectacular medieval epic with battle scenes shot in Carcassonne, more impressive, according to Kevin Brownlow, than its model, D. W. Griffith's *Intolerance* (1916). *Le Joueur d'échec/The Chess Player* (1927), set in Poland, was equally successful. Bernard skilfully made the transition to sound, joining Pathé*-Natan. *Les Croix de bois/The Wooden Crosses* (1931, based on Roland Dorgelès' best-selling novel), a haunting World War I story starring Pierre Blanchar*, was lent authenticity by the fact that Bernard, Blanchar and other members of the cast were themselves war veterans. Bernard directed probably the best version of *Les Misérables* (1933, in three parts), starring Harry Baur* and Charles Vanel*. His 1930s films also include the excellent populist melodrama *Faubourg-Montmartre* (1931) and the spy story *Marthe Richard au service de la France/Marthe Richard* (1937), with Edwige Feuillère* and Erich von Stroheim. With the exception of the war years, Bernard worked until the late 1950s. GV

Other Films Include: *Tarakanova* (1930); *Tartarin de Tarascon* (1934); *J'étais une aventurière* (1938); *Adieu chérie* (1946); *La Dame aux camélias* (1953); *La Belle de Cadix* (1953).

BERNHARDT, Kurt [US: Curtis]   Worms 1899 – Pacific Palisades, California 1981

German director. Coming from the stage, Bernhardt entered film as the director of the anti-war picture *Namenlose Helden/Nameless Heroes* in 1924, helped Marlene Dietrich* to stardom (*Die Frau nach der man sich sehnt/Three Loves*, 1929) and by 1930 had sufficiently established himself with a number of socially aware dramas to direct Conrad Veidt* in *Die letzte Kompagnie/The Last Company* (1930), one of Ufa's* very first sound films. In 1934 he left Germany for France, where he specialised in atmospheric thriller-melodramas such as *Carrefour* (1938). In 1939 Bernhardt went to the US where, thanks to the American distribution of *Carrefour*, he received offers from Warner Bros and MGM, signing a seven-year contract with Warner. He shot his first American picture, *My Love Came Back*, in 1940, followed by a series of melodramas (such as *Possessed*, 1947) and *films noirs* (such as *High Wall*, 1947) for which he is justly famous. After numerous visits to Germany in the 1950s, he eventually directed *Stefanie in Rio* (1960) for Artur Brauner's CCC-Film, which also brought back Fritz Lang* and other émigrés. A film directed in Italy was followed by Bernhardt's last film (*Kisses for My President*, 1964), made back in the US. MW

Other Films Include: *Qualen der Nacht/Agonies of Night, Die Waise von Lowood* (1926); *Kinderseelen klagen euch an, Das Mädchen mit den 5 Nullen* (1927); *Schinderhannes/The Prince of Rogues, Das letzte Fort* (1928); *Der Mann, der den Mord beging* (1931); *Der Rebell/The Rebel* (1932, co-dir. Luis Trenker*); *Der Tunnel* (1933); *L'Or dans la rue* (1934, Fr.); *The Beloved Vagabond* (1936, UK); *The Lady With the Red Hair* (1940, US); *Juke Girl* (1942, US); *Conflict* (1944, US); *My Reputation, Devotion, A Stolen Life* (1946, US); *The Doctor and the Girl* (1950, US); *Payment on Demand, Sirocco, The Blue Veil* (1951, US); *The Merry Widow* (1952, US); *Miss Sadie Thompson* (1953, US); *Beau Brummell* (1954, US); *Interrupted Melody* (1955, US); *Il tiranno di Siracusa/Damon and Pythias* (1961, It./US).

BEROLINA-FILM

German production company founded by Kurt Ulrich (1905–67) and Kurt Schulz (1912–57) in 1948. Berolina was one of the most prolific and commercially successful postwar German production companies, completing about seventy films between 1948 and 1962. Like other companies at the time it financed its films through guarantees from distributors such as Herzog, Gloria* and Constantin*. Berolina launched the successful genre of the *Heimatfilm** with *Schwarzwaldmädel* (1950) and *Grün ist die Heid* (1951), produced operettas like *Das Land des Lächelns* (1952) and *Der Vogelhändler* (1953), and put together star vehicles for Heinz Rühmann*, for instance *Wenn der Vater mit dem Sohne* (1955), *Charleys Tante* (1955) and *Der Pauker* (1958). Berolina had its own talent scout department and gave future stars Romy Schneider* and Götz George* their first chance. The first German production company after World War II to use colour, it often shot outdoors, using particularly scenic locations, partly to compensate for not owning a studio. The company was dismantled in 1967 after the death of Kurt Ulrich. JG

BERRI, Claude   Claude Langman; Paris 1934

French director, producer and actor, internationally famous as the director of *Jean de Florette* and *Manon des sources* (1986), the lyrical and nostalgic recreations of Marcel

Pagnol's* Provençal universe [> HERITAGE CINEMA IN EUROPE]. Berri started with an Oscar-winning short, *Le Poulet/The Chicken* (1963), and semi-autobiographical films such as *Le Vieil homme et l'enfant/The Two of Us* (1967), *Mazel Tov ou le mariage/Marry Me! Marry Me!* (1968) and *Sex-shop* (1972). There followed 'socio-comic' films, notably *Le Maître d'école/The Schoolmaster* (1981) and *Tchao Pantin* (1983), both starring Coluche, and the Catherine Deneuve* vehicle *Je vous aime* (1980). Since the triumph of *Jean de Florette* and *Manon des sources*, Berri has continued to make high-budget literary adaptations with *Uranus* (1990) and a lavish version of *Germinal* (1993), the latter released in France at the same time as Steven Spielberg's *Jurassic Park* and a totem in the battle to defend European audio-visual culture against American 'cultural imperialism' during the GATT negotiations. Across the different genres he has worked in, Berri's cinema is populist and popular, recalling, as in the title of his 1971 film *Le Cinéma de papa/Daddy's Cinema*, a classic heritage of realism, high production values, solid plots and popular stars.

Berri is also an important producer. He has worked with film-makers like André Téchiné*, Jacques Rivette* and Roman Polanski* (*Tess*, 1979), and produced two French 'super-productions' of the 1990s: *L'Amant/The Lover* (1991) and *La Reine Margot* (1994). His sister, Arlette Langman, is a scriptwriter and editor. GV

BERRY, Jules   Jules Paufichet; Poitiers 1883 – Paris 1951

French actor. Berry's flourishing career in Parisian *boulevard* theatre was paralleled by appearances in almost a hundred films, mostly in the 1930s. He transposed to the screen his elegant cad in countless examples of *théâtre filmé* (filmed theatre), such as *Arlette et ses papas* (1934) or *L'Habit vert* (1937), brilliantly reciting – and sometimes improvising – sparkling dialogue in a blur of frenetic gestures. But Berry's comic persona could also take on sinister tones, as in his most celebrated dramatic films, Jean Renoir's* *Le Crime de Monsieur Lange* (1935), Marcel Carné's* *Le Jour se lève* (1939) and *Les Visiteurs du soir* (1942, as the devil), and Albert Valentin's* *Marie-Martine* (1943). Whatever the genre or quality of the film, Berry's performances were always a delight, making him one of the most popular and instantly recognisable French film actors. GV

BERTA, Renato   Bellinzona, 1945

Swiss cinematographer, who trained at the Centro Sperimentale* in Rome and after working for Swiss-Italian television gained international recognition in the post-1968 years as favourite cameraman of many leading Swiss directors such as Alain Tanner*, Claude Goretta*, Michel Soutter*, Daniel Schmid* and Thomas Koerfer*. Equally valued by other European art and avant-garde directors, Berta did the camerawork on Jean-Marie Straub's* *Othon* (1969) and *Fortini/Cani* (1976) among other films, as well as for Jean-Luc Godard's* *Sauve qui peut (la vie)/Slow Motion* (1980), Eric

Rohmer's* *Les Nuits de la pleine lune/Full Moon in Paris* (1984), and Alain Resnais'* *Smoking/No Smoking* (1993). MW

BERTOLUCCI, Bernardo   Parma 1941

Italian director. The son of the renowned poet Attilio Bertolucci, Bernardo Bertolucci was himself awarded the Viareggio Prize for a first poetry work in 1962.

Bertolucci began his career in the cinema as assistant director on Pier Paolo Pasolini's* *Accattone* (1961); his own first film, *La commare secca/The Grim Reaper* (1962), was heavily indebted to his mentor's style. His next film, *Prima della rivoluzione/Before the Revolution* (1964), contained all the ideological and aesthetic tensions that would play themselves out during the course of his career. Set in his native Parma, this semi-autobiographical work is a coming-of-age story about a young man, Fabrizio, who is radicalised sexually by his aunt, and ideologically by his Marxist teacher, but who ultimately abandons the ideal of the revolution to accept his bourgeois birthright. Like Fabrizio, Bertolucci has struggled throughout his career to negotiate the rival claims of his high-cultural, materially privileged patrimony and the ideological imperatives of the left. The arena for this struggle has frequently been the cinema's built-in tendency towards spectacle, which Bertolucci has sometimes resisted but more often embraced with varying degrees of ambivalence. The cerebral, Godard*-inspired *Partner* (1968), for example, forgoes the pleasures of cinematic spectacle, whereas his brilliant version of Moravia's novel, *Il conformista/The Conformist* (1970), brings back those pleasures, albeit in the service of a politically responsible message (the denunciation of Fascism). The made-for-television film *Strategia del ragno/The Spider's Stratagem* (1970), an adaptation of José Luis Borges' short story 'The Theme of the Traitor and the Hero', foregrounds the relationship between political identity and spectacle by having the anti-Fascist hero-turned-traitor decide to transform his execution into public martyrdom during a performance of the opera *Rigoletto*.

In 1972, Bertolucci abandoned politically committed filmmaking for eroticism. *Ultimo tango a Parigi/Last Tango in Paris*, the story of two strangers (Marlon Brando and Maria Schneider) whose sexual encounters in a Parisian apartment serve as a metaphor for the psychodynamics of human relations, was a clamorous *succès de scandale*, banned in Italy until 1987 and accorded an 'X' rating in the US. Its box-office earnings made possible the ambitious *Novecento/1900* (1976), a panoramic vision of Italian political, social and cultural history from the beginning of the century to the present, filtered through the parallel and intersecting lives of a peasant (Gérard Depardieu*) and a land-owner (Robert De Niro). In this extravaganza (311 min., reduced to 245 min. for commercial distribution, and re-released in 1991 in its full-length version) Bertolucci indulges his love of spectacle, while trying, at the same time, to balance it with his ideological concerns. Political spectacle is the theme of the Academy-award-winning *The Last Emperor* (1987), the story of China's twentieth-century evolution, ending with Mao's cultural revolution of the late 1960s. At the centre of this grand epic resides the supreme paradox of an absolute ruler who is powerless, the ostensible maker of history who becomes the dupe of historical processes.

Bertolucci returned to literary adaptation in *The Sheltering Sky* (1990, UK/It.), based on the existentialist novel by Paul Bowles. The story of a couple seeking 'authenticity' on a journey to the remote reaches of the Sahara desert, the film finds its own authenticity in its nearly wordless, visually dazzling second half, as the young wife, newly widowed, assimilates into desert existence. With *Little Buddha* (1993, Fr./UK, starring Keanu Reeves) a new tranquillity has entered Bertolucci's work, unexpected in an author whose characters have generally been driven by a violent restlessness. MMo

Bib: Donald Ranvaud and Enzo Ungari, *Bertolucci by Bertolucci* (1987).

Other Films Include: *Amore e rabbia* (1969, ep. *L'agonia*); *I poveri muoiono prima* (1971, documentary); *La tragedia di un uomo ridicolo/Tragedy of a Ridiculous Man* (1981).

BESS, Jane   1894–?

German scriptwriter. The popular but critically ignored Beß had her first success as a writer when she invented Detective Morten (played by Harry Frank, and later by Olaf Storm), and the attractive woman detective Madge Henway (played by Edith Posca). By 1926 she was said to have written 126 scripts in almost every popular genre: apart from adventure and detective films she wrote treatments for *Straßenfilme** ('street' films) such as *Das Kind der Straße/Child of the Street* (1921, dir. Wolfgang Neff), *Der Aufstieg der kleinen Lilian/ The Ascent of Little Lilian* (1924, dir. Fred Sauer) and *Die Moral der Gasse/Morals of the Streets* (1925, dir. Jaap Speyer), for comedies, costume dramas and operetta films. From the mid-1920s she (co-)wrote the scripts of more prestigious films by directors such as Mihály Kertesz [Michael Curtiz in the US] (*Der goldene Schmetterling/The Golden Butterfly*, 1926), Richard Oswald* (*Funkzauber*, 1928), Joe May* (*Dagfin*, 1926) and, most often, Victor Janson. The coming of sound brought her career to an abrupt end. In 1933 she appears to have left Berlin, possibly for the Netherlands, where a screenplay of hers (*De Kribbebijter*) was directed by Herman Kosterlitz (Henry Koster) in 1935. MW

BESSON, Luc   Paris 1959

French director. Besson served his assistantship in film, advertising and music videos, shooting the critically successful *Le Dernier combat/The Last Battle* (1982) at the age of twenty-three. Gaumont* then lined up stars Isabelle Adjani* and Christophe Lambert and gave him a huge budget for his first major feature, *Subway* (1985). This modish mix of thriller and post-modern *cinéma du look**, set in a Paris métro recreated by Alexandre Trauner*, was disliked by critics but won huge popular acclaim, particularly among the young. This was echoed by Besson's next feature, *Le Grand bleu/The Big Blue* (1988), one of the French film events of the 1980s. If *Le Grand bleu* was almost pure image and no plot in its celebration of the ecstasy of deep-sea diving, *Nikita* (1990)

heralded a return to narrative, in science-fiction thriller mode. The tensions in Besson's work are emblematic of a strand in late 1980s/early 1990s French cinema: the youth appeal of US genres (rock music, thriller) is balanced by the iconography of Frenchness (restaurants, fashion, Paris métro), while the much-feared contamination of cinema by 'impure' forms (video, advertisements) is offset by an insistence on spectacular techniques which demand – so far successfully – that audiences actually sit in a cinema to appreciate them. Besson's latest film, *Leon* (1994), shot in English in New York, was a major international success. GV

BEYER, Frank   Nobitz, Thuringia 1932

German director. Beyer studied direction at FAMU* in Prague, assisting Kurt Maetzig* among others. In 1958, he joined DEFA* features studio in Potsdam-Babelsberg, and had his first success with *Fünf Patronenhülsen/Five Shell Casings/Five Bullets* (1960), the story of a difficult friendship between five members of the International Brigade during the Spanish Civil War. In *Königskinder/Invincible Love* (1962), he combined traditional realistic story-telling with a complex flashback structure. The same year, he adapted Bruno Apitz's autobiographical *Nackt unter Wölfen/Naked Among Wolves* (1963), based on the author's experiences at the Buchenwald concentration camp. Beyer's career was halted by the reception of *Spur der Steine/Traces of the Stones* (1966), which, except for a single preview shortly after its completion, was never publicly shown in the GDR. It became, however, a respectable box-office success in East and West Germany when re-released in 1989, spearheading the exhibition of a whole group of previously undistributed 1960s films. It was eight years before Beyer was allowed to direct another film, *Jakob der Lügner/Jacob, the Liar* (1974), the only DEFA film ever to be nominated for an Oscar. From the early 1980s Beyer worked for West German production companies and television, but returned to DEFA to direct the thriller *Der Bruch/The Break* (1989). His first post-unification film was *Der Verdacht/The Suspicion* (1991). MW

BFI – see BRITISH FILM INSTITUTE

BIGAS LUNA, Juan José   Barcelona 1946

Spanish director, who won international recognition for *Jamón, jamón/Ham, Ham* in 1992. A former artistic designer, he had also worked in publicity and documentary films. His first feature was *Tatuaje/Tattoo* (1976), and his next two, *Bilbao* (1978) and *Caniche/Poodle* (1979), established him as a cult director. In these works, he explored the social and sexual mores of the Catalan bourgeoisie. *Lola* (1985), a story of jealousy and death, was more commercial, still centred around sexual passions but losing some of the social analysis that also characterised Bigas Luna's earlier films, and with a more conventional narrative structure. After *Angustia/ Anguish* (1986), an experimental suspense thriller, he returned in even more commercial vein with *Las edades de Lulú/The Ages of Lulu* (1990), an adaptation of a novel by

Almudena Grandes which had won an award for erotic literature. Surprisingly moralistic in tone, the film was popular, probably because of its sexual explicitness. *Jamón, jamón*, Bigas Luna's next film, became one of the most popular Spanish films of the 1990s. Sprinkled with references to Lorca, Buñuel* and Dalí, *Jamón, jamón* casts an ironic look at Spanish stereotypes, especially traditional masculinity. However, the combination of symbols of Spanishness and Italian actresses Stefania Sandrelli* and Anna Galiena suggests the uneasy attitude of recent Spanish cinema towards its own cultural positioning. Bigas Luna attempted to exploit the success of his 'new style' and of his male protagonist, Javier Bardem, in *Huevos de oro/Golden Balls* (1993), but audience indifference suggests the formula may be exhausted. CDe

BINGER, Maurits Herman
Haarlem 1868 – Wiesbaden, Germany 1923

Dutch producer and director. As a sideline to his printing business, Binger opened a film studio in Haarlem in 1912. Hollandia Filmfabriek produced about fifty features between 1912 and 1923, over half the total Dutch silent film output. He formed a stock company of actors, of whom Annie Bos* was the undisputed star, and hired Louis H. Chrispijn (1854–1926) to direct the Hollandia stable in films like *Weergevonden/Lost and Found* (1914), a melodrama about an orthodox Jewish family. At the same time Hollandia produced educational documentaries about Dutch industry and short fictional subjects, the so-called 'wooden shoe-and-windmill' films. World War I (in which the Netherlands remained neutral) provided a stimulus to production because of the decline in foreign competition. Binger himself became principal director when Chrispijn left the studio in 1915, directing eighteen of the twenty-one Hollandia features released during the war. But while Chrispijn had focused on popular Dutch themes and characters, Binger preferred society dramas and the rich settings of the international elite, assuming that this would be more attractive to foreign audiences. This meant a loss of topicality: while Europe was engulfed in warfare, Binger omitted all allusion to it, even in his trilogy *Oorlog en vrede/War and Peace* (1918). His most successful production, however, was an indictment of capitalist society, *Op hoop van zegen/The Good Hope* (1918), the screen version of a well-known Dutch play by Herman Heijermans. The end of the war marked Hollandia's final phase. As a result of growing competition the studio nearly went broke in 1919. Binger obtained British financial backing for his feature films, while the non-fiction branch was turned into an independent company, Polygoon*, soon a major producer of newsreels and industrial films. An increasing number of British directors, stars and writers staffed Hollandia. For example, B. E. Doxat-Pratt directed *Hard tegen hard/The Skin Game* (1920), F. A. Richardson *In den nacht/In the Night* (1920), Oscar Apfel *Bulldog Drummond* (1922). However, while the British did not like Binger's 'continental touch', Dutch contemporaries described the studio's output as 'boring British films'. Between 1920 and his death in 1923, Binger directed eleven Hollandia features, often screen adaptations of popular Dutch plays, including *Schakels/Links* (1920), *De Jantjes/The*

Jack Tars (1922) and *Mottige Janus/Pocked Janus* (1922). When he died, the most prolific Dutch production company ceased to exist. KD/AvB

Bib: Ruud Bishoff, *Hollywood in Holland: de geschiedenis van de Filmfabriek Hollandia, 1912–1923* (1988).

BINOCHE, Juliette
Paris 1964

French actress. After a spell in theatre and television, Binoche emerged around 1985 with small parts in Jean-Luc Godard's* *Je vous salue, Marie/Hail Mary!* (1984) and Jacques Doillon's* *La Vie de famille* (1985), and the lead in André Téchiné's* *Rendez-vous* (1985). Her gamine looks and seductive combination of spontaneity and sensuality recalled New Wave* actresses, especially in Leos Carax's* *Mauvais sang/The Night is Young* (1986) and *Les Amants du Pont-Neuf* (1991). Lately, she has moved towards more 'mature' parts and a European career, with Philip Kaufman's *The Unbearable Lightness of Being* (1987, US), Louis Malle's* *Damage/Fatale* (1992, UK/Fr.), and Krzysztof Kieślowski's* *Trois couleurs bleu/Three Colours: Blue* (1993). GV

BIRGEL, Willy
Cologne 1891 – Dübendorf, Switzerland 1973

German actor, who started his screen career relatively late, in Paul Wegener's* *Ein Mann will nach Deutschland/A Man Wants to Go to Germany* (1934) and in his first years predominantly featured in shady roles. From 1937, after Birgel had become a '*Staatsschauspieler*' (state actor) in Nazi Germany, he turned to playing severe, cold masculine types. With ... *Reitet für Deutschland/Riding for Germany* (1941), he perfected his style as the '*Herrenreiter des deutschen Films*' (gentleman rider of the German film). Despite facing tough questions from the Allies after the war, Birgel returned to the cinema thanks to Erich Pommer*. After a disappointing directorial debut with *Rosenmontag* in 1955, he increasingly worked for the theatre. From the 1960s to his death, he also played in countless television productions. MW

BLACK BRITISH INDEPENDENT FILM

British movement. In his introduction to *Questions of Third Cinema* (Pines and Willemen, eds., 1990) Paul Willemen argues that black film-makers 'now constitute the most intellectually and cinematically innovative edge of British cultural politics'. Institutionally, black independent film-making in Britain owes its existence to a combination of factors in the late 1970s and early 1980s – 'race riots' and inner city unrest, resulting in a politics of containment on the part of local authorities and more focused demands for access and representation from the black communities; the enlightened cultural policies of the Greater London Council before its dissolution; the commitment of the new Channel 4* to previously unfranchised cultural voices; and the development of the Workshop Movement*. The Workshop Movement in particular established the infrastructure for the emergence of black workshops such as Sankofa and Black Audio Film/Video Collective, whose films – *Territories* (Sankofa, 1984), *Passion of Remembrance* (Sankofa, 1986) and *Handsworth Songs* (Black Audio, 1986) – formed canonical reference points, and whose founders – Isaac Julien*, Maureen Blackwood, Martine Attille, Nadine Marsh-Edwards, Lina Gopaul, John Akomfrah – were identified as the directors, producers, writers and theorists within what was essentially a collective movement. Aesthetically, black film-making was influenced by a conjunction of 'Third World' debates around Third Cinema, debates about representation and subjectivity developed by *Screen**, and debates about race, identity, hybridity and diasporic cultures articulated by such black theorists as Stuart Hall, Paul Gilroy and Homi K. Bhabha. In the 1990s, the collective spirit has been replaced to some extent by an attention to individual directors like Isaac Julien and feature films like *Young Soul Rebels* (1991). New voices, however, continue to emerge – Gurinder Chadha, whose first film, *I'm British But...* (1989), was supported by the BFI New Directors scheme, went on to make the first Asian feature film in Britain, *Bhaji on the Beach* (1993) – and black filmmakers associated with the workshops continue to develop a debate about a multicultural British cinema. JC

Bib: *Black Film, British Cinema*, ICA Documents no. 7 (1988).

BLACK, Cathal   born 1952

Irish director and writer. Though Black has made only a few films, they have displayed a visual richness which is not always evident in the work of other Irish film-makers. His first film, *Wheels* (1976), was an adaptation of a short story by Irish writer John McGahern. It explores the relationship of a son to his father who remains on the family farm after the son has migrated to the city. *Our Boys* (1980) was the first sustained look at Irish Catholic education. Using actuality material, documentary interviews and drama sequences, Black examined the often brutal legacy of Christian Brothers education. Sensitivity to its subject matter led RTE*, one of the film's backers, to shelve the film for a decade before broadcasting it. *Pigs* (1984) focuses on a disparate group of outsiders, including the first representation of a gay man in an Irish film, who live in a Dublin squat. Black's visual resonances are within the European art cinema tradition, with few concessions to mainstream commercial cinema. KR

BLACK WAVE – see YUGOSLAV 'BLACK WAVE'

BLANC, Anne-Marie   Vevey 1921

Swiss actress. Already a national icon in the late 1930s and early 1940s through leading parts in some of the most successful Swiss films directed by Leopold Lindtberg* (*Wachtmeister Studer*, 1939; *Die missbrauchten Liebesbriefe*, 1940; *Landamman Stauffacher*, 1941; *Marie-Louise*, 1943),

Blanc continued to be popular throughout the next three decades in over thirty films made in Switzerland and Austria, but also in Britain (*White Cradle Inn*, 1947), France (*On ne meurt pas comme ça*, 1946, co-starring Erich von Stroheim), and Germany (*Roman eines Frauenarztes*, 1954, *Via Mala*, 1961). A celebrated stage actress, she toured Europe with partners such as Albert Bassermann (1948), Oskar Werner* (1959), Axel von Ambesser (1972), Sonja Ziemann and Charles Régnier (1975). Through her collaboration with a new generation of film-makers, Blanc served as an important recognition factor for audiences in the 1970s and 1980s, helping to integrate the 'new Swiss cinema' into the international mainstream and contributing a strong sense of continuity to Swiss national cinema. MW

Other Films Include: *Gilberte de Courgenay* (1941); *Maturareise* (1942); *Palace Hotel* (1951); *Hoheit lassen bitten* (1954); *S.O.S. Gletscherpilot* (1959); *La Blonde de Pékin* (1966); *Riedland* (1975); *Violanta* (1977); *Séverine* (1980); *L'Allégement* (1983); *Der Pendler* (1985).

BLANCHAR, Pierre   Pierre Blanchard; Philippeville [Skikda], Algeria 1892 – Paris 1963

French actor. Like many French actors of the classical period, Blanchar pursued a dual career on stage and screen. He shared with Jean-Louis Barrault* piercing eyes and a feverish, mannered acting style, well suited to tormented heroes such as Raskolnikov in Pierre Chenal's* *Crime et châtiment/Crime and Punishment* (1935, for which he was awarded a prize at Venice). His good looks won him romantic leads, often in costume, as in *L'Affaire du courrier de Lyon/The Courier of Lyons* (1937). His powerful incarnation of the tragic World War I hero of Raymond Bernard's* *Les Croix de bois/The Wooden Crosses* (1931) gave him a powerful aura of authenticity (he had himself been wounded in the trenches). During World War II, Blanchar played the emblematic Pontcarral in Jean Delannoy's* *Pontcarral, colonel d'Empire* (1942), a film widely considered as obliquely 'resistant'. At the liberation he headed the film industry's Liberation Committee and read the voice-over commentary for the collective *Libération de Paris* (1944–45). With a few exceptions, such as Delannoy's *La Symphonie pastorale* (1946), he then mostly devoted himself to the theatre. GV

BLASETTI, Alessandro   Rome 1900

Italian director and scriptwriter. Blasetti began as a film critic and theorist and as a spokesperson for the revitalisation of the flagging Italian film industry during the 1920s. In 1925 he became a film critic for the newspaper *L'Impero*, and in 1927 editor of the magazines *Cinematografo* and *Lo spettacolo d'Italia*. In 1928, Blasetti and journalist friends formed the production company Augustus, with the aim of putting into practice their critical ideals of a cinema that would be 'organically Italian' and at one with current cultural politics. The first product of this company was *Sole/Sun* (1929), for which Blasetti received directing credit, though it was very much a collective effort and Blasetti's formal training as director consisted of a brief excursion to the Ufa* studios in Germany. *Sole* was seen by critics as heralding a new type of consciously 'Italian' film – an ideal most evident in Blasetti's use of non-professional actors in the role of the 'people'. Unfortunately the film had very limited distribution (no complete copy of it seems to have survived) and Augustus ran into financial difficulties. Blasetti went on to work for Cines*, the company owned by Stefano Pittaluga*, whom Blasetti had previously attacked as an enemy of his ideals. For Cines he made *Resurrectio* (1931), an urban melodrama involving the struggle of a disillusioned orchestra conductor to return to the stage, and *Nerone* (1930), a film organised around parodic sketches by the Italian stage comedian Ettore Petrolini. More central to his concerns was a third film made later the same year – *Terra madre/Mother Earth*, the story of a son who inherits a rural estate and rediscovers the power and fertility of the land (a metaphor for the nation). Subsequent films made for Cines by Blasetti include *Palio* (1932, set around the historic horse race in Siena), *1860* (1933, a historical film about the Italian Risorgimento, set in Sicily), and *Assisi* (a documentary on the medieval Umbrian town). Like *Terra madre*, these films involve returns to provincial settings where 'popular' causes (a working-class hero's ride to victory in *Palio*; the struggle of inhabitants of rural Sicily to expel foreign mercenaries in 1860) form the basis of myths of national political awakening.

In 1934, after the demise of Cines, Blasetti made *Vecchia guardia/Old Guard*, a film that reworks many of his Cines motifs, but through the story of a group of Fascists attempting to restore order in a small town destabilised by striking workers. This was followed by *Aldebaran* (1935), on the call to duty of a young submarine officer. Despite the fact that the film's hero is a Fascist soldier, *Aldebaran* was picked up for distribution by MGM. By the late 1930s, Blasetti had come to be Italy's most famous stylist of epic costume films (such as *La corona di ferro/The Iron Crown*, 1941), many loosely based on nineteenth- and early twentieth-century historical novels and melodramas, but from the early 1940s he adapted to changing circumstances with a group of pre- or quasi-neo-realist* films, including *Quattro passi fra le nuvole/Four Steps in the Clouds* (1942, about the efforts of a petit-bourgeois patriarch to defend the honour of a husbandless pregnant woman), *Nessuno torna indietro/Nobody Goes Back* (1943, on the love affairs of young women sharing a boarding house in Rome), and *Un giorno nella vita/A Day in the Life* (1946, about a group of partisans who take refuge in a remote convent while pursued by German soldiers). After the war Blasetti continued to make historical costume films such as *Fabiola* (1948), *La fiammata* (1952) and *Altri tempi/Infidelity* (1952, the first of many episodic films made in Italy). In the 1950s, Blasetti also made fairly successful films in the style of the *commedia all'italiana*, including *Peccato che sia una canaglia/Too Bad She's Bad* (1954) and *La fortuna di essere donna/Lucky to Be a Woman* (1956), films that launched Sophia Loren*.

Besides feature films, Blasetti directed documentaries, plays and television programmes. He also appears (playing himself) in Luchino Visconti's* *Bellissima* (1951). While he enjoyed more success after World War II than any other Italian director from the 1930s, he (like Mario Camerini*) could never quite overcome his association with the Fascist period. JHa

Other Films Include: *La tavola dei poveri* (1932); *Ettore Fieramosca* (1938); *Un'avventura di Salvator Rosa* (1939); *La cena delle beffe* (1941); *Prima comunione* (1950); *Tempi nostri/A Slice of Life* (1953); *Amore e chiacchiere* (1957); *Io amo, tu ami ...* (1960); *Liolà/A Very Handy Man* (1964); *Io, io, io ... e gli altri* (1966); *La ragazza del bersagliere* (1967); *Simon Bolivar* (1969).

BLIER, Bernard   Buenos Aires, Argentina 1916 – Paris 1989

French actor. Blier was the archetype of the character actor who, despite few leading roles, ranked high in the French star firmament (he was tenth in the overall postwar French box-office popularity rankings). Blier trained in the theatre with Louis Jouvet*, a relationship portrayed in Marc Allégret's* *Entrée des artistes/The Curtain Rises* (1938), though his first important part was in *Gribouille* (1937). With his unglamorous physique, he cornered the market in sympathetic humiliated husbands, as in *Hôtel du Nord* (1938) and *Quai des Orfèvres* (1947). He ventured into dramatic parts as well as sinister ones, epitomised by his excellent Inspector Javert of *Les Misérables* (1958). Generally, though, he played comic roles and became a pillar of French postwar comedies, such as those of Georges Lautner and Jean Yanne, appearing in over 200 films [> COMEDY (FRANCE)].

Blier also appeared in films directed by his son Bertrand Blier*, in particular *Buffet froid* (1979). He received a César* for life achievement in 1988. GV

BLIER, Bertrand   Boulogne-Billancourt 1939

French director, son of actor Bernard Blier*. Blier made his first feature, *Hitler, connais pas!*, in 1963, but his career took off with the spectacularly successful *Les Valseuses/Going Places* (1973). Inspired by the libertarian *café-théâtre*, *Les Valseuses* also launched Gérard Depardieu*, Miou-Miou* and Patrick Dewaere. This picaresque saga of two hoodlums on the run encapsulates the features of Blier's subsequent (and self-referential) work: an ability to capture '*l'air du temps*' – here post-1968 societal changes – a desire to shock, and a misogyny 'justified' by women's extravagant sexual demands and men's fear of inadequacy (as in *Calmos/Femmes Fatales*, 1975, and *Préparez vos mouchoirs/Get Out Your Handkerchiefs*, 1977, which won an Oscar for best foreign film). Technically accomplished and by turns brilliantly funny and gruesome, Blier's cynical, absurdist and comic cinema is often popular at the French box office, in particular *Tenue de soirée/Ménage* (1986, special jury prize at Cannes and Best film César*). The more arty *Trop belle pour toi* (1989) was an international hit. GV

Bib: Jill Forbes, *The Cinema in France After the New Wave* (1992).

Other Films: *Si j'étais un espion/If I Was a Spy* (1967); *Buffet froid* (1979); *Beau-père* (1981); *La Femme de mon pote/My Best Friend's Girl* (1983); *Notre histoire/Our Story* (1984); *Merci la vie* (1991); *Un, deux, trois soleil* (1993); *Mon homme* (1995).

BLOKKER, Jan Andries Amsterdam 1927

Dutch scriptwriter and critic (also television producer), who began as a film critic in 1952 and became the intellectual guide to a new generation of Dutch film-makers in the 1960s. Blokker wrote the scripts for two successful films, *Fanfare* (1958, dir. Bert Haanstra*) and *Makkers staakt uw wild geraas/That Joyous Eve* (1960, dir. Fons Rademakers*), which marked the beginning of a new era in Dutch cinema. Between 1968 and 1978 he headed the broadcasting organisation VPRO, which introduced unconventional forms of journalism to television. In the 1980s Blokker headed the Production Fund for Dutch feature films, while still writing articles for national newspapers on a wide range of subjects, making his reputation as the scourge of both left-wing and right-wing philistinism. He resumed his scriptwriting activities in the 1990s, adapting Dutch novels for several outstanding television mini-series directed by Frans Weisz* and Harry Kümel*. He has published several books on the history of reading and printing in the Netherlands. KD

BLOM, August Copenhagen 1869–1947

Danish director, one of the great pioneers of Danish cinema. Blom began his career as an actor and opera singer and made his screen debut in 1909 in a Sherlock Holmes film produced by Nordisk Films*. The following year he began directing, and in 1911 became artistic director at Nordisk, where he worked until 1924.

Blom directed around 125 films, making a name for himself in 1910 with *Den hvide Slavehandel/The White Slave*. His productions include *Hamlet, Dr Jekyll and Mr Hyde* (1910), *Balletdanserinden/The Ballet Dancer* (1911) and *Et Revolutionsbrullup/A Revolutionary Marriage* (1914), but three films stand out: *Ved Fængslets Port/Temptations of a Great City* (1911), *Atlantis* (1913) and *Verdens Undergang/ The End of the World* (1916). *Ved Fængslets Port*, starring Clara Pontoppidan*, is an erotic melodrama, a genre which became a Danish speciality. Danish erotic melodrama*, set among the urban middle class, gave prominence to women characters who were permitted to display their sensuality with numerous lingering kisses. Taking advantage of his position, Blom ensured that he and his colleagues made a large number of such films. *Ved Fængslets Port* is one of the archetypes of the genre as well as an artistic masterpiece, with subtle performances, a clear narrative, sharp editing, and sets which show off the characters well.

Blom's other two important films were in a different genre altogether. Featuring hundreds of actors, *Atlantis* was his most ambitious work. No expense was spared in this adaptation of Gerhardt Hauptmann's novel, for which shooting took place in Copenhagen, Berlin and New York. The central shipwreck scene is especially memorable, using dramatic edit-ing unusual at the time. *Verdens Undergang* was another super-production, a science-fiction epic about a disaster which ends all life on earth (only one young couple survives). It demonstrated once more Blom's ability to control large and complicated compositions. ME

BLOMBERG, Erik Helsinki 1913

Finnish director, cinematographer and producer. Though Blomberg directed only five features, he is one of the few major figures in Finnish cinema. He studied photography in London in the early 1930s and worked for a local photographic studio before travelling to Paris to work with George Saad, a prominent fashion photographer. Offered a position as cinematographer in Suomi-Filmi, he became one of Finland's key cinematographers. His first assignment was Risto Orko's* *VMV 6* (1936). He then worked on three melodramas directed by Teuvo Tulio*: *Taistelu Heikkilän talosta/ Struggle for the House of Heikkilä* (1936), *Silja, nuorena nukkunut/Silja, Fallen Asleep When Young* (1937), and *Kiusaus/Temptation* (1938). After World War II he worked in Sweden, with Ivar Johansson among others. As a producer Blomberg did his most influential work with the leftist intellectual Nyrki Tapiovaara*. Three of the five films he directed in the 1950s form a group of their own: *Valkoinen peura/The White Reindeer* (1953), *Kun on tunteet/When There Are Feelings* (1954) and *Kihlaus/The Engagement* (1955). All three star Mirjami Kuosmanen* (Blomberg's wife), who also co-wrote the scripts. *Valkoinen peura* was one of Finnish cinema's greatest international successes, garnering many prizes. It is set in Lapland, where Blomberg had made several short documentaries in the 1940s. He also directed *Miss Eurooppaa metsästämässä/Looking for Miss Europe* (1955) and *Hääyö/ Wedding Night* (1959). HS

BÓDALO, José José Bódalo Zúffoli; Córdoba, Argentina 1916 – Madrid 1985

Spanish actor of Argentinian origins. Bódalo's deep voice and craggy, slightly overweight appearance made him a much sought-after character actor from 1947. He appeared in key postwar films such as *La colmena/The Beehive* (1982, dir. Mario Camús*), *El crack/The Crack* (1980) and *El crack II/The Crack II* (1983), where his aura of world-weariness was used to excellent effect. Earlier notable films include *Locura de amor/Love Crazy* (1948), *El pecador y la bruja/The Sinner and the Witch* (1964) and *Ambiciosa/Ambitious Woman* (1976). PWE

BÓDY, Gábor Budapest 1946–85

Hungarian film director. Bódy was the only internationally renowned Hungarian experimental director, and he was by far the most controversial figure of the third postwar generation of film-makers. He studied philosophy and later graduated from the Academy of Theatre and Film Arts in Budapest. In the mid-1970s he created an experimental section in the Balázs Béla Stúdió* and complemented his experimental film-making with intensive theoretical research and teaching. In the 1980s his interest turned to other visual media, and during a stay in Germany he created an international video-periodical for distribution of video art called 'Infermental'. He used extended video and Super-8 footage in his last feature film, *Kutya éji dala/The Dog's Night Song* (1983), in which he took on the main role. Bódy made three feature films and a number of experimental films and video-tapes, and all his work is characterised by the systematic dissection of the surface of visual forms and the conventions of representation. Although he did not face problems of political censorship – his interest in cinema was of a different nature – his kind of film-making activity became increasingly difficult to sustain in the mid-1980s. His last film, representing different contemporaneous avant-garde and underground sub-cultures, was viewed by studio officials as an anarchistic and destructive work and funds were not forthcoming for further video-art experiments. Bódy committed suicide on 24 October 1985. KAB

Other Films Include: *Amerikai anzix/American Postcard* (1975); *Nárcisz és Psyché/Narcissus and Psyche I-II-III* (1980).

BOGARDE, (Sir) Dirk   London 1921

British actor, whose strikingly varied career makes him both a figure of unique respect in British cinema and a critical problem. The popular view is of a 1950s male pin-up, reaching stardom in such films as *Doctor in the House* (1954), who was rescued from a crippling seven-year contract with Rank* to become a serious actor in the European art cinema* of Joseph Losey* – *The Servant* (1963), *Accident* (1967) – and Luchino Visconti* – *La Caduta degli Dei/The Damned* (1969), *Morte a Venezia/Death in Venice* (1972). Certainly, the respect which he commands has something to do with his surprising ability to reinvent himself. More systematic criticism (notably by gay critics) recognises in this ability a testing of male sexuality which extends across his work – a striking feature in a national cinema which is apparently so certain its masculinity. It appears in the sexualised delinquency of *The Blue Lamp* (1950), it is explicit in the homosexuality of *Victim* (1961) – both 'social problem' films directed by Basil Dearden* – and it is most playfully camp in *Modesty Blaise* (Losey, 1966). It also surfaces in a consistent strain of erotic sadism which is exploited by Losey in *The Servant*, by Visconti in *The Damned*, and by Liliana Cavani* in *Il portiere di notte/The Night Porter* (1974). If there is a case for considering actors as *auteurs*, Bogarde is probably one of the more interesting and complex of British *auteurs*.

For a leading British actor he has made remarkably few American films – *Song Without End* (1960), *The Fixer* (1968) and *Justine* (1969) – but since the 1970s he has become one of the most European of British actors, with important roles in films by Visconti, Cavani, Henri Verneuil* (*Le serpent/The Serpent/Night Flight from Moscow* (1973, Fr.), Alain Resnais* (*Providence*, 1977, Fr.), Rainer Werner Fassbinder* (*Despair/Eine Reise ins Licht*, 1978, Ger.), and Bertrand Tavernier* (*Daddy Nostalgie/These Foolish Things*, 1990, Fr.).

Bogarde received British Film Academy awards for *The Servant* and for *Darling* (1965), and a BAFTA award for 'outstanding contribution to world cinema' in 1990. He was knighted in 1992. JC

Bib: Andy Medhurst, 'Dirk Bogarde', in Charles Barr (ed.), *All Our Yesterdays* (1986).

Other Films Include: *Dancing with Crime* (1947); *Esther Waters, Once a Jolly Swagman* (1948); *So Long at the Fair* (1950); *Blackmailed* (1951); *Hunted, The Gentle Gunman* (1952); *The Sleeping Tiger* (1954); *Simba, Doctor at Sea* (1955); *Ill Met by Moonlight* (1956); *Doctor at Large, Campbell's Kingdom* (1957); *A Tale of Two Cities* (1958); *The Doctor's Dilemma, Libel* (1959); *The Mind Benders* (1962); *Doctor in Distress* (1963); *King & Country* (1964); *A Bridge Too Far* (1977).

BÖHM, Karlheinz [Karl Heinz BOEHM]
Darmstadt 1928

German actor. The son of a famous conductor, Böhm started out as the elegant young lover of Arthur Maria Rabenalt's* *Alraune* (1952) and in the film operetta *Der unsterbliche Lump* (1953). He featured in over thirty films during the following decade, still typecast as the stiff juvenile hero in Ernst Marischka's* hugely popular *Sissi* trilogy (1955–57), leaving him with a serious image problem. Böhm attempted a change in British, French and American films, and succeeded almost too well as the self-conscious serial killer in Michael Powell's* *Peeping Tom* (1960). He subsequently appeared in the striptease thriller *Too Hot to Handle* (1959, UK), the lynch-law drama *La Croix des vivants* (1960, Fr.), as a Nazi officer in Vincente Minnelli's *The Four Horsemen of the Apocalypse* (1962, US) and as a sadistic agent in *The Venetian Affair* (1966, US). A second German career began in 1972, when Rainer Werner Fassbinder* made full use of Böhm's by now many-layered star image, first as the worldly-wise Prussian councillor Wüllersdorf in *Fontane Effi Briest/Effi Briest* (1974), then as the sadistic husband in *Martha* (1974), the homosexual art dealer in *Faustrecht der Freiheit/Fox and His Friends* (1975), and finally the arrogant, middle-class communist Tillmann in *Mutter Küsters Fahrt zum Himmel/Mother Kuster's Trip to Heaven* (1976). Apart from occasional appearances on stage and television, Böhm has devoted much of the last fifteen years to promoting charities for starving children in Central Africa and Ethiopia. TE/MW

BOIS, Curt   Berlin 1901–91

German actor. With a film debut in *Klebolin klebt alles* (1909) and a final appearance in Wim Wenders'* *Der Himmel über Berlin/Wings of Desire* in 1987, Bois has had the longest career in German film history. He starred in the comedy *Der Jüngling aus der Konfektion* (1926), followed by *Der Fürst von Pappenheim* (1927, dir. Richard Eichberg*), famous for his transvestite scenes, later maliciously used to travesty the film's meaning and to tar Jewish actors in the compilation propaganda film *Der ewige Jude* (1940). In his few German sound films before emigrating to the US in 1933, Bois recreated the Jewish '*schlemihl*' made famous by Ernst Lubitsch* in the 1910s. Appearing in many émigré films in Hollywood in the late 1930s and 1940s, Bois is best remembered for his nimble-fingered pickpocket in Michael Curtiz's *Casablanca* (1942). In 1950 he returned to East Germany, where he was associated with Bertolt Brecht's theatre and acted sporadically in DEFA* films, before moving to West Berlin in 1954 and concentrating on his stage career. Appropriately for someone so closely identified with Berlin, Bois rendered eloquent homage to its past in Wenders' romantic masterpiece, *Der Himmel über Berlin*. MW

BOISSET, Yves   Paris 1939

French director, a graduate of IDHEC*, former film critic and admirer of American cinema, who started making films in the late 1960s. Boisset worked in the *policier** genre from the start, but in his most interesting work of the 1970s he used it to raise topical social issues in the manner of André Cayatte, but also of the politicised cinema of the period in France and especially Italy [> ITALIAN POLITICAL CINEMA]. He dealt, for instance, with corruption in the police (*Un Condé/The Cop*, 1970) and in government (*L'Attentat/The French Conspiracy*, 1972), with racism in *Dupont Lajoie* (1975), with the Algerian war in *R.A.S.* (1973), and with fascist secret police groups in *Le Juge Fayard dit 'Le Shérif'* (1976) – films that presented their argument in a direct, clear-cut (some say overly black-and-white) and entertaining way. They were often subject to political censorship, Boisset acquiring a solidly left-wing reputation. *La Femme flic/Female Cop* (1980), about a policewoman (played by Miou-Miou*), added the impact of feminism and signalled a move to more psychological subject matter. Boisset is a prolific director, making films at the rate of almost one a year, though except for *Allons z'enfants* (1980) and *Bleu comme l'enfer* (1986) none has lately achieved the success of his earlier work. In 1994 he replaced Costa-Gavras* as director of *L'Affaire Dreyfus*. GV

BOLEN, Francis   Chimay 1908–81

Belgian critic, writer and director. One of the most prolific critics in the history of Belgian cinema. Bolen's self-appointed role as *documenteur* of Belgian film history often included participating in its events (he appeared in Gaston Schoukens'* first sound film *La Famille Klepkens*, 1929). Bolen also held various positions of importance, such as cinema attaché at UNESCO (1949–51), founder and president of the Comité National Belge des Travailleurs du Film, and secretary of the *Revue Belge du Cinéma*, Belgium's leading film journal.

His dedication to Belgian cinema forms the basis of his most famous publication, *Histoire Authentique du Cinéma Belge* ('An Authentic History of the Belgian Cinema'), which he described as 'anecdotal, folkloric and critical' [> GENERAL BIBLIOGRAPHY]. As well as encouraging the likes of Charles Dekeukeleire*, Henri Storck* and André Cauvin*, Bolen

made several shorts from 1933 to 1960, few of which were widely seen. CF

BOLVARY, Geza von   Budapest 1897 – Rosenheim, Germany 1961

Hungarian director of musical comedies in the prosperous German and Austrian cinemas of the 1930s and 1940s. Already known for his silent melodramas and comedies, Bolvary became hot property after his first sound film, the Willy Forst* vehicle *Zwei Herzen im 3/4 Takt* (1930), which made him the specialist of a new musical sub-genre, the Viennese film operetta. The film's huge international success led to a number of follow-ups centred on popular German actors – Forst again (*Ein Tango für Dich*, 1930; *Die lustigen Weiber von Wien*, 1931), Zarah Leander* (*Premiere*, 1937), and Willy Fritsch* (*Die Fledermaus*, 1945). Most notable among his postwar films, apart from other musicals, were a number of entertaining but historically and politically intriguing portraits of musicians, including the classic *Ein Lied geht um die Welt* (1958). MW

Other Films Include: *Champagner/Champagne, The Vagabond Queen* [UK], *The Wrecker* [UK] (1929); *Der Herr auf Bestellung* (1930); *Der Raub der Mona Lisa* (1931); *Wiener G'schichten* (1940); *Schicksal* (1942); *Schrammeln* (1944); *Fritz und Friederike* (1952); *Mein Leopold* (1955); *Schwarzwaldmelodie* (1956); *Was die Schwalbe sang* (1956), *Zwei Herzen im Mai* (1958).

BOND FILMS

British film series. Somewhat predictably, the package for the most commercially successful series of films in postwar British cinema was put together by an Italian-American ('Cubby' Broccoli) and a Canadian (Harry Saltzman, who had previously been involved in Woodfall*) with American money (United Artists). The success itself was less predictable: Ian Fleming's James Bond novels, though Philip Larkin and Kingsley Amis were fans, had not been best-sellers, Sean Connery* was an unknown, and United Artists were only prepared to invest $900,000 in *Dr No* (1962). Connery, however, brought to the part an accent which was foreign to the embarrassments of English class, and a style which allowed space for the audience to share the joke; the one-liners and double entendres of the dialogue allowed the audience not to take the violence too seriously ('sado-masochism for all the family'); Ken Adam's design chimed with the pop culture and pop art of the 1960s; and the narratives were based on routines on which infinite variations could be played, rather than on logical or psychological development. (Bond films are like *Carry On* films* in that people remember incidents rather than stories.) More fundamentally, James Bond offered playful fantasies to men, 'an assembly kit for fantasists' (Alexander Walker). While the 'angry young men' were vituperating against women as the agents of conformity, Bond offered sublimation and conquest. The formula ran on into the 1980s, surviving changes of cast with increasing self-reflexiveness, measuring the political temperature after the Cold War, and charting a history of male fantasy from sex to technology to techno-sex, and from playful sadism (the golden girl of *Goldfinger*, 1964) to body horror with special effects (the exploding of Grace Jones in *A View to a Kill*, 1985). JC

Bib: Tony Bennett and Janet Woollacott, *Bond and Beyond: The Political Career of a Popular Hero* (1987).

BONDARCHUK, Sergei F.   Belotserka, Ukraine 1920 – Moscow 1994

Soviet director and actor. Graduate of VGIK*, who first appeared in Sergei Gerasimov's* *Molodaya gvardiya/The Young Guard* in 1948. He subsequently became one of the leading actors in Soviet cinema but is best known in the West for directing a four-part version of Tolstoy's *Voina i mir/War and Peace* (1966–67), which won an Oscar, and *Waterloo* (1970, a Soviet-Italian co-production), both notable for their large-scale battle scenes and the quality of their acting. Vasili Shukshin*, Orson Welles and Rod Steiger have appeared in his films, as has Bondarchuk himself, from his directorial debut, a film version of Sholokhov's *Sud'ba cheloveka/The Fate of a Man* (1959). Bondarchuk also filmed Sholokhov's *Oni srazhalis' za rodinu/They Fought for Their Country* (1977). RT

BONNAIRE, Sandrine   Clermont-Ferrand 1967

French actress. Picked out of hundreds of adolescent hopefuls, Bonnaire was an overnight sensation in Maurice Pialat's* *A nos amours/To Our Loves* (1983). Her lack of training and working-class origins added authenticity to her talented performance as the unruly heroine, and to her portrayal of a tragic drop-out in Agnès Varda's* *Sans toit ni loi/Vagabonde* (1985). Bonnaire (who received a César for both films) has become a major figure among young French actors, injecting into her heroines a toughness recalling the young Jeanne Moreau*. GV

Other Films Include: *Blanche et Marie* (1984); *Police* (1985); *Sous le soleil de Satan/Under Satan's Sun* (1987); *Monsieur Hire, Peaux de vaches* (1989); *Jeanne la pucelle* (1994).

BOORMAN, John   Shepperton 1933

British director. 'For me,' says John Boorman, 'movie-making is a way of exploring the hidden places.' Despite coming from television documentary (he was head of BBC television documentaries from 1960 to 1964), Boorman is interested in a cinema of myth, a mythic interest which focuses on the Grail legend, and leads at its most interesting to modern 'quest' films like *Point Blank* (1967, US) and *Deliverance* (1972, US), or, more traditionally, to *Excalibur* (1981, US). It can also lead to *The Exorcist II: The Heretic* (1977, US), which Boorman describes as a 'human and healing film' but

which others thought a disaster. His autobiographical film, *Hope and Glory* (1987), gives a rather cute but visually dazzling account of boyhood in the London Blitz, and won Best Director and Best Screenplay awards from the New York Film Critics.

Taking up residence in Ireland, Boorman was made Chairman of the Board of the National Film Studios of Ireland (formerly Ardmore Studios*) in 1975 until it went into receivership in 1982, and was a member of the Irish Film Board* from 1980 to 1982. He was Executive Producer of Neil Jordan's* first feature, *Angel* (1982). JC

Bib: John Boorman, *Money into Light: The Emerald Forest, A Diary* (1985).

Other Films: *Catch Us If You Can* (1965); *Hell in the Pacific* (1968, US); *Leo the Last* (1970); *Zardoz* (1974); *The Emerald Forest* (1985); *Where the Heart Is* (1990, US).

BORAU, José Luis   José Luis Borau Moradell; Zaragoza 1929

Spanish director, best known for *Furtivos/Poachers* (1975), released shortly before Franco's death. *Furtivos* focused sensationally on political and sexual repression in Spain, satirising the institutions of a regime whose dissolution was adumbrated in countless scenes of menace and eventual rebellion against the constraints of incest and tradition. Earlier in his career Borau had trained at the IIEC* in Madrid, where he made his cinematic debut with the short *En el río/At the River* (1960), followed by *Brandy* (1963), a Western, and *Crimen de doble filo/Double-edged Crime* (1964), in which he transferred the conventions of the thriller to a Spanish urban setting. In *Hay que matar a B./B. Must Die* (1973) Borau dramatised the insidious appeal and blinding effects of nationalism, a key theme of his work, to which he returned in later films such as *Río Abajo/On the Line* (1984) and *Tata mía/Dear Nanny* (1986). The circumscribing of woman's freedom by social forces is a second recurrent concern, linking *Río Abajo* and *Tata mía* with *La Sabina* (1979) and the Borau-scripted *Mi querida señorita/My Dearest Señorita* (Armiñán*, 1971). RF

Bib: Agustín Sánchez Vidal, *José Luis Borau* (1990).

BORD SCANNAN NA hEIREANN (IRISH FILM BOARD)

Irish organisation. Bord Scannan na hEireann is the statutory body, established in 1981, charged with aiding Irish film production. With the exception of minimal amounts from the Irish Arts Council, it was the first state body to invest directly in indigenous productions. It made culturally significant investments in pre-production and took minority stakes through loans in films from an annual budget of only about IR£500,000 until 1987 when the Board was wound down as part of government cutbacks. It was reactivated in 1993 under Lelia Doolin, with an initial budget of IR£1.1m, rising to annual sums of £2–3 million in subsequent years. The Board membership includes film director Neil Jordan*. Films supported by the Board include Jordan's first feature, *Angel* (1982), Pat Murphy's* *Anne Devlin* (1984), and Joe Comerford's* *Reefer and the Model* (1987). KR

BOROWCZYK, Walerian   Kwilcz 1923

Polish director. Borowczyk studied fine art and worked in lithography and poster design before turning to animation. His first films, made with Jan Lenica*, revealed a bizarre and dark vision with a satirical edge influenced by surrealism. The success of *Dom/House* (1958) launched his European career and in 1959 Borowczyk moved to France. Here his macabre wit came to the fore in films like *Renaissance* (1963). Switching to live action, Borowczyk made impressively original features, especially *Goto, l'île d'amour/Goto, Isle of Love* (1969) and *Blanche* (1971). Films such as *Contes immoraux/ Immoral Tales* (1974) and *La Bête/The Beast* (1975) established Borowczyk as something of an 'eroticist', but subsequent features moved to sexploitation, using material largely unworthy of his talents. AW

Other Films Include: *Les Jeux des anges* (1964, anim.); *Le Théâtre de Monsieur et Madame Kabal* (1967, anim.); *Dzieje Grzechu/Story of a Sin* (1975); *La Marge* (1976).

BOS, Annie   Johanna Bos; Amsterdam 1886 – Leiden 1975

Dutch actress. After a short stage career, Bos became the first and only Dutch actress with star status in the silent period; starting in films in 1912, she reached the peak of her fame between 1915 and 1920. She played a great variety of characters in more than twenty features and many shorts, specialising in unconventional women in dramatic situations. A great admirer of the Italian *diva* Francesca Bertini [> DIVISMO], she developed a minimalist, understated performance style. Most of her films were produced, and often directed, by Maurits Binger* for Hollandia in Haarlem. When the studio was reorganised in 1920 under British supervision, she featured in three films under the name of Anna Bosilova. She moved to the US in an unsuccessful attempt to further her career, appearing in at least one American film, *Without Fear* (1922) with Pearl White. Her last film was *Mooi Juultje van Volendam/Beautiful July of Volendam* in 1924. KD

Bib: Geoffrey Donaldson, 'Annie Bos: de Hollandsche filmdiva', *Skrien*, vol. 76–77 (1978).

BOSÉ, Lucia   Milan 1931

Italian actress, who won the title of Miss Italy in 1947, competing against such outstanding finalists as Gina Lollobrigida*, Gianna Maria Canale and Eleonora Rossi Drago. After appearing in *1848* (1948), a short film by Dino

Risi*, she was given a leading part in *Non c'è pace tra gli ulivi* (1950), directed by Giuseppe De Santis*, who then cast her in a longer and more dramatic role in *Roma, ore 11* (1952). But it was in the early films of Michelangelo Antonioni*, *Cronaca di un amore/Story of a Love Affair* (1950) and *La signora senza camelie/The Lady Without Camelias* (1953), that her stylish brunette elegance was most dramatically revealed. Working with Luciano Emmer*, she showed a quality of self-confident freshness in *Parigi è sempre Parigi* (1951) and again in *Le ragazze di Piazza di Spagna* (1952). With Walter Chiari*, her fiancé at the time, she played in a number of mediocre romantic comedies. In 1955 Bosé married the famous bullfighter Luis Dominguin, giving birth to two daughters and a son, Miguel Bosé, who has become a moderately successful singer and an actor in films by Pedro Almodóvar* among others. In Spain she starred in Juan Antonio Bardem's* *Muerte de un ciclista/Death of a Cyclist* (1955), where she reverted to her Antonioni character of the 'thoroughbred' middle-class woman, immersed in existentialist sadness. This was further reflected in Francesco Maselli's* *Gli sbandati* (1955), Luis Buñuel's* *Cela s'appelle l'aurore* (1955, Fr./It.), and Jean Cocteau's* *Le Testament d'Orphée* (1960, Fr.). After a ten-year break, she returned to the cinema in 1968 to make three Spanish films and in 1969 she went back to Italy, appearing in the Taviani* brothers' *Sotto il segno dello Scorpione/Under the Sign of Scorpio* (1969) and Federico Fellini's* *Fellini Satyricon* (both 1969). A number of other films followed, including Mauro Bolognini's *Metello* (1970) and *Per le antiche scale/Down the Ancient Stairs* (1975); in France, Marguerite Duras'* *Nathalie Granger* (1972) and Jeanne Moreau's* *Lumière* (1976); and in Switzerland, Daniel Schmid's* *Violanta* (1977), in which she displayed a new, strong dramatic presence, as she had already done in Liliana Cavani's* *L'ospite/The Guest* (1971). After another ten-year absence, she made further appearances in television dramas and in the film version of a successful novel, *Volevo i pantaloni* (1990). MMo

BOSNIA and HERZEGOVINA – see (former) YUGOSLAVIA

BOST, Pierre – see AURENCHE, Jean

BOSTAN, Elisabeta   Buhuşi 1931

Romanian director and scriptwriter, specialising in children's and youth films. One of the earliest graduates of the Bucharest Theatre and Film School, she made innovatory shorts, and achieved prominence with her sensitive evocation of childhood in a series about a boy called *Naica* (1963–67). Her first feature, *Puştiul/The Kid* (1961), was followed by a skilful effort to adapt and film for a wide audience the highly literary work of Ion Creanga – *Amintiri din copilărie/ Childhood Memories* (1965). *Veronica* (1972) and *Mama/ Rock'n'Roll Wolf* (1977) provide flights of intelligent fantasy in which music plays a key role. The latter film initiated a number of features and series for children co-produced with the USSR, notably *Salţimbanci/Clowns* (1981). *Unde eşti* *copilărie?/Where Did You Go, My Childhood?* (1988) is an eloquent rites of passage film. As the most resilient Romanian woman film-maker, Bostan continues to work at home and abroad, and lectures at the Institute of Theatre and Film. MM

BOTELHO, João   Lamego 1949

Portuguese director. Joining the new Lisbon film school in 1974, Botelho became one of the founders of *M*, a film magazine. His positions were highly theoretical, coloured by the influence of Jean-Luc Godard* and Jean-Marie Straub*. He also became a distinguished graphic designer, this talent being used to good effect in his first feature, *Conversa Acabada/The Other One* (1981), about the correspondence between the two great Portuguese modernist poets, Pessoa and Sá Carneiro. Almost entirely shot in a studio using back projections, the film suggests a flat, graphic space. In *Um Adeus Português/A Portuguese Goodbye* (1985), Botelho recalled the colonial wars (a rare occurrence in Portuguese cinema) through the story of a family migrating from the country to Lisbon. Increasingly, the family became an essential element in his films. He has said that he makes his films for his children and that, in contrast to large-scale American productions, he prefers to make a 'local' – sometimes almost 'home-made' – cinema (shots taken in his house appear in his films, and formed the basis of *Três Palmeiras/Three Palm Trees*, 1994).

Botelho's is also a moral position, finding in contemporary Portugal similarities to Dickens, whom he adapted in a modern black-and-white version of *Tempos Difíceis/Hard Times* (1988). Nevertheless, his characters, however rooted in his perception of Portuguese reality, move in a fragmented and abstract filmic world, physical but also metaphysical, Botelho contrasting the new bourgeoisie with those who look for redemption and grace. This opposition is extreme in *Aqui na Terra/Here on Earth* (1993), a film with two stories, one set in the city, the other in the country, where elements such as land and sky and air are symbolically contrasted. *Acqui na Terra* was made between two commissions for portmanteau films, the first called *The Four Elements*, in which Botelho's subject is air (*O Dia dos Meus Anos/The Day of My Birthday*, 1992), the second a film about Lisbon in 1994, for which he filmed a segment covering the hours from 6 a.m. to 2 p.m. (*Três Palmeiras*). In both cases, against time limitations (an hour to represent a day in one film or eight hours in the other), Botelho stressed fragmentation, a feature which has become a distinctive element of his cinema. AMS

BOULTING, Roy   Bray 1913
and
BOULTING, John   Bray 1913 – Sunningdale 1985

British directors, writers and producers, and twin brothers, who produced most of their films together. During the war, John directed *Journey Together* (1945) for the RAF Film Unit, and Roy directed *Desert Victory* (1943), *Tunisian Victory* (1944) and *Burma Victory* (1945) for the Army Film Unit. In Charter Films, which they established in 1937, roles were fluid. 'As producers and directors,' said John Boulting, 'we generally worked on the basis that the one who wrote the script should direct the film and be the arbiter of the film's creative development.' In the 1940s they produced such tough dramas and melodramas as *Pastor Hall* (1940), *Thunder Rock* (1942), *Fame is the Spur* (1947), and, probably their best film, *Brighton Rock* (1947). From the 1950s they switched to comedy, social satire and farce, producing one classic in *I'm All Right Jack* (1959), and a few amusing swipes at British manners and institutions in such films as *Private's Progress* (1956), *Brothers in Law* (1957) and *Carlton-Browne of the F.O.* (1959). JC

Other Films Include: *The Guinea Pig* (1948); *Seven Days to Noon* (1950); *The Magic Box* (1951); *Seagulls over Sorrento* (1954); *Lucky Jim* (1957); *Suspect* (1960); *Heavens Above!* (1963); *The Family Way* (1966); *Twisted Nerve* (1968); *There's a Girl in my Soup* (1970).

BOURVIL   André Raimbourg; Petrot-Vicquemare 1917 – Paris 1970

French actor. One of the best-loved popular French film comedians, Bourvil started as an accordionist in Normandy dance halls and later sang in Parisian cabarets and on the radio, where he was discovered. From his first lead in *La Ferme du pendu* (1945), a peasant melodrama, he drew on his origins as a farmer's son to develop his early persona of the 'village idiot'. He emerged as a star in Claude Autant-Lara's* *La Traversée de Paris/A Pig Across Paris* (1956), for which he won a prize at Venice. From then on he broadened his comic peasant to embody the 'average Frenchman' duped by more aggressive middle-class partners (Jean Gabin* in *La Traversée*, Louis de Funès* in the hits *Le Corniaud/The Sucker*, 1965, and *La Grande vadrouille/Don't Look Now, We're Being Shot At*, 1966).

Like many comics, Bourvil had ambitions to play serious roles, which he did as the brilliantly sinister Thénardier of *Les Misérables* (1958) and in Jean-Pierre Melville's* thriller *Le Cercle rouge/The Red Circle* (1970), made shortly before his death. But for French audiences his enduring appeal was comic, the not-so-simple peasant and epitome of the man in the street, vindicated through stardom. GV

Other Films Include: *Miquette et sa mère* (1950); *Le Passe-muraille* (1950); *Le Trou normand* (1952); *Si Versailles m'était conté* (1954); *Le Miroir à deux faces* (1958); *Le Chemin des écoliers* (1959); *Tout l'or du monde* (1961); *La Cuisine au beurre* (1963); *Les Grandes gueules* (1965); *Le Cerveau* (1969).

BOUWMEESTER, Theo – see FRENKEL, Theo

BOX, Muriel   Violette Muriel Baker; Tolworth 1905 – London 1991,

Sydney   Beckenham 1907 – Perth, Australia 1983

and

Betty   Beckenham 1920

British directors, producers and writers. Muriel and Sydney Box began as a prolific husband and wife writing team, writing one-act plays in the 1930s, and formed a company during the war, with Sydney's sister Betty as assistant, to produce government instructional films. Moving to feature film writing, Sydney and Muriel received an Oscar in 1945 for the original script of *The Seventh Veil*. In 1946, Sydney was placed in charge of Gainsborough by J. Arthur Rank*, with Muriel in charge of the script department, and Betty in charge of Islington Studios. Together they were responsible for almost forty films in a four-year period. In the early 1950s, Muriel began directing, and has directed more films than any other British woman, *Sight and Sound** condescendingly describing them as 'women's pictures ... part of the magazine fiction of the screen – and no less competently organised than most magazine fiction.' Sydney and Muriel's working partnership broke up in 1958 when Sydney became a television executive. They separated in 1969. Betty has had a director-producer relationship with Ralph Thomas, resulting in over thirty films, including the *Doctor ...* series, since 1954. She is married to Peter Rogers, who produces the *Carry On* series with Ralph's brother, Gerald Thomas. Of the trio, Muriel has a particularly strong claim to a place in British film history as one of an extremely small group of women feature film directors; her work has recently been reassessed by feminist critics. JC

Films Directed By Muriel Box: *The Happy Family* (1952); *A Prince for Cynthia* [short], *Street Corner* (1953); *The Beachcomber, To Dorothy a Son* (1954); *Simon and Laura* (1955); *Eyewitness* (1956); *The Passionate Stranger* (1957); *The Truth About Women* (1958); *Subway in the Sky, This Other Eden* (1959, Ir.); *Too Young to Love* (1960); *The Piper's Tune* (1962); *Rattle of a Simple Man* (1964).

BOYANA STUDIOS

Bulgarian film studios. When one considers that back in 1953 only one feature film was produced in Bulgaria, the growth of Bulgarian cinema since then is nothing short of sensational. The quality of film production rose with the increased sophistication of the home audience. Before World War II, there were only 165 movie theatres scattered across the entire country; by the end of the 1960s there were more than 3,000. The Boyana Studios, constructed in the 1950s at the foot of Mount Vitoša overlooking Sofia, and expanded in the 1960s into 'Film City Boyana', include five separate and independent sections: the Boyana Feature Film Studio, the Sofia Animation Studio, the paired Vreme Popular Science and Documentary Film Studios, and the Boyana Film Laboratory.

Until 1983, the Boyana Feature Film Studio was composed of four creative groups, each with its own artistic director. Beginning in 1983, however, when an ill-fated reform was in-troduced by the newly appointed general director Nikolai Nennov, the four creative groups were disbanded and feature film production placed under the double management of Zako Heskija and Ljudmil Kirkov*. However, as the quality of feature film production noticeably decreased during the 1980s, the worldwide reputation of the Sofia Animation Studio correspondingly increased. Todor Dinov (*Jabolkata/ The Apple*, 1963; *Margaritkata/The Daisy*, 1965), the father of Bulgarian animation, inspired a 'school' of highly talented film cartoonists who quickly won world recognition: Donju Donev (*Trimata glupazi/The Three Fools*, 1970; *De Facto*, 1973), Stojan Dukov (*En Passant*, 1975), Ivan Vesselinov (*Naslednici/The Heirs*, 1970), Henri Kulev, Slav Bakalov, Ivan Andonov, Rumen Petkov, Radka Bačvarova, Hristo Topuzanov, Zdenka Dojčeva, Genčo Simeonov, Georgi Čavdarov, Asparukh Panov, Nikola Todorov, Proiko Proikov, Penčo Bogdanov, Velislav Kozakov, and Vlado Šomov. The philosophical parables of Dinov, Donev and Dukov became the trademark of Bulgarian animation during the 1970s, supported to a great extent by the biennial Varna World Animation Film Festival.

On the documentary and popular science side, it was Zahari Žandov* who first signalled a new Bulgarian cinematography when his documentary *Hora sred oblacite/Men amid the Clouds* (1946) won a prize at the Venice festival. Hristo Kovačev, whose *Ot edno do osem/From One to Eight* (1966) also won a prize at Venice, chronicled the history of the Bulgarian working class at the Documentary Film Studio from 1950 onwards. And Januš Vazov, whose career at the Popular Science Studio began in 1951, made more than forty films on art and folklore (*Narodno vajatelstvo/Folk Sculpture*, 1956), history and biology, and occasionally feature films with documentary elements, such as *Stepni hora/Steppe People* (1985). RH

BOYER, Charles   Figeac 1897 – Phoenix, Arizona 1978

French actor. Boyer, along with Maurice Chevalier*, was one of the only French stars to make a really successful career in Hollywood. A cultured and classically trained actor, Boyer possessed distinguished looks, dark eyes and a famous velvety voice. He emerged in the 1920s, but fame came with sound. He appeared in proletarian roles in Franco-German productions such as *Tumultes* (1931) and Fritz Lang's* French film *Liliom* (1934). However, his real register was that of the lover in romantic (often costume) melodrama; notably with Danielle Darrieux* in *Mayerling* (1936) and Michèle Morgan* in *Orage* (1937), embodying a man consumed by love, the object of desire of the heroine and of the camera. This is also his Hollywood image, in melodramas such as *All This and Heaven Too* (1940) with Bette Davis and *Back Street* (1941) with Margaret Sullavan. He also conveyed the sinister aspect of male seduction, especially in *Gaslight* (1944, with Ingrid Bergman*). Boyer took American citizenship in 1942 and was active in promoting Franco-American relations. The antithesis of Chevalier's caricatural Frenchman, Boyer nevertheless owed much of his success in Hollywood to a romantic notion of 'Frenchness'. He kept up French connections, acting in films directed by exiles such as Julien Duvivier* (*Tales of Manhattan*, 1942) and remakes of French films (*Algiers*, 1938, after *Pépé le Moko*; *The Thirteenth Letter*, 1951, after *Le Corbeau*). He continued his international career after the war, with notable parts in Max Ophuls'* *Madame de...* (1953), Christian-Jaque's* *Nana* (1954) and Alain Resnais'* *Stavisky...* (1974). He killed himself two days after the death of his wife of forty-four years, the British actress Pat Paterson, perhaps his most romantic gesture. GV

BRAKEL, Nouchka van   Amsterdam 1940

Dutch director and scriptwriter. After graduating from the Dutch Film Academy (Amsterdam), van Brakel initially worked in youth films, but subsequently concentrated on films about women struggling against social conventions, for which she has attracted a great deal of popular interest. Her first feature, *Het debuut/The Debut* (1977), about a fourteen-year-old girl seducing a forty-year-old man, was a hit. *Een vrouw als Eva/A Woman Like Eve* (1979) is a lesbian romance which provoked heated controversy (radical lesbians criticised the fact that it was not made or acted by lesbians) and much media attention, boosting its box-office success. *Van de koele meren des doods/Hedwig/The Cool Lakes of Death* (1982) is a psychological portrait of a young woman at the turn of the century, while *Een maand later/One Month Later* (1987) presents the fantasies of a housewife who wants to change places with a single woman for a month. As in van Brakel's previous films, the main roles are played by Renée Soutendijk* and Monique van de Ven. KD

BRANAGH, Kenneth   Belfast 1960

British/Irish actor and director, whose significance for British cinema may be in his revival of the tradition of popular Shakespeare on film. His first film as actor/director, *Henry V* (1987), offered an opportunity to reassess the patriotism of Laurence Olivier's* 1945 version in the age of Thatcherite English nationalism, but the political edge was blunted by what Branagh has called 'life-enhancing populism'. *Much Ado About Nothing* (1993) plays out the Olivier/Vivien Leigh* fantasy of the 'fabled couple' with a rather 'laddish' Branagh playing Benedict to the Beatrice of his wife, Emma Thompson (who in her own right won an Oscar for *Howards End* [1992], and has appeared with Branagh in all his films to date). The film's undoubted popularising success relies on its charm, its settings and its all-star cast (including Hollywood's Keanu Reeves and Denzel Washington), rather than its challenge or new perception. While the comparison with Olivier may be too obvious, it allows us to chart a shift in stardom from heroism and dangerous romance to a rather resistible brashness, and from Shakespeare as national myth to Shakespeare as national theme park.

Branagh has also directed and acted in three non-Shakespearean films, the sub-Hitchcockian *Dead Again* (1991), the sub-*Big Chill*, *Peter's Friends* (1992), and the not completely sub-Coppola *Mary Shelley's Frankenstein* (1994). *Frankenstein*, his most recent adaptation of the classics, had Branagh as the scientist and many of the usual directorial

mannerisms (a lot of running actors and wheeling cameras), but something awesome was preserved from the relentless gothic horror of the book – and not all the credit can go to Coppola, who produced, De Niro, who played the monster, or even Mary Shelley, who put it there in the first place. JC

Bib: Alison Light, 'The Importance of Being Ordinary', *Sight and Sound* (September 1993).

BRANCO, Paulo   Lisbon 1950

Portuguese producer. In 1974 Branco began programming for art-house cinemas in Paris and four years later he founded the distribution company Hors-Champs. His release of Manoel de Oliveira's* *Amor de Perdição/Ill-Fated Love* (1977) in Paris re-established a link between France and Portugal. Branco was associate producer on Marguerite Duras'* *Aurélia Steiner – Vancouver* (1979) and produced Jean-Claude Biette's *Loin de Manhattan/Far from Manhattan* (1981); he also founded V.O. Filmes with António-Pedro Vasconcelos in Portugal. The company's first achievements were completion of Vasconcelos's *Oxalá/God Willing* (1981), production of Oliveira's *Francisca* (1981), João Botelho's* *Conversa Acabada/The Other One* (1982) and João César Monteiro's* *Silvestre* (1980), and co-production of Raul Ruiz's* *Território/Le Territoire/The Territory* (1981). Branco also acted as associate producer on Wim Wenders'* *The State of Things* (1982). For the first time since António da Cunha Telles* in the 1960s, Portuguese cinema had a real producer, one with international connections who attracted foreign productions to Portugal and made it possible for Portuguese technicians to work with experienced craftsmen, creating, as Serge Daney wrote in *Cahiers du Cinéma*, a 'Portuguese pole'. Portuguese cinema suddenly had a new visibility on the international art-house circuit.

As often in Portuguese cinema, the euphoria was short-lived, however; none of the structural problems (dependence on state subsidy, split between production and distribution) was solved, and V.O. Filmes faded, the partners going their separate ways. Nevertheless, fifteen years and many companies later, Branco still produces both in Portugal and France. He is most noted for his nine films with Oliveira: *Francisca* (1981), *O Sapato de Setim/Le Soulier de satin/The Satin Slipper* (1985), *O Meu Caso/Mon Cas* (1986), *Os Canibais/The Cannibals* (1988), *Non ou a Vã Glória de Mandar/No, or the Vain Glory of Command* (1990), *A Divina Comédia/The Divine Comedy* (1991), *O Dia do Desespero/Day of Despair* (1992), *Vale Abraão/The Valley of Abraham* (1993) and *A Caixa/Blind Man's Bluff* (1994). He has also produced feature films by young directors such as João Mário Grilo and João Canijo; the anthology *The Four Elements* (1992) directed by Botelho, Joaquim Pinto*, Monteiro and Grilo; Botelho's *Três Palmeiras/Three Palm Trees* (1994); and Pedro Costa's *Casa de Lava* (1994). Another important collaboration was with Ruiz, with whom he worked between 1980 and 1985. This partnership was revived in 1994 with *Fado Majeur et Mineur*. Other distinguished film-makers Branco has produced are Alain Tanner*, Wenders, Jacques Rozier, Werner Schroeter* and Peter Handke. In France he collaborated with directors of the younger generation such as

Olivier Assayas, Danielle Dubroux and Laurence Ferreira Barbosa. In 1989, Branco moved back into Portuguese distribution and exhibition, creating a permanent link between national production, distribution and exhibition for the first time in almost forty years. His companies Atalanta (distribution) and Medeia (exhibition) offered new possibilities for independent films in a market dominated by American products and where European films had become increasingly rare. Branco played a leading role as an actor in Ruiz's *Point de fuite* (1983) and a cameo in Telles's *Vidas* (1983). AMS

BRANDAUER, Karin   Alt Aussee 1946 – Vienna 1992

Austrian director, notable for documentaries and adaptations of Austrian literature, mainly for television. After *Der Weg ins Freie* (1982, a Schnitzler adaptation) and *Erdsegen* (1986, based on Peter Rosegger), Brandauer came to international festival attention with *Einstweilen wird es Mittag/Marienthal* (1988), a docu-drama about a mining village during a strike in 1930, based on a celebrated sociological study of unemployment. Observing the role of women in traditional communities confronted with industrialisation and social change (*Verkaufte Heimat*, 1989), Brandauer's films are strongly committed to rural values while showing an acute historical sense, as in a television series on the South Tyrol referendum in 1939, and *Sidonie* (1990, adapted from a novel by Erich Hackl). She was married to actor Klaus Maria Brandauer*. TE

BRANDAUER, Klaus Maria   Bad Aussee 1944

Austrian actor. After work in theatre and television, Brandauer's career took off when he starred in István Szabó's* *Mephisto* (1981), *Redl Ezredes/Colonel Redl* (1985) and *Hanussen* (1988), where he specialised in power-hungry, self-tormented and contradictory characters. Brandauer has won a variety of film awards, including a 1982 Academy Award for *Mephisto*, which led to major roles in British and American productions. He directed his first film in 1989, *Georg Elser – Einer aus Deutschland*, with himself in the title role of the lone would-be assassin of Hitler. MW

Other Films Include: *The Lightship* (1985, US); *Streets of Gold* (1986, US); *Burning Secret* (1988, UK); *Das Spinnennetz* (1989; dir. Bernhard Wicki*).

BRASILLACH, Robert – see BARDÈCHE, Maurice

BRASSEUR, Pierre   Pierre-Albert Espinasse; Paris 1905 – Brunico, Italy 1972

French actor. A 'sacred monster' of stage and screen, whose immense filmography (over 130 titles) includes few leading parts, yet who left his mark on French cinema, especially in *Les Enfants du paradis* (1943–45). Brasseur trained at the Paris Conservatoire; he acted in, and wrote plays for, *boulevard* theatre. From the late 1920s he appeared indiscriminately in minor roles in popular movies, gradually specialising in depraved rogues (Marcel Carné's* *Quai des brumes*, 1938) and demented bohemians (Jean Grémillon's* *Lumière d'été*, 1943). Close to the Surrealists, he appeared in Pierre Prévert's* fantasy *Adieu Léonard* (1943, written 1932). He developed a baroque, rather menacing persona of seducer and/or *bon viveur* (as in Denys de la Patellière's *Les Grandes familles*, 1958). He appeared in René Clair's* *Porte des Lilas* (1957), Georges Franju's* *Les Yeux sans visage/Eyes Without a Face* (1960) and Walerian Borowczyk's* *Goto l'île d'amour/Goto, Isle of Love* (1969). But the glory of his career remains his flamboyant incarnation of the actor Frédérick Lemaître in *Les Enfants du paradis*. His subversion of an over-the-top melodrama rehearsal is one of the great moments of French cinema.

Brasseur was once married to the actress and novelist Odette Joyeux (born Paris, 1917), who played intense young women, notably in Marc Allégret's* *Entrée des artistes/The Curtain Rises* (1938) and Claude Autant-Lara's* *Douce* (1943). Their son Claude Brasseur (Claude Espinasse, born Paris 1936) has pursued a successful career on stage and in the cinema since the late 1950s. GV

BRAUN, Harald   Berlin 1901 – Xanten 1960

German director, who began at Ufa* in 1937 thanks to Carl Froelich* and made his directorial debut in 1942 with *Zwischen Himmel und Erde/Between Heaven and Earth*. He was granted a producer's licence by Erich Pommer* in 1947. With *Nachtwache* (1949), one of the biggest box-office hits of the time, came Braun's first real postwar success. A kind of ecumenical *Heimatfilm**, *Nachtwache* tells the story of a doubting woman doctor brought back to the church by the determined efforts of a priest. In a similar vein, Braun's subsequent films often revel in symbolism, betraying his religious upbringing and highbrow education. His biopic of the Nobel prize-winning pacifist Bertha von Suttner, *Das Herz der Welt* (1951), earned him several awards. MW

BRAUNBERGER, Pierre   Paris 1905–90

French producer, associated with the new breed of independent producers who supported the New Wave* (see also Georges de Beauregard* and Anatole Dauman*). Braunberger, however, was by then already a veteran, with experience of the 'first wave' of *auteur* cinema in France [> FRENCH AVANT-GARDE] during which he produced such films as René Clair's *Entr'acte* (1924), Luis Buñuel's *L'Age d'or* (1930) and Jean Renoir's* *La Chienne* (1931), as well as more mainstream films, through his company Etablissements Braunberger-Richebé. His New Wave involvements include François Truffaut's* *Tirez sur le pianiste/Shoot the Pianist* (1960) and Jean Rouch's* *Moi, un noir* (1959). He went on to produce films by Maurice Pialat* and Claude Lelouch*, among others. In 1969 he co-founded the GREC (Groupe de recherches et d'essais cinématographiques), an organisation devoted to financing short, 'uncommercial' projects.

Braunberger recounted his eventful life and work in an entertaining and informative autobiography, *Cinémamémoire* (1987). GV

BRAZZI, Rossano   Bologna 1916 – Rome 1994

Italian actor and director. Considering his active participation in the anti-Fascist movement, it is ironic that Rossano Brazzi found his early film roles in classic examples of Mussolini's Fascist cinema such as *La forza bruta* (1941). An international star in the 1950s, the dashingly handsome Brazzi was initially signed up by David O. Selznick, but his talent was hardly extended as the distinctly unromantic German professor in the 1948 version of *Little Women*. It was 1954 before Brazzi was given a chance to prove his potential as a Hollywood leading man, when he had his first stock part as a 'Latin lover' opposite Jean Peters in *Three Coins in the Fountain*. Despite newspaper speculation about his relationships with a succession of female co-stars, Brazzi was much more than a handsome foil. Katharine Hepburn was so impressed with his acting that she suggested Brazzi's name should accompany hers above the titles of *Summertime/Summer Madness* (1955, US/UK). Apparently his singing voice was not quite as attractive; the musical parts of Brazzi's role in *South Pacific* (1958) were dubbed by Giorgio Tozzi. Falling out of favour with Hollywood in the 1960s, Brazzi returned to Italy, also turning his hand to directing (sometimes under the pseudonym of Edward Ross). Perhaps revelling in his cameo as the criminal mastermind of *The Italian Job* (1969, UK), Brazzi was notoriously arrested in 1984 for his alleged involvement in an arms-smuggling conspiracy. He ended his long career with television appearances, notably in the British productions *The Far Pavilions* (1984) and an episode of the *Ruth Rendell Mysteries* (1990). SH

Films as Director: *The Christmas That Almost Wasn't/Il natale che quasi non fu* (1966, US/It.); *Sette uomini e un cervello* (1968); *Salvare la faccia/Psychout for Murder* (1969, Argentina/It.); *Cappucetto rosso, Cenerentola ... e voi ci credete* (1972).

BREIEN, Anja   Oslo 1940

Norwegian director, who studied at IDHEC* in Paris. After several shorts, Breien made her first feature, *Voldtekt/Rape*, in 1971. Her international breakthrough came with the successful *Hustruer/Wives* (1975), a witty feminist answer to John Cassavetes' *Husbands* (1970) which, in its spontaneous style, recalled the French New Wave*. *Hustruer* explores the role of women in contemporary Norwegian society through the story of three housewives who break free from their husbands and families for a few days to experience freedom, albeit temporarily. The plot is minimalist and the dialogue was improvised by the three actresses, who toured Norway with Breien to promote and discuss the film. In the 1980s Breien's work broadened to other genres, such as drama and the thriller, while still concentrating on female identity and social critique, especially of women's lives. Her latest film,

Smykketyven/Twice upon a Time (1990), portrays a middle-aged man driven to the edge of madness. KS

Other Films Include: *Den alvarsamma leken/The Serious Game of Love and Loneliness* (1977); *Arven/Next of Kin* (1979); *Forfølgelsen/The Witch Hunt* (1981); *Papirfuglen/Paper Bird* (1984); *Hustruer ti år etter/Wives Ten Years After* (1985).

BREJCHOVÁ, Jana   Prague 1940

Czech actress. Jana Brejchová was the leading female star of Czech cinema in the postwar period. Although she lacked formal training, her physical beauty and grace were soon noticed in her early films, *Štěňata/Puppies* (1957), co-scripted by Miloš Forman*, and Jiří Weiss's* *Vlčí jáma/The Wolf Trap* (1957). Parts in key films such as Vojtěch Jasný's *Touha/Desire* (1958) and Jiří Krejčik's *Vyšši princip/A Higher Principle* (1960) led to major acting roles in Evald Schorm's* *Každý den odvahu/Everyday Courage* (1964) and *Návrat ztraceného syna/Return of the Prodigal Son* (1966). Equally at home in comedy and drama, she continued to lend distinction to Czech films in the 1970s and 1980s, notably in Vladimír Drha's study of mother-daughter relations, *Citlivá místa/Sensitive Spots* (1988). Her sister, Hana Brejchová, was cast in the leading roles of Forman's *Lásky jedné plavovlásky/A Blonde in Love* (1965) and Jaroslav Papoušek's *Nejkrásnější věk/The Best Age* (1968). PH

Other Films Include: *Žižkovská romance/A Local Romance* (1958); *Baron Prášil/Baron Münchhausen* (1961); *Bloudění/Wandering* (1965); *Ženu ani květinou neuhodiš/Never Strike A Woman – Even with a Flower* (1966); *Noc nevěsty/Night of the Bride* (1967); *Farařův konec/End of a Priest* (1968); *Zabil jsem Einsteina pánové/Gentlemen, I Have Killed Einstein* (1969); *Luk královny Dorotky/The Bow of Queen Dorothy* (1970); *Slečna Golem/Miss Golem* (1972); *Mladý muž a bílá velryba/Young Man and the White Whale* (1978); *Útěky domů/Escapes Home* (1979); *Schůzka se stíny/A Meeting with Shadows* (1982); *Zánik samoty Berhof/The End of the Lonely Farm Berghof* (1983); *Vlastně se nic nestalo/Killing with Kindness* (1988).

BREL, Jacques   Brussels 1929 – Bobigny, France 1978

Belgian singer, actor and director. Known internationally for his singing and, later, his acting, Brel also directed two films in his native Belgium.

Brel's poetic songs expressed his revolt against the bourgeois world, or paid homage to Belgium. When he gave up singing for acting in 1966, he brought the same sense of intensity and tragedy to films by such directors as Marcel Carné* and André Cayatte (in the latter's *Les Risques du métier/The Risks of the Job*, 1967, he was a schoolteacher accused of raping a pupil), though he also played a comic part in Edouard Molinaro's successful *L'Emmerdeur* (1973), remade in Hollywood as *Buddy, Buddy* (1981). In 1972 Brel directed (and starred in) his first film, *Franz*, a tragi-comic love story. Despite good reviews, *Franz* failed at the box office. Brel's next film, *Le Far West* (1973), was a comedy about two men who play at being cowboys at weekends. Although it represented Belgium at Cannes in 1973 and starred Lino Ventura* and Michel Piccoli*, *Le Far West* was criticised for its portrayal of American Indians. Brel retired from film-making after these two discouraging attempts. CF

BRESSON, Robert Bromont-Lamothe 1907

French director. One of the most respected *auteurs* of world cinema, described by admirer Paul Schrader as 'the most important spiritual artist' and as a 'Jansenist' by his detractors. Bresson's originality within French cinema is twofold. First, he is almost unique in pursuing a religious discourse; second, his dislike of actors and use of unknown amateurs runs counter to the great French tradition of performance- and dialogue-based cinema.

Bresson studied philosophy and was a photographer and painter before working in film. Startlingly, he began as a scriptwriter on mainstream comedies in the 1930s. His first feature, *Les Anges du péché* (1943), was a naturalistic convent drama with established actors, qualified by Bresson as 'a bit naive, too simple'. He emerged as a force in independent cinema with *Les Dames du Bois de Boulogne* (1945) and *Le Journal d'un curé de campagne/The Diary of a Country Priest* (1951), adapted from a novel by the Catholic writer Georges Bernanos. Apart from the themes of redemption and divine grace which inform all his work, *Le Journal* exemplified the power of Bresson's austere black-and-white *mise-en-scène*, in which extreme sparseness combines with an almost hyper-realist use of locations and soundtrack. Bresson's next two films, *Un condamné à mort s'est échappé/A Man Escaped* (1956) and *Pickpocket* (1959), are understated yet lyrical, offering minute observation of the gestures and sounds of a prison escape in the former, and of the techniques of picking pockets in the latter (Schrader reprised the ending of *Pickpocket* in his *American Gigolo*, 1979). Bresson went on to produce one of the most consistent bodies of films in French cinema, introducing colour in *Une femme douce/A Gentle Creature* (1969), also noteworthy for the fact that its principal 'model', Dominique Sanda, became a star in her own right (as did Anne Wiazemsky, the protagonist of *Au hasard, Balthazar*, 1966) – a phenomenon said to irritate Bresson.

Bresson's cinema, while critically acclaimed, does not attract large audiences and he has made relatively few films, putting his difficulties, not unreasonably, down to his refusal of 'performance'. His opposition to mainstream cinema, the coherence of his themes and *mise-en-scène* and his self-scripted films made him one of the models for the future New Wave* in the early 1950s. Bresson's quest for a 'pure' cinema – 'I want to be as far from literature as possible, as far from every existing art' – actually relates him to an even earlier tradition, that of the French avant-garde* of the 1920s. GV

Bib: Paul Schrader, *Transcendental Style in Film: Ozu, Bresson, Dreyer* (1988).

Other Films: *Le Procès de Jeanne d'Arc/The Trial of Joan of Arc* (1962); *Mouchette* (1967); *Les Quatre nuits d'un rêveur/Four Nights of a Dreamer* (1971); *Lancelot du lac* (1974); *Le Diable probablement/The Devil Probably* (1977); *L'Argent* (1983).

BRIALY, Jean-Claude Aumale [Sour El-Ghozlan], Algeria 1933

French actor and director. Brialy was one of the totem actors of the New Wave*. Claude Chabrol's* *Le Beau Serge* (1957) and *Les Cousins* (1958) and Jean-Luc Godard's* *Une femme est une femme/A Woman is a Woman* (1961) fixed his persona as the spoilt young man roaming the streets of Paris in his sports car in search of women and fun. Though he acted in many other films – including Eric Rohmer's* *Le Genou de Claire/Claire's Knee* (1970) and Claude Miller's *L'Effrontée/ An Impudent Girl* (1985) – he never regained such prominence. He is, however, a well-known stage actor, theatre owner and media personality. He has directed a number of films, including adaptations of classic French children's fables such as *Les Malheurs de Sophie* (1980) and *Un bon petit diable* (1983). GV

BRITISH BOARD OF FILM CENSORS (BBFC) [now BRITISH BOARD OF FILM CLASSIFICATION]

British institution. 'This film is so cryptic as to be meaningless. If there is a meaning it is doubtless objectionable.' Thus the 1930 BBFC examiner in rejecting Germaine Dulac's* *La Coquille et le clergyman/The Seashell and the Clergyman* (1928). The Board was established in 1913 as an industry response to the eccentricities of the Local Authority licensing of films. Technically, it was an industry-run advisory body, financed by the fees levied on applications, 'advising' Local Authorities on the suitability of films for public exhibition, and the submission of a film for certification was voluntary. In effect, it was virtually impossible for a film to be shown commercially without a BBFC certificate. The Board has been served in its time by some legendary 'old duffers' (though John Trevelyan, BBFC Secretary in the 1960s and 1970s brought a more liberal approach) and the archives are full of equally legendary inanities which reflect at best a conservative and at worst a dangerously reactionary view of class relations, sexual relations, religion, and international affairs. In 1975 a more 'rational' system of regulation was introduced when films were removed from the common law offence of indecency and brought under the Obscene Publications Act, which allowed a defence of context (on the grounds, for example, of artistic context) and gave some protection from arbitrary prosecution. In 1982, the BBFC changed its name to the British Board of Film Classification, and in 1985, in response to anxieties about 'video nasties', it was given statutory authority for the certification of videos under the Video Recording Act. JC

Bib: James C. Robertson, *The Hidden Cinema: British Film Censorship in Action 1913–1975* (1989) and *The British Board of Film Censors: Film Censorship in Britain, 1895–1950* (1985).

BRITISH DOCUMENTARY MOVEMENT

British movement. Internationally, the documentary movement is frequently identified as Britain's major contribution to world cinema, while domestically its influence on both the aesthetics and the institutions of cinema is regarded as decisive. As a movement, its home base lay in a sequence of state-sponsored bodies in the 1930s and 1940s: the Empire Marketing Board (EMB) Film Unit (1927–33) established by John Grierson* and Stephen Tallents; the General Post Office (GPO) Film Unit (1933–39), which operated from the disbandment of the EMB until it became the Crown Film Unit (1939–52) under the Ministry of Information, with responsibilities for wartime and postwar propaganda. The movement, however, had loose boundaries, and incorporated at various points the Shell Film Unit, the British Transport Film Unit, the Realist Film Unit, the Strand Film Unit, and Films of Scotland. Grierson was the driving force throughout, recruiting to the various units such personnel as Basil Wright*, Edgar Anstey*, Arthur Elton, Stuart Legg, Paul Rotha*, Harry Watt*, Humphrey Jennings*, Alberto Cavalcanti*, Len Lye*, Norman McLaren*, Pat Jackson, and his two sisters, Ruby and Marion Grierson.

Institutionally, the continuing significance of Grierson's achievement in the establishment of a government-sponsored sector was in blurring the lines between state and independence, where independence came to mean dependence on the state as a way of ensuring independence from commerce. It was the same achievement, with the same contradictions, which another Scot, John Reith, was simultaneously negotiating with the incorporation of the BBC. In both, there were ideological and moral values at stake as well as institutional ones: institutionally, non-commercial cinema and broadcasting were established within the framework of public service in opposition to commerce; ideologically, cinema and broadcasting with a serious purpose were regarded as morally superior to the Hollywood dream factory. In this way, the documentary movement gave institutional form to a bias against 'mere' entertainment which came to define what was meant by 'quality' cinema.

Aesthetically, the 'documentary attitude' is credited with (or blamed for) the dominance of social realism and an ambivalence towards 'artiness' in British cinema. Certainly, a reading of Grierson might confirm such a view: the origins, he declares, 'lay in sociological rather than aesthetic ideas'. Michael Balcon* extended the influence of social realism when he claimed the patrimony of the documentarists for Ealing*: 'More and more,' he said, the feature film 'makes use of characters and action arising out of contemporary problems, such as were handled by the documentarists: labour problems, class problems, problems of psychology. More and more it is prepared to break away from the studio and its hot-house plots, to use real places and real people.' All this, however, is to create a myth of the documentary movement, unifying a set of diverse practices and aesthetic strategies under a homogenised 'realism', collapsing together the reportage of *Housing Problems* (1935) with the lyricism of *Song of Ceylon* (1934) and the modernism of *Night Mail* (1936), *Pett and Pott* (1934), or Len Lye's experiments in animation. While Grierson himself undoubtedly had little time for aesthetic debate, it is reasonable to conjecture that had it not been for the pressures of wartime propaganda, he might not have been able to keep the lid on experimentation and debate for ever. It is the mythology of the documentary movement, a mythology which Grierson promoted, which has formed the decisive critical discourse in British film culture rather than an attentiveness to the films themselves. JC

Bib: Ian Aitken, *Film and Reform: John Grierson and the Documentary Film Movement* (1990).

BRITISH FILM INSTITUTE (BFI)

British institution, established in 1933 to 'encourage the use and development of the cinematograph as a means of entertainment and instruction'. From the beginning, the BFI occupied an uncertain territory between culture, education and industry. As a potential instrument of cultural regulation, it evoked the suspicion of the industry, who attempted to restrict its sphere of influence to instructional films, and of educationalists, who resented its subservience to the industry. By the late 1940s its future was in doubt, but the Radcliffe Committee of 1947 attempted to give it a more clearly cultural remit.

An information service was established in 1934, particularly for the support of education and culture, and the National Film Archive (initially the National Film Library) in 1935, with a distribution library from 1938. The Scottish Film Council was established in 1934, initially as a committee of the BFI but subsequently as an autonomous body. In 1952, the BFI took over the Festival of Britain's Telekinema as the National Film Theatre, building its own theatre in 1957, and instituting the London Film Festival the same year. In the 1960s it began to build up a chain of Regional Film Theatres. The Education Department reached the peak of its influence in the 1970s, when it was central to many of the debates in film culture and initiated the development of Film Studies in higher education, and in the 1980s, when it made important advances in establishing Media Studies in the school curriculum. By the 1980s the BFI Library was the largest collection of books and periodicals on film and television in the world. The Institute has published *Sight and Sound** since 1933, and BFI Publishing has become a major force in media publishing. In production, the BFI Experimental Film Fund was established in 1951 under the chairmanship of Michael Balcon*, changing its name to the BFI Production Board in 1966.

Recession and the contortions demanded of cultural institutions by a market economy have left their mark on the BFI, and it still occupies the same uncertain territory between culture, education and industry, attempting to address an increasing number of constituencies with decreasing resources, torn between a new entrepreneurial desire to be a major player in the British film and television industries and old public service responsibilities to research, archives, education and culture. Its record of achievement, however, is impressive, and it has been one of the few resources of British film culture which might be envied from outside. JC

BRITISH NEW WAVE

British movement. The films usually associated with a 'British New Wave' between 1959 and 1963 had their roots in Free Cinema*, in the journal *Sequence**, and in the documentaries of Humphrey Jennings* and the neo-realism* of Roberto Rossellini* and Vittorio De Sica*. More immediately, they had their roots in British theatre and literature. Woodfall, the main production company, was formed by Tony Richardson*, John Osborne and the producer Harry Saltzman, with the explicit intention of exploiting the success of the Royal Court Theatre, and the films are – without exception – adaptations of novels, stories or plays, mostly written in the mid-1950s. The new wave in the cinema can be read as the backwash of a wave which had happened elsewhere. (Lindsay Anderson* attributed this dependence on adaptation to the reluctance of British backers to put money into anything which had not proven its success elsewhere.)

What was new, however, was that the key directors (Anderson, Tony Richardson, John Schlesinger*, Karel Reisz*) all directed their first features between 1959 and 1963, translating to the cinema some of their generation's revolt against the complacency of the older generation and the metropolitan bourgeoisie, and finding in the northern working class a vitality and toughness which the postwar cinema of Ealing* had not reflected. They brought with them a new sense of place and observation – 'the poetry of everyday life' – which they had learned from their own documentary experience. What was not new about the new wave was that the directors were all 'Oxbridge' men. Their identification with northern working-class men was from the outside, characteristically refracted through a romantic individualism (which they shared with the French New Wave*) which sought out rough, alienated heroes at odds with their society, and punished the women who trapped them into conformity. In translating the celebrated anger and vitality of the new culture they also translated some of the misogyny which fuelled it.

The British New Wave was short-lived, most of its directors working in America from the mid-1960s. Its descendants might be traced in television rather than cinema, where the progressive realist drama of the 1960s and 1970s kept a small domestic flame alive. JC

Bib: John Hill, *Sex, Class and Realism: British Cinema, 1956–1963* (1986).

Films Include: *Room at the Top, Look Back in Anger* (1959); *The Entertainer, Saturday Night and Sunday Morning* (1960); *A Taste of Honey* (1961); *The Loneliness of the Long Distance Runner, A Kind of Loving* (1962); *This Sporting Life, Billy Liar* (1963).

BROODTHAERS, Marcel   Brussels 1924 – Cologne, Germany 1976

Belgian director, photographer, poet and artist, whose creations can be read as a critique of the official art scene of his time, which he saw as snobbish and bourgeois. He was influenced by René Magritte and Marcel Duchamp, as well as by minimal art, conceptual art and pop art. Magritte's influence shows in *La Pipe/The Pipe* (1968–70), filmic variations on the painter's 'Ceci n'est pas une pipe'.

Broodthaers directed some thirty-three short films on 16mm, 35mm and Super-8. These include documentaries, animation films and short fiction pieces. Broodthaers' films, mostly screened in museums and art galleries, offer a reflection on his own artistic enterprise, and the relationship of the work of art to the world. *La Clef de l'horloge/The Watchkey* (1957–58), a complex art documentary, pays homage to Kurt Schwitters, who inspired the Dada movement, through a combination of montage, camera movement and movement of objects in front of the camera. *Le Corbeau et le renard/The Raven and the Fox* (1967), after La Fontaine's fable, was accompanied by a book and an exhibition, all interconnected on an aesthetic and semantic level. This was Broodthaers' first integration of film-making into his artworks. *La Pluie/Rain* (1969) documents his transition from literary to visual artist. Words written on paper are erased by the rain, leaving the writer (Broodthaers) with something that resembles more a painting than a written text. The camerawork for most of his films was done by Jean Harlez or Paul de Fru. SS

BROOKS, Louise   Cherryvale, Kansas 1906 – Rochester, New York 1985

American actress, who made brief but significant appearances in European cinema. In Germany she rose in G. W. Pabst's* films from a beggar in *Tagebuch einer Verlorenen/The Diary of a Lost Girl* to a siren in *Die Büchse der Pandora/Pandora's Box* (both 1929), while in France she was a celebrated beauty queen in *Prix de beauté/Miss Europa* (1930, dir. Augusto Genina*, script by René Clair*). Subsequently, she virtually disappeared from the screen after returning to Hollywood. Consigned to oblivion for some three decades, she became the object of French cinephilia in the 1960s and since then has enjoyed iconic status as one of Weimar cinema's* archetypal *femmes fatales*. But unlike the inner soulfulness of an Asta Nielsen*, she became the signifier of an unsettling sexual androgyny and impetuous naivety, which created exactly the 'modernist' impression Pabst was looking for to move beyond expressionism*. MW

BRÜCKNER, Jutta   Düsseldorf 1941

German director, with an academic background. Brückner was a scriptwriter before making her first film, about her mother: *Tue recht und scheue niemand!/Be Upright and Walk without Fear* (1975). The semi-autobiographical *Hungerjahre – in einem reichen Land/Hunger Years – In a Rich Country* (1979) depicts growing up in the repressive Adenauer era. Women's experiences, hopes and desires are Brückner's themes, and her characters a means to engage with historical processes from a feminist perspective. Attention to realistic details, including stills and documentary footage, characterised her approach in the 1970s. However, she turned towards performance art for *Ein Blick – und die Liebe bricht aus/One Glance – and Love Breaks Out* (1986), a compulsive and stylised re-enactment of women's enslavement to passionate love. *Kolossale Liebe/Mighty Love* (1984–92), about the Romantic writer Rahel Varnhagen, employs video technology to create fantasy images. Brückner is also a prolific film theorist and an activist for greater women's representation in European cinema. Her video *Lieben Sie Brecht?/Do you Love Brecht?* (1933) is leading to a film project about the writer, *Es Hat Zähne/It Has Teeth*. US

BRUSENDORFF, Ove
Kolding 1909 –
Copenhagen 1986

Danish film historian. Brusendorff wrote *Filmen I–III* ('The Film, I–III') from 1938 to 1941, the first history of world cinema in Danish. Impressed by the need to preserve films and related material, in 1941 he founded Det Danske Filmmuseum (the Danish Film Museum), of which he was managing director until 1960. Later he ran a cinema. ME

BRUSSE, Kees
Rotterdam 1925

Dutch actor and director, who made his first appearance as a child star in 1936 in *Merijntje Gijzen's jeugd/The Youth of Merijntje Gijzen*, directed by Kurt Gerron*. After the war Brusse became one of Holland's most valued stars, playing lead roles in many films, from *De dijk is dicht/The Dyke is Sealed* (1950) directed by Anton Koolhaas. His naturalistic acting was well received abroad when *Ciske de Rat*, directed by Wolfgang Staudte* in 1955, was released in a German-language version. Bert Haanstra* and Wim Verstappen* relied on him as their principal actor. In the 1960s Brusse began to make his own films and television programmes, using his experience as an actor and stage director. He directed two feature films, *Kermis in de regen/Kermess in the Rain* (1962) and *Mensen van morgen/People of Tomorrow* (1964). KD

Other Films as Actor Include: *Jenny* (1959); *De Zaak MP* (1960); *De overval/The Silent Raid* (1962); *Blue Movie* (1971); *VD* (1972); *Dakota* (1974); *Dokter Pulder zaait papavers/ When the Poppies Bloom Again, Rooie Sien* (1975); *Mysteries* (1978); *Een pak slaag/Mr Slotter's Jubilee* (1979); *Vroeger kon je lachen* (1983).

BUCHANAN, Jack Helensburgh, Scotland 1891 –
London 1957

British actor associated with the top-hat-and-tails school of musical comedy in the 1930s. Following success on both sides of the Atlantic in musical revue (including a Broadway success with Jessie Matthews*), Buchanan made his first talkies in Hollywood, where he partnered Jeanette MacDonald in Ernst Lubitsch's* *Monte Carlo* (1930, US), before returning to Britain to become one of the most popular and debonair leading men of the sophisticated British musical. He part-

nered Anna Neagle* in *Goodnight Vienna* (1932), Fay Wray in *When Knights Were Bold* (1936), and starred with Maurice Chevalier* in René Clair's* *Break the News* (1938), a film which Buchanan also produced. Unfortunately for the British musical, he never partnered Jessie Matthews on film. He was often claimed as Britain's answer to Fred Astaire, and the two can be seen together to excellent effect in Vincente Minnelli's *The Band Wagon* (1953, US). JC

BUCHHOLZ, Horst
Berlin 1933

German actor. After a spell dubbing foreign films into German, Buchholz became a 1950s pop icon, the German James Dean, playing the young rebel with the soulful eyes in *Die Halbstarken* (1956) and *Endstation Liebe* (1957), both directed by Georg Tressler*. A number of romantic leads in international productions followed, most notably in *Tiger Bay* (1959, UK), *The Magnificent Seven* (1960, US) and Billy Wilder's Cold War satire *One, Two, Three* (1961, US). Unsuccessfully trying his hand at direction, he eventually found, from the mid-1970s, a more mature acting identity in television and theatre. He returned to the screen as a heavy with a past in Wim Wenders'* *In weiter Ferne, so nah!/Far Away, So Close* (1993). TE/MW

Other Films Include: *Himmel ohne Sterne, Regine* (1955); *Herrscher ohne Krone, Robinson soll nicht sterben* (1956); *Montpi* (1957); *Nasser Asphalt* (1958); *Das Totenschiff* (1959); *Fanny* (1960); *Nine Hours to Rama* (1962, US); *Johnny Banco* (1966); *... aber Jonny!* (1973); *Frauenstation* (1975).

BUFTEA (BUCUREŞTI/Bucharest) STUDIO

Romanian feature film studio at Buftea, a 'film city' sixteen kilometres outside Bucharest. Mostly built between 1952 and 1958 on a 30-hectare lakeside, Buftea represents a highly centralised film industry started almost from scratch. Nationalisation of production in 1948 led directly to plans for Buftea, with workshops, labs, housing, a power plant, etc. The four original sound stages extended to 1,000 sqm – among the largest in eastern Europe – and by the 1970s there were five stages with a total area of 3,000 sqm. There are impressive permanent sets, including a castle, and forty trained thoroughbred horses on site. The original equipment, from all over Europe, was of good quality, and Buftea is still reasonably equipped. In 1968 Orson Welles, while working at Buftea, flattered the studio with the compliment that 'there are very few in the world that can compete'. Responsible for all except documentary and animation films, Buftea has produced nearly 500 features and many television series. In addition to regular contacts with east European countries, there have been co-productions with the West – primarily France and West Germany – at their highest in the 1970s. Many, like Sergiu Nicolaescu's French-Romanian series 'William the Conqueror', were epics, and a massive French television series was finished in 1987. Before the 1989 revolution the management had already decided that viability lay in providing facilities for foreign producers, but the economic crisis facing feature production and the ending of political commitment to cinema threatens the very existence of Buftea. MM

BUGAJSKI, Ryszard — Warsaw 1943

Polish director. Bugajski studied philosophy at Warsaw University and graduated from Łódź* in 1973. He translated and produced plays for television before co-directing his debut feature, *Kobieta i Kobieta/A Woman and a Woman* (1980) with Janusz Dymek. In 1980 he joined Andrzej Wajda's* prestigious Film Unit 'X' and in 1981 made *Przesłuchanie/The Interrogation* (released 1989). This harrowing tale of the political arrest of a young woman and her subsequent torture by the authorities was set in the Stalinist era. Even so, the film was considered too inflammatory by the cultural apparatchiks of Jaruzelski's Poland and was banned. Although a pirate video circulated widely in Poland, the film was only seen internationally in 1990, winning the Best Actress award at Cannes for Krystyna Janda* as well as international distribution and acclaim. With no work prospects in Poland, Bugajski emigrated to Canada in 1985, where he is currently directing for the cinema and television (as Richard Bugajski). AW

BULAJIĆ, Veljko — Nikšič, Montenegro 1928

Montenegran director whose debut film in 1959, *Vlak bez voznog reda/Train Without a Timetable* (about the mass migrations after World War II), won two Golden Arenas at the annual national film festival in Pula*. The 'good guy' of Yugoslav cinema, privileged by the authorities and hated by colleagues, he directed two of the biggest spectacular epics of the 1960s dealing with the partisan struggle during World War II: *Kozara* (1962) and *Bitka na Neretvi/Battle on the River Neretva* (1969) [> YUGOSLAV 'PARTISAN FILMS']. For the latter he acquired an international cast (including Franco Nero and Oleg Vidov) and won Oscar nominations. In 1980 he directed a television series of interviews with Tito, *Tito's Memoirs*. He was deeply involved in another huge project, *Veliki transport/Great Transport/The Courageous* (1983). Although thematically close to his successful debut, the film was a disaster, both artistically and financially, drawing Bulajić into a series of court cases, newspaper polemics and scandals. SP

Other Films: *Rat/War* (1960); *Uzavreli grad/When the Fires Started/Smouldering City* (1961); *Skopje 1963* [doc] (1964); *Pogled u zjenicu sunca/A Glance at the Pupil of the Sun* (1966); *Atentat u Sarajevu/Assassination in Sarajevo/The Day that Shook the World* (1975); *Čovjek koga treba ubiti/A Man to Kill* (1979); *Visoki napon/High Voltage* (1981).

BULGARIA

River traffic on the Danube brought the Lumière* Cinematographe to Bulgaria. The first presentations took place in February 1897 in the port town of Ruse, and a few months later in Sofia. When Vasil Gendov, a pioneer of Bulgarian cinema, opened his modern theatre in Sofia in 1908, he could depend on a regular flow of movies from France and Germany by way of Vienna and the Danube. To save his enterprise when World War I broke out, he turned to film production and starred himself in a self-directed Max Linder* copy: *Balgaran e galant/The Bulgarian is Gallant* (1915). Its immediate box-office success launched a primitive Bulgarian national cinema. Between 1915 and 1948, when the film industry was nationalised, fifty-five feature films were made, eleven of them produced by Gendov-Film and many starring the director himself and his wife Žanna Gendova.

One minor silent masterpiece, Boris Grežov's *Sled požaka u Rusija/After the Fire over Russia* (1929), the story of White Russians who emigrated to Bulgaria to work in the mines, is recognised as the high point of the pioneer days of Bulgarian cinema. Grežov also directed the first Bulgarian sound film, *Beskrăstni grobove/Graves without Crosses* (1931), a production all the more remarkable for lamenting the victims of the military 'White Terror' of 1923. The first 'art film' – featuring actors from the National Theatre – was Nikola Larin's *Pod staroto nebe/Under the Old Sky* (1922), based on Tsanko Tserkovski's drama. During the interregnum period, Bulgarian productions by private companies – Gendov-Film, Rila-Film, Balkan-Film, Kubrat-Film and Rex-Film – had to contend with more attractive imported fare: by the mid-1920s, German films had cornered an estimated 45 per cent of the home market, followed by American films with 29 and French with 18 per cent. Against these commercial giants, the Bulgarian film industry survived mostly by filming popular folk legends and well-known literary classics: Gendov's *Bay Ganjo* (1922), Grežov's *Momina skala/Maiden Rock* (1923), Peter K. Stojčev's adaptation of Elin Pelin's novel *Zemya/Land* (1930) and his *Planinska pesen/Song of the Mountains* (1934), Aleksandar Vazov's *Gramada/Cairn* (1936), and Yossip Novak's *Strahil Vojvoda/Strahil the Voyvoda* (1938). Unfortunately, most of these films were lost in an air raid on Sofia during World War II.

Following the liberation of Sofia in September 1944, private companies produced eight more films – until 5 April 1948, when the film industry was nationalised. Boris Borozanov, himself a film pioneer, wedded Bulgarian patriotism to the schematic formula of Socialist Realism* in *Kalin orelăt/Kalin the Eagle* (1950), a heroic tale about a nationalist rebel set at the end of Ottoman rule. But the real beginning of modern Bulgarian cinema is marked by documentarist Zahari Žandov's* first venture into fiction film, *Trevoga/Alarm* (1951), aided by screenwriter Angel Wagenstein*, who was able to inject some flesh-and-blood passion into Orlin Vassiliev's schematic drama. Until the death of Stalin* in 1953, and the subsequent end of the harshly restrictive, Moscow-dictated 'Žandov Years' in 1955, Bulgarian cinema was noteworthy only for the shooting-between-the-lines segments in historical epics and contemporary social films: Dako Dakovski's *Pod igoto/Under the Yoke* (1952) and *Nespokoen păt/The Troubled Road* (1955), Borislav Šaraliev's *Pesen za čoveka/Song of Man* (1954), Žandov's *Septemvrijci/Septembrists* (1954) and his remake of Elin Pelin's *Zemya/Land* (1957), and Nikola Korabov's *Dimitrovgradci/People of Dimitrovgrad* (1956).

With the coming of the 'thaw' following the Twentieth

Party Conference in the Soviet Union and the April Plenum of 1956, Bulgarian cinematography came into its own as a prominent national movement in Eastern Europe. Rangel Vălčanov* collaborated with screenwriter Valeri Petrov* on *Na malkija ostrov/On a Small Island* (1958), Binka Željazkova* with Hristo Ganev on the politically oriented and subsequently banned *Partizani (Životăt si teče tiho...)/Partisans (Life Flows Quietly By)* (1958), and East German director Konrad Wolf* with Wagenstein on *Zvezdi/Sterne/Stars* (1958), a Bulgarian-East German co-production. Despite the evident 'revolutionary' messages in all three films, their [Bulgarian] 'poetic realism'* and the psychological analysis of the leading characters made them stylistically distinctive. A third Bulgarian director was added to the 'poetic cinema' group when cameraman-documentarist Vălo Radev*, a VGIK* graduate, made his first feature film, *Kradecăt na praskovi/The Peach Thief* (1964), a Bulgarian-Yugoslav co-production. Radev was also instrumental in launching major technical innovations at the Boyana* Studios, notably widescreen production and colour.

With the downfall of Nikita Khrushchev in October 1964, the screenplay for Vălčanov's *Lachenite obuvki na neznajnija voin/The Unknown Soldier's Patent Leather Shoes* was put on hold indefinitely, and it wasn't until fifteen years later that the film could be made. Vălčanov left Bulgaria to work in Czechoslovakia (*Ezop/Aesop*, 1970), while screenwriters Ganev and Petrov chose 'spiritual exile'. Over the next few years Bulgarian cinema faced a nearly ruinous crisis under four successive dictatorial general directors, until 1971 when Pavel Pissarev was appointed to the post to win back the confidence of exiled and alienated film-makers. Three important films on contemporary social themes were immediately banned upon completion: Hristo Piskov and Irina Aktaševa's *Ponedelnik sutrin/Monday Morning* (1966), Binka Željazkova's* *Privărzanijat balon/The Attached Balloon* (1967), and Ljubomir Šarlandjiev's *Prokurorat/The Prosecutor* (1968). In addition, several other screenplays were doctored, while even completed films were re-edited to conform with nebulous production formulas. Despite the severe restrictions, however, promising directorial talent continued to surface at the Boyana Studios: Zako Heskija (*Gorešto pladne/Torrid Noon*, 1966), the team of stage director Griša Ostrovski and cameraman Todor Stoyanov (*Otklonenie/Sidetrack*, 1967), documentarist turned fiction film-maker Eduard Zahariev* (*Nebeto na Veleka/The Sky over the Veleka*, 1968), Ljudmil Kirkov* (*Švedski krale/Swedish Kings*, 1968), Metodi Andonov* (*Bjalata staja/The White Room*, 1968), the team of stage director Hristo Hristov* and animation film-maker Todor Dinov (*Ikonostasăt/Iconostasis*, 1969), and Georgi Stojanov (*Ptici i hrătki/Birds and Greyhounds*, 1969).

The turning point came in 1972 with the release back-to-back of Andonov's *Kozijat rog/The Goat Horn*, the biggest box-office success in Bulgarian film history, and Ljudmil Staikov's* *Obič/Affection*, winner of the Gold Prize at the 1973 Moscow festival. Aided again by novelists, scriptwriters and playwrights – Jordan Radičkov*, Nikolai Haitov* and Georgi Mišev* – a Bulgarian 'new wave' of socially conscious films by talented directorial newcomers became the talk of international festivals: Zahariev and Mišev's *Prebrojavane na divite zajci/The Hare Census* (1973) and *Vilna zona/Villa Zone* (1975), Ivan Terziev and Nikolai Nikiforov's *Măže bez rabota/Men Without Work* (1973), Hristov and Radičkov's *Posledno ljato/The Last Summer* (1972–74), Georgi Djulgerov's* *Avantaž/Advantage* (1977), and the reunited Vălčanov and Petrov's *S ljubov i nežnost/With Love and Tenderness* (1978).

The movement was curtailed somewhat by the state's enormous financial investment in a series of epic spectacles produced on the occasion of the 1,300th anniversary of the founding of Bulgaria in 681: Žandov's *Bojanskijat majstor/Master of Boyana* (1981), Djulgerov's *Mera spored mera/Measure for Measure* (1981), Staikov's *Khan Asparuh* (1981), Šaraliev's *Boris părvi/Boris I* (1985) and Stojanov's *Konstantin Filosof/Constantine the Philosopher* (1986). Towards the end of the 1980s the political reforms that swept across Eastern Europe inspired some veteran directors to re-examine the Stalinist past (Djulgerov's *Lagerăt/The Camp*, 1989), while young graduates of the Sofia Film and Theatre School (VITIS) probed failings in the socialist system: Ljudmil Todorov's *Bjagašti kučeta/Running Dogs* (1988), Krassimir Krumov's *Exitus* (1988), Čaim Cohen's *Zasčitete drebnite životni/Protect the Small Animals* (1988), and Peter Popzlatev's *Az, grafinjata/I, the Countess* (1989).

Today, following the downfall of Todor Živkov and subsequent democratic elections in 1990, state funding for national film productions has been cut to the bone. From an average of twenty or so feature films annually in Bulgaria a decade ago, and approximately the same number of television films, only half a dozen domestic film and television productions were scheduled in the Boyana Studios for the 1993–94 season. Without co-production input from the West, contemporary Bulgarian cinematography is for all practical purposes non-existent. A stark contrast with the heyday of the 1970s under Pavel Pissarev, when the Boyana Studios turned out nearly one feature film a week for cinemas and television. RH

BULGARIAN 'POETIC REALISM'

Bulgarian stylistic trend of the 1950s and 1960s, particularly evident in the work of cinematographers but also due to the vision of scriptwriters and directors. The primary influence came from Soviet cinema in the wake of the Twentieth Party Congress in 1956, when new guidelines for film production were laid down by Khrushchev. Bulgarian 'new wave' directors Rangel Vălčanov* (*Na malkija ostrov/On a Small Island*, 1958), Binka Željazkova* (*A bjahme mladi/We Were Young*, 1961) and Vălo Radev* (*Kradecăt na praskovi/The Peach Thief*, 1964) were heavily influenced by Soviet cameraman Sergei Urusevsky's work on Mikhail K. Kalatozov's* *Letyat zhuravli/The Cranes Are Flying* (1957), winner of the Palme d'Or at the 1958 Cannes festival. Other influences came from Italian neo-realism* (Vittorio De Sica*, Luchino Visconti*, Roberto Rossellini*) and from the poetic short films of French experimentalist Albert Lamorisse (*Le Ballon rouge/The Red Balloon*, 1956), rather than the prewar French Poetic Realism*. The movement subsided significantly after Khrushchev's fall from power in 1964, although 'poetic realism' was to remain an essential trait in the best of Bulgarian cinema for some time after. RH

BUÑUEL, Luis
Luis Buñuel Portolés; Calanda, Teruel 1900 – Mexico City, Mexico 1983

Spanish director of international standing who worked in Spain, France and Mexico. Buñuel's first films, *Un chien andalou* (1929) and *L'Âge d'or* (1930), were made in Paris with Salvador Dalí (though the latter's input on *L'Âge d'or* was minimal). Both masterpieces of Surrealist cinema, they established Buñuel as a key figure of the European avant-garde*. They revealed his taste for shocking images (such as an eye being slit by a razor blade), as well as anti-clerical and anti-bourgeois provocations which would reverberate throughout his entire *oeuvre*. His first Spanish film, *Las Hurdes/Land Without Bread* (1932), however, was a grim documentary on poverty in rural Extremadura. In the last years of the Republic, Buñuel produced and partially directed a handful of films for one of Spain's more liberal production companies, Filmófono.

Following the Nationalists' victory in the Civil War (1939), Buñuel left for America but moved to Mexico in 1947 after failing to make headway in Hollywood. His Mexican films included popular melodramas such as *Susana* (1950) and *El bruto/The Brute* (1952) and more personal works like *Los Olvidados/The Dispossessed/The Young and the Damned* (1950), *El/This Strange Passion* (1952) and *Nazarín* (1958), which re-established his international reputation. Buñuel went back to Spain for *Viridiana* (1961, Palme d'or at Cannes), but the film was banned there as blasphemous. Though he would later return to Spain to film *Tristana* (1970) and parts of *Cet obscur objet du désir/That Obscure Object of Desire* (1977), Buñuel spent the postwar years in Mexico and France where, in the 1960s and 1970s, he made a series of caustic, witty and elegant films in collaboration with scriptwriter Jean-Claude Carrière and producer Serge Silberman. *Le Journal d'une femme de chambre/Diary of a Chambermaid* (1963), *Belle de jour* (1966) and *Le Charme discret de la bourgeoisie/The Discreet Charm of the Bourgeoisie* (1972), starring the likes of Jeanne Moreau*, Catherine Deneuve*, Stéphane Audran* and Fernando Rey*, represent both the best of Buñuel's second French career and an important strand of the European art cinema* of the time.

Despite Buñuel's geographically split career, strong continuities appear: all his films are marked by a fascination with Surrealism, especially in its exploration of the poetry of dreams, desire and *amour fou*, and imbued with a desire for release from childhood repression. The Surrealists, the Marquis de Sade – his 'master' – along with major figures from Spanish culture (above all, the picaresque writers, Goya, Galdós and Valle-Inclán) were his key inspirations. At the same time, an early interest in Marxism prompted his repeated exposures of social injustice. Although in a sense *sui generis*, Buñuel's films are indebted to German Expressionism* and Italian neo-realism* as well as to popular Mexican and Spanish melodrama. His obsessions (religion, the bourgeoisie, marginalised individuals, sexual desire) are expressed in ways that explore the limits of experience without sacrificing tolerant understanding of human folly, though they are not always free from misogyny. Buñuel films, however, are graced with a distinctive brand of corrosive wit and sardonic humour. PWE/GV

Bib: Peter William Evans, *The Films of Luis Buñuel: Subjectivity and Desire* (1994).

Other Films Include: *Subida al Cielo/Mexican Bus Ride* (1951, Mex.); *Ensayo de un crimen/The Criminal Life of Archibaldo de la Cruz* (1955, Mex.); *La Mort en ce jardin/La muerte en este jardín/Death in the Garden* (1956, Fr./Mex.); *El angel exterminador/The Exterminating Angel* (1962, Mex.); *Simón del desierto/Simon of the Desert* (1965, Mex.); *La Voie lactée/The Milky Way* (1969, Fr./It.); *Le Fantôme de la liberté/The Phantom of Liberty* (1974, Fr.).

BURIAN, Vlasta
Liberec [then Austria-Hungary] 1891 – Prague 1962

Czech comedian. Regarded as the genius of Czech cabaret, Burian lived for the theatre and appeared on stage regularly, making films during the day. As with music hall and vaudeville performers elsewhere, his films were closely linked to theatrically inspired routines, with visual comedy allied to verbal humour and an inspired mimicry. He was often compared to Groucho Marx, but his thin, angular body and mournful moustache produced quite a different resonance. Between 1923 and 1956 he appeared in thirty-seven features, many directed by Karel Lamač* and Martin Frič,* opposite leading stars such as Anny Ondra*, Josef Rovenský and Theodor Pištek. Two typical films of the 1930s were *Funebrák* (1932), in which he played an undertaker's assistant, and *Lelíček ve službách Sherlocka Holmese/Lelíček in the Service of Sherlock Holmes* (1932), both directed by Lamač. For Frič, he starred in an adaptation of Gogol's *The Inspector-General* (*Revizor*, 1933) and as the Baron in *Baron Prášil/Baron Münchhausen* (1940). Tricked into parodying the exiled foreign minister, Jan Masaryk, during World War II, he was subsequently tried and forbidden to act, but returned to the screen in the early 1950s. PH

Other Films Include: *Tu ten kámen/Tutankhamun/This is the Stone* (1923); *C. a K. polní maršálek/C. and K. Field Marshal, On a jeho sestra/He and his Sister* (1931); *Anton Špelec, ostrostřelec/Anton Špelec, Sharpshooter* (1932); *Pobočník Jeho Výsosti/His Majesty's Adjutant, U snědeného krámu/The Ruined Shopkeeper* (1933); *Hrdina jedné noci/Hero of a Single Night* (1935); *Tři vejce do skla/Three Eggs, Soft-boiled* (1937); *Katakomby/The Catacombs* (1940); *Zaostřit, prosím!/Close Up, Please!* (1956).

BURTON, Richard
Richard Jenkins; Pontrhydfen, Wales 1925 – Switzerland 1984

British actor. Burton's career is rather too conveniently divided into two periods: Before and After *Cleopatra*. Before *Cleopatra* (1963, US) he is characterised as an actor of great power and passion; after, he is a merely a celebrity. The fact that the Fall turns around a woman – and not merely *a* woman, but Elizabeth Taylor – and around an abandonment of theatrical integrity in favour of Hollywood stardom, strengthens the suspicion that Burton may be the most mythologised of British actors. Certainly, his stage career in the 1940s and 1950s suggests a theatrical potential never fully realised. But his cinema career was always uneven, and much of the best was saved to the last. In his prelapsarian phase, he was suitably heroic (if unchallenged) in a number of Hollywood epics, notably *The Robe* (1953, US) and *Alexander the Great* (1956, US); he was miscast in *Look Back in Anger* (1959) in an attempt to bring some of his acquired Hollywood glamour to the 'kitchen sink'; while Nicholas Ray in *Amère victoire/Bitter Victory* (1957, Fr./UK) perhaps recognised a kindred spirit in Burton's characteristic blend of insolence, sensitivity and sadness. After the Fall, he produced some of his best cinematic performances in roles which were far removed from the heroism of his youth – the disillusioned, self-destructive and weary cynicism of *Who's Afraid of Virginia Woolf?* (1966, US), *The Night of the Iguana* (1964, US) and *The Comedians* (1967, US). He played the aging Trotsky in Joseph Losey's* *L'Assassinio di Trotsky/The Assassination of Trotsky* (1972, It/Fr); and in *The Spy Who Came in from the Cold* (1965) and, poignantly, in his last film, Mike Radford's *Nineteen Eighty-Four* (1984), completed just before his death, he exposed some of the more fragile qualities which the strength of his famous theatrical voice had often concealed. JC

Bib: Melvyn Bragg, *Rich: A Biography of Richard Burton* (1988).

BUYENS, Frans   Temse 1924

Belgian director. Thought of as an idealist, a humanist and a rebel, Buyens (who worked also as literary critic and writer) is considered the best documentary film-maker of the post-Storck* and Dekeukeleire* generation, with films about Frans Masereel (1970) and Auguste Vermeylen (1963).

His controversial first film, *Vechten voor onze rechten/ Fighting for Our Rights* (1961), a compilation of television and press material on the nationwide strikes of 1960–61, was criticised by the socialist party and trade unions, while praised by workers. Though awarded prizes internationally, it was banned from the Antwerp festival. *Deutschland, Terminus Ost/Germany, Terminus East* (1965), about the Berlin Wall, won a prize at Venice, as one of the finest examples of *cinéma-vérité*. Buyens' most interesting work includes documentary portraits that confront the viewer with complex intellectual issues. His films on art, for instance on cartoonist Frits Van den Berghe, demonstrate his skills as editor. Buyens also made fiction films, for example *Het Dwaallicht/ Le Feu follet/The Will-o'the-wisp* (1973) based on Willem Elsschot's well-known novel, and *Minder dood dan de anderen/Less Dead than the Others* (1991).

Touching upon controversial subjects, loyal to his cause against commercial cinema, Buyens always had to work under the most difficult financial conditions, in spite of his in-ternational recognition. His frustration over this situation led him to publish an open letter to the Belgian government in 1989, denouncing the lack of policy towards film and especially documentary. SS

Other Films Include: *De Schietschijf/The Target* (1962); *Auguste Vermeylen* (1963); *Mijn moedertaal/My Native Tongue* (1965); *Plus ou moins homme/More or Less a Human Being* (1967); *Open Dialoog/Open Dialogue, Ieder van ons/Each of Us, Frans Masereel* (1970); *Henri De Braekeleer* (1977); *Un jour les temoins disparaîtront/One Day the Witnesses Will Disappear* (1980); *Tango, tango* (1993).

BYRNE, Eddie   Dublin 1911–1981

Irish actor. Byrne was already an experienced variety theatre performer at Dublin's premier venue, the Theatre Royal, before playing in *I See a Dark Stranger* (1946), the first of more than twenty films he acted in. He usually played Irish character roles in British films, having the lead in only one film, *Time Gentlemen Please!* (1952), in which he was a tramp who disturbs the equanimity of a sedate English village. His later career included roles in *Mutiny on the Bounty* (1962, US) and *Star Wars* (1977, US), his last film. KR

Other Films Include: *Captain Boycott* (1947); *The Gentle Gunman* (1952); *Happy Ever After* (1954); *Rooney* (1958).

BYRNE, Gabriel   Dublin 1950

Irish actor, who began his career at the Dublin Shakespeare Society in 1974 and thereafter worked at the Project Theatre when Jim Sheridan* was in charge. His first television appearances were in *The Riordans*, a rural soap, and its successor, *Bracken*. His first film role was in Thaddeus O'Sullivan's* *On a Paving Stone Mounted* (1978), and his first commercial cinema roles in *The Outsider* (1979) and *Excalibur* (1981, US). Thereafter, he began to carve out a career as an international star through memorable roles as an investigative journalist in *Defence of the Realm* (1985), an Irish-American gangster in the Coen brothers' *Miller's Crossing* (1990, US), and as a traveller/gypsy in *Into the West* (1992). His good looks and screen presence would seem to make him ideal material as a potential commercial cinema star, but his career has yet to achieve megastar status, a result perhaps of a string of less than memorable roles in such films as Michael Mann's *The Keep* (1983, US), Costa-Gavras'* *Hanna K* (1983), Ken Russell's* *Gothic* (1986), and Frank Deasy and Joe Lee's *The Courier* (1987). He has continuing theatrical interests, and was executive producer of *Into the West*. Byrne lives mainly in the USA and was married until 1993 to actress Ellen Barkin, opposite whom he starred in *Siesta* (1987, US). KR

C

CACOYANNIS, Michael   Limassol, Cyprus 1922

Greek Cypriot film director, also theatre director, editor and producer. After law studies in Britain, Cacoyannis became a producer for the BBC's wartime Greek-language broadcasts, simultaneously attending drama school and acting on stage. He went to Greece in 1952, where he directed his first feature, *Kiriakatiko xipnima/Windfall in Athens* (1954). He worked with facility in both the theatre and the cinema, directing critically acclaimed films such as *Stella* (1955) and *To koritsi me ta mavra/The Girl in Black* (1956). These films were distinguished by their sensitive treatment of contemporary Greek issues, use of authentic locations and promising new actors (Elli Lambeti*, Giorgos Foundas, and Melina Mercouri*, who made her screen debut in *Stella*). With those of Nikos Koundouros*, Cacoyannis' films were the first independent Greek productions to attract international attention. In 1962 he directed *Ilektra/Electra*, the first of a trilogy of adaptations of Euripides tragedies, and in 1964 he achieved international fame with the US production of *Zorba the Greek*, starring Anthony Quinn and based on the novel by Nikos Kazantzakis. *Zorba the Greek* remains his biggest success. His next film, *The Day the Fish Came Out* (1967), an international production, was by comparison an anti-climax. Cacoyannis returned to Greek productions without the results his early career had seemed to promise. TNe

Other Films Include: *To telefteo psema/A Matter of Dignity* (1958); *Eroica* (1960); *The Trojan Women* (1971, US); *Attila 74* (1975); *Iphigenia* (1976); *Sweet Country* (1986); *Pano, kato ke plagios/Up, Down and Sideways* (1993).

CAHIERS DU CINÉMA

French film journal, the best-known and probably the most influential in the world, founded in April 1951 by Lo Duca and Jacques Doniol-Valcroze, and joined by André Bazin* for the second issue. *Cahiers'* fame comes from its glorious cinephile 'first period' when the *politique des auteurs** was developed, and when many of its star critics – François Truffaut*, Eric Rohmer* and Jean-Luc Godard* among them – became the film-makers of the New Wave*. *Cahiers* has known many tribulations since, which can be divided into its second and third phases. In the second period, the '*pures et dures*' post-1968 years, theories were developed under the triple aegis of Althusser, Lacan and Foucault and photographs were banned from the cover; this phase also influenced Anglo-American theory via *Screen**. The third and last period, from the late 1970s, has seen a return to cinephilia, precisely at a time when cinema was coming under threat. The critical theories debated in *Cahiers* over these years have been concerned with the status of the cinematic image in relation to television, to 'new images' and to painting, as well as, in a neat return to origins, with the place of the *auteur* in contemporary (especially French) cinema. These debates have not so far had the resonance of the earlier ones, though forth-coming translations of works by one-time editor Serge Daney, the most important film critic of the 1980s, as well as by Pascal Bonitzer and Jacques Aumont, should remedy this.

Cahiers never existed in a vacuum. Bazin wrote for the earlier *L'Ecran français*, and in the postwar years new journals appeared, some still in existence. But while its greatest critical rival remains *Positif**, competition has also emerged from glossy magazines such as *Première* (since 1976), prompting the creation of a news section (1980), with more topical items. In 1984, *Cahiers* diversified into book publishing with Editions de l'Etoile. However much these changes may owe to economic necessity, the continued existence of *Cahiers* (and *Positif*) is testimony to the relative health of French film culture. GV

CAINE, Michael   Maurice Micklewhite; London 1933

British actor, who came to prominence as one of the representative figures of London's 'swinging 1960s' (when he shared a flat with Terence Stamp* in the King's Road). A graduate of Joan Littlewood's Theatre Workshop, he played bit parts in such films as *Carve Her Name with Pride* (1958) and *The Wrong Arm of the Law* (1962), attracted attention in *Zulu* (1963), and achieved stardom as Harry Palmer in *The Ipcress File* (1965). His persona as a crafty Cockney Lothario was established in *Alfie* (1966), a film which was surprisingly successful in the US and which won him his first Oscar nomination. Never a romantic star, marked indelibly as basically an 'ordinary bloke' by his accent (a trademark as well as a mark on which he trades), Caine is an intensely professional cinematic actor, whose performances are carefully measured and whose stardom is based on craft as much as charisma. 'In a play,' he says, 'the person who's speaking is getting all the attention. You're not looking at the other person. But in a movie, the person who's speaking doesn't exist unless someone reacts. Movies are about reacting, and that's what I do particularly well.' He did it well enough to steal the Oscar nomination from Laurence Olivier* in their two-hander, *Sleuth* (1973), and to win an Oscar for Best Supporting Actor in Woody Allen's *Hannah and Her Sisters* (1986, US). Not always wise in his choice of films, he gave one of his best performances in partnership with Sean Connery* in John Huston's *The Man Who Would Be King* (1975, US). JC

Bib: Michael Caine, *Acting in Films: An actor's take on movie making* (1990).

Other Films Include: *The Wrong Box, Funeral in Berlin, Hurry Sundown* [US] (1966); *Billion Dollar Brain* (1967); *The Magus* (1968); *The Italian Job* (1969); *Get Carter* (1970); *Kidnapped, Zee & Co* (1972); *The Black Windmill* (1974); *The Romantic Englishwoman/Une Anglaise romantique* (1975, UK/Fr.); *California Suite* (1978, US); *Dressed to Kill* (1980, US); *Victory/Escape to Victory* (1981, US); *Deathtrap*

(1982, US); *The Honorary Consul* (1983); *Educating Rita* (1983); *Mona Lisa* (1986); *On Deadly Ground* (1994, US).

CALVERT, Phyllis   London 1915

British actress, who became a star in the Gainsborough* melodramas of the 1940s. Previously she had played an effective lead to George Formby* in *Let George Do It!* (1940), and had worked with Carol Reed* on *Kipps* (1941) and *The Young Mr Pitt* (1942), but it was *The Man in Grey* (1943) which brought wide popular appeal. Typecast as the virtuous victim, and caught between Margaret Lockwood's* scheming, James Mason's* cruelty and Stewart Granger's* swashbuckling, Calvert was able to make virtue interesting, and, in *Fanny by Gaslight* (1944) in particular, there is nothing insipid about her femininity. By the 1950s she was playing more varied dramatic parts, with her performance as the mother in *Mandy* (1952) her most satisfying role. JC

Other Films Include: *Two Thousand Women, Madonna of the Seven Moons* (1944); *They Were Sisters* (1945); *Men of Two Worlds, The Magic Bow* (1946); *Time Out of Mind* (1947, US); *The Golden Madonna* (1949); *Appointment with Danger* [US], *Mr Denning Drives North* (1951); *The Net* (1953); *Indiscreet* (1958, US); *Twisted Nerve* (1968).

CAMERINI, Mario   Rome 1895 – Gardone Riviera 1981

Italian director. Alongside Alessandro Blasetti*, Camerini was one of the most successful, influential, innovative and popular film-makers in 1930s Italy. He began his film career after World War I as a scriptwriter, assistant director and director at Cines*, where he often worked for his cousin Augusto Genina*. His early collaboration with Genina included *Marito, moglie, e …* (1922, co-dir.), *Cyrano de Bergerac* (1923, co-dir. and co-scriptwriter), *Jolly, clown da circo* (1924), a film Camerini claims to have directed, though only Genina's name appears as director, and *Kiff Tebbi* (1927), a silent film Genina is reputed to have begun but left to Camerini. In the 1920s Camerini also directed two films involving the popular film 'superheroes' Maciste* and Saetta. Significantly, *Maciste contro lo sceicco* (1925) and *Kiff Tebbi* take place in Africa, a setting that had as much to do with Italian colonialism as with the popularity of Rudolph Valentino's *The Sheik*. After *Kiff Tebbi*, Camerini worked briefly as an editor and subtitler before going on to direct *Rotaie/Rails*, shot in 1929 as a silent film with a musical score and released in 1931 with a soundtrack. Along with Blasetti's *Sole/Sun* (1929), *Rotaie* was widely heralded as signalling the revival of the Italian film industry. Throughout the 1930s Camerini worked in various genres, but he is perhaps best known for his 'populist' light comedies that always verged (as in the German *Kammerspielfilm*) on 'dark' realist melodrama. For this reason, films such as *Rotaie, Gli uomini, che mascalzoni …* (1932), *T'amerò sempre* (1933), *Il signor Max/Mr Max* (1937), *Grandi magazzini* (1939) and *Batticuore* (1938) have led film historians to compare Camerini with such

diverse directors from that period as René Clair*, Ernst Lubitsch*, Frank Capra and F. W. Murnau*. All these films concerned petit-bourgeois protagonists who struggled amid the artifice of a decadent upper class, a society given to consumerism, and the modern urban landscape of Italy. Many of them also launched two new matinee idols, Vittorio De Sica* and Assia Noris*, Camerini's wife. Despite his success and popularity during the Fascist years, only one of Camerini's films, *Il grande appello/The Last Roll-call* (1936), overtly depicts a project of the Fascist state, namely the military activities of the Italians in North Africa, a return to a setting Camerini had mythologised in his 1920s films.

Although neither Camerini nor his films were directly attacked after 1945, his style was dismissed as 'escapist' and denigrated as contrary to the aesthetics of neo-realism* (though his 1945 film *Due lettere anonime* has much in common with 'neo-realist' films). Like Blasetti, he was never quite able to overcome being associated with the Fascist period, particularly by younger critics. JHa

Other Films Include: *Voglio tradire mio marito, Saetta principe per un giorno* (1925); *Figaro e la sua gran giornata, L'ultima avventura* (1931); *Giallo* (1933); *Il cappello a tre punte/The Three-Cornered Hat, Come le foglie* (1934); *Ma non è una cosa seria/But It's Nothing Serious* (1936); *Il documento* (1939); *Centomila dollari, Una romantica avventura* (1940); *I promessi sposi/The Spirit and the Flesh* (1941); *Una storia d'amore* (1942); *L'angelo e il diavolo/The Angel and the Devil* (1946); *La figlia del capitano/The Captain's Daughter* (1947); *Molti sogni per la strada/The Street Has Many Dreams* (1948); *Il brigante Musolino* (1950); *Moglie per una notte* (1952); *Gli eroi della domenica* (1953); *Ulisse/Ulysses* (1954); *Suor Letizia* (1956); *Primo amore/First Love* (1959); *Via Margutta/Run with the Devil, Crimen/Killing at Monte Carlo* (1960); *I briganti italiani/Seduction of the South* (1961); *Kali Yug la dea della vendetta* (1963); *Il mistero del tempio indiano* (1964); *Delitto quasi perfetto/Imperfect Murder* (1966); *Don Camillo e i giovani d'oggi* (1972).

CAMINO, Jaime   Jaime Camino Vega de la Iglesia; Barcelona 1936

Spanish director. Though from Barcelona, Camino was only loosely connected to the Barcelona School* (which he considered too uncommercial and marginalised to warrant his involvement). He began by writing film criticism and making documentaries. His first feature was *Los felices 60/The Happy 60s* (1963), followed by *Mañana será otro día/Tomorrow's Another Day* (1967), a comedy of manners. His next films were *España otra vez/Spain Again* (1968), a reassessment of the Spanish Civil War within the framework of a conventional love story; *Un invierno en Mallorca/Winter in Majorca* (1969), a dramatisation of the time spent in Majorca by George Sand and Chopin; and *Mi profesora particular/My Private Teacher* (1973). Although he has worked since, Camino's most significant film – recalled in *El largo invierno/The Long Winter* (1991) – remains *Las largas vacaciones del 36/The Long Holidays of 1936* (1976), a narrative about two bourgeois Barcelona families holding out in the hills as the Civil War is waged all around them. PWE

CAMPOS, António
Leiria 1922

Portuguese director. An 'amateur' in the best sense, Campos acquired some reputation among film societies with two 8mm shorts, *Um Tesouro/A Treasure* and *Um Segredo/A Secret* (1958), remarkable films for someone almost completely untutored in any aspect of cinema. In 1961, Campos shot the equally extraordinary *Almadabra Atuneira/The Tuna Fishery* about fishermen on the tuna boats. By then his talent and individuality as a film-maker were obvious. He obtained a grant from the Gulbenkian Foundation to study in London, but soon returned to Portugal. Contemporary with, yet never really part of, the New Portuguese Cinema*, Campos worked basically for Gulbenkian, making some thirty short documentaries for educational and archive purposes. His first feature was *Vilarinho das Furnas* (1971), about a village soon to disappear below the waters of a dam. In *Falamos de Rio do Onor* (1973), a title that can mean *We Speak From* or *About Rio de Onor*, he filmed a part-Portuguese, part-Spanish village still united by an old communitarian system. These films, more or less coinciding with the revolution of 1974, established Campos's international reputation as an ethnographic film-maker. Again in archival mode, he made *Paredes Pintadas da Revolução Portuguesa/Graffiti of the Portuguese Revolution* (1976), having the previous year shot *A Festa/The Festivities* (1975, a short), and *Gente da Praia da Vieira/People from Praia da Vieira* (1976, a feature), both in the seaside village near his home town where he had made *Um Tesouro*. Containing another amazing sequence on a fishing boat, this film, though not overtly political, is one of the best documents on the 'hot summer' of unrest in 1975. Campos then tried fiction with *Ti Miséria*, a short for television, and *Histórias Selvagens/Wild Stories* (both 1981). Virtually retired, he re-emerged with *Terra Fria/Cold Land* (1991) and the short *A Tremonha de Crital/The Crystal Hopper* (1993). Focusing once again on farmers and fishermen, these are ambiguously fictional works, their most interesting elements being those in which the documentary approach predominates. AMS

CAMÚS, Mario
Mario Camús García; Santander 1935

Spanish director and scriptwriter, responsible for one of the most impressive genre-defying bodies of work in modern Spanish cinema. A pupil of Carlos Saura's* at IIEC*, Camús co-scripted the latter's first two features, *Los golfos/The Hooligans* (1959) and *Llanto por un bandido/Lament for a Bandit* (1963), before directing three neo-realist allegories [> SPANISH NEO-REALISM], *Los farsantes/The Actors* (1963), *Young Sánchez* (1963) and *Con el viento solano/With the East Wind* (1965), as well as more accessible features with box-office stars such as Sara Montiel* and Jose Luis López Vázquez*. During the late 1970s and 1980s, Camús' work took an altogether more sombre direction as he embarked on a series of critically acclaimed glossy adaptations of literary works both for film – for instance *La Colmena/The Beehive* (1982) – and television.

More recently, he has produced screenplays for other directors, including a version of Ramón del Valle-Inclán's

Luces de Bohemia/Bohemian Lights (1985, dir. Angel Díez), and *El pájaro de la felicidad/The Bird of Happiness* (1993) for his partner, Pilar Miró*, with whom he co-scripted *Werther* (1986) and *Beltenebros/Prince of Shadows* (1991). MD

CANNES

French film festival, founded in 1938, originally to counter fascist influences thought to contaminate Venice*. The planned opening on 1 September 1939 was cancelled because of the war, and the first Cannes festival actually took place six years later. Cannes soon became one of the top world festivals: the cinema was popular, the Côte d'Azur glamorous, and the beach provided endless photo opportunities for starlets. The showbiz factor has always been high at Cannes, whether it was Sophia Loren* causing a near-riot in 1958 or Quentin Tarantino's appearance in 1994. As in all such events, the list of prizes over the years reveals both masterpieces and duds. More serious arguments have agitated Cannes periodically, such as German protests over the screening of Alain Resnais'* *Nuit et brouillard/Night and Fog* in 1955 and the closure of the festival by the 'events' of May 1968. François Truffaut* called Cannes 'a failure dominated by rackets, compromises and blunders' in 1957, but two years later he was awarded the *mise-en-scène* prize for *Les Quatre cents coups/The 400 Blows*. Increasing officialdom and suspected 'corruption' has led to the creation of several parallel sections over the years – the 'Semaine internationale de la critique' in 1962 and the 'Quinzaine des réalisateurs' in 1969, generally devoted to independent and *auteur* cinema. Despite the controversies Cannes still fulfils two major functions. It is an important film market, and its awards guarantee distribution rather than oblivion for some non-mainstream, non-Hollywood films. GV

CANUDO, Ricciotto
Gioia del Colle, Italy 1879 – Paris 1923

Italian-born French film writer. Canudo moved to Paris in 1902 and joined the avant-garde of the 1910s and 1920s [> FRENCH AVANT-GARDE] in which intellectuals, artists and film-makers attempted to define the specificity of the moving image and struggled to assert the legitimacy of the medium. Canudo's main claim to fame is to have coined the phrase 'the seventh art', but he also edited and wrote for a number of early film publications, such as *La Gazette des sept arts*, and headed the group responsible for the first actual cine-club in 1920. In Richard Abel's words, he was 'the most flamboyant prophet of the new art'. GV

Bib: Richard Abel, *French Cinema, The First Wave, 1915–1929* (1984).

ČAP, František
Čachovice, [then Austria-Hungary] 1913 – Piran, Slovenia 1972

Czech/Slovene director and scriptwriter. After his debut in 1939, it took Čap only a year to become 'the most appreciated and the best paid director in Czechoslovakia', when he made *Babička/Grandmother* (1940), his adaptation of a famous Czech novel by Božena Němcová. Čap's international reputation was confirmed by awards in Venice (*Noční motyl/Night Butterfly*, 1941) and Cannes (*Muži bez křídel/Men Without Wings*, 1946). He rejected several offers from Italy and Germany during World War II; but, his films being judged 'too patriotic' by the Czech authorities in 1948, he escaped with his mother – to Munich. After two films in Germany, he was offered work in Yugoslavia in 1952, and brought some life to the heavy, literature-based Slovene cinema of the time. His teen-comedy *Vesna* (1953) and its sequel *Ne čakaj na maj/Don't Wait for May* (1957) are still among the most popular films ever made in Slovenia, while *Trenutki odločitve/Moments of Decision* (1955) touched upon the sensitive subject of the attribution of guilt between collaborators and partisans. Too different for the small Slovene setting, he died a solitary figure in Piran. SP

Bib: Zdenko Vrdlovec, Jože Dolmark: *František Čap* (1981).

Other Films Include: *Ohnive leto/Fiery Summer* (1939); *Devčica z Bezkyd/Girl from Bezkyd* (1944); *Bila tma/White Darkness* (1948); *Die Spur fuhrt nach Berlin/Adventure in Berlin* (1952); *Am Anfang war es Sünde/The Sin* (1954); *Harte Männer – Starke Liebe/Salt and Bread* (1957); *Vrata ostaju otvorena/The Door Remains Open* (1959); *X-25 javlja/X-25 Reports* (1960); *Sreščemo se večeras/We'll Meet Tonight, Naš avto/Our Car* (1962).

CAPRINO, Ivo
Kristiania [Oslo] 1920

Norwegian director and producer, working mostly in animation and famous for his films featuring dolls. Caprino patented his own system for animating dolls in front of the camera, before turning to more traditional animation. His dolls are charming creatures with large, clear moving eyes and distinct character traits, sometimes representing people, sometimes animals or fantastic beings. Caprino mostly made short films, starting with *Tim og Tøffe/Tim and Tøffe* (1948). In the 1950s and 1960s he adapted Norwegian folk tales for a series of doll films each lasting about twenty minutes. These films, known and loved by generations of children, have become central to Norwegian children's culture and are still frequently shown on television and in cinemas. *Ugler i mosen/Mischief* (1959), a feature for children, combines animation and live action. Caprino's fully animated feature *Flåklypa Grand Prix* (1975) tells the story of an inventor living with a crow and a hedgehog on a distant Norwegian mountain. His revolutionary car, with the backing of an oil sheik, wins the 'Flåklypa' grand prix race. *Flåklypa Grand Prix* is the most popular Norwegian film ever. KS

Other Films Include: *En dukkedrøm/A Doll's Dream, Musikk*

på loftet/Music in the Attic* (1951); *Veslefrikk med fela/Veslefrikk and his Fiddle* (1952); *Den standhaftige tinnsoldat/The Steadfast Tin Soldier* (1954); *Karius og Baktus/Karius and Baktus* (1955); *Askeladden og de gode hjelperne/Askeladden and His Good Helpers* (1961); *Reveenka/The Fox Widow* (1962); *Sjuende far i huset/The Seventh Father in the House* (1965); *Gutten som kappåt med trollet/The Boy Who Competed in Eating with a Troll* (1966).

CARAX, Leos
Alex Dupont; Paris 1960

French director, hailed as a prodigy in the 1980s. With his tortured personality, instant success through his first feature, *Boy Meets Girl* (1984), and regular use of alter ego actor Denis Lavant, Carax has been seen as the carrier of the New Wave* inheritance. *Boy Meets Girl*, shot in black and white on location in Paris, combined New Wave romanticism with post-modernism (especially in the use of music). *Mauvais Sang/The Night is Young* (1986) added overt references to Jean-Luc Godard* with the use of primary colours and a Juliette Binoche* made to look like Anna Karina*. The extravagant (in all senses) *Les Amants du Pont-Neuf* (1991), starring Lavant and Binoche, is a sumptuous and romantic tribute to Paris, *amour fou* and Binoche. Carax figures controversially in debates over the *cinéma du look*, his cine-literacy and 'neo-baroque' *mise-en-scène* earning criticism for a beautiful but supposedly 'empty' cinema, but also passionate admiration. GV

CARDIFF, Jack
Great Yarmouth 1914

British cinematographer and director, who became an expert on colour cinematography with Technicolor in the 1930s. He was a camera assistant at the age of 13, graduating to camera operator for René Clair's* *The Ghost Goes West* (1936), and for Europe's first Technicolor film, *Wings of the Morning* (1937). In the late 1930s he made a series of documentary shorts, shot mainly in India, to gain experience of the new colour system, returning to Britain as co-cinematographer on *The Great Mr Handel* (1942). He was snapped up by Michael Powell and Emeric Pressburger* for *The Life and Death of Colonel Blimp* (1943), *A Matter of Life and Death* (1946), *Black Narcissus* (1947) – for which he won an Academy Award – and *The Red Shoes* (1948). For Alfred Hitchcock*, he photographed *Under Capricorn* (1949), with its exceptionally long takes. Cardiff turned to directing in the late 1950s, with *Sons and Lovers* (1960) as his most successful film, but he remained primarily a cinematographer. JC

Other Films Include: **As Cinematographer** – *Western Approaches* (1944); *Scott of the Antarctic* [co-ph] (1948); *The African Queen* (1952); *The Barefoot Contessa* (1954, US); *War and Peace* (1956, US); *The Prince and the Showgirl* (1957); *The Vikings* (1958, US); *Death on the Nile* (1978); *Conan the Destroyer* (1984, US); *Rambo First Blood Part II* (1985). **As Director** – *Intent to Kill* (1958); *Young Cassidy* [completed for John Ford] (1965).

CARDINALE, Claudia
Tunis, Tunisia 1939

Italian actress. At the age of seventeen Cardinale won a contest for the most beautiful girl of Italian origin in Tunis. Rewarded with a trip to the Venice festival, she later moved to Italy to prepare for a career as a film actress. Although initially chosen for her physical charms rather than her acting prowess, she soon developed into an intelligent and versatile actress, equally at home in serious and comedy roles. Her early career was fostered by producer Franco Cristaldi*, whom she married. Cristaldi gave her roles in films he produced, beginning with Mario Monicelli's* *I soliti ignoti/Persons Unknown* (1958), but also looked after her career in general. She gave fine performances for a number of major directors, notably Luchino Visconti* (*Rocco e i suoi fratelli/Rocco and His Brothers*, 1960; *Il gattopardo/The Leopard*, 1963; *Vaghe stelle dell'orsa/Sandra*, 1964), but also for, among others, Valerio Zurlini*, Francesco Maselli* (*Gli indifferenti/Time of Indifference*, 1963), Luigi Comencini* (*La ragazza di Bube/Bebo's Girl*, 1963), and Federico Fellini* ($8\frac{1}{2}$, 1963). After her divorce from Cristaldi her career went into decline and she mostly made undistinguished films until the early 1980s, when she re-emerged in a number of international productions, including Werner Herzog's* *Fitzcarraldo* (1982, Ger.) and Diane Kurys'* *Un Homme amoureux/A Man in Love* (1987, Fr./It.). She went on to give proof of a new maturity as an actress with superbly modulated performances in Marco Bellocchio's Pirandello adaptation *Enrico IV* (*Henry IV*, 1984) and in Luigi Comencini's* *La storia/The Story* [or *History*], 1986). She also gave a moving performance as the mother in Henri Verneuil's* autobiographical films *Mayrig* (1991, Fr.) and *588, rue Paradis* (1992, Fr.) GNS

CARETTE, Julien
Paris 1897 – Le Vésinet 1966

French actor, usually known simply as 'Carette'. One of the archetypal character actors or, as Raymond Chirat put it, 'eccentrics' of French cinema: never a star, yet instantly recognised and appreciated by a devoted audience. Carette, who had a long career in theatre and music hall and acted in dozens of comic films, would be just one of these talented bit-players, along with Pauline Carton, Saturnin Fabre, Marguerite Pierry, Sylvie and many others, were it not for his parts in four Jean Renoir* films – *La Grande illusion, La Marseillaise* (both 1937), *La Bête humaine* (1938) and *La Règle du jeu/Rules of the Game* (1939) – to which he brought his inimitable working-class Parisian accent and a capacity to move and amuse at the same time. The Prévert* brothers and Claude Autant-Lara* also employed him frequently. Carette's death, set alight by his cigarette in a wheelchair, was a sad final scene for such a likeable actor. GV

Bib: Raymond Chirat and Olivier Barrot, *Les Excentriques du cinéma français (1928–1958)* (1983).

CAREY, Patrick
London 1917

Irish director and cameraman. From a theatrical family, Carey worked for several years on the Dublin stage, but from 1945 he began working in films in Britain, shooting his first film, a documentary, in 1947. Working mainly in Asia during the following six years, he was one of the crew that filmed the 1953 ascent of Mount Everest. Continuing to work in Britain, and for the National Film Board of Canada, he specialised in 'nature documentaries'. He won an Oscar in 1967 for his photography on *Wild Wings* (1967), after three earlier films had been nominated for the award. One of these was Carey's most admired film, *Yeats Country* (1965), which drew on the Sligo landscape to evoke W. B. Yeats' poetry. Carey rarely worked in feature production, though he was second unit director-cameraman on *A Man for All Seasons* (1966). KR

CARLSEN, Henning
Ålborg 1927

Danish director. Carlsen began his career as assistant director to the documentary film-maker Theodor Christensen* at Minerva Film, working there from 1948 to 1953. Thereafter he worked for Nordisk Film* until 1957, as a freelance director and from 1960 also as a producer. From 1968 to 1981 he managed Copenhagen's Dagmar cinema. He has also directed for theatre and television and taught at the Danish Film School. His first feature was the semi-documentary *Dilemma* (1962). In all, he has directed forty-five documentaries and thirteen features.

Dilemma, based on a novel by Nadine Gordimer, was perhaps the first film treatment of the racial problems of South Africa (the film was shot there clandestinely). *Sult/Hunger* (1966), Carlsen's most successful film, was also the most truly Scandinavian. Carlsen and fellow-Dane Peter Seeberg wrote the script from the novel by the Norwegian writer Knut Hamsun; Per Oscarsson, a Swedish actor, played the lead, and the cast included Danish and Norwegian actors. The film, shot on location in Oslo, was a superb adaptation of Hamsun's turn-of-the-century autobiographical portrait of a writer's disintegration. Carlsen's later films failed to live up to the critical and box-office achievement of *Sult*. He made some comedies and a number of co-productions, especially with France, notably *Un Divorce heureux/En lykkelig skilsmisse/A Happy Divorce* (1975), and *Oviri/Gauguin, le loup dans le soleil* (1986), a film about the painter Paul Gauguin. ME

Other Films Include: *De gamle/Old People* (1961); *Kattorna/The Cats, Ung/Being Young* (1965); *Hør, var der ikke en, som lo?/Did Somebody Laugh?* (1978).

CARNÉ, Marcel
Paris 1909

French director. Carné's place in film history is assured as the foremost exponent of Poetic Realism*, especially in his collaborations with the poet/scriptwriter Jacques Prévert*.

Carné trained as a photographer and started in film as a journalist (for *Cinémagazine*) and assistant director to René Clair* and especially Jacques Feyder*. His first film, *Nogent, Eldorado du dimanche* (1930), was a documentary on working-class leisure, heralding his interest in 'ordinary people'; during the Popular Front* period he worked briefly with the left cooperative Ciné-Liberté. With *Jenny* (1936, starring Françoise Rosay*), Carné established his poetic-realist universe: stylised urban decors, a cast of workers and marginals, a dark and pervasive atmosphere of doom shot through with the genuine poetry of the everyday. It was followed by *Hôtel du Nord, Quai des brumes* (both 1938) and *Le Jour se lève* (1939). These films showcased the work of Carné's brilliant team: set designer Alexandre Trauner*, composers Maurice Jaubert* and Joseph Kosma*, émigré cameramen Eugen Schüfftan* and Curt Courant*, actors like Jean Gabin*, Louis Jouvet*, Michel Simon* and Michèle Morgan*. Last but not least was Prévert, who contributed sardonic humour (as in the surreal-burlesque *Drôle de drame*, 1937) and romantic fatalism, especially in *Quai des brumes* and *Le Jour se lève*, for which he wrote the dialogue.

In the constrained context of the German occupation, Carné, with Prévert, switched to costume dramas. *Les Visiteurs du soir* (1942) was a medieval fable, and *Les Enfants du paradis* (1943–45) an exuberant reconstruction of the Parisian theatre of the 1830s, with a remarkable performance by Arletty*. While these two films drew on the 'poetic' side of poetic realism, *Les Portes de la nuit* (1946) seemed the swan-song of its dark populism. Carné, without Prévert, switched to natural decors (*La Marie du port*, 1950) and contemporary subjects, such as the much criticised but highly popular *Les Tricheurs* (1958), a portrait of the young generation, but he never regained his prewar status. However, *Thérèse Raquin* (1953, starring Simone Signoret*) and *L'Air de Paris* (1954, with Arletty and Gabin) show that Carné still excelled at evoking, respectively, doomed passion and a nostalgic popular Paris. GV

Bib: Edward Baron Turk, *Child of Paradise* (1989).

Other Films: *La Fleur de l'âge* (1947, unfinished); *Juliette ou la Clé des songes* (1951); *Le Pays d'où je viens* (1956); *Terrain vague* (1960); *Du mouron pour les petits oiseaux* (1963); *Trois chambres à Manhattan* (1965); *Les Jeunes loups* (1967); *Les Assassins de l'ordre* (1971); *La Merveilleuse visite* (1974); *La Bible* (TV, 1976).

CAROL, Martine
Marie-Louise Mourer; Biarritz 1920 – Monaco 1967

French actress. The most popular French female star before Brigitte Bardot*, Carol has been unjustly disparaged for her acting and for the unfashionable genres she worked in, especially the costume film. Carol began in true starlet mode, bleaching her hair and doing publicity stunts, including throwing herself into the Seine. After small parts on stage (as Maryse Arley) and in film, her career took off with *Caroline Chérie* (1950), directed by Richard Pottier from Cécil Saint-Laurent's 'scandalous' novel. This set Carol on her path as the 'ooh-la-la' star of a series of comic-erotic adventures (actually aimed at a family audience), in which period costumes showed off her ample curves – *Nana* (1955), directed by her then husband Christian-Jaque* from Zola's novel, is a good example. Criticised as 'pandering to the fantasies of Fourth Republic men', she was very popular with women, who appreciated her light touch in contemporary romantic comedies such as Christian-Jaque's *Adorables créatures/Adorable Creatures* (1952). Her sex-goddess image was to be her down-

fall. In the new era ushered in by Bardot she seemed old-fashioned; the disastrous reception of Max Ophuls'* *Lola Montès* (1955), in which she is presented as a fairground attraction, also affected her badly. Her last years were a sad tale of failed marriages, drink and drugs, leading to suicide. Carol was a vibrant popular performer, the first to challenge the male hegemony at the French box office. GV

Other Films Include: *Les Belles de nuit, Un caprice de Caroline Chérie* (1952); *Lucrèce Borgia/Sins of the Borgias* (1953); *Madame du Barry* (1954); *Nathalie, agent secret/The Foxiest Girl in Paris* (1957); *Austerlitz* (1960); *Vanina Vanini* (1961, It./Fr.).

CARROLL, Madeleine
Marie Madeleine Bernadette O'Carroll; West Bromwich 1906 – Marbella, Spain 1987

British actress, who became one of a few British stars to achieve international stardom in the 1930s. Originally a French teacher, she made her stage debut in 1927, only a year before she appeared in film. Her lack of the usual theatrical background may account for her unmannered performances. She made an international impact in Victor Saville's* *I Was a Spy* (1933), in which she played the Belgian nurse Marthe Cnockhaert, who simultaneously spied for the Allies and tended the German wounded. Alfred Hitchcock* ensured her stardom, pairing her, as one of the first of his cool blondes, with Robert Donat* in *The 39 Steps* (1935) and with John Gielgud* in *Secret Agent* (1936). Her particular appeal was more attuned to Hollywood, and it is no surprise that she moved there in 1936, starring with Ronald Colman* in *The Prisoner of Zenda* (1937, US). She retired from film in 1949, and subsequently worked for UNESCO. JC

Other Films Include: *The Guns of Loos, The First Born* (1928); *The Crooked Billet, L'Instinct* [Fr.], *The American Prisoner, Atlantic* (1929); *The 'W' Plan, Young Woodley, French Leave, Escape, The School for Scandal* (1930); *Fascination* (1931); *Sleeping Car* (1933); *The Dictator* (1935); *White Cradle Inn* (1947).

'CARRY ON . . .' FILMS

British series, which began unthreateningly with *Carry On Sergeant*, intended as a one-off in 1958, initiated the series with *Carry On Nurse* (1959), continued with up to four films a year through the 1960s, appeared intermittently in the 1970s until *Carry On Emmannuelle* (1978), and then reappeared in 1992 with its salute to the quinquennial celebrations, *Carry On Columbus*. The thirty films in the series were produced by Peter Rogers and directed by Gerald Thomas, with a core cast which included Kenneth Williams, Sid James, Kenneth Connor, Charles Hawtrey, Joan Sims, Hattie Jacques and Barbara Windsor. The films belong in the music-hall tradition of George Formby* and Max Miller, and their humour is in the tradition of the seaside postcard ('pinched bums, big tits, screaming queens and henpecked husbands are the conditions of their existence'; 'their most celebrated feature, their great comic glory, is the reliance on innuendo' – Andy Medhurst). In the early films, the objects of the carryings on were institutions, but by the mid-1960s the series had discovered a rich seam in the send-up of film genres – Bond movies* (*Carry On Spying*, 1964), epics (*Carry On Cleo*, 1964), and empire (*Carry On . . . Up the Khyber*, 1968). By the end of the permissive 1970s cinemagoers were harder to scandalise, and the 'Carry On . . .' films were consigned to endless repeats on weekend afternoon television. JC

Bib: Andy Medhurst, 'Carry On Camp', *Sight and Sound* (August 1992).

CASTELLANI, Renato   Finale Ligure 1913 – Rome 1985

Italian director. After studying architecture in Milan, Castellani entered cinema first as a journalist and then as a scriptwriter for films by Augusto Genina*, Mario Camerini*, Mario Soldati* and in particular Alessandro Blasetti* (*La corona di ferro/The Iron Crown*, 1941). At the time of his directorial debut with *Un colpo di pistola* (1941) and *Zazà* (1942), both written by Alberto Moravia but not signed by him because of racial laws, Castellani was one of the leading exponents of the 'calligraphy' movement, whose narrative formalism was trying to counter Fascist rhetoric. His postwar trilogy about the poor – *Sotto il sole di Roma/Under the Sun of Rome* (1948), *È primavera/It's Forever Springtime* (1949) and *Due soldi di speranza/Two Cents Worth of Hope* (1951) – added to the *commedia romanesca* ('Roman-style comedy') elements of realism such as actors taken from the street. This lively, vibrant and optimistic vision of popular life led to the so-called 'rose-tinted' neo-realism*, as opposed to the pessimism of a film like Vittorio De Sica's* *Umberto D.* (1952). An intelligent craftsman and sharp observer of social reality, Castellani has also often been charged with formalism. Such controversial qualities can be seen in films like *Giulietta e Romeo/Romeo and Juliet* (1954), the bitter *I sogni nel cassetto* (1957), and the prison film *Nella città l'inferno/And the Wild, Wild Women* (1958), starring Anna Magnani* and Giulietta Masina*. An affected but sincere account of land occupation in Calabria, *Il brigante* (1961) can be seen as a late tribute to a neo-realism which Castellani had been accused of trying to bury. His cinema career ended in the 1960s with a number of mediocre films. He then worked for television, making popular and historically accurate serials such as *Leonardo da Vinci* (1971) and *Verdi* (1982). GVo

Other Films Include: *La donna della montagna* (1943); *Mio figlio professore/Professor, My Son* (1946); *Mare matto* (1963); *Controsesso* [ep. *Una donna d'affari*], *Tre notti d'amore/Three Nights of Love* [ep. *La vedova*] (1964); *Questi fantasmi* (1967); *Una breve stagione* (1969).

CASTRO, Estrellita   Estrella Castro Navarrete; Seville 1914 – Madrid 1983

Spanish actress and singer, one of the most famous Spanish *folklóricas** actresses. She made her first film appearance in *Rosario la cortijera/Rosario the Farmhouse Girl* (1935), but her most characteristic role is as *Mariquilla Terremoto/ Mariquilla the Earthquake* (1940). Here, her whining, high-pitched, rapid-speaking style and cheerful homely facial expression, complete with trademark kiss-curl, are given their folksiest expression in an enormously popular musical. Other major films include *Suspiros de España/Sighs of Spain* (1939) and *La gitanilla/The Little Gypsy Girl* (1940). PWE

CAVALCANTI, Alberto   Rio de Janeiro, Brazil 1897 – Paris, France 1982

British/Brazilian director. Educated in law in Brazil, and in art in Geneva, Cavalcanti became an art director in Paris in the 1920s, associating himself with the avant-garde* art movement, and particularly with Surrealism. His first major film was *Rien que les heures* (1926), a 'city film' which anticipated Walther Ruttmann's* *Berlin: Symphony of a Great City* (1927). In 1934 he was invited by John Grierson* to join the GPO Film Unit, to which he brought a concern with technical innovation and experiment that often ran counter to Grierson's more social reformist agenda. Relations between the two were strained. Harry Watt*, however, credits him with training his generation of documentary film-makers: 'I believe fundamentally,' he said, 'that the arrival of Cavalcanti in the GPO Film Unit was the turning point of British documentary.' Cavalcanti's best known directed films with the Unit, *Pett and Pott* (1934) and *Coal Face* (1935), are distinctive in their intricate editing of sound and image, and his productions (for which he also supervised sound) include *Night Mail* (1936), *North Sea* (1938) and *Spare Time* (1939).

Cavalcanti left the Grierson group when it became the Crown Film Unit and joined Ealing Studios, where he directed two of the studio's best films of the early 1940s, *Went the Day Well?* (1942) and the 'Ventriloquist's Dummy' episode of *Dead of Night* (1945). But his real importance at Ealing was in training and developing new directors like Robert Hamer*, Charles Frend and Charles Crichton*, and in production. Michael Balcon* credits Cavalcanti with a special role in establishing the 'trademark' of Ealing*: 'The whole of the Ealing output had a certain stamp on it. Whether I would have done it on my own I don't know. But most certainly I acknowledge . . . that of all the help I got his is the help that was most important.' From 1949, Cavalcanti divided his time between Brazil, where he founded the Brazilian Film Institute; Europe, where he directed in Britain, France, Italy, Austria and Romania; and the US, where he taught at UCLA. JC

Bib: Elizabeth Sussex, 'Cavalcanti in England', *Sight and Sound* (August 1975).

Other Films Include: *Le Train sans yeux* (1925, Fr.); *La P'tite Lilie* (1927, Fr.); *La Jalousie du barbouillé* (1928, Fr.); *Le Petit*

Chaperon rouge (1929, Fr.); *Coralie et Cie* (1933, Fr.); *We Live in Two Worlds, The Line to Tschierva Hut* (1937); *The Chiltern Country* (1938); *La Cause commune* [made in UK for showing in France] (1940); *Champagne Charlie, Trois Chansons de la résistance/Soup Before Sunrise* [made in UK for Free French Army] (1944); *Nicholas Nickleby, They Made Me a Fugitive* (1947); *Simão o coalho/Simon the One-Eyed* (1952, Brazil); *Herr Puntila und sein Knecht Matti* (1955, Aus.); *La Prima notte* (1958, It.); *Thus Spake Theodor Herzl* (1967, Israel).

CAVANI, Liliana   Capri 1937

Italian director. Cavani's work, in both documentary and fiction, represents a significant response to the revolutionary social and political changes in Italy since the 1960s. Her dramatisation of socio-historical concepts has led her to create cinematic character who are 'rebels', 'visionaries' or 'madmen', experiencing in acute form the conflict between historical and spiritual reality, past and present.

After studying at the Centro Sperimentale* in Rome, Cavani became a freelance television director for RAI*. Her first major assignments were documentaries on the Third Reich (1962), Stalin* (1962) and women in the Resistance (1965), followed by the 1965 Venice prize-winner, *Philippe Pétain, Processo a Vichy/Philippe Pétain, Vichy on Trial*. Her first feature, *Francesco d'Assisi* (1966), starring Lou Castel (the schizophrenic hero of Marco Bellocchio's* *I pugni in tasca/Fists in the Pocket*), was based on the meticulous observation of everyday reality mastered during her apprenticeship as a documentarist, and became an emblem of emerging Catholic dissent. Her commitment to a visionary expression of social issues continued with *Galileo* (1968), *I cannibali/The Cannibals* (1969) and *L'ospite/The Guest* (1971), which all focus on repressive mechanisms and challenge traditional assumptions about authority. The turning point in her career came with *Il portiere di notte/The Night Porter* (1974), starring Dirk Bogarde* and Charlotte Rampling, whose huge box-office success made her reputation as one of the most provocative (not least within feminist circles) film-makers of the 1970s. Her choice of controversial themes, graphic use of sexuality and forceful apolitical stance underline a complex vision of the contemporary world. Her German trilogy continued with *Al di là del bene e del male/Beyond Good and Evil* (1977) and *Interno Berlinese/Berlin Interior* (1978), in which games of erotic enslavement and domination reflect a complex historical situation (Nazism). Her most recent films – *Francesco* (1989, with Mickey Rourke in the role of Saint Francis) and *Dove siete? Io sono qui/Where Are You? I Am Here* (1993) – continue to place individuals in extreme situations. In 1979 Cavani added opera to her repertoire, directing Berg's *Wozzeck* for the Maggio Musicale Fiorentino. Since then she has worked for the Paris opera and for La Scala, Milan. GM

Other Films Include: *Milarepa* (1974); *La pelle/Skin* (1981); *Oltre la porta/Beyond the Door* (1982).

CBA (Centre de l'Audiovisuel à Bruxelles)

Belgian workshop, supporting and producing audiovisual work. Founded in November 1978 as the Centre Belge de l'Audiovisuel, the CBA was the combined inspiration of Henri Storck* and Jean-Claude Batz with the help of Kathleen de Béthune and François Persoons (Minister of Culture). It was the first workshop to be created with French help, after long discussions over what could be done to support cinema in Belgium, in particular in the Francophone community. The CBA is seen as a workshop space where film-makers can meet free from bureaucracy, and where decisions can be made fast enough to keep new independent cinema alive. After several years, the CBA was renamed *Centre de l'Audiovisuel à Bruxelles*, to indicate a wider remit, which includes both French and 'Flemish' directors, and co-productions with private and foreign producers as well as television (RTBF). In its first ten years the CBA produced or co-produced more than a hundred films, ranging from those of well-known directors such as Chantal Akerman* (*Toute une nuit*, 1982) to the work of a new generation of directors such as Michèle Blondeel, Luc and Jean-Pierre Dardenne, and Michel Khleifi. CF

CECCHI D'AMICO, Suso   Rome 1914

Italian scriptwriter. The daughter of Emilio Cecchi and wife of music critic Fedele D'Amico, Suso Cecchi D'Amico must count as Italy's most distinguished scriptwriter. Starting as a script translator, she made her first original contribution as co-scriptwriter (with her father) on Renato Castellani's* *Mio figlio professore/Professor, My Son* in 1946. Her contribution to Luigi Zampa's* *Vivere in pace/To Live in Peace* (1946) won her a Silver Ribbon (Italy's equivalent of an Oscar). She worked with Cesare Zavattini* and Ennio Flaiano* on the scripts of *Ladri di biciclette/Bicycle Thieves* (1948) and *Roma città libera* (1946) respectively. She soon emerged as a writer with a style of her own, first on neo-realist* subjects and then social and moral satire. She was scriptwriter on many important films by distinguished directors, including Vittorio De Sica's* *Miracolo a Milano/Miracle in Milan* (1951), Alessandro Blasetti's* *Altri tempi/Infidelity* (1952), Michelangelo Antonioni's* *Le amiche/The Girlfriends* (1955), Francesco Rosi's* *Salvatore Giuliano* (1962), Franco Zeffirelli's* *The Taming of the Shrew* (1967, US/It.), Luigi Comencini's* *La storia/The Story* [or *History*] (1986), and most recently Nikita Mikhalkov's* *Oci ciornie/Ochi chërnye/Dark Eyes* (1987). Many of her collaborations were long-standing, the most celebrated with Luchino Visconti*, for whom she was the major scriptwriter on almost all his films from *Bellissima* (1951) to *L'innocente/The Innocent* (1976). Particularly when working with Visconti, the depth of her culture, her sense of realism and attention to the text enabled her to play a major creative role. MMo

CECCHI, Emilio   Florence 1884 – Rome 1966

Italian producer, scriptwriter, critic and director. Although Cecchi worked in various capacities in the Italian film industry from the 1930s to the 1950s, he is mostly remembered for his early 1930s work. Cecchi was hired by Cines*, first as artistic director in March 1931, and then as director of production in April 1932, a position he held only until November 1933; his tenure occurred, however, at the height of the revival of Italian cinema (depleted since the 1920s) and at a time when Cines was responsible for most Italian film production. Before working at Cines, Cecchi had little direct experience of film production. He had been a successful writer, had published film criticism (1930–31), and spent some time in Hollywood while lecturing in California. As director of production, he came to embody the multiple aims and contradictions surrounding an Italian cinema attempting to produce 'art for the people'. He is credited with having encouraged a cosmopolitan film style congruent with the European avant-garde [> AVANT-GARDE CINEMA IN EUROPE] by attracting directors such as Walther Ruttmann* and Carlo Bragaglia and writers such as Luigi Pirandello; a modernist formalism is also evident in many of the documentaries he produced. On the other hand, the 'Cecchi era' brought Italian film production closer to a 'popular' style that, as never before, emphasised Italian locations and everyday life. Significantly, Cecchi's vision of film as a popular art was bound up with his admiration for Hollywood films, whose virtues he had extolled in his first film reviews.

In the early 1940s, Cecchi worked as scriptwriter on such films as *Piccolo mondo antico/Old-Fashioned World* (1941), *Sissignora* (1941) and *Giacomo l'idealista* (1943). He revised the scripts of *I promessi sposi/The Spirit and the Flesh* (1941) and *Vespro siciliano* (1949). He wrote commentaries for documentaries and directed short features such as *Vita e morte degli etruschi* (1947) and *Anatomia del colore* (1948). In 1949 he returned to the reorganised Cines as 'artistic consultant' and in 1952 as part of its administrative council. Throughout the 1950s and 1960s he was mostly engaged in writing literary criticism and history. JHa

CECCHI GORI, Mario   Brescia 1920 – Rome 1993

Italian producer. Throughout his long career, in association with Dino De Laurentiis* from 1948 and with his son Vittorio from the 1970s, Cecchi Gori produced some 170 films. After the creation of his own production house in 1957, he opened an important phase for Italian cinema by 'inventing' *commedia all'italiana*, the genre which exploded during the years of the 'economic boom'. He demonstrated a remarkable commercial intuition, typical of a 'salesman' according to his detractors but in fact the result of the skills of a great artisan. He produced Luigi Zampa's* popular comedies, as well as those of Ettore Scola* and many others, including especially many directed by Dino Risi*: *Il mattatore/Love and Larceny* (1960), *Il sorpasso/The Easy Life* (1962), *La marcia su Roma/The March to Rome* (1962), *I mostri/The Monsters* (1963), *Il gaucho* (1964), *Il tigre/The Tiger and the Pussycat* (1967), all starring Vittorio Gassman*. Gassman embodied the company's image in over twenty films, being eventually replaced in this role by Ugo Tognazzi*, Nino Manfredi, and the singer Adriano Celentano (the latter starring in 'lighter' pro-

ductions). In the 1970s and 1980s Cecchi Gori's name was linked to the 'new Italian comics'*, particularly Paolo Villaggio. He addressed his films to a middle-brow audience, although he also produced a series of ambiguous political/judiciary movies (such as Damiano Damiani's *L'istruttoria è chiusa: dimentichi*, 1971). His presence within Italian cinema grew even larger with the creation in 1989 of Penta, a joint venture with Silvio Berlusconi [> FININVEST], which produced many run-of-the-mill films as well as more prestigious ones such as those of Carlo Verdone (*Borotalco*, 1982; *Perdiamoci di vista*, 1994), Roberto Benigni* (*Il piccolo diavolo/The Little Devil*, 1988; *Johnny Stecchino*, 1991), Gabriele Salvatores (*Mediterraneo*, 1991), Giuseppe Tornatore*, and Marco Risi, and films by *auteurs* such as Ermanno Olmi* (*La leggenda del santo bevitore/The Legend of the Holy Drinker*, 1988), Gianni Amelio* (*Lamerica*, 1994) and Federico Fellini* (*La voce della luna/The Voice of the Moon*, 1990). Penta has recently suffered from the effects of its rapid and excessive growth and from internal dissensions, especially over risky endeavours such as the creation of Pentamerica, an American subsidiary, and participation in the Italian pay-TV channel Telepiú. GVo

CENSORSHIP in SPAIN

The major restraining force on Spanish cinema under Franco, not only stifling elementary freedoms of speech, but also, from the 1960s, disarming Spain's attempt to compete in a world film market of increasing erotica. Censorship was introduced in November 1937, with the creation of the Junta Superior de Censura Cinematográfica (Supreme Film Censorship Board). This led to the prohibition of the public use of the Catalan language (June 1939), censorship of films at the script stage (July 1939) and the compulsory dubbing of all foreign film imports (April 1941). The driving force behind censorship was the Catholic Church, which, scandalised by such films as Rafael Gil's* *La fe/Faith* (1947), set up the Oficina Nacional clasificadora de Espectáculos (National Board of Classification of Spectacles), whose dictates were followed strictly by many cinemas, parents and teachers. It is a mark of the arbitrariness of Francoist film censorship that exactly what the censor could proscribe was not defined until the Censorship Norms of 1963. Respect was to be shown to 'our institutions', to the Catholic Church's 'dogma, morals and cult', and to 'the Head of State'. Banned were justifications of suicide, divorce, illicit sexual relations and even contraception. Censorship crippled the attempt of Luis García Berlanga*, Juan Antonio Bardem*, and the New Spanish Cinema* directors to introduce neo-realism* into Spain. Censorial decisions also illustrated the administrative torpor of the Franco establishment. The Spanish dubbed version of John Ford's *Mogambo* (1953) transformed its married couple (Grace Kelly and Donald Sinden) into brother and sister to justify the wife's liaison with Clark Gable. Censorship even endowed Spanish films with certain stylistic strategies: a delight in allegory, ellipsis, metaphor and symbol (Carlos Saura's* *La caza/The Hunt* [1965] and *Ana y los lobos/Ana and the Wolves* [1972]), the diffusion of sense (Martín Patino's* *Nueve cartas a Berta/Nine Letters to Berta* [1965]), subversive literary adaptations (*La leyenda del Alcalde de*

Zalamea/The Legend of the Major of Zalamea [1972]) and the ostentatious modishness of the so-called Barcelona School*. Censorship was abolished in 1977, ushering in one of the most liberal cinemas in Europe. JH

CENTRO SPERIMENTALE

Italian institution. The Centro Sperimentale di Cinematografia is Italy's oldest national film school. It was created in 1934 through the re-formation of the much smaller National School of Cinematography, established (in 1932) and headed by director Alessandro Blasetti*. Although its formation was the direct result of initiatives by the Fascist government, it operated quasi-independently from state control and without precise political objectives. While there were earlier models of national film schools outside Italy, such as the Soviet VGIK*, the Centro grew out of very specific conditions in 1930s Italy: a shared interest among some filmmakers, theorists and the state to centralise, institutionalise and promote cinema as a form of national culture, and to guarantee a future for the Italian film industry, whose production had fallen to just a few films a year during the late 1920s. Throughout the 1930s the Centro Sperimentale was directed by film-maker and critic Luigi Chiarini*. It was situated in a school in Rome until 1939, when it was relocated to its current site in the new cinema complex adjacent to Cinecittà* on the via Tuscolana in the southern suburbs of Rome. Since its inauguration, the Centro has offered professional training in all areas of film production. It has also served as a forum for film theory and criticism, producing a series of books that ranged from translations of S. M. Eisenstein* and Béla Balázs* to writings by Italian intellectuals. JHa

CERVI, Gino   Bologna 1901 – Castiglione della Pescaia 1974

Italian actor. Cervi was one of the most famous protagonists of Italian action-adventure films during the late 1930s and early 1940s. His prolific career spanned five decades. A stage actor since 1923, he started working in film in the early 1930s, appearing as a supporting character actor in several unsuccessful low-budget films before being given the lead in Alessandro Blasetti's* *Aldebaran* (1935), one of the first military dramas of the period. Between 1935 and 1942 he made five films with Blasetti, including *Ettore Fieramosca* (1938), *Un'avventura di Salvator Rosa* (1939), *La corona di ferro/The Iron Crown* (1941) and *Quattro passi fra le nuvole/Four Steps in the Clouds* (1942). In many respects, Cervi's screen persona became as inextricable from Blasetti's adventure films as Vittorio De Sica's* was from Mario Camerini's* romantic comedies. But whether for Blasetti or Camerini, with whom he also made two films in the early 1940s (*Una romantica avventura* in 1940 and *I promessi sposi/The Spirit and the Flesh* in 1941), Cervi became a familiar presence in Italian historical films. Although he appeared in various film genres and international productions until 1972, he was best known in the postwar years for his role as Peppone, the Communist

mayor in the very popular Franco-Italian *Don Camillo* comic series, co-starring Fernandel* as Don Camillo (except in the last film made after Fernandel's death): *Le Petit monde de Don Camillo* (1952) and *Le Retour de Don Camillo* (1953), both directed by Julien Duvivier*, were followed by four other sequels, two (in 1955 and 1961) directed by Carmine Gallone* and two (in 1965 and 1972) by Luigi Comencini*. JHa

CÉSARS

French institution. Césars, the French Oscars, were created in 1975 by advertising executive Georges Cravenne. Awards in twenty categories are determined by nomination and secret voting by members of the Académie du Cinéma (created at the same time), composed of some 2,400 French film professionals. Initially greeted with derision, and not just in the US, the Césars have proved extremely successful and are much sought after by the profession; half the French population watches the 'Nuit des Césars' on television. GV

CHABROL, Claude   Paris 1930

French director. One of the stable of *Cahiers du cinéma* critics, Chabrol inaugurated the New Wave* with *Le Beau Serge* (1957), *Les Cousins* (1958) and *Les Bonnes femmes* (1960). Like other early New Wave films, these were characterised by independent production, location shooting, new stars (Jean-Claude Brialy*, Stéphane Audran*) and a focus on a young, disaffected generation. Chabrol soon departed from this idiom to enter on a prolific and varied career embracing comedies (*Marie-Chantal contre le docteur Khâ*, 1965), thrillers (*A double tour/Web of Passion*, 1959), war films (*La Ligne de démarcation*, 1966), political thrillers (*Les Noces rouges/Blood Wedding*, 1973, *Nada*, 1974), a 'lesbian' drama (*Les Biches/The Does*, 1968), and more; his filmography runs to over forty features. If there is unity in Chabrol's work, it can be found along two axes. The first is his work with his main star (and for a long time, wife) Stéphane Audran, especially *Le Boucher* (1970) and their superb 'dramas of adultery': *La Femme infidèle/The Unfaithful Wife* (1969), *La Rupture/The Breakup* (1970) and *Juste avant la nuit/Just Before Nightfall* (1971). The second is Chabrol's dissection of the French bourgeoisie, which ranges from the incisive to the affectionate, usually in the thriller format. At the incisive end are *Que la bête meure/Killer!* (1969) and *Violette Nozière* (1978); more affectionate are *Poulet au vinaigre/Cop au vin* (1984), *Masques* (1987) and *Le Cri du hibou/The Cry of the Owl* (1987). With his lush adaptation of *Madame Bovary* (1991, with Isabelle Huppert*), Chabrol made an excursion into the Heritage cinema* genre, though *Betty* (1992) and *L'Enfer* (1994) signal a return to the bourgeois thrillers. Ironically, given Chabrol's critical beginnings, there is a comfortable 'quality' to his films, which is, however, far from unpleasurable. GV

Other Films Include: *Les Godelureaux* (1961); *Landru* (1963); *Paris vu par ...* (1965, ep. 'La Muette'); *Le Scandale/The Champagne Murders*, *La Route de Corinthe* (1967); *La*

Décade prodigieuse/Ten Days Wonder (1971); *Docteur Popaul* (1972); *Une partie de plaisir* (1974); *Le Cheval d'orgueil* (1980); *Les Fantômes du chapelier/The Hatter's Ghosts* (1982); *Le Sang des autres/The Blood of Others* (1984); *Inspecteur Lavardin* (1986); *Une affaire de femmes* (1988); *Jours tranquilles à Clichy/Quiet Days in Clichy, Docteur M* (1990).

CHAGOLL, Lydia   Voorburg 1931

Belgian director and editor; also dancer and choreographer, who has worked in opera and theatre, and for 'Flemish' and Francophone public television. From the 1960s, she also published books evoking her memories as a prisoner in World War II Japanese camps.

Her films attack injustice, violence and ill-treatment. *De stille getuigen/The Silent Witnesses* and *In naam van de Führer/In the Name of the Führer* (both 1977) are two of her most valuable documentaries, confronting us with the horrors of the Holocaust. The latter was especially controversial. Given awards at some festivals, it was boycotted by others. *Voor een glimlach van een kind/For a Child's Smile* (1982) denounces ill-treatment of children through an imaginative combination of reconstruction and interviews. SS

CHANNEL 4

British institution, whose establishment in 1982 signalled a change in the relationship between British cinema and television. Channel 4 was conceived as a publisher-broadcaster rather than a producer-broadcaster like the BBC or the ITV companies, with the Channel commissioning its original work rather than producing programmes itself. Under this system, the series 'Film on Four' was established, commissioning films for television from independent producers, with investment set at around £500,000. In operation the system became a form of patronage for the low- to medium-budget feature film, with Channel 4 holding back transmission of some films to give them life in the cinema, entering into partnerships with the BFI* Production Board or British Screen, or investing in (continental) European films. Out of this came such films as *The Draughtsman's Contract* (1982), *A Letter to Brezhnev* (1985), *My Beautiful Laundrette* (1985), and investment in, for example, *Paris, Texas* (1984, Ger./Fr.). In addition, the legislation which established Channel 4 wrote into its remit that it should experiment and innovate and cater for audiences not previously addressed. Accordingly, the commissioning editor for Independent Film and Video had the responsibility of seeking new production from oppositional groups like Cinema Action, from small regionally based companies, and from the Workshop Movement* which the Channel helped to develop. The remit was extended to include investment in Third World cinema. At the beginning of the 1980s, at one level Channel 4 seemed to provide the context for a medium-budget art cinema, and at another level it was creating a diversity of access to film production – and, as a national broadcaster, to film viewing. Government legislation in 1991 made Channel 4 more dependent than it had been on advertising revenue, and the accountants had to count the costs of patronage more carefully. While support of the Workshops was cut off at the beginning of the 1990s, and much of the radical excitement soured into scepticism, Channel 4 still deserves credit for fostering such directors as Terence Davies*, Isaac Julien* and Derek Jarman*. In the 1990s, it has surprised many by its success in an increasingly commercial broadcasting environment, and it is still a major part of the infrastructure of a new British art cinema. JC

Bib: John Pym, *Film on Four: A Survey, 1982–1991* (1992).

CHAPLIN

Swedish film magazine. Founded in 1959 by Bengt Forslund and published by the Swedish Film Institute, the bimonthly *Chaplin* is the leading Swedish film magazine, containing popular interviews and reviews as well as essays and articles about film politics, film theory and film technique. During the 1960s it was a forum for politically committed debate, the nearest thing Sweden had to *Cahiers du cinéma*. *Chaplin* is published in both Swedish and English. LGA

CHAPLIN, Geraldine   Santa Monica, California 1944

American actress prominent in Spanish and French cinema; Charlie Chaplin's eldest daughter. Her international reputation grew after David Lean's* *Doctor Zhivago* (1965). Appearing as a child actress, notably in her father's *Limelight* (1952), she trained in ballet before resuming a career in cinema. Her dark long hair, fragile androgynous beauty and fluency in French and Spanish have been used to interesting and sometimes incongruous effect by a range of *auteurs*, especially Carlos Saura*, with whom she enjoyed a personal and professional relationship between 1967 and 1979 (their films include *Ana y los lobos/Ana and the Wolves*, 1972; *Cría cuervos/Raise Ravens* 1975; and *Elisa, vida mía/Elisa, My Love,* 1977), as well as Jacques Rivette* (*Noroit*, 1977; *L'Amour par terre*, 1984) and Alain Resnais* (*La Vie est un roman*, 1983; *I Want to Go Home*, 1989). Chaplin has also worked in television and American cinema (with directors such as Robert Altman and Alan Rudolph). She appeared as her own grandmother Hannah in Richard Attenborough's* *Chaplin* (1992). MD

CHÁVARRI, Jaime   Madrid 1943

Spanish director, who studied at the Escuela Oficial de Cinematografía*, and made shorts and Super-8 films before his first feature, *Los viajes escolares/School Trips* (1973), which, like *El desencanto/Disenchantment* (1976), exposes the repressiveness of conventional family structures in a way that alludes to contemporary politics and institutions. His next two films, *A un Dios desconocido/To an Unknown God* (1977) and *Dedicatoria/A Dedication* (1980), retained a polemical focus. Their treatment of homosexuality and incest reflects Chávarri's broader interest in dissident sexual relationships, also taken up in the later, more commercial *Las cosas del querer/The Things of Love* (1989). His most popular film is *Las bicicletas son para el verano/Bicycles are for the Summer* (1984), an account of the Spanish Civil War through its effects on an ordinary Madrid family, particularly the son, played by the then novice Gabino Diego*, who also stars in Chávarri's latest film, *Tierno verano de lujurias y azoteas/A Tender Summer of Lust on the Rooftops* (1993). IS

CHENAL, Pierre
Philippe Cohen; Brussels 1904 – La Garenne-Colombes 1991

French director, one of the most interesting yet least known of the classical French film-makers. A talented draughtsman and poster designer, close to the Surrealists, and a communist sympathiser, Chenal started with documentaries, including on the cinema. His first feature was the extraordinary *Le Martyre de l'obèse* (1932), on the amorous tribulations of an extremely fat man. His second, *La Rue sans nom* (1933), based on Marcel Aymé's novel about a derelict Parisian street, was the first to attract the label of Poetic Realism*. Chenal's subsequent work included prestigious literary adaptations (*Crime et châtiment/Crime and Punishment*, 1935, *L'Homme de nulle part/The Late Mathias Pascal*, 1936, *L'Affaire Lafarge*, 1937) and populist films like *La Maison du Maltais/Sirocco* (1938). *L'Alibi* (1937) – starring a great Louis Jouvet*/Erich von Stroheim duo – and the (first) adaptation of James Cain's *The Postman Always Rings Twice* as *Le Dernier tournant* (1939) mark Chenal as a pioneer of French *film noir*. Chenal spent the war years in Argentina, where he made several films, returning to France to direct the classic comedy of French provincialism, *Clochemerle* (1948), and several excellent *policiers*, in particular *Section des disparus* (1956) based on David Goodis and *Rafles sur la ville/Sinners of Paris* (1958), which were praised by Jean-Luc Godard*. He also made the anti-racist *Sangre Negra/Native Son* (1949–51, Argentina/US), based on, and starring, the novelist Richard Wright. GV

Bib: Pierrette Matalon, Claude Guiguet, Jacques Pinturault, *Pierre Chenal* (1987).

CHERKASOV, Nikolai K.
St Petersburg 1903 – Leningrad 1966

Russian Soviet actor. After a career on stage in Leningrad, Cherkasov began playing small comic roles in films, such as Vladimir Gardin's* *Poet i tsar'/The Poet and the Tsar* (1927). His first major dramatic roles were the leading part in Iosif Kheifits's* and Natan Zarkhi's *Deputat Baltiki/Baltic Deputy*, and that of the tsarevich Alexei in Vladimir Petrov's* *Pëtr I/Peter the Great* (both 1937). He has played Gorky, Pavlov, Rimsky-Korsakov and Mayakovsky, but shot to international prominence with his title roles in Sergei Eisenstein's* *Aleksandr Nevskii/Alexander Nevsky* (1938) and *Ivan Groznyi/Ivan the Terrible* (1944–45, Part Two released 1958). Cherkasov accompanied Eisenstein when he was summoned to see Stalin*, Molotov and Zhdanov in 1946 to discuss the 'errors' of Part Two of the latter film. After Stalin's death,

Cherkasov made his last major film appearance in Grigori Kozintsev's* *Don Quixote* (1957). He was also a deputy to the USSR Supreme Soviet. RT

Bib: Nikolai Cherkasov, *Notes of a Soviet Actor* (n.d.).

CHEVALIER, Maurice
Paris 1888–1972

French singer and actor. The leading French male music-hall star of the twentieth century, Chevalier long embodied the international stereotype of the Frenchman. After an impoverished Parisian childhood, 'Momo' quickly graduated from local *cafés-concerts* to stardom in the great Parisian music halls. A superstar in 1920s Paris, he led stage revues with hit songs like 'Valentine', his stage persona a winsome mixture of cocky *gavroche* and dandy. He was soon signed by Paramount. Chevalier, who had already appeared in many French shorts, made sixteen US movies between 1928 and 1935. *Innocents of Paris* and *The Love Parade* (both 1929) were his first hits, followed by many others; the best – *The Smiling Lieutenant* (1931), *One Hour With You* (1932) and *The Merry Widow* (1934) – were directed by Ernst Lubitsch*. In the make-believe universe of these musicals, Chevalier epitomised the frivolously sexy Parisian, with emphatic gestures and heavy French accent. Returning to Europe in 1935, he made a few films which were (surprisingly) only moderately successful, his Hollywood glamour clashing with French populism in the underrated *L'Homme du jour* (1936, dir. Julien Duvivier*), *Avec le sourire/With a Smile* (1936, dir. Maurice Tourneur*) and *Pièges/Personal Column* (1939), Robert Siodmak's* last French film. He also starred in René Clair's* *Break the News* (1938, UK) and Curtis (Kurt) Bernhardt's* *The Beloved Vagabond*, made in London in 1936. A performing tour for French prisoners of war in Germany caused Chevalier problems at the Liberation. However, he went on singing and acting, notably in René Clair's* *Le Silence est d'or/Man About Town* (1947) and Vincente Minnelli's *Gigi* (1958). Both are nostalgic pieces in which Chevalier incarnates an aging beau, symbolising a vanishing era of popular entertainment. GV

Bib: Gene Ringgold and DeWitt Bodeen, *Chevalier, The Films and Career of Maurice Chevalier* (1973).

CHIARI, Walter
Walter Annichiarico; Verona 1924–91

Italian actor. The very young Chiari gained wide popularity at the end of the war through variety shows and musical comedies. Throughout the 1950s and 1960s, his persona of the boasting lovable rogue, his ability to improvise and his brilliant talkativeness made him one of the first Italian television stars. As man and artist, Chiari was inclined to dissipation, living 'some hundred real and imaginary lives'; like many other 'kings' of variety shows (Erminio Macario*, Ugo Tognazzi*, among others), he 'wasted' his film acting, confining his roles to parody and character sketches (*Totò al giro d'Italia*, 1948; *Mogli e buoi ...*, 1956; *Gli zitelloni*, 1958; *Un* dollaro di fifa, 1960; Walter e i suoi cugini, 1961; I magnifici tre, 1962), sometimes playing doubles or twins (I cadetti di Guascogna, 1950; I gemelli del Texas, 1964). From 1947 to 1968 he made eighty-five films. Among his few dramatic roles, some consideration must be given to Giorgio Pastina's Vanità (1947), where he plays a 'tough' guy living in early twentieth-century Milan, and to Luchino Visconti's* Bellissima (1951), where he is the unforgettable Annovazzi, a mean trickster trying to take advantage of Anna Magnani*. Indeed, there was in Walter Chiari a really dramatic (if clownish) vein, a hidden and perhaps more authentic dimension, hinted at in films such as Mario Monicelli's* Donatella (1956), Alessandro Blasetti's* Io, io, io ... e gli altri (1966), Nanni Loy's Made in Italy (1965), and fully exploited only by Dino Risi's* Il giovedí (1962), the story of a clumsy divorced father who spends a gloomy afternoon with his son, and by Damiano Damiani in La rimpatriata (1963). Apart from Orson Welles' Campanadas a medianoche/Chimes at Midnight (1966), where he plays a hilarious Silence, in the last years of Chiari's life only a few young directors were able to exploit his melancholy histrionics: Peter del Monte in Tracce di vita amorosa (1990) and especially Massimo Mazzucco in Romance (1986). GVo

CHIARINI, Luigi   Rome 1900–75

Italian critic and director. During the 1930s and 1940s Chiarini, along with Umberto Barbaro*, played an important role in the promotion of Italian cinema. From its foundation in 1934, he directed the Centro Sperimentale* in Rome, contributing to its magazine Bianco e nero as well as writing his book Cinque capitoli sul film (1941). Influenced by the idealist philosophy of Giovanni Gentile, he insisted on the need to consider cinema in all its complexity, saying that 'film is an art, cinema is an industry'. He called for the expressive specificity and autonomy of cinema, summed up in his formula 'film as an absolute form', a formula he developed in the five films he directed: Via delle Cinque Lune (1942), La bella addormentata/Sleeping Beauty (1942), La locandiera (1943), Ultimo amore (1947) and Patto col diavolo (1950). These are highly theoretical, erudite, 'literary' movies, sophisticated from a figurative point of view but ultimately academic. During the postwar period Chiarini became a crucial presence in the Italian cultural landscape. He was then influenced by the Marxist Gramsci, although still within a Gentilian perspective, and published his most mature books: Il film nei problemi dell'arte (1949), Il film nella battaglia delle idee (1954), Cinema quinto potere (1954), Arte e tecnica del film (1952), all of which were attentive to the problems of the media and culture industries. After leaving the Centro Sperimentale in 1951, Chiarini was the first person in Italy to teach film history, first at the University of Pisa (1961–66) and eventually at the University of Urbino. His ideas may today appear a little outdated, but he remains an important figure for the affirmation of cinema as an art form and a language. From 1964 to 1968 he was director of the Venice* Film Festival, a position from which he was displaced both by the political radicalism of 1968 and changes in the media industries. GVo

CHIAURELI, Mikhail E.   Tbilisi, Georgia [Russian Empire] 1894 – USSR 1974

Georgian Soviet director and actor. Chiaureli graduated from art school in Tbilisi and made his first screen appearance in the title role in the first Georgian feature film, Ivan Perestiani's* Arsen Dzhordzhiashvili/The Murder of General Gryaznov (1921). He appeared in several Georgian features during the 1920s and made his directorial debut with V poslednii chas/At the Last Moment (1928), set in the Civil War. He made an experimental satire, Khabarda (1931), co-scripted with Sergei Tretyakov, and the first Georgian sound feature, Poslednii maskarad/The Last Masquerade (1934), followed by two works devoted to Georgian history, Arsen (1937) and Georgii Saakadze (1942–43). Chiaureli is best known, however, for the three films that constituted the kernel of Stalin's* 'personality cult': Velikoe zarevo/The Great Dawn (1938), Klyatva/The Vow (1946) and Padenie Berlina/The Fall of Berlin (1949), Mosfilm studio's seventieth birthday present to Stalin. The last of these, made on Agfacolor stock taken from Nazi Germany as war booty, constitutes the apotheosis of the Stalin cult and defines the postwar 'Empire style' of Soviet propaganda. Unsurprisingly, Stalin awarded all three films the Stalin Prize. RT

CHOMÓN, Segundo de   Segundo de Chomón Ruiz; Teruel 1871 – Paris, France 1927

Spanish director. One of the pioneers of Spanish cinema, Chomón set up his own workshop in Barcelona for making cameras, and for shooting and distributing films. His first film, Choque de trenes/Train Crash (1902), is an early example of juxtaposition and of the use of models for special effects. Chomón was fascinated by the possibilities of the medium and, in Gulliver en el país de los gigantes/Gulliver and the Giants (1903), he developed superimposition techniques allowing him to show giants and the conventionally sized Gulliver simultaneously. Other important experiments and discoveries developed by Chomón include the use of the tracking shot, animation and backdrops. His reputation earned him a contract with Pathé* in Paris, from where he eventually moved on to Turin. His talents were used by many others, including Abel Gance* for Napoleon (1926), in an uncredited sequence. He made over 150 films. PWE

CHRISTENSEN, Benjamin   Viborg 1879 – Copenhagen 1959

Danish director and actor, who began his career as an opera singer. He made his screen debut in 1912 and the following year bought a film company, Dansk Biograf. Here he directed Det hemmelighedsfulde X/The Mysterious X/Sealed Orders (1914), of which he was also producer, set designer, lead actor and distributor. He fulfilled the same multiple roles for his second film, Hævnens Nat/Blind Justice (1916). Christensen's talent was already evident: it was characterised by sharp editing, sophisticated lighting and mobile camerawork. His third film, Häxan/Witchcraft Through the Ages (1922), was produced by the Swedish company Svensk Filmindustri, though shot in Danish studios with Danish actors (Christensen himself had a major part as the Devil) and Danish technicians, among them the cameraman Johan Ankerstjerne*. *Häxan* is one of the most bizarre and intriguing movies in film history, an early masterpiece of the horror genre. Planned as an educational film about witchcraft, it developed into a passionate, sensuous but also horrific description of the perception of witchcraft through the Middle Ages and the Renaissance. The film provoked admiration for its daring subject and visual mastery (finding some of its inspiration in Renaissance painting), but also scandal for its sexual theme and scenes of nudity. Banned in several countries, it earned Christensen an invitation to work for Ufa* in Germany, where he directed several films, including *Seine Frau, die Unbekannte/His Mysterious Adventure* (1923), and played a lead role in Carl Theodor Dreyer's* German film *Michael/Mikaël/Chained* (1924). In 1925 he moved to Hollywood; in a stay of a decade he directed mostly thrillers, among them *The Haunted House* (1928) and *Seven Footprints to Satan* (1929).

When Christensen returned to Denmark in 1934, Danish cinema was at a low ebb. He made his directorial comeback with *Skilsmissens Børn/Children of Divorce* (1938), a film advanced both in theme – the effects of divorce on children – and *mise-en-scène*. However, the three subsequent films he directed before retiring in 1943 (to manage a cinema), including *Damen med de lyse Handsker/The Lady with the Light Gloves* (1942), failed to re-establish his earlier reputation. ME

CHRISTENSEN, Theodor   Holbrek 1914 – Copenhagen 1967

Danish director and theoretician. Theodor Christensen directed his first documentary, *C – et Hjørne af Danmark/C – a Corner of Denmark,* in 1938, beginning a long career in the genre. Besides practical film work, he became the best Danish film theoretician of his generation, co-writing one of the earliest Danish theoretical works on film (*Film*, 1936, with Karl Roos). An inspiring teacher, he lectured at the Cuban Film School and the Danish Film School, of which he was a leading light until his death.

Christensen was influenced in his practice both by theoreticians such as Béla Balázs*, Rudolf Arnheim* and Sergei Eisenstein*, and by the British documentary movement*, especially the John Grierson* school. One of his earliest films, *Iran, Det ny Persien/Iran, The New Persia* (1939), shows the clear influence of Basil Wright* and Harry Watt's* *Night Mail* (1936). During the German occupation Christensen made documentaries clandestinely. His *Denmark Fights for Freedom* (1944), a record of the Danish resistance, was smuggled out of the country to publicise the efforts of the movement. After the war Christensen directed *Det gælder din Frihed/Your Freedom is at Stake* (1946), a historical account of the war period as seen through the eyes of the resistance. He also made *Her er banerne/This is the Railway* (1948) and *Enden på legen/The End of the Game* (1960). ME

CHRISTIAN-JAQUE   Christian Maudet; Paris 1904–94

French director, one of the most versatile and successful French film-makers. After poster design and art direction he worked for Paramount in Joinville in 1931. A French-style Michael Curtiz, Christian-Jaque succeeded in virtually all genres. After *Les Disparus de Saint-Agil/Boys School* (1938), a boarding-school story starring Erich von Stroheim, his 1940s films are considered his best: costume dramas (*La Symphonie fantastique*, 1942, *La Chartreuse de Parme/La certosa di Parma*, 1948), literary adaptations (*Boule de suif/ Angel and Sinner*, 1945), bourgeois dramas (*Un revenant/A Lover's Return*, 1946). However, his Fernandel* vehicles of the 1930s – especially *Un de la Légion* (1936) – deserve re-evaluation, as do the swashbuckler *Fanfan la Tulipe* (1952, best director at Cannes 1952) and some of his films with his then wife Martine Carol*: *Adorable créatures/Adorable Creatures* (1952), *Nana* (1955), *Nathalie/The Foxiest Girl in Paris* (1957). From the 1960s he continued in genre films with some success – for instance, *La Tulipe noire/The Black Tulip* (1964) with Alain Delon*, and the spoof Western *Les Pétroleuses/The Ballad of Frenchie King* (1971), with Brigitte Bardot* and Claudia Cardinale*. He also worked in television. GV

CHRISTIE, Julie   Chukua, India 1941

British actress, who emerged as a star in the 1960s, representing the liberated woman before women's liberation was formally recognised. In *Billy Liar* (1963), in her first major role, she is the free spirit in the grim northern city who cuts through the male dreams of leaving, and actually escapes, leaving Tom Courtenay's bags on the station platform as monuments to lost desire. 'With Julie Christie,' says Alexander Walker, 'the British cinema caught the train south.' The train was heading for the swinging 1960s, for which Christie became an icon. In *Darling* (1965), the iconic movie of the period, her character is both celebrated for her freedom and punished for her independence, playing out the ambivalence of the sexual revolution. Her performance won her an Oscar, and awards from the New York Critics and the British Film Academy. Carrying her independence into her personal life and career, Christie has been discriminating and her filmography contains few of the clunkers which pepper the careers of most British stars of her generation. She has been as successful in Hollywood as in Britain in securing interesting projects, including her role in Altman's *McCabe & Mrs. Miller* (1971) for which she received an Oscar nomination. Her recent work has included a number of voice commentaries on television documentaries on political issues, and her commitment to feminism led her to accept a lead role in Sally Potter's* *The Gold Diggers* (1983), a low-budget film with an all-women crew on which all participants were paid the same wage. JC

Other Films Include: *Young Cassidy, Doctor Zhivago* (1965); *Fahrenheit 451* (1966); *Far from the Madding Crowd* (1967); *Petulia* (1968, US); *In Search of Gregory* (1969); *The Go-*

Between (1970); *Don't Look Now* (1973); *Shampoo* (1974, US); *Nashville* [cameo as herself] (1975, US); *The Demon Seed* (1977, US); *Heaven Can Wait* (1978, US); *Memoirs of a Survivor* (1981); *The Return of the Soldier, Heat and Dust* (1983); *Power* (1986, US); *Miss Mary* (1987, Argentina); *La Mémoire tatouée/Secret Obsession* (1988, Fr/Tunisia); *Fools of Fortune* (1990).

CHUKHRAI, Grigori N.   Melitopol, Ukraine 1921

Soviet director. Graduated from the workshop run by Mikhail Romm* and Sergei Yutkevich* at VGIK* in 1953 and began making films for Mosfilm in 1955. His first film, *Sorok pervyi/The Forty-first* (1956), won a Special Prize at Cannes in 1957, but he is best known for two war films: *Ballada o soldate/Ballad of a Soldier* (1959, prizes at Cannes and Venice, and Lenin Prize in 1961), and *Chistoe nebo/Clear Sky* (1961), a prize-winner at the Moscow Film Festival. He continued making films into the 1980s and taught at VGIK from 1966 to 1971. His films reflect a concern for individuals caught up in the tide of historical events. RT

CHYTILOVÁ, Věra   Ostrava 1929

Czech director. Věra Chytilová worked as a draughtswoman, fashion model and continuity person before studying at FAMU* (1957–62). Her commitment to experiment was already apparent in her student films, and her graduation film, *Strop/Ceiling* (1962), the study of a fashion model, was a defiant mixture of *cinéma-vérité** and formalism. There were echoes of this in her first feature, *O něčem jiném/Something Different* (1963), which told the parallel stories of a woman gymnast and a housewife, the first as documentary, the second as fiction. Working with her husband, the cinematographer Jaroslav Kučera, and writer/designer Ester Krumbachová, Chytilová directed the two most inventive films of the Czech New Wave*, *Sedmikrásky/Daisies* (1966) and *Ovoce stromů rajských jíme/The Fruit of Paradise/We Eat the Fruit of the Trees of Paradise* (1969). The first was a nonnarrative montage of the destructive antics of two female teenagers which demonstrated that an avant-garde film could also be funny, while the second was an allegorical portrait of male/female relations presented in images of remarkable formal beauty. After the Soviet invasion of 1968, such excesses were not encouraged and Chytilová found herself unable to work. In 1976, she wrote an open letter to President Husák and was surprisingly reinstated, returning with a lively parable of sexual relations, *Hra o jablko/The Apple Game* (1976), and the unusually abrasive moral tale *Panelstory/Prefab Story* (1981). She renewed her collaboration with Krumbachová for a comic portrayal of a middle-aged Don Juan, *Faunovo velmi pozdní odpoledne/The Very Late Afternoon of a Faun* (1983). In recent years she has derived much of her inspiration from theatre, directing a film version of the mime play *Šašek a královna/The Jester and the Queen* (1987), and working with the avant-garde theatre group Sklep (The Cellar) on *Kopytem sem, kopytem tam/Tainted*

Horseplay/Snowball Reaction/A Hoof Here, A Hoof There (1988). A retrospective of her films was shown on French television in 1989, but she has still to receive similar recognition from the English-speaking world. PH

Other Films: *Pytel blech/A Bagful of Fleas* [short, released together with *Strop* as *U stropu je pytel blech/There's a Bagful of Fleas at the Ceiling*] (1962); *Perličky na dně/Pearls of the Deep* [episode *Automat 'Svět'/At the World Cafeteria*] (1965); *Čas je neúprosný/Inexorable Time* [short] (1978); *Kalamita/Calamity* (1980); *Chytilová versus Forman* [short] (1981, Belgium); *Praha, neklidné srdce Evropy/Prague, Restless Heart of Europe* [short] (1984); *Vlčí bouda/Wolf's Cabin* (1986); *T.G.M. – osvoboditel/Tomáš G. Masaryk – The Liberator* [short] (1990); *Mí Pražané mi rozumějí/My Inhabitants of Prague Understand Me* (1991); *Dědictví aneb Kurvahošigutntag/Inheritance or Shit-Boys-Gutntag* (1992).

CIFESA (Compañía Industrial de Film Español/Industrial Company of Spanish Film)

Spanish production company, founded in Valencia by Vicente Casanova in 1932. Cifesa's comedies* and historical films* provided the Franco regime with a useful publicity machine for over a decade. Cifesa was the closest thing to a Hollywood studio in Spain, with its roster of creative personnel and stars. The historical melodramas at first concentrated on male (e.g. Juan Antonio Arévalo's *¡Harka!*, 1941) and subsequently on female heroics (e.g. Juan de Orduña's* *Agustina de Aragón/Agustina of Aragon*, 1950). In these films Spanish history was rewritten as the triumph of Nationalist beliefs over native or foreign forms of 'decadence'. The common surface celebration of regional difference merely camouflages an ideology of national unity developed by a regime ruthlessly determined to disavow regionalist sensibilities. Foreigners are usually cardboard cut-out figures of ridicule or villainy, or both. Cifesa's most neurotically chauvinistic film was Orduña's *Alba de América/Dawn of America* (1951), made in reply to Gainsborough* studios' *Christopher Columbus* (1948). The latter's representation of Spain as a land riddled with disease, corruption and bloodshed is replaced by Cifesa's transformation of the country into a haven of moral and spiritual nobility, while Fredric March's opportunist adventurer is replaced by Antonio Vilar's Messianic great discoverer. Even so, for all their compromises with dictatorship ideology, Cifesa's enormously popular films were often surprisingly characterised by contradiction. The lyricising of traditionalist forms of masculinity in *¡Harka!*, a military narrative set in North Africa, amazingly raises through its dynamics of male bonding taboo questions about homosexuality. Equally, in the female-centred narratives, the representation of heroic femininity through the commanding presence of stars like Aurora Bautista* or Amparo Rivelles*, Cifesa's Crawford and Stanwyck, allows for some problematising of apparently conformist narratives and stereotypical characters. These films, as well as Cifesa's screwball-style comedies (such as Orduña's *Tuvo la culpa Adán/Adam's Fault*, 1943), distracted the population from the hardships of the postwar years. Eventually, with foreign imports taking their toll of home-grown products, Cifesa switched from production to distribution in 1952, before closing down in 1964. PWE

Bib: Félix Fanés, *Cifesa: la antorcha de los éxitos* (1982).

CINE NEGRO

Spanish film genre. Drawing from Hollywood *film noir* and French *policier** traditions in melodramas and crime thrillers like *Brigada criminal/Criminal Brigade* (1950), *Los atracadores/The Robbers* (1961) and *Crimen de doble filo/Double-edged Crime* (1964), Spanish *cine negro* was one of the few film cycles to dramatise the social discontent characteristic of Franco's Spain in the 1950s and 1960s. Exploited in equal measure, as Marsha Kinder has observed in *Blood Cinema*, by both ends of the political spectrum, *cine negro* shaped equally the melodrama of the right-wing *Surcos/Furrows* (1951, dir. José Antonio Nieves Conde*) and the left-wing *Muerte de un ciclista/Death of a Cyclist* (1955, dir. Juan Antonio Bardem*). Eschewing the American *noir* tradition of focusing on the transgressive woman, these films tended to be critiques of patriarchy (and by implication of Franco's dictatorship), foregrounding the violation of the law by young men in need of a suitable role model. The post-Franco revival of *cine negro*, however, in such contemporary films as *El crack/The Crack* (1980, dir. José Luis Garci*), *Matador* (1986, dir. Pedro Almodóvar*), *Amantes/Lovers* (1990, dir. Vicente Aranda*), and *Beltenebros/Prince of Shadows* (1991, dir. Pilar Miró*), is more clearly aligned with the American tradition, particularly with the postmodern offerings of the 1980s and 1990s which have witnessed a hyperbolic return to the figure of the *femme fatale*. Aranda's *Fanny Pelopaja/Fanny Straw Top* (1984), a violent and erotic study of sado-masochism, is possibly the most fascinating of the recent examples of the form. RM

Bib: Marsha Kinder, *Blood Cinema* (1993).

CINECITTÀ

Italian studio. This complex of film studios in Rome, opened in 1937, has served as a major centre of Italian film production for decades. After a mysterious fire destroyed Carlo Roncoroni's Cines* studios in 1935, Roncoroni and Luigi Freddi* struck an agreement to construct, with state subsidies, a new production complex on a large site on the outskirts of Rome. The facility, envisioned as a new 'cinema city' ('Cinecittà'), was designed by Freddi and architect Gino Peresutti. Its construction began in January 1936, with Mussolini ceremonially laying the cornerstone, and it was opened, again by Mussolini, in 1937. Government subsidies for its construction were spread over four years (1935–39), during most of which Cinecittà was technically owned and operated by Roncoroni. After his death in September 1938, it was taken over by the government and run by a senator and former industrialist, Giovanni Tofani. By 1939, Cinecittà had become the largest cinema complex in Italy, centralising Italian film production more than it had ever been. Between 1937 and 1939, Cinecittà's ten sound stages became the production sites for almost two-thirds of all films made in Italy. By 1942, the number of sound stages had grown to twelve (with two additional ones at the nearby Centro Sperimentale*), as compared to twelve other sound stages in Rome, four in Turin, and three in Tirrenia.

With the fall of Fascism, Cinecittà came to symbolise for many Italian film-makers a kind of film too closely associated with the regime. In 1945 its facilities were briefly taken over by the Allies for use as a refugee camp. But in the 1950s Cinecittà once again became one of the most important sites for Italian film production, whether by producers of genre films such as the peplum* or *auteur* films such as Federico Felllini's* *8½* (1963). JHa

CINÉMA *BEUR*

French film genre of the 1980s. '*Beur*' is French slang – a play on *arabe* – for second-generation North Africans in France, children of the 1950s and 1960s immigrants. As this generation came of age and immigration made its way up the political agenda in the mid-1980s, a number of them made films featuring *beur* characters as part of post-colonial, multi-ethnic urban France. Unlike the authors of experimental British black cinema such as Isaac Julien*, *beur* film-makers chose mainstream narratives and realism to dramatise the lives of their heroes.

Though minimising racism (in contrast to the militant cinema of the earlier generation), the world of *beur* films is embedded in poverty and unemployment (Abdelkrim Bahloul's *Le Thé à la menthe/Mint Tea*, 1984; Mehdi Charef's *Le Thé au harem d'Archimède/Tea in the Harem*, 1985, and *Miss Mona*, 1987; Rachid Bouchareb's *Bâton Rouge*, 1985, and *Cheb*, 1991). Dominant themes are a desire for integration and the difficulty of belonging to either French or Arabic culture. *Beur* cinema's focus on young men is not devoid of misogyny and homophobia, and its lack of militancy arguably dilutes its impact. It nevertheless shows, in accessible form, a complex and sympathetic representation of ethnic identity in modern France, challenging traditional negative stereotypes. It is difficult to say if the fading of *beur* cinema in the early 1990s – one exception being Malik Chibane's *Hexagone* (1994) – is a function of integration (Charef's last two films, *Camomille*, 1988, and *Au pays des Juliets*, 1992, are not concerned with specific *beur* issues), or a symptom of political backlash. GV

CINÉMA DU LOOK

French film genre, which arose with Jean-Jacques Beineix's* *Diva* in 1981, designating youth-oriented films with high production values. Subsequent titles include Beineix's *37°2 le matin/Betty Blue* (1986), Luc Besson's* *Subway* (1985) and *Nikita* (1990), and Leos Carax's* *Mauvais Sang/The Night is Young* (1986). Another possible candidate is Jean-Pierre Jennet and Marc Caro's *Delicatessen* (1991). The 'look' of the *cinéma du look* refers to the films' high investment in non-naturalistic, self-conscious aesthetics, notably intense colours and lighting effects. Their spectacular (studio-based) and technically brilliant *mise-en-scène* is usually put to the service of romantic plots. The *cinéma du look* is popular at the box office but hated by critics who dislike its calculated borrowings from advertising, music videos and cartoons, summarised by *Cahiers du cinéma** as 'postcard aesthetics'. *Cahiers,* and in its wake many Anglo-American critics, see the films as typical of a post-modern, 'image for image's sake' style in their lack of social or ideological substance; other French critics more positively label them 'neo-baroque'. These debates reveal both an uneasiness about the status of cinema in the age of other media and a deep reluctance to accept forms of French cinema which do not follow the norms of *auteur* cinema. After *Nikita,* and with the failure of Beineix's *IP5* (1992), it looked like the moment had passed, but the international success of Besson's *Leon* (1994), shot in English, may yet give the *cinéma du look* a second life. GV

CINÉMA-VÉRITÉ

French film term, designating an international trend in postwar documentary film-making; in Europe, a type of film making extensive use of interviews. A literal translation of Dziga Vertov's* *Kino-Pravda,* the expression originated with the sociologist Edgar Morin, who, with Jean Rouch*, directed the key *cinéma-vérité* work: *Chronique d'un été/Chronicle of a Summer* (1961), in which Parisians respond to personal questions and the film-makers appear in the film, reflecting on their own practice. Other important films are Rouch's *Moi, un noir* (1959) and Chris Marker's* *Le Joli mai* (1963). *Cinéma-vérité* is indebted both to Vertov and to Robert Flaherty*, a dual heritage indicative of the splits at the centre of the concept: on the Soviet side spontaneity but montage, on the American side a non-interventionist observation of the subjects' lifestyles shot in long takes. *Cinéma-vérité* raises wider issues about objectivity and 'manipulation', touching on a question central to all documentary, that of authenticity, although on the whole it aimed to reveal rather than capture 'truth'. *Cinéma-vérité* was made possible by new technologies – sensitive film stock, portable cameras and sound equipment – and coincided with the advent of television and a growing interest in sociology. Perhaps more than in the films themselves, its importance resides in its hybrid use in fiction films such as those of the New Wave*. GV
[> DOCUMENTARY; FREE CINEMA]

CINÉMATHÈQUE FRANÇAISE

French film archive. Founded in September 1936, the Cinémathèque was not the first film archive in the world, nor even the largest; but it is probably the most famous, its place in history secured by its educational function as a 'school' for generations of *cinéphiles*, including the New Wave*. For a long time, its history overlapped with that of director and co-founder Henri Langlois*, whose idiosyncratic methods and lack of administrative skills were legendary. Langlois preferred accumulation of prints and screenings to cataloguing, restoring and housekeeping; two fires destroyed important collections. The attempt by André Malraux, Minister for Culture, to impose an administrator in 1968 caused a celebrated furore in which international film personalities flocked to Langlois' defence. Partly in response, the Service

des Archives du Film was created in 1969 at Bois d'Arcy for the deposit (a legal obligation since 1977), storage and restoration of film prints. Since 1981 the Socialist Ministry for Culture has funded a thorough programme of cataloguing and restoration. It has also planned a massive 'image palace' in the Palais de Tokyo, next to the Palais de Chaillot where the Cinémathèque moved in 1962, to include the Cinémathèque, the FEMIS* film school and the BIFI library (Nouvelle Bibliothèque de l'Image-Filmothèque) as well as a new museum. Since Langlois' death, presidents of the Cinémathèque have included Costa-Gavras*, Jean Rouch* and Dominique Païni.

Other major French cinémathèques are the Cinémathèque de Toulouse, headed by founder Raymond Borde, the Cinémathèque Universitaire at Paris III University, and the Musée du cinéma de Lyon [> LUMIÈRE]. GV

CINÉMATHÈQUE ROYALE DE BELGIQUE / KONINKLIJK FILMARCHIEF VAN BELGIE

Belgian archive, cine-club and museum. The origins of the Cinémathèque were as *Le club de l'écran de Bruxelles,* formed by André Thirifays, Henri Storck* and Pierre Vermeylen in the early 1930s. The club originally provided a meeting place for young and enthusiastic journalists, directors and technicians. Inspired by the initiative of Henri Langlois*, creator of the Cinémathèque Française*, the group decided to turn their cine-club into a Cinémathèque in 1938. After the war it was housed in the Palais des Beaux Arts where it has remained ever since, becoming a member of the International Federation of Film Archives (FIAF) in 1946. Its most important curator, Jacques Ledoux*, was appointed in 1948.

One of the Cinémathèque Royale's early projects was a survey of the 'Ten best films of all time' in 1958, the first of its kind, and it also initiated the festival of experimental films at Knokke-le-Zoute in 1949 (the next festivals were in 1958, 1963, 1967, 1971 and 1974). Granted a state subsidy in l960, the Cinémathèque expanded into a film museum. Nowadays its archive collection, estimated at more than 80,000 films, and its specialist book library draw film critics and researchers from around the world. CF/SS

CINÉMATHÈQUE SUISSE

Swiss film archive, situated in Lausanne. A member of the International Federation of Film Archives (FIAF), and the only Swiss film archive of national standing, the Cinémathèque Suisse started in Basle in 1943, as the Schweizerisches Filmarchiv/Archives Suisses du Film, thanks to the initiative of 'Le Bon Film', the oldest film club in Switzerland (from 1931), and to three of its members: Georg Schmidt, Peter Bächlin and Harry Goldschmidt. The beginnings were difficult, and the archive closed in 1948, to be reopened in Lausanne the following year at the initiative of the Ciné-club de Lausanne, under the name of the Cinémathèque Suisse. Despite difficult circumstances it continued to expand, becoming the life work of Freddy Buache, its director since 1951. Receiving annual subsidies from the city of Lausanne since 1950 and from the Swiss Confederation since 1963, the archive's non-commercial existence was finally assured in 1981 when it was transformed into a state institution. The Cinémathèque Suisse was originally modelled on the Cinémathèque Française* (especially in the early years, when Henri Langlois* served as an invaluable source of advice). Its activities include collecting films (17,000 features, 14,500 shorts, of which 90 per cent are of foreign origin), restoration, daily screenings, and storage of film-related material. Since 1972, in the absence of a *dépôt légal* (automatic deposit of film prints), the Cinémathèque keeps a copy of every film awarded state subsidies (some 600 titles up to 1994). The *Ciné-journal suisse* (national newsreel, 1924–75) is also preserved, in a separate collection. MW

Bib: *La Cinémathèque Suisse 1943–1981: Livre d'or* (1981).

CINES

Italian production company. The name Cines has, for some fifty years, been linked with a succession of quite different enterprises. The original company was founded in Rome in 1906 by Filoteo Alberini, a pioneer of Italian silent cinema, with support from the Banco di Roma. It started by imitating Pathé*, and then specialised in historical and costume films with Mario Caserini and Enrico Guazzoni as its most prominent directors. It was a diversified company with studios in Rome in Via Vejo and a film stock production facility near Padua. In 1919 it joined the UCI consortium put together as a response to the postwar crisis but collapsed in 1924. In 1929 the Via Vejo studio was taken over by Stefano Pittaluga's* company Cines-Pittaluga, which made the first Italian sound film, *La canzone dell'amore* (1930), and produced films by Mario Camerini*, Goffredo Alessandrini* and others. After Pittaluga's death in 1931 control passed to the banker Ludovico Toeplitz, who made Emilio Cecchi* his director of production. This was a period of great success for Cines. But in 1935 Cines was restructured as part of the state-owned holding company IRI; its distribution and exhibition arms came under the state-run ENIC (Ente Nazionale Industrie Cinematografiche) while studios and production were taken over by Carlo Roncoroni under the name Cines-SAISC. A mysterious fire destroyed the Via Vejo studio in 1935 and Cines ceased to exist until 1941, when it was reconstituted in the name of the corporate state by Luigi Freddi* and subsequently produced films by Luigi Chiarini*, Carmine Gallone*, Alessandro Blasetti*, Mario Camerini* and Roberto Rossellini* (*L'uomo dalla croce*, 1942). Transferred briefly to Venice during the German occupation, the new Cines was put into liquidation in 1945. Cines returned, still as a state company, in 1949, and produced a number of films, most of them (with the exception of some by Pietro Germi* and by Luigi Zampa*) undistinguished. Deeply in debt, Cines was definitively liquidated in 1957. GVo

CINTRA, Luís Miguel   Madrid, Spain 1949

Portuguese actor, the leading Portuguese performer and theatrical director of the last twenty years. From 1970 to 1972,

Cintra attended the Old Vic theatre school in Britain. Returning to Portugal in 1973, he joined the future filmmaker Silva Melo to co-found the Teatro da Cornucópia, a company he still heads and for which he has so far directed thirty-nine productions. He also staged opera (*L'Enfant et les sortilèges, Dido and Aeneas, Le Nozze di Figaro, The Bear*). Before his stay in Britain he had acted in film, appearing in João César Monteiro's* *Quem Espera por Sapatos de Defunto...Morre Descalco/He Who Waits for the Dead Man's Shoes Dies Barefoot* (1970) and Paulo Rocha's* *A Pousada das Chagas/The Stigmata Inn* (1971); for both directors he later became their favourite actor. In 1978 began the adventure of Rocha's *A Ilha dos Amores/The Island of Loves* (completed 1983) in which Cintra plays the part of a Portuguese writer in Japan who begins to live like the locals. He was reunited with Monteiro in *Silvestre* (1980), playing the knight opposite Maria de Medeiros* in her debut part as the maiden. Again with Rocha he was a cynical politician in *O Desejado ou As Montanhas da Lua/The Desired One or the Mountains of the Moon* (1987). In the meantime his theatrical experience made him Manoel de Oliveira's* choice for the leading part in the 1985 film version of Paul Claudel's play *O Sapato de Setim/Le Soulier de satin/The Satin Slipper* (1985). From then on Cintra was present in all the old master's films, in leading or supporting roles (once even just as a voice), from *Meu Caso/Mon Cas* (1986) to *A Caixa/Blind Man's Bluff* (1994), making him a regular visitor to the Cannes and Venice film festivals and bringing him international recognition. In recent years he has appeared in first features such as Joaquim Pinto's* *Uma Pedra no Bolso/Tall Stories* (1988) and Pedro Costa's *O Sangue/Blood* (1990). He has been heard in Portuguese, French, Italian, English, Chinese and Japanese, but more unforgettable even than this rare screen polyglotism is his voice: the ability to turn 'the pleasure of the text' into sound, using language to build up his persona as the seducer who is in turn mysterious and frightening. It was through language and in particular Japanese (which he learnt phonetically) that he became the complex charactor of Moraes in *A Ilha dos Amores*, changing not only his gestures but also his body and personality in what remains his most extraordinary film performance. AMS

Other Films: *Ninguém Duas Vezes/Not Once, Twice* (1984); *O Bobo/The Jester* (1987); *A Morte do Príncipe/The Prince's Death, Aqui na Terra/Here on Earth* (1993).

CLAIR, René   René Chomette; Paris 1898–1981

French director, writer and actor. One of the first *auteurs* of world cinema, Clair epitomised a certain idea of 'Frenchess', with his light, witty and elegant films which ranged from farce to sentimental comedy. Although Jean Renoir* now stands as the greatest French director of the classical era, at the time Clair had a higher standing: André Bazin* could write in 1957, 'René Clair is probably, after Chaplin, the most esteemed director in the world' (an opinion not shared by other writers at *Cahiers du cinéma*). Clair was an actor and film critic before becoming assistant to Jacques de Baroncelli and joining the French avant-garde*. *Entr'acte* (1924) and *Paris qui dort/The Crazy Ray* (1924–25) wedded formal experimentation with Surrealist fantasy and a touch of the populism which characterised his later work. He injected movement into two Labiche farces, *Un chapeau de paille d'Italie/The Italian Straw Hat* (1928) and *Les Deux timides* (1929), especially with the comic chases inherited from early cinema which became his trademark. *Sous les toits de Paris* (1930), *Le Million* (1931) and *Quatorze juillet* (1932), all brilliantly designed by Lazare Meerson*, fixed an iconography of popular Paris – a 'sweet' version of the darker Poetic Realism*, full of street singers, irate concierges and neighbours, and pretty *midinettes* (like Annabella* in the latter two films). At the same time, *Sous les toits de Paris*, one of the first French talking pictures, was a remarkable experiment in sound, both technically and in its discourse on the *possibilities* of the new dimension. As a social satire on modernisation, *A nous la liberté* (1931) foreshadowed Chaplin's *Modern Times* (1936). By 1934, the failure of *Le Dernier milliardaire* (another social satire, about an imaginary dictatorship) hinted that Clair's style was going out of fashion. He left for Britain, where he made *The Ghost Goes West* in 1936 (lots of chases in a Scottish castle), and *Break the News* (1938) with Maurice Chevalier* and Jack Buchanan*, before going on to Hollywood for another successful career (including *The Flame of New Orleans*, 1940, and *It Happened Tomorrow*, 1943). He returned to France in the 1950s, when he made elegant (and popular) costume films such as *Le Silence est d'or/Man About Town* (1947), *Les Belles de nuit* (1952) and *Les Grandes manoeuvres* (1955) [> TRADITION OF QUALITY]. Clair wrote many plays and novels and his film essays have been collected. He also wrote one of the classic texts on the coming of sound, *Cinema Yesterday and Today* (1972). As Bazin put it, Clair's work manifested a rare 'meeting of intelligence and popularity'. GV

Bib: R. C. Dale, *The Films of René Clair, I: Exposition and Analysis; II: Documentation* (1986).

Other French Films: *Le Fantôme du Moulin Rouge* (1925); *Le Voyage imaginaire* (1926); *La Proie du vent* (1927); *La Tour* (1928, short); *Air Pur* (1939, unfinished); *La Beauté du diable/Beauty and the Devil* (1950); *Porte des Lilas* (1957); *La Française et l'amour* (1960, ep. 'Le mariage'); *Tout l'or du monde* (1961); *Les Quatre vérités* (1962, ep. 'Les Deux Pigeons'); *Les Fêtes galantes* (1965).

CLARKE, T. E. B. Thomas Ernest Bennett Clarke; Watford 1907 – Surrey 1989

British scriptwriter, who was a contract writer at Ealing from 1943 until 1957, responsible for a number of the films by which Ealing* comedy came to be defined: *Hue and Cry* (1947), *Passport to Pimlico* (1949), *The Lavender Hill Mob* (1951) and *The Titfield Thunderbolt* (1953). Clarke was mainstream Ealing, the Ealing of the self-regulating community in its 'gentle revolution' (Michael Balcon's* phrase) against postwar bureaucracy, as opposed to the sharper comedy of Robert Hamer* or Alexander Mackendrick*. Though his characteristic form was comedy, he also co-wrote for Basil Dearden* the moralising fantasy *The Halfway House* (1944),

and the police drama *The Blue Lamp* (1950) which created the character of P.C. George Dixon for Jack Warner*. Clarke won an Oscar and an award at Venice for *The Lavender Hill Mob*. JC

Bib: T. E. B. Clarke, *This is Where I Came In* (1974).

Other Films Include: *For Those in Peril* (1944); *Who Done It?* (1956); *Barnacle Bill* (1957); *A Tale of Two Cities, Gideon's Day, Law and Disorder* (1958); *Sons and Lovers* (co-sc., 1960).

CLAUS, Hugo Bruges 1929

Belgian novelist, dramatist, poet, scriptwriter and director. Claus is the dominant figure in Belgium's postwar Dutch-language literature, his books being widely translated. He is frequently cast as an *enfant terrible* in his own country, mainly because of his consistently anti-authoritarian, anti-clerical and anti-fascist brand of humanism. His place in Belgian cinema is primarily as a writer, for example of commentaries for documentaries by Charles Dekeukeleire*, Paul Haesaerts and Patrick Ledoux. His longest collaborations, though, are with Roland Verhavert*, for whom he wrote the screenplay for *Pallieter*, and Fons Rademakers*, for whom he adapted Stijn Streuvel's novel *De Teleurgang van de Waterhoek*, which became the celebrated *Mira* (1971). Adapting his own work for the screen has brought Claus less success. In 1967 he directed *De Vijanden/Enemies* (produced by Verhavert), and in 1980 *Vrijdag/Friday*. Both these films were regarded as scandalous, thanks to Claus' characteristic anti-conformist stance as well as their eroticism and bluntness. Together with a few further attempts at direction (*Het Sacrament/The Sacrament*, 1989), Claus has published several screenplays. CF

CLEESE, John Weston-super-Mare 1939

British actor. It is difficult to dissociate Cleese, a graduate of the Cambridge Footlights comedy revue, from his television work on *Monty Python's Flying Circus* (1969–74) and *Fawlty Towers* (1975, 1979). His comic brilliance in those series, owing as much to physical routines as to the nuances of dialogue or character development, makes it difficult to see him without expecting the hysteria to burst through, a funny walk to take over, or a dead parrot to be slapped on the table. Many of his most popular film performances derive from routines – the Monty Python films or *The Secret Policeman's Ball* (1980) – but in *A Fish Called Wanda* (1988), which he scripted and on which he collaborated with Charles Crichton*, he showed the potential of his basic persona for more sustained comic development with a performance that won him a BAFTA Best Actor award. JC

Other Films Include: *Interlude* (1967); *The Best House in London, The Rise and Rise of Michael Rimmer, The Magic Christian* (1969); *And Now for Something Completely*

Different (1971); *Monty Python and the Holy Grail* (1975); *Monty Python's Life of Brian* (1979); *Time Bandits* (1981); *The Secret Policeman's Other Ball, Monty Python Live at the Hollywood Bowl; Monty Python's The Meaning of Life* (1983); *Silverado* [US], *Clockwise* (1985); *The Secret Policeman's Third Ball* (1987); *Erik the Viking* (1989).

CLÉMENT, René · Bordeaux 1913

French director, one of the most successful yet least celebrated postwar French film-makers. Clément studied architecture, made an animation film, directed several shorts – including *Soigne ton gauche* (1936) with Jacques Tati* – and documentaries before making his first feature, the remarkable Resistance film *La Bataille du rail/Battle of the Rails* (1946), with non-professional actors and photography by Henri Alekan*. He also acted as 'technical consultant' on Jean Cocteau's* *La Belle et la bête* (1946). Although *Le Père tranquille/Mr Orchid* (1946) and *Jeux interdits/Forbidden Games* (1952) return to the war, there is little common thread through Clément's films: 'I want to explore all genres and in each of my films I look for a new tone, a different style.' But if there is no thematic link between *Au-delà des grilles/Le mura di Malapaga/The Walls of Malapaga* (1949, a populist drama which attempts to rewrite the prewar Jean Gabin* myth in a postwar environment), *Jeux interdits* (the war through children's eyes), *Gervaise* (1956, a costume Zola adaptation) and *Plein Soleil/Purple Noon/Lust for Evil* (1960, a Patricia Highsmith adaptation with Alain Delon*), there is the impeccable *mise-en-scène*, care for detail and solid scripts of the Tradition of Quality*, which ensured Clément a large audience and numerous prizes (including Oscars for *Au-delà des grilles* and *Jeux interdits*). Towards the end of his career he turned to large-scale productions with international stars, such as *Paris brûle-t-il?/Is Paris Burning?* (1966). GV

Other Films Include: *Les Maudits/The Damned* (1947); *Le Château de verre/The Glass Castle* (1950); *Knave of Hearts/Monsieur Ripois* (1954, UK/Fr.); *Les Félins/The Love Cage* (1964); *Le Passager de la pluie/Rider on the Rain* (1970).

CLOSAS, Alberto · Alberto Closas Lluró; Barcelona 1921

Spanish actor, whose popularity as a stage actor led to a long and successful career in films. After a period in Argentina, he returned to Spain to star in one of the Spanish cinema's landmarks, Juan Antonio Bardem's* *Muerte de un ciclista/Death of a Cyclist* (1955). His limpid, compassionate eyes suited his role as the adulterer who cannot ultimately endure the strain of evading responsibility for his part in a hit-and-run accident. His popularity greatly increased also through the innumerable comedies he made in the 1950s and 1960s, where he characteristically played the handsome, elegant, leading man. PWE

CLOSE UP

British/Swiss film journal, published in English in Switzerland from 1927, edited by Kenneth Macpherson and Winifred Bryher, with articles in the early issues by H. D. (Hilda Doolittle), Dorothy Richardson, Gertrude Stein and Eisenstein*, and contributions to the later issues from John Grierson*, Ralph Bond and Paul Rotha*. Financed by Bryher's personal fortune, *Close Up* was aimed at a cinephile readership. Intellectually, it belonged to the same contradictory current of English modernism as the London Film Society*, arguing passionately for the art of the film and the avant-garde, pessimistic about the arrival of sound, but defending the right of the masses to entertainment ('as long as they desire eyewash and bunk they must have it'). *Close Up* was against censorship and cosmopolitan in its interests, with a special issue on 'Black cinema and race' in 1929, and sophisticated articles on psychoanalysis and the cinema. In 1930, Macpherson directed what Peter Wollen* calls 'the one outstanding British avant-garde film of the period', *Borderline*, starring H. D., with Paul and Eslanda Robeson in the cast. The journal folded in 1933.

The interest of *Close Up* for an intellectual history of the cinema was revived in the 1980s by feminist work (especially by Anne Friedberg) that looked in particular at the work of H. D., Bryher and Richardson on psychoanalysis and issues of spectatorship. JC/RC

CLOUZOT, Henri-Georges · Niort 1907 – Paris 1977

French director and scriptwriter, one of the most controversial film-makers of the postwar period. Clouzot's early activities were devoted to writing. After an early short (*La Terreur des Batignolles*, 1931), he began adapting thrillers in the 1940s, a genre he pursued throughout his career. The first was his debut feature *L'Assassin habite ... au 21* (1942). *Le Corbeau* (1943, produced by the German-owned Continentale) turned him into both a celebrity and an object of scandal. Its vicious portrait of a strife-ridden small town was deemed 'anti-French' and Clouzot was suspended from the film industry in 1944. Ironically, historians now read the film as anti-German. Clouzot resumed film-making in 1947, shooting a small but significant and highly successful body of films epitomising (with such directors as Yves Allégret*) the French *noir* tradition. Most, like *Quai des Orfèvres* (1947) and *Les Diaboliques* (1955), combine tight, suspenseful crime narratives with critical depictions of bourgeois milieux. *Le Salaire de la peur/The Wages of Fear* (1953), the ultra-tense story of two men delivering a lorry-load of nitro-glycerine, was a triumph at home and abroad. Clouzot directed one of Brigitte Bardot's* best films, *La Vérité* (1960). His films also include *Manon* (1949) and *Les Espions* (1957), and a documentary on Picasso, *Le Mystère Picasso* (1955). Ironically for a film-maker who wrote all his scripts and insisted that a director 'be his own *auteur*', Clouzot suffered at the hands of New Wave* critics, who saw him as a mere '*metteur-en-scène*' [> POLITIQUE DES AUTEURS] and disliked the black misanthropy of his vision. A reassessment of his work is long overdue. GV

COCTEAU, Jean
Maisons-Lafitte 1889 – Milly-la-Forêt 1963

French artist, writer and director. Cocteau's artistic output was prodigious – poems, plays, opera libretti, essays, drawings, church murals – and the cinema was only one aspect of it. Yet on account of their beauty and singularity his relatively few films have had a disproportionate impact. Cocteau introduced a rare element of the fantastic in French cinema, reworking myths and fairy tales which he rendered with a 'magic' imagery of mirrors, baroque objects and architecture and fabulous creatures. Apart from his avant-garde short feature *Le Sang d'un poète/The Blood of a Poet* (1930), Cocteau's cinematic activity was confined to the 1940s and 1950s. *La Belle et la bête*, starring Jean Marais* (1946, 'technical consultant' René Clément*, cinematographer Henri Alekan*), is one of the most beautiful French films ever made, a cult movie for *cinéphiles* and children alike. Cocteau pursued two main avenues in his films: myth, with *L'Eternel retour* (1943, dir. Jean Delannoy*), *Orphée* (1950) and *Le Testament d'Orphée* (1960); and Oedipal drama, with *Les Parents terribles/The Storm Within* (1948, described by André Bazin* as Cocteau's most theatrical *and* most cinematic work) and *Les Enfants terribles/The Strange Ones* (directed by Jean-Pierre Melville*, 1950). GV

Other Films as Director: *L'Aigle à deux têtes* (1948); *La Villa Santo-Sospir* (1952, short). **As scriptwriter**: *La Comédie du bonheur* (1942; dir. Marcel L'Herbier*); *Le Baron fantôme* (1943; dir. Serge de Poligny); *Les Dames du Bois de Boulogne* (1945; dir. Robert Bresson*); *Ruy Blas* (1948; dir. Pierre Billon).

COHL, Emile
Emile Courtet; Paris 1857–1938

French animation pioneer. After studying drawing, Cohl did political cartoons. He belonged to 'The Incoherents', an iconoclastic avant-garde artists' group, and was also variously a stage costume designer, vaudeville author, photographer and inventor of games. Noticing that a Gaumont* film had 'stolen' one of his ideas, he secured a contract in 1905 and began a fruitful new career in 'animated cartoons'. Although the American James Stuart Blackton had made an animated film, *The Haunted Hotel*, in 1906, historians agree that Cohl, starting with *Fantasmagorie* (1908), was the real father of animation, developing it both technically and aesthetically. He created characters such as the 'fantoche' (puppet) and built comically anarchic series round them, experimenting with techniques: movable cut-outs, three-dimensional animation, single-frame exposure. While at Gaumont he also wrote scripts and directed live-action films and animated scenes for other films. He moved to Pathé* in 1910 and Eclair in 1912, and in September 1912 to Eclair's New York premises. There he made more series (including the 'Newlyweds') and, it appears, had his equipment and methods widely copied. Back in Paris in 1914, he experienced difficulties in the face of increased competition; as he said, 'Father of animated cartoons, today I see my offspring returning from America resurfaced, gilded, thanks to the fabulous dollar.' Increasingly marginalised, he died destitute. Though Walt Disney always acknowledged his debt to Cohl, it is only recently that scholars have recognised his importance as a pioneer and his influence on all subsequent animation. GV

Bib: Donald Crafton, *Emile Cohl, Caricature, and Film* (1990).

COLETTE
Sidonie-Gabrielle Colette; Saint-Sauveur en Puisaye 1873 – Paris 1954

French novelist and film critic, one of the most popular writers of the twentieth century. Many of her works focusing on women – *La Vagabonde*, *Chéri* – have been adapted for the cinema: by Musidora* in the 1910s, Simone Bussi in the 1930s and Jacqueline Audry* in the 1940s and 1950s; *Gigi* (her portrait of the archetypal gamine) was filmed by Audry (1949) and Vincente Minnelli (1958). Colette wrote film criticism from 1914 to 1939, and contributed scripts and dialogues, notably for Marc Allégret's* *Lac aux dames* (1934) and Max Ophuls'* *Divine* (1935), the latter based on her own experience of the music-hall stage. She was the subject of Yannick Bellon's documentary *Colette* (1950). GV

COLMAN, Ronald
Richmond, Surrey 1891 – Santa Barbara, California 1958

British actor. Colman emigrated to America in 1920 and his most popular starring roles belong to the history of Hollywood cinema, but while his British cinema career was brief, it is noteworthy. He was recruited for film from the London stage, and was one of the actors placed under contract by Cecil Hepworth* in his attempt to develop a stable of British stars. He made two films with Hepworth: *Sheba* (1919) and *Anna the Adventuress* (1920). His career in Hollywood was slow to start, but after he was chosen by Lillian Gish to star opposite her in *The White Sister* (1923, US), it never looked back. One of the most popular stars of both the silent and the sound screen over three decades, he was, after Chaplin, the cinema's best loved Englishman. 'Ronald Colman,' wrote one of his contemporaries, 'is good for humanity. Doctors might prescribe a dose of him for depressed patients or for those with acute melancholia. He should be encouraged for a world that is too humdrum and too respectable.' JC

Other British Films: *The Toilers, A Daughter of Eve, Snow in the Desert, A Son of David* (1919); *The Black Spider* (1920). **American Films Include**: *Stella Dallas* (1925); *Beau Geste* (1926); *Bulldog Drummond* (1929); *Bulldog Drummond Strikes Back* (1934); *Clive of India, A Tale of Two Cities* (1935); *Lost Horizon, The Prisoner of Zenda* (1937); *The Light That Failed* (1940); *The Talk of the Town, Random Harvest* (1942); *Kismet* (1943).

COLOMO, Fernando
Fernando Colomo Gómez;
Madrid 1946

Spanish director associated with the 'Nueva comedia madrileña' ('New Madrid Comedy') [> COMEDY (SPAIN)], who rose to popularity with the low-budget Tigres de papel/Paper Tigers (1977), a bitter-sweet look at democracy's mixture of ideological chaos and hedonistic exultation – soft drugs, sex – that challenged the radical postures of the 'progre' generation (1960s/1970s anti-establishment liberals, also explored in Estoy en crisis/I'm Having a Crisis, 1982). This generation's evolution and assimilation into the socialist 'establishment' is depicted in the more accomplished La vida alegre/A Happy Life (1987), where Verónica Forqué's* philanthropic installation of a centre for the treatment of venereal diseases unveils a chain of sexual affairs, political schemes and comic situations. Like Forqué's, Antonio Resines's* acting provides the film with a spontaneity also characteristic of his earlier performance in Colomo's La línea del cielo/Skyline (1983), where his heavy Spanish accent, together with the 'Manzanita' flamenco score, presage the hero's impossibility of melting into the (otherwise demythified) American dream. Colomo's last film to date is Alegre ma non troppo (1994). IS

COMEDY

Comedy has undoubtedly been the most prominent popular genre in European cinema, each country developing its own versions and sub-genres (e.g. 'Commedia all'italiana'*). Information is disseminated throughout the Encyclopedia, under national, generic and personnel entries. Texts below focus on Austria, France, Germany, Greece, Poland, Portugal and Spain.

Austria
The most common type of Austrian cinematic comedy is the cabaret film. In the 1930s, a special form of protest against Austrian fascism developed on small stages. A brilliant game of coding and decoding among actors and audience, it was a common struggle against censorship. Dramatic and terpsichorean bravado, wordplay in the Jewish tradition, improvisation, political and sexual suggestion, and sharp-tongued criticism of current events characterised Viennese cabaret and were influential on comic actors who then crossed over to film: Fritz Grünbaum (Mädchen zum Heiraten, 1932), Karl Farkas (In der Theateragentur, 1930 [short]), Fritz Imhoff (Episode, 1935; Opernring, 1936; Schrammeln, 1944; Der Feldherrnhügel, 1953), Hans Moser* (Ungeküßt soll man nicht schlafen gehen, 1936), Hugo Gottschlich, Josef Meinrad, Helmut Qualtinger*, and others. They all learned the art of using a pointedly raised brow, deft wordplay and grotesque expressions, though the explosive power of the political humour from the stage was substantially toned down in the films; this genre was gradually abandoned in favour of more harmless and less topical subjects in the postwar period. The cabaret traditions were, however, revived in the so-called 'New Austrian Film' of the 1980s and 1990s, to great popular success, since the most successful productions either borrowed from cabaret or were cabaret numbers adapted to film:

Müllers Büro (1986, dir. Niki List*), Muttertag (1993, dir. Harald Sicheritz) and Indien (1993, dir. Paul Harather). AL

France
Alice Guy's* La Fée aux choux/The Cabbage Fairy (1896) was a farce about babies popping out of cabbages. Almost a century later, Les Visiteurs (1993, dir. Jean-Marie Poiré*) demolished all previous box-office records. Between these two titles, comedy has consistently been the most popular genre in France. Yet despite its high cultural status in literature (Rabelais, Molière), comedy has also been the most despised and ignored French film genre, with the exception of a few star-auteurs: Max Linder*, René Clair*, Sacha Guitry*, Jacques Tati*, Pierre Etaix. Auteur-oriented critics mistrust a genre based on performers, who moreover often come from other media (theatre, music hall, radio, song), and consider French comedy to be socially irrelevant, undemanding and lacking in subversiveness.

Comics sustained a large amount of silent French cinema, especially during the 'golden age' of 1907–15 when numerous series were produced, dominated by André Deed* and Max Linder*. If the 1920s saw the rise of the avant-garde and of bourgeois melodrama, sound firmly re-established comic genres, deriving either from the theatre (directors Clair, Guitry, Marcel Pagnol*; actors Raimu*, Michel Simon*, Jules Berry*) or the music hall (actors/singers Fernandel*, Bach and Georges Milton*, Arletty*), and included sub-genres such as the comique troupier*. French directors also emulated American-style light comedy (directors Marc Allégret*, Christian-Jaque*, Henri Decoin*; actors André Luguet, Fernand Gravey, Danielle Darrieux*, Micheline Presle*, Edwige Feuillère*). The postwar period saw the even greater popularity of Fernandel, while dramatic actors like Jean Gabin* joined the ranks of comedy alongside new ones such as Noël-Noël, Darry Cowl, Robert Lamoureux, Bernard Blier*, Francis Blanche, Jean Poiret, Michel Serrault, and especially Bourvil* and Louis de Funès*, the latter surpassing all others at the box office and causing most critical consternation. Directors such as Yves Robert (especially with La Guerre des boutons/War of the Buttons, 1962), Georges Lautner, Gilles Grangier and Gérard Oury achieved huge success. While these comics and their films were for domestic consumption only, Jacques Tati's success was international, his humour built on universal sight gags. Later Pierre Etaix took up the Linder–Tati tradition in such films as Le Soupirant/The Suitor (1963), although his fame was mainly national. The 1960s and 1970s saw the rise of a fresh generation of comic stars such as Jean Yanne, Michel Galabru, Annie Girardot and Jean-Paul Belmondo* (L'Homme de Rio/That Man from Rio, 1964), the worldwide success of Edouard Molinaro's La Cage aux folles/Birds of a Feather (1978), and the appearance of the 'flaky' Pierre Richard, often in a duo with Gérard Depardieu* (in films directed by Francis Veber). A new generation of stars, scriptwriters and directors from the libertarian café-théâtre also appeared, bringing a sexually more explicit and stylistically more naturalistic humour, and a sharper social mockery (though the films toned down the politics of the original plays): directors such as Coline Serreau* (whose Trois hommes et un couffin/Three Men and a Cradle, 1985, was a huge hit), stars such as Coluche, Michel Blanc, Thierry Lhermitte, Christian

Clavier, Miou-Miou* and Josiane Balasko*. Directors Patrice Leconte and Jean-Marie Poiré* popularised this tradition, while Bertrand Blier's* early work represented its *auteur* manifestation. From the 1980s, other influences shaped French comedy, notably television, with comics such as 'Les Nuls', and advertising (for instance Etienne Chatiliez's *La Vie est un long fleuve tranquille/Life is a Long Quiet River*, 1988, and *Tatie Danielle*, 1990).

Three aspects of French film comedy may explain its lasting popularity: its overwhelming maleness, which has gone hand in hand with the hegemony of male stars at the box office (with a few exceptions: Annie Girardot, Josiane Balasko, Anémone, Valérie Lemercier); the importance of language and word-play in French culture [> JACQUES PRÉVERT, HENRI JEANSON, MICHEL AUDIARD]; and the taste for deriding social and regional types. Although the conventional image of French cinema is centred on dramatic trends such as Poetic Realism* and *auteur* cinema, the importance of comedy shows that the construction of national identity by French cinema should rather be sought in comedy – the only domestic genre to resist Hollywood. GV

Germany

The financial backbone of the German film industry throughout its history was the continuous national popularity and success of light entertainment comedies, or *Lustspielfilme*. Until the early 1910s, German film comedy derived from variety, cartoon and slapstick traditions. As the few surviving films prove, the comic one-, two- or three-reelers revealed strong elements of subversive, grotesque and surrealist humour, as in the films of Heinrich Bolten-Baecker, Leo Peuckert, Karl Valentin, or the early Ernst Lubitsch*. While both Lubitsch (*Die Austernprinzessin,* 1919) and Reinhold Schünzel* (*Hallo Caesar*, 1927) took up the episodic cinema of attractions and grotesquerie, they also incorporated strong elements from operetta (*Madame Dubarry*, 1919, *Der Juxbaron*, 1926), which were to become of considerable importance in musical comedies after the introduction of sound in 1929.

With the hitherto strong Jewish contribution (Max Mack, Victor Janson, Lubitsch, Schünzel among the directors, Felix Bressart, Julius Falkenstein, Paul Biensfeldt and Curt Bois* among the actors) vanishing from the German screen by the mid-1930s, Nazi comedy lacked its previous surreal and self-ironic dimension. Instead it was dominated by musical comedies* and revue films, watered down versions of contemporary American screwball comedies along with characteristically a-political – though ideologically by no means neutral – comedies centred on the everyday problems of the petit-bourgeois male, whose most successful screen incarnation became Heinz Rühmann* in films such as *Der Mustergatte* (1937) and *Hauptsache glücklich* (1941).

The first postwar years produced a few comedies notable for their satirical treatment of contemporary social issues (*Berliner Ballade*, 1948; *Herrliche Zeiten*, 1950), but by the 1950s, with Germany's economic recovery under way, the film industry returned to politically non-committal entertainment, in line with a public taste unchanged since sound was introduced in the 1930s. Heading the popularity stakes among directors was Kurt Hoffmann, and among the actors (apart from Rühmann) was Heinz Erhardt*, who became notorious for his bad puns and nonsense repartee. Musical comedies

starring contemporary pop idols Peter Kraus and Conny Froboess also enjoyed a brief but significant vogue. When the cinema first tried to compete with television in the late 1960s and 1970s, a number of hugely popular series emerged by directors such as Harald Reinl* and Werner Jacobs, following an ever more rigid formula which reinforced innocuous nostalgia for monstrously stupid teachers and classroom pranks (modelled initially on one of Rühmann's greatest hits, *Die Feuerzangenbowle*, 1944). Equally successful at that time were regionally differentiated, but more often than not Bavarian, sex comedies.

After a long period of stagnation, German comedy once more gained national and international attention with Doris Dörrie's well-crafted romantic-farcical love triangle *Männer.../Men* (1985). Keeping up the momentum, if in a somewhat less sophisticated direction, are a number of contemporary star comedians ('Otto' Waalke, 'Loriot'), crossing over from television into features which were among the most successful German film productions of the 1980s, usually thought of as the decade of the New German Cinema*. While the 1990s promise to be a lean period for German cinema generally, it is once more the comedies, such as *Schtonk* (1992), about the persistence of the Nazi past, or the East/West comedies by Detlev Buck which are likely to determine the predominant filmic image of the period. MW/TE

Greece

Popular Greek comedy developed into a genre after World War II, reaching its peak after 1955. It was influenced by numerous sources, such as theatre (revues, variety, farce, travelling troupes), cinema ('commedia all' italiana'*), ancient Greek comedy (Aristophanes), circus, country fairs and shows, shadow puppet theatre, etc.

The major aesthetic characteristic of popular Greek comedy is the development of specific comic types. These types used improvisation to transcend the limits of conventional scripts based on stereotypical themes (usually elements from contemporary lower middle-class society) and conventional direction. Improvisation occasionally reached the point where performers in effect played their roles in parallel with, or even against, the director of the film. This 'self-direction' usually involved exaggerated emphasis on some bodily or mental characteristic (baldness, stature, posture, speech defect, neurotic behaviour). Accordingly, the genre produced excellent comic performers, outstanding among them being Vassilis Logothetidis, Nikos Stavridis, Vassilis Avlonitis, Kostas Hadjihristos, Dinos Iliopoulos, Mimis Fotopoulos, Georgia Vassiliadou, Nikos Rizos and, of a younger generation, Thanassis Vengos* and Kostas Voutsas.

From the early 1960s Greek comedies lost their farcical elements, becoming initially light sentimental comedies and later musicals. As the films became less dependent on performers, elements such as music, stars, colour, choreography and spectacle came to the fore. Of less interest artistically, this sub-genre was sometimes more popular than the earlier farces. Some of the first Greek musicals, *Kati na kei/ Something Hot, Koritsia ya filima/Girls for Kissing* and *Rendez-vous ston aera/Meeting in the Air,* were the most popular films of the 1963–64, 1964–65 and 1965–66 seasons respectively.

In the mid-1970s Greek comedy virtually disappeared,

along with commercial Greek cinema in general, victim of the growth of television. However, the comedies continue to touch Greek audiences today: they are among the most popular programmes on television, where they are shown repeatedly. AM

Films Include: *Kalpiki lira/The Counterfeit Coin* (1955, dir. Yorgos Tzavellas); *Laterna ftohia ke filotimo/Barrel Organ, Poverty and Dignity* (1955, dir. Alekos Sakellarios); *I kafedjou/The Coffee Fortune Teller* (1956, dir. Alekos Sakellarios); *I thia apo to Chicago/The Aunt from Chicago* (1957, dir. Alekos Sakellarios); *Na zissoun ta ftohopeda/Long Live the Poor Fellows* (1959, dir. Orestis Laskos); *Zitite pseftis/Liar Wanted* (1961, dir. Yannis Dalianidis); *O atsidas/The Ace* (1961, dir. Yannis Dalianidis); *O Hadjihristos taxidsis/The Taxi Driver* (1962, Kostas Hadjihristos); *Fonazi o kleftis/The Thief is Crying Out* (1965, Andreas Andreadakis).

Italy – see 'COMMEDIA ALL'ITALIANA' and NEW ITALIAN COMICS

Poland

Polish film has a reputation for being tragic, philosophical, romantic, intellectual, political – everything, it seems, except funny. Despite the popularity of Hollywood comedies, and strong comic theatre and cabaret traditions, Polish film comedies and directors are hard to find. It seems that the strictures of Socialist Realism* and script censorship have worked to the detriment of the genre.

Comedy did flourish, though, in the silent and prewar sound years, with the popular actor Adolf Dymsza in the Chaplinesque persona of 'Dodek', and the antics of Eugeniusz Bodo. The most popular film was Michal Waszyński and Jan Nowina-Przybylski's *Cham/Roughneck* (1931), sold to thirteen countries. The major directors who worked consistently in the genre in the postwar period were Tadeusz Chmielewski, whose 1958 hit *Ewa chce Spać/Eve Wants to Sleep* combined light farce with serious reflection on teenage delinquency, and Stanisław Bajera, who made the cross-dressing *Poszukiwany-Poszukiwana/On the Run* (1973).

Some of the best comedies were of course those that annoyed the authorities – Marek Piwowski's *Rejs/Trip Down the River* (1970) was limited to one release print and Antoni Krauze's* *Prognoza Pogody/Weather Forecast* (1983) was banned outright. One success story was the futuristic *Seksmisja/Sexmission* (1984) by Juliusz Machulski*, starring one of the best contemporary comic actors, Jerzy Stuhr*. In the 1990s, with the censor gone and society ripe for ridicule, the material is there for the kind of black humour and political satire that Polish audiences enjoy. *Kraj Świata/Edge of the World* (1993) by Maria Zmarz-Koczanowicz, based on Janusz Anderman's short stories, has the rare courage to laugh heartily at the late 1980s. AW

Portugal

The most important genre in Portuguese cinema, if not the only one – at least according to public perception. Portuguese comedy is actually Lisbon comedy, the representation of the city being one of its main characteristics. The urban space is presented as a collection of neighbourhoods, sometimes mentioned in film titles, such as Estrela and Castelo. The genre was born with the first sound film shot in Portugal, *A Canção de Lisboa/Song of Lisbon* (1933), directed by Cottinelli Telmo. The *revista* (revue), a theatrical genre consisting of humour, topical satire, song and dance, was the basis of the film genre, and from the stage came scriptwriters and stars. The great flowering of Portuguese comedy came in the 1940s with António Lopes Ribeiro* (*O Pai Tirano/The Tyrannical Father,* 1941), his brother Francisco Ribeiro, known as 'Ribeirinho' (*O Pátio das Cantigas/Song of the Courtyards,* 1942), and Arthur Duarte, who had previously worked at Ufa* in Germany (*O Costa do Castelo/Costa of the Castle,* 1943, *A Menina da Rádio/The Radio Girl,* 1944, *O Leão da Estrela/The Lion from Estrela,* 1947, and *O Grande Elias/Big Elias,* 1950, already a pale rendition of the genre). António Silva, Beatriz Costa and Vasco Santana, who respectively played the father, the daughter and the beloved in *A Canção de Lisboa,* were the genre's greatest stars, later working with 'Ribeirinho' and the veteran actress Maria Matos; younger pretenders to stardom appeared in the films of the 1940s, perhaps the only period when an attempt at a 'star system' was made in Portugal. Importantly, the most sustained efforts in the genre were made during World War II. The title of *O Pai Tirano,* 'the tyrannical father', though it refers to a play-within-the-film, can be read as symptomatic: Salazar was the father figure/tyrant, but while he was in charge people could be happy and sing – as in *O Pátio das Cantigas,* in which he is actually referred to as the man who saved Portugal from the war. Much more successful than the explicit propaganda of the time, *O Pátio das Cantigas* is the most influential film of the conservative and authoritarian ideology of the Salazar regime. Repeatedly shown since, these 1940s comedies are the most popular Portuguese films ever, generating the ideology of a 'golden age' that never existed. However, after producing *O Pai Tirano* and *O Pátio das Cantigas* (as well as Manoel de Oliveira's* *Aniki-Bóbó,* 1942), Ribeiro went bankrupt. AMS

Spain

Spanish comedy arguably has its origins in the pioneering work of Segundo de Chomón* and his experiments with animated photo-montage, exemplified in the silent, machine-age comedy *El hotel eléctrico/The Electric Hotel* (1905). In the 1920s and 1930s, film comedy in Spain developed through the adaptation of traditional Spanish theatrical forms and popular entertainments, in particular the *sainete* and the *zarzuela*. In the 1930s, Republican Spain saw the rise of new production companies such as Cifesa* (1932) and Filmófono (1935), both responsible for a string of highly successful comedies. In the 1940s, comedy was integrated into film panegyrics of the Spanish military, as in Juan de Orduña's* *¡A mí la legión!/Follow Me, Legion!* (1942), which sought to mythify the army as the (anti-semitic) essence of Spanish nationalism. Comedy also fulfilled a similarly edifying purpose in Rafael Gil's* *Huella de luz/A Sight of Light* (1944) and Luis Marquina's *Malvaloca/Hollyhock* (1942), in which role-playing fantasies and role reversals are mixed with strict observation of Catholic morality. Comedy also made possible some of the pioneering attempts at an ideologically oppositional cinema during the early part of the dictatorship. Luis García Berlanga's* *¡Bienvenido, Mr Marshall!/Welcome, Mr*

Marshall! (1952) satirised stereotypical images exploited by the regime for opportunist export as well as home consumption. The most popular comedic genre of the late 1960s and early 1970s was the so-called 'sexy Spanish comedy', a comedy of manners and customs reflecting major issues of Spain in the 1960s: tourism, consumerism and above all sexual repression. These were a compensation for viewing tastes enjoyed abroad but not in Spain, a kind of ersatz soft pornography for a sexually repressed public. Formula comedies such as Tito Fernández's *No desearás al vecino del quinto/Thou Shalt Not Covet Thy Fifth Floor Neighbour* (1971) and Vicente Escrivá's *Lo verde empieza en el Pirineo/Smut Starts at the Pyrenees* (1973) were among the biggest grossing films of the 1970s.

In general, Spanish comedies of the late 1970s and 1980s capitalised on the new freedoms of the post-Franco era, signalling a break with the past in films which celebrated sexual experimentation, such as Fernando Colomo's* *¿Qué hace una chica como tú en un sitio como éste?/What's a Girl Like You Doing in a Place Like This?* (1978). Comedy then took several directions. One developed out of the so-called *Escuela de Madrid* (Madrid School) of the late 1970s and presented a wry, satirical look at youth and popular culture, and a growing disenchantment with democracy, as seen in the work of Colomo, Fernando Trueba* and, most provocatively, in the early work of Pedro Almodóvar* and Juan José Bigas Luna*. Another trend saw the satire and black humour of Luis García Berlanga, continued by Carlos Mira Franco and José Luis García Sánchez. Meanwhile, as new legislation in the 1980s authorised special theatres to screen hard-core pornography, the 'sexy Spanish comedy' of the 1970s gradually faded away, to be replaced by the '*comedia militante de derechas*' (militant right-wing comedy), personified by veteran director Rafael Gil* and his adaptations of novels by Vizcaíno Casas, as well as the anti-democratic diatribes of Pedro Lazaga* and Mariano Ozores*. At present, Spanish comedy is perhaps best known internationally through the work of the 1994 Oscar-winner Trueba (*Belle Epoque*, 1992), Bigas Luna and, of course, Almodóvar. BJ

COMENCINI, Luigi   Salò 1916

Italian director. After spending his childhood in France, Comencini returned to Italy and graduated in architecture from Milan, where he became one of the founders of the Italian Film Library. A film critic as well as a scriptwriter for Mario Soldati*, Alberto Lattuada*, Pietro Germi* and Dino Risi*, he made several noteworthy short films before his first feature, *Proibito rubare* (1948), a sort of *Boys Town* with a Neapolitan setting and an interest in childhood, a dominant theme in his subsequent films. Important landmarks of Comencini's career are the excellent *La finestra sul Luna Park* (1957) in which, in a post-neo-realism* scenario, he subtly alludes to the drama of emigration and affirms the supremacy of affection over blood ties, as well as *Incompreso* (1967); he also made a philosophical 'Casanova' for children: *Infanzia, vocazione e prime esperienze di Giacomo Casanova veneziano* (1969), and a utopian 'Pinocchio' for adults: *Le avventure di Pinocchio* (1971). A highly versatile artist and a great storyteller, Comencini moved easily from populism to

'rose-tinted' neo-realism (*neorealismo rosa*), and from social drama to thriller and to opera and episode film. It was, however, with two early examples of what was to become *commedia all'italiana** – *Pane, amore e fantasia/Bread, Love and Dreams* (1953) and *Pane, amore e gelosia/Bread, Love and Jealousy/Frisky* (1954), starring Gina Lollobrigida* and Vittorio De Sica* – that he first left an important and identifiable mark. This propensity was refined during the 1950s in light comedy works and reached its peak in *Tutti a casa/Everybody Go Home!* (1960), which, alongside Mario Monicelli's* almost contemporary *La grande guerra/The Great War* (1959), introduced history to the comic film and vice versa. PV

Other Films Include: *L'imperatore di Capri* (1949); *Persiane chiuse/Behind Closed Shutters* (1950); *La bella di Roma* (1955); *Le sorprese dell'amore* (1959); *A cavallo della tigre/Jail Break* (1961); *La ragazza di Bube/Bebo's Girl* (1963); *Lo scopone scientifico* (1972); *Delitto d'amore, Mio Dio, come sono caduta in basso!/Till Marriage Do Us Part* (1974); *La donna della domenica/The Sunday Woman* (1976); *L'ingorgo/Bottleneck* (1979); *Voltati Eugenio* (1980); *La Bohème* (1987), *La storia/The Story* [or *History*] (1986).

COMERFORD, Joe   Born 1949

Irish director and writer. Comerford is one of the main contributors to recent developments in Irish cinema. His films have brought to the screen previously ignored or excluded marginal social groups: drug addicts in *Withdrawal* (1974), working-class teenagers in *Down the Corner* (1978), travellers in *Traveller* (1982), and IRA renegades in *Reefer and the Model* (1988), a film which won the Europa prize for best film in 1988. Comerford's films are often informed by a gloomy, dark image of the Irish, with the inarticulate incest victim, Angela, in *Traveller* an extreme example. Among his other films is *High Boot Benny* (1993). KR

COMIQUE TROUPIER

French genre. The *comique troupier*, or military comedy, once one of the most popular French genres, reached its peak in the 1930s. It remained strictly for national consumption, addressing barrackfuls of conscripts and family audiences. With roots in the music hall and the theatre (in particular the plays of Georges Courteline, whose *Les Gaietés de l'escadron/The Joys of the Squadron* was filmed twice, in 1912 and 1932), the genre depended on songs and comic routines by the likes of Bach, Carette*, Roland Toutain and Raimu*. Its undisputed star, however, was Fernandel*, whose prototypical *Ignace* was the most popular French film of 1937 (alongside, ironically, the war drama *La Grande illusion*). *Comique troupier* humour is regressive, chaotic and bawdy; it relies on male ineptitude and ritual humiliation, transvestism and petty rule-breaking. Though order eventually prevails, the attraction of the *comique troupier* is to offer ordinary soldiers the brief chance to outwit or annoy their superiors. It was also the only genre which could mock the French army, 'serious' war films being subjected to the close scrutiny of the censors. Though it waned with World War II, the *comique troupier* had a revival in the 1970s, thanks to singers Les Charlots (especially in Claude Zidi's* *Les Bidasses en folie/Soldiers Freaking Out*, 1971), to Robert Lamoureux's *Mais où est donc passée la 7e compagnie?/Whatever Happened to the 7th Company?* (1973) and its sequels, and to the soft porn boom. Such films as *Les Filles du régiment/The Girls of the Regiment* (1979) can occasionally be seen on European cable channels. GV

[> COMEDY (FRANCE), FINNISH MILITARY FARCE]

'COMMEDIA ALL'ITALIANIA'

Italian genre. *Commedia all'italiana*, or 'Comedy – Italian style', a satirical form spiced with elements of social and moral criticism and originally a mixture of comedy and drama, emerged in the late 1950s. Its distant origins lay in the popular cinema of the Fascist period (notably the work of Mario Camerini*), and an element of continuity can be found in the career of Vittorio De Sica*, both as an actor for Camerini in the 1930s and as a director (and again actor) in the 1940s and 1950s. But a more important source was the 'rosy' or 'rose-tinted' neo-realism* (*neo-realismo rosa*) which appeared in the late 1940s and early 1950s when films like Luigi Zampa's* *L'onorevole Angelina* (1947), Luciano Emmer's* *Domenica d'agosto/Sunday in August* (1950), Renato Castellani's* *Due soldi di speranza/Two Pennyworth of Hope* (1951) and indeed De Sica's *L'oro di Napoli/The Gold of Naples* (1954) signalled the first symptoms of a move towards a more indulgent notion of neo-realism, inclined to dwell on the minor misfortunes of daily life, materially poor but rich in optimism and hope. Also important were the films of Totò*, and the contributions made to them by writers like Age* and Scarpelli and directors Steno* (Stefano Vanzina) and Mario Monicelli*, future stalwarts of the fully developed *commedia all'italiana*.

A watershed in the development of the genre came with *Pane, amore e fantasia/Bread, Love and Dreams* (1953), directed by Luigi Comencini* and starring Vittorio De Sica* and Gina Lollobrigida*, and Dino Risi's* *Poveri ma belli/Poor but Beautiful* (1956). The rustic style of *Pane, amore e fantasia* (and its sequel) was complemented, and eventually replaced, by a more incisive type of urban humour, typified by actor Alberto Sordi's* versatile characterisations of the 'average Italian' in the changing society of the 1950s economic boom: *Il seduttore/The Seducer* (1954), *Il moralista/The Moralist* (1959), *Mafioso* (1962). A shift to a more complex and mature form was achieved with Monicelli's *I soliti ignoti/Persons Unknown* (1958), starring Vittorio Gassman* with a full supporting cast including Totò. This marked the beginning of the golden age of the genre. Some of the films combined comic characters, actors and language with a reinterpretation of Italian history (Monicelli's *La grande guerra/The Great War*, 1959) and Comencini's *Tutti a casa/Everybody Go Home!*, 1960). In others, such as Risi's *Il sorpasso/The Easy Life* (1962), changes in social customs and the new status symbols favoured by the emerging classes were put under the microscope: the 'modernity' of sexual liberation, the enthusiasm for the motor car, mass travel, tourism,

beach life, popular music and the consumer goods foisted on the public by television advertising were relentlessly mocked. Central to the genre were actors Sordi, Gassman, Ugo Tognazzi* and (later) Nino Manfredi, with roles also played by emerging stars Marcello Mastroianni* and Monica Vitti*. Writers including Rodolfo Sonego*, Leo Benvenuti, Piero De Bernardi and Ruggero Maccari contributed to the genre, as did Ettore Scola*. Among the directors who entered its orbit were Nanni Loy, Antonio Pietrangeli*, Lina Wertmüller* and Pasquale Festa Campanile. Important titles include Monicelli's *L'armata Brancaleone* (1966), Pietro Germi's* *Signore e signori/Ladies and Gentlemen* (1966), Loy's *Il padre di famiglia/The Head of the Family* (1967), Risi's *Straziami ma di baci saziami/Hurt Me, but Cover Me With Your Kisses* (1968), Manfredi's *Per grazia ricevuta/For Grace Received* (1971), Wertmüller's *Mimì metallurgico ferito nell'onore/The Seduction of Mimi* (1972), and Franco Brusati's *Pane e cioccolata/Bread and Chocolate* (1974).

By this time, however, the capacity of the genre to keep up with social change, particularly the new youth movements, was blunted. The army of comedians from the 'boom' years was ageing and began to disperse. The last great exponent of the *commedia all'italiana* was Scola, with *C'eravamo tanti amati/We All Loved Each Other So Much* (1974) and *La terrazza/The Terrace* (1980), which combine a wealth of familiar motifs with a rare narrative skill. Meanwhile the genre was falling apart. Although the intervening generation supplied important comedians, such as Giancarlo Giannini and Mariangela Melato, there is really no continuity between the classic *commedia all'italiana* and the 'New Italian comics'* who emerged in the 1980s. PDA

Bib: Enrico Giacovelli, *La commedia all'italiana* (1990).

CONNAUGHTON, Shane   Born 19[?]

Irish writer. Connaughton trained as an actor, but became a writer of stage and television plays and films. He was nominated, with Jim Sheridan*, for Best Adapted Screenplay for the Oscar-winning *My Left Foot* (1989). Though he did not win an award for that film, he had already collected an Oscar in 1981 for writing the short, *The Bottom Dollar*. His writing, especially in the linked stories published as *A Border Station* (1989), and in his original script for *The Playboys* (1992), centres on his own childhood. Connaughton's work is usually set in and near the village of Redhills, Co. Cavan, where he was brought up and where *The Playboys* was shot. KR

Bib: Kevin Rockett, 'From Atlanta to Dublin', *Sight and Sound* (June 1992).

CONNERY, Sean   Edinburgh 1930

British actor. The accepted myth of Connery casts him as an Edinburgh milkman, body builder and art school model, entering a stage career through the chorus line of *South Pacific*, appearing in films from 1956, and becoming a star 'accidentally' when he was chosen to play James Bond* in *Dr No* (1962). There is, however, a concealed history in his career in television drama in the late 1950s. Among a number of distinguished roles, including Vronsky in an adaptation of *Anna Karenina* and Hotspur in *The Age of Kings*, Connery played the demanding lead role of the derelict boxer in a live BBC version of Rod Serling's *Requiem for a Heavyweight* (1957), a role created by Jack Palance in one of the key plays of American live television drama.

Bond, however, made Connery a star, and the association was so strong that he could have been trapped in the part. Always unpretentious as an actor, he seemed destined to play interesting variations on the theme of sardonic sexuality. What is remarkable, however, is the increasing depth which his basic persona has acquired with age. Always good to look at, with enough irony to translate good looks into playful sexual danger, his later screen presence has developed the contours of a landscape embedded with history. Since *Robin and Marian* (1976, US), and increasingly in films like *Highlander* (1986), *Der Name der Rose/The Name of the Rose* (1986, Ger./It./Fr.), *The Untouchables* (1987, US) and *Indiana Jones and the Last Crusade* (1989, US), he has claimed, like Clint Eastwood and John Wayne, the prerogative of the aging male star to play against his own legend. Liberated from the romantic lead, he has been able to counterpoint age and experience against youth and vigour, using his own mythic persona to give the counterpoint an elegiac tone.

Connery won an Oscar as Best Supporting Actor for *The Untouchables*, and a BAFTA award as Best Actor for *The Name of the Rose*. JC

Other Films Include: *No Road Back, Hell Drivers* (1957); *Darby O'Gill and the Little People* (1959, US); *The Longest Day* (1962, US); *From Russia with Love* (1963); *Marnie* [US], *Goldfinger* (1964); *The Hill, Thunderball* (1965); *A Fine Madness* (1966, US); *You Only Live Twice* (1967); *Shalako* (1968); *La tenda rossa/Krasnaya palatka/The Red Tent* (1969, It./USSR); *The Molly Maguires* (1970, US); *The Anderson Tapes* [US], *Diamonds are Forever* (1971); *The Offence* (1973); *Zardoz, Murder on the Orient Express* (1974); *The Wind and the Lion* (1975, US); *A Bridge Too Far* (1977); *The First Great Train Robbery* (1978); *Time Bandits, Outland* (1981); *Five Days One Summer* (1982); *Never Say Never Again* (1983); *The Russia House, The Hunt for Red October, Highlander II – The Quickening* (1990, US); *Robin Hood: Prince of Thieves* (1991, US); *Rising Sun* (1993, US).

CONSTANTIN

German production and distribution company, founded in 1949. Constantin enjoyed a meteoric rise because of its dominant role as a small to medium production unit, its exclusive distribution contracts with producers Horst Wendlandt and Wolf C. Hartwig and, finally, its ability to create a market niche based on product differentiation. Constantin's owner, Waldfried Barthel, developed a double strategy for capturing dwindling audiences. He attracted the younger, more mobile moviegoers with film series targeted at teenagers and he took sex films out of the porn shops, making them respectable to adult movie audiences. Barthel also enhanced his production values, strategically deploying technological advances unavailable on television, such as colour and wide-screen.

Constantin commissioned the most successful commercial film series of the postwar period, especially the thirty-six-part Edgar Wallace series produced by Wendtland (1959–72) and the seventeen-part Karl May series, also produced by Wendtland (1962–68). Constantin's other strategy was to adapt series or make clones from rival distributors' one-off hits, cashing in, for instance, on the success of the sex education film *Helga* (1967).

When American films overtook German films at the box office in the early 1970s, Constantin went bankrupt (1977). Neue Constantin, founded to retain the brand name, has been managed by Bernd Eichinger, who changed the company's production and distribution strategies, specialising in blockbuster genres for worldwide distribution: action films such as *Das Boot* (1981), or adaptations of literary best-sellers like *Der Name der Rose/Le Nom de la rose/The Name of the Rose* (1986, dir. Jean-Jacques Annaud*). JG/TE

CONSTANTINE, Eddie
Edward Constantine; Los Angeles, California 1917 – Wiesbaden, Germany 1993

French actor and singer, American by birth. Like Yves Montand*, Constantine launched a singing career through a meeting with the singer Edith Piaf. He became a French film star in a series of parodic thrillers based on Peter Cheyney, initiated by Bernard Borderie's *La Môme vert-de-gris/Poison Ivy* (1953). As Lemmy Caution, Constantine embodied the French idea of a hard-boiled American hero: tall, handsome, cynical, hard-drinking and irresistible to women. He appeared in many films subsequently, as Caution or Caution-clones, as in émigré John Berry's skilful *noir* thriller *Je suis un sentimental* (1955). Michel Deville's* *Lucky Jo* (1964) was a departure, as was Jean-Luc Godard's* *Alphaville* (1965), a typical Godardian commentary on the star's image, which actually marked the end of his popular career. He tried unsuccessfully to work in the US, finishing his career as a nostalgic icon for European art film directors such as Rainer Werner Fassbinder*, Ulrike Ottinger* and Chris Petit. GV

CORDEIRO, MARGARITA – see REIS, António

CORK FILM FESTIVAL

Irish film festival. Established in 1956, the Cork Film Festival was the first film festival in Ireland. Its traditional strength has been its eclectic selection of short films. After a period of indecisiveness in the 1970s, it began to engage more fully with the changing Irish film cultural environment of the 1980s. It was for thirty years the only Irish film festival, but there are now five others: the successful Dublin Film Festival, which began in 1986, the pleasurable Galway Film Fleadh (Festival), the modest Derry Film Festival, and two children's film festivals, in Dublin and Belfast. KR

CORNEAU, Alain   Orléans 1943

French director. An IDHEC* graduate, Corneau was always interested in music, the subject of his international hit *Tous les matins du monde* (1992, winner of seven Césars*). Previously, however, Corneau was one of the main exponents of the French thriller of the 1970s and 1980s, which he employed in the style of the period to diagnose the ills of French society [> POLICIER]. *France, société anonyme* (1974), *Série noire* (1979), *Le Môme* (1986), *Police Python 357* (1975) and *Le Choix des armes* (1981) continued this trend, although moving towards the mainstream, with more schematic narratives, larger budgets and major stars. Apart from the more personal *Nocturne indien* (1989), which combines a thriller format with an unusual Indian setting, Corneau seems to have opted for Heritage cinema*, with *Fort Saganne* (1984), a colonial saga starring Depardieu, *Tous les matins du monde*, the story of baroque composer Marin Marais, and arguably *Le Nouveau monde* (1995), which recreates French relationships with American culture of the 1950s. GV

CORTI, Axel   Paris 1933 – Vienna 1993

Austrian director. Corti worked for Austrian radio and theatre before directing feature films for Austrian television in the 1960s, mainly docu-dramas and ambitious literary adaptations. He was the last director to make a film with actor Hans Moser* (*Kaiser Joseph und die Bahnwärterstochter*, 1962). His trilogy *Wohin und zurück* (1982–85), about an emigrant who escapes the Nazi regime in 1938, makes it to America and returns as a US soldier to his home country in 1945, received critical acclaim and prizes abroad, including the (German) Adolf Grimme Prize in 1987, for its sensitive treatment of the experience of forced emigration. IR

Other Films Include: *Der Fall Jägerstätter* (1971); *Eine blaßblaue Frauenschrift* (1984); *The King's Whore/Die Hure des Königs* (1990).

COSTA-GAVRAS, Constantin   Konstantinos Gavras; Athens 1933

French director of Greek origin. A graduate of IDHEC*, Costa-Gavras' first feature *Compartiment tueurs/The Sleeping Car Murders* (1965), based on Sébastien Japrisot's popular thriller, is usually considered routine. However, it already heralds two characteristics of his later work: gripping narrative and major stars (here Yves Montand* and Simone Signoret*). His greatest critical and popular success came with three of his next films, *Z* (1969), *L'Aveu/The Confession* (1970) and *Etat de siège/State of Siege* (1973). All three star Montand; all three combine the clarity, pace and drama of popular cinema with political issues (respectively Greek dictatorship, Communist totalitarianism and American imperialism) in the manner of the French *film à thèse* and the Italian 'political cinema'* of the time. As is often the case with 'liberal' films, the ideological positions are clear-cut and unobjectionable. Nevertheless, the films exposed huge audiences to important topical issues. Costa-Gavras' subsequent career in France has been uneven, but in the 1980s he made successful Hollywood films, in particular *Missing* (1982), *Betrayed* (1988) and *Music Box* (1989). In contrast to the male world of his French films, these are movies distinguished by an emphasis on women. Costa-Gavras and his wife Michèle Ray are producers. Between 1982 and 1987 he was director of the Cinémathèque française*. GV

Other Films: *Un Homme de trop/Shock Troops* (1967); *Section spéciale* (1975); *Clair de femme* (1979); *Hanna K* (1983); *Conseil de famille/Family Business* (1986); *Petite apocalypse* (1993); *A propos de Nice* (1994, one ep.); *L'Affaire Dreyfus* (1994, taken over by Yves Boisset); *Raspoutine* (1995).

COTTAFAVI, Vittorio   Modena 1914

Italian director. Although he worked in many genres, Cottafavi is celebrated as the *auteur* of the peplum*. With relatively large budgets, films like *La vendetta di Ercole/The Vengeance of Hercules* (1960) and *Ercole alla conquista di Atlantide/Hercules Conquers Atlantis/Hercules and the Captive Women* (1961) forge coherent worlds out of disparate classical and fantasy elements, rendered with a kitsch finesse, filling the wide screen with brilliant colour effects. Some of Cottafavi's films, such as *Messalina, Venere imperatrice/Messalina, Imperial Venus* (1960), have a tragic tone, but his Hercules is an amiable hero, reluctantly drawn into conflict and amused at the world about him. RD

Bib: 'Vittorio', *Présence du Cinéma* (special issue, 1961).

COURANT, Curt   Berlin 1899 – Los Angeles, California 1968

German cinematographer, who began his career in Italy and entered German film as cameraman on Joe May's* *Hilde Warren und der Tod* (1917). At first a craftsman rather than a creative force in his own right, his name could be found on the credits of films by virtually all the major commercial directors of the Weimar years, such as Rudolf Biebrach and Reinhold Schünzel*, Georg Jacoby* and Ludwig Berger*, Kurt Bernhardt* and Carl Froelich*. His most prestigious German assignment came in 1929, when he did principal cinematography on Fritz Lang's* *Die Frau im Mond/Woman on the Moon*. His stint with Lang stood him in good stead after he was forced into exile in 1933: in Britain, he worked with Alfred Hitchcock* (*The Man Who Knew Too Much*, 1934), and Berthold Viertel (*The Passing of the Third Floor Back*, 1935). In France, where his reputation was highest, he shot Jean Renoir's* *La Bête humaine* (1938), Marcel Carné's* *Le Jour se lève* (1939), a film by Abel Gance* (*Louise*, 1939), and Max Ophuls'* *De Mayerling a Sarajévo* (1940). In the US he photographed Chaplin's *Monsieur Verdoux* (1947) and, at the height of his fame, seems virtually to have retired, for not much is known of him thereafter, though he did shoot another film in 1961. TE

COUTARD, Raoul
Paris 1924

French cinematographer, celebrated for his New Wave* work, especially with Jean-Luc Godard*. Coutard started as a photographer-reporter, then became a cinematographer with Pierre Schoendorffer, whose producer Georges de Beauregard* introduced him to Godard. Coutard was a key element in Godard's first feature *A bout de souffle/Breathless* (1960), using a hand-held camera to achieve the improvised look of the film, pushing the unorthodox black-and-white Ilford stock to its limits and making imaginative use of natural and ceiling light. Coutard lit most Godard films until the late 1960s, and again worked with him on *Passion* (1982) and *Prénom Carmen* (1983), as well as with other New Wave directors such as François Truffaut*. Though Coutard is associated with the black-and-white luminosity of *A bout de souffle*, *Jules et Jim* (1962) and *Alphaville* (1965), he also worked in colour, for instance on *Le Mépris* (1963), in which he appears in the credit sequence. He has directed a few features, including *Hoa-Binh* (1970) and *SAS à San Salvador* (1982). GV

COWARD, Noël
Teddington 1899 – Blue Harbor, Jamaica 1973

British playwright, actor, scriptwriter and producer. An actor since the age of 12, Coward is primarily known as a leading actor and writer of the prewar British theatre. Many of his plays were adapted for the screen in the 1930s: *Cavalcade* (1933), *Bitter Sweet* (1933 and 1940) and *Design for Living* (1933). His first screen acting credit was for two bit parts in D. W. Griffith's *Hearts of the World* (1918), and in the 1950s and 1960s he played cameo roles in such films as *Our Man in Havana* (1960) and *The Italian Job* (1969). Conventionally identified in the theatre as a writer of sparkling dialogue and sophisticated society comedy, a musical lyricist of wit and brilliance, and an actor who took haughtiness to the brink of self-parody, Coward's work in the cinema shows a range of craft, sensitivity and technique. His most significant contribution was in the four films on which he worked with David Lean*: *In Which We Serve* (1942), co-directed with Lean, for which he wrote the screenplay and the music, and played a lead part; *This Happy Breed* (1944) and *Blithe Spirit* (1945), both adapted from his stage plays; and *Brief Encounter* (1945), co-written by Lean and Coward and based on Coward's original stage play, *Still Life*. Coward received a Special Academy Award for *In Which We Serve*. JC

Bib: Sheridan Morley, *A Talent to Amuse: A Biography of Noël Coward* (1969).

CRETEIL (Festival International de Films de Femmes)

French film festival. Originally held in Sceaux from 1979, the French International Women's Film Festival moved to Créteil (another suburb of Paris) in 1985, where it is now housed in the Maison des Arts, part-financed by local funds. This annual ten-day event takes place in late March/early April and has become the world's largest women's film festival; in 1994 it drew a mixed audience of over 50,000 spectators and showed over a hundred films whose common denominator was a woman director. Créteil's trajectory reflects that of women's cinema in Europe since the 1970s: from an explicitly feminist ethos, the event has moved towards more mainstream film, privileging art-house, *auteur*-oriented cinema over experimental and video work. Despite the toning down of its feminism, the festival has met with limited success in its aim of improving women's standing in the film industry. Professional and media resistance to feminism, strong in France, makes the continued existence and scope of the festival all the more impressive. GV

CRETINETTI – see DEED, André

CRICHTON, Charles
Wallasey 1910

British director, best known for his three classic Ealing comedies*, *Hue and Cry* (1947), *The Lavender Hill Mob* (1951) and *The Titfield Thunderbolt* (1953). He began his career as an assistant editor at London Films, where he cut such films as *The Private Life of Henry VIII* (1933), *Elephant Boy* (1937) and *The Thief of Bagdad* (1940). He began directing at Ealing with *For Those in Peril* (1944) and continued to direct with the studio until *The Man in the Sky* (1957). He made one successful comedy after Ealing closed, *The Battle of the Sexes* (1959), and a low-key thriller, *He Who Rides a Tiger* (1965), but his career in the 1960s was not particularly distinguished. In 1988, however, John Cleese*, with whom he had made a number of training videos, persuaded him to co-script and direct the very successful comedy *A Fish Called Wanda*. JC

Bib: Charles Barr, *Ealing Studios* (1977).

Other Films Include: *Dead of Night* ['The Golfing Story'] (1945); *Against the Wind* (1948); *Dance Hall* (1950); *Hunted* (1952); *The Divided Heart* (1954); *Law and Disorder* (1958).

CRISTALDI, Franco
Turin 1924 – Monte Carlo, Monaco 1992

Italian producer. The son of a lawyer and partisan, Cristaldi founded his own production company, Vides, in Turin in 1947, initially concentrating on documentaries and newsreels. He later moved into fiction with an unusual film on the Risorgimento, *La pattuglia sperduta* (1954) by Piero Nelli. He moved to Rome but maintained links with the northern industrial capitals, imposing a new style of work on the Italian cinema of the 1960s. For him cinema should be dominated by the director, but also by the highly professional producer. His view was that 'we don't have to produce films which sell, but we do have to sell the films that we produce'. He considered plots more important than stars and he chose films for their ability to capture the 'mood of a particular period'. He produced works by, among others, Luchino Visconti* (*Le notti bianche/White Nights*, 1957; *Vaghe stelle dell'Orsa/Sandra*, 1965); Pietro Germi* (the Oscar winner *Divorzio all'italiana/*

Divorce – Italian Style, 1961; *Sedotta e abbandonata/Seduced and Abandoned*, 1964); Mario Monicelli* (*I soliti ignoti/Persons Unknown, 1958; I compagni/The Strikers*, 1963); and Luigi Comencini* (*La ragazza di Bube/Bebo's Girl*, 1963). He produced all Francesco Rosi's* films from *I magliari* (1959) to *Cristo si è fermato a Eboli/Christ Stopped at Eboli* (1979), including *Salvatore Giuliano* (1962), which he pushed through to completion in spite of ostracism by the authorities and the banks. He was particularly dedicated to the discovery of such talents, which he regarded as part of his duty. He thus promoted the early careers of Gillo Pontecorvo*, Francesco Maselli*, Elio Petri*, Ugo Gregoretti (*Omicron*, 1964), Nanni Loy (*Un giorno da leoni*, 1961) and Marco Bellocchio*. He was a 'padre padrone' (despotic father) figure, as seen in the case of Giuseppe Tornatore* and his *Nuovo Cinema Paradiso/Cinema Paradiso* (1988), which was cut, reassembled and brought out several times before achieving worldwide success and winning many prizes, including an Oscar. His – contradictory – respect for *auteurs*' wishes and for meeting estimated budgets earned him a love-hate attitude from many directors, including Federico Fellini*, for whom he produced *Amarcord* (1973, another Oscar) and *E la nave va/And the Ship Sails On* (1983). Winner of a record number of awards, Cristaldi was forced to compromise increasingly during the 1980s as a result of the overpowering influence of television. He nevertheless continued to produce international successes, including Jean-Jacques Annaud's* *Der Name der Rose/The Name of the Rose* (1986). GVo

CROATIA – see YUGOSLAVIA (former)

CRUZ, Penélope   Born 1970

Spanish actress, who has shot to fame over the last few years after performances in *Jamón, jamón/Ham, Ham* (1992, dir. Juan José Bigas Luna*), *Belle Epoque* (1992, dir. Fernando Trueba*) and *Alegre ma non troppo* (1994, dir. Fernando Colomo*). Her dusky, coltish beauty projects an image of fresh, uninhibited sexuality crossed with a kind of Swiss finishing school girlish innocence. Her adolescent appeal is given a more earthy definition in *Jamón, jamón*, where she plays the local prostitute's daughter. PWE

CUADRADO, Luis   Luis Cuadrado Encinar; Toro
                                           1934 – Madrid 1980

Spanish cinematographer of impressive versatility who, after studying at the Escuela Oficial de Cinematografía* in the early 1960s, worked with the most prominent directors of the New Spanish Cinema* and the Barcelona School* between 1965 and 1975. Cuadrado's striking photography of the bleached arid landscape around Aranjuez in Carlos Saura's* *La caza/The Hunt* (1965) won him the first of a series of awards, and immediate recognition as a bold and resourceful cinematographer. Although a vociferous advocate of the virtues of black and white, from 1967 Cuadrado did work in colour, creating the distinctly painterly chiaroscuro of such contemporary classics as Victor Erice's* *El espíritu de la col-*

mena/The Spirit of the Beehive (1973) and José Luis Borau's* *Furtivos/Poachers* (1975). Blindness cut Cuadrado's career prematurely short, but his imaginative cinematography strongly marks over thirty films, many of them Elías Querejeta*-produced landmarks of the modern Spanish cinema. MD

CUSACK, Cyril   Durban, South Africa 1910 –
                                                Dublin 1993

Irish actor. Though born in South Africa, Cusack lived most of his life in Ireland. His first film role was as an evicted child in the Film Company of Ireland's* *Knocknagow* (1918), but he did not come to prominence as a film actor until he played a member of an IRA gang in Carol Reed's* *Odd Man Out* (1947). By then he was a well-established actor at the Abbey Theatre, where he had worked since 1932. He appeared in more than fifty film and television productions. Like most Irish actors, he was rarely given the lead role in films, and his theatrical career was more important artistically. KR

Other Films Include: *Shake Hands with the Devil* (1959); *A Terrible Beauty* (1960); *Fahrenheit 451* (1966); *Poitín* (1978).

CUTTS, Graham   Brighton 1885–1958

British director, who began his career as a northern exhibitor and moved into direction with the apparently sensational *Cocaine* (which had to be retitled *While London Sleeps*) in 1922. Cutts formed a partnership with Herbert Wilcox* and his brother Charles in the early 1920s, before moving to Gainsborough where he was Michael Balcon's* main director at Gaumont-British before the emergence of Alfred Hitchcock. Cutts was a stylist, achieving success with Ivor Novello* on *The Rat* (1925) and its sequel, *The Triumph of the Rat* (1926), with Jack Buchanan* on *Confetti* (1927), and with Betty Balfour* on *The Sea Urchin* (1926). He did not manage the transition to sound with equal success. JC

Other Films Include: *Paddy the Next Best Thing, Woman to Woman* (1923); *Die Spielerin/Chance the Idol* [Ger.], *The Queen was in the Parlour* (1927); *Return of the Rat* (1929); *The Sign of Four* (1932); *Three Men in a Boat* (1933); *Just William* (1939); *Combined Operations* [doc], *Food Manufacture* [doc] (1946).

CYBULSKI, Zbigniew   Zbyszek Cybulski; Kniaze,
                                     Ukraine 1927 – Wrocław 1967

Polish actor. Cybulski trained in the Stanislavsky method at the Cracow Theatre School and on graduating formed the satirical theatre company Bim Bom, with fellow actor Bogumił Kobieła. Although an accomplished actor and theatre director, Cybulski is best remembered for his film role as Maciek, the increasingly disillusioned nationalist militant hired to kill a local communist leader, in Andrzej Wajda's* *Popiół i Diament/Ashes and Diamonds* (1958). The film was an international success and Cybulski heralded as the 'Polish James Dean' for his portrayal of tough yet vulnerable youth. Indeed, his expressive and handsome face, half hidden by thick dark glasses, came to symbolise a whole generation of Polish youth to international audiences. Unlike James Dean, Cybulski aged in front of his fans, continuing to work in theatre and film. His comic talent is preserved in Wojciech Has'* *Rękopis Znaleziony w Saragossie/The Saragossa Manuscript* (1965). Cybulski's death at the age of 40 remains a mystery; it was never clear whether he committed suicide or whether alcohol or fatigue made him fall under a departing train. Wajda's tribute to Cybulski, *Wszystko na Sprzedaż/Everything for Sale* (1969), with its disconcerting mixture of fact and fiction, was widely acclaimed. AW

CZECH NEW WAVE

Czech film movement. The term is used to describe the group of Czech directors who emerged in the early 1960s and spearheaded an extremely varied group of films that regularly won awards at international festivals (as well as two Oscars), marking the first significant inroads of Czech and Slovak cinema into international markets. Technically, it refers to those directors who graduated and/or made their debuts in the early 1960s, including Miloš Forman*, Věra Chytilová*, Jiří Menzel*, Jan Němec*, Evald Schorm*, Jaromil Jireš* and Ivan Passer*. The only time they banded together for a group photograph was to defend Chytilová's *Sedmikrásky/Daisies* against charges of formalism in 1967. The photograph also includes fellow new wave directors Pavel Juráček, Hynek Bočan and Antonín Máša.

The importance of the new directors was considerable but the innovations of the 1960s were more crucially linked to structural changes within the industry and a progressive liberalisation in most areas of culture (the theatre saw productions of Beckett, Ionesco, Albee and Havel; Kafka and Hašek were reassessed and republished). All generations of filmmakers participated in the changes, including Otakar Vávra*, Karel Kachyňa*, Ján Kadár* and Elmar Klos*, Vojtěch Jasný* and František Vláčil*, as well as Slovak contemporaries such as Štefan Uher* and Juraj Jakubisko*. While the directors themselves point to the simplifications implicit in the term, which did not reflect a single theoretical position, they constituted a closely-knit group and frequently collaborated. Their production of innovative and critical work between 1963 and 1969 made it longer-lived than most comparable movements, including the French New Wave*. The styles of the 'wave' range from realism to surrealism, from improvisation to classical narrative, but there are many stylistic and thematic connections. The problems faced by youth in a hostile environment were touched on by virtually all the directors in the early 1960s and the influence of *cinéma-vérité** is noticeable in a wide range of films (most obviously those by Forman, Passer and Chytilová). While there were nods in the direction of Jean-Luc Godard*, Michelangelo Antonioni*, Federico Fellini* and the British New Wave*, the importance of Czech literature should also be noted: the comic tradition deriving from Hašek, the return to avant-garde writers such as Vančura* and Nezval. Novelists Bohumil Hrabal, Josef Škvorecký, Milan Kundera and Arnošt Lustig collaborated

on adaptations of their work, while writers such as Ester Krumbachová (who worked with Němec, Chytilová and Jireš) and Jan Procházka wrote important original screenplays.

The term *Czechoslovak* New Wave is used to include the work of Slovak directors such as Uher and Jakubisko. There was frequent interaction and their films were no less radical. At the end of the 1960s, the focus seemed to shift to Slovakia with the appearance of directors such as Dušan Hanák* and Elo Havetta. They joined Jakubisko in films that drew on Slovak inspiration and literature (Ladislav Ťažký, Ján Johanides) as well as the (West) 'European art film'* (two Alain Robbe-Grillet films were co-productions with Slovakia).

The 'New Wave' was effectively ended by the Soviet invasion of 1968, when cultural freedoms were identified with the forces that led to the 'Prague Spring' and the threat to the Soviet model of communism. Forman, Passer, Kadár, Jasný, Weiss* and Němec were among those who left the country. Others such as Juráček and Schorm were unable to work in the cinema, and many did not resume their careers until the middle or late 1970s. The film-makers' cohesion was broken, increased vetting of scripts ensured the absence of significant social criticism, and all formal experiment was stifled. PH

Bib: Peter Hames, *The Czechoslovak New Wave* (1985).

CZECHOSLOVAKIA

Czechoslovakia has an important place in the prehistory of the cinema by virtue of the work of the physiologist J. E. Purkyně (1787–1869), who wrote on persistence of vision as early as 1818 and in 1850, with the optician Ferdinand Durst, created the Kinesiscope, with which he used animated images to demonstrate the beating of the heart and the flight of butterflies. The first Czech films were made in 1898 by the photographer Jan Kříženecký, who was the first motion picture producer in Austria-Hungary.

A permanent film theatre was opened in Prague in 1907 by the conjuror Ponrepo, and regular film production began in 1910. Fiction films were centred on the Asum company (1912–17), founded by the architect Max Urban and his wife, the popular stage actress Andula Sedláčková; the first venture was a prestigious production based on Smetana's *Prodaná nevěsta/The Bartered Bride* (1913). At the outbreak of World War I, more than a third of the 700 cinemas in the Austro-Hungarian Empire were on Czech territory. Despite wartime difficulties, the Prague building contractor Vácslav Havel, grandfather of President Havel, established Lucernafilm in 1914, with other companies following at the end of the war, including Weteb, Praga, Excelsior and Poja. In 1919, Czechoslovakia scored its first foreign success with Karel Degl's *Stavitel chrámu/The Builder of the Cathedral*, released in France as *La Cathédrale*. The first Slovak film, *Jánošik*, was made by Jaroslav Siakel and František Horlivý in 1921 with American financing.

The formation of the independent Czechoslovak republic in 1918 furthered attempts to develop film as part of a national culture and, despite strong competition from German and American films, feature production averaged over twenty-six films a year in the silent period. One of the most popular films of the late 1920s was Karel Lamač's* adaptation of Jaroslav Hašek's anti-war novel *Dobrý voják Švejk/The Good Soldier Švejk* (1926), which was rapidly followed by three sequels. Films of social commitment included Přemysl Pražský's *Battalion* (1927) and Karl Junghans' *Takový je život/Such is Life* (1929), while Gustav Machatý* attracted attention with the artistically ambitious *Kreutzerova sonáta/The Kreutzer Sonata* (1926) and *Erotikon* (1929).

The introduction of sound brought inevitable problems of language, but a demand for Czech-language films on the domestic market ensured a rise from only eight features in 1930 to an average of over forty in the late 1930s. The studios at Barrandov*, built in 1932–33, were originally designed as a centre for international production and were the most advanced in central Europe. The first significant international interest in Czech cinema followed the success of three films at the 1934 Venice festival: Josef Rovenský's *Řeka/The River/Young Love* (1933); the Karel Plicka/Alexander Hammid* feature documentary on Slovak folklore, *Zem spieva/The Earth Sings* (1933); and Machatý's *Extase/Ecstasy* (1932), starring Hedy Kiesler (later Lamarr). All three films had a pastoral context and privileged the image as a primary component, giving birth to the notion of 'Czech lyricism'. The importance of cinematography in Czech and Slovak films was established by cinematographers such as Jan Stallich (*Řeka*, *Extase*), Václav Vich (*Erotikon*) and Otto Heller (*Před maturitou/Before the Finals*, both 1932), an influence still evident in the 1960s work of Jaroslav Kučera (*Všichni dobří rodáci/All My Good Countrymen*, 1968) and Jan Čuřík (*Holubice/The White Dove*, 1960).

Attempts to establish an art cinema were centred, in particular, on the novelist Vladislav Vančura*, who made an impressive debut with *Před maturitou*, co-directed by Svatopluk Innemann. However, the more radical forms of *Na sluneční straně/On the Sunnyside* (1933) and *Marijka nevěrnice/Faithless Marijka* (1934) failed to meet with commercial success. The 1930s also saw the debuts of the popular stage comedians Jiří Voskovec* and Jan Werich*. Two of their films were directed by the prolific Martin Frič*, who made a series of films starring comic actors such as Vlasta Burian*, Hugo Haas*, and Oldřich Nový. Attacks on the rise of fascism were apparent in the Voskovec and Werich film *Svět patří nám/The World Belongs to Us* (1937) and in Hugo Haas' film of Karel Čapek's play *Bílá nemoc/The White Sickness* (1937).

The period of the Nazi occupation had its effect on film-making, with the number of films dropping from forty in 1939 to nine in 1944. Nonetheless, there were films of note from Frič and from Otakar Vávra*. The National Film Archive was formed in 1943, and a group that included Vančura, Vávra and Elmar Klos* planned the future nationalisation of the film industry. The film school, FAMU*, was founded in 1947, and in the same year a separate Slovak cinema, with its own studios at Koliba in Bratislava, was established. Nationalisation also paved the way for the international success of Czech and Slovak animation with the establishment of studios in Prague and Zlín (Gottwaldov) [> ANIMATION (CZECHOSLOVAKIA)]. Czech films again attracted attention when Karel Steklý's *Siréna/The Siren/The Strike* (1947) and Jiří Trnka's *Špalíček/The Czech Year* (1947) won major awards at Venice in 1947 and 1948.

Following the Communist takeover in 1948, there was a fairly swift adherence to the moribund formulae of Stalinist cinema, and another plunge in production combined, somewhat paradoxically, with international recognition in the field of animation. In addition to Jiří Trnka*, the work of Karel Zeman*, Hermína Týrlová, Břetislav Pojar, Jiří Brdečka and others soon acquired a world following. There was a real sense in which animated film kept alive visual traditions at a time when 'formalism' was officially condemned. Following Khrushchev's 'de-Stalinisation' speech of 1956, a limited 'thaw' set in, reflecting similar developments in Poland and the Soviet Union. Older directors such as Jiří Weiss*, Ján Kadár* and Elmar Klos were able to tackle more ambitious topics, while the first FAMU graduates, such as Vojtěch Jasný* and Karel Kachyňa*, made their debuts. Together, the new films became the focus for the 1959 conference at Banská Bystrica attacking 'remnants of bourgeois thought'. However, the new repression was short-lived and soon challenged by a second generation of FAMU graduates, now described as the <Czech New Wave>*. Miloš Forman*, Věra Chytilová* and Jaromil Jireš* all made their debuts in 1963 and combined with older and younger colleagues in the period 1963–69 to promote a period of extraordinary creative diversity in which film-makers sometimes appeared to escape the demands of both the market and ideology. Of course, films were banned (Chytilová's *Sedmikrásky/Daisies*, 1966, Jan Němec's* *O slavnosti a hostech/The Party and the Guests*, 1966), and innovative films were only made by pushing against the system, but the achievements were considerable. Other directors of note to make their debuts included Jiří Menzel*, Ivan Passer*, Evald Schorm*, Pavel Juráček and Jan Schmidt, and, in Slovakia, Štefan Uher* and Juraj Jakubisko*.

The development of creative ideas in the film industry was but one aspect of a wider phenomenon – the growth of ideas in economics, politics, literature and the arts that made up the Czechoslovak reform movement. It was a movement that led directly to the 'Prague Spring' of 1968 and plans to introduce 'socialist democracy'. It was this threat to the Soviet model of centralised power ('the leading role of the Communist Party') that led to the Warsaw Pact invasion of August 1968. The policies of 'normalisation' that followed were designed to liquidate the reforms of the late 1960s and led to exile, silence or accommodation in all walks of life. Kadár, Forman, Passer, Jasný and Němec were among those who went into exile, while other directors such as Ladislav Helge, Schorm and Juráček were unable to work. Well over a hundred films from the 1960s were banned and directors, after appropriate acknowledgment of the correctness of the 1968 invasion, were forced to make films that were either naive or conformed to a bland and officially sanctioned image of popular entertainment. In 1973, four films were banned 'for ever' – Forman's *Hoří, má panenko!/The Firemen's Ball* (1967), Němec's *O slavnosti a hostech*, Jasný's *Všichni dobří rodáci/All My Good Countrymen* (1968), and Schorm's *Farářův konec/End of a Priest* (1968). In these circumstances, the search for minor elements of criticism or formal dissent became a precise art. Menzel, Chytilová and Jireš continued to make films, although most film-makers were kept unemployed until 1976. Some of their achievements are still notable. Menzel made *Na samotě u lesa/Seclusion Near a Forest* (1976), continued his collaboration with the country's leading novelist, Bohumil

Hrabal, with *Postřižiny/Cutting It Short* (1980) and *Slavnosti sněženek/The Snowdrop Festival* (1983), and gained an Oscar nomination for *Vesničko má, středisková/My Sweet Little Village* (1985). Chytilová made the critically abrasive *Panelstory/Prefab Story* (1979), while in Slovakia directors such as Uher, Dušan Hanák*, and Martin Hollý frequently transcended the norms of the time.

In the post-1969 situation, animated film again permitted a freedom denied to features. The work of Adolf Born, Jaroslav Doubrava and Miloš Macourek provided a critical edge, while the 'militant surrealism' of Jan Švankmajer* followed a path totally at variance with official ideology. The tradition of puppet film found new expression in the work of Jiří Barta (*Krysař/The Pied Piper*, 1986).

Czechoslovakia is a pioneer of children's films and in the mid-1980s they made up as much as 15 per cent of the annual production of around forty features. Based principally in the Zlín (Gottwaldov) studios, many directors worked in the genre, and children's films have been a major element in film exports. The most notable specialist directors have included Věra Plívová-Šimková and Ota Koval.

In the late 1980s, there was evidence of a new generation of directors coming to the fore with feature films that presented a more direct challenge to current orthodoxies, notably Irena Pavlásková (*Čas sluhů/Time of the Servants*, 1989), Petr Koliha (*Něžný barbar/Tender Barbarian*, 1989), Miloš Zábranský (*Dům pro dva/A House for Two*, 1988), and Zdeněk Tyc (*Vojtěch, řečený sirotek/An Orphan Called Vojtěch*, 1989). These signs of a system noticeably fraying were confirmed by the 'Velvet Revolution' of November 1989. External forces like the Gorbachev reforms and the general crisis of Eastern Europe were matched by an internal situation where resistance to change had made collapse virtually inevitable.

The best post-revolutionary film is Jan Svěrák's Oscar-nominated *Obecná škola/The Elementary School* (1991), one of the last productions of the soon to be privatised Barrandov Studios. Many of the post-revolutionary films have been disappointing, showing a crudity and tastelessness that is partly a settling of past accounts and partly commercial necessity in a market now open to Hollywood penetration. After a drop in production from 1990, the number of features rose again in 1993 to twenty-two, with several Czech titles outperforming their US rivals on the home market. International co-productions supported projects ranging from the commercial (Menzel's *Život a neobyčejna dobrodružství vojáka Ivana Čonkina/The Life and Extraordinary Adventures of Private Ivan Chonkin* [rel. 1994 in US]) to the art cinema (Švankmajer's *Lekce Faust/Faust*, Drahomíra Vihanová's *Pevnost/The Fortress*). Czech television replaced Barrandov as the major producer, supporting ambitious projects such as the award-winning adaptation of Eva Kantůrková's novel *Přítelkyně z domů smutku/My Companions in the House of Anguish* (1993), directed by Hynek Bočan, and *Pomsta/Revenge* (1994), by the exiled Yugoslav director Lordan Zafranović.

The prospects for an independent Slovak cinema are uncertain, although Slovak television backed a second feature by the talented Martin Šulík (*Všetko čo mám rád/Everything I Like*, 1992). With the division of Czechoslovakia into separate states in 1993, this is now a history that must be written separately. PH

CZIFFRA, Geza von
Arad 1900 – Dießen, Bavaria 1989

Austrian director. After his debut with the puppet movie *Gullivers Reisen* (1922), Cziffra went to Berlin in 1923, where he published literary and political articles and worked as an assistant director. A major figure in the Hungarian cinema after 1933, he was contracted by Wien-Film in 1941, for which, two years later, he directed the box-office hit *Der Weisse Traum* (1943), a melodramatic musical-on-ice. Immediately after the war he returned to Vienna and established the first production company licensed by the American forces in liberated Austria. In 1952 he set up his second and more successful company, Arion-Film, and was able to re-establish his reputation as a director of popular revue films. His twelve Peter Alexander* movies (including *Das haut hin*, 1957; *Schlag auf Schlag*, 1959; *Charleys Tante*, 1963) decisively shaped the German musical and light entertainment cinema of the 1950s and 1960s. MW

CZINNER, Paul
Budapest 1890 – London 1972

Hungarian-born director, who began his career with Expressionist* films (*Homo immanis*, 1919; *Inferno*, 1919). From 1924 he worked regularly with his future wife Elisabeth Bergner* and with Carl Mayer*, making popular variations of the *Kammerspielfilm** (*Nju*, 1924; *Fräulein Else*, 1929; *Der träumende Mund/Dreaming Lips*, 1932), as well as the occasional historical costume drama (*Liebe*, 1926), cross-dressing comedy (*Der Geiger von Florenz/Impetuous Youth/The Violinist of Florence*, 1926), or a mixture of both (*Dona Juana*, 1927). All his German films contained exceptional star casts, including Bergner, Emil Jannings*, Conrad Veidt*, Rudolf Forster, Max Schreck and Alfred Bassermann, around each of whom Czinner knew how to create an appropriate cinematic frame, notable for its exceptional mobility.

In 1933, Czinner and Bergner emigrated to Britain, where they tried to adapt their brand of bitter-sweet melodrama to English tastes, with limited success. In 1939 they went to Hollywood, but were unable to work on further co-productions. In 1949 Czinner returned to Europe, directing ballet and opera films (*Don Giovanni*, 1955) and documentaries on European music and dance theatres. MW

Other Films Include: *The Woman He Scorned* (1929, UK); *Ariane* (1931); *As You Like It* (1936, UK).

D

DAGOVER, Lil
Java 1897 – Munich 1980

German actress, one of the international stars to emerge from the German cinema in the 1920s and 1930s. She had her screen debut in Fritz Lang's* exotic costume drama *Harakiri* (1919), in which she first practised her unfocused offscreen look. An abstract element in Lang's *mise-en-scène*, but also capable of connoting emotional turmoil and nameless dread, this look was Dagover's most memorable acting contribution to her best-known part as Jane in Robert Wiene's* *Das Cabinet des Dr Caligari/The Cabinet of Dr Caligari* (1920), adding greatly to the film's ambiguous tone, somewhere between horror and fascinated desire.

Dagover's skill with ocular excess gave depth to the mostly melodramatic roles she played in other Lang films, such as *Der müde Tod/Destiny* (1921) and *Dr Mabuse, der Spieler/Dr Mabuse, the Gambler* (1922), and F. W. Murnau's* *Phantom* (1922), making her an actress at once typically 'expressionist' and at the threshold of the transition from Henny Porten* to the *femmes fatales* of Weimar* cinema, such as Louise Brooks* and Marlene Dietrich*. In the 1970s, on talk shows and in interviews, she credibly represented Weimar cinema, giving its blessing to the neo-romantics of the New German Cinema*. TE/MW

Other Films Include: *Die Spinnen* (1919); *Tartüff* (1926); *Orient Express* (1927); *Der Kongress tanzt* (1931); *Schlußakkord* (1936); *Buddenbrooks* (1959); *Der Richter und sein Henker/End of the Game* (1976).

DALGARD, Olav
Folldal 1898 – Jar 1980

Norwegian director, who also worked in theatre. Dalgard was a member of the Norwegian Labour Party, which made extensive use of film for propaganda purposes in the 1930s. Dalgard made films for election campaigns, but also semi-documentaries about important events in the history of the Norwegian labour movement. In 1936 a grant allowed him to go to Moscow and study film and theatre, and his 1938 film *Det drønner gjennom dalen/Thunder Through the Valley* reflects his increased professionalism. The film was made for the tenth anniversary of the forestry workers' trade union, and shows how a labour dispute makes the men understand the necessity of unionisation. Dalgard's best-known film is *Gryr i Norden/Nordic Dawn* (1939), on a workers' strike in an Oslo match factory in 1889. *Vi vil leve!/We Want to Live!* (1946) explores the resistance to the German occupation. Dalgard is also the author of the first Norwegian scholarly book on film history and theory, *Filmskuespillet* ('The Film Play', 1951). KS

Other Films Include: *Samhold må til/Solidarity is Necessary* (1935); *Vi bygger landet/We are Building the Country* (1936); *By og land hand i hand/City and Countryside Hand in Hand* (1937); *Lenkene brytes/Breaking the Chains* (1938); *Om kjærligheten synger de/They Sing about Love* (1946).

DALIO, Marcel
Israel Moshe Blauschild; Paris 1899–1983

French actor. Dalio came from the music hall and theatre and was typecast in most of his huge 1930s filmography (thirty films in 1936–38 alone) in minor roles which exploited his Semitic features – a casting which was both racist and a source of employment. The cowardly L'Arbi in Julien Duvivier's* *Pépé le Moko* (1936) and Mattéo in Pierre Chenal's* *La Maison du Maltais* (1938, a rare leading part) are the epitome of this stereotyping. His role as the rich and generous Jewish prisoner in Jean Renoir's* *La Grande illusion* (1937), clearly meant as positive, still appeared as racist to some. As the cultured Marquis de la Chesnaye in Renoir's *La Règle du jeu/Rules of the Game* (1939), Dalio at last escaped the stereotype. But when the war forced him to emigrate to Hollywood, he found himself playing another: the 'Frenchie' in US films which, however, included distinguished titles such as *Casablanca* (1942) and *To Have and Have Not* (1944). Dalio acted in small parts in many popular French and US movies until 1980. GV

DALLE, Béatrice
Brest 1964

French actress. Dalle was 'discovered' on the streets of Paris and cast by Jean-Jacques Beineix* as Betty in *37°2 le matin/Betty Blue* (1985). The film was a massive success, and Dalle the most explosive revelation of a new generation of actresses. With her blatant sensuality and popular wit (on and off the screen), Dalle projects provocative sexuality, insolence and spontaneity in the Brigitte Bardot* mould. Like BB, she has found it hard to escape typecasting. Her subsequent films, including Claire Devers' intelligent *Chimères* (1989), which works against her *Betty Blue* image, and Diane Kurys'* *A la folie* (1994), have failed at the box office and so far she remains, unfortunately, a one-film star. GV

DALRYMPLE, Ian
Johannesburg, South Africa 1903 – London 1989

British writer, director and producer, described by Roger Manvell as 'one of several enlightened and highly educated young British university men attracted to adopt film-making as a profession during the 1920s and 1930s'. Dalrymple wrote screenplays – many of them adaptations – for some of the most significant films of the 1930s, including two of Michael Powell's* 'quota quickies', *Her Last Affaire* (1935) and *The Brown Wallet* (1936), *The Good Companions* (1933) and *South Riding* (1938) for Victor Saville*, *The Citadel* (1938) for King Vidor, and *Pygmalion* (1938), for which he received an Academy Award. He also co-directed with Saville the excellent *Storm in a Teacup* (1937), which he adapted from James Bridie's stage play. During the war, after scripting *'Pimpernel' Smith* (1941) for Leslie Howard*, he became head of the Crown Film Unit, his productions including *London Can Take It!* (1940), *Target for To-night* (1941) and *Listen to Britain* (1942). He formed his own company, Wessex, in 1946, where he directed one of his most interesting adaptations, *Esther Waters* (co-dir. Peter Proud, 1948), from George Moore's novel, and continued to produce until the late 1960s. JC

DAMIANOS, Alexis   Crete 1919

Greek director and actor. Damianos, considered one of the major Greek film-makers, has directed only three films. *Mehri to plio/To the Ship* (1966) and *Evdokia* (1971) were brave attempts to create an independent discourse at a difficult period just before and during the military dictatorship, when the Greek commercial film industry was at its peak. The films deal with emigration and prostitution, placing the two issues on a timeless, universal and tragic level, even though the *mise-en-scène* is naturalistic. They investigate the play between fate and people's conditions and desires, the limits of personal freedom and the ability to transcend social and cultural barriers [> NEW GREEK CINEMA]. Damianos's latest film, *Iniohos/The Charioteer*, took several years to make; it was finally released in 1995. Damianos has also had a very successful acting career. TN

DANELIA, Georgi N.   Tbilisi, Georgia [USSR] 1930

Russian director and scriptwriter, who studied at the Moscow Architectural Institute and the Higher Courses for Directors, which he completed in 1959. Danelia's first film was *Tozhe lyudi/People Too* (1959), a short taken from an episode in *War and Peace*. His first feature was *Seryozha* (1960), co-directed with Igor Talankin, from a popular story by Vera Panova. In *Ya shagayu po Moskve/I Walk Around Moscow* (1963), Danelia used humour, the charm of his actors and a popular song to describe the adventures of a group of young people centred on Kolya, played by the young Nikita Mikhalkov*. Among Danelia's other films are *Sovsem propashchii/Quite Lost* (1973), a version of Mark Twain's *The Adventures of Huckleberry Finn*, and *Osennii marafon/Autumn Marathon* (1979), a 'sad comedy' in which the hero, an academic, can never quite catch up with all his obligations (the title alludes to his enforced jogging sessions with a Danish professor). *Osenii marafon* won the main prize at the 1979 San Sebastian Film Festival. In Danelia's 1986 science-fiction comedy *Kin-Dza-Dza*, two Soviet citizens are transported to a distant planet. His next film, *Pasport/Passport* (1990), is a comedy of errors about a Georgian nationalist and his Jewish half-brother who wants to emigrate. JGf

DANELIUC, Mircea   Hotin 1943

Romanian director, scriptwriter and actor, often considered the strongest of the younger Romanian film-makers. A student of French literature, he graduated from film school in 1972, and worked as assistant director to Mircea Dragan. His first feature, *Cursă/The Long Drive* (1975), about the unfulfilled dreams of two truck drivers and a young woman they pick up, achieved both box-office success and critical acclaim, thereby helping to create space for contemporary movies by young directors. *Editie specială/Special Issue* (1978) used the stereotypical form of the anti-fascist war thriller to create a tightly edited psychological art movie. The highly original *Probă de microfon/Microphone Test* (1979) analysed relationships between the media and society through the stilted world of Romanian television journalism, with Daneliuc starring as a cameraman. Equally politically complex, *Croazieră/The Cruise* (1981) is a parable about a boat journey organised as a reward for good conduct. *Glissando* (1984), the first feature in which Daneliuc did not star, is an ambitious and disturbing parable of human decay set in the gambling house of a Dante-esque asylum. At the Venice festival it was compared to the films of Federico Fellini* and Ingmar Bergman*. *Jacob* (1988), a powerful social drama, won similar international acclaim. *Patul conjugal/Conjugal Bed* (1993) hilariously and sarcastically conveys the emotional deprivation of post-Ceaușescu Romania. MM

DANISH CHILDREN'S FILMS

Popular Danish genre. As a large section of the Danish audience is composed of young children and teenagers, films have been regularly produced for these two age groups, especially after World War II, when Astrid and Bjarne Henning-Jensen* began to make children's films. The couple co-directed *De Pokkers unger/Those Blasted Kids* in 1947; *Palle alene i verden/Palle Alone in the World* (1949) was made by Astrid Henning-Jensen* alone. Both films combine social reality with amusing story-telling. The same cannot be said of the 1950s series of children's films, *Far til Fire/The Father of Four*. Based on a Danish comic strip, these were sentimental and old-fashioned in outlook, although their popularity helped sustain interest in the genre through the 1960s and the 1970s. In 1982 legislation helpfully decreed that 25 per cent of state subsidies to film production should go to children's films, with the result that several interesting films were made in 1983: Bille August's* *Zappa*, Nils Malmros'* *Skønheden og udyret/The Beauty and the Beast*, and Rumle Hammerich's *Otto er et næsehorn/Otto is a Rhino*. Subsequent examples include *Skyggen af Emma/Emma's Shadow* (1988) and *Drengene fra St. Petri/The Boys from St Petri* (1991), both directed by Søren Kragh-Jacobsen. ME

DANISH EROTIC MELODRAMA

Danish film genre. The erotic melodrama, or 'domestic drama', as it was coyly labelled in Britain at the time, was the most popular Danish film genre before World War I. Danish cinema was unique in dealing openly with questions of sexuality and desire, a circumstance which historians have related to the unusually liberal climate (including an important women's movement) which then prevailed in Denmark, especially Copenhagen, the 'Paris of Northern Europe', and to the influx into the city of a new class of women shop assistants and office workers. The genre's sophisticated narratives took place among the contemporary urban upper and middle classes and focused on women's fantasies and desires. The extraordinarily successful *Afgrunden/The Abyss* (1910), starring Asta Nielsen*, both launched and typified the genre, containing most of its key elements, especially the extravagantly long-drawn-out kiss – a Danish innovation soon eagerly copied all over the world. Other representative films are *Ved Fængslets Port/Temptations of a Great City* (1911), *Expeditricen/In the Prime of Life* (1911) and *Den Stærkeste/ The Strongest/Conquered* (1912). ME

Bib: Marguerite Engberg, 'The Erotic Melodrama in Danish Silent Films 1910–1918', *Film History* (March 1993).

DANSK KULTURFILM

Danish institution ('Danish Cultural Film') established in 1932 out of a growing concern with cinema's cultural effects. The institution's purpose was to produce educational and children's films and films about Denmark. Many of the best-known Danish documentary directors have worked for it, including Astrid and Bjarne Henning-Jensen*, Søren Melson and Theodor Christensen*. Major films produced by Dansk Kulturfilm are *Føllet/The Colt* (1943) by Bjarne Henning-Jensen, *Her er Banerne/This is the Railway* (1948) by Theodor Christensen and *Palle alene i verden/Palle Alone in the World* (1949) by Astrid Henning-Jensen. With the reorganisation of various film institutions in 1958, Dansk Kulturfilm came under the administration of the State Film Centre, Statens Filmcentral. ME

DARRIEUX, Danielle   Bordeaux 1917

French actress. The embodiment of the 'sophisticated Frenchwoman', Darrieux has had one of the longest and most distinguished film careers of all French actresses. While studying music and singing, she was cast from a newspaper advertisement in Wilhelm Thiele's* *Le Bal* (1931, the French version of his *Der Ball*) at the age of fourteen. Her part as the unruly daughter who throws her parents' invitations in the Seine rather than post them set the foundations of her early persona: the pretty, bubbly and impertinent young woman, her heart-shaped mouth in a permanent pout. A successful career followed in comedies and musicals, such as Robert Siodmak's* *La Crise est finie* (1934), Billy Wilder's *Mauvaise graine* (1934), and in *Battement de coeur* (1939, directed by Henri Decoin*, her first husband). Unusually, she alternated between this light tradition and melodrama – *Mayerling* (1936), co-starring Boyer*, *Katia* (1938). Darrieux's dominant 1930s image, however, was that of the modern young woman: a lawyer in *Un mauvais garçon* (1936), wearing up-to-date swimsuits in the extraordinary *Club de femmes* (1936, in which no man appears except her transvestite boyfriend) or fashionable berets and shiny raincoats in the melodramatic *Abus de confiance* (1937). Her success attracted the attention of Hollywood, but her American career was lacklustre. Her postwar films capitalised on her melodramatic, sophisticated

image. In Max Ophuls'* *La Ronde* (1950) and *Madame de.../The Earrings of Madame de...* (1953), she epitomised another stereotype of French femininity: the elegant and knowing adulteress. She starred in other popular costume films like *Le Rouge et le noir* (1954) and *Pot-Bouille/The House of Lovers* (1957), both with Gérard Philipe*. Her post-1950s film career was less successful, with exceptions such as Jacques Demy's* *Les Demoiselles de Rochefort* (1967) and *Une chambre en ville* (1982), and André Téchiné's* *Le Lieu du crime/The Scene of the Crime* (1986). Meanwhile she has pursued a very successful career on television and on stage. GV

DASSIN, Jules   Middletown, Connecticut, 1911

American director and actor. After studying drama in Europe (1934–36), Dassin worked for the theatre and radio in New York. In 1941 he worked as an assistant director at RKO and subsequently as a director at MGM, Universal and 20th Century-Fox. Dassin's creative work is divided into two periods, the American and the European/Greek. To the first belongs *Brute Force* (1947), *The Naked City* (1948) and *Night and the City* (1950, shot in London), forming the director's cycle of films of social concern: violence, popular milieux and the city. In 1950, having become implicated in the House Un-American Activities Committee witch-hunt, he left for Europe. He was never to return permanently to the US. In France, Dassin directed one of the key *policiers** of the mid-1950s, *Du Rififi chez les hommes/Rififi* (1955, best *mise-en-scène* prize at the 1955 Cannes Film Festival), a tale of loyalty and betrayal among a male 'family' of gangsters, with striking black-and-white photography. In this film, as in a few others, Dassin also acted under the pseudonym Perlo Vita. *Rififi* is especially celebrated for its extraordinarily long, tense central sequence depicting the heist, with meticulous observation of gesture and no dialogue. *Rififi* began Dassin's European period, characterised by broad ideological concerns and formal variations. Moving to Greece, he made *Pote tin Kiriaki/ Never on Sunday* (1959), a pleasing morality tale. The film's star, Melina Mercouri* (Dassin's wife), was propelled to world fame, aided by Manos Hadjidakis's* inspired music. Subsequent films attempted, less successfully, to incorporate classical drama into contemporary Greek reality. Now living permanently in Greece, and a passionate advocate of its culture, Dassin works mainly for the stage. NK/GV

Other Films Include: *The Tell-Tale Heart* (1941, US); *Thieves' Highway* (1949, US); *Celui qui doit mourir/He Who Must Die* (1956, Fr.); *La Legge/La Loi/Where the Hot Wind Blows* (1958, It./Fr.); *Phaedra* (1962, Gr.); *Topkapi* (1964, US); *La Promesse de l'aube/Promise at Dawn* (1971, Fr./US); *Kravgi Ginekon/A Dream of Passion* (1978, Gr.); *Circle of Two* (1980, Canada).

DAUMAN, Anatole   Warsaw, Poland 1925

French producer. With Georges de Beauregard* and Pierre Braunberger*, Dauman is a key figure in French *auteur* cinema. His company, Argos Film (founded 1951 with Philippe Lifchitz), was notable for taking on 'risky' and 'difficult' films, including Alain Resnais'* *Nuit et brouillard/Night and Fog* (1955) and *Hiroshima, mon amour* (1959), Robert Bresson's* *Mouchette* (1967), and Chris Marker's* *La Jetée* (1962). Since the 1970s Argos has taken on an international dimension, producing Nagisa Oshima's *Ai no corrida/In the Realm of the Senses* (1976, Jap./Fr.), Andrey Tarkovsky's* *Offret/The Sacrifice* (1986) and several films by Wim Wenders* among many others. GV

DAVIDSON, Paul   Loetzen, East Prussia 1867 – Berlin [?] 1927

German producer, who could scarcely know, when he founded the Allgemeine Kinematographen in Frankfurt in 1906, that it would make him one of the fathers of the German film industry. From equipment to theatres, from theatres to film exchanges, and from exchanges to studios, Davidson's rapid progress shows how thoroughly he had grasped the logic of the film business, which rests on the interlocking cogs of exhibition, distribution and production.

Davidson's early objective was to build up a chain of cinemas. Profits from his Union-Theater (UT), the largest in Germany at the time, and sited in prime locations in many regional industrial centres as well as Berlin and Brussels, gave him the capital to reorganise, by 1909, his different activities into the Projektions AG 'Union' (PAGU*), Germany's first vertically integrated film company. Moving operations to Berlin in 1913, he remodelled his UT at Berlin's Alexanderplatz into the country's biggest *Filmpalast*, with a capacity of 1,200 seats, and also converted his 1911 distribution contract with Asta Nielsen* (and her director-husband Urban Gad) into a production agreement for eight films per year, building for her the necessary studio space. Aware of the debates around the *Autorenfilm** and the need for cultural legitimacy, Davidson offered Max Reinhardt* a three-year contract in 1913 worth an astounding 200,000 Marks.

In 1914, Davidson 'discovered' Ernst Lubitsch*, starting a collaboration which lasted for nearly ten years and over thirty-five films. In 1917, Davidson sold PAGU to the newly founded Ufa*, retaining producer's rights and a seat on the board. Lubitsch's epic spectaculars such as *Madame Dubarry* (1919) and *Anna Boleyn* (1920) were all produced by Davidson, who was instrumental in the director getting his offer from Hollywood. Lubitsch's departure proved fatal: the Ufa subsidiary Paul Davidson-Film, set up in 1924, never found its stride and had ceased trading by spring 1927. A few months later, Davidson committed suicide. TE/MW

DAVIES, Terence   Liverpool 1945

British director, whose small but perfectly formed output over an almost twenty-year period – three shorts and two features between 1974 and 1992 – is one more testimony both to the aesthetic possibilities and the financial difficulties of a British art cinema. Davies' work to date has been largely autobiographical. Both his trilogy, released in 1984 and com-

prising *Children* (1974), *Madonna and Child* (1980) and *Death and Transfiguration* (1983), and his two features, *Distant Voices, Still Lives* (1988) and *The Long Day Closes* (1992), return to the experience of growing up in Catholic, working-class Liverpool in a family which was both nurturing (the mother) and brutalising (the father). The films are highly formal in their composition, recreating the past like a family album, using studio settings to maintain control, and evoking memory with a soundtrack of radio voices and popular songs. Davies' celebration of the working-class community and the enduring 'mam' has been criticised for its sentimentalising nostalgia, but has been defended as a highly formalised and self-reflexive exploration of male memory. *The Neon Bible* was shown in Cannes (1995) to a mixed reception. JC

DAY-LEWIS, Daniel   London 1957

British actor. Son of the poet Cecil Day-Lewis and Jill Balcon and grandson of Michael Balcon*, Daniel Day-Lewis' film career is marked by a remarkable range and a willingness to take risks in his choice of roles. Apparently carved out for the effete or brooding masculinity of an earlier age, which he plays in *A Room with a View* (1987) and Martin Scorsese's *The Age of Innocence* (1993, US), or for the unrestrained eroticism of *The Unbearable Lightness of Being* (1987, US), Day-Lewis stretches his physical versatility from the athletic dash of Hawkeye in Michael Mann's *The Last of the Mohicans* (1992, US) to his Oscar-winning performance as Christy Brown, the writer confined to a wheelchair by cerebral palsy, in Jim Sheridan's* *My Left Foot* (1989). First achieving recognition as the gay punk in Stephen Frears'* and Hanif Kureishi's* *My Beautiful Laundrette* (1985), Day-Lewis, now on the edge of international stardom, took the same risks with public and box-office acceptability when he played the not particularly attractive Gerry Conlon, one of the Guildford Four who were wrongly imprisoned as IRA bombers, in Sheridan's *In the Name of the Father* (1993). JC

DEAN, Basil   Croydon 1888 – London 1978

British producer and director, who founded Associated Talking Pictures in 1929 and extended Ealing* studios in 1931. Dean was a major figure in London theatre in the 1920s, coming to film as an extension rather than a replacement of his theatre activities. He adapted his own co-authored play, *The Constant Nymph*, twice (in 1928 and 1933), and directed adaptations of Galsworthy's *Loyalties* (1933) and Dodie Smith's *Autumn Crocus* (1934). He also saw the potential of music hall as popular entertainment, signing up Gracie Fields* and George Formby*. He produced Gracie Fields' first film *Sally in Our Alley* (1931) and directed several others, including her best, *Sing As We Go* (1934). For Formby, he established the director/producer team of Anthony Kimmins and Jack Kitchin. Dean was committed to a national cinema, and was opposed to the internationalism which Korda* sought: 'Better that the vulgarity should be our own,' he said, 'and not someone else's.' He returned to the theatre in 1938, handing over Ealing studios to Michael Balcon*. JC

Bib: Basil Dean, *Seven Ages: An Autobiography 1888–1927* (1970), and *The Mind's Eye: An Autobiography 1927–1972* (1972).

Other Films Include: As Director and Producer – *The Return of Sherlock Holmes* (1929); *Escape, Birds of Prey* (1930); *Lorna Doone, Look Up and Laugh* (1935); *The Show Goes On, The First and the Last* (1937).

DEARDEN, Basil
Basil Dear; Westcliffe-on-Sea 1911 – London 1971
and
RELPH, Michael
Broadstone, Dorset 1915

British director, producer, writer team, who worked together from the mid-1940s until Dearden's death in a car accident in 1971. Basil Dearden had joined Basil Dean* as a stage manager in the West End theatre, and accompanied him to Ealing in 1936. At Ealing, he assisted on George Formby* films and co-directed Will Hay* comedies with Hay. His solo directorial debut was *The Bells Go Down* (1943), a film on which Michael Relph was art director. Relph had entered films in 1932 as an art director for Michael Balcon*. He joined Ealing in 1942, working as designer on all Dearden's films and as associate producer on others. Their director-producer-writer team was formed in 1949.

Dearden and Relph, both at Ealing and after, are associated with the social problem film, dealing with issues such as delinquency (*Violent Playground*, 1958), race (*Sapphire*, 1959) and closeted homosexuality (*Victim*, 1961). Critical commentary has tended to treat them as decent but dull, and certainly the cautious narrative form of their films often cocoons the problem they are addressing. But it also throws up difficulties in the way of resolution, and the social (and sexual) tensions in their films are often more interesting than the Big Moral Statement they are trying to make. *Frieda* (1947), directed by Dearden with Relph as associate producer, about a small postwar community adjusting to the idea of a good German, is one of the most interesting, and least discussed, Ealing films, and a brilliant dissection of postwar society. JC

Bib: 'Dearden and Relph: two on a tandem', *Films and Filming* (July 1966).

Other Films Include: Dearden – *The Black Sheep of Whitehall* [co-dir. Hay] (1941); *The Goose Steps Out* [co-dir. Hay] (1942); *My Learned Friend* [co-dir. Hay] (1943); *The Halfway House, They Came to a City* (1944); *Dead of Night* ['The Hearse Driver'] (1945). **Dearden/Relph** – *The Captive Heart* (1946); *Saraband for Dead Lovers* (1948); *The Blue Lamp* (1950); *Pool of London* (1951); *The Gentle Gunman* (1952); *The Square Ring* (1953); *The Ship that Died of Shame* (1955); *The Smallest Show on Earth* (1957); *Rockets Galore* (1958); *The League of Gentlemen* (1960); *The Secret Partner* (1961); *The Mind Benders* (1962); *Woman of Straw* (1964); *Khartoum* (1966); *The Assassination Bureau Limited* (1969); *The Man Who Haunted Himself* (1970).

DECOIN, Henri
Paris 1896–1969

French director. Prolific director of the classical period, known especially for a series of films starring Danielle Darrieux*. Decoin was also a sports journalist and scriptwriter and worked on French versions of multi-language films. His long and varied filmography – forty-nine titles as director – makes it difficult to categorise his work generically. The 1930s, however, are dominated by bitter-sweet comedies and melodramas with Darrieux, then his wife. The former are epitomised by *Mademoiselle ma mère* (1937) and *Battement de coeur* (1939), in which Decoin successfully blended the American-style light comedy at which Darrieux excelled (and on the strength of which she was invited to Hollywood) with classic performances from French character actors such as Saturnin Fabre and Carette*. *Abus de confiance* (1937), on the other hand, belonged to the tradition of the French populist drama, a trend Decoin pursued during the war, notably with a first-class adaptation of Georges Simenon's* *Les Inconnus dans la maison/Strangers in the House* (1942), starring Raimu* and scripted by Henri-Georges Clouzot*. Decoin's two notable postwar films are another Simenon adaptation, *La Vérité sur Bébé Donge* (1952), with Darrieux and Jean Gabin*, a sombre psychological drama, and *Razzia sur la chnouf* (1955), an excellent *policier*, in which Gabin and Lino Ventura* haunt Parisian cabarets and the drugs underworld. Decoin's last film, *Nick Carter va tout casser*, starring Eddie Constantine*, was made in 1964. GV

DEED, André
André [de?] Chapuis, Le Havre 1884 – Paris 1938 [some sources: 1879–1931]

French actor, one of the major comic stars of early world cinema. Like many comics, Deed `came from the music hall, where he had been a singer and an acrobat. At Pathé*, he starred in a popular comic series as the character Boireau (1906–09). His fame greatly increased when he was lured to Giovanni Pastrone's* Itala studios in Turin in 1909, where under the pseudonym of Cretinetti he starred in more than a hundred films, some directed by himself (in Spain he was Torribo or Sanchez, in English-speaking countries Foolshead or Jim). Typical of early farce and chase films, his humour was physical and violent, based on a character who gets into trouble and makes things worse in his struggle to escape the consequences. He is described by Richard Abel as 'a grotesquely bewildered clown and a skilful practitioner of physical gags'. As the popularity of the early comic genres waned, so did Deed's and he died in neglect and poverty. GV

Bib: Richard Abel, *The Ciné Goes to Town: French Cinema 1896–1914* (1994).

DEFA

East German production company, licensed by the Soviet Allies on 17 May, 1946 as a film-makers' collective headed by Kurt Maetzig*. Relaunched the following year as a production-distribution company (with shares held by German and Soviet authorities), DEFA (Deutsche Film AG) was nationalised in 1953, and thus became the GDR's official film (and later television) conglomerate. By the mid-1960s DEFA was producing feature films, popular science films, short films and documentaries, newsreels, children's cartoons and animation films. Since it had at its disposal the full Ufa* studio capacities in Babelsberg, it was not only the first, but also the largest German postwar production company, administering a complex and paradoxical inheritance. The new company's avowed ideological orientation was socialist, while at the same time it relied on the technical facilities and professional expertise of Babelsberg's politically compromised Ufa past (Günther Rittau, Erich Waschneck, Arthur Maria Rabenalt*, among others). Although the presence of ex-Nazi personnel was by no means as conspicuous as in the West, with DEFA opening the studio to returning exiles (Wilhelm Dieterle*) as well as international directors (Roberto Rossellini*) some historical continuities were symptomatic: Hans Heinrich, for instance, as the studio's chief editor, was responsible for *Die Drei Coronas* (1940) and *Ohm Krüger* (1941) as well as for the first DEFA production *Die Mörder sind unter uns/The Murderers Are Amongst Us* (1946) and *Rotation* (1949), both directed by Wolfgang Staudte*.

The early 1950s saw a determined effort by DEFA to eliminate the 'disruptive effects' of both its expressionist heritage (*Wozzeck*, 1947) and its socio-critical-satirical tendency (*Der Untertan/The Kaiser's Lackey*, 1951), signalling that ideological correctness was to be more important than the expertise of veterans such as Erich Engel, Gerhard Lamprecht* or Staudte, all of whom were shed or left in the course of the decade. Those who stayed, among them Slatan Dudow, who directed *Kuhle Wampe oder Wem gehört die Welt?/Kuhle Wampe* (1932), Kurt Maetzig and Andrew Thorndike, subscribed more or less readily to the aesthetic doctrine of 'Socialist Realism'*, and put their considerable talents at the service of the young GDR state. The political 'thaw' of the late 1950s and early 1960s saw DEFA venture into popular genres, while a new generation of DEFA directors began to claim a share of the radicalism of Italian neo-realism* and the young East European cinemas. Films such as Gerhard Klein's *Berlin – Ecke Schönhauser* (1957) and Maetzig's *Septemberliebe* (1961) laid the foundations for a new DEFA tradition, which was taken up in the 1970s and early 1980s by other directors such as Hermann Zschoche (*Sieben Sommersprossen*, 1978), Helmut Dziuba (*Erscheinen Pflicht*, 1984) and Lothar Warneke (*Leben mit Uwe*, 1974). Aided by a new generation of actors, writers and technical personnel, the DEFA films from the 1960s onwards will stand as enduring testimony to a film-making practice that attempted to reflect depressing socialist realities while still trying to keep faith in a political ideal. This more critical view, often glimpsed from behind the veil of comedy and literary adaptations, demanded its price. As the state's official film company, occupying a monopoly position and trading under the name of the Ministry of Culture, DEFA was tethered to the party line: the 11th Plenary of the Central Committee of the SED ('Sozialistische Einheitspartei Deutschlands'), held in December 1965, resulted in the banning of nearly the entire annual feature film output, variously branded as 'modernistic', 'nihilistic', 'anarchistic' and 'pornographic'.

After the fall of the GDR regime in 1990, DEFA facilities and personnel were put under the administration of the 'Treuhand' which, in December 1992, sold the Babelsberg studio complex to the French business conglomerate Compagnie Générale des Eaux (CGE), who hired Volker Schlöndorff* to oversee the remodelling of Babelsberg into a European media centre. MW

DE FILIPPO, Eduardo   Naples 1900 – Rome 1984

DE FILIPPO Peppino   Naples 1903 – Rome 1980

DE FILIPPO, Titina   Annunziata De Filippo; Naples 1898 – Rome 1963

Italian film and theatre family. (Eduardo: playwright-director-actor; Peppino: actor-playwright; Titina: actress). Eduardo De Filippo was unquestionably, alongside Luigi Pirandello, the greatest Italian playwright of the twentieth century, raising the Neapolitan tradition to the level of European high culture. Son of actor-playwright Eduardo Scarpetta, Eduardo made his stage debut with his father's company at the age of four. Having started in variety, in the late 1920s he founded, with his brother and sister, the 'Teatro umoristico', and shortly afterwards the family moved hesitantly into film. Eduardo and Peppino began their film career in Mario Bonnard's *Tre uomini in frac*. They were then invited by Mario Camerini* to star in his delightful adaptation of the Spanish story *Il cappello a tre punte/The Three-Cornered Hat* (1934), which Mussolini personally censored. Other films followed, including Raffaello Matarazzo's* *Sono stato io/I Did It* (1937), which marked Titina's film debut, but their films remained secondary to their theatrical work throughout the period.

In 1944 Peppino flamboyantly left the company, a breach that was never healed. An author of lightweight comedy and farce, he was perhaps the better actor, with an extraordinary comic presence. He flourished in minor films, starring opposite Totò* in a series of films with titles like *Totò, Peppino e la malafemmina/Totò, Peppino and the Wicked Woman* (1956) and also opposite Aldo Fabrizi*. He created the hugely popular television character Pappagone and was marvellously used by Federico Fellini*, for instance in *Luci del varietà/Variety Lights* (1950). Eduardo was never a spectacular film actor, but his achievements were more varied. Declaring that his ambition was 'not to turn the man in the street into an actor, but the actor into a man in the street', he created an original style in parallel with that of neo-realism*, aided by the talents of his sister Titina and of Totò. He directed and acted in a number of films, including adaptations of his theatrical masterpieces of the late 1940s, most notably *Napoli milionaria* (film: 1950; English title: *Side Street Story*). Other film acting credits include Vittorio De Sica's* *L'oro di Napoli/The Gold of Naples* (1954) and Luigi Comencini's* *Tutti a casa/Everybody Go Home!* (1960). For her part Titina continued to act in her brother's plays and films, creating the title role in *Filumena Marturano* (play: 1946; film: 1950), and in films by other directors (for instance in Luchino Viscont's* *Bellissima*, 1951), until forced by illness to give up the stage. GVo

DEKEUKELEIRE, Charles
Brussels 1905 – Werchter 1971

Belgian director, described in *Close Up** as 'a self-made man of the cinema, the undisputed leader of the Belgian school'. Dekeukeleire worked as a film critic, denouncing the way the cinematic institution was ruled by money and mediocrity. In one of his theoretical studies clearly influenced by Soviet writings, *Le Cinéma et la pensée* ('Cinema and Thought', 1947), he maintains that cinema should be a reflection of our industrial society's cultural and social base. His first experimental films were part of the international avant-garde* of the time. Three of his most acclaimed early works are *Combat de boxe/Boxing Match* (1927), *Impatience* (1928) and *Histoire de détective/Detective Story* (1929). *Impatience* is an abstract film, with rhythmic editing; *Histoire de détective*, applying Soviet montage*, hints at a potential narrative situation and then breaks it down. As was the case for most avant-garde film-makers in Europe, Dekeukeleire's anti-establishment position, and the new working conditions brought by the coming of sound, jeopardised his career in the 1930s. He turned to commissioned documentaries, and between 1930 and 1962 directed over a hundred films inspired by liberal humanism, on industrial or civic themes, starting with *Terres brûlées/Verschroeide Aarde/Burnt Earth* (1934). *Thèmes d'inspiration/Inspirational Themes* (1938) is one of his most remarkable documentaries, a mixture of Belgian landscapes and human faces with paintings by Ensor, Permeke and Meunier. SS

Bib: Kristin Thompson, '(Re)discovering Charles Dekeukeleire', *Millennium Film Journal* (Fall/Winter 1980/81).

Other Films Include: *Witte Vlam/Flamme blanche/White Flame* (1930); *Het kwade oog/Le Mauvais oeil/The Evil Eye* (1936); *Le Diamant/The Diamond* (1948); *L'Abbaye de Maredsous* (1953).

DE KUYPER, Eric
Brussels 1942

Belgian director (based in the Netherlands); also novelist, choreographer, critic and academic. He has lectured on film at the University of Nijmegen, edited a Dutch theoretical film journal (*Versus*) and engages in many publishing and operatic ventures. De Kuyper's experimental film work displays a complex range of influences, from semiotics and underground cinema to flamboyant Hollywood musicals and melodramas. While *Casta Diva* (1982) relates to the underground, *Naughty Boys* (1983), awarded the De Sica Prize at Venice, is an experimental musical cast with non-professionals. *A Strange Love Affair* (1985, co-directed by Paul Verstraeten) draws on Sirk and Minnelli. De Kuyper, who also directed *Le Pierrot lunaire* (1988) and *Pink Ulysses* (1990), has described his film practice as patchwork and has claimed the status of amateur, working at weekends and during holidays, often with non-professional actors and on low budgets. Across the diversity of De Kuyper's work, a recurrent concern is the exploration of the human (male) body in its tempting beauty, combined with a profound sensitivity. SS

DELANNOY, Jean
Noisy-le-Sec 1908

French director, who began as an actor and editor in the late 1920s and worked as an assistant director before making his directing debut in 1935. His real prominence came during the war with *L'Eternel Retour* (1943), from a script by Jean Cocteau, and the costume drama *Pontcarral, colonel d'Empire* (1942); both were extemely successful, as was the prize-laden *La Symphonie pastorale* (1946), from the novel by André Gide and starring Michèle Morgan*. Delannoy continued working successfully in mainstream genres through the 1940s and 1950s (in fact until the early 1990s, though never regaining the status of the earlier decades). His reliance on literary texts (and often dialogues by Jean Aurenche* and Pierre Bost*) and major stars, and his elegant though impersonal *mise-en-scène*, situated him within the tradition of quality*, earning him the contempt of the New Wave* critics. Among his most interesting films, *Les Jeux sont faits/The Chips Are Down* (1947), *La Minute de vérité/The Moment of Truth* (1952), *Chiens perdus sans collier* (1955), *Notre-Dame de Paris/The Hunchback of Notre Dame* (1956) and *Maigret tend un piège/Inspector Maigret* (1958) are testimony to a high degree of professionalism and understanding of popular tastes. GV

DE LAURENTIIS, Dino
Torre Annunziata 1919

Italian producer. After acting classes at the Centro Sperimentale* in Rome and appearing in Mario Camerini's* *Batticuore* (1938), De Laurentiis became a producer. He set up Real Cine in Turin in 1941 and then became production manager for Riccardo Gualino's Lux*. Among the films he produced there were Alberto Lattuada's* *Il bandito* (1946), and Giuseppe De Santis'* *Riso amaro/Bitter Rice* (1949), which launched the career of Silvana Mangano* (who soon became his wife). Owner of the Farnesina studios in Rome with Carlo Ponti*, De Laurentiis founded Ponti-De Laurentiis in 1950, which produced films by Lattuada as well as by Roberto Rossellini*, Vittorio De Sica*, Luigi Zampa* and Federico Fellini*, and historical epics such as Camerini's *Ulisse/Ulysses* (1954) and King Vidor's *War and Peace* (1956, US). But it was the more lowbrow productions, particularly films starring Totò*, which achieved spectacular box-office success. Totò and De Laurentiis in fact set up a company, DDL, to exploit their success. In 1957 Ponti and De Laurentiis went their separate ways, the latter to pursue his own dream of becoming a great international producer. He set up a large production unit called Dinocittà on the outskirts of Rome, where films such as Richard Fleischer's *Barabba* (1961) and John Huston's *La Bibbia/The Bible In the Beginning ...* (1966) were shot, together with Mario Monicelli's* *La grande guerra/The Great War* (1959), Alberto Sordi's* films and others. A man with a genuine passion for the cinema and for taking risks, he was forced to sell Dinocittà in 1971 for financial reasons. He moved to the US, where he worked as executive producer on *Serpico* (1973), *Death Wish* (1974) and *Three Days of the Condor* (1975). He set up his own company, De Laurentiis Entertainment, and worked once again with super-productions like *King Kong* (1976), *Hurricane* (1979), *Flash Gordon* (1980) and *Dune*

(1984), the last-named directed by David Lynch and on which the executive producer was De Laurentiis' own daughter Raffaella. But he also remained committed to prestige *auteur* cinema, producing films directed by Robert Altman, Ingmar Bergman*, Miloš Forman* and Michael Cimino among others. In the early 1980s he invested part of his capital in a chain of Italian fast food restaurants. In the early 1990s, in a changed Hollywood climate, he had more failures than successes but remained determined not to abandon the field. MMo

DEL GIUDICE, Filippo
Trani, Italy 1892 – Florence, Italy 1961

British producer, who arrived in Britain as a refugee from Mussolini in 1932, established the Two Cities production company with the director Mario Zampi in 1937, and produced some of the most critically acclaimed films of the 1940s. In an article in *The Quarterly Review of Film and Television* (Summer 1952), Geoffrey Wagner writes, 'It can be claimed that one man [...] effectively created the British prestige cinema. This was Filippo del Giudice who, over a very few years, produced thirty-five films, including *In Which We Serve* (1942), *The Way Ahead* (1944), *The Way to the Stars* (1945), *Odd Man Out* (1947), *Men of Two Worlds* (1946), *School for Secrets* (1946), *Blithe Spirit* (1945), *Henry V* (1945), and *Hamlet* (1948) ... Including *Henry V*, all these films, constituting a remarkable record of quality, were made for an average of £200,000, about half the amount spent by most English producers operating at that time [...]. All these movies were powerful commercial successes; *Henry V* has grossed fifteen million dollars in its limited specialised release in the United States.'

Del Giudice retired to a monastery in 1958. JC

DELLUC, Louis
Cadouin 1890 – Paris 1924

French theoretician and director. Inspired by Cecil B. DeMille's *The Cheat* (1915), Delluc (originally a literary critic) became a key figure in the French avant-garde*, especially for his writing. He edited a number of film journals, including the ambitious *Cinéa*, and pioneered film criticism in his regular column for *Paris-Midi*; his essays were the first to be collected in France, in *Cinéma et cie* (1919), *Photogénie* (1920), and other volumes. A great admirer of Hollywood, Delluc also advocated a specifically French cinema: 'Let French cinema be real cinema, let French cinema be really French.' Like the future practitioners of the New Wave*, he moved on to film-making, writing scripts for Jean Epstein* and Germaine Dulac*, and directing seven films between 1920 and 1923. Of these the best are *Fièvre* (1921), an atmospheric drama set in a studio-reconstructed Marseilles bar, and *La Femme de nulle part* (1922), an exploration of subjectivity past and present; both star his wife Ève Francis. Contemporary critic Léon Moussinac's description of *Fièvre* encapsulates Delluc's 'impressionist' cinema: 'From faces and gestures, from expressive movements in a completely integrated decor, [Delluc] can produce emotional effects of real power ... even poetry.'

The Louis Delluc Prize was created in 1937, awarded annually to a French film considered an artistic achievement (that year it went to Jean Renoir's* *Les Bas-fonds/The Lower Depths*). GV

DELON, Alain
Sceaux 1935

French actor, director and producer. When the exceptionally handsome young Alain Delon started acting in the 1950s, he bypassed the New Wave*, unlike his contemporary Jean-Paul Belmondo*. Instead, he came to prominence in René Clément's* *Plein Soleil/Purple Noon/Lust for Evil* (1960), based on a Patricia Highsmith novel, and his career took off in prestigious Italian *auteur* films (*Rocco e i suoi fratelli/Rocco and His Brothers*, 1960, *L'eclisse/The Eclipse*, 1962, *Il gattopardo/The Leopard*, 1963), in which he combined charismatic but ambiguous sex appeal with a hint of corruption. His success in the thriller *Mélodie en sous-sol/The Big Snatch* (1963, with Jean Gabin*) steered him away from playboys towards increasingly tough and monosyllabic gangsters or *flics* in films directed by Jean-Pierre Melville* (*Le Samouraï*, 1967, *Le Cercle rouge/The Red Circle*, 1970), Henri Verneuil* (*Le Clan des Siciliens/The Sicilian Clan*, 1969), Jacques Deray (*Borsalino*, 1970), or himself (*Pour la peau d'un flic/For a Cop's Hide*, 1981, *Le Battant/The Cache*, 1983). Delon failed in Hollywood but reigned over French cinema in the 1960s and 1970s, sharing top box-office ranking with Belmondo and Louis de Funès*, his image apparently unaffected by off-screen liaisons, scandals and right-wing politics. He also founded his own production company. Delon's popularity then declined with that of the traditional *policier**, prompting, perhaps, his return to art cinema: *Un Amour de Swann/Swann in Love* (1984), *Notre histoire/Our Story* (also 1984, for which he won a César*), and, ironically, Jean-Luc Godard's *Nouvelle Vague* (1990). GV

Other Films Include: *Sois belle et tais-toi, Christine* (1958); *Faibles femmes, Le Chemin des écoliers* (1959); *Che gioia vivere* (1961, It./Fr.); *La Tulipe noire/The Black Tulip, L'Insoumis, Les Félins/The Love Cage* (1964); *Les Aventuriers* (1966); *Adieu l'ami, La Piscine/The Swimming Pool* (1968); *La Veuve Couderc* (1971); *L'Assassinio di Trotsky/The Assassination of Trotsky* [It./Fr.], *Un flic/Dirty Money* (1972); *Traitement de choc, Les Granges brûlées, Deux hommes dans la ville* (1973); *La Race des 'seigneurs', Les Seins de glace, Borsalino & Co* (1974); *Flic story* (1975); *Mr Klein* (1976); *Armaguedon, L'Homme pressé* (1977); *Le Toubib* (1979); *Trois hommes à abattre* (1980); *Le Choc* (1982); *Parole de flic* (1985); *Le Passage* (1986); *Dancing Machine* (1990); *Le Retour de Casanova* (1992).

DEL POGGIO, Carla
Maria Luisa Attanasio; Naples 1925

Italian actress. Carla Del Poggio was discovered at the Centro Sperimentale* in Rome by Vittorio De Sica*, who cast her as the whimsical heroines of *Maddalena ... zero in condotta* (1940) and *Un garibaldino al convento* (1942). After these lighter roles, she became a dramatic actress, epitomising the 'tragic young woman' in the films of Alberto Lattuada*, whom she married in 1945: as sister and prostitute in *Il bandito* (1946); as the cursed lover of a black soldier in *Senza pietà/Without Pity* (1948); as frustrated bride in *Il mulino del Po/The Mill on the Po* (1949); and as the aspiring artiste in *Luci del varietà/Light of Variety/Variety Lights* (1950, co-dir. Federico Fellini*). Her parts in Giuseppe De Santis'* *Caccia tragica/Tragic Hunt* (1947) and *Roma ore 11* (1952) were no less troubled. More unusual but less successful were her digressions into the imaginary (in Mario Camerini's* *L'angelo e il diavolo/The Angel and the Devil*, 1946) and melodrama (Pietro Germi's* *Gioventù perduta/Lost Youth*, 1947). After a number of minor roles, particularly in France, and a disappointing *Cose da pazzi/Das Bekenntnis der Ina Kahr* (1954), directed by a weary G. W. Pabst*, Carla Del Poggio's career came to an end alongside Peter Ustinov in Hugo Fregonese's *I girovaghi/The Wanderers* (1956), a 'chaotic and absurd' film belonging to the 'Hollywood on the Tiber' period of Italian cinema. GVo

DELVAUX, André
Heverlee 1926

Belgian director; also teacher, musician and linguist. Despite sustained international success, Delvaux remains close to Belgium, which he sees as his continuing source of inspiration. While many of his films use Belgium as their setting, Delvaux's 'Belgian-ness' has most frequently been associated with two dominant themes in the traditions of Walloon and Flemish painting. From surrealists such as Paul Delvaux and René Magritte, and from the magic realist novelist Johan Daisne, he is said to take a preoccupation with the blurred border between reality and imagination. He also shares with Flemish painters such as Bosch and Breughel an obsession with beauty linked to death and decay. Such cultural duality may go some way towards explaining why Delvaux is one of the few Belgian film-makers to have equal success at home and abroad, and with both Francophone and Dutch-language films.

Delvaux's first feature, *De Man die zijn haar kort liet knippen/L'Homme au crâne rasé/The Man Who Had His Hair Cut Short* (1965), based on Daisne's classic novel, brought him international critical acclaim. Delvaux's style can be characterised by a musical approach to direction, influenced perhaps by his early training as a pianist. His films are typically constructed around key motifs – a haircut (*De Man...*), a train (*Un Soir, Un Train*, 1968), a house (*Rendez-vous à Bray*, 1971) – whose significance is often only available in retrospect. His male characters undertake journeys which blur the distinctions between imagination and reality, or past and present. Meanwhile his female characters, even when central as in *Een Vrouw tussen Hond en Wolf/Femme entre chien et loup/Woman in a Twilight Garden* (1979), are sources of mystery and confusion, whose presence inevitably precipitates the hero deeper into his black (mind) hole.

Delvaux began his film career relatively late in life. As a lecturer in languages, he had made short films with his college students. As a trained pianist, he accompanied silent films at the Cinémathèque Royale*. He also lectured on film theory at the film school INSAS. As well as features and short films, he has made series for television, and acted, in Marion Hänsel's* film *Sur la terre comme au ciel/On Earth as it is*

in Heaven (1992). He was awarded the Plateau* Life Achievement Award at the 1991 International Film Festival in Ghent. CF

Other Films: *Nous étions treize/There were Thirteen of Us* [short, co-dir. with his students] (1955); *Forges* [co-dir. Jean Brismée and André Bettendorf] (1956); *Cinéma bonjour/Hello Cinema* [TV, short, co-dir. Jean Brismée] (1958); *La Planète fauve/The Fauve Planet* [short, co-dir. Jean Brismée] (1959); *Yves boit du lait/Yves Drinks Milk* [short], *Fellini* [four-part series for RTB] (1960); *Jean Rouch* [five-part series for RTB], *Le Temps des écoliers/Haagschool/Primary School Time* [short] (1962); *Le Cinéma polonais/The Polish Cinema* [nine-part series for RTB] (1963); *Derrière l'écran/Achter het Scherm/Behind the Screen* [six-part series for RTB] (1966); *Les Interprètes/The Cast* (1968); *Belle* (1973); *Met Dieric Bouts/Avec Dierick Bouts* [short] (1975); *To Woody Allen, from Europe with Love* (1980); *Benvenuta* (1983); *Babel Opera* (1985); *L'Oeuvre au noir/The Abyss* (1988); *1001 Films* [short] (1989).

DEMY, Jacques
Pontchâteau 1931 – Paris 1990

French director. One of the outstanding film-makers of post-war France, Demy is best known for his first feature *Lola* (1961) and for *Les Parapluies de Cherbourg/The Umbrellas of Cherbourg* (1964), his first musical proper.

Demy was brought up in Nantes, a city he loved (the affection is well captured in Agnès Varda's* moving film portrait *Jacquot de Nantes*, 1991), and where he made his earliest amateur movie. He studied cinema in Paris, training in short films with Georges Rouquier* and later in animation with Paul Grimault*. *Lola*, a lyrical poem to Nantes and the cabaret artiste played by Anouk Aimée, shared some of the aesthetic concerns of the New Wave* (although Demy was not strictly part of it): location shooting, exuberant *mise-en-scène* – especially stunning camerawork by Raoul Coutard* – and love for the American cinema. *Les Parapluies de Cherbourg* inaugurated the 'bitter-sweet' Demy universe, with sentimental music by Michel Legrand*, pastel colour-scheme, and the innovation of all-sung dialogue. The film turned Catherine Deneuve* into a star and was awarded a prize at Cannes, but Demy never matched its popular success in his subsequent chequered career, although *Peau-d'Ane/Donkey Skin* (1970), a sumptuous adaptation of the Perrault fairy tale, came near. Nevertheless, *Les Demoiselles de Rochefort* (1967) and *Une chambre en ville* (1982), like *Les Parapluies*, beautifully illustrate Demy's original, if not totally satisfactory, pursuit of a specifically French musical genre. GV

Other (Feature) Films: *Les Sept péchés capitaux/The Seven Deadly Sins* (1962, ep.); *La Baie des Anges* (1963); *Model Shop* (1969, US); *The Pied Piper* (1972, UK); *L'Événement le plus important depuis que l'homme a marché sur la lune/A Slightly Pregnant Man* (1973); *Lady Oscar* (1978); *Trois places pour le 26* (1988). GV

Dr. No (UK, 1962; Terence Young):
Ursula Andress, Sean Connery

Die Nibelungen I (Germany, 1924;
Fritz Lang)

Ni liv/Nine Lives (Norway, 1957;
Arne Skouen)

La Violetera (Spain, 1958; Luis-Cesar Amadori): Sara Montiel

Deutschland, bleiche Mutter/Germany, Pale Mother (Germany, 1980;
Helma Sanders-Brahms): Eva Mattes

The Third Man (UK, 1949; Carol Reed):
Alida Valli, Joseph Cotten

37°2 le matin/Betty Blue (France, 1985; Jean-Jacques Beineix):
Jean-Hugues Anglade, Béatrice Dalle

Amphitryon (Germany, 1935; Reinhold Schünzel): Willy Fritsch

Hej rup!/Heave Ho! (Czechoslovakia, 1934; Martin Frič):
Jiří Voskovec and (left) Jan Werich

La Maternelle (France, 1933; Marie Epstein/Jean Benoît-Lévy):
Madeleine Renaud (right) and Mady Berry

Häxan/Witchcraft Through the Ages (Denmark, 1922;
Benjamin Christensen): Clara Pontoppidan

DENEUVE, Catherine
Catherine Dorléac; Paris 1943

French actress. Declared by *Newsweek* 'the most beautiful woman in the world', and like Bardot* a model for Marianne, the effigy of the Republic, Catherine Deneuve has embodied, on and off screen, an ideal of elegant French womanhood since the early 1960s. With Isabelle Adjani*, she is France's top female star of the 1980s and early 1990s.

After small parts in comedies with her sister Françoise Dorléac and a short spell with Roger Vadim*, Deneuve triumphed in Jacques Demy's* *Les Parapluies de Cherbourg/ The Umbrellas of Cherbourg* (1964). This entirely sung melodrama popularised her image of the demure middle-class *jeune fille*, solidified in Demy's *Les Demoiselles de Rochefort* (1967) and other light comedies such as *La Vie de château* (1965). Roman Polanski's* *Repulsion* (1965, UK) and Luis Buñuel's* *Belle de jour* (1967) added a layer of 'perverse' sexuality, producing the figure of the ice maiden, a bait for sadistic male fantasies. This was further exploited in the 1970s in Buñuel's *Tristana* (1970, Sp.) and Marco Ferreri's* *Liza/La cagna* (1971, It.). Deneuve's Italian and Hollywood films (*Hustle*, 1975, *The Hunger*, 1984), and her role as ambassador of French chic (Saint-Laurent clothes, Chanel perfume) internationalised her. In France in the 1980s she continued an active career in mainstream (*Je vous aime*, 1980, *Fort Saganne*, 1984) and *auteur* cinema (with François Truffaut*, André Téchiné*, Jean-Pierre Mocky*, François Dupeyron), evolving towards figures of independence and stoic suffering, of greater appeal to women and more in tune with her off-screen feminism. But although her status remained intact in the 1980s, her parts tended to become symbolic rather than actual leads. Her success in *Indochine* (1992), a popular colonial melodrama [> HERITAGE CINEMA IN EUROPE], may herald more substantial mature roles. GV

Other Films Include: *Les Portes claquent* (1960); *Les Parisiennes* [ep.] (1962); *Le Vice et la vertu* (1963); *Les Créatures* (1966); *Benjamin ou les mémoires d'un puceau, La Chamade* (1968); *La Sirène du Mississipi/The Mississipi Mermaid* (1969); *Peau-d'Ane* (1970); *Ça n'arrive qu'aux autres* (1971); *Un flic/Dirty Money* (1972); *L'Événement le plus important depuis que l'homme a marché sur la lune/A Slightly Pregnant Man* (1973); *Touche pas la femme blanche* (1973); *Le Sauvage* (1975); *L'Argent des autres* (1978); *Le Dernier métro/The Last Metro* (1980); *Hôtel des Amériques, Le Choix des armes* (1981); *Le Bon plaisir, Paroles et musique* (1984); *Le Lieu du crime/The Scene of the Crime, Speriamo che sia femmina/Let's Hope It's a Girl* (1985, It.); *Drôle d'endroit pour une rencontre/A Strange Place to Meet* (1988); *La Reine blanche* (1991); *Ma saison préférée* (1993).

DENMARK

Silent films knew no barriers – actors spoke with their bodies, and (translated) intertitles helped the narrative along. This 'portability' was one reason why tiny Denmark could produce and export films so successfully. Another was the extraordinary activity of Nordisk Films*, which in the decade up to 1920 single-handedly made Danish cinema one of the most important national cinemas in the world.

Like other Europeans, Danes first marvelled at Lumière's* Cinematograph and Skladanowsky's* Bioscope in 1896. The earliest Danish films were the work of Peter Elfelt*, who turned out some 200 reportage films on the royal family and the life of the Danish middle classes from 1896 to 1912. The first Danish cinema, the Kosmorama, was an instant success, soon copied by many others, including Ole Olsen's* Biograf-Theatret in 1905. In 1906 Olsen founded Nordisk Films Kompagni, the first and soon the most powerful Danish production company. Olsen's genius was to recognise before almost anyone else the potential of export; by the end of 1906 he had set up six overseas offices, at a time when he was still unchallenged in the domestic market. By 1909, when other Danish film firms came on the scene, they found Nordisk difficult to dislodge.

Despite the attentions of the censor from 1907 (censorship was finally abolished, except for children's films, in 1960), the years from Nordisk's foundation to the start of World War I were the golden age of Danish cinema. Production was numerically high and artistically remarkable, and the whole world was its market. Danish cinema's international success derived partly from a stream of sophisticated dramas set among the upper and middle classes, especially the daring 'domestic' or 'erotic' melodramas [> DANISH EROTIC MELODRAMA], notable examples of which include *Ved Fængslets Port/Temptations of a Great City* (1911), directed by August Blom* – who also made spectaculars such as *Atlantis* (1913) – and Urban Gad's *Afgrunden/The Abyss* (1910), starring Asta Nielsen*. As well as pioneering themes and genres, Danish film-makers also won international renown for their technical mastery, especially in cinematography (for instance, the outstanding Johan Ankerstjerne*).

Another Danish innovation was the shift to longer movies. Until 1910, films everywhere were limited to one reel, or about fifteen minutes running time. In the spring of that year a minor Danish production company called Fotorama* astonished audiences with the novelty of a half-hour film entitled *Den hvide Slavehandel/The White Slave*. Its immediate success prompted other Danish companies to produce multi-reel films, and from 1911 Nordisk focused exclusively on producing 'long' dramatic features, a move from which it derived substantial commercial benefit. The switch to longer films was also of great importance aesthetically, allowing actors to give more detailed performances. The first to employ the possibilities imaginatively was Asta Nielsen*, who in September 1910 made her remarkable debut in *Afgrunden/The Abyss*, produced by Kosmorama*. This immediately turned her into European cinema's very first star and *femme fatale*. She appeared in two more Danish films in 1911 before leaving for Germany.

In 1913, despite acute competition in multi-reelers from all the major European film companies, Danish films still enjoyed a considerable reputation. World War I, however, would change that. The war years saw the rise of Hollywood to international pre-eminence, while closer to home Denmark faced increasing competition from Germany and Sweden. When the war ended and borders reopened, Danish films had lost their freshness and with it their appeal for world markets. It was, however, in the immediate postwar period that Carl Theodor Dreyer* directed his first films, *Præsidenten/The President* (1918) and *Blade af Satans Bog/ Leaves from Satan's Book* (1919), both produced by Nordisk. With the latter in temporary decline, Dreyer later had to turn to other production companies either at home or abroad. Palladium*, founded in 1921, was Nordisk's earliest domestic rival. Its artistic director, Lau Lauritzen*, is credited with first using the comic duo in cinema: Fyrtaarnet og Bivognen* won huge worldwide success long before Laurel and Hardy. With the proceeds from these films, Palladium produced Dreyer's *Du skal ære din Hustru/The Master of the House* (1925). Earlier, another pioneering Danish director, Benjamin Christensen*, had stunned the world with *Häxan/Witchcraft Through the Ages* (1922), a visually sumptuous, highly controversial account of witchcraft in the Middle Ages. The first Danish animated film, meanwhile, had been made in 1920. *De 3 smaa mænd/The 3 Little Men* was produced and directed by Robert Storm-Petersen, who had also written the comic strip on which it was based.

By erecting language barriers to export, the advent of sound made life difficult for the Danish film industry, effectively restricting distribution of its products to Scandinavia. However, the end of the 1930s saw the rise of the Danish documentary, particularly influential during the German occupation and the early postwar years. Key directors were Theodor Christensen* and Bjarne Henning-Jensen*.

The years of the German occupation (1940–45) brought radical changes to the cinema. On the exhibition side, audiences initially increased as people sought respite from everyday life. But having reached a peak in 1943, attendances began to decline as the exigencies of war – including strict censorship – took their toll. When the occupying forces took over the functions of the Danish police in August 1943, people decided to stay at home.

For producers, too, the early years of the occupation proved deceptively lucrative. Output rose from ten features a year before the war to twenty-two in 1942. Dwindling German imports eased distribution of Danish films on the home market. From 1943, however, production was squeezed by shortages of raw materials and German sabotage, and in 1945 only five films were made. A year later all five Nordisk studios were bombed, halting production until the end of the war.

On the whole, however, Danish cinema ended the 1940s in credit. Carl Theodor Dreyer* directed his masterpiece *Vredens dag/Day of Wrath* in 1943. And documentary prospered. During the occupation the state-founded Ministeriernes Filmudvalg produced almost seventy documentaries, while Dansk Kulturfilm* too remained active. In 1946 Theodor Christensen released his homage to the Danish resistance, *Det gælder din frihed/Your Freedom is at Stake*, and in 1955 Bjarne Henning-Jensen directed *Hvor bjergene sejler/Where Mountains Float* in Greenland. Many talented documentarists followed, including Jørgen Roos*, Henning Carlsen* and Jørgen Leth.

The decade produced another successful genre in the Danish children's film*, inaugurated by Astrid Henning-Jensen's* *Palle alene i verden/Palle Alone in the World* (1949), based on a popular Danish children's book. The 1940s also saw the first Danish experimental films. The earliest, *Flugten/The Escape* (1942), was directed by Jørgen Roos and

the painter Albert Mertz. Subsequent examples of the genre were often likewise directed by painters or sculptors. In 1946, *Fyrtøjet/The Tinder Box*, the first Danish feature-length animation film, was released, directed by Svend Methling* from a story by Hans Christian Andersen. Det Danske Filmmuseum (the Danish Film Museum) was set up in 1941.

These innovations were not matched in Danish mainstream cinema of the 1940s. Fiction films of the war years were largely escapist entertainment harking back to 'the good old days' (the title of one movie). Comedies and musicals predominated, the latter a new genre in Denmark. A rare excursion into overt patriotism was provided by *Sommerglæder/A Summer's Joy* (1940), from Herman Bang's famous novel. Good financial conditions encouraged some producers to be a little more daring, Nordisk, for instance, giving Bjarne Henning-Jensen the chance to direct his first feature, *Naar man kun er ung/While Still Young* (1943). Palladium tried its hand at sophisticated comedy in the shape of *Tak, fordi du kom, Nick/Thanks for Coming, Nick* (1941).

The 1950s brought new changes. A vogue for trivial, second-rate films began in 1950 with *De røde heste/The Red Horses*, and 1951 marked the launch of Danish television. By the end of the decade its power was manifest: the first Danish cinema closed in 1959, and many more followed. Declining attendances meant that Danish films were increasingly difficult to finance. State support helped, but could not prevent a number of Danish production companies from closing down. Only Nordisk survived unaided, but in 1981 it too asked for help. Since then, all Danish feature films have needed full or partial state support.

The Danish Film School, Den danske Filmskole, was founded in 1966, and in 1967 a film department opened at the University of Copenhagen; cinema began to be taught in primary and secondary schools. A Film Act of 1982 earmarked 25 per cent of state film support for children's films, resulting in a series of excellent films such as *Tro, håb og kærlighed/ Twist and Shout* (1984) by Bille August*, who directed the award-winning *Pelle Erobreren/Pelle the Conqueror* in 1987. Other notable directors of children's films are Søren Kragh Jacobsen and Nils Malmros*, whose ability to emphathise with the young is particularly evident in *Kundskabens Træ/ The Tree of Knowledge* (1983). The 1980s also offered ambitious films for grown-ups, above all those of Lars von Trier*, who made his directorial debut in 1984 with *Forbrydelsens element/The Element of Crime*, a deeply felt personal work, and made *Europa/Zentropa* in 1991.

With the advent of television and later video, and given the small size of its internal market, the fact that Danish cinema survives at all is to be marvelled at. That it does so is due to state help, Denmark's specialised genres, and the work of ambitious *auteurs* such as Bille August, Gabriel Axel* and Lars von Trier. ME

DEPARDIEU, Gérard   Châteauroux 1948

French actor, the biggest star in France since the mid-1970s. With more than fifty leading roles under his belt at the age of 47, Gérard Depardieu has also achieved worldwide stardom.

Depardieu's adolescence in working-class Châteauroux

was marked by delinquency, which later haunted him when (unresolved) allegations of rape ruined his chances of an Oscar for *Green Card* (Aust./Fr.) in 1990. The theatre (a continuing passion) led him to the straight and narrow and to Paris, where he briefly joined the libertarian *café-théâtre*, meeting fellow actors Coluche, Patrick Dewaere and Miou-Miou*. After a dozen minor film parts, his co-starring role in Bertrand Blier's* *Les Valseuses/Going Places* (1973) turned him into France's young male sensation. Since then, his star has hardly stopped rising. Apart from exceptional talent and energy, a key to Depardieu's success is his versatility. Equally at ease in broad farce and romantic leads (despite unconventional features), he has been a mainstay of popular cinema (*Préparez vos mouchoirs/Get Out Your Handkerchiefs*, 1977, *Inspecteur La Bavure/Inspector Blunder*, 1980, *Les Fugitifs*, 1986, etc.), a supporter of *auteur* films by Marguerite Duras*, Marco Ferreri* and Maurice Pialat*, and of major art films like *1900* (1976), *Le Dernier métro/The Last Metro* (1980) and *Cyrano de Bergerac* (1990). Out of this diversity a strong star persona has emerged, made up of an intensely male physical presence, combined with surprising and, according to him, 'feminine' gentleness. Depardieu's bulky physique and earthy off-screen activities (tending a vineyard) evoke a popular longing for ancestral roots (crystallised in *Jean de Florette*, 1986), while his cultural aura projects a modernist personality. Like Jean Gabin* before him, Depardieu sums up an idealised French masculinity, merging working-class virility with romanticism. Exporting himself has meant losing some of these complexities, since Depardieu's global stardom is, so far, dependent (as was Maurice Chevalier's*) on playing a rather clichéd Frenchness, as in *Green Card*, or even Europeanness, as in Ridley Scott's* *1492 Conquest of Paradise* (1992, UK/Fr./Sp.). Already a star of 'heritage' cinema* with *Jean de Florette* and *Cyrano*, Depardieu has moved increasingly to this type of film in the 1990s, notably with *Germinal* (1993) and *Le Colonel Chabert* (1994), while retaining an interest in *auteur* cinema, as shown by his starring role in Jean-Luc Godard's *Hélas pour moi* (1993). GV

Bib: Paul Chutkow, *Gérard Depardieu* (1994).

Other Films Include: *L'ultima donna/The Last Woman, Barocco* (1976); *Le Camion* (1977); *Mon oncle d'Amérique/ My American Uncle* (1980); *La Femme d'à côté/The Woman Next Door, Le Retour de Martin Guerre/The Return of Martin Guerre* (1981); *Danton* (1982); *Fort Saganne, Le Tartuffe* (1984); *Police* (1985); *Tenue de soirée* (1986); *Sous le soleil de Satan/Under Satan's Sun* (1987); *Camille Claudel* (1988); *I Want to Go Home, Trop belle pour toi* (1989); *Tous les matins du monde* (1992); *Raspoutine* (1995).

DEPPE, Hans   Berlin 1897–1969

German director, whose first film, *Der Schimmelreiter* (1934), has become a film adaptation classic (based on Theodor Storm). In a diverse pre-World War II output, including a masterpiece of observational cinema (*Straßenmusik*, 1936), it was Deppe's two Ludwig Ganghofer adaptations – *Schloß Hubertus* (1934) and *Der Jäger von Fall* (1936) – that an-

nounced the genre on which the director's fame would eventually rest: the *Heimatfilm**. Skilfully modulating between the rural pantheism favoured by Nazi blood-and-soil epics and nostalgic, picture-postcard sentiment, Deppe became, with the phenomenal success of his 'panorama picture' *Schwarzwaldmädel* (1950) and *Grün ist die Heide* (1951), postwar Germany's foremost director of the *Heimatfilm*, inaugurating the genre's vigorous and long-lasting renaissance. The Deppe era, synonymous with the ideological mix that made the genre so popular, coincided with the Adenauer era in politics. TE/MW

DE SANTIS, Giuseppe   Fondi 1917

Italian director. After studying philosophy, De Santis made a name for himself as a short story writer, then as a critic for the magazine *Cinema*. He was assistant director to Luchino Visconti* (*Ossessione*, 1942), Aldo Vergano and Roberto Rossellini* and wrote a number of scripts. In 1945 he assisted Mario Serandrei on a documentary on the Resistance, *Giorni di gloria/Days of Glory*. Starting with *Caccia tragica/Tragic Hunt* (1947) and *Riso amaro/Bitter Rice* (1949; his best-known film, starring Silvana Mangano*), De Santis set out to create a new form of neo-realism*. His films were popular-populist, baroque melodramas influenced both by classical American cinema and by Soviet Socialist Realism*, and making suggestive use of landscapes as well as eroticism. From the farmers' co-operatives of the lower Po to the rice fields of Vercelli and the sheepfolds of his native Latium countryside in the hieratic *Non c'è pace tra gli ulivi* (1950), he offered an epic cross-section of rural Italy, embracing its confused post-Resistance aspirations. De Santis then turned his attention to urban environments with two admirable films, *Roma ore 11* (1952), based on a dramatic news event (the collapse of a staircase on which hundreds of young women were queuing for a job interview), and *Un marito per Anna Zaccheo* (1953), a strikingly modern portrait of a woman (Silvana Pampanini*) seeking an impossible balance between her desires and societal constraints. Later works, such as the Fordian *Cesta duga godinu dana/La strada lunga un anno/The Road a Year Long* (1958), an Italian-Yugoslav co-production filmed in Yugoslavia, the bourgeois drama *La Garçonnière* (1960) and the unusual war film *Italiani brava gente/Attack and Retreat* (1964), are not without interest, but De Santis remains a director tied to the immediate postwar period of Italian film history. PV

Other Films Include: *Giorni d'amore* (1954); *Uomini e lupi/ Men and Wolves* (1956); *Un apprezzato professionista di sicuro avvenire* (1972).

DE SICA, Vittorio   Sora 1901 – Neuilly-sur-Seine, France 1974

Italian actor and director. De Sica's career exemplifies the heights as well as the banalities of four decades of Italian film-making, progressing from the so-called 'white telephones' of the 1930s, to neo-realism* and later 'rose-tinted' comedies [>

'COMMEDIA ALL'ITALIANA'], and to the romantic realism of the 1970s. De Sica's film career began in 1918 when he appeared as young Clémenceau in Bencivenga's *Il processo Clémenceau*. He continued working in the theatre, including with his own acclaimed company, ZaBum. Although by 1932 he had appeared in two more films (*La compagnia dei matti*, 1928, and *La vecchia signora*, 1931), he was still mainly known as a stage actor. However, *Gli uomini, che mascalzoni ...* (1932), his first film for director Mario Camerini*, turned him into the most popular male star in 1930s Italian cinema. He appeared in four more Camerini films during that period: *Darò un milione* (1935), *Ma non è una cosa seria/But It's Nothing Serious* (1936), *Il signor Max/Mr Max* (1937) and *Grandi magazzini* (1939), romantic comedies which firmly established his screen persona as the petit-bourgeois hero and (as one critic put it) the 'bravo ragazzo' (the nice guy).

The 1940 romantic comedy *Due dozzine di rose scarlatte/Two Dozen Red Roses* launched a brief series of films, including *Maddalena ... zero in condotta* (1940) and *Teresa Venerdì/Doctor Beware* (1941), for which De Sica is credited as both actor and director. The last two films, as well as *Un garibaldino al convento* (1942), all concern the 'coming of age' of a young female character who becomes romantically attracted to an older man, played by De Sica in two of the films. The films, however, evolved gradually away from the conventions of 1930s romantic comedy. In *Teresa Venerdì* and *Un garibaldino al convento*, the female protagonists are caught in oppressive youth institutions (orphanage, boarding school), themes that form a bridge to De Sica's later neo-realist films. *Sciuscià/Shoeshine* (1946), *Ladri di biciclette/Bicycle Thieves* (1948), *Miracolo a Milano/Miracle in Milan* (1951) and *Umberto D.* (1952), all scripted by Cesare Zavattini*, placed De Sica at the forefront of the neo-realist movement, along with Roberto Rossellini* and Luchino Visconti*. While each film is constructed around a specific postwar social problem (respectively: juvenile crime, unemployment, homelessness, and the plight of the aged), De Sica's lyricism departs from the purely didactic by inviting a powerful emotional engagement. With *Umberto D.*, neo-realism reached a state of 'terminal purity' in its rigorous adherence to Zavattini's 'poetics of immediacy', and the film's box-office failure ushered in a period of commercial compromise for the financially strapped director. His next project, *Stazione Termini/Indiscretion of an American Wife* (1953), indeed involved concessions to David O. Selznick, who financed the production provided it showcased his wife, Jennifer Jones. De Sica resumed his acting career, appearing in France in Max Ophuls'* *Madame de .../The Earrings of Madame de ...* (1953) with Danielle Darrieux* and Charles Boyer*, and in Italy with Gina Lollobrigida* in Luigi Comencini's* immensely popular *Pane, amore e fantasia/Bread, Love and Dreams* (1953) and *Pane, amore e gelosia/Bread, Love and Jealousy/Frisky* (1954); he also delivered a brilliant performance as the lead in Rossellini's *Il generale Della Rovere* (1959). After a five-year hiatus, De Sica returned to directing with *La ciociara/Two Women* (1960), a well-crafted adaptation of the Moravia novel set in a ravaged World War II Italy and starring Sophia Loren*. De Sica launched the lucrative team of Loren and Marcello Mastroianni* in several 'rose-tinted' hits, including *Ieri, oggi, domani/Yesterday, Today and Tomorrow* (1963) and

Matrimonio all'italiana/Marriage – Italian Style (1964), followed by undistinguished commercial ventures such as *Sette volte donna/Woman Times Seven* (1967) and *Amanti/A Place for Lovers* (1968), starring Shirley MacLaine and Faye Dunaway respectively. With *Il giardino dei Finzi-Contini/The Garden of the Finzi-Continis* (1970), De Sica made a conscious return to committed film-making, incorporating the lessons of commercial cinema into an unflinching account of Jewish persecution under the Fascist regime and the Nazi occupation of Ferrara. 'I am happy that I made it,' he said, 'because it brought me back to my old noble intentions.' JHa/MMa

Other Films as Director: *I bambini ci guardano* (1943); *La porta del cielo* (1944); *L'oro di Napoli/The Gold of Naples* (1954); *Il tetto/The Roof* (1956); *Il giudizio universale/The Last Judgment* (1961); *Boccaccio '70* (ep. *La riffa*), *I sequestrati di Altona/The Condemned of Altona* (1962); *Il boom* (1963); *Un mondo nuovo/A Young World* (1965); *Caccia alla volpe/After the Fox* (1966); *Le streghe* (1967, ep. *Una sera come le altre*); *I girasoli/Sunflower* (1969); *Le coppie* (1970, ep. *Il leone*); *Lo chiameremo Andrea* (1972); *Una breve vacanza/A Brief Vacation* (1973); *Il viaggio/The Journey* (1974).

DEVILLE, Michel   Boulogne-sur-Seine 1931

French director. Although contemporary with the New Wave*, Deville (trained as an assistant) worked parallel to it. He made light comedies, including, with Anna Karina*, *Ce soir ou jamais* (1961) and with Brigitte Bardot*, *L'Ours et la poupée* (1970); thrillers, either 'classic', such as *Lucky Jo* (1964, with Eddie Constantine*), or 'political', such as *Le Dossier 51* (1978); and erotic costume films, like *Benjamin ou les mémoires d'un puceau* (1968) and *Raphaël ou le débauché* (1970), many co-written by Nina Companeez. His career took a different course in the 1980s and 1990s with a series of glossy art-house hits: *Péril en la demeure* (1985, awarded a César*), *Le Paltoquet* (1986), and *La Lectrice* (1988), in which he developed a cool, mannered style and a distanced eroticism. GV

DICKINSON, Thorold   Bristol 1903 – London 1984

British director, who had a richly varied career in the British film industry and in film culture over more than half a century. In the 1920s he was assistant director and editor for George Pearson*, and in the early 1930s he edited *Sing As We Go* (1934) for Basil Dean* and *Midshipman Easy* (1935) for Carol Reed*. He went to Spain during the Civil War and directed two short documentaries, *Spanish ABC* and *Behind the Spanish Lines* (both co-dir. Sidney Cole, 1938). He directed his first feature, *The High Command*, in 1937, and continued to direct feature films consistently though not prolifically throughout the 1940s. As a director, his films are marked by a strong visual imagination which places him outside the mainstream of British cinema of the period, but which at its richest, as in his adaptation of Pushkin, *The Queen of Spades* (1949), rivals the work of Michael Powell* and Emeric Pressburger. He was also programme controller of the London Film Society* throughout the 1930s, and Vice-President of the Association of Cine-Technicians (the industry trade union) from 1936 to 1953. He was an adviser on film in Israel in the early 1950s, and from 1956 to 1960 he directed the film service of the United Nations Office of Public Information. In 1960 Dickinson took up the post of Lecturer in Film Studies at the Slade School of Fine Art, and became Britain's first Professor of Film in 1967. He published *A Discovery of Cinema* in 1971. JC

Bib: Jeffrey Richards, *Thorold Dickinson: The man and his films* (1986).

Other Films Include: *The Arsenal Stadium Mystery* (1939); *Gaslight* (1940); *The Prime Minister* (1941); *The Next of Kin* (1942); *Men of Two Worlds* (1946); *Secret People* (1952); *Hill 24 Doesn't Answer* (1955, Israel).

DIEGO, Gabino   Gabino Diego Solís; Madrid 1966

Spanish actor, who rose to prominence after appearing in *Las bicicletas son para el verano/Bicycles are for the Summer* (1984, dir. Jaime Chávarri*). Further roles in *El viaje a ninguna parte/Voyage to Nowhere* (1986, dir. Fernando Fernán Gómez*), *¡Ay, Carmela!* (1990, dir. Carlos Saura*) and *El rey pasmado/The Stupefied King* (1991, dir. Imanol Uribe*) have established him as an unlikely star. His village idiot appearance, gangling posture, bulging crimson lips and dopey expression give him an endearing charm, highly suitable for roles in which he is either the clumsy simpleton (*¡Ay, Carmela!*) or knavish but still lovable self-seeker (Chávarri's *Tierno verano de lujurias y azoteas/A Tender Summer of Lust on the Rooftops*, 1993). PWE

DIEGO, Juan   Juan Diego Ruiz Montero; Berninjos, Seville 1942

Spanish actor, with early experience on stage. He achieved prominence in the early 1980s, appearing in such films as *Los santos inocentes/Holy Innocents* (1984, dir. Mario Camús*), *Los paraísos perdidos/Lost Paradises* (1985, dir. Martín Patino), *La corte de Faraón/Pharaoh's Court* (1985, dir. García Sánchez). After notoriously impersonating Franco in Jaime Camino's* *Dragon Rapide* (1986), he was even more in demand, appearing in *La noche oscura/Dark Night of the Soul* (1988, dir. Carlos Saura*), *El Rey pasmado/The Stupefied King* (1991, dir. Imanol Uribe*) and *Jamón, jamón/Ham, Ham* (1992, dir. Juan José Bigas Luna*), in all of which his somewhat histrionic style suited him well to the tormented, twisted roles demanded by these films. PWE

DIETERLE, Wilhelm   Ludwigshafen 1893 – Ottobrunn 1972

German director and actor. Managing a parallel career on stage (with Max Reinhardt's* Deutsches Theater) and in the cinema from 1913 onwards, Dieterle starred in numerous films, including E. A. Dupont's* *Die Geier-Wally* (1921), Paul Leni's* *Das Wachsfigurenkabinett/Waxworks* (1923), and F. W. Murnau's* *Faust* (1926). From 1923, he directed a string of hits, leading him to set up his own production company in 1927.

A bad debt on one of his theatre ventures obliged Dieterle to accept a contract with Warner Bros in 1930, directing their German-language versions of American pictures and doing remakes of European successes (*Madame Dubarry*, 1934). Classed as a reliable B-picture director, Dieterle made a Hollywood living with such films as *The Last Flight* (1931) and *Satan Met a Lady* (1936). When Max Reinhardt* went to Hollywood, Dieterle co-directed with him *A Midsummer Night's Dream* (1935), a prestige venture that upgraded him to A-director status and teamed him with Paul Muni on a highly successful series of biopics.

In 1939 he became the co-founder of the anti-fascist magazine *The Hollywood Tribune* (edited by Dupont) and of the English-speaking exile theatre group 'The Continental Players' (with Leopold Jessner as director), while together with his wife, the actress Charlotte Hagenbruch, he played a major part in securing work permits for German and Jewish refugees. Until 1956 Dieterle was employed by RKO, MGM, Selznick, Paramount and Columbia, and among many other films, made a classic gothic costume melodrama, *The Hunchback of Notre Dame* (1939), starring Charles Laughton*. He returned to Europe in 1958 where he retired from film after directing some Italian and German co-productions in 1960. MW

Bib: Marta Mierendorff, *William Dieterle: Der Plutarch von Hollywood* (1993).

DIETRICH, Marlene   Maria Magdalene von Losch; Berlin 1902 – Paris 1992

German actress, for some synonymous with movie glamour, for others epitomising Weimar culture. She began in film in Wilhelm Dieterle's* *Der Mensch am Abwege* and Joe May's* *Tragödie der Liebe* (both 1923), but still regarded herself as a theatre actress and cabaret singer. Seeing her in Georg Kaiser's comedy *Zwei Krawatten*, Josef von Sternberg offered her the role of Lola Lola in *Der blaue Engel/The Blue Angel* (1930): 'von Kopf bis Fuß auf Liebe eingestellt.' The rest, as they say, is history. Dietrich left for Hollywood in 1930 and worked on six films by Sternberg which turned her into a legend she was careful to nurture for the next half-century. After films for Ernst Lubitsch* (*Desire*, 1936, *Angel*, 1937), Rouben Mamoulian (*Song of Songs*, 1933), Tay Garnett (*Seven Sinners*, 1940) and, reputedly, a string of lovers from Maurice Chevalier* and Jean Gabin* to Ernest Hemingway, she was officially 'box-office poison', but not short of roles, including a Western parody (*Destry Rides Again*, 1939), before playing tongue-in-cheek comments on her own star image in Fritz Lang's* *Rancho Notorious* (1952), Orson Welles' *A Touch of Evil* (1958) and Billy Wilder's *A Foreign Affair* (1948) and *Witness for the Prosecution* (1958). An American citizen, she worked for the US Entertainment Organization during World War II, touring the front in Europe and earning her stripes as a staunch anti-Nazi. Back in Berlin in 1945, for her mother's funeral, she 'also buried the Germany she once knew and loved'. In later years, living in Paris, she worked for radio and, until an accident on stage in 1975, as a successful *diseuse*. She is buried in Berlin, where the Stichtung Deutsche Kinemathek has acquired her estate. TE/MW

Bib: Maria Riva, *Marlene Dietrich* (1992).

DIJK, Gerrit van   Uden 1938

Dutch animator. After training at the Academy of Arts, van Dijk began a career as a painter, later becoming involved in film-making. Since 1971 animation films, which he calls 'moving paintings', have formed the bulk of his work. Van Dijk calls himself a visualiser, and his films are innovative, provocative and moving at the same time. They often express strong social and political commitment, as in the 'Jute' series (twelve films, 1978–79). By contrast, *Janneke* (1990) presents a personal reflection on the origins of human life. Van Dijk also experimented with animation techniques – in *Pas à deux* (1988, co-dir. Monique Renault) he used 'rotoscoping', a technique which consists of transforming live-action footage into animated scenes. Like other Dutch animators (Borge Ring, Co Hoedeman, Paul Driessen, Paul de Nooyer, Monique Renault, Hans Nassenstein), van Dijk is the recipient of many international awards; indeed, Dutch animation perhaps enjoys a better international reputation than Dutch feature films. Van Dijk and his wife Cilia helped found the Netherlands Institute of Animation Film in Tilburg in 1993. AMu

Other Films: *It's Good in Heaven* (1971); *De vlag/The Flag* (1972); *Butterfly* (1973); *CubeMenCube* (1975); *Sportflesh, Our House* (1976); *Quod libet* (1977); *Queen* (1978); *Alle Menschen werden Brüder, UN Soldiers, The Unexpectable, Holocaust, United Europe, Love Power, Holiday, Tanzen nach den Pfeifen von Franz Josef Strauss, Tale of a 1001 Murder, Letter for Carter, The Fascinating World of Jan van Riebeeck* (1979); *The End* (1981); *He Almost Clutched His Hand* (1982, co-dir. J. Overtoom and P. Sweenen); *Music for the Millions, A Good Turn Daily* (1983); *Water* (1988, co-dir. P. Sweenen); *Snert* (1991; co-dir. P. Sweenen and J. Overtoom); *Frieze Frame* (1991).

DILLON, Carmen   London 1908–95

British art director. Trained as an architect and working mainly with Two Cities, Rank and Disney, Dillon established her reputation with the Laurence Olivier* Shakespeare adaptations: *Henry V* (asst. art dir., 1945), *Hamlet* (1948) and *Richard III* (1955). She won an Oscar for *Hamlet* and an Art

Direction award at Venice for *The Importance of Being Earnest* (1952). Associated particularly with period reconstruction, she was flexible in her approach. She breaks exuberantly with historical naturalism in *Henry V*, where she combines theatricality with a vivid colour scheme drawn from illuminated manuscripts, but in Joseph Losey's* *The Go-Between* (1970) or Fred Zinnemann's *Julia* (prod. des., 1977) she builds the feel of the period out of closely researched detail. JC

Other Films Include: *The Gentle Sex* (1943); *The Way to the Stars* (1945); *School for Secrets* (1946); *The Browning Version* (1951); *Doctor in the House* (1954); *The Prince and the Showgirl* (1957); *A Tale of Two Cities* (1958); *Sapphire* (1959); *Kidnapped, Carry On Constable* (1960); *Accident* (1967); *Lady Caroline Lamb* (1973); *Butley* (1976).

DINDO, Richard   Zurich 1944

Swiss director. A former office worker from a working-class background, Dindo spent three formative years in Paris where he witnessed the May 1968 events and saw hundreds of films at the Cinémathèque Française*. Self-taught, he started film-making at the age of 26, with a documentary about two juveniles which also traces the history of the Swiss labour movement (*Die Wiederholung*, 1970). He next shifted his attention to another blind spot in his country's political history, the Swiss legal system, in *Die Erschiessung des Landesverräters Ernst S.* (1976). After two documentaries about the Spanish Civil War (*Schweizer im spanischen Bürgerkrieg*, 1973, and *Raimon – Lieder gegen die Angst*, 1977), he made his first feature, *El Suizo – Un amour en Espagne* (1985), which investigates the same topic from the point of view of the younger generation. After taking a critical look at the Zurich youth movement in *Dani, Michi, Renato & Max* (1987), Dindo – in a reprise of his earlier films about Swiss writer Max Frisch in *Max Frisch, Journal I–III* (1978–80) and actor Max Haufler in *Max Haufler, der Stumme* (1981) – made documentary essays about the French poet Arthur Rimbaud (*Arthur Rimbaud, une biographie*, 1991) and the Jewish painter Charlotte Salomon (*Charlotte – c'est toute ma vie*, 1992). Despite their attention to facts, these documentaries radically test the limits of the documentary genre in their exploration of subjectivity. MW

DI VENANZO, Gianni   Teramo 1920 – Rome 1966

Italian cinematographer. Di Venanzo started young as a camera assistant on some of the most important neo-realist* films, including Luchino Visconti's* *Ossessione* (1942), and films directed by Roberto Rossellini* and Vittorio De Sica*. He was director of photography for the first time on Carlo Lizzani's* *Achtung! Banditi!* (1951) and *Cronache di poveri amanti/ Stories of Poor Lovers* (1954) and went on to work with directors such as Francesco Maselli*, Mario Monicelli*, Lina Wertmüller* and Luigi Comencini*. His fame, however, is mostly due to his work with Michelangelo Antonioni* on such films as *Le amiche/The Girlfriends* (1955), *Il grido/The Cry* (1957), *La notte/The Night* (1961), *L'eclisse/The Eclipse* (1962), and with Francesco Rosi* on *La sfida* (1958), *Salvatore Giuliano* (1961), *Le mani sulla città/Hands Over the City* (1963). Di Venanzo significantly influenced lighting techniques: he challenged classical schemes and revolutionised black-and-white cinematography by eliminating 'theatre light' (*luce teatro*) in favour of 'light everywhere' (*luce dovunque*). He pioneered the use of soft lights known as 'photo-flood' and 'photo-spot' (although Antonioni claimed that Enzo Serafin was the first to use them on his early feature *Cronaca di un amore/Story of a Love Affair* in 1950). All of this contributed to a distinctive style '*à la* Di Venanzo', which at the same time was flexible enough to adapt to the directors' own styles: Rosi's dramatic realism, Antonioni's 'visual ambiguity', Fellini's avant-gardist '*mise-en-scène* of light' in $8\frac{1}{2}$ (1963) and orchestration of visions and ghosts in *Giulietta degli spiriti/Juliet of the Spirits* (1965), one of Di Venanzo's rare ventures into colour. GVo

DIVISMO

Italian star phenomenon. *Diva* in Italian means goddess and by extension other objects of worship such as (female) film stars. *Divismo* describes the phenomenon of star worship (and star power), with particular reference to the silent period. It acquired currency in terms of the role of operatic prima donnas and lead actresses of theatre companies in Italy in the early years of the century. In these companies not only was the *diva* the star attraction around which the performance of the rest of the company revolved, but often she was also formally or informally the head of the company and able to determine the repertoire. Actresses like Eleonora Duse and Emma Gramatica enjoyed great power as well as great reputation, and the practice soon spread to the cinema. Lyda Borelli and Francesca Bertini emerged as film stars first and foremost around 1914, to be joined by Pina Menichelli and Leda Gys. In a meteoric film career lasting only five years, Borelli's intense appearance, striking poses and sinuous movements provide the central focus of all her films, notably *Ma l'amor mio non muore/But My Love does not Die* (1914), *Fior di male/Flower of Evil* (1915) and *Malombra* (1917), and the whole *mise en scène* and the performances of the rest of the cast are little more than supporting elements as she goes through her routines of joy and (more often) suffering. Bertini was a more accomplished actress, able to interpret a variety of roles, and she had a longer career. She performed alongside Leda Gys as a pantomime character in *Histoire d'un pierrot* (1914), becoming a star with *Assunta Spina* in 1915. The post-1918 crisis in the Italian cinema brought an abrupt end to the *diva* genre. Bertini and Borelli both married aristocrats and were able to retire, although Bertini returned sporadically to the screen as late as the 1950s. Her career (and that of other *dive*) is commemorated in a documentary by Gianfranco Mingozzi, *L'ultima diva; Francesca Bertini/The Last Diva; Francesca Bertini* (1982). GNS

DJULGEROV, Georgi

Burgas 1943

Bulgarian director and writer. Widely recognised as the most talented director of the middle generation of Bulgarian film-makers. After winning a prize at the Oberhausen festival for his diploma film at the Moscow Film School (VGIK*), *Bondar/The Cooper* (1969), based on a story by Nikolai Haitov* and filmed in Armenia, Georgi Djulgerov returned home and shot the same short feature again in the author's native Rhodope mountains. The remake, *Izpit/The Test*, appeared as an episode in the two-part *Šaren cvjat/Colourful World* (1971). He followed this with a widely praised feature film on the resistance movement, *I dojde denjat.../And the Day Came...* (1973), based on the personal experiences of scriptwriter Vassil Akyov. Djulgerov's breakthrough on the international scene occurred when his next feature, *Avantaž/Advantage* (1977), won the Best Director award at the 1978 Berlin film festival; it is the story of a petty conman living on the edge of society during the Stalinist years. Although less successful, his next film, *Trampa/Swap* (1978), continued the director's socio-political probing into the troubled era of the personality cult.

Djulgerov then spent three years working on *Mera spored mera/Measure for Measure* (1981), a three-part spectacle produced for the 1,300th anniversary of the founding of Bulgaria and dealing with the Ilinden uprising of 1903 in Greek Macedonia, a project that won him praise abroad but displeasure among the authorities at home because of his unbiased approach to the sensitive political issue of Macedonia. Prevented from directing feature films at the Boyana* Studios, Djulgerov soon made his mark as a director of fiction-like documentaries on sports, while at the same time teaching a new generation of film-makers at the Sofia Academy of Dramatic Art (VITIS). Upon Mikhail Gorbachev's rise to power, Djulgerov was allowed to work again in the feature film department at the Boyana Studios; he responded with another statement on the Stalinist period: *Lagerăt/The Camp* (1989), an autobiographical account of his own youth in a pioneer camp of the 1950s. RH

DOCUMENTARY

All national cinemas in Europe have produced documentaries, discussed under national entries, individual film-maker's entries (e.g. Robert Flaherty*, Jean Rouch*), and generic entries such as the British Documentary Movement*. Texts below focus on Belgium, Denmark, Germany, Greece, Hungary, Norway and Poland.

Belgium
Belgian cinema is often said to have been influenced more by the pictorial model than by the cinematographic one, and this shows in the prominence of the documentary film, and especially of the *film sur l'art**. Henri Storck*, Charles Dekeukeleire* and André Cauvin were especially responsible for international awareness of this Belgian school of art documentary, which started in the 1930s. Another, equally strong, Belgian tradition, partly rooted in early documentation of Belgium's colonial history (especially the Congo, now Zaire), is the ethnographic, socio-political and industrial

documentary, which has produced such classics as Storck's and Joris Ivens'* *Misère au Borinage/Borinage* (1933). Up to the late 1960s, Belgian documentaries were sponsored mainly by the Ministry of Economy (tourist films) and the Ministry of Education (films on art, sociological films). Three important figures in socio-political film of the 1960s are Paul Meyer*, Jean Brismée and Frans Buyens*.

New regulations passed in 1964 and 1967 divided Belgian film production into 'Flemish' and Francophone components. From then on, 'Flemish' (i.e. Dutch-speaking) and Francophone documentaries ran on different tracks. A new and strong generation of documentary film-makers grew up in Francophone Belgium: Christian Mesnil, Boris Lehman*, Patricia and Etienne Verhaegen and others, helped by the creation of the CBA* in 1978. In recent years, a close relationship with television stations has been life-saving for the documentary film. RTBF (Francophone public television) has a solid tradition in this respect, most recently with the programming of their Channel Arte 21.

On the 'Flemish' side, several interesting figures have continued to work in documentary: Frans Buyens*, Robbe De Hert and other members of the Fugitive Cinema* group, though all have struggled with financial difficulties. Some found support in the documentary film department of BRT (Dutch-language public television), but this department was abolished in 1975. So documentary film-making was segmented between the cultural, art, science, leisure and information departments. Interesting names in this context are: Maurice de Wilde (historical series); Jan Neckers (on Zaire); Paul Bottelberghs (educational television), Stefaan Decostere (video documentaries). 'Flemish' commercial television (VTM) has chosen the path of 'infotainment' (Paul Jambers) but also screened an impressive series on survivors of the Holocaust called *De laatste Getuigen/The Last Witnesses* (1992), by a gifted young documentarist, Luckas Van der Talen. SS

Denmark

Discounting the many reportage films made in the silent era, notably by pioneer Peter Elfelt*, the Danish documentary movement was launched in 1935 by architect Poul Henningsen (1894–1967). *Danmark* was produced by the Foreign Ministry with the aim of presenting a picture of Denmark and the Danes to the outside world. 'P.H.' (as he was often called) did not, however, provide the bland portrayal the Ministry had anticipated. Henningsen's film heralded the coming of a documentary style which found its greatest exponent in Theodor Christensen*, who made his first film, *C – et hjørne af Danmark/C – a Corner of Denmark*, in 1938. Paradoxically, the Danish documentary movement received a major boost, and benefited from relatively favourable working conditions, during the German occupation of 1940–45. The government's film committee was ostensibly set up to fight unemployment, in reality to counter German influence. The Ministeriernes Filmudvalg (Film Committee of the Ministries) produced almost seventy documentaries between 1941 and 1945. Particularly worthy of note are Bjarne Henning-Jensen's* *Brunkul/Lignite* (1941), Søren Melson's *Kutter H 71/Cutter H.71* (1943) and Hagen Hasselbalch's *Kornet er i fare/The Crop is in Danger* (1944). Dansk Kulturfilm* continued to produce work, including

Bjarne Henning-Jensen's *Føllet/The Colt* (1943); and the resistance movement too managed to produce films clandestinely, the best known of which is *Denmark Fights for Freedom* (1944). In 1946 the great epic of the resistance movement, *Det gælder din Frihed/Your Freedom is at Stake*, was released, to the initial resentment of many – particularly politicians, singled out for special criticism for their behaviour during the occupation. After the war many documentary film-makers moved on to fiction films, to be succeeded by a new generation of documentarists. Among them were Jørgen Roos*, who made many documentaries in the 1950s and 1960s, including notable films on Greenland, and Henning Carlsen*, who made an excellent film about old age, *De gamle/The Old*, in 1961, before going to South Africa to shoot *Dilemma* (1962), a feature-length semi-documentary about racial tension. ME

Germany

Kulturfilme. As in other European countries and in the US, the earliest years of the German film industry were dominated by documentaries or *actualités*. The transition to narrative fiction film around 1910 motivated opponents of the young industry to organise the Kino Reform Movement*, which was partly responsible for an oppositional, distinctively German documentary practice, the *Kulturfilm* ('cultural film'), which included films for training and educational uses that, like newsreels (see below), mostly accompanied feature films. The war saw the almost total appropriation of documentary for military, industrial and nationalist propaganda purposes. Documentaries were produced in large numbers during the Weimar years at Ufa* and other major companies. Often feature-length and making up a complete programme, *Kulturfilme* in the 1920s ranged in scope from the 'naturist' manifesto *Wege zu Kraft und Schönheit* (1925, dir. Wilhelm Prager and Nicholas Kaufmann) and industry-sponsored science and technology films, to the two-part, heavily nationalist compilation film *Der Weltkrieg* (1927, dir. Leo Lasko).

Socialist documentaries tried to oppose the conservative *Kulturfilm*, emphasising political mass education; they reached their peak in the late 1920s with *Blutmai* (1929) and Piel Jutzi's *Unser täglich Brot/Our Daily Bread/Hunger in Waldenburg* (1929). While this documentary tradition played an important role in the development of the *Arbeiterfilme* of the late Weimar period, it was able neither to establish an alternative form nor engage a wider public. These goals were better served by a genre of experimental documentary known as the 'cross-section' films, such as Walther Ruttmann's* *Berlin die Sinfonie der Großstadt/Berlin – Symphony of a City* (1927) and *Melodie der Welt* (1929), which, together with Hans Richter's *Alles dreht sich, alles bewegt sich* (1929), combined an awareness of the technical and artistic implications of film with the social-political commitment of the 'Neue Sachlichkeit'. Ruttmann's films, along with Ufa's feature-length *Kulturfilme*, make up the tradition that Leni Riefenstahl* drew on for her ultimate symbiosis between newsreels, avant-garde experiment and political appropriation. *Sieg des Glaubens* (1933), *Triumph des Willens/Triumph of the Will* (1935), and *Olympia* (1938) represent a peculiar continuity in personnel and style between the documentary avant-garde of the late 1920s and the Nazi propaganda-compilation films.

Although personnel active before 1945 still dominated *Kulturfilm* production in the first decade after World War II, the documentaries made in the 1950s soon dissociated themselves from the *Kulturfilm* tradition by making use of new technical developments such as the 16mm hand-held camera and synchronous sound. Preparing the ground for a new generation of documentary film-makers, television directors such as Klaus Wildenhahn and Peter Nestler also used the financial opportunities of the new medium to expand its aesthetic and ideological boundaries. Wildenhahn adopted a *cinéma-vérité** approach of long-term observation (*In der Fremde*, 1968; *Heiligabend auf St. Pauli*, 1968; *Emden geht nach USA*, 1976). This model soon became the norm, both because of Wildenhahn's teaching at the Berlin film school, and because other politically committed documentary film-makers (Rolf Schübel, Theo Gallehr, Eberhard Fechner, Jutta Brückner*, Helke Sander*) were in sympathy with this practice. A comparable mode of 'participatory observation', carried out over often very extended periods of time, was used in the GDR to counter the ideological manipulation of official television (directors: Jürgen Böttcher, Volker Koepp, Winfried Junge). A distinct documentary approach also helped articulate the style and ideological orientation of much of the New German Cinema*. Film essays, montage films and observational documentaries mounted a critique of commercial fiction film and explored social reality, landscape and human interaction in what came to be known as the 'new sensibility'. Elsewhere, documentary as an autonomous genre gained a new self-confidence, with the films of Klaus Wyborny, Vlado Kristl, Helmut Herbst and Werner Nekes, as well as more overtly political films such as Hartmut Bitomsky's reworking of Germany's audiovisual past and present in *Deutschlandbilder* (1983) and *Reichsautobahn* (1985), and Harun Farocki's television-financed critiques of television's power of incorporation, *Bilder der Welt und Inschrift des Krieges* (1988) and *Videogramm einer Revolution* (1993). German documentary has recently diversified, without a distinctive strategy yet emerging out of the new realities of unification. The very diverse and competitive media 'landscape' puts pressure on but also preserves niches for film-makers continuing to investigate their countries' history, constituting, at their best, a counter-memory to the dominant industrialised image machinery they are nevertheless part of. MW

Newsreels (*Wochenschau*). A product of the pioneering efforts of cinematic innovator Oskar Messter*, who put out the first *Wochenschau* (Messter Woche) in 1910, the German newsreel rose to be the one effective competitor to the French companies Pathé* and Gaumont* which dominated the European market, and it became the most effective arm of National Socialist ideological manipulation in the 1930s and 1940s [> NATIONAL SOCIALISM AND GERMAN CINEMA]. During World War I, the state seized upon the propaganda potential of the newsreel, Messter Woche providing the first footage of the front in October 1914. In 1917 Messter Film was integrated into the new state-controlled Ufa*, designed explicitly to raise the standards of German film-making and improve the national image abroad. Messter's film personnel formed the core of Ufa's news propaganda office, Bufa (*Bild und Filmamt*). In 1920, Messter Woche was absorbed by Deulig Wochenschau, which produced the first German sound newsreel in January 1932, as Deulig Tonwoche. In 1927, Alfred Hugenberg, a right-wing nationalist media mogul, saved Ufa from bankruptcy. He brought his political persuasion to bear most markedly on the production of newsreels, Ufa owning 80 per cent of the market. Capitalising on the situation, Nazi Propaganda Minister Goebbels assumed administrative control of both Ufa and Deulig in 1933 (the Party finally buying out Hugenberg in 1937). A product of all existing *Wochenschau* resources (Tobis, Deulig, Deutsche and Ufa), the Nazi newsreel – Deutsche Wochenschau – not only reported on Party activity, but represented the German *Volk* as a unified mass spectacle, simultaneously valorising the technical superiority of German film-making and finding its greatest refinement in the documentaries of Leni Riefenstahl*.

The postwar/Cold War newsreel in both West and East Germany was almost totally dependent on state subsidy and subject to censorship by the occupation forces. The few privatised services of the 1950s and 1960s, like the American-sponsored Fox Tönende Wochenschau, remained allied to Western and capitalist state interests in underwriting the *Wirtschaftswunder*. Across the border, the transformation of Ufa into DEFA* (Deutsche Film Aktiengesellschaft, 1946), granted the Soviets 80 per cent control of East German film-making, guaranteeing that the DDR newsreel, *Der Augenzeuge*, toed the Party line. Although the newsreel's function was eventually undermined by television, the *Wochenschau* was (and still is) a significant archival source for compilation film-makers. In the DDR, for example, Andrew and Annelie Thorndike's *Wilhelm Pieck: das Leben unseres Präsident* (1951), *Du und mancher Kamerad* (1956), and the *Archive sagen aus* series effectively exploited the newsreel's claim to authenticity to valorise the political hegemony of the time. JM

Greece

The first film made in Greece was a newsreel of the interim Olympics of 1906, possibly shot by a French cameraman. In 1909 the Hungarian cameraman Josef Hepp, considered the founder of Greek documentary, started working in Greece. In 1916, Hepp was exiled for his political film *Anathema tou Venizelou/Anathema of Venizelos*. The first newsreels were glorifications of political figures. By 1922, however, the painter Yorgos Prokopiou and the Gaziadis brothers recorded soldiers' everyday life at the front during the Greek–Turkish war. Prokopiou's work marks the move from newsreel to documentary. Greek newsreels traditionally functioned as shop windows for government propaganda, while documentaries attempted to disclose the undesirable facts behind the facade. For this reason no documentary movement was allowed to develop in the 1930s.

In 1953, Roussos Koundouros founded the first professional institute for the production of documentaries, making a series of films on scientific subjects and producing many films for the state. In 1960, all the short films shown at the first Thessaloniki* Film Festival were documentaries; the period of development and consolidation which followed was cut short by the military coup in 1967. Independently produced documentaries, investigating social realities and relationships, inevitably tended to social criticism. Along with an alternative political position, the film-makers of this period, working outside the official production circuit, attempted to formulate a new aesthetic approach [> NEW GREEK CINEMA]. Under the dictatorship (1967–74), censorship did not permit social criticism and film-makers turned towards ethnographic subjects requiring a more descriptive approach. The number of documentaries increased, but there was a marked decline in quality. After 1974 feature-length political documentaries were produced for the first time in Greece. A more liberal regime gave film-makers the opportunity to address the seven-year dictatorship in critical terms. By the 1980s documentary had declined along with the New Greek Cinema. It is currently exiled to television, where it is synonymous with reportage. AD

Films and Directors Include: Kostas Aristopoulos: *Gramma ston Nazim Hikmet/Letter to Nazim Hikmet* (1976). **Alexis Grivas**: *750,000* (1966). **Takis Kanellopoulos**: *Makedonikos gamos/Macedonian Wedding* (1960). **Menelaos Karamagiolis**: *Rom* (1989). **Nikos Kavoukidis**: *Martyries/Evidence* (1975). **Lambros Liaropoulos**: *Gramma apo to Charleroi/Letter from Charleroi* (1965). **Vassilis Maros**: *I tragodia tou Egeou/The Tragedy of the Aegean* (1961). **Kostas Sfikas**: *Engenia/The Opening* (1962), *Anamoni/Waiting* (1963), *Thiraikos orthros/ Thira Matins* (1968, co-dir. Stavros Tornes). **Dimos Theos**: *Ekato ores tou Mai/100 Hours in May* (1963, co-dir. Fotos Lambrinos). **Yorgos Tsemperopoulos**: *Megara* (1974, co-dir. Sakis Maniatis). **Kostas Vrettakos**: *To stroma tis katastrofis/Disaster Layer* (1980); **Lena Voudouri**: *O Karaghiozis/ Karaghiozis* (1975).

Hungary: the 'documentary-fiction' film

Hungarian film genre of the 1970s and early 1980s. The Hungarian *documentary-fiction* is close to the Jean Rouch* kind of *cinéma-vérité*. Parts are played by non-professional actors, often from the same profession as the characters they portray. The storyboard is more or less written in advance, but dialogue is improvised by the actors. Directors mostly work with two or more hand-held cameras. The first appearance of the genre was István Dárday's *Jutalomutazás/Holiday in Britain* in 1974. The narratives usually have some basis in Hungarian social reality, though two themes have predominated: the representation of everyday life and petty conflicts among lower middle-class people – Dárday-Szalay-Vitézy's *Filmregény/Film Novel* (1976) and Béla Tarr's* *Családi tűzfészek/Family Nest* (1977) – or conflicts between people of that social class and the political leadership – Dárday-Szalay's *Harcmodor/Stratagem* (1980), Vitézy's *Békeidő/Time of Peace* (1980). Film-makers within this genre had no particular artistic ambitions, considering their films primarily as political acts. The genre had a considerable impact on the representation of everyday life in mainstream Hungarian film, though it lost its momentum in the early 1980s as a consequence of a general disillusionment with the political impact of such films. KAB

Norway

The silent era offered travelogues and 'Norwegian views', but the first important director of Norwegian documentaries was Per Høst, a famous nature photographer. Some of his films, such as *Equador* (1954) and *Galapagos* (1955), were theatri-

cally distributed. Høst also documented the Lapp culture in 1957 with *Same Jakki/Jakki, the Lapp*, an artistic as well as a commercial success, followed by *Same Ællin/Ællin, the Lapp* (1971). Norwegian feature documentary has also gained international fame with Thor Heyerdahl's carefully detailed filmed archeological expeditions; the Swedish-produced *Kon-Tiki* won an Oscar in 1950. In the 1970s there was a wave of radical documentaries made for cinema distribution, as a protest against the public service conservatism of NRK, the sole Norwegian television channel. Oddvar Einarson protested against hydro-electric power with *Kampen om Mardøla/ The Struggle for Mardøla* (1972) and *Prognose Innerdalen/ The Innerdalen Prognosis* (1981). Sølve Skagen and Malte Wadmann portrayed workers' conflicts in *Hvem eier Tyssedal?/Who Owns Tyssedal?* (1975) and *Tvers igjennom lov/In Spite of the Law* (1979). Sigve Endresens gained cinema distribution for *For harde livet!/For Your Life!* (1989), about young drug addicts fighting their addiction. KS

Poland

Poland enjoys a world-class reputation for documentary film-making. Despite – or perhaps because of – political restrictions, the documentary genre has been important to both film-makers and the cinema-going public at various points in the history of Polish cinema.

In the mid-1950s a group of documentaries known as the 'black series' looked at social problems officially considered nonexistent. In the films of Jerzy Hoffman, Jerzy Bossak and W. I. Borowik, prostitution, alcoholism and homelessness were brought to light through a mixture of staged and real situations. Many of Poland's finest directors began their careers making documentaries. Andrzej Munk's* first medium-length films, *Gwiazdy Muszą Płonąć/The Stars Must Shine* (1954) and *Błękitny Krzyż/Men of the Blue Cross* (1955), are 'docu-dramas', and he used his documentary experience to create a style reminiscent of Italian neo-realism* in his later features. In the 1970s the documentary form was explored anew by young film-makers like Antoni Krauze*, Marcel Łoziński, Krzysztof Kieślowski* and Marek Piwowski. A manifesto published by the Cracow Group of documentary film-makers – Kieślowski, Tomasz Żygadło, Krzysztof Wojciechowski, Grzegorz Królikiewicz – declared that documentary should inform fictional work, and this concept prevailed in the 'cinema of moral unrest' of the 1970s and 1980s. Some film-makers, like Piwowski in *Rejs/Trip Down the River* (1970), mixed documentary and fiction, while in other cases the documentary ethos imbued fictional accounts of contemporary issues with a sense of integrity and authenticity. Not all film-makers, however, saw documentary merely as a schooling for feature films. Marcel Łozinski, Irena Kamieńska and Andrzej Titkow have continued to work exclusively in this form. Indeed the popularity of documentaries in Poland at the end of the 1980s can be attributed to their exposure of previously hidden historical and political events. With the economic crisis of the 1980s, many young film-makers who were unable to make features turned to documentary and short films. Among these, the amusing and well regarded films of Maria Zmarz-Koczanowicz, dealing with Polish youth sub-cultures, stand out. As Polish cinemas are now dominated by Hollywood, documentaries claim a strong following in art-house cinemas, unlike in western Europe where they are largely confined to festivals and television. With Polish society ripe for observation and comment, documentaries may well retain their popularity. AW

DOILLON, Jacques   Paris 1944

French director. Since the early 1970s, Jacques Doillon has occupied a marginal yet not negligible place in French *auteur* cinema. He co-directed *L'An 01* (1973) with Jean Rouch* and Alain Resnais*, and came to prominence with his first feature, *Les Doigts dans la tête* (1974). His intimate, small-scale films are marked by recurrent themes of oedipal and gender conflicts – especially between fathers and daughters – which, although not strictly autobiographical, often rework events from his life. Doillon tends to concentrate on female characters and prefers working with actresses; he is also a gifted director of young actors, as in the excellent *Le Jeune Werther* (1993). Doillon's *mise-en-scène* favours pared-down, claustrophobic settings and situations, contrasting with the violent emotions depicted. His films have a steady, if restricted, appeal; as he aptly said, 'I'm afraid I will remain an unsettling film-maker interested in complexity.' GV

Other Films: *Un sac de billes* (1975); *La Femme qui pleure* (1978); *La Drôlesse* (1979); *La Fille prodigue* (1981); *La Pirate, La Vie de famille, La Tentation d'Isabelle* (1985); *La Puritaine* (1986); *Comédie!* (1987); *L'Amoureuse* [TV] (1987, rel. 1993); *La Fille de quinze ans, La Vengeance d'une femme, Le Petit criminel* (1990); *Amoureuse* (1992); *Un homme à la mer, Du fond du cœur* (1994).

DONAGGIO, Giuseppe [Pino]   Bruano 1941

Italian composer. Donaggio's prolific career has been marked by a high number of international productions, second only in this respect to Ennio Morricone*. In particular, his professional partnership with American director Brian De Palma covers over twenty years and includes, among others, popular films such as *Carrie* (1976), *Dressed to Kill* (1980) and *Body Double* (1984). Although his scores were mostly composed for horror films and thrillers (apart from the De Palma films, there was Joe Dante's *Piranha*, 1978, and *The Howling*, 1981), Donaggio has also worked on more 'intimate' scores for films ranging from the family melodrama of Liliana Cavani's* *Oltre la porta/Beyond the Door* (1982) to the political cinema of Giuseppe Ferrara's *Il caso Moro/The Moro Affair* (1986). GLS

DONAT, Robert Manchester 1905 – London 1958

British actor. Gaining international recognition for his supporting role as Culpepper in Alexander Korda's* *The Private Life of Henry VIII* (1933), Donat's performance as Edmond Dantès in *The Count of Monte Cristo* (1934, US) confirmed his stardom. His wry wit in *The 39 Steps* (1935) and *The Ghost Goes West* (1936), combined with the affectionate idealism of *The Citadel* (1938) and *Goodbye, Mr. Chips* (for which he won an Oscar in 1939), made him the most popular male

romantic lead of the late 1930s in Britain. Reviewing his performance in Jacques Feyder's* *Knight Without Armour* (1937), Graham Greene* said, 'Mr Donat is the best film actor – at any rate in star parts – we possess; he is convincing, his voice has a pleasant roughness and his range is far greater than that of his chief rival for film honours, Mr Laurence Olivier*.' During the war he gave one of his finest performances in Carol Reed's* *The Young Mr. Pitt* (1942), and he continued to extend his range after the war with *The Winslow Boy* (1948). A chronic asthmatic throughout his career, he was only able to complete his last film, *The Inn of the Sixth Happiness* (1958), with the aid of oxygen, and was given a Special Citation by the Academy 'for the valour of his last performance'. JC

Bib: Jeffrey Richards, *The Age of the Dream Palace: Cinema and Society in Britain, 1930–1939* (1984).

DONNER, Jörn   Helsinki 1936

Finnish director, producer, writer and actor. Donner began his career as a film critic in the early 1950s, publishing pamphlets, novels and travel books as well as a biography of Ingmar Bergman*. He co-founded the Finnish Film Archive* in 1957, established his own production company in the 1960s, and worked as head of the Swedish Film Institute* and the Finnish Film Foundation in the 1970s and 1980s. Donner is now an active film producer, award-winning novelist and a member of the Finnish Parliament (representing the Swedish People's Party). Donner's first Finnish feature as a director was *Mustaa valkoisella/Black on White* (1968), in which he also played the leading male role. In *69* (1969), *Naisenkuvia/Portraits of Women* (1970) and *Anna* (1970), Donner used women's predicaments to underline his criticisms of the Finnish welfare system. His later features are 'case studies' of sexual harassment (*Män kan inte våldtas/Men Can't be Raped*, 1978) and corruption in the business world (*Dirty Story*, 1984). In Sweden, Donner produced, among other films, Bergman's *Fanny och Alexander/Fanny and Alexander* (1982). JS

DONSKOI, Mark S.   Odessa, Ukraine [Russian Empire] 1901 – Moscow 1981

Soviet director and scriptwriter, who graduated in law and practised as a defence lawyer in the Ukraine before starting in film in 1926. His first two films, *V bol'shom gorode/In the Big City* (1928) and *Tsena cheloveka/The Price of a Man* (1929), were attacks on the 'bourgeois influences' of the 1920s New Economic Policy and paeans to the new Soviet morality. Donskoi achieved prominence through his 'Gorky trilogy' – *Detstvo Gor'kogo/The Childhood of Maxim Gorky* (1938), *V lyudyakh/Into the World* (1939) and *Moi universitety/My Universities* (1940), in which the life of the writer was offset against a backdrop of stultifying pre-Revolutionary Russian provincial life. *Raduga/The Rainbow* (1944) was an epic tale of the heroic exploits of a Ukrainian woman partisan against the German occupiers, for which Donskoi won both an Oscar and a USSR State Prize. He made two further Gorky adaptations – *Mat'/The Mother* (1956) and *Foma Gordeyev* (1959) – but his career declined into predictable hagiography with two films about Lenin's mother: *Serdtse materi/The Heart of a Mother* (1966) and *Vernost' materi/A Mother's Devotion* (1968). RT

DÖRRIE, Doris   Hanover 1955

German director, who studied drama and film at the University of the Pacific, Stockton, California, and at the New School of Social Research, New York. In 1975 she returned to Germany, where with Wolfgang Berndt she co-directed the documentary *Ob's stürmt oder schneit* (1976). She worked for television (ZDF), wrote and directed *Paula aus Portugal* (1979) and other film portraits of women, which combined humour and sensitivity (*Katharina Eiselt*, 1980; *Von Romantik keine Spur*, 1981; *Mitten ins Herz*, 1983). Dörrie achieved national and international acclaim in 1985 with *Männer.../Men*, a tragi-comic love triangle which, according to *Der Spiegel*, 'exactly captures the *Zeitgeist*' – post-feminist disenchantment making way for a new acceptance of the foibles and fallibilities of the human heart. While *Männer* might be accused of indulging its (male) protagonists, and ultimately lacking satirical bite, *Paradies* (1986), another *ménage à trois* story, this time with an *amour fou* ending, is more agonisingly bleak and failed to find an audience. With *Happy Birthday, Türke* (1992) Dörrie returned to the semi-documentary style of her earlier work. KP

DORS, Diana   Diana Fluck; Swindon1931 – London 1984

British actress. 'I was the first sex symbol this country ever had,' Diana Dors claimed in 1966. 'Before me female stars were either pretty or matronly. Sex was just an incidental – best left to the Continentals.' Dors' career began with Rank with an underage debut in *The Shop at Sly Corner* (1946), cameos in the Huggetts series, and appearances in one or two social problem films – notably *Good-time Girl* (1948) and *I Believe in You* (1952) – in which her sexual precociousness was one of the problems. She was a memorably unglamorous kitchen maid in Lean's* *Oliver Twist* (1948), but her most satisfying and critically successful performance was as the condemned murderer Ruth Ellis in *Yield to the Night* (1956). The success of the film failed to ignite the Hollywood career she sought, and her career as a star effectively ended in the 1960s. She returned in 1984 for one final sensitive performance in Losey's* *Steaming*, a film released (in 1985) after the death of both Losey and Dors.

Christine Geraghty compares Dors' sex symbol role to that of Marilyn Monroe and Brigitte Bardot*, finding in the construction of each the same public private life, the difficult marriages, the emphasis on the body and body parts (the pout, the lips, the wiggle), the same mixture of knowingness and vulnerability, and the same final retreat – into suicide, privacy, or, in Dors' case, bankruptcy, professional decline and tours of working men's clubs to maintain her lifestyle. The peculiarly British characteristic which Dors added to the sex goddess was humour and a knowing kind of vulgarity.

In an interview, she claimed to have turned down the Shirley Ann Field part in *Saturday Night and Sunday Morning* (1960), a piece of casting which might have left its mark on the masculinity of the social realist cinema. JC

Bib: Christine Geraghty, 'Diana Dors', in Charles Barr (ed.), *All Our Yesterdays: Ninety Years of British Cinema* (1986).

DOUGLAS, Bill   Newcraighall, Scotland 1937- Barnstaple 1991

British director. Douglas made only four features: the autobiographical trilogy, *My Childhood* (1972), *My Ain Folk* (1974) and *My Way Home* (1979), and his film on the Tolpuddle Martyrs, *Comrades* (1986). The films, however, give evidence of a major European director whom the British film industry was unable to support. *My Childhood* lasts fifty minutes and cost around £4,000 to make. It is, however, one of the most intense and artistically condensed expressions of experience in British cinema. Almost painful in the unsentimental rigour of its style, the trilogy, in the semi-autobiographical tradition of the Soviet director much admired by Douglas, Mark Donskoi*, traces Douglas' childhood in a mining village in Scotland during and immediately after the war, through institutionalisation in a children's home and relative liberation in the inanities of National Service, to his first glimpses of a sustaining male relationship. The merits of the films were recognised by critics both at home and overseas, but Douglas failed to gain financial support for further projects until Channel 4* put up the balance to make *Comrades* four years after the script had been completed. Douglas's script of James Hogg's *Confessions of a Justified Sinner*, on which he had worked for twelve years and which was believed by those who had read it to be his best work, had failed to find financial backing at the time of his death at the age of 54. JC

Bib: Eddie Dick, Andrew Noble and Duncan Petrie (eds.), *Bill Douglas: A Lanternist's Account* (1993).

DOVZHENKO, Alexander [Oleksandr] P.   Sosnitsa, Ukraine [Russian Empire] 1894 – Moscow 1956

Ukrainian Soviet director and writer. Trained as a teacher, Dovzhenko worked as a civil servant and diplomat, then studied painting in Munich and became a newspaper cartoonist. He began film work in Odessa in 1926, directing the comedies *Vasya-reformator/Vasya the Reformer* (his first feature film) and *Yagodka lyubvi/The Fruit of Love*, and the thriller *Sumka dipkur'era/The Diplomatic Bag*. His major films, beginning with *Zvenigora* (1928), are characterised by a unique combination of lyricism, social commentary, gentle satire and powerful echoes of Ukrainian folklore. *Arsenal* (1929) was his first film to achieve widespread recognition outside the Ukraine. His next film, *Zemlya/The Earth* (1930), a highly poeticised version of collectivisation and a powerful evocation of nature and landscape, made his international reputation.

His first sound film, *Ivan* (1932), traced the transformation of the hero from an unenlightened peasant to a committed Communist shock worker against the background of the construction of the Dnieper dam, one of the key projects of the first Five Year Plan. After this Dovzhenko's career went downhill, as he became little more than a loyal 'servant of the state'. *Aerograd* (1935) affirmed his faith in the future of the Soviet Far East; *Shchors* (1939), set in the Civil War, was made at Stalin's* suggestion as a 'Ukrainian *Chapayev*' and won a State Prize in 1941. *Osvobozhdenie/Liberation* (1940) celebrated the reunification of western Ukraine with Ukraine proper following the Nazi-Soviet pact, while *Bitva za nashu sovetskuyu Ukrainu/The Battle for Our Soviet Ukraine* (1943) and *Pobeda na pravoberezhnoi Ukraine/Victory on the Ukrainian Right Bank* (1945) dealt with World War II. A number of Dovzhenko's unfilmed scripts were later made by his widow Yulia Solntseva. Dovzhenko also taught at VGIK* and wrote articles on film. RT

DRACULA – see TRANSYLVANIA

DRAVIĆ, Milena   Belgrade, Serbia 1940

Serbian actress, probably the only real star of Yugoslav cinema, discovered as a teenage girl by František Čap* for his film *Vrata ostaju otvorena/The Door Remains Open* (1959). This successful start led her to enter the Film Academy in Belgrade. By 1962 she had already gained her first Golden Arena at the national film festival in Pula*, for Branko Bauer's* *Prekobrojna/Superfluous* (1962). Since then she has appeared in over seventy films by more than thirty directors, among whom Puriša Djordjević and Dušan Makavejev* were the most important for her career. For international audiences she will be remembered as the radical activist proclaiming the sexual revolution in Makavejev's *W. R. – Misterije organizma/W. R. – Mysteries of the Organism* (1971), while Yugoslav television viewers recall her as the host of one of the best nightclub shows (together with her husband Dragan Nikolič), *Licem u lice/Face to Face*. SP

DREYER, Carl Theodor   Copenhagen 1889–
                                                              1968

Danish director, a towering figure in Danish film and one of the key directors of European art cinema*, making films in Denmark, Sweden, Norway, France and Germany. After an unhappy childhood, Dreyer began his career as a journalist. He wrote his first film script in 1912 and the following year was hired by Nordisk Films*, where until 1918 he wrote intertitles and scripts, read manuscripts and adapted novels and plays for the cinema. In that year he directed his first film, *Præsidenten/The President* (released in 1920), a melodrama about illicit love. In 1919 he began his second film for Nordisk, *Blade af Satans Bog/Leaves from Satan's Book* (released in 1921). This coincided with a decline in Nordisk's fortunes, causing Dreyer to seek a producer abroad. After making films in Sweden and Germany, he returned to Denmark in 1925 to direct *Du skal ære din Hustru/The Master of the House* for Palladium*.

These early films already exhibit key Dreyerian features: a quasi-documentary recreation of material details combined with a spirituality brilliantly evoked through lighting; anti-bourgeois attitudes; a pronounced interest in martyrdom; and strong women characters. *Du skal ære din Hustru* attracted the attention of a French producer, and in 1927 Dreyer began working on the project often considered his masterpiece, *La Passion de Jeanne d'Arc/The Passion of Joan of Arc*. In the making of the film, claimed by the critics for the French avant-garde*, Dreyer sought maximum authenticity, using extreme close-ups on the unmade-up faces of the actors (including Marie Falconetti and the writer Antonin Artaud), and taking the intertitle dialogue from the official transcripts of Joan of Arc's trial. Dreyer declared: 'We must truly give the audience the feeling that they see life through the keyhole of the cinema. I do not seek anything . . . but life.' The film had its world premiere in Copenhagen in April 1928 and was a resounding critical success; it was released in France in a version censored by the Church. Dreyer's first sound film, *Vampyr/The Vampire* (1932), also made in France, was a commercial failure, however, and he spent the next ten years working as a journalist. In 1942 he was offered the chance to direct a documentary, *Mødrehjælpen/Helping Young Mothers*, and the following year a fiction film, *Vredens Dag/Day of Wrath*, produced by Palladium. Set in seventeenth-century Denmark, the film's narrative of witchcraft and intolerance had obvious contemporary resonances for a country under German occupation, and Dreyer was forced to flee the country at the end of 1943. He directed *Två människor/Two People* in Sweden in 1944. Returning to Denmark at the end of the war, in 1952 he was granted a state licence to run one of Copenhagen's most lucrative cinemas, allowing him to direct *Ordet/The Word* (1955), a sombre religious drama. In 1964 Dreyer released his last feature, *Gertrud*, the powerful tale of a woman repressing her desires but asserting her spiritual independence.

Besides features, Dreyer directed a number of documentaries. After *Mødrehjælpen*, the best known of these is *De nåede færgen/They Caught the Ferry* (1948). He also made a film on a famous Danish sculptor, Bertil Thorvaldsen. During the last twenty years of his life Dreyer worked on many different projects which remained unrealised, in particular a film version of *Medea* with Maria Callas in the main role, and a film on Christ which he hoped to make right up to his death. He completed the script but his American producer withdrew. ME

Bib: David Bordwell, *The Films of Carl-Theodor Dreyer* (1981).

Other Films (As Director): *Prästänkan/The Parson's Widow* (1920, Swe.); *Der var engang/Once Upon a Time*, *Die Gezeichneten/Love One Another* (1922, Ger.); *Michael/Mikaël/Chained* (1924, Ger.); *Glomdalsbruden/The Bride of Glomdal* (1926, Nor.); *Landsbykirken/The Danish Village Church, Kampen mod Kraeften/The Struggle Against Cancer* (1947, shorts); *Thorvaldsen* [short] (1949); *Storstrømsbroen/The Bridge of Storstrøm* [short] (1950); *Et Slot i et Slot/Castle Within a Castle* [short] (1954).

DULAC, Germaine
Germaine Saisset-Schneider; Amiens 1882 – Paris 1942

French director, and key figure in the 'first' avant-garde [> FRENCH AVANT-GARDE] of the 1920s. Dulac started as a photographer and wrote for two feminist journals, *La Fronde* and *La Française*. In her thirties she began her own production company, Delia Film. Her first films were conventional melodramas, but a chance meeting with theoretician Louis Delluc* led to them formulating the tenets of the avant-garde. Dulac was at the heart of this group of intellectuals devoted to the promotion of art film-making, film education and film criticism.

From *Ames de fous* (1917), Dulac increasingly privileged the representation of impressions and inner feelings over narrative. Her first critical success was *La Fête espagnole* (1920), but her major work is *La Souriante Mme Beudet/The Smiling Mrs Beudet* (1923), a sympathetic portrayal of the frustrations, desires and revolt of a bourgeois housewife, which uses superimpositions, dissolves and slow motion. Dulac alternated avant-garde productions with mainstream films like *Gossette* (1923), but aspired to a more abstract style, 'the integral film ... a visual symphony made of rhythmic images'. A supreme expression of this is the controversial *La Coquille et le clergyman/The Seashell and the Clergyman* (1928), a rare attempt at rendering the unconscious on screen. She went on to make abstract and documentary films, including *Germination d'un haricot* (1928), the stop-motion record of the germination of a seed, and she also lectured on film. She was head of Gaumont* newsreels until her death. Dulac was deeply committed to both feminist issues and the search for a new cinematic language. GV

Bib: Sandy Flitterman-Lewis, *To Desire Differently: Feminism and the French Cinema* (1990).

Other Films Include: *Les Soeurs ennemies, Vénus victrix* (1917); *La Cigarette* (1919); *La Belle dame sans merci* (1920); *La Mort du soleil* (1922); *Ame d'artiste* (1925); *La Princesse Mandane, Thèmes et variations* (1928).

DUNAYEVSKY, Isaak O.
Lokhvitsa, Ukraine [Russian Empire] 1900 – Moscow 1955

Russian composer. Dunayevsky composed the music for Grigori Alexandrov's* popular musical comedy films *Vesëlye rebyata/The Happy Guys* (1934), *Tsirk/The Circus* (1936), *Volga-Volga* (1938), *Svetlyi put'/The Radiant Path* (1940) and *Vesna/Springtime* (1947). He also scored Ivan Pyriev's* *Bogataya nevesta/The Rich Bride* (1938) and *Kubanskie kazaki/The Kuban Cossacks* (1950). His catchy tunes combined elements of folk and popular music, marches and dances, and were very popular. RT

DUPONT, Ewald André
Zeitz 1891 – Los Angeles, California 1956

German director. One of Germany's first regular film critics (from 1911), he began scriptwriting numerous detective film series in 1916, making the switch to directing in 1918 with twelve episodes of the *Max Landa* detective series. Two Henny Porten* pictures – *Die Geier-Wally* (1921) and *Das alte Gesetz* (1923) – as well as *Der Demütige und die Tänzerin* (1925) made Dupont the most commercially promising director of his generation. But it was *Varieté/Variety* (1925), produced by Erich Pommer*, which brought him world fame. Featuring Emil Jannings* and Lya de Putti*, the film has remained a stylistic and dramatic *tour de force*, combining innovative camerawork (Karl Freund*) and lighting with a feel for eroticism and violence. Like so many who tried to repeat a German success in Hollywood, Dupont came unstuck. *Love Me and the World is Mine* (1927), his first US picture, was a commercial flop, and the studio unforgiving. His ventures in Britain were more promising: for British International Pictures, Dupont directed *Moulin Rouge* (1928) and *Piccadilly* (1929) two night-club films worthy of the director of *Varieté* and minor masterpieces of the British silent cinema. Still in Britain, but as a radical departure, Dupont made *Atlantic/Atlantik* (1929), Europe's first sound film, shot in three languages, as a highly profitable novelty, even if it is stylistically cramped and marred by stilted dialogue. Dupont made several more multi-language films starring Conrad Veidt* and Fritz Kortner*, before returning to BIP's German partner firm, Emelka, for which he made a circus film, *Salto Mortale/Trapeze* (1931). Sent to Los Angeles in 1932 for a film about the Olympics, Dupont decided to stay, accepting B-picture assignments, working as a press agent, editor of an émigré journal, and finally eking out a meagre existence on television series. TE/MW

Bib: Jürgen Brettschneider (ed.), *Ewald André Dupont: Autor und Regisseur* (1992).

DURÁN, Rafael
Rafael Durán Espayaldo; Madrid 1911 – Seville 1994

Spanish actor from the stage who attained huge popularity after his second film, *La tonta del bote/The Prize Idiot* (1940). His pairing with Josita Hernán led to a successful partnership in a series of 1940s films, many made at Cifesa*. Suaveness and class characterised his leading-man roles in comedies and melodramas like *Eloisa está debajo de un almendro/Eloísa is Underneath an Almond Tree* (1943), *Tuvo la culpa Adán/Adam's Fault* (1943), *Ella, él y sus millones/She, He and Their Millions* (1944). By the 1950s these qualities had become too mannered and thereafter he was relegated to supporting roles. PWE

DURAS, Marguerite
Marguerite Donnadieu; Gia-dinh, Indo-China [now Vietnam] 1914

French novelist, playwright and director, a major figure in French and feminist culture. Duras wrote screenplays, notably for Alain Resnais* (*Hiroshima mon amour*, 1959), and co-directed an adaptation of her play *La Musica* (1967, with Paul Seban), before directing *Détruire, dit-elle/Destroy She Said* in 1969. She has since engaged in writing and film-making as parallel and cross-referencing activities: *La Femme du Gange/Woman of the Ganges* (1974) and *India Song* (1975) rework the same events and characters as her novels *The Vice-Consul, The Ravishing of Lol V. Stein* and *L'Amour*.

Duras is a modernist who works on sound and image with equal intensity; her lyrical soundtracks – sometimes featuring her own mesmerising voice, as in *Le Camion* (1977) – may even assume a separate identity: *Son nom de Venise dans Calcutta désert* (1976) matches a new set of images to the soundtrack of *India Song*. Duras' approach is minimalist and allusive, and she has been criticised for her a-historical characters. While her vision of women's 'suicidal' condition is bleak, her films nevertheless concentrate on female desire and women's experience. She strongly disapproved of Jean-Jacques Annaud's* lavish adaptation of her Goncourt prize-winning autobiographical novel *L'Amant/The Lover* (1991). GV

Bib: Lesley Hill, *Duras* (1993).

Other Films (as Director) Include: *Jaune le soleil* (1971); *Nathalie Granger* (1972); *Des journées entières dans les arbres/Whole Days in the Trees* (1976); *Baxter, Vera Baxter* (1977); *Le Navire night, Aurélia Steiner – Vancouver* (1979); *Les Enfants* (1984).

DUVANEL, Charles-Georges   Aarau 1906 – Geneva 1975

Swiss cinematographer and director. The youngest camera operator on the first *Ciné-journal suisse* newsreels (1924–34), Duvanel was one of the most productive Swiss documentary film-makers in the inter-war period. Like most of his early work, his best-known films – *Les Ailes en Suisse* (1929) and *Pionniers* (1936) – create an intense Swiss iconography of the everyday that was fully exploited (including by Duvanel himself) in the cinema of the 'spiritual defence of the nation' during World War II [> LINDTBERG]. In addition to his official propaganda films (including productions for the national tourist office), Duvanel pursued a long and varied independent career, going back to *La Vocation d'André Carel* (1925) with Michel Simon*, and the 1930 Dyrenfurth expedition film *Himatschal, der Thron der Götter* (1931). He went on making films until 1970, with *Le Cadeau des Incas*. MW

Other Films Include: *Das weisse Stadion* (1928); *Le Défilé de la 1ère Division* (1937); *Vivre, une oeuvre, un peuple* (1939); *L'Année vigneronne* (1940); *Il neige sur le Haut-Pays* (1943); *Le Simplon* (1956); *Croix rouge sur fond blanc* (1963); *Poésie du rail* (1965).

DUVIVIER, Julien   Lille 1896 – Paris 1967

French director. One of the great French directors of the classical era, Duvivier was revered in the 1930s but later un-favourably compared with Jean Renoir*. Assistant to André Antoine*, he started making silent films in 1919, mostly melodramatic literary adaptations such as *Poil de carotte* (1926, which he remade with sound in 1932). From his prolific 1930s output, four films stand out: an excellent early Simenon adaptation, *La Tête d'un homme* (1932), in which Harry Baur* stalks shady bars in Montparnasse as Inspector Maigret; and (especially) three films which created and fixed the Jean Gabin* 'myth', *La Bandera* (1935), *La Belle équipe* (1936) and *Pépé le Moko* (1936). Beyond their different genres (respectively a foreign legion drama, a tale of male solidarity at the time of the Popular Front*, and a thriller set in Algiers), these films illustrate the dominant Duvivier universe of that period: pessimistic proletarian tales of loyalty and betrayal, 'men's stories', as he put it. Also characteristic was his extraordinary technique, especially his signature virtuoso camera movements combined with extremely long takes. Duvivier's two other notable 1930s films are *Un carnet de Bal* (1937), a series of episodes around an actress (Marie Bell) and a galaxy of male stars (including Raimu* and Pierre Blanchar*), and *La Fin du jour* (1938), about an actors' retirement home (with, among others, Michel Simon*), both displaying his skilled use of stars. Duvivier also worked in Hollywood, making (among other films) *The Great Waltz* (1938), *Tales of Manhattan* (1942) and *The Imposter* (1944, with Gabin). *Panique* (1947) continued his 1930s pessimistic vein, as did the virulently misogynist *Voici le temps des assassins* (1956), which is partly redeemed by the presence of Jean Gabin. Duvivier's postwar career was distinguished by the immense success of the Franco-Italian *Don Camillo* series starring Fernandel* and Gino Cervi* (five films from 1952 to 1965, of which Duvivier directed the first two, with a sixth in 1972 with Cervi alone), and by the Zola adaptation *Pot-bouille/The House of Lovers* (1957, with Gérard Philipe*). GV

DYKHOVICHNY, Ivan   Moscow 1947

Russian director, actor and scriptwriter. In 1979, after ten years' work as a theatrical actor, Dykhovichny entered the Higher Courses for Directors, where he was taught by Eldar Ryazanov* and, briefly but influentially, by Andrey Tarkovsky*, graduating in 1982. Tarkovsky's influence is apparent in Dykhovichny's early shorts, including *Elia Isaakovich i Margarita Prokof'evna/Elia Isaakovich and Margarita Prokofevna* (1981), from a story by Isaak Babel. Dykhovichny found international success with his 1988 version of Chekhov's story *Chërnyi monakh/The Black Monk*, which he co-scripted with Sergei Solovyov*. Dykhovichny's most recent film is *Prorva/Moscow Parade* (1992), a Franco-Russian co-production starring the German singer Ute Lemper. *Prorva*'s achievement was to capture the glamour of the facade of 1930s Stalinist Moscow as well as the decay and corruption beneath. JGf

E

EALING COMEDY

British genre. While Ealing comedy should include the films which Basil Dean* produced with George Formby* and Gracie Fields* in the 1930s, the term usually refers to those comedies made under Michael Balcon* in the postwar period – from *Hue and Cry* (1947) to *Barnacle Bill* (1957) – directed mainly by Charles Crichton*, Henry Cornelius, Charles Frend, Alexander Mackendrick* and Robert Hamer*, and scripted most characteristically by T. E. B. Clarke*. Nostalgia has often imposed a unity on Ealing comedy which misses the variations between the films themselves, and the term 'Ealing comedy' has a certain mythical status, identifying not simply a collection of films but a way of being English. Charles Barr relates this to Michael Frayn's distinction between Herbivore and Carnivore elements in British culture around the time of the Festival of Britain in 1951: 'Festival Britain was the Britain of the radical middle-classes – the do-gooders; the readers of the *News Chronicle*, the *Guardian* and the *Observer*; the signers of petitions; the backbone of the BBC. In short, the Herbivores, or gentle ruminants.' Ealing comedies belonged with the Herbivores.

The ingredients of the mythical genre involve a set of oppositions between settled communities and soulless progress. The herbivorous communities can be represented by the crew of a West Highland puffer, a small business, or a London borough; carnivorous progress can be represented by an American, big business, or Whitehall: respectively, *The 'Maggie'* (1954), *The Man in the White Suit* (1951), *Passport to Pimlico* (1949). The outcome is invariably a triumph of community and consensus over capitalism and bureaucracy. Identified in spirit with the memory of the Blitz and the herbivore Attlee Labour government in its early years, the Carnivores were coming, and by the time of *The 'Maggie'* (1954) the opposition has developed sharp edges.

The genre may have died with Ealing, but the spirit lives on. JC

Bib: Charles Barr, *Ealing Studios* (1977).

ECHANOVE, Juan
Juan Echanove Labanda;
Madrid 1961

Spanish actor. A comic Spanish version of Charles Laughton. Beer-bellied, lips glistening, his fat man persona takes on a more than Sancho Panza-like earthy innocence. His essential contribution to films like *Tiempo de silencio/A Time of Silence* (1986), *La hora bruja/The Witching Hour* (1985) and *Bajarse al moro/Going Down to Morocco* (1989) seems to embody the new democracy's consumerist, physical indulgences. PWE

EDINBURGH INTERNATIONAL FILM FESTIVAL

British festival, established in 1947 as the first British film festival and then only the third in the world (after Venice and Cannes). It was established by Norman Wilson, editor of *Cinema Quarterly*, the journal of the British Documentary Movement*, and Forsyth Hardy, John Grierson's biographer. Its first advisory committee included Basil Wright* and Paul Rotha*, and its early focus was on screening and discussing world documentary. Under the direction first of Murray Grigor and then of Linda Myles, in the 1970s and early 1980s the festival became an important focus of theoretical discussion, with the first Women and Film conference in 1972; retrospectives and publications on Sam Fuller, Roger Corman, Douglas Sirk and others; special events on psychoanalysis and cinema, history/popular memory, and avantgarde cinema; and 'Scotch Reels', an influential debate on Scottish film culture. In the 1980s, other festivals appeared in Britain – Tyneside, Leeds, Birmingham, Nottingham, for example – with their own distinctive edge and equal claims on subsidy. It remains to be seen whether Edinburgh will discover a distinctive direction for the latter part of the 1990s. JC

EGGELING, Viking
Lund 1880 – Berlin 1925

Swedish painter and director, one of the pioneers of European experimental cinema. Eggeling left Sweden in his early years to go to France and Switzerland, where he was greatly influenced by Cubism, Dadaism and the new avantgarde [> AVANT-GARDE CINEMA IN EUROPE]. With Hans Richter he made experimental films based on non-figurative, Chinese-type, picture scrolls. His only surviving film is the remarkable little piece *Diagonalsymfoni/Diagonal Symphony*, which he completed in Berlin in 1923–24, and which can be seen as an effort to create an equivalent to music on screen by means of abstract moving images. LGA/BF

Bib: Louise O'Konor, *Viking Eggeling, Artist and Filmmaker, Life and Work* (1971).

EGGERT, Konstantin V.
1883–1955

Russian director, actor and entrepreneur. Eggert worked on the stage, including the Moscow Art Theatre, from 1912 and in cinema from 1924, when he appeared in Yakov Protazanov's* *Aelita*. His career is closely associated with the Mezhrabpom studio*, in which he became a major shareholder and for which (with Vladimir Gardin*) he directed his first film *Medvezh'ya svad'ba/The Bear's Wedding* (1926), an adaptation by Anatoli Lunacharsky* of a gothic horror story by Prosper Mérimée, which starred Eggert and Lunacharsky's wife Natalya Rozenel and proved to be far more popular at the Soviet box office than Eisenstein's*

Bronenosets Potëmkin/The Battleship Potemkin. He directed four more features, culminating in a Balzac adaptation in 1937. He was arrested, and ended his artistic career as an actor in the Gulag. RT

EICHBERG, Richard   Berlin 1888 – Munich 1952

German director, who was extremely popular for two decades. Eichberg's success as a director prompted him to start a production company in 1916 (Eichberg Film). Featuring turbulent and sensational action and employing a number of optical effects, his films were recognised by what the trade, in a half-derogatory, half-admiring tone, referred to as the 'Eichberg style'. From the early 1920s he was equally adept at comedy (*Der Fürst von Pappenheim*, 1927), and offered Lilian Harvey* (*Leidenschaft*, 1925) as well as Hans Albers* (*Der Greifer*, 1930) their first major roles. In the mid-1920s, he made big international production films for British companies, such as the astonishing melodrama *Song* (1928) with Anna May Wong and Heinrich George*. In the years following the Nazi takeover, Eichberg preferred working in Paris, and in India where he made versions of *Der Tiger von Eschnapur* and *Das indische Grabmal* (both 1938; silent versions by Joe May*). An émigré to the USA between 1938 and 1949, Eichberg, ironically one of the most 'American' of all German directors, was unable to find employment in Hollywood. MW

Other Films Include: *Strohfeuer* (1915); *Das Skelett* (1916); *Im Zeichen der Schuld* (1918); *Kinder der Landstraße* (1919); *Der Fluch der Menschheit* (1920); *Die schönste Frau der Welt* (1924); *Die keusche Susanne* (1926); *Das Girl von der Revue* (1928); *Die unsichtbare Front* (1932); *Die Reise nach Marrakesch* (1949).

EISENSTEIN [EIZENSHTEIN], Sergei M.   Riga, Latvia [Russian Empire] 1898 – Moscow 1948

Soviet director and film theorist. Eisenstein trained as a civil engineer but abandoned his courses and joined the Red Army after the Revolution. Assigned to a theatrical troupe during the Civil War, he gained valuable experience designing and painting sets and producing plays. In 1921, with his childhood friend Maxim Strauch*, he joined the Proletkult Theatre and staged a series of experimental agitational plays, using the techniques of circus, music hall and cabaret in what he termed a 'montage of attractions' [> SOVIET MONTAGE], which was intended to galvanise audiences into an ideologically motivated reaction. One of his productions included a short film, *Dnevnik Glumova/Glumov's Diary* (1923), a spoof of an American thriller. But he was slowly becoming aware of the limitations of theatrical realism, especially when he staged *Protivogazy/Gas Masks* (1924) in a gas works. The experiment failed and Eisenstein, as he put it, 'fell into cinema'. He had already worked with Esfir Shub* re-editing imported films for Soviet audiences and in his first full-length film, *Stachka/The Strike* (1925), he applied the montage of attractions to cinema for the first time. Unlike Lev Kuleshov*,

Eisenstein thought that the essence of montage lay in the *conflict* between different elements, chosen for their effectiveness, and from this conflict a new synthesis would arise. The actors' role was diminished to that of representing 'types', while the director became supreme. Although he used professional actors in all his films, he chose people for their physical type rather than their acting ability, at least in his silent films. Hence an unknown worker played Lenin* in *Oktyabr'/October* (1928). Eisenstein achieved international recognition with his second feature, *Bronenosets Potëmkin/ The Battleship Potemkin* (1926). The fictitious sequence of the massacre on the Odessa steps proved so powerful that it became embedded in the popular consciousness as an actual historical event, as did the storming of the Winter Palace in *Oktyabr'*. This film had to be re-edited because of Trotsky's fall from grace, and all Eisenstein's subsequent work was dogged by political difficulties. His film about collectivisation, begun as *General'naya liniya/The General Line*, was re-cut and eventually finished as *Staroe i novoe/The Old and the New* in 1929. Eisenstein did not even wait for its Moscow premiere: he had already left with Grigori Alexandrov* and Eduard Tisse* for the West, ostensibly to learn about the new medium of sound. Eisenstein had already theoretically investigated the possibility of incorporating sound into montage, devising the notion of orchestral counterpoint, proclaimed in the 1928 'Statement on Sound' signed with Alexandrov and Vsevolod Pudovkin*. The idea of 'attractions' gave way to that of 'stimulants', which would provoke a complex series of associations in the audience, setting them thinking along a line predetermined by the director. He called this 'intellectual cinema', and *Oktyabr'* represents his first experiment in this direction. Critics accused him of making films that were 'unintelligible to the millions'.

Eisenstein eventually went to Hollywood: the projects he put forward were rejected and he ended up in Mexico, shooting his first sound film, *¡Que viva México!* However the money ran out and he returned to Moscow in 1932. Boris Shumyatsky* rejected a number of Eisenstein's projects but in 1935 allowed him to start working on a new film about collectivisation, *Bezhin lug/Bezhin Meadow*. After two years this was stopped for financial and political reasons, and it was only after Shumyatsky's own fall from grace in 1938 that Eisenstein was able to complete his next, and most accessible, film *Aleksandr Nevskii/Alexander Nevsky*, starring Nikolai Cherkasov*. In this film he was also, for the first time, able to realise his ideas on audio-visual montage and orchestral counterpoint in a remarkable collaboration with Sergei Prokofiev*, especially in the famous 'Battle on the Ice' sequence. The film marked his rehabilitation and he was awarded the Order of Lenin in 1939. Eisenstein's last film, *Ivan Groznyi/Ivan the Terrible* (1943–46) was never completed. The first part, released in 1945, was an instant critical success and it earned the Stalin Prize for Eisenstein and Cherkasov. In the second part, however, the deliberate historical parallels between Ivan and Stalin* became all too apparent and, although completed, the film was not shown, its existence not officially acknowledged until 1958. In it Eisenstein extended his exploration of montage into the use of colour. The third part of *Ivan* was never finished.

Eisenstein's work in film theory and practice made him the towering figure in Soviet cinema history, referred to by all others simply as 'The Master'. His major theoretical works have been translated into English as *The Film Sense* (1942); *Film Form* (1949); *Film Essays and a Lecture* and *Notes of a Film Director* (both 1970); *Writings, 1922–34* (1988); *Towards a Theory of Montage* (1991); *Beyond the Stars* (1995) and *Writings, 1935–48* (1996). RT

EISNER, Lotte   Berlin 1896 – Paris 1983

German historian, who in 1927 became a film critic for the daily *Film-Kurier*. She left Berlin for Paris in 1933, working as a correspondent for *World Film News* and other publications. Temporarily interned in the concentration camp of Gurs, she began working at the Cinémathèque Française* in 1945, where she was curator until 1975, programming festivals and lectures, and scouring the globe for films and documents that decisively shaped the inspiring Cinémathèque approach. Besides studies of F. W. Murnau* (1965) and Fritz Lang* (1976), Eisner is the author of *L'Ecran démoniaque* (1952; in English: *The Haunted Screen: Expressionism in the German Cinema and the Influence of Max Reinhardt*, 1973). With its attention to pertinent art-historical connections between film, theatre, literature and the visual arts, the book remains the seminal aesthetic study of Expressionist film*. In 1975 she concluded the German edition of her book (*Die dämonische Leinwand*) with a salute to the young directors of the New German Cinema*, who idolised her as an incarnation of the history of their national cinema. MW

EKK, Nikolai V. Nikolai Ivakin; Riga, Latvia [Russian Empire] 1902 – Moscow 1976

Soviet director, actor and scriptwriter. Ekk graduated from Vsevolod Meyerhold's Directing Workshop and worked in his theatre until 1927 when he graduated from the GTK film school, where he had worked under Pavel Tager, one of the pioneers of sound in the USSR. Ekk directed the first Soviet sound film, *Putëvka v zhizn'/The Path to Life* (1931), which dealt with the communal re-education of the homeless orphans left after the 1917–21 Civil War. The film was highly regarded at the first Venice film festival in 1932. He also directed, and starred in, the first Soviet colour film, *Grunya Kornakova* (1936), and made another colour feature, *Sorochinskaya yarmarka/Sorochintsy Fair*, based on the Gogol story, in 1939. He was then sent into internal exile in Tashkent and left unemployed and unemployable for nearly two decades. Among subsequent works was a stereoscopic (3-D) film, *Chelovek v zelënoi perchatke/The Man in the Green Gloves* (1968). He also worked as a stage director and scripted all his films. RT

EKMAN, Gösta (Jr.)   Stockholm 1939

Swedish actor. Gösta Ekman Jr., son of Hasse Ekman* and grandson of Gösta Ekman Sr.*, played small parts and worked as a continuity person in the 1950s for both his father and Ingmar Bergman*. In 1960 he began acting at the Stockholm Municipal Theatre. Fame came with comic roles

in the films and cabaret shows of Hans Alfredson and Tage Danielsson – for example *Mannen som slutade röka/The Man Who Gave Up Smoking* (1972) and *Picassos äventyr/The Adventures of Picasso* (1978). In a series of shorts directed by Mats Arehn for television, Ekman developed the slapstick character 'Papphammar' (1980). His comic character is that of a person out of step with reality, a sort of Swedish Jacques Tati*. A highly versatile performer, in addition to numerous popular films Ekman has appeared in prestigious art cinema productions, making him one of the most skilled actors in Sweden. LGA/BF

EKMAN, Gösta (Sr.)   Stockholm 1890–1938

Swedish actor. Gösta Ekman Sr. is one of the greatest stage actors in the history of the Swedish theatre. He was also a distinguished and versatile film actor, capable of creating gentle, well-mannered characters as well as passionate ones. He made his film debut in 1911 in *Blott en dröm/Only a Dream*. Thereafter he acted in about forty films in Sweden, with such directors as Victor Sjöström* (*Vem dömer?/Love's Crucible*, 1922) and Gustaf Molander*, with whom he made *Swedenhielms/The Family Swedenhielms* (1935), but especially *Intermezzo* (1936, co-starring the young Ingrid Bergman*). He also worked outside Sweden, appearing notably in Germany, in F. W. Murnau's* *Faust* (1926, where he plays Faust to Emil Jannings's* Mephisto), and in Denmark, in Anders Wilhelm Sandberg's* 1926 version of *Klovnen/The Clown*. LGA/BF

EKMAN, Hasse [Hans]   Stockholm 1915

Swedish director, scriptwriter and actor. The son of actor Gösta Ekman Sr.* and father of Gösta Ekman Jr.*, Hasse Ekman is one of the most versatile and popular film directors of the Swedish postwar scene, noted for his 'continental touch' combining elegance, irony and light humour. At one stage he was considered a principal rival to Ingmar Bergman*, directing psychological dramas such as *Banketten/The Banquet* (1948) and *Flicka och hyacinter/Girl with Hyacinths/The Suicide* (1950). The latter, which investigates a young woman's suicide through the diverse perceptions of her neighbours and friends, is a 'disguised' episode film, a genre in which Ekman also excelled. He also made successful war films such as *Första divisionen/First Division* (1941) and *Excellensen* (1944). With *Fram för lilla Märta/Three Cheers for Little Märta* (1945), he won great popular acclaim, and he has been most successful as a comedy director. He has directed altogether over forty features. As an actor, he appeared in many of his own films and in Ingmar Bergman's* *Törst/Thirst* (1949) and *Gycklarnas afton/Sawdust and Tinsel* (1953). LGA/BF

EKRAN

Slovene monthly film magazine, established in 1962 in Ljubljana with the intention of providing a critical evaluation of modern cinema. Initially relying on translations from

126

French, Italian and American authors, *Ekran* reached its first peak at the end of the 1960s with original contributions centred on the Yugoslav 'Black Wave'*. In the 1980s, the magazine was closely linked with a strong local school of Lacanian psychoanalysis and it opened its pages to French film theory (Raymond Bellour, Pascal Bonitzer, Michel Chion), creating an inter-disciplinary field of humanist and cultural studies. This theoretical focus prompted the organisation of an annual autumn film school and the creation of a book series, Imago. Recent circulation was 2,000. SP

ELFELT, Peter   Copenhagen 1866–1931

Danish film pioneer, who trained as a photographer. Elfelt opened his own photographic establishment in 1890 and in 1900 became photographer to the royal family. Elfelt was the original Danish film pioneer, making nearly 200 reportage films up to 1914, starting with *Kørsel med grønlandske Hunde/Driving with Greenlandic Huskies* in 1896, in which a park in Copenhagen on a snowy day stood in for Greenland. In the following years Elfelt specialised in films on royalty and the middle classes. In 1903 he made the first Danish fiction film, *Henrettelsen/The Execution*, with a running time of eight minutes. ME

Other Films Include: *De Kongelige skal fotograferes/The Royal Family Have Their Photograph Taken, Juletræet/The Christmas Tree* (1899); *Skiløb, Holmenkollen/Ski Race, Holmenkollen* (1900); *Badende Damer. Fri Strand/Ladies Bathing on the Beach* (1901); *Kong Edwards og Dronning Alexandras Kroning/The Coronation of King Edward and Queen Alexandra* (1903).

ELLIOTT, Denholm   London 1922 – Ibiza, Spain 1992

British actor, distinguished as a consistently watchable supporting actor since his film debut in 1949. Elliott's characterisation of the vulnerable, and sometimes shifty, loser was played with enough sensitivity to win him sympathy. He was rewarded with recognition in the 1980s, winning BAFTA awards for his supporting roles in *Trading Places* (1983, US), *A Private Function* (1984), and *Defence of the Realm* (1985). He became part of the Merchant-Ivory* stable in *A Room with a View* (1985) and *Maurice* (1987), and had fun in cameo roles in the Hollywood blockbusters *Raiders of the Lost Ark* (1981, US) and *Indiana Jones and the Last Crusade* (1989, US). JC

Other Films Include: *The Sound Barrier* (1952); *The Cruel Sea, The Heart of the Matter* (1953); *King Rat* (1965); *Alfie* (1966); *A Doll's House* (1973); *Robin and Marian* (1976, US); *Bad Timing* (1980); *Killing Dad* (1989).

ELVEY, Maurice   William Seward Folkard; Darlington 1887 – Brighton 1967

British director, distinguished more for the quantity of his work than its quality. Between 1913 and 1957, with around 300 features and innumerable shorts, he is reputed to have made more feature films than any other director in Britain, and may have few rivals anywhere in the world. 'Elvey's position,' says Rachael Low, 'as one of the most important film-makers in England cannot be questioned, whatever the artistic qualities of his work. [...] Although not an originator himself, he was quick to adopt new ideas and to sense what the public liked.' JC

Bib: Rachael Low, *The History of British Film, 1914–1918* (1950), and *The History of British Film, 1918–1928* (1971).

Films Include: *Maria Marten* (1913, also *The Murder in the Red Barn*); *When Knights Were Bold* (1916); *Dombey and Son* (1917); *Adam Bede, Hindle Wakes* (1918); *Comradeship* (1919); *Bleak House* (1920); *The Hound of the Baskervilles* (1921); *The Passionate Friends* (1922); *The Sign of Four* (1923); *Hindle Wakes* (1927); *Sally in our Alley* (1931); *This Week of Grace* (1933); *The Gentle Sex* [co-dir., Leslie Howard], *The Lamp Still Burns* [completed by Elvey after Howard's death] (1943); *Is Your Honeymoon Really Necessary?* (1953); *You Lucky People* (1955).

EMIGRATION AND EUROPEAN CINEMA

The phenomenon of emigration both within Europe and from Europe greatly affected the cinema throughout its first century. Social factors (poverty and racism, especially anti-semitism) and historical events such as wars, revolutions and totalitarian regimes drove people from their home countries, usually west, towards Germany and the Netherlands, then France and the UK, and massively to the US. Economic and cultural factors specific to the film industry have also repeatedly drawn European film personnel to North America. There has been a small movement in the opposite direction, with American directors such as Joseph Losey* and Jules Dassin*, and stars like Eddie Constantine* and Paul Robeson* making a career in Europe.

Many Hollywood pioneers and movie moguls came from central Europe. Subsequently, Hollywood attracted film people who went either of their own volition or as a result of the studios' systematic policies of talent-scouting. Some made a first or second career there (Charlie Chaplin, Mihály Kertész [Michael Curtiz], Jean Negulescu [Negulesco], Ernst Lubitsch*, Greta Garbo*, Ingrid Bergman*, Douglas Sirk [Detlef Sierck*]) while for others Hollywood was a – more or less extended and more or less successful – episode: Victor Sjöström*, Mauritz Stiller*, Max Ophuls*, Fritz Lang*, René Clair*, Julien Duvivier*, Jean Renoir*, S. M. Eisenstein*, Louis Malle*, Nestor Almendros* and many others. The country most affected has been Germany. While directors, actors, scriptwriters, art directors and cameramen were forced to leave Germany when the Nazis came to power in 1933, others had already left. Those tempted, apart from

Lubitsch, Sirk and Lang, included F. W. Murnau*, William Dieterle*, E. A. Dupont*, Paul Leni*, Ludwig Berger*, Emil Jannings*, Marlene Dietrich*, Robert Siodmak*, Pola Negri*, Lya de Putti*, Erich Pommer*, Carl Mayer*, Karl Freund*, Joe May*, Richard Oswald*, Otto Preminger, Billy Wilder and Reinhold Schünzel*. From 1 April 1933, Jews were systematically excluded from public life in Germany and consequently almost a third of Germany's film industry personnel fled to neighbouring countries and the US. France and Britain were especially important for émigré film-makers, since their film industries were then experiencing a period of dramatic growth. Consequently, producers like Pommer, Seymour Nebenzal* and Alexander Korda* set up new production companies which provided work for fellow émigrés. Between 1933 and 1940, Lang, Siodmak, Ophuls, Kurt Bernhardt*, G. W. Pabst*, Anatole Litvak* and others made nearly fifty films in France, including box-office hits such as *Mayerling* (1936), *Carrefour* (1938) and *Pièges* (1939), while in Britain Korda and Max Schach produced highly successful costume films for the international market.

Most émigrés resettled in the US, though few of those who arrived in Hollywood between 1933 and 1938 had a studio contract. After 1938–39, the number of refugees to the US increased dramatically. Altogether, about 500 German film-makers lived in Hollywood. In the 1920s–30s the German émigrés in Hollywood worked on films with a 'European flavour' and from the early 1940s film-makers such as Wilder, Siodmak and Lang contributed greatly to the development of *film noir* with such films as *Double Indemnity* (1944), *Phantom Lady* (1944), *Scarlet Street* (1945) and many others. German émigrés are also known for the sub-genre of the anti-Nazi film, of which about 180 were produced between 1939 and 1945 in the US, transmitting an anti-fascist message in traditional genre films such as spy thrillers (*Confessions of a Nazi Spy*, 1939), melodramas (*The Mortal Storm*, 1940) and comedies (*To Be or Not to Be*, 1942). In addition, German actors and their accents were much sought-after, ironically often to play Nazis (or their victims) in anti-Nazi films; Schünzel, Peter Lorre* and Conrad Veidt* were particularly successful in this respect. Only a handful of film-makers returned to Germany after World War II; most had settled permanently in the US and, furthermore, the German film industry was still run by those who had been successful in the Third Reich. Though it is impossible to speculate on what might have happened otherwise, there is no doubt that German film production suffered incalculably from this drain of talented film personnel.

Less visible because of the shared language has been the drain from the British film industry. Among the most famous British émigrés (or British personnel who worked substantially in Hollywood), apart from Chaplin, are: Julie Andrews, Cecil Beaton, Ronald Colman*, Alfred Hitchcock*, Vivian Leigh*, James Mason* and David Niven*. The important migrations mentioned above slowed down somewhat in the postwar period, as Hollywood itself went through a crisis and started investing in European productions [> EUROPEAN CINEMA AND HOLLYWOOD]. Since the 1980s, however, a renewed migration has taken place, with European film-makers seeking work abroad as their own national cinemas weaken; examples include Andrei Mikhalkov-Konchalovsky*, Miloš Forman*, George Sluizer*, Wolfgang Petersen*, Paul Verhoeven*, Roman Polanski* and Bernardo Bertolucci*, as well as actors such as Rutger Hauer*.

During the same period many other film-makers have turned to France, following another long tradition. In the 1920s, the French cinematic avant-garde was international, with film-makers such as Alberto Cavalcanti*, Carl Theodor Dreyer* and Luis Buñuel* among others [> FRENCH AVANT-GARDE; AVANT-GARDE CINEMA IN EUROPE]. A significant group of émigrés had already arrived from Russia in the wake of the October revolution. The old Pathé* studios in Montreuil became the centre of an active community. Iosif Yermolev [Joseph Ermolieff in France], an ex-Pathé employee, founded Ermolieff-film in 1920, with a team of prestigious directors including Yakov Protazanov* [Jacob Protazanoff], Alexandre Volkov [Volkoff], Vjačelav Turžanskij [Victor Tourjansky], actor Ivan Mozzhukhin [Mosjoukine*], set designers and cinematographers. Yermolev produced a dozen films before leaving for Berlin in 1922, and Ermolieff-film became Les Films Albatros, specialising in literary adaptations of French and Russian classics, with emphasis on nostalgia and exoticism, and producing prestigious films by Marcel L'Herbier*, Jacques Feyder*, René Clair*, and others. Other firms, such as Ciné-France-Film, had a strong Russian contingent and produced French films, including Abel Gance's* *Napoléon* (1926) and Volkov's *Casanova* (1927, starring Mosjoukine). The Russian influence continued in the 1930s when personnel included directors Fyodor Otsep* [Fédor Ozep], Nicolas Farkas and Tourjansky and many others, as well as gifted cinematographers and set designers, generating the popular French genre of the 'Slav melodrama'. Lazare Meerson* revolutionised set design and taught other designers such as Alexander Trauner* and Georges Wakhevitch. New directors from Russia emerged, such as Litvak, and Władysław Starewicz [Ladislav Starevitch]. There were, during the same period, significant exchanges between France and Italy. Franco-Italian bilingual films were made, and several Italian directors worked in France: Mario Bonnard*, Carmine Gallone* and Augusto Genina*.

Meanwhile, despite the threatening political climate, the attraction of better conditions in German studios remained strong, and French stars and directors became frequent travellers between Paris, Berlin and Munich. The coming of sound also contributed to the acceleration of cross-European journeys, with the making of multi-language versions by Ufa* in Germany, Paramount in Paris and British International in London, between 1929 and 1932. Films were made in sometimes as many as a dozen versions (especially at Paramount) but more often in two or three, with German, French and English the most common languages, usually using the same decor but native stars (it was also at that time that Hollywood initiated the practice of remaking European films, especially French films, a phenomenon renewed with particular vigour in the 1980s and 1990s). As mentioned above, Paris in the 1930s also saw a major influx of German and central European personnel, the result of both economic and political emigration. During World War II, while some French film personnel left for Hollywood (Renoir, Duvivier, Jean Gabin*, Michèle Morgan* and others), French cinema lived in virtual autarchy.

In the postwar period, emigration to France took an individual character, with a wide range of personnel (Buñuel, Luis Mariano*, Roman Polanski*, Walerian Borowczyck*, Eddie Constantine*) working in Paris, though two strands can be detected. First, the intense programme of co-productions (especially with Italy) in the 1940s and 1950s brought many actors to France: Antonella Lualdi, Lea Massari, Gina Lollobrigida*, Raf Vallone, Romy Schneider* and Maria Schell* among others. Secondly, the combination of generous French aid and of the break-up of the Eastern block, has produced another wave of eastern Europeans in France, among them Andrzej Wajda*, Krzysztof Kieślowski* and Otar Iosseliani*, and, from other countries, directors such as Pedro Almodóvar* and Manoel de Oliveira*. No doubt the increasing 'Europeanisation' of European cinema, through co-productions and EU-backed projects, will further increase this transnational movement of personnel [> EUROPEAN COMMUNITY AND THE CINEMA]. JG/GV

EMMER, Luciano   Milan 1918

Italian director. Emmer started his film career in the 1940s, first in collaboration with Enrico Gras and then on his own, as a maker of innovative short landscape films and documentaries about art and artists. He branched out into feature film-making in the 1950s, beginning with the appealing *Una domenica d'agosto/Sunday in August* (1950), based on a story by Sergio Amidei* (who also produced). But he continued to make films about artists, notably *Leonardo da Vinci* (1952) and the very striking *Picasso* (1954). Finding fewer opportunities to make cinema films, either documentary or feature, since the 1960s he has worked mainly for television. GNS

ENGEL, Erich   Hamburg 1891 – Berlin 1966

German director. A close friend of Brecht and one of his preferred theatre directors, Engel (with Brecht) directed the Karl Valentin* film *Mysterien eines Friseursalons* (1923). With the coming of sound, he began producing his own films (such as *Wer nimmt die Liebe ernst?*, 1931). During the 1930s Engel was a sought-after comedy director who, without falling foul of the regime, kept alive some of the genre's subversive potential, always upholding the right of the individual against society and the state (*... nur ein Komödiant*, 1935; *Der Maulkorb*, 1938; *Nanette*, 1940). His favourite actress was Jenny Jugo, who benefited most from his skill with actors, appearing in eleven of his films before 1945, which included, apart from comedies, the psychological *Kammerspiel**, *Pechmarie* (1934), and costume dramas. Among his ten post-war films, the best-remembered is *Die Affäre Blum* (1948), a historically acute DEFA* production about anti-semitism, a topic rarely treated by German film-makers. MW

Bib: Herbert Holba, Günter Knorr, Helmut Dan, *Erich Engel: Filme 1923-40* (1977).

Other Films Include: *Fünf von der Jazzband* (1932); *Ein Hochzeitstraum, Mädchenjahre einer Königin, Die Nacht mit dem Kaiser* (1936); *Hotel Sacher* (1939); *Altes Herz wird wieder jung, Man rede mir nicht von Liebe* (1943); *Es lebe die Liebe* (1944); *Der Biberpelz* (1949); *Die Stimme des Anderen* (1952); *Konsul Strotthoff* (1954); *Liebe ohne Illusion, Vor Gott und den Menschen* (1955); *Geschwader Fledermaus* (1958).

EPSTEIN, Jean   Warsaw, Poland 1897 – Paris 1953

French director and theoretician. Epstein moved to Paris in 1921, after studies in Switzerland and Lyons. Like his contemporary Louis Delluc* he was first a film theoretician, publishing several books (including *Bonjour cinéma*, 1921); he became a prominent director of the French avant-garde*. Although best known for his experimental films, such as *La Chute de la maison Usher/The Fall of the House of Usher* (1928), Epstein was also interested in realism – his first film was a documentary on *Pasteur* (1922). For Pathé*, he made three fiction films which combine melodramatic narratives with formal concerns: *L'Auberge rouge, Cœur fidèle* (both 1923) and *La Belle Nivernaise* (1924). *Cœur fidèle*, described as a 'symbolic melodrama', is the most original, with fast editing and unusual use of close-ups. After a spell at the Russian émigré studio Albatros, where he made popular films, Epstein ran his own production company (1926–30), giving free rein to his formal preoccupations. In its complex narrative structure *La Glace à trois faces* (1927) anticipates Alain Resnais*. It was one of the earliest films made for the new 'art' cinema circuit, and is considered the culmination of the French narrative avant-garde. *La Chute de la Maison Usher*, which employs slow motion, illustrated Epstein's theories of time in the cinema. On the other hand *Finis terrae* (1929), filmed on a remote Brittany island, anticipated neo-realism* and inaugurated Epstein's 'Breton cycle'. His career in the 1930s and 1940s was difficult, alternating commercial features and documentaries.

His sister, the film-maker Marie Epstein*, wrote scripts for him, co-directed and acted in some of his early films. GV

EPSTEIN, Marie   Marie-Antonine Epstein; Warsaw, Poland 1899 – Paris 1995
and
BENOÎT-LÉVY, Jean   Paris 1888–1959

French directors and scriptwriters. When not ignored by film history, the Polish-born Epstein is overshadowed by her collaborators, her brother Jean Epstein*, and Jean Benoît-Lévy. Marie and her brother were part of the French avant-garde* of the 1920s. She was assistant director and acted in Jean's *Cœur fidèle* (1923) and wrote scripts for some of his best films. Her major work, however, was as scriptwriter and co-director with Benoît-Lévy in sound films, starting with *Le Coeur de Paris* (1931). Their second film, *La Maternelle* (1933), adapted from Léon Frapié's populist novel, is one of the best early French sound films, an extraordinary combination of social propaganda (for state nursery education), naturalism and lyricism, with a luminous performance by Madeleine Renaud*. Epstein worked with Benoît-Lévy throughout the 1930s. Their work shows concern for popular milieux and for the young – as in *Peau de pêche* (1929), *La Maternelle*, and *Altitude 3200* (1938) – as well as, unusually for the period, women (*Hélène*, 1936, *Le Feu de paille*, 1939). Epstein made a documentary on atomic energy in 1953 and worked at the Cinémathèque Française* restoring silent films, including some of her brother's and Abel Gance's* *Napoléon*. GV

Bib: Sandy Flitterman-Lewis, *To Desire Differently: Feminism and the French Cinema* (1990).

ERHARDT, Heinz   Riga, Latvia 1909 – Hamburg 1979

German actor. A gifted cabaret comedian in the 1940s, Erhardt showed off his film talent in *Der Müde Theodor* (1957). He perfected a typical, often ironically archaic use of language in a prodigious number of comedies [> COMEDY (GERMANY)] such as *Witwer mit fünf Töchtern* (1957), *Der Haus-Tyrann* and *Natürlich die Autofahrer* (both 1959), creating a unique screen persona, a bulky patriarch without authority but also without resentment. His wit was sometimes infantile but always innocent and anti-establishment, and his most characteristic part was that of the eponymous hero of *Willi Winzig/Bill Tiny* (1962). Later, Erhardt specialised in comic cameos in the Karl May series – cantor Hampel in *Der Ölprinz* (1965), Professor Morgenstern in *Das Vermächtnis des Inka* (1966) – as well as in filmed operettas like *Frau Luna* (1964). Towards the end of his career, Erhardt returned to his first screen alter ego Willi Winzig (four films), taking advantage of the vogue for series. By the 1970s he served as an apt reminder of some of the continuities that run through the German popular cinema, despite all the breaks and ruptures. TE/MW

Bib: Rolf Thissen, *Heinz Erhardt und seine Filme* (1986).

Other Films Include: *Kauf dir einen bunten Luftballon* (1961); *Appartment-Zauber* (1963); *Die große Kür, Die Herren mit der weißen Weste* (1969); *Was ist denn bloß mit Willi los?*, *Das kann doch unseren Willi nicht erschüttern* (1970); *Der Opernball, Unser Willi ist der Beste* (1971); *Willi wird das Kind schon schaukeln* (1972).

ERICE, Victor   Victor Erice Aras; Carranza, Vizcaya 1940

Spanish director, the most respected but least prolific of his time. Erice has made only three features in thirty years, yet his reputation has never been higher in Spain and abroad. Educated at the Escuela Oficial de Cinematografía*, Erice was prominent in attacking the Francoist cinema of his youth. His first work, an episode in the collective *Los desafíos/The Challenges* (1969), already features the elliptical narrative typical of the so-called Francoist aesthetic which he would take to new heights. The full-length *El espíritu de la colmena/The Spirit of the Beehive* (1973), the story of a fragmented family, a child obsessed with Frankenstein, and a Civil War escapee, brought him fame. The film is uncompromisingly al-

lusive and evocative, marked by long takes of barren Castilian landscapes and the luminous photography of Luis Cuadrado*. Self-consciously artistic, it was also resolutely – if obliquely – political, with cinematic horror standing for the disasters of Spanish history which had not been addressed directly. *El sur/The South* (1983) retains characteristic themes and techniques, with a young girl meditating on the cause of her father's suicide. Silent for the next decade, Erice concentrated on television commercial spots. *El sol del membrillo/The Quince Tree Sun* (1992) grew from a short to a full feature. Chronicling the pursuit of perfection by the painter Antonio López, this 'dream documentary' rehearses Erice's theme of the necessity, and the impossibility, of art. But like the earlier films it is also, if less obviously, historical in its incidental depiction of contemporary Madrid. The moving last sequence shows a camera juxtaposed with a pile of rotting fruit. It is an appropriate emblem of a career which has combined a rigorous critique of the cinematic apparatus with an unfashionable concern for transcendental issues such as mortality. PJS

ERMLER, Fridrikh M.   Rechitsa, Latvia [Russian Empire] 1898 – Moscow 1967

Soviet director. A member of the Communist Party from 1919, Ermler served in the Civil War in both the Red Army and the secret police. After training as an actor and working as a scriptwriter, he directed his first film, the short comedy *Skarlatina/Scarlet Fever* (1924). His subsequent silent films depicted problems of everyday life, rather than heroics: *Kat'ka – bumazhnyi ranet/Katka's Reinette Apples* (1926), *Dom v sugrobakh/The House in the Snowdrifts* and *Parizshkii sapozhnik/The Parisian Cobbler* (both 1928). Ermler's last silent film was also his best: *Oblomok imperii/A Fragment of Empire* (1929) contrasted the old world with the new through the story of an amnesiac Civil War soldier returning to the new Soviet Union. His first sound film, made with Sergei Yutkevich*, *Vstrechnyi/Counterplan* (1932), was a psychologically well-judged account of the problems of the first Five Year Plan period, while *Krest'yane/Peasants* (1935) represented a defence of collectivisation. He then made the two-part *Velikii grazhdanin/A Great Citizen* (1938–39), devoted to the life of Stalin's* murdered rival Sergei Kirov, and, among other works, a film version of the Battle of Stalingrad, *Velikii perelom/The Great Turning Point* (1946), which won a prize at Cannes. His films demonstrated a strong sense of realism and a measure of creative independence that their subject matter often belied. RT

ESCAMILLA, Teo   Teodoro Escamilla Serrano; Seville 1940

Spanish cinematographer and director, who worked as apprentice camera operator to Luis Cuadrado* for ten years before succeeding him as a key member of Elías Querejeta's* production team in the 1970s, and enjoying a thirteen-year association with Carlos Saura*, beginning with *Cría cuervos/Raise Ravens* (1975). As well as regularly collaborating with

Manuel Gutiérrez Aragón* and Jaime de Armiñán*, Escamilla emerged as the key cinematographer of the transition period through his adventurous flair and his experiments with colour. *Tú sólo/You Alone* (1984) is his only full-length film to date as director. MD

ESCUELA OFICIAL DE CINEMATOGRAFÍA (EOC)

Spanish film school, founded in 1962 (replacing the Instituto de Investigaciones y Experiencias Cinematográficas*) under the aegis of Manuel Fraga Iribarne's Ministry of Information and Tourism, with increased grants, a new statute and professorship. The EOC formed part of José María García Escudero's grand design to create a liberal, Europeanised 'New Spanish Cinema'*. Former EOC students include many of Spain's leading 1970s and 1980s film-makers: Manuel Gutiérrez Aragón*, Victor Erice*, José Luis García Sánchez, Jaime Chávarri*, and Pilar Miró*. The appointment in 1969 of the conservative Juan Julio Baena as director of the EOC, following Fraga's fall, sparked the collective resignation of most of its staff, strikes by students, their mass expulsion, and the closure of the EOC in 1972. JH

ESTESO, Fernando   Zaragoza 1945

Spanish actor, famous as a television comedian, who made a stage debut at the age of two. His persona as an unsophisticated, pie-faced, bulging-eyed 'man in the street' enlivened many comedies co-starring Andrés Pajares* and directed by Mariano Ozores* [> COMEDY (SPAIN)]. These films portrayed him as an unlikely would-be Don Juan, his paunchy frame and doltish air hardly equipping him for his lady's man ambitions which, unsurprisingly, usually ended in fiasco. His most popular films include *¡Caray con el divorcio!/Hooray for Divorce!* (1982) and the characteristically bawdily titled *El soplagaitas/The Prick* (1980) and *Agítese antes de usarla/Shake Before Use* (1983). PWE

EUROPAFILM

Swedish film company. Europafilm was founded as a production company in 1930 by Gustaf Scheutz. Its initial success, in competition with the rival Svensk Filmindustri*, was based on the popularity of comedian Edward Persson, and the company set up its own studios and cinema chain. A period of growth and diversification into the wider entertainment industry in the 1970s was followed by decline; Europafilm was bought by Svensk Filmindustri, its trademark finally disappearing in 1985. LGA

EUROPEAN ART CINEMA

We think we know what we mean by 'art cinema'. Yet in the European cinema of the 1990s, when directors as diverse in their preoccupations and styles as Krzysztof Kieślowski*, Leos Carax* and Pedro Almodóvar* can be united by the same term, it would be more accurate to talk of 'art cinemas' to indicate the national and historical plurality concealed by the term. While being a means of defining and marketing a certain kind of European film, art cinema is also the institutional and aesthetic space into which the work of directors from beyond Europe has been integrated: for example, Kenji Mizoguchi from Japan, Satyajit Ray from India and, more recently, Zhang Yimou from China. Art cinema operates as a means of merging aesthetic and national 'difference', and of encouraging both.

Two moments can be loosely identified as having contributed to the formation of what Peter Lev calls 'a continuing impulse in film history', and to its association with Europe: the European avant-gardes of the 1920s and the New Waves that flourished from the late 1950s to the early 1970s [> BRITISH, CZECH AND FRENCH NEW WAVE, AVANT-GARDE CINEMA IN EUROPE]. The first of these moments includes the schools of Soviet montage*, surrealism, French impressionism [> FRENCH AVANT-GARDE] and German expressionism*, all sharing a common search for creative and conceptual liaisons between the then silent medium and painting, music and poetry. In its earliest incarnation, then, art cinema implied an aesthetic project based in formal experimentation and innovation. Equally, as Steve Neale has observed, the concept of art cinema as an institutional space was developed by the national cinemas of Europe from the 1920s as 'attempts to counter both American domination of their indigenous markets in film and to foster a film industry and a film culture of their own'. The second, postwar, flourishing of art cinema can thus be seen as a consolidation of characteristics established in the 1920s.

The crucial role of Italian neo-realism* in the development of postwar European art cinema is, as David Bordwell notes, in its being 'a transitional phenomenon' between the prewar and wartime national cinemas and those that were to develop after the war. The demise of the American studio system and the Paramount anti-trust decrees of 1948 created a shortage of films for international distribution. Equally, television was emerging both as a competitor for audiences and as a new market for films. This combination of factors meant that, from the mid-1950s onwards, films were increasingly made for international distribution. Italian neo-realism, then, can be seen as the forerunner of the art cinemas of the 1950s and 1960s, wherein the themes, styles and authorial address specific to a national cinema would find international audiences. 'The fullest flower of the art cinema paradigm', as Bordwell has called the postwar New Waves, 'occurred at the moment that the combination of novelty and nationalism became the marketing device it has been ever since'. The late 1950s/early 1960s thus brought the cinematic 'shocks' of the French New Wave*, of Michelangelo Antonioni's* *L'avventura* (1960), Federico Fellini's* *La dolce vita* (1960) and the international discovery of Ingmar Bergman*, for many the archetypal European art cinema director.

The stylistic modes of art cinema – as opposed to Hollywood popular genres – traditionally privilege realism and ambiguity, two registers generally unified through the appeal to authorial expressivity. The notion of the *auteur* director as developed in *Cahiers du cinéma** in the 1950s, and then modified by Andrew Sarris in the US during the 1960s, speaks both of the critical support system that comes into being around art cinema and of the complexity of art cinema's internationalism. After all, the French New Wave defined itself positively in relation to American cinema and negatively in relation to the French cinema of the 1950s. Similarly, the New German Cinema* of the late 1960s and 1970s established the *auteur* as 'public institution' in order to mark out a space for a national cinema founded on a combination of art cinema precepts: an aesthetics of personal expressivity supported by state funding. This tendency to 'institutionalise' the idea of the *auteur*, and with it an idea of a national art cinema, reached its apogee in the cultural policies of the French Minister for Culture, Jack Lang, in the 1980s when French *auteur* cinema was regarded as a significant part of the national cinematic patrimony. Perhaps the most high-profile example of this particular strategy is the French co-production of the French/Swiss/Polish *Trois couleurs/Three Colours* trilogy: *Bleu/Blue, Blanc/White* (both 1993) and *Rouge/Red* (1994) directed by Kieślowski, who represents the paradigm of the European *auteur*.

While Kieślowski, Carax and Almodóvar serve as significantly different versions of contemporary European art cinema directors, the specificity of European art cinema is increasingly unclear. Since the 'New American Cinema' of De Palma, Scorsese and Cimino took part of its inspiration from the European cinema of the 1960s, the idea of the *auteur* has become a critical/industrial commonplace. Yet since its heyday in the 1960s, art cinema has been understood, in some European film industries at least, as both a generic and an institutional option that, if no longer guaranteeing international visibility, at least preserves some of the cultural cachet associated with its past. CDa

Bib: David Bordwell, *Narration in the Fiction Film* (1985).

EUROPEAN CINEMA AND HOLLYWOOD

Before 1914, France and Italy were the two main exporters of film. Between 1913 and 1925, however, American exports of film to Europe increased fivefold. If Hollywood secured its position as the world leader in film exports at the expense of a war-ravaged Europe, there was little American production involvement in Europe until 1945. European concern over the extent of the influx of American films began to take shape in the 1920s, with Germany the first major industry to take action against American films in the form of the Film Europe* initiative spearheaded by Erich Pommer*. Following the German example – whereby distributors were issued a permit to release a foreign film each time they financed and distributed a German one – France and Italy began to impose import restrictions, quotas, tariffs and quid pro quo conditions that sought to secure screen time for domestic production. In the UK, the 1927 Cinematograph Films Act instituted a quota on foreign film imports, which resulted in a flurry of British 'quota quickies' to satisfy quota demands. The Motion Picture Producers and Distributors of America (MPPDA; renamed the Motion Picture Association of America, MPAA, in 1945) gave what was to become the conventional American response to attempts by European countries to protect their industries, claiming that 'This government had adopted no re-

strictive regulations similar in any way to those enforced in certain foreign countries.' Nearly seventy years later, the same disingenuous free-trade rhetoric would be repeated in the 1993 Uruguay Round of the General Agreement on Tariffs and Trade (GATT).

American production involvement in Europe increased dramatically after World War II, the devistated continent now reliant on American aid and having little capacity or will to dictate strict import quotas. Equally, there were hundreds of American films, unreleased in Europe during the war, with which Hollywood could saturate European markets. At the same time, as Peter Lev has pointed out, 'European markets became a necessity, not a luxury, to American film companies in the 1950s, because the American audience for motion pictures was rapidly shrinking.' The Paramount decrees of 1948 which signalled the end of the vertical integration of Hollywood led to a drop in the number of films produced, and thus the increasing importance of the export market. In the face of the American strategy of market saturation, European countries returned either to quota systems or to a system of 'blocked funds' to try to counter American domination of domestic markets. The 1948 Anglo-American Film Agreement allowed US companies to withdraw only $17 million of their earnings, leaving over $40 million each year to accumulate in blocked accounts, the proviso being unlimited American access to the British market. The 1948 Franco-American Film Agreement allowed US firms to withdraw up to $3.6 million of their funds annually, leaving around $10 million blocked to be used for joint production with French companies and the construction of new studios, among other things. This latter agreement replaced the 1946 Blum-Byrnes trade agreement that had given America generous terms to export their films to France. Both 1948 agreements laid the ground for what became known as 'runaway productions', one of the three sorts of production that came to characterise the postwar relationship between Hollywood and Europe, the others being co-productions and what Peter Lev calls 'the Euro-American art film'.

With high unemployment in Hollywood in the 1950s and 1960s, and with lower production costs and more flexible labour regulations in Europe – especially Italy and Spain – the two immediate postwar decades saw a spate of European-American film production. 'Runaway productions' relied on a combination of European and American personnel and stars, were financed through blocked funds and tended towards the spectacular epic, films like *Alexander the Great* (1955), *Ben-Hur* (1959), *Lawrence of Arabia* (1962) or *55 Days at Peking* (1964); the ground-breaking Italian (so-called) 'Spaghetti' Westerns* of the mid-1960s should also be included here. Co-production agreements were increasingly part of the production structure of such films; although they had been tried in the 1920s, they became common practice only after World War II. Jean-Luc Godard's* *Le Mépris/Contempt* (1963) is both a satire on the exigencies of co-production – Georgia Moll as the harassed interpreter caught between Jack Palance's overbearing American producer, Fritz Lang's* urbane European director, Michel Piccoli's* French screenwriter and Brigitte Bardot's* alienated sex goddess – and the very incarnation of the Euro-American art film. Such a film, according to Lev, 'attempts a synthesis of the American entertainment film (large budget, good production values, internationally known stars) and the European art film (auteur director, artistic subject and/or style) with the aim of reaching a much larger audience than the art film normally commands'. While the 1960s can be seen as the high point of such ventures, a nominal list of some of the more celebrated examples of the Euro-American art film indicates the longevity of this production style: *Blowup* (1967), *Ultimo tango a Parigi/Last Tango in Paris* (1972), *Paris, Texas* (1984), *The Last Emperor* (1987).

The 1993 GATT talks illustrated the extent to which the relationship between Europe and Hollywood remains 'a two-way fascination and a one-way exploitation', to use Godard's phrase. American objections to European film subsidies and 'protectionist' measures resulted in a piece of concerted brinkmanship by the French government – supported by a prestigious group of film-makers and stars – over the issue of 'cultural exception', which threatened to scupper the entire GATT agreement, of which film and audiovisual issues constituted only a small part. 'Cultural exception' was the idea that films and audiovisual material – because of their 'cultural specificity' to a particular nation – should not be governed by the same terms applied to foodstuffs, minerals, cars, etc. At the eleventh hour this principle was effectively acknowledged in a piece of EU/US political legerdemain: in order to save the GATT treaty, it was agreed simply to exclude film and audiovisual material from its terms. That the French government was so active in facing down American *laissez-faire* petitioning was accounted for by the French film critic Michel Ciment in December 1993 as follows: 'If French cinema has survived it is because of two measures that an American interpretation of GATT could decide were illegal. The first is the quota imposed on films shown on televison (60 per cent of them must be European). The second is a 13 per cent tax on all tickets sold at the box-office, which is used to subsidise innovative films, art-house cinemas, independent distributors, film festivals, film schools and East European and African production.' In retrospect, this aspect of GATT looks less resolved than simply put on hold, and the proliferation of cable and satellite channels promises to pose questions of broadcasting territory and intellectual property rights as well as to challenge definitions of the 'national' that underwrite positions such as those adopted by the French over their film industry.

Aesthetically speaking, the relay between Europe and Hollywood has had complex and diverse consequences, from the fascination and support evinced in the 1920s by American studios for German directors such as F. W. Murnau*, Ernst Lubitsch* and Paul Leni*, to the sometimes uncomfortable exile that Hollywood offered to émigré European directors such as Lang, Jean Renoir*, Douglas Sirk (Sierck*) and Robert Siodmak* in the 1930s and 1940s. A prime example of this international cross-pollination of film style can be seen in critical approaches to *film noir* as a hybridisation of American generic structures, German Expressionism* and French Poetic Realism*. The European New Waves* and art cinemas of the 1950s and 1960s were often fascinated by Hollywood, a fascination epitomised by Godard's films, and in turn can be seen to have fed into the stylistics of American directors such as Martin Scorsese, Francis Ford Coppola and Brian De Palma of the 'New American Cinema' of the 1970s. This traffic of influence and mutual acknowledgment has been evident

more recently in the American vogue for remaking successful European, and particularly French, films, for example Coline Serreau's* *Trois hommes et un couffin/Three Men and a Cradle.* (1985) as *Three Men and a Baby* (1988), Luc Besson's* *Nikita* (1990) as *The Assassin* (1993) and Daniel Vigne's *Le Retour de Martin Guerre* (1981) as *Sommersby* (1993). CDa

Bib: Peter Lev, *The Euro-American Cinema* (1993).

EUROPEAN COMMUNITY [NOW EUROPEAN UNION] AND THE CINEMA

While European cinema production had previously fallen under general EC legislation and directives on trade and industry, it was not until the 1980s that the Brussels authorities developed a coherent policy specifically concerning film and other European media. The issue had been brought to a head by a 1984 proposal from French president François Mitterand to establish a pan-European co-production fund for work in cinema and television. Mitterand's plan was rejected but it had started the ball rolling.

In 1986 the Commission's Directorate for Information, Communication and Culture put forward its *Mesures pour Encourager le Développement de l'Industrie de Production Audio-Visuelle* (or MEDIA for short). Once accepted by the Council, MEDIA began a pilot phase in 1987, to last until 1990, under the control of the EC Ministers for Cultural Affairs. As a symbol of the EC's commitment to its MEDIA programme, 1988 was designated European Cinema and Television Year. Events included the first ever European Film Awards*, although somewhat ironically the Berlin ceremony garnered very little media attention. During the same year, in an attempt to emphasise the economic implications of MEDIA, the suffix '92' was added to the programme's acronym. MEDIA 92 was to be a high-profile test case for the new EC internal market, encouraging collaboration between the twelve member states.

The full MEDIA programme was adopted by the Council of Ministers of the EC in December 1990 and was retitled MEDIA 95. From 1991 to 1995, MEDIA was awarded a budget of 200 million ECU (roughly £340 million). Most of this money was designated as 'seed' funding, a system of repayable advances with the programme's initiatives sharing in any profit they had helped to create. Thus it was hoped that the MEDIA budget would largely become self-perpetuating in years to come. In an attempt to broaden the scope of MEDIA (and its funding), European states from outside the EC have been encouraged to join the programme's activities. In 1992 MEDIA initiatives were opened to five members of the European Free Trade Association (EFTA) – Austria, Finland, Iceland, Norway and Sweden – as well as to Poland, Hungary and Czechoslovakia.

MEDIA is made up of an ever-increasing programme of initiatives which support the development, production and distribution of European audiovisual culture. Of these, nineteen are partly or wholly concerned with film. The remit of the respective initiatives can usually be gleaned from their catchword titles. CARTOON, for example, comprises a package of measures to support European animation production, including a database of contacts and incentives to encourage cooperation between studios. The most important MEDIA initiative with regard to development is the European Script Fund (SCRIPT). Recognising that securing finance for the development of projects is often the biggest hurdle faced by European film-makers, SCRIPT provides loans and advice to help get proposals up and running. The loans, averaging 50 per cent of a project's pre-production budget, become reimbursable if the project goes into production. Completed films which have benefited from assistance by SCRIPT include *Acción Mutante* (1992, Spain), *Daens* (1992, Belgium/ France/Netherlands) and *Naked* (1993, UK). For projects that have made it to the production stage, Euro Media Garanties (EMG) provides film-makers with a measure of financial security. Supporting ventures that involve producers from at least three Council of Europe members, EMG will guarantee up to 70 per cent of the loan finance taken out on the project.

Perhaps the biggest success story of the MEDIA programme, the European Film Distribution Office (EFDO) has helped many films reach wider markets, both within the continent and around the world. EFDO's main remit is to support distribution between EU member states, but through 'EFDO Abroad', which presents films at festivals outside Europe, it now also promotes European cinema to countries worldwide. With the vast majority of European cinema consisting of low-budget projects which are only ever distributed in their country of origin, EFDO has been particularly beneficial to smaller productions. In fact 80 per cent of EFDO's available funds are set aside for films costing no more than 2.25 million ECU (£3.825 million). Covering up to 50 per cent of distributors' pre-costs, EFDO offers interest-free loans to films which have secured a distribution deal for no less than three EU countries. Moreover, the loan is only repayable if the release is successful. Conversely, if a supported film does especially well at the box-office, EFDO becomes entitled to a small share of the profits, or 'success dividend', which can then be reinvested. Among the well-known films to have received support from EFDO are *Babettes gaestebud/Babette's Feast* (1987, Denmark), *Spoorloos/The Vanishing* (1987, Netherlands/France) and *Volere volare* (1991, Italy).

Another film to have benefited from EFDO money, *Toto le héros/Toto the Hero* (1991, Belgium/France/Germany), serves as a testament to the package of MEDIA initiatives and the spirit of cooperation they have fostered within European cinema. A co-production of three member states, *Toto* was aided at every stage by European funding, beginning with support from SCRIPT and ending with the promotion of the video release by Espace Vidéo Européen (EVE). Yet one of the film's major sources of funding came from outside the MEDIA programme, via an initiative of the Council of Europe, EURIMAGES.

Set up in 1988, EURIMAGES is a co-production fund in the mould of that proposed by François Mitterand four years earlier. Providing financial support for films made by production partners from at least three member countries, the fund initially comprised twelve Council countries. A notable absentee from the final agreement, though, was the UK. Displaying the all too prevalent combination of ignorance about what is happening in Europe and a belief that the

British still lead the way, the UK government soon established its own European Co-Production Fund (ECF). In the meantime EURIMAGES has gone from strength to strength and the UK finally joined in 1993.

European government initiatives aimed at the media industries are completed by the Audiovisual EUREKA programme (AVE). Again proposed by Europe's prime mover in this field, François Mitterand, AVE's remit is somewhat less specific than those of MEDIA or EURIMAGES. AVE exists primarily to encourage the development and application of advanced audiovisual technology. It also differs from the other major programmes in that it has a wider membership base of nearly thirty countries and responds to specific proposals from the industry rather than attempting to initiate projects itself.

At the time of writing (early 1995), the MEDIA programme is preparing to enter a new phase, MEDIA 2. Although details are still to be confirmed, MEDIA 2 looks quite different from its predecessor, reducing the nineteen initiatives to three strands: training, development and distribution. MEDIA 2 should also have a considerably larger budget for its next five-year programme, but the decision not to provide any specific measure in favour of exhibition has already proved controversial.

Each EU country now has a Mediadesk to provide information and answer queries about the MEDIA programme. SH

EUROPEAN FILM AWARDS (FELIX)

Established in 1988 as part of the European Community's Cinema and Television Year, the FELIX awards were intended as a European rival to the Oscars. Yet their initial impact can be measured from the challenge made by Sean Day-Lewis after the first ceremony in Berlin went almost unnoticed: 'Hands up anybody who can name one of the winners or, come to that, anybody who knows whether the epoch-making occasion happened at all.'

FELIX largely follows the format of its Hollywood counterpart, awarding its major prizes in the categories of Best Film, Best Actor/Actress and so on. One innovation is the prise for Best Young Film, recognising the achievements of up-and-coming talents in European cinema. Suitably, the first recipient of this award was the *enfant terrible* of Spanish film, Pedro Almodóvar, for his *Mujeres al borde de un ataque de nervios/Women on the Verge of a Nervous Breakdown* (1988). As if to emphasise the 'European-ness' of the awards, the annual FELIX ceremony does not have a permanent home, visiting Berlin, Paris and Glasgow in its first three years. Reinforcing FELIX's identity, the prefix 'European' was added to the award categories from 1990, Best Film becoming European Film of the Year, etc. In 1991 responsibility for FELIX was assumed by the newly founded European Film Academy (EFA), bringing with it the respected name of the Academy's president, Ingmar Bergman*. But perhaps the most significant change was made to the awards in 1993. While the European Film of the Year continues to be judged on artistic merit, potential winners now have to achieve a designated amount of box-office revenue before qualifying for nomination. FELIX thus recognises that commercial viability is as important as critical acclaim if European cinema is to resist Hollywood's continued domination of the market.

Although the European Film Awards have undoubtedly made significant progress since their inception, FELIX has a long way to go before it can hope to compete with the Oscars in the popular imagination. In the words of EFA chairman Wim Wenders*, 'our handicap is that the awards should have started at least twenty years ago'. SH

The winners in the major FELIX categories so far are as follows:

Best Film (European Film of the Year from 1990)
1988 *Krótki Film o Zabijaniu/A Short Film About Killing* (Krzysztof Kieślowski; Poland)
1989 *Topio stin Omichli/Landscape in the Mist* (Thodoros Angelopoulos; Greece/France/Italy)
1990 *Porte aperte/Open Doors* (Gianni Amelio; Italy)
1991 *Riff-Raff* (Ken Loach; UK)
1992 *Il ladro di bambini/Stolen Children* (Gianni Amelio; Italy/France)
1993 *Urga. Territoriya lyubvi/Urga. Territory of Love* (Nikita Mikhalkov; Russia/France)
1994 *Lamerica* (Gianni Amelio; Italy)

Best Young Film (Young European Film of the Year from 1990)
1988 *Mujeres al borde de un ataque de nervios/Women on the Verge of a Nervous Breakdown* (Pedro Almodóvar; Spain)
1989 *300 Mil do Nieba/300 Miles to Heaven* (Maciej Dejczer; Poland/Denmark)
1990 *Henry V* (Kenneth Branagh; UK)
1991 *Toto le héros/Toto the Hero* (Jaco van Dormael; Belgium/France/Germany)
1992 *De Noorderlingen/The Northerners* (Alan van Warmerdam; Netherlands)
1993 *Orlando* (Sally Potter; UK/Russia/France/Italy/Netherlands)
1994 *Le Fils du requin* (Agnès Merlet; France) and *Woyzeck* (Janos Szasz; Hungary)

Best Actor (European Actor of the Year from 1990)
1988 Max von Sydow for *Pelle Erobreren/Pelle the Conquerer* (Denmark)
1989 Philippe Noiret for *La Vie et rien d'autre/Life and Nothing But* (France) and *Nuovo Cinema Paradiso/Cinema Paradiso* (Italy)
1990 Kenneth Branagh for *Henry V* (UK)
1991 Michel Bouquet for *Toto le héros/Toto the Hero* (Belgium/France/Germany)
1992 Matti Pellonpää for *La Vie de bohème/Bohemian Life* (Finland/France/Sweden)
1993 Daniel Auteuil for *Un Cœur en hiver* (France)
[1994: no award]

Best Actress (European Actress of the Year from 1990)
1988 Carmen Maura for *Mujeres al borde de un ataque de nervios/Women on the Verge of a Nervous Breakdown* (Spain)
1989 Ruth Sheen for *High Hopes* (UK)
1990 Carmen Maura for *¡Ay, Carmela!* (Spain)
1991 Clothilde Coreau for *Le Petit Criminel* (France)
1992 Juliette Binoche for *Les Amants du Pont-Neuf* (France)
1993 Maia Morgenstern for *Balanta/Le Chêne/The Oak* (Romania/France)
[1994: no award]

EUSTACHE, Jean   Pessac 1938 – Paris 1981

French director. A peripheral yet important figure in *auteur* cinema, Eustache was an editor and worked for television; he made several films, including *Les Mauvaises fréquentations/Bad Company* (1967, made up of two episodes, one being *Le Père Noël a les yeux bleus/Father Christmas Has Blue Eyes*, 1965), *La Rosière de Pessac* (1969, a documentary), *Mes Petites amoureuses* (1975) and *Une sale histoire/A Dirty Story* (1977). His outstanding film, however, was the extraordinary *La Maman et la putain/The Mother and the Whore* (1973), the intense, epic yet intimate story of one man (Jean-Pierre Léaud*) and two women (Bernadette Lafont and Françoise Lebrun). Characteristic of the sexual utopias and dystopias of the 1970s, it remains one of the best cinematic documents of that decade, not least in its awareness of, and complicity with, male self-centredness. A film 'as autobiographical as fiction can be', in Eustache's words, it had serious repercussions for at least two people: the woman on whom the 'whore' was based committed suicide the day after the premiere, and Eustache himself took his own life in 1981. GV

EVANS, (Dame) Edith   London 1888 – Cranbrook, 1976

British actress, and theatrical dame, who made relatively few films but left her mark as a character actress on those she made. She secured her place in history (and the place of handbags) with her Lady Bracknell in Anthony Asquith's* *The Importance of Being Earnest* (1952). The almost operatic nature of her performance was well suited to Thorold Dickinson's* expressionistic *The Queen of Spades* (1949), and she gave a memorable cameo in *Tom Jones* (1963). Her performance in Bryan Forbes'* *The Whisperers* (1966) as an eccentric old woman, down but not quite out, won her Best Actress awards from the Berlin festival, the British Academy and the New York Film Critics. JC

EVENSMO, Sigurd   Hamar 1912 – Oslo 1978

Norwegian film personality, a film critic from 1948 to 1962 in both the written press and broadcasting. A member of the labour movement, he recognised people's desire for entertainment but also sought to develop taste and a critical attitude to Hollywood. From 1962 to 1978, Evensmo worked at the Norwegian Board of Film Censors, where he fought the increase in screen violence from the late 1960s. A humanist and strong pacifist, he believed profit-seeking in the film industry led to depictions of violence, and to him this was the main justification for censorship; 'the masses' needed protection. He discussed censorship in his books *Vold i filmene* ('Film Violence', 1968) and *Den nakne sannhet* ('The Naked Truth', 1971), and wrote what is still the most important book on Norwegian film history, *Det store tivoli* ('The Great Funfair', 1967). Evensmo also scripted six Norwegian features: *Lenkene brytes/Breaking the Chains* (1938), *Blodveien/Road of Blood* (1955), *Line* (1961), *Afrikaneren/The African* (1966), *Det støste spillet/The Biggest Game* (1967), *Bare et liv – historien om Fridtjof Nansen/Just a Life – the Story of Fridtjof Nansen* (1968). KS

EXPORT, Valie   Waltraut Lehner; Linz 1940

Austrian director. Also a photographer, video and performance artist, Export successfully moved from experimental shorts to features. She called her *Tapp und Tastfilm/Grope-and-Feel Film* (1968) 'the first real woman's film'. It involved a 'cinema' strapped to her chest 'with the performance taking place in the dark as usual, but in a somewhat smaller hall. There is room only for two hands. In contrast to the dominant cinema where the viewer is a mere voyeur, here the spectator can finally grasp reality with both hands.' Like her other 'film happenings', such as *Cutting* (1967–68) and *Der Kuss* (1968), *Tapp und Tastfilm* is an attempt to redefine the audience-performer relation and to extend cinematic conventions. Export's first feature, *Unsichtbare Gegner/Invisible Adversaries* (1978), about female identity, representation and the environment, was a 'feminist science-fiction' film which managed to be theoretically and visually challenging as well as entertaining and humorous. Together with her *Die Praxis der Liebe/The Practice of Love* (1984), *Unsichtbare Gegner* has become a classic of international women's cinema, and shows that Export has been able to address a wider audience without compromising her political and aesthetic positions. US/TE

EXPRESSIONIST FILM

German genre. Expressionist films such as *Das Cabinet des Dr Caligari/The Cabinet of Dr Caligari* (1920) and *Das Wachsfigurenkabinett/Waxworks* (1924) were produced in Germany between 1919 and 1923 by important companies such as Decla Bioscop, Ilag-Film and Neumann Produktion, complete with generous budgets and premiered after extensive advertising campaigns. Two goals were to be achieved with expressionist films: to regain export territory closed to German films because of World War I, and to attract new, socially and artistically more sophisticated audiences to the cinema without scaring away traditional viewers. For this reason, the films mix popular, romantic and thriller fantasies based on novels by Hanns Heinz Ewers, E. T. A. Hoffmann and Dostoevsky with elements derived from the vogue (which had already peaked) for expressionist motifs in the established arts such as painting and the theatre. Examples of these motifs were stylisation of the decor, extreme artificial-

ity, effective lighting design (lights and shadows), stereotypical characters and exaggerated acting. Unlike expressionist drama, the films did not feature idealistic-rebellious protagonists protesting against inhumane demands – with the exception of *Von morgens bis mitternachts* (1920), not widely shown at the time – but instead seemed driven by strange urges and violent passions, and haunted by nameless phantoms and fears. Expressionist films used the contemporary German theatre's sophisticated stagecraft selectively, often turning it into mere signals of pathological states, but also, in the process, developing a fascinating poetic film language of mood, gesture and atmosphere.

Hollywood craftsmen and directors were much taken by German expressionist cinema, developing its different elements and integrating them into more specific generic contexts (low-key lighting for mystery, distorted perspectives for horror). While not all the German films from the 1920s thus labelled should be regarded as expressionist, there can be no doubt that their peculiar amalgam of primitive emotion and sophisticated film technique tapped deeply into the roots of cinematic pleasure, ensuring that the term has retained its currency ever since. JG/TE

Bib: John D. Barlow, *German Expressionist Film* (1982).

Other Films Include: *Genuine, Das Haus zum Mond* (1920); *Torgus* (1921); *Raskolnikow* (1923); *Der Golem, wie er in die Welt Kam/The Golem* (1920); *Nosferatu – Eine Symphonie des Grauens/Nosferatu the Vampire* (1922).

EYCK, Peter van   Steinwehr 1913 – Maennedorf, Switzerland 1969

German actor, one of the few German-speaking film stars of the immediate postwar era with a durable international career. The tall blond Nordic type, he received his first film role in Hollywood in the early 1940s. Van Eyck (who had acquired American citizenship and served in the US Army from 1943 to 1945) initially played German officers of the Prussian type (in Billy Wilder's *Five Graves to Cairo*, 1943, and Douglas Sirk's [Sierck*] *Hitler's Madman*, 1943). Starring in more than eighty American, German, French, Italian and British productions after the war, he personified positive heroes as well as arrogant cynics and powerful villains. MW

Other Films Include: *The Wife Takes a Flyer, Once Upon a Honeymoon* (1942, US); *Hallo Fräulein!, Königskinder* (1949); *Die Dritte von rechts* (1950); *The Desert Fox* (1951, US); *Le Grand jeu/Il grande giuoco* (1954, Fr./It.); *Attack* (1956, US); *Der gläserne Turm/The Glass Tower* (1957); *Der Rest ist Schweigen/The Rest is Silence* (1959); *Liebling der Götter* (1960); *Le Salaire de la peur/The Wages of Fear* (1953, Fr.); *Mr. Arkadin* (1955, Sp./Swi.); *Die tausend Augen des Dr. Mabuse/The Thousand Eyes of Doctor Mabuse* (1960); *The Longest Day* (1962, US); *The Spy Who Came in from the Cold* (1965, UK); *The Bridge at Remagen* (1969, US).

F

FABRIZI, Aldo
Rome 1905–90

Italian actor and director. A man of modest background, Fabrizi started his career in 1931 in variety theatres, bringing in the warm and 'human' vein of Roman dialect comedy. In his many film parts he was tolerant and gently ironic but also imbued with petit-bourgeois moralism, for example as the tram driver in *Avanti c'è posto* (1942) and the fishmonger in *Campo de' Fiori/The Peddler and the Lady* (1943), both directed by Mario Bonnard. Roberto Rossellini* discovered his dramatic talent, casting him as Don Pietro in *Roma città aperta/Rome Open City* (1945), a symbol of the new Italy. With his down-to-earth common sense and a touch of sentimentality, Fabrizi bridged the period of reconstruction and neo-realism*, embodying a peasant under the Occupation in Luigi Zampa's* *Vivere in pace/To Live in Peace* (1946), a grumpy but sympathetic police inspector in Mario Monicelli's* *Guardie e ladri/Cops and Robbers* (1951) and a janitor in Renato Castellani's* *Mio figlio professore/Professor, My Son* (1946). However, his greatest successes are perhaps those in which he played more grotesque roles, such as the tyrant Nicolao in Rossellini's *Francesco giullare di Dio/The Flowers of St Francis/Francis, God's Jester* (1950), or when he demonstrated pathos, as in Alberto Lattuada's* *Il delitto di Giovanni Episcopo/Flesh Will Surrender* (1947). During these early years he also directed a number of films which exploited his previous screen characters. Notable are *Emigrantes/Gli emigranti* (1949), made in Argentina, and the episode *Marsina stretta* (from a Pirandello short story) in *Questa è la vita/Of Life and Love* (1954). His good-humoured characters occasionally gave way to a somewhat unsympathetic cynicism. This was fully exploited by Ettore Scola* in *C'eravamo tanto amati/We All Loved Each Other So Much* (1974), Fabrizi's last performance of some quality, given that throughout the 1960s he had turned to more indulgent comedies, such as *I tartassati* (1959), *Totò, Fabrizi e i giovani d'oggi* (1961), *I quattro monaci* (1963) and *Frà Manisco cerca guai* (1964). GVo

Other Films as Director Include: *Benvenuto, reverendo!* (1950); *La famiglia Passaguai* (1951); *La famiglia Passaguai fa fortuna* (1952); *Papà diventa mamma* (1952); *Una di quelle* (1953); *Hanno rubato un tram* (1954); *Il maestro* (1958).

FAINZIMMER, Alexander M.
Yekaterinoslav [now Dnepropetrovsk], Ukraine [Russian Empire] 1906 – USSR 1982

Soviet director. Graduated from Pudovkin's* workshop at the GTK (later VGIK*) film school in 1928 and made films from 1930 to 1980, but is best known for his first sound film, the satirical grotesque *Poruchik Kizhe/Lieutenant Kijé* (1934), for which Sergei Prokofiev* wrote the score. The Belorussian studio which produced the film, Belgoskino, was closed down shortly afterwards for politically suspect activi-

ties. Fainzimmer also directed *Ovod/The Gadfly* (1955) from a script by Viktor Shklovsky* and with a score by Dmitri Shostakovich*. RT

FALK, Feliks
Stanisławów, Ukraine 1941

Polish director and scriptwriter. Falk graduated from Łódź in 1974, after which he joined Andrzej Wajda's* 'X' Production Unit and became part of the 'cinema of moral unrest', rising to prominence with *Wodzirej/Top Dog* (1978). Set in a small town, the film follows Danielak, portrayed by the brilliant comic actor Jerzy Stuhr*, as he ruthlessly plays the system to get a coveted job. The popular sequel, *Bohater Roku/Hero of the Year* (1987), expressed a more general disenchantment, showing Danielak in the early 1980s trying to make a comeback but finding a new official mentality resilient to his manipulations. AW

Other Films Include: *Był Jazz/And There Was Jazz* (made 1981, rel. 1984); *Kapitał, Czyli Jak Robic Pieniądze w Polsce/Capital, or How to Make Money in Poland* (1989); *Koniec Gry/The End of the Game* (1991).

FAMU

Prague Film School (FAMU: the Film Faculty of the Academy of Music and Dramatic Arts) formed in 1947, and one of the first of the national film schools. It initially comprised seven departments: dramaturgy, direction, photography, documentaries, reportage, techniques, production and theory. Starting with less than half a dozen teachers, the staff was considerably expanded in the 1960s. The first graduates appeared in 1949–50, and virtually all subsequent Czech and Slovak film-makers trained there.

The FAMU system of education was closely identified with the figure of Otakar Vávra*, who characterised its approach as a balance between theory and practice. The importance of literature was recognised and the novelist Milan Kundera lectured there in the 1960s (before the publication of *The Joke*). The dearth of good scripts in the 1980s has been linked to a diminished role for literature in training rather than to ideology as such, although the two were linked. A high proportion of students come from abroad and some of the best-known graduates have included Aleksandar Petrović*, Frank Beyer, Agnieszka Holland* and Emir Kusturica*. The former Dean, František (Frank) Daniel, took the FAMU 'system' to the US in the 1970s. The appointment of film theorist Jan Bernard as Dean in 1993 signalled a desire to maintain the school's founding principles. PH

FANCK, Arnold
Frankenthal, Rheinpfalz 1889 – Freiburg 1974

German director. Fanck entered film in the early 1920s with spectacular documentaries about skiing, mountaineering and glacier hikes, almost single-handedly inventing the genre of the mountain film [> HEIMATFILM] at a time when German film was dominated by studio-made productions. With *Der Berg des Schicksals* (1924) Fanck began casting professional actors, among them Luis Trenker* and Leni Riefenstahl* (*Der Heilige Berg*, 1926), who sometimes shared directorial credits. In *Die weisse Hölle vom Piz Palü/The White Hell of Piz Palu* (1929), G. W. Pabst* was in charge of the interior scenes. Refusing to become a Party member, Fanck was unable to make feature films in Germany after *Der ewige Traum* (1934). In Japan, he directed *Die Tochter des Samurai* (1937) and several documentaries; *Ein Robinson* (1940) was shot in Chile. Back in Germany during the war, he made a living by directing documentaries about public works projects, while his film portraits of the monumentalist sculptors Breker and Thorak remained uncompleted. TE/MW

Bib: Herbert Linder (ed.), *Arnold Fanck* (1976).

FASSBINDER, Rainer Werner
Bad Wörishofen 1945 – Munich 1982

German director and probably the most important film-maker of postwar Germany. Born into a bourgeois family and raised by his mother as an only child, he claimed that ('five times a week, often three films a day') from a very early age 'the cinema was the family life I never had at home.' After amateur directing-scripting-acting efforts – *Der Stadtstreicher/The City Tramp* (1965) and *Das kleine Chaos/The Little Chaos* (1966) – Fassbinder joined the Munich 'action-theatre'. There he worked with Peer Raben* and Kurt Raab, Hanna Schygulla* and Irm Hermann, who subsequently became the most important members of his cinematic stock company.

The years 1969–76 were Fassbinder's most prodigious and prolific period. An outstanding career in the theatre (productions in Munich, Bremen, Bochum, Nuremberg, Berlin, Hamburg, and Frankfurt, where for two years he ran the 'Theater am Turm' with Kurt Raab and Roland Petri) was a mere backdrop to a relentless outpouring of films (up to six a year, totalling sixteen feature films, and, for television, eleven feature films, a five-part series, two two-part adaptations, and a variety show). During the same period he also did four radio plays and took on ten roles in other directors' films, among them the title part in Volker Schlöndorff's* Brecht adaptation *Baal* (1970). His major international successes began with *Der Händler der vier Jahreszeiten/The Merchant of Four Seasons* (1972) and *Angst essen Seele auf/Fear Eats the Soul* (1974), and by the time of *Faustrecht der Freiheit/Fox and His Friends* (1975) and *Despair/Eine Reise ins Licht* (1978) he had become an international figure. Meanwhile his work often received mixed notices from national critics, many of whom only began to take Fassbinder seriously after the foreign press had hailed him as a genius. Much of

Fassbinder's work was financed by television. Thanks to the producer Peter Märthesheimer at WDR, Fassbinder in the late 1970s turned to recognisably German subject matter. Together they made *Die Ehe der Maria Braun/The Marriage of Maria Braun* (1979), Fassbinder's commercially most successful film and the first in his 'postwar German trilogy', followed by *Lola* (1981) and *Die Sehnsucht der Veronika Voss/Veronika Voss* (1982). His testament film was the controversial fourteen-part television adaptation *Berlin Alexanderplatz* (1980), which is still one of the unrecognised masterpieces of world cinema. His sudden death from a drug overdose in June 1982 symbolically marked the end of the most exciting and experimental period the German cinema had known since the 1920s [> NEW GERMAN CINEMA]. TE

Bib: Thomas Elsaesser, *Fassbinder's Germany* (1995).

Other Films Include: *Liebe ist kälter als der Tod/Love Is Colder than Death, Katzelmacher* (1969); *Götter der Pest/Gods of the Plague, Warum läuft Herr R. Amok?/Why Does Herr R. Run Amok?* [co-dir. Michael Fengler], *Das Kaffeehaus/The Coffee House* [TV version of stage production], *Die Niklashauser Fart/The Nicklehausen Journey* [TV], *Der Amerikanische Soldat/The American Soldier* (1970); *Rio das Mortes, Whity, Warnung vor einer heiligen Nutte/Beware of a Holy Whore, Pioniere in Ingolstadt/Pioneers in Ingolstadt* [TV] (1971); *Bremer Freiheit/Bremen Coffee* [TV version of stage production], *Die bitteren Tränen der Petra von Kant/The Bitter Tears of Petra von Kant, Wildwechsel/Jailbait* (1972); *Acht Stunden sind kein Tag/Eight Hours Are Not a Day* [five-part TV series], *Welt am Draht/World on a Wire* [two-part TV series] (1973); *Nora Helmer* [TV version of stage production], *Martha* [TV], *Fontane Effi Briest/Effi Briest* (1974); *Wie ein Vogel auf dem Draht/Like a Bird on a Wire* [TV show with Brigitte Mira] (1975); *Mutter Küsters Fahrt zum Himmel/Mother Kuster's Trip to Heaven, Angst vor der Angst/Fear of Fear* [TV] (1975); *Satansbraten/Satan's Brew, Ich will doch nur dass ihr mich liebt/I Only Want You to Love Me* [TV], *Chinesisches Roulette/Chinese Roulette* (1976); *Bolwieser/The Station Master's Wife* [two-part TV film], *Frauen in New York/Women in New York* [TV version of stage production] (1977); *Deutschland im Herbst/Germany in Autumn, In einem Jahr mit dreizehn Monden/In a Year of Thirteen Moons* (1978); *Die dritte Generation/The Third Generation* (1979); *Lili Marleen, Lola, Theater in Transe/Theater in a Trance* [video production of international theatre festival] (1981); *Querelle*, 1982.

FELIX – see EUROPEAN FILM AWARDS

FELLINI, Federico
Rimini 1920 – Rome 1994

Italian director and scriptwriter. Fellini's extravagant inventiveness and carnivalesque style, and his authorship of ground-breaking films such as *La strada* (1954), *La dolce vita* (1960) and *Amarcord* (1973), have made him synonymous in the popular imagination with Italian cinema itself.

Fellini was born and raised in Rimini, the setting of *I vitelloni/The Spivs* (1953) and *Amarcord*. He moved to Florence in 1938 and to Rome in 1939, where he joined the editorial staff of the humorous magazine *Marc'Aurelio*. After the war, he worked in The Funny-Face Shop, drawing caricatures of American G.I.s. He also wrote gags and scripts for film and radio, including the show *Cico e Pallina* about a young married couple, whose co-star Giulietta Masina* became his wife in 1943. Through a friend, the actor Aldo Fabrizi*, Fellini met Roberto Rossellini* and contributed to the screenplay of *Roma città aperta/Rome Open City* (1945). In addition to four other collaborations with Rossellini, *Paisà* (1946), *Il miracolo/The Miracle* (1948), *Francesco giullare di Dio//The Flower of St Francis/Francis, God's Jester* (1950) and *Europa '51* (1952), Fellini wrote scripts for such directors as Alberto Lattuada*, Pietro Germi*, Luigi Comencini* and Eduardo De Filippo*. Lattuada gave the aspiring film-maker his start as co-director of *Luci del varietà/Lights of Variety/Variety Lights* (1950), a film which anticipates Fellini's lifelong fascination with the tackiness and glitz of the vaudeville stage. But it was *Lo sceicco bianco/The White Sheik* (1952), his first solo effort, which established important elements of his *auteurism*: the collaboration with playwright Tullio Pinelli and scriptwriter Ennio Flaiano* until 1965, and with the composer Nino Rota* until Rota's death in 1979; the thinly veiled autobiography (the provincial newly-weds' arrival in Rome as a replay of his own recent past), and a fondness for popular culture (here photo-romance). The paradigm was repeated in *I vitelloni*, an even more transparently autobiographical film about Fellini's hometown peer group whose fantasies kept them in a state of permanent adolescence. The Giulietta Masina trilogy – *La strada* (1954), *Le notti di Cabiria/Cabiria/Nights of Cabiria* (1957), and *Giulietta degli spiriti/Juliet of the Spirits* (1965) – explored her characters' drive to transcend the constraints of everyday life. Gelsomina (in *La strada*), a simpleton sold into slavery to a sideshow strongman, Zampanò, has 'breakthrough' experiences of a preternatural order; Cabiria, a spunky prostitute, seeks redemption through religion and romantic love; Giulietta, a middle-class housewife abandoned by her husband, discovers her own spiritual resources.

Though highly original, Fellini's 1950s films were still bound to realist codes. *La dolce vita* (1960) signalled a quest for a radical new film language reflecting the breakdown of traditional values in the Italy of the postwar 'boom'. $8\frac{1}{2}$ (1963), with its mixture of lived experience, dream, memory and fantasy, went even further. Both films added important chapters to Fellini's cinematic autobiography; Marcello Mastroianni* played the alter ego figure of the artist newly arrived from the provinces and attempting to adjust to metropolitan life in *La dolce vita*, and was the director in the throes of a mid-life crisis in $8\frac{1}{2}$. Two decades later, Mastroianni resumed this role in Fellini's encounter with feminism, *La città delle donne/City of Women* (1980) and in *Ginger e Fred/Ginger and Fred* (1985), a nostalgic look at a lifetime of performance in the context of televised vulgarity. Other transparently autobiographical films include *Roma/Fellini's Roma* (1972), a pastiche of personal impressions of the Eternal City, and *Amarcord* (1973), a poetic return to the film-maker's adolescence in Rimini during the Fascist era. Two highly self-referential films merge personal reminiscences with reflections on the cinematic apparatus: *I clowns* (1970), a documentary about the director's quest for the world's great clowns, and *Intervista* (1987), a celebration of Cinecittà's* fiftieth anniversary in the form of an extended interview for Japanese television.

Though opposed in principle to literary adaptations, Fellini has adapted a series of texts, beginning with Edgar Allan Poe for *Tre passi nel delirio/Histoires extraordinaires/Tales of Mystery* (1968, ep. *Toby Dammit*). Petronius' *Satyricon* attracted him as a series of fragments whose gaps begged to be filled in (*Fellini-Satyricon*, 1969), and the lists of sexual conquests in Casanova's *Memoirs* (which Fellini found as boring as a telephone directory) invited his demystification (*Casanova*, 1976). Finally, Ermanno Cavazzoni's story of a simpleton's odyssey in *Poema dei lunatici* prompted Fellini to survey a postmodern landscape through the astonished eyes of Roberto Benigni* in *La voce della luna/The Voice of the Moon* (1990).

In 1993, Fellini was given an Oscar for Lifetime Achievement, a fitting tribute to his ability to create a filmic mythology both intensely private and universal in its reach. MMo

Bib: Peter Bondanella, *The Cinema of Federico Fellini* (1992).

Other Films as Director: *Amore in città/Love in the City* (1953, ep. *Agenzia matrimoniale*); *Il bidone/The Swindlers* (1955); *Boccaccio '70* (1962, ep. *Le tentazioni del dottor Antonio*); *Block-notes di un regista/Fellini: A Director's Notebook* (1969); *Prova d'orchestra/Orchestra Rehearsal* (1978); *E la nave va/And the Ship Sails On* (1983).

FEMIS (formerly IDHEC)

French film school (Institut de Formation et d'Enseignement pour les Métiers de l'Image et du Son/Institute for the training and teaching of audio-visual professions), which incorporated and replaced IDHEC (Institut des Hautes Etudes Cinématographiques) in 1986. Situated in the Palais de Tokyo in Paris, near the Cinémathèque Française*, and endowed with enviable resources, FEMIS takes on fifty to sixty students a year to study theoretical film analysis alongside practical work. The present (1994–95) President is the scriptwriter Jean-Claude Carrière. The so-called Vaugirard school, officially the Lycée Louis Lumière, provides more technically oriented training. IDHEC/FEMIS and Vaugirard have produced many noted French and European film-makers and technicians (Alain Resnais*, Louis Malle*, Jacques Demy*, Anja Breien*, Henri Decae, Claude Zidi*), although plenty of great film-makers did not attend such schools, and the practice of assistantship has remained the accepted way for people (whether school-trained or not) to gain entry to film-making. GV

FERNÁN GÓMEZ, Fernando
Fernando Fernández Gómez; Buenos Aires, Argentina 1921

Spanish actor and director. After a career on stage from 1938, his first screen appearance in *Cristina Guzmán* (1943) initiated a series of largely comic leading roles first in mainstream cinema and later in the films of *auteurs* such as Juan Antonio Bardem*, Luis García Berlanga* and Edgar Neville*. His persona in the 1940s and 1950s is typified by his role in *El último caballo/The Last Horse* (1950) as the demobbed serviceman who refuses to allow the horse which has faithfully served him during his military period to be ridden, perhaps to death, by bull-ring *picadores*. The Quixotic aura of the part was retained in later films – many directed by Manuel Gutiérrez Aragón*, such as *Maravillas/Marvels* (1980), *Feroz/Wild* (1984), *La noche más hermosa/The Most Beautiful Night* (1984) – where he toned down the more farcical elements of his character. In two of the most important films in his career as an actor – Carlos Saura's* *Ana y los lobos/Ana and the Wolves* (1972) and Victor Erice's* *El espíritu de la colmena/The Spirit of the Beehive* (1973) – the elements of farce have disappeared, even though his role as the religious maniac in the former has a sinister comic dimension, and in *El espíritu de la colmena* the drift towards a graver presence fails to eradicate totally a lingering impression of comedy.

Fernán Gómez is also a major writer and director, whose credits include, as writer, *Las bicicletas son para el verano/Bicycles are for the Summer* (1984, dir. Jaime Chávarri*), and, as director, *El mundo sigue/Life Goes On* (1963), *Mi hija Hildegart/My Daughter Hildegart* (1977), as well as the very successful *Mambrú se fue a la guerra/Mambru Went to War* (1986), *El viaje a ninguna parte/Journey to Nowhere* (1987) and *El mar y el tiempo/The Sea and the Weather* (1989). PWE

FERNANDEL
Fernand Contandin; Marseilles 1903 – Paris 1971

French actor. One of the great French comic stars, with over 150 films from 1930, Fernandel started in the Marseilles music hall, singing and clowning in soldier disguise, and exploiting his two greatest assets: his horse-like features, especially his huge teeth, and a strong southern accent.

In over forty movies in the 1930s alone, Fernandel evolved two types familiar from Provençal folklore. On the one hand he was the poignant simpleton of Marcel Pagnol's* *Angèle* (1934), *Regain/Harvest* (1937) and *Le Schpountz* (1937). On the other, he played (and sang) the idiotic proletarian of countless farces, especially the military vaudevilles of the *comique troupier**, of which the epitome was *Ignace* (1937). His humour was a mixture of physicality and innuendo, well illustrated by *Le Rosier de Madame Husson/The Virtuous Isidore* (1931), in which, lauded as the virgin of the village, he celebrates by (accidentally) visiting the brothel. The public adored him while officials were appalled by the success of his 'despicable vulgar comedies which are the shame of our production'. He continued working with Pagnol in *La Fille du puisatier/The Well-Digger's Daughter* (1940) and *Topaze* (1951) and made countless other successful comedies, including *L'Auberge rouge/The Red Inn* (1951), *Le Mouton à cinq pattes/The Sheep Has Five Legs* (1954) and *La Vache et le prisonnier/The Cow and I* (1959). His popularity reached new heights with *Le Petit monde de Don Camillo/The Little World of Don Camillo* (1952), directed by Julien Duvivier* in Italy

and followed by four sequels up to 1965 (a last film in 1972 starred Gino Cervi* alone). As Don Camillo, the priest who 'talked to God' and fought with Cervi's Communist mayor, Fernandel capitalised on his irrepressible grin and his accent. He directed three films, and in the 1960s co-founded a production company, Gafer, with Jean Gabin*. One of his sons, Franck Fernandel, was a moderately successful pop star in the 1960s. GV

FERRANDIS, Antonio
Antonio Ferrandis Monrabal; Paterna, Valencia 1921

Spanish actor with a stage background who, since 1963, has appeared in films in highly effective supporting roles as a quiet, self-possessed character, and is much admired for his clear enunciation. His appearances have been in popular as well as *auteur* films. Examples of the former include *Sor Citroen/Sister Citroen* (1967) and *No desearás la mujer de tu prójimo/Thou Shalt Not Covet Thy Neighbour's Wife* (1968), both directed by Pedro Lazaga*; of the latter, Vicente Aranda's* *Fata Morgana/Morgan Le Fay* (1966), Jaime de Armiñán's* *Mi querida señorita/My Dearest Señorita* (1971) and *El amor del Capitán Brando/The Love of Captain Brando* (1974), and a cameo in Luis Buñuel's* *Tristana* (1970). PWE

FERRERI, Marco
Milan 1928

Italian director who also worked in Spain and France. In Italy, Ferreri began working in advertising and film production and then experimented with newsreels. While selling film equipment in Spain, he met the comedy writer Rafael Azcona*, who was to contribute to many of his films. Two of his features became milestones of the Spanish cinema: *El pisito/The Little Flat* (1958) and *El cochecito/The Wheelchair* (1960). Anticipating the black humour of Luis García Berlanga's* films, *El pisito* shows a young couple postponing their wedding until they find a flat. Out of desperation, the young man (José Luis López Vázquez*) marries an aged woman, hoping for her early death. Marriage, however, revitalises the old woman and the young couple's plans are frustrated. *El cochecito* covers a similarly grotesque territory.

Ferreri split the rest of his career between Italy and France, producing one of the most original and disturbing bodies of work of the European art cinema* of the 1960s and 1970s, a startling blend of socio-political critique (sex, consumerism, alienation), black humour and misogyny. *Una storia moderna: l'ape regina/The Conjugal Bed* (1963) ends with Ugo Tognazzi* reduced to a wheelchair by women's sexuality. Ferreri reflected on male obsessions in *Break-up* (1965, uncensored version released 1969); in *Dillinger è morto/Dillinger is Dead* (1969), he portrayed a fetishistic and alienated world. His attention focused increasingly on changing sexual roles, culminating in *L'ultima donna/The Last Woman* (1976), where Gérard Depardieu*, in a celebrated scene, emasculates himself with an electric knife (as a response to feminism). Undoubtedly, though, Ferreri's 'scandalous' reputation rests principally on *La grande abbaffuta/La Grande bouffe* (1973), an allegory of the ravages of consumerism, in which a team of European stars (Marcello Mastroianni*, Tognazzi, Philippe Noiret*, Michel Piccoli*) literally eat themselves to death. His films of the 1980s reflected the intellectual weariness both of Italy and of the director himself, who seemed to be simply pandering to an audience waiting to be provoked (*La carne*, 1991). However, with *La casa del sorriso* (1992), and above all *Diario di un vizio* (1993), Ferreri seems to have returned to his most scathing vein. PWE/PM

Other Films Include: *Los chicos* (1960); *Le italiane e l'amore* (1961, ep.); *La donna scimmia/The Ape Woman* (1963); *Controsesso* (1964, ep.); *Marcia nuziale* (1966); *L'harem* (1967); *L'udienza* (1971); *Liza/La cagna* (1972); *Touche pas la femme blanche* (1975); *Ciao maschio/Bye Bye Monkey, Il seme dell'uomo/The Seed of Man* (1978); *Chiedo asilo* (1979); *Storie di ordinaria follia* (1981); *Storia di Piera* (1983); *Il futuro è donna* (1984); *I Love You* (1986); *Come sono buoni i bianchi* (1987).

FEST

International film festival. Established in Belgrade in 1970 as a 'festival of festivals', FEST soon became an important gathering point for film-makers from around the world. A special attraction of the early years was a midnight programme called 'Brave New World', organised by Dušan Makavejev*. Some of the rebellious mood of the early 1970s was captured in the film *Nedostaje mi Sonia Heine/I Miss Sonja Henie*, for which each of FEST's famous guests (Miloš Forman*, Tinto Brass, Sergio Leone*, Paul Morrissey) directed one episode with the same cast and the same text – based only on the words of the title. In the 1980s, the audience was still coming (over 200,000 visitors in the best years) but the guests were not. FEST became a kind of distributors' fair and finally collapsed under the economic and cultural embargo of Serbia in 1993. SP

FESTIVALS

Film festivals gather films (as well as film-makers and stars) in one venue for the purpose of promotion and information. Although such events have taken place since the 1910s, the first festival in the modern sense of the term was Venice*, opened in 1932, followed by Cannes* in 1946 and Berlin* in 1951. These three constitute the major league of European film festivals, joined by Karlovy Vary* and Locarno* in 1946, Edinburgh* in 1947, London in 1957, and a host of others. Festivals' *raison d'être*, apart from media and tourist appeal, is to be a market place for new product and, incidentally (and often controversially), a forum for critical evaluation. Many award prizes and a Cannes, Venice or Berlin prize carries promotional value. Since the early 1980s, as the theatrical market for film has shrunk, festivals in Europe have taken on a vital role, as the *only* place of exhibition for an increasing number of films, at worst creating the ghetto of the 'festival circuit', but at best a springboard for media exposure and occasional release: the films of Emir Kusturica* and Kira Muratova* are two examples of the latter. Concurrently a veritable explosion of smaller festivals has taken place, es-

pecially in western Europe, where they are substantially supported by central and local state funds, catering for a wide variety of specialisms (animation, horror, shorts, thrillers, women's films, gay and lesbian films, children's films, silent cinema, realist cinema, national cinemas, etc.). While the market value of the smaller events is negligible, they perform a crucial cultural function, continuing and to some extent replacing the work of film clubs as a forum for discovery and debate, and providing an opportunity to circulate other European and non-American films. GV

Below is a *selective* list of film festivals. When not attributed to a writer, information is from British Council and British Film Institute documentation. For further details, see: *Directory of International Film Festivals*, published by the British Council, and the *BFI Handbook* (both yearly).

Albania hosts a biennial national film festival in Tirana [> ALBANIA]. **Austria** has three main annual film festivals. The Viennale – Internationale Filmfestwochen Wien (Vienna international film festival, every autumn) is subsidised by the Vienna City Council and a private sponsor, and includes symposia and publications. The other two festivals are dedicated to Austrian cinema: the Österreichische Film Tage Wels (Austrian Film Days, in Wels) since 1984, and the Diagonale – Festival des Österreichischen Films (festival of Austrian cinema) held in Salzburg since 1993 and organised by the Austrian Film Commission. (MW) **Belgium**'s most famous, though short-lived, festival was Exprmntl (experimental films) at Knokke-le-Zoute which ran in 1949, 1958, 1963, 1967, 1971 and 1974, and remains legendary for both its films and its passionate climate of debates and 'happenings'. Out of the country's large number of festivals should be mentioned the Brussels international film festival (January), the Brussels international festival of fantasy and science-fiction film and thrillers (March), and, also in Brussels, Cinédécouvertes (cine-discoveries) in July and Filmer à tout prix ('To film no matter what') in October. In November, a festival of European film is held in Virton. Ghent holds the Internationaal Filmgebeuren (international film festival) in October and an art film festival in February. (CF/SS) **Bulgaria**'s main festival is the international festival of comedy films in Gabrovo in May (odd years). There is also an animation festival in Varna in October (odd years). **Czechoslovakia**: see Karlovy Vary* (now Czech Republic). Bratislava (now Slovakia) holds several festivals, including the Forum (festival of first feature films, November–December). **Denmark**. The main festival is the Odense international film festival (August, odd years). There are also a film and video festival in Copenhagen (June, even years) and the Copenhagen gay and lesbian film festival (September, annually).

Finland. The Midnight Sun festival takes place every June (since 1986) in Sodankylä, a small Lapland community, focusing on new Finnish cinema and silent films. Espoo ciné, in southern Finland, started in 1990. Kettupäivät ('The Foxdays') in Helsinki in early November is a forum for new Finnish shorts, documentaries and videos. The international children's film festival (launched in 1982) takes place in Oulu in late November. The Tampere short film festival in early March (since 1970) is an important forum for new Finnish film-makers. MuuMedia in early March in Helsinki (since

1991) concentrates on video and the new media. (JS) **France**. While the major event remains Cannes* (May), the most important specialist events are: the Annecy festival (January), the Clermont-Ferrand short film festival, the Cognac festival of thrillers, the Créteil* international women's film festival (March–April), the Cinéma du réel (documentary) festival in Paris (March) and the Deauville festival of American cinema in September (notoriously boycotted in the early 1980s by French Minister of Culture Jack Lang). The Institut Lumière in Lyons and the Cinémathèque Française* organise regular retrospective festivals, the latter in particular with Cinémémoire (Paris, November), which shows newly restored prints. (GV) **Germany**. The most important German Festival is in Berlin. The Internationale Kurzfilmtage Oberhausen (Oberhausen international short film festival), held annually since 1955 (in April), exhibits a wide variety of short films. The Internationales Film-Festival Mannheim (November), established in 1952, emphasises debut features and documentaries. The Internationale Hofer Filmtage (Hof International Film Days) has since 1967 been a meeting place for younger German film-makers, especially film school graduates. The Leipzig festival (November–December), launched in 1957, is a forum for politically committed documentary film-making. Although its political focus has shifted since the end of the GDR to Third World film, it still functions as a window for central and eastern Europe. Germany has two major women's film festivals, Feminale (Cologne, May, since 1984) and Femme totale (Dortmund, since 1987). The Stuttgart animation festival has been running since 1982. (MW) **Greece**: see Thessaloniki*. **Hungary**. The main festival is the Hungarian Film Week, which provides a survey of Hungarian cinema, including documentary, experimental and student films. It is usually held in February, a week before Berlin*. (KAB) **Ireland**: see Cork*.

Italy. For many years Venice* was Italy's sole major film festival. Since the early 1960s many smaller festivals have emerged. A pioneering role was played, from 1960, by the Festival del Cinema Libero at the Apennine resort of Porretta Terme, for films made outside or on the fringes of the system. This was followed in 1965 by the Mostra del Nuovo Cinema at Pesaro (June). Founded by critic Lino Miccichè, Pesaro has devoted itself to the discovery or re-discovery of *auteurs*, movements and national cinemas, promoted conferences, and produced a steady stream of important publications. Throughout the 1970s and early 1980s numerous local initiatives followed. Among the most important were the Salso Film and TV Festival at Salsomaggiore, devoted (until its demise in the 1990s) to research and experiment; Filmmaker in Milan, dedicated to independent production; the Festival Cinema Giovani in Turin, with retrospectives of the 'New Waves' of the 1960s; and the Bergamo Film Meeting, a festival-market for quality films awaiting distribution. Among specialist festivals the most noteworthy are Mystfest at Cattolica, near Rimini, for thrillers, and the Pordenone festival of early cinema (October). (GVo) **Netherlands**. The three main festivals are the Netherlands Film Festival (formerly Dutch Film Days), in Utrecht (September), where an independent film festival (Cinemanifestatie) ran 1966–71; the documentary festival in Amsterdam (December); and the Rotterdam festival (January–February) (KD). **Norway**. The main Norwegian

film festival is held in Haugesund annually (August–September). In addition, a festival takes place in Oslo in November, and a short films festival in Trondheim in June. **Poland** has four annual festivals. The festival of Polish feature films in Gdansk/Gdynia (September) presents Poland's latest productions, and holds the annual meeting of the Association of Polish Film-makers. The Cracow festival of short films (late May) celebrated its thirty years as the major Polish short film festival in 1993. The Warsaw International Film Festival has grown in recent years from a student film club event to a well organised festival of recent international releases (modelled on London). The Lubuskie Lato Filmowe, run by the Association of Film Societies (Dyskysyjne Kluby Filmowe) at Lagow in western Poland, presents the latest films produced in Poland and eastern and central Europe. (AW)

Portugal. Among Portugal's numerous festivals are the Espinho festival (November) for animation, the Encontros Internacionais de Cinema Documental (documentaries) in Odivelas, the Fantasporto (fantasy films) in Oporto in February, the Figueira da Foz festival (September) and the Troia festival (June–July). **Romania**. There is a biennial animation festival in Mamaia; the national film festival has taken place at Costinesti since 1976, but its future is in doubt. (MM) **(Former) Soviet Union**. The major film festival of the Soviet Union has been Moscow, in July (odd years, alternating with Karlovy Vary*), traditionally the showcase for Soviet and eastern European socialist cinema; other festivals are held in St Petersburg (June), Sochi (May–June) and Tashkent (May–June). Among other festivals in the ex-Soviet states are the International Film Forum 'Arsenal' in Riga (Latvia) in September, for experimental film, the 'Golden Taurus' festival in Kaunas (Lithuania) in June and the 'Molodost' international film festival in Kiev (Ukraine) in October. **Spain**. The San Sebastián Film Festival (annually in September, since 1953) initially contributed glamour and an indirect legitimacy to Franco's regime, showcasing films which were then further cut or prohibited in Spain. After the transition to democracy, it is still Spain's premier film event; under Pérez Estremera, San Sebastián presents a competitive section built around the pick of Spanish autumn releases and the best new Latin American films, plus major international titles. Under Fernando Lara, festival director since 1983, the Valladolid International Film Festival (October) premieres major art films, complemented by tributes and retrospectives. Spain's other large festivals are Sitges (October) for fantasy and horror, and Valencia for Mediterranean cinema. (JH)

Sweden's main festivals are in Stockholm (November) and Uppsala (October, specialising in short films); there is also a festival in Gothenburg (February). **Switzerland**. Apart from Locarno*, the main festivals in Switzerland are Nyon and Solothurn. Emerging from the 'Festival du film amateur' (Rolle 1963–64, Nyon 1965–68), Nyon is concerned with documentary. Its director was Moritz de Hadeln (also Locarno's director 1972–77) until 1980, when Erika de Hadeln took over, pursuing the festival's remit of showing politically and socially committed films. Solothurn, or the Solothurner Filmtage (Solothurn Film Days), held annually in the last week of January since 1966, is the most important venue for domestic productions, together with theme-specific films by foreign directors, exhibitions and round-tables on issues of national film policy. Solothurn has since the early 1990s opened up towards video, television and co-productions. Video art finds a place at the Internationale Film- und Videotage in Lucerne, the International Video Week in Geneva and the Video Festival at Locarno. (MW)

UK. Apart from Edinburgh* the major event is the London Film Festival (November), held at the National Film Theatre and other London cinemas, created as a non-competitive 'festival of festivals' to present material shown at other festivals earlier in the year, as well as films released in their own country but not in Britain. The National Film Theatre also hosts the London lesbian and gay film festival (March) and the Jewish film festival (October). Smaller film festivals in the UK include Aberystwyth (November), Birmingham (October), Brighton (May), Cambridge (July), Leeds (October), the Norwich Women's Film Weekend (May), Nottingham ('Shots in the Dark', a thriller film festival, May–June) and Southampton (September). (GV) **(Former) Yugoslavia**. There is an international festival of animated films in Zagreb (Croatia) in June (even years) [> ZAGREB SCHOOL OF ANIMATION]. See also entries on Fest* (Belgrade, Serbia) and Pula* (Croatia).

FEUILLADE, Louis   Lunel 1873 – Nice 1925

French director. One of the great pioneers of French cinema, Feuillade started out as a wine merchant, wrote poetry and journalism on topics ranging from a defence of Catholicism to bull-fights and created a short-lived satirical magazine, *La Tomate*. He was hired by Alice Guy* at Gaumont* in 1905 and became artistic director in 1907 when Guy left France. He wrote and directed hundreds of comic films, melodramas, biblical scenes, trick films, etc. His stupendous activity encompassed the long-running children's series *Bébé* and *Bout-de-Zan*; the ambitious art series 'Le Film esthétique', based on original subjects and with sophisticated decors; and the realist series 'La Vie telle qu'elle est' ('Life as it is'), meant to give 'an impression of truth never seen before'. This 'impression of truth', based on location shooting, informs Feuillade's most famous films, the extraordinary *Fantômas* (five feature-length films, 1913–14), a baroque crime series set in Paris which mixes the everyday with the delirious, based on phenomenally successful novels by Marcel Allain and Pierre Souvestre. *Fantômas* combines anarchist and bourgeois sensibilities, a duality which also informs *Les Vampires* (1915–16), starring Musidora*. Both series were immensely popular, an object of fascination for artists, and the target of Establishment disapproval. Feuillade responded with *Judex* (1917), another series in which the hero was, nominally, on the side of the law. He also made *Vendémiaire* (1919), *Tih-Minh* (1919) and *Barrabas* (1920). His filmography includes almost 400 titles. GV

FEUILLÈRE, Edwige   Caroline Cunati; Vesoul 1907

French actress. Trained in classical theatre and a member of the Comédie Française, Feuillère, as Cora Lynn, appeared in-itially in films chiefly interested in her statuesque body. She made some American-style sophisticated comedies, such as *Mister Flow* (1936) and *L'Honorable Catherine* (1943), but specialised in costume dramas like *Lucrèce Borgia* (1935), *De Mayerling à Sarajévo* (1940), *L'Idiot* (1946) and *L'Aigle à deux têtes* (1948), in which she excelled with her majestic beauty and deep, melodious voice. By the early 1950s she was a *grande dame* of French cinema, epitomising for François Truffaut* the staginess of the tradition of quality*, but appealing to a popular audience, especially women, with her erotically charged portrayals of mature women, as in *Olivia/The Pit of Loneliness* (1951) and *Le Blé en herbe/The Game of Love* (1954). She still pursues a successful stage career. She received an honorary César* in 1984. GV

FEYDER, Jacques   Jacques Frédérix; Ixelles, Belgium 1885 – Prangius, Switzerland 1948

French director of Belgian origin. Feyder worked as an actor in and director of mainstream French silent films. Three of them raised him to the status of a major director. *L'Atlantide* (1921), based on Pierre Benoît's melodramatic novel, was an unusually long film for the time, shot on location in North Africa; *Crainquebille* (1923), a dramatic tale set in popular Paris, prefigured Poetic Realism*; and *Visages d'enfants* (1923–25, shot in Switzerland) was praised for its realism, especially in its use of children and the Swiss countryside. Feyder was hired by MGM and went to Hollywood, directing *The Kiss* (1929) with Greta Garbo* and foreign versions of American films, including *Anna Christie* (1930), also with Garbo. His reputation, back in France, traditionally rests on *La Kermesse héroïque/Carnival in Flanders* (1935), a humorous though formal costume drama starring Françoise Rosay* and Louis Jouvet*; nowadays *Le Grand jeu* (1933) and *Pension Mimosas* (1934) seem more interesting with their 'poetic realist' sensibility – their seedy decors and world-weary characters, greatly enhanced by wonderful performances, especially by Rosay. GV

FIELDS, (Dame) Gracie   Grace Stansfield; Rochdale 1898 – Capri, Italy 1979

British actress. By the time she made her film debut in 1931, 'Our Gracie' was already a star of the music hall and a major recording star, with an audience that had followed her progress since 1915 when she left Rochdale and the Lancashire cotton mills to join musical revue. By 1936 she was the most popular British film star and remained among the top three until 1940. Though her popularity dipped during the war, when she elected to remain in Hollywood (where she made three modestly successful films), it recovered afterwards and she continued into retirement abroad as a British national institution, created Dame of the British Empire in 1979, the year of her death.

The secret of her popularity can be heard most clearly in the recordings of her live performances. She plays an audience, goading it into enjoyment, feeding it the kind of cheek that passes for affection, and appealing to a shared contempt for pretension. Even her own claims to be taken seriously as an 'artiste' are constantly undermined by physical and vocal clowning. In the films, she creates the same solidarity with her working-class audience but also functions as the bridge to a national community which crosses class boundaries. As 'consensus personified' (Jeffrey Richards' phrase), Gracie tends not to have a plot or a romance of her own but facilitates the plots and the romances of others, her own romantic inclinations only hinted at with a glance and quickly suppressed with a shrug or a funny face. In *Sing As We Go* (1934), probably her best film, it is she who mediates with management on behalf of the workers, and when her mediation fails (despite the benign good intentions of the managers) it is Gracie who leads the redundant workforce into a rousing chorus of 'Sing As We Go' as they march jauntily into unemployment, the Depression and the hunger marches. The films are sentimental and reassuring, but they also tap into real social anxieties, and the sentiment is sometimes laced with vinegar. As the 1930s progressed, the national interest asserted itself and the films, while retaining their class roots, increasingly served the needs of a cheerful patriotic consensus. JC

Bib: Jeffrey Richards, *The Age of the Dream Palace: Cinema and Society in Britain, 1930–1939* (1984).

Other Films: *Sally in Our Alley* (1931); *Looking on the Bright Side* (1932); *This Week of Grace* (1933); *Love, Life and Laughter* (1934); *Look Up and Laugh* (1935); *Queen of Hearts* (1936); *The Show Goes On* (1937); *We're Going to be Rich, Keep Smiling* (1938); *Shipyard Sally* (1939). **In the US**: *Stage Door Canteen* [cameo], *Holy Matrimony* (1943); *Molly and Me, Paris Underground* (1945).

FILM COMPANY OF IRELAND

Irish production company. The Film Company of Ireland was the most important Irish production company of the silent period. Between 1916 and 1920 it made more than twenty fiction films, including three features. Eight of the first year's nine short films were directed by the Abbey Theatre's J. M. Kerrigan, who later became a Hollywood character actor. The most important films were *Knocknagow* (1918), a landlord/tenant drama set in 1848 during the Great Famine, and *Willie Reilly and his Colleen Bawn* (1918), set in the 1740s and 1750s and centred on the relationship between a Catholic man and a Protestant woman. Other personnel associated with the company, especially producer James M. Sullivan, and director John MacDonagh, who had been sentenced to death for his role in the 1916 Rising, were closely associated with the radical nationalist movement and, as a result, were targeted by the British authorities. KR

Bib: Kevin Rockett, Luke Gibbons, John Hill, *Cinema and Ireland* (1988).

FILM D'ART

French movement and production company. 'Le Film d'Art' designates: (1) a company founded in February 1908, partly with funds from Pathé*. The company acquired a studio in Neuilly and hired playwright Henri Lavedan and Comédie Française actor Charles Le Bargy to produce quality filmed drama. *L'Assassinat du Duc de Guise* (1908) remains the classic Film d'Art product, and the symbol of the strategy to move the cinema firmly into the realm of 'bourgeois' narrative. High production costs pushed the company into debt, however, and it closed in 1911. Meanwhile Pathé created a similar company, SCAGL (Société cinématographique des auteurs et gens de lettres), which produced such films as *L'Arlésienne* (1908). Other companies or departments within companies (such as Gaumont*) were created with similar aims. (2) The Film d'Art as a genre, and more specifically the historical film, set in place new trends for French cinema: bringing in and promoting well-known stage actors, introducing more sober performance styles, and developing more sophisticated narratives and film language. GV

Bib: Richard Abel, *The Ciné Goes to Town: French Cinema 1896–1914* (1994).

FILM EUROPE

German-led European film initiative. Erich Pommer* seems to have been the first to develop the idea of making 'continental' and 'pan-European' films to expand film markets beyond national borders, leading to two European-wide film congresses, one held in Paris in 1926 and the other in Berlin in 1928. Cultural topics were the most discussed, while economic questions stayed largely off the agenda, possibly so as not to offend American guests but also ensuring that the events had few practical results. Beginning in 1924, film companies from various European countries entered into reciprocal distribution agreements. They also promoted exchanges of creative talent, hoping to develop products aimed at an international market. E. A. Dupont* and Olga Tschechowa* were under contract to the British film industry, resulting in films such as *Moulin Rouge* (1928) and *Piccadilly* (1929), while Alfred Hitchcock* also worked briefly in German studios. The German-Dutch company Tobis-Klangfilm succeeded in creating a European cartel from 1929 to 1930 by monopolising the patent for sound film in Europe, and for a short time the pan-European market was protected against the American film industry more strongly than had ever been the case. French film personnel especially felt the pull of Ufa, but a great number of Italians also worked in Berlin during the 1930s.

A much more effective co-operation between European countries began at the end of the 1950s. Of all films produced in Germany in the 1960s around 40 per cent were co-productions with European partners, without, however, bringing about an integration of European film markets. This to some extent happened in the 1970s, though predominantly as a consequence of American movies' box-office strength and Hollywood distribution strategies. The frequently launched initiatives to defend Europe's markets against

American domination seem doomed, since such attempts, however worthy, concentrate on promoting low-budget art films with limited popular appeal and few infrastructural benefits [> EUROPEAN COMMUNITY AND THE CINEMA, EUROPEAN FILM AWARDS]. JG/TE

FILM INSTITUTE OF IRELAND

Irish organisation. Originally established in 1945 as the National Film Institute of Ireland, a Catholic propagandist organisation, it was taken over and secularised in the 1980s under the name Irish Film Institute. Following the establishment of the Irish Film Centre*, a project initiated by the Irish Film Institute, it was renamed again (as the Film Institute of Ireland), though its policies remain those of the IFI. These include the development of the Irish Film Archive, which houses the largest collection of Irish film material held anywhere, two successful art cinemas, the promotion of media education, and occasional publications. Its involvement in the European Union's* MEDIA programmes [> EUROPEAN COMMUNITY AND THE CINEMA] has included the establishment of Espace Vidéo Européen, which is housed at the Film Centre. KR

FILM OG KINO

Norwegian film magazine, started as *Norsk filmblad* in 1930 and changed to *Film og kino* in 1965. The main film periodical in Norway, it is published by the Kommunale kinematografers landsforbund (National Association of Municipal Cinemas). The magazine has seen many editorial changes through its long history. In the 1950s it promoted Hollywood blockbusters and reported on the modernisation of Norwegian cinemas. In the 1960s the magazine focused on art films by famous directors, and had lengthy reports on international film festivals. More recently, *Film og kino* has been committed to covering Norwegian film culture and it features detailed film reviews. KS

FILM POLSKI

Polish film institution. Film Polski was established in 1945 with Aleksander Ford* as chief. Administered by filmmakers, it was responsible for every area of the industry, from film stock manufacture to production, distribution and exhibition. The political relaxation of the mid-1950s allowed the formation of the 'zespoły' or film units, devolving the production function from the institutional centre and to groups of film-makers. With a leading director heading each unit, comprised of like-minded colleagues, a large degree of autonomy could be achieved. The best example is the famous 'X' unit, under Andrzej Wajda's* direction, which produced some of the finest and most politically challenging films of the 1970s. Although scripts were vetted, there was relatively little interference during filming, and it was left to Film Polski and its control of distribution and exhibition to determine the fate of completed films. It was common practice to delay distribution, or print only a limited number of politically 'unpopu-

lar' films. By failing to exploit films to their full commercial potential, Film Polski contributed to the economic malaise of the industry. In matters of international promotion, filmmakers were at its mercy since all submissions to foreign festivals were made through Film Polski.

Film Polski entered the post-communist era with a reputation tainted by corruption and inefficiency. Its staff, however, had experience of, and good contacts in, the international film community. Film Polski is now a government-sponsored cooperative and functions in two distinct areas. Firstly, it continues to deal with the international promotion of Polish film as a whole and of Poland as a co-producer/location for filming. Its second (privately financed) function is to make international film sales for the independent film producers and film units now operating in Poland. AW

FILM SOCIETY, The

British institution, established by Ivor Montagu* and others to show artistic films which, because of censorship or lack of commercial appeal, would not be shown in other cinemas. The Society catered to the growing band of intellectuals who saw the cinema as a new art form, were attracted to modernist forms, and could afford the subscription. Early members included Roger Fry, Keynes, Shaw, Ellen Terry and H. G. Wells, and the first council included Montagu, Sidney Bernstein, Iris Barry, Thorold Dickinson* and Basil Wright*. The Film Society established the model for a number of regional film societies. It angered those on the left who resented socialist films being restricted to an elite, provoking the moves which led to the Federation of Workers' Film Societies. Iris Barry, film critic and early member of the Film Society council, emigrated to New York in 1931 and became the first film curator of the Museum of Modern Art. JC

Bib: Don Macpherson (ed.), *Traditions of Independence: British cinema in the 1930s* (1980).

FILM SUR L'ART

Belgian genre. A privileged genre in Belgian film, the *Film sur l'art*, defined as 'between didacticism and documentary', takes an artist or an art form as its subject, often focusing on Belgian painting (René Magritte, James Ensor, Dieric Bouts, etc). Some established directors have repeatedly worked within the genre (Luc de Heusch*, Henri Storck*, Charles Dekeukeleire*), while it has provided others with an apprenticeship – for example Thierry Zeno and Chris Vermorcken.

After three conferences (Paris in 1949, Brussels in 1950 and Amsterdam in 1951), the Federation Internationale du Film d'Art (FIFA) was set up in Brussels, followed by a rival but short-lived organisation in Florence in 1955. FIFA occasionally presided over international festivals devoted to films about art and artists and published a catalogue sponsored by UNESCO, where Francis Bolen*, one of its main organisers, worked at the time. The Bergamo festival continued the tradition of art-film festivals until it changed policy, after which (from 1971 onwards) San Remo became the venue.

In 1980 the importance of the genre in Belgium was affirmed by the creation of the CFA (Centre du Film sur l'Art) in Brussels, a branch of the CBA*. The CFA was founded by Storck, with the support of art critics, curators, historians and collectors, and is presided over by Jean-Pierre Van Tieghem. It is largely funded by state aid from the French-speaking community. The aim of the centre is to buy, exhibit, promote and produce *films sur l'art*. Ten years after its creation it has become a specialised cinémathèque, possessing over 120 titles to which at least ten are added every year. Defined only by its subject matter, the *Film sur l'art* provides Belgian film-makers with a unique space for active research into the relation between cinema and the other arts, free from formal constraints. CF/PW

FILMINOR

Finnish production company. Founded in 1962 by a group of film club activists and the Students' Union of the Helsinki Polytechnic, Filminor has played a central role in Finnish production ever since. Its objective has remained the same over the decades: to provide a framework for young directors to make their first films. Filminor is partly financed by state subsidies, partly by producing sponsored short films, documentaries and commercials. Launched in the spirit of the New Wave*, the company has promoted both collective and *auteur* works. Its first feature production, *Yö vai päivä/Night or Day* (1962), deconstructive of representations of 'Finnish nature', was co-directed by Risto Jarva* and Jaakko Pakkasvirta*, both key figures in the early stages. In the 1960s and 1970s Filminor was particularly associated with Jarva, along with a group of followers, among them Peter von Bagh*. The late 1980s was a productive period, with several features by new male directors such as Jaakko Pyhälä, Ville Mäkelä, Olli Soinio, Matti Ijäs and Ilkka Järvi-Laturi (Filminor has never produced any features by women). In the early 1990s Filminor co-operated with the Helsinki School of Design in teaching practical film-making. AK

FILMSKE SVESKE

Yugoslav film magazine, established at the Belgrade Film Institute in 1968. The fact that the French translation of the title would be 'Cahiers du cinéma' is not the only link between the two magazines: from the beginning, *Filmske sveske* was concerned with Marxism, semiotics and structuralism. It managed to widen its views and to maintain a high level of film theory through translations of French and American authors and original contributions. Although it gradually changed from a monthly magazine to a yearbook of film theory, it had a great impact on theoretical film studies in the former Yugoslavia. SP

FILMVERLAG DER AUTOREN

German distribution co-operative. Modelled on the literary 'Verlag der Autoren' (and Hollywood's 'United Artists'), the 'Filmverlag der Autoren' ('Publishing House of Authors') was founded in 1971 by a group of directors wishing to enter

the market. Initially a co-operative between Wim Wenders*, R. W. Fassbinder*, Hans W. Geissendörfer, Uwe Brandner and Laurens Straub, the Filmverlag's guiding idea was for 'name' directors to act as a distribution company and take maximum advantage of the German subsidy system. The Filmverlag's shares were acquired in 1985 by former manager Theo Hinz and, despite chronic financial problems, the company continues to distribute innovative German films [> NEW GERMAN CINEMA]. MW

FILMVILÁG

Hungarian film magazine. The most important Hungarian magazine of film theory and criticism, founded in 1958. In the 1980s *Filmvilág* provided an important forum for intellectuals from many diverse fields, allowing them to debate issues (under the 'cover' of film) which would otherwise be censored. This role was inherited from another monthly, *Filmkultúra*, a magazine which had the same critical function in the 1960s and early 1970s until its editor, Yvette Bíró, was dismissed for political reasons. While remaining primarily a film magazine, *Filmvilág* has always placed cinema within a wider cultural context; more recently, it has expanded to include general media issues. KAB

FININVEST

Italian production company. Silvio Berlusconi's television networks developed an interest in film production in the mid-1980s, first by acquiring broadcasting rights and then by participating directly in production itself through the production house, Reteitalia. The money invested in this operation was considerable: in 1986, out of a total national investment in film production of 220 billion lire (*c.* £100 million), Berlusconi's company was responsible for some 90 billion, and in 1990, together with the Cecchi Gori* company, 180 billion out of a total 240 million. Initially, the results failed to attract large television and cinema audiences. In 1989, after Fininvest declared a 'loss' of 200 billion lire on its investment in Italian cinema, an agreement with the Cecchi Goris led to the creation of a joint production and distribution venture, Penta. In addition to a large number of 'low/middle-brow' productions and some 'quality' films directed by the likes of Marco Risi* and Bernardo Bertolucci*, Penta came to promote the majority of Italian films by both young and established directors. However, the death of Mario Cecchi Gori* in November 1993, the expiry of Penta's five-year agreement and Berlusconi's election as Prime Minister of Italy in 1994 slowed down Fininvest's activity, although its role within Italian cinema remains significant. GVo

FINLAND

A delineation of a strictly Finnish cinema is complicated by socio-historical circumstances before World War I when Finland was still a Russian Grand Duchy. During this period moviegoers could be divided into three categories according to their mother tongue: Swedish (55 per cent), Finnish (35 per cent) and Russian (15 per cent). Film production and distribution rights were largely monopolised by a Swedish-speaking minority based in Helsinki. The 'Finnishness' of the cinema of this period is therefore predominantly a matter of geography rather than language or a shared Finnish identity. However, Finnish film culture took its first tentative steps before the declaration of independence in December 1917. The Lumière* Cinematograph was demonstrated in Helsinki in June 1896, and the first screening by Finnish pioneer Karl Emil Ståhlberg* took place in January 1887. In 1904 the first permanent cinema appeared in Helsinki. From 1906 to 1913, Ståhlberg made many short documentaries through his studio, Atelier Apollo. The first Finnish fiction films, directed by Teuvo Puro, were *Salaviinanpolttajat/The Moonshiners* (1907) and *Sylvi* (1913). After Finland gained independence, a national production company called Suomen Filmikuvaamo (later Suomi-Filmi) was established. From 1915, the state levied a 10 per cent tax on filmgoing, alcohol, telephones and train tickets in support of the Russian war effort in the Crimean. After World War I and the Finnish civil war, and with independence secured, Finnish film production lost its momentum. Public screening of German films came to a halt, to be replaced by restricted import of Swedish and Russian films, along with American cinema, which enjoyed a new popularity thanks mostly to Chaplin. Seeking to rebuild a Finnish cinema from scratch, cinephiles looked to the successful Swedish and Danish national film production companies for models. However, it took more than ten years for the Finnish cinema to reach wider audiences.

From the founding of Suomi-Filmi in 1920 until the 1940s, Finnish cinema history can be summarised by a few significant events. The first of these is the shooting of Erkki Karu's* film *Nummisuutarit/The Village Shoemakers* (1923). The story (written by Aleksis Kivi some fifty years earlier) has been filmed twice since; as a sound film directed by Wilho Ilmari in 1938 and later in colour by Valentin Vaala* in 1957. In Karu's film two recurring themes of Finnish cinema, the forest and alcohol, received their first notable cinematic expression. Karu and Suomi-Filmi also produced one of the first widely successful films, *Tukkipojan morsian/The Logroller's Bride* (1931). Risto Orko*, who joined the company in 1933, became one of the major producer-directors of Finnish cinema, one of his early films, a rural love story called *Siltalan pehtoori/The Steward of Siltala* (1934), being the first Finnish film to attract more than one million spectators. In 1935 T. J. Särkkä* took over as head of Oy Suomen Filmiteollisuus Ab (SF), Suomi-Filmi's rival. After Mauno Mäkelä's* Fennada-Filmi was founded, with the merging of two smaller companies in the late 1940s, Finnish film production remained almost exclusively controlled by these three concerns until the early 1960s. In 1939, as the Winter War broke out, both Orko and Särkkä directed and produced their major spectacles, *Aktivistit/The Activists* (Orko) and *Helmikuun manifesti/The February Manifesto* (Särkkä and Yrjö Norta). Both films deal with Finland's struggle for independence in the early years of the twentieth century. Public screening of these films was later forbidden because of their openly political and anti-Russian sentiments. Thematically the films are linked by an extremely forceful national ethos which aimed to unite the people against the common enemy from the east. Ideological and economic contradictions were hidden beneath the larger and more important issue of the nation's independence.

In contrast to the situation twenty-five years earlier, World War II caused an economic boom for small national cinemas such as that of Finland. Again Finland was left isolated from wider international influences but instead of German films, this time it was Hollywood which became the central issue in a lengthy conflict. Under Särkkä's leadership, Finnish film producers accommodated German demands to restrict European imports of American movies. The consumption of national entertainment forms greatly increased during the crisis but again became a target for state taxation to benefit war initiatives. War and its image, perhaps more than any other motif in Finnish cinema, generated an audience. For example, *Tuntematon sotilas/The Unknown Soldier* (1954, dir. Edvin Laine*) is still the most successful Finnish film to date both at home and abroad. This interest in the 'attractions of war' remains strong: Rauni Mollberg* directed a remake of *Tuntematon sotilas* (1986) and Pekka Parikka recycled similar motifs in *Talvisota/The Winter War* (1989). While war has been seen as a source of national and collective trauma, since the 1930s a rich tradition of Finnish military farce* has acted as a medium for dealing with loss, death and contradiction through innocent humour and childish gags. *Juha*, the first colour feature film (in Sovcolor), was produced by SF and directed by Särkkä in 1956. Other companies promptly followed suit: Suomi-Filmi produced yet another version of *Nummisuutarit* (1957, dir. Vaala), and Fennada another vagabond story, *Kulkurin masurkka/The Vagabond's Mazurka* (1958, dir. Aarne Tarkas*). Nevertheless it was several years before colour films outnumbered black and white. The end of the decade marked the last stand of the 'old-fashioned' Finnish studio films. A new generation and a 'new wave' of film-makers (Risto Jarva*, Maunu Kurkvaara*, Mikko Niskanen*, among others) began to emerge, energetically promoted by the author, scriptwriter, producer, director, and later member of parliament, Jörn Donner*, who was also co-founder of the Finnish Film Archive* (1957).

In the early 1960s Finnish cinema reached a new low, after which it entered on a necessary period of transformation. The most prosperous years of film production (1952–56) had passed, marked by the failure of SF, long the largest production company. Television invaded Finnish homes in 1958 and within four years was reaching almost 80 per cent of the population. The state began giving film awards, indicating an acceptance of cinema as an important cultural form. Simultaneously it became evident that the film industry could not progress without state subsidies. The main function of the Finnish Film Foundation (Suomen elokuvasäätiö, or SES, established in 1969) is to distribute grants (provided by the Ministry of Culture and Education) to support domestic film production. SES also functions as the official promoter of Finnish cinema both at home and abroad.

There are approximately 250 cinemas in 180 towns and cities in Finland. In 1990, there were some 6.2 million cinema admissions (for a population of 5 million). In addition, there are forty municipal cinemas and seven film centres administered by local government and mostly financed by the Ministry of Culture and Education. The biggest distributors and importers are Finnkino and the American companies, Warner and United Pictures. The alternative circuit is concentrated mostly around communal film centres and film societies, which wielded some influence over exhibition in the 1960s and 1970s. However, the Union of Film Societies in Finland later lost status as a result of poor financial management, and film centres have begun to expand into their traditional territory. The oldest film centre, Oulun Elokuvakeskus, was established in 1973 and soon became a model for others. It runs a programme of film screenings with an emphasis on cinema for children. It has its own library and film archive, second only to the Finnish Film Archive*. Oulun Elokuvakeskus played a key role in establishing the annual International Children's Film Festival in Oulu. Similar centres were set up in the 1980s in major cities such as Tampere, Turku, Lahti, Iisalmi, Jyväskylä and Kajaani, each with its own local flavour. The Tampere centre runs a cinema, publishes a popular magazine and organises an annual Short Film Festival [> FESTIVALS (FINLAND)]. The Turku centre puts on an annual festival of classic Finnish films and co-publishes a scholarly film periodical with the department of Cinema and Television Studies at the University of Turku and the Finnish Society for Cinema Studies. Other organisations in the alternative field include the Finnish Film Contact (Suomen Elokuvakontakti), which rents experimental and documentary films and is the main organiser of the Kettupäivät film festival. AVEK, the Centre for the Development of Audiovisual Culture (Audiovisuaalisen Viestintäkulttuurin Edistämiskeskus), was set up in 1987 with funds derived from a sales tax on blank audio and videotapes with the aim of supporting Finnish audiovisual production. Finnish film culture is also alive through its magazines. *Filmihullu* ('Film-buff') is Finland's oldest, beginning life in the late 1960s as a radical counterpoint to established trends in Finnish film culture, and closely reflecting New Wave* movements elsewhere in Europe. *Filmihullu*, a bi-monthly, is still edited by founder Peter von Bagh*. *La Strada*, published four times a year by a film centre in Tampere, concentrates on new films and film-makers, especially popular American cinema. *Lähikuva* ('Close-Up') is a scholarly quarterly published in Turku by the Finnish Society for Cinema Studies and local film organisations. The bi-monthly *Peili* ('Mirror') foregrounds issues of film, television and video education and is practically the only forum for discussion of children's cinema and television. *Lähikuva* publishes English summaries of its articles.

Since the early 1920s, Finnish cinema has traversed the country's various landscapes, from the wilderness to the fields, from the village to the city, following the movement of culture in general. Each of these environments has its own powerful dualisms. The forest is a haven of escape and shelter but also a frightening and threatening place which can easily be destroyed [> LUMBERJACK FILMS]. Similarly, the rural landscape of villages and fields is equally conducive to the flame of romance, even eroticism [> NISKAVUORI FILMS], and impulsive acts of violence. It often seems to be the same dream that drives characters to acts of love or crime, with a correspondingly similar result – loss of freedom. Countless illustrations of the theme can be found among the classic films of Hannu Leminen*, Teuvo Tulio* and others, and in the newer cinema, especially that of Aki and Mika Kaurismäki*. In addition to the Kaurismäki brothers, contemporary Finnish cinema has produced several promising young directors, including Veikko Aaltonen (*Tuhlaajapoika/The*

Prodigal Son, 1992; *Isä meidän/Pater Noster*, 1993), Ilkka Järvilaturi (*Kotia päin/Homebound*, 1989; *Tallinnan pimeys/Darkness in Tallinn*, 1993), and Markku Pölönen (*Onnenpäivä/The Happy Day*, 1993). Their films represent both an attempt to recycle essential characteristics of the Finnish cinematic tradition and a renewal of international, especially European influences.

Finnish cinema is a masculine cinema, not only because of its major themes and environments, narrative style and world-view, but also because most of its film-makers have been (and still are) men. Likewise popular comic genres, such as the Puupää* and Uuno* films, are male-centered. Finnish cinema is defined by various dual constructions and insurmountable contradictions, which nevertheless provide a powerful source of energy for attempts to bridge the extremes. Finnish cinema may strive to liberate itself from the burden of its contradictory past, but its undeniable richness lies in its ability to express fundamental dualities in many and varied ways. JS

FINNEY, Albert   Salford 1936

British actor. A leading member of the generation of northern actors which took the British theatre by storm in the mid-1950s, and gained prominence in cinema in the social realism of the British New Wave*. Finney made his film debut in 1960 in *The Entertainer*. It was, however, the other role he created that year – that of Arthur Seaton in *Saturday Night and Sunday Morning* (1960) – which stamped a new image on British cinema. A bookie's son from Salford, Finney's characterisation seemed to come from inside the new, young, dissatisfied working class, and with its insolent defiance, aggressive sexuality and self-absorbed cockiness dispelled the dreams of a decent and contented class community left over from Ealing. Finney's performance in the title role of *Tom Jones* (1963) carried some of the same class insolence and a lot of the sexuality, and the success of the film made him an international star. With hints of autobiography, in 1967 he directed and starred in *Charlie Bubbles*, a film from a Shelagh Delaney script about the disenchantments of success. The loss of youth was also at the centre of Stanley Donen's *Two for the Road* (1967), in which he starred with Audrey Hepburn. His career did indeed stall after *Gumshoe* (1971), and films like *Murder on the Orient Express* (1974) added very little to his stature as an actor. In the 1980s and 1990s, however, he has re-emerged, often with a kind of dissipated grandeur, in *Shoot the Moon* (1982, US), *The Dresser* (1984), *Under the Volcano* (1984, US), and *Miller's Crossing* (1990, US). He continues to work in theatre and on television. JC

FINNISH FILM ARCHIVE (Suomen elokuva-arkisto, SEA)

Finnish institution, member of the International Federation of Film Archives (FIAF). Set up as a private enterprise in 1957, SEA became a state institution in 1979 administered by the Ministry of Culture and Education. In addition to films, SEA maintains a collection of photographs, posters and manuscripts. Since 1972 the principal focus has been the preservation of Finnish films. SEA directs a research unit centred on national cinema. With the Finnish Film Foundation, SEA publishes the proposed ten-volume *Suomen Kansallisfilmografia* (Finnish National Filmography), of which four volumes have so far appeared. The Archive's screenings take place in its Orion theatre in Helsinki, and at matinee screenings in major cities elsewhere in Finland. SEA has the largest library of film-related printed material in Finland. JS

FINNISH MILITARY FARCE

Finnish film genre, which boomed in the late 1930s when *Rykmentin murheenkryyni/The Black Sheep of the Regiment* (1938) became one of the most popular films of the decade. The roots of military farce are in literature, foreign military comedies – imported from Sweden, France [> COMIQUE TROUPIER] and the USA – and most of all in the tradition of folk theatre. The central focus in military farce was to play with the limits of hierarchy, bending, twisting or turning it upside down. During the war years the genre attained new dimensions when it was widely adapted for indirect propaganda purposes – 'mental therapy' for ordinary soldiers and people on the home front. Finnish military farce experienced another boom in the 1950s when earlier ideological burdens were erased by an admixture of elements from other genres, such as the musical and adventure films, and there was a more radical self-reflexivity. The earlier attempt to test the limits of the military hierarchy gave way to exploration of gender relations. In this sense, the genre reworked a favourite theme of Finnish cinema of the 1950s: the re-evaluation of traditional masculinity. When the studio system collapsed in Finland in the early 1960s, military farce – like most other established genres – was forgotten. During the past ten years, however, there have been several spirited attempts to breathe fresh life into the tradition: the most popular Finnish film of the decade was *Uuno Turhapuro armeijan leivissä/Numbskull Emptybrook in the Army* (1984), which adapted the conventions of the genre to the world of the Uuno* films. Ere Kokkonen has since directed *Vääpeli Körmy ja Marsalkan sauva/Sergeant Körmy and the Marshal's Stick* (1990), *Vääpeli Körmy ja vetenalaiset vehkeet/Sergeant Körmy and the Underwater Vehicles* (1991) and *Vääpeli Körmy ja etelän hetelmät/Sergeant Körmy and the Southern Fruits* (1992), which can be seen as contemporary re-creations of the military farce. The protagonist is an old-time military man whose methods constantly clash with modern military ways, producing a number of comic situations. KL

FINOS FILM

Greek production company. Finos Film, founded by Filopimin Finos, produced its first film, *I foni tis kardias/The Voice of the Heart*, in 1943, and reached its peak in the 1960s. Until the death of its founder in 1977 it was the most successful production company in Greece. Finos Film was modelled on Hollywood, owning film studios, laboratory facilities and a distribution network, developing a local star system, employing a large number of artists and technicians and producing films continuously. Its production standards were exceptionally high, in contrast to other Greek commercial studios, whose output was mainly low-budget, quickly made films of indifferent quality. Like other studios, the company produced mainly melodramas and comedies [> COMEDY (GREECE); GREEK MELODRAMA]. But it also adapted Hollywood genres such as musicals (*I thalassies i handres/Glass Beads from the Sea*, 1967), Westerns (*To homa vaftike kokkino/Blood on the Land*, 1965), and other styles to the requirements of a Greek audience, producing high-quality copies of the original but in familiar settings and in Greek. Finos Film was also noted for adaptations of popular contemporary plays and revues. It produced some art films too, for instance *To potami/The River* (1960, dir. Nikos Koundouros*) and *Ilektra/Electra* (1962, dir. Michael Cacoyannis*). Finos Film was responsible for the three most popular films in Greek cinema history: *Ipolohagos Natassa/Lieutenant Natassa* (1970), *I arhontissa ke o alitis/The Lady and the Pauper* (1968), and *I daskala me ta xantha mallia/The Teacher With the Blonde Hair* (1969), all three starring Aliki Vouyouklaki*. TN

FISCHER, Gunnar   Ljungby 1910

Swedish cinematographer. Gunnar Fischer has worked with directors such as Carl Theodor Dreyer*, Hasse Ekman* and Hampe Faustman, but is probably best known for the lyrical black-and-white cinematography of Ingmar Bergman's* key films of the 1950s: *Sommaren med Monika/Summer with Monika* (1952), *Smultronstället/Wild Strawberries* (1957), *Det sjunde inseglet/The Seventh Seal* (1957), and others. Fischer's mastery of black-and-white technique is particularly evident in outdoor sequences, for instance the scenes on the island in *Sommaren med Monika*. His virtuosity and versatility are perhaps best displayed in *Smultronstället*, in which he brilliantly evokes both the sparkling idyllic childhood landscapes remembered by the hero (Victor Sjöström*) and the surreal nightmare at the beginning of the film. He has also directed short films. LGA/BF

FISCHER, Otto Wilhelm   Klosterneuburg 1915

Austrian actor. After training at Max Reinhardt's* school, Fischer played both light and serious parts on Viennese stages and at the Munich Kammerspiele. From 1936 to 1945 he appeared on screen as harmless young artist or aristocrat in a number of films, but his fame rose with his increasing specialisation in melodrama, which turned him into the most popular male star of postwar Germany. In contrast to the Nazi ideal of male decisiveness, Fischer represented a new type of man, suffering from inner conflicts: like female melodramatic characters, his heroes yearned, sacrificed and cried. Their struggle to act morally can be seen as symbolic of the dilemma faced by Germany and the Germans during the immediate postwar period of reconstruction and *Wirtschaftswunder* (economic miracle). Fischer imbued these unconventional melodramatic characters with the elegance, discreet charm and even geniality of his earlier roles, but he added excess and unpredictability: elegance became artificial (especially in his way of talking), and charm, eccentricity and geniality turned to cynicism. Outside German cinema, Fischer gained some popularity through 1960s international co-productions such as *Axel Munthe, der Arzt von San Michele/La Storia di San Michele/Le Livre de San Michele* (1962, Ger./It./Fr.). KU

Bib: Dorin Popa, *O. W. Fischer: Seine Filme, sein Leben* (1989).

Other Films Include: *Sieben Briefe* (1944); *Bis wir uns wiedersehen* (1952); *Tagebuch einer Verliebten* (1953); *Bildnis einer Unbekannten, Ludwig II. Glanz und Elend eines Königs* (1954); *Skandal in Ischl* (1957); *Es muß nicht immer Kaviar sein/Pourquoi toujours du caviar* (1961); *Teerosen* (1976, TV).

FISHER, Terence   London 1904 – Twickenham 1980

British director, whose name is most closely associated with the series of horror films he made at Hammer*, beginning with *The Curse of Frankenstein* in 1957. Before Hammer, Fisher had been an editor since 1933, and a director since 1948, but it is in the relatively low-budget horror genre that he most clearly laid claim to the status of *auteur*, a claim which was honoured in France before it was considered seriously in Britain. Criticised by some British critics of the time for being 'disgusting' and by others for lacking the expressionist touches of European horror or the Universal cycle of the 1930s, Fisher's technique is, as Robert Murphy describes it, 'almost pedantically disciplined'. The camera follows the action with a realistic restraint which gives a cool objectivity to the sexual fantasies, body horrors and oedipal nightmares which are being enacted. Fisher left Hammer briefly in the early 1960s and made *Sherlock Holmes und das Halsband des Todes/Sherlock Holmes and the Deadly Necklace* (1962, Ger./It./Fr.) in Germany, before returning to home base to make such films as *The Gorgon* (1964), *Dracula – Prince of Darkness* (1965) and *Frankenstein Must be Destroyed* (1969). JC

Bib: David Pirie, *A Heritage of Horror* (1973).

Other Films Include: *The Astonished Heart* [co-dir.], *So Long at the Fair* [co-dir.] (1950); *Stolen Face* (1952); *Four-Sided Triangle* (1953); *Face the Music* (1954); *Dracula, The Revenge of Frankenstein* (1958); *The Hound of the Baskervilles, The Mummy* (1959); *The Brides of Dracula* (1960); *The Curse of the Werewolf* (1961); *The Phantom of the Opera* (1962); *Frankenstein Created Woman* (1967); *The Devil Rides Out* (1968); *Frankenstein and the Monster from Hell* (1974).

FITZGERALD, Barry   William Joseph Shields; Dublin 1888–1961

Irish actor. While a civil servant, he played in amateur theatrical productions and changed his name to Barry Fitzgerald to avoid dismissal from employment (his brother, actor

Arthur Shields, kept his name). Fitzgerald occasionally played at the Abbey Theatre from 1916 before becoming a full-time actor in 1929. His first film role was in the Irish-produced *Land of Her Fathers* (1924). He played the Orator in Alfred Hitchcock's* version of O'Casey's *Juno and the Paycock* (1929), while his stage role of Captain Boyle was given to the inexperienced British actor Edward Chapman. Contracted by RKO to play one of his most famous roles, that of Fluther Good in O'Casey's *The Plough and the Stars*, in John Ford's 1936 film version of the play, he thereafter worked mainly in Hollywood, where he won an Oscar for his role as Father Fitzgibbons in *Going My Way* (1944). He returned to Ireland frequently and played his most memorable role as the impish matchmaker in John Ford's *The Quiet Man* (1952). KR

Other Films Include: *The Long Voyage Home* (1940, US); *How Green Was My Valley* (1941, US); *Happy Ever After* (1954); *The Catered Affair* (1956, US); *Broth of a Boy* (1959).

FLAHERTY, Robert   Iron Mountain, Michigan 1884 – Dummerston, Vermont 1951

American director, who spent four years in Britain between 1933 and 1937 and played an important part in the development of the British Documentary Movement*. His reputation had been established with *Nanook of the North* (1922, US), *Moana* (1926, US) and *Tabu* (1931, US). In Britain, *Industrial Britain* (1933), made with John Grierson's* support, left behind a great deal of footage which was subsequently edited by, among others, Marion Grierson. He spent three years in the Aran Isles making *Man of Aran* (1934), and went to India with Zoltan Korda to make *Elephant Boy* (1937). Returning to the US, he received an International Prize from the Venice Festival for *Louisiana Story* (1948, US). Flaherty was a romantic rather than an ethnographer, but he set many of the problems of ethnographic film in motion. Grierson admired his lyrical poetry 'with its emphasis of man against the sky', but was inclined to add, 'I hope the neo-Rousseauism implicit in [his] work dies with his own exceptional self.' JC

Bib: Arthur Calder-Marshall, *The Innocent Eye: The Life of Robert J. Flaherty* (1963).

FLAIANO, Ennio   Pescara 1910 – Rome 1972

Italian scriptwriter. A prominent name in Italian journalism and literature, Flaiano started as a film reviewer, first on the weekly *Oggi*, beginning immediately before the war, and later on *Il Mondo*. After a few experiments in film writing, he wrote the wittily unorthodox text of *Roma città libera* (1946, dir. Marcello Pagliero) which examines the bewilderment of Romans under the Allied occupation. His talents were diverse: comedy of manners, in Alessandro Blasetti's* films such as *Tempi nostri/A Slice of Life* (1953), in Gianni Franciolini's *Villa Borghese/It Happened in the Park* (1953), and in Mario Monicelli's* much-censored *Totò e Carolina* (1953); caustic humour in films by Luis García Berlanga* such as *El verdugo/The Executioner* (1963), where he collaborated with Rafael Azcona*; the world of the fantastic, little explored by Italian cinema, with *Camilla* (1954), *Fortunella* (1958) and *Fantasmi a Roma/Phantom Lovers* (1961). However, Flaiano's true comic inspiration as a disillusioned moralist was mostly linked (in collaboration with the more 'metaphysical' Tullio Pinelli) to the films of Federico Fellini*, beginning with *Luci del varietà/Lights of Variety/Variety Lights* (1950, co-dir. Lattuada*), and continuing through *I vitelloni/The Spivs* (1953), *La strada* (1954), *La dolce vita* (1960), $8\frac{1}{2}$ (1963) and *Giulietta degli spiriti/Juliet of the Spirits* (1965). Flaiano also specialised in 'made-to-measure' subjects, for instance for a particular actor, some of which were collected posthumously. A great source of original subjects and witticisms, he was a great 'squanderer' of ideas, some of which remained unacknowledged; *Roman Holiday* (1953), for example, devised by Ben Hecht for Audrey Hepburn's debut, was written by Flaiano and Suso Cecchi D'Amico*. Flaiano's plans to film his novel *Melampus* came to nothing, though the story eventually became the basis of Marco Ferreri's* *Liza/La cagna*, made in 1972, the year of Flaiano's death. GVo

Other Films Include: *Pastor Angelicus* (1942); *La freccia nel fianco* (1943); *Fuga in Francia/Flight into France* (1948); *Guardie e ladri/Cops and Robbers* (1951); *Lo sceicco bianco/The White Sheik* (1952); *Peccato che sia una canaglia/Too Bad She's Bad* (1954); *Il bidone/The Swindlers* (1955); *La donna del fiume/Woman of the River* (1955); *Le notti di Cabiria/Cabiria/Nights of Cabiria* (1957); *La notte* (1961); *La decima vittima/The 10th Victim* (1965); *I protagonisti* (1968).

FLORES, Lola María de los Dolores Flores Ruiz; Jerez de la Frontera 1925 – Madrid 1995

Spanish actress, singer and dancer, legendary *diva* of the *folklóricas**, as famous for her problems with the taxman as for her singing and dancing. Often referred to as 'La Faraona' after the title of her starring vehicle of 1955, she made her stage debut at fifteen and shortly after appeared on screen in *Martingala/Excuse* (1941). Her rise to stardom was slow, her 1940s film appearances restricted to supporting roles. Her stage partnership with Manolo Caracol was transferred to the screen in *Embrujo/Bewitchment* (1948), lasting through four films and finally achieving great success with *La niña de la venta/The Girl at the Inn* (1951). Flores reached her peak as a solo star in the 1950s. JA

FOLKLÓRICAS (musicals): The *españolada*

Spanish musical genre. The *españolada* (or *andaluzada* as those set in Andalusia were commonly referred to) originated in the late 1920s and drew from the indigenous *sainete* (one-act farce) and *zarzuela* (operetta), as well as Hollywood musicals, whose colour schemes were later often crudely imitated. The genre's ideological possibilities were avidly exploited by the Nationalist government in the aftermath of the Civil War. The nurturing of flamenco as a tourist cliché during the Franco years facilitated the export of the *españoladas*

to the lucrative Latin American market as well as bolstering its national consumption. *Españoladas* were based on flimsy formulaic plots on which catchy songs were obtrusively hung, and were often star vehicles for well-known performers like Peret, Estrellita Castro*, Imperio Argentina*, Lola Flores*, Sara Montiel* and Antonio Molina. They were characterised by xenophobia, a glorification of the Spanish male as a paragon of virtue and desirability, and a warning of the dangers and vices lurking in the city. Folkloric interludes – often diegetically integrated into the narrative – functioned as a crucial component of the *españolada*. Protagonists were frequently professional performers, as in the backstage *cuplé* musicals of Montiel, or amateur performers, as in the folk musicals of Marisol, whose spontaneous bursts into song served to draw attention to the exquisite performing abilities of the Spanish. The socio-political problems of the country were erased from the screen and dismissed as trivial concerns easily surmounted by those with fortitude of character.

The post-Francoist musical – most significantly Carlos Saura's* flamenco trilogy and Jaime Chávarri's* *Las cosas del querer/The Things of Love* (1989) – has functioned as an inquiry into the phenomenon of the *españolada*. Once reviled as the epitome of regressive Francoist cinema, the genre has recently been critically re-evaluated. MD

FORBES, Bryan John Theobald Clarke; London 1926

British actor, **writer**, **director and producer**. Forbes began as a film actor in *The Small Back Room* (1949) and became a familiar figure in such male bonding films of the 1950s as *The Wooden Horse* (1950) and *The Colditz Story* (1955). Since the mid-1950s he has written a number of original screenplays, including *The League of Gentlemen* (1960), in which he also played a part, and *The Angry Silence* (1960), which he wrote for Beaver, the company he formed with Richard Attenborough* in 1959. His directorial debut was *Whistle Down the Wind* (1961), and he directed, wrote and often produced such well-known films of the 1960s as *The L-Shaped Room* (1962), *Seance on a Wet Afternoon* (1964) and *The Whisperers* (1966). In 1969 he was appointed head of production in EMI's attempt to crack the nut of British film production at Elstree, but despite commercial success with *The Railway Children* (1970) and critical success with Joseph Losey's* *The Go-Between* (1970), the attempt failed and he resigned in 1971. His subsequent career has included directing *The Stepford Wives* (1975, US) and co-scripting – with William Boyd and William Goldman – Attenborough's *Chaplin* (1992). JC

Bib: Bryan Forbes, *A Divided Life: Memoirs* (1992).

FORD, Aleksander Łódź 1908 – Florida, USA [Copenhagen, Denmark?] 1980

Polish director. Ford's career began in the silent era, with several shorts and a feature, *Mascotte/Mascot* (1930). One of the founding members of START (Society of Devotees of

Artistic Film) in 1930 and of the film-makers' cooperative SAF in 1935, he became a leading figure in the development of the postwar film industry; he was head of Film Polski* between 1945 and 1947 and artistic director of the Studio Film Unit from 1955 to 1968. He directed the first Polish epic, *Krzyżacy/Knights of the Teutonic Order* (1960), based on the classic novel by Nobel laureate Henryk Sienkiewicz, which celebrated Poland's victory at the battle of Grunwald (1410). A blockbuster, later considered essential patriotic and educational viewing, the film still tops the Polish box-office charts. Ford was one of the victims of the communist anti-semitic drive of 1968. He lost his administrative job and emigrated shortly afterwards, working in Scandinavia, Germany and the US until his death. AW

Other Films Include: *Ulica Graniczna/Border Street/So That Others May Live* (1949); *Piątka z Ulicy Barskiej/Five from Barska Street* (1954); *Ósmy Dzień Tygodnia/The Eighth Day of the Week* (1958, rel. 1983); *Sie sind frei, Doktor Korczak/Dr Korczak, the Martyr* (1973, Ger./Israel).

FORMAN, Miloš   Čáslav 1932

Czech director and scriptwriter educated at FAMU* (1951–56), where he studied scriptwriting. Forman worked as an assistant to Alfred Radok on *Dědeček automobil/Old Man Motor Car* (1956) and directed productions for Radok's Laterna Magika theatre. He co-scripted *Nechte to na mně/Leave it to Me*, directed by Martin Frič* (1955), and *Štěňata/Puppies* (1958), directed by Ivo Novák, before making his debut as writer/director with *Konkurs/Talent Competition/Competition* and *Černý Petr/Black Peter/Peter and Pavla* in 1963. Together with his colleagues Ivan Passer* and Jaroslav Papoušek, he worked with non-professional actors and semi-improvised dialogue to present a view of working-class life free from the stereotypes of Socialist Realism*. *Černý Petr* and *Lásky jedné plavovlásky/A Blonde in Love/Loves of a Blonde* (1965) had obvious links with late neo-realism* and *cinéma-vérité*, as well as with classic comedy. Focusing on the impermanence of young love, the confusion of middle age and the gulf between generations, they also provide a profound social analysis. When Passer and Papoušek made their own directing debuts with *Intimní osvětlení/Intimate Lightning* (1965) and *Nejkrásnější věk/The Best Age* (1968), they produced works in very much the same style. Forman's satire on bureaucracy, *Hoří, má panenko/The Firemen's Ball* (1967), was interpreted as a direct assault on the Communist Party and banned 'for ever' in 1973, only to be re-released a few months before the collapse of the Jakeš government in 1989.

Forman was already abroad, working on the script for his first American film, when Czechoslovakia was invaded by the Warsaw Pact countries in 1968. *Taking Off* (1971, US) continued the improvised, group-centred approach of his Czech films, but he has subsequently opted for literary subjects and a conventional approach to narrative. His Oscar-winning *One Flew Over the Cuckoo's Nest* (1975, US), clearly a comment on totalitarianism, gained much from his emphasis on ambiguous characterisation and ensemble playing, while *Amadeus* (1984, US), filmed in Prague with a mainly Czech

team under conditions of press blackout, had much to say on the relationship of the artist to patronage and bureaucracy. In 1975 he became co-director of the Film Department at Columbia University, New York and, in 1993, a board member of the newly privatised Barrandov* studios. PH

Bib: Miloš Forman and Jan Novák, *Turnaround* (1994).

Other Films: *Laterna magika II/Magic Lantern II* [co-d] (1960); *Dobře placená procházka/A Well-Paid Stroll* [TV] (1966). **In the US**: *Visions of Eight* [episode *The Decathlon*] (1972); *Hair* (1979); *Ragtime* (1981). **In France**: *Valmont* (1989).

FORMBY, George   Wigan 1904 – Preston 1961

British actor. Coming from the northern music hall (his father George Formby Sr. was a music-hall favourite before him), and gaining a national audience through radio, Formby became the most popular male domestic star with British audiences in the late 1930s, alternating at the top of the polls with Gracie Fields*. While Hollywood attempted to woo most other British box-office favourites of the period, including both Fields and Jessie Matthews*, it is hard to imagine what they could have done with Formby. Like his French counterpart, Fernandel*, with whom he was often compared, his particular appeal resisted translation. His characters are based on sexual innocence: romantically inept, they nevertheless aspire to the girls of their dreams. His songs, which he sang to a symbolically small ukulele, are based on a complicit game with the audience about how far you can take sexual innuendo: while Gracie could be coy, George could be smutty. But however smutty it got, it was safe. George was just being naughty, and the audience could permit itself the joke because, coming from George, it could never be seriously offensive or sexually threatening. The game is peculiarly English, drawing both from the seaside postcards of Donald McGill and from the northern music-hall tradition, and surfacing again in the *Carry On** films.

Formby made his most popular films under contract to Basil Dean* at Ealing, providing a voice of populist consensus immediately before the war and during its early years. He never recovered the popularity of those years, and when *George in Civvy Street* (1946) flopped, he returned to the music hall. JC

Bib: Jeffrey Richards, *The Age of the Dream Palace: Cinema and Society in Britain, 1930–1939* (1984).

Other Films: *By the Shortest of Heads* (1915); *Boots! Boots!* (1934); *Off the Dole, No Limit* (1935); *Keep Your Seats Please* (1936); *Keep Fit, Feather Your Nest* (1937); *It's in the Air, I See Ice!* (1938); *Trouble Brewing, Come On George!* (1939); *Let George Do It!, Spare a Copper* (1940); *South American George, Turned Out Nice Again* (1941); *Much Too Shy* (1942); *Get Cracking, Bell-Bottom George* (1943); *He Snoops to Conquer* (1944); *I Didn't Do It* (1945).

FORMER SOVIET UNION – see SOVIET UNION

FORQUÉ, Verónica
Verónica Forqué Vázquez; Madrid 1955

Spanish actress. Comic leading lady in films since 1971, and daughter of film director José María Forqué, in whose films she made her earliest appearances. Her first major film not directed by him was *¿Qué he hecho yo para merecer esto?/What Have I Done to Deserve This?* (1984), and from then she continued to work with Pedro Almodóvar* among other directors, typically as a dizzy dame, an ingenuous, heart-of-gold scatterbrain. Usually dressed in 'tarty' clothes, this screwball heroine gives fullest expression to her role as the uneducated Rita with the high-pitched voice and the low-brow peroxide intellect in Almodóvar's *Kika* (1993), a film that more colourfully reprises appearances in films such as *¿Por qué lo llaman amor cuando quieren decir sexo?/Why Do They Call It Love When They Mean Sex?* (1992). PWE

FORST, Willi
Wilhelm Frohs; Vienna 1903–80

Austrian actor and director. A specialist of stage comedy and operetta from 1919, Forst appeared in various Austrian silent films, starting with *Der Wegweiser* (1920). He rose to international recognition in two sound films by E. A. Dupont* (*Atlantic/Atlantik*, 1929; *Peter Voss, der Millionendieb*, 1932) and worked for directors such as Robert Siodmak*, Geza von Bolvary* and Karl Hartl*. Forst was already a popular star of the sound cinema when he directed his first film, *Leise flehen meine Lieder* (1933). He was subsequently often scriptwriter, producer and star as well as director of his films, his exceptional vocal qualities making him one of the most popular stars of Austrian and German musical comedies and film operettas of the 1930s and 1940s (together with Lilian Harvey* and Willy Fritsch*) in such films as *Zwei Herzen im 3/4 Takt* (1930), *Der Prinz von Arkadien* (1932), *Ein blonder Traum* (1932), *Königswalzer* (1935), *Mazurka* (1935), *Serenade* (1937), *Operette* (1940) and *Wiener Blut* (1942). *Maskerade/Masquerade in Vienna*, which he directed in 1934, made Paula Wessely* into a major film star. Enjoying his greatest successes between 1938 and 1945, Forst proved an expert craftsman and master of the 'Viennese film', establishing a stylistic quality which other directors and other films in the genre failed to attain, as he depicted a carefree Viennese dream world set to waltzes. This led to later accusations that he had turned a blind eye to the atrocities of the Nazi regime and the war. Forst himself described his work as a 'silent protest', arguing that he made 'Austrian films' at a time 'when Austria had ceased to exist'; he also refused to act in Veit Harlan's* *Jud Süss* (1940) and incurred Nazi disapproval.

Forst's postwar films did not match his pre-1945 successes, either artistically or commercially. The sole exception, *Die Sünderin/The Sinner* (1951), is the story of a young woman (Hildegard Knef*) who becomes a prostitute to make a living and support her artist lover and who later commits suicide with him. The Catholic Church's protests turned the film into a *succès de scandale*. Forst's last film as director was *Wien, Du Stadt meiner Träume* (1957). FM

Bib: Robert Dachs, *Willi Forst: Eine Biographie* (1986).

FORSTER, Rudolf
Gröbming 1884 – Bad Aussee 1968

Austrian actor, who developed a range of expressive performances in his characteristic role as the urbane and charming aristocrat. His talent for pantomime, which was noted for its precision, helped him give his characters often diabolically ambivalent features. He surprised his audience in his first sound film, G. W. Pabst's* version of Bertolt Brecht's *Die Dreigroschenoper/The Threepenny Opera* (1931), playing Mackie Messer as an unexpected 'gentleman gangster'. In 1937 Forster emigrated to the US, but he returned to Germany in 1940 to play the former Viennese mayor Lueger in *Wien 1910* (1942), an openly anti-fascist film. In the course of his career Forster worked with directors such as Paul Czinner*, Willi Forst*, Otto Preminger and Helmut Käutner*. His film persona lost almost all its former popularity after 1945, however, having by then flattened into a cliché. FM

FORSYTH, Bill
Glasgow 1946

British director and writer, who spent fifteen years working in Scottish-sponsored documentaries before making *That Sinking Feeling* (1980). The film, a 'no-budget' comedy using members of the Glasgow Youth Theatre, was, he claims, the first fiction narrative feature to be made in Scotland by a native Scot living in Scotland. Its success at the Edinburgh Film Festival* led to funding for an earlier script for *Gregory's Girl* (1981), using many of the same actors for a comedy of teenage manners (and lack of them) in Cumbernauld New Town. *Local Hero*, made for Goldcrest* in 1982 (released 1983), was his entry into the Big Time. Set again in Scotland, but with Burt Lancaster adding star appeal, the film revisits some of the territory of Alexander Mackendrick's* *The 'Maggie'* (1954), with the twist that the 'innocent' villagers are eager participants in their own sell-out to international capitalism. After *Comfort and Joy* (1984), Forsyth found it impossible during the rest of the 1980s to get the backing to make films in Scotland. His work in Hollywood has included one excellent and under-recognised film, *Housekeeping* (1987, US), adapted from Marilynne Robinson's novel, and *Breaking In* (1989, US), starring Burt Reynolds from a John Sayles script. Forsyth's skills are in localised, eccentric observation and idiosyncratic detail rather than in seamless narrative: skills which he struggles to maintain as the stars sparkle and the budgets rise. *Being Human* (1994), starring Robin Williams, with a budget of $20 million from Warner Bros, struggled under the weight of studio expectations, but may have convinced Forsyth that Hollywood is not the best place for a European eccentric. JC

Bib: Alan Hunter in Eddie Dick (ed.), *From Limelight to Satellite: A Scottish Movie Book* (1990).

FOSS, Wenche
Kristiania [Oslo] 1917

Norwegian actress in film and theatre. Since her first feature in 1940, Foss has played leading roles in more than thirty films. A versatile actress who can also sing and dance, she has performed in dramas and comedies, though she is mainly known for the latter. Laughter and joy being central elements of Norwegian popular culture, she is adored by audiences who have turned her into a celebrity. Norwegian film magazines of the 1940s and 1950s glamorised her and lovingly scrutinised her films, as well as her marriage, home and children. Today she is still the object of intense fascination in women's magazines. She was, and still is, a beautiful woman, though not in any ethereal way. Indeed, her 'ordinariness', the sense that she is 'one of us', is central to her appeal and status as a living Norwegian legend. KS

Films Include: *Tørres Snørtevold* (1940); *Den farlige leken/ The Dangerous Game, En herre med bart/A Gentleman with a Moustache, Jeg drepte!/I Killed!* (1942); *Rikard Nordraak* (1945); *Et spøkelse forelsker seg/A Ghost Falls in Love* (1946); *Trollfossen/The Magic Waterfall* (1948); *Kranes konditori/ Krane's Coffee Shop* (1951); *Det kunne vært deg/It Could Have Been You* (1952); *Ung frue forsvunnet/A Young Wife has Disappeared, Brudebuketten/The Bridal Bouquet* (1953); *Portrettet/The Portrait* (1954); *Herren og hans tjenere/The Lord and his Servants, Støv på hjernen/The Obsessive Housewife* (1959); *Tonny* (1962); *Episode, Om Tilla/About Tilla, Vildanden/The Wild Duck* (1963); *Afrikaneren/The African* (1966); *Operasjon V for vanvidd/Operation M for Madness* (1970); *Song of Norway* (1970, US); *Bør Børson jr.* (1974); *Liv & død/Life & Death* (1980); *Julia Julia* (1981); *Leve sitt liv/Living one's Life* (1982); *Åpen framtid/Open Future* (1983); *Adjø solidaritet/Goodbye Solidarity* (1985); *På stigende kurs/In Great Demand* (1987); *Begynnelsen på en historie/The Beginning of a Story* (1988).

FOTORAMA

Danish production company, founded in 1909 in the provincial town of Århus. During its first year, Fotorama made only one film, but in April 1910 it released the ground-breaking melodrama *Den hvide Slavehandel/The White Slave*, directed by Alfred Lind* (and immediately copied by August Blom*, the leading Nordisk Films* director). With a running time of some forty minutes, it was the first true European multi-reel film. (Some foreign companies had made films of more than one reel but always as serials, released one reel at a time.) Contrary to the expectations of many exhibitors, the public loved *Den hvide Slavehandel*, forming long queues to see it.

Fotorama had another box-office hit in 1911 with *Den sorte Drøm/The Black Dream*, which gave roles to two famous Danish film stars, Asta Nielsen* and Valdemar Psilander*. Thereafter several Fotorama directors were poached by Nordisk, and Fotorama survived mainly as a distribution company. It closed down in 1940. ME

FRANCE

'Let French cinema be real cinema, let French cinema be really French.' (Louis Delluc*)

Silent cinema

Louis and Auguste Lumière's* first public (and paying) screening of films at the Grand Café in Paris on 28 December 1895 remains the reference point for the beginning of world cinema (despite the numerous inventions and experimentations leading up to that moment, including those of Max Skladanowsky* among many others). The key to the historic success of the Lumière Cinematograph was its ability to project images to an audience (as opposed to Edison's single-viewer Kinetoscope), creating cinema as a *social* activity, at a time of rising popularity for a new 'image culture', notably with postcards, illustrated magazines, and world exhibitions (the Paris World Exhibition of 1900 was instrumental in promoting the new cinema).

Early French cinema was, as elsewhere, a fairground entertainment presenting novelties: short 'realist views' such as the Lumière films – *L'Arrivée d'un train en gare de La Ciotat, La Sortie des usines Lumière, Le Déjeuner de bébé* (all 1895) – comic scenes such as *L'Arroseur arrosé* (1895) and Alice Guy's* farce *La Fée aux choux/The Cabbage Fairy* (1896), inspired by contemporary cartoons and music-hall shows. It is customary to oppose the documentary impulse of the Lumières' cinema to the fiction of Georges Méliès*, who imported the tricks of his stage phantasmagorias to the screen, though the distinction now appears less clear-cut. Apart from its popular success and creative ferment, the distinctiveness of early French cinema was the business acumen of its practitioners. The Lumières promptly took their Cinematograph to all corners of the globe, fixing for posterity the term 'cinema'. While Méliès also expanded, Charles Pathé's* and Léon Gaumont's* newly created companies were extraordinarily successful at producing, distributing (switching from selling to renting in 1907) and exhibiting their films, both at home and abroad; Pathé's Gallic cockerel and Gaumont's daisy became household symbols the world over, holding sway until World War I. Films were exhibited in fairgrounds and in theatres, *cafés-concerts* and department stores, until permanent cinemas became the main sites of exhibition between 1906 (the Omnia-Pathé) and 1911. Major distribution companies such as Etablissements Aubert and AGC were also set up. In June 1916 the first centralised censorship body was instituted, for the granting of exhibition certificates, a system which formed the basis of most subsequent censorship legislation.

Pathé and Gaumont (joined from 1907 by Eclair, Eclipse, Lux and smaller companies) and Méliès (until 1911) developed a multitude of early genres: *actualités*, comic chase and trick films, *féeries*, religious scenes, historical films, erotic films, realist films, melodrama, animation (Emile Cohl*), even 'Westerns' (shot in the Camargue). Although initially it did not matter much who 'directed', emerging personalities included, after Guy and Méliès, Ferdinand Zecca, Léonce Perret, Albert Capellani and Victorin Jasset. The years preceding World War I saw the move to longer films and a rich field of detective series (*Nick Carter*), and especially comic series: *Bébé, Bout-de-Zan, Calino, Onésime, Pétronille*, etc., dominated by actors André Deed* (*Boireau, Cretinetti*), Max Linder* (*Max*) and 'Prince'* (*Rigadin*). Concurrently, the Film d'Art* and SCAGL (a branch of Pathé) crystallised the process of 'embourgeoisement' of the cinema, or, in historian Tom Gunning's words, its transition from the 'cinema of attractions' to the 'cinema of narrative integration', by adapting literary works (though the traditional view that all pre-1908 French cinema was 'primitive' has been challenged by Richard Abel [> BIBLIOGRAPHY]). Between 1909 and 1911 there was a move to even longer films, partly to get ahead of American competition. Like Italy and Denmark, France moved to features, with a preference for realist films (*Les Victimes de l'alcool*, 1911), including historical films and Louis Feuillade's* crime serials (*Fantômas*, 1913–14).

The rise of an increasingly organised Hollywood film industry and the outbreak of World War I dealt a fatal blow to the French world hegemony, and French cinema entered a state of crisis until the coming of sound. Whereas France had dominated the pre-1914 world market, by 1925 only seventy-three French films were shown on the French market, compared to over 500 American films. Pathé and Gaumont were dismantled in the 1920s, leading to an endemic 'atomisation' of the French film industry, though both resurfaced later in different guises. The long and arduous struggle against Hollywood had begun, although, in a now familiar phenomenon, American films – Chaplin, Keaton, Cecil B. DeMille, Griffith – also found their most enthusiastic audiences in France. A 'first wave' of passion for the cinema as an art developed with the French avant-garde*, whose interests were both formal and cultural: defining the specificity of film in theory and in practice, exploring (already) authorship, setting up film clubs, art cinemas and film journals. Louis Delluc* and Ricciotto Canudo* were the movement's first critics; Delluc (*Fièvre*, 1921), Marcel L'Herbier* (*El Dorado*, 1921), Jean Epstein* (*Cœur fidèle*, 1923), Germaine Dulac* (*La Fête espagnole*, 1920) were at the centre of its film-making experiments, though all also worked in narrative film; Abel Gance* in particular (*La Roue*, 1921–23, *Napoléon*, 1927) combined formal experiments with great popular epics. More cosmopolitan and politically motivated practitioners joined them, including René Clair*, Jean Grémillon*, Man Ray, Luis Buñuel*, Jean Vigo*, Marcel Carné*, Alberto Cavalcanti* and others. Popular genres continued to flourish, even though production had declined. These included comedies and serials (Feuillade's *Judex*, 1917), bourgeois melodramas, realist films (Jacques Feyder's* *Crainquebille*, 1923), 'modern studio spectaculars' (L'Herbier's *L'Argent*, 1929), colonial melodramas (Feyder's *L'Atlantide*, 1921) and historical epics (Raymond Bernard's* *Le Miracle des loups*, 1924), this last genre greatly influenced by the important group of Russian émigrés at the Albatros studio of Alexandre Volkoff. [> EMIGRATION AND EUROPEAN CINEMA]

Although the coming of sound signalled the end of some avant-garde practices, continuity was evident in the carrying over of some silent preoccupations into the sound era, especially realism; many avant-garde film-makers also continued or began a successful career in the 1930s (L'Herbier, Gance, Clair, Feyder, Julien Duvivier* and Jean Renoir*).

1930–1960: the classical age

The French film industry was ill-prepared for the coming of sound (although French scientists had invented sound systems as early as 1900, none had been patented) and technically the transition was anything but smooth: American and German systems were imported, short-lived methods such as multi-language versions were tried (1929–32), especially at the Paramount studios in Joinville ('Babel-on-Seine'), and the first French sound films (*L'Eau du Nil*, *Le Collier de la Reine*, 1929) were little more than silent films with sound passages. René Clair's populist *Sous les toits de Paris* (1930), on the other hand, shot for the powerful German firm Tobis at the Epinay studios near Paris, became a worldwide hit. It used sound and music imaginatively and fixed for decades to come a nostalgic vision of old Paris and its 'little people'.

French film-makers quickly adapted to the talkies, and the early 1930s saw a rapid increase in features – up to 157 in 1931, settling down eventually at 100–120 films a year, a figure which with the exception of the 1940s has been maintained to the present day. Studios around Paris (Epinay, Boulogne-Billancourt, Joinville) and in the south of France (Marseilles, Nice) invested in equipment and expertise. Many new large cinemas were built in city centres and a classification system for film exhibition was put in place in 1931. Though they occasionally clashed with conservative local censorship (town mayors had the power to ban film exhibition), the decisions of the Commission de contrôle were characterised by liberalism towards depictions of morality, adultery, etc. – contributing to the perennial 'naughty' reputation of French film outside France – and repressiveness towards political issues; criticism of major institutions was severely sanctioned (a *cause célèbre* of the decade was Jean Vigo's* *Zéro de conduite*, 1934). The booming film scene was swelled by more émigrés, from Germany and central Europe, including Fritz Lang*, Anatole Litvak*, Max Ophuls* and Robert Siodmak* (provoking xenophobic and anti-semitic attacks from the right). Apart from Gaumont-Franco-Film-Aubert (GFFA) and Pathé-Natan, production was in the hands of numerous individual producers, some with shaky finances. Scandals and bankruptcies, aggravated by the recession, were common; GFFA and Pathé-Natan collapsed. Government attempts at putting the industry in order came to little, and the industry had to cope with strong competition from Hollywood (for every French film shown, there were two to three American films; distribution was now largely in US hands). However, with few exceptions, the top box-office successes of the decade were French.

The novelty of sound prompted the two most popular genres of the early 1930s: musicals and filmed theatre. Apart from Clair's films, musicals tended to be filmed operettas, often French versions of German films starring Annabella*, Albert Préjean*, Henri Garat* or Lilian Harvey*, or pictures with comic singers, especially Georges Milton*, Bach, and Fernandel*, the star of the *comique troupier**. Other music-hall performers – Josephine Baker*, Mistinguett, Maurice Chevalier*, Tino Rossi and Charles Trenet – also appeared frequently in films. This was the typical fare of the '*cinéma du sam'di soir*', when people went regularly to their local flea-pit or to the new picture palaces built in city centres. Filmed theatre, based on *boulevard* comedies, showcased star performances and sparkling dialogue (by scriptwriters like Jacques Prévert*, Henri Jeanson*, Charles Spaak and Marcel Achard). These films' investment in the French language and in performance were adored by the audience and did much to shore up a specifically French cinema in the face of the Hollywood 'threat'; their genres, traditionally considered socially and aesthetically of little worth, constitute a fascinating testimony to the period. Key directors included Yves

Mirande, Louis Verneuil, Pière Colombier, Marcel Pagnol* and Sacha Guitry*, and among the main stars were Raimu*, Harry Baur*, Arletty*, Jules Berry*, Louis Jouvet* and Michel Simon*.

In contrast to the light-hearted genres which dominated the box office, the dark realist-melodramatic current in French cinema, usually referred to as Poetic Realism*, was favoured by critics. Based on realist literature or original scripts and set in working-class milieux, the films featured pessimistic narratives and night-time settings, prefiguring American *film noir*. Many great *auteurs* of the time chose this idiom: Duvivier, Feyder, Grémillon, Renoir, Jean Vigo, Pierre Chenal*, Albert Valentin*. The Poetic Realist drama was that of the male hero, best embodied by Jean Gabin*; it was also that of the Parisian *faubourgs*, beautifully recreated by Lazare Meerson* and Alexander Trauner* and lit by Curt Courant*, Eugen Schüfftan*, Jules Kruger and Claude Renoir, among others. Other melodramatic genres were important: classic melodramas were (re)made, such as Raymond Bernard's *Les Misérables* (1933), and new ones emerged: military or navy melodramas, high society dramas (by L'Herbier and Gance among others), and the 'Slav' melodramas associated with the Russian émigrés (stars included Danielle Darrieux*, Charles Boyer*, Pierre Richard-Willm*, Pierre Fresnay* and Pierre Blanchar*).

There is some justification in seeing Jean Renoir as the towering figure in French cinema of the 1930s, not so much because he was set apart from the rest but because he encompassed the practices of his time, making avant-garde films, comedies, popular melodramas, committed Popular Front* and poetic realist films all within one decade. His last film of the 1930s, *La Règle du jeu/Rules of the Game* (1939, for many his masterpiece, though a flop at the time), ended a decade of both great artistic achievement and vital popular cinema. Film culture was thriving; the Cinémathèque Française* was founded in 1936, popular magazines like *Pour Vous* and *Cinémonde* were read weekly by millions; Maurice Bardèche* and Robert Brasillach*, and later Georges Sadoul*, began writing film history. The Cannes* film festival was planned.

The German occupation had a paradoxical effect on French cinema. Some film-makers and actors – Renoir, Duvivier, Gabin, Michèle Morgan* – emigrated to the US, while others, like Alexander Trauner and Joseph Kosma*, went into hiding, and the industry framework changed. On the other hand, the majority of film personnel remained in France and worked relatively smoothly under the new regime, and historians have argued for an aesthetic and generic continuity between the 1930s and 1940s. Pétain's Vichy government created a new ruling body (COIC), which introduced a sounder financial framework, box-office control, a boost to short film production, and a new film school (IDHEC*). A few films (such as *Les Visiteurs du soir* and *Lumière d'été*, both 1943) were made in the 'free' zone, but lack of means hampered production and the majority of the 220 films made during the war came out of Paris, often from the German-owned firm Continentale. Despite material hardship, French cinema prospered. Films were closely monitored by German and Vichy censorship, prompting directors to avoid contemporary subjects, but few films were actual propaganda. British and American films were banned, French movies dominated screens. Cinemas were warm, attendance had never been higher.

The dominant genres of the war years were escapist: light comedies (*L'Honorable Catherine*, 1943); thrillers (*L'Assassin habite ... au 21*, 1942); musicals, costume dramas (*Pontcarral, colonel d'Empire*, 1942; *Les Enfants du paradis*, 1943–45), including a rare 'fantastic' trend: *La Nuit fantastique* (1941), *L'Eternel retour* (script by Jean Cocteau*). Although the films were on the whole 'just entertainment', some have been read as critiques of the Germans and of Pétain's regime, an ambiguity which perhaps characterises most Vichy cinema: Henri-Georges Clouzot's* *Le Corbeau* (1943), found offensive by the Germans, was criticised at the Liberation as anti-French and pro-Nazi. An interesting generic development of the time was the rise of the 'woman's film', with melodramas like Gance's *Vénus aveugle* (1940), Pagnol's *La Fille du puisatier/The Well-Digger's Daughter* and Jean Stelli's *Le Voile bleu* (1942). While these films may have been vehicles for the reactionary Vichy ideology, they featured strong women characters and weak father figures who can be understood in relation to a defeated collective masculinity. However, when *Les Enfants du paradis* came out on 9 March 1945, to huge popular and critical acclaim, its two central characters, Baptiste (Jean-Louis Barrault*) and Garance (Arletty), were seen as the embodiment of the indestructible 'spirit of France'.

A Committee for the Liberation of French Cinema was set up at the Liberation, and a journal, *L'Ecran français*, founded. Jewish personnel returned, while as part of the *épuration* Guitry, Clouzot, Arletty, Chevalier and others were punished for fraternising with the Germans. French cinema briefly dealt with the war trauma. Documentaries and fiction films were made to glorify the Resistance, notably René Clément's* 1945 *La Bataille du rail/Battle of the Rails*, while others, such as Christian-Jaque's* *Boule de suif/Angel and Sinner* (1945), Claude Autant-Lara's* *Le Diable au corps/Devil in the Flesh* (1946) and Clément's *Jeux interdits/Forbidden Games* (1951) dealt with the topic more obliquely. Soon, however, the war theme receded, with exceptions such as Alain Resnais'* *Nuit et brouillard/Night and Fog* (1955) and *Hiroshima mon amour* (1959), partly as a result of censorship. Significantly, though, the war became a favourite subject of comedies for the next four decades.

The cinema of the Fourth Republic started off on a platform of change. The Centre National de la Cinématographie (CNC), founded in 1946, laid the foundations of modern French cinema, including the principle of a degree of state control, box-office levies and aid to non-commercial cinema which, in the long run, ensured its livelihood. Substantial efforts were made to rebuild and modernise French cinemas. Film culture prospered with the revival of the ciné-clubs under the aegis of André Bazin*, new analytical film journals such as *Les Cahiers du cinéma*, and popular screenings at the Cinémathèque. The French film industry, however, had to face a flood of American films. As part of the settlement of the French war debt to the US, the 'Blum–Byrnes agreements' of 1946 granted generous import quotas to American films in return for US imports of French luxury goods – anticipating the GATT negotiations of 1993.

French production returned to its 100–120 films yearly average in 1950, helped by co-productions, especially with

Italy. From the late 1940s to the late 1950s, French cinema experienced its period of greatest stability and popularity. Audiences peaked between 1947 (423m) and 1957 (400m), after which permanent decline set in (television was not a significant rival until the 1960s). The industry was highly organised and well equipped, with a large reserve of experienced professionals. There were twelve sound stages in 1950; art directors such as Alexander Trauner, Jean d'Eaubonne, Léon Barsacq, Max Douy and Georges Wakhévitch created decors in every style; cinematographers like Henri Alekan*, Armand Thirard, Christian Matras and Louis Page were in great demand, their polished photography one of the hallmarks of what came to be known as the 'tradition of quality'* (the period also saw the introduction of colour and wide screen). This was also the era of scriptwriters Jean Aurenche* and Pierre Bost*, and later Michel Audiard*. Prewar directors like Clair, Duvivier, Renoir, Carné and Ophuls were back at work, joined by the 'war generation': Jacques Becker*, Yves Allégret*, Autant-Lara, Christian-Jaque, Clouzot and Clément. The French film industry was at its peak.

As in the 1930s, a 'dark' and a 'light' tradition divided popular French cinema of the 1940s and 1950s. Dark became excessively *noir*, especially in the films of Yves Allégret and Clouzot, in Carné and Prévert's epitaph to Poetic Realism, *Les Portes de la nuit* (1946), and in the 'social problem' films of André Cayatte (*Avant le déluge*, 1954). The *noir* idiom fed into the *policier**, partly inspired by the success of crime literature, as well as the popularity of Eddie Constantine* spoof thrillers (directed by Bernard Borderie). Becker's 1954 masterpiece *Touchez pas au grisbi/Honour Among Thieves* initiated a true renaissance of the genre, in which aging gangsters (typically Gabin or Lino Ventura*) and their male 'families' roamed the cobbled streets of Montmartre in black Citroëns. But if, as in the 1930s, the *noir* tradition is the best known, the 'light', in the shape of costume dramas and comedies, was the mainstay of the popular cinema. Sumptuous period reconstructions, often based on literary classics, demanded studio work and careful planning as well as big stars (Gérard Philipe*, Martine Carol*, Danielle Darrieux, Michèle Morgan*, Micheline Presle*, Maria Schell*). Many directors – mainstream and *auteurs* – worked in costume drama (Renoir, Clair, Ophuls, Jacqueline Audry*, Christian-Jaque). Martine Carol, then the biggest female star, smouldered in 'risqué' costume films like *Caroline chérie* (1950) and *Nana* (1955). But changes were afoot; in the mid-1950s, Carol was displaced as top French sex goddess by Brigitte Bardot* in *Et Dieu... créa la femme/And God Created Woman* (1956). The prominence of Carol and Bardot at the box office is noteworthy, as both *policiers* and comedies were male-oriented. Comic stars included, apart from Fernandel, Noël-Noël, Darry Cowl and Francis Blanche, the two biggest new postwar comics, Bourvil* and Louis de Funès*. While these comics were strictly for home consumption, Jacques Tati* became a much loved international star with *Jour de fête*, 1949, *Les Vacances de Monsieur Hulot/Mr Hulot's Holiday*, 1951, and *Mon Oncle*, 1958.

Tati was not just a comic; his originality was that he worked on the margins of the industry. Other such independent figures began to appear in the postwar period: Agnès Varda*, Alain Resnais*, Robert Bresson*, Jean-Pierre Melville*,

Roger Leenhardt, Georges Rouquier, Louis Malle*. These directors were disparate aesthetically and ideologically, but they were united in their distance from the mainstream. Their independence, their emphasis on personal 'vision' and the relative austerity of their practice marked them as *auteurs*, the precursors of (Varda, Resnais, Malle) or models for (Bresson, Melville) the forthcoming New Wave*. *Auteur* cinema was increasingly recognised by the French film industry as a vital aesthetic and marketing category, as able to compete with Hollywood as, on a different terrain, the 'tradition of quality'. A series of government measures, starting with the *loi d'aide* (1948) and culminating in the *avance sur recettes** (1960), institutionalised *auteur* cinema as a vital force in France, paving the way for the New Wave.

The New Wave, May 1968 and after

During the years 1959 to 1962, spearheaded by François Truffaut's* *Les Quatre cents coups/The 400 Blows* (1959) and Jean-Luc Godard's* *A bout de souffle/Breathless* (1960), there appeared a 'New Wave' of stylistically innovative (though on the whole 'a-political') films directed by former critics of *Cahiers du cinéma* (Truffaut, Godard, Eric Rohmer*, Jacques Rivette*, Claude Chabrol*, Pierre Kast, Jean Daniel Pollet) and classically trained independent film-makers like Varda, Resnais, Malle, Jacques Demy* and others. Several reasons explain the 'newness' of the phenomenon: the advent of de Gaulle's Fifth Republic, heralding a desire for modernity and renewal; changes in film technology (lightweight cameras, Nagra sound, location shooting); new producers (Georges de Beauregard*, Pierre Braunberger*, Anatole Dauman*, Alexandre Mnouchkine) who saw the financial possibilities in making small-budget films for small audiences. Film practice also fitted the new *politique des auteurs**. One of the New Wave's lasting achievements was to initiate new modes of spectatorship; another was to create new kinds of stars: the directors themselves, and those in front of the camera: Jean-Paul Belmondo*, Jean-Claude Brialy*, Jean-Pierre Léaud*, Jeanne Moreau*, Anna Karina*, Stéphane Audran*.

Contrary to the legend which sees the New Wave wiping the slate clean, popular genres continued successfully. However, the impact of the new *auteur* cinema was such that one history of French cinema could be written as geological layers of individual film-makers who won critical recognition and public sponsorship, if not always popular approval: those of the New Wave itself who continued to work; those in the 'spirit' of the New Wave who started later: Nelly Kaplan*, Jacques Rozier, Luc Moullet, Philippe Garrel, Jacques Doillon*, André Téchiné*; the 'classical *auteurs*': Bertrand Tavernier*, Claude Sautet*, Michel Deville*; finally, the inevitable 'unclassifiables': Maurice Pialat*, Jean Eustache*, Luis Buñuel*, Georges Franju*, Marguerite Duras*. A new generation of producers supported them (Paulo Branco*, Jean-Pierre Rassam, Margaret Menegoz, Marin Karmitz*), as did film journals *Cahiers du cinéma*, *Positif** and *Cinématographe*.

Even though initially its impact appeared limited (the events have been the subject of very few films, one being Romain Goupil's *Mourir à trente ans*, 1982), the political and social upheaval of May 1968 brought changes to both French cinema and film theory. The 1970s saw a continued decline in audiences and numbers of cinemas. Mainstream genres continued to flourish, however, especially the *policier* and comedy. Belmondo and Alain Delon* were the major stars of the former, Bourvil and de Funès of the latter (especially in the films of Gérard Oury), followed by the *café-théâtre* generation [> COMEDY (FRANCE)]. At the same time, societal changes (libertarianism, feminism) found an echo in the increased naturalism of French cinema, especially after the virtual abolition of censorship from 1967. At the two extremes appeared pornographic and militant cinema. Porn films flooded cinemas for a few years (in 1975 the 'X' category was created which instituted a heavy financial penalty for porn, though there was no official censorship), and were for a time distinguished by extremely witty titles, if nothing else. The plainly titled *Emmanuelle* (1973) and its sequels represented the mainstream end of that market, the films of Walerian Borowczyk* its *auteur* manifestation. On the militant side, film cooperatives sprang up, such as Godard's Dziga Vertov group and Chris Marker's* SLON. A generation of women film-makers emerged, as did women's festivals [> CRÉTEIL], and several of these film-makers have now built important careers (Yannick Bellon, Diane Kurys*, Coline Serreau*). Militant cinema found its popular expression in the political thrillers of Costa-Gavras* and Yves Boisset*, and in many less commercial productions. There was also a renewed interest in history, especially that of the German occupation, initiated by two key films, Marcel Ophuls' *Le Chagrin et la pitié/The Sorrow and the Pity* (1971) and Malle's *Lacombe Lucien* (1974). Directors such as René Allio, Tavernier and Téchiné participated in this movement, which was connected to the popularisation of the 'new history' in social sciences and the media. As World War II began finally to be talked about openly, so (timidly) was the Algerian war, for instance in René Vautier's *Avoir vingt ans dans les Aurès* (1972).

The 1980s and 1990s are marked by schizophrenia. With television viewing at a maximum, expansion of the video market, development of multi-screens and quick rotation of films (making it increasingly difficult for small, marginal *auteur* productions to survive), and with, for the first time, an audience market share for Hollywood higher than for French films, a sense of doom set in. On the other hand, an unparalleled amount of state help under the Socialist government (1981–95), the continued strength of both popular and learned film culture, maintained production in contrast to collapsing film industries in the rest of Europe, the (perhaps temporary) success of the GATT negotiations to preserve the 'cultural exception' of the cinema, and the international success of a number of French films and stars – all this gave rise to optimism and celebration, symbolised by the Césars* awards. French reactions to the numerous Hollywood remakes of French films epitomise this split: anger at being stolen from, pride at being copied. French initiatives in television production, especially with the rise of Canal Plus, proved imaginative and fruitful. In the early 1990s, over 60 per cent of films were financed with some television input, although the vast majority were for theatrical release. Three major generic trends have emerged.

First, the continuity of *auteur* cinema. Most New Wave film-makers are still at work, as well as many from subsequent generations: Tavernier, Téchiné, Sautet, Alain Cavalier,

Jean-Pierre Mocky, Jean-Charles Tacchella, Jean-Claude Brisseau, Claude Miller, Andrzej Zulawski, Leos Carax*, Claire Denis, Catherine Breillat, Euzhan Palcy, Diane Kurys, Tonie Marshall, Eric Rochant, and more recently Cedric Kahn, Patricia Mazuy, Marion Vernoux and Olivier Assayas (many trained at FEMIS*). A notable trend in the younger generation is a return to the New Wave's detachment from social and political issues, with some exceptions provided by the second-generation immigrant directors of the *cinéma beur**. The commercial, critical and symbolic importance of *auteur* cinema in 1990s France is best illustrated by the extraordinary media attention given to young directors such as Carax and Cyril Collard, whose *Les Nuits fauves/Savage Nights* (1992), released shortly before he died of AIDS, was one of the film events of these years. Secondly, popular genres and especially comedy have proved their durability. Serreau's *Trois hommes et un couffin/Three Men and a Cradle* (1985), Jean-Marie Poiré's* *Les Visiteurs* (1993) and Josiane Balasko's* *Gazon maudit* (1995) were popular triumphs, as have been films by Francis Veber, Patrice Leconte and Claude Zidi*. Thirdly, what might be called 'new spectacular cinema' is French cinema's response to the threat of television, making use of increasingly large budgets, major stars, highly skilled technicians and technologies. The new spectacular cinema takes two major forms: the *cinéma du look** on the one hand (glossy, youth-oriented; dirs. Jean-Jacques Beineix*, Luc Besson*) and, on the other hand, costume 'super-productions' [> HERITAGE CINEMA IN EUROPE], films such as Claude Berri's* *Jean de Florette* (1986), Yves Robert's *La Gloire de mon père* (1990), Jean-Paul Rappeneau's* *Cyrano de Bergerac* (1990) and Jean-Jacques Annaud's* *L'Amant* (1991). Often critically disparaged, the 'heritage' films combine popularity at home with exportability.

A century of 'real' cinema, a century of 'French' cinema

Co-productions are a characteristic of French production in the 1990s, together with a new internationalism; Krzysztof Kieślowski*, Nikita Mikhalkov*, Manoel de Oliveira*, Raul Ruiz*, Pedro Almodóvar* and others make films in France or with French money. Conversely, Besson and Malle have made 'French' films in English. Has Delluc's notion of a 'really French' cinema been forgone? Perhaps not entirely. French cinema, across its breadth and diversity, still occupies some spaces where its national identity may be found. One is realism, according to Jean Grémillon 'the grandeur, the meaning, the significance of French cinema', a national cinema which never really developed non-realistic genres (horror, science-fiction, the fantastic, the peplum*); another is its continued foregrounding of performance (if there is no European star system, there is arguably a French one); and finally there is the lasting popularity of indigenous comedy. Though some would argue that key to the identity of French cinema – both institutionally and aesthetically – are its *auteurs*, the true exponents of the 'real cinema' advocated by Delluc, the strength of its popular traditions also underpins – though for how long? – its survival. GV

[> COMEDY (FRANCE); POLICIER; FRENCH AVANT-GARDE; POPULAR FRONT CINEMA; TRADITION OF QUALITY; POLITIQUE DES AUTEURS]

FRANCHI, Franco
Franco Benenato;
Palermo 1922 – Rome 1992
and
INGRASSIA, Ciccio
Palermo 1923

Italian actors. In the 1960s and the early 1970s, Ciccio and Franco were the only surviving representatives of *commedia all'italiana**. These 'two cine-idiots most cine-watched in the country', as they were once defined, started in open-air theatre in Sicily, working their way through variety shows. They were discovered by the popular singer Domenico Modugno and offered small parts in Mario Mattoli's *Appuntamento a Ischia* (1960) and De Sica's* *Il giudizio universale/The Last Judgment* (1961). They finally starred in *L'onorata società* (1961), directed by the Neapolitan writer and comedian Riccardo Pazzaglia.

Franchi and Ingrassia were a perfect duo. 'Dividing us', they used to say, 'would be like tearing a photograph in two.' Their film roles and plots were rigidly set, endlessly reproducing the patterns of the popular variety shows of the day. Franco, the plebeian with rough working-class appearance, exaggerated gestures and expressions and sardonic/idiotic laugh, embodied basic instinctive needs, while Ciccio, whose physique recalled that of a gaunt decaying aristocrat, displayed a mature dignity, pushed to the limits of hysteria by the surreal foolishness of his companion. Together they made more than a hundred films whose titles point to their symbiotic relationship: *002 agenti segretissimi/00-2 Most Secret Agents* (1964), *I due mafiosi/The Two Mafiosi* (1964), *I due pompieri/The Two Firemen* (1968) and, inevitably, *Don Chisciotte e Sancho Panza* (1968). They revelled in parody, mimicking successful films by means of titles (many, alas, untranslatable) such as *Sedotti e bidonati* (1964), *Le spie vengono dal semi-freddo/Dr Goldfoot and the Girl Bombs* (literally 'The spies who came in from the semi-cold', directed by Mario Bava* in 1966), *Brutti di notte* (1968), *Satiricosissimo* (1970), and two 'low-grade' cult movies, *Ultimo tango a Zagarol/The Last Italian Tango* (1973) and *Farfallon* (1974). Eventually, they made it to art cinema, playing in the puppets episode, *Che cosa sono le nuvole?*, directed by Pasolini* for *Capriccio all'italiana* (1968), in the 'jar' episode of the Tavianis'* *Kaos* (1984) and, as the Cat and the Fox, in Luigi Comencini's* *Le avventure di Pinocchio* (1972). In 1974, Ciccio on his own wrote, directed and played *Paolo il freddo* and *L'esorciccio/The Exorcist – Italian Style*. He was also the unforgettable Teo, the mad uncle of Fellini's* *Amarcord* (1973). But in spite of these solo ventures and some furious quarrels they stayed together, united 'first by hunger and then by success'. GVo

FRANCIS, Freddie
London 1917

British cinematographer and director. After serving as a camera operator in the 1950s on a number of Powell* and Pressburger films, including *The Small Back Room* (1949), *Gone to Earth* (1950) and *The Tales of Hoffmann* (1951), and as second unit photographer on John Huston's *Moby Dick* (1956), Francis received his first cinematographer credit on *A Hill in Korea* (1956). He photographed *Room at the Top* (1959), *Saturday Night and Sunday Morning* (1960), and won an Oscar for *Sons and Lovers* (1960), directed by another cinematographer, Jack Cardiff*. He went to Hammer* Films in 1962, and somewhat reluctantly became a noted director of horror films such as *The Evil of Frankenstein* (1964), *The Skull* (1965) and *Dracula Has Risen from the Grave* (1968). He gave up directing in 1975 and returned to cinematography for David Lynch's *The Elephant Man* (1980, US/UK), working with Lynch again on *Dune* (1984, US). In 1991, he shot the remake of *Cape Fear* (US) for Martin Scorsese. JC

FRANJU, Georges
Fougères 1912 – Paris 1987

French director. An original figure in French cinema, Franju worked in set design and scientific film and was one of the co-founders of the Cinémathèque Française*. His first documentary short, *Le Sang des bêtes* (1949), shot in a Parisian slaughterhouse, had an enormous impact, revealing Franju's acute perception of the cruel and the uncanny within a realistic setting, as did *Hôtel des Invalides* (1952). This prepared the terrain for his best-known features which, rarely for French cinema, worked within the genre of the 'fantastic', especially *Les Yeux sans visage/Eyes Without a Face* (1960) and *Judex* (1963), a tribute to Louis Feuillade's* 1917 series (Franju also directed a film on Georges Méliès* in 1952). Among his other features are some distinguished literary adaptations, notably *Thérèse Desqueyroux* (1962, based on François Mauriac) and *Thomas l'imposteur/Thomas the Imposter* (1965, based on Jean Cocteau*). He also worked in television. GV

FRANKS, Herz
Born 1926

Latvian documentary director and scriptwriter. After working as a photographer and journalist, Frank wrote scripts for documentaries. Since 1965 he has scripted and directed over twenty films. Among the most important are *Zapretnaya zona/Forbidden Zone* (1975) and *Vysshii sud/Supreme Court/ [Last Judgment]* (1987), which traces the life of a young man from his trial and conviction for murder to his execution. In 1989, together with Vladimir Eisner, he directed *Zhili-byli sem' Simeonov/Once There Lived Seven Simeons*, the story of a doomed attempt by a Siberian family jazz ensemble to hijack a plane and escape from the Soviet Union. JGf

FRAUEN UND FILM

Founded by film-maker Helke Sander* in 1974, *Frauen und Film* is the first and only feminist film journal in Europe. The primary concerns of *Frauen und Film* are a continuing analysis of the workings of patriarchal culture in cinema and the concomitant demand for radically improved opportunities for women in film and television. In January 1984, the Berlin editors decided to cease publication, arguing that the recognition *Frauen und Film* had attained among fellow film journalists would run counter to the journal's radical ethos.

However, the Frankfurt editors – Karola Gramann, Gertrud Koch and Heide Schlüpmann – took over, and *Frauen und Film* continues to publish two issues a year, emphasis having shifted from political engagement with contemporary issues of film production to historical and theoretical concerns, with special issues devoted to women's experience of film in the 1950s, psychoanalysis and film, avant-garde and experimental film-making, masochism, female desire and early film history. In its present form *Frauen und Film* is the only film journal of such high theoretical standards in Germany, having in this respect taken on the task once briefly fulfilled by *Filmkritik*. MW

FRAUENFILM

German women's film movement (the term means 'Women's cinema'). Until the mid-1970s there were very few women directors in West Germany. Ula Stöckl and Erika Runge, whose careers started in the mid-1960s, were notable exceptions. The state- and television-subsidised New German Cinema* of the 1970s, though dominated by male *auteurs* such as R. W. Fassbinder* and Wim Wenders*, provided an institutional framework and an – albeit limited – space for women. Television, in particular, offered many first-time film-makers, and therefore women, a chance. Recognising the need for an infrastructure, in 1973 Claudia von Alemann and Helke Sander* organised the first International Women's Film Seminar; in 1974 the feminist film journal *Frauen und Film** was founded. The journal became an important forum for discussing ideas and organising distribution, exhibition and film festivals (such as the Feminale in Cologne, from 1984); the Association of Women Film Workers was founded in 1979. Most women film-makers involved being politically committed, both to the Left and to the Women's Movement, their prime concern was initially with didactic socialist/feminist agitation and information, dealing with such issues as domestic violence – Christina Perincioli's drama-documentary *Die Macht der Männer ist die Geduld der Frauen/The Power of Men is the Patience of Women* (1978) – and motherhood – Helga Reidemeister's prize-winning documentary *Von wegen 'Schicksal'/This is 'Destiny'* (1979). The early films of Sander, Jutta Brückner*, Helma Sanders-Brahms* and Margarethe von Trotta* also dealt with such political issues. From the 1980s the concern shifted from realism and 'positive' images of women towards theoretical and aesthetic interests. This led to a preoccupation with formal elements, such as sound; Alemann's *Die Reise nach Lyon/Blind Spot* (1980) literally traces the footsteps of Flora Tristan in the city of Lyons. Film-makers also became increasingly concerned with fantasy and psychic reality, for example Ulrike Ottinger* and Brückner in her 1980s films. Elfi Mikesch, a prize-winning cinematographer, directed a variety of films, from documentaries to stylised sexual fantasies.

Although most women worked in low-budget features – and thus remained marginal – von Trotta's and Sanders-Brahms' move towards international art cinema paid off in terms of public recognition, and paved the way for other successes: Marianne Rosenbaum's *Peppermint Frieden/Peppermint Freedom* (1982), a light-hearted autobiographical account of growing up in the 1950s, and Alexandra von Grote's *Novembermond/November Moon* (1985), a romantic love story between two women caught up in the turmoil of World War II. Doris Dörrie's* 1980s comedies showed a new tendency towards popular cinema, and similarly, in the 1990s, Monika Treut's* cheerful engagement with sexual politics is a far cry from the didactic films of the 1970s. US

Bib: Julia Knight, *Women and the New German Cinema* (1992).

FREARS, Stephen   Leicester 1941

British director, whose early film credits include assistant director on *Morgan a Suitable Case for Treatment* (1966), *If....* (1968) and *O Lucky Man!* (1973). He made his first feature film, *Gumshoe*, in 1971, but between 1971 and 1984, when he made *The Hit*, he worked in television drama. *My Beautiful Laundrette* (1985) was also made for television, but its surprise success earned it a cinema release in the United States and an Oscar nomination. This film and *Sammy and Rosie Get Laid* (1987), both made collaboratively with the writer Hanif Kureishi*, are key films of the 1980s, unpicking the social fabric of Thatcherism into its multicultural and multisexual threads. Since 1987, Frears has built up a successful Hollywood career with *Dangerous Liaisons* (1988, US), from a Christopher Hampton script; *The Grifters* (1990, US), produced by Martin Scorsese from a Jim Thompson novel; and *Hero/Accidental Hero* (1992, US). Described in a *Guardian* interview as neither a jobbing director nor an *auteur* (and despite his elevation to *auteur* status in France), Frears characterises himself as 'an old BBC drama department man', willing to implement the writer's intentions rather than to express his own personality. JC

Bib: Jonathan Hacker and David Price, *Take 10: Contemporary British Film Directors* (1991).

FREDA, Riccardo   Alexandria, Egypt 1909

Italian director. A master craftsman of popular films in many different genres, Freda began his directing career making 'heroic' epic films such as *Don Cesare di Bazan* (1942), *Aquila nera/The Black Eagle* (1946) and a version of *Les Misérables*, *I miserabili* (1947). An admirer of classical American cinema, he persevered with various types of historical and costume pictures, from *Beatrice Cenci* (1956) to *Roger-la-Honte* (1966, Fr./It.), including peplum* films such as *I giganti della Tessaglia/The Giants of Thessaly* (1960). In the 1960s he turned his attention to the horror genre with *L'orribile segreto del Dottor Hichcock/The Terror of Doctor Hichcock* (1962) and *Lo spettro/The Spectre* (1963), well-crafted claustrophobic films displaying a dark and sadistic aspect [> ITALIAN HORROR FILM]. With time his perspective became increasingly disenchanted, as he struggled to express his considerable talents and culture in the face of inadequate budgets and shoddy scripts. He co-wrote but did not direct (as planned) the comic 1994 swashbuckler *La Fille de D'Artagnan/D'Artagnan's Daughter*, shot by Bertrand Tavernier*. GF

FREDDI, Luigi   Milan 1895 – Sabaudia 1977

Italian producer. The most important political and entrepreneurial figure in the Italian cinema in the 1930s, Freddi was put in charge of the state-sponsored sector of the industry after it was 'corporatised' by the Fascist government in 1934. As General Director of Cinematography, Freddi pursued a rigorously commercial policy, helping to make Italian films competitive with Hollywood imports. He was responsible for centralising the industry, concentrating on efficient studio production, and for the construction of the Cinecittà* studios (1935–37). He fell from favour because of his outspoken opposition to the protectionist proposals in the government's 'Alfieri law' of 1938, which led to the withdrawal of the Hollywood majors from the Italian market, but returned to take over the revived Cines* company in 1941. A dedicated (but non-ideological) Fascist, his close associations with the regime led him to be made a scapegoat in 1945, when he was stripped of his powers and even, for a while, deprived of his pension rights. GNS

FREE CINEMA

British movement. Free Cinema consisted of six programmes of films shown at the National Film Theatre between 1956 and 1959. More broadly, it refers to a movement which linked the journal *Sequence** with the British New Wave*. What made the films 'free' was an attitude to 'the poetry of everyday life', an engagement (in the existentialist sense), and a free expression of personality which escaped the routines of commercial cinema or the standard British documentary. 'These films are free,' declared a programme leaflet, 'in the sense that their statements are entirely personal.' The programmes were assembled by a group which included Lindsay Anderson*, Karel Reisz*, John Fletcher and Walter Lassally, and included films – mainly documentaries, with a few animations – by Anderson: *O Dreamland* (1953), *The Wakefield Express* (1952), *Every Day Except Christmas* (1957); Reisz: *Momma Don't Allow* (1956), *We Are the Lambeth Boys* (1959); Tony Richardson*: *Momma Don't Allow* (1956); Norman McLaren*: *Neighbours* (1953); Georges Franju*: *Le Sang des bêtes* (1949); Jan Lenica* and Walerian Borowczyck*: *Once Upon a Time* (1957), *Dom* (1958); Roman Polanski*: *Two Men and a Wardrobe* (1958); Claude Goretta* and Alain Tanner*: *Nice Time* (1957); François Truffaut*: *Les Mistons* (1957); and Claude Chabrol*: *Le beau serge* (1957). Appearing in 1956, Free Cinema was the first expression in the cinema of the generational shift that was occurring in the Royal Court Theatre around *Look Back in Anger*. JC

Bib: Alan Lovell and Jim Hillier, *Studies in Documentary* (1972).

FRENCH AVANT-GARDE

Film movement(s) of the 1920s. From World War I to the coming of sound, Paris witnessed an extraordinary explosion of artistic and intellectual interest in the cinema, constituting a series of 'avant-gardes' which, following the pioneering work of Georges Sadoul*, it is customary to divide into three waves. First, the 'impressionist school' around Germaine Dulac* (*La Fête espagnole*, 1920), Louis Delluc* (*Fièvre*, 1921), Jean Epstein* (*Cœur fidèle*, 1923), Marcel L'Herbier* (*El Dorado*, 1921) and Abel Gance* (*La Roue*, 1921–23). Although these film-makers' formal concerns varied substantially, they shared a desire to develop a specific film language made of 'impressionist' or 'pointillist' notations to express subjectivity, using techniques such as slow motion and superimposition, but also, importantly, natural locations and natural light – a major difference from German expressionist* film. The 'impressionists' were concerned with authorship, loved American cinema (and generally disliked French popular genres) and at the same time wanted to create a specifically French (art) cinema – thus anticipating the concerns of the French New Wave*. Their concentration on subjectivity gave rise to the accusation of 'navel-gazing' by the more cosmopolitan and iconoclastic members of what is regarded as the 'second' avant-garde, influenced by Cubism, Dadaism and Surrealism. These include Fernand Léger (*Ballet mécanique*, 1924), René Clair* (*Entr'acte*, 1924, in which artists Marcel Duchamp and Man Ray, among others, appear), Dulac with *La Coquille et le clergyman/The Seashell and the Clergyman* (1928), from a script by Antonin Artaud, Luis Buñuel* (*Un Chien andalou*, 1929, made with Salvador Dali, and *L'Age d'or*, 1930) and Jean Cocteau* (*Le Sang d'un poète*, 1930). The 'third' avant-garde had a more socially oriented agenda, making important use of documentary, and includes Alberto Cavalcanti's* *Rien que les heures* (1926), Marcel Carné's* *Nogent, Eldorado du dimanche* (1930) and Jean Vigo's* *A propos de Nice* (1930).

Neat as these distinctions are, they are complicated by several factors. First, these French developments took place within international movements [> AVANT-GARDE CINEMA IN EUROPE]. Secondly, film-makers such as Dulac moved between different 'waves'; in her case, as Sandy Flitterman-Lewis has shown, a commitment to feminism unites her work. Thirdly, as Richard Abel has pointed out, French avant-garde practitioners combined their experiments with narrative cinema, and many moved frequently between avant-garde and mainstream genres. Finally, there were many interconnections in the period's extraordinary cultural activities; the creation of film clubs, art cinemas, film theory, specialised film journals and regular film columns in the press truly elevated the cinema to the status of the 'seventh art' [> CANUDO], but also inscribed it firmly within a wider cultural field in France and outside. GV

Bib: Richard Abel, *French Cinema: The First Wave, 1915–1929* (1984).

FRENCH NEW WAVE – see NEW WAVE (FRANCE)

FRENKEL, [BOUWMEESTER] Theo

Theodorus Maurits Frenkel;
Rotterdam 1871 – Amsterdam 1956

Dutch director and actor. Theo Frenkel preferred to call himself Theo Bouwmeester after his mother, who came from a well-known theatrical family. Starting as a director at Cecil Hepworth's* studio in Walton-on-Thames (England) in 1908, he soon had his own troupe of actors and made more than fifty pictures in a variety of genres, mostly writing the scripts himself. In 1910 he became head of Charles Urban's studios in Hove near Brighton (England) and in Nice (France), where he directed more than 120 films in two years, many of them in colour, using one of the earliest colour systems, Kinemacolor. To enhance the spectacular aspect of his films, he selected stories that demanded glamorous costumes and monumental landscapes, preferably Greek myths, biblical tales and historical romances. Frenkel cast his wife Julie Meijer (1878–1963) in many leading roles and himself seized every opportunity to appear with her in front of the camera. These films never made a profit, however, and Frenkel had to move on. He worked for the British Pathé* studios in 1912, moved to Berlin in 1913, and finally returned to neutral Holland at the outbreak of World War I. In his own country he was by far the most experienced all-round film-maker of the time, and he wasted no time creating several sensational dramas, such as *Het wrak van de Noordzee/The Wreck of the North Sea* (1915), *Genie tegen geweld/Genius Against Violence* (1916) and *Pro domo* (1918). He returned to Berlin to direct German-Dutch co-productions such as *Alexandra* (1922) and *Frauenmoral/Women's Morals* (1923), but his international career was over. Since the Netherlands could not support his ambitions either, he retired from film-making in 1925, only returning to direct his last feature in 1928.

Though Frenkel made more than 220 films, only a few have survived, making it impossible properly to assess his artistic importance. This is a pity since he was a director on a European scale, producing a vast body of work spanning Britain, France, Germany and the Netherlands. KD

Bib: Geoffrey Donaldson, 'Theo Frenkel Sr.', *Skrien*, vol. 129–130 (1983).

FRESNAY, Pierre

Pierre Laudenbach; Paris
1897 – Neuilly-sur-Seine 1975

French actor. Though Fresnay started in film as early as 1915, he made his mark when sound allowed his urbane and distinguished voice, polished at the Comédie Française, to be heard. Ironically, it was a put-on southern accent that made him famous. Though surrounded by real Provençal actors, Fresnay was credible as Marius in Marcel Pagnol's* Marseilles trilogy, *Marius* (1931), *Fanny* (1932) and *César* (1936). The films' triumph launched him on a career as a matinée idol, including in costume dramas with his wife, the singer Yvonne Printemps (*Trois valses* and *Adrienne Lecouvreur*, both 1938). The gentlemanly formality of Fresnay's acting was brilliantly used by Jean Renoir*, who cast him as the aristocrat de Boieldieu in *La Grande illusion* (1937). A versatile

actor, Fresnay was excellent as a detective in *L'Assassin habite ... au 21/The Murderer Lives at Number 21* (1942) and as the cool doctor of *Le Corbeau/The Raven* (1943). He continued playing doctors and other figures of authority in less distinguished but popular films in the 1950s. Fresnay's (and Printemps') postwar career was increasingly slanted towards theatre. They acted on stage and co-managed a theatre. GV

FREUND, Karl

Königsdorf 1890 – Santa Monica,
California 1969

German cinematographer, who began in 1906 as a projectionist in Berlin before graduating to newsreel cameraman for Pathé* and technical operator for Oskar Messter* in 1908 [> DOCUMENTARY (GERMANY)]. In the 1920s, he worked at Ufa* and gained an international reputation as a master of extreme camera angles, camera movements and bold lighting effects. Freund worked with directors such as Fritz Lang* (*Metropolis*, 1927), F. W. Murnau* (*Der brennende Acker/Burning Soil*, 1922; *Der letzte Mann/The Last Laugh*, 1924), Paul Wegener* (*Der Golem, wie er in die Welt kam/The Golem*, 1920) and E. A. Dupont* (*Variété/Variety*, 1925), helping to create some of the most influential and highly regarded films of Weimar* cinema. In 1927 he co-produced and co-scripted Walther Ruttmann's* landmark documentary, *Berlin die Sinfonie der Großstadt/Berlin, Symphony of a City*. Three years later Freund went to the US to work on an experimental colour programme for Technicolor. He filmed classical fantasy and horror pictures for Universal Studios, including *Dracula* (1931) and *The Mummy* (1933, which he also directed), and won an Academy Award for cinematography on *The Good Earth* in 1937. In 1944 he founded the Photo Research Corporation in Burbank, California. Among other Hollywood films he shot *Undercurrent* (1946, Vincente Minnelli) and *Key Largo* (1948, John Huston). In 1954 he was given a technical award by the American Academy for designing and developing the direct-reading light meter. MW

FRIČ, Martin

Mac Frič; Prague [then
Austria-Hungary] 1902 – Prague 1968

Czech director. Czechoslovakia's most prolific film-maker, Martin Frič directed eighty-five films, working in most genres but specialising in comedy. After leaving school, he was an actor, screenwriter and cameraman before beginning a collaboration with Karel Lamač* in 1924. He made a series of comedies with leading comic actors of the 1930s and 1940s, including Vlasta Burian*, Hugo Haas*, Jiří Voskovec* and Jan Werich*, and Oldřich Nový. Apart from his films with Voskovec and Werich, his outstanding comedies were probably *Kristián* (1939) and *Pytlákova schovanka/The Poacher's Ward* (1949), respectively a delightful comedy about fake identity and a satire on kitsch. Frič also directed *Jánošík* (1936), an international success and the second film about the legendary Slovak folk hero. During the 1950s, at the height of the Stalinist repression, he renewed his association with Werich for *Císařův pekař – Pekařův císař/The Emperor's Baker – The Baker's Emperor* (1951). Never an *auteur* in the accepted sense, Frič deserves credit for producing films of quality and as a mediator between stage, cabaret and screen. The role of his films in the preservation of popular culture is confirmed by their success in times of political adversity and again after his death. PH

Other Films Include: *Páter Vojtěch/Father Vojtěch* (1928); *Varhaník u sv. Víta/The Organist at St Vitus' Cathedral* (1929); *Dobrý voják Švejk/The Good Soldier Švejk* (1931); *Anton Špelec, ostrostřelec/Anton Špelec, Sharpshooter* (1932); *Život je pes/A Dog's Life, Revizor/The Inspector-General* (1933); *Hej rup!/Heave Ho!* (1934); *Ulička v ráji/A Street in Paradise* (1936); *Svět patří nám/The World Belongs to Us* (1937); *Baron Prášil/Baron Münchhausen, Katakomby/Catacombs* (1940); *Valentin Dobrotivý/Valentine the Kind-hearted* (1942); *Návrat domů/The Return Home* (1948); *Medvěd/The Bear* [TV] (1961); *Král Králů/King of Kings* (1963); *Hvězda zvaná Pelyněk/A Star Called Wormwood* (1964).

FRICKER, Brenda   Dublin 1944

Irish actress. Fricker has worked on stage and in television, including roles in the first Irish television soap in the 1960s, *Tolka Row*, the British television hospital series, *Casualty* (1986–90), and the *Brides of Christ* mini-series (1992). Her television films have included Pat O'Connor's* *The Ballroom of Romance* (1982), in which she played an unmarried woman in search of a husband in 1950s rural Ireland, and *Utz* (1991). She came to international prominence through winning an Oscar for her role as Christy Brown's mother in *My Left Foot* (1989). She continued to work with *My Left Foot* director Jim Sheridan* on *The Field* (1990, UK/Ir.), in which she again played a long-suffering woman, a characterisation which has become something of a trademark. KR

FRITSCH, Willy   Wilhelm Egon Fritz; Kattowitz 1901 – Hamburg 1973

German actor. After minor roles at the Deutsches Theater Berlin, his film debut, *Seine Frau, die Unbekannte* (1923), established Fritsch as a juvenile lead. He is best remembered, however, for his screen partnership with female star Lilian Harvey*. Dating back to the 1920s (*Die keusche Susanne*, 1926; *Ihr dunkler Punkt*, 1928), their on-screen romances made them the dream couple of the 1930s. The immensely popular Fritsch came to incarnate the optimistic hero of Ufa's* depression era comedies (*Die Drei von der Tankstelle*, 1930) and operetta films (*Der Kongress tanzt*, 1931). Also partnered with Käthe von Nagy (*Ihre Hoheit befiehlt*, 1931), Fritsch later played more serious roles in melodramas (*Die Geliebte*, 1939), eventually maturing into fatherly parts (*Wenn der weiße Flieder wieder blüht*, 1953). KU/TE

Other Films Include: *Spione* (1928); *Amphitryon* (1935); *Glückskinder* (1936); *Fanny Elßler* (1937); *Capriccio* (1938); *Frau am Steuer* (1939); *Film ohne Titel* (1947); *Was macht Papa denn in Italien?* (1961).

FROELICH, Carl   Berlin 1875–1953

German director, cameraman and film pioneer, who as early as 1903 joined Oskar Messter's* technical department, before becoming cameraman for Henny Porten's* 1906 debut film *Meissner Porzellan*. As co-director, he created the special effects in *Richard Wagner* (1913), which was distributed successfully in the US. During the war he was one of only eight licensed film correspondents at the front, shooting material for the 'Messter Woche', making him one of the fathers of the German newsreel [> DOCUMENTARY (GERMANY)].

In the first years after the war Froelich directed, among other films, *Arme Thea* (1919), starring Lotte Neumann, *Der Tänzer* (1919) with Lil Dagover*, and *Die Brüder Karamasoff* (1920) with Emil Jannings* and Fritz Kortner*. Shortly after the huge success of *Mutter und Kind* (1924, again starring Porten), Froelich, Porten and her husband Wilhelm von Kaufmann set up Porten-Froelich Produktion, Berlin, which produced fifteen films before 1929, most of them enormously popular and professional star vehicles for Porten. Froelich directed one of the first German talkies, *Die Nacht gehört uns* (1929, starring Hans Albers*), which, because of its enormous budget, was shot in London as a German-French co-production. Two years later, Froelich supervised Leontine Sagan's* *Mädchen in Uniform/Maidens in Uniform* (1931). In 1933 he became a member of the National Socialist Party, and directed *Ich für Dich – Du für mich* (1934) for the Reichspropaganda Ministry. He directed two major Zarah Leander* films (*Heimat*, 1938; *Das Herz der Königin*, 1940), and, once more, Porten in the nostalgic two-part romance, *Familie Buchholz/Neigungsehe* (1944). Imprisoned immediately after the war, he was 'rehabilitated' in 1953, on the occasion of his fiftieth anniversary in the movie business and the year of his death. MW

FRÜH, Kurt   St. Gallen 1915 – Boswil 1979

Swiss director. A left-wing writer, actor, cabaret artist, stage director as well as industrial and advertising film-maker, Früh worked at the *Ciné-journal suisse* newsreels during World War II and between 1949 and 1953 was assistant director to Leopold Lindtberg* at Lazar Wechsler's* Praesens-Film. He started his own career as a feature film director at Gloria-Film with two urban dialect comedies – *Polizischt Wäckerli* (1955) and *Oberstadtgasse* (1956). His next film, *Bäckerei Zürrer* (1957), drew a very personal and accurate picture of a petit-bourgeois milieu but also managed to introduce some ambiguity into its straightforward narrative. For a long time, *Bäckerei Zürrer*'s slightly ironic dimension remained the only deviation from popular genre forms in Früh's work, as neither the Heinz Rühmann* vehicle *Der Mann, der nicht nein sagen konnte* (1958), nor the Max Haufler pictures *Hinter den sieben Gleisen* (1959) and *Der Teufel hat gut lachen* (1960), nor the musical *Der 42. Himmel* (1962) revealed a particular talent for subverting comic and melodramatic stereotypes.

When Früh turned to television, radio and film teaching in the 1960s, it seemed as if his career in cinema had come to an end. In the early 1970s, however, he made an astonishing comeback with two films said to have inspired the younger generation of Swiss film-makers. *Dällebach Karl* (1971) is the portrait of an authentic regional character living in complete social isolation, while *Der Fall* (1972) traces the financial and mental decline of a down-at-heel private detective. Despite considerable critical acclaim, both films were financial failures, and, funds having dried up, they remained Früh's last. MW

Other Films Include: *Café Odéon* (1959); *Es Dach überem Chopf* (1961); *Im Parterre links* (1963).

FUGITIVE CINEMA

Belgian film collective, founded in Antwerp in 1964 by former members of Filmgroup 58, including the poet and critic Paul Vree. They were joined two years later by Robbe De Hert, who has been the central figure ever since. Other prominent members have included Guido Henderickx and Patrick Le Bon. Fugitive Cinema was a reaction against the popular comedies of Jan Vanderheyden* with which 'Flemish' cinema had until then been associated. Its aim was to produce and distribute realistic, committed films, which looked critically at the political, social and cultural reality of Belgium. Often labelled as subversive, Fugitive Cinema works rarely gained financial support from either government or Dutch-language public television (BRT). Although successful at international festivals, the early short films were not released on the commercial circuit, and by the end of the 1980s Fugitive Cinema was in financial trouble. While Henderickx and Le Bon chose to go their own way, Robbe De Hert continued to be the group's most critical if not anarchist member, with films such as *Camera Sutra ou les visages pâles/Camera Sutra of de bleekgezichten/Camera Sutra* (1973). Although he now works in a more commercial style, Robbe De Hert's critique of Belgian film policy and production system is still voiced regularly, for example in *Les Fabricants des rêves/De Droomproducenten/Dream Merchants* (1989), a documentary which asks what is to become of the Belgian audio-visual industry. SS/CF

FUNÈS, Louis de   Louis Germain de Funès de Galarza; Courbevoie 1914 – Nantes 1983

French actor. It may surprise many outside France who never got the chance to see his films that Louis de Funès was the biggest French box-office star of all time. He trained in music hall and appeared in small parts in over seventy films before his first leading roles. These came with *Ni vu, ni connu/Incognito* (1958), *Pouic-Pouic* (1963) and especially *Le Gendarme de Saint-Tropez* (1964) and its sequels, which made him the French king of comedy. Throughout the 1960s and 1970s, in contrast to Alain Delon's* and Jean-Paul Belmondo's* flatteringly virile heroes, de Funès, with his slight physique and ultra-mobile face, portrayed Frenchmen as irascible and bumbling petit-bourgeois. He was often paired with contrasting male stars like Yves Montand* and Bourvil*, with the latter in *Le Corniaud/The Sucker* (1965) and *La Grande vadrouille/Don't Look Now, We're Being Shot At* (1966), two of the biggest French box-office hits. His

hallmark was barely contained rage – against authority, domineering wives, foreigners (his films were regrettably often sexist and racist). But overblown and incompetent as his characters were (the gendarme was the archetype), they still triumphed, and that is one secret of his immense popularity. The other was his great comic talent, unfortunately not always matched by his films. GV

Other Films Include: *Le Mouton à cinq pattes/The Sheep Has Five Legs* (1954); *La Traversée de Paris/A Pig Across Paris* (1956); *Oscar* (1967); *La Folie des grandeurs* (1971); *Les Aventures de Rabbi Jacob* (1973); *L'Aile ou la cuisse* (1976); *La Zizanie* (1978).

FUSCO, Giovanni   Sant'Agata dei Goti 1906 – Rome 1968

Italian composer. Although his name is not as immediately recognisable as that of more popular Italian composers such as Ennio Morricone* and Nino Rota*, Fusco was a very influential figure whose name appears on the credits of such landmark films as Michelangelo Antonioni's* *L'avventura* (1960) and Alain Resnais'* *Hiroshima mon amour* (1959) and *Le Guerre est finie/The War Is Over* (1966). A graduate of the prestigious Accademia di Santa Cecilia, Fusco was notably eclectic, his skills and experience ranging from chamber music to the theatre, and in film from documentaries to fiction. Such an openness to experimentation marked his career and his ability to create new musical 'landscapes' was an invaluable help to the exploration of the relationship between images and sounds in the cinema of *auteurs*. Although Fusco worked with several directors such as Damiano Damiani, Mario Bolognini and the Taviani* brothers, he will be particularly remembered for his collaboration with Antonioni, for whom he wrote most of his scores. GLS

FUTURISM

Italian avant-garde circle, from 1909 through the 1930s, whose most famous spokesperson was F. T. Marinetti. Between 1909 and 1916, the Futurists published numerous manifestos decrying everything traditional about Italian art and culture, celebrating instead signs of modernity: urban landscapes, mechanisation and speed, war and its new technologies. Their wide range of artistic production included painting, theatre, poetry, musical performance, prose texts, sculpture, assemblages, architecture, furniture, ceramics, clothing and culinary preparations. Individual productions often co-opted techniques from different media. While the Futurists' manifestos often valorised cinema for its potential to the movement, their actual output of films and photography was minimal, and none of it is known to exist today.

Between 1909 and 1912, Futurists Bruno Corra and his brother Arnaldo Ginna are reputed to have made a sepia-tone photograph entitled 'Christus' and a series of coloured designs conceived as 'chromatic tunes'. Corra wrote in 1912 of having made a film of these designs, *Musica cromatica*, in which the designs were filmed as sequences – a technique that anticipated other avant-garde theories and practices of montage and animation. Concurrently, Anton Giulio Bragaglia linked Futurism to a new kind of photographic 'synthesis', which he described as 'photodynamism' and which he demonstrated through his own experiments with photographic superimposition, collage and (by the mid-1920s) film. For the most part, though, Futurists saw cinema as a potential trope or toy for their theoretical and rhetorical arsenal. Giacomo Balla, for instance, venerated cinema for its use of image, while Marinetti saw in cinematic montage the apotheosis of his literary ideal of 'word montage'. In 1916, Marinetti and five other Futurists wrote the first manifesto about cinema, *Cinematografia futurista*. This brief treatise proclaimed that cinema fulfilled their ideal of a Futurist 'synthetic theatre', while being a completely new art. That the Futurists described cinema as 'synthetic theatre' had as much to do with their effort to transform art and culture through provocative syntheses and performance as with their belief that a Futurist film was itself a performance. Significantly, the 1916 manifesto was written the same year as a group of Futurists made what is now believed to be the only Futurist film – *Vita Futurista* (dir. Arnaldo Ginna) – initially shown between other Futurist performances at the Niccolini Theatre in Florence in 1917 and reputed to have involved eight sequences running roughly 1,200 metres.

After World War I, the context of such film productions and of the Futurist project changed significantly. While Futurism re-emerged during the 1920s, increasingly supportive of Italian Fascism, its members saw less potential in the progressively industrialised cinema. Film remained of interest to this generation of Futurists less in itself than in its 'copenetration', to use Balla's term, with other forms. Significantly, there is evidence of Futurism's impact on mainstream Italian cinema after 1916, particularly in Enrico Prampolini's set designs for Anton Giulio Bragaglia's *Thais* (1916) and *Perfido incanto* (1916), and later in Carlo Ludovico Bragaglia's *O la borsa o la vita* (1933), and Guido Brignone's *La voce lontana* (1933). Several Futurists, including Marinetti, were appointed alongside Fascist political figures to the first national film council in 1926. [> AVANT-GARDE CINEMA IN EUROPE] JHa

FYRST, Walter
Kristiania [Oslo] 1901 – Oslo 1993

Norwegian director, who moved to features from advertising with *Trollelgen/The Magic Elk* (1927), a film portraying nature in the style characteristic of 1920s Norwegian cinema. Fyrst made two other features, an urban crime story entitled *Cafe X* (1928) and the second Norwegian sound film, *Prinsessen som ingen kunne målbinde/The Princess That No One Could Silence* (1932), based on a Norwegian folk tale. During the German occupation of 1940–45 he made two overt Nazi propaganda films, *Vi er Vidkun Quislings hirdmenn/We are the Soldiers of Vidkun Quisling* (1942) and *Unge viljer/Young Wills* (1943). The first is a documentary modelled on Leni Riefenstahl's* *Triumph des Willens/Triumph of the Will* (1935), the latter a fictional narrative about evil Marxist trade union leaders and a young couple who join a Nazi organisation. Fyrst was condemned for treason at the end of the war, but returned to film production after serving his sentence. In the 1950s he made commercials and a feature, *Hjem går vi ikke/We're Not Going Home* (1955), a film dealing with the topical issue of a young couple beset by housing problems. From the 1960s on, Fyrst worked in television. KS

Other Films Include: *Brudekronen/The Bridal Crown*, *Bagateller for en sjømann/A Sailor's Trifles* (1944).

FYRTAARNET og BIVOGNEN

Danish comic duo of the silent cinema, played by Carl Schenstrøm (Copenhagen 1881–1942) and Harald Madsen (Silkeborg 1890 – Copenhagen 1949). Schenstrøm, a former stage actor, started acting in film in 1909 at Nordisk Films*. In 1914 director Lau Lauritzen* joined Nordisk and cast Schenstrøm in numerous films until the end of 1919, when he and Schenstrøm left for Svensk Palladium in Sweden. Back in Denmark in 1921, Lauritzen became artistic director of the new (Danish) Palladium* with Svend Nielsen, and created the comic couple 'Fyrtaarnet og Bivognen' (literally 'The Lighthouse and the Endwagon', credited as Pat and Patachon in their English, German and Austrian films), with Schenstrøm as Fyrtaarnet and Madsen, a former circus clown, as Bivognen. The duo proved a tremendous hit and made Palladium's fortune. Schenstrøm and Madsen were ideal for the parts of, respectively, the tall and lean Fyrtaarnet and the small and round Bivognen. Schenstrøm wore clothes one size too small to appear even taller and concealed his handsome face under a mask with protruding nose, drooping moustache and long hair. Madsen wore his clothes tight around his stout little torso. Like all comic duos they played on contrasts, within a symbolic father-son relationship: Fyrtaarnet was pleasant and helpful, Bivognen the naughty boy. Among their best films are *Takt, Tone og Tosser/Bilberries/Misplaced Highbrows* (1925) and *Vester – Vov – Vov/People of the North Sea* (1927). Also worth mentioning are *Film, Flirt og Forlovelse/Film, Flirt and Engagement* (1921, their first film) and *I de gode gamle Dage/In the Good Old Days* (1940).

Fyrtaarnet og Bivognen were cinema's first comic duo to achieve international fame, long before the likes of Laurel and Hardy in Hollywood. Lauritzen also cast the pair in his most ambitious film, *Don Quixote* (1926), with Schenstrøm as Quixote and Madsen as Sancho Panza. In the late 1920s and the 1930s Schenstrøm and Madsen also appeared in British, German and Austrian films. They made their last film together in 1940. ME

Bib: Marguerite Engberg, *Fy og Bi* (1980).

G

GABIN, Jean
Jean Alexis Moncorgé; Paris 1904–76

French actor. The greatest male star in classic French cinema, Gabin is known primarily as the embodiment of the 1930s proletarian hero in such classics as Julien Duvivier's* *La Belle équipe* (1936), Jean Renoir's* *La Bête humaine* (1938) and Marcel Carné's* *Le Jour se lève* (1939), although he had a long and prolific career until his death in 1976.

Gabin started out as a music-hall singer, and his early films – *Chacun sa chance* (1930), *Paris-Béguin* (1931), *Les Gaietés de l'escadron/The Joys of the Squadron* (1932) – deploy theatrical aesthetics. With *La Bandera* (1935), which made him a star, he switched to (melo)dramatic roles, combining the signs of French working-class masculinity with those of a tragic, and often criminal, hero ('Oedipus in a cloth cap', as André Bazin* put it), epitomised in Duvivier's *Pépé le Moko* (1936). His minimalist, naturalistic acting and tremendous charisma smoothed over the contradictions inherent in this dual persona. Thus he symbolised both the hopes of the Popular Front* and the gloom of the approaching war, which he spent first in Hollywood (making *Moontide*, 1942, and *The Imposter*, 1944) and then in the Free French forces, earning a decoration. Gabin's postwar career was more uneven, films like *Martin Roumagnac* (1946, with Marlene Dietrich*) and Carné's 1950 *La Marie du port* failing to achieve the expected success. But he resoundingly regained his prewar popularity in 1954 with Jacques Becker's* *Touchez pas au grisbi/Honour Among Thieves* (1954) and Renoir's *French Cancan* (1955). From then on he was a pillar of mainstream cinema, alternating between populist dramas (*L'Air de Paris*, 1954, *Rue des prairies*, 1959, *Le Chat*, 1971), comedies (*Le Baron de l'écluse*, 1960) and thrillers (three Maigret films, *Mélodie en sous-sol/The Big Snatch*, 1963, and others). Often accused of betraying his prewar proletarian image in his roles, Gabin in the 1960s and 1970s nevertheless retained his popular audience, who identified with both his social rise and his enduring working-class identity. A Gabin museum opened in September 1992 in his childhood village of Mériel, north of Paris. GV

Bib: Claude Gauteur and Ginette Vincendeau, *Jean Gabin, Anatomie d'un mythe* (1993).

Other Films Include: *Cœur de Lilas* (1931); *Du haut en bas* (1933); *Zouzou* (1934); *Les Bas-fonds/The Lower Depths* (1936); *La Grande illusion, Gueule d'amour* (1937); *Quai des brumes* (1938); *Remorques/Stormy Waters* (1939–41); *Au-delà des grilles* (1949); *Le Plaisir, La Vérité sur Bébé Donge* (1952); *Razzia sur la chnouf, Chiens perdus sans collier, Gas-oil* (1955); *Des gens sans importance, Voici le temps des assassins, La Traversée de Paris/A Pig Across Paris* (1956); *Le Rouge est mis* (1957); *Les Misérables, Maigret tend un piège/Maigret Sets a Trap, En cas de malheur/Love is My Profession, Les Grandes familles* (1958); *Le Président* (1961); *Un singe en hiver/A Monkey in Winter* (1962); *Monsieur* (1964); *Le Tonnerre de Dieu* (1965); *Le Pacha* (1968); *Sous le signe du taureau, Le Clan des Siciliens/The Sicilian Clan* (1969); *La Horse* (1970); *Le Tueur* (1972); *L'Affaire Dominici* (1972); *Deux hommes dans la ville* (1974).

GADES, Antonio
Antonio Estevez Rodenas; 1936

Spanish actor, dancer and choreographer, who has worked extensively on stage. Discovered by the legendary dancer Pilar López in 1952, Gades forged an unprecedented career as one of the most innovative exponents of flamenco. A vocal opponent of the Franco regime, he worked abroad for long periods during the late 1960s and early 1970s, before returning to Spain to take over the artistic directorship of the Spanish National Ballet in 1978. A productive collaboration with Carlos Saura*, both as actor and choreographer, resulted in the much admired flamenco trilogy of *Bodas de sangre/Blood Wedding* (1981), *Carmen* (1983) and *El amor brujo/Love the Magician* (1985). MD

GAINSBOROUGH MELODRAMA

British genre, which appeared at Gainsborough Studios during and immediately after World War II, offering an escape from the proprieties of wartime propaganda and realism. The series of films was ushered in with *The Man in Grey* (1943), released as part of the varied programme which Edward Black had been developing at the studio since 1931. The box-office success of this film, and of *Fanny by Gaslight* (1944), another costume melodrama, encouraged the more entrepreneurial Maurice Ostrer to give the audience the 'escape' it wanted, and, recognising where his wartime market lay, to concentrate on women's pictures. Predictably, the policy brought critical contempt hand-in-hand with huge commercial success, establishing James Mason*, Stewart Granger* and Margaret Lockwood* as top box-office stars. Recent feminist criticism has rediscovered the Gainsborough melodramas, in particular the costume films. The interest lies in their difference from the overwhelmingly masculine wartime and postwar cinema. They may not offer correct, positive heroines, but they leave space for female fantasy, with Margaret Lockwood masquerading as a highwayman in *The Wicked Lady* (1945) and offering a seductive alternative to the moral probity of Phyllis Calvert's* version of femininity in *The Man in Grey* – 'I don't care for sugary things,' she says. The wicked ladies are punished in the end, but not before they have left their mark and cut a dash through decency and emotional restraint. The brief cycle of Gainsborough melodramas offers feminist criticism one of the few examples of the woman's film as a genre in postwar British cinema. JC

Bib: Sue Aspinall and Robert Murphy (eds.), *Gainsborough Melodrama*, BFI Dossier 18 (1983).

GALLONE, Carmine   Taggia 1886 – Rome 1972

Italian director. The most consistent feature of Gallone's long career as a director (from the 1910s to the 1960s) is an enduring interest in opera and a distinctively Italian operatic and melodramatic aesthetic. He began directing films for the rapidly expanding Cines* company in 1914. Often starring the *diva* Lyda Borelli [> DIVISMO], and sometimes his wife Soave Gallone, his early films were closely aligned with the tradition of stage melodrama, with a mainly static camera allowing full play to the *diva*'s eye-catching performance.

Along with Augusto Genina*, Gallone was one of the few Italian film-makers to find work in Italy's crumbling film industry in the early and mid-1920s. But after his costly and critically unacclaimed remake of the successful silent epic *Gli ultimi giorni di Pompei/The Last Days of Pompeii* (1926, co-dir. Amleto Palermi), he, like many Italian silent film directors, went to work abroad. After making films in Germany, France and Britain, Gallone returned to Italy to make *Casta diva/Chaste Goddess* (1935), a lavish historical melodrama about the life and times of the composer Vincenzo Bellini, which was awarded the Mussolini Cup for best Italian film at the Venice film festival. For the Italian film industry under Fascism, Gallone represented both the Italian cinema's heroic legacy and its potential international appeal, and in 1937 he was chosen to be co-writer and director of the epic *Scipione l'africano/Scipio Africanus*. Operatic in style and harking back to a silent film aesthetic, *Scipione l'africano* is one of the most vivid examples of the revival of the early historical epic during the 1930s and one most often linked to Fascist ideals; its central character has often been likened to Mussolini. Not all Gallone's films were so backward-looking. Although similar to Hollywood boxing films and family melodramas from the early 1940s, *Harlem* (1943) evinces many traits later valorised by neo-realism*. In the postwar years, however, he confined himself largely to 'film opera' – a flourishing Italian genre of the late 1940s and 1950s of which he was the major exponent. Gallone directed films about the lives of four famous composers – Verdi, Bellini (*Casta Diva*), Mozart (*Melodie eterne*, 1940), and Puccini – as well as *Casa Ricordi/House of Ricordi*, about the famous music publishing house, told through episodes from the lives of Rossini, Donizetti, Bellini, Puccini and Verdi. In the years following World War II, he also directed eight operatic adaptations. Gallone's consistency and adaptability are most vividly exemplified in his 1946 film *Davanti a lui tremava tutta Roma/Tosca* (1946), wherein performers of *Tosca* become embroiled in anti-Fascist activities. JHa

Other Films Include: *La donna nuda/The Nude Woman* (1914); *La falena/The Moth, Malombra* (1916); *Rendenzione/ Maria di Magdala/Redemption/Mary Magdalen* (1918); *Amleto e il suo clown/Hamlet and His Jester* (1920); *Nemesis* (1921); *Marcella* (1922); *I volti dell'amore/The Faces of Love, Il corsaro/The Corsair* [co-dir.] (1923); *La cavalcata ardente/ The Fiery Cavalcade* (1925); *Das Land ohne Frauen/Land without Women* (1929, Ger.); *Le Chant du marin* (1930, Fr.); *Un Soir de rafle* (1931, Fr.); *Giuseppe Verdi* (1938); *Il sogno di Butterfly/The Dream of Butterfly* (1939); *Manon Lescaut, Oltre l'amore/Beyond Love, Amami, Alfredo!/Love Me, Alfredo!* (1940); *L'amante segreta/The Secret Lover, Primo amore/First Love* (1941); *La regina di Navarra/The Queen of Navarre, Le due orfanelle/The Two Orphans, Odessa in fiamme/Odessa in Flames* (1942); *Harlem, Tristi amori/Sad Loves* (1943); *Il canto della vita/The Song of Life* (1945); *Rigoletto* (1946); *La signora dalle camelie/La traviata, Addio Mimì* (1947); *Il Trovatore, La leggenda di Faust/The Legend of Faust* (1949); *La forza del destino/The Force of Destiny* (1949); *Messalina* (1951); *Puccini, Cavalleria rusticana, Senza veli/Without Veils* (1953); *Casta diva* [remake], *Madame Butterfly* (1954); *Don Camillo e l'onorevole Peppone* (1955); *Michele Strogoff, Tosca* (1956); *Polikuska* (1958); *Cartagine in fiamme/Carthage Burning* (1959); *Don Camillo monsignore ... ma non troppo* (1961); *Carmen di Trastevere, La monaca di Monza/The Nun of Monza* (1962).

GANCE, Abel   Paris 1889–1981

French director, who worked as a scriptwriter (notably for Gaumont*) and actor before directing his first film in 1915. Many of his early works were war propaganda. With *Mater dolorosa* (1917) and especially *La Dixième symphonie* (1918), *J'Accuse* (1919) and *La Roue* (1921–23), Gance became a leading member of the French avant-garde*. His work was characterised by melodramatic excess (*La Dixième symphonie*), formal inventiveness (*La Roue*), and technical innovation (split screens, complex camera movements, experiments with sound), all trends which find their apotheosis in *Napoléon vu par Abel Gance/Napoléon* (1927), a five-hour epic comparable to Griffith's *The Birth of a Nation* (1915) in its combination of reactionary ideology and formal brilliance. *Napoléon* became an international art-house success in the early 1980s thanks to a restored version by British film historian Kevin Brownlow (shown with live music), which also helped revive early cinema studies.

Film history loses interest in Gance after the coming of sound, as he seemed to content himself with making sound versions of his earlier films (*Mater dolorosa*, 1932, *Napoléon Bonaparte*, 1934, and *J'accuse*, 1937) and directing Georges Milton* in the reactionary *Jérôme Perreau, héros des barricades* (1935). Yet he also made sumptuous melodramas, including the remarkable *Paradis perdu* (1939) and *La Vénus aveugle* (1943), whose qualities have been overshadowed by the fact that Gance was an avowed admirer of Pétain. In the 1950s, Gance turned to epics and swashbucklers, with *La Tour de Nesle* (1955), *Austerlitz* (1960) and *Cyrano et d'Artagnan* (1964). He also made historical epics for television. The importance of Gance, as Norman King put it, is not just as an innovator, but as a film-maker 'who blurred the distinction between the "artistic" and the "popular" '. GV

Bib: Norman King, *Abel Gance: A Politics of Spectacle* (1984).

Other Films Include: *La Folie du Docteur Tube* (1915); *Au secours!* (1923, with Max Linder*); *Le Roman d'un jeune homme pauvre* (1935); *Un grand amour de Beethoven/The Life and Loves of Beethoven* (1936); *Louise* (1939); *Le Capitaine Fracasse* (1943); *Magirama* (1956, short); *Bonaparte et la Révolution* (1971).

GANZ, Bruno
Zurich 1941

Swiss-born German actor. Working with Peter Stein's prestigious Berlin Schaubühne from 1970, Ganz became one of the most acclaimed young actors of German theatre. He left the ensemble to star in Eric Rohmer's* *Die Marquise von O/La Marquise d'O* (1976) and achieved international recognition in the role of Jonathan in Wim Wenders'* *Der amerikanische Freund/The American Friend* (1977). A key actor of the 1970s and 1980s, he became, along with Hanna Schygulla* and Klaus Kinski*, the international face of the New German Cinema*. After co-directing a documentary on his actor colleagues Bernhard Minetti and Curt Bois*, *Gedächtnis* (1982, with Otto Sander), he worked mainly for television in the mid-1980s. He appeared as one of the angels in Wim Wenders' *Der Himmel über Berlin/Wings of Desire* (1987) and in the same director's *In weiter Ferne, so nah!/Far Away, So Close* (1993). MW

Other Films Include: *Der Herr mit der schwarzen Melone* (1960); *Chikita* (1961); *Die Wildente* (1976); *Die linkshändige Frau* (1977); *The Boys from Brazil* (1978, US), *Nosferatu – Phantom der Nacht/Nosferatu the Vampyre* (1979); *Die Fälschung* (1981); *Ręce do góry/Hands Up* (1967, Pol., rel. 1981; dir. Jerzy Skolimowski*); *System ohne Schatten* (1983).

GAOS, Lola
Dolores Gaos González-Pola; Valencia 1921–93

Spanish actress with experience in theatre before appearing in major films casting her as witch, go-between or otherwise suspicious, sinister or marginalised characters. Her rasping voice, parched, multi-furrowed skin and weasel-like appearance were used by Luis Buñuel*, who cast her as one of the more transgressive beggars in *Viridiana* (1961) and the colluding housekeeper in *Tristana* (1970). Above all, she was the monstrous Oedipal mother in José Luis Borau's* *Furtivos/Poachers* (1975), refusing to release her son from her overpowering influence, symbol of the regime's grip on the entire nation. PWE

GARAT, Henri
Henri Garascu; Paris 1902 – Hyères 1959

French actor and singer. Garat's immense popularity in the early 1930s is matched only by the critical contempt in which he was held (Henri Jeanson* called him 'the suburbs of Maurice Chevalier'*). After a spell as Mistinguett's partner in the 1920s Parisian music halls, Garat starred in French versions of German-filmed operettas (notably *Le Chemin du paradis* [*Die Drei von der Tankstelle*], 1930, dir. Wilhelm Thiele, and *Le Congrès s'amuse* [*Der Kongreß tanzt*], 1931, dir. Erik Charell, both co-starring Lilian Harvey). With his athletic matinée-idol looks, Garat became the new sentimental hero; women threw themselves at him, his kisses were auctioned for charity. A Hollywood-style French star whose life mirrored the fantasy world of his films, he failed in the US. As the popularity of filmed operettas declined, so did his. Apart

from the amusing *Un mauvais garçon* (1936, with Darrieux*), his career petered out. Garat slid into drugs, serial marriages and gambling; he died poor and forgotten. GV

GARBO, Greta
Greta Gustafsson; Stockholm 1905 – New York 1990

Swedish-born American actress. Greta Garbo is one of the great icons of film history, the epitome of stardom itself, indissolubly linked with the golden age of Hollywood. In a celebrated essay, Roland Barthes compared her face to a mask, 'an archetype of the human face', for its beauty but also for its uncanny perfection and mystery. Her short Swedish career started in different circumstances, though. From a poor background and orphaned at thirteen, she was chosen in 1921 to play in a publicity film for the department store where she worked. Another commercial appearance won her a lead in a short slapstick comedy, *Luffar-Petter/Peter the Tramp* (1922), directed by Erik Petschler, on the strength of which she gained a scholarship to acting school at Stockholm's Royal Dramatic Theatre. Here she was discovered by her mentor, Mauritz Stiller*, who took charge of her, changing her name to Garbo and launching her with a part in *Gösta Berlings saga (del I och II)/The Story of Gosta Berling (pts I and II)* (1924). Ironically, her subsequent career was changed by a project with Stiller in Turkey which never materialised; instead they went to Berlin, where Stiller persuaded G. W. Pabst* to hire his protégée for a role in *Die freudlose Gasse/Joyless Street* (1925, starring Asta Nielsen*). In Berlin they also met the talent-hunting Louis B. Mayer of MGM, who on Stiller's insistence reluctantly agreed to sign Garbo as well as her director-Svengali to a contract. In Hollywood their collaboration lasted through Garbo's first US vehicle, *The Torrent* (1926), in which Stiller, as he had done in *Joyless Street*, coached her off set, and just ten days of shooting of her second, *The Temptress* (also 1926), before he was replaced as director. But their paths had already decisively diverged, Stiller returning embittered and ill to Europe in 1928 while Garbo was slipping out of Swedish film history into the international pantheon of movie myths. LGA

Other American Films Include: *Flesh and the Devil* (1926); *Wild Orchids, The Kiss* (1929); *Anna Christie* (1930); *Mata Hari* (1932); *Queen Christina* (1933); *Anna Karenina* (1935); *Camille* (1936); *Ninotchka* (1939); *Two-Faced Woman* (1941).

GARCI, José Luis
José Luis Garci Muñoz; Madrid 1944

Spanish film critic, **writer**, **scriptwriter and director** of television and feature films. His directorial debut was *Asignatura pendiente/Unfinished Business* (1977), the story of two adults recalling their childhood and adolescence circumscribed by the restrictive atmosphere of Franco's Spain. The expression of the protagonists' resentment at their psychological and politically deprived youth, as well as their missed opportunities, addressed the sense of unfinished business of a whole generation of Spaniards during the period of transition to democracy. Garci's *Volver a empezar/Starting Over* (1982) won Spain its first Oscar for best foreign-language film. Strongly influenced by classical Hollywood, *Volver a empezar* is characterised less memorably by its critique of the past than by its sense of nostalgia, both in the musical score and in the story of the return to his native Spain of a Nobel prize-winning professor of literature exiled in the USA. RM

Other Films Include: *El crack/The Crack* (1980); *Sesión continua/Double Feature* (1984).

GARCÍA BERLANGA, Luis   Valencia 1921

Spanish director, whose popularity at home has not been matched abroad but who nevertheless stands with his one-time collaborator Juan Antonio Bardem* as a major figure in the Spanish cinema of the 1950s and 1960s, serving, as Katherine Kovács observed, as a 'link between the generation of Buñuel* and that of Carlos Saura*'. Between 1947 and 1950 Berlanga studied at the IIEC*. The formative influence of Italian neo-realism* [> SPANISH NEO-REALISM], in conjunction with his own politically motivated reaction against the American films that from the early 1950s dominated the Spanish market, was immediately apparent in his first two features, *Esa pareja feliz/That Happy Couple* (1951, co-dir. Bardem) and *¡Bienvenido, Mr Marshall!/Welcome Mr Marshall!* (1952). The latter is an intriguing reflection on questions of national and regional identity, and, despite its comic surface, a bitter indictment of Francoist policies. Perhaps Berlanga's most accomplished picture, however, was his 1963 slice of 'esperpento' (grotesque drama), *El verdugo/The Executioner,* which in 1992 was voted (with Buñuel's *Viridiana*) the best Spanish film ever in the film journal *Dirigido*. Co-scripted with Rafael Azcona* and Ennio Flaiano*, *El verdugo* is a catalogue of Berlangian themes (solitude, lack of community, the suppression of the individual, the need to compromise), capturing what José María Latorre has termed 'the tragi-comic sense of existence'. In the 1970s and 1980s Berlanga enjoyed popular success with *La escopeta nacional/The National Shotgun* (1977), which spawned two sequels, and *La vaquilla/The Heifer* (1985). In addition to film-making, Berlanga has lectured at the Escuela Oficial de Cinematografía* and, until 1983, was head of the Spanish Filmoteca. Recently he has worked in radio and publishing. RM

GARDIN, Vladimir R.   Moscow 1877 – Leningrad 1965

Russian director, actor and teacher. Gardin started a film career in 1913, directing with Yakov Protazanov* the popular romantic melodrama *Klyuchi schast'ya/The Keys to Happiness.* In the pre-Revolutionary period he was best known for adaptations of Russian literary classics, including Tolstoy's *Anna Karenina, Kreitserova sonata/The Kreutzer Sonata* (both 1914) and *Voina i mir/War and Peace* (co-directed with Protazanov), and Turgenev's *Nakanune/On the Eve* (both 1915). In 1919 Gardin helped found the State Film School (later VGIK*), where he taught for many years and which he later also headed. He continued directing after the Revolution but his films, made in the tradition of melodrama and popular with audiences, were criticised by the avant-garde for their artistic conservatism and the woodenness of their acting. Works such as *Slesar' i kantsler/The Locksmith and the Chancellor* (1924), *Krest i mauzer/The Cross and the Mauser* (1925), *Medvezh'ya svad'ba/The Bear's Wedding* (1926, co-dir. Konstantin Eggert*) and, above all, Gardin's version of the life of Pushkin, *Poet i tsar'/The Poet and the Tsar,* became synonymous with all that was supposedly wrong with the traditions of pre-Revolutionary Russian cinema. Nevertheless he continued teaching and appeared in several major films, including Fridrikh Ermler's* and Sergei Yutkevich's* *Vstrechnyi/Counterplan* (1932), Vladimir Petrov's* *Pëtr I/Peter the Great* (1937–39) and Mikhail Romm's* *Sekretnaya missiya/Secret Mission* (1950). RT

GASSMAN, Vittorio   Genoa 1922

Italian actor, who was established as one of Italy's best stage performers before his cinema career took off with his fourth film, Giuseppe De Santis'* *Riso amaro/Bitter Rice* (1949). Gassman has sometimes been criticised for overacting but, as David Thomson more generously puts it, his 'effusion seems quite natural and innocent'. His good looks, combined with a talent for comedy, led to many characterisations as handsome rogues and comic cads.

Never quite a star of international renown, Gassman attracted attention with his wedding to Shelley Winters in 1952. They made one film together, *Mambo* (It./US) in 1954, and divorced later that year. After a handful of films for MGM, including *Sombrero* (1952) and *Rhapsody* (1953), Gassman went back to Italy where he starred in, and co-directed with Francesco Rosi*, a film version of Jean-Paul Sartre's play *Kean* (1957). The theatre continued to play an important part in his professional life; he formed his own company, Teatro Popolare Italiano, in 1960. Mario Monicelli's* *I soliti ignoti/Persons Unknown* (1958) proved to be a watershed in Gassman's film career. Displaying a great talent for comedy, he then concentrated on humorous roles, notably in a brilliant series of films with Dino Risi*, including *Il sorpasso/The Easy Life* (1962) and *I mostri/The Monsters* (1963); he won the Best Actor award at Cannes in 1975 for his part in Risi's* *Profumo di donna/Scent of a Woman* (1974). He continued a regular collaboration with Risi, and made two films with Robert Altman in the US, *A Wedding* (1978) and *Quintet* (1979) as well as one with Alain Resnais*, *La Vie est un roman/Life is a Bed of Roses* (1982, Fr.). Gassman won the Nastro d'argento (Silver Ribbon, Italy's equivalent of the Oscars) for Best Actor on two occasions, first for *Kean*, then for *Lo zio indegno/The Uncle* (1989). He published a collection of poems, *Vocalizzi*, in 1988. SH

GAUMONT, Léon
Paris 1864 – Sainte-Maxime 1946

French pioneer. Léon Gaumont founded the Comptoir Général de la Photographie – later Gaumont et Cie – in 1895 to market equipment. His company, which he ran with an iron hand, expanded spectacularly until World War I, forming the other French 'empire' (symbolised by a daisy logo) to rival Pathé*. Gaumont's success was based on the successful development and marketing of others' inventions. With the backing of major financiers (including Gustave Eiffel), Gaumont developed the camera-projector Chronophotographe and in 1897 an improved version for 35mm film, the Chronographe. He experimented with sound (Chronophone), showing synchronised sound films as early as 1902. His sound experiments included a system used for *L'Eau du Nil* (1928), but all eventually failed. In 1905 Gaumont built the then largest studio in the world, a 'glass cathedral' with the most advanced technology of the time. From 1907, Gaumont worked on colour and expanded into distribution and exhibition, building a chain of Parisian and provincial cinemas; its jewel in the crown was the Gaumont-Palace in Paris (opened in 1911, demolished in 1972) which, with over 3,000 seats, was the largest in the world. By 1914 Gaumont had 2,100 employees and its capital was FF4m, both large figures by French standards (although Pathé employed 5,000). A studio was built in Nice (La Victorine), and subsidiaries established in Britain, eastern Europe and the US. Legend has it that Léon Gaumont was uninterested in films (there is some dispute over this) and delegated film production to his secretary Alice Guy*. As well as making her own films, Guy hired and trained a team of film-makers – including Louis Feuillade*, Victorin Jasset, Emile Cohl* and Léonce Perret, joined later by Jacques Feyder*, Marcel L'Herbier*, Henri Fescourt and Léon Poirier – who developed realist and crime series (especially Feuillade's), biblical scenes and comic series such as *Calino*, *Léonce* (Perret), *Zigoto* and *Onésime*. In addition, Gaumont shot newsreels (Gaumont-actualités) and educational films (Encyclopédie Gaumont).

Like Pathé, Gaumont suffered a crisis provoked by World War I and competition from Hollywood, although for a time it was supported by foreign capital. Foreign subsidiaries such as Gaumont-British maintained an independent existence. Gaumont retired in 1929; the firm merged with two others to form Gaumont-Franco-Film-Aubert (GFFA), which went bankrupt in 1938. A new injection of funds revived the firm during World War II, and Gaumont has been producing and distributing films since. Today Gaumont is still one of the most powerful names in French cinema. GV

GAUP, Nils
Kautokeino 1955

Norwegian-Lapp director and actor. One of the founders of a Lapp theatre in 1985, Gaup wrote one Lapp play and acted in several others, as well as in Norwegian films in the 1980s. His directorial breakthrough, *Veiviseren/Pathfinder* (1987), takes its inspiration from a twelfth-century Lapp legend about Aigin, a young boy who returns from a hunting expedition to find his sister and parents slaughtered by ruthless tribesmen known as Tschudes. Aigin takes his revenge by leading the Tschudes into a lethal trap. The boy responds intuitively to the symbols and supernatural signs that govern Lapp culture and earns the title of 'pathfinder' in another Lapp encampment saved from the Tschudes. The sparse dialogue is in Sami, the Lapp language. Erling Thurmann-Andersen's Panavision camera takes full advantage of the flat tundra landscape, evoking the classic Norwegian film theme of man's relationship to nature. The success of *Veiviseren* led to a contract with Disney and the co-production of *Håkon Håkonsen/ Shipwrecked* (1990), a family-oriented action film. *Hodet over vannet/Head Above Water* followed in 1994. KS

GAY CINEMA IN EUROPE – see LESBIAN AND GAY CINEMA IN EUROPE

GEBÜHR, Otto
Kettwig 1877 – Wiesbaden 1954

German actor, famous for his incarnation of King Frederick II of Prussia. His film debut in 1917 was in an Oskar Messter* production (*Der Richter*), where his striking physical resemblance to portraits of Frederick II was first noticed, leading to *Fridericus Rex* (1920–23). Although Gebühr portrayed other historical figures – Blücher in *Waterloo* (1928), the king of Saxony in *Bismarck* (1940) – his Frederick made him a legendary figure of the German cinema of the 1920s and 1930s. Putting in personal appearances, especially in small towns, dressed as the king and receiving standing ovations from a near-hysterical audience, he gratified the national craving for the 'spirit of Potsdam' and served the Right's propaganda machine. MW

GELABERT, Fructuoso
Fructuoso Gelabert Badiella; Barcelona 1874–1955

Spanish director, one of the pioneers of Spanish cinema. Having built his own camera and projector, he made his first film, *Riña en un café/Fight in a Café*, in 1897. In the same year, encouraged by the results of this venture, he made *Salida de la Iglesia Parroquial de Sans/Leaving the Church of St Maria de Sans* (1897) and *Salida de los trabajadores de 'la España Industrial'/Workers Leaving 'España Industrial'* (1897). He then directed newsreels and documentaries, as well as fiction films, including *La Dolores* (1908). Like Segundo de Chomón*, he experimented with models and miniature sets. His *Vuelta de la Reina Madre y del Rey Niño a Barcelona/Visit to Barcelona by Doña María Cristina and Don Alfonso XIII* (1898) was the first Spanish film sold abroad (to Pathé* in Paris). PWE

GELOVANI, Mikhail G.
Lasuria, Georgia [Russian Empire] 1893 – Moscow 1956

Georgian Soviet actor, who began his stage career at the Rustaveli Theatre in Tiflis (Tbilisi) in 1913 and later moved to the Moscow Art Theatre. He started acting in films in 1924

but is remembered for his virtual monopoly of the portrayal of Stalin in such central films of the personality cult as Sergei Yutkevich's* *Chelovek s ruzh'ëm/The Man with a Gun*, Mikhail Chiaureli's* *Velikoe zarevo/The Great Dawn* (both 1938), *Klyatva/The Vow* (1946) and *Padenie Berlina/The Fall of Berlin* (1949), Grigori Kozintsev's* and Leonid Trauberg's* *Vyborgskaya storona/The Vyborg Side* (1939), Mikhail Kalatozov's* *Valerii Chkalov* (1941) and the Vasiliev* brothers' *Oborona Tsaritsyna/The Defence of Tsaritsyn* (1942). He also directed a number of minor films. RT

GENINA, Augusto   Rome 1892–1957

Italian director, scriptwriter, and producer. Along with Carmine Gallone*, the prolific Augusto Genina was one of the few Italian directors of silent films to pursue a long career in sound cinema, in his case up to the 1950s. Like Gallone, too, he worked abroad during the 1920s and early 1930s.

Genina entered Italian film-making at the age of 20, peddling ideas to film companies. By 1913 he had sold stories to Celio Films, and soon after worked as writer and director for Cines*. He scripted most of the films he directed over this decade, including his first, *La moglie di sua eccellenza/His Excellency's Wife* (1913), shot in Barcelona and released by Cines as two separate films. After a series of films for Cines in 1914, he worked for a variety of companies throughout Italy. In 1920 he began co-producing many of his films and in 1922 he was appointed head of the new Unione Cinematografica Italiana, a trust that mediated subsidies from Italian banks to the film industry. Genina's films during the 1910s and early 1920s were romantic melodramas, many adapted from popular literature and drama, mostly about eccentric upper-class characters. His first major success, *La signorina Ciclone* (1916), involved the European escapades of a wealthy American heiress. During the middle and late 1920s, Genina increasingly developed contacts outside Italy. His next major success, *Cyrano de Bergerac* (1923, co-dir. Mario Camerini*), was released in France in a three-colour version. Genina's career really flourished between 1929 and 1937, when he worked mostly in Germany and France, his films influenced by the styles of these national cinemas. *Prix de beauté/Miss Europa* (1930) strikingly exemplifies the influence of a European modernist aesthetic, with a story by G. W. Pabst*, script by René Clair* and Genina, sets by Robert Gys, and Louise Brooks* in the lead. Its consonance with the artistic strategies of the avant-garde* cinema of Europe at the time is most evident in its self-reflexive use of sound and image and meta-narrative about cinema, stardom and mass culture; Brooks plays a rising film star whose death occurs during a screening of her first sound film, her gleefully singing on-screen image counterposed to her lifeless form just off-screen. Despite being offered a contract by Paramount in 1935, Genina returned to Italy, where the film industry had begun to revive, and became involved in films which valorised Italian nationalism. On the one hand were colonialist epics such as *Squadrone bianco/White Squadron* (1936), *L'assedio dell'Alcazar/The Siege of Alcazar* (1940) and *Bengasi* (1942). On the other hand, *Naples au baiser de feu* (1937, Fr.) and *Castelli in aria/Ins blaue leben/Castles in the Air* (1939,

Ger./It.) offered touristic visions of Italy as an enchanted land.

Genina directed relatively few films after World War II. The most famous was *Cielo sulla palude/Heaven over the Marshes* (1949), based on the life of Maria Goretti (beatified by the Catholic Church in 1947), and using neo-realist* techniques such as non-professional actors to accentuate the bleakness of Goretti's poor, rural community. However, as film critic Guido Aristarco noted in 1949, the characters' acceptance of their condition makes this film quite different ideologically from other neo-realist films. Furthermore, as André Bazin* observed, the contradictions inherent in the neo-realist treatment of a saint makes this one of the most curious Italian films of the period. JHa

Other Films Include: *La doppia ferita/The Double Wound, Lulu* (1915); *Il principe dell'impossibile/Prince of the Impossible, Femmina/Female, Addio giovinezza!/Farewell Youth!* (1918); *Lo scaldino/The Warming-pan* (1919); *I tre sentimentali/Three Sentimentals* (1920); *Marito, moglie, e ...* (1922, co-dir.); *Il corsaro/The Corsair* (1923, co-dir.); *Il focolare spento/The Cold Hearth* (1925); *L'ultimo lord/The Last Lord, Addio giovinezza!/Inconstant Youth* [remake] (1926); *Quartier Latin* (1928, Fr.); *Les Amours de minuit* (1930, Fr.); *Paris-béguin* (1931, Fr.); *La Femme en homme* [remake of *L'ultimo lord*] (1932, Fr.); *Ne sois pas jalouse, Nous ne sommes plus des enfants* (1934, Fr.); *Vergiss mein nicht/Forget Me Not* [Ger.], *Blumen aus Nizza, La gondala delle chimera/Phantom Gondola* (1936, Austr.); *Frauenliebe-Frauenleid* [Ger.]; *Naples au baiser de feu* [Fr.] (1937); **in Italy**: *Castelli in aria/Castles in the Air*, also Ger. version directed by Genina, *Ins blaue Leben* (1939); *L'edera/Devotion* (1950); *Tre storie proibite/Three Forbidden Stories* (1952); *Maddalena* (1953); *Frou-frou* (1955, Fr./It.).

GEORGE, Götz   Berlin 1938

German actor. Son of the actors Heinrich George* and Berta Drews, George made his screen debut in *Wenn der weisse Flieder blüht* (1953) and through the 1960s specialised in juvenile daredevils and young heroes in moral conflict, as in Wolfgang Staudte's* *Herrenpartie* (1964). His huge popularity, however, is chiefly due to his long-running performance as the unconventional Inspector Schimanski in the television crime series *Tatort* (1981–91). He continued to work in film, transferring Schimanski to the screen in *Zahn um Zahn* (1985). In Helmut Dietl's satirical look at the public scandal around the faked Hitler diaries, *Schtonk* (1992), George demonstrated a previously unrevealed talent as a comic actor. MW

GEORGE, Heinrich   Heinz Georg Schulz; Stettin 1893 – Sachsenhausen 1946

German actor, epitome of bull-necked and bullying German masculinity. An extremely able man of the theatre, George acted on and produced for stage and screen from 1921. Also directing at Erwin Piscator's Volksbühne (1925–28), and at the Heidelberg Festspiele (1926–38), he was a member of the Communist Party until 1933, when he joined the National Socialists. In his films, George's characters hide sensitivity behind brutal behaviour (*Das Meer*, 1927, *Manolescu*, 1929, *Berlin-Alexanderplatz*, 1931), but they can also be ruthless (*Jud Süss*, 1940). Playing the Communist father in *Hitlerjunge Quex* (1933), he might have been dramatising his own political confusion, but thereafter George became one of the Nazi cinema's key dramatic actors (*Der Biberpelz*, 1937, *Heimat*, 1938), in charge of his own production unit at Tobis from 1942. Arrested by Soviet troops in 1945, he died in the Sachsenhausen camp of appendicitis. He was honoured with a commemorative stamp for the centenary of his birth. KP/MW

Bib: Erich M. Berger, *Heinrich George im Film seiner Zeit* (1975).

GERASIMOV, Sergei A.   Sarafanovo, Russia 1906 – Moscow 1985

Soviet director and scriptwriter. Gerasimov began his career in 1924 as an actor with FEKS (Factory of the Eccentric Actor) and appeared in all the silent films made by Grigori Kozintsev* and Leonid Trauberg*. His most important films as director were: *Semero smelykh/The Brave Seven* (1936), *Komsomol'sk* (1938), *Bol'shaya zemlya/The Great Earth* (1944), *Molodaya gvardiya/The Young Guard* (1948) and *Tikhii Don/And Quiet Flows the Don* (1957–58). As a teacher at VGIK* he exerted a major influence on younger directors, and between 1944 and 1946 he headed the Central Studio of Documentary Films, even though his own career was in features. RT

GERMAN EXPRESSIONISM – see EXPRESSIONIST FILM

GERMAN MOUNTAIN FILMS – see HEIMATFILM

GERMAN STREET FILMS – see STRASSENFILME

GERMAN WOMEN's CINEMA – see FRAUENFILM

GERMAN, Alexei Yu.   Leningrad 1938

Russian director. The son of writer Yuri German, he graduated in 1960 from the Leningrad State Institute of Theatre, Music and Cinema, where he had studied with Grigori Kozintsev*. From 1964 he worked at Lenfilm, where in 1968 he co-directed *Sed'moi sputnik/The Seventh Companion* with Grigori Aronov. During the next twenty years German made only three feature films, each of them beset by delays, censorship and shelving, but they have brought him a reputation as one of the key directors of the period. *Proverka na doro-*

gakh/Trial on the Road/Roadcheck was made in 1971 originally as *Operation 'Happy New Year!'*, from a story by German's father. It describes the partisans' struggle against the Nazis without false heroics and gives a sympathetic portrait of an ex-deserter who eventually dies bravely with the partisans. It was immediately attacked by artistic censors for its lack of 'heroism', and banned, despite praise from Kozintsev, Iosif Kheifits* and the writer Konstantin Simonov. The film was not released until 1986. *Dvadtsat' dnei bez voiny/Twenty Days Without War*, from a story by Simonov about a war correspondent's leave from the front in Tashkent, was made in 1976, and its unconventional picture of the war also led to attacks. It was called 'the shame of Lenfilm' but surreptitiously released after being shelved for a year. German's most ambitious film, *Moi drug Ivan Lapshin/My Friend Ivan Lapshin*, also from a story by his father, had a long and tortuous history. The screenplay was written in 1969, but German was not allowed to make it until 1979. Though the story, about a criminal investigator, was set in Leningrad, German moved it to a remote provincial town and introduced other changes, setting the film in 1935. 'The main thing for us,' he later said, 'was not the detective intrigue, nor the love story, but the time itself. It was the time we were making the film about.' *Moi drug Ivan Lapshin* also succeeds extraordinarily in capturing the ambiguity of the period, the contrast between buoyant sloganising and the bleak horror seeping in from the margins, with visually stunning black and white photography and remarkable acting. It, too, caused scandals at Lenfilm and was shelved until 1984. When eventually released, it proved a major popular and critical hit. In a 1987 poll, nine out of ten Soviet film critics selected it as the best Soviet film of all time, and its aesthetic influence can be seen in such works as Yevgeny Tsymbal's* *Zashchitnik Sedov/Defence Counsel Sedov* and Vitaly Kanevsky's* *Zamri, umri, voskresni/Don't move, Die and Rise Again!* German, however, made no new films in the 1980s. At the end of the decade he was very influential as head of a unit at Lenfilm dedicated to advancing the careers of young film-makers. In the early 1990s he began work on *Khrustalev, mashinu!/Khrustalev, My Car!*, a project set in 1953, just before the death of Stalin. JGf

GERMANY

I – THE GERMAN CINEMA AS IMAGE AND IDEA
Germany can look back on as long a film history as any other country, and yet, more often than not, its cinema has seemed ambivalent even in its achievements. The disasters of German history this century have left their mark on the cinema, and even more so on the image and idea we have of it. With political unification, the moment may have come also to stress the continuities: of personnel, genres and film policy, as well as of the industry's and the state's role in creating a 'national' cinema, across the divides of popular cinema and art cinema, but also bridging the post-World War II developments in East and West Germany. Thus, looking back at a hundred years of cinema today requires rather more radical a shift of accent and perspective than would have seemed either possible or necessary even twenty years ago, when the phenomenon of

L'Argent (France, 1929; Marcel L'Herbier):
Brigitte Helm

Leningrad Cowboys Go America (Finland, 1989;
...ki Kaurismäki)

Cronaca di un amore/Story of a Love Affair
(Italy, 1950; Michelangelo Antonioni):
Lucia Bosé

Ferne, so nah!/Far Away, So Close (Germany, 1993;
Wim Wenders): Otto Sander

Tristana (Spain/France, 1970; Luis Buñuel): Catherine Deneuve,
Fernando Rey

Misère au Borinage/Borinage (Belgium, 1933; Henri Storck/
Joris Ivens)

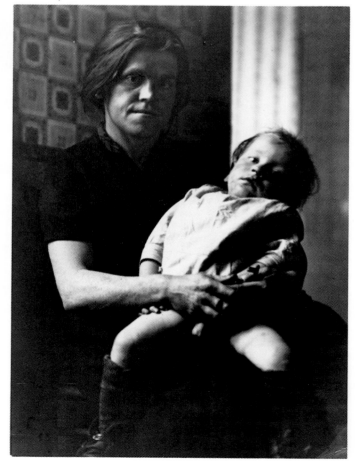

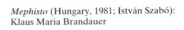
Mephisto (Hungary, 1981; István Szabó):
Klaus Maria Brandauer

Aniki-Bóbó (Portugal, 1942; Manoel de Oliveira)

Dom za vešanje/Time of the Gypsies (Yugoslavia, 1989; Emir Kusturica):
Ljubica Adzovic

Intermezzo (Sweden, 1936; Gustaf Molander): Ekman Gösta (Sr),
Ingrid Bergman

Ingeborg Holm (Sweden, 1913; Victor Sjöström)

Ossessione (Italy, 1942; Luchino Visconti):
Massimo Girotti

The Crying Game (UK/Ireland, 1992; Neil Jordan)

the 'New German Cinema'* briefly focused international attention on a film tradition which seemed to have taken leave of its – and our – senses a long time ago. We now can look with fresh eyes at the beginnings of the cinema, and adopt an outlook that spans the whole of German cinema, reintroducing its technicians and crafts(wo)men as well as its directors. We can give due weight to the institutions and their often remarkable continuity across the historical breaks, and one needs to find the right balance between the stars-and-genre cinema and the art-and-*auteur* cinema. Now that more material has become available on the early period, we can afford to pay a little less attention to the best-known periods: the 1920s and the 1970s.

The beginnings up to 1917

Although it seems perverse to argue that the cinema was not inaugurated in France, it is nonetheless true that the brothers Max and Emil Skladanowsky* showed projected moving images on their 'Bioskop' to a paying public at the Berlin Wintergarten on 1 November 1895, almost two months earlier than the Lumière* brothers. But the Wilhelmine cinema's first pioneer was Oskar Messter*, the first universal movie man: inventor-director-producer-distributor-exhibitor all in one. Messter's production companies were eventually absorbed by Ufa* in 1917, but by then he had covered the entire range of popular film subjects and genres: scenic views and *actualités*, detective films and social dramas, domestic melodrama and historical epic, romantic comedies, operas and operettas. Actors who started with Messter were among the leading names of the German silent era: Henny Porten*, Lil Dagover*, Ossi Oswalda, Emil Jannings*, Harry Liedke, Harry Piel*, Reinhold Schünzel*, Conrad Veidt*. Messter shaped much that would remain the bedrock of the German commercial cinema. Its other pioneer was Paul Davidson*, starting from the opposite end. On his way up from distribution to production, he acquired the first chain of picture palaces, the first international star (Asta Nielsen*), the first purpose-built glasshouse studio, and he also gave Germany's first world-class director, Ernst Lubitsch*, his start in pictures. His outlook was international, trading with Pathé* and Gaumont* and closing deals with Nordisk* and Cines*.

An art cinema (the *Autorenfilm*) has existed since 1913, thanks to Nordisk and other Danish imports, and in the films of Paul Wegener*, a first (neo-romantic, literary) notion of national cinema made its appearance, already fixing the topics, moods and styles which to this day are most persistently associated with the German cinema, under the somewhat misleading name of 'Expressionism' [> EXPRESSIONIST FILM]. With Wegener's massive bulk and scowling face, the brooding male entered the German cinema, setting the example for many other actors: Jannings, as well as Werner Krauß*, Fritz Kortner* and Heinrich George*.

Expressionism, Weimar cinema and Ufa

The expressionist cinema of the early 1920s is regarded as the isolated pinnacle of German screen art, yet the films are often judged severely, by historians such as Siegfried Kracauer* and Lotte Eisner*, for the political message they are said to convey. Paul Wegener's* *Der Golem/The Golem* (1915), Robert Wiene's* *Das Cabinet des Dr. Caligari/The Cabinet of Dr. Caligari* (1920), Fritz Lang's* *Der müde Tod/Destiny*

(1921), Paul Leni's* *Das Wachsfigurenkabinett/Waxworks* (1924), F. W. Murnau's* *Nosferatu – Eine Symphonie des Grauens/Nosferatu the Vampire* (1922) and *Der letzte Mann/The Last Laugh* (1924), Henrik Galeen's *Der Student von Prag/The Student of Prague* (1926) and Lang's *Metropolis* (1927) have all been variously interpreted as products of frustrated impulses and social unrest, foreshadowing future monsters or reflecting a troubled body politic. Clearly, German national cinema is more than a history of successive styles or directors' masterpieces: it belongs to the complex and intriguing phenomenon known as Weimar*, lasting from 1919 to 1933. Its defining style could also have been 'New Objectivity', and not merely for the latter half of the decade. The sexually and socially explicit films of Richard Oswald*, Reinhold Schünzel's* naturalist *Das Mädchen aus der Ackerstrasse* (1920), Fritz Lang's 'reflection of the times' *Dr. Mabuse, der Spieler/Dr Mabuse, the Gambler* (1922), Joe May's *Tragödie der Liebe* (1923), E. A. Dupont's* *Varieté/Variety* (1925), whose atmospheric and romantically sordid realism was equalled in America only by Stroheim, and the sardonic, gritty films of G. W. Pabst* (*Die freudlose Gasse/Joyless Street*, 1925, *Die Liebe der Jeanne Ney/The Loves of Jeanne Ney*, 1927, and *Die Büchse der Pandora/Pandora's Box*, 1929) are as convincing a German national tradition, leading to the proletarian films of Piel Jutzi's *Mutter Krausens Fahrt ins Glück/Mother Krause's Journey to Happiness* (1929), the *Straßenfilme**, and 'cross-section' films like Walther Ruttmann's* *Berlin die Sinfonie der Großstadt/Berlin – Symphony of a City* (1927) and *Melodie der Welt* (1929).

At the time, national cinema was defined by neither of these styles. The question was, rather, how to create a viable film industry which could break the boycott against German film exports after the war in Europe, and perhaps break into the US market. Setting up Ufa was a national(ist) attempt at a massive concentration of capital and resources, in order to pursue a strategy of product differentiation between the domestic market, the international commercial market and the international art cinema (also a market). Its champion was Erich Pommer*, who helped create a production and distribution network which, however briefly, seemed to pose the only challenge to Hollywood hegemony in Europe. While Ufa's overall strategy might not have been achieved, despite a mixture of legislative, film-diplomatic (Film Europe*) and financial measures, the German film industry in the 1920s built up an impressive technical infrastructure, with geniuses like Guido Seeber* and other crafts(wo)men (cinematographers, art directors, composers) forming a professional and creative avant-garde much envied and emulated elsewhere, and leading to emigration*. The competitively weakest aspect of German films was felt by American critics to be story construction, despite scriptwriters as notable as Carl Mayer* and Thea von Harbou*: an absence of linear narrative causality, obliquely motivated characters, complicated flashback structures made German films seem slow, murky, confused – the reverse side of its virtues: psychologically subtle, introspective, atmospheric, moody and uncanny.

The conversion to sound

The coming of sound seemed set to dispel the peculiarities of the German style. Initially developed by German engineers

(Tri-Ergon) but not exploited until the Americans had shown the way, optical sound was introduced relatively quickly, thanks to the new management at Ufa under Ludwig Klitzsch having injected capital into the ailing giant in 1927–28, and astute deals with rivals both at home (Tobis-Klangfilm) and abroad preventing costly patent wars. While critical successes like *Der blaue Engel/The Blue Angel* (1930), *Die Dreigroschenoper/The Threepenny Opera* (1931) and *M – Eine Stadt sucht ihren Mörder/M* (1931) may be remembered as the best examples of early German sound cinema, Ufa's international hits were musicals and comedies, usually shot in multi-language versions (German, French and English), such as *Der Kongreß tanzt* (1931), *Die Drei von der Tankstelle* (1930), *Bomben auf Monte Carlo* (1931), *Ich bei Tag und du bei Nacht* (1932). Fast-paced and witty, they carried across the world an image of Germany as youthful, sporty and vital. The sound cinema also profiled new faces, with female stars such as Renate Müller*, Lilian Harvey*, Marika Rökk* beginning to draw level with their male colleagues (Willy Fritsch*, Heinz Rühmann*, Hans Albers*) and not only ensuring that the German film industry was by far the strongest in Europe (with over 500 films produced between 1930 and 1933), but also drawing talents away from Rome and Paris to Berlin throughout the 1930s.

The Nazi years
The major break in German film history is unquestionably 1933. Yet despite the political changes brought about by Hitler's seizure of power, and the exodus it imposed on Jewish film personnel [> EMIGRATION AND EUROPEAN CINEMA], Nazi film policy only gradually transformed the business into an instrument of direct state propaganda. The German film industry's reputation as sophisticated, technically innovative and perfectionist did not cease in 1933, but continued right until 1945. The best propaganda, according to Joseph Goebbels, was popular entertainment which could express the regime's populist ideology as an attainable ideal, while making no mention of the totalitarian reality. A new generation of often gifted directors embraced (or as they would later claim, braced themselves for) the task, such as Veit Harlan*, Wolfgang Liebeneiner*, Gustav Ucicky*, Hans Steinhoff*, Karl Hartl* and Geza von Bolvary*, while their erstwhile colleagues Billy Wilder, Robert Siodmak*, Max Ophuls*, Kurt Bernhardt*, Edgar Ulmer and many others had to try their luck in France, Britain or, towards the latter half of the 1930s, in Hollywood, helped by the deft survivor's skills of German-Jewish producers like Pommer and Seymour Nebenzal*, or Austro-Hungarians like Alexander Korda* and Arnold Pressburger.

The films made in Germany during the Nazi years are still the object of critical controversy. For the most part, they continued popular genres already established at the time of the Weimar cinema: costume dramas, comedies, films of national history, social problem films, literary adaptations, biopics, melodramas. While often considered artistically worthless, many of them were not only box-office successes at the time, but have become secret classics of the subsequent fifty years for Sunday matinee spectators and television viewers in both Germanies and across the generations. Zarah Leander*, Adele Sandrock*, Kristina Söderbaum*, Sybille Schmitz*, Willy Birgel*, Willy Forst*, Rudolf Forster, Carl Raddatz*,

Theo Lingen have remained household names to this day, a fact that raises issues which have never been adequately answered, about the continuity of forms and their political uses, about popular culture as mass deception or as reservoirs of resisting energy. Parallel to the entertainment feature films, the Nazi cinema dubiously distinguished itself in the genre of the formally often experimental but ideologically coloured documentary* (*Kulturfilm*), whose most famous practitioner was Leni Riefenstahl*. Her films had also helped train scores of cameramen and editors, who played a crucial function in the demagogic but, especially during the last war years, also shockingly realistic newsreels.

Postwar divisions and continuities
The German cinema as a film industry ceased to exist in 1945, with the collapse of the Third Reich and the Allied Forces' decision not only to dismantle Ufa and its vertically integrated structure, but also to prevent a different kind of studio system from emerging. Given the fact that large parts of the industrial infrastructure and most of the actual studios came under Communist control, the West German commercial cinema continued a kind of ghostly afterlife of the Nazi genre cinema, while for the East German, state-controlled company DEFA* directors such as Erich Engel, Kurt Maetzig* and Wolfgang Staudte* tried to give a somewhat less shadowy afterlife to the realist traditions of the *Straßenfilme**, by reinventing the proletarian film (*Arbeiterfilm**). Both Germanies contributed to the brief life of the *Trümmerfilme* 'ruin films', halfway between Weimar's sordid realism and Hollywood's *film noir*. Since the vast majority of film directors, actors and technicians active in the cinema of the 1950s had either been successful professionals or had learnt their craft during the Ufa years, this ghost image of the cinema was no return of the repressed, but merely the outward signs of the continuity and conservatism typical of popular culture almost everywhere.

German film criticism had always had difficulties in coming to terms with the 'escapist' tendencies of the mass media, demanding from cinema a commitment either to art and innovation or to (critical) realism. The disappointment was particularly vivid when films in the 1950s and early 1960s failed to pass these tests, preferring, like their audiences, Romy Schneider* in *Sissi* (1955) or Hans Deppe's* *Heimatfilme**, which were often remakes of titles from the 1920s, 1930s and 1940s. More recently, a younger generation of critics, writing also in feminist film journals like *Frauen und Film**, have rediscovered many of the melodramas, pop musicals (*Schlagerfilme*) and social problem films of the 1950s, once more alert to the kinds of contradictions worked out in the films, or fascinated by their own love-hate relationship to these spectacles of damaged masculinity, where hysterical wives are obliged to prop up self-tormented husbands and stagger with them towards the happy end. A cinema based on stars, it made a whole generation of men and women cling to the tight-lipped faces of Dieter Borsche, O. W. Fischer, Curd Jürgens* and O. E. Hasse*, or dissolve in the tear-stained eyes of Maria Schell*, Ruth Leuwerick* and Hildegard Knef*.

From the 1960s to the 1980s
For the generation of short-film directors, however, who were

trying to break into the closed shop of the German film business, such a cinema of stars and genres was anathema. They distrusted the commercial instincts of producers like Artur Brauner, or distributors turned producers like Ilse Kubaschewski of Gloria*, seeing their hugely successful series (Karl May films, Edgar Wallace films) merely as a symptom of the bankruptcy of commercial movie-making. The Oberhausen Manifesto insisted on a complete break with the German cinema's past, but also wanted a European outlook, following the lead that the French New Wave* and the 'new' cinemas in Britain, Czechoslovakia or Poland had given. Thanks to the tactical skills and publicity efforts of Alexander Kluge*, the New German Cinema* came also to stand for a conception of film-making where the government acted as patron, providing film-makers with the kind of funds given to the other arts like theatre, opera and music, with the film-maker, as writer-director-producer, enjoying the same recognition as other artists and authors (*Autorenkino*).

The cinematic benefits of the film funding system were more easily detectable in the second generation, when directors like Rainer Werner Fassbinder*, Werner Herzog*, Wim Wenders*, Margarethe von Trotta* and Helma Sanders-Brahms* made films that came to be noticed abroad. They also helped actors, mainly from the theatre, such as Klaus Kinski*, Bruno Ganz*, Hanna Schygulla* and Barbara Sukowa*, to become, if not stars, then at least the recognised faces of this cinema. The increased film-making activity, especially around Fassbinder, also professionalised traditional crafts such as cinematography, with cameramen (Michael Ballhaus*, Xaver Schwarzenberger, Thomas Mauch, Jörg Schmidt-Reitwein, Robby Müller*) winning international recognition. Next to the *auteurs*, another New German cinema emerged which turned towards the exploration of social issues and political dilemmas. It was largely funded via co-productions with television, which wanted topical and even controversial material, but presented with a personal signature or autobiographical slant, in order to bypass the requirement of 'balanced' reporting applied to politically sensitive issues. This 'niche' between current affairs television and committed or experimental film-making gave many women film-makers a first opportunity, making the German cinema of the 1970s and 1980s a centre of the European women's film.

Decline and new beginning: unification and beyond

With the death of Fassbinder in 1982, and a change of funding policy under the conservative government of Chancellor Kohl, the German cinema seemed to have entered into a period of rapid decline, following a classic pattern, where a much-trumpeted national 'new wave' leaves, as it ebbs away, a few *auteurs* who have to succeed on the international art cinema and festival circuits. Such is the uncertain fate of Wenders, Herzog and von Trotta. On the other side, a transfer of power from cinema to television occurred, which at first absorbed a considerable number of as yet unaffiliated directors, cameramen and related personnel, before this labour market achieved saturation, as it did in the mid-1980s. With it, the New German Cinema vanished like a mirage, having never been popular with domestic audiences, and having produced too many one-off films and film-makers.

With unification in 1990, a whole new pool of potential talent emerged from the other part of Germany, as did new subjects, not least unification itself, and its many tragic, brutally absurd and tragi-comic consequences for the lives of people both east and west (Dani Levy, Detlef Buck). So far, however, it is difficult to see new genres or new personalities, either among directors or actors. Rather, it seems as if the long association of the German cinema with television has finally shifted the balance, and made the comedians familiar from television the only film stars the German cinema audience still recognises: Otto Waalke, Loriot, Gerhard Pohl. By chance and coincidence, in 1992 the old Ufa studio in Babelsberg celebrated its 75th anniversary just in time to see its site and premises sold to a French conglomerate, who nominated former 'New German Cinema' director turned international independent (and only postwar German Oscar-winner) Volker Schlöndorff* as (caretaker) director. Whether this was the signal for the German cinema to become its own museum, or the start of a whole new cycle, making Berlin once more the heart of a film-making nation, remains to be seen. TE

II – THE GERMAN CINEMA: POPULAR GENRES

The German cinema's international image (like that of other European cinemas) has been based on great *auteurs* and privileged 'movements' (such as the 'New German cinema'*). Yet a wealth of popular genres sustained its industry and audience interest at least until the 1970s. Some, such as the *Heimatfilm**, *Straßenfilme**, *Kammerspielfilme** and *Arbeiterfilme** attained some celebrity. Others, equally important, are listed below (in alphabetical order).

Arztfilme **(Doctors' films)**, loved by audiences from the late 1930s to the 1960s, and especially in the early 1950s. The biggest successes were melodramas such as *Robert Koch, der Bekämpfer des Todes* (1939), *Nachtwache* (1949), *Dr. Holl* (1951) and *Sauerbruch – Das war mein Leben* (1954), where physicians (especially surgeons) represented selfless, heroic fighters striving to save lives or battle with bureaucracies. Doctors' films clearly played on the audience's need for strong, helpful father figures, inevitably suggesting parallels to the Führer's cult, and idealised via the profession's high ethical standards. Stories went all out for tears, while nostalgically affirming a value system that had never existed: a caring community, undivided by class, held together by a belief in the nation and an all-powerful deity. While the genre's popularity during the Nazi period is easily explained, its even greater resonance in the immediate postwar period hints at a compensation mechanism, a desire to make up for collective disappointment and replace the disgraced idols with more trustworthy ones. Apart from the comedy *Frauenarzt Dr. Prätorius* (1949) and a sex film such as *Mädchen beim Frauenarzt* (1971), few doctors' films went for laughs, or traded on the audience's voyeurism, in contrast to films of this genre elsewhere, for instance, Britain's *Carry On* *Nurse*, or the American *MASH*. TE/JG

Ausstattungsfilme **(Costume films)**. Inspired by successful Italian and US spectaculars, costume films became popular under the label of *Großfilm* at the end of the 1910s. During the period of hyper-inflation (1918–23) the young Ufa* could afford to invest in Joe May's* gigantic *tour de force*, *Veritas*

Vincit, and his costly eight-part series *Die Herrin der Welt/The Mistress of the World* (both 1919). However, it was the historical films directed by Ernst Lubitsch*, beginning with *Madame Dubarry/Passion* (1919) and culminating in *Das Weib des Pharao/The Loves of Pharaoh* (1921), that finally assured international profitability and brought further forays into the genre. German costume films were exercises in international grandiloquence (the French Revolution, the Italian and Spanish Renaissance, oriental adventures), but from the mid-1920s some of the most expensive and most popular of these *Austattungsfilme* ('films with production values') showed a penchant for national history and nationalist mythology (e.g. Fritz Lang's* *Die Nibelungen*, 1924). Using typically melodramatic devices, they were preferably set in the days of Prussia's glory (a sub-genre known as *Preußenfilme*), from the reign of Frederick the Great to the Vienna Congress of 1814 (*Fridericus Rex*, four parts, 1922–23; *Der Kongress tanzt*, 1931), but also included musicals and comedies set in turn-of-the-century Vienna. With World War II, the historical costume film proved to be most suitable for promoting nationalism, allowing the Nazi film industry to turn already well-established patterns to overtly propagandist purposes (e.g. *Jud Süss*, 1940). Throughout the 1950s costume films continued to make money, fostering a new generation of stars, such as Karlheinz Böhm* and Romy Schneider*. The latter's *Sissi* trilogy (1955–57) kept European audiences in thrall. Well into the 1960s remakes like Lang's *Das indische Grabmal/The Hindu Tomb* (1959) proved attractive, before the appeal of costumes and period decor moved to television and in the cinema was largely replaced by technical special effects. MW/TE

Musicals have always been among the most successful genres in Germany, producing different sub-genres to follow changing fashions in popular music. Operetta films, common from the mid-1910s to the early 1950s, were based on stage versions and presented romantic love stories often played out in an aristocratic milieu. The most popular operettas adapted the works of turn-of-the-century Viennese composers such as Franz Lehár and Ralph Benatzky. A new type of operetta film, the *Filmoperette*, emerged in the 1930s, with original libretti and scores, combining traditions drawn from operetta, comedy, cabaret and music-hall revue. It generally featured ordinary people, and its songs often became popular recording hits. Many composers being Jewish, Ufa* changed the formula after 1933, switching to *Revuefilme* (modelled on Hollywood 'backstage musicals'): *Hallo Janine!* (1939), *Der weiße Traum* (1943). The *Revuefilme* songs also often became hits. Films featuring Ufa* star Marika Rökk* were the most popular, while among the successful composers were Franz Grothe, Peter Kreuder and Michael Jary*. When the average age of German cinemagoers fell during the 1960s, *Schlagerfilme* (pop-music films) were introduced. As a rule, leading parts were played by pop stars using the film as promotion for their latest record. Among the best remembered *Schlagerfilme* are those with Peter Alexander*, Peter Kraus, Conny Froboess (*Wenn die Conny mit dem Peter*, 1958) and Freddy Quinn (*Freddy, die Gitarre und das Meer*, 1959). As German popular music made way for American pop at the beginning of the 1970s, so did the *Schlagerfilme*, bringing to

an end one of the most typical and long-lasting German film genres. JG

***Problemfilme* (social problem films)**, where the individual confronts social contradictions (class difference, moral conventions, poverty) beyond his/her control and/or comprehension. The social problem film covered several types of narrative, and can be distinguished by setting: the *Gesellschaftsfilm* (bourgeois melodrama) and the *Problemfilm* (petit bourgeois/working-class milieu), itself subdivided into *Straßenfilme**, *Kammerspielfilme** and *Arbeiterfilme**, which all emerged in the 1920s. The Nazis banned films too openly alluding to social realities as 'defeatist', and demanded uncompromising optimism. However, there were exceptions, such as Werner Hochbaum's* *Morgen beginnt das Leben* (1933). The aftershocks of Nazism and the war once more marked a return to the *Problemfilm*, under the stylistic traits of *film noir*, as in the *Trümmerfilme* (see below). In the late 1950s and early 1960s it was the bourgeois *Gesellschaftsfilm* that came to prominence, now emphasising emotional misery and moral isolation in the increasingly materialist world of opportunism during the 'economic miracle' (*Das letzte Rezept*, 1951; *Teufel in Seide*, 1956). The early 1960s also saw a return to working-class themes, although now focused on the disorientation of male adolescents, as in Wolfgang Staudte's* *Kirmes* (1960) and in a string of films by Will Tremper (*Flucht nach Berlin*, 1960), Georg Tressler (*Die Halbstarken*, 1956; *Endstation Liebe*, 1958) or Frank Wysbar (*Nasser Asphalt*, 1958). This last cycle converged with another trend, where under the East German label of *Gegenwartsfilme* (at DEFA*: Frank Beyer*, Konrad Wolf, Egon Günther*, and others), and under the West German label of *Junger deutscher Film* (Young German Cinema), directors like Alexander Kluge*, Edgar Reitz*, and others such as Jean-Marie Straub* and Danièle Huillet* (*Machorka Muff*, 1963) and Peter Schamoni (*Schonzeit für Füchse*, 1966), began to investigate the rigidities and dogmas of a social landscape whose official ideology seemed seriously out of step with what they perceived as the realities of people's lives. The *Problemfilm* can also be recognised in what came to be a distinctive feature of the 'New German cinema'*, namely its emphasis on issue-oriented film-making, covering every conceivable topic from abortion (*Es/It*, 1965) to vagrancy (*Abschied von gestern/Yesterday Girl*, 1966), from social prejudice against homosexuality (*Jagdszenen aus Niederbayern/Hunting Scenes from Lower Bavaria*, 1969) to unemployment and ethnic minorities (*Angst essen Seele auf/Fear Eats the Soul*, 1973). The genre eventually became so broad in range as to all but disappear into the many forms of docudrama cultivated by public service television. TE/MW

Series and serials. A prototype of German series (copied from French and Danish models) was Joe May's* thirty-part 'Stuart Webb' detective series, featuring the star actor Ernst Reicher (from 1914 to 1923). Once originality and cultural prestige came to be prized in film-making, film genres took over their function from the 1930s into the 1950s. It was not until the German film industry experienced an economic crisis in the late 1950s that German studios hit once more on the idea of producing films in series, such as the Edgar Wallace series (1959–72), the Karl May series (1962–68) and several sex film* series. Successful for a while, they signalled the final demise of a popular national cinema as it was replaced by television, which has of course always thrived on series. JG/TE

Sex films. While pornographic film goes back to the beginnings of the cinema, the first wave of sex films in Germany appeared just after World War I, in the period between the abolition of military censorship and the reintroduction of the centralised censorship of the Weimar Republic in May 1920. In the last years of the war sex-education films were often made in collaboration with medical experts; sex researchers such as Magnus Hirschfeld worked on films about syphilis (*Es werde Licht!*, four parts: 1916/17–1918) and homosexuality (*Anders als die anderen/Different from the Others*, 1919). So-called *Sittenfilme* ('sexual mores' films) by contrast were more openly pornographic, as in *Opium* (1919), where the viewer was 'warned' of the consequences of taking drugs by being shown the trancelike dreams of an abuser, with bare-breasted women suggestively beckoning. Sex films did not appear (at least overtly) during the Nazi regime, which did not tolerate 'smut'. It was German film distributors, especially Constantin*, who initiated the second wave of sex films between 1967 and 1973 in order to lure back diminishing audiences. The strategy worked: domestically produced sex films managed, for the last time (1968–70), to yield larger profit margins for German distributors than American films. This wave of sex films went through three cycles. Firstly, sex-education films were made from 1967 onwards, the statements of experts legitimising erotic scenes showing undressing and simulated intercourse. *Helga* (1967) enjoyed national and international success and was the prototype for this cycle, of which Oswald Kolle was the undisputed champion. Secondly, 'report films' appeared in 1970. Alluding to the Kinsey Reports, they showed sexual episodes based on data allegedly collected in sociological studies. The thirteen-part series* *Schulmädchenreport* (1970–80) set the conventions. Thirdly, sex comedies emerged around 1972, abandoning the educational pretence. Legitimising voyeurism by making sex a subject of laughter, they harked back to the folk and carnivalesque forms of bawdy entertainment. Sex comedies often feature local settings, as in the six-part series *Liebesgrüße aus der Lederhos'n* (1973–82), parasitic on *Heimatfilms** and travelogues. More ethnographically intriguing was the popularity of a series set in the mining region of the Ruhr (*Laß jucken, Kumpel*, 1972–81). Production of mainstream sex films fell during the late 1970s as hard-core porn films and videos became socially acceptable. At first shown in special cinemas, they were absorbed into the general video market during the 1980s. JG/TE

***Trümmerfilme* (Ruin films).** Ruin films are German *films noirs* produced during the immediate postwar years (1946–49). The nickname derived from the films' setting in the ruined cityscapes of postwar Germany, and their appeal was based on presenting German viewers with protagonists who shared their recent experience. *Film ohne Titel* and *Zwischen gestern und morgen* were the most popular films of 1948. Though they are set in the present, the outcome of the stories featured in *Trümmerfilme* is usually decided by past events which, although unnamed, would at the time have been readily identified as referring to the Nazi period. Moral dilemmas became psychological states, depicted by complex flashbacks or low-key lighting. In contrast to American *films noirs*, the plots of *Trümmerfilme* distinguished clearly between good and evil. In DEFA*-produced ruin films, made under Soviet control, didactic anti-fascist messages were obligatory (*Die Mörder sind unter uns/The Murderers are Amongst Us*, 1946). JG

***Kriegsfilme* (war films).** As nationalist propaganda, the war film in Germany goes back to the Navy League's travelling cinemas of 1901–07, showing off the military might of modern warships while organising the German cinema's first distribution circuit. In the early 1910s, the Franco-Prussian War of 1870–71 served as background for melodramas of separated families, or moral conflicts. *Die Verräterin* (1911) and *Madeleine* (1912) were only two examples that represented war unheroically, challenging conventional norms. War-weariness and the demand for escapist films generally excluded the war film from the move to full-length feature films (an exception was Paul Leni's* *Der Feldarzt/Das Tagebuch des Dr. Hart/The Doctor/Diary of Dr. Hart*, 1916). Such was the shock of defeat that the first anti-war films, G. W. Pabst's* *Westfront 1918* and Victor Trivas' *Niemandsland*, were not made until 1930 and 1931, respectively. With the Nazis in power, it fell to Karl Ritter to polish the image of the military with his *Soldatenfilme* (soldier films): their message was that patriotism rather than victory makes a soldier's life and death important. In the 1950s, the Cold War and West Germany's anti-Nato debate found its parallel in the discussions around the 'revisionism' of popular anti-war films such as *08/15* (1955), *Haie und kleine Fische* (1957), and *Unruhige Nacht* (1955). Closest in spirit to Pabst and Trivas was Bernhard Wicki's* *Die Brücke/The Bridge* (1959), while the U-boat films of the 1930s and 1950s inspired a recent foray into a psychologically complex war film, Wolfgang Petersen's* technical *tour de force*, *Das Boot/The Boat* (1981). TE/KU

GERMI, Pietro   Genoa 1914 – Rome 1974

Italian director. Federico Fellini* once described Germi as a 'great carpenter' in recognition of his unique mastery of film craft; he was also a very effective actor both in his own films and in those of others. Germi made his debut with *Il testimone/The Witness* (1946), the beginning of the early, 'dramatic' phase of his work which ended with *Un maledetto imbroglio/A Sordid Affair* (1959). Two films about the problems of southern Italy, *In nome della legge/In the Name of the Law* (1949) and *Il cammino della speranza/Road to Hope* (1950), were great box-office successes but caused controversy, many critics objecting to the extravagant, Hollywood-style approach taken by this 'fellow traveller' of neo-realism*. A similar fate awaited *Il ferroviere/Man of Iron* (1956) and *L'uomo di paglia/Man of Straw* (1958), in which Germi created two powerful portraits of men in a state of crisis, corrupted by their own moralism, superficiality and sentimentality. With his surly humanism and rejection of ideology, Germi was something of a nineteenth-century man. His later films – *Divorzio all'italiana/Divorce – Italian Style* (1961), *Sedotta e abbandonata/Seduced and Abandoned* (1963) and *Signore e* signori/*The Birds, the Bees and the Italians* (1965) – established him as one of the masters of *commedia all'italiana**, helped by first-rate scripts from Age* and Scarpelli*, Ennio De Concini and Luciano Vincenzoni. His satirical comedy of manners of this period is infused with a bitterness which falls just short of invective. His last films were less successful; he died during the preparation of *Amici miei*, a sharply malicious comedy eventually made by Mario Monicelli*. MMo

Other Films Include: *Gioventù perduta/Lost Youth* (1948); *La città si difende/Passport to Hell* (1951); *La presidentessa/The Lady President* (1952); *Il brigante di Tacca del Lupo/The Brigand of Tacca del Lupo* (1952); *Amori di mezzo secolo, Gelosia* (1953); *L'immorale/The Climax* (1966); *Serafino* (1968); *Le castagne sono buone/Pocketful of Chestnuts* (1970); *Alfredo Alfredo* (1972).

GERRON, Kurt
Kurt Gerso; Berlin 1897 – Auschwitz 1944

German actor and director, associated with one of the most tragic and shameful incidents of German film history. Gerron was trained as an actor by Max Reinhardt*, but had his first stage recognition under director Erich Engel*, playing in Brecht plays. A big man, he became typecast in the cinema, often in bit parts (as in E. A. Dupont's* *Varieté/Variety*, 1925), and in scores of films directed by Richard Oswald*, Reinhold Schünzel*, G. W. Pabst* and Hans Steinhoff*, and perhaps most memorably in *Der blaue Engel/The Blue Angel* (1930) as the magician, coldly observing Emil Jannings'* slide into self-humiliation. Essentially a comic actor, Gerron in 1928 teamed up with the famous Jewish comedian Sigi Arno, in an (unsuccessful) attempt to create a German Laurel and Hardy (as 'Beef and Steak').

Gerron directed his first film in 1926, but came into his own as a director in the sound period. An expert at comedies, Gerron directed two of the genre's stars, Heinz Rühmann* (*Meine Frau die Hochstaplerin*, 1931) and Willi Fritsch* (*Ein toller Einfall*, 1932); he also made a thriller with Hans Albers* (*Der weiße Dämon*, 1932). Politically as well as racially persecuted, Gerron left for France, then settled in Amsterdam in 1933, making several films there but concentrating on theatre and radio. Arrested by the SS in 1943 and interned at Westerbork, Gerron was sent to Theresienstadt in 1944, in order to direct a staged documentary intended to persuade world public opinion that the Jews were well-treated in concentration camps (*Der Führer schenkt den Juden eine Stadt/ The Führer Donates a City to the Jews*). His job done, Gerron, along with his crew, was put on a train to Auschwitz and murdered there. TE

Bib: Barbara Felsmann, *Kurt Gerron gefeiert und gejagt* (1992).

GEYER, Karl A.
Ilmenau 1880 – Hamburg 1964

German technician and industrialist, who turned laboratory technology into an independent branch of the German film industry. In 1908 he constructed a perforator whose principles are still in use today, and in 1921–22 he automated film developing (as did the Americans at the same time), as well as print production. His film laboratory equipment was sold throughout Europe via his own company, founded in January 1918. The introduction of sound created economic hardship in the German film industry as Tobis-Klangfilm tried to maintain a stranglehold over the patent for sound reproduction, but Geyer overcame this problem by founding his own company, the Deutsche Filmgemeinschaft, which produced Leontine Sagan's* *Mädchen in Uniform/Maidens in Uniform* (1931). After the war, Geyer-Werke went on to become West Germany's leading firm in laboratory technology, broadening its area of operations to include sound dubbing, video and photography. The majority of the company's shares are still owned by the Geyer family. JG

GHIONE, Emilio
Fiesole 1879 – Rome 1930

Italian actor, producer and director, who first appeared in films as a double and in walk-on parts for Aquila Films in Turin, where he grew up. He later moved on to Giovanni Pastrone's* Itala Films, and then to Cines* in Rome, where he was given a part in *Il poverello d'Assisi* (1911). Eventually he was hired by Celio, where, with Francesca Bertini and Alberto Collo, he acted in his first three films, including *Histoire d'un Pierrot* (1914) [> DIVISMO]. In 1913, he directed *Idolo infranto*, and, in 1914, *Nelly la Gigolette* (co-starring Bertini), where he created the character of Za la Mort, the romantic and noble-minded 'apache' gangster, to whom his reputation is inextricably linked. The character was, with Za la Vie (played by Kally Sambucini, his real-life companion), the hero of two serials inspired by Louis Feuillade's* *Fantômas* (1913–14) and *Judex* (1917): *Il triangolo giallo/The Yellow Triangle* (1917, four episodes) and *I topi grigi/The Grey Mice* (1918, eight episodes), both outstanding successes. Ghione's performance style was unusual in Italian terms: expressionistic rather than naturalistic, dependent on facial expressions and the use of his body. His outdoor scenes were set in squalid, starkly illuminated peripheral areas of the city. Ghione acted in over a hundred films, among which are some of the most popular mystery and adventure films of the Italian silent cinema. In 1920, he founded Ghione Film but his success waned in an industry undergoing a severe crisis. In the mid-1920s, he emigrated like many others to Germany, where he revived Za la Mort in two films with Fern Andra. In 1926 he played in Carmine Gallone's* and Amleto Palermi's remake of *Gli ultimi giorni di Pompei/The Last Days of Pompeii* and directed a rustic drama, *Senza padre*, his last work. After trying to overcome the crisis by founding the short-lived Compagnia delle Maschere e del Colore, he moved in poverty to Paris, where he tried a new career as a writer. He wrote a long article on cinema in Italy, published in *L'Art cinématographique* in 1929. The same year he was repatriated, by then seriously ill with tuberculosis. MMo

GIELGUD, (Sir) John
London 1904

British actor. Of the leading trio of 'theatrical knights' – with Ralph Richardson* and Laurence Olivier* – Gielgud has remained most firmly wedded to theatre, seeming most at ease in direct stage adaptations such as Olivier's *Richard III* (1955) or Joseph Losey's* *Galileo* (1976). While his theatrically modulated delivery resists the naturalism of extended film characterisation, his cameo appearances are always a delight to watch. Although, like Olivier's, his later career has included some routine bread-and-butter work, since the 1930s he has also appeared in distinctive films by Victor Saville*, Alfred Hitchcock*, Thorold Dickinson*, Otto Preminger, Orson Welles, Andrzej Wajda* and David Lynch, and his is the unmistakable voice of Humphrey Jennings'* *A Diary for Timothy* (1945). More recently, he has given extended performances in Alain Resnais'* *Providence* (1977) and Peter Greenaway's* *Prospero's Books* (1991). JC

Other Films Include: *The Good Companions* (1933); *Secret Agent* (1936); *The Prime Minister* (1941); *Julius Caesar* (1953, US); *The Barretts of Wimpole Street, Saint Joan* (1957); *Becket* (1964); *Campanadas a medianoche/Chimes at Midnight* (1966, Sp./Switz.); *The Charge of the Light Brigade* (1968); *Oh! What a Lovely War* (1969); *Dyrygent/The Conductor* [Pol.], *The Human Factor* (1979); *The Elephant Man* (1980, US/UK); *Arthur, Chariots of Fire* (1981, US); *Gandhi* (1982).

GIL, Rafael   Rafael Gil Alvarez; Madrid 1913–86

Spanish director. Gil's vast output, stretching from 1941 to 1982, inhibited consistency of style. His 1940s films reveal a skill for taut, pacey narratives, and a talent for comedy. This is evident in *Eloísa está debajo de un almendro/Eloisa is Underneath an Almond Tree* (1943), based on Jardiel Poncela's farcical thriller. The film's setting and cast of crazy characters expressed through comedy the darker side of the prevailing ideology. In contrast, *El hombre que se quiso matar/The Man Who Wanted to Kill Himself* (1941), a sort of *criticón* (satirical) narrative in which a man cuts himself off from the world so as to speak plainly, seems partly aimed at satirising the '*palabrería*' (verbiage) and hypocrisies usually associated by the regime with liberalism and democracy. Gil was not untouched by the 1940s taste for Spanish historical films* and he made several, for instance *El clavo/The Nail* (1944), whose triumphalist prejudices are barely hidden. PWE

GILDEMEIJER, Johan Hendrik   Alkmaar 1871 – Amsterdam 1945

Dutch director and scriptwriter, who entered the film trade in 1908 as a distributor, soon opening a cinema as well. He began writing scripts for producer Maurits Binger* in 1913 and went into production at the outbreak of World War I. He wrote and produced his first feature, *Fatum*, directed by Theo Frenkel*, in 1915, after which he directed his own scripts. His greatest success was *Gloria Transita* (1917), a melodrama about the rise and fall of an opera star. The picture was screened accompanied live by four singers who synchronised their voices to the opera scenes in the story. The power of the film was still evident when it was revived seventy years later. Gildemeijer used a similar playback method in *Gloria fatalis* (1922). He will also be remembered as the initiator of the Internationale Kino Tentoonstelling in Amsterdam in 1920, the first post-World War I European film trade exhibition, organised to bring together the former enemies on neutral ground. It included the first international film contest in which a jury awarded a prize for a film's artistic merits; the winner was Abel Gance's *La Dixième symphonie* (1918, Fr.). KD

Bib: Geoffrey Donaldson, 'Film, opera and Johan Gildemeijer', *Griffithiana* (1987).

Other Films as Director: *Koningin Elizabeth's dochter/Queen Elizabeth's Daughter* (1915); *Diamant/Diamond, Een danstragedie/A Dance Tragedy* (1916); *Romance Impromptu* (1933); *Fantasia Musica* (1937).

GILLIAM, Terry   Minneapolis, USA 1940

American/British director, who moved to Britain in 1967 and became part of the Monty Python's Flying Circus team, contributing a series of uncharacteristically bleak animation sequences to the television series. He directed *Monty Python and the Holy Grail* (1975) with the same team, and has subsequently established an independent existence as a director of eccentric and sometimes unsettling mythologies and fantasies, including the wonderfully dystopic *Brazil* (1985). Gilliam had a struggle to retain the dystopia in Hollywood, and *The Fisher King* (1991, US) returns to the Grail legend with a gentler ending. Responding to a Toronto Festival award for the film, Gilliam wrote, 'Thank you very much for justifying my decision to sell out.' JC

Other Films Include: *Jabberwocky* (1977); *Time Bandits* (1981); *The Adventures of Baron Munchausen* (1988, UK/Ger.).

GILLIAT, Sidney – see LAUNDER, Frank

GIMPERA, Teresa   Teresa Gimpera Flaquer; Barcelona 1936

Spanish actress, a well-known model who became one of the muses of the Barcelona School* after her debut in Vicente Aranda's* *Fata Morgana/Morgan Le Fay* (1965). She achieved a difficult transition from pop icon to sought-after actress for television and cinema, and the films in which she has starred range from the commercial 'sexy Spanish comedy' [> COMEDY (SPAIN)] to Victor Erice's* masterpiece *El espíritu de la colmena/The Spirit of the Beehive* (1973). Slim, blonde and with northern features, her hallmark is a certain formality and poise which singles her out from the Spanish norm. XR

GIROTTI, Massimo
Mogliano 1918

Italian actor. Before his first film role in Mario Soldati's* *Dora Nelson* (1939) Girotti was a professional swimmer, and his early casting had more to do with his athletic body than with training as an actor. For the first three years of his film career, his screen persona was shaped through swashbuckler and costume adventure films. His first major role was as the young hero of Alessandro Blasetti's* lavish medieval fantasy, *La corona di ferro/The Iron Crown* (1941). The same year, he starred as the same character (Tremal-Naik) in two adventure films, *Pirati della Malesia* and its sequel *Le due tigri*. Soon, however, Girotti was increasingly cast in contemporary melodramas. He played a wounded Italian pilot in Roberto Rossellini's* *Una pilota ritorna* (1942), and an Italian boxer in New York in Carmine Gallone's* *Harlem* (1943), but was especially notable as the vagrant mechanic of *Ossessione* (1942), Luchino Visconti's* version of *The Postman Always Rings Twice*. The complexity of his eroticised anti-hero in *Ossessione* resulted in part from his being cast both with and against the athletic and romantic persona of the adventure films. After the war, Girotti appeared in adventure films, peplums* and melodramas, and delivered noteworthy performances for such major directors as Giuseppe De Santis* (*Caccia tragica/Tragic Hunt*, 1947), Pietro Germi* (*In nome della legge/In the Name of the Law*, 1949), Michelangelo Antonioni* (*Cronaca di un amore/Story of a Love Affair*, 1950), Visconti (*Senso*, 1954), and Alberto Lattuada* (*Lettere di una novizia*, 1960). Roles in two Pasolini* films brought him renewed prominence in the art cinema of the late 1960s: as the paradigmatic bourgeois father in *Teorema/Theorem* (1968) and as Creon in *Medea* (1970), he played dignified and sacrificial patriarchs.

Girotti has worked extensively in theatre, including in Visconti's very successful production of *The Cherry Orchard* (1965), and in Italian, French and German television. Girotti's longevity as a performer and his association with Italy's major cinematic movements established him as a living relic, and film-makers began to direct him self-consciously. Thus Bertolucci included Girotti in the line-up of older stars of neo-realism* as part of his iconoclastic strategy in *Ultimo tango a Parigi/Last Tango in Paris* (1972), while Ettore Scola* in *Passione d'amore/Passion of Love* (1981) cast him as a colonel whose performance deliberately recalled that of Ussoni in *Senso*. JHa/MMa

GLADTVET, Ottar
Kristiania [Oslo] 1890 – Oslo 1962

Norwegian film pioneer, who began working as a projectionist in his father's cinemas in 1906, and directed his first feature, *Overfaldet paa postaapnerens datter eller Kampen om pengebrevet/The Assault on the Postmaster's Daughter or The Fight about the Money Letter*, in 1913. Gladtvet made four more features, politically reactionary melodramas (in which, for instance, crooks are trade unionists), before joining an expedition to Venezuela and Colombia in 1920, out of which came his documentary *Blant Syd-Amerikas urskovsindianere/Among the Indians of South America's Jungle* (1922). Back

home he directed commercials in the 1920s and 1930s, including animated ones. His last feature as director was also a documentary, *Til Vesterheimen/Westwards – Homewards* (1939), a report on the visit of the Norwegian crown prince and his wife to the US. He stopped directing in the 1940s but continued to work as a cameraman. KS

Other Films as Director Include: *Revolutionens datter/The Daughter of the Revolution* (1918).

GLASNOST AND THE CINEMA

The Russian word *glasnost*, which literally means 'giving voice', attained international currency during the late 1980s, along with *perestroika*, meaning 'restructuring', as the main slogans of the attempt during the Gorbachev years to reform Soviet society. *Glasnost* was seen by Soviet politicians as the handmaid of the more important *perestroika*, but when the economic and political restructuring of the Soviet Union was shown to be impossible, this was mainly because of the spectacular success of *glasnost*. As a policy allowing greater freedom of expression in the media and the arts, it was introduced gradually and not unequivocally after Gorbachev's accession in 1985. In the press it allowed adventurous publications such as the weekly newspaper *Moskovskie novosti* ('Moscow News') and the illustrated weekly magazine *Ogonek* ('The Little Flame') to delve into the Soviet (and pre-Soviet) past and provide a more nuanced and polyphonic version of Russian history. Gradually they were allowed to turn their attention to the present, and expose the enormous economic, political and moral problems that beset the country. In the later 1980s, Soviet television joined in the process, though there were regular applications of the ideological brakes. In literature, most daring was shown by the so-called 'thick journals', monthly magazines that combine publication of works of literature with serious journalism, and which have been in the forefront of Russian intellectual life for over a century. Such journals as *Novyi mir* ('New World') and *Znamya* ('The Banner') brought (or in some cases returned) to Soviet readers writings by émigré writers from Nabokov and Zamyatin to Brodsky and, eventually, Solzhenitsyn, as well as hitherto banned works by writers who remained in Russia. Pasternak's *Doctor Zhivago*, for example, was finally published in the Soviet Union in 1988. This process boomed in 1988, with journals reaching hugely inflated print runs: the young people's monthly *Yunost'* ('Youth'), for instance, was printing over 3 million copies. But perhaps inevitably, boom was followed by decline. Readers became sated with 'revelations'; additionally, the withdrawal of state subsidies and the harsh intrusion of market economics led to paper shortages and huge inflation in book and magazine prices. In the former Soviet Union the situation for serious publishing is precarious indeed.

In the area of cinema, the first hints of *glasnost* were provided by the release in the mid-1980s of shelved films, such as Alexei German's* *Moi drug Ivan Lapshin/My Friend Ivan Lapshin*, a trickle which turned into a flood after the inauguration of a Conflict Commission at the Fifth Congress of the Union of Cinematographers* of the USSR, held in May 1986. Among the scores of films released with the active intervention of the Commission were Tengiz Abuladze's* *Monanieba/Repentance*, Alexander Askoldov's* *Komissar/The Commissar*, Andron Mikhalkov-Konchalovsky's* *Istoriya Asi Klyachinoi/The Story of Asya Klyachina*, Irakli Kvirikadze's* *Plovets/The Swimmer*, and a number of important works by Kira Muratova* and Alexander Sokurov*. The appearance of these films substantially altered our understanding of the Soviet cinema of the Brezhnev period.

The new board of the Union also took measures to encourage younger film-makers, and it is notable that most of the key films of the next decade were made by new directors. The loosening of ideological control was soon apparent in a wave of hard-hitting documentaries on both historical and contemporary topics. Remarkable among the former is Marina Goldovskaya's *Vlast' solovetskaya/Solovki Power* (1988), a history of the notorious northern labour camp complex. Contemporary documentaries covered a range of hitherto taboo issues from ecological neglect to drugs, prostitution and AIDS. The ambitious work of such directors as Herz Franks*, Stanislav Govorukhin*, Iosif Pasternak* and Jūris Podnieks* opened a window on a parallel Soviet reality long known to exist but scarcely acknowledged officially.

The new freedom of expression allowed to film-makers also led to polemical new readings of the Soviet past in the work of such directors as Yevgeni Tsymbal* and Vitali Kanevsky*, and films like Alexander Proshkin's *Kholodnoe leto pyat'desyat tret'ego/The Cold Summer of '53* (1987). Nor did the version of the lives of contemporary Soviet young people revealed in Vasili Pichul's* *Malen'kaya Vera/Little Vera*, Valeri Ogorodnikov's* *Vzlomshchik/The Burglar*, Rashid Nugmanov's* *Igla/The Needle* or, most notably, Muratova's *Astenicheskii sindrom/The Asthenic Syndrome* conform to official stereotype. But by the end of the decade the ideological and aesthetic free-for-all that characterised the move to the 'market economy' in Russian film-making was responsible for the release of a torrent of sub-American gangster films and 'sex thrillers'. Ambitious examinations of contemporary Russian life continued to be made, but the simultaneous breakdown of the old Soviet distribution system and a popular yearning for hitherto inaccessible cinematic Americana made their path to the audience increasingly fraught. JGf

GLORIA

German distribution company of the post-World War II period. Founded in 1949 by Ilse Kubaschewski, Gloria also opened first-run cinemas in 1955. Following the trend in the 1950s German cinema, Gloria subsequently extended its activities to include production, through its own company Divina, founded in April 1953, which produced three of the most successful films of the 1950s: *08/15* (released in three parts from 1954 to 1955), *Die Trapp-Familie* (1956) and *Der Arzt von Stalingrad* (1958). The company also made money on their *Heimatfilme** such as *Grün ist die Heide* (1951), *Weißer Holunder* (1957) and *Adieu, Lebewohl, Goodbye* (1961). In 1957, when German film attendance dropped, Gloria failed to develop a new market strategy. Despite an early investment in youth movies in the 1960s, Kubaschewski had to sell to an American company in 1973. JG

GLÜCK, Wolfgang   Vienna 1929

Austrian director. Glück has directed film and television series since the 1950s, as well as *Heimatfilme** such as *Der Pfarrer von St. Michael* (1957, Ger.) and movies with moral lessons, including *Gefährdete Mädchen* (1957, Ger.) and *Denn das Weib ist schwach* (1961, Ger.). Many of his works are adaptations of contemporary Austrian literature, such as *Wunschloses Unglück* (1974, based on Peter Handke) and *Die kleine Figur meines Vaters* (1979, based on Peter Henisch). Glück lay a cornerstone of the 'New Austrian Cinema' with *Der Schüler Gerber* (1981, based on a novel by Friedrich Torberg), which won several prizes. *38 – Auch das war Wien* (1986) was, however, his greatest success. This sentimental treatment of another Torberg novel was strongly criticised as 'anti-fascist kitsch' but was nominated for a best foreign film Oscar in 1986; it received the Austrian Film Prize in 1987. Glück also works as a stage director. IR/AL

Other Films Include: *Die Gigerln von Wien* (1965); *Das Gebell* (1976); *Anleitung zum Unglücklichsein* (1986).

GODARD, Jean-Luc   Paris 1930

French director. Originally a film critic at *Cahiers du cinéma**, Godard was the most radical director of the New Wave*; his body of work is central to modern *auteur* cinema. The son of a Franco-Swiss bourgeois family, Godard briefly studied anthropology before he began writing on film. His first feature, *A bout de souffle/Breathless* (1960), with its jagged editing, references to American cinema and casual male lead (Jean-Paul Belmondo*), was an instant success. It initiated Godard's lifelong reflection on the image, which in his 'first period' combined a search for modernist cinema with romanticism and cinephilia, most lyrically in *Le Mépris/Contempt* (1963, starring Brigitte Bardot*) and *Pierrot le fou* (1965, with Anna Karina*, Godard's first wife). Godard's 1960s work scrutinised France in the grip of the consumer boom, with its spreading housing estates, computers and advertisements, as in *Alphaville* (1965) and *Masculin féminin* (1966). It also posited prostitution as the – literal and metaphorical – condition of women (*Vivre sa vie/My Life to Live*, 1962, *Une femme mariée/The Married Woman*, 1964, *2 ou 3 choses que je sais d'elle/Two or Three Things I Know About Her*, 1967) and, by extension, of the human condition under capitalism. Anticipating the events of May 1968, *La Chinoise* and *Weekend* (1967) launched Godard's 'second period' of increasingly experimental work. With Jean-Pierre Gorin he founded the 'Dziga Vertov* group', making films (*Le Gai savoir*, 1968, *Pravda*, 1969, *Vent d'Est/Wind from the East*, 1970) aimed at smaller, militant audiences. Most starred Anne Wiazemsky, his second wife. Godard now developed an extreme countercinema informed by Marxist/Maoist ideology. His aim, as he famously put it, was not to make 'political films' but to 'make films politically'. *Tout va bien* (1972), starring Yves Montand* and Jane Fonda, angled these concerns towards a more accessible format. Godard subsequently worked in video with his third partner, Anne-Marie Miéville (a photographer and film-maker), most powerfully in *Numéro Deux* (1975), returning to film with *Sauve qui peut (la vie)/Slow Motion*

181

(1980), a pessimistic self-reflexive account of male-female collaboration, again crossed with questions of prostitution. This film marked Godard's return to Switzerland, where he has since lived. In this 'third period', Godard has pursued narrative film – *Prénom Carmen* (1983), *Je vous salue, Marie/Hail Mary!* (1984), *Détective* (1984), and video/documentary work, for instance the idiosyncratic *Histoire(s) du cinéma* (1989, made for television). Godard's later films have often disappointed, with the exception of *Passion* (1982), a reflection on the specificity of the cinematic image. The ironically titled *Nouvelle vague* (1990), while continuing such investigation, is typical of the pared-down narratives and desultory melancholy of his late work.

Godard's films have been a site of contradictions. While regularly predicting the 'end of cinema', they are romantically cinephile. His use of women is both critical of and complicit with patriarchal representations: evidence, in Laura Mulvey's* words, of his 'deep-seated but interesting misogyny'. Godard's cinema, while politically motivated, has alienated audiences; his relationship with Hollywood has moved from adoration to rejection to collaboration (*King Lear*, 1987). At the same time, the tensions have been productive and are transcended by the brilliance of Godard's use of image and sound. Godard's key role in developing modernist and postmodernist cinema can be felt not only directly in the work of such film-makers as Chantal Akerman* and Leos Carax*, but throughout postwar world cinema. He was awarded a César* for life achievement in 1986. GV

Bib: Raymond Bellour and Mary Lea Bandy (eds.), *Jean-Luc Godard, Son + Image* (1992).

Other Films Include: *Le Petit soldat* (1960, rel. 63), *Une Femme est une femme/A Woman is a Woman* (1961); *Les Carabiniers* (1963); *Bande à part/Band of Outsiders* (1964); *Made in USA* (1967); *One Plus One (Sympathy for the Devil), British Sounds (See You at Mao), Luttes en Italie/Lotte in Italia/Struggle in Italy* (1969); *Vladimir et Rosa* (1971); *A Letter to Jane* (1972). **With Anne-Marie Miéville**: *Ici et ailleurs* (1974–76), *France/tour/détour/deux/enfants* (1979, TV); *Soft and Hard* (1985); *Soigne ta droite, Aria* [ep.] (1987).

GODFREY, Bob   West Maitland, Australia 1921

British animator, of Australian parentage, who attracted attention with *The Do-It-Yourself Cartoon Kit* (1961), and whose 30-minute film *Great* (1975), a comic musical treatment of Brunel, won an Academy Award. Godfrey's work, in films like *Polygamous Polonius* (1960), *Henry 9 Till 5* (1970) and *Kama Sutra Rides Again* (1971), is admired for its surreal visual imagination and is notorious for its sexism. He provided animation sequences for Roman Polanski's* *Dance of the Vampires* (1967). He has recently begun a collaboration with the *Guardian* cartoonist Steve Bell. JC

GODINA, Karpo   Skopje, Macedonia 1943

Slovene director and cinematographer. After several successful short films (of which *Zdravi ljudi za razonodu/Healthy People for Entertainment/Litany of Healthy People* won the Grand Prix at Oberhausen in 1971) and more than 200 commercials, Godina directed his first feature film, *Splav Meduze/The Raft of Medusa*, in 1980. The famous painting by Géricault not only provided the title and the opening sequence, but was also used as a metaphor for the story itself: a road movie about a group of young artists gathered round Ljubomir Micić, a founder of 'Zenitism', an anarchist avant-garde art movement based in the Balkans of the 1920s. Visually stunning (Godina was director of photography for more than twenty films between 1960 and 1980), the film uses silent movie features such as iris shots and intertitles. *Rdeči boogie/Red Boogie* (1982) repeated the theme of misunderstood artists on the road: a group of jazz musicians travels around Slovenia during the postwar socialist reconstruction. *Umetni raj/Artificial Paradise* (1990), Godina's most ambitious project to date, is based on the discovery of several sculptures made by Fritz Lang* as a young officer of the Austrian army during World War I, while he was stationed with a pioneer of Slovene cinema, Karol Grosmann*. The film, although somewhat pretentious in suggesting the importance of this period for Lang's development, was shown at a special tribute screening at the 1991 Cannes film festival on the occasion of the centenary of Lang's birth. SP

GOETZ, Curt   Kurt Walter Götz; Mayence 1888 – Grabs, Switzerland 1960

German actor, playwright and director, who began as scriptwriter on, among other films, Ernst Lubitsch's* *Ich möchte kein Mann sein* (1918). His directorial debut was the ambitious *Friedrich Schiller* (1923), but he subsequently worked in the theatre. Returning to film in the mid-1930s, Goetz wrote *Glückskinder* (1936), *Land der Liebe* (1937) and *Sieben Ohrfeigen* (1937). In 1938 he emigrated to Hollywood, later settling in Switzerland (1946), where he wrote, directed and acted in *Frauenarzt Dr. Prätorius* (1950) and co-directed *Das Haus in Montevideo* (1951). After scripting and acting in Kurt Hoffmann's* *Hokuspokus* (1953), adapted from his play of the same name and co-written with his wife Valérie von Maertens, Goetz adapted another of his plays for Wolfgang Liebeneiner's* *Ingeborg* (1960). His (and Maertens') brand of witty dialogue and understated but lethal critique of petit-bourgeois double standards makes them rare masters of German film comedy, whose importance exceeds their comparatively modest screen credits. TE/KU

GOGOBERIDZE, Lana L.   Tbilisi, Georgia [USSR] 1928

Georgian director, a graduate of VGIK*. Gogoberidze's first film was a co-directed documentary, *Tbilisi 1500 let/Tbilisi is 1,500 Years Old* (1959). She began directing features in 1961, and her greatest success was *Neskol'ko interv'yu po lichnym voprosam/Several Interviews on Personal Problems* (1979), the story of a Tbilisi journalist whose professional success is soured by her errant husband's complaints of neglect (professional women also figure strongly in *Krugovorot/The Whirlwind*, 1987). This film has an autobiographical strand, in scenes in which the heroine recalls being reunited with her mother, returned from the camps – scenes which, in their stillness and concentration, contrast with the energetic visual style of the rest of the film. Gogoberidze has approached this material directly in her most recent film, *Valsi Pecoraze/Waltz on the Pecora River* (1992). Set in the late 1930s, it tells the parallel stories of a mother exiled as the wife of an 'enemy of the people', and her daughter, who runs away from an orphanage to find the family flat now occupied by a KGB officer. JGf

GOLDCREST

British production company, which symbolised renaissance for the British film industry after *Chariots of Fire* in 1981, and despair following the failure of *Revolution* in 1985. Goldcrest was started by Jake Eberts in 1977 as a film development company. Following the international success of *Chariots of Fire* and *Gandhi* (1982), Goldcrest became an independent production company with David Puttnam* and Richard Attenborough* on the Board. It had an ambitious slate aimed at the American market with smaller budget productions for television and cable. Success and prestige continued with *Local Hero* (1983) and *The Killing Fields* (1984), and it seemed that Goldcrest could do no wrong. In 1985, James Lee, Chief Executive after Eberts left in 1983, declared, 'Hopefully, this will be the last year we find ourselves quite as vulnerable to one film.' The one film was the commercially disastrous *Revolution* (1985), with *Absolute Beginners* (1986) to follow. *A Room with a View* (1985) and *The Mission* (1986) continued to win Oscars for the company but could not save it, and it was sold in 1987. The ambitions of Goldcrest, and their failure, concentrated minds on the nature of a British national cinema. JC

Bib: Jake Eberts and Terry Ilott, *My Indecision is Final: The Rise and Fall of Goldcrest Films* (1990).

GONZÁLEZ, Agustín   Agustín González Martínez; Madrid 1930

Spanish actor. After Juan Antonio Bardem's* *Felices Pascuas/Happy Christmas* in 1953 González appeared in many supporting roles, usually as a hard man. His powerful build and grim features made him highly suitable for tough guys: a *cacique* (petty tyrant) in *Los santos inocentes/Holy Innocents* (1984, dir. Mario Camús*), and corrupt figures of authority in *El aire de un crimen/Scent of a Crime* (1988) and *La corte de Faraón/Pharaoh's Court* (1985). His forceful performances were an important feature of Luis García Berlanga's* trilogy, *La escopeta nacional/The National Shotgun* (1977), *Patrimonio nacional/National Heritage* (1980) and *Nacional III/National III* (1982). PWE

GORETTA, Claude   Geneva 1929

Swiss director, with Alain Tanner* the best-known director of the 'new Swiss cinema' of the late 1960s and the 1970s.

Goretta was educated in law at Geneva University before going to London with fellow student Tanner, where both worked at the British Film Institute* and – in the context of 'Free Cinema'* – made their first short documentary, *Nice Time* (1957), an impressionistic though sociologically acute view of London's Piccadilly Circus on a Saturday night. Goretta returned to Switzerland where he worked for television on documentaries and literary adaptions through the 1960s. He made his first feature about a character's decline into madness, the highly acclaimed *Le Fou/The Madman*, voted best Swiss film of 1970. *L'Invitation/The Invitation* (1973), a mischievous comedy about an office party which goes awry, was influenced by, among others, Jean Renoir* – to whom Goretta had paid tribute three years earlier in a loose television remake of *Partie de campagne* (original made in 1936) – and fared even better internationally, earning an Oscar nomination and a jury prize at Cannes. *Pas si méchant que ça/Not as Wicked as That* (1974), a French-Swiss co-production, though less successful, confirmed Goretta's growing international reputation, partly because of the casting of Gérard Depardieu* and Marlène Jobert in the lead roles. Inspired by a true story, this was a comedy about the head of a small firm (Depardieu) who has recourse to petty crime to keep his ailing firm afloat. Underneath the charm, though, there was, as Depardieu put it, 'a dark, contained violence'. Winning greater acclaim than these gentle comedies, *La Dentellière/The Lacemaker* (1977) was the portrait of a naive provincial beautician and her unhappy liaison with a young bourgeois intellectual. It became Goretta's best-known film, and launched Isabelle Huppert* as an international star. While praised at the time for its authenticity, the film's investment in such a melancholy, passive heroine (despite Huppert's intense performance) is not unproblematic. *La Dentellière* prefigured a return to the more intimate style of Goretta's early television work, as seen in *Les Chemins de l'exil ou Les Dernières années de Jean-Jacques Rousseau* (1978). *La Provinciale/A Girl from Lorraine* (1980) occupied similar territory to that of *La Dentellière*, with its 'sad' heroine, played this time by Nathalie Baye*. Goretta has continued to work regularly, but none of his films has acquired the reputation or the distribution of his 1970s work. MW/GV

Other Films Include: *Tchékhov ou Le Miroir des vies perdues* (1965); *Vivre ici/To Live Here* (1968); *Le Jour des noces/The Wedding Day* (1970); *Jean Piaget/The Epistemology of Jean Piaget* (1977); *La Mort de Mario Ricci/The Death of Mario Ricci* (1983); *Si le soleil ne revenait pas* (1987); *L'Ombre* (1991).

GORRIS, Marleen   Roermond 1948

Dutch director and scriptwriter. After literary and theatre studies, Gorris made a spectacular debut in 1982 with *De stilte rond Christine M/A Question of Silence*, which she wrote and directed. The film tells the story of three 'ordinary' women who kill a male shop-keeper, apparently without motive; their trial reveals, with the help of a woman lawyer, the extent of patriarchal oppression and the women's deep solidarity. *De stilte rond Christine M* gained immediate international recognition, though its militantly feminist content and approach sharply divided audiences. It also set the trend for Gorris' next films, with their metaphorical narratives of a world governed by men's destructive drives and of the need for women's solidarity. The sharp contrast between the sexes lends itself to a clear display of power relations. Gorris' resolute tone expresses itself through classical forms and transparent narration: *De stilte rond Christine M* is structured like a detective story, while *Gebroken spiegels/Broken Mirrors* (1984) is a modern Jack the Ripper tale. Both films were produced by Matthijs van Heijningen*. *The Last Island* (1990) was a – commercially – less successful account of the strained relations of a group of people stranded on a desert island. Since 1990 Gorris has also worked for television, directing a drama series written by young scriptwriters. She directed *Antonia* in 1995. KD/AN

GOVORUKHIN, Stanislav S.   Born 1936

Russian actor and director of feature films and documentaries. Govorukhin completed his studies at VGIK* in 1966, and began work in the Odessa studios. His first film, co-directed with V. Durov in 1967, was *Vertikal'/Vertical*, an adventure film starring the legendary actor and singer Vladimir Vysotsky. Among features directed by Govorukhin are *Zhizn' i udivitel'nye priklyucheniya Robinzona Kruzo/The Life and Extraordinary Adventures of Robinson Crusoe* (1973) and *Priklyucheniya Toma Soyera/The Adventures of Tom Sawyer* (1981), but his best-known feature was the five-part television film *Mesto vstrechi izmenit' nel'zya/The Meeting Place Cannot be Changed* (1979). A police thriller set at the end of World War II, and again starring Vysotsky, it was one of the most popular films of the era. In recent years, Govorukhin has been active both as an actor, notably in Sergei Solovyov's* *ASSA*, and as a polemical journalist, but his greatest fame is as director of documentaries. *Tak zhit' nel'zya/We Cannot Live Like This* (1990) was a combative assessment of the failures of Soviet Communism. *Rossiya, kotoruyu my poteryali/The Russia We Have Lost* (1991) offered an enthusiastic portrait of pre-Revolutionary Russia. *Alexander Solzhenitsyn* (1992), a television film, relates a journey by the director to the writer's Vermont home. JGf

GRAATKJÆR, Axel   Axel Sørensen; Velling-Koller 1885 – Århus 1969

Danish cinematographer. Graatkjær began his career as a programme seller in Ole Olsen's* Copenhagen cinema Biograf-Theatret in 1905. The following year he started as a cameraman in Olsen's new company, Nordisk Films*, for which he shot most of their fiction films until 1911, when expansion led to the hire of other cameramen. Graatkjær left Nordisk for Germany in 1913, as cameraman on the Asta Nielsen* films directed by Urban Gad. He remained in Germany, working for Ernst Lubitsch*, Robert Wiene* and Friedrich Wilhelm Murnau* among others, until the coming of sound, when he retired. The international reputation of early Danish films for their outstanding camerawork was in great part due to Graatkjær, especially his pioneering work on deep-focus cinematography, and Johan Ankerstjerne*. One of the best examples of Graatkjær's work is August Blom's* *Ved Fængslets Port/Temptations of a Great City* (1911). ME

GRANGER, Stewart   James Leblache Stewart; London 1913 – Santa Monica, USA 1993

British actor, who, with James Mason*, was one of the top British box-office attractions as a romantic lead in the Gainsborough melodramas* of the 1940s. Less dangerous than Mason, in *The Man in Grey* (1943) and *Fanny by Gaslight* (1944) he played the chivalrous champion of damsels placed in distress by Mason's aristocratic villainy. In *Love Story* (1944), a contemporary melodrama, he played a gallant RAF pilot threatened by blindness, while in the exotic *Madonna of the Seven Moons* (1944) he was a gypsy brigand offering Phyllis Calvert* a romantic alternative to respectablity with a rich Italian banker. Outside the Gainsborough series, but still a romantic genre actor, he starred in Frank Launder's* *Captain Boycott* (1947) and Basil Dearden's* *Saraband for Dead Lovers* (1948), before moving to Hollywood in the 1950s for a series of swashbuckling adventurer roles under contract to MGM: *King Solomon's Mines* (1950), *Scaramouche* (1952), *The Prisoner of Zenda* (1952), *Beau Brummell* (1954), *Moonfleet* (1955) and *Bhowani Junction* (1956) [all US]. In realistic vein, Sidney Gilliat cast him as a predatory spiv in *Waterloo Road* (1945) and Dearden exploited his moral ambiguity in *The Secret Partner* (1961). His film career declined in the 1970s, and he later worked mainly for American television. JC

GREAT BRITAIN

'... the English cinema remains utterly amorphous, unclassified, unperceived.' (Peter Wollen*, 1969)

The history of British cinema begins promisingly. Victorian enterprise and invention primed the first generation for the new technology, and Victorian entertainment and social improvement prepared an audience in the music halls and the magic lantern shows. Both before and after the first demonstration of the Lumière Cinematograph* in Paris in December 1895, moving picture patents were taken out, and Birt Acres had demonstrated his system for the projection of motion pictures on 15 January 1896 to members of the Royal Photographic Society, a month before the first demonstration of the Lumière system to a paying public in Britain on 20 February 1896 at the Regent Street Polytechnic in London. The early cinematographers were portrait photographers, lanternists, instrument makers and businessmen, and they established bases not only in London, but in Yorkshire (Bamforth & Company, the Sheffield Photo Company), Lancashire (Mitchell and Kenyon), and, most famously, in Brighton. From the so-called 'Brighton school', G. A. Smith* corresponded and shared tricks with Georges Méliès*, and both he and James Williamson* developed close-ups and multi-shot scenes before Edwin Porter in America.

Britain, then, shares with France many of the pioneering initiatives of early cinema, and by 1900, given its access to an imperial world market, could have been expected to become a (if not the) world leader. The fact that it did not may have more to do with the economic, legislative and cultural conditions in which British cinema developed than with something inherent in the British character. *Pace* Satyajit Ray ('I do not think the British are temperamentally equipped to make the best use of the movie camera') and François Truffaut* ('Isn't there a certain incompatibility between the terms "cinema" and "Britain"?'), the amorphousness which Peter Wollen notes in British cinema may be better understood as a product of history than as a state of nature.

Britain and Hollywood

All European cinemas live in the shadow of Hollywood. Britain, however, like Ireland, lives in the same linguistic market. In one transatlantic flow, this has meant that British audiences receive Hollywood films in their own language, without the mediation of dubbing or subtitling, allowing the Hollywood cinema to compete with the national cinema on equal terms. In the other direction, it has meant that major British producers from Alexander Korda* to David Puttnam* have looked to the North American market as the nut they have to crack. In either direction, it gives a particular turn of the screw to the notion of a national cinema in Britain, and gives Britain a particular place in European cinema.

Historically, the American domination of the British market was already in place by the beginning of World War I. The war itself, with many European cinemas out of action, established Hollywood's hegemony, its large domestic market enabling it to construct at an early stage a modern, Fordist mode of production capable of providing mass entertainment for a world market. By 1926, with around 3,500 cinemas operating in Britain and approximately 40 per cent of cinemagoers attending twice a week, only 5 per cent of the films shown in Britain were produced in Britain, and Britain represented over a third of Hollywood's foreign earnings.

During the silent period the possibility of Britain being part of a European cinema was still open. It was an easy matter to retitle or remake films for different national languages and French films were popular in the cinemas. Alfred Hitchcock* directed his first films for Michael Balcon* in Germany, Michael Powell* had his first job with Rex Ingram in the south of France, directors like Victor Saville* and Graham Cutts* worked in France and Germany, and even a star like Betty Balfour* made films with Louis Mercanton and Marcel L'Herbier*. The arrival of sound, however, reshaped the world market around language, placed Britain firmly in the same linguistic market as Hollywood, and severed the links with the European mainland.

But British audiences' infatuation with Hollywood was not simply a matter of markets, and Jeffrey Richards in *The Age of the Dream Palace* (1984) suggests some of the irrational, cultural reasons which shaped preferences. Of particular relevance is a split which emerged in the audience not around language but around accent, with a marked preference for American films among the working-class audience and satisfaction with British films among the middle classes. Richards quotes a 1937 survey of exhibitors in *World Film News* which reports on the difficulties that exhibitors in working-class areas had with British films:

> British films, one Scottish exhibitor writes, should rather be called English films in a particularly parochial sense: they are more foreign to his audience than the products of Hollywood, over 6,000 miles away. Again and again exhibitors of this category complain of 'old school tie' standards inherent in so many British films. They describe the 'horse laughs' with which the Oxford accents of supposed crooks are greeted and the impatience of their patrons with the well-worn 'social drama' type of filmed stageshow.

This working-class audience (which most surveys put at around 80 per cent of the total) preferred 'the more vigorous American films'. Exhibitors from middle-class areas, however, reported a preference for British films, 'especially in places like Bournemouth, Dorking, the Isle of Wight etc.'

> Good clean comedy and society drama with interesting dialogue, something people can think about and discuss afterwards, seems to sum up the most frequent attitude to what is wanted. The Gaumont (Matthews–Hitchcock) and Wilcox (Anna Neagle) type of British film seems to go down particularly well. History is often stated to be popular, as are mystery films. American gangster, crime or police films are frowned upon.

In a country as divided as Britain by class and region, with their separate tastes, preferences and prejudices, American films may have occupied neutral territory for the mass market on which the box office depended, and Jimmy Cagney may have been more recognisable as a working-class hero than Michael Redgrave. The popular British films with the working-class audience of the 1930s were, of course, those of George Formby* and Gracie Fields* with their roots in northern music hall. Critics, on the other hand, voted with Bournemouth and Dorking, and the opposition was established between a 'quality' British cinema, based on the supposedly 'English' characteristics of reality and restraint, and the frivolities and melodramas of the Hollywood dream factory, an opposition which revolved around Michael Balcon's* distinction of 'realism and tinsel'.

World War II provided the conditions for such a quality cinema. Feature film output dropped and imports were restricted, but audiences increased, and, in the Crown Film Unit and the Ministry of Information, the government had established a support mechanism not only for documentaries and information films, but also for feature production, as part of the war effort at home and overseas. The war also provided British themes and narratives which offered an emotional intensity to a British audience primed for patriotism. Films like *Target for Tonight* (1941) and *49th Parallel* (1941) were top box-office draws, and in the early stages of the war, realism with its roots in documentary established itself not only as a quality cinema, but also as a popular national cinema.

Much of the history of Britain's immediate postwar relations with Hollywood concerns a series of negotiations by Rank for a share of the American market, and a series of bunglings by government on the imposition and repeal of import taxes on films, which resulted in boycott skirmishes across the Atlantic. The requirement for American companies to remit more of their profits for investment in British production intensified the pressure on them to form subsidiaries in Britain, advancing the process of turning

British commercial cinema into a branch industry dependent on American investment and distribution.

Domestically produced feature films clearly targeted at British audiences continued to be produced by teams like Basil Dearden* and Michael Relph, Frank Launder* and Sidney Gilliat, or the Boulting Brothers*, well into the 1960s, the British New Wave* continued to send out echoes into the 1970s, and the *Carry On** films went on until 1978. But as Margaret Dickinson and Sarah Street suggest in *Cinema and State* (1985), 'After 1961 it became increasingly difficult to define any part of the industry as British rather than Anglo-American', and the generation of successful film-makers which emerged in the late 1970s and 1980s – Ridley Scott*, Alan Parker*, David Puttnam* – have been explicit, with varying degrees of satisfaction, that their kind of success is dependent on the American market.

The impact of Hollywood on British culture has been by no means wholly negative, and there have been good reasons for audiences to prefer American films. Its economic dominance in mass entertainment, however, in production, distribution and, increasingly, exhibition, has progressively closed down the possibilities of a national popular cinema in Britain, while the lure of the American box office has shaped the possibilities which remain, commodifying culture as marketable images.

Regulation and support

For most other European countries the arguments for a national cinema could be bound up with the defence of a national culture in the national language. In many countries, these were arguments which governments could recognise, producing systems of legislation and support that provided the conditions for some kind of relatively coherent cultural strategy. In Britain, the language argument did not apply, and culture was not regarded as a proper concern of government. British government policy towards cinema has been dedicated much more significantly to the regulation of the market and the protection of the manufacturing industry than to the sustenance of a national film culture.

The first significant legislation of cinema in Britain was the 1927 Cinematograph Films Act, which instituted a quota on foreign imports. The quota provision required exhibitors to increase the percentage of domestic product shown in the cinemas from the 5 per cent of 1927 to 20 per cent by 1935. The initial effect was indeed to boost production: new companies appeared, large companies like Gaumont-British and Gainsborough reorganised to take advantage of quota requirements, and the largest company, British International Pictures, built its studios at Elstree. The later effect, when it was discovered that audiences still preferred American films, was to produce 'quota quickies' at minimum cost to satisfy the quota requirement. Very little critical work has been done on the 'quota quickie', and the judgment that they were uniformly dreadful may be the result of assumption rather than analysis. They did achieve at least some of the requirements of an industrial quota by maintaining employment levels in the industry, and they provided conditions in which directors like Carol Reed* and Michael Powell*, and actresses like Margaret Lockwood* and Googie Withers*, could work on a large number of films in a relatively short space of time. They did not, however, win over audiences to British films.

The quota was a protective measure, designed to create a market for British films. Without investment, however, it was apparent that the only market which would be created was the British one, and that was not sufficient to guarantee the quality which critics increasingly demanded. In the postwar period, government, and particularly the Attlee Labour government with future Prime Minister Harold Wilson at the Board of Trade, began to develop systems of economic support for the production of 'quality' British films.

The first such initiative was the establishment in 1949 of the National Film Finance Corporation (NFFC) with a rolling fund of £5 million from the Treasury. While the NFFC was a limited resource in an increasingly difficult climate, over the thirty-five years of its existence it helped to fund over 750 films, including *The Third Man* (1949), *The Small Back Room* (1949), *The Happiest Days of Your Life* (1950), *Saturday Night and Sunday Morning* (1960) and *Gregory's Girl* (1981). It also supported the establishment of the short-lived Group 3, which produced twenty-two feature films between 1951 and 1955 with John Baxter* as managing director and John Grierson* as executive producer, a unique Griersonian attempt to develop a government-supported feature film production company.

In much the same spirit of doing something for the film industry, in 1951 the Labour government introduced the Eady Levy, a levy of one-twelfth of the ticket price at the box office, which was to be returned mainly to the producers of eligible British films but with some funds reserved for the British Film Institute* Experimental Film Fund (later the BFI Production Board), the National Film School and the Children's Film Foundation. While the support of the Experimental Film Fund (under the chairmanship of Michael Balcon*) clearly recognised the cultural dimension of film, as far as the return to producers was concerned there was no requirement as to the type of film, and the definition of a British film was a version of the one which had been developed for quota regulation: a film 75 per cent of whose production costs was spent on British labour and British materials. The Eady Levy did indeed provide an incentive to production, making the difference between profit and loss for many films and attracting overseas production to Britain. By the 1970s, the Hollywood majors were making increasing use of British studio space, exploiting British special effects skills to make a number of the new space age spectaculars. The result was that films like *Superman*, *Star Wars* and *Batman*, which were made in British studios with 75 per cent of their production costs going to British labour and materials, were defined by the Department of Trade and Industry as British films and qualified for Eady support. Both the logic and the absurdity of the situation are apparent. Following an industrial logic, the Levy attracted production to Britain which provided a continuation of skilled employment. The absurdity was that, while indigenous British producers struggled to survive, a government levy was subsidising what were already hugely successful films made by competitors in the linguistic market. The industrial logic produced a cultural absurdity.

By the end of the 1970s, a major difficulty for domestic production was in securing investment for British films which seemed increasingly to be high-risk investments. The brief flurry of renaissance at the beginning of the 1980s, associated mainly with Goldcrest* and hailed at the time as a resurgence of the national spirit, is attributable, at least in part, to a change in tax law. The Inland Revenue Statement of Practice SP9/79 was a tax arrangement, introduced in 1979, which allowed such institutions as banks and pension funds to consider films as the equivalent of industrial machinery, and claim tax relief against investment in films. It offered an incentive to financial houses and holding companies like Pearson-Longman and Crédit Lyonnais to invest in the film industry. The most visible result of this was *Chariots of Fire* (1981), much of whose initial funding came from the National Union of Mineworkers' Pension Fund. The success of *Chariots of Fire* was followed by that of *Gandhi* (1982), *Local Hero* (1983) and *A Passage to India* (1985), and the renaissance was on. The flurry looked like a change in the climate.

Unfortunately the climate changed again in 1986, and the late 1980s and early 1990s were marked by more traditional British weather. In line with removing public support from sections of industry which the Thatcher government thought should be 'liberated', the budget of 1985 not only withdrew tax incentives, it also terminated the Eady Levy and closed down the NFFC. It replaced the NFFC with British Screen, a consortium of major film and television interests – including Channel 4, Rank and Granada Television – with at least pump-priming support from the Treasury. While the initial record of British Screen under Simon Relph was impressive and often enlightened, funding sources which were themselves exposed to the uncertainties of the market were not capable of protecting the film industry from the devastations of recession. The number of films produced has fluctuated, but the levels of investment have shown a fairly steady downward trend: more films are struggling to find less money.

The historic lack of long-term forms of public support for cinema, either through subsidy or incentives, may not be unique to Britain in Europe, but it is a major determining condition. The discourse of economic liberalism proclaims that if British people freely choose to support American films, then they are exercising their sovereignty as consumers and it is not for governments to intervene. But without effective government intervention there is a narrowing range of popular British cinema to exercise choice upon, and mainstream British cinema is driven more and more into dependence on American investment.

Television

Since at least the early 1980s it has been impossible to discuss British cinema without also discussing British television: the 'least worst television in the world', as Milton Schuman tagged it; or in another tag popular at the beginning of the 1980s, 'British cinema is alive and well, and its name is television.' The most apparent and dramatic effect of television has been the wooing of the mass audience away from public forms of entertainment towards private, domestic entertainment. In Britain this happened more dramatically than elsewhere in Europe, partly because British television was able to meet the need for native forms of entertainment which cinema had failed to satisfy, and partly because postwar cinema was in the stranglehold of near monopolistic or duopolistic conditions in distribution and exhibition. The two factors together created a downward spiral in which cinema admissions declined from a peak of 1,635 million in 1946 to a low of around 70 million in 1984. In weaning the audience

from public entertainment, television also prepared the way for video, with Britain, by the beginning of the 1980s, running second only to Japan in per capita ownership of video recorders, demonstrating that Britain had not lost its appetite for films but had transferred its affections to the small screen.

The initial reaction of the film industry to television's popularity was self-protection and non-cooperation. Since 1982, however, with the arrival of Channel 4 and increasingly with the Films Act of 1991 – which requires all broadcasters to commission at least 25 per cent of their domestically produced programmes from independent producers – the film industry and the television industry have been on converging tracks. In particular, television has become the one remaining hope of an indigenous low to medium-budget feature film industry.

The increasing interdependency of television and cinema transforms not only the economics of British film but also the cultural and aesthetic expectations which the national audience and the international market have of it. Directors like Ken Loach* and Mike Leigh* have brought what is essentially a British television aesthetic into cinema, to considerable international acclaim, challenging to some extent the critical antipathy to British cinema and chipping away at its amorphousness. More insidiously, television has primed the world audience for the prestige of Britain's literary and theatrical heritage, finding a market through such sumptuous literary adaptations as *Brideshead Revisited* (1981) and *The Jewel in the Crown* (1984) for the 'Heritage' film*, one of Britain's more dubious contributions to world culture. The rediscovery in the films of Merchant/Ivory* *et al.* of Edwardian England and its waning Empire – the ironic ambivalence towards class and sexuality of E. M. Forster or Evelyn Waugh softened by the warm, elegiac tones of national nostalgia – seems to have reshaped what is meant by 'quality' in British cinema into period detail, melancholic languor and the evocation of loss. At a time when Britain has difficulty selling much else, it has been remarkably successful at selling its past.

An art cinema?

These are some of the conditions which give shape to the 'official' British cinema, and particularly to the British 'quality' cinema. The place of the art cinema, however, as a component of the national culture like Italian neo-realism* or the French New Wave*, was occupied by the British Documentary Movement*. It is somehow appropriate to the empirical and utilitarian traditions of British thought that documentary should be its contribution to world art cinema: an art cinema, as Alan Lovell suggests (*Studies in Documentary* [1972]), which was ambivalent about art. The Documentary Movement is, however, a more complex phenomenon than critical discourses have sometimes supposed, and the experimentalism of Len Lye* or Norman McLaren*, the lyricism of Basil Wright*, or the links to Surrealism through Humphrey Jennings* and Alberto Cavalcanti*, were not wholly suppressed by the no-nonsense Calvinism of John Grierson*. Parallel to the 'official' art cinema of the Documentary Movement, there was an 'unofficial' cinema in the avant-gardism of the group around *Close Up*, the internationalism of the London Film Society*, and the political radicalism which developed around the Progressive

Film Institute, the Workers' Film and Photo League, and Kino. This latter constituted a Workers' Film Movement which shadowed the official Documentary Movement through the 1930s, offering a less consensual critique of British society and politics during the Depression, and engaging directly in the politics of class, the international arms industry, the international working-class movement, and the Spanish Civil War. The documentary attitude which was appropriated by critics and producers during and after the war for the discourse of quality cinema contained the official Documentary Movement and forgot the rest.

What was contained or forgotten in particular was modernism, and the documentary as art cinema which was promoted after the war (after the death of Jennings, with Lye in New York, McLaren in Canada and Cavalcanti back in Brazil) was an art cinema without the avant-garde* impulse of much European modernism. This lack of sustained engagement with modernism makes Britain's art cinema almost unique in Europe, and provides the distinction between an art cinema and a 'quality' cinema.

The currents of modernism and the avant-garde present in the unofficial cinema of the 1930s seem to have been extinguished by the patriotic needs of wartime cinema, and there is no continuous tradition. The current resurfaced, however, in the 1960s and 1970s in the Workshop Movement*, the London Film-makers Co-op, and the Independent Film-makers Association. This very heterogeneous movement emerged from the aesthetics of the American avant-garde, pop art, the politics of 1968 and feminism as both an alternative cinema and an oppositional cinema; it was fostered by the BFI* Production Board, the Arts Council and the Greater London Council; and it was given an infrastructure by Channel 4* in the 1980s. Placed, and placing itself, on the margins, with no intention of being absorbed into the mainstream, it was nevertheless a remarkably vigorous and vigorously diverse current. In the 1980s and 1990s, with the emergence out of this current of directors like Peter Greenaway*, Derek Jarman*, Sally Potter* and Isaac Julien*, there is the first appearance of a British art cinema which has engaged not only with modernism, but with popular culture, pop art and the other avant-garde movements of American and European culture, combining them with a more localised politics of race, gender and sexuality. With the continuing infirmity or uncertainty of indigenous mainstream cinema, the eddies on the edge of the mainstream begin to suggest what a national cinema might look like, the amorphousness which Wollen complains of beginning to redefine itself more positively as diversity.

Critical perspective
It seems possible that some of the shapelessness of British cinema is a trick of critical perspective. Certainly, it is not a cinéma d'auteurs, and many of those who have been quickest to bury it – Truffaut*, Movie* – have been those who are most committed to the creative, self-expressive auteur as the guarantee of value. In a cinema which lacks stable systems of support, the producer has to create the structures in which expression can happen, continually reinventing the wheel, and it may be those structures, rather than the individual artist, which give the cinema its shape. If, as Andrew Sarris claims, the history of American cinema is a history of direc-

tors, then the history of British cinema is one of producers and producer-directors – Hepworth*, Balcon*, Korda*, Grierson*, Puttnam*, Attenborough* – and of production teams – Powell* and Pressburger, Dearden* and Relph, Launder* and Gilliat, Muriel and Sidney Box*, the Boulting Brothers*, Merchant-Ivory*. The individual director as auteur, the self-expressive artist who allowed critics to shape American popular cinema and European art cinema, is a more elusive figure in British film culture. This is not to suggest that all that is required to make British cinema fall into place is a substitution of the producer for the director, or even the replacement of one critical paradigm by another – genre studies, say, instead of authorship. No single paradigm seems adequate to the specificities and diversities of a national cinema. Without a means of classification or a test of value, criticism is faced with the choice of abandoning the theory or abandoning the cinema. It may be, however, that it is not the shape of the cinema which is the problem but the shape of the criticism.

In the 1990s, in a Britain which is no longer Great and a Kingdom which is no longer United, there are again signs of a cinema staggering towards resurgence, still without consistent support and still uncertain about what constitutes success. Like Dr Johnson's walking dogs, it is not always that they do it well but that they do it at all that seems to invite – and deserve – attention. Four Weddings and a Funeral (1994) is undoubtedly an international phenomenon, but it does not in itself constitute a renaissance: it may, in fact, be an example of a film which is only famous for being famous. More significant is the tentative emergence of an infrastructure which allows films to be produced in unexpected places and at a variety of levels. If British cinema as a complex whole begins to seem something more than a contradiction in terms, and if criticism finds new ways of charting its history, it may be because both cinema and criticism are beginning to recognise and reflect the fault lines, divisions and diversities which disunite the culture into differences and identities rather than imposing on it the unity implicit in the desire for a National Cinema. JC

[> BOND FILMS, EALING COMEDY, FREE CINEMA, GAINSBOROUGH MELODRAMA, HAMMER HORROR, CLOSE UP, SCREEN, SEQUENCE, SIGHT AND SOUND].

GREECE

The beginnings of cinema in Greece are still not well documented. The first public film screening took place in 1897 or 1898 in Athens, probably of Lumière* films. Public reactions reportedly ranged from wonderment to uproar and the stoning of the screen. By 1903, however, there was permanently installed projection equipment, showing mainly French films.

The first film made in Greece was a newsreel of the 1906 interim Olympics held in Athens, possibly shot by a French cameraman, Gaumont's* representative in Egypt. Subsequently a number of short Greek subjects (newsreels and fictional) were filmed, often by foreign cameramen, notably the Hungarian Josef Hepp. The first production company, Athene Films, was set up in 1910 by Spiros Dimitrakopoulos, a slapstick comedian. Only stills of his films survive. In 1911, Hepp filmed the medium-length I mikri *pringipes ston kipo tou palatiou/Young Princes in the Royal Garden*, a kind of royal home-movie, and *I issodos tou ellinikou stratou stin Thessaloniki/The Entry of the Greek Army into Salonika* (1912) in the first Balkan War. During the same period, Evangelos Mavrodimakis opened cinemas in Smyrna and Athens and established the first distribution company. *Golfo*, the first full-length Greek feature, was produced in 1914 and premiered on 22 January 1915. It was based on a bucolic popular play, a well-established melodramatic sub-genre which took its subjects from nineteenth-century country life, and was produced by Kostas Bahatoris and directed by an Italian, Filippo Martelli. From 1912 to 1922, Greece was embroiled in a series of regional conflicts which hampered the film industry's development. In 1916, in the first case of political censorship, Hepp was sent into internal exile for two years after making a documentary in support of the monarchy.

The first commercially successful Greek films were short comedies made by Vilar and Mihail Mihail in the 1920s. The Gaziadis brothers (Dimitris, Kostas and Mihalis) formed the production company DAG Film, which between 1927 and 1929 produced three feature-length films, all of them major commercial successes. The third, *Astero*, a bucolic melodrama directed by Dimitris Gaziadis, was the first Greek film to register in export markets, appealing to both Greek immigrants in the US and foreign audiences. The coming of sound in 1929 had dire repercussions. Lacking capital to adapt to the new technology, the Greek film industry collapsed, and during the 1930s very few films were made. DAG Film produced just two more films before going out of business. The first sound film was made in 1932, once more a bucolic melodrama, *O agapitikos tis voskopoulas/The Shepherdess' Lover*, by Dimitris Tsakiris. In the 1930s some Greek films were shot in Cairo and Istanbul, where technical facilities were available, but with indifferent results. Production restarted in 1939, but World War II and the ensuing German occupation (1941–44) put a stop to attempts to revive the industry. However, in 1939 Filopimin Finos made his first film and in 1943 formed the production company Finos Film*, which was to become the country's major studio. Its first film was one of the few made during the German occupation.

The ensuing civil war notwithstanding, the Greek film industry relaunched active production in 1945, producing films that attracted growing audiences despite strict censorship, casualties suffered in the hostilities and the acute poverty of the postwar years. Its cause was helped by the high level of illiteracy, the cost and technical difficulty of dubbing foreign films and the exodus from the countryside to the urban centres. By the late 1950s the film industry was at its most dynamic, exeriencing explosive (and profitable) growth. Within fifteen years Greece was making the highest number of films per capita in the world. For several years it produced around a hundred feature films a year: 101 Greek films were released in 1965–66, 117 in 1966–67, and 108 in 1968–69.

The early 1950s saw the first independent film productions, heavily influenced by Italian neo-realism* – Grigoris Grigoriou's *Pikro psomi/Bitter Bread* (1951) and Stelios Tatassopoulos' *I mavri yi/Black Earth* (1952). These were shot on location using amateur actors and tackled social issues. Nikos Koundouros* (*O drakos/The Ogre of Athens*, 1956) and Michael Cacoyannis* (*Stella*, 1955) attracted

international attention. In 1966 several other independent film-makers attempted to break the stranglehold of the commercial industry, proposing a committed and *auteur* cinema. The military dictatorship of 1967 effectively halted this trend until 1970, when Thodoros Angelopoulos* made his first film (*Anaparastassi/Reconstruction*), and the situation changed dramatically after the collapse of the dictatorship in 1974. Committed and political film-makers were able to work unhindered with, initially, considerable commercial success. In the new ideological climate, almost all pre-1974 films were condemned as 'old' and reactionary. The New Greek Cinema* emerged, a lively and innovative movement which attracted substantial popular interest. However, by 1974 Greek television was already reaching the majority of households, claiming an ever increasing audience. Greek television serials started to use the conventions and casts of the commercial cinema, producing small-screen versions of older movies. At the same time vintage Greek films provided television with some of its most popular programming. State television in the 1980s produced television films which were relatively successful in attracting audiences but were deemed too expensive to be continued. The combination of these developments plunged the film industry into a crisis from which it never recovered. Just sixteen Greek films were released in the 1976–77 season and seventeen in 1977–78, all commercial failures. The virtual elimination of censorship meant that one of the last attempts at survival would centre on pornographic films. The viability of these, too, collapsed after the deregulation of television and the proliferation of new channels in the late 1980s.

One of the perennial problems of the New Greek Cinema was lack of funds. To meet this, substantial resources were channelled to art cinema through the Greek Film Centre* during the 1980s, when Melina Mercouri* was the Socialist government's Minister of Culture. Otherwise, state involvement has been mainly through awards at the Thessaloniki* (Salonika) Film Festival and the annual State Cinema Awards. Despite support from the Film Centre, New Greek Cinema lost touch with its audience and stagnated in repetitive motifs and themes. Greece now produces only around ten films a year, few of interest or commercial significance except those by well-known directors such as Angelopoulos and Pandelis Voulgaris*. A sign of the times was the 1992 transformation of the Greek Film Festival in Salonika into an international event.

In the heyday of the commercial cinema, Greek films accounted for 16 per cent of the total and a 25 per cent share of the national box office; Hollywood provided 45 per cent of the films and took about the same market share. Most of the remainder came from France, Italy and the UK. Since 1975, American films have strongly increased their share of the market (88 per cent in 1991) at the expense of the rest; Greek films in 1991 took just 7 per cent of total box office. In the 1960s, before the advent of Greek television, a very strong secondary market of second-run and suburban cinemas operated, often showing films that were not released in first-run cinemas. Most of these films, which do not appear in the official statistics, were Greek, Turkish and Indian.

Legislation on cinema production and exhibition has been both spasmodic and repressive. A 1920s law stipulated that no film scene could be shot anywhere in Greece without the permission of the police; this has been relaxed only to the extent that the authority is now the Ministry of State. Very strict censorship regulations were introduced by the German occupation forces in 1942 and were never subsequently repealed. After 1974 censorship was liberalised in practice but not in law. In some cases the regulations are still used, as in the case of Martin Scorsese's *The Last Temptation of Christ* (1988), banned after strong protests by the Greek Church.

The first Greek film magazine, called *Kinimatografos* ('Cinema'), was launched in 1923 and lasted for twenty issues. 1924 saw the start of the bi-weekly trade journal *Kinimatografikos Astir* ('Film Star'), which survived until 1970. The first book on cinema, by film-maker Dimitris Gaziadis – *Pos boro na pexo ston kinimatografo* ('How Can I Act in the Cinema?') – was published in 1926, while in 1927 Mihail Mihail issued his autobiography, *Istoria enos paliatsou* ('History of a Clown'). The first journal to treat cinema in aesthetic and artistic terms was *Synchronos Kinimatografos** ('Contemporary Cinema'), published from 1969 to 1985. The 1970s saw the launch of about ten other journals (*Film, Kinimatografika Tetradia, Proodeftikos Kinimatografos*, etc.) of which only one, *Othoni** ('Screen'), survives. Since 1983 the publishing company Egokeros has issued numerous books on the cinema. 1989 saw the first successful launch of a commercial monthly, *Cinema*.

Major genres and themes

The output of commercial Greek cinema consisted mainly of quickly made low-budget films aimed exclusively at the domestic market. A few films attempted to meet 'European' or Hollywood standards but met with little success abroad. Only Greek sex films had some impact on foreign markets. The industry operated under strict formulas and intense production schedules that left little room for experimentation. Only a small corpus of films produced independently after the war can be considered part of the European art cinema* of the period.

Commercial Greek cinema drew its inspiration from the major popular entertainment forms of the time: shadow puppet plays (*Karaghiozis*), satirical musical revues and sentimental novels. It used only a small number of plots, either comic or melodramatic. Within these two broad approaches there were a number of sub-generic variations: family melodramas, courtroom and crime dramas, pastoral melodramas, light sentimental comedies, satires, broad comedy. A few films can be classified under other genres, but these too borrow heavily from melodrama and comedy: musicals, war movies, sex films, adaptations of ancient Greek tragedies [> COMEDY (GREECE); GREEK MELODRAMA]. The central theme of most films, whether melodramas or comedies, is a socially ill-matched love affair. Invariably opposed by the richer families, it usually ends well. The melodramas present the problematic of the fulfilment of desire, the pain and hurt of the struggle to claim what is 'rightfully' one's own. The consoling message of the comedies is that 'ordinary' people possess the humour and humanity to see off difficulties.

It is not hard, however, to see the deep insecurity of the postwar years reflected in these films. Their intensity, labyrinthine plotting and abrupt changes of gear often leave narrative gaps where explanations cannot be accommodated. The acting is exaggerated, sometimes to the point of hysteria

– witness Thanassis Vengos*, Greek commercial cinema's comic superstar. Despite its peculiarities, the 'old' Greek cinema has played a most important role in the formation of Greek popular culture. Legendarily popular, the films have retained their appeal over the years, as their endless recycling on television shows. And their catch-phrases, jokes, mannerisms and songs have entered everyday life, recognised and used by people unborn when the films were made and often unaware of their origin. TN

GREEK FILM CENTRE

Greek institution. The Greek Film Centre (GFC) was set up in 1970 as a profit-making subsidiary of the Greek Industrial and Development Bank. It took its present name after the fall of the dictatorship in 1974. In 1982 the Ministry of Culture intervened to provide substantial loans and to make the Centre's principal objective the production and promotion of quality Greek films at home and abroad. In 1982 the GFC invested in thirteen feature and an equal number of short films, providing up to 50 per cent of the invested capital. It also improved the terms of its financial aid, allowing co-producers (often the directors of the film) to recoup their investment first. In 1983, the GFC began to finance scriptwriting. In 1986 a special department called 'Hellas Film' was created to promote Greek films abroad. By 1988 the GFC was the only Greek film production company in existence. Notwithstanding arguments about its role, it helped to preserve the national cinema. Almost all 'New' Greek film-makers received funds from its co-production programme [> NEW GREEK CINEMA], and it remains today the main Greek producer of new films (some of them international co-productions). Funds are raised through a percentage of cinema receipts, under the jurisdiction of the Ministry of Culture. NF

GREEK MELODRAMA

Greek film genre. Melodrama forms the core of mainstream Greek cinema, all of whose output, comic [> COMEDY (GREECE)] or tragic, contains large elements of the melodramatic. The key theme is relationships, both between the sexes and within families, especially mothers and sons.

The first feature-length Greek films belonged to a melodrama sub-genre much favoured by Greek cinema, the bucolic or pastoral melodrama. Here the major theme was the conflict between rich landowners and poor peasants, usually channelled through a liaison between members of the two opposing sides. The most important film in this sub-genre is *Dafnis ke Chloi/Daphnis and Chloe* (1931, dir. Orestis Laskos). After World War II, audiences developed a taste for treatments of contemporary urban experience. Now liaisons were the medium through which the urban poorer classes met the richer ones; examples are *To koritsi me ta paramithia/The Girl with the Tales* (1956, dir. Andreas Lambrinos), or *O nikitis/The Winner* (1965, dir. Maria Plita). Melodrama, especially the low-budget, high-speed 'melo' formula, successfully exploited the audience's desire for social mobility. Other themes included the suffering experienced by mothers in bringing up their children, especially their sons – *Amartissa ya to pedi mou/I Sinned for My Child* (1950, dir. Christos Spentzos) – and the search for identity: *I odissia enos xerizomenou/Odyssey of the Uprooted* (1969, dir. Apostolos Tegopoulos).

Greek melodrama can be divided into three categories: 'art', 'high' and 'melo'. 'Art' and 'high' melodramas were less common but carried more critical prestige. Their stories were more sophisticated versions of the themes used by the cheaper 'melo', which was dismissed out of hand by the cultural establishment. 'High' melodrama was influenced by Hollywood (*Lola*, 1964, dir. Dinos Dimopoulos), 'art' melodrama by Italian neo-realism* (*To koritsi me ta mavra/The Girl in Black*, 1956, dir. Michael Cacoyannis*; *Mayiki poli/Magic City*, 1954, dir. Nikos Koundouros*), while the 'melo' built on aspects of the Middle Eastern and Asian – Turkish, Indian and Arab – cinemas. TN

GREENAWAY, Peter   London 1942

British director, whose highly intellectual films, described by Chris Auty as 'beautiful butterflies trapped down by drawing pins', have moved from the seclusion of the avant-garde cinema of the 1970s to success with art-house audiences since *The Draughtsman's Contract* in 1982. A product of a 1960s art school training, influenced by John Cage and serialism, Greenaway is a neo-classical rather than a neo-romantic modernist, structuring his films around classificatory systems and numbers, splitting and doubling his characters, and distracting his narratives in red herrings, puns, non sequiturs and verbal disquisitions. Greenaway offers his art-house aficionados the pleasures of the puzzle rather than the satisfactions of resolution, and offers to more sceptical spectators a *mise-en-scène* of sumptuous cleverness which teeters on the brink of the ridiculous and lends itself easily to parody. The visual pastiche and narrative repetitions of the films are echoed in the tuneful minimalism of Michael Nyman's scores. 'At heart,' says Peter Wollen*, 'Greenaway, like R. B. Kitaj, is a collagist, juxtaposing images from some fantastic archive, tracing erudite coincidental narratives within his material, bringing together Balthus and Borges in a bizarre collocation of bizarre eroticism and trompe-l'oeil high modernism.' *The Baby of Mâcon* (1993), a co-production involving the UK, Netherlands, France and Germany, maintains the virtuosity, but suggests a director badly in need of a new idea. JC

Bib: Peter Wollen, 'The Last New Wave', in Lester Friedman (ed.), *British Cinema and Thatcherism* (1993).

Other Films Include: *Five Postcards from Capital Cities* (1967); *H is for House* (1973); *Dear Phone* (1977); *1–100, A Walk Through H, Vertical Features Remake* (1978); *The Falls* (1980); *Zandra Rhodes* (1981); *Four American Composers* (TV, 1983); *A Zed & Two Noughts* (1985); *The Belly of an Architect* (1987); *Drowning by Numbers* (1988); *The Cook the Thief His Wife & Her Lover* (1989); *A TV Dante – Cantos 1–8* [TV] (1990); *Prospero's Books* (1991).

GREENE, Graham   Berkhamsted 1904 – Vevey, Switzerland 1991

British novelist, scriptwriter and critic. Graham Greene is identified with the 'literary tradition' of British cinema, dealing in Paul Rotha's words with 'complex themes of great importance'. His early contact with cinema was as film critic for the *Spectator* from 1935 to 1940. His criticism was often caustic, but in his advocacy of a 'poetic cinema' he anticipated Lindsay Anderson* and the critics of *Sequence*. A collection of his film criticism, *The Pleasure Dome*, was published in 1972, and a Graham Greene Film Reader, *Mornings in the Dark*, in 1993. He is probably the most adapted of the major contemporary British novelists, with his novels or short stories forming the basis for Alberto Cavalcanti's* *Went the Day Well?* (1942), Fritz Lang's* *Ministry of Fear* (1944, US), John Ford's *The Fugitive* (1947, US) and George Cukor's *Travels with My Aunt* (1972, US), among others. His own experience of writing for the cinema has been uneven, and he writes of it with some scepticism. His collaboration with Carol Reed* did, however, produce three distinctive films: *The Fallen Idol* (1948), *The Third Man* (1949) and *Our Man in Havana* (1960); and for John Boulting* he adapted his own novel, *Brighton Rock* (1947). JC

Bib: *Mornings in the Dark: Graham Greene Film Reader* (1993).

Other Films As Scriptwriter Include: *La mano dello straniero/The Stranger's Hand* [from his own short story] (1954, It./UK); *Loser Takes All* [from his own novel] (1956); *Saint Joan* (1957); *The Comedians* [from his own novel] (1967).

GREENWOOD, Joan   London 1921–87

British actress, whose particular contribution to postwar cinema was to introduce a genteel eroticism to the English upper classes, playing off an unmistakable husky voice against 'English rose' respectability. In *Kind Hearts and Coronets* (1949) there is an unambiguous sexuality in her performance, suggesting a delight in adultery unexpected in an Ealing* comedy. Her performance as Gwendolen in *The Importance of Being Earnest* (1952) confirmed her strength in high theatrical comedy. Ealing was probably not the place to develop her particular erotic potential, though she played winsome leads for Alexander Mackendrick* in *Whisky Galore!* (1949) and *The Man in the White Suit* (1951), and the British cinema in general offered her very little after another sexy cameo in *Tom Jones* (1963). She continued to work in theatre, and returned to television in 1981 to play a wonderfully dotty, husky and still sexy aunt in Trevor Griffiths' *Country*. JC

GRÉMILLON, Jean   Bayeux 1901 – Paris 1959

French director. One of the least known of the great French directors of the 1930s, Grémillon is possibly the most 'classic' in his combination of realism and popular genres. While

191

studying music, Grémillon played the violin in cinemas. His first films were documentaries, and his first features, *Maldone* (1928) and *Gardiens de phare* (1929), critical successes. The popular success of the latter led to a contract with Pathé*-Natan, but *La Petite Lise* (1930), judged too black, displeased the company and Grémillon was fired; *Daïnah la métisse* (1931) was mutilated by its producer, GFFA. After a fallow period, success returned with *Gueule d'amour* (1937, one of Jean Gabin's* best films), lasting until *Le Ciel est à vous* (1943–44), and including *L'Etrange Monsieur Victor* (1938), *Remorques/Stormy Waters* (1939–41) and *Lumière d'été* (1943). His postwar career was chequered. But among documentaries and aborted projects the excellent *Pattes blanches* (1948) and *L'Amour d'une femme* (1954) stand out.

Grémillon's atmospheric realism, especially his depictions of social milieux (typographers, seamen, the provincial bourgeoisie), echoed his definition that 'it is a question not of mechanical naturalism, but, rather, of the beauty in achieving the maximum of expression within the maximum of order.' He also, unusually, offered portraits of remarkably strong and complex women in *Le Ciel est à vous* and *L'Amour d'une femme*, feminist heroines *avant la lettre* (respectively Madeleine Renaud* and Micheline Presle*), struggling equally with work and love. There as in *Gueule d'amour*, Grémillon made explosive use of melodrama, subverting (as Geneviève Sellier has noted) dominant cinema from inside, reaching a wide audience without compromising his own ideas. GV

Bib: Geneviève Sellier, *Jean Grémillon, Le Cinéma est à vous* (1989).

Other Features: *Pour un sou d'amour* (1931, uncredited); *La Dolorosa* (1934, Sp.); *La Valse royale* [French version of *Koenigswalzer*, Ger.], *Pattes de mouche* (1936); *L'Etrange Madame X* (1951).

GRETLER, Heinrich   Zurich 1897–1977

Swiss actor, who started his career on the Zurich stage in 1919 and five years later made his screen debut in the Swiss-American co-production *Die Enstehung der Eidgenossenschaft/William Tell*. After a seven-year interlude on the Berlin stage during which he also appeared in several German films, he returned to Switzerland in 1933. His exceptionally deep voice and aged looks while still in his thirties destined him to portray fatherly characters, notably in numerous dialect comedies (including *Wie d'Warret würkt/The Effects of Truth*, 1933, and *Jä-soo!*, 1935), political apologias for national independence (*Füsilier Wipf*, 1938; *Landammann Stauffacher*, 1941, dir. Leopold Lindtberg*), and in Max Haufler's *L'Or dans la montagne* (1939) and Lindtberg's adaptions of Friedrich Glauser's popular novels *Wachtmeister Studer* (1939) and *Matto regiert* (1947). After the war he once more worked in Germany and Austria, his popular screen image inextricably bound up with weather-beaten, good-natured Swiss mountain folk, whose ultimate expression Gretler probably gave as Alp-Oehi in Johanna Spyri's *Heidi* (1952) and *Heidi and Peter* (1955). MW

Bib: Werner Wollenberger, *Heinrich Gretler: Der grosse Schweizer Schauspieler* (1981).

Other Films Include: *Die mißbrauchten Liebesbriefe* (1940); *Steinbruch* (1942); *Herz der Welt* (1952); *Die Sonne von St. Moritz, Rosen-Resli, Uli, der Knecht* (1954); *Der 42. Himmel* (1962); *Kohlhiesels Töchter* (1962).

GRIERSON, John   Deanston, Scotland 1898 – Bath 1972

British producer, director and critic, founder of the British Documentary Movement* and one of the most influential figures in the development of British film culture. Grierson was born near Stirling in Scotland and educated in Literature and Philosophy at the University of Glasgow. He travelled on a scholarship to the United States, where he studied mass communications and wrote on cinema. On his return to Britain, he joined the Empire Marketing Board (EMB) as Assistant Films Officer in 1927, and produced and directed *Drifters*, which was premiered at the London Film Society with *Battleship Potemkin* in 1929. He persuaded Stephen Tallents to form the EMB Film Unit, and began to assemble a team of young film-makers who formed the Documentary Movement, moving to the General Post Office (GPO) Film Unit when the EMB was disbanded in 1933. Grierson left the GPO in 1936, and was appointed Film Adviser to the Imperial Relations Trust and to the governments of Australia, New Zealand and Canada. In 1938 he formed Film Centre with Arthur Elton, Basil Wright* and Stuart Legg to explore the possibilities of the sponsored documentary independent of government, and became Production Adviser to Films of Scotland. He advised on the establishment of the National Film Board of Canada and became its first Commissioner in 1939. Similar Film Boards were established in New Zealand and Australia in the 1940s. In 1945, based in New York, he was investigated for Communist sympathies. Visiting Britain in 1947, he was refused a re-entry visa to the US, and worked for UNESCO in Paris. Returning to Britain, he was Controller of the Films Division of the Central Office of Information from 1948 until 1950, and from 1951 until 1954 he was Executive Producer of Group 3, a body established by the newly formed National Film Finance Corporation to produce feature films. In 1955 he joined Scottish Television (STV), producing and presenting *This Wonderful World*, a selection of international documentaries, until 1965.

The reach of Grierson's influence is less in the films he directed (which are uncertain as credits were a matter of little concern), or even produced, than in the institutions he established, the careers he began, the production opportunities he opened, the aesthetics he promoted, and the critical values he advocated. Taken together, these gave a material reality to the discourse of a cinema of public service, civic responsibility and the 'creative treatment of reality'. 'I regard cinema as a pulpit,' he famously declared, and the word which he preached has left an inheritance of social democratic values that still underpins many of the critical discourses which seek to define British cinema. JC

Bib: Ian Aitken, *Film and Reform: John Grierson and the Documentary Movement* (1990).

GRIMAULT, Paul
Neuilly-sur-Seine 1905 – Yvelines 1994

French animation director. A draughtsman and designer, Grimault was close to the Surrealists and a friend of Jacques Prévert*, with whom he later collaborated; he appeared briefly in *L'Atalante* (1934) and *Le Crime de Monsieur Lange* (1935). Learning animation techniques, he made *Phénomènes électriques* for the 1937 Paris Exhibition, using the French Hypergonar system (a precursor of CinemaScope) and Technicolor. Subsequently, Grimault made poetic and humorous animated shorts, including *Le Petit soldat* (1947) with Prévert. In the same year he began the first French animated feature, *La Bergère et le ramoneur/The Shepherdess and the Sweep*, a libertarian fairy tale from a Prévert script. Grimault disowned the butchered version released in 1953 but bought the negative in 1967 and reworked it with Prévert. The beautiful final version, mixing old and new footage, was released in 1980 as *Le Roi et l'Oiseau/The King and Mister Bird* (awarded the Prix Louis Delluc*). Grimault's last film, *La Table tournante* (1989), combines old animated films and live action by Jacques Demy*. Along with Emile Cohl*, Grimault was the key figure in French animation film and a great influence on younger generations. GV

GROSMANN, Karol
Drakovci, Slovenia 1864 – Ljutomer, Slovenia 1929

Pioneer of Slovene cinema. His two-minute 17.5 mm *Sejem v Ljutomeru/Ljutomer's Fair* (1905) is the first known Slovene movie. *Odhod od maše/Return from the Church* (1905) and *Na domačem vrtu/Home Garden* (1906) later confirmed his Lumière*-like vision of cinematographic views as fragments of everyday life. A lawyer and intellectual, Grosmann was well known for his fascination with modern techniques. A pure coincidence brought a slightly wounded German soldier named Fritz Lang* into his house during World War I. Lang stayed for a few weeks and made some sculptures, visible in Karpo Godina's* *Umetni raj/Artificial Paradise* (1990). SP

GRUBČEVA, Ivanka
Sofia 1946

Bulgarian director. Best known internationally for her award-winning films for children and youth. Upon graduating from the Babelsberg Film School in Potsdam (GDR) with the diploma film *Hlapeto/The Brat* (1968), based on a Georgi Mišev* story, Grubčeva worked as assistant director for Metodi Andonov* and Ivan Terziev before embarking on an antifascist theme in *Edin mig svoboda/A Moment of Freedom* (1970). The film's failure, both artistically and commercially, prompted a return to the world of children to make a string of highly praised films, as well as television productions such as *Deca igrajat văn/Children Play out of Doors* (1972), *Izpiti po nikoe vreme/Exams at Any Odd Time* (1974), *Pri niko-go/With Nobody* (1975), and the five-part television serial *Vojnata na taraležite/The Hedgehogs' War* (1979). Working principally with scriptwriters Georgi Danailov and the Mormarev brothers, who often used the children's film to deal critically with general social problems, Grubčeva was instrumental in raising the Bulgarian children's film to a high standard. In 1987, with Gorbachev's rise to power in the USSR, she was appointed artistic director of the newly formed Alfa production unit at the Boyana* Studios. RH

GRÜNDGENS, Gustaf
Düsseldorf 1899 – Manila 1963

German actor and director, whose life was immortalised as the 'Mephisto' of Klaus Mann's book and Istvan Szabó's* film (1981). In 1920 Gründgens worked in the theatre, acting and directing in the classic repertoire (Shakespeare, Büchner, Wilde, Shaw) while also doing cabaret and opera. His film career began in 1929, when he played gentleman thieves and criminals (*Der Brand in der Oper*, 1930, *Die Gräfin von Monte Christo*, 1932, *M – Eine Stadt sucht ihren Mörder/M*, 1931). After acting in musical comedies (*Die Finanzen des Großherzogs*, 1934, *Tanz auf dem Vulkan*, 1938), historical epics (*So endete eine Liebe*, 1934, *Das Mädchen Johanna*, 1935), and propaganda films (*Ohm Krüger*, 1941), he was put in charge of a production unit at Terra-Filmkunst in 1938, where he directed a string of highly successful melodramas (such as *Der Schritt vom Wege*, 1939). Heavily compromised by his prominent role during the Nazi period, he nonetheless worked as director of several theatres after the war (Städtische Bühnen Düsseldorf, Deutsches Schauspielhaus Hamburg, 1947–63). KP

Bib: Heinrich Goertz, *Gustaf Gründgens* (1982).

GUBENKO, Nikolai N.
Odessa, Ukraine [USSR] 1941

Russian actor, director and screenwriter. Gubenko graduated from the acting faculty of VGIK* in 1964, and from the directing faculty, where he studied in the workshop of Sergei Gerasimov* and Tamara Makarova*, in 1970. His acting debut was as Kolya Fokin in Marlen Khutsiev's* *Zastava Il'icha/The Ilyich Gate*. Gubenko directed his first feature, *Prishël soldat s fronta/A Soldier Returns from the Front*, in 1972. Among his best films are *Podranki/Orphans* (1977), which considers the lives of children orphaned by World War II; the satirical comedy *Iz zhizni otdykhayushchikh/Holiday People* (1981); and *I zhizn', i slëzy, i lyubov'/Life, Love, Tears* (1984), the story of a group of pensioners living in an old people's home. In 1987 Gubenko directed *Zapretnaya zona/Forbidden Zone*, about the devastating effect of a hurricane on the inhabitants of a small Volga village. In 1987 he also became the director of the legendary Taganka Theatre in Moscow. In the last years of the Soviet Union he served as Minister of Culture. JGf

GUERRA, Tonino
Santarcangelo di Romagna 1920

Italian scriptwriter. One of the finest Italian dialect poets of the twentieth century, Guerra was also a gifted prose writer who used ironic and concise simplicity in his somewhat grotesque and fairytale-like depictions of reality. His scriptwriting career started with Giuseppe De Santis'* *Uomini e lupi/Men and Wolves* (1956). He made notable contributions to the work of Michelangelo Antonioni* by creating his suspenseful atmospheres and increasingly free forms from *L'avventura* (1960) to *Identificazione di una donna/ Identification of a Woman* (1982). He wrote a series of 'fairytales' for Federico Fellini*, which include *Amarcord* (1973), *E la nave va/And the Ship Sails On* (1983) and *Ginger e Fred/Ginger and Fred* (1985). He worked for some considerable time with Elio Petri* (*L'assassino/Assassin*, 1961; *Un tranquillo posto in campagna/A Quiet Place in the Country*, 1968), with Francesco Rosi* (for example on *Cadaveri eccellenti/Illustrious Corpses*, 1975, and *Carmen*, 1984) and on many of the Taviani* brothers' finest films, including *La notte di San Lorenzo/The Night of San Lorenzo* (1982) and *Kaos* (1984). Guerra added poetry to the work of 'prose' *auteurs* such as Rosi and the Tavianis, but was not afraid to superimpose his own style on more 'poetic' directors. His versatility is evidenced by his work for such diverse directors as Andrey Tarkovsky* (*Nostalghia*, 1983), Thodoros Angelopoulos* (*Taxidi sta Kithira/Voyage to Cythera*, 1984; *O melissokomos/The Beekeeper*, 1986; *Topio stin omihli/Landscape in the Mist*, 1988) and Marco Bellocchio* (*Enrico IV/Henry IV*, 1984). He even produced some outstanding scripts for less popular directors, such as Franco Indovina (*Lo scatenato/ Catch as Catch Can*, 1967, and *Tre nel mille*, 1970), and adapted some of his own stories for the four-episode film *La domenica specialmente/Especially on Sunday* (1992). MMo

Other Films Include: *La strada lunga un anno* (1957); *La notte* (1961); *I giorni contati*, *L'eclisse/The Eclipse* (1962); *Deserto rosso/The Red Desert* (1964); *La decima vittima/The 10th Victim* (1965); *Blowup* (1966); *C'era una volta/More than a Miracle* (1967); *Zabriskie Point* (1969, US); *Uomini contro* (1970); *Il caso Mattei/The Mattei Affair* (1972); *Un papillon sur l'épaule* (1973, Fr.); *Il mistero di Oberwald/The Oberwald Mystery* (1980); *Il frullo del passero/The Sparrow's Flutter* (1988).

GUILLÉN, Fernando
Fernando Gallego Guillén; Barcelona 1932

Spanish actor, whose rakish leading-man roles have become ironised in recent films, especially through his paedophile priest in Pedro Almodóvar's* *La ley del deseo/The Law of Desire* (1987) and as Carmen Maura's* feckless lover in *Mujeres al borde de un ataque de nervios/Women on the Verge of a Nervous Breakdown* (1988). Heavily eye-browed, he projects a feral sexuality that has remained undimmed in films like Gonzalo Suárez's* *Don Juan en los infiernos/Don Juan in Hell* (1991). PWE

GUINNESS, (Sir) Alec
Alec Guinness de Cuffe; London 1914

British actor, distinctive in his ability to combine the skills of character actor and realistic performance in the same role. Although he is identified with the school of acting which works from the outside in rather than from the inside out, accumulating external details rather than revealing inner truths, the virtuosity of his impersonations does not seem to damage the credibility of his characterisations. His Fagin in David Lean's* *Oliver Twist* (1948), though physically a caricature, is emotionally a character of some depth. In the Ealing comedies*, *Kind Hearts and Coronets* (1949), in which he plays all eight of the doomed d'Ascoynes, gives full scope to his playful virtuosity, while *The Man in the White Suit* (1951) gives him a role of appealing but dangerous innocence. Guinness won an Oscar, a New York Film Critics award and a British Academy award for his performance as the insanely uncompromising Captain Nicholson in Lean's *The Bridge on the River Kwai* (1957), a theme on which he played variations in *Tunes of Glory* (1960). Since the 1960s, his performances have been a little more predictable, though his role as Obi Wan Kenobi in the *Star Wars* series almost stole the movies from the action men. His most satisfying and complete characterisation in recent years was as George Smiley in the BBC television serialisations of John Le Carré's *Tinker, Tailor, Soldier, Spy* (1979) and *Smiley's People* (1982).

Knighted in 1959, he was given a Special Academy Award in 1979 for 'advancing the art of screen acting through a host of memorable and distinguished performances'. JC

Other Films Include: *Great Expectations* (1946); *The Mudlark* (1950); *The Lavender Hill Mob* (1951); *Father Brown* (1954); *The Ladykillers* (1955); *The Horse's Mouth* (1959); *Our Man in Havana* (1960); *Lawrence of Arabia* (1962); *Doctor Zhivago* (1965); *Fratello Sole, Sorella Luna/Brother Sun Sister Moon* (1973, It./UK); *Star Wars* (1977, US); *The Empire Strikes Back* (1980, US); *Return of the Jedi* (1983, US); *A Passage to India* (1985); *A Handful of Dust* (1987); *Kafka* (1991, US/Fr./UK).

GUITRY, Sacha
Alexandre Guitry; St Petersburg, Russia 1885 – Paris 1957

French director, actor and playwright, son of stage star Lucien Guitry. Sacha spent his youth among artistic celebrities (Cézanne, Auguste Renoir, Sarah Bernhardt, etc.), who feature in his documentary *Ceux de chez nous* (1915). He became one of the acclaimed playwrights and actors of the *boulevard* theatre, creating a glittering and frivolous world in which he and his successive wives figured prominently (he married five actresses). Guitry's main assets were his wit and his voice; after much publicised contempt for the cinema, he began filming his own plays in record time and with huge success. Films like *Désiré* and *Quadrille* (both 1937) attracted critical scorn, but recent writers, following François Truffaut*, have re-evaluated Guitry's work precisely because its distanced theatricality was so *modern*. Frivolous, misogynist and reactionary, Guitry's films are saved by his humour and his devastating verbal flow, as in the famous seventeen-minute telephone monologue of *Faisons un rêve* and his voice-over in the brilliant *Le Roman d'un tricheur/The Story of a Cheat* (both 1936). He created his own humorous historical genre, a unique amalgam of history textbook and music-hall revue, in *Les Perles de la couronne/The Pearls of the Crown* (1937) and *Remontons les Champs-Elysées* (1938). As collaborator and writer of the chauvinistic *De Jeanne d'Arc à Philippe Pétain* (published 1944), Guitry was jailed in August 1944. He continued making idiosyncratic historical films, such as *Si Versailles m'était conté/Royal Affairs in Versailles* (1953) and *Napoléon* (1955), and comedies, notably the vicious *La Poison* (1951, starring Michel Simon*). Guitry's populist spectacles had a modernist edge. Before Orson Welles, he invented the narrated credit sequence, parading the cinematic apparatus. He was a model for New Wave* *auteurs*; as Truffaut observed, 'he was always Sacha Guitry; that is, he embroidered on themes that were personal to him.' GV

GÜNTHER, Egon
Schneeberg 1927

German director, who is, together with Konrad Wolf*, Frank Beyer* and Heiner Carow, the best-known representative of the 'second' generation of GDR directors. Günther began in 1958 as a script editor at DEFA*, directing his first film in 1965 (*Lots Weib*). His second feature, *Wenn du groß bist, lieber Adam*, made in 1965, was banned, following the clampdown ordered by the eleventh SED Party Congress on all stirrings of a cultural 'thaw' (it was premiered in 1990). Undaunted, Günther turned to literary adaptations, choosing a founding father of the GDR (Johannes Becher) but filming his most youthfully revolutionary work; *Abschied* (1968) was a major national and international success. A second adaptation, *Junge Frau von 1914* (1970), also based on a canonical GDR author, Arnold Zweig, showed Günther's acute eye for period, free of nostalgia. KP

Other Films Include: *Der Dritte* (1972); *Erziehung von Verdun* (1973); *Die Schlüssel* (1974).

GUTIÉRREZ ARAGÓN, Manuel
Torrelavega, Santander 1942

Spanish director. Student of the Escuela Oficial de Cinematografía* and co-scriptwriter for García Sánchez, José Luis Borau*, Jaime Camino* and Gonzalo Suárez*. Across the range of his widely different films there is a marked interest in fable and myth, often coded with political allusion and combined with ironic treatment of the material. His first feature, *Habla, mudita/Speak, Little Mute Girl* (1973), turns an exploration of the power-play of education and communication into a political allegory of Francoist censorship*. His next film, *Camada negra/Black Brood* (1977), initially banned for its portrayal of the violence of Spanish fascism, remains his most controversial work. Here, as in films such as *Demonios en el jardín/Demons in the Garden* (1982) and *La mitad del cielo/Half of Heaven* (1986), the family reflects the tensions of institutional and social structures. Disillusionment with the father figure and exorcism of the 'inner demons' characterise *Demonios en el jardín*, whose combination of accurate, evocative '*costumbrismo*' (depiction of regional customs and manners) and popular stars – Angela Molina*, Ana Belén*, Imanol Arias* – ensured box-office success. After the commercial failure of the ironic but tender fable about a half-human, half-bear wild boy, *Feroz/Ferocious* (1984), Gutiérrez Aragón enjoyed relative success with the star-studded *La noche más hermosa/The Most Beautiful Night* (1984), a comedy of romantic intrigue which symbolically dramatises post-Franco Spain: Luis's (Fernando Fernán Gómez*) longing for a truly exceptional experience (to see a comet that passes over Spain only once in a hundred years) is frustrated by the less sublime demands of down-to-earth, sexual desires. In *La mitad del cielo*, his last film to date, Gutiérrez Aragón recaptures the blend of fantasy and reality, fable and social criticism that was so successful in *El corazón del bosque/The Heart of the Forest* (1978). As in his other films, part of the impact of *La mitad del cielo* derives from powerful narrative situations and boldly defined characters, played here by Fernán Gómez, Molina and Margarita Lozano. IS

GUY [GUY-BLACHÉ], Alice
Saint-Mandé 1873[5?] – Mahwah, New Jersey 1968

French director, arguably the world's first fiction film-maker. As a secretary fascinated by the Lumière* cameras, she sought her boss Léon Gaumont's* permission to direct her own sketches. The earliest (arguably the first fiction film ever, now lost), *La Fée aux choux/The Cabbage Fairy* (1896), was a comic fairy tale; a later version, *Sage-femme de première classe/First Class Midwife* (1902), still exists. Gaumont delegated his growing production department to Guy, and there followed intense activity until 1906, during which she directed about 200 one-reelers, acting also as scriptwriter, producer and wardrobe assistant. This heady, anarchic period gave Guy great scope and power: she experimented with photography, sound and tinting, and spanned the spectrum of popular genres from slapstick and melodrama to historical epics. Ferdinand Zecca, Victorin Jasset and Louis Feuillade* – France's future leading directors – were all her apprentices. In 1907 she married Herbert Blaché and emigrated to the US. After the birth of her first child in 1909, Guy founded the Solax film company, releasing over 300 titles, up to fifty of them directed by herself. Solax became Blaché Features, specialising in four-reelers; later the Guy-Blachés founded various short-lived companies before being driven out of business in 1917. Guy stopped making films after *Tarnished Reputation* (1920), her seventieth American picture. Divorced, she returned to France with her two children, unsuccessfully trying to revive her film career and struggling (with equally little success) to correct histories which regularly attributed her French films to male directors such as Jasset and Emile Cohl*.

Alice Guy was belatedly celebrated by the Cinémathèque Française* and awarded the Legion of Honour in 1953, but her pioneering role was only widely recognised in the 1970s. She gave credence to her own statement that 'there is nothing connected with the staging of a motion picture that a woman cannot do as easily as a man.' GV

Bib: Anthony Slide (ed.), *The Memoirs of Alice Guy-Blaché* (1986).

H

HAANSTRA, Bert
Holten 1916

Dutch director. Coming from a family of visual artists, Haanstra was involved in painting, drawing and photography from an early age, and he entered film-making relatively late. He applied his talents to different genres and a wide range of subjects, but pictorial sophistication always remained at the heart of his films. This quality was recognised internationally when his second documentary, *Spiegel van Holland/Mirror of Holland* (1950), won the Grand Prix for short films at the Cannes festival. Its lyrical camerawork shows the Dutch landscape as reflected in, and seen from, its waterways. This interest in the Dutch environment inspired many of Haanstra's later films. At the same time he introduced irony as another characteristic element of his visual style: in *Spiegel van Holland* we see an upside-down world in which the observation of nature becomes an observation of the human condition.

In the early 1950s Haanstra made a series of instructional films for the Shell Film Unit in London: *Strijd zonder einde/The Rival World* (1955), about man's fight to control insects, is a documentary as sensational as the best science-fiction. In the same vein he analysed the Dutch struggle to control the sea in *En de zee was niet meer/And There Was No More Sea* (1956) and other films, before producing his grand synthesis of this national theme, *De stem van het water/The Voice of the Water*, a feature-length documentary, in 1966. *Glas/Glass* (1958), a poetic interpretation of the art of glass-blowing, won an Oscar for the best short film in 1959.

Haanstra's first fiction film, *Fanfare* (1958), is a comedy in the Ealing* studios tradition, though in a very Dutch setting, turning the divisions in a small farming community into farce. The film, written by Haanstra in cooperation with Jan Blokker*, broke all box-office records in Holland at a time when local film production was almost non-existent; Haanstra thus paved the way for new generations of Dutch film-makers. As entertaining in a quite different way was *Alleman/The Human Dutch* (1963), a feature-length documentary on the Dutch as they leave home and show themselves in public. Using a candid camera technique, Haanstra documented a national intimacy that would not survive the new liberties of the 1960s. The film won a Golden Bear in Berlin as well as an Oscar nomination. It was scripted by Anton Koolhaas, who became Haanstra's chief scriptwriter until 1980, considerably improving the dramatic and rhetorical impact of his films. Haanstra made another feature-length documentary for theatrical release, *Bij de beesten af/Ape and Superape* (1972), before returning to fiction with *Dokter Pulder zaait papavers/When the Poppies Bloom Again* (1975) and *Een pak slaag/Mr Slotter's Jubilee* (1979), both starring Kees Brusse*, in which his tragic view of human life becomes more prominent. KD

Other Films: *De Muiderkring herleeft* (1949); *Nederlandse beeldhouwkunst tijdens de late middeleeuwen, Panta rhei* (1951); *Dijkbouw/The Dyke Builders* (1952); *Ontstaan en vergaan/The Changing Earth, De opsporing van aardolie, De verkenningsboring/The Wildcat, Het olieveld* (1954); *God Shiva* (1955); *Rembrandt, schilder van de mens/Rembrandt Painter of Man* (1957); *Over glas gesproken* (1958); *De zaak MP/The MP Case* (1960); *Delta Phase 1, Zoo* (1962); *Retour Madrid* (1968); *Nationale parken ... noodzaak* (1978); *Nederland, Vroeger kon je lachen* (1983); *Chimps onder elkaar* (1984); *Monument voor een gorilla* (1987).

HAAS, Hugo
Brno [then Austria-Hungary] 1901 – Vienna, Austria 1968

Czech actor, director and scriptwriter. Haas studied music and acting, and was a member of several theatre companies. He became a popular comic actor in films such as *Muži v offsidu/Men in Offside* (1931) and *Život je pes/A Dog's Life* (1933, part of a sequence of seven films directed by Martin Frič*). He turned to direction in the late 1930s, notably with his film version of Karel Čapek's anti-fascist play *Bílá nemoc/The White Sickness* (1937), in which he also played the part of Doctor Galén. The film was withdrawn after Nazi protests but the Jewish-born Haas completed two more films before leaving for Hollywood, where he played cameos and became a B-movie director/writer/lead actor in a sequence of nine films. *Pickup* (1951) and *One Girl's Confession* (1953) were based on Czech novels, and *Edge of Hell* (1956) was a remake of Frič's *Ulička v ráji/A Street in Paradise*, in which Haas had starred. Haas's last films were made in Austria, but plans to return to his home country in 1968 were thwarted by the Soviet invasion and he died the same year. PH

Other Films Include: **As Actor** – *Dobrý voják Švejk/The Good Soldier Švejk* (1931); *Načeradec, král kibiců/Načeradec, King of the Kibitzers* (1932); *Ulička v ráji/A Street in Paradise* (1936). **As Actor/Director** – *Velbloud uchem jehly/Camel through the Eye of a Needle* [co-dir.] (1936); *Děvčata, nedejte se!/Girls, Defend Yourselves!* [co-dir.], *Kvočna/Mother Hen* [dir. only] (1937); *Co se šeptá/What is Whispered* (1938). **As Actor/Writer/Director in the US** – *Girl on the Bridge* (1951); *Strange Fascination* (1952); *Thy Neighbour's Wife* (1953); *Bait, The Other Woman* (1954); *Hold Back Tomorrow* [writer/director only] (1955); *Hit and Run, Lizzie* (1957); *Night of the Quarter Moon* [dir. only], *Born to be Loved* (1959); **In Austria** – *Der Nachbar/The Neighbour* (1966); *Verrückt/Crazy Idea* (1967).

HADJIDAKIS, Manos
Xanthi 1925 – Athens 1994

Greek composer; also orchestra director and conductor. Hadjidakis was one of the leading contemporary Greek composers, writing music for numerous Greek and international films. He was instrumental in the 1950s in creating a new style of Greek popular music whose appeal was greatly reinforced by its use in films and plays. His film music of that period has attained permanent cultural value and popularity independent of the films it was written for. Hadjidakis' best film music is considered to be his score for Dušan Makavejev's* *Sweet Movie* (1974). He won an Academy Award for the music and lyrics of the title song in Jules Dassin's* *Pote tin Kiriaki/Never on Sunday* (1959). *O megalos erotikos/The Great Love Songs* (1973, dir. Pandelis Voulgaris*) was based on a Hadjidakis composition of the same name. Hadjidakis managed and conducted his own symphony orchestra. TN

Other Films Include: *Laterna ftohia ke filotimo/Barrel Organ, Poverty and Dignity, Stella* (1955); *O drakos/The Ogre of Athens* (1956); *I paranomi/The Outlaws* (1960); *It Happened in Athens* (1962, US); *America, America, Topkapi* (both 1964, US); *Blue* (1968, US); *Taxidi tou melitos/Honeymoon* (1979); *Eleftherios Venizelos* (1980); *Memed my Hawk* (1983, UK); *Enas erodios ya tin Germania/Heron for Germany* (1987); *Issihes meres tou Avgoustou/Quiet August Days* (1991).

HAITOV, Nikolai   Javorovo 1919

Bulgarian scriptwriter and dramatist, whose tales about rustic life in his native Rhodope mountains provided the materials for several commercially successful film productions, most notably Georgi Djulgerov's* *Izpit/The Test* (1971). By the 1970s, Haitov was one of the most sought-after scriptwriters at the Boyana* Studios. When *Izpit* was paired with another Haitov adaptation, Milen Nikolov's *Gola săvest/Naked Conscience*, and released as the two-part *Šaren svjat/Colourful World* (1971), the combined message of proving one's manhood and safeguarding natural resources appealed to the sensibilities of a people forced to abandon its rural roots and migrate to industrial centres during the postwar period. At the same time, another Haitov story, *Krajat na pesanta/The End of the Song* (1971), was adapted by Nikolov, and his play *Lamjata/The Dragon* – filmed by Todor Dinov in 1974 – was enjoying a popular run in the theatres as a fairy tale set in medieval Bulgaria.

It was a stage director turned film-maker, Metodi Andonov*, who then collaborated with Haitov on *Kozijat rog/The Goat Horn* (1972), the most successful film in the history of Bulgarian cinema. Set in the Middle Ages, this tale of vengeance drew on familiar mountain ballads and folk traditions for its action-packed story. But in Haitov's hands the screenplay was also honed to a legend along the lines of an ancient myth – a tale handed down through the centuries from ancient Thrace, in much the same manner as the more familiar legend of Orpheus had originated. Later, Haitov and director Eduard Zahariev* were to rework the same legends of manhood and valour in their *Măžki vremena/Manly Times* (1977).

Not all of Haitov's stories made successful film productions. But his respect for the outsider, his deeply moral attitude to nature, and his belief that even a lonely 'fight for right' has its own rewards raised him to the eminence of a national balladeer. RH

HALAS, John – see BATCHELOR, Joy

HAMER, Robert   Kidderminster 1911 – London 1963

British director, who, on the basis of three and a bit feature films at Ealing in the 1940s, has claims to being one of the distinctive *auteurs* of British postwar cinema. His signature, as Charles Barr has pointed out, is the mirror worlds played out in 'The Haunted Mirror' episode of *Dead of Night* (1945), in which a world of dull respectability is undermined by a world in which passion slips from control. In *Pink String and Sealing Wax* (1945) the world of the chemist shop is mirrored in reverse by the world of the public house. In *Kind Hearts and Coronets* (1949) the dignified restraint of Louis' commentary is in comic counterpoint to the lust and murder which he is commenting upon. *It Always Rains on Sunday* (1947) is almost an attack on Ealing itself, the world of the self-regulating community disintegrating in its conflict with a mirror world of criminality and repressed sexual desire. Hamer has a reputation as a 'woman's director' and indeed, unusually for Ealing, strong women are at the centre of each of the films: most characteristically, Googie Withers*. But the women pay for their strength, and there is something at least ambivalent if not sadistic in the way female desire is punished.

Hamer fought a losing battle with alcoholism, and died at the age of 52. JC

Bib: Charles Barr, *Ealing Studios* (1977).

Other Films Include: As Editor – *Jamaica Inn* (1939); *The Foreman Went to France* (1942). **As Director** – *The Loves of Joanna Godden* [Hamer directed some sections while Charles Frend was ill] (1947); *Father Brown* (1954); *School for Scoundrels* (1960).

HAMMER HORROR

British genre, developed by Sir James Carreras' Hammer Films between 1954 and 1968 at Bray Studios. Hammer went into production in 1948, taking over a large country house at Bray, west of London, as its studio. Carreras was unashamedly commercial, working in 'B' features with tightly controlled budgets and going wherever public taste took him. In 1955, he exploited the success of the BBC serialisation of *The Quatermass Experiment* (1953) and produced *The Quatermass Xperiment* (1955) with the emphasis on the X. Its success encouraged him to pursue the horror genre, and in 1957 he released *The Curse of Frankenstein*, which was made for £65,000 and grossed around £2 million, with £1 million coming from America. The horror films which followed continued the box-office success, particularly in the overseas market, earning Carreras the contempt of British quality critics and a 1968 Queen's Award for Industry.

Dave Pirie suggests that the horror genre 'remains the only staple cinematic myth which Britain can claim as its own and which relates to it in the same way as the Western relates to America.' At its best, Hammer horror, like Gainsborough melodrama* before it, brought to the genre a stylistic approach which played off the restraint characteristic of British cinema against the excess of the conventions, the decency of Peter Cushing against the monstrous sexuality of Christopher Lee, exposing the familiar myths of class and sexuality to the uncanny and the undead. JC

Bib: Dave Pirie, *Hammer: A Cinema Case Study* (1980).

HAMMID, Alexander
Alexander Hackenschmied; Linz, Austria 1907

Czech director, cinematographer and editor. The principal exponent in Czechoslovakia of what he called the 'independent film', Hammid originally studied graphics before moving to architecture and photography. In 1930 he organised the first week of avant-garde films in Prague as well as a New Photography exhibition. His first film, *Bezúčelna procházka/ Aimless Walk* (1930), was shown alongside René Clair's* *Entr'acte* and Jean Vigo's* *A Propos de Nice*. An unusual view of Prague, reflected in its title, it hinged on the idea of the separation of one human being into two. In *Na Pražskem hradě/Prague Castle* (1932) he sought the relationship between architectonic and musical form. His interest in the relation between image and music is further evidenced in the Venice award-winner *Zem spieva/The Earth Sings* (1933), where he edited Karel Plicka's footage of Slovak folklore to a specially commissioned score. He took a major credit as 'artistic collaborator' on Gustav Machatý's* *Ze soboty na neděli/From Saturday to Sunday* (1931), and in the late 1930s worked as photographer and editor of Herbert Kline's *Crisis* (1939), a documentary on Czechoslovakia from the Anschluss to the German invasion. In the US, where he changed his name from Hackenschmied to Hammid, he continued to follow an idiosyncratic path, co-directing *Meshes of the Afternoon* (1943) with Maya Deren and *The Medium* (1950) with Gian-Carlo Menotti, as well as many documentaries, and pioneering films using multi-screen and IMAX. PH

Other Films Include: *Listopad/November* [short, ph] (1934); *Poslední léto/The Last Summer* [short, co-ph, co-ed] (1937). **In the US**: *Lights Out in Europe* [ph, ed] (1939); *The Forgotten Village* [co-d, ph, ed] (1940); *At Land* [short, co-ph, co-ed], *Valley of the Tennessee* [d], *Toscanini: Hymn of the Nations* [short, d] (1944); *A Study in Choreography for the Camera* [co-ph, co-ed], *The Private Life of a Cat* [short, d] (1945); *Ritual in Transfigured Time* [short, co-ph, co-ed] (1945–6); *To Be Alive* [short, co-d, ph] (1964); *We Are Young* [short, co-d, ph] (1967); *US* [short, co-d, ph] (1968); *To Fly* [sup. ed] (1976).

HANÁK, Dušan
Bratislava 1938

Slovak director. One of the leading Slovak directors to emerge in the late 1960s, Hanák graduated from FAMU* in 1965 and made his feature debut with *322* (1969), which won the Grand Prix at Mannheim. A visionary but pessimistic film, it was banned until 1988. His remarkable documentary *Obrazy starého sveta/Pictures from an Old World* (1972), a compelling portrait of peasant life, suffered a similar fate,

while his comedy *Ja milujem, ty miluješ/I Love, You Love* (1980, released 1988) also proved too abrasive for the authorities. In those films that were released, *Ružové sny/Rose-tinted Dreams* (1976) and *Tichá radost'/Silent Joy* (1985), he treated, respectively, Slovak-gypsy relations and the problems of the independent woman. In neither film did a more accessible surface compromise his fundamental honesty of treatment. He also directed *Súkromné životy/Privatlieben/ Private Lives* in 1990. PH

HANEKE, Michael
Munich, Germany 1942

Austrian director and scriptwriter. A stage director, scriptwriter and director of television films since 1970, Haneke emerged in the 1990s as Austrian cinema's most significant talent internationally, with his bleak but compelling vision of the end of civilisation. He made his mark early on with a number of television films which portray isolated individuals and understated relationships in a style reminiscent of Robert Bresson* – such as *Sperrmüll* (1976), *Lemminge* (1979, two parts) and *Wer war Edgar Allen?* (1984). In 1989, he introduced a new aesthetic paradigm in Austrian cinema with his first feature *Der Siebte Kontinent/The Seventh Continent* (1989), which depicts with relentless logic the journey to collective suicide of a middle-class Viennese family. It was followed by *Benny's Video* (1992) and *71 Fragmente einer Chronologie des Zufalls* (1994), forming a trilogy around the theme of narcissism, abjection and the coldness of personal contacts in the age of video, and portraying – through a disciplined, sparse style – what he has called 'my country's emotional glaciation'. AL

Bib: Alexander Horwath (ed.), *Der Siebente Kontinent* (1991).

HÄNSEL, Marion
Marseilles, France 1948

Belgian director and actress of French origin. Settling in Belgium after acting work in Paris and New York, Hänsel formed her own production company Man's Films in 1977. Her first feature, *Le lit/The Bed* (1982), which centres on the pain and suffering of a wife and her dying artist husband, announced her potential, and was nominated for a French César* for best foreign film.

Hänsel's cinema attempts to treat powerful and emotive subjects in an accessible way, and her films are flavoured with a certain 'European-ness' through their use of Euro-stars (Jane Birkin in *Dust*, 1985), locations (Italy in *Il Maestro*, 1989), and adaptations of European literature, for example *Les Noces barbares/Cruel Embrace* (1987), based on Yann Queffelec's novel (1985 Goncourt prize). In *Sur la terre comme au ciel/On Earth as in Heaven* (1992, also scripted by Hänsel), the subject of an unborn child speaking to its mother introduces a new warmth and tenderness into Hänsel's conflictual cinema. CF

HANSON, Lars
Gothenburg 1886 – Stockholm 1965

Swedish actor. A distinguished and handsome stage actor, Hanson was involved in film during the Golden Age of Swedish silent film. Probably the best-known actor of the period, he became the prototype of the virile and romantic hero. He had major roles in Mauritz Stiller's* *Dolken/The Dagger* (1915), *Vingarne/The Wings* (1916), *Sången om den eldröda blomman/Song of the Scarlet Flower* (1919), *Erotikon/The Bonds That Chafe* (1920) and *Gösta Berlings saga (del I och II)/The Story of Gosta Berling (pts I and II)* (1924), and in Victor Sjöström's* *Thérèse* (1916) and *Tösen från Stormyrtorpet/The Lass from Stormyrtorpet* (1917). He went to Hollywood with Sjöström, starring (in both cases opposite Lillian Gish) in *The Scarlet Letter* (1926) and *The Wind* (1928), among other films. The film historian Georges Sadoul* praised Hanson's performance particularly in the latter, for his convincing embodiment of the 'initially gormless, scruffy village idiot, transformed by love into a hero worthy of love'. Despite Hollywood success, Hanson returned to Sweden and thereafter worked mainly on the stage. He did, however, act in some significant war films, for example Gustaf Molander's* *Rid i natt!/Ride Tonight!* (1942) and *Det brinner en eld/There Burns a Flame* (1943). LGA/BF

HARBOU, Thea von
Tauperlitz 1888 – Berlin 1954

German scriptwriter. A best-selling author of romance novels (*Die nach uns kommen*, 1910) and popular pamphlets (*Der Krieg und die Frauen*, 1913), she was hired by Joe May* Film in 1919. During pre-production on *Das indische Grabmal* (filmed by Joe May in 1921 and remade in 1959 by Fritz Lang), based on one of her novels, she met Fritz Lang*. Between 1920 (*Das wandernde Bild*) and 1933 (*Das Testament des Dr. Mabuse*) Harbou wrote the scripts for all Lang's films, and for other directors; she was Weimar cinema's top writer, second only to Carl Mayer*. Intelligent and inquisitive, she had a unique gift for melodramatic confrontations, for pace and pitch, and a good understanding of what moved the new mass audience.

While Lang emigrated in 1933, Harbou stayed in Germany, continuing her thriving career. In 1933 she was elected chair of the Association of German sound film authors, becoming a member of the Nazi Party and acting as script doctor on overt propaganda films. She also tried her hand at directing, with less success. In the late 1940s she wrote dubbing scripts for Deutsche London Film, before rounding off her unusually long career with such commercial pot-boilers as *Es kommt ein Tag* (1950) and *Dr. Holl* (1951). TE

Bib: Reinhold Keiner, *Thea von Harbou und der deutsche Film bis 1933* (1991, 2nd ed.).

Other Films Include: *Die heilige Simplicia* (1920); *Der müde Tod/Destiny* (1921); *Der brennende Acker/The Burning Earth, Phantom* (1922); *Die Austreibung* (1923); *Die Nibelungen. 2 Teile, Die Finanzen des Großherzogs, Michael* (1924); *Zur Chronik von Grieshuus* (1925); *Metropolis* (1927); *Frau im Mond/Woman on the Moon* (1929); *Elisabeth und der Narr, Hanneles Himmelfahrt* (1934); *Der alte und der junge König, Ein idealer Gatte* (1935); *Eine Frau ohne Bedeutung* (1936); *Der Herrscher* (1937); *Jugend, Verwehte Spuren* (1938); *Hurra! Ich bin Papa!* (1939); *Via Mala, Fahrt ins Glück* (1948); *Dein Herz ist meine Heimat* (1953); *Das indische Grabmal/The Indian Tomb* (1959).

HARLAN, Veit
Berlin 1899 – Capri, Italy 1964

German director of melodramas and historical spectaculars, notorious for some of the most overtly propagandist (*Der große König*, 1942; *Kolberg*, 1945), anti-semitic (*Jud Süss/Jew Süss*, 1940; not to be confused with the British version directed by Lothar Mendes in 1934) and tear-jerking (*Die goldene Stadt*, 1942; *Opfergang*, 1944) films of the Nazi regime. Harlan's film career started in 1926 when he acted in some twenty films for directors such as Ludwig Berger* (*Der Meister von Nürnberg*, 1927), Kurt Bernhardt* (*Das Mädchen mit den fünf Nullen*, 1927), Gustav Ucicky* (*Yorck*, 1931; *Flüchtlinge*, 1933; *Das Mädchen Johanna*, 1935), Richard Eichberg* (*Die unsichtbare Front*, 1932), Robert Wiene* (*Taifun/Polizeiakte 909*, 1933) and Geza von Bolvary* (*Stradivari*, 1935). From 1935 to 1958 Harlan produced his own films, except for a five-year break between 1945 and 1950. He was charged with war crimes but later cleared, and returned to film-making despite protests from the German left. His ideologically less blatant literary adaptations (*Die Kreutzersonate*, 1937; *Der Herrscher*, 1937; *Die Reise nach Tilsit*, 1939; *Immensee*, 1943), comedies (*Krach im Hinterhaus*, 1935; *Kater Lampe*, 1936; *Der müde Theodor*, 1936), and melodramas (*Maria, die Magd*, 1936; *Jugend*, 1938; *Verwehte Spuren*, 1938; *Das unsterbliche Herz*, 1939) nonetheless show a predilection for myth and heavy symbolism which associate Harlan with the ideals of Nazism. MW

Bib: Siegfried Zielinski, *Veit Harlan: Analysen und Materialien zur Auseinandersetzung mit einem Film-Regisseur des deutschen Faschismus* (1981).

HARRIS, Richard
Limerick 1933

Irish/British actor. Trained at the London Academy of Music and Dramatic Art, and a graduate of Joan Littlewood's Theatre Workshop, Harris appeared in a number of British films in the late 1950s (often associated with Ireland). His performance as Frank Machin in *This Sporting Life* (1963) gave him international recognition, a Best Actor award from Cannes and an Oscar nomination. A landmark performance in the British New Wave*, his representation of masculinity owes more to the individualism of the American Method school than to the social naturalism of Albert Finney*, with Marlon Brando lurking behind Machin's inarticulate physicality. It was a level of performance he did not repeat, though it revealed a current of masochism in Harris' career (and his life) which he drew on more graphically in *A Man Called Horse* (1970, US). His career in the 1970s and 1980s was more marked for its boozy scandals than for his acting. Since his recent return to Ireland, however, he has won an Oscar nomination for his part in Jim Sheridan's* *The Field* (1990, UK/Ireland), was memorably masochistic in Clint Eastwood's *Unforgiven* (1992, US), and has been praised for his West End stage performance in the title role of Pirandello's *Henry IV* (1992). JC

Other Films Include: *Shake Hands with the Devil* (1959); *A Terrible Beauty* (1960); *The Guns of Navarone, Mutiny on the Bounty* (1962); *Il Deserto rosso/The Red Desert* (1964, It.); *Major Dundee* (1965, US); *Camelot* (1967, US); *The Molly Maguires* (1970, US); *Robin and Marian, The Return of a Man Called Horse* (1976, both US); *El triunfo de un hombre llamado Caballo/Triumphs of a Man Called Horse* (1982, US).

HARRISON, (Sir) Rex   Huyton, Lancashire 1908 – New York, USA 1990

British actor. Never an actor of hidden profundities, Harrison's natural environment was theatrical light comedy in which elegance was preferred to depth, and urbanity to rough edges. Though, in keeping with the mood of the late 1930s, he plays an idealistic reporter in Victor Saville* and Ian Dalrymple's* *Storm in a Teacup* (1937) and appears in King Vidor's socially conscious *The Citadel* (1938), he seems more at home in Herbert Wilcox's* *I Live in Grosvenor Square*, David Lean's* *Blithe Spirit*, or Sidney Gilliat's* *The Rake's Progress* (all made in 1945). His career on stage was as successful as his career in film, and the two came together in his performance as Professor Higgins in *My Fair Lady* on Broadway (1956–8) and in George Cukor's film adaptation (1964, US), for which he won an Oscar. It was one of those parts in which character and actor come to define each other, and though Harrison continued to give good performances (in, for example, *The Yellow Rolls-Royce*, 1964; and in the US: *The Agony and the Ecstasy*, 1965, *Doctor Dolittle*, 1967, and *Staircase*, 1969), they tended to live under the shadow of Henry Higgins. JC

HARTL, Karl   Karl Anton Hartl; Vienna 1899–1978

Austrian director and producer. Hartl's first two films, *Ein Burschenlied aus Heidelberg* (1930) and *Berge in Flammen/The Doomed Battalion* (1931, co-dir. Luis Trenker*), led to Ufa* entrusting him with more substantial (multi-lingual) productions. His preferred genres were science fiction: *F.P.1 antwortet nicht/I.F.1 ne répond plus/Secrets of F.P.1* (1932, Ger./UK/Fr.), *Gold/L'or* (1933–34. Ger./Fr.); and comedy: *Die Gräfin von Monte Christo* (1932) and the crime comedy *Der Mann der Sherlock Holmes war* (1937). As chief producer at Wien-Film during the 1938–45 period, Hartl's merit was the large number of typical 'Viennese films' he produced (directed for instance by Willi Forst*) in comparison to an unusually small number of propaganda films. During his management of Wien-Film, Hartl also wrote many scripts but directed only one film: *Wen die Götter lieben* (1942). After the war he continued to work as a producer, writer and director of light entertainment films. His most successful projects were

Der Engel mit der Posaune (1948), *Weg in die Vergangenheit* (1954) and *Mozart* (1955). After 1963 Hartl worked as a film consultant. KU

Bib: Goswin Dörfler, 'An Austrian Director: Karl Hartl', *Focus on Film*, no. 29 (March 1978).

HARVEY, Lilian   Helene Lilian Pape; London 1906 – Juan-les-Pins, France 1968

British-born German actress, arguably the most popular musical star of the German cinema. She was contracted by Richard Eichberg*, who also hired Willy Fritsch* as her partner (*Die keusche Susanne*, 1926), creating the 'dream couple' of the German film. From 1928 she worked for Ufa*, advertised as 'the sweetest girl in the world', in such successes as *Hokuspokus, Die Drei von der Tankstelle* (both 1930), *Der Kongreß tanzt* (1931), *Zwei Herzen und ein Schlag, Ein blonder Traum* (both 1932) and *Ich und die Kaiserin* (1933). In 1932, she signed a contract with 20th Century-Fox, but none of her Hollywood films made much of an impact and she returned to Europe in 1935, to star in one of the most delightful but also most brazenly derivative Nazi comedies, *Glückskinder* (1936, dir. Paul Martin), a covert remake of *It Happened One Night*. More double acts with Fritsch followed (*Fanny Elßler*, 1937; *Capriccio*, 1938). After helping choreographer Jens Keith escape to Switzerland, she was questioned by the Gestapo and emigrated to France, then to the US, where she briefly made a living as a nurse and in radio and theatre. In 1946 Harvey returned to France, worked on the music-hall revue 'Paris s'amuse', toured the provinces and Belgium, and in 1957 retired to the Côte d'Azur. KP

Bib: Christiane Habich (ed.), *Lilian Harvey* (1990).

HAS, Wojciech Jerzy   Cracow 1925

Polish director. Among the leading directors of the 1950s and 1960s, but distinct from the 'Polish School' in his rejection of World War II themes and heroic action. His alienated and solitary protagonists are more likely to be passive than heroic. In *Pętla/The Noose* (1958), Has has adapted a story by Marek Hłasko (Poland's answer to Jack Kerouac) about a day in the life of an alcoholic. Has is known for his transpositions of 'impossible' literary classics, in particular the hugely successful *Rękopis Znaleziony w Saragossie/The Saragossa Manuscript* (1965), starring Zbigniew Cybulski*. His 1988 feature, *Niezwykła Podróz Baltazara Kobera/The Fabulous Journey of Balthazar Kober*, explores the territory of epic quests and magical medieval worlds. Has is currently director of the Łódź* Film School. AW

Other Films Include: *Lalka/The Doll* (1968); *Sanatorium pod Klepsydrą/The Hourglass Sanatorium* (1973); *Piśmak/Write and Fight* (1985); *Osobisty Pamiętnik Grześnika... Przez Niego Samego Spisany/Memoirs of a Sinner* (1985).

HASSE, O(tto) E(duard)
Obersitzko 1903 – Berlin 1978

German actor, famous for characters in uniform with a strong personality and individualist code of honour. He began his career at Max Reinhardt's* acting school in Berlin and appeared as extra in F. W. Murnau's* film *Der letzte Mann/The Last Laugh* (1924). Between 1930 and 1939 he worked in Munich (at the Münchner Kammerspiele), and collaborated on a film with Karl Valentin* (*Der verhexte Scheinwerfer*, 1934); during the war he featured in prestige productions like *Stukas* (1941) and *Rembrandt* (1942). Hasse found ready roles after 1945, in the *Trümmerfilme* 'ruin film' genre, for instance *Berliner Ballade* (1948) and *Epilog* (1950), while also playing Nazis and ex-Nazis in international productions such as Anatole Litvak's* *Decision Before Dawn* (1950, US) and Alfred Hitchcock's* *I Confess* (1952, US). His greatest acting triumphs in Germany are in two anti-war films: as Admiral Canaris (*Canaris*, 1954) and in *Der Arzt von Stalingrad* (1958). He also worked frequently in France, where Jean Renoir* used him in *Le Caporal épinglé/The Vanishing Corporal* (1962), before settling for German television, where he was instantly recognised and much loved by millions. KP

Bib: Hans Knudsen, *O. E. Hasse* (1960).

Other Films Include: *Peter Voß, der Millionendieb* (1932); *Peer Gynt* (1934); *Der letzte Walzer* (1953); *Les Aventures d'Arsène Lupin* (1956, Fr.); *Les Espions* (1957, Fr.); *Der Maulkorb* (1958); *Die Ehe des Herrn Mississippi* (1961); *Le Vice et la vertu/Vice and Virtue* (1963, Fr.); *Trois chambres à Manhattan* (1965, Fr.); *Etat de siège/State of Siege* (Fr./It., 1973).

HASSELBLADS FOTOGRAFISKA AKTIEBOLAG

Swedish film company. Hasselblads Fotografiska Aktiebolag was a Gothenburg company whose managing director, Nils Bouveng, started small-scale film production in 1915. Close collaboration with the distribution company Victoria Filmbyrå helped Hasselblad develop into an important rival to Svenska Bio*, its output exceeding that of its competitor for a couple of years. With Georg af Klercker* as director, Hasselblad concentrated on a broad commercial repertoire often based on popular literature, with melodrama as its main genre, in contrast to Svenska Bio's policy of drawing on more established literature. The firm launched actors such as Mary Johnson, Dagmar Ebbesen and Karl Gerhard. In 1918 a merger of Hasselblad, Victoria Filmbyrå and four other small companies created a new company, Filmindustri AB Skandia, which a year later merged with former rival Svenska Bio to form Svensk Filmindustri*. BF

HATHEYER, Heidemarie
Villach 1918 – Zurich, Switzerland 1990

Austrian actress. Hatheyer gained her first acting experience in Viennese cabaret before performing in theatres in Vienna and Munich; she enjoyed a successful stage career for the rest of her life. As Friedrich Luft put it, 'Hatheyer was not beautiful but she exuded life, never played sentimentally, always honestly.' In 1937 she was discovered by Luis Trenker*, who cast her in *Der Berg ruft/The Challenge* (1937) as the 'wild, young girl of the mountains', which she played also in *Die Geierwally* (1940, dir. Hans Steinhoff*), her greatest success, fixing her persona as a strong, charismatic woman. Throughout the Nazi period she appeared in leading roles in films such as *Ich klage an*, *Die Nacht in Venedig* (both 1941), *Der große Schatten* (1942) and *Man rede mir nicht von Liebe* (1943). In the postwar period and until the end of the 1950s she continued acting on stage and starred in some of the more popular films of the time (*Mein Herz darfst Du nicht fragen*, 1952, *Pünktchen und Anton*, 1953, *Der Meineidbauer*, 1956, *... und führe uns nicht in Versuchung*, 1957). She remained active on stage until 1983 but failed to attract film offers until the 1980s. Her last film dates from 1988 (*Martha Jellneck*, dir. Kai Wessel), where she was once more praised for her candour and strong personality. FM/KP

Bib: Cinzia Romani, *Tainted Goddesses: Female Film Stars of the Third Reich* (1992).

HAUER, Rutger O.
Breukelen 1944

Dutch actor. The son of professional stage actors, Hauer rose to fame when Paul Verhoeven* directed him as the hero of a popular television children's series, *Floris* (1969–70), a Dutch equivalent of *Ivanhoe*. Hauer played leading roles in five other films by Verhoeven: *Turks fruit/Turkish Delight* (1973), *Keetje Tippel/Cathy Tippel* (1975), *Soldaat van Oranje/Soldier of Orange/Survival Run* (1977), *Spetters/Hunks* (1980), and *Flesh and Blood* (1985, US). His persona developed as the rogue who can switch from charming to ice-cold in an instant. International recognition came in the 1980s when Hauer starred in American films directed by Ridley Scott* (*Blade Runner*, 1982), Nicolas Roeg (*Eureka*, 1982) and Sam Peckinpah (*The Osterman Weekend*, 1983), and in European films by Ermanno Olmi* (*La leggenda del santo bevitore/The Legend of the Holy Drinker*, 1988) and Lina Wertmüller* (*In una notte di chiaro di luna/Crystal or Ash, Fire or Wind, as Long as It's Love*, 1989). In Britain he became well-known for his Guinness beer commercials. KD/FW

HAWKINS, Jack
London 1910–73

British actor, whose distinctive persona seemed to remain constant across a range of parts and genres. A child actor from the age of thirteen, he made his film debut in 1930 in Basil Dean's* *Birds of Prey*. He appeared mainly in supporting roles in the 1930s and early 1940s when his first love was still theatre, but came into prominence in the postwar cinema as one of the stalwarts of well-bred and stiffly backboned English middle-class manhood. His role as the Captain in *The Cruel Sea* (1953) called upon his qualities of decent concern and moral decisiveness, while *Mandy* (1952) offered him a sensitive and caring role as a teacher of deaf children. During the 1950s he became the acceptable image of the British police in, for example, *Home at Seven* (1952), *The Long Arm* (1956) and John Ford's *Gideon's Day* (1958), while simultaneously playing lead roles, somewhat surprisingly, in such Hollywood epics as Howard Hawks' *Land of the Pharoahs* (1955, US) and William Wyler's *Ben-Hur* (1959, US). Always in demand, he continued to act, with dubbing, after an operation for cancer of the larynx in 1966. JC

Other Films Include: *The Good Companions* (1933); *The Next of Kin* (1942); *The Fallen Idol, The Small Back Room* (1949); *The Elusive Pimpernel* (1950); *Fortune is a Woman, The Bridge on the River Kwai* (1957); *The League of Gentlemen* (1960); *Lawrence of Arabia* (1962); *Zulu* (1963); *Guns at Batasi* (1964); *Lord Jim* (1965); *Shalako* (1968); *Oh! What a Lovely War* (1969); *The Adventures of Gerard, Waterloo* [It./USSR] (1970); *Nicholas and Alexandra* (1971, US); *Kidnapped, Young Winston* (1972).

HAY, Will   Stockton-on-Tees 1888 – London 1949

British actor, who was one of the northern music-hall performers popular in Britain between 1936 and 1940. Like Gracie Fields* and George Formby*, his performances adapted his music-hall style to film rather than simply transferring stage routines. His screen character developed around the theme of incompetence rewarded and official pomposity overthrown. With his pince-nez as his standard prop, his most familiar role was as the schoolmaster desperately trying to cover up his own incompetence with verbal pretentiousness, inconsequentiality, and a bemused double take which was all his own. Like Karl Valentin or W. C. Fields, he did not share in the joke, nor was he romantically inclined – in *Where There's a Will* (1937) he almost puts his hand on a young woman's knee, but it is absent-mindedness rather than lechery and he thinks better of it. Hay made a series of comedies with Gainsborough before moving to Ealing. He was directed by Marcel Varnel between 1937 and 1941, and co-directed three films with Basil Dearden*: *The Black Sheep of Whitehall* (1941), *The Goose Steps Out* (1942) and *My Learned Friend* (1943). JC

Other Films Include: *Those Were the Days* (1934); *Boys Will Be Boys* (1935); *Good Morning, Boys, Oh, Mr Porter!* (1937); *Convict 99* (1938); *Ask a Policeman* (1939); *The Ghost of St Michael's* (1941); *The Big Blockade* (1941).

HEER, Johanna   Vienna 19[?]

Austrian cinematographer. Heer began her career as a director of photography in the US, where she worked on, among other films, *Subway Riders* (1979–81). Her work is characterised by her use of colours and light, which she calls 'painterly camerawork', developed to its most elaborate de-

gree in Percy Adlon's *Zuckerbaby* (1985, Ger.). Since 1991 she has directed documentaries together with Werner Schmiedel: *Der andere Blick* (1991), an essay on G. W. Pabst* and the responsibility of the artist during the Third Reich, and a tribute to Simon Wiesenthal, *Die Kunst des Erinnerns – Simon Wiesenthal* (1994). AL

HEIFITS, Josef – see KHEIFITS, Iosif E.

HEIJNINGEN, Matthijs van   Alphen aan de Rijn 1944

Dutch producer, who worked as a pantomime artist and theatre company manager before entering film production. Heijningen founded his company Sigma Films in 1974 and became one of the leading producers of Dutch art cinema in the 1980s. Several Dutch film-makers made their debut under his auspices, for instance Ate de Jong, Nouchka van Brakel*, Paul de Lussanet, George Schouten, Frouke Fokkema, Marleen Gorris* and Willeke van Ammelrooy*. He has also produced films by other European directors such as Harry Kümel* (*Eline Vere*, 1991) and Sally Potter* (*Orlando*, 1992). JR

Bib: Joyce Roodnat, 'Matthijs van Heijningen', *Nederlands Jaarboek Film 1986* (1986).

HEIMAT FILM and MOUNTAIN FILMS

German genres. The *Heimatfilm* is unique to Germany. Several films produced during the Weimar Republic (such as *Die Geier-Wally*, 1921) and the Third Reich may be categorised as *Heimatfilme*, but the apogee of the genre comes in the 1950s. *Heimatfilme* depict a world in which traditional values prevail: love triumphs over social and economic barriers, and the story is usually set in an idyllic German countryside, highlighting maypoles and other folkloric traditions. Many *Heimatfilme* take their titles from folk songs, such as *Grün ist die Heide* (1951) and *Am Brunnen vor dem Tore* (1952). The genre produced its own directors (Hans Deppe*) and stars (Sonja Ziemann and Rudolf Prack, for instance). As the popularity of the *Heimatfilm* waned in the late 1950s, films appeared which cross-bred it with other generic conventions, such as the musical and sex comedies. *Heimatfilme* died out after the mid-1960s, just as a number of New German Cinema* films (*Jagdszenen in Niederbayern/Hunting Scenes from Bavaria*, 1969, *Jaider – der einsame Jäger*, 1971) began to be critical of their social message and covert xenophobia. When Edgar Reitz* made his epic *Heimat*, fully aware of the word's resonance, he was implicitly commenting on both the genre and the genre's critical ripostes, preferring to refer to Carl Froelich*/Zarah Leander's* *Heimat* (1938) and the ecological movement's rediscovery of regionalism and agrarian roots. Other prominent *Heimatfilme* include: *Schwarzwaldmädel* (1950), *Wenn die Abendglocken läuten* (1951), *Ferien vom Ich* and *Tausend rote Rosen blühn* (both 1952), and *Die Trapp-Familie* (1956).

Mountain films (*Bergfilme*) designate a popular German

genre of the 1920s and 1930s which should not be confused with the *Heimatfilm*, despite some superficial similarities. Mountain films used simple, melodramatic plots, spendidly highlighting the snow-covered mountains, and often involving accidents and dangerous last-minute rescues. Arnold Fanck* and Luis Trenker* set its formula; Fanck's films – *Im Kampf mit dem Berge* (1921), *Die weisse Hölle vom Piz Palü/The White Hell of Piz Palu* (1929) – presented the struggle between the (usually male) protagonist(s) and the mountains in powerfully elemental and pantheistic terms. Franck's cameramen used special lenses and camera speeds to capture natural phenomena (sudden weather changes, avalanches or rock-falls), celebrating film technology along with nature. Trenker's films tended to feature more heroic, patriotic individuals in spectacular adventures undergoing trials of strength and conviction, as in *Berge in Flammen* (1931) and *Der Rebell* (1932). JG/TE

Bib: Willi Höfig, *Der deutsche Heimatfilm 1947–1960* (1973); Eric Rentschler, 'Relocating the Bergfilm', *New German Critique*, no. 51 (1990).

In Austria, the 'New *Heimatfilm*' designates alternative, critical attempts to deal with life in the Austrian countryside, in films and television series of the late 1970s and early 1980s. The New *Heimatfilm* deals with the country's Nazi past, its rigid morality based on Catholicism, and the intellectual aridity of village life. Documentary style, sparing use of dialogue and the use of dialect characterise the Austrian New *Heimatfilm*, as do counter-touristic landscape shots which dispense with idyllic scenes and kitsch.

The Austrian Broadcasting Company, ORF, produced *Alpensaga*, a six-part series (1976–80) written by Wilhelm Pevny and Peter Turrini and directed by Dieter Berner, which focused on life in a small village between 1899 and 1945, providing an account of the 'forgotten' past – the decline of the empire, and the rise and fall of Nazism. Another series, *Das Dorf an der Grenze* (dir. Fritz Lehner; script by Thomas Pluch), centred on the controversial situation of a bilingual village on the Slovenian border from 1918 to the present day (three parts, 1979–83; part four directed by Peter Patzak*, 1992). Lehner was also responsible for the film adaptation of *Schöne Tage* (1981, based on Franz Innerhofer's novel), a quasi-documentary on rural traditions, rendered in impressive yet not romanticising or picturesque images. Apart from realistically showing the ordinary life of mountain farmers, *Schöne Tage* also points to the devastating effects of a strict (Catholic) set of moral standards. Confrontations with these moral codes recur in other films, such as *Raffl* (1984; dir. Christian Berger) and *Heidenlöcher* (1985; dir. Wolfram Paulus*), which place such moral codes in a social and political context. Films associated with the New *Heimatfilm* (such as Angela Summereder's *Zechmeister*, 1981), often deal with film-makers' experiences or with historical events. However, as in Paulus' second feature, *Nachsaison* (1987), they can also simply record daily routines and the struggle for economic survival. A 'representation of one's own world' (Alexander Horwath), the New *Heimatfilm* can therefore introduce diversity and authenticity into images of Austria otherwise often subject to the demands of tourism and the heritage industry [> HERITAGE CINEMA IN EUROPE]. IR/SS

HELISMAA, Reino
Helsinki 1913–65

Finnish scriptwriter, actor and singer. Helismaa was one of the key figures in postwar Finnish popular culture. He wrote song lyrics, short parodies for radio, dramas, musical transcriptions and film scripts. Of his 5,000 songs, some 1,500 have been recorded, most to the music of Toivo Kärki. During the 1950s, Helismaa wrote twenty-nine screenplays. The major reason for this productivity was the immense financial success of *Tuntematon sotilas/The Unknown Soldier* (1954, directed by Edvin Laine*), which impelled production company SF to invest heavily in new films. As a quick writer, Helismaa was much in demand. His first script was a loosely assembled story of three tramps on their way to Lapland in search of gold: *Rovaniemen markkinoilla/At the Rovaniemi Fair* (1951) was directed by Jorma Nortimo and produced by T. J. Särkkä*. It started a stylistic trend in Finnish cinema known as 'rillumarei' (tra-la-la). One of the wanderers was played by Esa Pakarinen, who became famous as Pekka Puupää [> PUUPÄÄ FILMS]. *Rovaniemen markkinoilla* radically shifted the direction of Finnish film comedy towards lush and unashamed folk farce. In the postwar atmosphere of toil and rebuilding, Finnish audiences wholeheartedly accepted the throwaway optimistic nonsense of *rillumarei*. Film critics, on the other hand, have always had great difficulties with these films: as one of them put it, *rillumarei*'s basic tendency was 'to blur the artistic instinct of underdeveloped audiences'. More recently, *rillumarei* has been defined as the carnivalesque genre of Finnish cinema. Nonetheless, T. J. Särkkä continued to produce the films, Helismaa wrote the scripts, and audiences kept laughing. HS

HELM, Brigitte
Berlin 1906

German actress, famous for her double role as Maria in her first film, Fritz Lang's *Metropolis* (1927). A ten-year contract with Ufa* secured her leading parts as the vamp in films by Karl Grune, Marcel L'Herbier* (*L'Argent*, 1929) and G. W. Pabst*, usually as the icy queen of someone's heart; she was especially eerie as the usurer's blind daughter in Pabst's *Die Liebe der Jeanne Ney/The Loves of Jeanne Ney* (1927) and genuinely moving in *Die wunderbare Lüge der Nina Petrowna* (1929). Navigating the change to the talkies in *Die singende Stadt*, 1930, she also worked in France and Britain. Her contract with Ufa completed, she retired from film, apparently miffed by bad publicity, but possibly also because she herself recognised that, as Ephraim Katz puts it: 'Her acting range never matched her exceptional beauty, a fact that became more evident with sound.' TE

Other Films Include: *Alraune* (1929); *Manolescu, Der König der Hochstapler* (1929); *Die Herrin von Atlantis* (1933); *Gold* (1934).

HENNING-JENSEN, Astrid
Astrid Smahl; Copenhagen 1914

Danish director. A stage actress in Copenhagen from 1935, Astrid Henning-Jensen worked from 1941 in documentary together with her husband Bjarne Henning-Jensen*. She directed her first solo film, *Palle alene i verden/Palle Alone in the World*, in 1949 with her son Lars in the lead. The script was based on a popular Danish children's book by Jens Sigsgaard. Unlike so many films in this popular Danish genre [> DANISH CHILDREN'S FILMS], *Palle alene i verden* was rooted in realism; it was awarded a prize at Cannes in 1950. In the following years Henning-Jensen mostly collaborated with her husband, for instance on their children's film *De Pokkers unger/Those Blasted Kids* (1947) and on *Paw* (1959). In 1954 she directed *Ballet Girl*, describing the life of a ballet student at the Copenhagen Royal Theatre. After a period of reduced activity, *Vinterbørn/Winter Born* (1978, on childbirth) and *Øjeblikket/The Moment* (1980, about a cancer sufferer) made her the most popular director of her generation, the films becoming box-office hits in spite of their subject matter. Astrid Henning-Jensen's work is characterised by a combination of humanism, social engagement and poetic charm. ME

HENNING-JENSEN, Bjarne   Copenhagen 1908–95

Danish director. Bjarne Henning-Jensen was a stage actor from 1931; as a director of documentaries he worked at Nordisk Films* from 1940 to 1950 and then independently. Among his films *Papir/Paper* (1942) is outstanding for its sense of rhythm. In 1943 he directed his first feature, *Naar man kun er ung/While Still Young*, a realistic story of 'ordinary' young people, an unusual topic in Denmark at the time. *Ditte Menneskebarn/Ditte, Child of Man* (1946), directed with his wife Astrid Henning-Jensen* and based on a well-known Danish novel by Martin Andersen Nexø, is the study of an outcast orphan living in a hostile farming community. Ditte was played by a newcomer, Tove Maës, who later became a well-known actress. *De Pokkers unger/Those Blasted Kids* (1947) was another successful children's film. *Kort er sommeren/Short is the Summer* (1962) was made with Norwegian and Swedish actors. Bjarne Henning-Jensen's masterpiece, *Hvor bjergene sejler/Where Mountains Float* (1955), depicted in strikingly beautiful images cultural tensions among the people of Greenland. It was awarded the Golden Lion in Venice in 1955. ME

HEPWORTH, Cecil   London 1874–1953

British director and producer, who formed the Hepworth Manufacturing Company at the Walton-on-Thames Studios in 1904 and went on to become the most important film producer in the early history of British cinema. 'Throughout its quarter century of existence,' says Rachael Low, the Hepworth Manufacturing Company 'gave the British film industry its greatest and sometimes its only source of pride.' Hepworth entered the film industry with a patented electric arc lamp in 1896, and by 1897 had published the first handbook on cinematography, *Animated Photography: The ABC of the Cinematograph*. For the first decade of the century, he produced, directed and photographed short subjects, both factual and fictional, most notably *Rescued by Rover* (1905)

and *John Gilpin's Ride* (1908). He then concentrated on producing and building up a stable of successful contract stars, including Chrissie White, Alma Taylor and Stewart Rome. In 1910 he patented a primitive sound system, Vivaphone. By 1911 the Hepworth Company was producing longer features, and Hepworth returned to directing in 1914, releasing his two best-known films, *Annie Laurie* and *Comin' Thro' the Rye* in 1916. *Comin' Thro' the Rye* was remade in 1923, with Chrissie White. He was a meticulous craftsman with a feel for natural setting, but his conservativeness became apparent in the 1920s when he failed to keep up with the way cinema was developing. His company went into bankruptcy in 1924, and he released only one more feature, *The House of Marney* (1926) with Alma Taylor. He published his autobiography in 1951. JC

Bib: Cecil Hepworth, *Came the Dawn: Memories of a Film Pioneer* (1951).

HERITAGE CINEMA IN EUROPE

The term describes period films made since the mid-1970s. Characteristic, successful examples include *Jean de Florette* (1986, France), *A Room with a View* (1985, UK), *Babettes gæstebud/Babette's Feast* (1987, Denmark) and *Belle Epoque* (1992, Spain). The term suggests an affinity with what has been called the heritage industry, notably retro fashion and the popularisation of museums and historical sites through the use of simulacra, lighting and sound effects and actors in period costume. Films may be characterised by use of a canonical source from the national literature, generally set within the past 150 years; conventional filmic narrative style, with the pace and tone of '(European) art cinema'* but without its symbolisms and personal directorial voices; a museum aesthetic, period costumes, decor and locations carefully recreated, presented in pristine condition, brightly or artfully lit; a performance style based on nuance and social observation.

It is arguable whether this is a distinct phenomenon. There are precedents (for example, the French costume dramas of the 1950s such as *Les Misérables*, 1958), but heritage films may be distinguished from many period films in a number of ways. While displaying high production values, they are generally small-scale and intimate, not spectacular; they do not (on the whole) deal with the great events of history, as conventionally understood, or even, like *Senso* (1954, Italy) or *Angi Vera* (1978, Hungary), treat such events through their impact on personal lives; much less do they address the construction of historical representation, like *Ludwig – Requiem für einen jungfräulichen König/Ludwig – Requiem for a Virgin King* (1972, Germany) or *Amarcord* (1974, Italy). However, it is not a uniquely European genre, except perhaps in the sense of Eurocentric, since it has been important to the cinema of most white settler nations, notably Australia, Argentina and Canada.

The focus of the films is, typically, on attractively presented everyday bourgeois life. Critically they are an interesting case study. Often hugely popular in their country of origin, they tend to be sold as art cinema outside it. Though the market research is not available, it seems likely that they are especially popular with middle-class audiences, in a period when this class has become the majority or at least a significant minority in many European countries. They are thus embraced by the same class from which the critical establishment is drawn, yet the latter has generally viewed them negatively. Often characteristics such as nostalgia or attention to fixtures and fittings are criticised without considering the potential of the former to be a critique of the present or the sensuousness of the latter and its iconographic expressivity (typically requiring the skilled reading of a female spectator). Equally, the genre has provided a space for marginalised social groups, a sense of putting such people back into history, for instance women: *Rouge Baiser* (1985, France), *Rosa Luxemburg* (1986, Germany), *Howards End* (1991, UK); lesbians and gay men: *El diputado/Congressman* (1978, Spain), *Ernesto* (1979, Italy), *Avskedet/The Farewell* (1980, Finland); even ethnic minorities (*Cheb*, 1990, France) and the disabled (*My Left Foot*, 1989, Ireland). None of this argues for the merit of the genre, but suggests a critical issue of some complexity that warrants exploration. RD

Bib: Andrew Higson, 'Re-presenting the National Past: Nostalgia and Pastiche in the Heritage Film', in Lester Friedman (ed.), *British Cinema and Thatcherism* (1993).

HERMANSEN, Hugo   Kristiania [Oslo] 1879 – Oslo 1939

Norwegian film pioneer, owner of the first Norwegian cinema, which opened in Oslo in 1904, Hermansen controlled twenty-six cinemas by 1907 before going into film production. His successful 1905 and 1906 documentaries on the accession of King Carl drew large audiences to his cinemas. Hermansen's company, Norsk Kinematograf, also produced the first Norwegian fiction film, *Fiskerlivets farer – Et drama paa havet/The Dangers of a Fisherman's Life – An Ocean Drama*, in 1906 (released 1908). In the following years Hermansen concentrated on his profitable cinema business, but in 1909, at the age of thirty, he suffered a severe stroke. He eventually recovered but gave up his position as head of the cinema chain. He produced three films in the 1920s. KS

HERZOG, Werner   Werner Stipetic; Munich 1942

German director of international reputation and one of the figureheads of the New German Cinema*. Herzog made shorts and documentaries (*Herakles*, 1962; *Spiel im Sand*, 1964; *Die beispiellose Verteidigung der Festung Deutschkreutz*, 1966) before directing his award-winning script *Lebenszeichen/Signs of Life* (1968). An *auteur* with a strong personal signature even when doing remakes (*Nosferatu – Phantom der Nacht/Nosferatu the Vampyre*) and literary adaptations (*Woyzeck*, 1979), Herzog has a single subject, which he varies according to the central character's self-image as over-reacher and prophet or underachiever and holy fool: the impossible self-determination of the male individual, best embodied by Klaus Kinski* (five films) and Bruno S (two films). Herzog's trademark is the search for

extreme locations, outlandish situations and excessive characters, but often in order to let a strange and touching humanity emerge from impossible odds. Herzog's best-known films are the megalomaniac quests of *Aguirre, der Zorn Gottes/Aguirre, Wrath of God* (1972), *Fitzcarraldo* (1982) and *Cobra verde* (1987), all starring Kinski. TE

Bib: Timothy Corrigan (ed.), *The Films of Werner Herzog: Between Mirage and History* (1986).

Other Films Include: *Auch Zwerge haben klein angefangen/Even Dwarfs Started Small* (1970); *Fata Morgana, Land des Schweigens und der Dunkelheit/Land of Silence and Darkness* (1971); *Die große Ekstase des Bildschnitzers Steiner, Jeder für sich und Gott gegen alle/Every Man for Himself and God Against All/The Enigma of Kasper Hauser* (1974); *Herz aus Glas/Heart of Glass* (1976); *Stroszek* (1977); *Wo die grünen Ameisen träumen* (1984); *Echos aus einem düsteren Reich/Bokassa Ier – Echos d'un sombre empire* (1990); *Schrei aus Stein/Scream of Stone* (1991).

HEUSCH, Luc de   Brussels 1927

Belgian director, who was assistant to Henri Storck* from 1947 to 1949 and took part in the postwar internationalist and experimental art movement Cobra. With Cobra and Storck's support, he made his first film, *Perséphone*, in 1951. The same year he founded the Comité International du Film Ethnographique et Sociologique with Jean Rouch*, a major influence on his work. In 1954, de Heusch started teaching ethnography at the Brussels Free University. He has published several books on the subject, and his *Cinema and Social Science* (1962) is a classic within the field of visual anthropology. Luc de Heusch directed documentaries on both African and European societies. *Sur les traces du renard pâle, Recherches en pays Dogon/On the Trail of the Pale Fox* (1983), on the anthropologist Marcel Griaule, won the Prix du Public at Cannes. Apart from making a fiction film (*Jeudi on chantera comme dimanche/Tell Me the Difference Between Thursday and Sunday*, 1967, produced by Storck), de Heusch has been especially committed to the *Film sur l'art**: he has directed films on famous painters, including the celebrated *Magritte ou la leçon de choses/Magritte or the Object Lesson* (1960), and *Je suis fou, je suis sot, je suis méchant/I'm Mad, I'm Foolish, I'm Nasty* (1991), a penetrating portrait of James Ensor.

Luc de Heusch presides over the Henri Storck Foundation, is a board member of the Belgian National Film Archive and Museum, and vice-president of the Centre du Film sur l'Art. SS

HICKEY, Kieran   [?]1936 – Dublin 1993

Irish director and writer. Hickey was one of only a few Irish film-makers of his generation to study film formally. He began his career as a director of documentaries with his partners, cameraman Sean Corcoran and editor Pat Duffner. They made sponsored documentaries for state agencies, while also producing films on writers Jonathan Swift and James

Joyce. In the 1970s Hickey was one of the first film-makers, along with Bob Quinn*, to help carve out an indigenous Irish cinema. His film *Exposure* (1978), about the suppressed sexuality of three male surveyors who come into contact with a foreign woman, identified an interest in the middle class. This concern was pursued in *Criminal Conversation* (1980), written, like *Exposure*, in collaboration with Philip Davison, which explores the world of Dublin's nouveaux riches. KR

Other Films Include: *A Child's Voice* (1978); *Attracta* (1983); *Short Story: Irish Cinema 1945–1958* (1986); *The Rockingham Shoot* (TV, 1987).

HILLER, (Dame) Wendy   Bramshall, Cheshire 1912

British actress. A bright shining star of British cinema, Wendy Hiller has made only around twenty films since her debut in the 1937 quota quickie *Lancashire Lass*, and the particular affection which she seems to inspire can be laid at the door of only three of these twenty: Anthony Asquith's* *Pygmalion* (1938), Gabriel Pascal's *Major Barbara* (1941), and *I Know Where I'm Going!* (1945), directed by Michael Powell* and Emeric Pressburger. What inspires the affection is an unmannered directness, a shyness, an aloofness from seduction, and an economy of performance which makes restraint seem like a positive value rather than an absence of passion. Her alert intelligence in *I Know Where I'm Going!* may be blown a little off course by romance, but she falls in love with dignity and retains a sense of herself. After 1945 much of her work was in theatre, and though she won an Oscar for her supporting role in *Separate Tables* (1958), and was memorable as Gertrude Morel opposite Trevor Howard* in *Sons and Lovers* (1960), her appearances in film were intermittent and succumbed to the 'British disease' of anthology casting: *Murder on the Orient Express* (1974), *Voyage of the Damned* (1976). *The Elephant Man* (1980, US, UK) and *The Lonely Passion of Judith Hearne* (1987) offered her small but rewarding parts, and television gave her some excellent roles – perhaps most notably as the steely matriarch of Trevor Griffiths' *Country* (1981). JC

Other Films Include: *To Be a Woman* [co-narrator] (1951, dir. Jill Craigie); *An Outcast of the Islands* (1952); *Single-handed* (1953); *Something of Value* (1957, US); *Toys in the Attic* (1963, US); *A Man for All Seasons* (1966); *David Copperfield* (1970); *Making Love* (1982, US).

HITCHCOCK, (Sir) Alfred   London 1899 – Los Angeles, California 1980

British director. Hitchcock's contribution to British cinema in the 1920s and 1930s is well documented. Starting as a title card designer with Famous Players–Lasky at Islington Studio, he served as scriptwriter, assistant director and art director to Graham Cutts* on such films as *The Prude's Fall* and *The Passionate Adventure* (both 1924). In 1926, he directed his first two features for Michael Balcon* in Germany, *The*

Pleasure Garden/Irrgarten der Leidenschaft and *The Mountain Eagle/Der Bergadler*, absorbing influences from German Expressionism* and Soviet montage* which would inform his later style. After *The Lodger* (1926), he was one of Britain's most commercially successful directors, and *Blackmail* (1929), though shot silent, was released as Britain's first synchronous sound feature. Its creative and expressive use of sound was greeted in the avant-garde journal *Close Up** as a welcome departure from the 'photographs of people talking' of early sound cinema. In general, Hitchcock's British films, while remaining firmly within a popular tradition of film narrative, show the more diverse and experimental influences of a European art cinema in relation to visual style. After the success of *The Man Who Knew Too Much* (1934) and *The 39 Steps* (1935), however, it was apparent that the future lay in Hollywood. Hitchcock was signed to Selznick in 1938, and moved to America to make *Rebecca* (1940), which won Best Picture and Best Director Academy Awards. It is worth quoting at length the editorial of *Film Weekly* for 16 July 1937, both to indicate the standing which Hitchcock had in Britain, and to show a level of awareness in the trade press which was missing from most other areas of film criticism until the 1960s:

> So Alfred Hitchcock has decided to make a film in Hollywood after all [...]. I do not always applaud these Hollywood captures; but in Hitchcock's case I am sure experience of Hollywood's mass-production methods will improve his work. Hitchcock, still probably Britain's most talented director, certainly the most individualistic, has suffered for too long from being unchallenged in his own field and from being allowed to make his pictures almost exactly as he pleases.
>
> There is a strain of wilfulness in Hitchcock which has become more and more apparent with every picture he has made. He is a man with a cold and sardonic eye. He sees the grotesque side of his fellow men. And he is always more than ready to include one scarifying, impish touch even at the risk of sacrificing the mood of a scene or a whole picture. He pleases himself.
>
> Hitchcock is an individualist. Most of us believe him to be a genius in his own line. But he has always lacked restraint. In America he will come in contact with the producer system – the firm guiding hand that has seldom been felt in British studios. That system should curb his waywardness, and give his peculiar talent a more universal feel.

The possibility that Hitchcock might remain in Britain and become a great European director was beyond contemplation. Hitchcock returned to Britain to make two Ministry of Information shorts during the war, *Aventure Malgache* and *Bon Voyage* (both 1944); he supervised the editing of Harry Watt's* *Target for To-night* (1941) for American release, and was supervising director of the first documentary on the opening of the concentration camps, *Memories of the Camps* (1945). He made *Under Capricorn* in Britain in 1949, and returned in 1972 for *Frenzy*.

He was knighted in 1980. JC

Bib: Tom Ryall, *Alfred Hitchcock and the British Cinema* (1986).

Other British Films: *Number Thirteen* [uncompleted] (1922); *Always Tell Your Wife* [dir. Croise; completed direction]

(1923); *Downhill, Easy Virtue, The Ring* (1927); *The Farmer's Wife, Champagne* (1928); *The Manxman, Juno and the Paycock* (1929); *Elstree Calling* (dir. Brunel; completed direction], *Murder, An Elastic Affair* [short] (1930); *The Skin Game, Rich and Strange* (1931); *Number Seventeen* (1932); *Waltzes from Vienna* (1934); *Secret Agent, Sabotage* (1936); *Young and Innocent* (1937); *The Lady Vanishes* (1938); *Jamaica Inn* (1939).

HOCHBAUM, Werner Paul Adolph   Kiel 1899 – Potsdam 1946

German director, rediscovered after his film *Brüder* (1929) was found in the GDR film archive in 1974. Hochbaum entered film-making with political propaganda movies for the Social Democratic Party (SPD). *Brüder* was initiated by the leftist group Volksverband für Filmkunst and aimed at establishing a German socialist-revolutionary cinema that could derive political profit from the contemporary popularity of Soviet cinema. Developing a distinctly oppositional aesthetic programme, Hochbaum succeeded for a while even during the Nazi regime. Barred from film work in 1939, he spent the war years scripting an anti-fascist film which he planned to direct immediately after, but died before he could put it in production. KU

Other Films Include: *Vorwärts* (1929, short documentary); *Razzia in St. Pauli* (1932); *Morgen beginnt das Leben/Life Begins Tomorrow* (1933); *Die ewige Maske/The Eternal Mask* (1935); *Schatten der Vergangenheit/Shadows of the Past* (1936); *Ein Mädchen geht an Land* (1938).

HOFER, Franz   Saarbrücken 1883 – ?

German director. Recently rediscovered as a true *auteur* of early German cinema, Hofer's work is marked by stunning formal qualities and bizarre twists of plot. Hofer began as a theatre actor and playwright, before turning to film as a scriptwriter in 1910 (*Das Geheimnis der Toten*, starring Henny Porten*), directing his first film, *Des Alters erste Spuren*, in 1913. The years 1913–14 marked his most productive phase, when he worked in almost every genre, directing some of the most famous actors and actresses of the period in comedies such as *Hurrah! Einquartierung* (1913), detective dramas like *Der Steckbrief* (1913), and the *Sensationsfilm* (sensational film) *Die schwarze Natter* (1913). Among his surviving films of the middle and late 1910s the melodramatic *Heidenröschen* (1916) is the most remarkable, not only for its extravagant lighting and decors but also for its complex use of cinematic space, point-of-view editing and narrative structure. After the war Hofer temporarily ran his own company, Hofer-Film. He apparently slowed down in the 1920s, remaking one of his earliest films, *Das rosa Pantöffelchen*, in 1926. His last two films as director about which something is known are *Madame Lu, die Frau für diskrete Beratung/The Woman for Discreet Advice* (1929) and the populist sound film *Drei Kaiserjäger* (1933). MW

Bib: Heide Schlüpmann, 'The sinister gaze: Three films by Franz Hofer from 1913', in Paolo Cherchi Usai and Lorenzo Codelli (eds.), *Before Caligari: German Cinema 1895–1920* (1990).

HOFFMANN, Carl   Neisse an der Wobert 1881 – Berlin 1947

German cameraman and director, along with Karl Freund* and Fritz Arno Wagner* the most famous photographer of Weimar* cinema. In 1916 he became chief cameraman for Decla-Film, mainly working for director Otto Rippert (particularly on the six-part series *Homunculus*, 1916), where he experimented with trick photography. His close relation with Decla-Bioscop was sustained through his collaboration with Fritz Lang*. Hoffmann worked as photographer on several films by Joe May*, Paul Leni*, Richard Oswald*, F. W. Murnau*, Karlheinz Martin and Arthur Robison. His photography for *Der Kongress tanzt* (1931) offered an early example of mobile camera and sound film working well together. In 1927 he directed his first film, *Der Geheimnisvolle Spiegel* (1928), and from then on worked as director and camera operator on a dozen more films until his last pictures as director (*Ab Mitternacht*, 1938) and as cinematographer (*Via Mala*, 1945). His son Kurt Hoffmann* is a director. MW

HOFFMANN, Kurt   Freiburg i. Breisgau 1910

German director, son of Carl Hoffmann*. Beginning in 1939, with a series starring Heinz Rühmann*, he became one of Germany's most prolific directors of the postwar years. He directed almost forty films between 1948 and 1971, including remakes and a successful series with Liselotte Pulver*. Hoffmann was a conservative at heart though intellectually a radical, a surefooted professional with auteurist ambitions, torn between sentimentality and satire. His most ambitious films are *Ich denke oft an Piroschka* (1955), *Die Bekenntnisse des Hochstaplers Felix Krull/The Confessions of Felix Krull* (1957) and *Wir Wunderkinder* (1958). TE

Bib: Ingo Tornow, *Piroschka und Wunderkinder oder Von der Vereinbarkeit von Idylle und Satire: Der Regisseur Kurt Hoffmann* (1990).

HOLLAND, Agnieszka   Warsaw 1948

Polish director and scriptwriter. Holland graduated from FAMU* in Prague in 1971 and began her career as assistant to Krzysztof Zanussi* on *Iluminacja/Illumination* (1973). A member of Andrzej Wajda's* 'X' film unit, she was a prominent exponent of the 'cinema of moral unrest'. Her distinctive personal style, influenced by the Czech New Wave* and reflecting strong political views, was evident from her first feature, *Aktorzy Prowincjonalni/Provincial Actors* (1979), which received the FIPRESCI (international film critics) award at Cannes. While Holland was not popularly perceived as a feminist in Poland, her *Kobieta Samotna/A Woman Alone* (1981), the story of a middle-aged postwoman, was critically acclaimed for its perceptive portrayal of women in Poland. She scripted several of Wajda's films, including *Człowiek z Żelaza/Man of Iron* (1981) and *Korczak/Korczak* (1990). Holland's international reputation failed to shield her from adverse repercussions for her pro-Solidarity stance, and she was forced to emigrate when martial law was imposed. Based in Paris since 1981, she is one of the few Polish directors to have forged a successful European career, with the commercial and critical successes of *Bittere Ernte/Angry Harvest* (1984, nominated for an Academy Award for Best Foreign Film) and *Europa, Europa* (1990). Her first wholly 'French' film, the intense *Olivier Olivier* (1991), is based on the true story of a young boy who disappears from home and is 'found' six years later wandering the streets of Paris, his true identity in question. For her first Hollywood production, *The Secret Garden* (1993), Holland joined forces with scriptwriter Caroline Thompson to adapt the popular British children's novel by Frances Hodgson Burnett. AW

Other Films Include: *Gorączka/Fever* (1980); *To Kill a Priest* (1988, US/Fr.).

HOPKINS, (Sir) Anthony   Port Talbot, Wales 1937

British actor, who achieved international recognition for strong dramatic acting in the 1970s and 1980s, and notoriety for the monstrous credibility of his Hannibal Lecter in *Silence of the Lambs* (1990, US). A respected theatre and television actor, his best film performances are those which allow him a little scope for theatricality. His Captain Bligh in the 1984 version of *The Bounty* rivalled Charles Laughton's*; Richard Attenborough* discovered his sinister qualities in *Magic* (1978, US); and David Lynch cast him effectively as Dr Treves in *The Elephant Man* (1980, US/UK). His more subdued acting skills are evident in *84 Charing Cross Road* (1986), which began life as a BBC television play. More recently, he has taken out a patent on the emotional reticence of the middle-aged English male with a restrained performance as a repressed Edwardian patriarch in *Howards End* (1991), as a butler struggling with feelings while the world turns in *Remains of the Day* (1993), and as the writer C. S. Lewis in *Shadowlands* (1993). More irrepressibly, he has punctuated this streak of constricted Englishness with a wonderfully over-the-top performance as the Dutchman Van Helsing in *Bram Stoker's Dracula* (1992, US).

He was knighted in 1993. JC

HOPPE, Marianne   Rostock 1911

German actress. From 1928 Hoppe worked as an actress in Berlin theatres, making a star debut in the cinema with *Der Schimmelreiter* and *Jäger Johanna* (both 1934). She often played opposite Gustaf Gründgens*, to whom she was married from 1936 to 1945, and acted in several films of the Nazi period (*Crepuscule*, 1937, *Der Schritt vom Wege*, 1939, *Lumière dans la nuit*, 1943). After the war she returned to the theatre but also made appearances in the films of Helmut Käutner*, Wolfgang Staudte*, Hans Deppe* and Erich

Engel*, and as Rüdiger Vogler's mother in the opening scenes of Wim Wenders'* *Falsche Bewegung/Wrong Movement* (1975). TE

HÖRBIGER, Paul   Budapest, Hungary 1894 – Vienna 1981

Austro-Hungarian actor, who began his career as a stage actor in 1919 and pursued a successful theatre career throughout his life. During the silent era he acted for Fritz Lang* (*Spione/The Spy*, 1928), playing a servant or a chauffeur, and was praised for his 'Chaplinesque' body language. In sound cinema, he specialised in musical comedies and film operettas (*Zwei Herzen im 3/4 Takt*, 1930; *Die lustigen Weiber von Wien*, 1931; *Der Kongress tanzt*, 1931; *Operette*, 1940), coming across as funny but also sentimental: his rhythmic speech-song, particularly appropriate for operetta films, contrasted with his melancholy facial expression. He thus fitted the image of the tragic yet light-hearted Viennese and was an ideal partner for Hans Moser*, Maria Andergast and Luise Ullrich* in the typical 'Viennese films', as well as in Max Ophuls' *Liebelei* (1933). In 1935 he founded Algefa-Film and went on personifying the Austrian *ancien régime* through his characterisations of waiters, servants, chauffeurs, porters, but also barons and dukes. His best-known postwar films are Carol Reed's* *The Third Man* (1949), where he plays an intimidated porter, *Das Tor zum Paradies* (1949), where he impersonates death, and *Mädchenjahre einer Königin* (1954, with Romy Schneider*). Later he became mostly known as a wine-loving singer in his own television shows. AL/MW

HORN, Camilla   Frankfurt 1903

German actress, who began her extraordinarily long life in film as an extra with Marlene Dietrich*, as well as substituting for Lil Dagover* in F. W. Murnau's* *Tartüff* (1926). After Lillian Gish withdrew from Murnau's *Faust* (1926), Horn had her breakthrough chance, playing next to Gösta Ekman (Sr)* and Emil Jannings* and convincing as the naive but passionate Gretchen. She signed a contract with Ufa* for four years and starred in *Der fröhliche Weinberg* (1927), but left for Hollywood the same year, working for United Artists in *Tempest* (1928) and *Eternal Love* (1929). She returned to Berlin in 1929; in the 1930s her career took her to Paris and London as well as Germany (*Die Drei um Edith*, 1929; *Moral um Mitternacht*, 1930). Horn played opposite many of the leading men of the time, such as Gustav Diessl and Louis Graveure, Hans Albers* and Gustav Fröhlich, Ivan Petrovich and Albrecht Schoenhals. From the Gretchen type she graduated to the blonde vamp, playing models, countesses, dancers and ladies of the *demi-monde*. In 1941–42 she went to Italy. After the war she continued to make stage and television appearances, appearing once again in films in the 1980s: *Frankies Braut* (1982), *Der Unsichtbare* (1987), *Schloss Königswald* (1987). KP/TE

Bib: Camilla Horn, *Verliebt in die Liebe: Erinnerungen* (1985).

HORNEY, Brigitte   Berlin 1911 – Hamburg 1988

German actress, whose first film role was in Robert Siodmak's* *Abschied* (1930). *Ein Mann will nach Deutschland* (1934) and *Liebe, Tod und Teufel* (1934) marked the beginning of her ambivalent film career in Nazi Germany. Though Horney's expressive eyes, spare gestures, strong-willed and gamine charm did not fit the fascistic stereotyping of women, the Nazis made use of her skills and popularity as an 'anti-star' by channelling her image of inner strength into patriotic fighting films, skilfully deploying her unconventional beauty in erotic and exotic adventures (*Savoy-Hotel 217*, 1936). In 1936–37 she made two British films: *The House of the Spaniard* (1936) and *Secret Lives* (1937). She fled Germany in 1945 and lived in Switzerland and the US thereafter. From the 1960s she frequently returned to Germany to work on her second, less spectacular career in German television series: among others, *Derrick* (1977–80), *Heidi* (1976–77), *Jakob und Adele* (1983–86) and *Das Erbe der Guldenburgs* (1986–88). KU

HOSKINS, Bob   Bury St Edmunds 1942

British actor, who received international recognition for his performance as an old-fashioned London gangster out of his depth against new Britons, new sexualities and new criminal forces in Neil Jordan's* *Mona Lisa* (1986). Hoskins received Best Actor awards from Cannes, the New York Film Critics, the Los Angeles Film Critics, and BAFTA. Short, stocky and balding, but nonetheless a romantic, Hoskins' ability to play the bewilderment of the common man had first emerged in Dennis Potter's BBC six-part serial, *Pennies from Heaven* (1978), and was developed in *The Lonely Passion of Judith Hearne* (1987). His tendency to express his bewilderment through violence had appeared in John MacKenzie's *The Long Good Friday* (1981). JC

Other Films Include: **As Actor** – *The National Health* (1973); *Pink Floyd The Wall* (1982); *The Honorary Consul* (1983); *The Cotton Club* (1984, US); *Brazil* (1985); *Who Framed Roger Rabbit* (1988, US). **As Director** – *The Raggedy Rawney* (1987).

HOUWER, Rob   The Hague 1937

Dutch producer and director. Houwer studied in Munich, where he soon established his own production company, Houwer Film Munich. He produced several projects for young German film-makers such as Peter Schamoni, Volker Schlöndorff*, Johannes Schaaf and Peter Fleischmann in the 1960s and was one of the twenty-six signatories of the Oberhausen Manifesto in 1962 [> NEW GERMAN CINEMA]. He also directed shorts such as the prize-winning *Aanmelding/Application* (1964), made in the Netherlands. He took risks in Germany by producing innovative films while making commercial pot-boilers and sex comedies at the same time. In the 1970s he returned to the Netherlands and made up a creative team with director Paul Verhoeven* and scriptwriter Gerard Soeteman, producing a series of very successful features: *Wat zien ik/Business is Business* (1971), *Turks fruit/Turkish Delight* (1973), *Keetje Tippe/Cathy Tippell* (1975), *Soldaat van Oranje/Soldier of Orange/Survival Run* (1977), and *De vierde man/The Fourth Man* (1983). Many more Dutch films were developed under his supervision, including a feature-length animation film, *Als je begrijpt wat ik bedoel/If You Understand What I Mean* (1983). Houwer commutes between Munich and his company in Amsterdam, Verenigde Nederlandsche Filmcompagnie. KD

HOWARD, Leslie   Leslie Howard Stainer; London 1893 – shot down over France 1943

British actor, who as a Hollywood and Broadway star in the 1930s represented the best of Englishness for Americans, and on his return to Britain came to represent England's ideals for the English. Jeffrey Richards identifies three components in Howard's Englishness: 'the mystic, the intellectual, and the gentleman amateur'. The three qualities come together in *'Pimpernel' Smith* (1941), which he also produced and directed. A Cambridge professor who uses archaeology as a cover for rescuing intellectuals and artists from Nazi Germany, Smith (Howard) evades his captors at the end by vanishing, quite literally, in a cloud of smoke. There is much in the film which suggests that Howard's identification with the struggle against fascism was idealistic rather than political, and when asked by an American student how he got into the racket Smith responds, 'When a man holds the view that progress and civilisation depend in every age upon the hands and brains of a few exceptional spirits it's rather hard to stand by and see them destroyed.' The film also throws light on Howard's platonic attractiveness: Smith's only love is for 'the one sublime woman', a Greek marble of Aphrodite. That he had a great deal of respect for real women, however, is demonstrated by his last film as a director, *The Gentle Sex* (1943, co-dir. Maurice Elvey), which centres on women's contribution to the war effort.

Howard's best known part may be as Ashley in *Gone With the Wind* (1939, US), but he was best loved as the ideal Englishman: patriotism with a light touch, often whimsical, sometimes comic, never too serious to be jingoistic. When he died in 1943 after his plane was shot down by the Luftwaffe, C. A. Lejeune* wrote, 'Howard was more than just a popular actor. Since the war he has become something of a symbol to the British people.' JC

Bib: Jeffrey Richards, *The Age of the Dream Palace: Cinema and Society in Britain, 1930–1939* (1984).

Other Films Include: *The Heroine of Mons* [short] (1914); *The Happy Warrior* (1917); *The Lackey and the Lady* (1919); *Outward Bound* (1930, US); *Service for Ladies*, *The Animal Kingdom* (1932, US); *Secrets*, *Berkeley Square* (1933, US); *Of Human Bondage*, *British Agent* (1934, US); *The Scarlet Pimpernel* (1935); *The Petrified Forest*, *Romeo and Juliet* (1936, US); *Pygmalion* [co-dir. Asquith] (1938); *Intermezzo: A Love Story* (1939, US); *49th Parallel*, *From the Four Corners* [short] (1941); *The First of the Few* [also dir.] (1942); *The Lamp Still Burns* [prod. only] (1943).

HOWARD, Trevor   Cliftonville 1916 – Bushey 1988

British actor, who worked in the theatre for ten years before making his film debut in 1944 in Carol Reed's* *The Way Ahead*. This was followed in 1945 with a role in Anthony Asquith's* *The Way to the Stars*, and with the part for which he is perhaps best remembered, that of the doctor in David Lean's* *Brief Encounter*. British cinema after the war generated a club of typical English men, of which Howard was one, his particular strength being to make English dullness interesting. His characters were typically restrained, but the restraint covered complex emotions and the typicality was finely nuanced. His success in films like Alberto Cavalcanti's* *They Made Me a Fugitive* (1947), David Lean's* *The Passionate Friends* (1949) and Reed's *The Third Man* (1949) made him one of the key actors of the postwar period, and he continued to deliver well-judged character parts for the next three decades. JC

Other Films Include: *I See a Dark Stranger, Green for Danger* (1946); *Odette* (1950); *Lady Godiva Rides Again, Outcast of the Islands* (1951); *The Heart of the Matter* (1953); *The Cockleshell Heroes* (1955); *The Key* (1958); *Sons and Lovers* (1960); *Mutiny on the Bounty* (1962); *Von Ryan's Express* (1965, US); *The Charge of the Light Brigade* (1968); *Ryan's Daughter* (1970); *Ludwig* [It./Fr./Ger.], *A Doll's House* [UK/Fr.] (1973); *Conduct Unbecoming* (1976); *Sir Henry at Rawlinson End* (1980); *Gandhi* (1982); *White Mischief* (1987).

HRISTOV, Hristo   Plovdiv 1926

Bulgarian director. Widely respected for tackling some controversial socio-political themes, Hristo Hristov graduated from the Sofia Academy of Dramatic Art (VITIS) in 1958. Until 1966 he worked as a stage designer and director of plays and operas, then spent two years at the Mosfilm studios in Moscow assisting Marlen Khutsiev*, Andron Mikhalkov-Konchalovsky* and Mikhail Romm*. His first feature, *Ikonostasăt/Iconostasis* (1969), co-directed by animation director Todor Dinov, was a breakthrough in Bulgarian cinema because of its original treatment of iconography and religious art as integral to Bulgaria's historical and cultural tradition. Then, after making a heavily theatrical epic on national hero Georgi Dimitrov and the infamous Leipzig trial, *Nakovalnja ili čuk/Anvil or Hammer* (1972), co-produced by the Soviet Union and East Germany, he broke another taboo by adapting Jordan Radičkov's* controversial novel *Posledno ljato/The Last Summer* (1972–74) for the screen; two years on the shelf and released only in a drastically edited version, the film mourned in surrealist style the passing of village life and peasant traditions.

Hristov strained the patience of the authorities again in the 1980s by making a series of gripping psycho-dramas on the ills of Eastern bloc socialism: *Kamionăt/The Lorry* (1980, about the transport of a worker's body to his native village for burial), *Edna žena na trideset i tri/A Woman at 33* (1982, about a divorced office secretary unjustly victimised), *Sabesednik po želanie/Question Time* (1984, about a popular actor suffering from cancer who reviews the options left to him), and *Harakteristika/Reference* (1985, about honesty versus corrup-

tion among taxi drivers) – all withdrawn from theatrical circulation after a token release.

During Hristov's years as First Secretary of the Bulgarian Film-makers union (1974–82), several talented directors and scriptwriters at the Boyana* Studios received his moral support to experiment with genres and challenge the fixed ideological formulas of socialist film-making. RH

HRUŠÍNSKÝ, Rudolf   Nový Etynk 1920 – Prague 1994

Czech actor. One of Czechoslovakia's leading stage and screen actors, Rudolf Hrušínský also exerted great moral authority. In 1989, when Russian troops were again assembling outside Prague, his radio appeal calmed the nation, and in 1990–92 he served as an MP in the newly resurrected democracy. Born of a touring theatrical family, he had no formal training but joined E. F. Burian's youth theatre group and was a member of the National Theatre from 1960, in recent years appearing as Falstaff and as Ekdal in *The Wild Duck*. His film career began in 1937 when he appeared as the youthful lead in a sequence of films, before consolidating his comic talents as Švejk in *Dobrý voják Švejk/The Good Soldier Švejk* (1957). He appeared opposite Anne Heywood in Jiří Weiss' Anglo-Czech *Třicet jedna ve stínu/90° in the Shade* (1965), but is best known to international audiences for the nonchalant comedy of his roles in Jiří Menzel's* *Rozmarné léto/Capricious Summer* (1967), *Postřižiny/Cutting it Short* (1980) and *Slavnosti sněženek/The Snowdrop Festival* (1983). The range of his abilities is represented by a terrifying portrait of evil in Juraj Herz's *Spalovač mrtvol/The Cremator* (1968) and his restrained and moving performance as the doctor in František Vláčil's* *Dým bramborové natě/Smoke on the Potato Fields* (1976). PH

HUILLET, Danièle   Born 1936
and
STRAUB, Jean-Marie   Metz 1933

French-born directors working in Germany. Huillet and Straub work as a co-scripting and co-directing team, their equal collaboration so close that it is scarcely meaningful to separate the roles (Huillet has, however, indicated that she tends to be in charge of sound and editing, while Straub does most of the camerawork). Huillet and Straub's work is modernist, oppositional, demanding – and rarely seen outside the film festival circuit. Their films have their roots in European (mostly German) high culture: literature (Brecht, Böll, Kafka) and music (Bach, Schoenberg) and are concerned with an exploration of history. They are politically committed, sometimes explicitly, as in *Fortini/Cani* (1976), which reworks material about the Israeli-Palestinian conflict, but more often in the approach to their material. It is a cinema which is, in Maureen Turim's terms, 'theoretical, elliptical, innovative, and challenging'. GV

Feature Films: *Nicht versöhnt, oder Es hilft nur Gewalt, wo Gewalt herrscht/Not Reconciled* (1965); *Chronik der Anna*

Magdalena Bach/The Chronicle of Anna Magdalena Bach (1968); *Othon (Les Yeux ne veulent pas en tout temps se fermer, ou Peut-être qu'un jour Rome se permettra de choisir à son tour)/Othon* (1969); *Geschichtsunterricht/History Lessons* (1972); *Moses und Aron/Moses and Aaron* (1975); *Dalla nube alla Resistenza/From the Cloud to the Resistance* (1979, It./Fr./Ger./UK); *Zu früh/Zu spät/Too Early Too Late* (1981, It.); *Klassenverhältnisse/Class Relations* (1984).

HUNGARY

The first film screening in Hungary took place just a few months after the Lumière* brothers' first public show in Paris. Starting in May 1896, a representative of the Lumière company organised regular screenings in a Budapest hotel café for almost a year. The first footage produced in Hungary was also made by the same company. However, regular film production started relatively late. The first Hungarian film – *A tánc/The Dance* by Béla Zsitkovszky – was made in 1901. It consisted of twenty-seven one-minute reels, each representing a different kind of folk dance, and was commissioned by a cultural-scientific society. For some time, production and distribution were not separated in the Hungarian film industry. The first independent production company was created in 1911, but it failed a year later. The first full-length feature film, *Ma és holnap/Today and Tomorrow*, was made by the biggest production and distribution company, Projectograph, in 1912. It featured Mihály Kertész (later Michael Curtiz in Hollywood) as an actor, and it is likely that Kertész was also the director.

In the following decade, film production developed quickly. While by 1913 only ten Hungarian feature films had been made, by 1918 this number had increased to 109, and there were as many as thirty-seven film production companies. Three names stand out as pioneers of early Hungarian cinema. Jenő Janovics, a former actor and theatre director, was one of the most important producers of the time; and both Sándor Korda (later Alexander Korda*) and Mihály Kertész began their apprenticeship as directors in his company. In 1918 Korda bought Janovics' company and founded a studio called Corvin, whose facilities became the basis of later Hungarian film production. The period 1918–19 was a high point in Hungarian silent film production since the revolutionary governments from the autumn of 1918 until the summer of 1919 strongly supported cinema. During the short period of communist dictatorship in 1919 more than thirty films were produced, of which only two have survived. Since virtually all important film-makers of the time supported the revolution, after its downfall many of them had to leave Hungary. Understandably, the counter-revolutionary government did not trust film industry people, which caused an almost total disintegration of Hungarian film production during the following decade.

The next boom period for Hungarian cinema began in the mid-1930s. It was assisted by a law requiring theatres to devote 10 (later 20) per cent of their programmes to Hungarian films. Most of the films produced in this period were light comedies written by popular playwrights of the time, which gave Hungarian cinema a domestic success it has never achieved since. A significant part of this popularity was due to

comedy and melodrama stars such as Gyula Kabos, Kálmán Latabár, Pál Jávor or Katalin Karády*. Film production continued to increase during the war, and in 1943 reached a peak of fifty-four films, a figure never since equalled. Hungarian cinema also achieved its first international artistic success in the early 1940s: István Szőts'* *Emberek a havason/Men on the Mountains* (1942), which won first prize at the Venice Biennale. The end of the war, however, brought a halt to significant popular film-making in Hungary.

The subjection of Hungarian film production to politics began in the immediate postwar period, though for a few years this did not mean a unilateral or monolithic influence. Independent private producers could find money for production, albeit with great difficulty, whereas the major political parties participating in the coalition government founded their own production companies, evidently obtaining finance quite easily. The Hungarian film industry was entirely nationalised in 1948, after the communist takeover. But during this short transitional period some remarkable films were made, such as Géza Radványi's *Valahol Európában/Somewhere in Europe* (1947) and Szőts' *Ének a búzamezőkről/Song of the Cornfields* (1947). These films signalled a new beginning for Hungarian cinema, moving away from popular genres and adopting an *auteur* film perspective. However, this opening was blocked by communist ideological control for at least eight years, and the impact that Italian neo-realism* had on Szőts' and Radványi's work did not extend to Hungarian cinema generally – Radványi left Hungary in 1948, Szőts in 1957. After 1948, production dropped to five or six films per year and it remained at that level until 1955. Most films of this period were made for direct propaganda purposes in the style of Socialist Realism*, and conformed to the ideological imperatives of the Communist Party. Political censorship was not institutional, but was built in at different levels of film production and distribution. All institutions were politically responsible for the product that went through them. Political authorities played an active role in initiating film scripts. Topics were designed at the highest level of cultural bureaucracy and directors were either selected by the political authorities themselves or approved by them. At this stage we cannot speak about censorship *per se*, since the highest level of political control was present right at the beginning of a film's production. Nevertheless, the popular comedy tradition of the 1930s and 1940s managed to survive in several communist propaganda films too. A number of musicals featuring fashionable songs and popular stars achieved considerable success even if the narratives concentrated on the ubiquitous communist hero fighting imperialist agents and saboteurs. Production began to increase after 1955, with a significant jump in 1961, to around twenty films annually, a level sustained over the next twenty-five years. Production dropped significantly again after 1988. In the early 1990s, in the wake of political democratisation and the introduction of a market economy, the volume of feature film production has fallen below ten films a year. On the other hand, the drop in feature film production has been accompanied by a boom in documentaries.

The year 1955 is considered a turning point in Hungarian film history. Films made in this year signal a considerable loosening of ideological control, and a chance for the neo-realist trend initiated in the early 1940s by István Szőts to continue. The key film in this respect is Zoltán Fábri's 'peasant film' *Körhinta/Merry-go-round* (1955), which achieved great international success. Other 1955 films, like Félix Máriássy's *Budapesti tavasz/Spring in Budapest* and *Egy pikkoló világos/A Glass of Beer*, or Károly Makk's* *9-es kórterem/Ward no. 9*, also show a re-emergence of *auteur* film in Hungary, though this trend was blocked again for a short period after the Soviet invasion of 1956.

In 1962, however, a 'new wave' of Hungarian art cinema began [> BRITISH, CZECH, AND FRENCH NEW WAVE]. Two generations came to film-making at virtually the same time. Some directors of the first postwar generation – Zoltán Fábri, Károly Makk, János Hersko and Félix Máriássy – had already made important films in the 1950s, but others, like Miklós Jancsó*, András Kovács*, Márta Mészáros* and Péter Bacsó, made their first feature film at the same time as the generation that graduated from the Film Academy in the early 1960s (Ferenc Kósa, István Szabó*, Judit Elek, Sándor Sára, István Gaál and others). While the 'new wave' of the younger generation mainly concentrated on personal problems, such as young people's difficulties in adapting to society or conflicts between the value systems of different generations, the older film-makers turned to history and politics. Perhaps not surprisingly, after the Hungarian uprising of 1956, the strongest theme evident centred on problems of national identity, the relationship between the individual and history, and the individual's moral autonomy in the face of political pressures and repression. In this period, Hungarian cinema and politics were inextricably linked. Film-making became the prototype of politically conscious activity in Hungary, for political censorship was less severe in the case of films than for other cultural forms. Topics were not prescribed as in the 1950s, and decisions about scripts were made by a middle-ranking official at the Ministry of Culture, though the final decision whether or not a film should be released was still in the hands of the highest political officer of cultural policy. Directors could consider themselves important agents of political liberties in another sense, many of them having direct contact with high-ranking political leaders, which allowed them to function as an intellectual pressure group. In this period began the practice of 'political bargaining' between directors and political authorities, to negotiate changes and the release of politically controversial films. Although popular genre films reappeared (the historical melodrama and comedy in particular), they were few in number compared to the *auteur* films made in this period.

In the 1970s the political-historical analysis of the *auteur* cinema of the 1960s permutated into a distinctive sub-genre: the historical allegory or parable. This form had been initiated by Miklós Jancsó in 1965 with *Szegénylegények/The Round-up*, as a way of circumventing censorship, and it was at first used only by him. Historical events were given a highly symbolic and abstract treatment and were used to exemplify moral conflicts caused by dictatorial oppression. After 1968, however, many directors who had never before treated political or historical themes directly also adopted and modified this genre, creating a realist trend of political and historical parables: András Kovács' *A magyar ugaron/Fallow Land* (1972) and *Bekötött szemmel/Blindfold* (1975); István Gaál's *Magasiskola/The Falcons* (1970); Ferenc Kósa's *Nincs idő/Beyond Time* (1972). Finally, in the late 1970s, the political

preoccupation of films centred on the Stalinist Hungary of the 1950s. These films were no longer allegorical; rather, they made more or less direct political allusions to the inevitable failure of the regime: Pál Gábor's *Angi Vera* (1978) and *Kettévált mennyezet/Wasted Lives* (1984); Kovács' *A Ménesgazda/The Stud Farm* (1978); Kósa's *Mérkőzés/The Match* (1980); Makk's *Egymásra nézve/Another Way* (1982); Péter Bacsó's *Tegnapelőtt/The Day Before Yesterday* (1981), among others. The period was also characterised, however, by the banning of several films, mainly those made in the Balázs Béla Stúdió*.

Meanwhile popular film production underwent a real crisis when old-fashioned popular genres (classical melodrama and historical adventure films) were overtaken by the vogue for modern action movies, science-fiction and horror films. However, Western mass cultural trends were out of favour with the conservative communist culture policy of the time, and in any event these genres were too expensive for the Hungarian film industry. Moreover, most Hungarian film-makers refused to 'prostitute' themselves by making popular films, and when some of them tried to initiate a Hungarian 'quality popular' genre, as György Szomjas did in the late 1970s, they were hampered by the lack of 'positive myths' of everyday life upon which to base it. In the early 1980s the international market became increasingly important for Hungarian cinema, partly as a consequence of the declining political significance of Hungarian films at home, although some films were still banned. On the other hand, growing economic problems led a number of directors to seek financial support for their films from abroad. The most successful in this respect was István Szabó, whose *Mephisto* (1981) won an Academy Award in 1982. The most successful attempts at popular film-making of the period were imitations of foreign movies, like István Bujtor's *Az Elvarázsolt dollár/Enchanting Dollar* (1985), a Hungarian version of an Italian series.

In the late 1980s and early 1990s, with the coming of a new film-making generation (more than a dozen first films were made in the early 1990s), and after the collapse of the communist regime and the ideologically controlled and state-supported production system, no single trend dominated. In the early 1990s, Hungarian cinema was characterised by a significant documentary film production dealing with contemporary political and social issues, as well as with historical investigation; by the advent of the low-budget, amateur-style film supported by professional studios (András Szőke, Miklós Ács, András Szirtes); by various kinds of lyrical-subjective forms (Attila Janisch, Can Togay, Ildikó Enyedi, Tibor Klöpfler); and by an abstract metaphysical or utopian style (Béla Tarr*, György Fehér, András Monory, Zoltán Kamondy). In a country where the intellectual tradition of *auteur* cinema remains such a powerful influence, and where resources for film production have been dramatically reduced, 'popular' film has come to be represented by foreign – almost exclusively American – films. KAB

HUPPERT, Isabelle   Paris 1955

French actress. One of the most prominent French art cinema actresses since the late 1970s, Huppert trained for the stage.

212

One of her early film parts was as a rebellious teenager in Bertrand Blier's* *Les Valseuses/Going Places* (1973); her first success was in Claude Goretta's* *La Dentellière/The Lacemaker* (1977). These two films established the dual features of her persona: sexual intensity on the one hand, victimised innocence on the other. This duality is epitomised in Claude Chabrol's* *Violette Nozière* (1978), the story of a real-life patricide, for which she won a Best Actress award at Cannes. Huppert's most interesting parts express resistance through sexuality, as in Maurice Pialat's* *Loulou*, Jean-Luc Godard's* *Sauve qui peut (la vie)/Slow Motion* (1980) and Diane Kurys'* *Coup de foudre/Entre nous/At First Sight* (1983). In others, she embodies a more conventional coolness: Bertrand Tavernier's* *Coup de torchon/Clean Slate* (1981), Joseph Losey's* *La Truite/The Trout* (1982), Blier's *La Femme de mon pote/My Best Friend's Girl* (1983). This last film, like Josiane Balasko's* *Sac de noeuds/All Mixed Up*, extended her range to comedy, though her register is predominantly dramatic. As in France, Huppert's international films have been more critically than commercially successful (Michael Cimino's *Heaven's Gate*, 1980, Werner Schroeter's* *Malina*, 1990). She has been supportive of women *auteurs* such as Kurys, Balasko and others, including her sister Caroline Huppert. Her performance as Emma in Chabrol's *Madame Bovary* (1991) may signal a move towards more popular, melodramatic, parts. GV

Other Films Include: *Aloïse* (1974); *Le Juge et l'assassin* (1976); *Les Soeurs Brontë/The Brontë Sisters* (1979); *Passion* (1982); *La Garce* (1984); *Cactus* [Australia], *The Bedroom Window* [US] (1986); *Les Possédés* (1987); *Une affaire de femmes* (1988); *La Vengeance d'une femme* (1989); *Après l'amour* (1992); *Amateur* (1994, US).

HURST, Brian Desmond   Castle Reagh 1900 – London 1986

Irish director. In 1925 Hurst went to Hollywood, where he worked as an assistant to John Ford, but he returned to England in 1934 and began directing films. One of his first films was *Irish Hearts* (1934), and though he made a number of other Irish-subject films during his career, including *Riders to the Sea* (1935), *Ourselves Alone* (1936), *Hungry Hill* (1946) and *The Playboy of the Western World* (1962), they are not among his best work. Working in a number of genres, including crime, musical, war, comedy, historical romance, and horror, Hurst's career was punctuated by hits and misses, mostly the latter. KR

Other Films Include: *Dangerous Moonlight* (1941); *Scrooge* (1951).

HURT, John   Chesterfield 1940

British actor. His career as leading victim of the British cinema was established with a brilliant characterisation of Timothy Evans, hanged in 1944 for crimes he did not commit, in Richard Fleischer's *10 Rillington Place* (1970). Hurt's image projects pain and vulnerability, and his distinctive voice quavers with sensitivity. Regularly cast for type, his performances have a strength which his characters may lack. He won a British Academy Best Supporting Actor award for his role in Alan Parker's* *Midnight Express* (1978) and a Best Actor award for his unsentimental performance in the title role of David Lynch's *The Elephant Man* (1980, UK/US). One of his most distinctive achievements was on television in *The Naked Civil Servant* (1975), where his Quentin Crisp responds to his victimisation with flamboyant eccentricity. His appearance in *Alien* (1979, US) is brief, but to the point; he gives a near definitive performance as Winston Smith in Mike Radford's *Nineteen Eighty-Four* (1984); and his performance in *The Field* (1990, UK/Ir.) is as grotesque and excessive as the character demands. JC

HUSZÁRIK, Zoltán   Domony 1931 – Budapest 1981

Hungarian film director and designer. Huszárik was the most original talent of his generation; his distinctive personal and artistic character, and the fact that he did not follow any major cinematic trend or current but created his own unique artistic universe, made him a legendary figure of modern Hungarian cinema. He started his studies at the Academy of Theatre and Film Art in 1949, but was considered politically unreliable by the school authorities and had to leave in 1952. He went back after 1956, graduating in 1961. For ten years he made only short films, which earned him an international reputation, beginning with *Elégia/Elegy* (1965), awarded the Oberhausen prize. He made only two full-length feature films in his lifetime. The first, *Szindbád* (1971), is a masterpiece of non-linear narration and pictorial composition. It is also a summary of the particular inspiration that can be found in all his works: a melancholia generated by the disappearance of an organic sense of life in which sensual pleasures and the consciousness of mortality are closely entwined. Huszárik was also unique in the Hungarian cinema of the 1960s and 1970s in that his work remained untouched by any political, social or historical involvement. In all his short films he favoured a non-narrative lyrical and pictorial style which expressed a nostalgia for a relationship to nature and to cultural traditions on the verge of extinction. KAB

Other Films Include: *Amerigo Tot* [short] (1969); *Tisztelet az öregasszonyoknak/Tribute to Old Women* [short] (1972); *Csontváry* (1979).

IBSEN, Tancred   Glausdal 1893 – Oslo 1978

Norwegian director, grandson of the playwright Henrik Ibsen. Tancred Ibsen worked in Hollywood with King Vidor and Victor Sjöström* in the mid-1920s and directed the first Norwegian sound film, *Den store barndåpen/The Big Baptism*, in 1931. In the 1930s he directed several comedies in Sweden before returning to Norway, where he shot the first film of the newly formed production company Norsk Film*, *To levende og en død/Two Living and One Dead* (1937), followed by *Fant/Tramp* the same year. *Fant*, an effervescent screen version of Gabriel Scott's novel about Norwegian fisherfolk, has become a Norwegian classic, known and loved by generations. Alfred Maurstad* stars as the amiably roguish tramp who takes advantage of a young woman aboard his tiny boat. His reckless behaviour, guitar-playing and practical jokes are contrasted humorously with the conventional tight-knit community. His death by drowning allows the young woman to return to the arms of her decent lover, but the tramp has enabled her to appreciate more keenly the sensual pleasures of open-air dances and the beauty of water and sky.

Through the 1940s and 1950s, Ibsen continued to work in different genres, such as comedy, drama and documentary, including a film on the 1952 Oslo Winter Olympic Games. His last film was *Vildanden/The Wild Duck* (1963), an adaptation of his grandfather's play. Ibsen's films were often based on works of literature, and he generally wrote his own scripts. As an *auteur*, Ibsen was both traditional and experimental, working within established genres but always seeking new forms.
KS

Other Films Include: *Norgesfilmen/The Norwegian Film* (1927); *Vi som går kjøkkenveien/We Who Take the Back Door* (1932); *Op med hodet/Raise Your Head* (1933); *Synnøve Solbakken* (1934); *Du har lovet mig en kone/You Promised Me a Wife, Kanske en gentleman/Maybe a Gentleman* (1935); *Å vi gifta?/Are We Married?, Stackars miljon rer/Poor Millionaire, Spøket på Bragehus/The Ghost at Bragehus* (1936); *Valfångare/Whalehunters, Gjest Baardsen* (1939); *Tørres Snørtevold* (1940); *Den farlige leken/The Dangerous Game* (1942); *Et spøkelse forelsker seg/A Ghost Falls in Love* (1946); *Den hemlighetsfulle leiligheten/The Secretive Flat* (1948); *To mistenkelige personer/Two Suspicious Persons* (1950); *Storfolk og småfolk/Rich and Poor* (1951); *Olympiafilmen/The Film of the Olympic Games* (1952); *Venner/Friends* (1960).

ICELAND

With its rich story-telling heritage, it might seem paradoxical that Iceland has only consistently embraced the medium of film in the last fifteen years. Easily the smallest country in Scandinavia, Iceland has a population only recently exceeding a quarter of a million. What is remarkable, then, is that it should have produced a significant film culture at all, let alone the vigorous and exciting cinema which has developed since 1979.

Iceland's first recorded public screenings took place in 1903, and a permanent cinema was established in Reykjavik three years later. It was some time, however, before the country saw any indigenous film production – indeed, film-makers from other Nordic countries would produce films based on Icelandic subjects long before Icelanders themselves. An early example is Swedish director Victor Sjöström's* *Berg-Ejvind och hans hustru/The Outlaw and His Wife* (1918). Based on an Icelandic play by Jóhann Sigurjónsson and strongly evocative of the Icelandic mountain landscape, *Berg-Ejvind* was ironically shot in northern Sweden, possibly because of the exigencies of war.

Three films were made in Iceland during the silent period, all produced by the Danish Nordisk Films Kompagni*. Importantly, though, all three were adapted from works by Icelandic writers and featured significant contributions from indigenous personnel. This split personality is evident from the first of the Nordisk* trio, *Saga Borgarættarinnar/The Saga of the Borg Family*, directed in 1919 by a Norwegian, Gunnar Sommerfeldt, but with a screenplay by Gudmundur Thorsteinsson (who also appeared in front of the camera). However, the next two productions were principally the work of a man who might justifiably qualify as Icelandic cinema's first *auteur*, Gudmundur Kamban, who both directed and wrote the adaptations of his own originals for *Hadda Padda* (1922) and *Det sovende hus/The Sleeping House* (1926).

From the introduction of sound to 1979, perhaps only a dozen Icelandic movies were completed, the most famous of these being co-productions with Scandinavian neighbours. Examples include *Rauda Sikkjan/Den røde Kappe/The Red Mantle* (1967), a joint Danish-Swedish-Icelandic production. A historical drama based on royal intrigues in eleventh-century Iceland, *Rauda Sikkjan* was directed by Gabriel Axel* and shown at Cannes.

While major productions generally relied on outside funding, the continued influence of Icelandic literature can clearly be seen in the films' subject matter – as for example in the 1954 Swedish-Icelandic collaboration *Salka Valka*, directed by a Swede, Arne Mattsson, with most of the cast and crew coming from Sweden or Denmark. That *Salka Valka* still managed to retain a strong Icelandic character was due to a script based on two 1930s novels by Iceland's most celebrated twentieth-century author, Nobel Prize laureate Halldór Laxness. Not all films shot in Iceland before 1979 were made with foreign money. Directors Oskar Gislason and Loftur Gudmundsson each managed to make several features without the benefit of a national cinema infrastructure. Gudmundsson, whose features include *Milli fjalls og fjöru/Between Mountain and Shore* (1948) and *Nidursetningurinn* (1951), had made the ground-breaking documentary *Island i lyfandi myndum/Iceland in Moving Pictures* (1925) at the start of his career. *Island* is an early example of a strong Icelandic documentary tradition which continues to the present day, other notable non-fiction directors being Porgeir Porgeirsson, Reynir Oddson and Osvaldur Knudsen. The latter's work on volcanoes in the 1950s and 1960s still provides tourist information today.

1966 saw the foundation of Icelandic Television (RUV), a fertile training ground for Icelandic film personnel. Jobs provided by RUV also acted as a catalyst in the creation of the Felag Kvikmyndagerdarmanna (Icelandic Film-makers' Association). Despite the influence of television, it was the late 1970s before there was another major development in Icelandic film. The Reykjavik Film Festival was founded in 1978 and has since become an annual event attracting entries from all over the world. However, it was the year following the establishment of the festival which is now seen as the single most important juncture in Iceland's film history.

Quite why 1979 came to represent such a watershed is far from clear; but during that year a number of factors combined to change Icelandic film culture beyond recognition. One of the most significant was the foundation of the Icelandic Film Fund (and with it the Icelandic Film Archive). Until then, the commitment of the Icelandic government to film production was minimal, to say the least. While the IFF did not have an enormous amount of money to put into production – its initial funds amounted to 300,000 krona (less than £100,000) – it nevertheless represented an unprecedented commitment on behalf of the Icelandic authorities.

Secondly, 1979 saw an Icelandic film achieve hitherto unparalleled success at the box office. Around a third of Iceland's population went to see August Gudmundsson's *Land og synir/Land and Sons*. While Icelandic audiences for imported (mainly American) product had already risen to higher per capita levels than their Scandinavian neighbours, *Land og synir* was the first film to benefit from the rebirth of Icelandic film culture. After *Land og synir*, Gudmundsson went on to make the first direct film adaptation of an Icelandic saga in *Utlaginn/Outlaw* (1981), a faithful cinematic rendition of *The Saga of Gisli* which has become a focus of recent debates surrounding the representation of Icelandic national identity. Some films have gone out of their way to address this issue, notably Hrafn Gunnlaugsson's *Hrafninn flygur/When the Raven Flies* (1984), which, in the words of Peter Cowie, 'demolishes the received image of Viking heroism that Icelanders are taught at school'. Gunnlaugsson has also questioned the identity of contemporary Iceland, most strikingly with a punk version of the national anthem in *Okkar á milli/Inter nos* (1982). Music plays a significant part in the work of the new Icelandic cinema's other *enfant terrible*, Fridrik Thor Fridriksson. In 1982 Fridriksson's documentary *Rokk i Reykjavik/Rock in Reykjavik* captured the essence of an explosion in Icelandic youth culture centred on several new rock bands. One of those featured was Björk Gudmundsdóttir, who has become Iceland's best-known cultural export.

Fridrik Thor Fridriksson is a central figure in the development of recent Icelandic film. He founded Iceland's first film journal, *Kvikmyndabladid*, in 1978, and in the same year was instrumental in establishing the Reykjavik Film Festival, of which he was the first director. Fridriksson is known for his love/hate relationship with the Icelandic film authorities. Having set up his own production company, Hugrennigur, and directed a number of challenging documentaries such as *Eldmidurin/The Blacksmith* (1981), Fridriksson found it increasingly difficult to raise funds for his projects. Then the

censors deemed the youth-oriented *Rokk i Reykjavik* unsuitable for viewing by under-14s because of references to drugs. Ironically Fridriksson later received the IFF's largest-ever grant to make *Börn náttúrunnar/Children of Nature* (1991), which, widely distributed on the European art-house circuit, was nominated for an Oscar as Best Foreign Film. Fridriksson has described the film as 'a road movie about elderly people'.

Women figure strongly in Iceland's new generation of film-makers. A list of significant Icelandic women directors would include Kristín Pálsdóttir, Gudny Halldórsdóttir (Halldór Laxness's daughter), and Kristín Johannesdóttir, who made the first film by an Icelandic woman director in 1983 with the lyrical and personal *A hjare veraldar/Rainbow's End*. Like many of her contemporaries, Johannesdóttir was educated and trained abroad (in France), but has returned to contribute to the vibrant domestic film scene.

Icelandic cinema today maintains a varied output in genres ranging from historical epics to comedy. Most of its films will almost certainly never travel outside Iceland, rendered inexportable by the culturally specific ways in which they address an indigenous audience. Práinn Bertelsson, for example, has made a series of popular comedies starring the same central cast in different, nationally recognisable contexts such as fishing and farming, an Icelandic equivalent of Britain's *Carry On** films. Iceland nevertheless provides a useful, not to say enviable, role model for other small (and not so small) countries in the rest of Europe. SH

Bib: *Icelandic Films* (Reykjavik: Icelandic Film Fund, periodically from 1980 to 1992) provides detailed information on Icelandic films and film personalities.

IDESTAM-ALMQUIST, Bengt
Åbo 1895 – Stockholm 1983

Swedish film scholar and critic. Idestam-Almquist, also known under his pen name 'Robin Hood', was the founding father of Swedish cinema studies. He was a film writer in the daily *Stockholms-Tidningen* for almost five decades, initiated the first Swedish society for cinema studies in the 1930s, and wrote books and essays on Mauritz Stiller*, Victor Sjöström* and other figures of the early Swedish cinema. His pioneering work has been followed up by scholars such as Rune Waldekranz, Gösta Werner, Leif Furhammar and Jan Olsson. LGA/BF

IDHEC – see FEMIS

IGLESIA, Eloy de la
Eloy Germán de la Iglesia; Zarauz, Guipúzcoa 1944

Spanish director, who started by directing theatre for children and writing for television. He first achieved popular success with *El techo de cristal/Glass Ceiling* (1970), a thriller. A member of the Spanish Communist Party, Iglesia in the early 1970s made violent social protest films such as *La semana del asesino/Assassin's Week* (1972). His work attempts to represent class relations and state and social oppression via extremely controversial sexual subject matter: a *ménage-à-trois* in *Juego de amor prohibido/Forbidden Love Game* (1975), bestiality in *La criatura/The Creature* (1977), homosexuality in *El diputado/The Congressman* (1978). From the mid-1970s his films fall into two categories: some, like *Los placeres ocultos/Hidden Pleasures* (1977), deal with homosexuality; others, like *Navajeros/Knife Fighters* (1980), are family melodramas about juvenile delinquency. The films are made for a popular audience, shot on location on minimal budgets, with non-professional or unknown actors. The narrative unfolds at breakneck speed and there is no fancy technique; major incidents and symbolic motifs are repeated or heavily underlined to drive the message home. Iglesia's work has been described as the film equivalent of the yellow press and as belonging to 'the aesthetic of the Y-front'. JA

IIEC (INSTITUTO DE INVESTIGACIONES Y EXPERIENCIAS CINEMATOGRÁFICAS)

Spanish film school, founded in 1947 under the aegis of the Escuela de Ingenieros Industriales. The IIEC suffered from severe budgetary restrictions, changes of location and the indifference of the Spanish film industry, which meant that, save for Luis García Berlanga*, Juan Antonio Bardem* and Carlos Saura*, few of its early students found work. In 1959 a student strike led to the appointment of Sáenz de Heredia* as director, and to showcase panoramas of IIEC student shorts at the San Sebastián film festival in 1960 and in Madrid, which in turn helped launch the 'New Spanish Cinema'*. JH

IKONEN, Ansa   St Petersburg, Russia 1913 – Helsinki 1989

Finnish actress, who became famous in Valentin Vaala's* 'modern comedies' such as *Kaikki rakastavat/All are in Love* (1935) and *Vaimoke/Substitute Wife* (1936). In these films, Ikonen and her co-star Tauno Palo* formed the first great star couple of Finnish cinema. In wartime films such as *SF-Paraati* (1940) and *Kulkurin valssi/The Vagabond's Waltz* (1941), audiences knew from the beginning how everything would end. While waiting for the final kiss, the stories concentrated on meaningful gazes, star performances and song and dance numbers. Ansa and Tauno belonged to everyone; their charm seemed eternal. They made comedies and melodramas, and their on-screen collaboration lasted over twenty years. Their last film together was *Ratkaisun päivä/Days of Decision* (1956). Ikonen also acted without Palo in a number of comedies and melodramas. Her star persona is complex, combining notions of goodness, purity, sensibility and morality. During World War II she embodied the ideal Finnish woman in *Oi kallis Suomenmaa/Oh, Dear Fatherland* (1940), *Rantasuon raatajat/The Toilers of Rantasuo* (1942) and *Tyttö astuu elämään/The Girl Goes Out Into the World* (1943). In the 1950s most of her roles were comic rather than dramatic. Ikonen also tried directing: in 1944 she made the comedy *Nainen on valttia/Woman is the Wild Card*, which was reasonably successful both critically and financially. AK

ILIU, Victor   Sibiu 1912 – Rome, Italy 1968

Romanian director, whose *Morea cu noroc/The Mill of Good Luck* (1955) is regarded as a pioneering achievement in Romanian film. Iliu attended Eisenstein's* lectures on direction in 1946–47, and learnt from veteran Romanian director Jean Georgescu. From 1951, starting with *In sat la noi/In Our Village*, he made a series of rural Socialist Realist* dramas reflecting the ruling party's priority of collectivisation of agriculture in the semi-literate countryside. *Morea cu noroc*, a tale of Transylvanian peasants' poverty in the nineteenth century, shows Iliu transcending political diktat through creative film-making, looking to many European influences and fully utilising Romanian technical and acting talents. His next and last film – *Comoara din Vadul Veche/The Treasure of Vadu Vechi* (1963) – is a sombre psychological drama of sabotage. Until his early death he was a leading influence on the industry as president of the Association of Film-Workers, editor of *Cinema* and head of the I. L. Caragiale Institute for Theatre and Film Art (IATC), where he taught another generation, including Dan Pița* and Mircea Veroiu*. MM

ILLÉS, György   Eger 1914

Hungarian cinematographer, teacher and mentor of many generations of Hungarian cinematographers. He started in the film industry in 1935 and made his first film as a cinematographer in 1949. The same year, he became a teacher at the Academy of Theatre and Film Arts, and later was appointed director of the cinematography department, a post he still occupies. In the 1950s, Illés initiated a new realist style of cinematography, using natural lighting and flexible camera handling. He always considered that the cinematographer's work does not start with shooting, but at the script stage. Illés has shot more than fifty films, and many important Hungarian and international cinematographers – Vilmos Zsigmond, László Kovács, Jean Badal, Lajos Koltay – consider themselves his disciples. It is commonly held in Hungary that the worldwide reputation of Hungarian cinematography is primarily due to Illés' teaching and professional influence. KAB

Films Include: *9-es kórterem/Ward no. 9, Budapesti tavasz/Spring in Budapest* (1955); *Husz ora/Twenty Hours* (1965); *141 perc a befejezetlen mondatból/141 Minutes from the Unfinished Sentence* (1975).

ILYINSKY, Igor V.   Moscow 1901–87

Soviet actor. Ilyinsky was for many years the leading comic actor in Soviet cinema. He worked in both the Moscow Art and Meyerhold Theatres and first appeared on screen in Yakov Protazanov's* *Aelita* (1924), in which he played a comic detective. He appeared in Fyodor Otsep's* *Miss Mend* (1926), played leading roles in Sergei Komarov's *Potselui Meri Pikford/The Kiss of Mary Pickford* (1927) and *Kukla s millionami/The Doll with the Millions* (1928), and also appeared in three other Protazanov silent films, including *Prazdnik svyatogo Iorgena/The Feast of St Jorgen* (1930). But he was probably best remembered by Soviet audiences for his portrayal of archetypal philistine bureaucrats, Byvalov in Grigori Alexandrov's* musical comedy *Volga-Volga* (1938) and Ogurtsov in Eldar Ryazanov's* *Karnaval'naya noch'/Carnival Night* (1957). RT

INGRASSIA, Ciccio – see FRANCHI, Franco

IOSELIANI, Otar D.   Tbilisi, Georgia [USSR] 1934

Georgian director. In 1965 Ioseliani graduated from VGIK*, where he had studied with Alexander Dovzhenko*. His 1962 short *Aprel'/April* is about a newly married couple; his documentary *Chugun/Cast Iron* (1964) observes a day in the life of a metal works. In 1968 Ioseliani made his first full-length feature, *Listopad/Falling Leaves*, also set in a factory. In *Zhil pevchii drozd/Once Upon a Time There Was a Singing Blackbird* (1970), the charming, feckless hero, a percussionist at the Tbilisi Opera, has not a care in the world and is at the disposal of his many friends until, in the film's shocking finale, he is knocked down by a car and killed. *Pastoral'/Pastoral* (1975) examines the effect of a summer visit by a string quartet on the inhabitants of a Georgian village.

Since 1984 Ioseliani has been based in Paris. His 1984 film *Les Favoris de la lune/Favourites of the Moon*, a charmingly idiosyncratic Parisian comedy, has been compared to the work of René Clair* and Jacques Tati*, and won the Jury Prize in Venice. The documentary *Un petit monastère en Toscane/A Little Monastery in Tuscany* (1988) was followed by *Et la lumière fut/And Then There Was Light* (1989), set in a Senegalese village in which a timber company cuts down the trees, and which is clearly informed by Ioseliani's concern with the disappearance of tradition. In the melancholy allegorical comedy *La Chasse aux papillons/The Butterfly Hunt* (1992), Ioseliani returns to Russian concerns. When an elderly émigrée dies in a French provincial town, her castle is inherited by a sister from Moscow who, with the help of her relations, promptly reduces life in the castle to that of a Russian communal flat, before selling it to Japanese buyers. JGf

IRELAND

Cinema in Ireland, in both its pre-colonial and post-colonial formations, has been dominated by foreign films. For some years films from Britain, France and Italy were the most frequently seen in Ireland, but since the early 1910s the vast majority of films screened have been American, while most of the rest have been British. Only rarely have indigenous Irish films had more than peripheral status. Indeed, the first fiction films made in Ireland were by the American company, Kalem, which visited Ireland between 1910 and 1912, and whose director, Irish-Canadian Sidney Olcott, returned during the following two years to produce the first fictional representations of Irish history and culture. These productions had more to do with the potential income from the urban ethnic Irish cinema audience in America than with the relatively modest income available from the still largely rural Irish population.

It was not until 1916 that professional indigenous film-making began with the Film Company of Ireland*, but this development did not encourage the independent Irish state, established in 1922, to support Irish films. Indeed, nationalist policies towards the cinema and popular culture in general were propelled by xenophobia and a conservative Catholic morality that was already clearly evident before independence. The new state expended its energies on a cultural protectionist policy that sought to exclude from Ireland any influences which might challenge the pre-modern official Gaelic and Catholic cultures. The cinema, music (especially jazz), literature and popular publications were restricted in a policy as much Catholic as it was 'Gaelic'.

The Official Film Censor operates under the Censorship of Films Act, 1923, which restricts any film from public exhibition if it is deemed indecent, obscene or blasphemous, or is 'contrary to public morality'. Subjective assessments by conservative censors led to a policy of restricting anything which infringed Catholic morality. As a result, films which dealt with contraception and abortion, or represented in any sympathetic way extramarital affairs or divorce (on which a constitutional ban was introduced in 1937), or depicted rape or homosexuality, were either banned or cut. The result was that during the first four decades of independence about 3,000 films were banned, while another 8,000 were cut, with many other films never submitted to the Official Film Censor, a government employee, as their fate would have been well known to the distributors. Among the films banned were *Brief Encounter* (1945, UK) and *The Postman Always Rings Twice* (1946, US). The adaptations of Tennessee Williams plays in the 1950s were also banned, while the cycle of British 'social problem' dramas of the late 1950s and early 1960s were either banned or severely cut. The administrative explanation for such extensive banning and cutting was that the censors pursued a policy, approved by the Minister for Justice, of rarely issuing limited certificates, such as the British 'X' which was introduced in 1951. Thus almost all films released could be seen by all age groups. This policy did not change until 1965 after a sustained campaign by distributors and exhibitors concerned about declining product availability, with the support of liberal journalists and other anti-censorship campaigners.

Against this background of official hostility to the foreign cinema the Irish state might have been expected to encourage an alternative indigenous Irish cinema. Far from it; but the reason for this is as much economic as it is cultural. Ireland occupies a peripheral economic space in world cinema, with box-office accounting for only about 0.5 per cent of the global market. In European terms, it represents 1.1 per cent of the market; its 2.3 admissions per person per annum puts it around the European average, but the ability to generate a surplus on a film within its own territory is not possible except for the most modestly budgeted films. Total box-office income in 1992 was a mere IR£21 million, while video wholesale was worth IR£15 million and video rental and sell-through about IR£40 million. As a result, private investors have only rarely put money into Irish films, while the Irish state did not commit any significant resources to an Irish cinema in the decades after independence. The policy that emerged was integrated within general economic parameters.

The decades after independence had seen an attempt to

build an Irish economic base through protecting the native bourgeoisie from foreign competition and through state intervention in unprofitable areas of the economy. While the state made significant strides in the development of natural resources and the building of an infrastructure, the bourgeoisie remained generally inefficient even in a protected home market. In the postwar years a gradual shift in policy occurred which led to the embracing of foreign capital as the means of developing an Irish industrial base. In this context film was viewed as another industry which could generate employment and produce foreign earnings. As a result, state policy for film production became firmly linked to industrial policy, with little or no concern with a cultural programme for film. When this policy culminated in the belated opening of Ardmore Studios* in 1958, no provision was made for an Irish, let alone a cultural, policy at the studios. The exception to this had been to utilise the players of the Abbey Theatre, the Irish National Theatre and other Irish theatres in film productions, though they were usually confined to supporting roles in non-Irish films. Thus players as various as Cyril Cusack*, Barry Fitzgerald*, Noel Purcell and Jimmy O'Dea combined their theatre work with often inconsequential film parts. Alfred Hitchcock*, John Ford and others adapted Abbey Theatre plays as films, though before the establishment of Ardmore these were usually studio productions made in Britain or the USA. The consequence of this policy of encouraging foreign capital to make films in Ireland, and of providing financial aid for the studios, was that support for indigenous production was minimal until the early 1980s.

By then the struggle had shifted from concern with the direct and indirect subsidising of foreign productions in Ireland towards debate within the Irish film community between those who favoured a committed indigenous cinema and those who championed a commercial Irish film 'industry'. The outcome of this debate is that all sides are now relatively satisfied: tax-based investments allow for large private investment in films, while the rejuvenated Bord Scannan na hEireann* (Irish Film Board), and increased sums from Irish television for independent productions, have resulted in such an expansion of native and foreign productions that 1994 was the most active year ever for film production in Ireland. This further shift in film policy is part of a broader redefining of the position of the native bourgeoisie in the international economy. It is in the context of these changes that the struggle for an Irish cinema can be most usefully viewed.

During the barren decades of the 1940s, 1950s and 1960s Irish film-makers were largely confined to servicing information campaigns for government departments and state agencies through making documentaries and drama-documentaries on public health, farming modernisation or tourism. Ironically, these campaigns were indirectly part of the modernisation process which was to lead to a dramatic shift from the inward-looking protectionist policies of the early decades of independence, to an outward-looking, international focus in Irish society and culture from the late 1950s onwards. However, it is Peter Lennon's documentary, *The Rocky Road to Dublin* (1968), that stands out as the most challenging film made in Ireland in the 1960s. Though based as a journalist in Paris, Lennon, working with French cinematographer Raoul Coutard*, interviewed a number of Irish 'modernisers', while adding an acerbic commentary which was highly critical of independent Ireland. When the film was adopted by activists during the May 1968 'Events' in France as evidence of a committed critical cinema, it was assured of both notoriety and extensive audience interest in Ireland.

In the inter-war period only a small handful of fiction films were made by Irish film-makers. Culturally and economically, the most successful of these were *Irish Destiny* (1926, retitled *An Irish Mother*) and *The Dawn* (1936), both set during the final military phases of the struggle for independence. These films, and their American and British counterparts like *The Informer* (1935), *Ourselves Alone* (1936) and *The Plough and the Stars* (1936), all proved popular with Irish audiences. But a film industry and the allegiance of audiences cannot be built on such (uncritical) nostalgia. It was not until the social and cultural effects of the internationalisation of Irish society began to manifest themselves in the late 1960s and early 1970s that a new generation of Irish film-makers began to look with a critical eye at aspects of Irish culture and society previously unexplored on film.

In this new cinema a more complex notion of the past was explored by such film-makers as Bob Quinn*, Pat Murphy*, Robert Wynne-Simmons (*The Outcasts*, 1982), and Tommy McArdle (*It's Handy When People Don't Die*, 1980), with the pious platitudes of nationalist historiography being interrogated for their simplistic formulations. The bastion of Catholic and state ideology, the family, was shown to have fissures at its heart: the fragmented family in all classes and in all periods was explored. Such film-makers as Kieran Hickey* (*Exposure*, 1978; *Criminal Conversation*, 1980), who looked at middle-class mores, or Joe Comerford*, who focused on the opposite end of the social spectrum, brought out themes such as infidelity and incest which had been long buried by Irish society. Catholic institutions – especially education, as in Cathal Black's* *Our Boys* (1980) – celibacy in Bob Quinn's *Budawanny* (1987) and *The Bishop's Story* (1994), and teenage pregnancy in Margo Harkin's *Hush-A-Bye-Baby* (1989), did not escape scrutiny. The city made its cinematic presence felt for the first time in films such as Comerford's *Withdrawal* (1974) and *Down the Corner* (1978), and in Black's *Pigs* (1984), where marginal social groups are represented.

Many of these films were informed by a realist aesthetic in their perhaps unconscious rejection of earlier romantic representations of Ireland by foreign film-makers. Some film-makers, however, by locating their films in the west of Ireland, have consciously sought to subvert that cinematic and cultural tradition. Quinn's *Poitín* (1978), where greed, drunkenness and attempted rape are centred in a traditional Irish lakeside cottage, and Comerford's *Reefer and the Model* (1988), in which two gay men dance at a ceilidh in a pub, suggest that the most powerful inheritances are being challenged. While many of these films posed a realist opposition to the romantic tradition, other film-makers were exploring new formal parameters, especially Thaddeus O'Sullivan*, whose innovative *On a Paving Stone Mounted* (1978) drew on avant-garde traditions to examine Irish migration. By contrast, those who try to work within mainstream commercial genres, such as City Vision's *The Courier* (1987), discover that Dublin's cityscape is not readily adaptable to the thriller format. This problematic of genre is most clearly evident in the formal schizophrenia of *Reefer and the Model*, where the first half of the film has the feel and resonance of a European art film but much of the rest is informed by Hollywood chase movies.

Reefer suggests that Ireland, like other European countries, is grappling with the dominance of American culture, as some of its film-makers embrace Hollywood while others search for a critical, subversive relationship to it. Among those who have chosen to embrace international commercial cinema, Neil Jordan* (*The Crying Game*, 1992), Jim Sheridan* (*My Left Foot*, 1989, and *In the Name of the Father*, 1993), and Pat O'Connor*, have opened up spaces and possibilities of which previous generations of Irish film-makers might only have dreamed: not least the total of nineteen Oscar nominations for Jordan's and Sheridan's films, with three wins, while Irish make-up artist Michelle Burke is the only contemporary Irish person to have won two Oscars, for *La Guerre du feu/Quest for Fire* (1981, Fr./Canada) and *Bram Stoker's Dracula* (1992, US). While Irish-born directors such as Herbert Brenon and Rex Ingram became successful in Hollywood, neither of them made a film in Ireland. The present generation of commercial cinema directors have successfully straddled the Irish and non-Irish cinema worlds and in the process have helped place indigenous Irish film-making in the international arena. KR
[> IRELAND AND OTHER CINEMAS, BORD SCANNAN NA hEIRE-ANN, IRISH-LANGUAGE FILMS, FILM INSTITUTE OF IRELAND]

IRELAND AND OTHER CINEMAS

Since regular indigenous Irish fiction film production only developed in the late 1970s, most films about the Irish have been produced by British and American film-makers. American cinema has largely constructed Ireland as a bucolic haven free from the rigours of American competitiveness and its capitalist ethos, with a particular celebration of the pre-modern virtues of the West of Ireland, as in *The Quiet Man* (1952). In these films, the work-shy, carefree Irish 'peasants' with their fondness for drink and sport are endorsed. By contrast, British cinema, when not imposing its particular form of racist humour on the Irish, has concerned itself with Irish history (*Captain Boycott*, 1947) or political violence in partitioned Ireland. The latter group of films, such as *The Gentle Gunman* (1952) and *A Prayer for the Dying* (1987), have tended to construct a view of the Irish where historical and political events are dehistoricised and desocialised. To this end, characters such as those played by John Mills* in *The Gentle Gunman* or Stephen Rea* in *The Crying Game* (1992) are endorsed, since their humanistic concerns lead them to a rejection of the increasingly irrational violence represented by Dirk Bogarde* in *The Gentle Gunman* and Miranda Richardson in *The Crying Game*. It has been argued by John Hill that Irish film-makers, in particular Pat O'Connor* in *Cal* (1984) and Neil Jordan* in *Angel* (1982), carry this British tradition into contemporary Irish cinema. KR

Bib: Kevin Rockett, 'The Irish Migrant and Film', in Patrick O'Sullivan (ed.), *The Creative Migrant* (1994).

IRISH FILM BOARD – see BORD SCANNAN NA hEIREANN

IRISH-LANGUAGE FILM-MAKING

The first Irish-language sound film was a short, *Oidhche Sheanchais/Storyteller's Night* (1935), made by American-born Robert Flaherty* shortly after his *Man of Aran* (1934). It was not until the late 1940s, however, that Irish-language film-making became more frequent. Government-sponsored information films began to be produced in both Irish and English versions, while the Irish-language organisation, Gael Linn, pioneered an Irish-language newsreel, *Amharc Eireann* (A View of Ireland), which was shown in Irish cinemas from 1956 until 1964. Gael Linn made a number of documentaries, the most notable being two directed by George Morrison* which remain key texts for their use of actuality footage and for historical exploration. Gael Linn continued producing documentaries until the early 1970s. These were usually directed by the prolific producer Louis Marcus. By then, the Irish public service broadcasting service, Radio Telefis Eireann* (RTE), had taken on this role, and in 1993 the government announced the establishment of Telefis na Gaeilge, a separate Irish-language television channel, which is due to begin broadcasting in 1995. KR

IRONS, Jeremy   Cowes 1948

British actor, a leading member of the generation of British film actors who emerged in the 1980s. With a distinguished stage career at the Royal Shakespeare Company in the 1970s, Irons first appeared as a star in 1981: on television in the international hit, *Brideshead Revisited*, and on film in Karel Reisz's* *The French Lieutenant's Woman*. A distinctly cool actor (with a chilly sexuality) who tends to work in flickers of expression and eloquent silences, he is quoted as saying, 'I dislike the vulgarity of excessive effort.' His most complex performance is as the psychologically indivisible twins in David Cronenberg's *Dead Ringers* (1988, Canada), for which he won a New York Film Critics award. Constantly in demand since his Oscar for *Reversal of Fortune* (1990, US), and increasingly threatened by typecasting, his acting – in, for example, Louis Malle's* *Fatale/Damage* (1992) – seems to depend more and more on a weak lower lip and an intense all-purpose gaze. JC

Other Films Include: *Nijinsky* (1980, US); *Moonlighting* (1982); *Betrayal, The Wild Duck* [Australia] (1983); *Un amour de Swann/Swann in Love* (1984, Fr./Ger.); *The Mission* (1986); *A Chorus of Disapproval, Danny the Champion of the World* (1989); *Kafka* (1991, US/Fr./UK); *Waterland* (1992); *The House of the Spirits* [Ger./Den./Port.], *M. Butterfly* [US] (1993).

José Ysbert Alvarruiz; Madrid
1886–1966

Spanish actor. After a long career in the theatre, he turned to film at the end of the Civil War, becoming one of the most prolific and popular Spanish character actors. He usually appeared as a caricature of the well-intentioned, uneducated, wily, often rural Spaniard. His most memorable performances were in Marco Ferreri's* El cochecito/The Little Car (1960) and Luis García Berlanga's* ¡Bienvenido, Mr Marshall!/Welcome, Mr Marshall! (1952) and El verdugo/The Executioner (1963). In El verdugo, his characteristically gravelly voice and rodent-like appearance added an extra dimension to the macabre narrative, whose black humour provided a sharp critique of life under Franco. PWE

ITALIAN HORROR FILM

Considered by some critics as an inferior imitation of American cinema, the Italian horror film is nonetheless remarkably rich and original. Furthermore, the outstanding level of craftsmanship of its practitioners has enabled it to overcome the limitations of its often ridiculously low budgets.

After a hesitant start, during which it was often influenced by other popular Italian genres such as the peplum*, Italian horror emerged as a category of its own. Films such as Riccardo Freda's* I vampiri/The Lust of the Vampire (1957) and Mario Bava's* La maschera del demonio/Mask of the Demon/Black Sunday (1960) and I tre volti della paura/Black Sabbath (1963) succeeded in integrating modern horror with traditional 'Mediterranean' themes, treating sexuality more openly than in more puritanical countries and creating mesmerising female characters, archetypally played by Barbara Steele*. One founding member of the genre is unquestionably Freda, who, as well as being a skilled creator of swashbucklers and adventure films, was an original explorer of the world of nightmares and fear, notably in L'orribile segreto del Dottor Hichcock/The Terror of Doctor Hichcock (1962) and Lo spettro/The Spectre (1963). The other is Bava; an accomplished cameraman for Freda's I vampiri, he directed films which quickly attained cult status: I tre volti della paura, and others such as La frusta e il corpo/Night is the Phantom (1963) and Operazione paura/Curse of the Living Dead (1966). All his films focus on sexual perversions and pathological states of mind, evoked through brilliant special effects and camera movements, creating a disorienting, nightmarish atmosphere. At the end of the 1960s, Pupi Avati* brought a personal approach to the Gothic and traditional horror themes in his directorial debut Balsamus, l'uomo di Satana/Blood Relations (1968) and Thomas ... gli indemoniati/Thomas ... The Possessed (1969), which he pursued with La casa dalle finestre che ridono/The House with the Laughing Windows (1976) and especially Zeder/Revenge of the Dead (1983). The theme of the 'returning dead' is dealt with within the framework of the macabre country fable, immersed in blood and grotesque humour. Through the 1970s the most prolific exponent of the genre was Lucio Fulci, whom many consider the inventor of Italian-style 'gore'. Fulci specialised in fantasy horror, beginning with Non si sevizia un paperino (1972) and Sette note in nero/Murder to the Tune of the Seven (1977). Defined as the 'poet of the macabre' by French critics and extolled by magazines such as the American Fangoria, the unusual Fulci favours menace, repulsion and delirious visionary horrors, reworked from American horror films (the living dead, cursed houses, the buried alive, demonic possession). Films such as Zombi 2/Zombi Flesh Eaters (1979), Paura nella città dei morti viventi/Fear (1980), Il gatto nero/Black Cat (1981), Quella villa accanto al cimitero/The House on the Edge of the Cemetery (1981), L'aldilà (1981), Lo squartatore di New York/New York Ripper (1982), L'occhio del male/Manhattan Baby (1983), Murderock uccide a passi di danza/Murderock (1984) and Il miele del diavolo (1986) exemplify Fulci's approach to the genre, executed with Corman-style limited budgets and fast shooting, with a loyal and well-trained crew. Some are filmed on location in the US with dialogue in English for rapid foreign distribution.

Dario Argento's* Suspiria (1977) brought a radical change to Italian horror film. The imaginary finally breaks free from narrative and Argento allows vision to take priority, in a kaleidoscope of glowing images which reflect an original poetry of the horrific. New directors in the genre have tended to take their cue from him. They include Bava's son Lamberto Bava, with Macabro/Macabre (1980), Shark-Rosso nell'oceano (1984), Demoni/Demons (1985) and Demoni 2 (1986); the promising young Michele Soavi (Deliria, 1987; La chiesa/The Church, 1989; La setta/The Sect, 1991); and lesser lights such as Gianfranco Giagni (Il nido del ragno, 1988), Marcello Avallone (Spettri/Specters, 1987) and Alessandro Capone (Streghe/Witch Story, 1989). GVo

ITALIAN POLITICAL CINEMA (1960–94)

In the 1960s and the 1970s, by virtue of its creative vitality and variety, Italian cinema was able to compete with Hollywood productions, both at a national and a European level. The political film in particular, although sometimes derivative of Hollywood action cinema, reached the distinctiveness of a real genre. Its origins can be traced to the first Mafia movies, such as Pietro Germi's* In nome della legge/In the Name of the Law (1949). Since then, almost two hundred others have been made, including the television serial La piovra/The Octopus, started in 1983 and reaching a peak of popular success with its fifth series in 1991.

Italian cinema dealing with the Mafia is like a house with a grand reception room on the first floor, a ground floor and a bargain basement packed with comedies, parodies, cheap detective movies, etc. The most renowned tenant of the first floor is Francesco Rosi* with his masterpiece Salvatore Giuliano (1962), as well as Cadaveri eccellenti/Illustrious Corpses (1975), adapted from Leonardo Sciascia's novel Il contesto. With Il caso Mattei/The Mattei Affair (1972), Lucky Luciano (1973) and Dimenticare Palermo/To Forget Palermo (1990), Rosi presented the two Mafias (Italian and North American) as one thing ('Cosa Nostra'), reaching a radically pessimistic and ultimately questionable conclusion: to be a Sicilian is not just an accident of birth but an inescapable question of fate. On the same grand first floor we find Elio Petri*, the first to bring Sciascia to the screen with A ciascuno il suo/To Each His Own (1967), Damiano Damiani, who directed Sciascia's *Il giorno della civetta/Mafia* (1968), and Paolo and Vittorio Taviani*, who started with *Un uomo da bruciare/A Man for Burning* (1962, co-dir. Valentino Orsini), the story of a Sicilian trade unionist (Gian Maria Volonté*, the key actor of the whole genre) murdered by the Mafia. With Damiani, however, and numerous other Mafia films (such as *Perché si uccide un magistrato*, 1975, and *Pizza Connection*, 1985) and the first series of *La piovra*, we move down to the ground floor. Its original tenant was Alberto Lattuada*, whose black comedy *Il mafioso* (1962), starring an irresistible Alberto Sordi*, had one fatal flaw: the Mafia is ubiquitous, so that, as Sciascia wrote, 'the spectator is no longer led to think what is the Mafia, but rather what is not the Mafia'. The ground floor is also occupied by Florestano Vancini's *La violenza: quinto potere/Violence: Fifth Power* (1972) and Giuseppe Ferrara's *Il sasso in bocca* (1970), a skilful 'faction' about the history of the Mafia after 1945 and its connections with the ruling political class. In 1984 Ferrara appeared to slide down to the basement with *Cento giorni a Palermo/A Hundred Days in Palermo* and, ten years later, *Giovanni Falcone* (1993). Still on the ground floor, a special place is held by Pasquale Squitieri: *Camorra* (1972), *I Guappi/Blood Brothers* (1974), and his best film, *Il prefetto di ferro* (1977). The continued power of the Mafia in Sicily and southern Italy means that younger Italian directors are also attracted to the topic; for example Emidio Greco with *Una storia semplice/A Simple Story* (1991) and Ricky Tognazzi with *La scorta* (1993).

Italian political cinema divides into four thematic groups: 1) Fascism and the Resistance; 2) the police, the judiciary, and Christian Democrat power; 3) class struggle and revolutionary utopias; 4) 1970s student revolts and terrorism. Attempts have also been made to deal with Third World and anti-imperialist issues, producing 'Spaghetti Western'-like movies [> ITALIAN WESTERNS] such as Damiani's *Quien sabe?/ A Bullet for the General* (1966), Carlo Lizzani's* *Requiescant* (1967), Sergio Corbucci's *Il mercenario/A Professional Gun* (1968), and others. Gillo Pontecorvo's* *La battaglia di Algeri/ The Battle of Algiers* (1966) and Giuliano Montaldo's *Sacco e Vanzetti/Sacco and Vanzetti* (1970) are other interesting examples. The first – and largest – group reached a high point with Bernardo Bertolucci's* *Il conformista/The Conformist* (1970) and the Tavianis' *La notte di San Lorenzo/The Night of San Lorenzo* (1982). It also includes, among others, Ettore Scola's* *Una giornata particolare/A Special Day* (1977), Gianni Puccini's *I sette fratelli Cervi* (1968), Giuliano Montaldo's *L'Agnese va a morire/And Agnes Chose to Die* (1976), and four documentaries on Mussolini (mainly based on the newsreels of the Istituto LUCE*). Ideologically, they range from the ambiguous right (Squitieri's *Claretta*, 1984), to the intransigent left (Pier Paolo Pasolini's* *Salò o le 120 giornate di Sodoma/Salò*, 1975). The most significant film in the second group is Petri's *Indagine su un cittadino al di sopra di ogni sospetto/Investigation of a Citizen Above Suspicion* (1969), scripted by Ugo Pirro*, who, together with Franco Solinas*, was at that time Italy's most politically committed scriptwriter. In the third group we find Francesco Maselli's* *Lettera aperta a un giornale della sera* (1970), about the crisis of left intellectuals; *Il sospetto* (1975), about the Italian Communist Party under Fascism; and Petri's *La classe operaia va in paradiso/Lulu the Tool* (1971). The fourth group

includes a dozen or so films, including Rosi's *Tre fratelli/Three Brothers* (1981), although the best examples come from younger directors like Gianni Amelio* (*Colpire al cuore/ Straight to the Heart*, 1983), Marco Tullio Giordana (*Maledetti vi amerò*, 1980), and Giuseppe Bertolucci (*Segreti segreti*, 1984). GVo

ITALIAN WESTERNS

Italian genre. The Italian Western, known in its home country as '*Western all'italiana*' but popularly (and slightly disparagingly) referred to abroad as the 'Spaghetti Western', emerged as a world phenomenon with the release of Sergio Leone's* *Per un pugno di dollari/A Fistful of Dollars* in 1964. Leone's film did not spring from nowhere. The preceding years had seen the making of a number of German-Yugoslav Westerns based on the popular novels of Karl May and some twenty Italian-French-Spanish co-productions in the Western genre. Between the mid-1960s and 1978, no fewer than 400 Italian Westerns (mostly co-produced) were made, involving various permutations of the formula, though as the 1970s wore on the genre went into decline. The Italian Western emerged out of the ashes of the peplum*, in which many of its first practitioners – Sergio Corbucci, Riccardo Freda*, Mario Bava* and others, including Leone himself – were trained. The crews, too, were often the same, many having also formed second units for American spectaculars shot in Rome or in Spain in the 1950s. Locations were mostly Spain (especially Almeria), but later Italy, Yugoslavia and Israel, with a brief foray into Monument Valley for Leone's *C'era una volta il West/Once Upon a Time in the West* (1968).

The Italian Western is both the most original and the most parasitic genre to emerge in Italy in the 1960s. It began as a counterfeit, not only an imitation of the foremost American genre, but under the pretence of being American, with directors, actors and technicians credited with English pseudonyms. It was bottom-drawer cinema, aimed at small-town audiences and churned out by small and medium-sized production companies, of which Alberto Grimaldi's PEA (which later used its profits to move upmarket) was the most prominent. From the beginning the genre was marked by violence, aggressivity and a fierce and hyperbolic element of male sadomasochism, pushed to the edges of parody but always with an eye to the market. Mannered and rootless, the Italian Western owed its success to its ability to function as pure, abstract, violent spectacle accessible to audiences regardless of nationality or culture, and it is no accident that it was the only form of Italian cinema to encounter no barriers to international diffusion. Gradually, there emerged something resembling the Western, though it was never quite *the* Western but rather a no-man's-land form of adventure. Five basic variations can be noted. First and most famous is the mannerist style pioneered in Leone's 'dollars' trilogy – *Per un pugno di dollari*, *Per qualche dollaro in più/For a Few Dollars More* (1965) and *Il buono, il brutto e il cattivo/The Good, the Bad and the Ugly* (1966) – and continued in films ranging from Tonino Valerii's *I giorni dell'ira/Days of Wrath* (1967) to Giulio Questi's off-the-wall *Se sei vivo, spara/If You Live, Shoot* (1967). Second, the picaresque, as exemplified by the 'Ringo' cycle starring Giuliano Gemma and directed by

Duccio Tessari (such as *Una pistola per Ringo/A Pistol for Ringo* and *Il ritorno di Ringo/The Return of Ringo*, both 1965), but also by Michele Lupo's *Arizona Colt* (1967). Third is the 'political' Western, with its ideological reading of the West and of a backward, Third-Worldist Mexico, from Damiano Damiani's *Quién sabe?/A Bullet for the General* (1967) to Carlo Lizzani's* *Requiescant* (1967, with Lou Castel and Pier Paolo Pasolini*), Sergio Corbucci's *Il mercenario/A Professional Gun* (1968) and Giulio Petroni's *Tepepa/Blood and Guns* (1969). Fourth is the macabre-funereal mode of the Sartana and Django series. And fifth are the lighter, neo-Fordian Westerns beginning with Franco Giraldi's *7 pistole per i MacGregor/Seven Guns for the MacGregors* (1966) and *Sugar Colt* (1967), and leading to the comedy cycle of the Terence Hill (Mario Girotti)/Bud Spencer (Carlo Pedersoli)/E. B. Clucher (Enzo Barboni) trio initiated by *Lo chiamavano Trinità/They Call Me Trinity* (1970).

So central was the Western to the Italian cinema of those years that it involved both specialists in popular genres and more 'serious' artists: scriptwriters Age* and Scarpelli*, Ugo Pirro*, Franco Solinas* and Franco Arcalli; writers like Ennio Flaiano*; established directors such as Tinto Brass and Gianni Puccini; emerging directors including Bernardo Bertolucci*, Gianni Amelio* and Dario Argento*; and, last but not least, composers of whom the best known is Ennio Morricone*. It also enlisted distinguished actors from outside Italy: Fernando Rey*, Jean-Louis Trintignant*, Yul Brynner, Charles Bronson, even Orson Welles. It made stars of Clint Eastwood, Gian Maria Volonté* and Klaus Kinski*. But its own special stars were Giuliano Gemma ('Ringo'), Lee Van Cleef, Tomas Milian, Franco Nero ('Django') and the Terence Hill/Bud Spencer duo of the 'Trinity' films. With these last, the violent excesses of the classic Italian Western softened into harmless knockabout for family audiences. After 1973 the genre ran out of steam, but continued to roll on its own inertia. It was a unique example of (almost) an entire film industry turned over to the production of a single genre. It was an original cinema, with distinct and personal characteristics, which produced at least one great *auteur* in the form of Sergio Leone. GVo

ITALY

The Italian cinema is one of the most important in Europe. Cinema has played a significant role in Italian national culture, particularly in the period 1930–80, and it has enjoyed international esteem and success – first in the years immediately preceding World War I, when Italian spectaculars such as *Gli ultimi giorni di Pompei/The Last Days of Pompeii* (1913, dir. Mario Caserini) took the world by storm, and then again after 1945 with neo-realism* and in the 1960s and 1970s with Italian contributions to international art cinema [> EUROPEAN ART CINEMA] and with the so-called 'Spaghetti' Western [> ITALIAN WESTERNS]. But unlike in France, cinema in Italy has been marked by severe discontinuity and the glorious years have been interspersed with periods in which both quantity and quality of production slumped to very low levels.

For convenience the history of Italian cinema can divided into three overlapping formations. The first of these occurs between 1900 and 1930, when film production was widely dispersed and 'Italian cinema' had no clear, stable identity. The second lasts from 1928 to 1980, when production became relatively centralised in Rome, film attendance generally increased or remained stable, and Italian cinema acquired both a domestic and a global identity. The third formation began to emerge around 1968 and is marked by increasing co-production with television, by a decline in the importance of Rome as the centre of Italian film-making, and by widespread laments that 'Italian cinema' was either passing away or becoming increasingly difficult to dissociate from television.

1900–1931

The first Italian fiction film – Filoteo Alberini's *La presa di Roma – 20 settembre 1870/The capture of Rome, 20 September 1870* – was not produced until 1905. But the years prior to 1905 nevertheless saw the emergence of a flourishing pattern of exhibition of (mainly French) films. Until 1915 dedicated movie theatres were mainly confined to the centres of a few large cities. Elsewhere, films were shown in existing cabarets and theatres, or as part of travelling carnivals.

Italian film production between 1905 and 1931 can hardly be described as an *industry*. The 500 or so production companies, mainly located in Rome, Milan, Turin and Naples, lacked a centralised structure and the localised nature of film-making contributed to stylistic variances among the films. Weather and lighting in the often cloudy northern cities, for instance, encouraged indoor shooting in glass-covered studios with artificial lighting, which film-makers in Rome or Naples were less quick to adopt. On the production side, the period before 1931 falls into two halves – rapid expansion before World War I, followed by decline and eventual collapse of the production system. The period of expansion was itself marked by contradictory and somewhat opposing impulses. Much of the early expansion, for example, was driven by motives other than profit. Film-making responded in many cases to local needs – a phenomenon particularly evident in Naples. It was often associated with traditional systems of artistic patronage (numerous Italian aristocrats subsidised early films) and with a traditional aesthetic culture, evident in the collaboration of famous Italian literary authors such as Gabriele D'Annunzio, Di Giacomo, Luigi Capuana and Giovanni Verga. There were, however, cases where the expansion of film production before 1915 was driven by a profit motive on a grand scale. The most famous and successful production company organised along those lines was Cines*; its principal backer, Adolfo Pouchain, secured investment capital from his industrialist relatives and the Banco di Roma, turning Cines into the most successful international distributor of Italian films before World War I.

By 1914, over fifty Italian production companies were distributing their films to movie theatres across Italy, but just as importantly Italy had become the most successful national distributor in an international market. Turin had developed a variety of production facilities, which attracted the most famous film-makers of the era and would only be rivalled (and eventually replaced) by those in Hollywood. Italian films were readily exportable because they worked within genres – primarily the drawing-room melodrama and the historical spectacular – already popularised in the West through theatre and literature. Consequently, the image of Italy in its early, internationally successful films had less to do with the public culture or the everyday landscape and life of contemporary Italy than with a mythic past and the private settings of bourgeois melodrama. The geographic and financial dispersal of film production, however, and the disorganised distribution practices made it difficult for Italian producers to overcome the difficulties generated by World War I. When the war ended, they also had to compete with the rapidly growing popularity of Hollywood films both in Italy and abroad. After 1921, Hollywood films dominated Italian film theatres, comprising nearly 80 per cent of films exhibited through the late 1920s. And by the late 1920s virtually every major Hollywood studio had distribution (and, in some cases, post-production) offices in Italy.

One of the strategies for maintaining competitiveness involved the creation in 1919 of the Unione Cinematografica Italiana, a trust made up of eleven of the largest production companies in Italy. Although this consortium helped increase film production between 1919 and 1921, its monopolistic structure also reduced competition, and by 1923 the consortium collapsed, exacerbating the instability of Italian production. By the late 1920s domestic film production amounted to less than ten films a year, and some of the most successful silent directors and actors went to work abroad [> EMIGRATION AND EUROPEAN CINEMA]. Throughout the 1920s, production companies attempted to compete with the increasingly successful Hollywood films by futilely relying upon prewar narrative formulas. Significantly, however, one genre – the peplum* – successfully reworked the conventions of the early historical spectacular. Whole series of remakes and retakes involving the escapades of muscular, Olympian-named heroes such as Maciste*, Ajax and Saetta achieved substantial popularity both in Italy and in parts of Europe.

1928–1980

Two major factors contributed to the centralisation of Italian film production and to the formation of a film culture with a national and nationalistic scope. One was the success of entrepreneur Stefano Pittaluga*. The other was the transformation of national, public, economic and cultural policy accompanying the rise to power of Fascism after 1922.

The Fascist government was instrumental in centralising film production in Rome through the setting up of the Istituto Nazionale LUCE* in 1926 and its subsequent support for the construction of the Centro Sperimentale* and Cinecittà*, adjacent to LUCE, in the mid-1930s. The government also supported a national film industry through (albeit feeble) protectionist policies limiting the import and exhibition of Hollywood (and, later, non-Axis) cinema. While this did little to curb the widespread distribution of Hollywood films in Italy or to diminish their appeal, it did help organise film distribution. Contemporaneously the government was involved in 'popular cultural' initiatives such as the mobile cinema caravans that exhibited movies across rural Italy. In the late 1930s, it also encouraged the export of Italian films. But despite its interest in centralising and protecting film production, in producing documentaries and newsreels for national and international distribution, and in nationalising cinema as part of a broad economic policy and cultural initiative, the Fascist government exercised little direct control over domestic feature-length films during the 1920s and 1930s. But

censorship was severe, and the government's insistence on having all foreign films dubbed in Italian studios (as a way of controlling what was on the soundtrack) caused dubbing to become a generalised practice in Italian film-making, even for Italian films.

The government was also able to build on the foundations created by Pittaluga in the 1920s. Starting as an exhibitor, Pittaluga had moved into distribution and then production, where he was responsible for the revival of Cines and the making of Italy's first sound films, including Alessandro Blasetti's* Sole/Sun (1929) and Mario Camerini's* Rotaie/Rails (1929). After Pittaluga's death in 1931, Cines was taken over by the industrialist Lodovico Toeplitz, who appointed Emilio Cecchi* as director of production. Under Cecchi's leadership, Cines embarked on an ambitious production programme which included innovative documentaries as well as comedies and melodramas. Even more important than the international prestige gained by films such as Walther Ruttmann's* Acciaio/Arbeit macht Frei/Steel (1934) was the steadily improving performance of Italian films at the domestic box office, making Italy less dependent on imports and able to plan further expansion.

When the Cines studio burned down in 1935, it was replaced by the Cinecittà facilities, which became the primary locus for Italian film production up to the 1970s. Cinecittà rapidly became identified with the genres characteristic of Italian cinema of the period, ranging from 'white telephone' (bourgeois) comedies to the historical costume dramas which became the most conspicuous affirmation of Fascism's epic vision of the nation. But by the time of Italy's entry into World War II in 1940 other tendencies were at work which were to change the face of Italian cinema. In the field of the historical film, a small group of scriptwriters and directors known as the 'calligraphers' (Alberto Lattuada*, Renato Castellani*, Mario Soldati* and Luigi Chiarini*) withdrew from nationalistic bombast and, with their elegant adaptations of late nineteenth and early twentieth-century naturalistic fiction, began to offer an alternative picture of Italian culture, one less oriented towards heroic hyperbole. Meanwhile a resurgence of small-scale production led to a more modest type of popular comedy, often using street locations – particularly evident in the work of Ferdinando Maria Poggioli (Le sorelle Materassi/The Materassi Sisters, 1943).

More importantly, major cultural changes were afoot, which came to fruition with the fall of Fascism in 1943 and the liberation in 1945. With Ossessione (1942, starring Massimo Girotti*), Luchino Visconti* drew on his prewar experience as an assistant to Jean Renoir* and on an unlikely literary source (James Cain's crime novel The Postman Always Rings Twice) to produce an unvarnished picture of Italian rural life which shocked the censors and proved a forerunner of neorealism*. In 1945, with Fascism discredited and the economy in ruins, a group of film-makers including Visconti, Lattuada, Vittorio De Sica* and Roberto Rossellini* set out to produce a new type of cinema, with a different relation to popular and national life. Unable or unwilling to use Cinecittà as a production site, they shot their films on location, often with non-professional actors, bringing their material back for editing and sound dubbing in such studio facilities as remained operational. Characteristically their subject matter was the current state of the nation and the recent past of German occupation and local resistance, epitomised by Rossellini's *Roma città aperta/Rome Open City* (1945).

The style pioneered in the immediate postwar years, and generically referred to as neo-realism*, was a product partly of material and economic conditions and partly of a cultural-political imperative to interrogate social conditions and look forward to the future. As such as it was part of a general climate of cultural regeneration which sought to sweep away the residues of Fascism and reaffirm alternative cultural traditions such as that of turn-of-the century realism, or *verismo*. In the turn towards realism the cinema was seen as having a privileged role to play, and the ideas put forward by film theorists such as Umberto Barbaro* and Luigi Chiarini* in the magazines *Cinema* and *Bianco e Nero* found wide acceptance, not only in film circles but in the culture at large. These ideas had been germinating in the last years of Fascism and came to fruition dramatically in the immediate postwar period.

By 1950, however, conditions had changed. American films had reappeared on the market, to the delight of the public. Cinecittà reopened and the domestic industry was beginning to revive. Production rose from twenty-five films in 1945 to 104 in 1950 and 201 in 1954, steadily increasing its box-office share. The Christian Democrat government elected in 1948 was hostile both to the makeshift production methods and to the leftist ideology of most neo-realist film-makers and favoured the rebuilding of an industry based on studio production. Neo-realism as a movement began to break up. Its stylistic features and socio-political ambitions, however, continued to influence Italian cinema, setting a notional standard against which subsequent Italian films were compared. Meanwhile, the former neo-realists were increasingly drawn to 'art cinema', while a bizarre legacy remained in the popular cinema in the form of 'rose-tinted' neo-realism (*neo-realismo rosa*). This treated the pleasures and miseries of everyday life in a generally optimistic, populist vein and was to become the basis of the *commedia all'italiana** ('comedy Italian-style') of the late 1950s and the 1960s. While neo-realism had stressed poverty and the hope for social change in the uncertain conditions of the 1940s, the 1950s were the years of economic boom, but also of political stagnation. *Commedia all'italiana* reflected these changing conditions, satirising both the survival of the 'old' Italy (its primitive sexual morality, for example) and the emerging 'new' Italy of vulgarity and consumerism.

Commedia all'italiana was but one of many genres that flourished in the 1950s revival. Historical, adventure and costume films continued to be popular, often displaying production values that belied their extremely low budgets. At the lower end of the market, the historical film spawned a distinctive variant, popularly known as the peplum*, based on the exploits of muscular heroes in mythical antiquity. In the mid-1960s, the popularity of the peplum began to wane, and it was replaced by the Italian or 'Spaghetti' Western, which lasted until the mid-1970s. Higher up the scale, a curious co-existence emerged between Italian cinema and Hollywood. Unable to repatriate the profits made by its films in Italy, in 1949 MGM began using Italian studios as a site for its own productions; by 1950 it had begun production of *Quo Vadis*, the first of many 'super-spectacles' produced or co-produced in Italy by Hollywood companies over the 1950s, garnering

for Cinecittà the dubious label of 'Hollywood on the Tiber' [> EUROPEAN CINEMA AND HOLLYWOOD]. Meanwhile Italian producers such as Dino De Laurentiis* and Carlo Ponti* attempted, with some success, to set themselves up in Hollywood. These exchanges affected art films as well as popular genres. As early as 1949, RKO had bankrolled Rossellini's *Stromboli, terra di dio/Stromboli*, while later Carlo Ponti contracted Michelangelo Antonioni* to make three English-language films, *Blowup* (1967, UK), *Zabriskie Point* (1969, US) and *Professione: Reporter/The Passenger* (1975).

1960 was the annus mirabilis for Italian cinema. The share of domestic box-office for Italian films reached 50 per cent for the first time since the war, and two of the films most responsible for this unprecedented development, Federico Fellini's* *La dolce vita* and Visconti's *Rocco e i suoi fratelli/Rocco and His Brothers*, achieved critical acclaim and further box-office revenues internationally as well. The success of those two films (and that of Antonioni's artistically ground-breaking if less commercial *L'avventura*) marked the definitive arrival of Italy's contribution to the European art cinema* of the 1960s. Stars such as Marcello Mastroianni*, Giulietta Masina* and Monica Vitti* became household names, joining those of Sophia Loren*, Gina Lollobrigida*, Anna Magnani*, Alberto Sordi*, Totò* and Vittorio Gassman* among others. New directors came on the scene, including Pier Paolo Pasolini* (*Accattone*, 1961), Bernardo Bertolucci* (*Prima della rivoluzione/Before the Revolution*, 1964), Marco Bellocchio* (*I pugni in tasca/Fists in the Pocket*, 1965) and Paolo and Vittorio Taviani* (*I sovversivi*, 1967). Italian cinema affirmed itself not only in the national culture but as Italy's major contribution to the general cultural ferment of the decade. Other successes in the early 1970s, notably Liliana Cavani's* *Il portiere di notte/The Night Porter* (1974) and Ettore Scola's* *C'eravamo tanto amati/We All Loved Each Other So Much* (1974), seemed a further confirmation of this upward trend.

1968–1995

As the 1970s wore on, however, it became clear that major changes were taking place in Italian cinema. Dependence on the international market was leading to a dissolution of its identity as more and more films took on foreign stars to boost their appeal and more and more directors were tempted into international co-productions. American and other actors had been used in Italian films of the 1950s – Anthony Quinn in Fellini's *La strada* (1954) being a conspicuous example. But in the 1970s the trend accelerated. A landmark in this respect was Bertolucci's *Ultimo tango a Parigi/Last Tango in Paris* (1972), set (as the title indicates) in Paris, and starring Marlon Brando, Maria Schneider, Jean-Pierre Léaud* and – as solitary Italian representative – the ageing Massimo Girotti. Continuation of this international trend can be found in Liliana Cavani's* *Il portiere di notte* (1974, starring Dirk Bogarde* and Charlotte Rampling), in Bertolucci's *Novecento/1900* (1976, with Burt Lancaster, Donald Sutherland, Robert De Niro and Gérard Depardieu*), and in the further use of Bogarde, Lancaster, Helmut Berger, Anna Karina* and others in Visconti's films from the late 1960s onwards.

While the 'art' film became increasingly international (and popular genre cinema increasingly inclined to recycle foreign models, developing the Italian horror film* and the Italian Western*), a distinctively Italian character was maintained throughout the 1970s in two areas. One was the contemporary political film [> ITALIAN POLITICAL CINEMA], usually about the threat to the social order represented by the Mafia on the one hand and terrorism on the other. The other was the revisionary historical film that looked back at the recent past and in particular the legacy of Fascism, a conspicuous absence in Italian film culture before the 1970s. The treatment of Fascism in films as diverse as Bertolucci's *Il conformista/The Conformist* (1970) and Fellini's *Amarcord* (1973) became a way of framing a discourse about nationhood and nationalism, of re-evaluating popular taste, memory and consciousness, and of underscoring the political mission of cinema in national culture and everyday life. Related to this cinematic dialogue with the national past were the growing number of films about the legacy of cinema itself. These include Fellini's *E la nave va/And the Ship Sails On* (1983) and *Ginger e Fred/Ginger and Fred* (1985), the Tavianis' *Good Morning, Babilonia/Good Morning, Babylon* (1987), Giuseppe Tornatore's* *Nuovo Cinema Paradiso/Cinema Paradiso* (1988), Scola's *C'eravamo tanto amati, Le bal* (1983) and *Splendor* (1988), and Maurizio Nichetti's *Ladri di saponette/Icicle Thief* (1989). Some of these acknowledge cinema's role in shaping a national consciousness and popular memory, and some (particularly *Ginger e Fred* and *Ladri di saponette*) involve nostalgic protagonists unable to cope with the ubiquity of television in contemporary Italy.

That cinema attendance and production dropped to dramatically low levels by the late 1970s cannot be attributed wholly to the increased centrality of television in everyday Italian life or entirely, for that matter, to conditions within Italy. Nevertheless, the rapid emergence of private Italian television networks after 1980 contributed to the way movies were produced and consumed and to the transformation of Italian culture. No longer was the Rome-based state-run RAI* the centre of broadcasting and made-for-television co-productions, as it had been in the 1970s; nor could it maintain its role, since the 1950s, of state-sanctioned arbiter of national culture and public taste. The private television networks, the most successful of which were formed by entrepreneur (and later Prime Minister) Silvio Berlusconi, were based in Milan, and they initially competed with the RAI networks by importing/recycling foreign (particularly American) films and television programmes. The proliferation of television channels brought an unprecedented number of movies to the television screens, which, combined with theatrically distributed films and the growing number of those released on video, kept film consumption in the 1980s high. The private networks relied largely upon relatively inexpensive ('B-production') older films – Italian or foreign (largely Hollywood). By the 1990s, however, Berlusconi's Milan-based Fininvest* company began to invest in film productions for domestic and international distribution.

While Italian film production had always been entrepreneurial, not since its earliest years had it been so decentralised. In this environment, even entrepreneurial film-making begat new trends. A number of young film-makers of the 1980s – most notably Roberto Benigni*, Carlo Verdone, and Maurizio Nichetti – made films involving personas they had already developed as performers in other media. Equally significant in this regard is Nanni Moretti*, whose films have adopted a highly confessional style; his *Caro diario/Dear Diary* (1994) is constructed as a nomadic narrative through Rome's neighbourhoods and backstreets and across parts of southern Italy. This 'nomadic' style is also evident in several recent Italian 'road movies' involving characters' alienation and unrequited searchings – again, not a new theme in Italian cinema, but one acquiring a different significance in relation to the decentralisation of national film production and the increased marginalisation of film as a cultural form in Italy. The ironic detachment/involvement of characters – and of film-makers as social 'actors' – from/with their material social, and symbolic environments (especially in the quasi-confessional and nomadic films) belies a deep uncertainty in Italian cinema about its mission and, above all, its *place* in contemporary Italian life. After decades of struggling to secure a 'national cinema', however, these practices also attest to the possibility of not envisioning the nation as Utopia, or as a unified space of cultural production. JHa/GNS

IVENS, Joris George Henri Anton Ivens; Nijmegen 1898 – Paris, France 1989

Dutch director, who played a crucial role in establishing the international reputation of Dutch documentary film-making. Nicknamed 'the Flying Dutchman', the cosmopolitan Ivens turned up with his camera at many of the hot spots of twentieth-century history. His political convictions may have provoked the anger of the authorities, but his films, militant but lyrical, and his warm personality inspired countless film-makers. He helped to found the World Union of Documentary in 1947 and the Association Internationale des Documentaristes in 1963. He directed and co-directed over sixty films.

Destined to succeed his father as the owner of a chain of photographic shops, Ivens studied at the Rotterdam business school from 1917 to 1921. His political conscience was awakened while he was studying photo-chemistry in Berlin and working in camera factories in Dresden and Jena (1922–26). Back in the Netherlands, he took charge of the Amsterdam branch of the family business and in 1927 was involved in the founding of Filmliga, a film society which screened avant-garde films, invited foreign film-makers, established critical standards and encouraged indigenous talent, and was to have a profound influence on Dutch film culture. In 1928 Filmliga screened Ivens' first short, *De brug/The Bridge*, a formalist study in rendering movement on celluloid. Impressed by this and later films, Vsevolod Pudovkin* invited Ivens to the Soviet Union in 1930, a trip that proved seminal for Ivens' political development. Films such as *Nieuwe gronden/New Earth* (1934) and *Misère au Borinage/Borinage* (1933, co-dir. Henri Storck*) indicted the capitalist system for its waste of human resources. This stand was received unfavourably in his native country and he was forced to pursue his career abroad. In 1936 he travelled to the US, in 1937 he filmed the Civil War in Spain (*Spanish Earth*, 1937), and in 1938 he covered the war in China. During World War II he lived and worked in the US. Towards the end of the war Ivens was appointed film commissioner for the Dutch East Indies. However, having become aware of the authorities' resistance to Indonesian independence, he resigned in November 1945 and made *Indonesia Calling* in support of the Australian dockers' struggle to prevent Dutch ships from sailing to Indonesia. This led to decades of official harassment, including a passport ban. Ivens spent the years 1947 to 1957 in Eastern Europe. His return to the West was marked by *La Seine a rencontré Paris/The Seine Meets Paris* (1957), a film poem on the interaction between the Seine and the people of Paris, with a commentary by Jacques Prévert*. In the 1960s Ivens supported struggles in Latin America and Vietnam. In the 1970s there followed his mammoth production on China, *Comment Yukong déplaça les montagnes/How Yukong Moves the Mountains* (1976, co-dir. M. Loridan). His last film, *Une histoire de vent/A History of the Wind* (co-dir. M. Loridan), 'covering the no man's land between fiction and non-fiction', was premiered at the Venice film festival of 1988. In 1985 the Dutch government offered Ivens its apologies, reconciling the king of Dutch documentary with his native country. BH

Bib: Rosalind Delmar, *Joris Ivens: Fifty Years of Film Making* (1979); Thomas Waugh, *Joris Ivens and the Evolution of the Radical Documentary, 1926–1946* (1981).

Other Films: *Regen/Rain* (1929, NL, co-dir. M. Franken); *Wij bouwen/We Are Building, Zuiderzee* (1930, NL); *Philips Radio* (1931, NL), *Creosoot* (1931, NL); *Pesn o gerojach/Komsomol/Song of Heroes* (1932, USSR); *The 400 Million* (1938, US); *Power and the Land* (1941, US); *Our Russian Front* (1941, US, co-dir. L. Milestone); *Action Stations* (1943, Canada); *Pierwsze lata/The First Years* (1949, USSR); *Pokoj zwyciezy swiat/Peace Will Conquer the World* (1951, Poland, co-dir. J. Bossak); *Freundschaft siegt/Friendship Wins* (1952, DDR/USSR, co-dir. I. Pyrjew), *Wyscig pokoju Warszawa–Berlin–Praha/Peace Tour* (1952, Poland/DDR); *Das Lied der Ströme/The Song of the Rivers* (1954, DDR); *Before Spring, 600 Million People Are With You* (1958, China); *L'Italia non è un paese povero/Italy is not a Poor Country* (1960, It.); *Demain à Nanguila/Nanguila Tomorrow* (1960, Mali); *Carnet de viaje/Travel Notebook* (1961, Cuba); *Pueblo armado/An Armed Nation* (1961, Cuba); *À Valparaiso* (1963, Chile/Fr.); *El tren de la victoria/Le Train de la victoire/The Train of Victory* (1964, Chile); *Pour le mistral/For the Mistral* (1965, Fr.); *Le Ciel, la terre/The Threatening Sky* (1965, Vietnam/Fr.); *Rotterdam Europoort* (1966, NL); *Loin du Viêtnam/Far from Vietnam* (1967, Fr., co-dir.); *Le 17e parallèle/The 17th Parallel* (1967, Vietnam/Fr.); *Le Peuple et ses fusils/The People and Their Guns* (1970, Laos/Fr., co-dir.).

IVORY, James – see MERCHANT-IVORY

J

JACKSON, Glenda   Hoylake 1936

British actress, who gained critical attention through her highly adventurous work with the Royal Shakespeare Company in Peter Brook's Artaud-inspired Theatre of Cruelty season in the 1960s. Her performance as Charlotte Cordier in Peter Weiss' *Marat/Sade* was translated to the screen in 1967, and the improvisatory Brook production on Vietnam, *U.S.*, was adapted as *Tell Me Lies* (1968). As in her theatre work, her work in the cinema has a thread of the dangerous running through it; and her career has been closely linked to Ken Russell's*, with an Oscar-winning performance in *Women in Love* (1969), and roles in *The Music Lovers* (1970), *The Boy Friend* (1972), *Salome's Last Dance* (1987) and *The Rainbow* (1988). A strong dramatic actress with an ability to play strong women, she received a British Academy Award for her performance in *Sunday Bloody Sunday* (1971), but showed herself adept at light comedy by winning a second Oscar for *A Touch of Class* (1973). In 1987, she appeared in Lezli-An Barrett's *Business as Usual*, one of the few British feature films directed by a woman. She became a Labour Member of Parliament in the 1992 election. JC

Other Films Include: *Mary Queen of Scots* [as Queen Elizabeth I] (1972); *Bequest to the Nation* (1973); *The Maids* (1976); *The Romantic Englishwoman/Une Anglaise roman-tique* (1975, UK/Fr.); *The Incredible Sarah* [as Sarah Bernhardt] (1976); *Hedda* (1977); *Stevie* [as Stevie Smith] (1978); *Hopscotch* (1980); *Strange Interlude* (TV, 1988); *A Murder of Quality* (TV, 1991).

JACOBY, Georg   Mainz 1882 – Munich 1964

German director, whose fifty-year career began in 1913 (*Buckelhannes*). In 1915 he signed a contract with PAGU*, directing propaganda films (*Durchhaltefilme*) such as *Die Entdeckung Deutschlands* (1917). After the war Jacoby developed a talent for social drama, melodrama and sex films; his adventure films (*Der Mann ohne Namen*, 1921), epics (*Quo Vadis*, 1923) and comedies* (*Der dumme August des Zirkus Romanelli*, 1926), blending action and social analysis with a sophisticated *mise-en-scène*, made him one of the German cinema's commercially most reliable professionals. Jacoby was a pillar of genre cinema during the Nazi period (*Heißes Blut*, 1936), in charge of Ufa's* hottest musical star Marika Rökk*. He directed *Eine Nacht im Mai* (1938), the first German musical modelled on the Hollywood 'production number' genre, as well as the first German (Agfa) colour film, *Frauen sind doch bessere Diplomaten* (1941). His career culminated with Germany's top-grossing musical ever, *Die Frau* *meiner Träume* (1944), again starring Rökk. In the 1950s, Jacoby mainly specialised in remakes. KU

Bib: Helga Belach (ed.): *Wir tanzen um die Welt: Deutsche Revuefilme 1933–1945* (1979).

Other Films Include: *Bogdan Stimoff* (1916); *The Fake* (1927, UK); *Die Lindenwirtin* (1930); *Die Csárdás-fürstin/Princesse Czardas* (1934); *Der Bettelstudent* (1936); *Gasparone* (1937); *Kora Terry* (1940); *Familie Schimek* (1957)

JADRAN FILM

Croatian studio. The company was established in Zagreb in 1946, but its real growth began in 1955 when huge, Cinecittà*-like studios were build in the Zagreb suburb of Dubrava. It soon became the biggest production studio in Yugoslavia, with more than a hundred national projects in total. It was also the main partner for international co-productions seeking untouched natural beauty and reasonably low production costs. Orson Welles' *The Trial* (1962), Alan Pakula's *Sophie's Choice* (1982) and the two-part television series *War and Remembrance* (co-produced with the US) are among some 200 international co-productions made at Jadran. SP

JAENZON, Julius   Gothenburg 1885 – Stockholm 1961

Swedish cinematographer. Jaenzon is one of the most important names in the history of Swedish cinematography, together with Gunnar Fischer* and Sven Nykvist*. Jaenzon belongs to the Golden Age of the silent cinema, when he filmed (sometimes under the pseudonym of J. Julius) many of the works of Victor Sjöström* and Mauritz Stiller*. The formal beauty of his often extravagant images was complemented by technical virtuosity, perhaps most famously in the superimpositions of Sjöström's *Körkarlen/The Phantom Carriage/Thy Soul Shall Bear Witness* (1921), greatly admired throughout the world at the time. He also directed a few films. LGA/BF

Other Films Include: *Äktenskapsbyrån/The Marriage Bureau* (1913); *Vingarne/The Wings, Balettprimadonnan/The Ballet Primadonna/Anjuta, the Dancer* (1916); *Berg-Ejvind och hans hustru/The Outlaw and His Wife* (1918); *Sången om den eldröda blomman/The Song of the Scarlet Flower/Flame of Life* (1919); *Vem dömer?/Love's Crucible* (1922); *Gösta Berlings saga (del I och II)/The Story of Gosta Berling (pts I and II)* (1924).

JAKUBISKO, Juraj   Kojšov 1938

Slovak director. Jakubisko graduated from FAMU* in 1965, where he made a number of internationally acclaimed experimental films, including his graduation film, *Čekají na Godota/Waiting for Godot* (1965). Coming from Eastern Slovakia, he was encouraged by his tutor, the director Václav

Wasserman, to draw on the resources and traditions of folk culture. His trio of films, *Kristove roky/Crucial Years* (1967), *Zbehovia a pútnici/Il disertore e i nomadi/The Deserter and the Nomads* (1968, released in Czechoslovakia 1990) and *Vtáčkovia, siroty a blázni/Les Oiseaux, les orphelins et les fous/Birds, Orphans and Fools* (1969, released in Czechoslovakia 1991), revealed the cruelty of peasant art (in *Zbehovia a pútnici*) and focused on alienated youth in an improvisatory style typical of the post-Godard* generation. After the Soviet invasion, he was unable to make features again until 1979, when he returned with *Postav dom, zasad' strom/Build a House, Plant a Tree*, and the international success *Tisícročna včela/Die tausendjährige Biene/The Thousand Year Old Bee* (1983), following this with an adaptation of Hans Andersen's *Perinbaba/Frau Holle/Mother Carey* (1985), featuring Giulietta Masina*, and *Frankensteins Tante*, for West German television. His unfinished *Dovidenia v pekle, priatelia/See You in Hell, Fellows!* (1970) was finally completed in 1990. He returned to his earlier style with *Sedím na konári a je mi dobre/I'm Sitting on a Branch and I Feel Well/Flying High* (1989), and its sequel *Lepšie byť bohatý a zdravý, ako chudobný a chorý/It is Better to be Rich and Handsome than Poor and Ugly* (1992). The latter satirised both the new world of capitalism and the delusions of Slovak nationalism. PH

JAKUBOWSKA, Wanda   Warsaw 1907

Polish director. Poland's first woman director, Jakubowska was prominent in the START (Society of Devotees of Artistic Film) movement established in 1930 and the filmmakers' cooperative SAF. In the 1950s she headed a production unit called START. *Ostatni Etap/The Last Stage* (1948), based on her own experiences as an Auschwitz internee, was the second film to be produced in postwar Poland and the first to receive international distribution. AW

Other Films Include: *Żolnierz Zwycięstwa/Soldiers of Victory* (1953); *Opowieść Atlantycka/Atlantic Story* (1955); *Koniec Naszegoswiata/The End of Our World* (1964); *150 na Godzine/At One Hundred and Fifty Km an Hour* (1971); *Zaproszenie/Invitation* (1985); *Kolory Kochania/Colours of Love* (1987).

JANCSÓ, Miklós   Vác 1921

Hungarian film director. In the 1960s and 1970s, Jancsó was synonymous with Hungarian cinema among international audiences. He studied law and anthropology, and graduated in direction from the Hungarian Film Academy in 1951. During the 1950s, Jancsó made Stalinist newsreels. His first feature, *A harangok Rómába mentek/The Bells Have Gone to Rome* (1958), reveals none of the qualities that were later to become associated with the celebrated 'Jancsó style'. The earliest film that is characteristic of this style is *Oldás és kötés/Cantata* (1963), primarily because of its very long takes. This is also Jancsó's first film made with scriptwriter Gyula Hernádi, with whom he still works. Jancsó claimed that he and Hernádi had watched Michelangelo Antonioni's* *La* *notte* ten times before making this film, and indeed, technically speaking, Antonioni was a tremendous influence. Jancsó, however, was to develop a style of his own, whose main features are extremely long takes (up to ten minutes), minimal dialogue, a continuously moving camera choreographed with actors moving within a scene, and recurrent symbolic motifs and gestures.

The symbolic rendering of Jancsó's narratives dates back to *Így jöttem/My Way Home* (1964), where time and space are hinted at rather than specifically demarcated, characters are given little psychological delineation, and the film's central relationship between a young Hungarian man and a Russian soldier has to be deciphered through gestures and movements rather than dialogue. In his next film, *Szegénylegények/The Round-up* (1965) – for many critics his unparalleled masterpiece – all the elements of his style come together in an abstract historical parable about the nature of revolution and counter-revolution. It is also in this film that Jancsó's emphasis on the intricate mechanisms of political oppression testing the moral integrity of individuals appears for the first time. Though the story deals with the persecution of rebel prisoners who fought for the liberation of Hungary during the 1848 revolution against Austrian oppression, the film was interpreted by many as an allegory of the retaliations that followed the 1956 revolution. Subsequent films continued this focus on oppressive power, though, in Jancsó's increasingly abstract stylistics, characters functioned less as representatives of particular historical forces than as the embodiments of conflicting ideas.

In the early 1970s, at the height of his international reputation, Jancsó made four films in Italy about the rituals of power. In the 1980s the main subject of his work was the dissimulating and mystical character of politics. More recently, the stories again derive from actual political events. Jancsó now makes increasing use of video techniques, primarily to intensify an atmosphere of spatial and temporal confusion. He has also directed plays, though his theatrical work has never achieved the same importance as his films. KAB

Other Feature Films: *Három csillag/Three Stars* (1960); *Csillagosok, katonák/The Red and The White* (1967); *Csend és kiáltás/Silence and Cry, Fényes szelek/The Confrontation* (1968); *Sirokkó/Winter Wind* (1969); *Égi bárány/Agnus Dei, La pacifista/The Pacifist* (1970, It.); *Még kér a nép/Red Psalm* (1971); *La tecnica ed il rito/The Technique and the Rite* (1972, It.); *Roma rivuole Cesare/Rome Wants Another Caesar* (1973, It.); *Szerelmem Elektra/Elektreia* (1974); *Vizi privati, pubbliche virtú/Private Vices, Public Virtues* (1976, It.); *Életünket és vérünket: Magyar rapszódia I./Hungarian Rhapsody* (1978); *Allegro Barbaro: Magyar rapszódia II./Allegro Barbaro* (1979); *A zsarnok szíve, avagy Boccaccio Magyarországon/The Tyrant's Heart, or Boccaccio in Hungary* (1981); *Hajnal/Dawn* (1986); *Szörnyek évadja/The Monsters' Season* (1987); *Jézus Krisztus horoszkópja/Jesus Christ's Horoscope* (1988); *Isten hátrafelé megy/God Goes Backwards* (1991); *Kék Duna keringő/Blue Danube Waltz* (1992).

JANDA, Krystyna — Starachowice 1952

Polish actress. Janda shot to stardom in her first film role as the assertive film student Agnieszka in Andrzej Wajda's* *Człowiek z Marmuru/Man of Marble* (1977). She has had a long association with Wajda, appearing in *Bez Znieczulenia/Rough Treatment* (1978) and *Człowiek z Żelaza/Man of Iron* (1981), among other films. She received the Best Actress award at Cannes in 1990 for her role in *Przesłuchanie/The Interrogation* (1981, released 1989), Ryszard Bugajski's* film, in which she plays a woman subjected to humiliating tortures by the Stalinist authorities of 1950s Poland. Her film career now extends to France and Germany. A popular theatre and television actress, she won popular and critical acclaim for her television portrayal of the nineteenth-century Polish actress, Helena Modrzejewska. AW

Other Films Include: *Polowanie na Muchy/Hunting Flies* (1972); *Mephisto* (1981, Hung.); *Laputa* (1986, Ger.).

JANNINGS, Emil — Rorschach, Switzerland 1884 – Strobl, Austria 1950

German actor. A theatre actor since 1900, Jannings worked with the Max Reinhardt* company in 1915–16. His first film role came in the war propaganda film *Im Schützengraben* (1914). From 1916 his film parts were more substantial, and as Louis XV in Ernst Lubitsch's* *Madame Dubarry* (1919) he became world-famous. After *Quo Vadis* (1924) he felt typecast in costume drama, and succeeded in new roles: *Der letzte Mann/The Last Laugh* (1924) and *Variété/Variety* (1925), both well-received in the US. A three-year contract with Paramount followed, and in 1928 Jannings received the very first Oscar ever, for *The Last Command* (1928; dir. Josef von Sternberg). A wealthy man, he returned to Germany in 1929, having persuaded Sternberg to direct him once more, as Professor Rath in *Der blaue Engel/The Blue Angel* (1930). Jannings resumed his career in the theatre, but also recaptured his earlier film stardom in such Nazi propaganda films as *Der alte und der junge König* (1935). In 1936 he joined the board of directors of Tobis and was involved in *Ohm Krüger* (1941), one of the most expensive anti-British propaganda productions of the Third Reich. In 1946 the US military officially 'denazified' him. TE/SG

Bib: Herbert Holba, *Emil Jannings* (1979).

Other Films Include: *Frau Eva* (1916); *Lulu* (1917); *Die Brüder Karamasoff* (1920); *Danton* (1921); *Das Wachsfigurenkabinett/Waxworks* (1923); *Tartüff* (1925); *Faust* (1926); *The Street of Sin* (1927, US); *Der Herrscher, Der zerbrochene Krug* (1937); *Robert Koch, der Bekämpfer des Todes* (1939); *Altes Herz wird wieder jung* (1943).

JAQUE-CATELAIN Jacques Guerin-Castelain; Saint-Germain-en-Laye 1897 – Paris 1965

French actor, star of the late silent cinema. Jaque-Catelain's career is closely linked to that of his favourite director and mentor Marcel L'Herbier*. He appeared in many of the director's classics – *Rose-France* (1919), *El Dorado* (1921), *L'Inhumaine* (1924) – and in films by other directors, such as Léonce Perret's *Koenigsmark* (1923). A delicately handsome young man, fabulously attired amid L'Herbier's art deco sets, he was France's first *jeune premier*, anticipating stars such as Pierre Richard-Willm*, Charles Boyer*, Gérard Philipe* and Vincent Perez. Despite parts in further films by L'Herbier, he was not favoured by the transition to sound. He devoted much of his subsequent career to the stage. GV

Bib: Pierre Cadars, *Les Séducteurs du cinéma français (1928–1958)* (1982).

JARMAN, Derek Northwood 1942 – London 1994

British director. Coming out of art school in the 1960s, set designer for ballet and opera and for Ken Russell*, working with Super 8mm and video on lower than low budgets, Jarman has often been placed unproblematically by both critics and admirers in the gay avant-garde, radically and scandalously 'other' to the traditions of British cinema. Certainly, his work with cheap, accessible technologies, though it may not have been of his own choosing, has added new and distinctive formal possibilities to British cinema, and films like *Jubilee* (1978), *The Tempest* (1980) and *Edward II* (1991) offer a political attack on the state of England. By his own account, however, he is a traditionalist, consigned to the margins rather than choosing to work there: 'The one thing I really regret about my career was that I was put into the position of being anything but the most traditional film-maker of my generation.' The tradition to which he belongs might be that of Humphrey Jennings*: the same romanticism, the same love of style, of landscape and of Englishness. Both men were painters who began their careers as set designers; both have a connection to surrealist observation. But there is something disingenuous about Jarman's appeal to the English tradition, and it is tradition refracted through the more camp sensibility of Andy Warhol, Kenneth Anger and David Hockney. The films play out a tension between an elegiac traditionalism which continually returns to lost Golden Ages – Shakespeare, Marlowe, Caravaggio – and a gay, pop sensibility on which traditions founder. Jarman's emblematic image is the garden which he created at Dungeness and memorialised in *The Garden* (1990) – an exquisite, miniature English garden on an extremely stony soil.

His last film *Blue* (1993), a sound track against a blue screen, reflected on his experience of Aids and remembered the friends who had died of it, but refused what he called 'the pandemonium of images'. He died of Aids-related illness in 1994. JC

Bib: Jonathan Hacker and David Price, *Take 10: Contemporary British Film Directors* (1991).

Other Feature Films Include: *Sebastiane* [16mm; in Latin with subtitles] (1976); *The Angelic Conversation* [Super 8mm] (1985); *Caravaggio* [35mm] (1986); *Aria* ['Depuis le jour' ep.; Super 8mm and 35mm], *The Last of England* [Super 8mm] (1987); *War Requiem* [35mm and Super 8mm] (1988); *Wittgenstein* [Super 8mm and 35mm] (1993).

JARVA, Risto Helsinki 1934–77

Finnish director and producer. Jarva was still at the Helsinki Technical School when he directed his first short documentaries. During the 1960s he became the spokesperson for a socially committed 'new wave'; in *Onnenpeli/Game of Chance* (1965) Helsinki serves as a lively backdrop for modern human relations. Industrial environments form a realistic basis for the marriage drama *Työmiehen päiväkirja/A Worker's Diary* (1966), which also analyses class differences. In subsequent films, Jarva examined the emotionally impoverished life of an imaginary future (*Ruusujen aika/Time of Roses*, 1969), the perversions of car culture (*Bensaa suonissa/Rally*, 1970), and the scandal-mongering press (*Kun taivas putoaa/When the Heavens Fall*, 1972). *Yhden miehen sota/One Man's War* (1973) marked the end of his 'serious' social period, after which he concentrated on social comedies. *Mies joka ei osannut sanoa ei/The Man Who Couldn't Say No* (1975) is a plea for a more human urban environment, while *Loma/Holiday* (1976) deals with misunderstandings on a Mediterranean beach. Jarva's last film was *Jäniksen vuosi/The Year of the Hare* (1977), based on Arto Paasilinna's novel, in which the protagonist withdraws to the northern woods, fleeing an over-organised and depressing society that has forgotten ecological values. Jarva died in a car accident on the way home from a preview of *Jäniksen vuosi*. AH-H

JARY, Michael Laurahütte, Austria 1906 – Munich 1988

Austrian-born German composer with a classical training and a penchant for jazz and swing, who worked initially as a Berlin bar pianist. Jary's first operetta, *Der Vizeadmiral*, premiered in 1934, and was followed in 1936 by the musical *Das Notwendige und das Überflüssige*. Offers from Ufa* led to his first film score for *Die unerhörte Frau* (1936) whose jazzy foxtrot 'Heut' bin ich glücklicher als glücklich' became an immediate hit and made a name for Jary in the burgeoning record industry. Between 1937 and 1945 Jary worked as film composer for several companies, among them Terra-Filmkunst. There, he soon formed a highly successful composer-songwriter team with Bruno Balz. Among their most popular numbers were 'Das kann doch einen Seemann nicht erschüttern', 'Davon geht die Welt nicht unter' (both classics to this day), as well as a waltz tune, written especially for Zarah Leander*, which is still probably her best-remembered song: 'Ich weiß, es wird einmal ein Wunder geschehen'. Jary's hit songs gave a whole generation of female singers their break, including Rosita Serrano, Evelyn Künneke and Kary Barnet. In 1939 he embarked on a second career, as band-leader of a swing band, recording jazz titles for the Odeon record label up to 1943.

After the war Jary built up the Radio-Dance Orchestra Berlin, but soon tired of it and returned to composing. With his unerring ear for what was in the air, he picked up on the changes in popular music, extending his range to pop songs for the first German rock 'n' rollers in the 1950s, thus continuing his career as tunesmith extraordinary until the late 1950s. His last big hit, 'Wir wollen niemals auseinandergehen', was featured in a 1961 pop music film. TE/SG

Other Films Include: *Abenteuer in Warschau* (1937); *Der Florentiner Hut, Paradies der Junggesellen* (1939); *Wunschkonzert* (1940); *Die große Liebe* (1942); *Karneval der Liebe* (1943); *Die Dritte von rechts* (1950); *Die verschleierte Maya* (1951); *Die Zürcher Verlobung* (1957); *Bei Pichler stimmt die Kasse nicht* (1961).

JASNÝ, Vojtěch   Kelč 1925

Czech director. One of the first graduates of FAMU* in 1951, Jasný began his career in conjunction with Karel Kachyňa*, with whom he directed a number of documentaries as well as their joint feature debut, *Dnes večer všechno skončí/It Will All Be Over Tonight* (1954). In the late 1950s his films *Zářijové noci/September Nights* (1956) and *Touha/Desire* (1958) were in the forefront of those challenging the status quo, while the allegorical *Až přijde kocour/That Cat/Cassandra Cat* (1963), featuring Jan Werich*, and *Všichni dobří rodáci/All My Good Countrymen* (1968) were among the most important Czech films of the 1960s. The latter (banned between 1969 and 1989) was considered the first Czech film to tell the truth about the collectivisation of the countryside. Yet it was also a lyrical hymn to nature which refused to demonise its villains. After 1969, Jasný pursued a less significant international career, making films in Austria, West Germany, Finland and Canada. His Austrian films included an adaptation of Heinrich Böll's *Ansichten eines Clowns/Face of a Clown/The Clown* (1975). He returned to Czechoslovakia in 1991 to make the documentary *Proč Havel?/Why Havel?* PH

Other Films Include: *Přežil jsem svou smrt/I Survived Certain Death* (1960); *Procesí k panence/Pilgrimage to the Virgin* (1961); *Dýmky/Pipes* (1966); *Česká rapsodie/Czech Rhapsody* [short] (1969); *Fluchtversuch/Attempt to Escape* (1976, Aust.); *Rückkehr/The Return* (1977); *Gospodjica/Das Fräulein/The Maiden* (1980, Yug.); *Eläköön itsemurhaaja/Bis später/The Suicide* (1984, Fin.); *The Great Land of Small* (1987, Canada).

JAUBERT, Maurice   Nice 1900 – Azerailles 1940

French composer. Jaubert wrote music criticism and was director of music at Pathé*-Natan (1930–34). As a composer he wrote the scores (songs and music) of some of the greatest French films of the 1930s, among them René Clair's* *Quatorze juillet* (1932), Jean Vigo's* *Zéro de conduite* and *L'Atalante* (both 1934) and Marcel Carné's* *Drôle de drame* (1937), *Quai des brumes* (1938) and *Le Jour se lève* (1939), perhaps his most affecting of all. As his biographer François

Porcile put it, Jaubert always refused 'illustrative redundancy'. Jaubert himself remarked, 'Three notes on the accordion, if they are what a particular image demands, will always be more stirring than the Good Friday music from *Parsifal*.' GV

JEANSON, Henri   Paris 1900 – Honfleur 1970

French scriptwriter. From the early 1930s to the late 1960s, Jeanson wrote some of the wittiest lines in French cinema. Like many French film writers, including Jacques Prévert* and Michel Audiard*, he was particularly good at dialogue, the withering joke or aphorism his trademark, especially on the lips of the top stars of the time. Unlike Prévert, who developed a coherent universe, but like Audiard, Jeanson did not pursue particular themes in his films. A glance at his filmography, however, reveals many popular classics, from *Pépé le Moko* (1936) to *Fanfan la Tulipe* (1952) and *La Vache et le prisonnier/The Cow and I* (1959). Jeanson also wrote plays, scripts, film reviews, and journalism, notably for the satirical weekly *Le Canard enchaîné*, where his wit could be vitriolic (he was involved in a number of controversies and occasionally in court cases). He directed one film, *Lady Paname* (1950). GV

JELES, András   Jászberény 1945

Hungarian film and theatre director. Next to Gábor Bódy*, Jeles is perhaps the most powerful and original Hungarian director of his generation. In common with many directors, his career began in the Balázs Béla Stúdió*, in the mid-1970s. In his first feature, *A kis Valentino/Little Valentino* (1979), he used the documentary-fiction film style [> DOCUMENTARY (HUNGARY)] in a very particular way. Rather than reinforcing the story's verisimilitude, Jeles deliberately pushed it in an absurd-surrealist direction, constructing by the film's end a gloomy atmosphere of reality. The film provoked both scandal and an enthusiastic reception. His next two films were no less controversial; *Álombrigád/The Dreambrigade* (1983, released 1987) achieved notoriety as the only Hungarian feature film to be banned in the 1980s. In this film Jeles deploys an esoteric, theatrical style to deal with the conflicts of political self-expression among Hungarian workers. Despite the esoteric form, the message contained in the film's depiction of the relationship between workers and political leaders was clear enough to offend Hungarian officialdom. *Angyali üdvözlet/The Annunciation* (1984) was even more obscure: an adaptation of a Hungarian classic drama performed entirely by children. Many viewed it as a travesty of Hungary's 'sacred' literary tradition. In the meantime, Jeles organised an amateur theatre group called the Monteverdi birkózókör (Monteverdi Wrestling Club), whose performances achieved considerable international success. Since 1984 he has devoted most of his energies to the theatre. His latest film, *Dieu n'existe pas/God Does not Exist* (1993), is a strange, visionary story about a young Jewish girl in Hungary during World War II, elements of which are taken from the diaries of Anne Frank and Dickens' *David Copperfield*. KAB

JENNINGS, Humphrey
Walberswick, 1907 – Poros, Greece 1950

British director. 'Humphrey Jennings,' wrote Lindsay Anderson* in 1954, 'is the only real poet the British cinema has yet produced.' An intellectual and artist of enormous range, Jennings was a theatre set designer, poet and painter; he was a member, with Herbert Read, Roland Penrose and André Breton, of the Organising Committee of the International Surrealist Exhibition held in London in 1936; with Tom Harrisson and Charles Madge he was one of the initiators of Mass Observation, a project whose observations of the everyday were not so far removed from surrealism as one might suppose; and his uncompleted book, *Pandaemonium*, attempts an archaeology of discourses before Michel Foucault had invented the discipline. Jennings joined the GPO Film Unit in 1934, where he directed, worked with Len Lye* on his early animations, and designed for Alberto Cavalcanti*. Jennings was at the centre of English modernism throughout the 1930s, an avant-gardism and 'artiness' which reputedly was met with some suspicion by John Grierson*. The war, however, and the intense, romantic patriotism which it evoked, made him a lyrical rather than a critical modernist. His greatest achievement is represented by the group of films he made during the war: in particular, *Words for Battle* (1941), *Listen to Britain* (1942), made with Stewart McAllister, *Fires Were Started* (1943), and *A Diary for Timothy* (1945).

Jennings died in 1950 at the age of 43, falling from the rocks of the Greek island of Poros while scouting locations. JC

Bib: David Parkinson (ed.), *The Humphrey Jennings Film Reader* (1993).

Other Films Include: *Post-Haste, The Story of the Wheel* (1934); *Spare Time, The First Days* [with Harry Watt and Pat Jackson] (1939); *Spring Offensive, London Can Take It!* [with Harry Watt] (1940); *Heart of Britain* (1941); *The Silent Village* (1943); *The True Story of Lili Marlene* (1944); *A Defeated People* (1946); *The Cumberland Story* (1947); *Dim Little Island* (1949); *Family Portrait* (1950).

JHABVALA, Ruth Prawer – see MERCHANT-IVORY

JIMÉNEZ, Mary
Lima, Peru 1948

Peruvian-born director, working in Belgium. Jiménez's often brutal scenarios of desire, pain and obsessive love have established a cinema which oscillates between autobiographical closeness (à la Marguerite Duras*) and (psycho)analytical distance. After studying architecture in Peru, Jiménez moved to Belgium in 1973, graduating from the Brussels Film School in 1977. Initially concentrating on scriptwriting, she eventually formed a production company, with Carole Courtoy as her producer and sometimes actress. The use of film as a purgative experience is suggested by Jiménez's documentary *Du verbe aimer/Spelling Love* (1984), in which her return to her childhood home prompts memories of the loss of a mother who submitted her child to analysis, mental institutions and electric shock treatment. Jiménez's feature films reflect the horror of this past, through a preoccupation with mutilation, realised visually in a series of cut-up, bleeding or wounded bodies, and formally in a denial of the comfort of a linear narrative. In her breakthrough film *21:12 Piano Bar* (1981), the fragmented story of a woman's death is evoked through the use of an elliptical visual and aural structure, which involves the spectator through an attack on the senses. Jiménez's *L'Air de rien* (1989), shows evidence of an increasing optimism in her vision, for while the film opens with a woman (Carole Courtoy) being told that she may have a terminal illness, it then takes us through a celebration of life. CF

Other Films: *A Propos de vous/About You* (1976); *La Version d'Anne/Anne's Version* (1977); *La Moitié de l'amour/Half of Love* (1983–84); *Fiestas* (1988).

JIREŠ, Jaromil
Bratislava 1935

Czech director. Jireš studied at FAMU*, graduating in photography in 1958 and in direction in 1960. His first feature, *Křik/The Cry* (1963), dealt with the life of a television repairman whose wife is expecting a baby. Its complex narrative, involving flashbacks and flashforwards, establishes a mental world in which past, present, the individual and society intermingle. The film established Jireš as one of the leaders of the Czech New Wave* but he was unable to gain approval for a second feature until 1968, when he made *Žert/The Joke* in conjunction with novelist Milan Kundera. Planned before the publication of Kundera's book, the film used similar techniques to *Křik* to juxtapose the absurdities and idealism of 1950s Stalinism with the compromises and defeats of the present. Jireš maintained his technique through two very different films, an adaptation of Vítězslav Nezval's surrealist novel *Valerie a týden divů/Valerie and Her Week of Wonders* (1970), and the World War II story *... a pozdravuji vlaštovky/... And My Greetings to the Swallows* (1972). Although *Žert* was banned in 1973 'for ever', Jireš maintained a continuity of production and, albeit working on a variety of simplistic subjects, produced notable documentaries focusing on Czech music. His adaptations of novels by Vladimír Páral (*Mladý muž a bílá velryba/Young Man and the White Whale*, 1978; *Katapult/Catapult*, 1983) and a series of social problem films showed something of his former talent, but this only re-emerged with his post-1989 film, *Labyrinth* (1992), German-financed and widely seen as a necessary counterbalance to Steven Soderbergh's *Kafka*. PH

Other Films Include: *Perličky na dně/Pearls of the Deep* [episode *Romance*] (1965); *Útěky domů/Escapes Home* (1980); *Opera ve vinici/Opera in the Vineyard* (1981); *Neúplné zatmění/Partial Eclipse* (1982); *Prodloužený čas/Extended Time* (1984); *Lev s bílou hřívou/Lion with a White Mane* (1986); *Antonín Dvořák* [TV] (1990); *Popis věčného zápasu/Beschreibung eines Kampfes/Description of a Battle* (1991); *Helimadoe* (1993); *Učitel tance/The Dance Teacher* (1994).

JOHNSON, (Dame) Celia
Richmond, Surrey 1908 – Nettlebed, Oxfordshire 1982

British actress. Celia Johnson has become so inextricably linked to the part of Laura in *Brief Encounter* (1945) that it is sometimes surprising to see her in other roles. Much of her career was in theatre, and since her acting is in any case quietly self-effacing she seems to invite her own invisibility. One only has to compare her role as the English suburban rose in *Brief Encounter*, however, with that of the respectable working-class mam in *This Happy Breed* (1944), made the year before, to recognise the skill and range she brought to her film performances. The British cinema of the 1960s and 1970s had little to offer her, other than a good supporting role in *The Prime of Miss Jean Brodie* (1969). In 1980 she partnered Trevor Howard* again, with passion spent but skill undiminished, in the BBC television adaptation of Paul Scott's *Staying On*. JC

JORDAN, Neil
Sligo 1950

Irish director and writer. Jordan was an established short story writer (*Night in Tunisia and Other Stories*, 1978) and novelist (*The Past*, 1980) before he made his first film, a documentary on the making of John Boorman's* *Excalibur* (1981). His first feature, *Angel* (1982), was funded by the Irish Film Board* and Channel 4* but since then, though continuing to live in Ireland, he has most frequently made films in Britain – *The Company of Wolves* (1984), *Mona Lisa* (1986) and *High Spirits* (1988) – and America – *We're No Angels* (1989). Despite using unconventional material, Jordan established himself as a commercial director with *The Crying Game* (1992), the most successful non-American film ever released in the USA, with cinema box-office takings alone in excess of $60 million.

The Irish themes in Jordan's work include a concern with the metaphysics of political violence, focusing on individuals involved with Northern Ireland's paramilitary organisations and their attempts to start a new life (*Angel*, *The Crying Game*). The legitimacy of the state is rarely questioned, and it has been argued that the representation of Ireland in these films is a continuation of a British tradition of dehistoricising and desocialising Irish political violence. The modest scale of *The Miracle* (1991) brought Jordan back to his Irish roots with a low-key but effective exploration of an American woman's rediscovery of her Irish son after a long absence. KR

Bib: Kevin Rockett, Luke Gibbons, John Hill, *Cinema and Ireland* (1987).

JOUTSENO, Lea
Helsinki 1910–77

Finnish actress, embodiment of the 'new woman' in comic films of the 1940s. She appeared in minor roles in the 1930s but did not become a star until Valentin Vaala's* 'modern comedies' a decade later. Joutseno's collaboration on the script of these films was not credited until 1945. Most of the wartime 'modern comedies' negotiate relations between the sexes. The central conflict pits an effervescent, intelligent and determined woman against an introverted, inflexible, routine-bound man. The plot's aim is to find a balance between aggression and inhibition. In *Morsian yllättää/Bride Wanted* (1941), *Tositarkoituksella/With Serious Intent* (1943), and *Viikon tyttö* (1946) Joutseno's character learns to give up some of her unconventionality and her partner to express his feelings. *Varaventtiili/The Safety Valve* (1942), *Dynamiittityttö/Dynamite Girl* (1944) and *Vuokrasulhanen/A Hired Fiancé* (1945) are stories about resisting authority. *Tositarkoituksella* doubles as a propaganda film about a responsible work force. Joutseno plays a minister's daughter who joins the armed forces and travels to the countryside to work in the fields; however, she treats the trip as a romantic vacation rather than a patriotic act, a frivolousness which did not go unnoticed by critics at the time. Yet Joutseno's star image of the 1940s offered a possibility for female spectators to negotiate traditional family roles and social change. Lea Joutseno could behave unconventionally and get away with it, even though she threatened social structures and conventions. AK

JOUVET, Louis
Crozon 1887 – Paris 1951

French actor. When Jouvet first appeared in Marcel Pagnol's* *Topaze* in 1932, well into his forties, the press remarked that 'such a complete artist, first-rate stage director, highly cultured theatre manager and scintillating actor is for the cinema a precious conquest'. Although for Jouvet the cinema was mainly a way of supporting his theatrical ventures, he gave memorable performances in such classics as *La Kermesse héroïque/Carnival in Flanders* (1935), *Entrée des artistes/The Curtain Rises* (1938, where he plays himself as Paris Conservatoire teacher), *La Marseillaise* (1937), *Un carnet de bal* (1937) and *Quai des orfèvres* (1947). Tall and elegant, Jouvet exuded phlegmatic distinction bordering on insolence and occasionally menace. His main feature was an inimitable voice, a syncopated diction, as Robert Brasillach* put it, 'at once aristocratic and sly, moving and funny'. In one of his best prewar films, *Les Bas-fonds/The Lower Depths* (1936), he condensed these qualities as the destitute 'Russian' baron; in *Hôtel du Nord* (1938), he and Arletty*, as pimp and prostitute, stole the film from the romantic leads. Jouvet endures in French popular memory in his mockingly threatening 'bizarre, bizarre', uttered in dark tones to Michel Simon* in the surreal *Drôle de drame* (1937). GV

JOYE, Joseph Alexis
Romont 1852 – Basle 1919

Swiss educational film exhibitor. A Jesuit priest who spent formative years in Germany (1869–70) and Britain (1879–84), Joye was put in charge of religious youth education and spiritual welfare in a Basle parish (1886–1919; except for a five-year break between 1911 and 1915 when he was director of the order's Germanic provinces), where he soon began to illustrate his weekly lectures with magic lantern slides and still projections. In the winter of 1902–03, he started to exhibit films to accompany his by now fairly popular moral and religious lectures, which is all the more remarkable considering the fact that the first professional stationary exhibition sites did not appear in Switzerland before 1906–07. He thus acquired an extensive collection of early films.

The Joye collection lay fallow except for single films occasionally being shown in the local Basle parish during the four decades following Joye's death in 1919, until in 1958 Stephan Bamberger SJ transferred the already detoriating material to Zurich and began to restore and catalogue the film stock, and, on Davide Turconi's initiative, the 'Associazione italiana di richerche di storia del cinema' struck some 200 film prints in the 1960s. The complete collection of nitrate originals, 150,000 metres of film that constitute a unique cross-section of international film production, particularly of the period 1907–12, was finally deposited in the National Film and Television Archive in London in 1976; since then, around 1,300 films have been restored and reprinted from nitrate to celluloid, in many cases the only preserved copy of a film that would otherwise have been lost for ever. MW

Bib: Roland Cosandey, *Welcome Home, Joye! Film um 1910* (1993).

JUGO, Jenny   Mürzzuschlag, Steiermark 1905

Austrian-born actress, who signed a three-year contract with Ufa* in 1924. From the very beginning she displayed a talent for self-irony (*Die Hose*, 1927). In the sound era a fruitful collaboration with Erich Engel*, the director of eleven of her films, made her a star. With her naturalistic performance style Jugo was able to highlight the grotesque in the quotidian (in so-called *Alltagskomödien* ['everyday life comedies'] such as *Pechmarie*, 1934) as well as in artificial worlds (as in the costume film *Die Nacht mit dem Kaiser*, 1936), which made her an ideal medium for Engel's 'enlighted humour'. Her portrayal of Eliza in *Pygmalion* (Engel, 1935) marked the peak of her success as a comedienne. After Helmut Käutner's* *Königskinder* (1950) she retired from the cinema. KU

Other Films Include: *Die Puppe vom Lunapark* (1924); *Wer nimmt die Liebe ernst?* (1931); *Allotria* (1936); *Die Gattin* (1943).

JULIEN, Isaac   London 1961

British director, the first of the new wave of Black British independent film-makers to score at least a critical success with a feature film. *Young Soul Rebels* (1991), made through the BFI* Production Board with a budget of £1.2 million, won the Critics' Prize at the 1991 Cannes Festival. Set in 1977, the film uses the Queen's Silver Jubilee, the musical subcultures around punk, soul, disco and Rock against Racism, and the realignments in youth culture around anti-fascism, anti-racism and the gay movement, to explore a politics and a sensibility of racial and sexual difference and identity. Julien was a founder member of the Black Workshop, Sankofa. He co-directed with Maureen Blackwood *The Passion of Remembrance* (1986), and directed *This is Not an AIDS Ad* (1987) and *Looking for Langston* (1989), a visually stunning evocation of Langston Hughes, the gay Afro-American poet of the Harlem Renaissance. JC

Bib: Isaac Julien and Colin MacCabe, *Diary of a Young Soul Rebel* (1991).

JÜRGENS, Curd   Munich 1915 – Vienna 1982

German actor and director. From the mid-1930s to the 1970s Jürgens enjoyed a parallel career in theatre and film. Willi Forst* gave him a first film role in *Königswalzer* (1935), establishing him as good-looking lover and carefree daredevil. With Helmut Käutner's* Zuckmayer adaption *Des Teufels General/The Devil's General* (1955) his persona acquired dimensions of psychological depth. In *Die Ratten* (1955) and *Les Héros sont fatigués/The Heroes Are Tired/Heroes and Sinners* (1955, Fr.), he continued to make his mark as a character actor, playing opposite Brigitte Bardot* in *Et Dieu ... créa la femme/And God Created Woman* (1956). In the 1960s he participated in a number of European and American film projects (often remakes of German prewar films) as well as the German *St. Pauli* series. He also directed four films: *Prämien auf den Tod* (1949), *Die Gangsterpremiere* (1951), *Ohne Dich wird es Nacht* (1956), and *Bankraub in der Rue Latour* (1960). SG/TE

Bib: Gregor Ball, *Curd Jürgens* (1982).

JUSTER, Leif   Kristiania [Oslo] 1910

Norwegian actor, primarily a comedian, whose career extended from 1933 to the late 1980s. He also worked in radio, theatre and television. Juster's long, comically thin shape was perfectly suited to the film farces he often appeared in. Arne Skouen's* *Bussen/The Bus* (1961), however, also gave him the opportunity to display his warm humanity in the leading role of the bus driver. He was loved by generations of Norwegians for his ability to make them laugh. KS

Films Include: *Op med hodet/Raise Your Head* (1933); *Morderen uten ansikt/The Murderer Without a Face* (1936); *Gullfjellet/The Mountain of Gold, Den forsvundne pølse-maker/The Lost Sausage-maker* (1941); *Det æ'kke te å tru/ Unbelievable* (1942); *Fjols til fjells/Fools in the Mountains* (1957); *Bustenskjold* (1958); *Bussen/The Bus* (1961); *Freske fraspark/Powerful Kicks Backwards* (1963); *Hjelp vi får leilighet/Help, We've Got an Apartment* (1965); *Musikanter/ Musicians* (1967); *Mannen som ikke kunne le/The Man Who Couldn't Laugh* (1968); *Balladen om Mestertyven Ole Høiland/The Ballad of the Masterthief Ole Høiland* (1970); *Skraphandlerne/The Junk Dealers* (1975); *Deilig er fjorden/ The Lovely Fjord* (1985); *Bryllupsfesten/The Wedding Party* (1989).

K

KACHYŇA, Karel   Vyškov 1924

Czech director. Educated at FAMU*, Kachyňa was trained as a cinematographer and was one of the first graduates to enter the industry. Between 1950 and 1955, he worked on a series of documentaries with co-director Vojtěch Jasný*. They made their first feature together but then followed separate paths. In the 1960s, Kachyňa began an important collaboration with the writer Jan Procházka, which was to test the limits of what was then permitted in Czech cinema. Perhaps the most impressive of their films were *Naděje/Hope* (1963), *At' žije republika/Long Live the Republic* (1965), *Kočár do Vídně/Coach to Vienna* (1966), and *Noc nevěsty/Night of the Bride* (1967), in which script, cinematography and music were matched in a kind of counterpoint. Approved themes such as the war, collectivisation or the revolution were given an unorthodox treatment, focusing on the complexity of human motivation and frequently critical of the Communist role. Procházka became head of the Writers Union during the 'Prague Spring', and his last two films with Kachyňa, *Směšný pán/Funny Old Man* (1969) and *Ucho/The Ear* (1969, released 1990), were banned in the aftermath of the Soviet invasion. Kachyňa filmed, as *Už zase skáču přes kaluže* (1970), Procházka's adaptation of Alan Marshall's *I'm Jumping Over Puddles Again*, with another writer taking the credit (Procházka died in 1971). Kachyňa continued to make films but never achieved quite the same standard again, insubstantial themes frequently collapsing under an excess of imagery. His most notable later films have included *Lásky mezi kapkami deště/Love Among the Raindrops* (1979), *Smrt krásných srnců/Death of the Beautiful Roebucks* (1986), and *Poslední motýl/The Last Butterfly/Le Cri du papillon* (1990), a co-production with Britain and France. In 1993, he successfully returned to another Procházka subject with *Kráva/The Cow* (1993), made for television. PH

KADÁR, Ján   Budapest, Hungary 1918 – Los Angeles, USA 1979
and
KLOS, Elmar   Brno [then Austria-Hungary] 1910 – Prague 1993

Slovak and Czech directors, writers and producers. Ján Kadár studied law and then photography in Bratislava in the 1930s. Imprisoned in Nazi concentration camps during the war, he made three films in Slovakia in the late 1940s before moving to Prague and beginning his career with Elmar Klos. Klos began in cinema by helping his scriptwriter uncle, Josef Skružný, in the late 1920s and acting in small parts. He was co-founder and directed films for the film unit set up by the Bať'a shoe company in Zlín (subsequently Gottwaldov, now Zlín again), which pioneered documentary and advertising films in the late 1930s.

Kadár and Klos took co-credits on eight features, with Klos as producer and Kadár as director. Their films were charac-terised by their critical stance and a variety of stylistic approaches, ranging from a modern fairy story such as *Tři přání/Three Wishes* (1958, released 1963), which attacked social hypocrisy and corruption, to an almost documentary assault on Stalinist justice in *Obžalovaný/The Accused* (1964). Their film about the partisan struggle in Slovakia, *Smrt si říká Engelchen/Death is Called Engelchen* (1963), intercut past and present in a way that provoked comparisons with Alain Resnais'* *Hiroshima, mon amour*, while their Oscar-winning *Obchod na korze/A Shop on the High Street/The Shop on Main Street* (1965) mixed comedy, tragedy and fantasy in a compelling portrait of the Jewish experience under fascism. In 1968, Kadár emigrated to the United States where he followed an uneven career, although the Canadian-made *Lies My Father Told Me* (1975) enjoyed both critical and commercial success. Klos remained at home in obscurity, emerging in 1989 to collaborate with the Syrian-born Moris Issa on *Bizon*. PH

Other Films Co-Directed, Written and Produced by Kadár and Klos: *Únos/Kidnapped* (1952); *Hudba z Marsu/Music from Mars* (1955); *Tam na konečné/House at the Terminus* (1957); *Touha zvaná Anada/Adrift/Desire is Called Anada* (1969, released 1971).

KAIDANOVSKY, Alexander L.   Leningrad 1946

Russian actor, director and scriptwriter. After studies at the Shchukin Theatre Academy, Kaidanovsky worked as an actor in both the Vakhtangov Theatre and the Moscow Art Theatre, while also appearing in such films as Nikita Mikhalkov's* *Svoi sredi chuzhikh, chuzhoi sredi svoikh/At Home Among Strangers, Alone Among Friends* (1974). Perhaps his greatest success as an actor was the title role in Andrey Tarkovsky's* *Stalker* (1979). As a director he has made the short films *Sad/The Garden* (1983), based on Borges, and *Iona, ili khudozhnik za rabotoi/Jonah, or the Artist at Work* (1984). His first feature, *Prostaya smert'/A Simple Death* (1987), was based on Tolstoy's *The Death of Ivan Ilich*, and starred Alisa Freindlich, who played Kaidanovsky's wife in *Stalker*. Kaidanovsky's most ambitious film is *Zhena kerosinshchika/The Kerosene Seller's Wife* (1988), from his own script. The film is set in a town in former East Prussia in 1953, the year of Stalin's death, and superficially concerns the efforts of a visiting investigator to pursue charges of corruption laid against the head of the town's Party Committee. But Kaidanovsky's range is considerably greater, taking in questions of history and myth, truth, chance and lies, in a febrile and often hallucinatory narrative that, along with the work of Alexander Sokurov*, is visually the most ambitious and exciting achievement of recent Russian cinema. JGf

KALATOZOV, Mikhail K.
Mihail Kalatozishvili; Tbilisi, Georgia [Russian Empire] 1903 – Moscow 1973

Georgian Soviet director, who began as a jack-of-all-trades in Georgian cinema in 1923. His first film as director, the poetic documentary *Sol' Svanetii/Salt for Svanetia* in 1930, portrayed the benefits brought by Soviet power and the construction of a new road to an isolated part of the Caucasian mountains. In 1936 he became director of the Tbilisi film studios, was Soviet cinema's representative in the USA from 1943 to 1945, and between 1945 and 1948 was in overall charge of Soviet feature film production. During this period he made *Muzhestvo/Courage* (1939), *Valerii Chkalov* (1941) and the Cold War propaganda vehicle *Zagovor obrechënnykh/The Conspiracy of the Damned* (1950), for which he was awarded the Stalin Prize in 1951. He gained an international reputation with *Letyat zhuravli/The Cranes Are Flying*, which won the Palme d'or at Cannes in 1958. His last film was *Krasnaya palatka/The Red Tent* (1970), a co-production with Italy which dealt with the polar expedition of the Italian explorer Nobile. RT

KAMMERSPIELFILM

German genre, designating films produced during the early 1920s which drew on the conventions of contemporary German theatre. *Kammerspielfilme* usually received critical acclaim but did not achieve commercial success. The scriptwriter Carl Mayer* created the genre's narrative model in his screenplays for *Scherben/Shattered* (1921), *Hintertreppe* (1921), *Sylvester – Tragödie einer Nacht* (1923) and *Der letzte Mann/The Last Laugh* (1924). Characteristically, the plot is a realist drama portraying servants or members of the lower middle class who meet with a tragic end through murder or suicide. Most *Kammerspielfilme* were set indoors and drew on innovative cinematic techniques, as exemplified in the minimal use of titles and expressive camera movements in *Scherben*, *Sylvester* and *Der letzte Mann*. The *Kammerspielfilm*'s central figure was often an anti-hero, typical of many German films of the post-World War I era, and anticipating the protagonists of American *film noir* and of the post-World War II German *Trümmerfilm* ('ruin film'). The leads went to well-known stage actors such as Werner Krauß*, Eugen Klöpfer* and Fritz Kortner*, ensuring that, despite minority appeal, the films were premiered in Ufa's* most prestigious Berlin first-run movie theatres. JG

Bib: Jo Leslie Collier, *From Wagner to Murnau: The Transposition of Romanticism from Stage to Screen* (1988).

KANEVSKY, Vitali
Suchan, Siberia [USSR], 1935

Siberian-born Russian director, who began studying at VGIK* in 1960 but was falsely accused of theft and sentenced to eight years' imprisonment in 1966. Released in 1974, he received his director's diploma and made a short film,

Chetvërtaya taina/The Fourth Secret, at the Belorusfilm studios. In 1989, encouraged by Alexei German*, he made the autobiographical film *Zamri, umri, voskresni/Don't Move, Die and Rise Again!* Set in 1947, it relates the experiences of twelve-year-old Valerka and his friend Galiya among 'enemies of the people' and Japanese prisoners of war. The film succeeded as miraculously as German's *Moi drug Ivan Lapshin/My Friend Ivan Lapshin* (1979; released 1984) in evoking provincial life in Stalinist Russia. Alan Parker* saw part of the film and persuaded the Cannes festival to accept it; and in 1990, at the age of 55, Kanevsky won the Caméra d'or prize for a first feature. His next film, *Samostoyatel'naya zhizn'/An Independent Life* (1992), continues Valerka's story, as an adult in a world of mundane violence and degradation. Kanevsky's documentary, *My, deti dvadtsatogo veka/We, the Children of the Twentieth Century* (1993), is a depressing series of interviews with juvenile criminals, of which the most shocking sequence is a conversation with Pavel Nazarov, the young actor who played Valerka, imprisoned for stealing a car. JGf

KAPLAN, Nelly
Buenos Aires, Argentina 1934

French director. Kaplan was a journalist and assistant to Abel Gance* before starting to make her own films, including several shorts on painters. She has also written Surrealist/erotic novels under the name of Belen, and worked for television. Her claim to fame is her first feature, *La Fiancée du pirate/Dirty Mary* (1969), a key film in early feminist film debates. The 'fiancée' is a young woman (the sensual and impertinent Bernadette Lafont) who takes her revenge on a whole village by selling herself to the men who maltreated her mother and then ruining their reputation. Harshly criticised for its politically incorrect use of prostitution and humiliation of other female characters, the film is nevertheless a joyful attack on misogyny, seen by Lafont as 'a libertarian act'. Kaplan's subsequent films have been less successful, perhaps because her libertarian sensitivity became outmoded, but they have been consistently interesting if controversial: for instance *Néa* (1976), an attempt at soft porn from a woman's point of view, and *Plaisir d'amour* (1991), a tale of three women (grandmother, mother and daughter) who exhaust a man sexually. GV

Other Films Include: *Abel Gance: hier et demain* (1963, short); *Papa les petits bateaux...* (1971); *Charles et Lucie* (1979); *Patte de Velours* (1987, TV).

KARÁDY, Katalin
Budapest 1912 – São Paulo, Brazil 1989

Hungarian actress, who became the only Hollywood-type movie star in Hungary. Karády's career as an actress was fairly short but nonetheless dazzling. She was already a well-known popular singer when she appeared in her first and most successful movie, *Halálos tavasz/Deadly Spring* (1939). The film scandalised the fascist authorities, who condemned its sentimentality and lack of patriotic feeling. Karády's alto voice and the erotic mood she generated made her the Hungarian equivalent of the Marlene Dietrich* type of *femme fatale*. Her unwillingness to take part in Nazi propaganda campaigns during the war led to rumours of her being a British spy, rumours that were reinforced by her arrest by the Gestapo in 1944. Her participation in the resistance is still not clear (she claimed to have hidden refugees in her apartment). Karády left Hungary after the communist takeover in 1949 and this ended her career as an actress. Her films could not be shown for thirty years, which only helped to nourish the mythology surrounding her. It was only in the late 1970s that her songs were re-released and her films shown theatrically, to huge acclaim. KAB

Other Films Include: *Erzsébet királynő/Queen Elizabeth, Hazajáró lélek/Haunting Spirit* (1940); *Ne kérdezd, ki voltam/Don't Ask Who I Was, Kísértés/Temptation* (1941); *Sziriusz/Sirius, Halálos csók/Deadly Kiss, Egy szív megáll/A Heart Stops Beating* (1942); *Valamit visz a víz/Something is in the Water, Szováthy Éva* (1943); *Forró mezők/Hot Fields* (1948).

KARAINDROU, Eleni
Tihio [?]

Greek composer. Before starting to compose for the cinema, Karaindrou was well-known for her work in ethnic music. She emerged as a major film composer in Greece in the 1980s, mainly through her collaboration with Thodoros Angelopoulos*. Since *Taxidi sta Kithira/Voyage to Cythera* (1984) she has written the music for all his films. Recently she has also launched an international career with recordings in Germany and a collaboration with Margarethe von Trotta* (*L'Africana/Die Rückkehr*, 1990). Her music is distinguished for its lyrical, limpid and atmospheric sound, combining elements from classical music, jazz, Greek popular songs and folk music. She collaborated with Jan Garbarek on the music of Angelopoulos's *O melissokomos/The Beekeeper* (1986). TN

KAREZI, Jenny
Evgenia Karpouzi; Athens 1936–92

Greek actress and producer. Jenny Karezi was one of the major stars of the commercial Greek cinema. She made her stage debut at the age of eighteen and a year later appeared in her first feature, *Laterna ftohia ke filotimo/Barrel Organ, Poverty and Dignity* (1956). Its immediate success established her as a star. Thereafter Karezi divided her activities between stage and screen. Initially, she appeared in comedies, specialising in witty, charming and mischievous young women who make life difficult for husbands-to-be and parents. In the 1950s and 1960s she was the only screen rival of the 'national' Greek star Aliki Vouyouklaki*. She made a successful switch to melodramas and serious films in the late 1960s. In 1968 she married stage actor and producer Kostas Kazakos, with whom she formed a theatre company which produced serious political plays. Her occasional appearances in the 1970s and 1980s were mostly confined to television serials. TNe

Other Films Include: *To koroïdaki tis despinidos/Miss's Fool* (1959); *I Hionati ke ta epta gerondopallikara/Snow White and the Seven Bachelors* (1960); *Ta kokkina fanaria/Red Lanterns* (1962); *Despinis diefthindis/Miss Boss* (1964); *Kontserto ya polivola/Machine Gun Concert* (1967); *Lissistrati/Lysistrata* (1972).

KARINA, Anna
Hanne Karin Blarke Bayer; Copenhagen, Denmark 1940

French actress of Danish origin. A former model, Karina appeared in commercials and a short film in Denmark before moving to Paris in 1959. Her meeting with Jean-Luc Godard* was decisive for both. Godard's 'Karina years' (during most of which they were married) include seven features: *Le Petit soldat* (1960, rel. 1963), *Une femme est une femme/A Woman is a Woman* (1961), *Vivre sa vie/My Life to Live* (1962), *Bande à part/Band of Outsiders* (1964), *Alphaville, Pierrot le fou* (1965) and *Made in USA* (1967). The stunningly beautiful Karina was central to Godard's (and the New Wave's*) vision of a 'new' femininity: sensual, but also sensitive and intellectual, epitomised in the dreamy close-ups of Karina in *Vivre sa vie*: smoking, reading, talking philosophy in cafés, crying at the cinema (Jeanne Moreau* embodied another version of the New Wave woman). Karina starred in a few other *auteur* films, such as Michel Deville's *Ce soir ou jamais* (1961) and Jacques Rivette's* *La Religieuse* (1965, rel. 1967). Her career lost momentum after the split with Godard, although she directed *Vivre ensemble* in 1973, a telling document on the libertarian ethos of the 1960s and early 1970s. GV

KARLOVY VARY

Czech film festival. The first international film festival in Czechoslovakia was held at Mariánské Lázně (Marienbad) and Karlovy Vary (Carlsbad) in 1946. It became competitive in 1948, with the venue moving permanently to Karlovy Vary in 1950. To accommodate the introduction of the Moscow Festival in 1959, it went bi-ennial, the two festivals alternating until 1992. Both Karlovy Vary and Moscow functioned as Eastern bloc alternatives to Cannes* and Venice* but, despite a blatant ideological role (juries were frequently told which politically acceptable film to vote for), Karlovy Vary often provided a genuine meeting-place for film-makers. Important films to win its major award include Jiří Menzel's* *Rozmarné léto/Capricious Summer* (1967) and Ken Loach's* *Kes* (1969). Long before Nantes and London took up the cause, Karlovy Vary was promoting 'Third World' cinema and it became one of the principal channels through which Latin American, Asian and African cinema reached audiences in Europe. The first 'post-revolutionary' festival in 1990 concentrated on the Czech and Slovak film-makers whose work had been banned during the previous twenty years. PH

Touchez pas au grisbi/Honour Among Thieves
(France, 1954; Jacques Becker):
Jeanne Moreau, Jean Gabin

Eroica (Poland, 1958; Andrzej Munk)

Los golfos/The Hooligans (Spain, 1959; Mario Camús)

De vierde man/The Fourth Man (Netherlands, 1983; Paul Verhoeven): Jeroen Krabbé, Renée Soutendijk

Triumph des Willens/Triumph of the Will (Germany, 1935; Leni Riefenstahl)

Blackmail (UK, 1929; Alfred Hitchcock): Anny Ondra

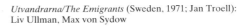

Utvandrarna/The Emigrants (Sweden, 1971; Jan Troell):
Liv Ullman, Max von Sydow

A bout de souffle/Breathless (France, 1960; Jean-Luc Godard):
Jean-Paul Belmondo, Jean Seberg

Sommaren med Monika/Summer with Monika (Sweden, 1953;
Ingmar Bergman): Harriet Andersson (left)

Ivan Groznyi/Ivan the Terrible (Soviet Union, 1944-45; S.M. Eisenstein):
Nikolai Cherkasov

Valkoinen peura/The White Reindeer
(Finland, 1953; Erik Blomberg)

La Grande illusion (France, 1937; Jean Renoir): (left to right) Jean Gabin,
Gaston Modot, Pierre Fresnay, Carette, Jean Dasté, Marcel Dalio

Marie-Louise (Switzerland, 1944; Leopold Lindtberg): Anne-Marie Blanc (right)

KARMITZ, Marin
Bucharest, Romania 1938

Romanian-born French producer, distributor and director. After studying at IDHEC* (1957–59) and working as an assistant director, he made a few shorts and features, of which the most interesting is *Coup pour coup* (1972), part of the militant cinema of the 1970s. After 1973, Karmitz switched to production and distribution through his company MK2. A passionate defender of *auteur* cinema, he also controls a cinema chain, which is still expanding. His production credits include films by Marco Bellocchio*, Jean-Luc Godard*, Louis Malle* and Claude Chabrol*, as well as Krzysztof Kieślowski's* high-profile pan-European venture *Trois couleurs Bleu/Three Colours Blue* (1993), *Trois couleurs Blanc/Three Colours White* (1993) and *Trois couleurs Rouge/Three Colours Red* (1994), a great success which seems to support Karmitz's claim that 'though financial conditions for production are better than they used to be, political conditions are not. We live in a world of slogans, appearances, stereotypes. [...] It is possible to do it differently, as I proved with Kieślowski's's trilogy.' GV

KARU, Erkki
Helsinki 1887–1935

Finnish producer and director, founder of the two biggest film studios in Finland, Suomi-Filmi in 1919 and Suomen Filmiteollisuus (SF) in 1933. Karu worked in theatre as an actor, stage decorator and director until 1918, after which he devoted his life to film, first as a cinema owner and then as a director of short comedies. As head of Suomi-Filmi, Karu was an autocrat. His theatre experience had equipped him with a sharp instinct for audience tastes, and in its early years Suomi-Filmi prospered. Among his successful films were *Koskenlaskijan morsian/The Logroller's Bride* (1923), and *Nummisuutarit/The Village Shoemakers* (1923), of which the first launched the uniquely Finnish genre of Lumberjack* films and the second was an adaptation of a well-known literary classic. As a director Karu was an experimenter, albeit one who aimed to reach as wide an audience as possible. As a producer he preferred folk topics and literary sources, with the occasional excursion into something new – for example, he allowed the Hollywood-trained Carl von Haartman to direct two visually astounding films, *Korkein voitto/The Highest Victory* (1929) and *Kajastus/The Dawn* (1930).

Under Karu, Suomi-Filmi was the largest, indeed only, significant production company during the silent era in Finland, turning out full-length features, shorts and documentaries. The company had its own laboratories and from 1926 its own exhibition network. Sound arrived in a Finland in full economic depression, hitting Suomi-Filmi hard. Karu left the company in 1933 and set up a new one, SF. Before his premature death Karu had time to direct three films: a dramatised documentary about the Finnish air force – *Meidän poikamme ilmassa – me maassa/Our Boys in the Air – We on the Ground* (1934) – and two comedies: *Syntipukki/Scapegoat* and *Roinilan talossa/In Roinila's House* (both 1935). Karu was the father of the Finnish studio system, his work being continued by Risto Orko* at Suomi-Filmi and T. J. Särkkä* at SF. AH-H

KASANDER, Kees
Gorinchem 1955

Dutch producer. Before becoming an independent producer Kasander worked in the early 1980s as assistant manager for Hubert Bals*, director of the Rotterdam film festival. He produced his first picture, *Le Toît de la baleine/On Top of the Whale*, directed by Raul Ruiz*, in 1982. Together with Denis Wigman, Kasander established a new production company, Allarts, with offices in The Hague and London (1984), specialising in international art cinema, documentary as well as fiction. Its first production was Peter Greenaway's* *A Zed & Two Noughts* (1985), followed by the same director's *Drowning by Numbers* (1988), *The Cook the Thief His Wife and Her Lover* (1989), *Prospero's Books* (1991), *Darwin* (1992), *The Baby of Mâcon* (1993) and *The Pillow Book* (1995). Allarts also worked with directors Eric de Kuyper*, Gabriel Axel* and the Argentinian Alejandro Agresti. When Allarts went into liquidation in 1993, its artistic record was outstanding. Activities were resumed under the name of Kasander & Wigman Productions. Between 1985 and 1990, Kasander organised the Image and Sound Festival in The Hague, showing artistic applications of new image technology. KD/FW

KASSILA, Matti
Keuruu 1924

Finnish director. Matti Kassila is the only film-maker of the Finnish 'studio era' still active. He started making short films at Suomi-Filmi in 1946 before moving to rival SF two years later. Kassila's career as a director began almost accidentally with a cheap comedy, *Isäntä soittaa haitaria/The Head of the House Plays the Accordion* (1949). His next film, *Professori Masa* (1950), broke new ground, propelling Finnish comedy into social polemics. It tells the story of a professor of politics who loses his professional status after an academic quarrel and becomes a worker. Kassila also directed comedies – *Radio tulee hulluksi/The Radio Goes Mad* (1952), *Hilmanpäivät/Hilma's Name Day* (1954), *Isän vanha ja uusi/Fathers Old and New* (1955) and *Pastori Jussilainen/Reverend Jussilainen* (1955). Later Kassila showed his talent in other genres. *Sininen viikko/The Blue Week* (1954), based on Jarl Hemmer's short story, is set on a workers' holiday island near Helsinki. *Elokuu/The Harvest Month* (1957), adapted from F. E. Sillanpää's novel, was a similar kind of psychological drama. *Elokuu* was chosen as the Finnish entry at the Cannes film festival in 1957 (the last Finnish film at Cannes until 1981). Kassila continued to adapt stories from Finnish national literature, among them *Punainen viiva/The Red Line* (1959). In the 1960s he made a series of entertaining crime films based on Mika Waltari's* novels: *Komisario Palmun erehdys/Police Inspector Palmu's Mistake* (1960), *Kaasua, komisario Palmu/Step on the Gas, Inspector Palmu* (1961), *Tähdet kertovat, komisario Palmu/It is Written in the Stars, Inspector Palmu* (1962), and *Vodkaa, komisario Palmu* (1969). Kassila also directed the last Niskavuori* film, aptly called *Niskavuori* (1984), and made *Jäähyväiset presidentille/Goodbye, Mr President!* in 1987. HS

KATOWICE FILM AND TELEVISION SCHOOL (WYDZIAŁ RADIA I TELEWIZJI, UNIWERSYTET ŚLĄSKI, KATOWICE)

Polish film school. The Department of Radio and TV at the University of Śląsk in Katowice, founded by Polish Television and intended as a television school, has become Poland's second film school, with many of its graduates working in cinematography. The student strikes and political manoeuvring in the faculty at Łódź* in the mid-1970s drew students and lecturers to Katowice, which also has better technical facilities. The department runs courses in cinematography for film and television, production management and direction, and promotes a strong documentary tradition with lecturers such as Krzysztof Kieślowski* and documentarist Irena Kamieńska. AW

KATRAKIS, Manos
Kastelli, Crete 1908 – Athens 1984

Greek actor. One of the most powerful Greek actors, distinguished for his wide acting range, improvisational abilities and expressive voice. Katrakis was exiled from 1947 to 1952 for his political activities. His major work was for the stage, where he first appeared in 1928. He ran his own company, the Greek Popular Theatre, from 1955 to 1967. His first film role was in *To lavaro tou 21/The 1821 Banner* (1928), a silent film about the Greek war of independence, his last for Thodoros Angelopoulos* in *Taxidi sta Kithira/Voyage to Cythera* (1984). In between he appeared in commercial films, mainly melodramas [> GREEK MELODRAMA], often lending them more weight than they deserved. Of note are his appearances in *Sinikia to Oniro/Dream Neighbourhood* (1961, dir. Alekos Alexandrakis) and *Ilektra/Electra* (1962, dir. Michael Cacoyannis*). TN

Other Films Include: *O agapitikos tis voskopoulas/The Shepherdess' Lover* (1932); *Mayiki poli/Magic City* (1954); *To homa vaftike kokkino/Blood on the Land* (1965); *To kanoni ke to aidoni/Guns and the Nightingale* (1968); *Kravgi Ginekon/A Dream of Passion* (1978); *Eleftherios Venizelos* (1980).

KAUFMAN, Mikhail A.
Białystok, Poland [Russian Empire] 1897 – Moscow 1980

Soviet director and cameraman, brother of Dziga Vertov* and Boris Kaufman (later cameraman on Jean Vigo's* films) and one of the founders of the Soviet school of documentary film-making. Kaufman was the cameraman for Vertov's silent newsreels and documentary films up to and including *Chelovek s kinoapparatom/The Man with the Movie Camera* (1929). He wrote, directed and shot the feature-length documentaries *Moskva/Moscow* (1927) and *Vesnoi/Springtime* (1929) and a series of documentaries in the 1930s, including *Nebyvalyi pokhod/An Unprecedented Campaign* (1931), *Bol'shaya pobeda/A Great Victory* (1933), *Aviamarsh/The Aviators' March* (1936) and *Nasha Moskva/Our Moscow*

(1939). From 1941 he concentrated on popular educational films and his career went into a decline with works such as *Kompozitor Tikhon Khrennikov/The Composer Tikhon Khrennikov* (1967), a study of the Stalinist head of the Composers' Union. RT

KAURISMÄKI, Aki
Orimattila 1957
and
KAURISMÄKI, Mika
Orimattila 1955

Finnish directors and producers. Brothers Aki and Mika Kaurismäki started their film careers together in the early 1980s with the highly experimental and entertaining *Valehtelija/The Liar* (Aki's script, 1980), *Saimaa ilmiö/The Saimaa Gesture* (1981) and *Arvottomat/The Worthless* (Aki's script, 1982). Subsequently they assisted each other but otherwise went their separate ways. It has been said that the first Kaurismäki films were the Finnish reflection of the European 'New Wave'*, with a twenty-year time lag. The 'Kaurismäki touch' was a compendium of the stylistic, narrative and thematic characteristics of the New Wave combined with typically Finnish ingredients such as moments of silence, melancholy, logical absurdities, unexpected and undeserved happiness, and violent deaths. In subsequent films produced by their company Villealfa, Aki and Mika Kaurismäki started developing parallel but separate careers. Aki made an adaptation of Dostoevsky's *Crime and Punishment* (*Rikos ja rangaistus,* 1983) set in modern Helsinki, and Mika directed *Klaani – Tarina Sammakoitten Suvusta/The Clan – Tale of the Frogs* (1984), also a literary adaptation. Signs of change were recognisable in Mika's *Rosso* (1985), about an Italian hit man who flies to Finland in search of his lost girlfriend. *Rosso* was made partly in Italy and partly in Finland, in Italian. Increasingly the Kaurismäki brothers looked abroad: Mika's next film, *Helsinki–Napoli – All Night Long* (1987) was shot in Berlin, *Amazon* (1991) in Brazil, *The Last Border* (1993) in Norway; Aki's *Leningrad Cowboys Go America* (1989) in Texas, *I Hired a Contract Killer* (1990) in English in London, and *La Vie de bohème* (1992) in French in Paris. The brothers' recent work sparks optimism for the possibility of a transnational European cinema in which the national roots of the film-makers provide the necessary spice; or, as the Finnish Film Foundation brochure puts it, 'The Finns have increasingly adopted the mentality and lifestyle of their western neighbours, yet their spirit remains influenced by the darker, more mystical nature of their neighbours to the east.' This duality lies at the heart of the films of Mika and Aki Kaurismäki. JS

Bib: Roger Connah, *K/K. A Couple of Finns and Some Donald Ducks: Cinema in Society* (1991).

Other Films Include: Aki Kaurismäki: *Calamari Union* (1985); *Varjoja paratiisissa/Shadows in Paradise* (1986); *Hamlet liikemaailmassa/Hamlet Goes Business* (1987); *Ariel* (1988); *Tulitikkutehtaan tyttö/The Match Factory Girl* (1990); *Leningrad Cowboys Meet Moses* (1993). **Mika Kaurismäki**: *Cha-Cha-Cha, Paperitähti/Paper Star* (1989); *Zombie ja kummitusjuna/Zombie and the Ghost Train* (1991).

KÄUTNER, Helmut
Düsseldorf 1908 –
Castellina, Italy 1980

German director (and former actor), whose first film, the sophisticated comedy *Kitty und die Weltkonferenz/Kitty and the World Conference* (1939), was banned by Goebbels at the outbreak of World War II because of its sympathetic portrait of a British diplomat. Käutner continued to deviate from the official Nazi formula with the Gottfried Keller adaptation *Kleider machen Leute/Clothes Make the Man* (1940), starring Heinz Rühmann*. Equally remarkable was his subsequent psychological melodrama, *Romanze in Moll/Romance in a Minor Key* (1943). Disliked by the Nazi officials for what they regarded as its escapist mood, the film enjoyed far greater popularity than many propaganda features. Also banned, but successful abroad, was *Große Freiheit Nr. 7/Port of Freedom/La Paloma* (1944, with Hans Albers*), which became a major hit in Germany after the war. Except for the prize-winning anti-war film *Die letzte Brücke/The Last Bridge* (1954) and the successful Zuckmayer adaptations *Des Teufels General/The Devil's General* (1955), *Der Hauptmann von Köpenick/The Captain from Köpenick* (1956) and *Der Schinderhannes* (1958), Käutner's postwar films met with an increasingly negative reception. From the mid-1960s he concentrated mainly on the theatre, opera and television. In 1974 he was given a German award for his performance in the title role of Hans Jürgen Syberberg's* *Karl May* (1974). MW

Bib: Wolfgang Jacobsen and Hans Helmut Prinzler (eds.), *Käutner* (1992).

Other Films Include: *Frau nach Maß* (1940); *Anuschka* (1942); *Unter den Brücken/Under the Bridges* (1946); *In Jenen Tagen/In Those Days* (1947); *Der Apfel ist ab* (1948); *Königskinder* (1950); *Käpt'n Bay-Bay* (1953); *Himmel ohne Sterne, Ludwig II: Glanz und Elend eines Königs* (1955); *Ein Mädchen aus Flandern* (1956); *Montpi* (1957); *Der Rest ist Schweigen/The Rest is Silence* (1959).

KAWALEROWICZ, Jerzy
Gwóździec,
Ukraine 1922

Polish director. Kawalerowicz is one of the leading figures of the 'Polish School' of the 1950s and early 1960s. He was born in Ukraine and graduated from the short-lived Cracow Film Institute, along with Wojciech Has*. His first solo features, *Celuloza/A Night of Remembrance* and *Pod Gwiazdą Frygijską/Under a Phrygian Star* (1954), were a two-part adaptation of I. Newerley's novel *A Night of Remembrance*. An epic tale of prewar Polish society, the films centre on one man's political development as a communist and his tempestuous romance with a fellow activist. In 1955 Kawalerowicz became head of the Kadr Film Unit with Tadeusz Konwicki* as his literary chief. Their work together on *Matka Joanna od Aniołów/Mother Joan of the Angels/The Devil and the Nun* (1961) won a Special Jury Prize at Cannes. Kawalerowicz was also prominent in the 'second wave' of Polish films of the 1960s. His taut psychological thriller, *Pociąg/Night Train* (1959), is comparable to the best of American B-movies, its reflections on mob violence and persecution adding a distinctly contemporary political overtone. Kawalerowicz's ambitious move into the epic genre with *Faraon/The Pharaoh* (1966), billed as the 'communist Cleopatra', is more memorable as an exercise in logistics and locations than for the film itself. Kawalerowicz turned again to Polish history with *Śmierć Prezydenta/Death of a President* (1977), which looked at the story of Gabriel Narutowicz, Poland's first elected president, and *Austeria/The Inn* (1983), dealing with World War I and the Hasidic Jewish community. His *Bronsteins Kinder/Bronstein's Children* (1990) is a German production about the revenge of three Jewish men on their German concentration camp warden many years after the war. AW

KERR, Deborah
Deborah Jane Kerr-Trimmer;
Helensburgh, Scotland 1921

British actress, with a distinguished record in some of the most vivid British films of the 1940s and some of the most memorable Hollywood melodramas of the 1950s and 1960s. Her role as the governess in *The King and I* (1956, US) is almost a parody of the qualities she brought to other dramatic roles: the spirited, independent woman, a little constrained by good breeding, up against a masculine force she had to bring under control. The 'breeding' was not always her hallmark. In her second film, John Baxter's* tough tragedy of the Depression, *Love on the Dole* (1941), she plays the working-class daughter who cynically sells herself to a rich spiv after the man she loved is killed in a demonstration. There were few parts for independent women in the patriotic films made during and after the war, and it was Michael Powell* and Emeric Pressburger* who offered Kerr her best parts, with striking roles in *The Life and Death of Colonel Blimp* (1943) and *Black Narcissus* (1947). She won a Best Actress Award from the New York Critics in 1947 for *Black Narcissus* and for Frank Launder* and Sidney Gilliat's* *I See a Dark Stranger* (1946). Offered a contract by MGM, she moved to Hollywood in 1949. She was nominated for the Best Actress Oscar for *Edward My Son* (1949), *From Here to Eternity* (1953, US), *The King and I*, *Heaven Knows, Mr Allison* (1957), *Separate Tables* (1958, US) and *The Sundowners* (1961, US/Australia). She was made a Fellow of the British Film Institute* in 1986. JC

Other Films Include: *Perfect Strangers* (1945); *King Solomon's Mines* (1950, US); *Quo Vadis* (1951, US); *Tea and Sympathy* (1956, US); *An Affair to Remember* (1957, US); *Bonjour Tristesse* (1958); *Beloved Infidel* (1959, US); *The Innocents* (1961); *The Night of the Iguana* (1964, US); *The Arrangement* (1969, US); *The Assam Garden* (1985).

KEUKEN, Johan van der
Amsterdam 1938

Dutch director, who proved his talent as a photographer at an early age before moving to Paris in 1956 to study at IDHEC*. He has been working in Amsterdam since 1960. While most of van der Keuken's films are non-fiction works made for television, they differ considerably from traditional documentaries. His work is firmly rooted in postwar modernism and developed in close affinity with experimental poetry, abstract expressionist painting and free jazz. Van der Keuken started with filmed portraits of modern poets, painters (*Een film voor Lucebert/A Film for Lucebert*, 1967) and jazz musicians (*Big Ben: Ben Webster in Europe*, 1967). His portrayals of a blind child in *Blind kind 1* (1964) and *Herman Slobbe: Blind kind 2* (1966) are gripping essays on the senses and how we imagine the world. *De tijd geest/The Spirit of the Time* (1968), a portrait of the 1960s, is a milestone in his development as well as a cinematic monument to the decade. Van der Keuken added a new element to his phenomenological approach when he introduced overt questions of ideology and politics into his films, as in *De snelheid 40–70/The Velocity 40–70* (1970). His preoccupation with the human condition on his doorstep expanded into a critical exploration of the global village as he began to travel widely. The relation between Europe and the Third World became a major theme, starting with the so-called North-South triptych: *Dagboek/Diary* (1972), *Het witte kasteel/The White Castle* (1973) and *De nieuwe ijstijd/The New Ice Age* (1974). But whatever their setting, van der Keuken's films are also contemplations on the state of our imagination in a changing culture, poetic comments on the function of our senses in the creation of identity, perhaps best shown in *Het oog boven de put/The Eye Above the Well* (1988) and *Bewogen koper/Brass Unbound* (1993). Van der Keuken's work is to some extent comparable to the radical project of the Russian film-maker Dziga Vertov* in the 1920s. Themes are arranged on the lines of a musical composition, in a finely structured collage of sounds and images. The soundtrack has an important function, particularly the music of Willem Breuker. Apart from his documentary work, van der Keuken has developed a strand of studio-made films, such as *Beauty* (1970), *De meester en de reus/The Master and the Giant* (1980) and *De Tijd/The Time* (1983). These staged and stylised fictions are less characterised by the poetic freedom of his other films but have the rigour of artistic manifestos. KD

Bib: Pauline Terreehorst, *Daar toen hier* (1988).

Other Films: *Paris à l'aube, Een zondag* (1960); *Yrrah, Tajiri, Opland, Lucebert: dichter, schilder* (1962); *Even stilte, De oude dame* (1963); *Indische jongen* (1964); *Beppie, Vier muren* (1965); *De poes* (1968); *Bert Schierbeek: De deur, Vietnam Opera, De muur, Het leesplankje* (1973); *Vakantie van de filmer* (1974); *De Palestijnen* (1975); *Voorjaar* (1976); *De platte jungle* (1978); *De weg naar het zuiden* (1981); *De beeldenstorm* (1982); *Speelgoed* (1984); *I Love Dollars, The Unanswered Question* (1986); *Face Value* (1991); *On Animal Locomotion* (1994).

KHANZHONKOV, Alexander A. [?] 1877 – Yalta, Crimea [USSR] 1945

Russian film producer. Khanzhonkov began importing films from France in 1906 and set up his own production company in 1908, concentrating mainly on Russian themes. He pro-

duced one of the first full-length feature films, *Oborona Sevastopolya/The Defence of Sebastopol* (1911), and employed most of the leading figures in pre-Revolutionary Russian cinema, including Evgeni Bauer*, Vera Kholodnaya*, Ivan Mosjoukine*, Lev Kuleshov* and Ivan Perestiani*. He became the major Russian film producer and his company owned cinemas and published film journals. In spring 1917 he moved to the Crimea for health reasons and later emigrated, returning, like Yakov Protazanov*, to work for Rusfilm (later Mezhrabpom*) in 1923. He became director of Proletkino, which, as its name implies, was supposed to produce films for the proletariat. When it failed, Khanzhonkov and others were charged with fraud in a sensational trial. He was never convicted but was thereafter forbidden to work in cinema as a 'disenfranchised person'. In 1934, on the fifteenth anniversary of Soviet cinema, he was rehabilitated and given a state pension. RT

KHEIFITS, Iosif E. [HEIFITS, Josef] Minsk, Belorussia [Russian Empire] 1905 – St Petersburg 1995

Soviet director and scriptwriter. Kheifits joined the Leningrad studios in 1928 and worked with Alexander Zarkhi on a Communist Youth League production brigade, making *Veter v litso/Wind in the Face* (1930) and *Polden'/Noon* (1931). Their best-known film in a long collaboration was undoubtedly *Deputat Baltiki/Baltic Deputy*, which portrayed the conversion of a professor to the revolutionary cause and won a Grand Prix at the 1937 Paris International Exhibition. Their other films included: *Chlen pravitel'stva/A Member of the Government* (1940), *Ego zovut Sukhe Bator/His Name is Sukhe Bator* (1942) and *Razgrom Yaponii/The Rout of Japan*, awarded a Stalin Prize in 1946. They achieved international recognition much later with three Chekhov adaptations: *Dama s sobachkoi/The Lady with the Little Dog* (1960), which won a prize at Cannes, *V gorode S/In the Town of S* (1967) and *Plokhoi khoroshii chelovek/The Duel* (1973). RT

KHOKHLOVA, Alexandra S. Berlin, Germany 1897 – Moscow 1985

Soviet actress and teacher, who began working in cinema in 1916, when she met her lifelong companion Lev Kuleshov*. Khokhlova studied at the State Film School (where she later taught, after it had become VGIK*) from 1919, and between 1920 and 1923 was a leading participant in the 'Kuleshov collective', appearing in his *Na krasnom fronte/On the Red Front* (1920). She appeared in most of his subsequent films, with leading roles in *Luch smerti/Death Ray* (1925), *Po zakonu/By the Law* (1926) and *Velikii uteshitel'/The Great Consoler* (1933), but is best remembered for her distinctive performance as the Countess in his *Neobychainye priklyucheniya Mistera Vesta v strane bol'shevikov/The Extraordinary Adventures of Mr West in the Land of the Bolsheviks* (1924). She exemplified the school of 'model' acting that Kuleshov tried to develop and was held up by Sergei Eisenstein* as a fitting contrast to the Hollywood female stereotype. RT

KHOLODNAYA, Vera V. Poltava, Ukraine [Russian Empire] 1893 – Odessa, Ukraine 1919

Russian actress. Trained as a ballerina at the Bolshoi, Kholodnaya began making films in 1914. After her appearance in Yevgeni Bauer's* *Pesn' torzhestvuyushchei lyubvi/ The Song of Love Triumphant* (1915), she became the most popular actress in pre-Revolutionary Russian cinema. She made five more films with Bauer, including *Deti veka/ Children of the Age* (1915) and her greatest screen triumph, *Zhizn' za zhizn'/A Life for a Life* (1916). Her portrayal of women's sadness and suffering gave her immense popularity in a Russia torn apart by war and revolution. In the summer of 1918, while filming in Odessa, Kholodnaya fell victim to the epidemic of Spanish influenza sweeping Europe. The funeral for this 'queen of the screen', as her contemporaries hailed her, was a Russian equivalent to the later obsequies for Rudolf Valentino in Hollywood. RT

KHUTSIEV, Marlen M. Tbilisi, Georgia [USSR] 1925

Russian director and scriptwriter. Khutsiev began work as an assistant director at the Tbilisi studios in 1944 and in 1952 he graduated from Igor Savchenko's* workshop at VGIK*. He directed his first film, *Vesna na Zarechnoi ulitse/Spring in Zarechnaya Street*, in 1956, and in 1959 made *Dva Fëdora/The Two Fyodors*, which saw Vasili Shukshin's* debut as an actor. Khutsiev's masterpiece is *Zastava Il'icha/The Ilyich Gate* (Ilyich is the patronym of Lenin), also known as *Mne dvadtsat' let/I am Twenty*, co-scripted with Gennadi Shpalikov. Work on this portrait of 1960s youth continued over five years, from 1959 to 1964, with constant harassment from the Soviet censors, and in the face of the disapproval of Khrushchev himself, who denounced the film in March 1963 for its failure to represent young people as builders of a Communist society. The version of the film which, as *Mne dvadtsat' let,* won the Special Jury Prize in Venice in 1964 had ninety minutes removed (including whole sections). The full film was not restored and shown until 1989, after a 1987 decision of the Conflict Commission set up by the Union of Cinematographers*. Despite his problems with *Zastava Il'icha*, Khutsiev made another film devoted to young people, *Iyul'skii dozhd'/July Rain*, in 1967, followed in 1970 by the war film *Byl mesyats mai/It Was the Month of May*, and in 1971 by the documentary *Alyi parus Parizha/The Red Sail of Paris*. In 1976, after the death of Mikhail Romm*, he joined Elem Klimov* and G. N. Lavrov in completing Romm's *I vsetaki ya veryu/And Nonetheless I Believe*, followed by *Posleslovie/Postscript* in 1983. His most recent project, also made over several years, is *Beskonechnost'/Infinitas* (1991). JGf

KIEŚLOWSKI, Krzysztof Warsaw 1941

Polish director. A distinctive voice in Polish cinema, known for his uncompromising moral stance, Kieślowski first came to attention in the early 1970s for his incisive (often shelved) documentaries and shorts on the political reality of life in Poland. His features of the late 1970s explored the relationship between the personal and the political with style, directness and a raw edge of realism, making him a key figure in the 'cinema of moral unrest'. Although the authorities banned *Przypadek/Blind Chance* (1981), Kieślowski was undeterred and made *Bez Końca/No End* in 1984. In the late 1980s he turned to television, directing *Dekalog*, a series of ten films thematically inspired by the Ten Commandments. The international release of one of these, *Krótki Film o Zabijaniu/A Short Film About Killing* (1988), and the subsequent massive success of the whole series, was greeted with surprise by Polish critics, who compared *Dekalog* unfavourably with Kieślowski's earlier work. His next feature, *Podwójne Życie Weroniki/The Double Life of Véronique* (1992), was a co-production between the Tor Film Unit and French producers; it enjoyed critical and commercial success, especially in France. Kieślowski's latest (and according to him, last) work is a trilogy based on the French flag: 'liberty' (*Trois couleurs Bleu/Three Colours: Blue*, 1993), 'equality' (*Trois couleurs Blanc/Three Colours: White*, 1993) and 'fraternity' (*Trois couleurs: Rouge/Three Colours: Red*, 1994). They have secured for Kieślowski – hailed as 'the most truly European director' – a place in the pantheon of European art cinema. AW

Bib: Danusia Stok, *Kieślowski on Kieślowski* (1993).

KILLANIN, (Lord) Michael Born 1914

Irish film producer. Though Lord Killanin's career covers an exceptionally broad range of activities, from journalist in China in the 1930s to President of the International Olympic Commission during one of its most turbulent times, the Moscow Olympics, his role as go-between and producer with John Ford in particular is of considerable importance. Befriending Ford in Hollywood in the 1930s, in part because he was from the same area of County Galway as Ford's ancestors, he acted as local liaison in Ireland during the making of *The Quiet Man* (1952). Killanin, with Ford and Tyrone Power, formed Four Provinces Films, with the intention of producing films in Ireland. Their first project was Ford's *The Rising of the Moon* (1957), but Power died shortly after its completion, thus effectively ending the partnership, though Killanin produced Ford's *Gideon's Day* (1958), a Scotland Yard story. He was also associate producer on *Young Cassidy* (1964), part of which was directed by Ford, and was co-producer of Brian Desmond Hurst's* *The Playboy of the Western World* (1962). Killanin's son, Redmond Morris, also works in film, having been associate producer of Thaddeus O'Sullivan's* *December Bride* (1990) and co-producer of Neil Jordan's* *The Miracle* (1991). KR

KINO REFORM MOVEMENT

German film movement. Cinema reform movements flourished in most European countries in the first decades of this century. In Germany one can distinguish two attempts by the cultural establishment (one around 1907, the other immediately after World War I, mainly represented by teachers and the clergy) to contain the nefarious influence of the new mass medium, seen to reside in its reliance on fiction and explicit body-language. However, the 'Kinematographische Reformvereinigung', founded in Berlin in 1907, had ultimately a rather ambivalent attitude towards the cinema: while it professed to protect women and children, whose exposure to narrative was regarded as a danger to public morality, the reformers were keen to enlist film as an educational tool in all manner of causes. In numerous pamphlets and articles (many published in the journal *Bild und Film* (1912–15) leading refomers such as Herrmann Häfker (born in Bremen 1873, died at the Mauthausen concentration camp in 1939) and Konrad Lange (1855–1921) tried to steer a path between advocating prohibition (fearing the power of moving images to incite imitation) and preventive measures (trusting the soothing effects of nature films, documentaries and uplifting patriotic subjects). An ambitious eight-volume monograph series, *Lichtbühnen-Bibliothek* (1913–15), also put forward the case for nationalising the film industry. Although this advice remained unheeded, the movement's regional associations were strong enough to produce and exhibit suitably 'cultural' films [> DOCUMENTARY (GERMANY)], and to lobby successfully for censorship and the protection of minors. Politically, reformers saw in the cinema the product of 'international capital' threatening the traditional values of the nation. One strategy advocated was to pre-empt the 'smut-merchants' by adapting literary works and persuading reputable stage actors to get involved in making films, paralleling the more commercially minded motives of the so-called *Autorenfilm* to widen audience appeal by addressing the middle-class viewer. The success of the *Autorenfilm* took the wind out of the reformers' sails, at least until the abolition of censorship in 1918 brought the first wave of sex films, when they were able to mount an effective parliamentary lobby, which led to the reintroduction of censorship in 1921. JG/MW/TE

Bib: Sabine Hake, *The Cinema's Third Machine: Writing on Film in Germany 1907–1933* (1994).

KINSKI, Klaus   Nikolaus Günther Nakszynski;
Zoppot, East Prussia (now Poland) 1926 –
Lagunitas 1991

German actor, whose expressive features, mannerisms and impossibly wide grin took him from subordinate parts in B-movies (such as the Edgar Wallace series), where he was typecast as a psychopathic eccentric, to art cinema stardom, via a stint as favourite villain in Italian Westerns*. After more second-rate productions in Italy and France, he was cast as the mad Spanish conquistador in Werner Herzog's* *Aguirre, der Zorn des Gottes/Aguirre, Wrath of God* (1972), which began a five-film collaboration that was to last until their parting quarrel in 1987 during the filming of *Cobra Verde* (1988). As the criminal, sex-mad director of a California health farm in Billy Wilder's *Buddy, Buddy* (1981), Kinski was able to combine the salient elements of all his acting careers. His daughter Nastassja Kinski (born 1961) has become an inter-

national film star, in such films as Roman Polanski's* *Tess* (1979) and Wim Wenders'* *Paris, Texas* (1984). TE

Bib: Philippe Rege, *Klaus Kinski* (1987).

Other Films Include: *A Time to Love and a Time to Die* (1958, US); *Das Geheimnis der gelben Narzissen/The Devil's Daffodil* (1961); *Der schwarze Abt, Das indische Tuch* (1963); *Winnetou, II Teil* (1964); *Doctor Zhivago* [US], *Per qualche dollari in più/For a Few Dollars More* (1965, It./Sp./Ger.); *Il grande silenzio* (1968, It.); *L'Important c'est d'aimer* (1974, Fr.); *Un genio, due compari, un pollo* (1975, It.); *Kinski – Paganini* (1989).

KIRKOV, Ljudmil   Vraca 1933

Bulgarian director, respected for his social themes and an ability to make films a young audience could easily identify with. After graduating from the Sofia Academy of Dramatic Art (VITIS), Kirkov enrolled in 1959 for a course in film direction at Moscow's VGIK* under Mikhail Romm*. After two insignificant feature films, he hit his stride with *Švedski krale/Swedish Kings* (1968), a social comedy contrasting Western tourists on the Black Sea coast with the native working class.

Kirkov's best films were made in collaboration with scriptwriter Georgi Mišev*: *Momčeto si otiva/A Boy Becomes a Man* (1972) and its sequel *Ne si otivaj!/Don't Go Away!* (1976) are about a youth coming of age; *Seljaninăt s koleloto/Peasant on a Bicycle* (1974) and *Matriarhat/Matriarchy* (1977) are nostalgic perspectives on fading village life. Kirkov also collaborated with dramatist-scriptwriter Stanislav Stratiev on three contemporary themes with a strong moral message: *Kratko slănce/Brief Sunlight* (1979), *Orkestăr bez ime/A Nameless Band* (1982), and *Ravnovesie/Balance* (1983). RH

KJÆRULFF-SCHMIDT, Palle   Esbjerg 1931

Danish director, who started directing in the theatre in 1953 and in film in 1957. *Bundfald/Dregs*, his first film, was a social melodrama about urban male prostitution. 1962 saw his breakthrough with *Weekend*, the story of seven friends, three married couples and a single man, who spend a weekend in the country. *Weekend* was influenced by the French New Wave*, attempting to capture reality without a strong plot line through unstudied performances from the actors. In form and content it was radically different from other Danish films. *Der var engang en krig/Once There Was a War* (1966), about the German occupation as seen through the eyes of a teenage boy, is still considered one of the best films on the subject. In the 1970s Kjærulff-Schmidt worked for Danish television. He returned to film in 1984, and made two films – *Tukuma* (1984) and *Peter von Scholten* (1987) – though they did not have the same appeal as his earlier works. ME

KLEIN-ROGGE, Rudolf Cologne 1888 – Graz, Austria 1955

German actor, originally from the stage, who obtained his first minor roles on screen in 1919. He appeared in a number of films by Weimar directors such as Franz Osten and Friedrich Zelnik, but is remembered for his impressively demonic villains in the title roles of Fritz Lang's* *Dr Mabuse, der Spieler/Dr Mabuse, the Gambler* (1922) and *Das Testament des Dr Mabuse* (1933), as well as for characters in other Lang films: the cruel Chinese emperor of *Der müde Tod/Destiny* (1921), King Etzel in *Die Nibelungen* (1924), Rotwang in *Metropolis* (1927), and Haighi in *Spione* (1928). Increasingly relegated to supporting roles – for instance in the Emil Jannings* star vehicles *Der alte und der junge König* (1935), *Der Herrscher* (1937) and *Robert Koch, der Bekämpfer des Todes* (1939) – Klein-Rogge seemed unable to add new dimensions to the screen image created by Lang. MW

KLERCKER, Georg af Kristianstad 1877 – Malmö 1951

Swedish director and actor. Long eclipsed by the greater renown of Victor Sjöström* and Mauritz Stiller*, the very prolific Klercker has lately come to be recognised as an important figure in Swedish silent film. He abandoned a military career for the stage. In 1911 he was hired by Svenska Bio*, where he acted and directed before moving to Göteborg in 1915 to work for Hasselblad*. Among his notable films, *Dödshoppet från cirkuskupolen/The Death Ride Under the Big Top* (1912), *Kärleken segrar/Love Will Conquer* (1916) and *Mysteriet natten till den 25:e/The Mystery of the Night Before the 25th* (1917) are conventional stories but skilfully made in the international melodramatic tradition of the time. Remarkable cinematography together with innovative formal devices, such as the use of off-screen space, mark Klercker's originality as a director. LGA/BF

Other Films Include: *Två bröder/Two Brothers, Jupiter på jorden/Jupiter on Earth* (1912); *Med vapen i hand/Weapon in Hand, Skandalen/The Scandal, Ringvall på äventyr/Ringvall in Search of Adventure* (1913); *För fäderneslandet/For the Fatherland* (1914); *Rosen på Tistelön/The Rose of Thistle Island, I kronans kläder/In Uniform* (1915); *I minnenas band/Tied to One's Memories, De pigorna, de pigorna!/Those Servant Girls, Those Servant Girls!, Högsta vinsten/The First Prize, Calles nya kläder/Calle's New Clothes, Ministerpresidenten/The Ministerial President, Svärmor på vift/Mother-in-law on the Spree, Calle som miljonär/Calle as a Millionaire, Trägen vinner eller Calle som skådespelare/Perseverance Does It or Charlie as an Actor, Nattens barn/Children of the Night, Fången på Karlstens fästning/The Prisoner at Karlsten Fort, Ur en foxterriers dagbok/From the Diary of a Fox Terrier, Aktiebolaget Hälsans Gåva/'Gift of Health' Ltd., Bengts nya kärlek eller Var är barnet?/Bengt's New Love/Where is the Child?, Vägen utför/The Way Downhill* (1916); *Mellan liv och död/Between Life and Death* (1917); *I mörkrets bojor/In the Fetters of Darkness, Förstadsprästen/The Suburban Vicar, Löjtnant Galenpanna/Lieutenant Madcap, För hem och härd/For Home and Hearth, Brottmålsdomaren/The Judge, Det finns inga gudar på jorden/There Are No Gods on Earth, Revelj/Reveille* (1917); *Nattliga toner/Night Music, Nobelpristagaren/The Nobel Prize Winner, Fyrvaktarens dotter/The Daughter of the Lighthouse Keeper* (1918); *Flickorna på Solvik/The Girls of Solvik* (1926).

KLIMOV, Elem G. Stalingrad, Russia [USSR] 1933

Russian director. After studies at the Higher Institute of Aviation, Klimov worked as an engineer and as a journalist before studying in the workshop of Efim Dzigan at VGIK*, graduating in 1964. His first two features, the satirical comedies *Dobro pozhalovat', ili postoronnim vkhod vospreshchen/Welcome, or No Unauthorised Admittance* (1964), set in a summer camp for Young Pioneers, and *Pokhozhdeniya zubnogo vracha/Adventures of a Dentist* (1965), set in a provincial town, both encountered censorship difficulties. *Sport, sport, sport* (1971) combined factual and feature material. *Agoniya/Agony*, Klimov's epic survey of the baleful influence of Rasputin on the last years of the tsarist regime, though completed in 1975, was not released in Russia until 1984. After the death of Mikhail Romm*, Klimov and Marlen Khutsiev* completed his film *I vse-taki ya veryu/And Nonetheless I Believe* (1976), a strident survey of negative aspects of twentieth-century life. In 1980 Klimov made *Larisa*, a short documentary about his wife, the director Larisa Shepitko*. His next project was *Proshchanie/Farewell* (1981), an anguished version of Valentin Rasputin's 1976 story about the flooding of a Siberian village, begun by Shepitko and taken over by Klimov after her untimely death. Like most of Klimov's films, it was initially shelved, this time because its desperate ecological warning did not please the Soviet authorities. *Idi i smotri/Come and See* (1985) is a savage epic about Nazi atrocities in Belorussia during World War II. Klimov was elected new First Secretary of the Soviet Union of Cinematographers* in May 1986, and he spent the following years presiding over the renewal of the Union and the industry. At the end of the decade he worked on a projected film of Mikhail Bulgakov's novel *The Master and Margarita*, but his plans did not come to fruition and the novel was eventually filmed by Yuri Kara. JGf

KLOPČIČ, Matjaž Ljubljana, Slovenia 1934

Slovene director, scriptwriter, art director and critic. After studying architecture, Klopčič began directing short films in 1959. His first feature, *Zgodba, ki je ni/On the Run/Non-existing Story* (1967), clearly influenced by the French New Wave*, established him as a typical *auteur*. In his later films, especially *Oxygen* (1970) and *Strah/Fear* (1974), he successfully deployed unusual narrative strategies, building up an impressive personal universe of split personalities and identity problems. While French critical acclaim (he was 'discovered' by *Positif** and the La Rochelle festival) opened the door to several important festivals, he seduced the Slovene public with a classical adaptation (both for film and television) of a famous Ivan Tavčar story, *Cvetje v jeseni/Autumn Flowers* (1973), about a tragic love affair between an elderly lawyer and a young country girl. *Iskanja/Search* (1979), based on a travel diary by Slovene writer Izidor Cankar, can be considered Klopčič's film manifesto: beautifully shot in Venice (by Tihomir Pinter), the film is full of metaphysical contemplations on art and life. Klopčič now teaches at the Ljubljana Film Academy, as well as writing for *Ekran** and occasionally directing for television. SP

Other Films: *Na papirnatih avionih/Paper Planes* (1967); *Sedmina/Funeral Feast/Regards to Maria* (1969); *Vdovstvo Karoline Žašler/The Widowhood of Karolina Žašler* (1976); *Dediščina/Heritage* (1984); *Moj ata, socialistični kulak/My Dad, the Socialist Kulak* (1988).

KLOS, Elmar – see KADÁR, Ján

KLUGE, Alexander   Halberstadt 1932

German director, who practised law before entering the cinema as assistant on Fritz Lang's* *Der Tiger von Eschnapur/ The Tiger of Bengal* and *Das indische Grabmal/The Indian Tomb* (both 1959) and director of art documentaries. From 1962, when he helped to draft the Oberhausen Manifesto [> NEW GERMAN CINEMA], Kluge became the chief ideologue of the Young and New German Cinema* whose success is difficult to conceive without his manifold activities.

One of the first post-Oberhausen films to obtain state subsidy and international recognition was Kluge's *Abschied von gestern/Yesterday Girl* (1966). Like all his best-known films, from *Die Artisten in der Zirkuskuppel: ratlos/Artists at the Top of the Big Top: Disorientated* (1968) to *Der Angriff der Gegenwart auf die übrige Zeit/The Blind Director* (1985), *Abschied von gestern* reveals a complex principle of narrative construction that uses the frictions (*Reibungen*) and fractions (*Bruchstellen*) – two of Kluge's favourite metaphors – between fragments of verbal and (audio)visual speech (public records, news, quotations, found footage) to produce distancing effects. A constant reference point in Kluge's films is the need to 'work on our history', carried over into his collective projects: *Deutschland im Herbst/Germany in Autumn* (1978), *Der Kandidat/The Candidate* (1980), *Krieg und Frieden/War and Peace* (1983), and culminating in *Die Patriotin/The Patriot* (1979). Kluge's film work is part of a larger cultural project encompassing political activism, fiction writing and television programmes, not to mention comprehensive sociological research published in collaboration with Hellmut Becker and Oskar Negt between 1961 and 1992. MW

Bib: Stuart Liebman, 'Alexander Kluge', *October*, no. 46 (1988).

Other Films Include: *Die unbezähmbare Leni Peickert/The Indomitable Leni Peickert* (1970); *Der große Verhau/The Big Dust-up* (1971); *Der starke Ferdinand/The Strong Ferdinand* (1976); *Die Macht der Gefühle/The Power of Emotion* (1983); *Vermischte Nachrichten* (1986).

KNEF, Hildergard [in US: NEFF, Hildegarde]   Ulm 1925

German actress whose adventurous life and career took her from Russia to Hollywood, and from draughtswoman for Ufa's* special effects department to Broadway. Her acting career began in earnest with Germany's first postwar film produced by DEFA*, *Die Mörder sind unter uns/The Murderers are Amongst Us* (1946). She created a sensation as a new type of *femme fatale*, more matter-of-fact and less sultry than Marlene Dietrich*, but also a complete break from the preferred erotic ideal of the Nazi entertainment film. After a (brief) nude appearance in *Die Sünderin/The Sinner* (1951) made her notorious, David Selznick brought her to Hollywood, with mixed results. Starring in German, French and British films, opposite Hans Albers,* Erich von Stroheim, Tyrone Power, Gregory Peck and others, she became one of the best-known European actresses of the 1950s and 1960s. Her film successes were complemented by stage appearances, for instance in the Broadway musical *Silk Stockings* (based on Lubitsch's* *Ninotchka*), but Knef also shone as a cabaret singer and wrote a best-selling autobiography. TE/SG

Other Films Include: *Zwischen gestern und morgen* (1947); *Fahrt ins Glück* (1948); *Decision Before Dawn* (1950, US); *Nachts auf den Straßen, Diplomatic Courier* [US], *The Snows of Kilimanjaro* [US], *Alraune, La Fête à Henriette* [Fr.] (1952); *The Man Between* (1953, UK); *Caterina di Russia* (1962. It.); *Landru* (1963; Fr.); *Jeder stirbt für sich allein* (1976); *Fedora* (1978, US); *Flügel und Fesseln/The Future of Emily* (1984, Ger./Fr.).

KOERFER, Thomas   Berne 1944

German-Swiss director. A graduate in economics, Koerfer began his film career as a volunteer with Alexander Kluge* at the Ulm Film Institute and with Brunello Rondi in Rome. From camera operator and editor on television documentaries he advanced to contributor on a political television magazine before making his first feature film, the Brechtian parable *Der Tod des Flohzirkusdirektors oder Ottocaro Weiss reformiert seine Firma* (1973). The use of intertitles, rhetorical commentaries, medium and long shots by Renato Berta*, interspersed with literary and philosophical disquisitions, made the film a textbook example of anti-illusionism. Thanks to a strong emphasis on performance, *Der Tod des Flohzirkusdirektors* established Koerfer as the most prolific intellectual talent among the young German-Swiss directors. He continued to pursue his complex and imaginative politics of form in variations on musical (*Konzert für Alice*, 1985) and literary themes from Robert Walser (*Der Gehülfe*, 1976), Rousseau, Voltaire (*Alzire oder der neue Kontinent*, 1978) and Gottfried Keller (*Der Grüne Heinrich*, 1993). While his films have been attacked as hermetic and cerebral, Koerfer has also tried his hand at more popular subjects in the big-budget family saga *Glut* (1983) and the road movie *Exit Genua* (1990). MW

Other Films Include: *Die Leidenschaftlichen* (1982); *All Out* (1990); *Die Liebe zum Tode* (1991).

KOKANOVA, Nevena
Stanke Dimitrov 1937

Bulgarian actress. A popular stage and screen actress, Kokanova is considered the 'first lady' of Bulgarian cinema. Having made her initial appearance on the screen as a nineteen-year-old in Jianko Jiankov's *Godini za ljubov/Years of Love* (1957), she achieved international fame in Vălo Radev's* *Kradetsăt na praskovi/The Peach Thief* (1964), in which she plays a prison commandant's wife who falls tragically in love with a Yugoslav POW. Married to actor-director Ljubomir Šarlandjiev, Kokanova appeared in almost all his films as the lead actress; upon his sudden death in 1979, she completed his last production: *Trite smărtni grjaha/Three Deadly Sins* (1980). RH

KOMOROWSKA, Maja
Warsaw 1937

Polish actress, originally trained with the world-famous experimental theatre director and theorist, Jerzy Grotowski. His approach to performance, emphasising the physical and the expression of emotion, clearly informs her work. She has worked closely with Krzysztof Zanussi*, notably in his early film *Bilans Kwartalny/Quarterly Balance/A Woman's Decision* (1975) and more recently in *Rok Spokojnego Słońca/The Year of the Quiet Sun* (1986). With her haunted and melancholy eyes and an air of physical and emotional vulnerability, Komorowska is typically cast as a victim of fate, as in Tadeusz Konwicki's* *Jak Daleko Stąd Jak Blisko/So Far, So Near* (1972), or as a willing female martyr. Komorowska is a popular and respected actress who works in theatre and television as well as film. She lectures at the Warsaw Drama School. AW

KONCHALOVSKY, Andrei – see MIKHALKOV-KONCHALOVSKY, Andron

KONINKLIJK FILMARCHIEF VAN BELGIE – see CINÉMATHÈQUE ROYALE DE BELGIQUE

KONWICKI, Tadeusz
Nowa Wilejka, Lithuania 1926

Polish writer and director. Konwicki is one of Poland's best known and highly regarded modern novelists. He was born in a small village near Vilnius, historical capital of Lithuania, then part of Poland but in the postwar period in the Soviet Union. The evocation of this homeland became a central theme in Konwicki's novels and films. For some time after the war his novels followed the style of Socialist Realism*, but with the post-1956 political and cultural liberation he employed a more individual style which attracted the disapproval of the authorities. His involvement in film dates back to the 1950s when he was literary head of the Kadr Film Unit and collaborated on screenplays for films such as *Matka Joanna od Aniołów/Mother Joan of the Angels* (1961) by Jerzy Kawalerowicz*. He made his directorial debut with *Ostatni Dzień Lata/The Last Day of Summer* (1958). An intimate and melancholy story about a chance meeting between a man and woman at the end of the war, the film was internationally acclaimed and won a prize at Venice in 1958. Konwicki's films offer personal reflections on the individual, and yearn for the mythical Lithuanian homeland of Polish literature. In *Jak Daleko Stąd Jak Blisko/So Far, So Near* (1972) Konwicki questioned the morality of war, creating a world where there was no 'absolute right' and individuals bore responsibility for their own actions. It was the first Polish film to take this critical standpoint. Other Polish directors have turned to Konwicki's novels for inspiration, most notably Andrzej Wajda*, who filmed *Kronika Wypadków Miłosnych/A Chronicle of Love Affairs* in 1986. AW

Other Films (as Director/Scriptwriter) Include: *Dolina Issy/The Issa Valley* (1982); *Lawa/Lava* (1989).

KORDA, (Sir) Alexander
Sándor László Kellner; Puszta Turpósztó, Hungary 1893 – London 1956

British producer and director of Hungarian origin. Korda entered the film industry in his native Hungary, where he directed his first film in 1914. After arrest under the Horthy regime, he fled to Vienna in 1919. He continued producing in Austria and Germany and spent three undistinguished years in Hollywood, before moving to Paramount's subsidiary in Paris in 1930, where he notably directed the classic *Marius* for Marcel Pagnol*. In 1932, he arrived in Britain, where he founded London Films, and worked with his brothers, Zoltan and Vincent*.

London Films' first features were 'quota quickies', but in 1933 Korda himself directed the hugely successful *The Private Life of Henry VIII*. The film cost £60,000 to make and grossed £500,000 in its first international run. In the US it broke box-office records for first-day admissions at Radio City Music-hall. This set Korda's course, a course which was decidedly bumpy in financial terms but pre-eminent in influence. He built Denham Studios near London in 1935 (though he was forced to sell in 1938). The same year he was made a partner, with Chaplin, Pickford and Fairbanks, in United Artists. During the war, he shuttled between Britain and America. Karol Kulik, in her biography of Korda, suggests that he may have been acting as a special envoy for his friend Winston Churchill, a task for which his knighthood in 1942 may have been the reward. He resumed directing briefly after the war, revamped London Films, which was responsible for such films as *The Third Man* (1949), *The Tales of Hoffmann* (1951), *Hobson's Choice* (1954) and *Richard III* (1955), took a controlling interest in British Lion in 1946 until it went into receivership in 1954, and founded the British Film Academy in 1947.

Like John Grierson*, Korda is less important for the individual films he directed or produced than for the influence he exerted and the context he framed. Like Grierson also, the influence is open to debate. Korda was determined that the British cinema should be an international cinema, and to be international it had to compete with Hollywood. Hence the rocky financial road. At the same time, he recognised that 'to be truly international a film must first of all be truly and intensely national', and hence the important careers which he encouraged, the projects he initiated, and the opportunities which he created. JC

Bib: Karol Kulik, *Alexander Korda: The Man Who Could Work Miracles* (1975).

Other Films Include: As Director (UK unless indicated) – *Tutyu és Totyo* (1914, Hung.); *Eine Dubarry von heute/A Modern Dubarry* (1927, Ger.); *The Private Life of Helen of Troy* (1927, US); *Service for Ladies, Wedding Rehearsal* (1932); *The Private Life of Don Juan* (1934); *Rembrandt* (1936); *That Hamilton Woman/Lady Hamilton* (1941, US); *Perfect Strangers* (1945); *An Ideal Husband* (1948). **As Producer** – *Catherine the Great* (1934); *The Scarlet Pimpernel* (1935); *Sanders of the River, The Ghost Goes West, Things to Come, The Man Who Could Work Miracles* (1936); *I, Claudius* [uncompleted], *Elephant Boy, Knight Without Armour* (1937); *The Divorce of Lady X, The Drum* (1938); *The Four Feathers, The Lion Has Wings* (1939); *Conquest of the Air* (1936–40), *The Thief of Bagdad* (1940); *Jungle Book* (1942, US); *Anna Karenina* (1948).

KORDA, Vincent
Puszta Turpósztó, Hungary 1897 – London 1979

British art director of Hungarian origin, who was an accomplished painter, studying in Budapest and Paris, before being brought to Denham Studios by his older brother, Alexander. He designed most of the memorable Korda productions of the 1930s, including *The Private Life of Henry VIII* (1933), *Things to Come* (1936) and, his masterpiece, *Rembrandt* (1936). He worked with Zoltan Korda on *Sanders of the River* (1935), *Elephant Boy* (1937) and *The Drum* (1938), and won an Oscar for *The Thief of Bagdad* (1940). Korda's designs are never simply backgrounds, and particularly in *Things to Come* and *The Third Man* (1949) they show the influence of his painterly training and of his interest in European modernism, expressionism and art deco. JC

Other Films Include: *Marius* (1931, Fr.); *The Girl from Maxim's* (1933); *Catherine the Great, The Private Life of Don Juan* (1934); *The Scarlet Pimpernel, Moscow Nights* (1935); *The Ghost Goes West, The Man Who Could Work Miracles* (1936); *The Spy in Black, The Lion Has Wings* (1939); *Lady Hamilton* (1941); *To Be or Not to Be, Jungle Book* (1942, both US); *Perfect Strangers* (1945); *An Ideal Husband, The Fallen Idol* (1948); *Outcast of the Islands* (1951); *The Sound Barrier* (1952); *Summer Madness, The Deep Blue Sea* (1955); *The Yellow Rolls-Royce* (1964).

KORNGOLD, Erich Wolfgang
Brünn (Brno), Czechoslovakia 1897 – Hollywood, California 1957

Bohemian-born composer of modern opera (*Die tote Stadt*), who toured as a conductor and in 1931 was named professor of music at the Akademie der Schönen Künste in Vienna. His second career as one of the great Hollywood composers started inconspicuously with his Strauss arrangements for Alfred Hitchcock's* *Waltzes from Vienna* (1934), continued with a Mendelssohn adaptation for *A Midsummer Night's Dream* (dir. Max Reinhardt* and Wilhelm Dieterle*, 1935, US), and finally earned him a generous contract with Warner Bros. Korngold received his first Oscar in 1936 for the score of *Anthony Adverse*, and his second for *The Adventures of Robin Hood* (1938). His film music was both an effective background for dramatic action and, where necessary, serious music in its own right, as with his 'Cello concerto in C-major, op. 37', featured in *Deception* (1946). From 1946, he composed again for concert halls in Europe while keeping his job in Hollywood. KU

Bib: Brendan G. Carroll, *Erich Wolfgang Korngold* (1984).

Other Films Include: *Captain Blood* (1935); *Give Us This Night* (1936); *The Private Lives of Elizabeth and Essex* (1939); *The Sea Wolf* (1941); *Devotion* (1943); *Between Two Worlds* (1944).

KORTNER, Fritz
Vienna 1892 – Berlin 1970

Austrian-born German actor and director, who appeared in films from 1915 and become a star in F. W. Murnau's* *Satanas* (1920), Reinhold Schünzel's* *Katharina die Große/Catherine the Great*, 1920), Carl Froehlich's* *Die Brüder Karamasoff/ The Brothers Karamasov* (1920) and Paul Leni's* *Hintertreppe/Backstairs* (1921, co-dir. Leopold Jessner). His virtuoso acting and use of changing facial expressions were best demonstrated as Dr Schön in G. W. Pabst's* *Die Büchse der Pandora/Pandora's Box* (1929), which made him one of the foremost German screen personalities. With the coming of sound, Kortner impressed with his voice in E. A. Dupont's* *Atlantic/Atlantik* (1929) and *Menschen im Käfig/Cape Forlorn* (1930), both multi-language films shot in Britain. Attacked by the Nazi press for being Jewish, Kortner emigrated to London. In 1941 he settled in Hollywood as a scriptwriter and character actor in films mostly with anti-fascist subjects (*The Strange Death of Adolf Hitler*, 1943; *The Hitler Gang*, 1944; *Berlin Express*, 1948). A naturalised American citizen since 1947, Kortner returned to Germany the same year to appear in Josef von Baky's* *Der Ruf/The Last Illusion* (1949). He soon regained his prewar prestige as an actor and director for cinema, theatre and television. MW

Bib: Walter Kaul and Robert G. Scheuer (eds.), *Fritz Kortner* (1970).

Other Films Include: *Manya, die Türkin, Im Banne der Vergangenheit* (1915); *Der Märtyrer seines Herzens* (1918); *Die Nacht der Königin Isabeau* (1920); *Beethoven, Maria Stuart* (1927, two parts); *Dreyfus* (1930); *Danton, Der Mörder Dimitri Karamasoff, Der brave Sünder* (1931); *Abdul the Damned* (1935, UK); *The Razor's Edge* (1946, US); *Sarajewo* (1955).

KOSMA, Joseph
Budapest, Hungary 1905 – Paris 1969

French composer of Hungarian origin. Kosma trained and worked in Budapest and Berlin, where he was influenced by Bertolt Brecht, Hanns Eisler and Kurt Weill, before moving to Paris in 1933. His meeting with Jacques Prévert* was decisive. Together they produced a huge number of songs, some of them for the films of Jean Renoir* (*Le Crime de Monsieur Lange*, 1935) and Marcel Carné* (*Les Portes de la nuit*, 1946), Kosma working in hiding during the war. He said, 'I put Jacques Prévert's poems to music without changing a comma – it was not easy but my enthusiasm for his poetry helped me surmount many technical obstacles.' Kosma's music contributed greatly to the identity and popularity of Poetic Realism*. He also composed scores for many films by Renoir, Carné and others, and wrote ballets, oratorios and an opera. GV

KOSMORAMA

Danish film magazine, published by Det Danske Filmmuseum (the Danish Film Museum) since 1954. The title is a tribute to the first permanent Danish cinema, which opened in Copenhagen in September 1904. In layout and contents, *Kosmorama* resembles the pre-1991 British *Sight and Sound** and the Swedish *Chaplin**. Initially published every two months, it has been a quarterly since 1975. In the early 1990s, *Kosmorama* had over 1,000 subscribers and sold 2,000 copies. ME

KOUNDOUROS, Nikos
Agios Nikolaos, Crete 1926

Greek director. Koundouros was the first major director to emerge from Greece. His life has been marked by political persecution: he spent four years in the Makronissos concentration camp after the civil war of 1946–49 and went into exile during the military dictatorship of 1967–74. His first film, *Mayiki poli/Magic City* (1954), set in a shanty district of Athens, was influenced by Italian neo-realism*. In 1956 he made *O drakos/The Ogre of Athens*, his best film and one of the greatest of Greek films. A bitter expressionistic comedy, it is a damning and poignant critique of the state of Greek politics and culture. Its commercial failure, despite international acclaim, was a blow for Koundouros' career. His next film, *I paranomi/The Outlaws*, was banned a week after its release and subsequently shown only at international festivals. In 1963 Koundouros won the Best Direction Award at the Berlin Film Festival for *Mikres Afrodites/Young Aphrodite*. Since his return to Greece in 1974, he has been prominent in Greek cinema both as director and as activist. Noting a tendency towards over-exaggeration, however, critics have given his later films mixed reviews. TN

Other Films: *To potami/The River* (1960); *Vortex i to prossopo tis Medoussa/Face of the Medusa* (1970); *Ta tragoudia tis fotias/Songs of Fire* (1974); *1922* (1978); *Bordel* (1985); *Byron, ballada ya ena demonismeno/Byron, Ballad for a Man Possessed* (1992).

KOVÁCS, András
Chidea, Romania 1925

Hungarian director. In the 1960s and 1970s, Kovács played an important role in Hungarian cinema both as a director and as president of the Association of Hungarian Film-makers, a vital organisation that mediated between political power and film-makers. He moved to Hungary from Romania in 1946 and graduated from the Academy of Theatre and Film Art in 1950. Between 1951 and 1957 he headed the Central Script Department of MAFILM, the state production company.

Kovács made his first film, *Zápor/Summer Rain*, in 1960, and his most important films were produced during this decade. His style is generally characterised by tight narrative structures and an abundance of dialogue; he also brought *cinéma-vérité** to Hungary in the 1960s. *Nehéz emberek/Difficult People* (1964) consists of parallel interviews based on part-fictional situations drawn from the lives of five Hungarian inventors who find it difficult to get their inventions approved by the authorities. Kovács' early films reveal a commitment to the idea that cinema should be the social and historical conscience of the nation. In his most important work, *Hideg napok/Cold Days* (1966), he deals with the atrocities committed by Hungarian fascists against Serbs and Jews during the war and raises the question of personal responsibility for historical events. During the 1970s, Kovács continued to make documentaries and *cinéma vérité*-type films, focusing on the political rigidity of the period and the powerlessness of socially conscious people. Though in the 1980s Kovács turned to more personal topics (such as the life of the wife of Count Károlyi, the first president of the Hungarian republic), in his latest film, *Két választás Magyarországon/Two Elections in Hungary* (1987), he returned to the more controversial political themes of his early works, here dealing with the abuse of the Hungarian parliamentary elections in 1985. KAB

Other Films Include: *Pesti háztetők/On the Roofs of Budapest, Isten őszi csillaga/Autumn Star* (1962); *Falak/Walls* (1968); *Extázis 7-10-ig/Ecstasy from 7 to 10* (1969); *Staféta/Relay Race* (1970); *A magyar ugaron/Fallow Land* (1972); *Bekötött szemmel/Blindfold* (1975); *Labirintus/Labyrinth* (1976); *A Ménesgazda/The Stud Farm* (1978); *Októberi vasárnap/A Sunday in October* (1979); *Ideiglenes paradicsom/Temporary Paradise* (1980); *Szeretők/Lovers* (1983); *A vörös grófnő/The Red Countess* (1985).

KOZINTSEV, Grigori M.
Kiev, Ukraine [Russian Empire] 1905 – Leningrad 1973

Soviet director and writer, who studied art with Alexandra Exter in Kiev and became involved in the production of street theatre after 1917. Kozintsev moved to Petrograd in 1920 and in 1921 co-founded FEKS with Leonid Trauberg*, with whom he worked closely until 1945, initially in theatre and from 1924 in cinema. Their joint films began with *Pokhozhdeniya*

Oktyabriny/The Adventures of Oktyabrina (1924) and ended with *Prostye lyudi/Simple People* (1945, released 1956). Whereas Trauberg's subsequent career as a film-maker went into severe decline, Kozintsev went on to make two biographical films, *Pirogov* (1947) and *Belinskii/Belinsky* (1953), and an adaptation of Cervantes' *Don Quixote* (1957), with Nikolai Cherkasov* in the title role. This prepared Kozintsev for the Shakespeare adaptations that initiated his international reputation: *Gamlet/Hamlet* (1964), starring Innokenti Smoktunovsky*, and *Korol'Lir/King Lear* (1971). Kozintsev also taught in various institutions, including VGIK* from 1922 until 1971, and published widely. His books include *Nash sovremennik Vil'yam Shekspi* (1962), published in English as *Shakespeare: Time and Conscience* (1966); *Prostranstvo tragedii* (1973), translated as *The Space of Tragedy* (1977); and *Glubokii ekran* ('The Deep Screen'). RT

KRABBÉ, Jeroen A.   Amsterdam 1943

Dutch actor and painter. After his education at the Amsterdam academy of dramatic art and some small film parts, Jeroen Krabbé entered the public eye in Paul Verhoeven's* *Soldaat van Oranje/Soldier of Orange/Survival Run* (1977). His charming looks and suave manner made him the 'ideal son-in-law' in light comedy, but he performs with equal facility in dramatic roles. He starred in other Dutch features such as Ate de Jong's *Een vlucht regenwulpen/A Flight of Curlews* (1981), but his role in Verhoeven's *De vierde man/The Fourth Man* (1983) made his international reputation. He moved to the USA and played major parts in Hollywood pictures such as *Jumpin' Jack Flash* (1986), *Crossing Delancey* (1989) and *Prince of Tides* (1991), and British films such as *Turtle Diary* (1985), the James Bond* film *The Living Daylights* (1987) and *Scandal* (1989), while continuing to appear in Dutch movies. KD/FW

Other Dutch Films: *Fietsen naar de maan* (1962); *Alicia* (1974); *Martijn en de magiër, Een pak slaag/Mr Slotter's Jubilee* (1979); *Spetters/Hunks* (1980); *Het verleden* (1982); *In de schaduw van de overwinning* (1986); *Sahara Sandwich* (1991); *Voor een verloren soldaat , Oeroeg* (1993).

KRACAUER, Siegfried   Frankfurt 1889 – New York 1966

German theorist, who published on a wide range of cultural phenomena. Between 1920 and 1933 Kracauer was also one of Weimar Germany's major film critics and cultural affairs editor of the renowned *Frankfurter Zeitung*. Kracauer was the first to analyse film from a sociological perspective, grounded on his extensive research in problems of epistemology (*Soziologie als Wissenschaft*, 1922) and class analysis (*Die Angestellten*, 1930). He left Germany for Paris in March 1933, and in 1941 fled occupied France to settle in the US. A commission to analyse Nazi film propaganda (*Propaganda and the Nazi War Film*, 1942) led to a comprehensive psychological history of German film, the influential *From Caligari to Hitler*

(1947), which argues that changes in style and content of Weimar* cinema resulted from changes in the psychological disposition of the nation's key social formation, the middle-class male. Frequently criticised for rigidity of method and selectivity of evidence, *From Caligari to Hitler* has nonetheless remained the classic account of the relationship between film and society in general.

Kracauer's *Theory of Film: The Redemption of Physical Reality* (1960) may one day claim the same position in the development of film theory*, but his posthumously published book on photography and history (*Of History: Last Things Before the Last*, 1967) has also renewed interest in his work. TE/MW

Bib: Thomas Y Levin (ed.), *Siegfried Kracauer* (1992).

KRÄLY, Hanns [US: KRALY, Hans]   Hamburg 1895 – Los Angeles, California 1950

German scriptwriter, who worked with Ernst Lubitsch* on all his German films and later followed him to Hollywood. His comic effects and brilliant dialogue full of Berlin humour contributed greatly to the erotic charm of Lubitsch's early Ossi Oswalda* and Pola Negri* pictures as well as to the sophisticated flair of Warner comedies such as *Three Women* (1924), *So This Is Paris* (1926) and *The Patriot* (1928). The collaboration with Lubitsch ended with *Eternal Love* (1929), and Kräly subsequently worked as the scenarist for Jacques Feyder's* *The Kiss* (1929) and co-wrote the story for Henry Koster's *It Started With Eve* (1941), before retiring in 1943. MW

KRAUSS, Werner   Gestungshausen 1884 – Vienna 1959

German actor, who entered the film business early in 1916 and appeared in popular genres such as sex education films (*Aufklärungsfilme*), detective stories, and melodramas. Krauß' fame began with Robert Wiene's* *Das Cabinet des Dr. Caligari/The Cabinet of Dr. Caligari* (1920), where he played the (mad?) Dr. Caligari. Although in many of his subsequent roles he continued to portray enigmatic and troubled figures (as in the Freudian melodrama *Geheimnisse einer Seele/Secrets of a Soul*, 1926), Krauß' various parts as the depressive gate-keeper in *Scherben/Shattered* (1921), Jack the Ripper in *Das Wachsfigurenkabinett/Waxworks* (1924), Scapinelli in *Der Student von Prag/The Student of Prague* (1926), and the lecherous butcher in *Die freudlose Gasse/Joyless Street* (1925) show a commendable range and resist typecasting. He also appeared as Count Muffat in Jean Renoir's* *Nana* (1926). A favourite actor of G. W. Pabst* and one of the most typical faces of the Weimar* cinema, he remained prominent during the Nazi era, playing a leading role in the infamous *Jud Süss/Jew Süss* (1940, dir. Veit Harlan*). The three films he starred in after the war were unremarkable. MW

Bib: Wolfgang Goetz, *Werner Krauß* (1954).

KRAUZE, Antoni   Warsaw 1940

Polish director, who studied Fine Art and was active in the Students' Satirical Theatre before graduating from Łódź* in 1966. He was assistant to Krzysztof Zanussi* on *Struktura Kryształu/The Structure of Crystal* (1969). Krauze was involved in the documentary movement of the late 1960s which gave rise to the 'cinema of moral unrest'. His debut feature, *Palec Boży/The Finger of God* (1973), the story of an individual's fight against the system in pursuit of his ambition to be an actor, is based on an autobiographical novel by Tadeusz Zamechura. Krauze's great talent for comedy was revealed in his second feature, *Prognoza Pogody/Weather Forecast* (1983). Set in an old people's home, this farce manages to avoid cliché while making both serious and hilarious points about the Polish welfare state. The film fell foul of the authorities and was shelved during the period of martial law. Krauze had to wait until the political thaw of the late 1980s to make his next film, *Dziewczynka z Hotelu Excelsior/Girl from the Hotel Excelsior* (1988), about the holiday romances and obsessions of a middle-aged couple at a seaside health spa. AW

KRÜGER, Hardy   Eberhard Krüger; Berlin 1928

German actor, with an international reputation. While still at school, Krüger was chosen to play in the propaganda film *Junge Adler* (1944). His first postwar film was *Diese Nacht vergeß' ich nie* (1949). Typecast as an easy-going teenager, he seemed unable to make his mark until *Solange du da bist* (1953). Dissatisfied with offers from German directors, he sought work abroad. His international career, unusually for a German actor, began in 1956 with the British war film *The One That Got Away* (1956). Under the direction of Joseph Losey*, Howard Hawks, Robert Aldrich and David Attenborough*, he profiled himself as an experienced character actor, often portraying taciturn, strong-minded protagonists. From 1961 onwards, Krüger occasionally worked as producer and director of nature and wildlife documentary films, but seems to have kept aloof from the next generation, since he appeared only once in a film of the New German Cinema*. TE/SG

Other Films Include: *Blind Date/Chance Meeting* (1959, UK); *Hatari!* (1960, US); *Les Dimanches de Ville d'Avray* (1962, Fr.); *The Flight of the Phoenix* (1965, US); *Barry Lyndon* [UK], *Potato Fritz* (1975); *A Bridge Too Far, The Wild Geese* (1977, both UK); *Blue Fin* (1979, Australia).

KUBELKA, Peter   Vienna 1934

Austrian director, who studied film at the Akademie für Musik und darstellende Kunst in Vienna and at the Centro Sperimentale* in Rome. Kubelka made his first film, *Mosaik im Vertrauen* (1955), in collaboration with Ferry Radax, before he developed in *Adebar* (1957), *Schwechater* (1958) and *Arnulf Rainer* (1958–60) what he called '*Metrischen Film*' ('metric film'), a radical technique that at times reduces the image to black and white abstract frames, anticipating later structuralist films. But his works are also very much *sound films*, and the soundtrack of *Arnulf Rainer* cannot be 'turned off' any more than its images, whose 'rhythm' is intended to penetrate even closed eyelids. The apparently more realistic *Unsere Afrikareise* (1961–66) is also built on a complex montage structure. Here, images record multiple 'systems' – white hunters, natives, animals, buildings – in a manner that preserves their individuality, but at the same time the editing of sound and image brings these systems into comparison and collision. In *Pause!* (1975–77), the artist Arnulf Rainer is once again the source of the film's imagery. Since the mid-1990s Kubelka has been working on *Denkmal für die alte Welt*. Kubelka's complete works, elaborated over twenty-five years, would not run for much longer than an hour. He was co-founder of the Austrian Filmmuseum in 1964 and assistant film librarian at the UN archive in New York. He is a member of the New York Film-makers Cooperative. MW

Bib: Christian Lebrat, *Peter Kubelka* (1990).

KUBRICK, Stanley   New York 1928

American director, who has made films in both Britain and America since the early 1960s, moving to England in 1974. The move was precipitated by a mixture of anglophilia and a desire for greater creative freedom, but unlike his compatriot Joseph Losey*, Kubrick has remained an American director in exile rather than a British or European director. *Lolita* (1962) and *2001: A Space Odyssey* (1968), though technically British films, are American in their conception; and *Barry Lyndon* (1975), based on a Thackeray novel, loses the sense of Thackeray's Englishness in an overlush visual style. Only the brilliant *A Clockwork Orange* (1972), from an Anthony Burgess novel, has a great deal to say about Englishness, projecting it to a futuristic decadence with a glossy, hard-edged violence which provoked the anxiety of the British Board of Film Censors*. JC

KULESHOV, Lev V.   Tambov, Russia 1899 – Moscow 1970

Soviet director and theorist. After studying art, Kuleshov joined Alexander Khanzhonkov's* studio in 1916 and worked as set designer for Yevgeni Bauer*. His first film as director was *Proekt inzhenera Praita/Engineer Prait's Project* (1918), which displayed elements of Constructivist machine worship. During the Civil War, he made newsreels and a feature combining documentary and acted footage, *Na Krasnom fronte/On the Red Front* (1920). In 1919 he organised his own workshop, the 'Kuleshov collective', at the State Film School (later VGIK*), which included Boris Barnet* and Vsevolod Pudovkin*. Since there was no film stock, they practised their ideas in a series of experiments called 'films without film' and developed the notion of the 'Kuleshov effect' in which, through montage*, each shot acquired a different shade of meaning according to its place in the sequence. But Kuleshov never believed in Sergei Eisenstein's* notion of 'typage', preferring instead to train actors or, as he called them, 'models' (*naturshchiki*), aiming for maximum screen expressivity with minimum gesture and effort. These ideas were further developed in *Neobychainye priklyucheniya Mistera Vesta v strane bol'shevikov/The Extraordinary Adventures of Mr West in the Land of the Bolsheviks* (1924), starring Alexandra Khokhlova*. Kuleshov next made a science-fiction film, *Luch smerti/Death Ray* (1925), and the Gold Rush drama *Po zakonu/By the Law/Dura Lex* (1926). His first sound film was *Velikii uteshitel'/The Great Consoler* (1933), a work of extraordinary complexity: superficially a biographical study of the American writer O. Henry, it examined the role of the artist in society, with clear implications for the Soviet artist under the new guidelines of Socialist Realism*. Subsequently his film-making career declined and his last film was *My s Urala/We Are from the Urals* (1944), but he continued to teach at VGIK until his death. Kuleshov was also a prolific writer, the first to use the term montage and to use it to define the specificity of cinema: his books include *Iskusstvo kino* ('The Art of Cinema', 1929), *Repetitsionnyi metod v kino* ('The Rehearsal Method in Cinema') and *Praktika kinorezhissury* ('The Practice of Film Direction', both 1935), and *Osnovy kinorezhissury* ('The Foundations of Film Direction', 1941). Kuleshov was the founding father of Soviet cinema: Pudovkin once remarked, 'We make films, Kuleshov made cinema.' RT

Bib: R. Levaco (ed., trans.), *Kuleshov on Film: Writings of Lev Kuleshov* (1974).

KULIDZHANOV, Lev A.   Tbilisi, Georgia [USSR] 1924

Soviet director. Kulidzhanov graduated from VGIK*, where he had studied with Sergei Gerasimov*, in 1955. His first film, *Damy/Ladies* (1955), based on Chekhov, was co-directed with G. Oganisyan. Among his later films were *Dom, v kotorom ya zhivu/The House I Live in* (1957), which extols the heroism of the mundane life of those far from the front during World War II, *Otchii dom/My Father's House* (1959), and *Kogda derev'ya byli bol'shimi/When the Trees Were Big* (1962). *Sinyaya tetrad'/The Blue Notebook* (1964) is about Lenin's life before the Russian Revolution. In 1969 Kulidzhanov made a version of Dostoyevsky's novel *Prestuplenie i nakazanie/Crime and Punishment*. The feature documentary *Zvezdnaya minuta/The Starry Minute* (1975) is about space flight and the first Soviet cosmonaut Yuri Gagarin. It was followed by the TV film *Karl Marks: Molodye gody/Karl Marx: The Early Years* (1980). Kulidzhanov's main claim to fame, however, is as one of the leading cinematic bureaucrats of the Brezhnev years, and proponent of the conservative tendency in Soviet cinema. The range of positions of authority that he occupied is indicative of the symbiotic relationship between the Soviet state and its 'loyal' artists. He was First Secretary of the Union of Cinematographers* of the USSR from 1965 until he was ousted in 1986, served as a deputy on the Supreme Soviet for several years, and was, after 1976, a candidate member of the Central Committee of the Communist Party of the USSR. He was the recipient of several official prizes and awards. JGf

KÜMEL, Harry   Antwerp 1940

Belgian director, who learned film-making by experimenting with his father's 8mm camera and co-founded the Filmgroup 58 (later Fugitive Cinema*). His *Anna la Bonne* (1958), based on a poem by Cocteau*, was awarded a prize at the Cannes amateur film festival. Several successful shorts followed, as well as documentaries made for BRT (Dutch-speaking public television) where he made pioneering cinema programmes. He left to work for the VPRO (Netherlands) television channel in 1967 and taught at the film school in Amsterdam. In 1968 he produced his first feature, *Monsieur Hawarden*, a Dutch-Belgian co-production. Kümel is best known internationally for his reworkings of the fantastic genre in the early 1970s, especially his idiosyncratic vampire film *Le Rouge aux lèvres/Les Lèvres rouges/Daughters of Darkness* (1971), starring Delphine Seyrig*, and his adaptation of Jean Ray's novel, *Malpertuis, histoire d'une maison maudite/Malpertuis* (1972). His subsequent work, including erotic tales, has been varied but less prominent internationally; in Belgium it has provoked a mixed reception, from unqualified enthusiasm to overt dismissal, especially in the case of *Eline Vere* (1991). SS

Other Films Include: *De komst van Joachim Stiller/The Return of Joachim Stiller* (1976); *The Secrets of Love* (1986).

KUOSMANEN, Mirjami   Keuruu 1915 – Helsinki 1963

Finnish actress and scriptwriter, known for her work in the 1940s and 1950s with her husband Erik Blomberg*. Though Kuosmanen is often credited solely as actress and co-writer, she also directed actors and dialogue scenes, with Blomberg responsible for technical aspects. Kuosmanen's first main roles were in *Miehen tie/The Way of Man* (1940) and *Yrjänän emännän synti/The Sin of the Mistress of Yrjänä* (1943). These established an openly sensual, even sexual image which was reinforced by many minor roles in the 'fallen woman' films of the 1940s. Critics used words such as 'lusty' and 'down-to-earth' to describe her tall, dark, proud presence, finding an interesting combination of sexuality and naturalness in her screen personality. In *Yrjänän emännän synti* she plays a wealthy farmer's daughter 'whose hips are crying out for a baby' which she cannot conceive because of her husband's infertility. She picks up the most handsome young man in the village, seduces him on midsummer's night and gets pregnant. Her husband (played by Edvin Laine*) cannot accept the baby until he rescues him from drowning in the nearby rapids. The theme of female sexuality is further developed in Kuosmanen's films of the 1950s, most of which she wrote with Blomberg. The best-known of these is *Valkoinen peura/The White Reindeer* (1953), in which she plays a Lapp woman who becomes a wild white deer, seducing and killing men. AK

KUREISHI, Hanif — London 1954

British writer and director, who scripted two of the most successful Channel 4* films of the 1980s: *My Beautiful Laundrette* (1985) and *Sammy and Rosie Get Laid* (1987), both directed by Stephen Frears*. *My Beautiful Laundrette* was a surprise success in both Britain and America, winning Kureishi an Oscar nomination for Best Screenplay. Centring on a mixed-race gay relationship in a Pakistani-owned laundrette, it ironically dissects the multicultural structure of Thatcherite London. *Sammy and Rosie*, less admired by the critics, offers a bleaker account of Britain in the context of the Brixton riots. In 1991, Kureishi directed *London Kills Me* (1991), a Dickensian fable of London street life and drug-dealing, from his own screenplay. His novel *The Buddha of Suburbia* (1990) has been dramatised by the BBC (first shown 1993). JC

KURKVAARA, Maunu — Viipuri 1926

Finnish director and producer. With Jörn Donner*, Risto Jarva*, Erkko Kivikoski, Mikko Niskanen*, Jaakko Pakkasvirta* and Eino Ruutsalo, Kurkvaara was one of a group of prominent Finnish film-makers who espoused the new trends running through European film in the late 1950s and early 1960s. Although they never properly constituted a Finnish 'New Wave'*, these film-makers nevertheless produced work in which the influence of modern European cinema is clearly identifiable. Kurkvaara was not satisfied with his first feature, *Onnen saari/Island of Happiness* (1954), re-releasing it two years later under the title *Ei enää eilispäivää/No More Yesterdays,* though the remake made little more impact than the original. His next film was the fantasy, *Tirlittan/Tweet Tweet* (1958), followed by *Patarouva/The Queen of Spades* (1959) and *Autotytöt/Car Girls* (1960). A stylistic change occurred in 1961 with *Rakas.../Darling...* (1961), a love story reflecting New Wave stylistic influences. The studio-based, producer-dominated cinema of the earlier decades in Finland was coming to an end and *auteurs* coming to the fore. Kurkvaara was one of the first of these new figures: he owned a small production company for which he wrote, photographed, directed and edited his own films. HS

KURYS, Diane — Lyons 1948

French director. Kurys was a stage and film actress before directing her first film, *Diabolo menthe/Peppermint Soda* (1977), an account of her adolescence in Paris in the late 1960s. A great popular and critical success, it contained the major elements of her work to come: naturalistic style, light humour based on social observation, an eye for period detail and the ability to rework aspects of her own life for a wide audience. However, *Cocktail Molotov* (1980), *Un homme amoureux/A Man in Love* (1987; an international production with Claudia Cardinale*) and *Après l'amour* (1992), though also reflecting personal concerns, did less well. Kurys' most successful films have been those which returned to her child-hood: *Coup de foudre/Entre Nous/At First Sight* (1983) and *La Baule-les-Pins/C'est la vie* (1990). *Coup de foudre*, with Isabelle Huppert* and Miou-Miou*, found a wide international audience for its seductive treatment of a close female friendship. Although Kurys refuses the label 'woman director', finding it 'negative, dangerous and reductive', the strength of her work is in exploring the family and emotions from a female-centred perspective. *A la folie* (1994), also about female friendship and starring the explosive duo of Anne Parillaud and Béatrice Dalle*, is a surprising and not altogether satisfying foray into a darker mood. GV

KUSTURICA, Emir — Sarajevo, Bosnia-Herzegovina 1955

Bosnian film director. The most successful film-maker of the former Yugoslavia. Awards for his amateur films during high school led him to the FAMU* film school in Prague, and his third-year film *Guernica* gained first prize at the 1977 Karlovy Vary* film festival. After two films for Sarajevo television (*Nevjeste dolaze/The Brides are Coming*, 1978, and *Buffet Titanic*, 1980), he was given his first chance to shoot a feature in 1981. His debut was a triumph: *Sjećaš li se Dolly Bell?/Do You Remember Dolly Bell?* (1981), a story of Sarajevo teenagers sampling the first taste of pop culture in the 1950s, was awarded the Golden Lion at Venice. With his second film, *Otac na službenom putu/When Father was away on Business* (1985), he stayed in Sarajevo but went back in time to 1948, mixing the political (Tito's break with Stalin) with a picturesque portrayal of old family traditions falling apart. Winning the 1985 Palme d'Or at Cannes and an Oscar nomination for Best Foreign Language Film established Kusturica as a film-maker of international standing. He turned down interesting offers in order to shoot *Dom za vešanje/Time of the Gypsies* (1989) in his typical slow-motion way: the production took almost two years. The film won the 1989 Best Director award at Cannes and established Kusturica as an 'oneiric' film-maker. Miloš Forman* invited him to teach at Columbia University in New York, where he turned a student's original screenplay into *Arizona Dream* (1993), dreamt up mostly for French money and combining his own stylistic tics with rather bizarre casting (Jerry Lewis, Faye Dunaway). His pro-Yugoslav position during the war in Bosnia made him 'unwanted' in his native city, Sarajevo. Kusturica now lives in Paris and directs European co-productions, such as *Bila jednom jedna zemlja/Once Upon a Time There was a Country/Il était une fois un pays*, a German-French co-production shot in Prague in 1994. SP

KUTZ, Kazimierz — Szopienice, Silesia 1929

Polish director. Kutz started his prolific career as assistant to Andrzej Wajda* on *Pokolenie/A Generation* (1955). One of the 'Polish School', his early features drew on his adolescence and on the war experience. In his debut feature, *Krzyż Walecznych/Cross of War* (1959), he linked three stories by Joseph Hen about society coming to terms with the end of the war. Kutz is best known for his 'Silesian' trilogy – *Sól Ziemi*

Czarnej/Salt of the Black Country (1970), *Perła w Koronie/ The Pearl in the Crown* (1972) and *Paciorki Jednego Różańca/ The Beads from a Rosary* (1980) – in which he examines different aspects of his native region and its long, troubled history (there have been disputes over ownership of Silesia, in western Poland on the border with Germany, for centuries). Kutz has worked extensively for theatre and television, as director of the Cracow Television Centre. His current cinema project is a film about the killing of striking miners in the Wujek mine by the authorities, a tragic postscript to the Silesian trilogy. AW

KVIRIKADZE, Irakli M.   Tbilisi, Georgia [USSR] 1939

Georgian director and scriptwriter. Kvirikadze studied in Grigori Chukhrai's* workshop at VGIK* (graduating in 1970), where he returned to teach in 1985. He wrote the scripts for his own films, including the short *Kuvshin/The Jar* (1971), *Gorodok Anara/The Little Town of Anara* (1976), *Plovets/The Swimmer* (1981) and *Vozvrashchenie Olmelsa/ The Return of Olmels* (1985), and for such films as *Robinzonada, ili moy angliiskii dedushka/Robinsonada, or My English Grandfather* (1987), directed by his wife, Nana Dzhordzhadze, and Valeri Ogorodnikov's* *Bumazhnye glaza Prishvina/Prishvin's Paper Eyes*. His most important film, *Plovets*, a tragi-comedy of great lyrical beauty, uses the experience of three generations of Georgian swimmers seen in 1913, 1947 and 1980, both to present a pointed allegory of life under three political regimes and to question our ability to represent the past adequately. It was shown in a version bereft of much of the central Stalin section, and not released as Kvirikadze made it until 1987. Kvirikadze returned to the subject of Stalin in 1991 with *Puteshestvie Tovarishcha Stalina v Afriku/Comrade Stalin Goes to Africa*. JGf

L

LADOIRE, Oscar   Oscar Ladoire Montero; Madrid 1954

Spanish actor, who came to films via film studies and critical writing for the journal *Casablanca*. A member of the 'Escuela de Madrid' generation [> COMEDY (SPAIN)], he mainly appears in *progre* (liberal) roles in these films. His radical image is expressed through a dishevelled appearance, distracted air and droopy mouth. Films as diverse as Fernando Trueba's* *Opera prima* (1980), Juan José Bigas Luna's* *Las edades de Lulú/The Ages of Lulú* (1990) and Fernando Colomo's* *Alegre ma non troppo* (1994) have also cast him as an individual trapped by the conflicting impulses of sexual desire. PWE

LAINE, Edvin   Iisalmi 1905 – Helsinki 1989

Finnish actor, director, scriptwriter and producer. Edvin Laine was one of the most productive craftsmen in Finnish cinema. Like many, he came to film from the theatre where he had been both actor and director. He continued to work in both theatre and film all his life. *Yrjänän emännän synti/The Sin of the Mistress of Yrjänä* (1943) was his first picture as director. He quickly became T. J. Särkkä's* favourite filmmaker, apparently most at home in melodramas, though he worked in other genres too: social realism (*Yhden yön hinta/The Price of One Night*, 1952), fantasy (*Prinsessa Ruusunen/Sleeping Beauty*, 1949), crime (*Kultainen kynttilänjalka/The Golden Candlestick*, 1948), folk comedy (*Aaltoska orkaniseeraa/Aaltonen's Missus Takes Charge*, 1949), and historical epic (*Sven Tuuva/Soldier Sven*, 1958). After the war Laine's films, which popularised national literature, played a key role in revising the historical notion of Finnish identity. He adapted all Väinö Linna's novels for the screen and directed three Niskavuori* films based on Hella Wuolijoki's dramas. His best-known film is *Tuntematon sotilas/The Unknown Soldier* (1954), based on Linna's novel – at the time the most expensive Finnish production. It was the third film, after Risto Orko's* *Siltalan pehtoori/The Steward of Siltala* (1934) and Särkkä's *Kulkurin valssi/The Vagabond's Waltz* (1941), to attract more than a million spectators in Finland alone. *Tuntematon sotilas* is also the most widely exported Finnish film, shown in more than forty countries. Särkkä tried to channel the money that *Tuntematon sotilas* brought to SF into new productions. Laine continued to adapt Linna's work with *Täällä Pohjantähden alla/Here Under the Northern Star* (1968) and *Akseli ja Elina/Akseli and Elina* (1970). These films can be considered the Finnish equivalent of Bertolucci's* *1900*: a family saga which deals with key events in the history of Finland from the beginning of the twentieth century to the end of World War II. HS

Other Films Include: *Ristikon varjossa/In the Shadow of the Prison Bars* (1945); *Laitakaupungin laulu/Song of the City Outskirts* (1948); *Musta rakkaus/Black Love, Niskavuori taistelee/Niskavuori Fights* (1957); *Myöhästynyt hääyö/The Delayed Wedding Night, Skandaali tyttökoulussa/Scandal in the Girls' School* (1959); *Akaton mies/How to Find a Wife for a Farmer* (1983).

LAMAČ, Karel also Karl or Carl; Prague [then Austria-Hungary] 1897 – Hamburg, West Germany 1952

Czech actor and director. Karel Lamač originally studied as a pharmacist, produced film reportage during the World War I, and subsequently gained employment as a film technician. Admired for his 'matinee idol' good looks, he was first famous as an actor, then as a prolific and cosmopolitan director, working, according to some estimates, on over 200 films. He built the independent Kavalírka film studios in 1926, and in conjunction with his then wife Anny Ondra* formed the Ondra-Lamač company in Berlin in 1930. Lamač directed the first two films based on Hašek's *The Good Soldier Švejk* in 1926: *Dobrý voják Švejk/The Good Soldier Švejk* and *Švejk na frontě/Švejk at the Front*. Working regularly in Western Europe, particularly Germany, he also made numerous multi-language versions and popular light comedies starring Vlasta Burian* and Ondra. During World War II, he directed features in Britain. PH

Films Include: *Gilly po prvé v Praze/Gilly's First Visit to Prague* (1920); *Chyt'te ho!/Catch Him!, Bílý ráj/The White Paradise* (1924); *Karel Havlíček Borovský* [co-d], *Lucerna/The Lantern* (1925); *Velbloud uchem jehly/Camel Through the Needle's Eye* (1926); *Saxophon Susi* (1928, Ger.); *Das Mädel mit der peitsche/The Girl with the Whip* (1929, Ger.); *On a jeho sestra/He and His Sister, Die Fledermaus* (1931, Fr.); *Funebrák, Leliček ve službách Sherlocka Holmese/Leliček in the Service of Sherlock Holmes, Baby* [Fr.] (1932); *Die Tochter des Regiments/Daughter of the Regiment* (1933, Aust.); *Polská krev/Polish Blood, Klein Dorrit/Little Dorrit* [Ger.], *Knock-Out* [Ger.] (1934); *Der Hund von Baskerville/The Hound of the Baskervilles* (1936, Ger.); *They Met in the Dark* (1943, UK); *It Happened One Sunday* (1944, UK); *La Colère des Dieux/Anger of the Gods* (1946, Fr.); *Die Diebin von Bagdad/The Thief of Bagdad* (1952, Ger.).

LAMBETI, Elli Elli Loukou; Attica 1926 – New York 1983

Greek actress. Lambeti was one of the major stage actresses of postwar Greece. Making her debut in 1942 at the age of fifteen, she continued to appear in the theatre, despite a long illness, until her death. Her screen debut was in *Adouloti sklavi/Unsubdued Slaves* (1946, dir. V. Papamihail), a resistance film. Her film career was mainly confined to the 1950s. She gave the impression of fragile sensitivity, combining a quiet charm with intense feelings of inner warmth. Her screen persona veered between realism and movie-star glamour. Her most memorable roles were in three of Michael Cacoyannis'* 1950s films: *Kiriakatiko xipnima/Windfall in Athens* (1954), *To koritsi me ta mavra/The Girl in Black* (1956) and *To telefteo psema/A Matter of Dignity* (1957). TN

Other Films Include: *Matomena Hristougenna/Bloody Christmas* (1951); *Kalpiki lira/The Counterfeit Coin* (1955).

LAMPREAVE, Chus María Jesús Lampreave; Madrid 1930

Spanish actress, playing increasingly important supporting roles. Early on identified with Luis García Berlanga* (*El verdugo/The Executioner*, 1963) and Marco Ferreri* (*El pisito/The Little Flat*, 1958), she has achieved greater prominence in the 1980s with a string of films, above all for Pedro Almodóvar* – *Entre tinieblas/Dark Habits* (1983), *¿Qué he hecho yo para merecer esto?/What Have I Done to Deserve This?* (1984), *Matador* (1986). She has also appeared in comedies such as Fernando Colomo's* *La vida alegre/A Happy Life* (1987) and Fernando Trueba's* *Sé infiel y no mires con quién/Be Wanton and Tread No Shame* (1985). Her strange, 'spinsterish' appearance lends itself well to benignly transgressive roles. PWE

LAMPRECHT, Gerhard Berlin 1897–1974

German director, who in the 1920s and 1930s was one of the mainstays of middle-class, middle-brow commercial cinema. Lamprecht's debut as director with *Es bleibt in der Familie* (1920) already revealed the theme connecting his oeuvre across different genres and political eras: a feel for characters in their social environment. He came to prominence as the adapter of Thomas Mann's *Die Buddenbrooks* (1923), but broke new ground with a number of *Problemfilme* ('social problem films') set in Berlin, also known as '*Milljöh*' or '*Zille*' films. For the Nazi regime he directed melodramas (*Barcarole*, 1935; *Die Geliebte*, 1939) and a biopic (*Diesel*, 1942). But Lamprecht remained a liberal with socialist sympathies, and after World War II he worked for DEFA*, making one of the best-known *Trummerfilme* 'ruin films' (*Irgendwo in Berlin/Somewhere in Berlin*, 1946). Intimate knowledge of Berlin is also the strength of his masterpiece, an adaptation of Erich Kästner's famous childrens' book *Emil und die Detektive/Emil and the Detectives* (1931).

From 1955 onwards, Lamprecht concentrated on his second career as a film historian and archivist: between 1962 and 1966 he ran the Deutsche Kinemathek (later Stiftung Deutsche Kinemathek), and between 1967 and 1970 compiled a ten-volume catalogue of German silent films (1903–31) which has remained the standard reference work for the period. TE/KU

Other Films Include: *Frauenbeichte* (1921); *Menschen untereinander* (1926); *Der schwarze Husar* (1932); *Der Spieler* (1938); *Meines Vaters Pferde* (1954).

LAMY, Benoît Arlon 1945

Belgian director. After several years of training, during which he worked alongside figures such as Pier Paolo Pasolini*, Pierre Laroche and Lucien Deroisy, Lamy became an independent writer/director/producer in the 1970s. He has produced and directed numerous short films and documentaries, with subjects as diverse as the religious divisions of an African community (*Ouagadougou, Sketches of Gods*, 1986) and lonely hearts advertisements (*Margrit Circus*, 1970).

Throughout his feature work, though, a consistency can be identified. *Home Sweet Home* (1973, which won awards in Moscow) and *Jambon d'Ardenne/Ham from the Ardennes* (1977) are both concerned with a clash between two communities, the staff and inmates of a retirement home in the former, and rival catering outfits in the latter – clear metaphors of Belgian cultural and linguistic divisions.

Lamy's mixing of professional with non-professional actors and his documentary observation of his cast invite comparisions with Paul Meyer*, yet ultimately his films are popular comedies, making use of local dialects (in *Home Sweet Home* both French and Flemish are spoken) and the Brussels humour popularised by Gaston Schoukens* in the 1930s–50s. In his most recent film, *La Vie est belle/Life is Rosy* (1987, co-written and directed by Ngangura Mweze), set in Zambia, this same comic formula prevails, with the addition of music. CF

LANDA, Alfredo   Alfredo Landa Areta; Pamplona 1933

Spanish actor. His film career, begun in 1962, has three stages. Firstly, as a supporting actor in minor films, with exceptions like Luis García Berlanga's* *El verdugo/The Executioner* (1963). Secondly, in innumerable and hugely popular comedies directed by Pedro Lazaga* or Mariano Ozores*, in which Landa was the 'ordinary' Spaniard of the late 1960s/early 1970s, motivated by voracious consumerism and sexual appetites, visually stressed by his beady eyes and full-fleshed cheeks – a character of such resonance that it became a trend known as '*Landismo*'. Thirdly, though still appearing in run-of-the-mill comedies, Landa has made more thoughtful ones which explore the softer, more congenial dimensions of his persona – Berlanga's *La vaquilla/The Heifer* (1985) and José Luis Borau's* *Tata mía/Dear Nanny* (1986) – as well as taking on dramatic roles in films like José Luis Garci's* *El crack/The Crack* (1980) and Mario Camús'* *Los santos inocentes/Holy Innocents* (1984). PWE

LANG, Fritz   Vienna 1890 – Beverly Hills, California 1976

German director, whose exceptional career in German and American cinema (with a short episode in France) spanned silent and sound film. Lang began as a scriptwriter for Joe May's* company, where he met his future wife and collaborator Thea von Harbou*. Joining Erich Pommer's* Decla in 1917 as a director, Lang applied a style at once austere and lyrical to romantic, sentimental, sensationalist and fantastic story material: *Der müde Tod/Destiny* (1921), *Die Nibelungen* (1924, two parts), *Metropolis* (1927), *Spione/The Spy* (1928). In his first German period (1919–33) he wrote most of his scripts, usually in collaboration with von Harbou. *Dr. Mabuse, der Spieler/Dr. Mabuse, the Gambler* (1922, two parts) is notable for its attempt to represent filmically psychological processes (in Mabuse's hypnotism of his victims); *Metropolis* (1927), the futuristic tale of a repressive technocratic society, is renowned for its special effects, its extravagant sets and even more extravagant budget, which caused

financial difficulties for Ufa*, while *M – Eine Stadt sucht ihren Mörder/M* (1931) subverts the conventional detective thriller by developing a deep psychological portrait of a serial killer and child molester. *Das Testament des Dr. Mabuse/The Testament of Dr. Mabuse* (1933) was banned by the Nazis and Lang emigrated to France, where he directed *Liliom* (1934, starring Charles Boyer*) before moving on to Hollywood.

Despite the success of his first American film, *Fury* (1936), Lang experienced some of the classic difficulties of European directors in Hollywood. Nevertheless he managed to build up a substantial career in America, working in different studios and genres, usually against established conventions. This is most noticeable in his Westerns: *The Return of Frank James* (1940), *Western Union* (1941) and especially *Rancho Notorious* (1952, with Marlene Dietrich*). He also contributed to the costume drama (*Moonfleet*, 1955) and the war film (*American Guerrilla in the Philippines*, 1950). His American career, however, is distinguished by his mastery of *film noir*, with films such as *Secret Beyond the Door...* (1948; his most underrated American film), *The Blue Gardenia* (1953), *The Big Heat* (1953) and the astonishingly Pirandellian *Beyond a Reasonable Doubt* (1956).

In 1958 Arthur Brauner invited Lang back to Germany to direct *Der Tiger von Eschnapur/The Tiger of Bengal* and *Das indische Grabmal/The Indian Tomb* (1959). Lang accepted, not least because he and von Harbou had written the script in 1920 for Joe May, who, breaking their agreement, had directed it himself. Another return to his earlier work, *Die Tausend Augen des Dr. Mabuse/The Thousand Eyes of Dr. Mabuse* (1960), concluded his work, although his final film gesture was to appear, as himself, in Jean-Luc Godard's* *Le Mépris/Contempt* (1963). WB

Bib: Stephen Jenkins (ed.), *Fritz Lang: The Image and the Look* (1981).

Other Films Include: *Die Spinnen/The Spiders* (two parts: 1919 and 1920); *Die Frau im Mond/Woman on the Moon* (1929); **In the US**: *You Only Live Once* (1937); *Man Hunt* (1941); *Hangmen Also Die!* (1943); *Ministry of Fear, The Woman in the Window* (1944); *Scarlet Street* (1945); *Clash By Night* (1952); *While the City Sleeps* (1956).

LANGLOIS, Henri   Smyrna [now Izmir], Turkey 1914 – Paris 1977

French film archivist. Although Georges Franju*, Jean Mitry and P. A. Harlé co-founded the Cinémathèque Française* (on 12 September 1936) with Langlois, it is the latter's personality which for better or worse was imprinted on the institution. Langlois' passion for the cinema and his catholic tastes created a collection of truly world dimensions. He collected everything – initially thanks to personal means – and in the early days notoriously stocked it anywhere he could (including, legend has it, in his bath). His priority of showing as many films as possible turned the Cinémathèque into a university for generations of film buffs and future film-makers, notably those of the New Wave*. But Langlois' lack of concern for administration and for conserving his prints clashed with the increasing professionalism of the Cinémathèque: when André Malraux, the Minister for Culture, tried to impose a new administrator in 1968 and film personalities flew to Langlois' defence, they were defending a romantic notion of cinephilia rather than a valid concept of film archiving. Nevertheless, Langlois' Cinémathèque was a central pillar of French film culture. Though his personality was dominant, his team of (often voluntary, usually female) helpers should be acknowledged, including Lotte Eisner*, Mary Meerson and Marie Epstein*. GV

Bib: Richard Roud, *A Passion for Films: Henri Langlois and the Cinémathèque Française* (1983).

LATINOVITS, Zoltán — Budapest 1931 – Balatonszemes 1976

Hungarian actor. From 1959 until his suicide in 1976, Latinovits played leading roles in forty-seven films and twenty-one television movies, acted in more than two dozen important stage productions, directed two plays, and published two books. He studied architecture, and though he never went to acting school he became the most employed actor in the Hungarian cinema of the 1960s. His talent was remarkably versatile, although he mostly played the energetic, impatient, non-conformist intellectual. His 'intellectual masculinity' was close to that of Marcello Mastroianni* (Latinovits dubbed Mastroianni's voice in *La dolce vita*, 1960) but he was more energetic and much more volatile. His powerful character led many directors to cast him in aggressive or negative roles, often as evil officers or other diabolical types.

Latinovits was a non-conformist, and he had many conflicts with Hungarian cultural bureaucracy. He tried to create his own theatre with selected actors and directors but the cultural and political authorities thwarted his plans. His suicide was a great shock in Hungary. Many poems were written in tribute, and he became a symbol of the intellectual and moral integrity of the artist. KAB

Films Include: *Gyalog a mennyországba/Walking to Heaven* (1959); *Oldás és kötés/Cantata* (1960); *Szegénylegények/The Round-up* (1965); *Hideg napok/Cold Days* (1966); *Falak/Walls, Fiúk a térről/Boys from the Square* (1967); *Csend és kiáltás/Silence and Cry* (1968); *Isten hozta őrnagy úr!/The Tót Family, Utazás a koponyám körül/Journey Round My Skull* (1969); *Szindbád* (1971); *A magyar ugaron/Fallow Land* (1972); *Az ötödik pecsét/The Fifth Seal* (1976).

LATTUADA, Alberto — Milan 1914

Italian director. Son of the musician Felice Lattuada, Alberto grew up in the lively cultural scene of 1920s Milan. He started as a photographer (publishing an album, *L'Occhio quadrato*, in 1941), as art critic for Fascist magazines such as *Corrente* (which was often critical of Fascism) and eventually as co-founder in 1940 (with Mario Ferreri and Luigi Comencini*) of the Cineteca Italiana, the Milan film archive. After a brief period as scriptwriter for Mario Soldati* (*Piccolo mondo antico/Old-Fashioned World*, 1941) and Ferdinando Poggioli (*Sissignora*, 1942), he made his directorial debut with *Giacomo l'idealista* (1942), which initiated his reputation as a 'literary' director, with a precisely observant, at times harsh style. A number of his films were indeed based on literature: *Il mulino del Po/The Mill on the Po* (1949) on Bachelli, *Il delitto di Giovanni Episcopo/Flesh Will Surrender* (1947) on D'Annunzio, *La lupa/The She-Wolf* (1953) on Giovanni Verga, *Lettere di una novizia/Rita* (1960) on Guido Piovene, and *Don Giovanni in Sicilia* (1967) on Vitaliano Brancati. Lattuada admired Russian film-makers and writers, from whom he drew his humiliated, oppressed characters and densely pathetic, grotesque situations: for instance *Il cappotto/The Overcoat* (1952, from Gogol) and *La steppa/The Steppe* (1962, from Chekhov). Lattuada was an eclectic film-maker, but all his films, including the neo-realistic* and original *Il bandito* (1946) and *Senza pietà/Without Pity* (1948), are robustly crafted and professionally acted; he had a gift for spotting talented actresses – Giulietta Masina*, Carla Del Poggio* (later to become his wife), Silvana Mangano* and Nastassja Kinski among others. Another constant element of his work is a strong erotic and romantic vein (*La spiaggia/The Beach*, 1954; *Guendalina*, 1957; *La cicala*, 1980) and in particular relationships between young women and older men (*Le farò da padre/Bambina*, 1974). He increasingly developed a streak of bitter irony which informs two of the best-known Italian comedies, *Il mafioso* (1962) and *Venga a prendere il caffé ... da noi/Come Have Coffee With Us* (1970), starring an unforgettable Ugo Tognazzi*. One the few professionals of the mid-1950s capable of adapting to technical and social change, Lattuada directed an Emmy award-winning, six-hour television film, *Cristoforo Colombo/Christopher Columbus* (1984). GVo

Other Films Include: *La freccia nel fianco* (1943–45); *La nostra guerra* (1945, doc.); *Luci del varietà/Variety Lights* (1950, co-dir. Fellini*); *Anna* (1951); *L'amore in città* (1953, ep. *Gli italiani si voltano*); *Scuola elementare* (1955); *La tempesta/The Tempest* (1958); *I dolci inganni/Les adolescents/Sweet Deceptions* (1960); *L'imprevisto/L'imprévu* (1961); *La mandragola* (1965); *Matchless* (1967); *Fräulein Doktor* (1968); *L'amica* (1969); *Bianco, rosso e .../White Sister* (1972); *Sono stato io/I Did It* (1973); *Cuore di cane* (1975); *Oh, Serafina!* (1976); *Così come sei/Stay as You Are* (1978); *Una spina nel cuore* (1985); *Due fratelli* (1988, TV).

LAUGHTON, Charles — Scarborough 1899 – Hollywood, California 1962

British actor, who became one of the most popular stars of the 1930s after his rumbustious, Oscar-winning performance in the title role of Alexander Korda's* *The Private Life of Henry VIII* (1933). He began on the stage, appearing with his wife, Elsa Lanchester, in London and on Broadway. In 1928 he made his film debut in two shorts, *Daydreams* and *Bluebottles*, directed by Ivor Montagu*. Following Broadway success in 1931, he was contracted to Paramount and throughout the 1930s he commuted between Britain and Hollywood, a star on both sides of the Atlantic. By 1939 he had taken up residence in Hollywood and became an American citizen in 1950.

A large actor in every sense, Laughton's appearance barred him from romantic leads, but the scale of his performance in character leads like Bligh in *Mutiny on the Bounty* (1935, US) or Ruggles in *Ruggles of Red Gap* (1935, US) left very little room on the screen for anyone else. Laughton's performance in *Henry VIII* (which had been conceived by Korda as a vehicle for Laughton and Lanchester) has been noted for the sexual innocence of its raunchiness, which John Grierson* attributed to the vitality and vulgarity of the music-hall tradition. The association with Korda continued in 1936 with *Rembrandt*, possibly a better film though a box-office failure, and with the ill-fated *I, Claudius* (1937), directed by Josef von Sternberg but unfinished. Laughton returned to Britain in 1954 to make *Hobson's Choice* with David Lean*.

Laughton continued his theatrical career throughout his life, collaborating for three years with Bertolt Brecht in the first production of *Galileo*, directed in 1947 by Joseph Losey*. He directed and co-scripted one film, which has acquired cult status, *The Night of the Hunter* (1955, US), a baroque and tense thriller starring Robert Mitchum. JC

Bib: Simon Callow, *Charles Laughton: A Difficult Actor* (1987).

Other Films Include (US unless stated): *The Sign of the Cross* (1932); *The Barretts of Wimpole Street* (1934); *Les Misérables* (1935); *Vessel of Wrath* [UK], *St. Martin's Lane* [UK] (1938); *Jamaica Inn* [UK], *The Hunchback of Notre Dame* (1939); *The Tuttles of Tahiti* (1942); *This Land is Mine* [dir. Renoir] (1943); *The Canterville Ghost* (1944); *The Paradine Case, The Big Clock* (1948); *The Man on the Eiffel Tower/L'Homme de la Tour Eiffel* [as Inspector Maigret] (1950, US/Fr.); *Young Bess* [as Henry VIII] (1953); *Witness for the Prosecution* (1958); *Spartacus* (1960); *Advise and Consent* (1962).

LAUNDER, Frank   Hitchin, 1906
and
GILLIAT, Sidney   Edgely 1908–1994

British directors, producers and writers. Their collaboration as screenwriters began in 1935, and included such films as *The Lady Vanishes* (1938) for Alfred Hitchcock* and *Night Train to Munich* (1940) and *The Young Mr Pitt* (1942) for Carol Reed*. Their first directorial credit was for *Millions Like Us* (1943), a documentary-style feature film on women factory workers during the war, which was followed in 1944 by *Two Thousand Women* (dir. Launder). Their collaboration continued until *The Great St Trinian's Train Robbery* in 1966. While they wrote together, they alternated between directing and producing, with Launder showing a tendency towards the eccentric farce of *The Happiest Days of Your Life* (1950) and the 'St Trinian's' series which followed it, and Gilliat favouring social comedies like *The Rake's Progress* (1945) and *Left, Right and Centre* (1959), with occasional black comedies like *London Belongs to Me* (1948). In the 1940s, both produced and directed effective and intricate thrillers such as *Green for*

Danger (Gilliat, 1946) and *I See a Dark Stranger* (Launder, 1946), but in the 1950s and 1960s they specialised more in distinctively British comedy, based on literate scripts, eccentric characters, and a mildly caustic glance. JC

Bib: Geoff Brown, *Launder and Gilliat* (1977).

Other Films (All Written Together) Include: **Director Launder, Producer Gilliat** – *Captain Boycott* (1947); *The Blue Lagoon* (1949); *Lady Godiva Rides Again* (1951); *Folly to be Wise* (1952); *The Belles of St Trinian's* (1954); *Geordie* (1955); *Blue Murder at St Trinian's* (1957); *The Bridal Path* (1959); *The Pure Hell of St Trinian's* (1960); *Joey Boy* (1965). **Director Gilliat, Producer Launder** – *State Secret* (1950); *The Story of Gilbert and Sullivan* (1953); *The Constant Husband* (1955); *Fortune is a Woman* (1957); *Only Two Can Play* (1962).

LAURITZEN, Lauritz   Silkeborg 1878 – Copenhagen 1938

Danish director. 'Lau' Lauritzen, as he preferred to call himself, began his career as an actor in 1907. In 1910 he wrote his first film script and he joined Nordisk Films* in 1914. He quickly acquired a reputation as a director of comedies, of which he made about 200 altogether. In late 1919 he left Nordisk to join the Swedish company Svensk Palladium. When this closed down in 1921, Lauritzen became the artistic head of the newly founded (Danish) Palladium*, where he created the enormously successful comic duo 'Fyrtaarnet og Bivognen'* with the actors Carl Schenstrøm and Harald Madsen, forerunners of film partnerships such as Laurel and Hardy. Over the following years Lauritzen directed many feature-length films with the duo, including his most ambitious, *Don Quixote* (1926), in which Schenstrøm convincingly incarnated the title role. Lauritzen did not adapt easily to the coming of sound. His *Han, Hun og Hamlet/He, She and Hamlet* (1932) with 'Fyrtaarnet og Bivognen' was not particularly successful, but between 1932 to 1938 he directed five successful comedies for Palladium, the most popular of which was *Barken Margrethe af Danmark/The 'Margrethe of Denmark'* (1935). ME

LAZAGA, Pedro   Pedro Lazaga Sabater; Valls, Tarragona 1918 – Madrid 1979

Spanish director, who also worked as an assistant director, scriptwriter and production manager. He started his directing career in 1948 with *Encrucijada/Crossroads*, and over the next thirty years made more than ninety films, mostly popular comedies [> COMEDY (SPAIN)]. In the 1960s his association with actor Paco Martínez Soria resulted in a series of warm-hearted comedies where the actor's impersonation of a good-natured rustic is the vehicle for criticism of the modern loss of moral values: for instance, *La ciudad no es para mí/City Life is Not for Me* (1965) or *Abuelo made in Spain/Old Man Made in Spain* (1968). In the late 1960s and the 1970s he directed Alfredo Landa* in many of the so-called 'sexy Spanish comedies', such as *Vente a Alemania, Pepe/Come to Germany, Pepe* (1970), where a village yokel's disillusionment with the dream of easy money and fast women in Germany brings him back to Spain, his old fiancée and social conformity. IS

LEAN, (Sir) David   Croydon 1908 – London 1991

British director. Lean began his long film career as a clapper boy with Maurice Elvey* in 1926. From 1930 he was an editor for Gaumont-British News, British Movietone News and British Paramount, editing such feature films as *Pygmalion* (1938) and *49th Parallel* (1941): 'the best editor I ever worked with,' says Michael Powell*, 'or should I say worked for.' His first film as a director, *In Which We Serve* (1942), was co-directed with Noël Coward*, and initiated a partnership which resulted in three more films from Coward scripts: *This Happy Breed* (1944), *Blithe Spirit* (1945) and *Brief Encounter* (1945). The next phase of his career, from 1946 to 1956, seems inflected by his encounter with Dickens – in the Dickensian atmosphere of *Hobson's Choice* (1954) as much as in the atmospheric adaptations of *Great Expectations* (1946) and *Oliver Twist* (1948). And the final phase, opened by *The Bridge on the River Kwai* (1957), is dominated by the wide-screen, 'big' theme, Oscar-winning epic – *Lawrence of Arabia* (1962), *Doctor Zhivago* (1965), *Ryan's Daughter* (1970) and, after a fourteen-year gap, *A Passage to India* (1985). The disparities of scale, from intimacy to epic distance, conceal any authorial consistency. There is a constant return from *Brief Encounter*, through *The Passionate Friends* (1949) and *Summer Madness* (1955), all the way to *A Passage to India*, of repressed passions and forfeited love, but the passions recede as the actors disappear into beautifully photographed landscapes. Roy Armes, discussing Lean, quotes John Grierson*: 'When a director dies, he becomes a photographer.'

Lean was knighted in 1984. JC

Bib: Gerald Pratley, *The Cinema of David Lean* (1974).

LEANDER, Zarah   Karlstadt, Sweden 1907 – Stockholm 1981

Swedish-born German actress and singer, who, after the departure of Marlene Dietrich*, became the German cinema's most famous *femme fatale*. After *Premiere* (1937), her first German-language film, proved a popular success, Leander signed a long-term contract with Ufa*. Her persona was crucially shaped in the films directed by Detlef Sierck* [Douglas Sirk] (*La Habanera, Zu neuen Ufern/To New Shores*, both 1937), melodramas in which a woman is ready to sacrifice herself for either man or child. Leander became, during the Nazi era, a highly paid icon of dangerous allure and female sophistication. She was both a composite of Hollywood glamour queens and a curiously 'Mediterranean' screen goddess. Irked by official disapproval (Hitler twice vetoed her nomination as 'state actress'), she broke her Ufa contract and returned to Sweden in 1943. Unable to resume her film career in postwar Germany, Leander made a modest comeback on stage, performing songs from her old films. TE/SG

Bib: Cornelia Zumkeller, *Zarah Leander: Ihre Filme, ihr Leben* (1988).

Other Films Include: *Heimat, Der Blaufuchs* (1938); *Es war eine rauschende Ballnacht, Das Lied der Wüste* (1939); *Der Weg ins Freie* (1941); *Die große Liebe* (1942); *Cuba Cabana* (1952); *Ave Maria* (1953); *Bei dir war es immer so schön* (1954).

LÉAUD, Jean-Pierre   Paris 1944

French actor, linked to the New Wave* and especially François Truffaut*. In their first film, *Les Quatre cents coups/The 400 Blows* (1959), the fourteen-year-old Léaud gave a remarkable performance as Antoine Doinel, his engaging spontaneity convincingly suggesting both the streetwise young Parisian and the lonely unloved child. The product of a close relationship with Truffaut was a Doinel saga (*L'Amour à 20 ans*, 1962, *Baisers volés/Stolen Kisses*, 1968, *Domicile conjugal/Bed and Board*, 1970, *L'Amour en fuite/Love on the Run*, 1978) in which he fell in love, got married and divorced. The candidness gave way to a mannered performance style, the adult personality a self-absorbed romantic, in love with 'magic' women but irresponsible with real ones (charming or exasperating depending on one's point of view). He successfully transferred this persona to non-Doinel Truffaut films (such as *La Nuit américaine/Day for Night*, 1973), several films by Jean-Luc Godard* (including *Masculin féminin*, 1966, *Made in USA*, 1967), and Jean Eustache's* extraordinary *La Maman et la putain/The Mother and the Whore* (1973). Léaud was badly affected by Truffaut's death in 1984. His later parts – small roles in films by, among others, Godard, Agnès Varda*, Catherine Breillat and Aki Kaurismäki* – have tended to refer back to his earlier image. GV

LECLERC, Ginette   Geneviève Menut; Paris 1912–92

French actress, typecast as an erotic vamp from the 1930s to the 1950s. She started in music hall and played in many light films of the 1930s which exploited her voluptuous physique rather than her talent. She was cast by Marcel Pagnol* in *La Femme du boulanger/The Baker's Wife* (1938) in a part allegedly intended for Joan Crawford, as the sultry wife who elopes but is eventually reconciled with her older husband (Raimu*) in a memorable scene in which he insults the cat instead. Leclerc enjoyed her greatest popularity in the 1940s, especially for her part in Henri-Georges Clouzot's* *Le Corbeau/The Raven* (1943), although the film, deemed 'anti-French', cost her a jail sentence in 1944. She resumed her career, but never really found the parts she deserved. Though Leclerc's talent and humour sometimes transcended the sluts and schemers she played, she was ultimately limited by sexist typecasting. GV

LEDOUX, Jacques
Warsaw, Poland 1922 – Brussels 1988

Belgian Director of the Cinémathèque Royale de Belgique*. Alongside Henri Storck* and Francis Bolen*, Jacques Ledoux is one of the most important figures in the development of Belgium's place in film history. After studying philosophy and engineering, Ledoux met André Thirifays, Pierre Vermeylen and Henri Storck, founders of the Cinémathèque Royale (in 1938). He was recruited as volunteer archivist, becoming curator of the film archive in 1948 and director of the Cinémathèque from 1960 to 1988.

Ledoux's passion for film extended to both the old and the new, the classic and experimental. Thus the old was collected and preserved, in the Cinémathèque's archives, and later shown in the Musée du cinéma which Ledoux founded in 1962. Meanwhile, the new was encouraged through the first experimental film festival at Knokke-le-Zoute (in 1949) and the creation in 1973 of the *Prix de L'Âge d'or*, given to a contemporary film which showed the promise of Luis Buñuel's* provocative work of 1930.

Accounts of Ledoux's life repeatedly emphasise two things: his privacy and his dedication. In appreciation of his achievements he was (posthumously) awarded the Erasmus prize, given by Holland to distinguished persons and institutions for their contributions to European cultural and social life. This was the first time the prize had been awarded in the area of film. CF

LEGRAND, Michel
Paris 1932

French composer and singer, the son of popular musician Raymond Legrand. Like his father, who had studied with Paul Whiteman in the US, Legrand specialised in fusing popular French *chanson* with jazz. A prolific composer and singer, he is particularly known for his work on New Wave* films, working with Jean-Luc Godard* and with Agnès Varda*, in whose *Cléo de 5 à 7/Cleo from 5 to 7* (1962) he appears – composing a song. Legrand also wrote the music for Jacques Demy's* *Lola* (1961) and his musicals *Les Parapluies de Cherbourg/The Umbrellas of Cherbourg* (1964) and *Les Demoiselles de Rochefort* (1967); his melancholy tunes contributed much to the bitter-sweet image of Demy's films. He has also had a successful international career and directed one film. GV

LEHMAN, Boris
Lausanne, Switzerland 1944

Belgian director. Boris Lehman's films centre upon the self and inhabit the margins of commercial and independent cinema. Over his twenty-year career, Lehman has directed, acted (in Samy Szlingerbaum's *Bruxelles/Transit*, 1980), collaborated (with Chantal Akerman*, Henri Storck* and Patrick Van Antwerpen, among others) and written for various journals. He also had a long-term commitment (from 1965 to 1983) to the Antonin Artaud centre for the mentally handicapped in Brussels.

Lehman's frequent appearance in his films may suggest self-obsession, and cinema does become a medium through which he can explore his identity as both a Belgian and a Jew (*Muet comme une Carpe/Silent as a Fish*, 1987), but solipsism is avoided through his ethnographic approach. Lehman's (unscripted) films are created from an observation of reality, using people who play themselves, to chronicle particular places and the passing of time, as in *Magnum Begynasium Bruxellense* (1978), a record of the Beguinage district of Brussels. Brussels is also the setting for his *tour de force*, *Babel* (1991), made over ten years and lasting more than eight hours. Once again, the real is mixed with the fictional, pushing the documentary form to its limits, as Lehman leads us on a journey from Brussels to Mexico and back. CF

LEIGH, Mike
Salford 1943

British director, most of whose work has been in theatre and television drama since the 1970s, with only four feature films to his credit, and a seventeen-year gap between his first feature film, *Bleak Moments* (1971), and his next, *High Hopes* (1988), which won the Critics' Award at Cannes. Since 1988, his films have attracted increasing international attention. His extensive work in theatre and television established a highly individual working method in which scripts were developed out of improvisation, the director/writer's role being to 'sculpt' characters and situations out of the material which the actors threw up. The detailed observation is often astonishing, but his aesthetic owes more to the *Carry On** tradition than to the critical realist tradition, a comedy of character which ruthlessly exposes vulnerability and social pretension but ends up assuring the audience of its own superiority. In his third feature film, *Life is Sweet* (1990), the revelation that people without taste are not necessarily people without feeling seems patronising and predictable, while in *Naked* (1993), which brings a new level of intensity to its performances, the lingering question of whether Leigh's misogyny is a thing in itself or just an aspect of misanthropy seems to be resolved on the side of misogyny. JC

Bib: Andy Medhurst, 'Mike Leigh: beyond embarrassment', *Sight and Sound* (November 1993).

LEIGH, Vivien
Vivien Mary Hartley, Darjeeling, India 1913 – London 1967

British actress, written of as the fragile 'Dresden shepherdess' of English acting until she snatched the part of Scarlett O'Hara in *Gone With the Wind* (1939, US) from under the noses of a number of American hopefuls. She received an Oscar for her performance. She made her film debut in 1934, and was placed under contract by Alexander Korda* in 1935. A well-publicised extra-marital affair with Laurence Olivier* after their appearance together in *Fire Over England* (1937) gave her the other ingredient of international stardom – romantic scandal. Always a delicate and graceful actress, in her British films she seemed exquisitely English, though when her Englishness was set against the grosser, un-English masculinity of Clark Gable or Marlon Brando, the steel within the delicacy became apparent. She won an Oscar and Best Actress awards from the New York Film Critics, the Venice Festival and the British Film Academy for her performance as Blanche du Bois in *A Streetcar Named Desire* (1952, US). Her delicacy extended to her health, and she suffered from tuberculosis through much of her career. JC

Other Films Include: *Things Are Looking Up, Gentleman's Agreement, Look Up and Laugh* [with Gracie Fields] (1935); *Dark Journey, Storm in a Teacup* (1937); *A Yank at Oxford, St. Martin's Lane* (1938); *Waterloo Bridge* (1940, US); *That Hamilton Woman/Lady Hamilton* [title role] (1941, US); *Caesar and Cleopatra* [title role] (1946); *Anna Karenina* [title role] (1948); *The Deep Blue Sea* (1955); *The Roman Spring of Mrs Stone* (1961); *Ship of Fools* (1965, US).

LEJEUNE, C. A.   Manchester 1897 – Pinner Hill 1973

British film critic, who wrote on cinema for almost forty years, in the *Manchester Guardian* from 1922 to 1928 and in the *Observer* from 1928 to 1960. She was also a regular broadcaster. Lejeune was a passionate advocate of a British cinema which celebrated British values. 'It is time,' she declared in 1931, 'that we began to be country-proud and empire-proud in the cinema, to boast a bit, to be a little swaggering for once. God knows, we have plenty to swagger about' – and she was clear that a British cinema of quality was a cinema of emotional restraint: Anthony Asquith's* *The Way to the Stars* (1945) had 'the great merit, rare in Hollywood pictures these days, of emotional restraint. [...] Again and again the audience is left to resolve its own tensions: an operation that is painful, unusual, and good for the soul.' Though she valued cinema's entertainment values – she enthused over Jessie Matthews*, for instance – she had little time for the bizarre or the excessive and no taste for the seamy. Strongly and conservatively moral, she retired because she did not approve of the growing trend of 'sex and savagery' in the cinema of the late 1950s and early 1960s.

Though no one would claim it as a victory for feminism, it is worth noting that there was a period in the 1950s when British film criticism was dominated by three women: C. A. Lejeune at the *Observer*, Dilys Powell* at the *Sunday Times*, and Penelope Houston, editor of *Sight and Sound**. JC

Bib: Anthony Lejeune, *The C. A. Lejeune Reader* (1991).

LELOUCH, Claude   Paris 1937

French director. Lelouch started his career as a film reporter, which explains his presence along with Godard*, Resnais* and Varda* (among others) as one of the directors of *Loin du Viêt-Nam/Far from Vietnam* (1967). The tone of his work, however, was set by *Un homme et une femme/A Man and a Woman* (1966), a glossy melodrama with a famous theme tune, one of the most successful and prize-bedecked French films ever, starring Anouk Aimée and Jean-Louis Trintignant*. Lelouch has made some thirty popular and

populist films, 'naive stories' as he puts it, overblown epics according to others, typically intercutting storylines from antiquity to the present day, and with programmatic titles such as *La Vie, l'amour, la mort/Life, Love, Death* (1968). His *Les Misérables* (1995, with Jean-Paul Belmondo*) characteristically alternates the nineteenth-century setting of Victor Hugo's novel with World War II. Some of his most interesting films are smaller in scale: *La Bonne année* (1973, with Lino Ventura* and Françoise Fabian) and *Edith et Marcel* (1983), a biopic of singer Edith Piaf. GV

LEMINEN, Hannu   Helsinki 1910

Finnish director. Stage manager, editor, scriptwriter and producer, Hannu Leminen directed twenty-nine feature films between 1937 and 1957, scripting, designing and editing many of them. He worked for all the major companies, starting at Suomi-Filmi as head of the stage department in 1937. His first films as stage manager were grand costume dramas directed by Risto Orko*, *Jääkärin morsian/The Infantryman's Bride* (1938) and *Aktivistit/The Activists* (1939). After his move to SF, he worked closely with Felix Forsman, a cinematographer who specialised in costume dramas; both were influenced by the French studio cinema of the 1930s. Leminen started his career as director at SF with *Täysosuma/Dead on Target* (1941). This was followed by a ten-year collaboration with his wife Helena Kara. Their best-known film is *Valkoiset ruusut/White Roses* (1943), based on Stefan Zweig's story and also filmed in Hollywood by Max Ophuls* five years later as *Letter from an Unknown Woman*. Together with Regina Linnanheimo*, Kara was a key star of Finnish melodrama. Under Leminen's direction, Kara's characters struggled with excessive love (*Valkoiset ruusut, Vain sinulle/For You Alone*, 1945), were shadowed by a shameful past (*Puck*, 1942), or were torn between desire and responsibility (*Soita minulle, Helena/Play for Me, Helena*, 1948, *Ratavartijan kaunis Inkeri/Beautiful Inkeri and the Railway Man*, 1950). A romantic, Leminen was interested neither in the realistic tradition of rural stories nor in adapting the national classics. His best-known films are melodramas of powerful emotions and moral contradictions. Leminen was also a pioneer in Finnish broadcasting; he was one of the founders of MTV (Finnish commercial television) in the 1950s, and in the 1960s and 1970s he headed the second public broadcasting channel (YLE2). AK

LENI, Paul   Stuttgart 1885 – Hollywood, California 1929

German director and set designer. A trained graphic artist and stage designer for Max Reinhardt*, Leni started his film career as a painter of film posters and then as set designer for Joe May*. Making his directorial debut with an impressive war melodrama (*Der Feldarzt/Das Tagebuch des Dr. Hart*, 1918), Leni continued to design the sets for big-budget productions at Ufa*. He co-directed and designed the *Kammerspielfilm** *Hintertreppe/Backstairs* (1921, script Carl Mayer*, co-dir. Leopold Jessner), which owes much of its atmosphere and visual power to his sets. Always an experimenter, he also worked with Guido Seeber* on semi-abstract shorts in the mid-1920s.

Early in 1922 Leni founded his own production company whose first venture was the menacing horror film *Das Wachsfigurenkabinett/Waxworks* (1924), which he directed himself, featuring Emil Jannings*, Conrad Veidt* and Werner Krauß*. A huge success and one of Weimar* cinema's enduring classics, *Das Wachsfigurenkabinett* earned Leni an invitation from Carl Laemmle to Hollywood, where he proved his visual flair for a new kind of horror film as the director of *The Cat and the Canary* (1927) and *The Man Who Laughs* (1928), before his career was abruptly cut short by a fatal case of blood poisoning. MW

Bib: Hans-Michael Bock (ed.), *Paul Leni: Grafik, Theater, Film* (1986).

Other Films Include: *Prima Vera, Dornröschen* (1917); *Die platonische Ehe, Prinz Kuckuck* (1919); *Die Verschwörung zu Genua* (1921); *The Last Warning* (1929, US).

LENICA, Jan   Poznań 1928

Polish animator and poster designer. A member of the left-wing avant-garde, Lenica was instrumental in establishing animation as an art form in Poland. Films like *Był Sobie Raz/Once Upon a Time* (1957, made with Walerian Borowczyk*) and *Nowy Janko Muzykant/Janko the Musician* (1960) used graphic techniques to create surreal and often darkly humorous parables of life. Winning international acclaim allowed Lenica to find finance in the West and maintain a relatively independent status. A growing political disillusionment is evident in his later films, for example *Landscape* (1975), where Lenica grapples with the totalitarianism that had seduced and betrayed him. AW

Other Films Include: *Dom/House* (1958); *Monsieur Tête* (1959, Fr.); *Labirynt/Labyrinth* (1963); *La Femme fleur* [Fr.], *A* [Fr.] (1964); *Adam II* (1969); *Ubu et la Grande Gidouille* (1979, Fr.).

LENIN, Vladimir I.   Simbirsk, Russia 1870 – Moscow 1924

Soviet revolutionary leader. Lenin, who led the October Revolution in 1917, was one of the first to realise the political potential of cinema in a backward and illiterate country like post-Revolutionary Russia, remarking: 'Of all the arts, for us cinema is the most important.' Unlike many of his contemporaries, he also appreciated that, as a successful propaganda medium, cinema would have to entertain its audiences as well as persuade them, hence his suggestion of a ratio between propaganda and entertainment films, later known as the 'Lenin proportion'. On 27 August 1919 he signed the decree creating the first nationalised film industry in the world. RT

LEONE, Sergio   Rome 1929–89

Italian director, the son of Roberto Roberti, a famous silent director (whose name Leone adapted as a pseudonym – Bob Robertson – for his first Western). Leone had a long apprenticeship as assistant director on a total of fifty-six films (including American super-productions filmed in Italy, such as *Ben-Hur*, 1959) and eventually made his debut with an unsigned peplum*, *Gli ultimi giorni di Pompei/The Last Days of Pompeii* (1959), which Mario Bonnard had abandoned for health reasons. Success came quickly, with *Il colosso di Rodi/The Colossus of Rhodes* (1961), another spectacular peplum, in which all is eventually resolved in the final catastrophe. After acting once again as a second unit director in *Sodoma e Gomorra/Sodom and Gomorrah* (1961, dir. Robert Aldrich), Leone achieved worldwide success with his 'dollar trilogy' – *Per un pugno di dollari/A Fistful of Dollars* (1964), *Per qualche dollaro in più/For a Few Dollars More* (1965) and *Il buono, il brutto e il cattivo/The Good, The Bad and the Ugly* (1966) – which inaugurated the genre of the Italian Western* (the so-called 'Spaghetti' Western), and brought instant fame to actors such as Clint Eastwood, Lee Van Cleef and Gian Maria Volonté*. The trilogy is highly mannerist (with rituals, expanded rhythms, majestic scenery, technical and linguistic exhibitionism), rich in imitations rather than citations and amplified by Ennio Morricone's* music, but it is also full of assertive vitality. *C'era una volta il West/Once Upon a Time in the West* (1968), written in conjunction with Bernardo Bertolucci* and Dario Argento*, shot no longer in Spain but in John Ford's Monument Valley, and starring Henry Fonda, attempted to produce an imaginary and mythical synthesis of the American frontier. *Giù la testa/A Fistful of Dynamite/Duck You Sucker!* (1971) is an anarchic and wittily ideological re-examination of the theme of traitors and heroes. Leone succeeded in creating a world that is both similar to the Western, yet is not the Western, a world with obscure, 'universal' roots, but which is also an exalted expression of love for, and obsession with, the cinema. When Leone returned to film-making, after more than a decade spent, among other things, launching the careers of Tonino Valerii and Carlo Verdone and directing memorable advertisements, the result was *C'era una volta in America/Once Upon a Time in America* (1983), a personal and unorthodox revisiting of the myths and archetypes of American cinema through a violent and eccentric gangster saga. GVo

LESBIAN AND GAY CINEMA IN EUROPE

It is generally assumed that European cinemas have a good track record on homosexuality: more images, sooner, less prejudiced, more often produced by openly lesbian/gay people. This account needs qualification and explanation, and more research.

Lesbian/gay representation has been all but entirely absent from East European cinemas. In Western Europe, lesbian/gay stereotypes are widely used, not only in popular comedies and thrillers but in canonical *auteur* works: *Die Büchse der Pandora/Pandora's Box* (1929, Germany); *Roma città aperta/Rome Open City* (1945, Italy), *La Fiancée du pirate/Dirty Mary* (1969, France). They are not necessarily the same as in

Hollywood, nor are stereotypes unambiguously negative, something radical gay/lesbian films have often taken up, as in *Un hombre llamado Flor de Otoño/A Man Called Autumn Flower* (1977, Spain), or *Madame X – eine absolute Herrscherin/Madame X – an Absolute Ruler* (1978, Germany). The greater number of lesbian/gay representations in Western European cinemas has much to do with identifying markets with which Hollywood did not compete: pornography and the educational film, not always firmly distinct genres. Soft-core heterosexual pornography has been a mainstay of many European industries and invariably includes lesbian sequences. Sex education films have treated male and female homosexuality and have often been enlightened as texts even when marketed as titillation, for instance *Anders als die Anderen/Different from the Others* (1919, Germany) or *Der Sittlichkeitsverbrecher/The Sex Criminal* (1962, Switzerland).

At the same time, European cinemas dealt with homosexuality in a serious manner much earlier than others. This did not only occur in films of blatant high seriousness: among the most cherishable early images of homosexuality are the male relationship in the highly strung melodrama *Geschlecht in Fesseln/Sex in Shackles* (1928, Germany) and the lesbian character in the French thriller *Quai des Orfèvres* (1947). The earliest known representation is in *Vingarne/The Wings* (1916, Sweden), with the earliest lesbian representation perhaps *Die Büchse der Pandora*. *Anders als die anderen* and *Mädchen in Uniform/Girls in Uniform* (1931, Germany) represent the earliest explicitly progressive treatments, a tradition taken up in the postwar years by *Victim* (1960, UK): the presence of contemporaneous, relatively strong homosexual rights movements in these countries is significant in accounting for these breakthroughs.

Government policies in many countries have facilitated *auteur* cinema, in which many more or less openly lesbian/gay directors have worked (Chantal Akerman*, Pedro Almodóvar*, Jean Cocteau*, Rainer Werner Fassbinder*, Marleen Gorris*, Derek Jarman*, Ulrike Ottinger*, Pier Paolo Pasolini*, Luchino Visconti*), as have (straight) women directors who treated homosexuality in a sympathetic, even at times envious, manner – among others, Mai Zetterling's* *Älskande par/Loving Couples* (1964, Sweden), Margarethe von Trotta's* *Das zweite Erwachen des Krista Klages/The Second Awakening of Krista Klage* (1977, Germany) or Diane Kurys'* *Coup de foudre/Entre Nous/At First Sight* (1983, France). In recent years, the European heritage* film has been remarkably hospitable to lesbian/gay themes, as for instance in *Novembermond/November Moon* (1984, Germany), *Maurice* (1987, UK), *Meteoro ke skia/Meteor and Shadow* (1962, Greece); one might consider Jacqueline Audry's* *Olivia* (1950, France) an important early example. *Auteur* and heritage cinema do not treat homosexuality as an issue or problem, but are not always lacking in anguish, as for instance in *Tystnaden/The Silence* (1962, Sweden), or melancholy, as in *Gli occhiali d'oro/The Gold-rimmed Spectacles* (1988, Italy), and few European films have had the (often bland) affirmative impulse of post-gay liberation cinema in the USA. RD

Bib: Richard Dyer, *Now You See It: Studies on Lesbian and Gay Film* (1990).

LESTER, Richard　　　　Philadelphia, USA 1932

American/British director, who has worked mainly in Britain since 1955. Coming out of music composition, television, and TV commercials, and passing through an association with Spike Milligan and Peter Sellers* on a television Goon Show spin-off called *A Show Called Fred* (1956), Lester brought a zany, pop sensibility to the cinema of the 1960s which set the style for the Beatles' first incursions into film, *A Hard Day's Night* (1964) and *Help!* (1965). In these films, and in his first feature, *It's Trad, Dad!* (1962) – starring Helen Shapiro – he brought the pacy editing and visual punch of television commercials to film, coining the vocabulary of early music video and catching the mood of the new music. *The Knack . . . and How to Get It* (1965) anticipated the more cynical *Alfie* (Lewis Gilbert, 1966), and *The Bed Sitting Room* (1969) links the Goons and Monty Python. Some of the pop sensibility can still be glimpsed in Lester's contribution to the sagas of *Superman II* and *III* (1981 and 1983) and *The Three* (and *Four*) *Musketeers* (1974 and 1975), but the exuberant flair began to show its age and many of the later films could have been made by someone else. JC

LETHEM, Roland　　　　Etterbeek 1942

Belgian director (also writer and critic of science fiction and fantasy literature). Lethem began making short experimental films in the mid-1960s. *Lili au lit/Lili in Bed* (1965) sets the agenda: heavy breathing is heard over a black screen, then in the final image a man is shown leaving the bed of a young girl. Sex and violence, obscenity and fantasy are the substance of Lethem's cinema, which often acts upon its audience through associational or surrealist images. Certain films are specific about their enemy, such as *Le Saigneur est avec nous/It's World War Three, Man* (1974), which condemns fascism, *Le Sexe enragé/The Red Sex* (1970), an attack on the bourgeoisie, and *Bande de cons/You Shits* (1970), a feature-length invective against film audiences. Lethem's anti-everything stance makes him a part of a venerable Belgian film tradition along with mavericks such as Noël Godin, Thierry Zeno, Michel Laitem and many others. CF/PW

LEUWERIK, Ruth　　　Ruth Leeuwerik; Essen 1924

German actress, who embodied the maternal ideal of the 1950s. Leuwerik's film career began in 1950 with *13 unter einen Hut*, establishing her as the mature and sensible companion whose passions are kept well hidden. In a period of social reconstruction, in need of moral uplift, she became (together with Maria Schell*) the most popular female star of the next two decades. At first teamed with the discreet and straightforward Dieter Borsche in family dramas (*Vater braucht eine Frau*, 1952) and comedies of manners (*Königliche Hoheit*, 1953), she formed the ideal couple with O. W. Fischer (*Bildnis einer Unbekannten*, 1954). Her biggest international success came with *Die Trapp-Familie/The Trapp Family* (1956) and *Die Trapp-Familie in Amerika* (1958), in which she convincingly moved from gracious nun to elegant aristocrat. The decline of the star system in the 1960s took Leuwerik 'down-market' (*Und Jimmy ging zum Regenbogen*, 1970) and into routine literary adaptations (*Unordnung und frühes Leid*, 1977, based on Thomas Mann). TE/KU

LEVENDE BILLEDER

Danish film magazine. *Levende billeder* ('Living Images'), a monthly, was founded in 1975 with a wider brief than *Kosmorama*'s*; besides film, subject matter embraced television, radio, music and later video. Financial difficulties forced closure in 1985, but the magazine was revived a few months later with support from Det Danske Filminstitut (the Danish Film Institute). ME

LE VIGAN, Robert
Robert Coquillaud; Paris 1900 – Tandil, Argentina 1972

French actor, who left a vivid mark on French cinema, despite rarely rating top billing in his sixty-odd films between 1931 and 1943. A brilliant, extravagant actor, Le Vigan specialised in louche, menacing or diabolical characters. He worked frequently with Julien Duvivier* (*Golgotha*, as Christ, and *La Bandera*, both 1935), and appeared in classics such as *Les Bas-fonds/The Lower Depths* (1936), *Quai des brumes* (1938) and *Goupi Mains-rouges/It Happened at the Inn* (1943). His career was curtailed at the Liberation because of his overt fascism. Condemned to forced labour, he escaped to Spain and then Argentina, abandoning his part (Jéricho) in *Les Enfants du paradis* (1943–45); he was replaced by Pierre Renoir*. GV

L'HERBIER, Marcel
Paris 1890–1979

French director (also novelist, scriptwriter poet and composer), whose career, like that of Abel Gance*, is split between a highly regarded silent phase and a neglected sound one. L'Herbier worked for the French army's film unit during the war and in 1919 made the patriotic *Rose France*. He shared the formal concerns of the French avant-garde*, deploying technical virtuosity (such as superimpositions) to express his characters' psychology, as in *El Dorado* (1921), considered by many his masterpiece. He published an early essay on film language, *Hermès et le silence* (1918), worked for Gaumont*, and set up his own production company, Cinégraphic, in 1923. *Feu Mathias Pascal/The Late Mathias Pascal* (1925), praised by Georges Sadoul* for its use of Italian locations, starred Ivan Mosjoukine*. L'Herbier's largest projects, *L'Inhumaine* (1924) and the brilliant *L'Argent* (1929, with Brigitte Helm*), display modernist architecture and production values lavish enough to compete with Hollywood while reflecting an image of European sophistication. L'Herbier worked successfully through the 1930s and 1940s, directing opulent melodramas such as *Le Bonheur* (1935), *Nuits de feu* (1937) and *Adrienne Lecouvreur* (1938), the wartime 'fantastic' costume drama *La Nuit fantastique* (1942) and the delightful Edwige Feuillère* comedy *L'Honorable Catherine* (1943); he also made pompous military dramas such *La Porte du large* and *Les Hommes*

nouveaux (both 1936), the latter an apology for French colonisation of Morocco. L'Herbier was an active participant in French film industry affairs, heading several professional associations throughout his career and co-founding IDHEC* in 1943. He published a collection of film essays, *L'Intelligence du cinématographe* in 1947 (revised 1977), and his autobiography *La Tête qui tourne* in 1979; he also worked for television. GV

Bib: Noël Burch, *Marcel L'Herbier* (1973).

LIEBENEINER, Wolfgang
Liebau, Schlesien 1905 – Vienna 1987

German actor, director and producer. From 1931, Liebeneiner played romantic screen lovers (in among other films, Ophuls'* *Liebelei*, 1933), and in 1937 he directed his first feature (*Versprich mir nichts!*). Although not a Party member, Liebeneiner held high office in the state bureaucracy and Nazi cultural life, becoming professor and director of the film academy as well as governor of the Reichsfilmkammer. His visual flair and professionalism served him on his propaganda assignments such as *Bismarck* (1940) and (as director and co-author) the notorious pro-euthanasia film *Ich klage an* (1941). Liebeneiner continued directing after the war, claiming he had used his position to protect opponents of the regime. As a key figure of Germany's postwar genre cinema (*Liebe 47*, 1949; *Die Trapp-Familie/The Trapp Family*, 1956; *Schwejks Flegeljahre*, 1964), Liebeneiner personified the continuities between late Weimar*, Nazi and postwar German cinema in all their ambiguities. TE/KU

Other Films Include: *Der Florentinerhut* (1939); *Auf der Reeperbahn nachts um halb eins* (1954); *Eine Frau für's ganze Leben* (1960); *Götz von Berlichingen* (1979).

LIEBMANN, Robert
Berlin 1890 – [?]

German scriptwriter. Before writing screenplays for Richard Oswald* in 1919, Liebmann worked with directors as different as Ludwig Berger*, Reinhold Schünzel*, Max Mack, Georg Jacoby* and Harry Piel*. Liebmann became chief script adviser for Erich Pommer's* unit at Ufa* in April 1929. His first sound film, the Lilian Harvey*–Willy Fritsch* comedy *Liebeswalzer* (1930), was a huge national and international success, giving rise to a wave of film operettas. With Carl Zuckmayer and Carl Vollmöller, Liebmann wrote perhaps the most famous Weimar sound film, *Der blaue Engel/The Blue Angel* (Josef von Sternberg, 1930). Equally adept at turning out thrillers (Robert Siodmak's* *Voruntersuchung*, 1931) or historical dramas (*Yorck*, 1931) Liebmann was nevertheless sacked by Ufa in March 1933 for being Jewish. He emigrated to Paris, where he adapted a Molnar play for Fritz Lang* (*Liliom*, 1934) and wrote *Carrefour* (1938, dir. Kurt Bernhardt*) and *Lumières de Paris* (1938, Richard Pottier). Little is known about his fate during or after the war. MW

LINDA, Bogusław   Toruń 1952

Polish actor and director. As one of the leading young actors associated with the 'cinema of moral unrest', Linda became an 'everyman' figure, the average young man trying to make his way in contemporary Polish society. His starring roles in films like Krzysztof Kieślowski's* *Przypadek/Blind Chance* (1987), Agnieszka Holland's* *Kobieta Samotna/A Woman Alone* (1981), Janusz Zaorski's* *Matka Królów/Mother of the Kings* (1982; first shown 1987) and a whole body of work which was finally seen in the political thaw of 1987, won him a popular following. Linda tried to move away from his politically symbolic roles in the mid-1980s, taking a diverse range of parts which were well received by the public. In 1990 he made his directorial debut with *Seszele/Seychelles*, about the longing to escape from everyday realities, as experienced by two psychiatric patients who subsequently take refuge in the labyrinthian passages of an opera building. The film was panned by Polish critics almost before it was finished, and was poorly distributed and promoted. However, *Seszele* soon became a cult hit with audiences, both in Poland and in Paris, where it won two student festival awards. AW

LINDER, Max   Gabriel Maximilien Leuvielle; Saint-Loubès 1883 – Paris 1925

French actor and director, the greatest comic genius of the French silent cinema. After theatre work in Bordeaux and Paris, Linder joined Pathé* in 1905 and acted in comic shorts, creating the character of 'Max' in 1907. When his rival André Deed* left for Italy, Linder's career took off in 1909 thanks to a prolific series with such titles as *Max aéronaute*, *Max toréador* and *Max virtuose*, many of which he himself directed after 1911. Linder's humour was theatrical, elegant and ironic, foreshadowing René Clair*. He created much-imitated gags, such as the 'fake mirror' (with someone else pretending to be him on the other side), and was a major influence on Chaplin, Harold Lloyd and others. Linder's handsome dandy – frock coat, striped trousers, spats, top hat and cane – courting women in Parisian salons, 'epitomised the leisured French bourgeois rentier [...] pursuing a life of "decadence"', as Richard Abel put it. His success was phenomenal and international, as he discovered on a tour of Europe. He obliged Pathé to raise his salary to FF1m in 1912, making him the world's highest-paid film star. He travelled to the USA in 1917 and 1922, on his second trip making successful films such as the parodic *The Three-Must-Get-Theres* (1922). Although shrouded in mystery, Linder's dramatic suicide (with his wife) may be traced to recurring illness and depression, war wounds and, arguably, the rising popularity of Hollywood comics. His reputation and some of his work survive, partly thanks to his daughter Maud Linder's documentaries, especially *L'Homme au chapeau de soie/The Man in the Silk Hat* (1983). His Paris cinema, the 'Max Linder' (built in 1924), was recently renovated. GV

Bib: Richard Abel, *The Ciné Goes to Town: French Cinema 1896–1914* (1994).

LINDTBERG, Leopold   Vienna 1902 – Sils Maria 1984

Austrian-born director and actor, who worked in both capacities in Germany under Wilhelm Dieterle*, Erwin Piscator and Leopold Jessner, but left for Zurich after the Nazis came to power in 1933. Alternately working for the stage, mainly at the Zurich Schauspielhaus, and for the cinema, he was associated for twenty years with the leading Swiss film producer of the time, Lazar Wechsler*. At Wechsler's Praesens-Film, Lindtberg became Switzerland's most prolific and popular director, with a number of dialect films and literary adaptations to his name. *Jä-soo!* (1935) is representative of the first category, with its fairly primitive *mise-en-scène* successfully put to the service of a cast of popular actors from the Zurich cabaret, Lindtberg apparently wishing to do for Zurich what Marcel Pagnol* was doing for Marseilles. Among his more ambitious, mostly literature-based films are *Füsilier Wipf* (1938), *Wachtmeister Studer* (1939), *Landammann Stauffacher* (1941), *Die mißbrauchten Liebesbriefe* (1942, awarded a prize at the Venice festival), *Der Schuß von der Kanzel* (1942), and *Matto regiert* (1947), which brought in remarkable box-office profits for Wechsler's company Praesens-Film and gave the Swiss film industry a hitherto unknown economic upswing. *Füsilier Wipf*, a national(ist) epic set during World War I but released in the threatening immediate pre-World War II years, was the greatest Swiss box-office hit ever (in Switzerland), and, in Hervé Dumont's words, 'a veritable catalogue of the ideas of the "spiritual defence of the nation"'. This notion, which would come into full force in 1939, was part of a federal government-sponsored cultural propaganda effort designed to promote a strong, unified sense of 'Swissness' in the face of the war threat, based on regionalism, on the literary heritage and on the army. At the end of the film, Wipf, turned into a man by the army, accepts his true place as the 'ideal Swiss' on a mountain farm, with his demure fiancée. *Die letzte Chance/The Last Chance* (1944–45, perhaps Lindtberg's most accomplished film) was a humanitarian story about a group of Jewish refugees seeking asylum in Switzerland, and a huge international success which shifted Praesens-Film towards an international strategy, to which also belong Lindtberg's less successful last three films, *Swiss Tour* (1949), *Die Vier im Jeep/Four in a Jeep* (1951) and *Unser Dorf/The Village* (1953). After leaving Praesens-Film in 1958, Lindtberg turned again to the stage and also made successful series for German, Austrian and Swiss television in the 1960s and 1970s. MW

Bib: Hervé Dumont, *Leopold Lindtberg et le cinéma suisse 1935–53* (1975).

LINNANHEIMO, Regina   Helsinki 1915–95

Finnish actress, best known for her performances in Teuvo Tulio's* melodramas and the wartime costume dramas of T. J. Särkkä*. Linnanheimo began her career in Valentin Vaala's* and Tulio's films in the 1930s and then worked for Särkkä's company, SF. The essence of Linnanheimo's star image is the tension between prodigality and purity. This was particularly reflected in Tulio's films, which had repeated difficulties with the censor. In the costume dramas, Linnanheimo often portrayed tragic heroines betrayed in cross-class love affairs. Her image as the ultimate 'fallen woman' of Finnish cinema derives from the Tulio films of the 1940s and 1950s. In *Rakkauden risti/The Cross of Love* (1946) she is a sheltered country girl seduced and abandoned by a sailor in the big city, where she ends up as a prostitute. A similar trajectory can be seen in *Levoton veri/Restless Blood* (1946), *Intohimon vallassa/In the Grip of Passion* (1947), *Hornankoski/The Rapids of Hell* (1949) and *Mustasuk-kaisuus/Jealousy* (1953). Linnanheimo also co-scripted some of Tulio's films, among them *Olet mennyt minun vereeni/You Have Got Into My Blood* (1956), in which she portrays a factory worker who finds a new lover while her fiancé is at sea. She starts drinking, is sent to prison, and ends up an alcoholic on the margins of the city. Regina Linnanheimo's eyes, in turn piercing and drowsy, became the erotic icon of Finnish cinema; symptomatically, the fallen women she played were often punished by going blind. AK

LIST, Niki

Vienna 1956

Austrian director, who started with short films. His first feature, *Malaria* (1982), was a huge box-office success; it won the Max Ophuls Prize in 1983 and the Austrian Film Prize in 1984. This stylish 'Zeitgeist' parody about a fashionable meeting place ('Café Malaria') and its eccentric customers was followed by *Mama lustig ... ?* (1984), a direct, sensitive documentary portraying a boy who suffers from Down's syndrome. In 1992 List continued this project with *Muß denken*. His *Müller's Büro* (1986), a *film noir*-comedy-musical, was again a box-office hit; it too received the Austrian Film Prize as well as the Golden Ticket (reward for commercial success) in 1986. List has also worked for television and as a press photographer. IR

Other Films Include: *Sternberg Shooting Star* (1988); *Werner Beinhart* (1990, Ger., co-dir.).

LITVAK, Anatole
Kiev, Russia 1902 – Neuilly-sur-Seine, France 1974

Russian-born director, whose international career took him to Germany, the UK, the US (he became an American citizen) and France. Litvak's French films show his remarkable ability to adapt to indigenous genres. His *Coeur de Lilas* (1931) is an atmospheric populist tale set in the Parisian 'lower depths' (with Jean Gabin*), which prefigures Poetic Realism*. With *L'Equipage* (1935) and *Mayerling* (1936), both 'women's melodramas', he made two of the most successful French films of the 1930s. Among his many Hollywood credits are remakes of his own *L'Equipage* as *The Woman I Love* (1937) and of Marcel Carné's* *Le Jour se lève* (1939) as *The Long Night* (1947), as well as the *noir* thriller *Sorry, Wrong Number* (1948). He made large-scale international productions such as *The Night of the Generals* (1967, UK); his last film was a French thriller, *La Dame dans l'auto avec des lunettes et un fusil/The Lady in the Car with Glasses and a Gun* (1970). GV

264

LIZZANI, Carlo
Rome 1922

Italian director. Formerly a militant critic (and early theoretician of neo-realism*), and a collaborator on early neo-realist films by Aldo Vergano, Giuseppe De Santis*, Alberto Lattuada* and Roberto Rossellini*, Lizzani began his directing career with a documentary on southern Italy, followed by two films about the Resistance, *Achtung banditi!* (1951, starring Gina Lollobrigida*) and *Cronache di poveri amanti/Stories of Poor Lovers* (1954), both infused with a sincere populism. Thereafter he moved eclectically but skilfully across a variety of genres, from historical drama (*Il processo di Verona/The Verona Trial*, 1962), to Italian ('Spaghetti') Western* (*Requiescant*, 1967), comedy of manners, and literary adaptation (*Fontamara*, 1980). His best films, though, were probably his popular films inspired by journalistic *faits divers*, such as *Svegliati e uccidi/Wake up and Kill* (1966, under the pseudonym of Lee W. Beaver) and *Banditi a Milano/The Violent Four* (1968). Lizzani wrote a well-known survey of Italian cinema, *Il cinema italiano*, in 1953 and was head of the Venice film festival from 1979 to 1982. GVo

LOACH, Ken
Nuneaton 1937

British director, whose work in political cinema and television over the past three decades has fuelled debate both about the content of political film and about its form. A former President of the Oxford University Dramatic Society, Loach joined the BBC in 1962. He directed early episodes of *Z Cars* (1962–), and the television play, *Up the Junction* (1965). In 1966, with producer Tony Garnett, he directed *Cathy Come Home* (1966), a documentary drama on the scandal of homelessness. 'Loach/Garnett' became a generic term for some of the best television drama of the 1960s and 1970s, raising debates on the left about the possibilities of 'progressive realism' and outrage on the right about the blurring of fact and fiction. Loach and Garnett adapted their approach to cinema in films such as *Kes* (1969) and *Family Life* (1971), concentrating on the apparent spontaneity of the actors (and non-actors) and a documentary camera style to create the effect of unrehearsed reality. Since 1981, Loach has worked independently of both Garnett and the BBC, though much of his work still retains a television involvement through Channel 4*. His film on the security forces in Northern Ireland, *Hidden Agenda*, won him a Special Jury Prize at the Cannes film festival in 1990, an award which he repeated in 1993 with *Raining Stones*. JC

Bib: Jonathan Hacker and David Price, *Take 10: Contemporary British Film Directors* (1991).

Other Films Include: *Poor Cow* (1967); *Black Jack* (1980); *Looks and Smiles* (1981); *Fatherland* (1986); *Riff-Raff* (1990); *Land and Freedom* (1995).

LOCARNO

Swiss film festival. Founded in 1946 as a showcase for the international film market, the Locarno International Film

Festival has been, at least since the 1980s, among the most important 'minor' European film festivals. It is divided between an international competition for fiction films, a retrospective of the work of a single director, accompanied by a publication (on, for instance: Boris Barnet* in 1985; Alberto Cavalcanti* in 1988; Lev Kuleshov* in 1990; Frank Tashlin in 1994), and a survey of Swiss films; it was temporarily supplemented with a short-lived section for television movies (1983–87). Under the direction of Vinicio Beretta (1953–65) the formula was to show politically committed *auteur* films in the afternoons and popular entertainment in the evenings, but it also gave a unique place to films from Eastern Europe. Under the direction of Sandro Bianconi and Freddy Buache (1967–70), the festival shifted its emphasis to *auteurs* from Western and Eastern 'new cinemas' as well as to emerging Third World productions. After a period of transition in the 1970s, David Streiff (1982–91) turned Locarno into the major cinema event in Switzerland with a secure position within the international festival circuit, by balancing the competition of first-run productions with many other sections, creating what has been described as a festival 'à la carte'. This policy was taken up by his successor, Marco Müller, with equally high attendance figures in the movie theatres as well as at the picturesque Piazza Grande, where every summer one of the biggest open-air screens in Europe is installed. MW

LØCHEN, Erik — Kristiania [Oslo] 1924 – Oslo 1983

Norwegian director, who started making short films in 1950; by 1977 he had directed twenty-five shorts of high quality, films which explored the nature of the medium. His first feature, *Jakten/The Hunt* (1959), about a woman and two men (ending with the death of one of the men during a hunting party in the mountains), is a Brechtian modernist film, stylistically one of the most interesting works in Norwegian cinema. Løchen's second feature, *Motforestilling/A Formal Protest* (1972) – a self-reflexive narrative about the making of a film – was both more experimental and politically motivated. Several versions of the film were made, its five reels combined in different ways. Towards the end of his life Løchen was artistic director of the production company Norsk Film*, inspiring many young Norwegian film-makers. KS

LOCKWOOD, Margaret — Margaret Day; Karachi, India 1916 – London 1990

British actress. Margaret Lockwood had appeared in around thirty films by 1943, many of them 'quota quickies', but the list includes a number of roles for Michael Powell* and Carol Reed*, the lead role in Alfred Hitchcock's* *The Lady Vanishes* (1939) and a role as the idealistic Michael Redgrave's* scheming wife in *The Stars Look Down* (1939). From 1965 she had a second career on television in the popular soap opera, *The Flying Swan*. But it was the period from 1943 to 1947, from *The Man in Grey* (1943) to *Jassy* (1947), which defined her image as the wicked lady of the Gainsborough melodramas, offering to postwar women an alternative image of womanhood. Rather than the proper and moving denial of desire of *Brief Encounter* (1945), the Lockwood character wanted it all and wanted it now. Her exchanges with James Mason* in *The Wicked Lady* (1945) make it unambiguous that her body has a market value, to be bargained for rather than innocently wooed with romantic love. Of course, she is punished in the end, but not before she has established that conquest and desire are not exclusively male pursuits. The popularity, particularly among women, of the melodramatic extravagance of the Lockwood character suggests an undercurrent to the restraint of British realism which recent feminist criticism has begun to recognise. JC

Bib: Sue Aspinall and Robert Murphy (eds.), *Gainsborough Melodrama*, BFI Dossier 18 (1983).

Other Films Include: *Lorna Doone, Midshipman Easy* (1935); *Melody and Romance* (1937); *Owd Bob, Bank Holiday* (1938); *Rulers of the Sea* [US], *Susannah of the Mounties* [US], *A Girl Must Live* (1939); *Night Train to Munich, The Girl in the News* (1940); *Quiet Wedding* (1941); *Dear Octopus* (1943); *Give Us the Moon, Love Story* (1944); *A Place of One's Own, I'll Be Your Sweetheart* (1945); *Bedelia* (1946); *Cardboard Cavalier* (1949); *Highly Dangerous* (1950); *Trouble in the Glen* (1954); *Cast a Dark Shadow* (1955); *The Slipper and the Rose* (1976).

ŁÓDŹ Film School (Państwowa Wyższa Szkoła Filmowa, Telewizyjna i Teatralna Im. Leona Schillera)

Polish film school. The Łódź Film School was established in 1947 after the dissolution of Poland's first film school in Cracow. It has a worldwide reputation for excellence and its graduates (among them Andrzej Wajda*, Roman Polanski*, Jerzy Skolimowski* and Krzysztof Zanussi*) have become some of the most accomplished directors and cinematographers of world cinema. For many years, attending the school was the only route into the profession in Poland, and graduation secured a place in one of the industry's film units. Some of Poland's finest film-makers lectured at the school: Aleksander Ford* (1948–68), Andrzej Munk* (1957–61) and Jerzy Kawalerowicz* (since 1980). The school's current director, Professor Wojciech Has*, has the difficult job of guiding it into the post-communist world. AW

LØKKEBERG, Vibeke — Bergen 1945

Norwegian director and actress, whose work is made from an explicitly feminist perspective. She first appeared as an actress in *Liv/Life* (1967) and *Exit* (1970), both directed by her then husband Pål Løkkeberg. Her own films depict women's experiences and have been described as 'feminine' in their use of circular narratives, lesser emphasis on dialogue and action, and attempts at portraying interiority. Her first feature, *Åpenbaringen/Revelation* (1977), is a powerful portrait of a wife and mother, played by the poet Marie Takvam, who as she approaches the age of sixty bitterly reflects on the choices she has made in her life. A prominent media personality,

Løkkeberg frequently plays the lead role in her films, which also feature members of her family. She is a controversial figure in Norwegian culture, her slow, contemplative films provoking criticism and praise in equal measure. KS

Other Films as Director Include: *Løperjenten/Betrayal* (1981); *Hud/Skin* (1986); *Måker/Seagulls* (1991); *Der gudene er døde/Where the Gods are Dead* (1993).

LOLLOBRIGIDA, Gina   Rome 1927

Italian actress. Lollobrigida's film career began in the American-style beauty pageants that were the rage in Italy in the immediate postwar years. Though she failed to win the titles of Miss Italy, or even Miss Rome, she obtained parts in Italian films and attracted the attention of American producer Howard Hughes, who offered her a contract in Hollywood (though no film). She soon returned to Rome, in 1951, and embarked on a successful career, earning international recognition for her performances in such Franco-Italian 'tradition of quality'* co-productions as Christian-Jaque's* *Fanfan la Tulipe* (1952) and René Clair's* *Les Belles de nuit* (1952) – both co-starring Gérard Philipe* – and in Jean Delannoy's* *Notre-Dame de Paris/The Hunchback of Notre Dame* (1956). At the end of Alessandro Blasetti's* episode *Il processo di Frine* in *Altri tempi/Infidelity* (1952), the concluding speech of the defence attorney (Vittorio De Sica*) gave rise to the witty designation that would come to signify a whole class of voluptuous young Italian starlets: 'If we absolve the *minorati psichici* (psychically under-endowed), why not the *maggiorate fisiche* (physically amply endowed)?' Lollobrigida's most memorable role was that of La Bersagliera – a feisty, dirt-poor, independent-minded young woman whose body may personify that of the impoverished rural South itself, but who manages to live happily ever after, in Luigi Comencini's* 'rose-tinted' realist diptych *Pane, amore, e fantasia/Bread, Love and Dreams* (1953) and *Pane, amore e gelosia/Bread, Love and Jealousy/Frisky* (1954) (both featuring De Sica as the slightly lecherous but ultimately good-hearted local police chief), two key precursors of *commedia all'italiana**. For a brief period, Lollobrigida was able to transcend her lightweight, sexy-populist persona in films which revealed some depth of dramatic talent, including Carlo Lizzani's* *Achtung banditi!* (1951) and two filmic adaptations of Moravia novels: Mario Soldati's* *La provinciale/The Wayward Wife* (1953) and Luigi Zampa's* *La romana* (1954). Aspiring to international recognition as a serious actress, Lollobrigida sought more prestigious roles as a *femme fatale*, even subsidising some productions. The titles speak eloquently of her ambitions: *La donna più bella del mondo/Beautiful but Dangerous* (1955), *Solomon and Sheba* (1959, dir. King Vidor; US), and *Vénus Impériale/Imperial Venus* (1962, dir. Jean Delannoy; Fr.).

Together with Sophia Loren*, Silvana Mangano*, Marisa Allasio and Silvana Pampanini*, Lollobrigida represented a *divismo** (stardom) of a totally physical sort. The discourse of the *maggiorate fisiche* has, as its sole sign and referent, the body itself – eloquent testimony to Italy's emergence from the devastations of war and entrance into the well-nourished arena of advanced consumer society. MMa

LONDON FILM-MAKERS CO-OP

British institution, which was established in 1966 on the model of the New York Film-makers' Co-op organised by Jonas Mekas in 1962. Its function was (and is) not simply to support the production of avant-garde film, but to set up mechanisms for distribution and exhibition and to provide a focus for theoretical debate. There has been no continuous avant-garde tradition in Britain, and the Co-op saw itself as part of an international movement. It did, however, develop a distinct national identity around 'structural film'. In the distinction which Peter Wollen* makes in his influential essay 'The Two Avant Gardes', the Co-op belongs to the painterly avant-garde deriving from explorations of the means of expression (time, repetition, space, duration) rather than from the more political traditions associated with Soviet cinema and Jean-Luc Godard*. The two traditions, of course, were never completely separate. The work of the Co-op, particularly through film-makers and writers like Malcolm Le Grice and Peter Gidal, is less a means of expression than a means of theoretical investigation through film of representation, meaning and film itself. JC

Bib: Peter Gidal, *Materialist Film* (1989).

LÓPEZ, Charo   María del Rosario López Piñuelas; Salamanca 1943

Spanish actress. After stage roles she appeared in some of the most significant Spanish films of the late 1960s. Early on she starred in a mixture of erotic movies, Italian Westerns* and *auteur* films. In the 1980s her many successes included Gonzalo Suárez's* *Epílogo/Epilogue* (1984) and Mario Camús'* *La colmena/The Beehive* (1982). Her most characteristic films of recent years are Suárez's *Don Juan en los infiernos/Don Juan in Hell* (1991) and Josefina's Molina's* *Lo más natural/The Most Natural Thing* (1990), where her projection of the long-suffering but capable modern woman is given a sharp focus. Her contralto voice, wide eyes and bony features give her beauty forceful definition. She appears in a cameo role in Pedro Almodóvar's* *Kika* (1993). PWE

LÓPEZ VÁZQUEZ, José Luis   José Luis López Vázquez de la Torre; Madrid 1922

Spanish actor, who has starred in over 200 films since his film debut in Luis García Berlanga* and Juan Antonio Bardem's* first feature, *Esa pareja feliz/That Happy Couple* (1951). A costume designer and assistant director in the 1940s, and a promising theatre actor, López Vázquez became widely known to the Spanish public of the 1950s and 1960s through his numerous appearances in popular comedies like Mariano Ozores'* *Chica para todo/A Girl for Everything* (1962). His persona was the naive, patriotic Spaniard exploited by less scrupulous individuals. In the late 1960s and early 1970s, Carlos Saura* followed Bardem and Berlanga in exploiting the taciturn veneer and endearing innocence suggested by López Vázquez's round, childlike face to dramatic effect in a succession of serious roles which ironised the benign 'natural' images of the Franco regime. López Vázquez has also worked with Mario Camús* and Josefina Molina*. MD

LOPUSHANSKY, Konstantin — Dnepropetrovsk, Ukraine [USSR] 1947

Russian director and screenwriter. After studying music at the Kazan and Leningrad Conservatoires, Lopushansky completed the Higher Courses for Directors at Goskino, and worked with Andrey Tarkovsky* on *Stalker* (1979). His first film, the short *Solo* (1983), about a performance of Shostakovich's Fifth Symphony, shows the influence of that work. It was followed by *Pis'ma mërtvogo cheloveka/Letters from a Dead Man* (1986), a vision of the world after nuclear war, on which one of the scriptwriters was Boris Strugatsky, also co-author of the source for *Stalker*. The dead man of the title is a professor, played by Rolan Bykov, who writes to his lost son of his despair at the hubris of modern science. Lopushansky returned to the subject of a post-catastrophic world in the religious and ecological fable *Posetitel' muzeya/A Visitor to a Museum* (1989). JGf

LOREN, Sophia — Sofia Scicolone; Rome 1934

Italian actress. Born in Rome but raised in Pozzuoli near Naples, Sophia Loren rose to stardom as one of the *maggiorate fisiche* (physically amply endowed women), along with others such as Gina Lollobrigida* and Silvana Mangano*. She soon transcended this typecasting, however, to become a fine actress and the apotheosis of idealised Italian womanhood.

Starting as an extra in Mervyn LeRoy's *Quo Vadis* (1951), Loren appeared in a series of B-movies until discovered by producer Carlo Ponti*, who married her and set about developing, safeguarding and marketing her image – which he has continued to do throughout her career. Typical of her early performances under his tutelage were her role as 'La pizzaiola' in Vittorio De Sica's* episode film *L'oro di Napoli/The Gold of Naples* (1954), and her starring role in Mario Soldati's* *La donna del fiume/Woman of the River* (1955). In 1956, a contract with producer/director Stanley Kramer took her to Hollywood where she performed in a number of films which exploited not only her beauty, but also her dramatic talent and considerable charisma. She co-starred with Cary Grant in Kramer's *The Pride and the Passion* (1957), with Alan Ladd in Jean Negulesco's *Boy on a Dolphin* (1957), with Anthony Perkins in Delbert Mann's *Desire Under the Elms* (1958), and with William Holden in Carol Reed's* *The Key* (1958). Back in Italy, she resumed her collaboration with De Sica with an Oscar-winning performance as the urbanised peasant Cesira whose strength enables her and her daughter to survive wartime privation and gang rape in an adaptation of Moravia's novel *La ciociara/Two Women* (1960). Her comic talents came to the fore playing opposite Marcello Mastroianni* in two other De Sica films: in the first episode of *Ieri, oggi, domani/Yesterday, Today and Tomorrow* (1963), she is a Neapolitan who continually becomes pregnant to avoid imprisonment for selling black-market cigarettes, and in *Matrimonio all'italiana/Marriage – Italian Style* (1964) she plays a prostitute who finally gets her rich lover to marry her and legitimise their three sons.

In the 1970s and 1980s she allowed her career to slow down, acting only in a few international productions such as De Sica's last film, *Il viaggio/The Journey* (1974). Ettore Scola's* *Una giornata particolare/A Special Day* (1977), set in Mussolini's Rome, has both her and Mastroianni act against type: she as a frumpish middle-aged housewife and he as a homosexual anti-Fascist intellectual. Now living in Switzerland, she emerged from semi-retirement in 1994 to play opposite Mastroianni in Robert Altman's *Prêt-à-porter*, and she and Mastroianni were jointly chosen in 1993 to present the Oscar for Lifetime Achievement to Federico Fellini* – who had never directed her in a film. MMa

LORRE, Peter — Rosenberg, Austria-Hungary 1904 – Hollywood, California 1964

Hungarian-born German actor and director, originally a stage actor (including for Bertolt Brecht), whose performance as the child murderer in Fritz Lang's* *M – Eine Stadt sucht ihren Mörder/M* (1931) made him an international star. Lorre's eloquent, sad face and distinctive voice singled him out for being typecast, a fate aggravated by emigration, at first to France in 1933 (where he worked for G. W. Pabst*), then to Hollywood via Britain (where he worked for Alfred Hitchcock*) in 1934. Lorre's Hollywood career began when Columbia offered him a contract in 1934 and he played a crazed scientist in *Mad Love* (Karl Freund*, 1935). Lorre's roles for the next decade alternated between psychopaths, Nazi spies, double agents and effete small-time crooks. At 20th Century-Fox, the Mr Moto series offered him a chance to give a comic inflection to his generally sinister persona. His second breakthrough came when he was partnered with Humphrey Bogart and Sydney Greenstreet in such classics as *The Maltese Falcon* (1941) and *Casablanca* (1942). Lorre returned to Germany to direct one of the great masterpieces of *film noir* (*Der Verlorene/The Lost One*, 1951). Disappointed by the lack of critical or commercial response to the film, he continued his acting career in Hollywood, mainly directed by Roger Corman in shock-horror spoofs, often opposite Vincent Price and Boris Karloff. TE/KU

Other Films Include: *Bomben auf Monte Carlo, Die Koffer des Herrn O. F.* (1931); *Du haut en bas* (1934, Fr.); *The Man Who Knew Too Much* (1934, UK); *Think Fast, Mr. Moto* (1937, US); *Arsenic and Old Lace, Passage to Marseille* (1944, both US); *Beat the Devil* (1953, US); *Tales of Terror* (1962, US); *The Raven, The Comedy of Terrors* (1964, both US).

LOSEY, Joseph — La Crosse, Wisconsin 1909 – London 1984

American/British director, who was blacklisted after his failure to attend the House Un-American Activities Committee in 1951, and moved to Britain where he established himself in the first rank of British and European directors. Losey's early career was in theatre, where he directed the Charles Laughton*/Bertolt Brecht collaboration on *Galileo* in 1947. He had attended film classes with Eisenstein* in Moscow in the 1930s, and in Hollywood, in the 1940s, he had established a reputation as a director of tight *noir* thrillers. His early work in Britain, much of it directed under pseudonyms to conceal his participation from American exhibitors, followed in the same line with such films as *The Sleeping Tiger* (1954), directed as 'Victor Hanbury', *Blind Date* (1959) and *The Criminal* (1960). The European influence remained strong, however, and it emerged in an anglicised form in the collaboration he formed with Harold Pinter* for *The Servant* (1963), *Accident* (1967) and *The Go-Between* (1970). In the two films he made with Elizabeth Taylor, *Boom* (1968), which also had Richard Burton*, and *Secret Ceremony* (1968), also with Mia Farrow and Robert Mitchum, he tried, and failed, to bring the star system to the art cinema – 'I was the first person to make a picture with the Burtons that lost money' – and in *Modesty Blaise* (1966) he created a pop art version of a Bond* film. Losey, much more than Stanley Kubrick* or even Richard Lester*, brought to British cinema the eccentric sensibility of the exile, belonging neither to America, Britain or Europe, a cineaste still loyal to theatre, creating an art cinema of refracted perspectives. JC

Bib: Michel Ciment, *Conversations with Losey* (1985).

Other Films Include: *The Boy with Green Hair* (1949, US); *The Prowler, M* (1951, both US); *Eva/Eve* (1962); *The Damned* (1962); *King & Country* (1964); *Figures in a Landscape* (1970); *L'Assassinat de Trotsky/The Assassination of Trotsky* (1972, Fr./It./UK); *A Doll's House* (1973, UK/Fr.); *The Romantic Englishwoman/Une Anglaise romantique* (1975, UK/Fr.); *Galileo* (1976, UK/Canada); *Mr Klein* (1977, Fr./It.); *Don Giovanni* (1979, It./Fr./Ger.); *Steaming* (1985).

LUBITSCH, Ernst   Berlin 1892 – Hollywood, California 1947

German director, actor and producer, and one of the great geniuses of comedy in the cinema. Joining Max Reinhardt's* ensemble in 1911, Lubitsch became successful as a film actor in 1913, creating the comic persona of the wily and lecherous shop assistant (for instance in *Die ideale Gattin* and *Die Firma heiratet*, both 1913), before also taking over direction (first film: *Fräulein Seifenschaum*, 1915). His international breakthrough came in 1919, with a string of hits: *Die Austernprinzessin/The Oyster Princess, Madame Dubarry/Passion, Die Puppe*. On the strength of the American success of *Madame Dubarry*, Lubitsch left for Hollywood in 1921, to direct Mary Pickford, and then a series of social satires which inaugurated the new genre of the 'sophisticated comedy' – *The Marriage Circle* (1923); *Lady Windermere's Fan* (1925); *So This is Paris* (1926) – which was to make him world-famous. The coming of sound did not diminish Lubitsch's talent or acumen (*The Love Parade*, 1929, starring Maurice Chevalier*; *Monte Carlo*, 1930), and in 1935 he became director of production at Paramount, though it was for them

that he made the sparkling political comedy *Ninotchka* (1939), with Greta Garbo*.

The famous 'Lubitsch touch' was a combination of sharp socio-psychological analysis and indirect comment, leaving out what the spectators could easily supply by way of erotic play or sexual innuendo. *To Be or Not to Be* (1942) is probably the blackest example of Lubitsch's satirical humour, unmasking the cruelty and barbarity of the Nazi regime by focusing on stupidity, illogicality and pompous make-believe. TE/KU

Bib: Sabine Hake, *Passions and Deceptions: The Early Films of Ernst Lubitsch* (1992).

Other Films Include: *Schuhpalast Pinkus* (1916); *Ich möchte kein Mann sein, Carmen* (1918); *Anna Boleyn* (1920); *Die Flamme* (1922). **In the US**: *Forbidden Paradise* (1924); *The Student Prince in Old Heidelberg* (1927); *Design for Living* (1933); *Heaven Can Wait* (1943); *Cluny Brown* (1946).

LUCAN, Arthur   Arthur Towle; Boston, Lincolnshire 1887 – Hull 1954

British actor and cross-dresser, who as Old Mother Riley made fourteen films between 1937 and 1952. A caricatural Irish 'washerwoman' in the tradition of British music hall, Mother Riley in the 1930s was the vituperative and populist scourge of capitalist enterprise, championing the working class, fulminating with malapropisms and maledictions against pretension and injustice, and transgressing all social niceties either by accident or design. 'Hers,' says Jeffrey Richards, 'is truly a case of body-language gone berserk, but it is an outward and visible sign of her refusal to be cowed or to conform.' During the war the character was taken over by the war effort, and spies and Nazis replaced the middle class as her/his adversaries. JC

Bib: Jeffrey Richards, *The Age of the Dream Palace: Cinema and Society in Britain, 1930–1939* (1984).

Films Include: *Old Mother Riley* (1937); *Old Mother Riley MP* (1939); *Old Mother Riley in Society, Old Mother Riley in Business* [both directed by John Baxter] (1940); *Old Mother Riley's Ghosts* (1941).

LUCE

Italian institution. The Istituto Nazionale LUCE (acronym for L'Unione Cinematografica Educativa) was the earliest of the para-state agencies created under Fascism. Its purpose was to produce newsreels and documentaries and to monitor the production and exhibition of feature films, both foreign and domestic. LUCE was set up in 1924–25 out of a private association for the development of cinema as a form of 'popular education'. Until 1943, it served as the most conspicuous presence of the Fascist government in film production, legislation and policy, and produced most of the official state newsreels and documentaries. From 1926, LUCE productions were required to be shown in all Italian cinemas, and by 1927 all other newsreels were prohibited. Throughout the 1930s, LUCE was headed by the outspoken Luigi Freddi*. Initially located in Rome, LUCE was moved in 1940 to its present location amid the newly constructed cinema complex on the outskirts of Rome, next to Cinecittà* and the Centro Sperimentale*. After World War II, the Institute's mission changed somewhat, but it continues to be a centre for the support and archival maintenance of Italy's national film culture. JHa

LUCIA, Luis Luis Lucia Mingarro; Valencia 1914 – Madrid 1984

Spanish director. He discovered child stars Marisol (directing her in three films between 1960 and 1962), Rocío Dúrcal and Ana Belén* [> SPANISH CHILD STARS], but is best remembered for his Cifesa* films, such as *La princesa de los Ursinos/The Princess of the Ursinos* (1947), *Currito de la Cruz/Currito of the Cross* (1948) and *Lola la piconera/Lola the Coalgirl* (1951). Lucia's Cifesa films canonise Spanish heroes prepared to sacrifice themselves for their country; whatever the narrative, their underlying project is the glorification of the Nationalists' victorious Spain. Women, too, sacrifice everything – even their sexuality – for the greater national glory. So, although in *Currito de la Cruz* Romerita (Jorge Mistral*) is by far the more promising prospect, Rocío eventually tears herself away from him, preferring the ideologised Currito, a decision motivated more by Cifesa's political affiliations than by verisimilitude. PWE

LUMBERJACK FILMS

Finnish genre, which foregrounds the relationship between masculinity and social development. The roots of 'forest romanticism' are in literature and theatre. In cinema the genre flourished twice, first during the 1920s and 1930s and then in the late 1940s and the 1950s. Most films of the first phase were based on famous novels: *Koskenlaskijan morsian/The Logroller's Bride* (1922, 1937), *Tukkijoella/The Log Drivers* (1928), *Laulu tulipunaisesta kukasta/Song of the Scarlet Flower* (1938). The second phase began with four films: two versions of *Hornankoski/The Rapids of Hell* (Finnish version directed by Roland af Hällström, Swedish version directed by Hällström and Teuvo Tulio*, both films 1949), *Kanavan laidalla/At the Edge of the Canal* (1949), and another version of *Tukkijoella* (1951). Lumberjack films problematise masculinity by positioning two modes of life – forest and agrarian culture – in relation to larger social developments seen as embodying a transformation from forests to fields, and then to the towns. Logging is represented as a crucial point in a man's life; 'wild nature', together with an unwillingness to settle down and start farming, drives young men from their homes to the forests. Finally, the spectacular ride on the logs down the rapids turns the heroes into 'real' men. Logging is a test of manhood, a rite of passage. In the forest comedies of the early 1950s the community is presented as a nostalgic paradise for city dwellers, in such films as *On lautalla pienoinen kahvila/Ferryboat Romance* (1952), *Me tulemme taas/We're Coming Back* (1953), *Lumikki ja seitsemän jätkää/Snow White and the Seven Loggers* (1953), *Taikayö/Enchanted Night* (1954), *Kaksi vanhaa tukkijätkää/Two Old Lumberjacks* and *Hei rillumarei/Heh, Tra-la-la* (both 1954).

The world of the Lumberjack films is thoroughly bipolar: urban and cultivated rural areas have strong feminine connotations and family ties, while the rapids and forest life are signified as a world structured by male bonding. The 'forest boom' of the late 1940s and early 1950s can be read in the context of masculine fears caused by the war and postwar social changes. Women in Lumberjack films are embodiments of responsibility or of corrupted values – or just those who prepare the coffee. Mikko Niskanen's* *Elämän vonkamies/Life's Hardy Men* (1986) and *Nuoruuteni savotat/ Lumbercamp Tales* (1988) are the latest phase in the development of the genre. Here, however, masculine heroism, romantic nostalgia and comic gags disappear beneath a documentary-like representation of the logging lifestyle. AK

LUMIÈRE, Louis Besançon 1864 – Bandol 1948
and
LUMIÈRE, Auguste Besançon 1862 – Lyons 1954

French pioneers. Louis and Auguste Lumière ran their father Antoine's photographic business in Lyons. Louis was the brilliant inventor of the Cinematograph (meaning 'writing in movement', later shortened to 'cinema'). He built on previous inventions such as Edison's Kinetoscope, but with the key addition of a mechanism allowing the intermittent motion of the film in the camera, based on the sewing machine. The Cinematograph was both camera and projector. The invention was patented in February 1895, first demonstrated on 22 March 1895 and then through the summer at various learned societies and congresses. Its hugely successful public screening on 28 December 1895 in Paris constitutes the official 'birth' of the cinema. The uncannily aptly-named Lumières (as Jean-Luc Godard* pointed out) were canny businessmen. To demonstrate their apparatus, they recorded trains entering stations (*L'Arrivée d'un train en gare de La Ciotat*), workers leaving (their) factories (*La Sortie des usines Lumière*), participants at conferences, etc. They showed a fascination for the trappings of modernity as well as idyllic views of bourgeois domesticity in sunlit gardens such as *Le Déjeuner de bébé*, and little comic scenes (*L'Arroseur arrosé*) [all films, 1895]. Meanwhile, their cinematographers travelled all over the world shooting *actualités*, world events and the European colonial expansion, building a catalogue of over a thousand films over the next two years. The Lumière documentary approach is often simplistically contrasted with the fantasy and invention of Georges Méliès*. But while even these earliest films show an attention to framing and narrative organisation, Lumière cameramen also produced religious scenes, such as the thirteen-tableau *La Vie et la passion de Jésus-Christ* (1897). The films having achieved their purpose, the Lumières stopped production to concentrate on technical developments such as wide-screen, colour and 3-D cinema.

The Lumière home in Lyons is now a museum at the splendid address of 1, rue du Premier Film. GV

LUNACHARSKY, Anatoli V.   Poltava, Ukraine
[Russian Empire] 1879 – Menton, France 1933

Soviet politician and writer. As People's Commissar for Enlightenment from 1917 to 1929, Lunacharsky held overall political responsibility for Soviet cinema in its formative period. A liberal by nature, he tolerated in his interpretation of Lenin's* views on cinema a wide variety of approaches, reminding film-makers that 'boring agitation is counter-agitation'. His wife, Natalia Rozenel, regularly appeared in vamp-like parts in films such as Konstantin Eggert* and Vladimir Gardin's* *Medvezh'ya svad'ba/The Bear's Wedding* (1926), which Lunacharsky co-scripted. He also wrote the scripts for a number of other popular melodramas, including Gardin's *Slesar' i kantsler/The Locksmith and the Chancellor* (1924, co-scripted by Vsevolod Pudovkin*) and Grigori Roshal's *Salamandra/The Salamander* (1928), in which he made a cameo appearance. He published a book, *Kino na zapade i u nas* ('Cinema in the West and Here', 1928), and numerous articles on cinema. RT

LUNGIN, Pavel S.   Moscow 1949

Russian director and scriptwriter. The son of the famous scriptwriter and playwright Semyon Lungin, Pavel Lungin studied structural linguistics at Moscow University, and completed the Higher Courses for Scriptwriters in 1975. He worked for several years as a scriptwriter before making his directorial debut with *Taksi-Blyuz/Taxi-Blues* (1989), a Franco-Russian co-production about the relationship between an alcoholic musician, played by Pyotr Mamonov, from the group 'Zvuki mu', and a Moscow taxi-driver. The film attracted attention for its bold if only partially successful attempt to blend Russian elements – an unblinking evocation of the poverty and misery of modern urban life – with an energy, rapid montage and excess familiar from American crime thrillers. Lungin attracted further controversy with his next feature, *Luna Park* (1992), in which a young anti-semitic Muscovite muscle-builder, whose group is devoted to achieving a racially pure Russia, discovers that he is half-Jewish. JGf

LUX

Italian production company. In 1934 Riccardo Gualino (1879–1961) founded in Turin the Compagnia Italiana Cinematografica Lux, which for thirty years stood out for its financial rigour and efficient organisation as well as for the cultural and technical quality of its productions. Gualino was an efficient businessman as well as a modern art connoisseur and promoter of avant-garde theatre. An anti-Fascist, he was involved in 1931 in an obscure financial scandal and interned by Mussolini. From 1935 to 1938 Lux did nothing but distribute foreign movies and it was not until 1941 that it started producing its own films (twenty-two in 1943–45) by directors such as Alessandro Blasetti* (*La corona di ferro/The Iron Crown*, 1941), Mario Camerini* (*I promessi sposi/The Spirit and the Flesh*, 1941), Goffredo Alessandrini*, Mario Soldati*, Raffaello Matarazzo*, Alberto Lattuada* and Renato

Castellani*. At the end of the war, Lux supported neo-realism* by producing Giuseppe De Santis'* *Caccia tragica/Tragic Hunt* (1947) and *Riso amaro/Bitter Rice* (1949), Lattuada's *Il bandito* (1946) and *Senza pietà/Without Pity* (1948), Luigi Zampa's* *Vivere in pace/To Live in Peace* (1946) and *L'onorevole Angelina/Angelina* (1947), as well as films by Soldati, Luigi Comencini* and Pietro Germi*. At the same time it also produced popular films such as Riccardo Freda's* *I miserabili/Les Misérables* (1947) and Lattuada's *Anna* (1951). Gualino's novel production system was to choose and finance a film, and then either entrust its making to his executive producers or put it out on 'fixed-price contract' to a co-production company. Lux's activity reached its peak in 1954 with Luchino Visconti's* *Senso*, and ended with Mario Monicelli's* *I compagni/The Strikers* (1963). In 1964 it was acquired (along with other companies) by the Rovelli SIR chemicals group. Over thirty years it had produced 170 films and distributed 300, and had been involved, through associate companies, in productions worldwide. GVo

LUXEMBURG

Until the 1980s there had been just two kinds of film made in Luxemburg, documentary and pornography. The former were mainly short indigenous productions, the latter produced by companies from other European countries taking advantage of minimal interference by Luxemburg's authorities.

Only in 1980 did Luxemburg produce its first feature, *Wât huet e gesôt/What Did He Say?*, directed by Paul Scheuer and produced by AFO Film. There was little further activity before the same director/producer team made *Congé fir e Mord/The Murderer Takes a Day Off* in 1983. Despite the fact that all Luxemburg's early features were made with minuscule budgets, a few films managed to compete with the Hollywood blockbusters which generally dominate the domestic box office. *Mumm Sweet Mumm* (1989), again directed by Paul Scheuer, this time for the Luxemburg Ministry of Culture, was among the top ten grossing films of that year, holding its own with the likes of *Batman* and *Lethal Weapon 2*. It was not until 1990 that the country produced its first picture on 35mm: *Schacko Klak* is also notable for obtaining half its $1 million budget from the Luxemburg government after its script won a Ministry of Culture/Centre National de l'Audiovisuel (CNA) competition for a project to celebrate the country's national identity. Directed by Paul Kieffer and Frank Feitleret, *Schacko Klak* is set in a Nazi-occupied village during World War II and is perhaps Luxemburg's most successful feature yet, having been selected for screening at film festivals in London, Montreal and Moscow.

Despite its relatively meagre record in film production, Luxemburg boasts a Cinémathèque which is the envy of larger European nations. Now boasting a stock of over 5,000 prints, the Cinémathèque Municipale was founded in 1977 and celebrated its tenth anniversary with visits from film-makers Claude Chabrol* and Samuel Fuller. Run by Fred Junck, it was a prime mover in the establishment of the Union des Cinémathèques de la Communauté Européenne, an organisation which co-ordinates the work of Europe's film archives.

The Luxemburg government has been responsible for several initiatives aimed at stimulating film culture, usually international rather than purely indigenous in character. While an attempt to establish a yearly festival of new German cinema foundered, generous tax-shelter incentives for foreign productions based in Luxemburg have proved extremely popular with foreign television companies, especially in Germany and France, since their announcement in 1988. The scheme, administered by the Ministry of Foreign Affairs and External Trade, has also attracted several features which were struggling to secure adequate finance in their own countries. A good example is *Elenya*, made by British director Steve Gough in 1992 with the help of German money and shot mainly in Luxemburg, standing in for North Wales. Gough described filming in Luxemburg as 'a very positive experience'. Ironically, the financial incentives offered by the Luxemburg government almost became a victim of their own success. In 1994 the Grand Duchy was so inundated with foreign film crews that the government decided to limit all film production under the incentives scheme to indoor shooting. Unfortunately, at that point Luxemburg only had one suitable studio and even this was only half-finished. Once completed, Delux benefited enormously from the change in regulations. Recent productions made on its stages include Steven Berkoff's *Decadence* (1994, UK).

Notwithstanding the establishment of the Film Fund in 1990, Luxemburg has yet to produce a director or star of international renown, although Andy Bausch, Luxemburg's most prolific film-maker, is well known in Germany where he is in constant demand by television. Bausch's innovative work, usually made on shoestring budgets, has occasionally failed at the box office. His 1989 film, *A Wopbopaloobob a Lopbamboom*, however, was seen by some 9,000 Luxemburg cinemagoers. Jean-Pierre Thilges has described it as '*American Graffiti* meets *On the Waterfront* in Smalltown, Luxemburg'. Bausch's 1993 comedy, *Three Shake-a-Leg Steps to Heaven*, should also be noted, if nothing else for the last performance by cult American star Eddie Constantine*.

While Luxemburg was crowned European Cultural Capital of the Year for 1995, cinema's centenary year, it seems likely that its films will only ever reach a small audience abroad, mainly via the international festival circuit. Here an encouraging precedent was set by Pol Cruchten, whose *Hochzaitsneucht/Wedding Night* won the Max Ophuls Prize at the Saarbrucken film festival in 1993. SH

LYE, Len   Christchurch, New Zealand 1901 – Rhode Island, USA 1980

British animator. Born in New Zealand, arrived in Britain in the 1920s, and emigrated to the US in 1944. Lye's animation work is chiefly associated with the British Documentary Movement* in the 1930s and early 1940s. He is remembered as an experimentalist in both form and technique, inventing a system of painting directly onto film which was used in the award-winning *Colour Box* (1935). The technique was later adopted by Norman McLaren*. Lye's career did not progress in America, and he left film-making for painting and sculpture in the late 1950s. JC

Other Films Include: *Tusalava* (1928); *Birth of a Robot* (1935); *Rainbow Dance* (1936); *The Lambeth Walk* (1941); *Kill or be Killed* (1942); *Color Cry* (1955, US); *Rhythm* (1957, US).

M

MAAS, Dick   Heemstede 1951

Dutch director and producer, one of the most successful Dutch film-makers of the 1980s. After graduating from the Dutch film academy, Maas made an interesting debut with *De lift* in 1983, a gripping thriller/horror movie that brought him international recognition. A passion for American genres and strong effects characterises his next films. *Flodder* (1986), a farce in which an anti-social family is offered a house in a wealthy neighbourhood, gave Maas an opportunity to mock the social security system as well as the behaviour of the privileged classes and was a box-office hit. *Amsterdamned* (1988) is a smooth action film with a memorable chase along the Amsterdam canals and a brief cameo by Dutch veteran filmmaker Bert Haanstra*. *Flodder in Amerika/Flodder Does Manhattan* (1992), a sequel to *Flodder*, confirmed Maas' status as one of the very few Dutch directors capable of attracting large audiences. Maas writes his own musical scores and works as a producer. With Laurens Geels he founded First Floor Features, a production company with studio facilities in Almere which has produced a number of feature films of artistic interest such as *Abel* (1986), directed by Alex van Warmerdam. RdK

McANALLY, Ray   Buncrana 1926 – Dublin 1989

Irish actor. Though McAnally began his theatrical career at a young age he did not come to international prominence until the 1980s, when he played the papal envoy in *The Mission* (1986) and Christy Brown's father in the Oscar-winning *My Left Foot* (1989). His work on television brought him an even wider audience. A much admired actor, he died just as his career was leading him to more prominent film and television roles. KR

Other Films Include: *Shake Hands With the Devil* (1959); *Billy Budd* (1962); *The Looking Glass War* (1969); *Fear is the Key* (1972); *Angel* (1982); *Cal* (1984); *Empire State* (1987); *The Fourth Protocol* (1987); *The Sicilian* [US], *Taffin, White Mischief* (1987); *High Spirits* (1988); *We're No Angels* (1989, US).

MACARIO, Erminio   Turin 1902–80

Italian actor. From the 1930s to his death, Macario was one of the kings of variety shows, famous for his ingenuous humour, often in dialect, and for his '*donne*' (little women) comperes such as Wanda Osiris. With his wide eyes, kiss-curl over his forehead, Harry Langdon-like face and short stature, he evoked figures such as the innocent, 'lunar' Pierrot of *commedia dell'arte*. '*Lo vedi come sei?*' ('*Can't you see what you're doing?*') was his disarmed and disarming lullaby as well as the title of one of his best-known films, made in 1939 by Mario Mattoli, the director who understood Macario's talent better than anyone. After his debut in 1933 in the mediocre *Aria di paese*, Macario became one of the most popular comic actors of 1930s and 1940s Italian cinema, alongside Totò*, Aldo Fabrizi* and Renato Rascel. His surrealist absent-mindedness is fully represented in *Imputato, alzatevi!* (1939), a sort of *Hellzapoppin*, directed with craftsman-like precision by Mattoli and written by a team of humorists from the weekly publication *Il Bertoldo*. After the war, Macario added an element of pathos to his humour in response to the difficult period of reconstruction which Italy was going through, and gained box-office success with three films by Carlo Borghesio: *Come persi la guerra/How I Lost the war* (1947), *L'eroe della strada/Street Hero* (1948) and *Come scopersi l'America/How I Discovered America* (1949). Later, Macario returned to 'lowbrow' films, relying mostly on jokes, sketches and *double entendre*, frequently working with actors such as 'straight man' Carlo Campanini, Totò (for example in *Lo smemorato di Collegno*, 1962), Peppino De Filippo* and Nino Taranto. In these productions Macario once again brilliantly embodied the bewildered vagabond. Mario Soldati's* *Italia piccola* (1957) was, however, a favourite with those critics who look for the serious, 'human' side in the comic actor. GVo

McDOWELL, Malcolm   Leeds 1943

British actor, who made his film debut in Ken Loach's* *Poor Cow* (1967), and became one of the representative figures of the 1970s through his roles in Lindsay Anderson's* Mick Travis trilogy, *If....* (1968), *O Lucky Man!* (1973) and *Britannia Hospital* (1982), and in Stanley Kubrick's* *A Clockwork Orange* (1972). McDowell brings a kind of innocent insolence to Mick Travis, a naivety which allows him to register experience while maintaining a critical distanciation in Anderson's mappings of the nation. Similarly, Kubrick's highly stylised Alex in *A Clockwork Orange*, though pathologically violent, allows McDowell to perform the character without becoming him. Apart from Schrader's *Cat People* in 1981, McDowell has not in recent years found films of similar interest. JC

MACEDONIA – see YUGOSLAVIA (former)

MACHATÝ, Gustav   Prague [then Austria-Hungary] 1901 – Munich, West Germany 1963

Czech director. Gustav Machatý worked as pianist in a movie theatre, actor and scriptwriter before directing the farce *Teddy by kouřil/Teddy'd Like a Smoke* (1919). He left for Hollywood in 1920, where he reputedly worked on films by D. W. Griffith and Erich von Stroheim. He returned to Czechoslovakia, and in 1926 made a highly acclaimed feature, *Kreutzerova sonáta/The Kreutzer Sonata*, based on the Tolstoy story and notable for its impressive sets and expressionist influence. He consolidated his reputation with the enormously successful *Erotikon* (1929), and his first two sound features, *Ze soboty na neděli/From Saturday to Sunday* (1931), and *Extase/Ecstasy* (1932), which earned the condemnation of the Vatican at the time and subsequent cult status for Hedy Lamarr's nude scene. His films brought together several talents, including the poet Vitězslav Nezval, one of the co-founders of Czech surrealism, who worked on all three of the latter films, Alexander Hammid*, the avant-garde director and future documentarist, as well as the key figures of the 'Czech school' of cinematography, Jan Stallich, Václav Vich and Otto Heller. The three films provide an often subtle analysis of male-female relations, given an added force through the poetic lyricism of Machatý's style. *Extase* marked the end of Machatý's Czech career and, after films in Italy and Austria, he was signed to a Hollywood contract. He did second unit work on *The Good Earth* (1936) and *Madame X* (1937), and directed *Jealousy* (1945). He also made a 'Crime Does Not Pay' short and the B feature *Within the Law* (1939). After directing *Suchkind 312/Missing Child 312* (1956) in West Germany, he was appointed professor at the Munich Film School. Attempts to negotiate further projects in Czechoslovakia came to nothing. PH

Other Films: *Švejk v civilu/Švejk in Civilian Life* (1927); *Načeradec, král kibiců/Načeradec, King of the Kibitzers* (1932); *Nocturno* (1934, Aust.); *Ballerine* (1936, It.); *The Wrong Way Out* [short] (1938, US).

MACHULSKI, Juliusz   Olsztyn 1955

Polish director and actor. Machulski graduated from film school in 1978 and heads the Zebra Film Unit. Poland's answer to a 'Hollywood Movie Brat', Machulski is known for his fast-paced popular comedies. His second feature, *Seksmisja/Sexmission* (1984), a sci-fi comedy starring Jerzy Stuhr*, attracted rave reviews and a large public in Poland, although his uninspired and stereotyped portrayal of women in a world without men was criticised abroad. His later films include *Kingsajz/Kingsize* (1987), a whimsical comedy/political allegory starring Stuhr and the new Polish sex symbol, Katarzyna Figura. AW

Other Films Include: *Vabank* (1981); *Vabank II czyli Riposta/Revenge* (1984); *Szwadron/Squadron* (1992).

MACISTE

Italian superhero. Maciste was the first, the most famous, and the most enduring in a cadre of 'muscle men' who appeared in mainstream Italian cinema virtually since its inception. Maciste was first performed by Bartolomeo Pagano, a stocky Genovese dockworker, in Giovanni Pastrone's* *Cabiria* (1914). In this historical film, set roughly on the eve of the Carthaginian wars, Pagano's Maciste accompanies a Roman patrician (Fulvio) on a mission to save a young girl who has been abducted and held captive by Numidians for their sacrificial rituals. He plays the brawn to the patrician's brain, appears shirtless throughout much of the film, and is involved in numerous physical challenges from man, beast and other forces. Largely as a result of the popularity of his character in *Cabiria*, Pagano was contracted by Pastrone to make *Maciste* in 1915 (though he had made a brief appearance as a corpulent policeman in one of the *Cretinetti* comedies [> DEED, ANDRÉ]). *Maciste* inaugurated a series in which the muscular hero is tested by various spectacular situations and through which the mask of Maciste became fused with the actor Pagano. Pagano's Maciste films include *Maciste alpino/Maciste in the Alpine Regiment* (1916), *Maciste atleta/Maciste the Athlete* (1918), *Maciste innamorato/Maciste in Love* (1920), a Maciste trilogy in 1920 (*Maciste contro la morte/Maciste Against Death, Il viaggio di Maciste/Maciste's Journey, Il testamento di Maciste/Maciste's Testament*), *Maciste in vacanza/Maciste on Holiday* (1921), *Maciste imperatore/Maciste Emperor* (1924) and *Maciste all'inferno/Maciste in Hell* (1926). The Maciste films opened the way for other superheroes, many with names from classical mythology, who appeared in their own film series. The most popular were Luciano Albertini's Sansone (Samson), who occasionally appeared with his wife Linda Albertini (as Sansonetta), Carlo Aldini's Ajax, Domenico Gambino's Saetta, and Alfredo Boccolini's Galaor. Most of their films were produced in Turin, and by the 1920s Albertini and Gambino had formed their own production companies (Albertini Films and Saetta Productions, respectively).

The figure of Maciste resurfaced in Italian cinema during the 1950s with the revival of the 'muscle man' epic or peplum*, performed by actors such as Kirk Morris, Alan Steel, Reg Lewis, Ed Fury, Mark Forrest and Reg Park. JHa

MACKENDRICK, Alexander   Boston, USA 1912 – California, 1993

British director. Born in Boston of Scottish parents, educated at Glasgow School of Art, Mackendrick joined Ealing* as a scriptwriter in 1946, having previously scripted a number of films for the Ministry of Information, including the Halas-Batchelor* '*Abu*' animation series. He began directing with *Whisky Galore!* (1949). The interest of his films lies in the ten-sion between Michael Balcon's* gentle smile at the English ('We had great affection for British institutions: the [Ealing] comedies were done with affection'), and Mackendrick's more caustic, destructive (and Scottish?) laughter ('Personally, I am very attracted by comedy . . . It lets you do things that are too dangerous'). Behind his version of the Ealing whimsy there are sharp edges, and anyone who is surprised by the venom of his first Hollywood movie, *Sweet Smell of Success* (1957, US), has missed the hardness of the Scottish comedies – the humiliating laughter at the end of *Whisky Galore!* or the relentless bewildering of the American in *The 'Maggie'* (1954). Mackendrick is more interested in generational disorder than in sexual disorder, and children figure importantly in his work. *Mandy* (1952), his only non-comedy at Ealing, is, as Charles Barr argues, both 'one of the most affecting of all British films' and one of the least sentimental about children, playing out the child's struggle to enter language, the family and society with an ending which is both positive and provisional. It is precisely the ambivalence of Mackendrick's vision that makes him the least dated of Ealing directors.

With the exception of *Sweet Smell of Success*, his directing career in Hollywood failed to ignite. In 1969, he became Dean of the Film Department at the California Institute of the Arts. JC

Bib: Philip Kemp, *Lethal Innocence: The Cinema of Alexander Mackendrick* (1991).

Other Films Include: *The Man in the White Suit* (1951); *The Ladykillers* (1955); *Sammy Going South* (1963); *A High Wind in Jamaica* (1965); *Don't Make Waves* (1967, US).

McKENNA, Siobhan   Belfast 1923 – Dublin 1986

Irish actress. Best known as a versatile and talented stage actress from 1940, she worked in both Irish and English-language theatre. She made her film debut in Brian Desmond Hurst's* Irish historical drama *Hungry Hill* (1947), then played a murderous Irish servant girl in a melodrama, *Daughter of Darkness* (1948). By the time she got to film one of her most celebrated stage roles, that of Pegeen Mike in the 1962 version of *The Playboy of the Western World*, she was already too old for the part. Her film career is of much less significance than her theatrical legacy. KR

Other Films Include: *The Lost People* (1949); *King of Kings* (1961, US); *Of Human Bondage* (1964); *Doctor Zhivago* (1965, US).

McLAREN, Norman   Stirling, Scotland 1914 – Montreal, Canada 1987

British animator, whose best-known British work, *Hell Unltd.* (1936), was made with his colleague at Glasgow Art School, Helen Biggar. (Stewart McAllister, who went on to become Humphrey Jennings'* editor and collaborator, was a contemporary.) Biggar and McLaren were members of the left activist film group Glasgow Kino, and their film is an attack on the growing arms trade of the 1930s coupled with an appeal for working-class solidarity. It attracted the attention of John Grierson*, who invited McLaren to join the GPO Film Unit (Biggar remained in Glasgow). Before joining the unit, McLaren went to Spain with Ivor Montagu* and was cameraman on *In Defence of Madrid* (1936). Again at the invitation of Grierson, McLaren joined the National Film Board of Canada in 1941 and became director of its animation unit. He continued to develop the technique of drawing directly on to film, the method invented by Len Lye*, producing both abstract and representational art animation. He also worked in live-action animation, and his film *Neighbours* (1952) received an Academy Award as well as a screening in the Free Cinema* season. JC

Other Films Include: **In Britain** – *7 till 5* (1933); *Camera Makes Whoopee, Colour Cocktail* (1935). **In US** – *Stars and Stripes* (1939); *Dots, Loops, Boogie Doodle* (1940). **In Canada** – *V for Victory* (1941); *Begone Dull Care* (1949); *Rhythmetic* (1956); *Mosaic* (1965); *Pas de Deux* (1968); *Spheres* (1969); *Striations* (1970).

MAETZIG, Kurt   Berlin 1911

German director, whose research in film technology and photochemistry protected him from deportation by the Nazis, who nevertheless banned him from film-making in 1937 because of his Jewish descent. In 1944 Maetzig joined the underground Communist Party (KPD) and after the war he became a main protagonist in East German film culture, not only through his work as a documentary and feature film director but also as co-founder of DEFA* and first head of the Deutsche Hochschule für Filmkunst (film school) in Potsdam.

Maetzig directed a great number of documentaries before making his first feature film, *Ehe im Schatten* (1947), a very successful *Trümmerfilm* ('ruin film'). After the programmatic change in GDR film-making around 1952–53, he directed the prototypical DEFA film, a two-part biopic of the socialist icon Ernst Thälmann: *Ernst Thälmann – Sohn seiner Klasse* (1954) and *Ernst Thälmann – Führer seiner Klasse* (1955). Trying to infuse East German film culture with new genres and topics, he made, with *Septemberliebe* (1960), one of the few DEFA productions touching on the division of Germany, a year before the Berlin wall went up. When his second so-called '*Gegenwartsfilm*' (*Das Kaninchen bin ich*, 1965) was withheld from exhibition, Maetzig returned to more conventional genres before retiring in the mid-1970s. TE/KU

Bib: Günter Agde (ed.), *Kurt Maetzig – Filmarbeit: Gespräche, Reden, Schriften* (1987).

Other Films Include: *Die Buntkarierten* (1949); *Der Rat der Götter* (1950); *Mann gegen Mann* (1976).

MAGNANI, Anna   Rome 1908–73

Italian actress. Anna Magnani, popularly known in Italy as Nannarella, was born in Rome (and not in Alexandria, as she herself claimed and is reported in many reference works),

daughter of Marina Magnani and an unknown father. She began as a theatre actress in 1929, and later, in 1969, returned to the stage for *La lupa/The She-Wolf* by Giovanni Verga. She became a revue artiste from 1934, and worked with Totò* during the war. In 1935 she had married the director Goffredo Alessandrini*, but the marriage was a failure. By the time it was annulled in 1950, she had had a child (who died of polio) by the actor Massimo Serato* and entered into a relationship with Roberto Rossellini* (who then deserted her for Ingrid Bergman*). She began her film career in 1934, with bit parts, and her first success was in Vittorio De Sica's* *Teresa Venerdì* in 1941. Probably the greatest of her triumphs was Rossellini's *Roma città aperta/Rome Open City* (1945), in which she became the tragic icon of Italy's suffering during the war and German occupation, but also of its renewal, in cinema and beyond.

Magnani was the greatest and deservedly the most popular film actress in Italy, a character worthy of the great Roman dialect poet G. G. Belli. Few figures in cinema since Garbo have so powerfully overlaid personality and acting. But unlike Garbo, Magnani was an actress first and a star second. And, while Garbo embodied a middle-class myth, Magnani was the incarnation of popular passion. Her loyalty to this character remained constant, even in her most mainstream films and those in which she was called upon to play unfamiliar parts. She made four films in Hollywood – one of which, *The Rose Tattoo* (1955), won her an Oscar. She played Anita Garibaldi in *Camicie rosse/Red Shirts* (1952), directed by her ex-husband Alessandrini and finished by Franco Rossi. She was a memorable Perichole in Jean Renoir's* *La carrozza d'oro/Le Carrosse d'or/The Golden Coach* (1953) and she performed a stunning monologue in *Una voce umana* (based on Jean Cocteau's* play *La Voix humaine*) in Rossellini's *L'amore* (1948). Though she was a naturalistic actress, her acting was based on more than mere instinct. According to Renato Castellani*, who directed her in *Nella città l'inferno/ ... And the Wild, Wild Women* (1958), Nannarella's technique was so refined that she transcended technique altogether. Two of her best performances vouch for this – in Luchino Visconti's* *Bellissima* (1951) and in Pier Paolo Pasolini's* *Mamma Roma* (1962) – as do the numerous awards she received. The secret of her immense popularity was that she was passionate but never sentimental. Her energy and lust for life were acknowledged when her coffin was carried out of the Santa Maria della Minerva church in Rome, two days after her death on 26 September 1973, and an all-engulfing roar rose up from the waiting crowd, from a sustained, frenetic, extraordinary round of applause. GNS

Other Films Include: *Davanti a lui tremava tutta Roma/Tosca, Il bandito* (1946); *Siamo donne/We the Women* (1953, Visconti ep.); *Roma/Fellini's Roma* (1972, cameo).

MAGNUSSON, Charles   Gothenburg 1878 – Stockholm 1948

Swedish producer. Magnusson was 'the creative producer' of Swedish silent film. He first became involved with Svenska Bio* as a newsreel photographer. Appointed managing director in 1909, he launched the company into large-scale film production and directed several movies himself. He moved Svenska Bio to Stockholm in 1911 and hired Mauritz Stiller* and Victor Sjöström*, who established the international reputation of Swedish cinema while making the company prosperous. In 1919 Svenska Bio merged with the rival Skandia company to form Svensk Filmindustri. The new company got into difficulties during the crisis of the 1920s, and Magnusson was fired in 1928. LGA/BF

MAKAROVA, Tamara F.   St Petersburg 1907

Soviet actress. Makarova started in film in 1927. Although she subsequently appeared in films by Vsevolod Pudovkin* (*Dezertir/The Deserter*, 1933) and Mikhail Chiaureli* (*Velikoe zarevo/The Great Dawn*, 1938, and *Klyatva/The Vow*, 1946), her career is closely associated with the director Sergei Gerasimov*, for whom she played leading roles in *Semero smelykh/The Brave Seven* (1936), *Komsomol'sk* (1938), *Bol'shaya zemlya/The Great Earth* (1944) and *Molodaya gvardiya/The Young Guard* (1947). Makarova usually embodied women in extremity and, with Lyubov Orlova*, was one of the key figures in defining the officially determined role of women in the Stalin* period. She taught at VGIK* from 1943 and shared a workshop with Gerasimov. RT

MAKAVEJEV, Dušan   Belgrade, Serbia 1932

Serbian film director and scriptwriter. The most controversial Yugoslav director began his film career with shorts after graduating in psychology and film and writing film criticism. From the beginning, his films were marked with a sweet smell of forbidden fruit, making him one of the most original members of the 'Black Wave'*: *Čovek nije tica/A Man is not a Bird* (1965) aimed to 'ironise the working class'; *Ljubavni slučaj ili tragedija službenice PTT/Love Affair, or the Case of the Missing Switchboard Operator/Switchboard Operator* (1967) focused on a love story between a rat exterminator and a telephone operator; *Nevinost bez zaštite/Innocence Unprotected* (1968) combined a 1942 semi-documentary of the same name with images of the participants twenty-five years later. But the real breakthrough came in 1971, with *W. R. – Misterije organizma/W. R. – Mysteries of the Organism*. This film collage, starring Milena Dravić*, and based on the theories of sexual psychologist Wilhelm Reich, was an international hit but was judged so 'subversive' in Yugoslavia that it was not officially shown there until 1986. Makavejev was forced to work abroad: he shot *Sweet Movie* (1974) in France and Holland, *Montenegro* (1981, also *Pigs and Pearls*) in Sweden, and *The Coca Cola Kid* (1985) in Australia. These films did not receive the critical acclaim of his early work, and *Manifesto* (1988, USA/Croatia) and *Gorilla Bathes at Noon* (1993, Ger.) failed to revive his fortunes. His latest film, *A Hole in the Soul* (1994, produced by his own company Triangle and the BBC), is an intimate self-portrait. SP

Bib: Daniel J. Goulding, 'Makavejev', *Five Film-makers* (1994).

MÄKELÄ, Mauno   Helsinki 1916–87

Finnish producer. Mauno Mäkelä was managing director and executive producer of Fennada-Filmi, set up in 1950, along with Risto Orko's* Suomi-Filmi and T. J. Särkkä's* Suomen Filmiteollisuus (SF) a leading company in the 1950s. An engineer by training, Mäkelä came to film in the footsteps of his father, Väinö Mäkelä. Initially Fennada's dual structure resembled that of SF. On one side the company put out cheaply and quickly made farces, often directed by Aarne Tarkas*, specialising in military vaudevilles of which it produced nearly one a year throughout the 1950s [> FINNISH MILITARY FARCE]. On the other, Fennada aspired to cultural prestige with adaptations of classic Finnish literature. The major director in this area was Roland af Hällström (*Putkinotko*, 1954; *Ryysyrannan Jooseppi/Joseph of Ryysyranta*, 1955). In addition to vaudeville and adaptations, Fennada produced films that could be seen as 'radical' compared to the output of its rivals. Ville Salminen's *Evakko/Evacuated* (1956), for example, is a sophisticated low-key counterpart to SF's war spectacular *Tuntematon sotilas/The Unknown Soldier* (1954). Production was rationalised into 'A' and 'B' films, with comedies premiered in the summer, traditionally a quiet period, primarily for rural audiences.

Mäkelä's personal power at Fennada was less central than Särkkä's at SF or Orko's at Suomi-Filmi, since he has no directing or writing credits. Towards the end of the 1950s Fennada was plunged into a crisis which severely affected the entire Finnish film industry. Unlike SF, which eventually went bankrupt, Fennada survived to make a few more films. Ritva Arvelo's *Kultainen vasikka/The Golden Calf* (1961) was one of the first beneficiaries of state awards. *Täällä Pohjantähden alla/Here Under the Northern Star* (1969), an epic based on Väinö Linna's trilogy of the same name, was the last Finnish film to reach over one million domestic viewers. Fennada's output declined further in the 1970s, and Mäkelä left the company. In the early 1980s the Finnish broadcasting company YLE bought Fennada's stock and exhibition rights to its films. The 'Mäkelä clan', however, still maintained a hold on Finnish cinema. Jukka Mäkelä (Mauno's nephew) was the managing director of Finnkino (established in 1986), which for a while controlled practically all national film production and exhibition in Finland. Finnkino, however, folded in early 1995. KL

MAKK, Károly   Berettyóújfalu 1925

Hungarian director. Makk is one of the most productive Hungarian directors of his generation. He graduated from the Academy of Theatre and Film Art in 1950 and has been an active and versatile film-maker for forty years. He tried his hand at many different genres and styles, including light comedy (*Liliomfi*, 1954), social drama (*Megszállottak/The Obsessed*, 1961), and lyrical psychological drama (*Szerelem/Love*, 1970). He has also made films for television. Whatever the genre, the distinctive features of Makk's work are his talent for directing actors and his ability to evoke the precise psychological atmosphere of a situation. His unquestionable masterpiece is *Szerelem*, which won several international prizes. This film was based on two autobiographical short stories by the Hungarian writer Tibor Déry, who spent four years in prison after 1956 for his activities in the revolution. During his prison years Déry wrote letters to his aged and ailing mother, and, to make his absence bearable for her, pretended he was abroad making a film. Makk's film is a moving testimony to the strength of emotion and loyalty in defiance of the humiliations imposed by a dictatorial power. KAB

Other Films Include: *9-es kórterem/Ward no. 9* (1955); *Mese a 12 találatról/Tale of the Twelve Scores* (1956); *Ház a sziklák alatt/House Under the Rocks* (1958); *Mit csinált a feleséged 3-tól 5-ig?/His Majesty's Dates* (1964); *Macskajáték/Cat Play* (1974); *Egy erkölcsös éjszaka/A Very Moral Night* (1977); *Két történet a félmúltból/Two Stories from the Recent Past* (1980); *Egymásra nézve/Another Way* (1982); *Játszani kell/Playing for Keeps* (1984); *Az utolsó kézirat/The Last Manuscript* (1987); *Magyar rekviem/A Hungarian Requiem* (1990).

MALLE, Louis   Thumeries 1932

French director. A graduate of IDHEC*, Malle co-directed with Jean-Yves Cousteau the prize-winning documentary *Le Monde du silence/The Silent World* (1956). His subsequent work is characterised by classicism, versatility and international success. Malle's early features place him in an odd position vis-à-vis the New Wave*; he was a precursor to it with *Ascenseur pour l'échafaud/Lift to the Scaffold* (1957), with his use of locations, Jeanne Moreau* and a Miles Davis score, and *Les Amants* (1958), and already marginal to it with the zany comedy *Zazie dans le métro* (1960, based on Raymond Queneau's novel). Malle's subsequent work combined classic *mise-en-scène* with 'risky' topics: suicide in *Le Feu follet/A Time to Live and a Time to Die* (1963), mother-son incest in *Le Souffle au coeur/Dearest Love* (1971), child sexuality in *Pretty Baby* (1978, US) and, most incisively, French collaboration during the Occupation in *Lacombe, Lucien* (1974). Unusually for a French director, Malle made a successful transition to the US with such films as *Atlantic City, U.S.A.* (1980, Can./Fr.) and *My Dinner with André* (1981), returning to France for his moving autobiographical wartime drama *Au revoir les enfants* (1987) and the Renoiresque *Milou en Mai* (1989). He made the glossy *Fatale/Damage* (1992) with Juliette Binoche* and Jeremy Irons*, shot in England and (controversially for the French) in English, and ironically returned to a more modest type of European art cinema* with the American *Vanya on 42nd Street* (1994). Malle has directed many documentaries on subjects ranging from the American Bible belt to the Tour de France. GV

Other Films Include: *Vie privée/A Very Private Affair* (1962); *Viva Maria!* (1965); *Le Voleur/The Thief of Paris* (1967); *Black Moon* (1975).

MALLESON, Miles Croydon 1888 – London 1969

British actor, scriptwriter and playwright. Malleson is probably most familiar as the genteel hangman of *Kind Hearts and Coronets* (1949) or as Canon Chasuble in *The Importance of Being Earnest* (1952), or in a wide range of small but distinc-

tive character parts in postwar films ranging from *Geordie* (1955) to *Peeping Tom* (1960). He was also, however, on the advisory council (along with George Lansbury, James Maxton and Sybil Thorndike) of the Masses Stage and Film Guild established by the Independent Labour Party (ILP) in 1929 to bring 'plays and films of an international character to working-class audiences'; he was the author of a play on the Tolpuddle Martyrs supported by the Trades Union Congress; and, simultaneously, he was one of Herbert Wilcox's* leading scriptwriters in the 1930s, with credits including such hits as *Nell Gwyn* (1934) and *Peg of Old Drury* (1935), the patriotic celebrations of monarchy, *Victoria the Great* (1937) and *Sixty Glorious Years* (1938), and, for Alexander Korda*, *The Thief of Bagdad* (1940), in which he also played the Sultan. JC

MALMROS, Nils   Århus 1944

Danish director. Malmros made amateur films at first, then – inspired by the French New Wave* – he made his professional debut with *Lars Ole 5c/Lars Ole from 5c* in 1973, demonstrating a talent for portraying the lives and attitudes of young people. He continued in this vein with *Drenge/Boys* (1976), while graduating in medicine; *Kundskabens træ/The Tree of Knowledge* (1981), which completed the trilogy, is probably his best work. *Skønheden og udyret/The Beauty and the Beast* (1983) dissects a father-daughter relationship, and *Kærlighedens smerte/Pain of Love* (1993) is a sensitive portrayal of a young woman. Malmros' films are poetic and personal, precisely located in his home town of Århus (*Århus by Night*, 1989). So far Malmros has directed six features and a charming television drama, *Kammesjukhul/Christmas among Pals* (1978) [> DANISH CHILDREN'S FILMS]. ME

MAMIN, Yuri   Leningrad 1946

Russian director, who graduated from the Leningrad State Institute of Theatre, Music and Cinema in 1969 as a theatrical producer. In 1982 Mamin completed the Higher Courses for Directors at Goskino, where he studied under Eldar Ryazanov*. His short comedy *Prazdnik Neptuna/Neptune's Feast* (1986) uses the device of Nikolai Gogol's play *The Inspector-General* – foolish provincials try to impress outsiders – to expose contemporary venality and bureaucratic incompetence. The satirical note prevails in his 1988 feature *Fontan/The Fountain*, in which events in a ghastly apartment block on the outskirts of Leningrad serve as a microcosm of all the absurdities and contradictions of the *perestroika* years. Mamin's next film, *Bakenbardy/Side Whiskers* (1990), provides a savage dissection of the forces threatening to tear Russia apart in its story of the clash between the social misfits of the 'Capella' gang and their enemies, the muscle-bound 'Bashers'. The 'Bashers' are then co-opted into a new grouping, the 'Side Whiskers', who sport Pushkinian facial hair as a sign of their Russianness. Mamin's films provide a picture of modern Russian life that is free of illusions, and his latest, *Okno v Parizh/Salades russes/A Window on Paris* (1992), in which a window in St Petersburg magically opens on to the rooftops of Paris, offers further scope for irony, this time over the unresolved ambivalence that Russians feel towards the rest of Europe. JGf

MANAKI, Milton
Avdela, Greece 1882 – Bitolj, Macedonia 1964

Macedonian photographer, pioneer of Yugoslav cinema. His brother Janaki taught Manaki photography and sent him a Bioscope No. 300 camera from London in 1905. His first views of family life, religious rituals and craftsmen's work still have great ethnological value. He later specialised in more structured documentary reportage of political visits and meetings, such as Sultan Reshad's visit to Bitolj in 1911. He was official court photographer to the Turkish sultan and the kings of Romania and Yugoslavia. In 1921 he opened, with his brother, the 'Manaki' film theatre in Bitolj, which was destroyed by fire in 1939. After World War II he was recognised as a pioneer of Yugoslav cinema and the press award given at the national film festival in Pula* was named after him. SP

MANGANO, Silvana
Rome 1930 – Madrid 1989

Italian actress. After training as a dancer, working as a model and winning the Miss Rome contest, nineteen-year-old Silvano Mangano shot to international stardom with her performance in Giuseppe De Santis'* *Riso amaro/Bitter Rice* in 1949. Striding through the rice paddy with her thighs exposed she brought a breath of glamour and fleshy sensuality – welcome to some, disapproved of by others – to neo-realism*. She married the film's producer, Dino De Laurentiis*, who fostered her career throughout the 1950s, giving her starring roles in big international productions shot in Italy such as *Ulisse/Ulysses* (1954, dir. Mario Camerini*), *Jovanka e le altre/Five Branded Women* (1960, dir. Martin Ritt) and *Barabba/Barabbas* (1961, dir. Richard Fleischer). Shunning the limelight and economically secure, she let her career lapse in the mid-1960s, but re-emerged, thinner but still extraordinarily beautiful, as the showcase star of De Laurentiis' episode film production *Le streghe/The Witches* (1966) and was thereafter much sought after by art cinema directors such as Pier Paolo Pasolini* (*Edipo re/Oedipus Rex*, 1967; *Teorema/Theorem*, 1968) and Luchino Visconti* (*Morte a Venezia/Death in Venice*, 1971; *Gruppo di famiglia in un interno/Conversation Piece*, 1974). Her final starring role was in Nikita Mikhalkov's* *Oci ciornie/Ochi chërnye/Dark Eyes* (1987). GNS

MAR, Fien de la
Josephine Johanna de la Mar; Amsterdam 1898–1965

Dutch actress. Popular film star of the 1930s, born into a family of actors and singers. She began her stage career at an early age and was already a star of the popular theatre when the Dutch film industry called on her talents as a comedienne and singer for the new sound films. She made her debut in *De Jantjes/The Jack Tars* (1934), the first popular Dutch film of the 1930s. Her strong, flamboyant and mature personality contrasted with other Dutch film stars of the 1930s such as Rini Otte and Lily Bouwmeester. She suffused her characters with life and satire and her songs became popular hits. Fien de la Mar played her last role in *Ergens in Nederland/Somewhere in Holland* (1940). KD/JR

Other Films: *Bleeke Bet/Pale Betty* (1934); *Op stap, De big van het regiment, Het leven is niet zo kwaad* (1935); *Klokslag twaalf* (Dutch version of *Quand minuit sonnera*, 1936, Fr.); *De spooktrein* (1939).

MARAIS, Jean
Jean Alfred Villain-Marais; Cherbourg 1913

French actor. There are two aspects to the career of the extravagantly good-looking Jean Marais: the critically acclaimed films he made as Jean Cocteau's* personal and professional partner, and the popular swashbucklers of the 1950s and 1960s. Marais trained for the stage and had small parts in films by Marcel L'Herbier*. In 1937 he met Cocteau, who propelled him into the limelight of Paris artistic circles, which led to a long and successful stage and film career. Cocteau used Marais' beautifully chiselled face and athletic body in his poetic-mythical fantasies, especially in *L'Éternel retour* (1943, scripted by Cocteau, directed by Jean Delannoy*), a reworking of the Tristan and Iseult legend, the fairy tale *La Belle et la bête* (1946), and *Orphée* (1950). Narratives, lighting and costumes turned on Marais' eroticism; he became one of France's top heart-throbs. When his partnership with Cocteau loosened (they remained friends), Marais starred in popular genre films of the 1950s, melodramas such as *Le Château de verre/The Glass Castle* (1950, with Michèle Morgan*), and costume dramas such as Jean Renoir's *Eléna et les hommes/Paris Does Strange Things* (1956). He found his niche in swashbucklers, the perfect setting for his dashing, muscular performances: *Nez de cuir* (1952), *Le Comte de Monte-Cristo* (1954), *Le Capitaine Fracasse* (1961), and many others, including a *Fantômas* series. These films, though critically scorned, made Marais one of the top ten stars of the French postwar box office. Alongside Gérard Philipe*, Marais represented an ambivalent masculinity which, as with Rudolf Valentino in Hollywood, combined the pleasures of feminine identification with 'male' narrative mastery. Marais' film career came to an end in the early 1970s. A prominent media personality in France, he has kept active in theatre, as well as painting and sculpture (he sculpted the head of Jean Gabin* displayed at the Gabin museum). GV

Other Films Include: *Carmen* (1943–45); *L'Aigle à deux têtes* (1948); *Les Parents terribles* (1948); *Dortoir des Grandes* (1953); *Napoléon* (1955); *La Princesse de Clèves, Le Miracle des loups* (1961); *Les Mystères de Paris, Le Masque de fer* (1963); *Peau d'Ane* (1970); *Parking* (1985); *Johanna d'Arc of Mongolia* (1988).

MARCEAU, Sophie
Paris 1966

French actress, who emerged as a cute adolescent in Claude Pinoteau's family comedy *La Boum* (1980), when she was barely fifteen. The phenomenal success of the film prompted

La Boum 2 (1982) and other comedies. Marceau was part of the 1980s fashion for pairing very young women with mature men such as Jean-Paul Belmondo* (*Joyeuses Pâques*, 1984). As she matured, her looks evolved into sultry sexiness, adorning for instance the historical epics *Fort Saganne* (1984, with Gérard Depardieu*), *Chouans!* (1988) and *La Fille de d'Artagnan/D'Artagnan's Daughter* (1994). Marceau has tried to move into *auteur* cinema, notably with Pialat's* *Police* (1985), but without much success so far. GV

MARCHESI, Marcello
Milan 1912 – S. Giovanni di Sinis 1977
and
METZ, Vittorio
Rome 1904–84

Italian scriptwriters and directors. Metz came from the theatre, worked for the weekly comic magazine *Marc'Aurelio*, and co-founded (in 1936) another magazine, *Bertoldo* – two publications which gave Marchesi and a whole generation of writers (Stefano Steno, Age* and Scarpelli*, Frattini, Continenza and, above all, Fellini*) their training ground. He came into the cinema through scriptwriting (*Imputato, alzatevi!*, 1939) and, together with Marchesi, wrote *Il pirata sono io* (1940) and *Non me lo dire*, both starring the great comic Erminio Macario*. From then until 1968, Marchesi and Metz wrote some sixty scripts for film comedies, often vehicles for such comic actors as Totò*, Macario, Renato Rascel, Walter Chiari* and Nino Manfredi. In addition, they themselves directed comedies, including *Sette ore di guai* (1951), *Mago per forza* (1952), *Lo sai che i papaveri* (1952), *Tizio, Caio e Sempronio* (1952), *Milano miliardaria* (1951) and others (on the whole less successful) in collaboration with Marino Girolami. They wrote variety shows (especially for Chiari) and musical comedies, and were prolific authors for radio and television – where Marchesi became a popular variety performer in the early 1960s. In addition, they turned out promotional slogans and hundreds of television advertisements.

Metz spent his entire career satirising political behaviour and ridiculing national fads. Marchesi published numerous books, including *Essere o malessere* (1962), *Il malloppo* (1972) and *Sette zie* (1977), in which he fully demonstrated his epigrammatic and disenchanted sense of humour. He drowned while swimming off the coast of Sardinia. He had written: 'The important thing is that death finds us alive.' MMo

MARCZEWSKI, Wojciech
Łódź 1944

Polish director. Marczewski finished his studies at Łódź* in 1969, making several television films before *Zmory/Nightmares* in 1979. Set in turn-of-the-century Poland, *Zmory* looks at a young boy's coming of age before World War I. Acclaimed for his visual style, Marczewski turned to his own childhood in the 1950s for inspiration in *Dreszcze/Shivers* (1981), which uses freeze-frames and camera angles to startling effect to elicit a child's perception of the world. Along with films like Feliks Falk's* *Był Jazz/And There was Jazz*

(1984) and Jerzy Domaradzki's *Wielki Bieg/The Great Race* (1987), *Dreszcze* is one of a series of films within the 'cinema of moral unrest', commenting on Poland in the Stalinist years. Although artistically acclaimed, *Dreszcze* was shelved for political reasons. Marczewski had to wait nine years to make *Ucieczka z Kina Wolność/Escape from Liberty Cinema* (1990), a homage to Woody Allen's *Purple Rose of Cairo* which skilfully comments on self-censorship in the new political regime while making fun of the old communist censorship. A subtle yet incisive film, the very successful *Ucieczka z Kina Wolność* upholds the promise of Marczewski's earlier work while bringing a new perspective to post-communist Polish cinema. AW

MARIANO, Luis
Mariano Eusebio González; Irun, Spain 1920 – Paris 1970

French singer and actor of Spanish origin. Mariano, a remarkable singer, started as an operetta star. Although his film persona was a continuation of his stage one, his phenomenal success was characteristic of popular French film genres of the 1940s and 1950s. In filmed operettas (*Violettes impériales/Violetas Imperiales/Imperial Violets*, 1952), or in musical comedies (*Le Chanteur de Mexico*, 1956), Mariano, his dark good looks enhanced by colourful costumes, epitomised the Latin lover. His huge popular appeal (especially to women) was matched by critical disdain. GV

MARISCAL, Ana
Ana María Rodríguez Arroyo; Madrid 1923

Spanish actress and director. A leading lady in the 1940s, she rose to stardom in José Luis Sáenz de Heredia's* *Raza/Race* (1941). From then on her demureness was used to great effect in films like *Vidas cruzadas/Crossed Lives* (1942) and Luis Lucia's* *La princesa de los Ursinos/The Princess of the Ursinos* (1947) and *De mujer a mujer/Woman to Woman* (1950). With her acting career sliding in the early 1950s, she set up a film production company and started directing. One of the very few women directors in Spain, her more personal work eventually gave way to routine narratives. PWE

MARISCHKA, Ernst
Vienna 1893 – Chur, Switzerland 1965

Austrian director, writer and actor. Marischka, who was to become one of the main purveyors of Austrian popular entertainment films, saw his first cinematic success as a director in 1912 with the full-length feature *Der Millionenonkel*. Subsequently he wrote numerous librettos and scripts for silent and sound films, such as *Wiener G'schichten* (1940, dir. Geza von Bolvary*), and directed successful films such as *Abenteuer im Grand-Hotel* (1943), with Hans Moser*, *Saison in Salzburg* (1952) and *Mädchenjahre einer Königin* (1954, with Romy Schneider*). His greatest fame, however, came from his *Sissi* trilogy (1955–57), one of the biggest successes in Austrian cinema. The three films – *Sissi* (1955), *Sissi – die* *junge Kaiserin* (1956) and *Sissi – Schicksalsjahre einer Kaiserin* (1957) – lavish sentimental costume dramas based on a romanticised portrait of Empress Elizabeth of Austria, turned Romy Schneider into a major international star. They also made an important contribution to the restoration of the Austrian concept of national identity, by recycling elements of the Habsburg myth; they are still popular hits both on television and video in Austria and in other continental European countries. Marischka's 1950s films stand out thanks to his masterful use of colour and flamboyant decor, as well as the great attention to detail that characterises their scripts. Marischka's brother **Hubert Marischka** (Vienna 1882–1959) had his roots as an actor in the theatre and operetta. He also worked as a scriptwriter and director of popular entertainment films, including *Wir bitten zum Tanz* (1941) with Paul Hörbiger* and Hans Moser, *Wiener melodien* (1947), *Du bist die Rose vom Wörther See* (1952, Ger.), and *Liebe, Sommer und Musik* (1956). FM/AL

MARKER, Chris
Christian François Bouche-Villeneuve; Neuilly-sur-Seine 1921

French director and photographer. Marker, who has been making documentaries since 1952, is considered a member of the 'Left Bank' of the New Wave* for his left-wing politics and the way his work combines social issues with formal experiment. He has shot films in many countries, but perhaps his most famous film, *Le Joli mai* (1963), is a portrait of Parisians in May 1962, a classic of *cinéma-vérité** in its blend of ethnographic interviews with auteurist self-portrait. For Marker as for Jean-Luc Godard*, 1968 marked a turning point; Marker turned to collective film-making with the founding of SLON. In the 1980s and 1990s, his films, especially *Sans soleil/Sunless* (1983) and *L'Héritage de la chouette/The Legacy of the Owl* (1988), were complex reflections on image culture (film, video, photography) in the postmodern era. Among his numerous films as director are *Lettre de Sibérie/Letter from Siberia* (1958), *Cuba Si!* (1961), *La Jetée/The Pier* (1964, composed mostly of still photographs), *Le Train en marche/The Train Rolls On* (1973, on Alexander Medvedkin*), *La Solitude du chanteur de fond/The Loneliness of the Long-distance Singer* (1975, on Yves Montand*), *Le Fond de l'air est rouge/The Air is Red* (1977), and *Le Tombeau d'Alexandre/The Last Bolshevik* (1993, also on Medvedkin). Versatile and cultured, Marker is also a writer and has worked at various times as editor, cameraman and producer. GV

MARMSTEDT, Lorens
Stockholm 1908–66

Swedish producer and director. Marmstedt worked both as a director and as a film critic, but he is best known as an important independent producer with the company Terra Film (1938–69). In the 1940s and 1950s he helped young directors when established film companies were reluctant to do so. He was responsible for the production of several films directed by Hasse Ekman*, Ingmar Bergman* and Hampe Faustman. LGA

MARTI, Walter
Zurich 1923
and
MERTENS, Reni
Zurich 1918

Swiss directors and producers, who began their collaboration in the mid-1950s, preparing for their first long documentary about the Swiss pedagogue Mimi Schreiblauer (*Ursula oder das unwerte Leben*, 1966) by making several short films: *Rhythmik* (1956), *Unsere Kleinsten* (1962), *Krippenspiel* (1962), *Le Pelé* (1963). Later films by Marti and Mertens (*Die Selbstzerstörung des Walter Matthias Diggelmann*, 1973, *Gebet für die Linke*, 1974) remained true to a method that combined the pedagogic aspect of Brechtian dialectics (they both met Brecht during his time in Zurich) with the representational politics of *cinéma direct*. Their style served as a rich source of inspiration for the younger Swiss directors of the 'new Swiss cinema' in the 1970s, which owes a great deal to Marti and Mertens in other ways too. Their independent production company, Teleproduction, backed Alain Tanner's* *Les Apprentis* (1964) and Rolf Lissy's *Eugen heisst wohlgeboren* (1968) – to name only the most prominent new film-makers – as producers and distributors at a time when neither official film funding (before the amendment of the Federal Film Act in 1969) nor alternative film distribution encouraged innovative feature films. MW

Bib: Erika and Moritz de Hadeln, *Walter Marti & Reni Mertens Teleproduction: 30 ans de cinéma suisse* (1982).

Other Films Include: *Héritage* (1980); *L'Ecole du flamenco* (1985); *Pour écrire un mot* (1988); *Requiem* (1992).

MARTÍNEZ SORIA, Paco
Zaragoza 1902 – Madrid 1982

Spanish actor. After many minor roles in a career that started in 1934, his appearance in Pedro Lazaga's* *La ciudad no es para mí/City Life is Not for Me* (1965) transformed him into a household name as the *paleto* (yokel) whose tradition-bound disapproval of modern city life chimed with Francoism's ambivalent attitudes towards modernity. The film led to a number of sequels on the '*menosprecio de corte, alabanza de aldea*' (preference for country over city life) theme, including *Abuelo made in Spain/Old Man Made in Spain* (1968), *El abuelo tiene un plan/The Old Man Has a Plan* (1972) and *¡Vaya par de gemelos!/What a Pair of Twins!* (1977), all directed by Lazaga. PWE

MASELLI, Francesco
Rome 1930

Italian director. After studying at the Centro Sperimentale* in Rome and working as an assistant for Luigi Chiarini* and Michelangelo Antonioni* – collaborating on the script of *Cronaca di un amore/Story of a Love Affair* (1950) and *La signora senza camelie/The Lady Without Camelias* (1953) – Maselli made his directorial debut with Cesare Zavattini*, with whom he directed the episode *La storia di Caterina* in the documentary *Amore in città/Love in the City* (1953). A

Communist, he told stories about bourgeois characters, analysing their problems (*Gli sbandati*, 1955), their failures (*I delfini*, 1960), their inability to make decisions (*Gli indifferenti/Time of Indifference*, 1964). He attempted, unsuccessfully, to break into comedy. In the wake of post-1968 political radicalisation, he was among the promoters of the Giornate del Cinema, the Venice* 'anti-festival' of 1973. As a film-maker he increasingly chose more overtly political themes: the crisis of a group of Communist intellectuals in the interesting if moralistic *Lettera aperta a un giornale della sera* (1970), or the myth of the party and the exaltation of militant commitment in *Il sospetto* (1975); the latter, a thorough reconstruction of the Fascist period, remains his most rigorous film. Because of his activity as president of the ANAC (the National Association of Cinema Authors) and his alienation from new public tastes, Maselli directed few films in the 1980s. In the current apolitical climate, he decided to turn back to 'private' stories. However, with the exception of a movie exploring the world of working-class suburbs, *Storia d'amore* (1986), enlivened by the rich characterisation of the female lead (emerging actress Valeria Golino), his subsequent films have been disappointing. PM

Other Films Include: *La donna del giorno/The Doll That Took the Town* (1956); *Le italiane e l'amore* (1961, ep. *Le adolescenti/Latin Lovers*); *Fai in fretta a uccidermi… ho freddo* (1967); *Ruba al prossimo tuo/A Fine Pair* (1968); *Tre operai* (1980, TV); *Avventura di un fotografo* (1982, TV); *Codice privato* (1988); *Il segreto* (1990); *L'alba* (1990).

MASINA, Giulietta   Bologna 1920 – Rome 1994

Italian actress. Though an artist in her own right, Masina is best known for her work with Federico Fellini* (her husband), as his feminised alter ego, a human screen on to which the film-maker projected his spiritual anxieties and creative concerns.

While still a student, Masina worked in theatre, moving on to radio during the war. She enjoyed considerable success as the co-star of *Cico e Pallina*, a show about a young married couple, scripted by Fellini (writer and actress married in 1943). After the war, Masina turned exclusively to the cinema, starting with a small part in the Florentine episode of Roberto Rossellini's* *Paisà* (1946), followed by a role in Alberto Lattuada's* *Senza pietà/Without Pity* (1948) which revealed her dramatic abilities. *Luci del varietà/Lights of Variety/Variety Lights* (1950), about a troupe of itinerant entertainers, co-directed by Lattuada and Fellini, marked the beginning of Masina's function as Fellini's tutelary genius. From this point on, her physical plasticity and psychological delicacy were put to the service of Fellini's art. Gelsomina in *La strada* (1954) is a simple-minded waif whose preternatural sensitivity underscores her extraordinary gift for mime. The protagonist of *Le notti di Cabiria/Cabiria/Nights of Cabiria* (1957), prefigured in Masina's cameo in *Lo sceicco bianco/ The White Sheik* (1952), is a spunky prostitute looking for redemption, which she finds neither in religion nor in romantic love, but in the world of performance and masquerade. A middle-aged, gentrified version of Gelsomina and Cabiria, the protagonist of *Giulietta degli spiriti/Juliet of the Spirits*

(1965) comes to terms with her inner demons, in a feminised re-enactment of Fellini's artistic quest in $8\frac{1}{2}$ (1963). Masina updated this character in *Ginger e Fred/Ginger and Fred* (1985), as the retired tap dancer/bourgeois matron reunited after forty years with her erstwhile dance partner and lover (Marcello Mastroianni*) for a Christmas television special.

Masina did work with other directors, including Rossellini in *Europa '51* (1952), Eduardo De Filippo* in *Fortunella* (1958), Renato Castellani* in *Nella città l'inferno/… And the Wild, Wild Women* (1958), Lina Wertmuller* in *Non stuzzicate la zanzara/Don't Tease the Mosquito* (1967), the British film-maker Bryan Forbes* in his adaptation of Giraudoux's *La Folle de Chaillot/The Madwoman of Chaillot* (1969), the Slovak Juraj Jakubisko* in the children's film *Perinbaba/Frau Holle/Mother Carey* (1985), and in France with Jean-Louis Bertuccelli in *Aujourd'hui peut-être* (1991). She appeared extensively on television, performing with great success in Tullio Pinelli's *Eleanora* (1972). With a physical expressivity reminiscent of Chaplin and Keaton, and a voice capable of conveying great ranges of emotion, Masina made an inestimable contribution to both the carnivalised exterior and the deeply serious interior of Fellini's film-making. MMa

MASON, James   Huddersfield 1909 – Lausanne, Switzerland 1984

British actor, and major British and American star, the softness of whose voice often belied the steel in his character's soul. Though he became respectable in *Odd Man Out* (1947), it was in the Gainsborough melodramas* that Mason emerged as a star, ousting George Formby* from the top of the British popularity charts in 1943. *The Man in Grey* (1943), *Fanny by Gaslight* (1944), *The Seventh Veil* (1945) and *The Wicked Lady* (1945) established him in the vein of erotic and aristocratic cruelty: most aristocratic in *The Man in Grey* and *Fanny by Gaslight*, most cruel in *The Seventh Veil* and most erotic in *The Wicked Lady*, where his taking of Margaret Lockwood* is conducted as a sexual transaction in which he is the loser. *Odd Man Out*, directed by Carol Reed*, offered him a more culturally prestigious role in a quality film. In 1949 he went to Hollywood, where he made two films with Max Ophuls*, *Caught* and *The Reckless Moment* (both 1949), played Rommel twice, in *The Desert Fox* (1951) and *The Desert Rats* (1953), played Brutus to Marlon Brando's Anthony in *Julius Caesar* (1953), and starred with Judy Garland in *A Star is Born* (1954). He returned to Britain in 1953 to make *The Man Between*, again with Carol Reed. He continued to play significant roles on both sides of the Atlantic until his death, winning a posthumous UK Film Critics award in 1985 for his part in *The Shooting Party*. JC

Bib: Sheridan Morley, *James Mason: Odd Man Out* (1989).

Other Films Include: *Blind Man's Bluff* (1936); *The Mill on the Floss, Fire Over England* (1937); *Hatter's Castle* (1941); *The Night Has Eyes, Thunder Rock* (1942); *The Bells Go Down* (1943); *They Were Sisters* (1945); *Madame Bovary* (1949); *Pandora and the Flying Dutchman* (1951); *Bigger Than Life* (1956, US); *North by Northwest* (1959, US); *The Trials of Oscar Wilde* (1960); *Lolita* (1962); *The Pumpkin*

Eater (1964); *Lord Jim* (1965); *Georgy Girl* (1966); *Age of Consent* (1969, Australia); *Child's Play* (1972, US); *Autobiography of a Princess, Mandingo* [US] (1975); *Voyage of the Damned* (1976); *Cross of Iron* (1977); *Heaven Can Wait, The Boys from Brazil* (1978, both US); *Salem's Lot* (1979, US); *The Verdict* (1982, US).

MASTROIANNI, Marcello — Fontana Liri 1923

Italian actor. In a varied and protean career spanning nearly five decades, during which he has starred in films by Federico Fellini*, Luchino Visconti*, Michelangelo Antonioni*, Vittorio De Sica* and others, Mastroianni has come to personify the entire evolution of postwar Italian cinema. His versatility, as both dramatic and comic actor, has produced a complex persona, a cross between Latin lover and tormented modern man.

As an amateur actor after the war, he joined Visconti's theatrical company and made an early screen appearance in Riccardo Freda's* *I miserabili/Les Misérables* (1947). He drew attention to himself in a series of 'rose-tinted realist' films by Luciano Emmer*, beginning with *Una domenica d'agosto/Sunday in August* (1950), and went on to perform serious roles in Carlo Lizzani's* *Cronache di poveri amanti/Stories of Poor Lovers* (1954) and Visconti's *Le notti bianche/White Nights* (1957). He rose to international stardom in two Fellini films, as the failed but idealistic journalist Marcello in *La dolce vita* (1960), and the film director Guido in $8\frac{1}{2}$ (1963). In the meantime he played a tormented intellectual in Antonioni's *La notte/The Night* (1961) and the scathingly satirical part of Baron Fefé Cefalù in Pietro Germi's* classic comedy, *Divorzio all'italiana/Divorce – Italian Style* (1961), and began a partnership with Sophia Loren* with two De Sica comedies, *Ieri, oggi, domani/Yesterday, Today and Tomorrow* (1963) and *Matrimonio all'italiana/Marriage – Italian Style* (1964). In the 1970s and 1980s his repertory expanded even further. The Taviani* brothers' *Allonsanfan* (1974) and Elio Petri's* *Todo modo* (1976) brought political cinema within his range [> ITALIAN POLITICAL CINEMA], and Ettore Scola* cast him in many memorable roles, most notably in *Una giornata particolare/A Special Day* (1977), where he plays Gabriele, an anti-Fascist homosexual, while Loren, in an equivalent reversal of their previous roles together, plays a frumpy housewife. As (once again) Fellini's alter ego, he found himself confronting the women's movement in *Città delle donne/City of Women* (1980) and lapsing into bitterness and nostalgia (opposite Giulietta Masina*) in *Ginger e Fred/Ginger and Fred* (1985). In the 1980s he returned to the theatre in Peter Brook's 1984 Paris production of the comedy *Cin-Cin* (filmed in 1991) and Nikita Mikhalkov's* *Pianola meccanica* (1984). He appeared in Mikhalkov's film *Oci ciornie/Ochi chërnye/Dark Eyes* (1987) and was reunited with Loren in Robert Altman's *Prêt-à-porter* (1994). He received a Golden Lion for lifetime achievement at the 1990 Venice Festival. His daughter (with Catherine Deneuve*) Chiara Mastroianni has begun a career as an actress in France, appearing notably in the films of André Téchiné*. MMa

MATARAZZO, Raffaello — Rome 1906–66

Italian director. A film critic for the magazine *Il Tevere*, Matarazzo began working for Cines* in 1931. He made an unsuccessful debut with *Treno popolare* (1933), an unusually realist film about ordinary people, entirely shot on location. For the next ten years he devoted himself to comedies and light thrillers, from *Kiki* (1934) and *Joe il rosso* (1936) through *Sono stato io!/I Did It* (1937, where Eduardo and Titina De Filippo* played together for the first time), to *Giorno di nozze* (1942) and *Il birichino di papà* (1943). In Spain during the war he made a film with silent *diva* [> DIVISMO] Francesca Bertini (*Dora, la espia*, 1943). Back in Italy, he directed a series of extraordinarily successful torrid melodramas for Titanus*: *Catene/Chains* (1950), *Tormento/Torment* (1951), *I figli di nessuno/Nobody's Children* (1951), *Chi è senza peccato/Who Is Without Sin* (1953), *Torna!* (1954) and *L'angelo bianco/White Angel* (1955), all starring as the 'cursed' couple Amedeo Nazzari* and Yvonne Sanson, often with Folco Lulli as the bad guy. With the rediscovery of these melodramas by critics in the 1970s, Matarazzo is now acknowledged as a master of popular psychology, adept at manipulating emotions; his characters, defenceless victims of legal injustice or fate, suffer and experience the 'truth' of everyday life, with the family at the centre of their universe. More personal movies include *La nave delle donne maledette/The Ship of Condemned Women* (1953), a colourful and lyrical sea adventure, and *La risaia/Rice Girl* (1956), a popular neo-realist* tale. When public taste changed, Matarazzo was soon marginalised, though he found the opportunity to produce and direct the elegiac *Amore mio* (1964), a love story about a married man and a young woman. Although this last film, like his first, was a commercial failure, he used to say that it was only for these two that he would claim all the credit. GVo

MATHIESON, Muir — Stirling, Scotland 1911 – Oxford 1975

British music director. Though hardly a household name, Muir Mathieson's name must surely appear on the credit lists of more British films than that of any other individual. A Scot, trained at the Royal College of Music, he joined Alexander Korda* at Denham in 1934, worked for various government film units during the war, and was musical director at Rank from 1945 until 1970. His first credit as music director was for *The Private Life of Don Juan* (1934); he persuaded Arthur Bliss to compose music for *Things to Come* (1936) and William Walton to compose the famous score for *Henry V* (1945). He also commissioned first scores from Vaughan Williams, Arnold Bax and Malcolm Arnold*. In all, it is estimated he initiated and conducted over a thousand scores. JC

MATTHEWS, Jessie — London 1907 – Pinner 1981

British actress, who made her film debut in 1923 at the age of sixteen, and became one of the top three British stars of the 1930s. Whereas Gracie Fields* and George Formby* had a predominantly working-class appeal derived from northern music hall, Matthews was the 'Dancing Divinity' of the sophisticated musical. She was the only one of the trio to achieve real success in America. While the ordinariness of the other two inspired affection in the domestic audience, Matthews offered fantasy and an extraordinary sexuality. In dance numbers, her pretty face and prim little mouth seemed unaware of what the rest of her body was doing in its slinky gowns and silky, liquid movements. She may not have had the choreography of Ginger Rogers, and she certainly lacked an adequate male partner, but she made up for it with the unselfconscious sensuality of her movement. In the three musicals she made with Victor Saville*, the fantasy was played out as masquerade flirting with the perverse: in *Evergreen* (1934) she poses as her own mother and falls in love with the young man who is posing as her son; in *First a Girl* (1935), based on the German film *Viktor und Viktoria* (1933), she double-cross-dresses and, of course, falls in love; and in *It's Love Again* (1936) she impersonates a celebrated adventuress. Matthews was at her best directed by Saville, her popularity declining towards the end of the decade when her direction was taken over by her husband, Sonny Hale. Her film career went into decline after the war, but she returned from relative obscurity in 1963 to play Mrs Dale in the BBC radio serial, *Mrs Dale's Diary*. JC

Bib: Jeffrey Richards, *The Age of the Dream Palace: Cinema and Society in Britain, 1930–1939* (1984).

Other Films Include: *Out of the Blue* (1931); *The Midshipmaid* (1932); *The Man from Toronto, The Good Companions* [Saville], *Friday the Thirteenth* [Saville] (1933); *Waltzes from Vienna* [Hitchcock] (1934); *Head over Heels* [Hale], *Gangway* [Hale] (1937); *Sailing Along* [Hale], *Climbing High* (1938); *Forever and a Day* (1943, US); *Victory Wedding* [short; dir. + role] (1944); *Tom Thumb* [cameo] (1958); *The Hound of the Baskervilles* [cameo] (1978).

MATTOLI, Mario   Tolentino 1898 – Rome 1980

Italian director. Mattoli came into contact with the cinema as a lawyer. In 1927 he set up an actors' company, Spettacoli Za-Bum, which worked with both dramatic theatre and music hall, bringing together the best-known actors of the period including Vittorio De Sica*. He made his directorial debut with *Tempo massimo* (1934), which fitted with a certain originality into the 'white telephone' vein of light (bourgeois) comedy. He made more than eighty films altogether, mainly in melodramatic and comic modes. An intelligent craftsman, he constructed his films by relying on his protagonists' fame outside the cinema, on stage or (later) television, never trying to impose his own authorial point of view (one critic wrote that his style was the very absence of style). Mattoli was therefore the ideal director for Totò*, with whom he made a memorable ensemble of skilful adaptations of classic stage comedies by Eduardo Scarpetta (*Un turco napoletano*, 1953; *Miseria e nobiltà*, 1954; *Il medico dei pazzi*, 1954), and intelligent evocations of the time (*Totò al Giro d'Italia*, 1948). He gained respect for his work in many genres: Camerini*-inspired comedy (*Ai vostri ordini, signora*, 1939), historical films (*Amo te sola*, 1935), 'Hellzapoppin'-type variety shows (*I pompieri

di Viggiù*, 1949), neo-realist* drama (*La vita ricomincia*, 1945), musicals (*Signorinella*, 1949), juvenile comedy (*Appuntamento a Ischia*, 1960) and parody (*Fifa e arena*, 1948). PV

Other Films Include: *La damigella di Bard* (1936); *Felicita Colombo* (1937); *La dama bianca* (1938); *Il pirata sono io* (1940); *Ore 9: lezione di chimica* (1941); *Stasera niente di nuovo* (1942); *L'ultima carrozzella* (1943); *Circo equestre Za-Bum* (1944); *I due orfanelli* (1947); *Cinque poveri in automobile* (1952); *Tipi da spiaggia* (1959); *Sua eccellenza si fermò a mangiare* (1961); *Per qualche dollaro in meno* (1966).

MAURA, Carmen   Carmen García Maura; Madrid 1945

Spanish actress. Though she worked widely in Spanish film and television before the 1980s, she is best known for her starring roles in Pedro Almodóvar's* films. She persuaded Almodóvar to make his first, anarchic feature, *Pepi, Luci, Bom y otras chicas del montón/Pepi, Luci, Bom and Other Girls in the Crowd* (1980), in which she played an unlikely teenage heiress turned vengeful sex kitten when raped by a policeman. She then contributed a bewildering variety of roles which helped establish Almodóvar as Spain's most controversial and commercially successful film-maker: a sentimental nun in *Entre tinieblas/Dark Habits* (1983); a murderous housewife in *Qué he hecho yo para merecer esto?/What Have I Done to Deserve This?* (1984); an amorous psychiatrist in *Matador* (1986); a transsexual actress in *La ley del deseo/The Law of Desire* (1987); and, the role that brought her international recognition, a desperate but defiant abandoned lover in *Mujeres al borde de un ataque de nervios/Women on the Verge of a Nervous Breakdown* (1988). Maura's versatility is evident; but beyond this her role was to humanise Almodóvar's sometimes far-fetched plots and to provide moments of pathos amid the furious farce. Lending a battered dignity to characters placed in absurd or impossible situations, she embodied the pride of the survivor, a recurrent theme in Almodóvar's work. Since a very public break-up with her maestro, Maura has continued to consolidate her position as one of Spain's most gifted actresses in films such as Carlos Saura's* hit Civil War musical *¡Ay, Carmela!* (1990) and Ana Belén's* gently feminist satire *Cómo ser mujer y no morir en el intento/How to Be a Woman and Not Die in the Attempt* (1991), the first film to be released abroad on the strength of her star name. PJS

Other Films Include: *La petición/The Engagement Party* (1976); *Tigres de papel/Paper Tigers* (1977); *La reina anónima/The Anonymous Queen* (1992).

MAURSTAD, Alfred   Nordfjord 1896 – Oslo 1967

Norwegian actor and director, who worked both in theatre and film. His first film role was in the 'national-romantic' *Brudeferden i Hardanger/The Hardanger Bridal Procession* (1926) [> NORWEGIAN RURAL MELODRAMAS]. He then played leading parts in several Norwegian and Swedish films, but is best known for portraying the heroes of Tancred Ibsen's* classic *Fant/Tramp* (1937), *Gjest Baardsen* (1939) and *Tørres Snørtevold* (1940). His strong masculine presence made him one of the most admired actors of his time. He tended to embody heroic characters, although his versatility enabled him to give convincing portraits of criminals as well. He directed two comedies during the occupation, *Hansen og Hansen/Hansen and Hansen* (1941) and *En herre med bart/A Gentleman with a Moustache* (1942). KS

Other Films as Actor Include: *Fantegutten/The Tramp Boy* (1932); *Styrmann Karlssons flamma/Sailor Karlsson's Passion* (1938, Sw.); *Trysil-Knut* (1942); *Jørund Smed/Jørund the Blacksmith* (1948); *Ukjent mann/Unknown Man, Valley of Eagles* [UK] (1951); *Ut av mørket/Out of Darkness, Laila* (1958); *Det store varpet/The Big Heist* (1960).

MAY, Joe
Vienna 1880 – Hollywood, California 1954

Austrian-born German director, who began as a scriptwriter and director in 1912, founded May-Film (1915–32), turned his wife Mia May into a popular serial queen, rose to singular pre-eminence in Weimar* cinema, and tragically failed to find a foothold in Hollywood after forced exile. In the 1910s and 1920s he directed and produced a number of very successful melodramas, detective thrillers and serials (four 'Stuart Webbs' and twenty-three 'Joe Deebs' detective films). His famous six-part epics (*Veritas Vincit*, 1919; *Die Herrin der Welt*, 1919; *Das Indische Grabmal*, 1921) were indicative of his prescience about the future of the feature-length film for the world market. May liked to work with a permanent team (M. Faßbender, R. Kurtz, M. Jacoby-Boy) and saw himself as a promoter of new talent (Thea von Harbou*, Fritz Lang*, E. A. Dupont*). Working with Erich Pommer* on *Asphalt* (1929), May visited Hollywood in 1928 to gather information on the techniques of sound film and returned to make the comedy *Ihre Majestät die Liebe* (1931).

In 1934 he arrived in Hollywood (via London and Paris) with a Paramount contract. His first two Hollywood films, *Music in the Air* (1934, produced by Pommer and scripted by Billy Wilder* and Robert Liebmann*) and *Confession* (1937), were unsuccessful. From 1939 he began to make B-pictures in various genres, but by the mid-1940s found himself bankrupt, trying with his wife to run a restaurant, appropriately called 'The Blue Danube'. TE/SG

Bib: Hans-Michael Bock and Claudia Lenssen (eds.), *Joe May: Regisseur und Produzent* (1991).

Other Films Include: *Vorgluten des Balkanbrandes* (1912); *Ein Ausgestoßener. 2 Teile, Entsagungen, Heimat und Fremde* (1913); *Die geheimnisvolle Villa* (1914); *Das Gesetz der Mine* (1915); *Tragödie der Liebe. 4 Teile* (1923); *Der Farmer aus Texas* (1925); *Dagfin* (1926); *... und das ist die Hauptsache* (1931); *Paris – Méditerranée/Zwei in einem Auto* (1932); *Ein Lied für Dich* (1933). **In the US**: *The House of Fear* (1939); *The Invisible Man Returns* (1940); *The Strange Death of Adolf Hitler* (1943); *Johnny Doesn't Live Here Any More* (1944).

MAYER, Carl
Graz, Austria 1894 – London 1944

Austrian-born German scriptwriter, who started his film career in 1919 with the scripts for the two archetypal expressionist* films, *Das Cabinet des Dr Caligari/The Cabinet of Dr Caligari* (1920, co-author Hans Janowitz) and *Genuine* (1920), both directed by Robert Wiene*. After these successes, his name became more closely associated with psychological dramas such as *Hintertreppe/Backstairs* (1921), *Scherben/Shattered* (1921), and *Sylvester* (1923) which helped initiate the *Kammerspielfilm**. After collaborating with F. W. Murnau* on *Der letzte Mann/The Last Laugh* (1924), *Sunrise* (1927, US) and *Four Devils* (1929, US), Mayer returned to Europe, first to France, where he co-wrote Paul Czinner's* *Mélo* (1932), and later to Britain, where his consultancy on *Pygmalion* (1938), the documentary *The Fourth Estate* (1939) and *Major Barbara* (1941) was uncredited. Because he was 'writing films' rather than merely writing for film, Mayer is not adequately described as 'scriptwriter' and it seems clear that the extraordinarily detailed specifications he gave did guide the hands and eyes of directors, cameramen and set designers. TE/KU

Bib: Jürgen Kasten, *Carl Mayer: Filmpoet* (1994).

Other Films Include: *Brandherd* (1920); *Der Gang in die Nacht* (1920); *Die Straße* (1923); *Tartüff* (1926).

MAYO, Alfredo
Alfredo Fernández Martínez; Barcelona 1911 – Palma, Majorca 1984

Spanish actor, originally in theatre. During the Civil War, Mayo enrolled in the Nationalist air force. His rugged features and resolute eyes brought him enormous success in *Raza/Race* (1941, dir. José Luis Sáenz de Heredia*), and other, stiffly heroic 1940s triumphalist roles at Cifesa* – for instance in *¡Harka!* (1941) and *¡A mí la legión!/Follow Me, Legion!* (1942) – which also made him one of the highest paid stars in Spain. After roles in melodrama and comedy and following a decline in the 1950s, his career was revitalised in the 1960s through appearances in Carlos Saura's* *La caza/The Hunt* (1965) and *Peppermint Frappé* (1967). These films knowingly gesture to the earlier ideologised image of his Cifesa roles, with *La caza* in particular using him to refer codedly to the legacy of the Civil War and its still unresolved issues. PWE

MEDEIROS, Maria de
Lisbon 1965

Portuguese actress. Medeiros became an actress by chance, when João César Monteiro* chose her to play the leading female role in *Silvestre* (1980), in which she already displays her two main characteristics: haunting eyes with an intense gaze, and an 'otherness', as if she were coming from 'elsewhere'. Medeiros went to Paris in 1984 to study philosophy, but soon started appearing on stage. Her strange and ageless qualities (is she a girl, is she a woman?) were again visible in *J'ai faim,* j'ai froid/I'm Hungry, I'm Cold, Chantal Akerman's* episode for *Paris vu par ... vingt ans après* (1984). Medeiros rapidly became involved in French cinema, but showed her remarkable versatility by also playing in American films, such as Philip Kaufman's *Henry and June* (1990; as Anaïs Nin) and Quentin Tarantino's *Pulp Fiction* (1994), and more recently in Spanish films. She returns occasionally to Portugal and has played in Manoel de Oliveira's* *A Divina Comédia/The Divine Comedy*, but especially important is her collaboration with the young Portuguese director Teresa Villaverde. Though already an international actress she played a small part in Villaverde's low-budget *A Idade Maior/Alex* (1991), and took the leading role in the director's second film, *Três Irmãos/Two Brothers, One Sister* (1994), an intense, almost hypnotic part for which she won a best actress award at Venice. She has also worked as a stage and film director. Her play *Fragment II* (1988) was based on Beckett, her film *A Morte do Príncipe* (1991) on Pessoa. In the latter, she acted with Luís Miguel Cintra*, who had directed an earlier stage production. AMS

Other Films Include: *Vertiges* (1984, Fr./Port.); *Paraíso Perdido/Lost Paradise* (1985); *Le Moine et la sorcière/The Monk and the Witch* (1987, Fr.); *1871* (1990); *L'Homme de ma vie/The Man in My Life* (1992); *Huevos de oro/Golden Balls* (1993, Sp.; dir. Bigas Luna*).

MEDEM, Julio   San Sebastián 1959

Spanish director, and young hope of post-democracy Basque cinema. Medem directed shorts before winning unexpected commercial and critical success with his first feature, *Vacas/Cows* (1992). Defined by Medem as a 'magical, atmospheric, surreal tale', the film stands as one of the most original and provocative products of recent Spanish cinema. A highly introspective and self-conscious use of the camera complements forceful treatment of issues concerning recent Spanish history, individual and national identity, and gender constructions and relations. Medem's visual style carries over to his second and, to date, last film – *La ardilla roja/The Red Squirrel* (1993) – which also deals with constructions of identity and the blurred frontier between reality and imagination. IS

MEDVEDKIN, Alexander I.   Penza, Russia 1900 – Moscow 1989

Soviet director and scriptwriter. A committed Communist from the day he joined the Party in 1920, Medvedkin participated in the Civil War of 1917–21 and from 1927 worked in the Gosvoyenkino army film studio. In 1932 he headed the film train that travelled to the major construction projects of the first Five Year Plan and used film to improve productivity: in one year the brigade shot seventy-two films. He made a number of films that used satire and grotesques to attack bureaucracy, and in 1935 his comic masterpiece *Schast'e/Happiness*, an attack on opponents of collectivisation, was released, followed in 1937 by *Chudesnitsa/Miracle Worker*.

During World War II Medvedkin worked at the front. In the early 1950s he filmed the agricultural campaign to conquer the Virgin Land, satirising that in turn in *Bespokoinaya vesna/The Unquiet Spring* (1956). He became a cult figure among left-wing intellectuals in the West in the 1970s and is the subject of two films by Chris Marker*, *Le Train en marche/The Train Rolls On* (1973) and *Le Tombeau d'Alexandre/The Last Bolshevik* (1993). RT

MEERSON, Lazare   Polish/Russian border 1900 – London 1938

French set designer of Russian origin, highly influential in French cinema. Meerson emigrated to Germany in 1917 and to France in 1924, where he joined the Russian personnel at the Albatros studios in Paris [> EMIGRATION AND EUROPEAN CINEMA]. In 1930 he worked for Tobis and began his celebrated collaboration with René Clair*, designing the sets of *Sous les toits de Paris* (1930) and creating an enduring image of popular Paris. Meerson designed Clair's other French films of the 1930s and many others, including Jacques Feyder's* *La Kermesse héroïque/Carnival in Flanders* (1935). His sets were characterised by a dialectic between stylisation and accurate naturalistic details; his assistants and disciples included Alexander Trauner* and Jean d'Eaubonne. GV

MEISEL, Edmund   Vienna 1894 – Berlin 1930

Austrian-born composer. Trained as a violinist and conductor, Meisel was active in film from 1926, when Prometheus-Film commissioned him to compose music for the German release in 1930 of Eisenstein's* *Bronenosets Potëmkin/The Battleship Potemkin* (1926). The premiere brought him unaccustomed recognition as a composer of avant-garde film and stage music. *Berlin die Sinfonie der Großstadt/Berlin, Symphony of a City* (1927; dir. Walther Ruttmann*) gave him the opportunity to develop to the full his harsh rhythms and atonal sound sequences, his score contributing much to the international acclaim that the film received. Meisel subscribed to the then current idea that sound and image should be contrapuntal, and critics sometimes complained that his music was trying to compete with the film for the audience's attention. In fact, Meisel's music was rejected in Moscow, and in 1928 he broke with Eisenstein. The first sound film he worked on, *Deutscher Rundfunk* (1928), seems to have been lost. Little is known about his time in Britain between 1928 and 1930, but when he returned to Germany, his style had altered, in line with the new norms of sound cinema: his film music had become more conventionally tonal and melodic. He died tragically early, aged 36. TE/SG

MÉLIÈS, Georges   Paris 1861–1938

French film pioneer. Georges Méliès was the inventor and populariser of the 'trick film' and one of the first all-round entrepreneurs of the cinema, heading his own 'empire' from 1896 to 1919. He learnt conjuring and worked as a magician

284

and puppeteer at the Musée Grévin (a wax museum) in Paris before taking over the Théâtre Robert-Houdin in 1888, where he presented spectacles of magic, fantasy and acrobatics. An enthusiastic spectator at Lumière's* first screening, he quickly acquired film and machinery from R. W. Paul* and began making films. After some Lumière-inspired documentaries, he moved on to the trick film in which the gimmicks of the theatre were supplemented by cinematic ones (jump cuts, double exposures, etc.), leading to an array of spectacular genres, from reconstructed current events to *féeries* (fantasies). Méliès founded his production company, Star-Film, in 1896, built a studio in Montreuil-sous-bois in 1897 and played all parts in the production process: make-up artist, actor, scriptwriter, director, editor, exhibitor and exporter (he opened a subsidiary in New York in 1902), producing over 500 films which he developed in his own laboratory. Among his best-known titles are *Le Voyage dans la lune/A Trip to the Moon* (1902) and *Voyage à travers l'impossible* (1904), drawing on the science fiction of Jules Verne; he also made a film about a Channel tunnel, *Le Tunnel sous la Manche/Tunnelling the English Channel* (1907). Méliès' decline was as swift as his rise. Changes in distribution patterns and the fading novelty of trick films caused him to lose control to Pathé* and eventually to stop producing in 1919. Star-Film went bankrupt and Méliès opened a kiosk at the Gare Montparnasse, where he was discovered in the late 1920s. Georges Sadoul* organised a gala evening in his honour in 1929.

In Méliès' films, the powers of imagination and humour were given full scope. As Claude Beylie put it, 'With Lumière, trains entered stations, with Méliès they got off the rails and flew into the clouds.' Theatrically inspired as they were, his films formed the basis of what early film historians call the 'cinema of attractions', a cinema of spectacle in which the spectator marvels at the possibilities of the medium itself. GV

Bib: Madeleine Malthête-Méliès (ed.), *Méliès et la naissance du spectacle cinématographique* (1984).

MELVILLE, Jean-Pierre   Jean-Pierre Grumbach; Paris 1917–73

French director, one of the most important independent filmmakers to emerge in the immediate postwar period and a great admirer of American culture, from which he derived his name, his sartorial style (Stetson hat, dark glasses) and his films, especially his *policiers**. Melville founded his production company (OGC) in 1945 and built a studio in Rue Jenner, Paris, in 1949. His first feature, *Le Silence de la mer* (1949, based on Vercors' novel), was an Occupation drama made on the margins of the French film industry; in 1950 he collaborated with Jean Cocteau*, filming the latter's *Les Enfants terribles/The Strange Ones* (1950). *Bob le flambeur* (1956) set the agenda for the rest of his career. It is a seductive, good-humoured tale of loyalty among male gangster clans, shot partly in the streets and cafés of Montmartre and Pigalle to a cool jazz score. Melville's subsequent work took the *policier* in the direction of increased abstraction and

bleaker masculinity: *Le Doulos* (1963), *Le Deuxième souffle/The Second Breath* (1966), and especially the remarkable *Le Samouraï* (1967), with its subtle colour range, pared-down decor and a laconic Alain Delon*. Melville used the thriller format for his Gaullist account of the Resistance, *L'Armée des ombres/Army in the Shadows* (1969). His work combined popular appeal (using stars like Delon, Jean-Paul Belmondo*, Serge Reggiani, Lino Ventura*) with formal images of modernity, one reason he is so admired by the American director Quentin Tarantino. Melville acted in a few films, notably as the 'novelist' Parvulesco in Jean-Luc Godard's* *A bout de souffle/Breathless* (1960). GV

Bib: Rui Nogueira (ed.), *Melville on Melville* (1971).

Other Feature Films: *Quand tu liras cette lettre...* (1953); *Deux hommes dans Manhattan* (1959); *Léon Morin, prêtre* (1961); *L'Aîné des Ferchaux* (1963); *Le Cercle rouge/The Red Circle* (1970); *Un flic* (1972).

MENZEL, Jiří   Prague 1938

Czech director and actor. Menzel graduated from FAMU* in 1962 and worked as an assistant to Věra Chytilová* before becoming a director. A self-proclaimed student of comedy (particularly the Czech comedies of Martin Frič*, and Jiří Voskovec* and Jan Werich*), his films are mostly based on collaborations with leading writers. Most of his best films have been in partnership with the novelist Bohumil Hrabal – *Perličky na dně/Pearls of the Deep* (1965, episode *Smrt pana Baltazara/The Death of Mr Balthazar*), *Skřivánci na niti/Skylarks on a String* (1969, released 1990, Berlin Golden Bear award), *Postřižiny/Cutting it Short* (1980), *Slavnosti sněženek/The Snowdrop Festival* (1983), and especially *Ostře sledované vlaky/Closely Observed Trains* (1966, Academy Award winner, 1967), the most popular abroad. Its story of a young station assistant more concerned with losing his virginity than promoting the Führer's New Order was very much in the Švejkian tradition of the little man finding his own ways of subverting dominant ideologies. Menzel also adapted two novels by Vladislav Vančura* and worked with Ladislav Smoljak* and Zdeněk Svěrák*. He was active in theatre as director of the Činoherní klub (Drama Club), and after the fall of the Communist government in 1989 he became head of the direction department at FAMU. In 1990 he made a film of his stage production of Václav Havel's *Žebrácká opera/The Beggar's Opera*. He has combined directing with acting, some of his best-known parts being the philandering doctor in Chytilová's *Hra o jablko/The Apple Game* (1976), Hrabal in Petr Koliha's *Něžný barbar/Tender Barbarian* (1989), and the leading role in Costa-Gavras'* *Petite apocalypse/A Minor Apocalypse* (1992). While always adopting a respectful attitude towards literary sources, Menzel's direction is distinguished by balanced ensemble playing, a gentle lyricism, and a humanist attitude to his characters reminiscent of Jean Renoir* and François Truffaut*. PH

Other Films as Director: *Zločin v dívčí škole/Crime in the Girls School* [title episode] (1965); *Rozmarné léto/Capricious Summer* (1967); *Zločin v šantánu/Crime in the Nightclub*

(1968); *Kdo hledá zlaté dno/Who Looks for Gold* (1974); *Na samotě u lesa/Seclusion Near a Forest* (1976); *Báječni muži s klikou/Those Wonderful Men with a Crank/Those Wonderful Movie Cranks* (1978); *Vesničko má, středisková/My Sweet Little Village* (1985); *Konec starých časů/The End of Old Times* (1989); *Život a neobyčejná dobrodružství vojáka Ivana Čonkina/The Life and Extraordinary Adventures of Private Ivan Chonkin* (1994).

MERCHANT–IVORY [IVORY, James] Berkeley, California 1928;
MERCHANT, Ismail Bombay, India 1936;
JHABVALA, Ruth Prawer Cologne, Germany 1927

American/Indian director-producer-writer team. Formed by an American director (Ivory), an Indian producer (Merchant), and a German-born writer of Polish descent who became Indian by marriage (Jhabvala), Merchant-Ivory during the 1980s has luxuriated in Englishness, becoming a brand-name for the 'heritage film'. The company was formed in the 1960s in India. Its first notable production was *Shakespeare Wallah* (1965, India), which dealt with the English in India through a travelling theatre company, and the partnership continued in the US in the 1970s, producing independent American films like *Roseland* (1977). In Britain, their series of adaptations began in 1979 with *The Europeans*, continued with *The Bostonians* (1984, US), turned to E. M. Forster with *A Room with a View* (1985), and followed its success with *Maurice* (1987) and *Howards End* (1991). The Forster cycle discovered a rich seam of English nostalgia which had already been mined on television with *Brideshead Revisited* (1981) and on film with *Chariots of Fire* (1981) and was revisited again by Charles Sturridge with adaptations of Forster's *Where Angels Fear to Tread* (1991) and Evelyn Waugh's *A Handful of Dust* (1987). The 'heritage film', which is now firmly identified with Merchant–Ivory, is characterised by a rich visual style and a loving recreation of the Edwardian period which replaces the irony of the original novels with a longing for England's past [> HERITAGE CINEMA IN EUROPE]. JC

Bib: Andrew Higson, 'Re-presenting the national past: nostalgia and pastiche in the heritage film', in Lester Friedman (ed.), *British Cinema and Thatcherism: Fires Were Started* (1983).

MERCOURI, Melina Athens 1923 – New York 1994

Greek actress, politician and singer, originally a stage actress. From her first screen appearance in *Stella* (1955), directed by Michael Cacoyannis*, Melina Mercouri commanded centre stage as actress or politician. Her passionate, charismatic personality established her as a star from her first role as a woman doomed for wanting to live in defiance of established moral codes. *Pote tin Kiriaki/Never on Sunday* (1959), directed by her husband Jules Dassin*, made her an international star, bringing to the world her husky voice and outsize personality. This performance won her an Oscar nomination and a share (with Jeanne Moreau*) of the Best Actress Award at the 1960 Cannes Festival. Her subsequent film career was less successful. She campaigned actively and courageously against the military dictatorship (1967–74), had her citizenship revoked and was forced into exile. She returned to Greece in 1974 and became actively involved in politics. She was elected to parliament in 1977 as socialist representative for Piraeus, the location for *Pote tin Kiriaki*. When the Socialist party came to power in 1981 she became Minister of Culture, a post she held from 1981 to 1989 and again from 1993 until her death, campaigning tirelessly for cultural causes. In 1990 she stood unsuccessfully for Mayor of Athens. TN

Other Films Include: *The Gypsy and the Gentleman* (1958, UK); *La Legge/La Loi/Where the Hot Wind Blows* (It./Fr., 1958); *Phaedra* (1962); *Topkapi* (1964, US); *La Promesse de l'aube/Promise at Dawn* (1971, Fr./US); *The Rehearsal* (1974, US); *Jacqueline Susann's Once is Not Enough* (1975, US), *Kravgi Ginekon/A Dream of Passion* (1978).

MESSTER, Oskar Berlin 1866 – Tegernsee 1943

German film pioneer, inventor, technician, producer and entrepreneur, who went into business as a manufacturer of film equipment, producing his first film projectors in 1896 and a film camera series in 1900. He secured nearly seventy patents, including one for a special Maltese cross, an optical printer and the synchronisation of projector and gramophone. Messter bought his first film theatre in Berlin in 1896, but produced films mainly for buyers of his projectors, only gradually making them to show in his own theatres and for Berlin's many variety halls. By 1897, Messter had equipped his studio with artificial lighting, and his October sales catalogue of that year lists eighty-four films. Among these were street scenes such as *Am Brandenburger Tor* (1896), films of current events, especially public appearances by Kaiser Wilhelm II (1897), and short narratives. Between 1903 and 1910 he produced 'Tonbilder' (sound pictures) with synchronised image and sound.

Messter founded Projektion and in 1913 Messters Projektion continued to manufacture film equipment while a new company, Messter Film, took over film production, acquiring a reputation in feature films and specialising in melodramas such as *Der Schatten des Meeres* (1912, with Henny Porten*) and *Die blaue Laterne* (1918). During World War I Messter worked on military applications of film technology (air reconnaissance, target practice, cameras for fighter planes). He established his own distribution company, Hansa Film-Verleih. The Messter business operated in a variety of areas, including newsreels (the 'Messter Woche' [> DOCUMENTARY (GERMANY)]). Ufa* took over Messter's companies in 1917 and he became a member of the Ufa board of directors as well as their chief technical adviser. JG

MÉSZÁROS, Márta
Budapest 1931

Hungarian director. Mészáros, one of Hungary's best-known film-makers, spent her early childhood in the Soviet Union where her family was exiled as communists. Her father was later arrested and 'disappeared' during Stalin's political purges. Mészáros studied film at VGIK* in Moscow and in the 1950s and most of the 1960s she made short films, news-reels and documentaries, some of them in Romania. Her career as a feature film director began in 1968 with *Eltávozott nap/The Girl*. In her early films Mészáros dealt with the fate of young women subjected to social and emotional deprivation. Her later films often focus on women's issues such as child-bearing and adoption and women's personal integrity, while most display an interest in the father-daughter relationship. At the same time, she is one of the few directors whose films have dealt openly and powerfully with the specific conditions faced by women in eastern Europe. It is perhaps symptomatic of this situation that her work is better known and appreciated abroad than in Hungary. In the 1980s Mészáros directed an autobiographical trilogy – *Napló gyermekeimnek/Diary for My Children* (1984), *Napló szerelmeimnek/Diary for My Loves* (1987), *Napló apámnak, anyámnek/Diary for My Mother and Father* (1990) – in which she analyses her childhood and adolescence as profoundly disturbed by Stalin's political atrocities, as well as repression in Hungary. KAB

Bib: Catherine Portuges, *Screen Memories: The Hungarian Cinema of Márta Mészáros* (1993).

Other Films Include: *Holdudvar/Binding Sentiments* (1969); *Szép lányok, ne sírjatok/Don't Cry, Pretty Girls* (1970); *Örökbefogadás/Adoption* (1975); *Kilenc hónap/Nine Months, Ök ketten/The Two of Them* (1977); *Olyan, mint otthon/Just Like Back Home* (1978); *Útközben/On the Way* (1979); *Örökség/The Heiresses* (1980); *Anna* (1981).

METZ, Vittorio – see MARCHESI, Marcello

MEYER, Paul
Limal 1920

Belgian director. After directing for the theatre and making several short films, Meyer made *Déjà s'envole la fleur maigre/Fall of Petals (Children of the Borinage)* (1960), originally commissioned as a short propaganda film for Dutch-language television (with whom Meyer has worked for many years). Meyer's decision to change both the focus and the format of the film halfway through filming was to leave him in financial ruin. The film mixes a Belgian setting (the southern Borinage region) with a European theme: the decline of the mining community. Yet the genre's standard dramatic ingredients of strikes, accidents and explosions are rejected, in favour of attention to the quotidian details of Italian immigrant life, and the use of ordinary people and locations, in the manner of neo-realism*. Winning four awards at the Antwerp film festival in 1960, the film has been described as a founding moment of a Wallonese cinematic imagination. Its importance for Belgian cinema history can be measured by its choice as the representative film for an exhibition of art in Belgium at the Musée d'Art Moderne in Paris, 1990–91. CF

Other Films: *L'Abbaye de la Cambre* (1955); *De Klinkaart/The Brick Works* [short] (1956); *Le Rétable de Notre-Dame de Lombeek* [short] (1957); *Stèle pour Egmont* [short], *Le Logement social* [short] (1958); *Borinage 61* [short for TV] (1961); *Le Nerf de la paix, Le Circuit de la mort/The Circuit of Death* [short for TV] (1962); *Ce pain quotidien/This Daily Bread* [13 programmes for TV] (1962-66); *Le Temps/Time* [TV] (1972); *Ça va, les Parnajon?* [TV] (1975); *L'Herbe sous les pieds/The Grass under Our Feet* (1977); *Introduction à Zone rouge* [collective video] (1989).

MEYER, Rudi
Ludwig Wilhelm Rudolf Meyer; Suhl, Germany 1901 – Amsterdam 1969

German-Dutch producer. Meyer began his career in 1919 at Decla in Berlin, the company of his famous uncle Erich Pommer*. When Decla merged with Ufa*, Meyer worked for Europe's largest studio in different capacities. On Pommer's departure for Hollywood in 1926, Meyer switched to a smaller studio, Aafa, and devoted his talents to production, publicity and international film distribution. When the Nazis came to power in 1933 he emigrated to the Netherlands. His arrival in Amsterdam had a strong impact on Dutch film culture, since Meyer brought expertise not only in distribution but also in production. The latter in particular was in great demand; Meyer introduced continuity and stability in Dutch film-making where *ad hoc* projects had been the rule. He also hired talented émigré directors to make quality pictures for a mass audience. In 1935 he presented his first production, *De kribbebijter/The Crosspatch*, directed by Herman Kosterlitz, who later made a Hollywood reputation as Henry Koster. Meyer also persuaded Ludwig Berger* to come to the Netherlands to direct *Pygmalion* (1937), a tremendous success. Friedrich Zelnik was imported to direct two further hits, *Vadertje Langbeen/Daddy Long-Legs* (1938) and *Morgen gaat het beter/Tomorrow is Another Day* (1939). Meyer made a star of Lily Bouwmeester, who featured in these last three pictures. He also cast her in the lead in Berger's *Ergens in Nederland/Somewhere in Holland* (1940). This touching film about marital relations during mobilisation was released shortly before the Germans occupied Holland, obliging Meyer to stop working. He was deported to Auschwitz but survived the camps, returning to Holland in 1947 and becoming a Dutch citizen. Postwar conditions in Holland were less favourable for film-making, however, and Meyer's network of émigrés had fallen apart. Even so, he produced the two most successful Dutch films of the 1950s, *Sterren stralen overal/Stars Are Shining Everywhere* (1953, dir. Gerard Rutten) and *Fanfare* (1958, dir. Bert Haanstra*). When he died, he was remembered as the producer who never failed to make a movie successful. KD

MEZHRABPOM (also Mezhrabpomfilm)

Soviet film studio. Originally founded in 1924 as an arm of the International Workers' Relief (for which Mezhrabpom is the

Russian acronym) and based on the pre-Revolutionary 'Rus' film-making co-operative, the studio remained outside direct centralised state control. It was organised as a limited company and run as a commercial operation, and therefore oriented its production towards a mass audience, notably in co-productions, especially with the similar German organisation Prometheus-Film, and films aimed at overseas markets. At the same time, Anatoli Lunacharsky* wrote a number of scripts for the studio, including *Salamandra/The Salamander* (1928). Among Mezhrabpom's leading directors were Vsevolod Pudovkin*, from *Shakhmatnaya goryachka/Chess Fever* (1925) to *Dezertir/The Deserter* (1933); Lev Kuleshov*, from *Vesëlaya kanareika/The Happy Canary* (1929) to *Krayzha zreniya/Theft of Sight* (1934; not released); Yakov Protazanov*, from *Aelita* (1924) to *Marionetki/The Marionettes* (1934); and Boris Barnet*, from *Miss Mend* (1926) to *U samogo sinego morya/By the Bluest of Seas* (1936), which was one of the studio's last productions.

From 1928 to 1936 the studio was renamed Mezhrabpom-film and brought under closer political and financial control. During this period one of its engineers, Pavel Tager*, developed the sound system used for the first Soviet sound films, including Nikolai Ekk's* *Putëvka v zhizn'/The Path to Life* (1931). But the studio's international and commercial orientations rendered it vulnerable to accusations of ideological deviation in the era of 'socialism in one country', and in 1936 it became the Soyuzdetfilm children's film studio, renamed again in 1948 after Gorky. RT

MIÉVILLE, Anne-Marie – see GODARD, Jean-Luc

MIKHALKOV, Nikita S. Moscow 1945

Russian actor and director. The son of Soviet writer Sergei Mikhalkov and younger brother of director Andron Mikhalkov-Konchalovsky* (Andrei Konchalovsky), Mikhalkov studied at the Shchukin Theatre Academy from 1963 to 1966 and then at VGIK*, where he graduated in 1971 from the workshop of Mikhail Romm*. Among his early acting roles was that of Kolya in Georgi Danelia's* *Ya shagayu po Moskve/I Walk Around Moscow* (1963). His first feature film as a director was *Svoi sredi chuzhikh, chuzhoi sredi svoikh/At Home Among Strangers, Alone Among Friends* (1974), an adventure story set during the Russian Civil War. It was followed by *Raba lyubvi/A Slave of Love* (1976), about the tribulations of a group of actors trying to complete a film melodrama in post-Revolution Odessa, and the political awakening of the star, played by Yelena Solovei. Also in 1976, Mikhalkov made *Neokonchennaya p'esa dlya mekhanicheskogo pianino/An Unfinished Piece for Mechanical Piano*, based on Chekhov's early play *Platonov*. The moving *Pyat' vecherov/Five Evenings* (1978), from the play by Alexander Volodin, is set in 1957, and chronicles the re-encounter of a couple separated at the outbreak of World War II. Mikhalkov's visually stunning but lugubriously (and inappropriately) sentimental version of Goncharov, *Neskol'ko dnei iz zhizni I. I. Oblomova/Several Days in the Life of I. I.*

Oblomov (also *Oblomov*; 1979), was followed by the family dramas *Rodnya/Kinfolk* (1981) and *Bez svidetelei/Without Witnesses* (also *A Private Conversation*; 1983). Mikhalkov continued his career as an actor, notably in Eldar Ryazanov's* *Vokzal dlya dvoikh/Station for Two* (1983) and *Zhestokii romans/A Cruel Romance* (1984). He was outspokenly sceptical about the changes in Soviet cinema introduced at the Fifth Congress of the Union of Cinematographers* in 1986, and his recent films have been made for Western companies. *Oci ciornie/Ochi chërnye/Dark Eyes* (1987) was made in Italy, and starred Silvana Mangano* and Marcello Mastroianni*, who won the Best Actor prize at Cannes in this confection loosely based on 'The Lady with the Little Dog' and other Chekhov stories. *Urga: Territoriya lyubvi/Urga: Territory of Love* (1991), a French co-production, was a glorious return to form, and won Mikhalkov the Golden Lion at Venice in 1991 and a European Film Award* in 1993. A film with an acute sense of history and geography, which captures the desolate, compelling grandeur of the steppes, it tells the story of a Mongol family's gradual accommodation to a modernity that will seemingly exclude Russians, and of the Russian protagonist's growing sense of his own anachronism. It was followed by the documentary *Anna: 6–18* (1993), a series of interviews filmed with his daughter on her successive birthdays, soliciting her opinions on questions both topical and eternal. *Bezuslovnyi effekt sharovoi molnii/Soleil trompeur/Burnt by the Sun* (1994), set in 1936, is Mikhalkov's belated contribution to the recent wave of historical investigations. It shared the Jury Prize at Cannes and won the Oscar for Best Foreign Film in 1995. In recent years Mikhalkov has run the highly successful Tritè film production company in Moscow. JGf

MIKHALKOV-KONCHALOVSKY, Andron S. [KONCHALOVSKY, Andrei] Moscow 1937

Russian director and scriptwriter. The son of Soviet writer Sergei Mikhalkov and elder brother of director Nikita Mikhalkov*, Mikhalkov-Konchalovsky studied at VGIK* in the workshop of Mikhail Romm*, graduating in 1965, the year in which his *Pervyi uchitel'/The First Teacher* was made at Kirgizfilm. Taken from a story by the Kirgiz writer Chingiz Aitmatov, it tells of a young man's struggle to impose Soviet ways in a distant Kirgiz village. His next film, *Istoriya Asi Klyachinoi, kotoraya lyubila, da ne vyshla zamuzh/The Story of Asya Klyachina, Who Loved But Did Not Marry* (also called *Asya's Happiness*; 1967), a starkly realistic view of life on a collective farm, was banned until 1988, when Konchalovsky belatedly won the Russian Nike award for best direction. He followed it with more conventional projects, adaptations of Turgenev's novel *Dvoryanskoye gnezdo/A Nest of Gentlefolk* (1969) and of Chekhov's *Dyadya Vanya/Uncle Vanya* (1971). *Romans o vlyublënnykh/Romance about Lovers* (1974) was followed by his last Soviet film, *Sibiriada/Siberiade* (1979), an inordinately long epic of life in a Siberian village from 1900 to the 1970s. Andrei Konchalovsky (as he signs his Western films) made his first American film, *Maria's Lovers*, in 1984. Starring Nastassja Kinski, Keith Carradine and Robert Mitchum, it successfully transposes a poignant love story by the Russian writer Andrei Platonov to a small town in Pennsylvania. This was followed by *Runaway Train* (1985), from a script by Akira Kurosawa; *Duet for One* (1986); *Shy People* (1987); *Homer and Eddie* (1989); and the Sylvester Stallone thriller *Tango & Cash* (1989), which Konchalovsky left halfway through shooting. With *The Inner Circle* (Russian title: *Blizhnii krug*; 1991), an Italian-Russian co-production, Konchalovsky returned to Russian material. Tom Hulce plays Ivan Sanshin, Stalin's cinema projectionist, and Bob Hoskins plays Beria in an unimaginative and cliché-ridden version of the Soviet 1930s, captured far more persuasively in Soviet films of the Gorbachev period. *Kurochka Ryaba/Riaba My Chicken* (1994) returns to the characters of *Istoriya Asi Klyachinoi* (Asya is now played by Inna Churikova, an actress who has achieved great renown playing in the films of her husband, Gleb Panfilov*), and finds them perplexed and defeated by the advent of the 'free market' in the Russian village. JGf

MILLS, (Sir) John   Felixstowe 1908

British actor, one of the more appealing representatives of British decency in wartime and postwar cinema. It is surely culturally significant that in 1947 the decent, unassuming and likeable John Mills displaced the wicked James Mason* from the top of the popularity charts.

Mills started in the chorus line of musical revue, and his screen debut was opposite Jessie Matthews* in *The Midshipmaid* (1932). In the 1930s, his association with the patriotic valour of the common man was established in the role of seaman Albert Brown in *Forever England* (1935). In *In Which We Serve* (1942), *This Happy Breed* (1944) and *Waterloo Road* (1945), Mills represented the 1940s version of the working-class hero: the little man caught up by war or the threat of war but with no aspiration to be other than he is, no imaginings other than to sort things out back home. Unlike Stanley Baker*, who also represents class difference in the war film, the Mills character seems to have no inner anger or spite. In civilian clothes, he is Mr Polly in *The History of Mr Polly* (1949) or Charles Laughton's* biddable son-in-law in *Hobson's Choice* (1954). As he grew older, Mills rose through the ranks and gained authority, a swagger stick and a moustache. He was, however, still able to return to his humble origins in *Ryan's Daughter* (1970), for which he received an Oscar as Best Supporting Actor. He was knighted in 1976. JC

Other Films Include: As Actor – *O.H.M.S.* (1937); *The Young Mr Pitt, The Big Blockade* (1942); *We Dive at Dawn* (1943); *Victory Wedding* [dir. Jessie Matthews, short] (1944); *The Way to the Stars* (1945); *Great Expectations* (1946); *Scott of the Antarctic* (1948); *Morning Departure* (1950); *The Colditz Story* (1954); *Above Us the Waves* (1955); *Ice Cold in Alex, I Was Monty's Double* (1958); *Tiger Bay* (1959); *Tunes of Glory* (1960); *King Rat* (1965, US); *The Wrong Box, The Family Way* (1966); *Oh! What a Lovely War* (1969); *Young Winston* (1972); *Lady Caroline Lamb, Oklahoma Crude* (1973, US); *The 'Human' factor* (1975); *Gandhi* (1982). **As Director**: *Sky West and Crooked* [+ prod.] (1965).

MILTON, Georges   Georges Michaud; Puteaux 1888 – Juan-les-Pins 1970

French actor and singer. Unknown outside France, Milton was an enormously popular comedian, first in the *café-concert* before and after World War I, and then in the cinema of the 1930s. His screen character, known as 'Bouboule', built on his stage work and his small, round physique. He was the *resquilleur* (eternal cheat), jovial and bawdy, who got the better of his social superiors through clowning and cunning in a series of hits, especially *Le Roi des resquilleurs/King of Cheats* (1930) and *La Bande à Bouboule/Bouboule's Gang* (1931). His only foray into *auteur* cinema was as the hero of Abel Gance's* politically ambiguous *Jérôme Perreau, héros des barricades* (1935), in which he plays the eponymous populist hero who befriends the great and the good and saves the country. GV

MIOU-MIOU   Sylvette Héry; Paris 1950

French actress, who rose to prominence alongside Gérard Depardieu* and Patrick Dewaere in Bertrand Blier's* *Les Valseuses/Going Places* (1973). Her first acting experience was in the *café-théâtre* [> COMEDY (FRANCE)]. From this libertarian tradition, she emerged as the strong but vulnerable independent woman of Yves Boisset's* *La Femme flic/Female Cop* (1980), Diane Kurys'* *Coup de foudre/Entre Nous/At First Sight* (1983) and Jacques Renard's *Blanche et Marie* (1985, a wartime story). It is a measure of her talent that she overcame the limitations of the comic nickname provided by Coluche to play moving dramatic parts, often using her erotic potential, as in Daniel Duval's *La Dérobade* (1979), Michel Deville's* *La Lectrice*, 1988, and Louis Malle's* *Milou en Mai*, 1989. She has also appeared in many comedies, such as those of Georges Lautner and Patrice Leconte. Miou-Miou has supported feminist projects like Claire Simon's *Scènes de ménage* (1991) but her limited room for manoeuvre in French popular cinema is illustrated by her humiliatingly misogynist role in Blier's successful *Tenue de soirée/Menage/Evening Dress* (1986). One of her latest roles is as the heroic mother of *Germinal* (1993). GV

MIRANDA, Isa   Inès Isabella Sampietro; Milan 1909 – Rome 1982

Italian actress. The elegant Isa Miranda, whose beauty recalled that of Marlene Dietrich*, was one of Italy's most celebrated film stars in the 1930s and 1940s. She appeared in several Italian films before her first lead role in Guido Brignone's *Tenebre* (1934). That same year she was launched into stardom by Max Ophuls'* *La signora di tutti*, which the German director made in Italy. Significantly, Ophuls' film drew upon her relative anonymity as an actress in a story that recounts the rise to stardom and eventual destruction of a film star. Between 1934 and 1937 Miranda was cast in five more Italian films – *Come le foglie/Like the Leaves* (1934), *Passaporto rosso/Red Passport* (1936), *Il fu Mattia Pascal/The Late Mathias Pascal* (1937; Miranda also appeared in the

French version, *L'Homme de nulle part*, 1936), *Scipione l'africano/Scipio Africanus* (1936) and *Una donna fra due mondi/Between Two Worlds* (1937) – before signing a contract with Paramount in Hollywood, where she made two films, *Hotel Imperial* (1939, a remake of a 1927 silent film) and *Adventure in Diamonds* (1940). Back in Italy she appeared in three films directed by her husband, Alfredo Guarini – *Senza cielo* (1940), *È caduta una donna* (1941) and *Documento Z 3* (1942) – and starred in Mario Soldati's* critically acclaimed *Malombra* (1942), based upon Antonio Fogazzaro's classic nineteenth-century novel, and in the title role of another turn-of-the-century romance, Renato Castellani's* *Zazà* (1942). After the war, Miranda appeared in many international co-productions, including René Clément's* *Au-delà des grilles/Le mura di Malapaga/The Walls of Malapaga* (1949), co-starring Jean Gabin*, and Max Ophuls' *La Ronde* (1950). One of her last appearances was in Liliana Cavani's* *Il portiere di notte/The Night Porter* (1974). JHa

MIRÓ, Pilar   Madrid 1940

Spanish director. Miró was the first woman director for Spanish television, specialising in drama and literary adaptations. Her film-making career has been surrounded by controversy, as she fell foul of the censor both during and after the Franco dictatorship. Her first feature, *La petición/The Engagement Party* (1976), a period melodrama, explores female sexuality and sadism. The ban on the film was lifted after a massive press campaign. The historical docudrama *El crimen de Cuenca/The Cuenca Crime* (1979) focuses on injustice, corruption and torture at the hands of the Civil Guard. Seized by command of the Military Tribunal, the film was only released following international pressure after its success at the 1980 Berlin Festival. Social and psychological alienation, existential frustration and the difficulties of communication are constant themes of Miró's films. *Beltenebros/Prince of Shadows* (1991), a dark-toned thriller in the tradition of *Cine negro**, recounts the return to Madrid of an erstwhile activist to eliminate a traitor from an underground cell. Both *Gary Cooper que estás en los cielos/Gary Cooper Who Art in Heaven* (1980) and *El pájaro de la felicidad/The Bird of Happiness* (1993) examine existentialist questions from a female perspective and reflect a change in mood from the early years of democracy to disillusionment with PSOE 'socialism' in the 1990s. In 1982 Miró became the films minister for the first socialist government after the end of dictatorship. She introduced changes in cinema legislation (1983), particularly in respect of film subsidies, which injected a major boost into the Spanish film industry. She resigned from this post in 1986 to return to film-making with a free adaptation of Goethe's *Werther* set in contemporary Spain (1986, co-scripted, like *Beltenebros*, by Mario Camús*). RM

MIRREN, Helen   London 1945

British actress, who has moved with equal success between theatre, film and television since the late 1960s. She was a member of the Royal Shakespeare Company, making her film debut in Peter Hall's *A Midsummer Night's Dream* (1968),

and accompanying Peter Brook on his tour of Africa with *The Conference of the Birds* in 1972. Mirren brings to her performances on film, and more recently on television, a combination of strength, sexuality and sheer skill. A strongly sensual actress in, for example, Michael Powell's* *Age of Consent* (1969, Australia), she could also burlesque sensuality in *O Lucky Man!* (1973) or in a superb performance as Titania in a television version of *A Midsummer Night's Dream* (1981). She received a Cannes film festival award for her performance in *Cal* (1984), and appeared with Harrison Ford in Peter Weir's underrated *The Mosquito Coast* (1986, US). In the 1990s she won a well-deserved BAFTA award for her performance in the television police serial *Prime Suspect* (1991). JC

Other Films Include: *Savage Messiah* (1972); *The Long Good Friday, Excalibur* (1981); *White Nights* (1985, US); *Pascali's Island* (1988); *The Cook the Thief His Wife & Her Lover* (1989); *Cortesie per gli ospiti/The Comfort of Strangers* (1990, It./UK); *Where Angels Fear to Tread* (1991); *The Hawk* (1992).

MIŠEV, Georgi   Yoglav 1935

Bulgarian scriptwriter. A prolific author of popular comedies and a highly skilled satirist, whose original stories and scripts helped to boost the fortunes of the Bulgarian cinema during its revival in the 1970s. Born and raised in a village, Mišev sometimes returns to memories of his youth for material, but for the most part his stories deal with the friction that results when rural traditions clash with the more impersonal and anonymous urban life.

As a scriptwriter, Mišev has collaborated mostly with three directors: Eduard Zahariev*, Ljudmil Kirkov* and Ivan Andonov. The best films are those with Zahariev, which reveal a penchant for the absurd in everyday life, particularly among ordinary people who strive to be better than they really are. In their first effort together, *Ako ne ide vlak/If the Train Doesn't Arrive* (1967), an absurd hunt takes place at night for a missing person about whom no one really knows anything. In *Prebrojavane na divite zajci/The Hare Census* (1973, winner of several festival awards), a government official appears suddenly in a village with nonsensical orders to count the number of wild hares in the district. And in *Vilna zona/Villa Zone* (1975) a suburban garden party on a summer night erupts into an out-of-control battle with the neighbours. Each of these films offered ample room for Zahariev and Mišev to satirise the conniving parvenu and the greedy petit bourgeois in contemporary socialist society.

Mišev collaborated with Ljudmil Kirkov on a series of nostalgic, yet quite bitter, films about disintegrating village life and the steady migration of rural populations to cities and industrial areas: *Momčeto si otiva/A Boy Becomes a Man* (1972), *Seljaninăt s koleloto/Peasant on a Bicycle* (1974), *Ne si otivaj!/Don't Go Away!* (1976), and *Matriarhat/Matriarchy* (1977). And although his screenplays for Ivan Andonov – *Samodivsko horo/Fairy Dance* (1976) and *Dami kanjat/Ladies' Choice* (1980) – reveal a mellowed Mišev, he can still poke some light-hearted fun at the foibles of the established middle class, the 'privileged' in a socialist society with a taste for ostentation.

Mišev's characters, carefully observed from everyday life, are readily recognisable to a home audience. However, as clearly delineated universal types, they also contributed to the acceptance of Bulgarian cinema abroad – and to the maturing of a now sophisticated national cinema. RH

MISTRAL, Jorge   Modesto Llosas Rosell; Aldaya 1920 – Mexico City, Mexico 1972

Spanish actor, who began in the theatre, moving to films after 1944 and signing an exclusive contract with Cifesa* in 1945. His swarthy good looks made him a matinee idol after he starred in Luis Lucia's* *Currito de la Cruz/Currito of the Cross* (1948) and Juan de Orduña's* *Locura de amor/Love Crazy* (1948). He moved to Mexico in 1949, appearing in many films there, including Luis Buñuel's* *Abismos de pasión/Wuthering Heights* (1953). His popularity was sustained throughout the 1950s in both Spain and Latin America, but at the end of the decade, with his looks beginning to fade, his career waned and he committed suicide. PWE

MODOT, Gaston   Paris 1887–1970

French actor. Though never a star, Modot has one of the most distinguished filmographies in French cinema. After many popular silent films, including French 'Westerns', Modot, who trained as a painter, was attracted to the avant-garde, notably the films of Germaine Dulac* and Louis Delluc*. His part in Luis Buñuel's* *L'Age d'or* (1930) brought him international notoriety (although the film was quickly banned). Modot then started a long collaboration with directors like Jean Renoir*, René Clair*, Marcel Carné* and Jacques Becker* which lasted until the 1960s. His most memorable parts are the engineer in *La Grande illusion* (1937) and the game-keeper in *La Règle du jeu/Rules of the Game* (1939), where he was characteristically laconic and reserved. GV

MOLANDER, Gustaf   Helsinki, Finland [then Russia] 1888 – Stockholm 1973

Swedish director and scriptwriter. Molander, who directed more than sixty films, started as a stage actor both in Sweden and Finland. He entered cinema as a scriptwriter for Mauritz Stiller* (*Herr Arnes pengar/Snows of Destiny/Sir Arne's Treasure*, 1919, and *Erotikon/The Bonds That Chafe*, 1920) and Victor Sjöström* (*Terje Vigen*, 1917). He directed his own first films during the Golden Age of silent Swedish cinema, but did not attain the same status as his illustrious colleagues. When they left for Hollywood he finally made his name as a director and became both the most productive and the most highly regarded Swedish film-maker of the 1930s. Molander worked in popular genre cinema, making high society comedies, such as *Vi som går köksvägen/We Who Use the Servants' Entrance* (1932), and bourgeois melodramas; most notable are those starring the young Ingrid Bergman*,

especially *Intermezzo* (1936), a major hit which brought her to international attention, *En kvinnas ansikte/A Woman's Face* (1938) (both films were remade in Hollywood – where Molander declined to go – respectively in 1939 with Bergman and 1941 with Joan Crawford) and *En enda natt/One Single Night* (1939). Molander's other major contribution to Swedish film history are his 1940s war films, including *Rid i natt!/Ride Tonight!* (1942) and *Det brinner en eld/There Burns a Flame* (1943), both with anti-totalitarian themes. He went on working until the 1950s, directing the third version of *Sången om den eldröda blomman/The Song of the Scarlet Flower* in 1956. His last film was an episode for *Stimulantia* (1967); entitled *Smycket/The Necklace*, it was based on a Guy de Maupassant short story ('La parure') and starred Ingrid Bergman, the actress he had helped make into a star. LGA/BF

Other Films as Director Include: *Bodakungen/The Tyranny of Hate* (1920); *Thomas Graals myndling/Thomas Graal's Ward, Amatörfilmen/The Amateur Film* (1922); *Mälarpirater/Pirates of the Mälaren* (1923); *33.333* (1924); *Polis Paulus' påskasmäll/Constable Paulus's Easter Cracker* (1925); *Ingmarsarvet/Ingmar's Inheritance* (1925); *Till österland/To the Orient, Hon, den enda/She, the Only One* (1926); *Hans engelska fru/His English Wife, Förseglade läppar/Sealed Lips* (1927); *Parisiskor/Parisian Ladies/The Doctor's Women, Synd/Sin* (1928); *Hjärtats triumf/The Triumph of the Heart* (1929); *Fridas visor/Frida's Songs, Charlotte Löwensköld* (1930); *En natt/One Night* (1931); *Svarta rosor/Black Roses, Kärlek och kassabrist/Love and Deficit* (1932); *Kära släkten/Dear Relatives* (1933); *En stilla flirt/A Quiet Flirt, Fasters millioner/My Aunt's Millions* (1934); *Ungkarlspappan/Bachelor Daddy, Swedenhielms, Under falsk flagg/Under False Flag* (1935); *På solsidan/On the Sunny Side, Bröllopsresan/The Honeymoon Trip, Familjens hemlighet/The Family Secret* (1936); *Sara lär sig folkvett/Sara Learns Manners* (1937); *Dollar* (1938); *Ombyte förnöjer/A Pleasant Change, Emilie Högqvist* (1939); *En, men ett lejon/One but a Lion* (1940); *Den ljusnande framtid/Bright Prospects, I natt eller aldrig/Tonight or Never, Striden går vidare/The Fight Goes On* (1941); *Jacobs stege/Jacob's Ladder* (1942); *Älskling, jag ger mig/Darling, I Surrender, Ordet/The Word* (1943); *Den osynliga muren/The Invisible Wall, Kejsarn av Portugallien/The Emperor of Portugal* (1944); *Galgmannen/The Gallows Man/The Talisman* (1945); *Det är min modell/It's My Model* (1946); *Kvinna utan ansikte/Woman Without a Face* (1947); *Nu börjar livet/Life Begins Now, Eva* (1948); *Kärleken segrar/Love Will Conquer* (1949); *Kvartetten som sprängdes/The Quartet That Split Up* (1950); *Fästmö uthyres/Fiancée for Hire, Frånskild/Divorced* (1951); *Trots/Defiance, Kärlek/Love* (1952); *Glasberget/The Glass Mountain* (1953); *Herr Arnes penningar/Mr Arne's Money* (1954); *Enhörningen/The Unicorn* (1955).

MOLINA, Angela   Angela Molina Tejedor; Madrid 1955

Spanish actress, who achieved renown by sharing the lead female role in Luis Buñuel's* *Cet obscur objet du désir/That

291

Obscure Object of Desire (1977) with Carole Bouquet. She already had a reputation for her roles in controversial films, such as Jaime Camino's* *Las largas vacaciones del 1936/The Long Holidays of 1936* (1976), a polemical study of the Civil War in Catalonia, and Manuel Gutiérrez Aragón's* *Camada negra/Black Brood* (1977), whose portrayal of right-wing violence in Spain led to bomb threats on the opening night. Such films established her as one of the key actresses of the transition period, the years following Franco's death. She has since appeared in films dealing with complex sexual situations, such as Jaime de Armiñán's *Nunca es tarde/It's Never Too Late* (1977) and Jaime Chávarri's* *A un Dios desconocido/To an Unknown God* (1977), and in films touching upon Spain's recent history. She has had a particularly fruitful professional relationship with Gutiérrez Aragón, starring in his *El corazón del bosque/The Heart of the Forest* (1978), *Demonios en el jardín/Demons in the Garden* (1982) and *La mitad del cielo/Half of Heaven* (1986), all studies of the Francoist and post-Franco periods. Some have criticised her 'wooden' acting style and slightly garbled diction, but her striking and somewhat austere looks have allowed her to bring power and dignity to her many roles in Spanish and other European films. SGHR

MOLINA, Josefina
Josefina Molina Reig;
Córdoba 1936

Spanish director, graduate of the Escuela Oficial de Cinematografía*, who started working in television in 1964 and made her first feature, *Vera ... un cuento cruel/Vera ... a Cruel Story,* in 1973. With Rosario Pi, Ana Mariscal* and, more recently, Pilar Miró*, Rosa Vergés and Ana Belén*, she is one of the very few women directors in Spanish cinema. She is often attracted to non-conformist characters, as in the star-studded *Esquilache* (1989, set in the reign of Charles III) and *Santa Teresa de Jesús* (1984, for television). *Lo más natural/The Most Natural Thing* (1990) again relied on stars – in this case Miguel Bosé (a heart-throb pop singer and actor) and Charo López* – to enliven a narrative about a woman's involvement with an ecology-conscious younger man, following the collapse of her marriage. In both cases the radical potential of the narratives (mutiny in *Esquilache*, feminism in *Lo más natural*) is balanced by tendencies less critical of political or institutional orthodoxies. PWE

MOLLBERG, Rauni
Hämeenlinna 1929

Finnish director and producer, who became internationally known with *Maa on syntinen laulu/Earth is a Sinful Song* (1973). In the late 1960s, Mollberg had been a stage actor and director. He also worked for Finnish television, where his literary adaptations were characterised by a combination of subjectivity and precise historical and social contexts. *Maa on syntinen laulu* was based on Timo K. Mukka's novel, published when the author was nineteen. Book and film are set in a remote village in Lapland, where people still live in close contact with 'earthly desires and heavenly aims', birth and death. The film brought elements of Mollberg's televisual

style to the big screen – extreme close-ups, amateur actors, and visually imposing landscapes. His penchant for literary adaptation is also reflected in *Aika hyvä ihmiseksi/Pretty Good for a Human Being* (1977). Mollberg's most ambitious project was a 1986 remake of Edvin Laine's* *Tuntematon sotilas/The Unknown Soldier* (1954). Mollberg interpreted the ordinary private soldier's point of view of Linna's novel more realistically than Laine, for whom patriotism took precedence. Mollberg used young amateur actors, hand-held camera and fast editing to create one of the most strongly pacifist war movies ever made. In his most recent film, *Ystävät toverit/Friends, Comrades* (1990), he combines his most personal themes, the landscapes of Lapland and the destruction of war. AH-H

MONICELLI, Mario
Viareggio 1915

Italian director. Brought up and trained in Milan in the 1930s, Monicelli made a precocious start as a film-maker when he won a prize at the 1935 Venice Festival as co-director of an amateur film, *I ragazzi della via Paal*. After apprenticeship with Mario Camerini* and Augusto Genina*, he made his professional debut in the late 1940s in partnership with Stefano Steno, with whom he made a large number of films as vehicles for the great comedian Totò* (notably *Totò cerca casa/Totò Wants a Home*, 1949; *Guardie e ladri/Cops and Robbers*, 1951; *Totò e Carolina*, 1953). He then made a key contribution to what became known as *commedia all'italiana*, starting with the brilliantly funny *I soliti ignoti/Persons Unknown* (1958). His most important films, while flattering audiences' tastes, were also moved by an acute – even fierce – critical spirit. In 1959 *La grande guerra/The Great War* shared the Golden Lion at the Venice Festival with Roberto Rossellini's* *Il generale Della Rovere* – the first time a popular and partly comic film was admitted to the ranks of art cinema. *I compagni/The Strikers* (1963) was an ambitious attempt to reclaim the history of the workers' and socialist movements in turn-of-the-century Turin. The film enjoyed some art-house success, especially abroad, but the general public in Italy was confused by its insertion of socio-political commitment into a basically entertainment genre. Monicelli had more success with a series of episode films, in particular *L'armata Brancaleone* (1965), starring an extraordinary Vittorio Gassman*. If *I soliti ignoti* had signalled the beginning of *commedia all'italiana*, *Amici miei/My Friends* (1975), a nihilistic critique of the years of consumerism and modernisation in Italy, is the swansong of the genre. The next chapter in Monicelli's life was *Un borghese piccolo piccolo/An Average Man* (1977), starring the comic actor Alberto Sordi*, whose tragic potentiality Monicelli had guessed in much the same way as twenty years before he had inspired a comic talent in dramatic actor Gassman. In *Speriamo che sia femmina/Let's Hope It's a Girl* (1985) – one of the many projects Monicelli inherited from someone else – he achieved a happy balance between traditional Tuscan 'malice' and an appealing sentimentality, and demonstrated an acute observation of new patterns of behaviour. PDA

Other Films Include: *È arrivato il cavaliere* (1950); *Totò e le donne* (1952, co-dir.); *Proibito* (1954); *Un eroe dei nostri tempi*

(1955); *Donatella* (1955); *Padre e figli/The Tailor's Maid* (1956); *Risate di Gioia* (1960); *Boccaccio 70* (1962, ep. *Renzo e Luciana*); *Casanova 70* (1965); *Capriccio all'italiana* [ep. *La Bambinaia*], *La ragazza con la pistola/The Girl with a Pistol* (1968); *Toh, è morta la nonna* (1969); *Brancaleone alle Crociate* (1970); *La mortadella/Lady Liberty* (1971); *Vogliamo i colonnelli* (1973); *Romanzo popolare* (1974); *Caro Michele* (1976); *I nuovi mostri/Viva Italia* (1977, co-dir.); *Viaggio con Anita/Lovers and Liars* (1978); *Temporale rosy* (1980); *Camera d'albergo* (1981); *Il marchese del Grillo* (1981); *Amici miei atto II* (1982); *Bertoldo, Bertoldino e Cacasenno* (1984); *Le due vite di Mattia Pascal* (1985); *I picari* (1987); *Il male oscuro* (1990); *Rossini! Rossini!* (1991); *Parenti serpenti* (1992).

MONTAGE – see SOVIET MONTAGE

MONTAGU, Ivor   London 1904 – Watford 1984

British producer, writer and director. Communist, aristocrat, son of the banker Lord Montagu, the Hon. Ivor Montagu was a leading figure in left-wing film activity in the 1930s. One of the founders of the London Film Society* in 1924, in 1934 he organised the Progressive Film Institute (PFI) as a producing and distributing body for the Communist Party. The PFI sent a crew (including Thorold Dickinson* and Norman McLaren*) to Spain during the Civil War, where Montagu produced and directed *In Defence of Madrid* (1936). *Peace and Plenty* (1939), directed by Montagu for the Communist Party, followed McLaren's *Hell Unltd.* (1936) in using graphics, puppets and animation to attack Chamberlain's appeasement policy. Montagu was editor and title writer for Alfred Hitchcock's* *The Lodger* (1926), associate producer of *The Man Who Knew Too Much* (1934) and *The 39 Steps* (1935), and first film critic of the *Observer* and the *New Statesman*. He was a friend and translator of Eisenstein*, and accompanied him on his visit to Hollywood and Mexico, recording the trip in his book *With Eisenstein in Hollywood* (1968). During World War II he worked for the Ministry of Information, and he was a scriptwriter at Ealing after the war. He was awarded the Lenin Peace Prize in 1959. JC

Bib: Ivor Montagu, *The Youngest Son: Autobiographical Sketches* (1970).

MONTAND, Yves   Ivo Livi; Monsummano Alto, Italy 1921 – Senlis 1991

French actor and singer. The son of poor Italian immigrants, Montand started his singing and film careers under the wing of the great singer Edith Piaf, with whom he co-starred in *Étoile sans lumière* in 1945. Replacing Jean Gabin* in *Les Portes de la nuit* (1946) brought him notoriety though not success; this came with Henri-Georges Clouzot's* *Le Salaire de la peur/The Wages of Fear* (1953), now a cult classic, which launched Montand's brand of tough virility. To this he later added the aura of his left-wing commitment, which found cinematic expression in Alain Resnais'* *La Guerre est finie/The War is Over* (1966), Jean-Luc Godard's* *Tout va bien* (1972) and a series of films directed by Costa-Gavras* (*Z*, 1969, *L'Aveu/The Confession*, 1970, *État de siège/State of Siege*, 1973). Montand achieved worldwide fame in George Cukor's *Let's Make Love* (1960, US), largely because of his relationship with co-star Marilyn Monroe. In the 1970s and 1980s, Montand's screen identity matured into a more melancholy masculinity; he widened his range, from thrillers like *Le Cercle rouge/The Red Circle* (1970) to comedy (*Le Sauvage*, 1975), to the intimate realist films of Claude Sautet* (*César et Rosalie*, 1972, *Garçon!*, 1983). Always a popular star, he crowned his career with huge success as the patriarch of *Jean de Florette* and *Manon des sources* (1986). Montand's overt political positions, increasingly anti-communist, made him one of France's most famous personalities; there was even talk of Montand for President. But he was equally popular as a singer (the subject of Chris Marker's* *La Solitude du chanteur de fond/The Loneliness of the Long-distance Singer* in 1974), and as Simone Signoret's* lifelong partner. He died while making his last film, Jean-Jacques Beineix's* *IP5* (released 1992). GV

Other Films Include: *Marguerite de la nuit* (1956); *Les Sorcières de Salem/The Crucible* (1957); *Compartiment tueurs/The Sleeping Car Murders* (1965); *Un soir, un train, On a Clear Day You Can See Forever* [US] (1970); *La Folie des grandeurs* (1971); *Vincent, François, Paul ... et les autres* (1974); *Police Python 357* (1975); *Le Choix des armes* (1981); *Trois places pour le 26* (1988).

MONTEIRO, João César   Figueira da Foz 1939

Portuguese director and actor. With a grant from the Gulbenkian Foundation, Monteiro studied at the London International Film School, graduating in 1963. Two years later he began *Quem Espera por Sapatos de Defunto ... Morre Descalço/He Who Waits for the Dead Man's Shoes Dies Barefoot*, soon to be interrupted and restarted in 1968, with Luís Miguel Cintra* in his first screen role. Monteiro had previously made a short, *Sophia de Mello Breyner Audreson* (1968, part of a series on artists), on the poet Sophia de Mello Breyner, his only completed film before 1974 (*Sapatos do Defunto* and *A Sagrada Família – Fragmentos de um Filme Esmola/The Holy Family – Fragments of a Begged Film*, 1972, are really segments of 'work in progress'). In a remarkable review of Manoel de Oliveira's* *O Passado e o Presente/Past and Present* (1971), Monteiro wrote: 'He [Oliveira] is, in the Portuguese context, part of the small minority of Catholic directors (the others being Paulo Rocha and, in a more modest way, the author of these lines), to whom the act of filming implies the awareness of a transgression. Filming is a violence of sight, a profanation of reality whose goal is to restore one sacred image.' The combination of the sacred and the transgressive became a distinguishing aspect of Monteiro's films, marked on the one hand by an obsession with literary quotation, painting and the cinema ('high culture'), and on the other by the abject, the sordid and the scatological ('low culture').

During the revolution, Monteiro made a militant film, *Que Farei Eu Com Esta Espada?/What Shall I Do with This*

Sword? (1975), a collage of images from F. W. Murnau's* *Nosferatu*, the American fleet approaching Lisbon, street demonstrations and the story of a prostitute speaking directly to the camera. With the end of the revolution and the defeat of the political project he had stood for, Monteiro went in search of traditional culture as a basis for a mythical Portuguese identity in *Veredas/Traditional Tales* (1977) and *Silvestre* (1980). *À Flôr do Mar/By the Seaside/Ultramarina* (1986) is more abstract, related in texture to his early film, *Sophia de Mello Breyner Audreson,* but this time a series of variations on sunshine and the colour blue.

After a variety of cameo parts, some in his own productions, Monteiro played the lead in *Recordações da Casa Amarela/Recollections of the Yellow House* (1989, winner of the Silver Lion at Venice). In this film, playing João de Deus (a common name which literally means John of God), the son of a Holy Family who is also a 'son of a bitch', Monteiro pursued his taste for transgression and thereby established himself as a cult figure. This was followed, with much less success, by *O Último Mergulho/The Last Dive* (1992), part of the anthology *The Four Elements*. AMS

Bib: João César Monteiro, *Morituri te salutant* (1974).

MONTENEGRO – see YUGOSLAVIA (former)

MONTESINOS, Guillermo   Guillermo José Montesinos Serrano; Castellón de la Plana 1948

Spanish actor whose career started in the early 1970s, though his first significant film was Luis García Berlanga's* *La vaquilla/The Heifer* (1985), which led to further successes in Fernando Trueba's* *Sé infiel y no mires con quién/Be Wanton and Tread No Shame* (1985), Fernando Colomo's* *La vida alegre/A Happy Life* (1987) and García Sánchez's *La corte de Faraón/Pharaoh's Court* (1985) – all films which identify him with the '*Escuela de Madrid*' (Madrid School) [> COMEDY (SPAIN)]. His most colourful recent appearance, however, was as the kitschy cabbie in Pedro Almodóvar's* *Mujeres al borde de un ataque de nervios/Women on the Verge of a Nervous Breakdown* (1988), where his usual role as nervous, lovable, comic sprite is overlaid with an alternative, subversive definition of masculinity in line with Almodóvar's aesthetics of transgression. PWE

MONTIEL, Sara (Sarita)   Marla Antonia Abad Fernández; Campo de Criptana 1928

Spanish actress and singer, who achieved legendary success in the *cuplé* musicals of the late 1950s and 1960s, such as Juan de Orduña's* *El último cuplé/The Last Song* (1957) and Luis-César Amadori's *La Violetera/The Violet Seller* (1958) and *Mi último tango/My Last Tango* (1960). Montiel had worked with Francoist directors in the 1940s without much public or critical success. A move to Mexico in the early 1950s produced a run of popular melodramas which led to contracts in Hollywood, where she appeared in six films including *Vera Cruz* (1954); she was married for a while to director Anthony

Mann. Back in Spain from 1957, she was habitually cast in her musicals as transgressive heroine, whose flamboyant performance and defiant voluptuous sexuality – overtly 'punished' – offered a nation in the grip of a puritanical dictatorship both an outlet and a metaphor for its own repression. She continues to perform in musical extravaganzas and her 1950s musicals are now highly valued out of affection, nostalgia or for their kitsch appeal. MD

MORE, Kenneth   Gerrards Cross 1914 – London 1982

British actor, one of the league of likeable gentlemen of post-war British cinema. He began in stage revue and worked in the mid-1930s at the Windmill Theatre. He retained his comic ability in his film career, and two of his most popular films were *Genevieve* (1953) and *Doctor in the House* (1954). In his dramatic roles, he projected a matter-of-fact heroism or an ability to get the job done. Like many British actors, he commuted between film and theatre, playing the lead in both the stage and screen versions of Terence Rattigan's play *The Deep Blue Sea* (1955), his screen performance winning him a Best Actor award at Venice. Very much an icon of decency in the 1950s in cinema, he moved into television in the 1960s, renewing his popularity with his role in the BBC serialisation of *The Forsyte Saga* (1967). JC

Other Films Include: *Look Up and Laugh* (1935); *Scott of the Antarctic* (1948); *Morning Departure* (1950); *The Franchise Affair* (1951); *The Yellow Balloon* (1952); *Reach for the Sky* (1956); *The Admirable Crichton* (1957); *A Night to Remember, The Sheriff of Fractured Jaw* (1958); *North West Frontier, The 39 Steps* (1959); *Oh! What a Lovely War* (1969).

MOREAU, Jeanne   Paris 1928

French actress and director. A key actress of the French New Wave*, Moreau had a solid training in the theatre (including the Comédie Française) and the popular French cinema of the 1950s, starring for example in *La Reine Margot* (1954). Her leading parts in Louis Malle's* *Ascenseur pour l'échafaud/Lift to the Scaffold* (1957) and *Les Amants* (1958) made her a focus of the emerging *auteur* cinema, a position confirmed by François Truffaut's *Jules et Jim* (1962). As the mesmerising Catherine in the latter, but also as Mme de Merteuil in Roger Vadim's* *Les Liaisons dangereuses* (1959), she crystallised the paradox of New Wave femininity: both cerebral and erotic, an authentically modern heroine who asserts her desire yet whose identity is ultimately confined to sexual icon. Moreau exported well and in the 1960s she became a fixture of international art cinema, playing in such films as Michelangelo Antonioni's* *La notte* (1960) and Orson Welles' *Le Procès/The Trial* (1962). Where Brigitte Bardot* was sex and Catherine Deneuve* elegance, Moreau incarnated 'intellectual' French femininity, with her lived-in looks and husky voice. Since the 1970s her star has waned, but her aura and talent have continued to fascinate film-makers, who tend to cast her in tragic cameo parts which she invests with more weight than they sometimes deserve, from Bertrand Blier's* *Les Valseuses/Going Places* (1973) to Luc Besson's* *Nikita* (1990). Lately, Moreau has developed the character of the scandalously sexy older woman, as in the delightful British television film *The Clothes in the Wardrobe* (1993), and the disappointing *La Vieille qui marchait dans la mer/The Old Lady who Walked on the Sea* (1991), an adaptation from the popular French writer San Antonio. Moreau has continued to work on stage and has directed three films, *Lumière* (1976), *L'Adolescente* (1979, starring Simone Signoret*) and *Lillian Gish* (1984). GV

Bib: Marianne Gray, *La Moreau* (1994).

Other Films Include: *Moderato Cantabile* (1960); *Eva/Eve* [It.], *La Baie des anges* (1962); *Le Feu follet/A Time to Live and a Time to Die* (1963); *Le Journal d'une femme de chambre/Diary of a Chambermaid* (1964); *Viva Maria!* (1965); *La Mariée était en noir/The Bride Wore Black* (1968); *Mr Klein* (1976); *Querelle* (1982, Ger.); *Le Paltoquet* (1986).

MORETTI, Nanni   Brunico 1953

Italian director and actor. Moretti sprang precociously to fame in 1976 with a Super-8 film, *Io sono un autarchico/I Am an Autocrat* (literally 'I am an autarchic', meaning something between anarchist, autonomist and autarkic in the old – and historically also Fascist – sense of self-sufficient), a witty, ironic immersion into the unreal feelings of a generation. This was followed by *Ecce bombo* (1978) and *Sogni d'oro/Golden Dreams* (1981), and a series of films throughout the 1980s which marked him out as an *auteur* with a highly personal approach and original style. Moretti's anti-naturalistic narrative discourse is an assault on the banality of the world and of the cinema, a desperate search for meaning in a violent and fragmented universe. His characters are paradoxical (the professor in *Bianca*, 1984, kills out of moralism); disturbing (the priest in *La messa è finita/The Mass is over*, 1985, renounces his calling out of his inability to help others); or bewildered (the amnesiac water-polo-playing Communist in *Palombella rossa/Red Lob*, 1989). His narration is disjointed, tending increasingly towards open-ended structures and a great economy of means, and making use of his own body as actor. *Caro diario/Dear Diary* (1993), a film in three episodes based on his own experience, is a light yet profound picture of contemporary Italy illuminated by the harsh gaze of a solitary humorist. In recent years Moretti has used his growing reputation to promote the work of talented newcomers such as Carlo Mazzacurati and Daniele Luchetti and has acted in their films (such as Luchetti's *Il portaborse/The Bagman*, 1991) as well as in his own. He has become a major public figure in Italy and a contributor to cultural and political debate – not least through his documentaries: *La cosa/The Thing* (1990), about Communist militants at the time the Party was changing its name, and the collective *L'unico paese al mondo/The Only Country in the World* (1994), a violent assault on Prime Minister and television entrepreneur Silvio Berlusconi and his 'telly-ocracy'. GVo

MORGAN, Michèle   Simone Roussel; Neuilly-sur-Seine 1920

French actress. With little training but an immensely photogenic face, the very young Morgan started with bit parts in the mid-1930s and the lead in Marc Allégret's* *Gribouille* and *Orage* (both 1937). It is as Jean Gabin's* partner in *Quai des brumes* (1938, Marcel Carné*), however, that her cool beauty entered film history. Wearing a shiny raincoat and a beret, she was the mythical 'lost girl', a persona carried over to Albert Valentin's* *L'Entraîneuse* (1938) and Jean Grémillon's* *Remorques/Stormy Waters* (1939–41). Contracted by RKO, she went to Hollywood in 1940, married actor William Marshall, had a son, took American citizenship and, in her own words, made five unmemorable films (with the honourable exception of Michael Curtiz's *Passage to Marseille*, 1944, a substitute for *Casablanca* which she had lost to Ingrid Bergman*). Back in France, Jean Delannoy's* *La Symphonie pastorale* (1946) inaugurated her second career as a leading star of the 'tradition of quality'*. Co-starring with Gabin, Gérard Philipe*, Jean Marais* and her then husband Henri Vidal, she graced costume dramas such as *Les Grandes manoeuvres* (1955) and *Marie-Antoinette* (1956), and psychological dramas such as *Les Orgueilleux/The Proud Ones* (1953), always the elegant, restrained and tragic Parisienne. Ignored by the New Wave* (except for Claude Chabrol's* *Landru/Bluebeard*, 1963) and by now handicapped by her age, she phased out her film career in the 1960s but successfully transferred to theatre. She has been awarded the Legion of Honour and many prizes, is a painter, and has written two volumes of memoirs. GV

MORLAY, Gaby   Blanche Fumoleau; Angers 1893 – Nice 1964

French actress. Primarily a stage actress, Morlay was a popular star of the French classical cinema. Equally talented in comedy (she started with Max Linder* in 1914) and drama (starring in Jacques Feyder's* *Les Nouveaux Messieurs* in 1929), she was a quintessential *boulevard* actress; most of her films were play adaptations. In comedies, like *Le Roi* (1936) and Sacha Guitry's* breathtaking *Quadrille* (1937), she bubbled (and sang too). However, one of her greatest successes was the tearfully patriotic wartime melodrama *Le Voile bleu* (1942, directed by Jean Stelli). GV

MORRICONE, Ennio   Rome 1928

Italian composer. One of the most influential and respected composers working in contemporary cinema, Morricone has provided music for an extraordinary 400 or so films in Europe and internationally. He has worked regularly with a host of renowned directors, including Bernardo Bertolucci*, Brian De Palma, Roland Joffé, Pier Paolo Pasolini* and Gillo Pontecorvo*. It was Morricone's innovative scores for the Italian Westerns* (or 'Spaghetti' Westerns) of Sergio Leone*, however, which brought the composer to prominence and which are seen as his trademark. The celebrated 'Man With

No Name' trilogy – *Per un pugno di dollari/A Fistful of Dollars* (1964), *Per qualche dollaro in più/For a Few Dollars More* (1965), *Il buono, il brutto e il cattivo/The Good, the Bad and the Ugly* (1966) – is marked by Morricone's original use of instrumentation, including cracking whips, bells, the jew's harp, and most strikingly, human whistling and chanting. His Western scores are also notable for their strong characterisation of individuals, whether Clint Eastwood's loner in the trilogy or Charles Bronson's stranger in *C'era una volta il West/Once upon a Time in the West* (1968), defined by a simple but haunting harmonica solo.

Classically trained at the Conservatorio di Santa Cecilia in Rome, Morricone has proved he can turn his hand to virtually any musical style. His range is easily demonstrated by comparing the rich pastorale score of Terrence Malick's *Days of Heaven* (1978, US) to the ragtime numbers, 'Prohibition Dirge' and 'Speakeasy', in *C'era una volta in America/Once Upon a Time in America* (1983). Morricone won British Academy Awards for his work on *Days of Heaven*, *The Mission* (1986, UK), *C'era una volta in America* and *The Untouchables* (1987, US), and four Oscar nominations. The score for *The Mission*, in which Morricone claims to take most pride, was awarded a Golden Globe in 1986. Morricone somehow manages to find time for work outside the cinema, writing, among other things, 'El Mundial', the official theme of the 1978 football World Cup in Argentina, as well as 'Chi Mai', the best-selling theme tune of the 1981 BBC television series *The Life and Times of David Lloyd George*. SH

Other Films Include: *Prima della rivoluzione/Before the Revolution* (1964); *I pugni in tasca/Fists in the Pocket* (1965); *Uccellacci e uccellini/Hawks and Sparrows* (1966); *La battaglia di Algeri/The Battle of Algiers* (1966); *Faccia a faccia/Face to Face* (1967); *Two Mules for Sister Sara* (1970, US); *Il Decamerone/The Decameron* (1971); *Giù la testa/A Fistful of Dynamite/Duck You Sucker!* (1971); *Novecento/1900* (1976); *La Cage aux folles* (1978, Fr./It.); *The Thing* (1982, US); *Ginger e Fred/Ginger and Fred* (1985); *Good Morning Babilonia/Good Morning Babylon* (1987); *Frantic* (1988, US); *Nuovo Cinema Paradiso/Cinema Paradiso* (1988); *Casualties of War* (1989, US); *Atame!/Tie Me Up! Tie Me Down!* (1989, Sp.); *Hamlet* (1990, UK); *Bugsy* (1991, US); *In the Line of Fire* (1993, US); *La Scorta* (1993); *Wolf* (1994, US); *Disclosure* (1994, US).

MORRISON, George Tramore 1922

Irish director and archivist. Morrison's film-making career is indelibly linked to two major actuality films, *Mise Eire/I Am Ireland* (1959) and *Saoirse?/Freedom?* (1961), which not only traced the struggle for Irish independence up to the outbreak of Civil War in 1922, but helped save a large portion of contemporary Irish newsreel film from being lost or destroyed. In the process, national consciousness was raised about this period of Irish history and the valuable use which could be made of archival material. The films are now viewed in a more critical light, and their often simplistic nationalist views and use of images of nature to naturalise historical difference are seen as representative of an earlier official Irish nationalist historiography. Morrison went on to make other docu-

mentaries, but none of them matched the impact of his first two films. KR

MOSER, Hans Johann Julier; Vienna 1880–1964

Austrian actor. After twenty-seven years of theatre and cabaret, Moser made his film debut in a supporting role in *Die Stadt ohne Juden* (1924); it took him nine more years and the coming of sound to find popularity as a folk comedian in Willi Forst's* 'Viennese films'. Moser created the character of the morose petit-bourgeois which was the foundation of his enormous popularity, setting the norm for the servants and bureaucrats typical of Austrian films until the 1950s. Always the underdog, he protested against his repressed social position with badly articulated recriminations in Viennese dialect. His chaotic and confusing manner (mumbling and flailing his arms, often to the point of near-hysteria) seldom solved his problems but made a sharp and funny counterpoint to the 'Prussian' Theo Lingen with whom he often played (for instance in *Ungeküßt soll man nicht schlafen gehen*, 1936). He also appeared in a few melodramas (*Maskerade/Masquerade in Vienna*, 1934), and his comic servants, always insisting on maintaining the order laid down by their masters, had a tragic quality. His appearances made even his most trivial films interesting. As Peter Handke said, 'You always wait impatiently until he appears.' Moser lost much of his poignancy in his postwar films, when he indulged in cosy Viennese charm (such as *Kaiserball*, 1956). KU/FM

Bib: Willibald Eser, *Hans Moser: 'Habe die Ehre'* (1981).

Other Films Include: *Der Dienstmann* (1928 and 1932); *Familie Schimek* (1935); *Einmal der liebe Herrgott sein* (1942); *Einen Jux will er sich machen* (1953); *Kaiser Joseph und die Bahnwärterstochter* (1962).

MOSJOUKINE [MOZZHUKHIN], Ivan I. Penza, Russia 1890 – Neuilly-sur-Seine, France 1939

Russian actor. After studying law Mosjoukine began acting, first in theatre and then from 1911 in comic roles in films such as *Domik v Kolomne/The House at Kolomna* (1913). He began playing lead roles in Yevgeni Bauer's* films for Alexander Khanzhonkov*, such as *Zhizn' v smerti/Life in Death* (1914), in which he first shed the 'Mosjoukine tears' that became his hallmark. After a disagreement with Bauer over casting, Mosjoukine left to make films for the rival Yermolev company under the direction of Yakov Protazanov*, frequently playing distraught demonic characters caught between duty and (usually) secret passion: *Nikolai Stavrogin, Chaika/The Seagull* and *Ya i moya sovest'/I and My Conscience* (all 1915), *Vo vlasti grekha/In the Realm of Sin, Pikovaya dama/The Queen of Spades* (one of his greatest popular successes), *Plyaska smerti/The Dance of Death* and *Sud Bozhii/Divine Judgment* (all 1916), *Prokuror/The State Prosecutor, Satana likuyushchii/Satan Triumphant* and *Malyutka Elli/Little Ellie* (all 1917), and *Otets Sergii/Father Sergius* (1918). The effectiveness of Mosjoukine's performances depended on his ability to communicate psychological states through expression and gesture, and this gave rise to the term the 'Mosjoukine style of screen acting', whose elements he himself attempted to define. He left Russia for France with Protazanov in 1920, starring in *Justice d'abord/Justice First* (1921, released in the USSR in 1923 as *Sluga slepogo dolga/The Servant of Blind Duty*), *L'Angoissante aventure/The Agonising Adventure* (1923, which he co-scripted) and *Le Brasier ardent*, which he directed himself and which is supposed to have persuaded Jean Renoir* to 'forget ceramics and try his hand at cinema'. He attempted to relaunch his career in Hollywood, then in Germany and again in France, but his later films never achieved the success that he had enjoyed earlier in Russia. RT

MOSKVIN, Andrei N.
St Petersburg 1901 – Leningrad 1961

Russian cameraman. The bulk of Moskvin's career as one of the leading Soviet cameramen was spent with Grigori Kozintsev* and Leonid Trauberg*, from their early FEKS days to their 'Maxim trilogy'. He is, however, probably best known internationally as the cameraman for the studio shots in Sergei Eisenstein's* *Ivan Groznyi/Ivan the Terrible* (1943–46), for which Eduard Tisse* worked on the outdoor shooting. RT

MOVIE

British journal. Established in 1962, *Movie* was responsible for translating the *politique des auteurs** from *Cahiers du Cinéma** to a British context, marrying it to the close textual reading of British literary criticism, and arguing for serious critical attention to be extended beyond the permissible range of 'quality' criticism to include *auteurs* like Frank Tashlin and Jacques Tourneur. *Movie* was motivated by 'a desire to investigate the way [films] worked ... the best antidote to the prevalent woolliness about the cinema seemed to us to lie in detailed, descriptive criticism.' The cinema which they championed was Hollywood, particularly those directors who were associated with *mise-en-scène*: Alfred Hitchcock*, Vincente Minnelli, Otto Preminger, Nicholas Ray. The cinema which came off worst was British cinema. In 1962, in the context of the British New Wave*, an editorial article declared, 'All we can see is a change of attitude, which disguises the fact that the British cinema is as dead as before. Perhaps it was never alive. Our films have improved, if at all, only in their intentions. We are still unable to find evidence of artistic sensibilities in working order.' *Movie* was most influential in the 1960s and early 1970s, and continues to appear intermittently. JC

MUELLER-STAHL, Armin
Tilsit 1930

German actor, with an increasingly international career. In the mid-1950s Mueller-Stahl transferred from stage to screen and got his breakthrough playing a legionnaire in a political thriller (*Flucht aus der Hölle*, 1962). He became one of DEFA's* most outstanding young actors and was offered many dramatic as well as comic roles. He worked for Frank Beyer*, and consolidated his popularity with frequent television appearances. In 1980 he fled to West Germany and quickly became internationally known after leading roles in, for instance, Rainer Werner Fassbinder's* *Lola* (1981) and George Sluizer's* *Utz* (1992). For Jim Jarmusch's episode film *Night on Earth* (1992, US) he played an East German taxi-driver stranded in New York, and in 1989 he starred in Costa-Gavras'* psychodrama *Music Box*, also shot in the US. TE/SG

MULLENS, Willy
Willebrordus Petrus Mullens; Weesp 1880 – The Hague 1952

Dutch film pioneer, who worked as director, producer, cameraman and exhibitor. The son of an itinerant showman, Mullens established a travelling cinema with his brother Bernard Albert (1879–1941) in 1900. As Alberts Frères they created one of the most attractive and well-known motion picture shows in the Netherlands, becoming legendary during the early days of the cinema. Their shows often included films shot by Mullens himself. Only one of these early shorts has survived, *De mésaventure van een Fransch heertje zonder pantalon op het strand te Zandvoort/Adventures of a French Gentleman Without His Trousers* (1905), a farce in which a seaside visitor, played by the director, loses his trousers. After settling in The Hague as a cinema owner, Mullens founded his own production house, Haghe Film, in 1914, specialising in educational, industrial and tourist films as well as newsreels. Well aware that the war provided a new reason to focus on national themes, he was among the first to explore the nation as a subject for documentary films. After the promotional *Mooi Holland/Beautiful Holland* (1915), he produced a propaganda film, *Neutraal Nederland/Neutral Netherlands* (1916), commissioned by the government to demonstrate to foreign states that the Dutch army was prepared to defend its territory. Mullens' remarkable social connections won him numerous assignments at a time when the cinema still had a dubious reputation. He also proved that documentaries were viable commercially and artistically. Two trips to the Dutch East Indies, in 1924 and 1926, produced a series of films about colonial life and work. In the 1930s Mullens' output diminished and his company began to specialise in subtitling. Mullens' approach had lost its appeal; his descriptive clarity could no longer compete with more dynamic styles, though he still enjoyed his status as a pioneer. Haghe Film continued to operate after his death in 1952, but the firm gradually went into decline and finally ceased operating in 1994. KD

Bib: Bert Hogenkamp, *De Nederlandse documentaire film, 1920–1940* (1988).

Other Feature Films: *Nederland* (1921); *Petroleum* (1924); *De Vrijheidsfilm, De Groene Kruisfilm, Achter de wolken schijnt de zon* (1925); *Volkenbond en vrede* (1926); *Tabakscultuur,*

Mooi Bandoeng, De Vrijheidsbond (1928); *Nederlandsche Kunstzijdefabriek Arnhem* (1929); *Verkade's bedrijf* (1930); *Waar een wil is, is een weg, De Zuiderzeewerken* (1931); *De Graal Pinksterzegen* (1932); *De Joodsche Invalide* (1933); *The Groene Kruisfilm* (1934); *Wit wint* (1939).

MÜLLER, Renate   Munich 1906 – Berlin 1937

German actress, who emerged in *Peter der Matrose* (1929), the first of seven comedies she starred in, all directed by Reinhold Schünzel*. Her skills as a singer and knowledge of foreign languages made her the ideal actress for the musical comedies of the early 1930s, appearing under Wilhelm Thiele's* direction in the German and English versions of *Die Privatsekräterin/Sunshine Susie* (1931) and *Mädchen zum Heiraten/Marry Me* (1932), and for Schünzel in the French version of *Saison in Kairo, Idylle au Caire* in 1933. Her best-known Schünzel film is *Viktor und Viktoria/Victor and Victoria* (1933), a cross-dressing comedy, shot in several versions (though not with Müller in the lead in the non-German versions) and remade in 1982 with Julie Andrews.

After Hitler's rise to power she continued to play coquettish and self-confident females in several light-hearted comedies (*Die englische Hochzeit*, 1934), also acting in a blatant propaganda vehicle (*Togger*, 1937). Her premature death at the age of 31 was officially due to epilepsy, but rumour had it that Müller came into conflict with the Nazis about her relationship with a Jewish emigrant and committed suicide. TE/KU

Other Films Include: *Liebling der Götter* (1930; a film about her life was made in 1960 under the same title); *Walzerkrieg* (1933); *Allotria* (1936).

MÜLLER, Robby   Willemstad, Curaçao 1940

Dutch cinematographer. After graduating from the Netherlands film academy, Müller followed the leading Dutch cinematographer Gerard Vandenberg to Germany, where he lit Hans W. Geissendörfer's first TV feature, *Der Fall Lena Christ* (1968). He would subsequently work on six other Geissendörfer films. Müller is best known for his camerawork on the films of Wim Wenders*, including *Summer in the City* (1970), *Alice in den Städten/Alice in the Cities* (1974), *Der Amerikanische Freund/The American Friend* (1977), *Paris, Texas* (1984), and *Bis ans Ende der Welt/Until the End of the World* (1991). Müller is highly esteemed by his peers, especially for his work in black and white. His eclectic career encompasses films by a large number of directors both in Europe and Hollywood, including Edgar Reitz* (*Die Reise nach Wien/Journey to Vienna*, 1973), Jim Jarmusch (*Down By Law*, 1986, *Mystery Train*, 1989), John Schlesinger* (*The Believers*, 1987), and Andrzej Wajda* (*Korczak/Dr Korczak*, 1990). Müller has periodically returned to the Netherlands to shoot films directed by Paul de Lussanet (*Mysteries*, 1978), Erik van Zuylen (*Opname/In for Treatment*, 1978), and Frans Weisz* (*Een zwoele zomeravond/A Hot Summer Night*, 1982 and *Hoogste Tijd/Last Call*, 1995), among others. HB

MULVEY, Laura   Oxford 1941 and
WOLLEN, Peter   London 1938

British directors and theorists. As independent avant-garde film-makers, Mulvey and Wollen are best known for two films which they co-directed in the 1970s: *Penthesilea: Queen of the Amazons* (1974) and *Riddles of the Sphinx* (1977). Both films use formal experiment to investigate theoretical and practical issues raised by the women's movement, addressing both the construction of sexuality through myth and history, and practical problems of child care. In *Amy!* (1980), a short film based on the life and legend of Amy Johnson, they address the myths of modernity, and in later work such as *Crystal Gazing* (1982) and *The Bad Sister* (1983) they use video to consider structures of fantasy. Their film-making is informed by their theoretical writing on semiotics, psychoanalysis, modernism and the avant-garde. Mulvey's 1975 *Screen** article, 'Visual Pleasure and Narrative Cinema' (probably the most cited article in feminist film theory), proved seminal for psychoanalytic debates about sexuality, subjectivity and cinema; Wollen's article 'The Two Avant Gardes' in *Studio International* (1975) was an important intervention in British avant-garde film theory and practice. Mulvey, with Claire Johnston and Linda Myles, organised the Women's Event at the Edinburgh Film Festival in 1972, and Wollen organised the Avant-Garde Event at the same festival in 1975. Laura Mulvey now teaches film studies in Britain. Her most recent film is *Fallen Idols* (1994). Peter Wollen teaches in California at UCLA, and continues to direct films and videos, including *Friendship's Death* (1987). JC

Bib: Laura Mulvey, *Visual and Other Pleasures* (1989); Peter Wollen, *Readings and Writings: Semiotic Counter-strategies* (1982).

MUNK, Andrzej   Cracow 1921 – Łowicz 1961

Polish director. One of the giants of the 'Polish School' of the 1950s, Munk studied architecture and law before going to Łódź*. After several fine documentaries, he made his first feature, *Człowiek na Torze/Man on the Track* (1957), which examines four different 'explanations' for a man jumping on to a train track (a structure echoed in Krzysztof Kieślowski's* 1987 *Przypadek/Blind Chance*). The film won Munk Best Director award at the 1957 Karlovy Vary* festival. His highly individual style and uncompromising analysis of the Polish nation – for example his ironic view of the Polish heroism cult in *Eroica* (1958) – signalled the emergence of the 'second wave' of Polish film-making. *Zezowate Szczęście/Bad Luck* (1960), his next film, continued exploring the concept of heroism in Poland with the same incisiveness and sarcasm. Munk taught at Łódź from 1957 until his untimely death in a car crash in 1961. This happened while he was shooting *Pasażerka/The Passenger*, a harrowing view of World War II and the concentration camps. The film was completed (using existing footage and stills) by Witold Lesiewicz and released in 1963. His influence on a generation of film-makers, among them Roman Polanski*, has earned him an important place in Polish film history. AW

Other Films Include: *Kolejarskie Słowo/A Railwayman's World* (1953); *Gwiazdy Muszą Płonąć/The Stars Must Shine* (1954); *Spacerek Staromiejski/A Walk in the Old City of Warsaw* (1958).

MURATOVA, Kira G.   Soroca, Romania 1934

Russian director, actress and scriptwriter. Muratova studied at VGIK* in the workshop of Sergei Gerasimov* (who, she says revealingly, taught her to listen to words and intonation), graduating in 1962. Her first two films, the short *U krutogo yara/By the Steep Ravine* (1962) and *Nash chestnyi khleb/Our Honest Bread* (1963), were co-directed with her then husband, Alexander Muratov. *Korotkie vstrechi/Short Meetings* (1967), her first film as solo director, concerns the triangular relationship between Valentina (Muratova), a woman who runs the water supply in a Soviet city, the geologist Maxim (Vladimir Vysotsky) and a young village girl. Goskino raised 'moral objections', and the film had a very limited release in film clubs. Her next film, the marvellously observant *Dolgie provody/Long Goodbyes* (1971), tells of the poignantly complex relationship between a feckless divorcée and her sixteen-year-old son. This film, about the ordinary lives of ordinary people, originally accepted by Goskino, was banned as 'non-socialist, bourgeois realism' (objections were made even to the way the characters danced). Muratova was deprived of her VGIK qualifications and banned from directing. After an abortive attempt to return to direction with a version of Lermontov's story 'Princess Mary', she was allowed to make *Poznavaya belyi svet/Getting to Know the World*, a romantic triangle set on a construction site, for Lenfilm in 1979. In *Sredi serykh kamnei/Among the Grey Stones* (1983), Muratova adapted a nineteenth-century story by Korolenko, but the film was heavily cut on completion. Muratova removed her name and the film was released as directed by 'Ivan Sidorov'. With the intervention of the Conflict Commission, set up by the Union of Cinematographers* in 1986, *Korotkie vstrechi* and *Dolgie provody* were released to lavish international praise, and Muratova was revealed as one of the most talented directors of the period.

Her next move was unexpected – she made *Peremena uchasti/Change of Fate* (1987), a version of Somerset Maugham's story 'The Letter', moving it to an unspecified Central Asian country. *Asteniceskii sindrom/The Asthenic Syndrome* (1989) can be seen as the key film dissection of the *perestroika* years. It begins in black and white, with the story of a troubled woman, reminiscent of Muratova's early work, but this time the woman is inconsolable in her bereavement and the tone is desperately bleak. Suddenly her tale is revealed to be a film, being shown at a Moscow cinema to an audience which includes the narcoleptic teacher hero of the 'main' film. Moscow is shown with unflinching, sometimes comic acuteness to be a place of hysterical, aggressive women and passive, inert men, all suffering from the syndrome of the film's title, a debility that provokes both these reactions to extreme stress. Muratova's vision of late Soviet life was so merciless that she achieved the by now rare distinction of having her film banned until it won the Special Jury Prize at Berlin in 1990. If *Asteniceskii sindrom* showed a society in moral agony, *Chuvstvitel'nyi militsioner/The Sensitive Policeman* (1992), made as the Soviet Union was collapsing, shows people as marionettes who spout a succession of Soviet clichés. The device of dialogue repetition familiar from Muratova's earlier films is here taken to absurd extremes. The bold formalism of *Chuvstvitel'nyi militsioner* offers a vision perhaps even darker than that of *Asteniceskii sindrom*. Both films show Muratova's continued aesthetic innovation, which she pushes even further in *Uvlechen'ia/Enthusiasms* (1994), a film about the hopes and dreams of a circus artiste and a jockey, which as good as dispenses with plot but is acutely alert to the passions (linguistic as well as physical) of its characters. Her recent work has cemented Muratova's reputation as, with Alexander Sokurov*, one of the two most challenging contemporary directors making films in Russian. JGf

MURER, Fredi M.   Beckenried 1940

Swiss director, who studied photography at the Zurich Kunstgewerbeschule. Seeing Robert Flaherty's* poetic documentaries inspired him to become a film-maker. Among his early films, for the most part 'home movies', anarchic observations of his surroundings and of Zurich artists (for instance *Bernehard Luginbühl*, 1966), *Vision of a Blind Man* (1969) was the most radical break with conventional film aesthetics. Filming on the longest day of the year but with his eyes covered by opaque glasses, with *Vision of a Blind Man* Murer attempted a film based on sound perceptions rather than sight. Later in 1969, Murer's contribution to the omnibus film *Swissmade*, a dark science-fiction story entitled *2069*, signalled his turn to the socio-political concerns that were also to inform his ethnographic documentary *Wir Bergler in den Bergen sind eigentlich nicht schuld, dass wir da sind* (1974). After a fiction film, *Grauzone* (1979), an apocalyptic *noir* parable exploring the blackest depths beneath the surface of the Swiss idyll, Murer made *Höhenfeuer/Alpine Fire* (1985), a complex narrative of incestuous love within the stifled environment of mountain farmers. In its ethnographic though highly poetic look at 'Heimat' [> HEIMATFILM] and nature, at generational conflicts and Oedipal relationships, it constituted a high point of the 'new Swiss cinema', summarising its dominant themes and formal obsessions. MW

Bib: Otto Ceresa and Irène Lambelet, *Fredi M. Murer* (1981).

Other Films Include: *Marcel – Tag eines Elfjährigen* (1962); *Pazifik – oder die Zufriedenen* (1965); *Sad-is-Fiction* (1969); *Passagen* (1972); *Christopher und Alexander* (1973); *Der grüne Berg* (1990).

MURNAU, Friedrich Wilhelm   Friedrich Wilhelm Plumpe; Bielefeld 1888 – Santa Monica, California 1931

German director. With Fritz Lang* and G. W. Pabst*, Murnau is one of the three directors on whose work rests the fame of the German cinema of the 1920s. Murnau, who gave himself the name of a famous artists' colony, studied philology, art history and literature before becoming a pupil of Max Reinhardt*, mainly as assistant director. He joined the air force, spent most of the war in Switzerland and upon his return to Berlin directed *Der Knabe in Blau* (1919). Much influenced by the Danish cinema of the time, *Der Gang in die Nacht* (1921), his first success, was a poignantly lyrical treatment of a melodramatic love triangle involving a blind painter. Meeting the leading 'film author' Carl Mayer* proved decisive for both, with Murnau producing five films scripted by Mayer, including *Der Bucklige und die Tänzerin* (1920), *Schloß Vogelöd* (1921) and *Der letzte Mann/The Last Laugh* (1924). But Murnau also worked with Henrik Galeen (*Nosferatu – Eine Symphonie des Grauens/Nosferatu the Vampire*, 1922) and Thea von Harbou* (*Der brennende Acker*, 1922, *Die Finanzen des Großherzogs/The Grand Duke's Finances*, 1924), a variety indicative of his ability to mould a film subject to his style. His plots show a preference for archetypal triangular human entanglements in order to explode them from within, surrounding every relationship – of love or power – with radiant ambivalences.

Three Murnau films have entered the canon of world cinema, all for different reasons. *Nosferatu*, still the classic film version of Bram Stoker's *Dracula*, founded one of the few undying film genres and, in the eponymous Count, one of the half dozen universally recognised movie icons [> TRANSYLVANIA]. *Der letzte Mann* is justly famous for its camerawork by Karl Freund* (his ingenious devices for making the camera mobile were dubbed '*entfesselt*' – unchained – a word connoting erotic licence at the time). But *Der letzte Mann* is also one of the most revealing parables of Weimar culture, with its fetishism of a uniform and Emil Jannings'* classic study of the self-tormented and yet monstrously autocratic male. Underrated in the Murnau canon are *Tartüff* (1926) and *Faust* (1926), again both with Jannings: one a *tour de force* of psychological perversity, the other a *tour de force* of spectacle and pyrotechnics, though neither was the commercial success Murnau and Erich Pommer* had expected (and needed).

By 1925 Murnau's reputation had reached Hollywood (thanks to Jannings' fame and the US distribution of *Der letzte Mann*), resulting in a four-year contract from William Fox. With a script by Mayer based on a Sudermann novel, Murnau embarked on what became his third acknowledged masterpiece: *Sunrise* (1927). Old-fashioned in its morality and sense of sin, but ultra-modern in its sensibility, it is one of the most cinematically sophisticated exercises ever about how to represent, precisely, the unrepresentable. What Lubitsch achieved in comedy, Murnau did for tragic subjects: thought and emotion, cleansed of ambiguity and stripped of moody vagueness. A commercial failure, *Sunrise* led to leaner budgets on Murnau's other Fox assignments, *Four Devils* (1929) and *City Girl* (1930). He severed his contract and took a skeleton crew (and Robert Flaherty*) to the South Seas, where he shot, under great difficulties, the independently produced *Tabu* (1931), a fairy tale of fate, eternal love and certain death in paradise. A week before its premiere, Murnau was killed in a car accident. TE

Bib: Lotte Eisner, *Murnau* (1972); Peter W. Jansen and Wolfram Schütte (eds.), *Friedrich Wilhelm Murnau* (1990).

Other Films Include: *Satanas, Sehnsucht, Der Januskopf* (1920); *Marizza, genannt die Schmugglermadonna* (1921); *Phantom* (1922); *Die Austreibung/Driven from Home* (1923); *Komödie des Herzens* (1924, script).

MURPHY, Pat   Dublin 1951

Irish director and scriptwriter. Murphy has made only two feature films: *Maeve* (1981), with co-director John Davies, and *Anne Devlin* (1984), but they are among the most culturally critical films of the new Irish cinema. *Maeve* explores the relationship between republicanism and feminism in Northern Ireland and poses this usually disguised problematic: even if republicans 'win', what type of society will it be for women as long as this male-dominated movement remains largely unengaged with women's concerns? In *Anne Devlin*, Murphy sought to uncover the 'hidden history' of a woman who was associated with the 1803 rebellion against British rule in Ireland, but whose role has been submerged by the elevation to mythic status of the rebellion's leader, Robert Emmet. In common with most independent Irish filmmakers in the late 1980s and early 1990s, she has faced extreme difficulty in continuing to make films. KR

Bib: Luke Gibbons, 'The Politics of Silence: *Anne Devlin*, Women and Irish Cinema', *Framework* 30–31 (1986).

MUSIDORA   Jeanne Roques; 1889–1957

French actress and director, one of silent cinema's greatest stars. Musidora owes her reputation to the part of Irma Vep (an anagram of vampire) in Louis Feuillade's* adventure serial *Les Vampires* (episodes 3–10, 1915–16), though she acted in more than sixty films up to 1926. She was France's first vamp, a sexy villainess in black leotards, a persona she carried (without the leotards) into Feuillade's *Judex* (1917) and exploited in contemporary stage acts. The Surrealists worshipped her 'subversive' eroticism and flamboyant life; she was a close friend of Colette*, Germaine Dulac*, Louis Delluc* and Marcel L'Herbier*. Musidora wrote a novel at fifteen, was a painter, dancer, songwriter and playwright, and a film-maker with her own production company. After adaptations of Colette's *Minne* (1916) and *La Vagabonde* (1917), and a film based on a Colette script (*La Flamme cachée*, 1920), she directed four films which showed her taste for real locations and stylistic experimentation; they rarely met with popular success. She was crowned 'queen of the cinema' in 1926, but her film career ended with sound (save for a short compilation film in 1951). She went on writing and from 1946 worked at the Cinémathèque Française*. Musidora's legend as sexual muse has endured, but her importance as a pioneer was recognised when her name was adopted by the women's group who organised the first women's film festival in Paris in 1974. GV

Other Films (as director) Include: *Vicenta* (1920); *Pour Don Carlos* (1921); *Sol y Sombra* (1922); *La Tierra de los Toros* (1924); *La Magique Image* (1951).

Det sjunde inseglet/The Seventh Seal (Sweden, 1957;
Ingmar Bergman): Max von Sydow (right)

W.R. Misterije organizma/W.R. Mysteries of the Organism (Yugoslavia, 1971;
Dušan Makavejev): Milena Dravič (right)

Trois couleurs Bleu/Three Colours Blue (Poland/France, 1993; Krzysztof Kieślowski): Juliette Binoche

Don't Lose Your Head (UK, 1966; Gerald Thomas): (left to right)
Kenneth Williams, Sidney James, Jim Dale

Scurtă istorie/Brief History (Romania, 1956;
Ion Popescu-Gopo)

Et Dieu . . . créa la femme/And God Created Woman (France, 1956;
Roger Vadim): Brigitte Bardot

Sissi (Austria, 1955; Ernst Marischka): Romy Schneider,
Karlheinz Böhm

Sedmikrásky/Daisies (Czechoslovakia, 1966; Věra Chytilová)

Szegénylegények/The Round-up (Hungary, 1965; Miklós Jancsó)

Les Visiteurs (France, 1993; Jean-Marie Poiré): Jean Reno, Valérie Lemercier

¿Qué he hecho yo para merecer esto?/What Have I Done to Deserve This? (Spain, 1984; Pedro Almodóvar): Carmen Maura (right), Verónica Forqué

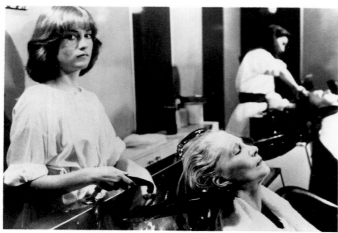

La Dentellière/The Lacemaker (Switzerland, 1977; Claude Goretta):
Isabelle Huppert (left)

Părvi urok/First Lesson (Bulgaria, 1960; Rangel Vălčanov)

Black Narcissus (UK, 1947; Michael Powell and Emeric Pressburger):
Deborah Kerr

Les Lèvres rouges/Daughters of Darkness (Belgium, 1971; Harry Kümel):
Delphine Seyrig (right)

Ostatni Etap/The Last Stage (Poland, 1948; Wanda Jakubowska)

Spoorloos/The Vanishing (Netherlands, 1987; George Sluizer): Johanna Jer Steege

N

NATIONAL SOCIALISM AND GERMAN CINEMA

Following the takeover by the National Socialist (Nazi) Party in January 1933, the Minister for Popular Enlightenment and Propaganda, Joseph Goebbels, exercised complete control over the film industry through: i) employment policy, ii) censorship, and iii) economic control mechanisms.

The Reichsfilmkammer (Reich Chamber of Film), dictated employment policy. With rare exceptions, only 'politically reliable' (and non-Jewish) members were admitted to the Chamber, and after 1938 the Nazis purged the few Jews who remained. Nazi employment policies caused an exodus of talent from the German film industry from 1933 onwards [> EMIGRATION AND EUROPEAN CINEMA].

To ensure that the films did not contradict film laws, pre-emptive censorship of screenplays by the Reichsfilmdramaturg became more important than censorship of the finished film, the standard practice since the Weimar Republic. After the first wave of purges, self-censorship became so effective that screenplays were, as a rule, only submitted for approval on a voluntary basis.

In 1934 the government introduced the categories of 'nationally and politically valuable' and 'nationally and politically especially valuable' films, which were exempt from tax. A financial incentive to tempt film companies into making films promoting Nazi ideology, it gave the government extra leverage without appearing to be interfering in the market. Additional economic control over the film industry was exercised by the state-run Filmkreditbank until 1937, when major portions of the industry were nationalised, such as Ufa*, and the distribution companies Terra and Tobis-Rota (amalgamated as Terra-Filmkunst). Independent film production was banned in June 1941, and the German film industry, consolidated into the giant Ufa Film, came under direct control of the Ministry of Propaganda. JG

Bib: Julian Petley, *Capital and Culture: German Cinema 1933–1945* (1979).

NAZZARI, Amedeo   Cagliari 1907 – Rome 1979

Italian actor. Arguably Italy's most popular male screen star in the late 1930s, Nazzari was often compared to Errol Flynn because of his undaunted coolness as adventure or romantic leading man and because his characters' trim moustaches or goatees bore some resemblance to Flynn's. His screen image was, however, quite complex. In Goffredo Alessandrini's* *Luciano Serra pilota/The Pilot Luciano Serra* (1938) he only becomes a 'Fascist hero' late in the film, having previously been a cynical expatriate living in South America. In *Montevergine/La grande luce/The Great Light* (1939) and *Harlem* (1943) he has underworld connections, while in *La cena delle beffe* (1941) and *Caravaggio, Il pittore maledetto/ Caravaggio, Painter with a Curse* (1941) he is cast as a

character whose heroic exploits seem driven, directly or indirectly, by madness. Meanwhile he also appeared, in sunnier guise, in light romances.

After the war his image was recast to suit the prevailing neo-realist* mode. He plays a partisan in Alessandro Blasetti's* *Un giorno nella vita/A Day in the Life* (1946), a returning P.O.W. in Alberto Lattuada's* *Il bandito* (1946), and a naval officer reduced to working on a dredger along the Tiber in *Fatalità* (1947). As he explains in *Fatalità* to his female co-star: 'The war is over. So many things have changed. Even I have changed.' In the early 1950s he starred in a series of hugely popular melodramas directed by Raffaello Matarazzo*, starting with *Catene/Chains* (1950). By the mid-1950s, however, he had lost his status as a leading man, though he continued to work in film until the 1970s. JHa

NEAGLE, (Dame) Anna   Florence Marjorie Robertson; London 1904 – Surrey 1986

British actress, whose career was developed almost exclusively from 1932 until 1959 by the director and producer Herbert Wilcox*, who became her husband in 1940. Associated with historical roles in the 1930s, she graduated from an irrepressible *Nell Gwyn* (1934) to become a dignified Queen Victoria in the patriotically popular *Victoria the Great* (1937) and its sequel, *Sixty Glorious Years* (1938). A top box-office star of the 1940s, she played a wide range of strong independent women, from Edith Cavell in *Nurse Edith Cavell* (1939, US) to Amy Johnson in *They Flew Alone* (1942), or from a spy in *The Yellow Canary* (1943) to a hero of the Resistance in *Odette* (1950). She is, however, most associated with the dramas and musical romances of the upper classes known as the 'Mayfair' cycle: *I Live in Grosvenor Square* (1945), *Piccadilly Incident* (1946), *The Courtneys of Curzon Street* (1947), *Spring in Park Lane* (1948) and *Maytime in Mayfair* (1949). She was made a Dame of the British Empire in 1969. JC

NEBENZAL [NEBENZAHL], Seymour   New York 1897 – Munich 1961

American-born German producer, who began his career in Berlin as co-founder (with Richard Oswald*) of Nero-Film in 1924. With generous budgets and the guarantee of unrestricted artistic freedom, Nebenzal was able to woo G. W. Pabst*, Fritz Lang* and Paul Czinner* (*Ariane*, 1931). The collaboration with Pabst was the most fruitful; after *Die Büchse der Pandora/Pandora's Box* (1929), Nebenzal produced Pabst's first five sound films. With Lang, he made *M – Eine Stadt sucht ihren Mörder/M* (1931) and the last German Nero production, *Das Testament des Dr. Mabuse/The Testament of Dr Mabuse* (1933), before going into exile in France, where he produced Anatole Litvak's* *Mayerling* (1936) and Max Ophuls'* *Le Roman de Werther/Werther* (1938). In 1940 he left for the US and produced Douglas Sirk's (Detlef Sierck*) *Summer Storm* (1944) and Joseph Losey's* remake of Lang's *M* (1950). KU

NEESON, Liam Ballymena, Northern Ireland 1953

Irish actor. Neeson's early career in Ireland included work at the Lyric Players Theatre, Belfast, and the Project and Abbey Theatres, Dublin. He made his feature film debut in John Boorman's* *Excalibur* (1981, US). Tall and ruggedly handsome, Neeson has mostly worked in the British and American film industries, where he has played a variety of roles, often as a lover: to Diane Keaton in *The Good Mother* (1988, US) and to Mia Farrow in *Husbands and Wives* (1992, US). His Irish roles have included *Lamb* (1985), in which he plays a Christian Brother who takes a boy away from a penal educational institution and goes on the run; an IRA hit man in *A Prayer for the Dying* (1987); and a ghost in Neil Jordan's* *High Spirits* (1988). Seeking to avoid being typecast as an 'Irish' actor, he has distanced himself from straight Irish roles. After a period in the doldrums, Neeson was rescued by the theatre through his performance in *Anna Christie* on Broadway, for which he won a Tony Award in 1993. This role also brought him to the attention of Steven Spielberg, who cast him in the title role in *Schindler's List* (1993, US), for which Neeson was nominated for an Oscar. KR

Other Films Include: *The Bounty* (1984); *The Innocent* (1985); *Duet for One* (1986); *The Mission* (1986); *Suspect* (1987, US); *The Dead Pool, Satisfaction* (1988, both US); *Next of Kin* (1989, US); *The Big Man* (1990); *Darkman* (1990, US).

NEGRI, Pola Pola Barbara Apollonia Chałupic; Lipno, Poland 1894 – San Antonio, Texas 1987

Polish-born actress. Emigrating from Poland during World War I, Negri advanced to stardom in Ernst Lubitsch's* films, personifying animal energy and cunning, and playing the man-crazy virgin as well as the man-eating vamp. In films such as *Carmen* (1918), *Die Augen der Mumie Mâ* (1918), *Madame Dubarry/Passion* (1919), *Sumurun* (1920) and *Die Bergkatze* (1921) she triggered murderous rivalries among her admirers. The first German actress to be offered a contract by Paramount (in 1922), she had her greatest American success with *Forbidden Paradise* (1924), directed by Lubitsch. Back in Europe by the late 1920s, Negri, despite her Polish accent, attempted a comeback in the German sound cinema (*Mazurka*, 1935), but in 1941 returned to the US, eventually reduced to parodying her silent screen image in *Hi Diddle Diddle* (1943). Film projects in postwar Germany came to naught, and Negri's last appearance was a cameo in *The Moon-Spinners* (1964, US). TE

Other Films Include: *Nicht lange täuschte mich das Glück* (1917); *Bella Donna* (1923, US); *A Woman of the World* (1925, US); *Barbed Wire* (1927, US); *Moskau-Shanghai* (1936); *Tango Notturno* (1937).

NĚMEC, Jan Prague 1936

Czech director. Jan Němec graduated from FAMU* in 1960, after studying direction under Václav Krška, a leading director of the 1940s and 1950s and advocate of the director's personal style. From the first, Němec was committed to a non-realist approach and his first feature, *Démanty noci/Diamonds of the Night* (1964), adapted from a novel by Arnošt Lustig, concerned the mental life of two young Jewish boys on the run from a Nazi death train. With *Mučedníci lásky/Martyrs of Love* (1966) and *O slavnosti a hostech/The Party and the Guests* (1966), both co-scripted by Ester Krumbachová, he produced, respectively, a romantic fantasy influenced by the traditions of Czech Poetism, and an absurdist political parable about a group of 'guests' and their adjustment to a system of absolute power. The latter was banned, reinstated, banned again, and banned 'for ever' in 1973. After filming the Soviet invasion of Czechoslovakia (*Oratorium pro Prahu/Oratorio for Prague*, 1968, banned), he emigrated in 1975 but was unable to sustain his career on a regular basis. He finally made a long-planned feature, *V žáru královské lásky/In the Heat of the King's Love/The Flames of Royal Love*, based on Ladislav Klíma's 'grotesque' novel *The Sufferings of Prince Sternenhoch*, in Prague in 1989, but it lacked the spontaneity of his earlier work. PH

Other Films Include: *Perličky na dně/Pearls of the Deep* [ep. *Podvodníci/The Impostors*) (1965); *Strahovskáudálosti/The Demonstration at Strahov* [short] (1968, released 1990); *Das Rückendekollete/The Low-cut Back* (1975, Switz.), *Metamorphosis* [TV, short] (1975, Ger.); *True Stories: Peace in Our Time?* [TV, co-dir.] (1988, UK); *The Poet Remembers* (1989, US).

NEO-REALISM

Italian film movement. Neo-realism is a generic term applied to the cinema which emerged in Italy in the years immediately following the liberation of Italy in 1943-45 and is associated with the names of Roberto Rossellini*, Luchino Visconti* and the director-writer team of Vittorio De Sica* and Cesare Zavattini*. Although the expression has been understood in many different ways, the core characteristics of neo-realism can be defined in terms of method (a preference for location filming and the use of non-professional actors), attitude (a wish to get close to everyday reality), subject matter (the life of the popular classes in the aftermath of war), and ideology/politics (the expression first of a hope of political renewal after the years of Fascist dictatorship and Nazi occupation, and then of a certain disillusionment when many aspects of the renewal failed to materialise). Not all neo-realist films necessarily shared all these characteristics, and neo-realism in the strong sense petered out in the early 1950s, its death knell sounded by the box-office disaster of De Sica and Zavattini's *Umberto D.* in 1952. Its main protagonists drifted away into other styles, while some of the attributes of the original neo-realism were taken up, in softer form, in the so-called *neo-realismo rosa* (rosy, or rose-tinted, neo-realism) of the 1950s. Curiously it was after neo-realism had already more or less died in Italy that it became a worldwide influence on film-makers as far apart as Spain [> SPANISH NEO-REALISM], India – *Ladri di biciclette/Bicycle Thieves* (1948) was shown in Calcutta in 1951 – and Latin America, where its simplicity and directness of means were greatly admired and widely imitated. GNS

NETHERLANDS, THE

Three key periods can be distinguished in feature film production in the Netherlands. The first coincided with World War I. The country's neutral status and the disruption of international trade created favourable opportunities for Maurits Binger* (and his Hollandia Filmfabriek), the most prolific producer and director of the silent era. At the same time, the country was discovered as a popular subject for documentaries by skilled cameramen like Willy Mullens*. The 1930s witnessed a second revival with the coming of sound and the arrival of refugee film-makers from Nazi Germany [> EMIGRATION AND EUROPEAN CINEMA]. Skilled émigré directors reshaped the ailing Dutch industry with films such as *Het meisje met den blauwen hoed/The Girl with the Blue Hat* (1934, dir. Rudolf Meinert), *Merijntje Gijzen's jeugd/The Youth of Merijntje Gijzen* (1936, dir. Kurt Gerron*), *Komedie om geld/A Comedy About Money* (1936, dir. Max Ophuls*), *Pygmalion* (1937, dir. Ludwig Berger*), and *Morgen gaat het beter/Tomorrow is Another Day* (1939, dir. Friedrich Zelnik). Two studios, Cinetone and Filmstad, and two producers, Loet C. Barnstijn and the émigré Rudi Meyer*, were responsible for the most successful films of this period. In the 1970s, the spectacular success of films directed by Paul Verhoeven*, written by Gerard Soeteman and produced by Rob Houwer* (*Wat zien ik/Business is Business* in 1971, *Turks fruit/Turkish Delight* in 1973, *Keetje Tippel/Cathy Tippel* in 1975, *Soldaat van Oranje/Soldier of Orange/Survival Run* in 1977) inaugurated a third 'golden age' in Dutch film-making which compensated for Hollywood's weakness at the box office; for the first time in their history, Dutch films grossed more than 10 per cent of domestic box-office receipts. Since the 1970s, the output of the Dutch film industry has averaged ten to fifteen feature films a year for theatrical release. At the same time, television is increasingly commissioning film-makers to direct mini-series, with outstanding results. Every year, the national output of fictional, documentary and animation films can be seen at the Netherlands Film Festival in Utrecht.

Though film production has always played a marginal role in the nation's film industry, several Dutch directors – notably Theo Frenkel*, Joris Ivens* and Paul Verhoeven* – have made impressive careers outside the Netherlands. Others, like Bert Haanstra*, Herman van der Horst, Fons Rademakers* and Johan van der Keuken*, have received critical recognition worldwide. Top cameramen Gerard Vandenberg, Robby Müller* and Jan de Bont are in demand for international productions. Dutch film stars – Willeke van Ammelrooy*, Rutger Hauer*, Jeroen Krabbé*, Sylvia Kristel and Renée Soutendijk* – are also respected abroad. Animation films by Marten Toonder, Borge Ring, Gerrit van Dijk* and Paul Driessen have won prizes on all continents.

Dutch films have always shown a certain fascination with the sea and the war. The sea has been an inspiration for documentary film-makers, from Joris Ivens' *Nieuwe Gronden/New Earth* (1934) to Bert Haanstra's *Stem van het water/The Voice of the Water* (1966) or Johan van der Keuken's *De platte jungle/The Flat Jungle* (1978). Before 1940, the sea and the coast were used for spectacular effect, exploiting the sea's dramatic function as a place of danger and death, for example in *Het wrak van de Noordzee/The Wreck of the North Sea* (1915, dir. Theo Frenkel) and *Jonge harten/Young Hearts* (1936, dir. Charles Huguenot van der Linden and Heinz Josephson). Curiously, there are no Dutch fiction films where the narrative is set at sea, or celebrates the nation's maritime past. Only very few films, such as *Dood water/Dead Water* (1934, dir. Gerard Rutten), explicitly link Dutch landscape to great national themes. Postwar fiction film-making, like Dutch literature, instead focused on the war. While historical films were an exception before 1940, the 1970s and 1980s saw much investment in the representation of this collective trauma, replacing former obsessions with the sea. The transition is marked by two fine pictures, produced on either side of the war, which interestingly assimilate both themes. Ludwig Berger's *Ergens in Nederland/Somewhere in Holland* (1940) dramatised the mobilisation of the navy on the eve of war, and Anton Koolhaas' *De dijk is dicht/The Dyke is Sealed* (1950) dealt with the war's aftermath in a coastal region. Later films focused on resistance activities, for instance Paul Verhoeven's *Soldaat van Oranje/Soldier of Orange/Survival Run* (1977), Wim Verstappen's* *Pastorale 1943* (1978), Ben Verbong's *Het meisje met het rode haar/The Girl with the Red Hair* (1981), and Fons Rademakers' *De aanslag/The Assault* (1986). A few pictures dealt with the fate of the Jews, such as *Charlotte* (1980, dir. Frans Weisz*) and *De ijssalon/The Ice Cream Parlor/Private Resistance* (1985, dir. Dimitri Frenkel Frank).

Dutch documentary film-making has attracted more attention abroad than at home, where audiences are more familiar with national fiction films which are rarely exported. Foreign critics like to describe Dutch documentarists as poets and observers rather than story-tellers and dramatists, and their films as showing a passion for pictorial sophistication and creative editing. To speak of a Dutch documentary 'school', however, ignores the idiosyncratic diversity of its protagonists. Artistic continuity, if it existed at all, was located in institutions such as the Polygoon* and Multifilm studios, for many years the backbone of documentary film-making in the Netherlands. Indeed, Polygoon's newsreels, portraying many sides of Dutch life between 1921 and 1980, leave an impressive visual documentation to posterity. In the meantime, television has modified the documentary tradition considerably. Its most recent developments can be followed at the annual International Documentary Film Festival of Amsterdam.

The Netherlands has a reputation for financing the international film industry. Dutch capital, for instance, played an important role in Europe's conversion from silent to sound cinema between 1929 and 1933, when Sprekende Films controlled Tobis, owner of the TriErgon sound patents and partner of the German sound film company Klangfilm. Sprekende Films not only slowed down the distribution of American sound films in Europe for two years, it also created sound film studios in Berlin (Tobis), Paris (Films Sonores Tobis) and London (Asfi). In the 1980s Dutch bankers financed the Cannon film company to the tune of hundreds of millions of dollars. Cannon ran into trouble when it tried to take over

Pathé Communications in the US and merged with MGM in 1991. However, important as these financial dealings have been internationally, they did nothing to support film-making at home.

By comparison with other European countries, Dutch cinema attendance per capita has always been low. This does not mean that the Dutch film market is unimportant internationally; its cinemas are among the top ten highest earners in the world, partly as a result of high ticket prices and a strong currency. Traditionally, however, the Dutch have never been avid moviegoers. In a population which has increased from 5 million in 1900 to 16 million today, film attendance grew from the handful who witnessed the first showing of Lumière* films in Amsterdam on 12 March 1896 to 65 million in the 1950s, but has dropped to 15 million in the 1990s – probably the lowest movie-going rate in the Western world. Moreover, in the absence of a strong production sector Dutch exhibitors and audiences have always been largely dependent on imports of foreign films, which are subtitled.

The film trade has been organised since 1918 into a national association of exhibitors and distributors, the so-called Nederlandse Bioscoopbond (since 1990 the Nederlandse Federatie voor de Cinematografie). Its main function is to regulate competition between members and to exclude all outsiders from the distribution and screening of films. This cartel arrangement has certainly benefited Dutch suppliers, but has done little to change the low level of film attendance. Could this structure be a cause rather than an effect of the stunted condition of Dutch movie-going? Since the 1980s, the trade has been dominated by a single large company, first Cannon, then its successor MGM.

In 1927, a new film society, Filmliga, laid the foundations for an independent and critical tradition by stimulating the import, screening and discussion of art films. Although Filmliga soon disintegrated, it had a lasting effect on film-making and criticism; without it, for instance, Joris Ivens' film-making career might have been quite different. Moreover, Filmliga produced a generation of film critics, in particular Menno ter Braak, Leo Jordaan, Janus van Domburg, Charles Boost and Ellen Waller, whose influence on public opinion was felt for decades. A similar movement appeared in the 1970s. An alternative infrastructure developed parallel to the official trade, its separate channels of production, distribution and exhibition largely supported by state subsidies. It offered an opportunity for young film-makers to direct their first projects and stimulated others to experiment with new narrative forms. The Rotterdam film festival, created by Hubert Bals* in 1972, is part of this independent tradition and has developed into a major international event.

The state showed little interest in film culture until the end of the 1950s. Taxes were high and aid non-existent. The Cinema Act of 1926 regulated censorship until 1977. Alongside the institution in the 1950s of small-scale subsidy to stimulate Dutch film-making, the state also financed the Netherlands Film and Television Academy to provide professional training, and the Netherlands Film Museum. In the 1970s further support was channelled into the import and exhibition of independent films. These infrastructural investments and production grants, boosted by funding from television, considerably improved conditions for the domestic film industry.

Three archives preserve the bulk of the audio-visual heritage. The Netherlands Film Museum in Amsterdam has a varied selection of national and international films; it also contains the Desmet collection, a company archive from the early 1910s consisting of hundreds of one-reelers and related documents. The collection of the Rijks Voorlichtings Dienst (national information office) in The Hague consists of the government's audio-visual output and other moving images documenting the nation's history. The archive of the national broadcasting centre, NOB, in Hilversum holds many film and video recordings from Dutch television productions; it also owns the Polygoon film collection of newsreels and documentaries.

As the century draws to a close, the production of audio-visual fiction has become a mature industry in the Netherlands, serving popular as well as highbrow tastes, and refuting the old complaint of Dutch indifference to drama. KD

NEVILLE, Edgar Edgar Neville de Romree; Madrid 1899–1967

Spanish director. An aristocrat, Neville had a first career in diplomacy before dubbing films in Hollywood. After three shorts and documentaries made during the Civil War for the Nationalists, his first feature was *La muchacha de Moscú/The Girl from Moscow* (1941). He then pursued a successful career in mainstream genres, such as the Spanish historical film* and the thriller. Mystery, fantasy, humour and irony characterise *La torre de los siete jorobados/The Tower of the Seven Hunchbacks* (1944) and *Domingo de carnaval/Carnival Sunday* (1945), the latter in some ways recalling Sternberg. In its panoramic survey of modern city life, *El último caballo/ The Last Horse* (1950) has a claim to be considered Spain's first neo-realist film [> SPANISH NEO-REALISM]. Other significant films include *Nada/Nothing* (1947) and *La ironía del dinero/The Irony of Money* (1955). PWE

NEW GERMAN CINEMA

German art film movement, *c.* 1965–82. Perhaps the only common characteristic of the New German Cinema was its rejection of German commercial cinema, first formulated in the 'Oberhausen Manifesto', drawn up and presented in 1962 at the Oberhausen festival of short films by young directors eager to make feature films. These directors identified the postwar commercial cinema with National Socialism, since many German directors of the 1950s had indeed begun their careers during the Third Reich. Refusing apprenticeship with such politically tainted directors and technicians, the Oberhausen generation either went abroad (Volker Schlöndorff*), taught themselves (Werner Herzog*), or, in a later phase, studied at film schools (Wim Wenders* and Helke Sander*). The only acceptable German cinema role models being directors who had died early (such as F. W. Murnau*) or had emigrated in 1933 (such as Fritz Lang*), it was German literature that provided subjects, from contemporary novels such as those of Peter Handke, Günter Grass and Heinrich Böll to the classically romantic works of Goethe, Kleist and Fontane. The directors' rejection of German commercial film was manifested in their refusal to follow established German film genre conventions and in their reluctance to hire well-known German stars or create their own. The (mediated) influence of American narrative conventions is more noticeable than any continuity with German cinema. Wim Wenders'* *Im Lauf der Zeit/Kings of the Road* (1976) and *Hammett* (1982, US) were clearly referring to the American road movie and *film noir* respectively, while the American melodramas of Douglas Sirk (Detlef Sierck*) became models for R. W. Fassbinder's* films: *Angst essen Seele auf/Fear Eats the Soul* (1974), *Die Ehe der Maria Braun/The Marriage of Maria Braun* (1979), *Lola* (1981), *Die Sehnsucht der Veronika Voss/Veronika Voss* (1982).

Although Alexander Kluge* (*Abschied von gestern/ Yesterday Girl*, 1966) and Jean-Marie Straub* and Danièle Huillet* (*Nicht versöhnt, oder Es hilft nur Gewalt, wo Gewalt herrscht/Not Reconciled*, 1965) show more radical breaks with both German and American classical narrative cinema when compared to the narrative techniques of Wenders and Fassbinder, the films of the New German Cinema do share common themes. Many concentrate on disadvantaged social groups or outsiders, especially people from lower- and middle-class backgrounds: a guest worker in Fassbinder's *Angst essen Seele auf,* a mentally ill woman in Helma Sanders-Brahms'* *Deutschland bleiche mutter/Germany Pale Mother* (1980), female alcoholics in Ulrike Ottinger's* *Bildnis einer Trinkerin/Ticket of No Return* (1979), social outcasts in Werner Herzog's* *Jeder für sich und Gott gegen alle/Every Man for Himself and God Against All/The Enigma of Kaspar Hauser* (1974), and a suicidal child therapist in Wenders' *Im Lauf der Zeit.* The New German directors' common stance outside Germany's commercial film industry gave rise to two trends. Firstly, the film-makers were constantly looking for new ways of financing their films. The Kuratorium Junger Deutscher Film was formed to fund the early productions of the New German Cinema, and directors hoped to take control of the distribution of their own films, through their Filmverlag der Autoren*. Secondly, the intransigent attitude to commercial film-making meant that New German directors (consciously drawing on literary precedents) considered themselves the film's sole authors and dispensed with professional producers or scriptwriters. Thus the films of the New German Cinema became identified with their directors, their names becoming the trademark of, and advertising for, the films, apart from promoting the label 'New German Cinema' at film festivals. Generally, New German Cinema films ran in art houses and were not commercially successful. New German Cinema was prized by critics for its cultural value and, for the first time since the 1920s, they argued that there existed German films which belonged to the realm of art [> EUROPEAN ART CINEMA].

Since the early 1980s the directors identified with the New German Cinema have gone in different directions: Kluge mainly produces short cultural reports for commercial broadcasting stations; Herzog has worked in other cultural areas (opera and television journalism); Wenders, Sanders-Brahms and Margarethe von Trotta* direct international film projects, and Fassbinder died in 1982. Other German filmmakers such as Wolfgang Petersen*, Doris Dörrie* and Klaus

Emmerich no longer share the blanket rejection of stars and genre films, but are involved in both German television and American film industry productions. JG/TE

Bib: Thomas Elsaesser, *New German Cinema: A History* (1989).

NEW GREEK CINEMA (NEOS ELLINIKOS KINIMATOGRAFOS, or NEK)

Greek film movement. The term Neos Ellinikos Kinimatografos (or NEK), emerged in the early 1970s to define a body of new films and differentiate them from mainstream Old Greek Cinema (Palios Ellinikos Kinimatografos, or PEK [> COMEDY (GREECE); GREEK MELODRAMA]). Commercial Greek cinema, then at the height of its popularity, was restricted to a very few film genres. The mid-1960s saw the release of a small number of innovative films – *Ouranos/Sky* (1962, dir. Takis Kanellopoulos), *Prossopo me prossopo/Face to Face* (1966, dir. Roviros Manthoulis), *Mehri to plio/To the Ship* (1968, dir. Alexis Damianos*) – but this tentative renewal came to an abrupt end with the military dictatorship of 1967. The journal *Synchronos Kinimatografos* and a few film societies kept the spark alive, however, and in the last years of the dictatorship a trickle of important, different, films began to appear. Thodoros Angelopoulos'* *Anaparastassi/Reconstruction* (1970) and Damianos' *Evdokia* (1971) are generally considered the starting points of New Greek Cinema. After the fall of the junta in 1974 and the ensuing liberalisation, the movement began to flourish, each year bringing a crop of new film-makers, though most made few films. Major newcomers were, along with Angelopoulos and Damianos, Pandelis Voulgaris*, Nikos Panayotopoulos and Nikos Nikolaidis. The most important figures to appear later were Stavros Tornes*, Vassilis Vafeas, Frida Liappa and Nikos Perakis. New Greek Cinema differed from the mainstream in three major respects:

a) Thematically, it focused on Greek social issues. Recurrent problems such as emigration, the abandonment of the countryside, political oppression and the civil war and its aftermath were dealt with openly for the first time. The role of history as a major force in the shaping of Greek society was an important theme.

b) Aesthetically. New Greek directors shunned mainstream narrative style in favour of forms influenced by militant, art and experimental cinemas [> EUROPEAN ART CINEMA]. Angelopoulos was especially successful in evolving a personal and influential film style.

c) Production. Film financing in the early period was exceptionally difficult and most productions were made possible by the dedicated, often voluntary, contributions of filmmakers to each other's films.

Audience response to the new approach was initially favourable, since in the early 1970s interest in political and experimental discourses was keen. Later, however, the movement lost its momentum, treading the same ground and losing touch with a public which turned with relief back to earlier mainstream Greek films, mainly comedies, regularly revived on the expanding television networks. In the late 1970s and the 1980s, New Greek Cinema was kept alive by subsidies from the Greek Film Centre*. The term lost currency in the mid-1980s, since when the public has almost completely abandoned the 'New' Greek cinema. TNe/TN

Films and Directors Include: Thodoros Angelopoulos: *Anaparastassi/Reconstruction* (1970); *Meres tou 36/Days of 36* (1972); *O thiassos/The Travelling Players* (1975); *Megalexandros* (1980). **Alexis Damianos**: *Evdokia* (1971). **Kostas Ferris**: *I fonissa/The Murderess* (1974); *Rebetico* (1983). **Frida Liappa**: *I dromi tis agapis ine nihterini/Love Wanders in the Night* (1981). **Tonia Marketaki**: *Ioannis o vieos/Violent John* (1973); *I timi tis agapis/The Price of Love* (1984). **Nikos Nikolaidis**: *Evridiki BA-2037/Eurydice BA-2037* (1975); *Takourelia tragoudane akoma/The Wretches are Still Singing* (1980); *Glikia simmoria/Sweet Bunch* (1983). **Nikos Panayotopoulos**: *Ta hromata tis iridos/The Colours of Iris* (1974); *I tembelides tis eforis kiladas/Idlers of the Fertile Valley* (1978); *Melodrama* (1980). **Yorgos Panoussopoulos**: *Taxidi tou melitos/Honeymoon* (1979); *I apenanti/A Foolish Love* (1981). **Lakis Papastathis**: *Ton kero ton Ellinon/When the Greeks* (1981). **Nikos Perakis**: *Arpa-Kolla/Patchwork-Cola* (1982); *Loufa ke parallagi/Loafing and Camouflage* (1984). **Tassos Psarras**: *Di' assimanton aformin/Reasons Why* (1974); *Mais/May* (1976). **Thanassis Rentzis**: *Mavro-aspro/Black-White* (1973; co-dir. Nikos Zervos); *Corpus* (1979); *Ilektrikos Angelos/Electric Angel* (1981). **Kostas Sfikas**: *To modelo/Model* (1974); *Mitropolis/Metropolises* (1975). **Dimos Theos**: *Kierion* (1974). **Stavros Tornes**: *Balamos* (1982); *Karkalou* (1984). **Vassilis Vafeas**: *Anatoliki periferia/Eastern Periphery* (1979); *Repo/Day Off* (1982); *O erotas tou Odissea/The Love of Ulysses* (1984). **Pandelis Voulgaris**: *To proxenio tis Annas/The Engagement of Anna* (1972); *Happy Day* (1976); *O megalos erotikos/The Great Love Songs* (1973).

NEW ITALIAN COMICS

In the late 1970s a new type of Italian film comedy emerged, which owed very little to the *commedia all'italiana** of the previous two decades or to any other comic tradition. The spur to the emergence of the 'new comics' ('*i nuovi comici*') was the ideological crisis provoked by the wave of terrorism of the 1970s and the intensification of government corruption scandals.

The new comics are a loose grouping of actors, directors and actor-directors, of whom the first to emerge were Roberto Benigni*, Massimo Troisi* and Nanni Moretti*. Moretti's Super-8 film *Io sono un autarchico/I Am an Autocrat* (1976) and his *Ecce bombo* (1978) have been cited as paving the way to the new comics, but Moretti is not typical. A director more than a performer, he owes nothing to cabaret and television, so important for the other comics (for example, the extraordinary television show *Non Stop*). However, Moretti does embody some characteristics of the new comics, especially the ability to connect with current cultural reality. The new comics created characters, situations and languages which constitute both a repertory and a synthesis of local slangs and sub-cultures: Moretti's apathetic youngsters of the 1960s, Troisi's young and up-and-coming Neapolitans, Paolo Villaggio's white-collar workers, Benigni's surrealist peasant Tuscany, Carlo Verdone's

Alberto Sordi*-like Rome, Abantantuono's southern dialect, Maurizio Nichetti's cartoon-like figures, and, finally, a whole 'bestiary' of character actors. The new comics also shared a search for new narrative modes, often 'contaminated' by other forms: cabaret, mime, animation, comic strips, and the verbal games of television entertainers and disc-jockeys, and it was this original mixture of performing modes that unified them for the audience throughout the 1980s. Emerging along the axis Naples–Rome–Milan (with some incursions into Tuscany), their wild and exhibitionist films constituted the leading edge of Italian cinema in terms both of 'quality' and of box-office. Throughout the 1980s the films of the new comics, usually released around Christmas, monopolised the national market and often out-performed Hollywood mega-productions. After the triumph in the late 1970s of the films of former rock singer Adriano Celentano, Troisi's *Ricomincio da tre/Starting Again at Three* (1981), Benigni and Troisi's *Non ci resta che piangere* (1984), Benigni's *Il piccolo diavolo/The Little Devil* (1988) and *Johnny Stecchino* (1991) were all major box-office hits. The success of Renzo Arbore's *Il pap'occhio* (1980) served as a powerful catalyst for many sub-cultures, opening up a space for Villaggio's *Fantozzi* series, Verdone's existential comedies (*Io e mia sorella*, 1987; *Maledetto il giorno che ti ho incontrato*, 1992), the surrealist games of Nichetti, the light-headed mime from Milan (*Ladri di saponette/Icicle Thief*, 1989, and *Volere Volare*, 1991), and Francesco Nuti's movies (*Io, Chiara e lo Scuro*, 1983, *Donne con le gonne*, 1991). There were also blatantly commercial spin-offs: Renato Pozzetto's *Culo e camicia* (1981), Abantantuono, Celentano, Enrico Montesano and Verdone's *Grand Hotel Excelsior* (1982), Jerry Cala and Christian De Sica's *Vacanze di Natale* (1983), Massimo Boldi, Cala, Ezio Greggio and De Sica's *Yuppies 2* (1986). The new comics seem to have lost their originality around the early 1990s, becoming either more radically personal (Troisi), or more abstract and self-indulgent. Some were absorbed into art cinema (like Benigni and Villaggio, the protagonists of Federico Fellini's* *La voce della luna/The Voice of the Moon*, 1990), though they continued to enjoy wide popular success. GVo

NEW PORTUGUESE CINEMA

In the early 1960s, a group of young Portuguese aspiring filmmakers attempted to make a *tabula rasa* of the 'old' Portuguese cinema, sparing only the venerated Manoel de Oliveira*. This was the time of the New Wave*, and the young pretenders knew their contemporary European cinema. António da Cunha Telles* and Paulo Rocha* had studied at IDHEC* in Paris, António-Pedro Vasconcelos attended Georges Sadoul's* classes at the Sorbonne and watched films at the Cinémathèque Française*; Seixas Santos, likewise a regular at the Cinémathèque, attended the London International Film School, as did Fernando Lopes and João César Monteiro*; José Fonseca e Costa, another frequent visitor to the Cinémathèque, trained as assistant to Michelangelo Antonioni* on *L'Eclisse* (1962). Their aim was to build a new cinema around Telles as producer. Rocha's *Os Verdes Anos/The Green Years* (1963) and Lopes' *Belarmino* (1964) were the first two features of the 'movement', heralding a new mood in Portuguese cinema. Particularly interesting was the distinctive representation of Lisbon, no longer an assemblage of separate neighbourhoods [> COMEDY (PORTUGAL)] but a tentacular space from which characters once arrived cannot escape, losing themselves in the labyrinth of the city and missing the opportunity of a different life elsewhere. This generation's fear of being prisoners in their own country is summed up in the story of the boxer Belarmino, the subject of Lopes' semi-documentary of the same name, who missed out on a great career abroad.

Unfortunately, the anticipated new audience for these films did not materialise. Moreover, the group was suspect to both regime and anti-fascist opposition, which criticised their lack of political comment and accused them of ignoring the great lessons of Italian neo-realism*. Only Fonseca e Costa was politically involved. Lopes, Rocha, Vasconcelos, Seixas Santos and Monteiro constituted the Vává group – named after the restaurant where they used to meet (and which formed the set of the last sequence of Os Verdes Anos) – whose positions were close to those of Cahiers du cinéma*. Telles attempted co-productions but without financial success. Mudar de Vida/Change of Life (1966) could be said to sum up the aim not only of the characters in Rocha's film (who end up emigrating to France) but also of the whole group of film-makers, some still waiting for an opportunity. By 1967, however, all hopes were gone. It was in an almost desperate situation that Lopes made the remarkable Uma Abelha na Chuva/A Bee in the Rain (completed only in 1971). After the documentary Belarmino, a fiction film; after a film on Lisbon, one set in the country – these contrasts would become the hallmark of Lopes' work, from Nós Por Cá Todos Bem/Everything Here is Fine (1977), in which a country-woman, his own mother, remembers her arrival in the city, to O Fio do Horizonte/On the Edge of the Horizon (1993), the story of a man's labyrinthine quest through the city to decipher the mystery of another person's past and present.

With no other prospects, the film-makers approached the powerful Gulbenkian Foundation, which eventually offered support to their cooperative, CPC (Portuguese Centre for Cinema). As a matter of honour, the old master Oliveira directed their first film, O Passado e o Presente/Past and Present, in 1971. In the same year Fonseca e Costa made O Recado/The Message, a more political work, as would be most of his subsequent features. Monteiro was working in a more experimental mode, while Vasconcelos shot the Godardian Perdido por Cem/100 Times Lost (1972), about a would-be escape from Portugal that fails at the last moment. After the revolution, and with its aftermath as background, Vasconcelos' Oxalá/God Willing (1981) was yet another film about staying in, leaving or returning to Portugal; later he would make more commercial projects such as O Lugar do Morto/Deadman's Shoes (1984). Seixas Santos, the most theoretical member of the group, directed Brandos Costumes/Sweet Habits (1975), a landmark. Although finished after the 25th of April (indeed it ends on the dawn of the coup), Brandos Costumes is a representation of, and an essay on, the supporting structures of the Salazar regime. Politically it can be considered the last film of the dictatorship. Ironically, even before the fall of the regime, the film-makers of the 'new cinema' were moving into a dominant position. Those cinéastes-cinéphiles who had wanted to represent

Portugal in a critical perspective were soon the men in power, henceforward often more concerned with politics than with films. AMS

NEW SPANISH CINEMA

Spanish film movement, referring to the work of a group of young directors (Mario Camús*, Miguel Picazo*, Martín Patino, Manuel Summers*, among others) who, following the Plan de Estabilización of 1959 and a token programme of liberalisation, availed themselves of new opportunities in production. They made a series of movies which, while displaying a politically critical attitude similar to that of their committed predecessors Luis García Berlanga* and Juan Antonio Bardem*, were characterised by a restrictive, elitist idiom: a corollary of the sidelining of commercial considerations. Nueve cartas a Berta/Nine Letters to Berta (1965, dir. Martín Patino), for instance, illustrates the claustrophobic inanity and hopeless inevitability of life in a country which, in contrast to its progressive neighbours, offered little opportunity for individual fulfilment. Camús' Con el viento solano/With the East Wind (1965) features a fugitive gypsy who encounters repression from all quarters. Eroticism is also presented with disconcerting awkwardness, a reflection of moral repression. Summers' Del rosa al amarillo/From Pink to Yellow (1963) considers the question of love in youth and old age – sections of society marginalised by the regime's insistence on the normalising institution of marriage. His Adiós, cigüeña, adiós/Goodbye, Stork, Goodbye (1971) again underlines with sensitivity the exclusion of adolescent sexuality from an officially imposed moral code. The protagonist of Picazo's La tía Tula/Aunt Tula (1964), who embraces the status of aunthood (maternal virginity), exemplifies an acquiescence in orthodox values, precluding any self-realisation. The depressing subject matters, unhappy endings, excessive naturalism and lack of stylistic innovation of these films confined them to an intellectual ghetto, and many of the films were box-office flops. More successful in aesthetic terms were the films of the contemporary Barcelona School*, which opted for a more eclectic idiom. Joaquín Jordá's Dante no es únicamente severo/Dante is Not Only Severe (1967), Carlos Durán's Cada vez que .../Each Time That ... (1967) and especially Vicente Aranda's* Fata Morgana/Morgan Le Fay (1966), less insular and generally more avant-garde in their conception, display a variety of influences from Italian neo-realism* to the French New Wave*. DK

Bib: Vicente Molina-Foix, New Cinema in Spain (1977).

NEW WAVE (FRANCE)

French film movement. While other European countries [> CZECH NEW WAVE, BRITISH NEW WAVE] saw important changes in film-making practices and styles in the late 1950s and early 1960s, it was in France that the Nouvelle Vague (New Wave) challenged most profoundly the established cinematic order and had the biggest international impact. The expression designates a 'freer' approach to film, outside traditional production and stylistic norms (professionalism, studios, literary sources, large budgets, stars), an approach which privileges spontaneity and the individual expression of the *auteur*-director. A number of factors account for the emergence of the New Wave: lighter and cheaper equipment allowed for location shooting, while the advent of television introduced new concepts of realism. Concurrently, the demise of the Hollywood studio system created opportunities to promote European national film styles on the world market. On a wider social front, the new regime of the Fifth Republic demanded 'new blood', while the rise of youth power helped shake older values and promote a younger generation of film-makers, as well as the increased presence of youth on screen.

In France, the New Wave was also preceded by a critical onslaught on classical French cinema – especially the 'tradition of quality'* – and by the development of the '*politique des auteurs*'* by the young critics at *Cahiers du cinéma**, under the sometimes reluctant aegis of André Bazin*. François Truffaut*, Jean-Luc Godard*, Eric Rohmer*, Jacques Rivette* and Claude Chabrol* were passionate *cinéphiles* who had learned their cinema history at the Cinémathèque Française*, a knowledge which would be seen in the high degree of self-reflexivity of their films. They championed their own pantheon of film-makers (Jean Renoir*, Alfred Hitchcock*, Howard Hawks) and posited the importance of a director's personal vision and of *mise-en-scène* over content and theme, paving the way for their own future practice.

The New Wave was neither a truly revolutionary nor a cohesive 'movement'. To opponents such as Bernard Chardère of *Cahiers'* rival *Positif**, it was 'rather vague and not that new'. There were antecedents in French silent cinema and in Renoir; closer in time there was Italian neo-realism*, the ethnographic cinema of Jean Rouch*, and the films of Agnès Varda*, Robert Bresson* and Jean-Pierre Melville*. Of the hundred first films made in France between 1958 and 1962, however, the central ones are clearly the *Cahiers* critics' own: Truffaut's *Les Quatre cents coups/The 400 Blows* (1959), Chabrol's *Le Beau Serge* (1957), Rohmer's *Le Signe du lion* (1959, rel. 1962), Rivette's *Paris nous appartient/Paris Belongs to Us* (1958–60) and Godard's *A Bout de souffle/ Breathless* (1960) – the Godard film a virtual manifesto with its location shooting, rule-breaking editing, casual acting and references to US *film noir*. While aesthetically innovative and exhilarating, these films generally lacked an interest in political or social issues, concentrating on personal angst among the (male) Parisian middle class (although another less media-prominent band of film-makers known as the 'Left Bank' group – Chris Marker*, Alain Resnais*, and Varda – showed greater political awareness). On the whole, the New Wave did not significantly challenge traditional representations of women. Although some films presented 'unconventional' heroines, mainly through the more spontaneous performances of a new breed of star (Jeanne Moreau*, Stéphane Audran*, Anna Karina*, Bernadette Lafont), others were downright misogynist (like Chabrol's *Les Bonnes femmes/The Girls*, 1960) or showed women as traditional muses or alluring temptresses, accessories to the tribulations of the young heroes.

The New Wave by no means achieved its aim of a complete revolution in French cinema; indeed Truffaut and Chabrol,

while pursuing recognisable personal themes, soon joined the mainstream. However, the promotion of the director as *auteur*/artist, as well as the creation of a new audience attuned to this type of cinema, greatly helped institutionalise *auteur* cinema and make it a lasting force in the French film industry. GV

Bib: Peter Graham (ed.), *The New Wave* (1968).

NEWTON, Robert   Shaftesbury 1905 – Beverly Hills, California 1956

British actor. Newton's career is dominated by two roles, Bill Sykes in David Lean's* *Oliver Twist* (1948) and Long John Silver in the Disney version of *Treasure Island* (1950). The wonderful hamming of the latter in particular became part of the cultural luggage of schoolboys in the 1950s, and was perpetuated in a sequel, *Long John Silver* (1955, Australia), and an Australian television series, *The Adventures of Long John Silver* (1955). The image of the shameless scene-stealer, however, belies the quiet control of his acting in other films. In *This Happy Breed* (1944), Newton's scrupulously economical performance is invisibly woven into the fabric of lower middle-class respectability between the wars. JC

Other Films Include: *Fire Over England* (1937); *Jamaica Inn* (1939); *Gaslight* (1940); *Major Barbara, Hatter's Castle* (1941); *Henry V* [as Pistol] (1945); *Odd Man Out* (1947); *Tom Brown's Schooldays* (1951); *Les Misérables, Blackbeard the Pirate* (1952, both US); *The Desert Rats, Androcles and the Lion* (1953, both US); *The Beachcomber* (1954); *Around the World in Eighty Days* (1956, US).

NICOLAESCU, Sergiu   Tirgu Jiu 1930

Romanian director and actor of great versatility and popular appeal, specialising in epics – often international co-productions. Nicolaescu worked as an engineer at the Sahia documentary studio, then as cameraman, scriptwriter and director of shorts, notably *Memoria trandafirului/Memory of the Rose* (1963), which took many international prizes. *Dacii/The Dacians* (1966), his first epic, is a mythic reinterpretation of Romanian history as a blending of the Roman and Dacian peoples 2,000 years ago, while *Mihai Viteazul/Michael the Brave/The Last Crusade* (1971) glorifies the fight for Romanian unity in the sixteenth century. These two films (in which he appeared) helped inspire a new emotional Romanian nationalism. Nicolaescu represented Romania in a series of European film co-productions, and has also worked with French and German television. He still directs and co-scripts (and until the 1980s regularly starred in) craftsmanlike thrillers, comedy and adventure films, historical epics and contemporary dramas. *Revanşa/Revenge* (1978) is a typical fast-paced quality thriller in which Nicolaescu plays an indestructible police chief involved in shootouts and an improbable plot. MM

NIELSEN, Asta
Copenhagen 1881–1972

Danish actress, who worked mainly in Germany. Nielsen was educated at the Royal Theatre school in Copenhagen. After her theatrical debut in 1902 and work in various Scandinavian theatres, she made her spectacular film debut in Urban Gad's *Afgrunden/The Abyss* (1910), an international success which aroused the attention of the German film industry. Nielsen was the earliest 'vamp' in world cinema, developing a strong, erotic persona which was central to the emerging genre of the Danish erotic melodrama*. She was equally at ease with tragedy and used the longer films pioneered in Denmark to develop a more naturalistic acting style. She made two more Danish films, *Den sorte Drøm/The Black Dream* and *Balletdanserinden/The Ballet Dancer* (both 1911), before leaving with Gad for Germany. There they made twenty-four films in three years, evolving into one of the director-star teams which would become familiar in European art cinema*. *Nachtfalter* (1911), *Die arme Jenny* (1912), *Der Totentanz/The Death Dance* (1912) and *Jugend und Tollheit/Youth and Madness* (1913), among others, ensured her both critical and popular success around the world. In 1912 her film *Die Kinder des Generals/Generalens Døtre/The General's Daughters* was chosen to inaugurate Copenhagen's giant 3,000-seater Paladsteatret cinema, the biggest in northern Europe.

Nielsen returned to Denmark during World War I and made *Mod Lyset/Towards the Light* (1918), but by then Danish cinema was on the decline and the film was a failure. The war over, she went back to Germany where she worked for the rest of the silent period, focusing on prestigious stage and literary adaptations with directors such as Ernst Lubitsch* and Carl Froelich*. Her own production company, Art-Film, produced *Hamlet* (1920), in which she played the prince, *Fräulein Julie/Miss Julie* (1921) and *Der Absturz* (1922). She made notable appearances in *Vanina/Vanina Vanini* (1922), *INRI* (1923), *Die freudlose Gasse/Joyless Street* (1925, dir. G. W. Pabst*) and *Dirnentragödie/The Tragedy of the Street* (1927). In 1932, she made her first sound film and last movie, *Unmögliche Liebe/Impossible Love* (1932). Rejecting Nazi overtures to stay, she returned to Denmark in 1937. Nielsen made over seventy films, about thirty of which are preserved. ME/MW

NIEVES CONDE, José Antonio
Segovia 1915

Spanish director. A film critic before becoming Rafael Gil's* assistant (1941–46). His first independently directed feature was *Senda ignorada/Path Unknown* (1947). From his early period, a particularly striking film is *Angustia/Anguish* (1947), a disturbing narrative about a man whose dreams predict actual crimes. Nieves Conde's reputation in Spain, however, rests on *Balarrasa/Reckless* (1950), *Surcos/Furrows* (1951) and *El inquilino/The Tenant* (1959). *Surcos* is the most significant of the three, on the grounds not only of its formal and thematic innovations but also of its impact on official attitudes to film-making in Spain at the time. Nieves Conde was instrumental in grafting on to Spanish cinema some features of Italian neo-realism*, above all the depiction of contemporary Spanish life [> SPANISH NEO-REALISM]. PWE

NISKANEN, Mikko
Äänekoski 1929 – Helsinki 1990

Finnish director, producer and actor, who also directed many television films. Niskanen trained as a director at VGIK* in Moscow in the early 1960s. Before making his first film, *Pojat/Boys* (1962), he had acted in various minor roles in studio pictures of the 1950s. Niskanen was a passionate actor and director in whose films the Finnish countryside and its social problems had a major role. The work which established his reputation outside Finland, as well as being very successful at home, was *Käpy selän alla/Skin, Skin* (1966), the first Finnish film to portray, and address, the generation born after the war. Niskanen's patriotic sincerity and empathy with rural life reached a 'neo-realist*' peak in *Kahdeksan surmanluotia/Eight Deadly Shots* (1972), originally a four-part television series. In the 1980s Niskanen made television adaptations of Kalle Päätalo's best-selling novels about life sixty years ago in the northern lumbering areas; *Elämän vonkamies/Life's Hardy Men* (1986) and *Nuoruuteni savotat/Lumbercamp Tales* (1988) can be seen as the latest phase in the Lumberjack* films genre. This time, however, the heroism, romanticism and comedy typical of the genre have been transformed into Niskanen's trademark near-naturalistic realism. JS

Other Films Include: *Sissit/The Partisans* (1962); *Asfalttilampaat/The Asphalt Sheep* (1968); *Syksyllä kaikki on toisin/In the Autumn It Will All Be Different* (1978); *Ajolähtö/Gotta Run!* (1982); *Mona ja palavan rakkauden aika/Mona and the Time of Burning Love* (1983).

NISKAVUORI FILMS

Finnish series of films based on Hella Wuolijoki's plays premiered between 1936 and 1953. Wuolijoki was a popular playwright, a socialist (friend of Bertolt Brecht), and later head of the Finnish broadcasting company. The films are a chronicle of the Niskavuori family and the mansion they inhabit in southern Finland from the 1880s to the end of World War II; conflicts between sexes, generations and classes are enacted against the historical context. The Niskavuori world is highly matriarchal, embodying the agrarian order. Paramount for the women are the farm and surrounding countryside, the extended family and its heritage – values against which everything else is measured. The men have problems living up to these values: they often fail, betray, and flee.

The first part of the saga, *Niskavuoren naiset/The Women of Niskavuori*, has been filmed three times, twice by Valentin Vaala* (1938 and 1958) and once by Matti Kassila* under the title *Niskavuori* in 1984. The story looks at the family immediately after Finland's independence in 1917: Aarne, the young head of the farm, is frustrated with his work, his wife Martta, and his aging mother, Loviisa, who still holds the real power in the family. He leaves Niskavuori and moves to the city with his new wife, Ilona, a teacher. Vaala's *Loviisa, Niskavuoren emäntä/Loviisa* (1946) moves back to the end of the nineteenth century and Loviisa's youth. The film shows power passing from the old matriarch to Juhani Niskavuori's wealthy young wife. *Niskavuoren Heta/Heta from Niskavuori* (1952, dir. Laine) tells the story of Juhani's sister, Heta, who marries a farm hand by whom she is pregnant. The film describes their life from the 1880s to the 1920s. Laine also directed *Niskavuoren Aarne/Aarne from Niskavuori* (1954), set in the 1930s, a chronological sequel to *Niskavuoren naiset*. Aarne, remarried in Helsinki, cannot forget Niskavuori and visits the farm secretly at night. When his ex-wife remarries, she sells her share of the farm to Loviisa, who talks Aarne into coming back. Ilona, Aarne's second wife, agrees to become the new woman of the house. *Niskavuori taistelee/Niskavuori Fights* (1957, dir. Laine) continues the saga into the war years. AK

NIVEN, David
Kirriemuir, Scotland 1910 –
Château-d'Œx, Switzerland 1983

British actor, who began his Hollywood career as an extra after resigning a commission with the Highland Light Infantry. His Sandhurst military school training and inherited membership of the officer class equipped him for many of the parts he was to play: charming, dapper and sophisticated with a dash of light-hearted sexual roguishness. He had parts in a number of notable Hollywood films of the 1930s: *The Charge of the Light Brigade* (1936), *Dodsworth* (1936), *The Prisoner of Zenda* (1937) and *The Dawn Patrol* (1938). Signed to Goldwyn, he followed a supporting role in *Wuthering Heights* (1939) with his first starring role as Raffles (*Raffles*, 1940) in a remake of the Ronald Colman* original. Returning to the British army during the war, he was given leave to appear in Leslie Howard's* *The First of the Few* (1942) and Carol Reed's* *The Way Ahead* (1944). On his discharge as a colonel he played the poet-airman caught between life and death in *A Matter of Life and Death* (1946), one of his most effective roles. He spent the rest of his career consistently in demand on both sides of the Atlantic, an international imaginary Englishman whose debonair dash occasionally slipped to reveal emotional vulnerability. He won an Oscar and a New York Film Critics award for his performance in Delbert Mann's *Separate Tables* (1958). JC

Bib: David Niven, *The Moon's a Balloon* (1971) and *Bring on the Empty Horses* (1975) (both republished 1985).

Other Films Include (UK Unless Indicated): *Bonnie Prince Charlie* (1948); *The Elusive Pimpernel* (1950); *Happy Go Lovely* (1951); *The Moon is Blue* (1953, US); *Carrington V.C.* (1954); *The King's Thief* (1955, US); *Around the World in Eighty Days* (1956, US); *My Man Godfrey* (1957, US); *Bonjour Tristesse* (1958); *The Guns of Navarone* (1961); *55 Days at Peking* (1963, US); *The Pink Panther* (1964, US); *Casino Royale* [as James Bond] (1967); *Paper Tiger* (1975); *Death on the Nile* (1978); *Rough Cut* (1980, US); *Curse of the Pink Panther, Trail of the Pink Panther* (1982).

NO-DO

Spanish documentary and newsreel company, whose pro-government films were compulsory viewing in cinemas from 1942 to 1975. This was something to which those attending the famous 'Conversaciones de Salamanca' conference (May 1955) profoundly objected. In the conference's published conclusions, Section IX called for the end of NO-DO's monopoly. Two months before Franco died the screenings did become optional, and by 1980 NO-DO's activities were absorbed by the Filmoteca. Although intended to serve as another instrument of Francoist ideology, NO-DO films lacked the uniformity of style and composition usually associated with National Socialist documentaries [> DOCUMENTARY (GERMANY)]. This reflects, firstly, Francoism's lack of cohesion and, secondly, perhaps a refusal by the NO-DO documentarists to be wholly ruled by ideology. Limited by technical deficiencies (no facilities for live sound recording and shortage of film stock) and internal as well as external censorship, NO-DO was nevertheless a school for technicians, scriptwriters and directors for almost forty years and it helped to shape audience interest in screen coverage of national and international news. IS

Bib: Vicente Sánchez-Biosca and Rafael R. Tranche, *No-Do: el tiempo y la memoria* (1993).

NOIRET, Philippe
Lille 1930

French actor. Neither a character actor nor a 'star', Noiret is one of the most popular male figures in French cinema. A stage and cabaret actor, Noiret's first notable films were Agnès Varda's* *La Pointe courte* (1956), Louis Malle's* *Zazie dans le métro* (1960) and Georges Franju's* *Thérèse Desqueyroux* (1962). His eclectic filmography of over a hundred titles includes films by French and Italian *auteurs* – among them Bertrand Tavernier's* *L'Horloger de Saint-Paul/The Watchmaker of Saint-Paul* (1973), *Coup de torchon/Clean Slate* (1981), and *La Vie et rien d'autre/Life and Nothing But* (1989), for which he won a César*; Marco Ferreri's* *La Grande bouffe/Blow Out* (1973); Francesco Rosi's* *Tre fratelli/Three Brothers* (1981, Italy) – and popular cinema, including Claude Zidi's* *Les Ripoux/Le Cop* (1984) and Giuseppe Tornatore's* *Nuovo Cinema Paradiso* (1988, It.). With his heavy-set figure and unctuous voice, Noiret embodies middle-aged patriarchal figures, ranging from the reassuringly avuncular to the deeply misogynist. GV

NORDISK FILMS KOMPAGNI

Danish production company. Founded in 1906 by Ole Olsen*, Nordisk was the oldest and most important Danish film producer. As early as 1910 it had developed into one of the largest firms in Europe, and was central to the 'golden era' of Danish cinema (1910–14), thanks to its pioneering of longer (multi-reel) films. This, combined with the emerging genre of the Danish erotic melodrama* and the star Asta Nielsen*, spread the popularity of Danish cinema all over the world. World War I put an end to all this. Danish film export became difficult, then virtually impossible. After vainly attempting to reconquer its foreign markets after the war, Nordisk was forced into liquidation in 1928. A few months later, however, it re-emerged, thanks to the Danish Petersen-Poulsen sound system which Carl Bauder, the new managing director, had bought and with which the first Danish sound feature, *Præsten i Vejlby/The Vicar of Vejlby* (1931), was released. The film was directed by George Schnéevoigt*, who became the company's leading director in the 1930s. During the German occupation Nordisk's five studios were bombed, and the company did not resume production until 1946. Several promising young directors made their debuts at Nordisk after the war, including Bjarne Henning-Jensen* and Ole Palsbo. Erik Balling* made his first film there in 1951 and soon progressed to production and artistic manager. In the late 1960s he began his hugely popular *Olsen Banden/Olsen Gang* series. These films were so profitable that Nordisk remained independent until 1981, when it had to join the rest of the Danish industry in dependence on the state for its continued existence. ME

NORIS, Assia   Anastasia Noris von Gerzfeld; St Petersburg, Russia 1912

Italian actress. Noris became a popular figure in Italian cinema during the 1930s and early 1940s. She most often appeared in romantic comedies, particularly those directed by Mario Camerini*, to whom she was married between 1940 and 1943. The films she made with Camerini include *Giallo* (1933), *Darò un milione* (1935), *Ma non è una cosa seria/But It's Nothing Serious* (1936), *Il Signor Max/Mr Max* (1937), *Batticuore* (1938), *Grandi magazzini* (1939), *Centomila dollari* (1940), *Una romantica avventura* (1940), and *Una storia d'amore* (1942). Her persona in these and other films from the 1930s was that of a wholesome, shy, idealistic, middle-class heroine struggling to find romance and career opportunity in contemporary urban Italy. Her screen image was also developed through her frequent pairing with Vittorio De Sica*. Declared best actress of 1939–40 by *Cinema* magazine, she was appropriately cast as a star in Mario Soldati's* *Dora Nelson* (1939). Her image, however, was anathema to the postwar neo-realist* cinema, and she emigrated to Egypt, making only two more films. JHa

NORSK FILM A/S

Norway's largest production company, jointly owned by central government and municipalities and financed by an annual government grant. The company was founded in 1932 and produced its first film, *To levende og en død/Two Living and One Dead*, in 1937, in the company's newly built studio (still the only one in Norway). Norsk Film has a prime role in Norwegian cinema, being required to implement a cultural policy which combines development of new talents with ensuring the highest possible artistic quality. Norsk Film produced 133 films between 1937 and 1990. KS

NORSTEIN [NORSHTEIN], Yuri B.   Andreyevka [USSR] 1941

Russian animator. Norstein studied at the Soviet animation studio Soyuzmultfilm and after 1961 worked there, participating in the making of dozens of films. His first film as a director was *25-e–pervyi den'/The 25th is the First Day* (1968). Together with Ivan Ivanov-Vano, one of the founders of Soviet animation, he directed *Secha pri Kerzhentse/The Battle of Kerzhenets* (1971), which used extracts from Rimsky-Korsakov's opera *The Tale of the Invisible City of Kitezh* and old Russian art. Norstein turned to the world of fable for *Lisa i zayats/The Fox and the Hare* (1973), *Tsaplya i zhuravl'/The Heron and the Crane* (1974) and *Ëzhik v tumane/The Hedgehog in the Fog* (1975). *Skazka skazok/The Tale of Tales* (1979), his most ambitious project of the period, made with the writer Lyudmila Petrushevskaya, was described as a 'poetic meditation on life and creativity'. Despite initial difficulties with censorship (the film was shelved for six months), it won several prizes, including citation by an international panel of experts in 1984 as the greatest animated film of all time. Norstein, who acknowledges debts to Dostoyevsky, Platonov and Kafka in his work, spent much of the early 1980s working on an animated film of Nikolai Gogol's *The Overcoat*, a story which he describes as like a chapter from the Bible, a 'storehouse of human conscience'. This film also encountered difficulties, first with Soviet bureaucrats, then with market conditions which were inimical to his slow working speed. Work on the film was interrupted in 1986, and in a recent interview Norstein suggested it would not be complete until 1997. JGf

NORTHERN IRELAND AND FILM

Northern Ireland is familiar to most people through the regular diet (especially in Britain) of television footage of bombings, shootings and funerals, or of a narrow range of films dealing with political violence: *Odd Man Out* (1947), *The Gentle Gunman* (1952), *Hennessy* (1975), *Angel* (1982), *A Prayer for the Dying* (1987). An indigenous independent film-making practice has developed since the 1970s, though films had been made prior to that, the most prolific period being the 1930s when a number of 'quota quickies' were produced by Donovan Pedelty and Richard Hayward. These films include the horse-racing comedy *The Luck of the Irish* (1935), and *The Early Bird* (1936), in which villagers rebel against a puritanical woman.

During the 1970s and 1980s a number of independent production companies were formed, such as those of documentarists John T. Davis – *Shell Shock Rock* (1979), *Power in the Blood* (1989), *Dust on the Bible* (1990) – and David Hammond, a prolific independent television producer. Fiction film-makers have included the late Bill Miskelly, whose feature, *The End of the World Man* (1985), won first prize at the Children's Festival at Berlin in 1985.

Channel 4* has played an important role in supporting independent production through its workshop programme. Formed in 1984, Derry Film and Video Workshop produced tapes and films, and out of this context Margo Harkin was able to make the incisive *Hush-A-Bye-Baby* (1989), which set a story of teenage pregnancy against the background of the British occupation of Northern Ireland and of conservative institutional and moral attitudes. Though produced through John Davies' Frontroom Productions, a London company, *Acceptable Levels* (1983) was also a Workshop project and remains one of the most interesting films to come out of the North. It follows the fortunes of a television documentary crew as they weave their way through political and institutional pressures and compromises to construct a version of the events in Northern Ireland which bears little relation to what they experience.

Financial support for film-making has been small-scale, with the Arts Council of Northern Ireland providing only limited support. With the extension of the British Film Institute's* charter to Northern Ireland, the North's marginal status in British and Irish film culture is changing. As significant has been the decision to establish the independent Northern Ireland Film Council, which is developing a broad range of film cultural activities. It was awarded production finance from the Arts Council in 1993, and is also being funded by the Northern Ireland Department of Education. KR

NORWAY

The first screening in Norway took place in April 1896, when pioneer Max Skladanowsky* demonstrated his Bioscope in Oslo. Films rapidly became a popular part of variety programmes and were shown in various locations before permanent cinemas – starting with Hugo Hermansen's* – were established in Oslo in 1904. *Actualités* (early newsreels) appealed to audiences, who in the early 1900s were offered films on topics such as the Boer War. Closer to home, Norwegian cinematographers recorded the succession (1905) and coronation (1906) of Carl, the new Norwegian king, formerly prince of Denmark. Being relatively expensive, such films were shown in more luxurious locations, attended even by members of the royal family.

Popular audiences, meanwhile, were keen on comedy and melodrama. The French comedian Max Linder* was a great star in Norway around 1910, and Danish erotic melodramas* also drew large audiences. The number of cinemas increased rapidly. All these factors caused a wave of moral panic in 1910. Members of the establishment worried about the damaging effect of movies, especially on children and teenagers. Guardians of morality claimed that movies led innocent viewers to theft and other immoral activities. This uproar led to the Film Theatre Act of 1913, still in place with minor changes. The Act states that film screenings must be approved by the Norwegian Board of Film Censors (Statens Filmkontroll, changed to Statens Filmtilsyn in 1994). The Board grades films by age category and may ban works deemed illegal, indecent, immoral or brutal; for most of the institution's history, censors have also had the right to order cuts. In the 1920s, kisses were shortened and 'indecent dance scenes' excised, as were shootings and fights, and some thirty films were forbidden every year. The figure went down to fewer than ten a year in the 1950s, increasing again at the end of the 1960s when Italian Westerns* were deemed overviolent. The 1960s saw important debates on censorship, triggered by the cutting of thirty-two minutes from Ingmar Bergman's* *Tystnaden/The Silence* (1963) because of 'indecent' sexuality. Some Norwegian critics demanded the abolition of censorship for adults, while others such as Sigurd Evensmo* argued in favour of censoring violence. In the early 1990s, four to five films were still banned every year.

Another key aspect of the Film Theatre Act was the decision to empower municipal councils to license film screenings within their jurisdiction. Between 1913 and 1926 most Norwegian local councils opened their own cinemas, and by 1930 municipal cinemas earned 90 per cent of the total cinema income. Of the 200 cinemas operating in Norway, more than half – the largest and most profitable ones – belonged to local councils. This system was still in place in the early 1990s and has given cinema exhibition a relatively strong position in Norway, even in the television and video era. In the early stages, municipal councils often invested the proceeds of film exhibition in other educational and cultural activities. As a result, the fledgling Norwegian film industry began to lag behind its Nordic neighbours: the first Norwegian fiction film, *Fiskerlivets farer – Et drama paa havet/The Dangers of a Fisherman's Life – An Ocean Drama*, was made in 1906 (released 1908), but by 1920 hardly twenty films had been made.

Though the 1920s were dominated by Hollywood, which accounted for up to 70 per cent of the Norwegian market, it was this decade that saw a Norwegian national cinema established, with nearly thirty features. The key genre was the Norwegian rural melodrama* in which hero and heroine – from different social backgrounds – struggle to express their love against a symbolic backdrop of fjords, mountains and waterfalls. Rural melodramas, shot on location and featuring national costumes, appealed to deep nationalistic sentiments in the culture. Rasmus Breistein directed the famous *Fante-Anne/Anne the Tramp* (1920) and *Kristine Valdresdatter/Kristine, Daughter of Valdres* (1930), both extremely successful at the box office.

Sound technology complicated film production and increased the cost of film-making for the small companies operating in Norway. Tancred Ibsen's* *Den store barnedåpen/The Big Baptism*, released in 1931, the first Norwegian sound film, was made with Swedish sound equipment and technicians. The twenty-nine Norwegian features made in the 1930s were produced by fifteen different companies, eight of which made only one film. The cinema-owning local councils had established strong national organisations, originally to control the powerful international distributors. But the same organisations also took an interest in film production, and urged the government to promote the development of Norwegian cinema. Cinema owners agreed to invest some of their income in the first Norwegian professional film studio, built outside Oslo. The studio itself belonged to a new film production company, Norsk Film*, established as a cornerstone of the national film industry. It produced four films in the late 1930s, the most successful of which was Ibsen's *Fant/Tramp*.

During the German occupation of 1940–45, a 'Film Directorate' was established, under which twenty-three features were made. These were mainly light farces with titles such as *Den forsvundne pølsemaker/The Lost Sausage-maker* (1941) and *En herre med bart/A Gentleman with a Moustache* (1942). Despite the German-dominated production structure, only very few Norwegian films of the period could be said to reflect National Socialist ideology – for instance *Vi er Vidkun Quislings hirdmenn/We are the Soldiers of Vidkun Quisling* (1942), an imitation of Leni Riefenstahl's* 1935 *Triumph des Willens/Triumph of the Will*, and *Unge viljer/Young Wills*

(1943). Both were directed by Walter Fyrst*. A tax on box-office receipts contributed to the production of domestic films, and at the end of the war a sizeable sum remained in the production fund.

The years following the war saw the emergence of the Norwegian occupation drama*, responding to a national fascination with the war experience; the most famous was Arne Skouen's* 1957 *Ni liv/Nine Lives* (an Oscar nominee for best foreign film in 1958). The occupation genre convinced the Norwegian authorities that film could serve nationalistic ends, and from 1947 onwards film production was considered a cultural priority by the government. A steady flow of state subsidies for film production, underpinned by patriotic arguments, has been in evidence ever since. Since the early 1960s all Norwegian feature films have received a subsidy equivalent to 55 per cent of gross box-office takings. This subsidy continues to be paid until the authorised production costs have been recovered. In addition, most Norwegian films receive a government-guaranteed loan granted by committees on which both film workers and producers are represented. Television broadcasting started in 1960, provoking a serious decline in cinema attendance, which sank from 35 million in 1956 (for a population of just over 3 million) to 19 million in 1968 and 4.2 million in 1991. While television was taking over as the leading audiovisual medium, it simultaneously left the road clear for cinema to try to become fully accepted as an art form. Norwegian film production from the 1960s comprised two categories: on the one hand, art films preferred by critics but rarely seen by larger audiences – such as *Jakten/The Hunt* (1959) and *Motforestilling/A Formal Protest* (1972), both directed by Erik Løchen* – on the other hand, farces and comedies starring popular Norwegian actors and actresses, despised by critics but popular at the box office; though when it comes to popularity in the 1960s, no Norwegian film compares with the James Bond* movies. Also on the popular side, the film series *Olsenbanden*/The Olsen Gang* drew large audiences. The series, which may be labelled 'crime-comedies' and was modelled on a Danish series, comprises thirteen films made between 1969 and 1984.

The 1970s saw Norwegian cinema widely espouse left-wing ideology. Social realism dominated film aesthetics, and it was thought that films should portray 'ordinary people' and social conflict – as in Oddvar Bull Tuhus's *Streik!/Strike!* (1975) or Pål Bang-Hansen's *Kronprinsen/The Crown Prince* (1979). Documentaries (often in 16 mm) were screened in factories, other workplaces and public gatherings. Sølve Skagen and Malte Wadman were central to this movement. Together they made *Bravo! Bravo!* in 1979, a 'satirical documentary' on the oil industry in Norway. They had already cooperated on *Hvem eier Tyssedal?/Who Owns Tyssedal?* (1975), about a Norwegian local community built around industry under foreign control [> DOCUMENTARY (NORWAY)]. Also significant in the 1970s was the breakthrough of several women directors, including Laila Mikkelsen, Vibeke Løkkeberg* and Anja Breien*. Breien made *Hustruer/Wives* (1975) as a response to John Cassavetes's *Husbands* (1970). This strong feminist tale about three old schoolfriends who decide to leave their husbands and families to experience freedom, at least for a few days, had an important impact. Director and actresses toured with the film, discussing it with audiences all over Norway. The most widely seen Norwegian film of the 1970s, on screen and video, was *Flåklypa Grand Prix* (1975), an animation film directed by Ivo Caprino*. It is a family-oriented narrative about life in a small Norwegian valley, where an inventor builds a sensational new car and wins the 'Flåklypa' grand prix race.

The 1980s saw a limited return to the trends of the 1960s. The flagship of high artistic aspirations was Oddvar Einarson's *X* (1986), which won the Silver Lion at Venice. *X* is a love story about a taciturn photographer and a fourteen-year-old homeless girl in Olso. Einarson's use in the film of the long take emphasises the slowly developing relationship between the two characters. The 1980s also produced a few successful adventure movies which found international distribution, for example Ola Solum's *Orions belte/Orion's Belt* (1985). Even more prominent was Nils Gaup's* *Veiviseren/Pathfinder* (1987), which won an Oscar nomination for best foreign film in 1989 and has been described as a 'Northern'– a Lapp equivalent of the American Western.

Ultimately, the most problematic aspect of Norwegian cinema in the 1990s is the low attendance at Norwegian films, which has triggered off a debate on the aims of national film production. Why should so much money be spent on Norwegian films when Hollywood is 'what people want'? As in the 1920s, Hollywood in the early 1990s dominates the box office. As in the rest of Europe, too, contradictory demands are made of a national cinema required to produce both artistic masterpieces and blockbusters. Against this background, Norwegian cinema has continuously to prove its own necessity. KS

NORWEGIAN FILM INSTITUTE (Det norske filminstitutt)

Norwegian institution, founded in 1955 in Oslo as the official Norwegian film archive and film museum. Other concerns have subsequently been added to its remit. Some subsidies to film production are administered by the Institute, which also promotes Norwegian film abroad. The Institute runs a well-equipped film library and has its own cinema offering archive screenings. KS

NORWEGIAN OCCUPATION DRAMAS

Norwegian film genre. The end of World War II in Norway brought with it a need to work through the war experience. Norwegian film-makers were eager to give expression to this need and audiences were drawn to their documentaries, semi-documentaries and fiction films. The nationalist drive of these films is clear, as they concentrate on the nation's sufferings, courage and strength. Whether documentary or fiction, occupation dramas purported to tell the 'true' story of the German occupation. But despite aspirations to realism, the films deployed a basically manichean mode, the Germans being exclusively evil crooks and the Norwegians paragons of courage and virtue. Sixteen such films were produced between 1945 and 1975, most of them between the late 1940s and the early 1950s. When the government decided to support film production in the late 1940s, it did so partly as a result of the contribution of the occupation genre to the formation of a national culture. Not until 1975, with *Faneflukt/Desertion*, was it possible to treat the Norwegian war experience in more nuanced ways. From that point on, German soldiers acquired individual traits and the Norwegians were not necessarily faultless; *Faneflukt*, for instance, portrays a love story between a Norwegian woman and a German soldier. Occupation dramas have, however, been rare since 1975. The new generation of filmgoers belongs to a youth culture that is both international and anti-establishment, and fundamentally out of sympathy with the kind of national identity embodied by the occupation dramas. KS

Films Include: *Englandsfarere/A Boat for England* (1946, dir. Toralf Sandø), *To liv/Two Lives* (1946, dir. Titus Vibe-Müller), *Vi vil leve/We Want to Live* (1946, dir. Olav Dalgard*); *Kampen om tungtvannet/La Bataille de l'eau lourde/The Struggle for Heavy Water* (1948, dir. Titus Vibe-Müller, supervised by Jean Dréville, Nor/Fr.); *Flukten fra Dakar/Flight from Dakar* (1951, dir. Titus Vibe-Müller); *Nødlanding/Emergency Landing* (1952, dir. Arne Skouen*); *Ni liv/Nine Lives* (1957, dir. Arne Skouen); *Omringet/Surrounded* (1960, dir. Arne Skouen); *Kalde spor/Cold Tracks* (1962, dir. Arne Skouen); *Blodveien/Blood Road* (1955, dir. Kåre Bergstrøm and Rados Novakovic); *Kontakt!/Contact!* (1956, dir. Nils R. Müller); *Stevnemøte med glemte år/Rendez-vous with Forgotten Years* (1957, dir. Jon Lennart Mjøen); *I slik en natt/On a Night Like This* (1958, dir. Sigval Maartmann-Moe); *Det største spillet/The Biggest Game* (1967, dir. Knut Bohwim); *Under en steinhimmel/Under a Stone Sky* (1974, dir. Knut Andersen, with Stanislav Rostotskij).

NORWEGIAN RURAL MELODRAMAS

Norwegian genre of the 1920s, which represented a breakthrough for indigenous Norwegian cinema. It was initiated by Rasmus Breistein's *Fante-Anne/Anne, the Tramp* (1920), which introduced the central element of the genre: the Norwegian countryside. Drawing on 'national romanticism', Norwegian landscape functioned since the mid-nineteenth century as a national symbol, together with other features such as national costumes and rural traditions, all present in the films. The genre's emphasis on tradition and the countryside, and its success, must be understood in the context of 1920s Norway, a country in the grip of modernisation and widespread industrial disputes. The appeal to national symbols and rural culture was a potent attempt to bind the nation together and smooth over social conflict.

The films of the genre, usually adapted from popular literature, are predominantly melodramas, though some contain elements of comedy. Plots usually focus on romantic love across social classes, with variously happy or unhappy resolutions. Rural melodramas drew large audiences, and their popularity is illustrated by the fact that, as late as 1931, *Kristine Valdresdatter/Kristine, Daughter of Valdres* (1930, dir. Rasmus Breistein), the last film in the genre, attracted larger audiences in Oslo than international masterpieces such as Charlie Chaplin's *City Lights* and Lewis Milestone's *All Quiet on the Western Front*. Nature and countryside have continued to play a central part in Norwegian film, but the advent of sound and the increased realism it produced (in Norway as

elsewhere) meant that in Norwegian sound film nature is no longer presented as the unique site for melodramatic love stories, but rather features in more varied ways – leading to a dilution of the genre. KS

Other Films Include: *Kaksen paa Øverland/The Landowner of Øverland* (1920, dir. G.A. Olsen); *Jomfru Trofast/Virgin Faithful* (1921, dir. Rasmus Breistein); *Til Sæters/To the Mountain Pastures* (1924, dir. Harry Ivarson); *Glomdalsbruden/The Bride of Glomdal* (1926, dir. Carl Theodor Dreyer*); *Brudeferden i Hardanger/Hardanger's Bridal Procession* (1926, dir. Rasmus Breistein); *Fjeldeventyret/The Mountain Story* (1927, dir. Leif Sinding), *Trollelgen/The Magic Elk* (1927, dir. Walter Fürst).

NOTARI, Elvira   Elvira Coda; Naples 1895–1946

Italian director and producer. The earliest and most prolific woman director in Italy, Notari made about sixty feature films, one hundred documentaries and numerous shorts for her own production house, Dora Film, between 1906 and 1930. She chose the stories, wrote the scripts, directed and co-produced all films at Dora. Her name was cancelled out of history, and her contribution to the history and development of Italian and world cinema has long remained unacknowledged.

Although not uneducated, Elvira Notari was of modest social origin. She founded Dora Film with her husband Nicola Notari, and the use of her husband's last name has added to the lack of acknowledgment of her authorship. Dora Film was a family enterprise, but it was unquestionably Elvira who wrote and directed all films, while Nicola worked as cameraman. The couple jointly supervised the whole production process from financing to editing. Their son Edoardo played 'Gennariello', an ever-present character whom scriptwriter Elvira kept modifying as he grew up. Her obscured contribution to the development of cinema presents several questions to the history of film, including that of the novelty and 'uniqueness' of Italian neo-realism*. In opposition to the contemporary Italian 'super-spectacles', Elvira Notari's cinema prefigures the aesthetic of neo-realism in its manner of direction, *mise-en-scène*, and subject matter. From the 1910s, her fictions were shot on location, in the streets and dwellings of Naples, often with non-professional actors. They documented, with stark realism, the conditions of urban living for the underclass. The suppression of female authorship is intertwined with that of historical forms of popular culture. Notari drew the subjects of her dark melodramas from the repertoire of Neapolitan popular culture, nineteenth-century popular novels as well as Italian popular romantic fiction directed at female audiences and centred on female characters. Her films offer insights into female viewpoints, desires and transgressive social behaviours. Dora Film 'silent' production specialised in colour and 'talking pictures'. Films were hand-painted frame by frame and synchronised 'live' with singing and music. Notari's films were distributed nationally as well as internationally, reaching Italian immigrants abroad. Some of the documentaries were produced specially for, and even commissioned by, such immigrants.

Notari's films encountered difficulties with Fascist censorship, which opposed her cinema's criticism of the law, its display of poverty and crime, and its use of regional popular culture and dialect. The coming of sound, together with Fascist censorship, put an end to her work. (A complete filmography can be found in the book below.) GB

Bib: Giuliana Bruno, *Streetwalking on a Ruined Map: Cultural theory and the city films of Elvira Notari* (1993).

NOUVELLE VAGUE – see NEW WAVE (FRANCE)

NOVELLO, Ivor
David Ivor Davies; Cardiff, Wales 1893 – London 1951

British actor, who, like Noël Coward*, with whom he is often compared, was also a director on stage and screen, a playwright, a scriptwriter and a songwriter whose most famous song is 'Keep the Home Fires Burning'. Elegantly and excessively beautiful, he was a matinee idol of the West End stage in the 1910s and 1920s, making his film debut in France under the direction of Louis Mercanton with *L'Appel du sang/The Call of the Blood* (1920). He played romantic leads throughout the 1920s, often adapting his films from his own plays. He created the character of Pierre Boucheron/The Rat in a series directed by Graham Cutts*: *The Rat* (1925), *The Triumph of the Rat* (1926) and *The Return of the Rat* (1929). *The Lodger* (1926), one of two Alfred Hitchcock* films in which he starred (the other being *Downhill*, 1927), is probably now his best-known film. Directed by D. W. Griffith in *The White Rose* in 1923, he failed to achieve Hollywood stardom. In 1934 he gave up cinema and returned to the theatre. JC

Other Films Include: *Miarka, la fille à l'ours/Miarka, Daughter of the Bear* (1920, Fr.); *Bonnie Prince Charlie, The Man Without Desire* (1923); *The Vortex* (1927); *The Constant Nymph* (1928); *Once a Lady* (1931, US); *The Lodger* [remake] (1932); *Sleeping Car, I Lived With You* [from his own play] (1933); *Autumn Crocus* (1934).

NOVOTNY, Franz
Vienna 1949

Austrian director. One of the exponents of the 'New Austrian Cinema', Novotny started with short films in the 1960s and trained at the Austrian state television broadcasting company as a reporter and director. His television film *Staatsoperette* (1977), a grotesque musical treatment of the Austrian First Republic, resulted in a condemnation by the Church, a scandal in Parliament and Novotny's dismissal from the television company. His cinema debut, *Exit – Nur keine Panik* (1980, Aust./Ger.), describes the excursions of an excessive male duo through the Viennese underworld, involving non-professional actors, slapstick action and 'local flavour'. Novotny's emphatically proletarian style, most obvious in his preference for vulgar language, made *Exit* a cult movie. His subsequent film, *Die Ausgesperrten/Locked Out* (1982), based on a script by Austrian writer Elfriede Jelinek, used a similar

formula in its trenchant account of a juvenile who kills his family and the events leading up to the murders. The subversion of 'family values', as well as explicit sexuality and violence, made the film very controversial. Novotny's forceful anti-establishment stance turned into farce in *Coconuts* (1985) and *Spitzen der Gesellschaft* (1990); in 1995 he made *Exit II – Verklärte Nacht*. He also writes and directs commercials. IR/AL

NUGMANOV, Rashid
Alma Ata, Kazakhstan [USSR] 1954

Kazakh director. One of the leading exponents of the Kazakh New Wave of film directors, Nugmanov began making films while a student of architecture in Alma Ata. *Ya-khkha/Ya-Ha-Ha* (1986), a short film made at VGIK*, where he studied in the workshop of Sergei Solovyov*, examines the Leningrad rock scene to a soundtrack of leading Russian rock groups, including 'Kino'. Kino's lead singer, the legendary Viktor Tsoi, stars, along with Pyotr Mamonov, from the group 'Zvuki mu', in Nugmanov's graduation film *Igla/The Needle* (1988), an eclectic thriller set in Alma Ata, in which the hero's drug addict girlfriend leads him into encounters with the sinister local underworld. Nugmanov's most recent film, *Dikii vostok/Wild East* (1993), combines Stalin and rock and roll in a futuristic parody of *The Seven Samurai*. JGf

NYKVIST, Sven
Moheda 1922

Swedish cinematographer, one of the world's leading directors of photography. After serving his apprenticeship with Julius Jaenzon* at Sandrews*, Nykvist worked as cinematographer with a number of Swedish directors, but is most famous for his work with Ingmar Bergman*, from *Jungfrukällan/The Virgin Spring* in 1960. Although he was awarded Oscars for his rich colour photography on Bergman's *Viskningar och rop/Cries and Whispers* (1973) and *Fanny och Alexander/Fanny and Alexander* (1982), his photographic style has tended towards the ascetic and intense, best seen in Bergman's *Persona* (1966), where the extraordinary (black-and-white) close-ups of actresses Bibi Andersson* and Liv Ullmann* set a new standard in modernist film-making. In the 1970s and 1980s Nykvist entered a more diverse and international phase, working on such films as Louis Malle's* *Black Moon* (1975, Fr.) and *Pretty Baby* (1978, US), Roman Polanski's* *Le Locataire/The Tenant* (1976, Fr.), Volker Schlöndorff's* *Un amour de Swann/Swann in Love* (1984, Fr./Ger.), Andrey Tarkovsky's* *Offret/The Sacrifice* (1986, Sw./Fr.), Philip Kaufman's *The Unbearable Lightness of Being* (1988, US) and Woody Allen's *Another Woman* (1988, US) and *Crimes and Misdemeanors* (1989, US), among others. He has directed several features, including *Lianbron/The Vine Bridge* (1965) and *Oxen/The Ox* (1991), as well as several shorts. LGA/BF

O

OBERON, Merle Estelle Merle O'Brien Thompson; Bombay, India 1911 – Los Angeles, California 1979

British actress of great beauty, whose British career is associated with Alexander Korda*, her husband from 1939 to 1945. Most famously, she played Anne Boleyn opposite Charles Laughton* in *The Private Life of Henry VIII* (1933), and it was her near fatal car crash in 1937 which caused the abandonment of *I, Claudius*. After playing Cathy to Laurence Olivier's* Heathcliffe in the Goldwyn production of *Wuthering Heights* (1939, US) she moved to Hollywood, where she starred in a number of films, notably Ernst Lubitsch's* *That Uncertain Feeling* (1941), *Forever and a Day* (1943) and Charles Vidor's *A Song to Remember* (1945). JC

O'CONNOR, Pat   Ardmore 1943

Irish director. O'Connor came to prominence as a television director, especially with *The Ballroom of Romance* (1982), for which he won a BAFTA award. The film recreated 1950s rural Ireland and explored the suppressed sexuality of the people attending the local dance-hall. His first feature film, *Cal* (1984), which was set in Northern Ireland, told of the relationship between the driver of an IRA unit and a widow whose policeman husband was killed by the unit. As John Hill observes, 'the film's inability to invest its view of the "troubles" with any degree of political complexity is confirmed by the retreat into metaphysics'. O'Connor's other Irish feature, *Fools of Fortune* (1990), is set among the Anglo-Irish in rural Ireland during the War of Independence. Their world is shattered as the events impinge on their lives, but as in *Cal*, O'Connor's concerns are less with the political and historical events than with an exploration of a love affair and the possibilities of redemption through retribution. O'Connor has worked most frequently in Britain and America, where he lives with his actress wife Mary Elizabeth Mastrantonio, who has also appeared in his films. KR

Bib: Kevin Rockett, Luke Gibbons, John Hill, *Cinema and Ireland* (1987).

Other Films Include: *A Month in the Country* (1987); *Stars and Bars* [UK], *The January Man* (1988, US).

OGORODNIKOV, Valeri   Born 1951

Russian director. A graduate of VGIK*, Ogorodnikov attracted attention with his first feature *Vzlomshchik/Burglar* (1986), a sympathetic portrait of the uncertainties of modern Soviet young people. The hero's punk brother was played by Konstantin Kinchev, a Soviet rock idol, leader of the group 'Alisa'. In *Bumazhnye glaza Prishvina/Prishvin's Paper Eyes* (1989), from a screenplay by the Georgian director Irakli Kvirikadze*, he attempted something much more complex. The protagonist is a contemporary television director who in the course of making a film about the 1940s finds himself torn between the personalities of the oppressed and their oppressors. After this, Ogorodnikov made *Opyt breda lyubovnogo ocharovaniya/Experiment in the Delirium of Love's Fascination* (1991). JGf

OLBRYCHSKI, Daniel   Łowicz 1945

Polish actor. Olbrychski was discovered by Andrzej Wajda*, who cast him as the lead in *Popioły/Ashes* (1965), an epic version of Żeromski's literary classic. With angelic good looks contrasted by a brooding persona, Olbrychski became an instant 1960s screen idol and successor to Zbigniew Cybulski* (a relationship explored in Wajda's *Wszystko na Sprzedasz/Everything for Sale*, 1969). Olbrychski's career flourished in Poland and abroad in films by Krzysztof Kieślowski*, Krzysztof Zanussi*, Margarethe von Trotta*, Claude Lelouch* and Volker Schlöndorff*, among others. Closely associated with Wajda, he is best known for his performances in *Panny z Wilka/The Young Ladies of Wilko* (1979) and *Wesele/The Wedding* (1972). AW

O'LEARY, Liam   Youghal 1910 – Dublin 1992

Irish actor, director, archivist. Legendary film activist who began his career as a civil servant and worked in theatre and film from the early 1930s. One of the founders of the Irish Film Society in 1936, he worked as a director in both independent theatre and at the Abbey Theatre, often directing Irish-language plays. He began making documentaries in the 1940s, some of which were sponsored by government departments. He also made one of Ireland's most effective propaganda films, *Our Country* (1948), which was widely distributed and helped defeat the powerful Fianna Fail party in the 1948 general election. O'Leary acted in a number of films, including *Stranger at My Door/At a Dublin Inn* (1950), a thriller, and as a missionary priest in *Men Against the Sun* (1953). In 1953 he moved to London, where he worked as Acquisitions Officer at the National Film Archive until 1965. During this time his interest in the silent cinema was activated and his book *Silent Cinema* (1965) was influential in drawing attention to this neglected area. He had already written the first Irish book on the cinema, *Invitation to the Film* (1945), and later wrote the first biography (1980) of the Irish-born director of the 1920s and 1930s, Rex Ingram. On returning to Ireland in 1965 he worked as a Viewing Officer at Radio Telefis Eireann* (RTE). During this time he began collecting Irish film memorabilia and gathering data for a history of the cinema in Ireland which was never completed. Donald Taylor Black made a documentary on his life, *At the Cinema Palace: Liam O'Leary* (1983). KR

OLEA, Pedro
Pedro María Olea Retolaza; Bilbao 1938

Spanish film-maker and producer, who belongs to the first generation of graduates of the Escuela Oficial de Cinematografía*. Olea has a long-standing career in Spanish television, where he has made series, documentaries and pop music programmes. The highlights of his cinema career have been period pieces such as *Tormento/Torment* (1974), based on Pérez Galdós's novel, and more recently *El maestro de esgrima/The Fencing Master* (1991), also set in nineteenth-century Spain, which was shortlisted for an Oscar. In both cases, excellent casting makes up for the blandness of the adaptations. Olea's *¡Pim, pam, pum ... fuego!/Ready, Aim ... Fire!* (1975), which recreates the Civil War's aftermath, heralded the vogue for post-Franco political melodramas. Olea reappeared in 1983, after six years in advertising, to direct one of the first films subsidised by the Basque government, *Akelarre*, a political parable in the supernatural mode of his earlier *El bosque del lobo/The Wolf's Forest* (1970). XR

OLIVEIRA, Manoel de
Manoel Candido Pinto de Oliveira; Oporto 1908

Portuguese director. In 1929, Oliveira was in the streets of Oporto making his first film, a short silent documentary entitled *Douro, Faina Fluvial/Hard Work on the River Douro* (completed in 1931). It was 1994 before he shot his first feature with international stars (Catherine Deneuve* and John Malkovich): *O Convento/The Convent/Pierre de touche*. Now universally considered a 'great master' of the cinema, Oliveira has had an extremely irregular and difficult career in his own country; only in the last two decades has he worked regularly, making twelve features (besides shorts) in twenty-three years, at a rate of one a year since 1990. In his youth, Oliveira was an athlete and racing driver. He then aspired to be an actor, and in *A Canção de Lisboa/Song of Lisbon* (1933), the first sound film made in Portugal, he appears as a matinée idol. However, influenced by Walther Ruttmann's* *Berlin, die Sinfonie der Großstadt/Berlin – Symphony of a City* (1927) and his contemporary Jean Vigo* (whom, many years later, he recalled in *Nice ... à propos de Jean Vigo*), he decided to go behind the camera with *Douro, Faina Fluvial*, made by himself and his cameraman, and edited on a billiard table.

Oliveira's first feature was *Aniki-Bóbó* (1942), set in the streets of Oporto (again) among a band of children. Perceived as a forerunner of Italian neo-realism*, *Aniki-Bóbó* is a sombre film threaded with a theme of temptation which recurs in later work. A contemporary box-office failure which has now become one of the most popular Portuguese films ever, *Aniki-Bóbó* forced Oliveira to quit cinema for almost fourteen years. With no official support but always curious about technique, he bought a camera in Germany and shot, alone and in colour, another short set in Oporto, *O Pintor e a Cidade/The Painter and the City* (1956). The focus was no longer 'the real' but its painted representation. *O Acto da Primavera/Rite of Spring/Passion of Jesus* (1963) was to prove seminal in his oeuvre. Overtly making a documentary on a performance of the Passion by peasants, Oliveira used

the film as a reflection on the theatrical within film. More or less at the same time, he shot a medium-length film, *A Caça/The Hunt* (1963); the two works (especially without the happy ending that censorship imposed on the latter) can be seen as symbolic visions of heaven and hell.

In 1970, the young film-makers of the New Portuguese cinema*, who recognised Oliveira as their only national role model, made a point of inviting him to direct the first film for their new cooperative CPC. This was *O Passado e o Presente/Past and Present* (1971), based on a play, and the first of what would be known as the 'Quartet of Frustrated Loves'. If this film is reminiscent of Luis Buñuel*, the next, *Benilde ou a Virgem-Mãe/Benilde or the Virgin Mother* (1975), is closer to Carl Theodor Dreyer*, Buñuel the iconoclast and Dreyer the Protestant being the favourite *auteurs* of the Catholic Oliveira. From the opening sequence of *Benilde ou a Virgem-Mãe*, with its amazing tracking shot between sets in a studio, the film is the first mature example of Oliveira's concept of the 'cinema as audiovisual preservation of the theatre', a concept far removed from that of 'adaptation'. But the camera and the film, if they do preserve a particular moment, bring us a moment that is already not just past but a phantom (as Oliveira would say later in Wim Wenders'* *Lisbon Story*). In this context, a key part of Oliveira's *oeuvre*, although never actually filmed (the script has been published), is *Angelica*, inspired by the actual event of the director having to photograph a dead woman. Already present in *O Passado e o Presente* (where a woman can only love her husbands when they are dead), this theme of death was to be essential to his films, especially from *Benilde ou a Virgem-Mãe*.

Amor de Perdição/Ill-Fated Love (1977), based on the most popular Portuguese romantic novel (by Camilo Castello Branco), was an obvious choice for the 'Frustrated Loves' quartet. It was first released as a four-part television series, to a stormy reception; the once-loved director of *Aniki-Bóbó* became the butt of jokes, a situation which would last for some years. Camilo Castello Branco appeared as a character in the subsequent *Francisca* (1981), perhaps Oliveira's masterpiece, and in *O Dia do Desespero/The Day of Despair* (1992), which depicts the day the writer shot himself. Oliveira followed the quartet with the massive adaptation of Paul Claudel's play, *Sapato de cetim/Le Soulier de satin/The Satin Slipper* (1985, special Golden Lion in Venice). *Meu Caso/Mon Cas* (1986), *A Divina Comédia/The Divine Comedy* (1991, special jury prize in Venice) and *A Caixa/Blind Man's Bluff* (1994), with the ever-present reflection on theatre and film, are meditations on humanity, whereas *Os Canibais/The Cannibals* (1988), an even more theatrical work (with an opera written especially for it), is a very black, hilarious comedy. Oliveira's most important projects in his late years have been *Non ou a Vã Glória de Mandar/No, or the Vain Glory of Command* (1990, which won a special tribute from the jury at Cannes), a reflection on Portuguese history through its defeats, and *Vale Abraão/The Valley of Abraham*, a modern adaptation of *Madame Bovary*, which ends with one of the most beautiful death scenes (and there are many to choose from) Oliveira ever did. AMS

Bib: Cinemateca Portuguesa, *Manoel de Oliveira* (1982); Cinémathèque Royale de Belgique (eds.), *95 ans de cinéma portugais, 'A Divina comédia', Manoel de Oliveira* (1995).

Other Films: *Já se Fabricam Automóveis em Portugal/Cars Are Already Made in Portugal, Miramar, Praia de Rosas/ Miramar, Beach of Roses* (1934, both shorts); *Famalicão* (1940); *O Pão/Bread* (1959, two versions, short and long); *As Pinturas do Meu Irmão Júlio/Paintings by My Brother Júlio* (1965, short); *Visita, ou Memórias e Confissões/Visit, or Memories and Confessions* (an autobiographical feature to be released after his death), *Lisboa Cultural/Cultural Lisbon* [TV] (1982); *Nice ... à propos de Jean Vigo* [TV] (1983); *Simpósio International de Escultura/International Symposium of Sculpture* [TV] (co-dir. Manoel Casimiro, his son), *A Bandeira Nacional/The National Flag* [short] (1985).

OLIVIER, (Sir) Laurence (Baron Olivier of Brighton)
Dorking 1907 – Steyning 1989

British actor and director. Already a star on Broadway and the West End in the 1930s (and for the next five decades), Olivier seemed destined for Hollywood stardom as well. Groomed by Hollywood in the early 1930s as a successor to Ronald Colman*, he was tested for *Queen Christina* (1933) but rejected by Garbo in favour of John Gilbert. In *Wuthering Heights* (1939), *Pride and Prejudice* (1940), *Rebecca* (1940) and *That Hamilton Woman/Lady Hamilton* (1941), however, he brought a troubled and austere romanticism to his roles which had all the marks of classic cinematic star quality. Returning to Britain during the war, Olivier put his romantic bravura at the service of patriotism in *Henry V* (1945), and continued after the war, sometimes to the dismay of purists, to bring his star quality to Shakespearean cinema. Like an old-fashioned actor-manager, he directed, produced and adapted *Henry V*, *Hamlet* (1948) and *Richard III* (1955) as star vehicles, creating popular cinema rather than simply filmed theatre.

Estimations of Olivier's acting vary, and critics are harsh on his playing to the gallery. Certainly, many of his appearances in the 1980s had the ring of the cash register about them. In his heyday, however, he brought a touch of glamour and slightly dangerous romance to a British cinema more used to geniality, restraint and responsibility.

Olivier was knighted in 1947, and received a life peerage in 1970. JC

Bib: Laurence Olivier, *Confessions of an Actor: An Autobiography* (1982).

Other Films (UK Unless Indicated): *Too Many Crooks* (1930); *Friends and Lovers* [US], *Potiphar's Wife* (1931); *Westward Passage* (1932, US); *Moscow Nights* (1935); *As You Like It, Conquest of the Air, Fire Over England* (1937); *The Divorce of Lady X* (1938); *Q Planes* (1939); *49th Parallel, Words for Battle* [commentary] (1941); *The Demi-Paradise* (1943); *The Magic Box* (1951); *Carrie* (1952, US); *The Beggar's Opera* [+ co-prod.] (1953); *The Prince and the Showgirl* [+ dir., prod.] (1957); *Spartacus* [US], *The Entertainer* (1960); *Term of Trial* (1962); *Bunny Lake is Missing, Othello* (1965); *Oh! What a Lovely War* (1969); *Three Sisters* [+ dir.] (1970); *Sleuth, Lady Caroline Lamb* (1973); *Love Among the Ruins* (1975, US); *Marathon Man* (1976, US); *A Bridge Too Far, A Long Day's Journey Into Night* [US] (1977); *The Boys from Brazil* (1978, US); *The Jazz Singer* (1980, US); *War Requiem* (1988).

OLMI, Ermanno
Bergamo 1931

Italian director. Unusual among Italian directors in being of working-class (originally peasant) origin, Olmi started his film career as a maker of in-house documentaries for the Edison Volta electric company of which he was an employee. After making documentaries in the 1950s he wrote and shot his first feature, *Il tempo si è fermato/Time Stood Still*, a delicate study of two men trapped in the mountains, in 1959. Still in the same documentary-influenced style he made *Il posto/The Job* (1961) and *I fidanzati/The Engagement* (1963), establishing himself as a sensitive and careful observer, not afraid to use a deliberately undramatic narrative rhythm. Another facet to his character – his Catholicism – emerged with *E venne un uomo/A Man Named John* (1965), a biopic of Pope John XXIII narrated by Rod Steiger. After a relatively fallow period in the mid-1970s he returned to prominence with *L'albero degli zoccoli/The Tree of Wooden Clogs*, a peasant family saga which won the Palme d'or at Cannes in 1978 and was widely interpreted as a Catholic and politically right-of-centre (so by implication Christian-Democrat) response to Bernardo Bertolucci's* Marxist epic *Novecento/1900* (1976), though a more pointed contrast could be made between the full-blown rhetoric of Bertolucci and Olmi's gentle under-statement. In the 1980s Olmi obtained commissions mainly from Italy's state-owned RAI* television network and reverted to documentary, but a deal struck with RAI, the pro-ducer Mario Cecchi Gori* and a French company enabled him to make a foray into international film with *La leggenda del santo bevitore/The Legend of the Holy Drinker* (1988), an adaptation of Joseph Roth's novel, enlivened by a marvellous performance by Rutger Hauer* as the eponymous drinker. A full-length documentary, *Lungo il fiume/Down the River* (1992), about the ecology of the Po valley, rich in pious senti-ment but short on analysis, revealed his limitations as a film-maker, but his early unpretentious films will secure his place in film history. GNS

OLSEN, Ole
Stareklint 1863 – Copenhagen 1943

Danish producer. Olsen began his career by peddling attrac-tions around the Scandinavian markets. From 1898 he made a fortune running a funfair in Malmö (Sweden); returning to Copenhagen, he opened a cinema, the Biograf-Theatret, in 1905. In 1906 he founded the Nordisk Films Kompagni*, the first and most important Danish film production company. His genius was to see the commercial possibilities of export, since he knew from experience that the supply of new films could not keep up with voracious demand. Within a year he had established six representative offices abroad, the most important in Berlin and Budapest. In 1914, as film distri-bution was changing from sales to renting, Olsen bought thirty-five first-run cinemas in Germany (which he was obliged to sell three years later when the German industry was nationalised). He remained manager of Nordisk until 1924, when he retired, spending the rest of his life collecting art. Like many early film pioneers, Olsen was a great entrepreneur but less adept at judging artistic talent. He allowed Asta Nielsen* to leave for Germany, and failed to persuade Benjamin Christensen* to work for Nordisk. ME

OLSENBANDEN

Norwegian film series. *Olsenbanden/The Olsen Gang* was the longest-running and most popular series in Norwegian cinema. The films are remakes of a Danish series of the same title [> NORDISK FILMS KOMPAGNI]. The thirteen 'crime-comedies' show the criminal Egon Olsen and his gang repeatedly planning a heist and failing to carry it out. In some of the films, the Olsen gang cooperates with Dynamite Harry, played by the Norwegian comedian Harald Heide Steen Jr. Gang members too are played by popular Norwegian comedians: Arve Opsahl, Sverre Holm and Carsten Byhring. All but the last of the *Olsenbanden* films, produced by Teamfilm, are based on Danish scripts, with the addition of the character of Dynamite Harry, who has no parallel in the Danish films. The Danish series was exported to Germany in a dubbed version, while the Swedes chose the Norwegian remake solution. As is typical of indigenous comedy in most European countries, *Olsenbanden*, while extremely popular with both adults and children, is detested by 'serious' critics. The series drew large audiences to the cinema and made substantial profits for Teamfilm; it is now equally popular on video. Such popularity is partly explained by the concept of the series format, audiences getting to know and appreciate characters over several films. But *Olsenbanden* also owes its success to the excellent cast, whose performances give life to simple characters and occasionally weak plots. KS

Films: *Olsenbanden/The Olsen Gang* (1969); *Olsenbanden og Dynamitt-Harry/The Olsen Gang and Dynamite Harry* (1970); *Olsenbanden tar gull/The Olsen Gang Takes Gold* (1972); *Olsenbanden og Dynamitt-Harry går amokkkkkk/The Olsen Gang and Dynamite Harry Run Wiiiiild* (1973); *Olsenbanden møter Kongen og Knekten/The Olsen Gang Meets the Jack and the King* (1974); *Olsenbandens siste bedrifter/The Last Achievements of the Olsen Gang* (1975); *Olsenbanden for full musikk/The Olsen Gang Make It Big* (1976); *Olsenbanden og Dynamitt-Harry på sporet/The Olsen Gang and Dynamite Harry Follow the Trail* (1977); *Olsenbanden og Data-Harry sprenger Verdensbanken/The Olsen Gang and Data-Harry Break the World Bank* (1978); *Olsenbanden og Dynamitt-Harry mot nye høyder/The Olsen Gang and Dynamite Harry Get Higher* (1979); *Olsenbanden gir seg aldri!/The Olsen Gang Never Gives In* (1981); *Olsenbandens aller siste kupp/The Olsen Gang's Very Last Heist* (1982); *...Men Olsenbanden var ikke død!/But the Olsen Gang Wasn't Dead!* (1984).

ONDRA, Anny Anny Ondráková; Tarnów, Galicia [then Austria-Hungary, now Poland] 1902 [3?] – Hamburg, West Germany 1987

Czech actress. After stage training in Prague, Anny Ondra became one of the leading stars of the inter-war European cinema, working principally with her first husband, the actor-director Karel Lamač*. Once described as 'Buster Keaton in skirts', she was the first female comic in Czech film, appearing in a wide range of comedies. Her appeal rested on a slightly coquettish naïveté, and she appeared in musicals as well as playing an obligatory range of orphans and abandoned women. She appeared in four British films and, in 1929, Alfred Hitchcock* put her fragile blonde beauty to rather different use in *The Manxman* and *Blackmail*, with her dialogue dubbed in the latter. Ondra-Lamač Film was founded in Berlin in 1930 and she played a central role in the production of most of her 1930s films. The second half of her career was based in Germany and she made her last screen appearance, for Helmut Käutner*, in 1957. PH

Films Include: *Dáma s malou nožkou/Woman with Small Feet* (1919); *Zpěv zlata/Song of Gold, Gilly po prvé v Praze/Gilly's First Visit to Prague* (1920); *Tu ten kámen/Tutankhamun/This is the Stone, Únos bankéře Fuxe/The Kidnapping of Banker Fuxe* (1923); *Bílý ráj/The White Paradise, Chyt'te ho!/Catch Him!* (1924); *Karel Havlíček Borovský, Lucerna/The Lantern* (1925); *Velbloud uchem jehly/Camel Through the Needle's Eye* (1926); *Der erste Küss/The First Kiss, Saxophon Susi* (1928, Ger.), *God's Clay* (1928, UK); *Blackmail, Glorious Youth, The Manxman* (1929, UK); *Die Fledermaus, Mamsell Nitouche* [German versions of *La Chauve-souris* and *Mam'zelle Nitouche*, shot in Fr.], *On a jeho sestra/He and His Sister* (1931); *Baby* (1932, Fr.); *Kiki* (1933, Fr.); *Die Tochter des Regiments/Daughter of the Regiment* (1933, Aust.); **In Germany**: *Klein Dorrit/Little Dorrit, Polská krev/Polish Blood, Knock-out* (1934); *Ein Mädel vom Ballett/A Girl from the Ballet, Donogoo Tonka* (1936); *Vor Liebe wird gewarnt/Beware of Love* (1937); *Himmel, wir erben ein Schloss/Heavens, We're Inheriting a Castle* (1943); *Schön muss man sein/One Has to Be Beautiful* (1951); *Die Zürcher Verlobung/Getting Engaged in Zurich* (1957).

OPHULS, Max Max Oppenheimer; Saarbrucken 1902 – Hamburg 1957

German director (sometimes spelt Ophüls; in the US occasionally Opuls). After a ten-year career in the theatre and in radio Ophuls joined Ufa* in 1931. His breakthrough came with the international success of *Liebelei* (1933; also French version, *Liebelei une Histoire d'amour*), based on a play by Arthur Schnitzler. Identified with Viennese charm and bitter-sweet world-weariness, Ophuls tried to extend his range after emigrating to Paris in 1933. Proving extremely versatile in putting together unlikely projects, between 1934 and 1940 he directed French, Italian, Dutch and English-language films, most of them exquisite evocations of a world of lost illusions, such as *La signora di tutti* (1934, It.) and *La Tendre ennemie* (1936, Fr.). Ophuls became a French citizen in 1938; nevertheless, he fled to America in 1941, but was unable to realise a film project until 1947. His first Hollywood film starred Douglas Fairbanks Jr. (*The Exile*, 1947), but he has become especially known for his three classic 'women's pictures', *Letter from an Unknown Woman* (1948), *Caught* (1949) and *The Reckless Moment* (1949), produced respectively for Universal, MGM and Columbia.

At the end of the 1940s Ophuls returned to Paris where he enjoyed a *succès de scandale* with *La Ronde* (1950), his second Schnitzler adaptation. Following *Madame de .../The Earrings of Madame de ...* (1953), featuring Danielle Darrieux*, he was commissioned to direct the French-German co-production *Lola Montès* (1955, with Martine Carol*), thought a failure at the time but now considered his masterpiece. Ophuls' stylistic trademarks are his intricate and extensive camera movements, functionally relating decor and music to the protagonists, and his films combine wit and an undaunted romanticism. His son Marcel Ophuls (born Frankfurt 1927) was his assistant on *Lola Montès* and himself became an international film-maker; he is especially noted for his remarkable *Le Chagrin et la pitié/The Sorrow and the Pity* (1971), a ground-breaking documentary on the complex, compromised and ambivalent attitudes of French people in a provincial town during the German occupation. He pursued the German occupation theme in *Hôtel Terminus/The Life and Times of Klaus Barbie* (1988, Fr.), on the Nazi war criminal Klaus Barbie. TE/GV

Bib: Max Ophuls, *Spiel im Dasein* (1963); Paul Willemen (ed.), *Ophuls* (1978).

Other Films Include: *Dann schon lieber Lebertran* (1931, Ger.); *Die verliebte Firma, Die verkaufte Braut/The Bartered Bride* (1932, Ger.); *Lachenden Erben* (1933, Ger.); *On a volé un homme* (1934, Fr.); *Divine* (1935, Fr.); *Komedie om geld/A Comedy About Money* (1936, Neth.); *Yoshiwara* (1937, Fr.); *Le Roman de Werther/Werther* (1938, Fr.); *Sans lendemain* (1940, Fr.); *De Mayerling à Sarajévo* (1940, Fr.); *Le Plaisir* (1952, Fr.).

ORDUÑA, Juan de   Juan de Orduña y Fernández-Shaw; Madrid 1907–74

Spanish director. Also actor, producer and scriptwriter, who rose to prominence at Cifesa*, where he directed many of the studio's major productions in the popular and lavishly made genre of the Spanish historical film*: for instance, *Locura de amor/Love Crazy* (1950), *Agustina de Aragón/Agustina of Aragon* (1958) and *Alba de América/Dawn of America* (1951). Based on the play by Tamayo y Baus, set in the reign of the Catholic kings, *Locura de amor* is at one level (like the other two films and many more made by Orduña) rather crude regime-inspired Cifesa propaganda. Foreigners, as in *Alba* and *Agustina*, are buffoonish or evil, and the natives heroic. The poster for *Agustina de Aragón* read: '*Superproducción racialmente hispana que triunfa apoteósicamente*' ('tremendously successful, racially Hispanic super-production'). Orduña went on making films until 1973, reprising Florián Rey's 1935 *Nobleza baturra/Aragonese Virtue* (1965), but scored his greatest hit with the Sara Montiel* musical *El último cuplé/The Last Song* (1957). PWE

ORKO, Risto   Rauma 1899

Finnish director and producer. Risto Orko was the managing director of Suomi-Filmi which, together with T. J. Särkkä's*

SF and (in the 1950s) Mauno Mäkelä's* Fennada-Filmi, was one of the three major studios in Finland. Orko went to Suomi-Filmi in 1933 to co-direct an educational feature about tuberculosis, *Ne 45000/Those 45,000* (1933). His co-director, Erkki Karu*, left Suomi-Filmi (which he had founded) before the film was finished, and Orko agreed to stay despite Suomi-Filmi's precarious financial position. With the help of loans, Suomi-Filmi held out until the much-needed financial success of *Siltalan pehtoori/The Steward of Siltala* (1934). In 1935 it was in a position to hire another director, Valentin Vaala*. In the 1920s, Suomi-Filmi had concentrated on national themes and folk stories, but under Orko's supervision the company began to build a more sophisticated image, in the style of European and especially French cinema. The films' protagonists came from the upper classes, and the stories were set in Helsinki or in country mansions and villas, aimed at the growing band of middle-class and urban viewers. The modern comedies produced by Suomi-Filmi in the late 1930s were also the first genre to target female viewers.

Both Suomi-Filmi and SF courted cultural acceptance with nationalist spectacles in the late 1930s. Orko himself directed the most lavish ones. *Jääkärin morsian/The Infantryman's Bride* (1938) and *Aktivistit/The Activists* (1939) deal with the Finnish fight for independence in World War I from a clearly anti-Russian stance – which is why they were banned from exhibition immediately after Finland lost the war with the Soviet Union in 1944. The film business in Finland divided into two camps during the war. Suomi-Filmi operated within Suomen Filmiliitto (The Finnish Film Alliance), part of the German-led International Film Chamber, which banned American films. Close relations with Germany guaranteed a supply of film-making material but spelled trouble for the company after the war. Although losing market share in feature films, Suomi-Filmi remained a major force in the industry because of its other activities as the dominant rental agency, producer of shorts and documentaries and owner of a large network of cinemas. After the war Suomi-Filmi went through an internal power struggle finally won by Orko, whose family acquired the company's entire stock. At the same time, however, Orko stopped directing to concentrate on production and administration. Only once did he return to film-making, directing *Tulitikkuja lainaamassa/Borrowing Matchsticks* (1980) with Leonid Gaidai, a co-production between Suomi-Filmi and Mosfilm. KL

ORLOVA, Lyubov P.   Moscow 1902–75

Soviet actress. Orlova graduated from the Moscow Conservatoire, acting on stage from 1926 and on screen from 1934. Although she appeared in films made by a number of directors, she made her reputation in a series of highly popular musical comedies directed by her husband Grigori Alexandrov*: they were known as the 'first couple' of Soviet cinema and Orlova was probably its most popular actress. She played what one critic has described as the 'ideal woman of the 1930s, the *femina sovietica*, a contemporary Valkyrie in a white sweater with a severe perm'. Her characterisations appealed to a contemporary willingness to be deceived, depicted a paradise that audiences could believe in, and were designed to illustrate the possibility of self-improvement through effort and the benign influence of the Party and Stalin. This is above all implicit in *Vesëlye rebiata/The Happy Guys* (1934), *Tsirk/The Circus* (1936), *Volga-Volga* (1938), *Svetlyi put'/The Radiant Path* (1940) and *Vesna/Spring* (1947). She also appeared in Alexandrov's *Vstrecha na El'be/Meeting on the Elbe* (1949), *Kompozitor Glinka/The Composer Glinka* (1952) and, her last film, *Russkii suvenir/A Russian Souvenir* (1960). After her death Alexandrov co-directed a film about her, *Lyubov Orlova* (1983). RT

OSTEN, Suzanne   Stockholm 1944

Swedish director. Osten studied art history and literature. A committed left-wing feminist, she joined a theatre group while still at school and has since worked extensively in experimental theatre in Stockholm, as playwright, director and manager. Like many Swedish film-makers, she combines theatre and film, for instance in using the same troupe of actors, including her leading man Etienne Glaser. Her first film, *Mamma/Our Life is Now* (1982), was a tribute to her mother, the film critic Gerd Osten. She attracted attention with her second film, *Bröderna Mozart/The Mozart Brothers* (1986), a comedy about staging Mozart's *Don Giovanni* (which won several international awards); her third film, *Livsfarlig film/Lethal Film* (1988), is about a horror movie director who awakens to more concrete horrors. Since then she has moved towards darker studies of characters (predominantly men) caught in intense psychological and historical conflicts, and her films have consistently reflected on violence: *Skyddsängeln/The Guardian Angel* (1989), set in 1910 and beautifully shot in luminous black and white, portrays a young revolutionary who infiltrates a bourgeois household in order to kill the head of the family. Though in colour, *Tala! Det är så mörkt/Speak up! It's so dark* (1993) is an even more sombre dissection of violence, through an intense confrontation between a young neo-Nazi and a middle-aged Jewish doctor who rescues him. Osten also works for Swedish television. GV

O'SULLIVAN, Thaddeus   Dublin 1948

Irish director and cameraman. Since the 1960s O'Sullivan has lived in London, where he trained as a cameraman, working in particular with experimental film-maker Stephen Dwoskin in the 1970s. His debut film, *A Pint of Plain* (1975), and his feature *On a Paving Stone Mounted* (1978) used an experimental form as they sought to explore the Irish migrant's experience in London and the migrant's relationship to Ireland. As Marc Karlin noted of *A Pint of Plain*, 'all things denoting British Realism were being unusually mobile ... It was hallucinating to see the props of British Cinema drifting from their moorings as if a poltergeist had invaded the land' (*BFI Productions Catalogue 1977–78*). O'Sullivan's formal challenge to Irish film-makers has not in general been taken up and he himself has gradually shifted towards mainstream commercial cinema and television. His first 35mm short, *The Woman Who Married Clark Gable* (1985), was about a woman, played by Brenda Fricker*, who fantasises that her husband, Bob Hoskins*, is transforming into Clark Gable, until the reality of their childless lives impinges on the cinematic imagination. O'Sullivan's most accomplished, and commercially popular, film, *December Bride* (1990), was set in Northern Ireland and concerns the relationships in a largely Protestant community between a housekeeper and two brothers. Having children in turn with both men she, and they, remain uncompromising in the face of the social opprobrium of the local community. O'Sullivan has also worked in television, making *In the Border Country* (1991), about the border area between Northern Ireland and the Republic. KR

Bib: *British Film Institute Productions Catalogue 1977–78* (1978).

OSWALD, Richard   Richard Ornstein; Vienna 1880 – Düsseldorf 1963

Austrian-born director, who made his first films in 1914 and founded his own company in 1916. In the post-World War I period Oswald took up current social debates around sexuality and crime to make a range of popular movies (such as the three-part *Es werde Licht!*, 1917–18; *Das Tagebuch einer Verlorenen*, 1918; *Anders als die Anderen/Different from the Others*, 1919; *Feme*, 1927). Along the way he 'discovered' stars such as Conrad Veidt*, Werner Krauß*, Lya de Putti* and Wilhelm Dieterle*. A sought-after director in almost every popular genre at least since his expensive costume drama *Lady Hamilton* (1921), Oswald did well in the first years of sound cinema, excelling in operetta films like *Wien, du Stadt der Lieder* (1930) or the historical panorama 1914, *Die letzten Tage vor dem Weltbrand* (1931), and making one of the many versions of the romantic tale *Alraune* (1930). A few months after the Nazi takeover he emigrated to Britain, then France, and finally the US. He was the father of the director Gerd Oswald (1919–89). MW

Bib: Helga Belach and Wolfgang Jacobsen (eds.), *Richard Oswald: Regisseur und Produzent* (1990).

Other Films Include: *Dida Ibsens Geschichte* (1918); *Die Reise um die Erde in 80 Tagen, Unheimliche Geschichten* (1919); *Nachtgestalten, Manolescus Memoiren* (1920); *Lucrezia Borgia* (1922); *Im weißen Rössl* (1926); *Frühlings Erwachen* (1929); *Dreyfus* (1930); *Der Hauptmann von Köpenick* (1931); *Unheimliche Geschichten* (1932).

OTHONI

Greek film magazine. *Othoni*, meaning 'Screen', was set up in Thessaloniki (Salonika) in 1979 and is now the longest continuously published Greek film journal. When it first came out, interest in cinema in Greece was high and many other film publications appeared. Initially *Othoni*'s contents leant heavily towards current theoretical issues – structuralism, Marxism, psychoanalysis, etc. Later, however, readers became disillusioned with these debates and interest declined.

While its rival journals succumbed, however, *Othoni* survived – at the price of diminishing the number of articles devoted to theory in favour of a more cinephile approach. *Othoni*'s austere stance, reflecting studied independence and distance from the Greek film establishment centred in Athens, sometimes provoked extreme reactions. Having covered the 1980s and the rise and decline of the New Greek Cinema*, *Othoni* is the only continuous record and reflection of the developments and changing trends of a critical period in Greek cinema history. TN

O'TOOLE, Peter — Connemara, Ireland 1932

British actor, born in Ireland, who made his film debut as Rob Roy in Disney's *Kidnapped* (1960). One of the new wave of actors to emerge in British theatre in the late 1950s, O'Toole came to critical attention in *The Long and the Short and the Tall* (1959), though the more bankable Laurence Harvey played the part in the film version. O'Toole leapt to fame in the title role of *Lawrence of Arabia* (1962), for which he won a British Academy award and an Oscar nomination, followed by starring roles in *Becket* (1964) and *Lord Jim* (1965). He has always been attracted to eccentric roles, and the eccentricity began to express itself in the 1970s in more mannered performances (unwisely in a musical version of *Goodbye, Mr. Chips*, 1959, with Petula Clark, and outrageously in *The Ruling Class*, 1972), and in a public persona which moved from star acting to scandalous celebrity. He received a US Film Critics award for *The Stunt Man* (1979, US), and gave a restrained performance as the tutor in Bertolucci's* *The Last Emperor* (1987, It.). JC

Other Films Include: *What's New Pussycat*; *La Bibbia/The Bible In the Beginning* ... [as three angels; It./US], *The Night of the Generals* (1966); *Casino Royale* (1967); *The Lion in Winter* (1968); *Under Milk Wood* (1971); *Man of la Mancha* (1972, US); *Rosebud* (1975, US); *Man Friday* (1976); *Caligula* (1980, US/It.); *My Favorite Year* (1982, US); *The Rainbow Thief* (1990).

OTSEP, Fyodor A. [OZEP, Fédor] — Moscow 1895 – Ottawa, Canada 1949

Russian director and scriptwriter. Coming to the cinema in 1916, Otsep jointly wrote scripts for a number of films, including *Polikushka* (1919), *Papirosnitsa iz Mosselproma/The Cigarette Girl from Mosselprom* and Yakov Protazanov's* *Aelita* (both 1924), *Kollezhskii registrator/The Station Master* (1925) and *Kukla s millionami/The Girl with the Millions* (1928). He directed the serial thriller *Miss Mend* (1926), *Zemlya v plenu/Earth in Captivity* (1928) and the Russo-German co-production of Tolstoy's *Zhivoi trup/The Living Corpse* (1929), after which he stayed in Germany, making *Der Mörder Dimitri Karamasoff/The Brothers Karamazov* (1931) as well as its French version *Les Frères Karamazoff* (also 1931). After the Nazis came to power he moved to France, where, under the name of Fédor Ozep, he contributed to the popular genre of exotic melodrama, making the French and

German versions of *Mirages de Paris/Großstadtnacht/Mirages of Paris* (1932), the Zweig adaptation *Amok* (1934), *La Dame de pique/The Queen of Spades* (1937), *Gibraltar/It Happened in Gibraltar*, and *Tarakanova/Betrayal* and its Italian version *La principessa Tarakanova* (all 1938). Interned as a displaced person, he was freed after the fall of France and fled to North America. He made his last film, *La Forteresse/Whispering City*, in Canada in 1947. RT

OTTINGER, Ulrike — Konstanz 1942

German director, whose training in fine art is reflected in her concern with the exploration of the image/sound relationship; her episodic narratives are conveyed through beautiful and stylised tableaux, underscored by a highly manipulated soundtrack. A major objective is to renegotiate visual pleasure for the female and lesbian spectator. Unlike many contemporary German feminist film-makers, though, Ottinger has rejected a realist treatment of women's issues, preferring exaggeration, artifice and parody. *Madame X – Eine absolute Herrscherin/Madame X – An Absolute Ruler* (1978), about a band of female pirates, though defended by Monika Treut*, provoked a hostile response from many feminists. In the context of postmodernist debates, however, Ottinger's aesthetics have become familiar enough, and are now better understood. *Bildnis einer Trinkerin/Ticket of No Return* (1979), only ostensibly about a couple of female alcoholics, aims to represent female desire and parodies the conventions of woman as spectacle; it again provoked fierce debate among feminists. *Freak Orlando* (1981), based on Virginia Woolf's novel and featuring Magdalena Montezuma, relates the mythology of the social/sexual outcast through the ages. With her lengthy documentaries *China – Die Künste – Der Alltag/China – The Arts – The Everyday* (1985) and *Taiga* (1992) – respectively six and eight hours long – and the feature film *Johanna d'Arc of Mongolia* (1988), Ottinger's recurring theme of exoticism was extended to her fascination with Oriental cultures. Ottinger's insistence on mythologising and aestheticising women's experience has retrospectively been validated by many critics as a more fruitful approach than one which focuses on subject matter. US

OVCHAROV, Sergei — Rostov, Russia [USSR] 1955

Russian director and scriptwriter. A student of the Higher Courses for Directors in the workshop of Gleb Panfilov*, Ovcharov came to prominence with *Nebyval'shchina/Believe it or Not* (1983) and *Levsha/Leftie* (1986), based on a story by the nineteenth-century Russian writer Nikolai Leskov. The ambitious *Ono/It* (1989) also has its source in nineteenth-century literature, Saltykov-Shchedrin's satire *The History of a Town*. But his reading of the novel includes all of Russian history, and finds roles for Lenin, Stalin, Beria, Khrushchev, Brezhnev and even Gorbachev on the way to an apocalyptic future. It was followed by *Barabaniada/Drum Rolls* (1993), a picaresque faux-naïf tale of the wanderings of a little drummer. JGf

OZEP, Fédor – see OTSEP, Fyodor

OZORES, Mariano   Mariano Ozores Puchol;
Madrid 1926

Spanish director. The son and brother of famous popular actors, Ozores directed his first film in 1959. With over eighty features, he became one of the most prolific directors of the Spanish cinema and a major exponent of the 'sexy Spanish comedy' [> COMEDY (SPAIN)]. Simple soft-porn narratives rely on farcical situations and performance by comic actors such as Fernando Esteso*, Andrés Pajares* (*Los bingueros/The*

Bingo Players, 1979, *¡Qué gozada de divorcio!/Divorce, What a Wonderful Thing!*, 1980) and Alfredo Landa* (*El reprimido/The Repressed Man*, 1974), as well as on visual gratification provided by the erotic icons of the *destape* (nudity) cinema, such as Nadiuska in *Manolo, la nuit* (1973) and Bárbara Rey in *Cuentos de las sábanas blancas/Tales of the White Sheets* (1977). With democracy, Ozores turned to political satire, in films like *El apolítico/The Apolitical Man* (1977), *¡Que vienen los socialistas!/The Socialists Are Coming!* (1982) and *Disparate nacional/National Nonsense* (1990). IS

P

PABST, Georg Wilhelm   Raudnitz 1885 – Vienna
1967

Austrian director, who epitomised the psychosexual realism of Weimar* cinema and late 1920s 'new sobriety'. After studying engineering in Vienna, Pabst moved to Berlin in 1921 as an actor, assistant director, and scriptwriter for Carl Froelich*. His reputation was made with *Die freudlose Gasse/The Joyless Street* (1925), which drew a pessimistic picture of Germany's social and moral situation after World War I [> STRASSENFILME]. He directed Brigitte Helm* in *Die Liebe der Jeanne Ney/The Loves of Jeanne Ney* (1927), but his best-known films are *Die Büchse der Pandora/Pandora's Box* (1929) and *Das Tagebuch einer Verlorenen/Diary of a Lost Girl* (1929), both featuring the quintessentially modern eroticism of Hollywood actress Louise Brooks*.

Pabst's first talkie, *Westfront 1918/Comrades of 1918* (1930), was an uncompromisingly frank anti-war film. Though Pabst was a convinced left-of-centre liberal, his political instincts often deserted him. His 1931 adaptation of the Bertolt Brecht–Kurt Weill piece *Die Dreigroschenoper/The Threepenny Opera* led to a law suit which Weill won. Political controversy embroiled his Franco-German co-production *Kameradschaft* (1931), a plea for solidarity among the international working class. In the 1930s Pabst worked regularly in France, where, apart from scriptwriting and 'technical supervision' on a number of projects, he directed some French versions of his German films and completed four French films – *Don Quichotte/Don Quixote* (1933), *Mademoiselle Docteur* (1936), *Le Drame de Shanghai* (1938) and *Jeunes filles en détresse* (1939) – before moving to Hollywood. After one unsuccessful picture and an aborted project, he returned to France and then to Austria at the outbreak of World War II. He spent the next six years in Germany, making three intriguing films under the Nazi regime (*Komödianten*, 1941; *Paracelsus*, 1943; *Der Fall Molander*, 1945), which severely damaged his international reputation. His first film after the war, however, was a denunciation of anti-semitism, and several of his subsequent melodramas probed the phenomenon

of Nazi Germany (*Der letzte Akt/The Last Ten Days*, 1955; *Es geschah am 20. Juli/Jackboot Mutiny*, 1955). MW/TE

Bib: Eric Rentschler (ed.), *G. W. Pabst: An Extraterritorial Cinema* (1990).

PAGNOL, Marcel   Aubagne 1895 – Paris 1974

French director, writer and producer, who contributed more than anyone to the promotion of Provençal culture. A young English teacher from Marseilles, he wrote successful plays and novels in the 1920s and launched his own short-lived magazine, *Les Cahiers du film*, to disseminate his enthusiasm for sound cinema. His first film, *Marius* (1931, based on his own play and directed by Alexander Korda*), was a triumph; *Fanny* (1932, directed by Marc Allégret*) and *César* (1936) likewise. The universe of this 'Pagnol trilogy', as it became known, was steeped in the humorous folklore of the 'little people' of Marseilles; the key to its success was nostalgia, but also wonderful performances by Raimu*, Pierre Fresnay*, Charpin and Orane Demazis, coupled with the primacy of dialogue and the southern accent. A darker side to Pagnol's work drew on an older Mediterranean culture, that of the rural drama reflected in *Jofroi* (1933), *Angèle* (1934) and *Regain/Harvest* (1937). These melodramas were grounded in the same archaic patriarchal values as the trilogy, but they swapped theatricality for location shooting and have been recognised as influential on neo-realism*. Pagnol's activities were awesome: not content with being a film-maker, writer and journalist, he was also a producer, studio and cinema owner. The populist universe of the trilogy was seen again in *La Femme du boulanger/The Baker's Wife* (1938) and *La Fille du puisatier/The Well-Digger's Daughter* (1940). There was a musical with Tino Rossi (*La Belle meunière*, 1948), but Pagnol's activities then slowed down. His penultimate rural drama, *Manon des sources* (1953), was remade by Claude Berri* in 1986.

Pagnol's work has often been criticised as 'filmed theatre';

323

in fact, like Sacha Guitry's*, it shows a sophisticated aware-ness of the relation between film and the stage. Pagnol received the highest cultural accolade of membership of the Académie Française in 1946, but his epitaph as popular entertainer comes from his own *Le Schpountz* (1937): 'The man who amuses those who have so many reasons to cry [...] is loved like a benefactor.' GV

PAGU (PROJECTIONS AG 'UNION')

German film company. Founded by Paul Davidson*, and the first fully integrated film company in Germany, PAGU started as a chain of cinemas all over Germany in 1906, and by 1911 had branched out into distribution, initially to secure the exclusive rights to Asta Nielsen's* films. In 1913 Davidson added a film studio near Berlin, specifically to produce the lucrative Nielsen films (directed by Urban Gad). Both Davidson's luxurious 'Union-Theaters' (UT) and his PAGU films, which relied heavily on subjects from literature, were designed to appeal to middle-class tastes. Attendance at UT movie theatres rose from 2.5 million to 6 million between 1911 and 1913 and the cinema chain was sold in 1917, later becoming part of Ufa*. His hands free, Davidson concentrated on production, picking a winner with Ernst Lubitsch*. In 1918, Ufa bought the majority of PAGU's shares but left Davidson to operate it as an independent company. Lubitsch and Davidson made lavish productions such as *Madame Dubarry/Passion* (1919) and *Anna Boleyn* (1920) under Ufa's auspices. Integrated into the Ufa empire in 1926, PAGU ceased to be registered as a separate company. JG/TE

PAJARES, Andrés   Andrés Pajares Martín; Madrid 1940

Spanish actor, working in theatre before appearing in films from the late 1960s onwards, often with Fernando Esteso*. His more regular leading man features make him less of a buffoon than Esteso in films like Mariano Ozores'* *El currante/The Worker* (1983). More recently, he has attempted to modify the farcical aspects of his persona in Luis García Berlanga's* *Moros y cristianos/Moors and Christians* (1987) and, especially, in Carlos Saura's* *¡Ay, Carmela!* (1990, co-starring Carmen Maura* and Gabino Diego*), where his portrayal of the entertainer caught in the crossfire of the Civil War elicited a moving dignity untapped in his earlier popular comedies. PWE

PAKKASVIRTA, Jaakko   Simpele 1934

Finnish director. An actor in the late 1950s, Pakkasvirta was a founding member of Filminor*, which produced his first two features (*Yö vai päivä/Night or Day*, 1962, co-dir. Risto Jarva*; *X-Paroni/Baron X*, 1963, co-dir. Jarva and Spede Pasanen). *Vihreä leski/Green Widow* (1968), a portrait of a suburban housewife, and *Kesäkapina/Summer Rebellion* (1970), a critique of consumerism, were both inspired by Jean-Luc Godard*. In the 1970s Pakkasvirta continued experimenting with modernist political cinema, making films for workers' unions and with workers themselves (*Punainen Helsinki/Red Helsinki*, 1971). His portrait of a construction worker, *Jouluksi kotiin/Home for Christmas* (1975), was in a more realistic idiom. *Runoilija ja muusa/Poet and Muse* (1978) and *Pedon merkki/Sign of the Beast* (1980) both comment on the 'national mythology', the former examining Eino Leino, the Finnish national poet, while the latter dealt with the Finnish struggle against Russia during World War II. *Ulvova mylläri/The Howling Miller* (1982), with Vesa-Matti Loiri as leading actor, projected a typical Finnish male escape fantasy of northern Finland as an 'authentic' world away from modern society. Male alienation was also the theme of Pakkasvirta's *Linna/The Castle* (1986), an adaptation of Kafka's novel. AK

PALLADIUM

Danish production company. Palladium was founded in 1921 by Svend Nielsen, with Lau Lauritzen* as artistic director. The same year, Lauritzen created the comic duo 'Fyrtaarnet og Bivognen'*, played by Carl Schenstrøm and Harald Madsen. From the very first film in the series, *Film, Flirt og Forlovelse/Film, Flirt and Engagement* (1921), the comics were a great hit both at home and abroad, and from then on the company concentrated exclusively on the Schenstrøm/Madsen films. Lauritzen himself directed three or four of them every year until 1925, when he and the actors went to Spain to shoot *Don Quixote* (released in 1926). Meanwhile Nielsen hired other directors, including Carl Theodor Dreyer*. After his return from Spain, Lauritzen continued to direct 'Fyrtaarnet og Bivognen' films while other directors such as Urban Gad experimented with them too (the last was made in 1940). With the coming of sound, the export of Danish films virtually ceased, and Palladium produced films mainly for the home market. The studio closed down in 1970, though the company still exists as a distributor. ME

PALO, Tauno   Hämeenlinna 1908 – Helsinki 1982

Finnish actor. Tauno Palo was the most popular male star of the Finnish studio era, acting in more than sixty films from the early 1930s to the 1970s. He was discovered in a Helsinki theatre, and his first major film role was in *Jääkärin morsian/The Infantryman's Bride* (1931). During the 1930s Palo's success developed in 'modern', sophisticated comedies such as *Vaimoke/Substitute Wife* (1936). His frequent co-star was Ansa Ikonen*, with whom he formed the classic Finnish screen couple. Their collaboration reached a high point in *Kulkurin valssi/The Vagabond's Waltz* (1941), a film full of glamour, gypsy romanticism and music for the deprived audiences of the war years. Singing was an essential part of the Palo–Ikonen star image, although both also performed in dramatic roles and on stage. Palo's exceptional status among Finnish male stars was due to his wide range: he could be the ideal hero (*Helmikuun manifesti/The February Manifesto*, 1939) or the cold-blooded criminal (*Hilja – maitotyttö/Hilja – The Milkmaid*, 1953), factory boss or shopfloor worker, settler or landowner, farmhand or city dweller. The complexity of his star image is reflected in the fact that he was an icon both of straightforward Finnish manhood *and* of 'Mediterranean' sexuality and exoticism. This contradiction is well developed in *Herra ja ylhäisyys/Lord and Master* (1944), in which he plays a Finnish-born officer fighting in the Mexican army. KL

PAMPANINI, Silvana   Rome 1925

Italian actress. Silvana Pampanini studied singing and piano at the Santa Cecilia Conservatory. In 1946 she was runner-up in the first postwar Miss Italy competition and was promptly offered her first (small) screen roles. She became one of the most popular actresses of the generation immediately preceding the so-called '*maggiorate fisiche*' ('physically amply endowed' women) actresses, such as Gina Lollobrigida* and Sophia Loren*. A lively and imposing brunette, she played vamps, courtesans and elegant ladies in a series of B-quality films churned out at the rate of about ten a year. Deploying a seemingly irrepressible sensuality, she had a talent for both dramatic roles (Luigi Zampa's* *Processo alla città*, 1952; Giuseppe De Santis'* *Un marito per Anna Zaccheo*, 1953; Abel Gance's* *La Tour de Nesle/La torre di Nesle*, 1955) and comedy (Mario Soldati's* *O.K. Nerone*, 1951; Luigi Comencini's* *La bella di Roma*, 1955). In 1958 she directed a twenty-minute documentary on Giuseppe Verdi, and in her honour the actor Totò* wrote one his most beautiful songs, 'Malafemmina' ('wicked woman'). Although still enjoying success abroad, especially in Spain, her popularity in Italy suddenly declined at the end of the 1950s; she returned as the ex-*diva* in Dino Risi's* *Il gaucho* (1964) and made a brief comeback appearance in Alberto Sordi's* *Il tassinaro* (1983). MMo

PANFILOV, Gleb A.   Magnitogorsk, Russia [USSR] 1934

Russian director and scriptwriter. While working as a chemical engineer after completing his studies at the Urals Polytechnic Institute, Panfilov saw Mikhail Kalatozov's* *Letyat zhuravli/The Cranes are Flying* (1957), and this led him to a correspondence course in cinema and work in Sverdlovsk [Yekaterinburg] television. From 1960 to 1963 he studied cinematography at VGIK*, and in 1966 he completed the Higher Courses for Directors. His first feature *V ogne broda net/No Crossing under Fire* (1967), the story of a young woman whose commitment to the Revolution leads to her discovery of a talent as a painter, gave a first starring role to Panfilov's wife, Inna Churikova. Churikova's remarkable talent is visible too in *Nachalo/The Debut* (or *The Beginning*, 1970), in which she plays an ordinary woman chosen to play Joan of Arc in a film; and in *Proshu slova/I Wish to Speak* (1973), in which she is the head of the soviet of a provincial town whose Party idealism is tested by the death of her teenage son. *Tema/The Theme* (1979), the story of a conformist writer forced to confront his own compromises, was shelved for seven years. During that time Panfilov shot *Valentina* (1981) from a play by Alexander Vampilov, about

the life of a young waitress in a Siberian village café. In recent years Panfilov has made two grandiose films from the work of Maxim Gorky, both starring Churikova. *Vassa* (1983), from the play *Vassa Zheleznova*, is a pre-Revolutionary family melodrama. It was followed by Panfilov's epic version of the novel *Mat'/The Mother* (1990). JGf

PAPAS, Irene   Irini Lelekou; Chiliomodion, Corinth 1926

Greek actress. Irene Papas is one of the few Greek actresses to have sustained a successful international career. She joined the Royal Drama School in Athens at the age of twelve, performed in variety at sixteen and made her film debut in 1948, in *Hameni angeli/Lost Angels*. Her striking features and vitality attracted the attention of foreign film-makers, and soon she was given parts in Italian and American films. Her international reputation was sealed by her appearance in *Zorba the Greek* (1964, dir. Michael Cacoyannis*). Papas has excelled in the interpretation of classical tragedy. However, she often carries her theatrical style into her other roles, resulting in caricatures of female 'Greekness' and Mediterranean mother-figures. Her best performance is still as the widow of the slain political activist in Costa-Gavras'* *Z* (1969). TNe

Other Films Include: *Nekri politia/Dead City* (1951); *Le Infideli* (1953, It.); *Tribute to a Bad Man* (1956, US); *Antigone, The Guns of Navarone* [UK] (1961); *Electra* (1962); *Anne of the Thousand Days* (1969, UK); *The Trojan Women* (1971, US); *Moses* (1975, It./UK); *Mohammad: Messenger of God/The Message* (1976, Lebanon); *Iphigenia* (1977); *Cristo si e fermato a Eboli/Christ Stopped at Eboli* (1980, It.); *Into the Night* (1985, US); *High Season* [UK], *Cronaca di una morte annunciata/Chronicle of a Death Foretold* [It.] (1988); *Pano, kato ke plagios/Up, Down and Sideways* (1993).

PAPATAKIS, Nikos   Addis Ababa, Ethiopia 1918

French-based Greek director; also nightclub owner. Papatakis started his film career in 1962, since when he has made just five films. A permanent resident in Paris, where he founded the left-bank nightclub 'La Rose Rouge', he divides his film activities between France and Greece. He collaborated with John Cassavetes on the latter's first film. Papatakis' films are essays on the drive to succeed (*I fotografia/The Photograph*, 1987) and power relations. Rebellion against authority is a running theme, from his first film, *Les Abysses* (1963), based on the case of the Papin sisters, two maids who savagely killed their employer, and on which Jean Genet based his play *Les Bonnes/The Maids*, to his latest (*Les Equilibristes*, 1991). The theme changed its form significantly over the thirty intervening years, however. By 1991, the open, explosive rebellion of *Les Abysses* had become impossible, and the only possibility seemed to be self-destructive implosion. TN

Other Films: *I voski tis simforas/The Shepherds of Confusion* (1968); *Gloria Mundi* (1975).

PARADZHANOV, Sergo Tbilisi, Georgia [USSR]
1924 – Yerevan, Armenia 1990

Armenian Soviet director. Graduated from VGIK*, where he studied with Igor Savchenko*, and made a number of Ukrainian-language films, which he described as 'justified failures'. He first achieved international recognition with *Teni zabytykh predkov/Shadows of Our Forgotten Ancestors* (1965). All his subsequent films were infused with the spirit of folklore and ethnography: *Sayat Nova*, also known as *Tsvet granata/The Colour of Pomegranates* (1969), *Legenda o Suramskoi kreposti/The Legend of Suram Fortress* (1984), and *Ashik Kerib* (1988). In 1974, because of his heterodoxy, all his film projects were blocked and he was imprisoned on various trumped-up charges and released in 1978 only after an international protest campaign. Describing cinema as a 'synthetic art', he developed Sergei Eisenstein's* concepts, using colour, rhythm, music, dancing and montage to move away from plot-constrained structures. RT

PAREDES, Marisa María Luisa Paredes
Bartolomé; Madrid 1946

Spanish actress, with much stage experience, who started her film career in 1960. Her varied films include Pedro Lazaga's* *Los económicamente débiles/The Less Well-off* (1960), Fernando Fernán Gómez's* *El mundo sigue/Life Goes On* (1963) and José Luis Borau's* *Tata mía/Dear Nanny* (1986). She has recently risen to renewed prominence through two films – Pedro Almodóvar's* *Tacones lejanos/High Heels* (1991) and Jaime Chávarri's *Tierno verano de lujurias y azoteas/A Tender Summer of Lust on the Rooftops* (1993) – in which her self-consciously histrionic mannerisms and aura of steely control suit roles of self-absorbed *divas* slightly past their prime. PWE

PARKER, Alan London 1944

British director. Parker is one of a group of directors and producers, which includes Ridley Scott* and Tony Scott, Adrian Lyne, Hugh Hudson and David Puttnam*, who graduated from the British advertising industry in the late 1960s. His first feature, *Bugsy Malone* (1976), was a musical gangster spoof with an all-children cast, and with the sweet smell of success in his nostrils he turned to Hollywood. His next feature, *Midnight Express* (1978), scripted by Oliver Stone, won Academy Awards for Screenplay and Music Score, and a nomination for Best Director. Like a number of Parker's films, it is stronger on action and visual dynamism than on political sensitivity. Most of Parker's subsequent work has been in America, though he still plays the role of the Islington 'turnip-head' (his contribution to a 1986 television series on British cinema was called 'A Turnip-Head's Guide to British Cinema'), and enjoys an occasional round of anti-intellectualism with anyone who regards cinema as an intellectual activity. JC

Bib: Jonathan Hacker and David Price, *Take 10: Contemporary British Film Directors* (1991).

Other Films Include: *Fame* (1980, US); *Shoot the Moon* (1981, US); *Pink Floyd The Wall* (1982); *Birdy* (1984, US); *Angel Heart* (1987, US); *Mississippi Burning* (1988, US); *Come See the Paradise* (1990, US); *The Commitments* (1991, UK/Ir.).

PASOLINI, Pier Paolo Bologna 1922 – Ostia
1975

Italian director and writer. Pasolini spent most of his childhood in Friuli in the far north-east of Italy. As a young man he joined the Communist Party, but was expelled from it in 1949 for alleged homosexuality. In spite of his expulsion and his many subsequent public disagreements with the Party and with the rest of the left he continued proudly to regard himself as a Communist to the end of his life. In 1950 he set out for Rome, where he soon established a reputation with two volumes of poetry, *Le ceneri di Gramsci* (1957) and *La religione del mio tempo* (1961), and two novels making creative use of Roman dialect and slang, *Ragazzi di vita* (1955) and *Una vita violenta* (1959). His skill with vernacular dialogue brought him work in the film industry, notably on the script of Federico Fellini's* *Le notti di Cabiria/Cabiria/Nights of Cabiria* (1957).

Pasolini's first two films as director – *Accattone!* (1961) and *Mamma Roma* (1962) – had Roman low-life themes, but were distinguished by a strong utopian current. A short film, *La ricotta* ('Curd-cheese' – episode of the 1963 compilation film *RoGoPaG/Laviamoci il cervello*), featured a hilarious but far from malicious parody of the Deposition from the Cross which led to charges of blasphemy. By contrast *Il Vangelo secondo Matteo/The Gospel According to Saint Matthew* (1964) was a stark and sober retelling of the Gospel according to Matthew, which earned him the inaccurate label of Catholic-Marxist – in fact his Marxism was as heterodox as his attitude to religion was ambivalent. He was interested in what he called 'the sacred' (*sacrale*), but increasingly located this quality in primitive religion and myth. In his 'unpopular' films of the late 1960s – *Edipo re/Oedipus Rex* (1967), *Porcile/Pigsty* (1969) and *Medea* (1970) – he explored mythic notions of the transition from primitivism to civilisation, to the implied disadvantage of the latter. His own utopias were located as far away as possible from the modern, capitalist, bourgeois world of which he felt himself a member and a victim – either downwards (among the peasantry and sub-proletariat), outwards (in southern Italy, Africa, the Arab world, India), or backwards in time (in the Middle Ages or pre-classical Greece).

In the 1960s his longstanding interest in language drew him to semiotics, and he attempted to theorise his approach to cinema in a number of essays (available in English in *Heretical Empiricism*, 1988). He argued that film language has a natural base in reality, which is endowed with meaning when the film-maker turns it into signs. But his own film work is far from naturalistic. Eschewing narrative continuity, Pasolini concentrates on single, powerful images whose expressivity seems independent of 'reality' as ordinarily conceived. What underlies them, however, is a desperate search for a pre-symbolic emotional truth which modern man can no longer grasp. From the mid-1960s onwards Pasolini's films were mostly set either in the past or, in the case of *Appunti di viaggio per un film sull'India* (1968) and *Appunti per un'Orestiade africana* (1970), in far-off places. The exceptions are *Teorema/Theorem* (1968), a brutal dissection of the bourgeois family, the 'modern' section of *Porcile*, and a few shorts. In 1970 he embarked on a series of films based on medieval tales – *Il decamerone/The Decameron* (1971), *I raconti di Canterbury/The Canterbury Tales* (1972), and *Il fiore delle mille e una notte/The Arabian Nights* (1973). Though all three films (especially *The Canterbury Tales*) have their darker side, this so-called 'trilogy of life' was widely interpreted as a celebration of a lost world of joyful and innocent sexuality. Pasolini, however, repudiated this interpretation and indeed the films themselves. Increasingly convinced that 'sexual liberation' (including gay liberation) was a sham, he turned in his journalism to a fierce denunciation of contemporary sexual mores. Having courted unpopularity on the left for his criticisms of the radical students of 1968, he compounded it with his opposition to the liberalisation of Italy's archaic abortion law, though he had to beat a hasty retreat. Then in 1975 he made *Salò o le 120 giornate di Sodoma/Salò*, setting de Sade's novel in the last years of Fascism in Italy, explicitly linking fascism and sadism, sexual licence and oppression. *Salò* was to be his last film. On the morning of 2 November 1975, his battered body was discovered on waste ground near the seaside resort of Ostia (a site revisited in Nanni Moretti's* *Caro diario/Dear Diary*, 1993), outside Rome. Controversy continues to surround this brutal murder, for which a young male prostitute was tried and convicted in 1976. GNS

Bib: Maurizio Viano, *A Certain Realism: Making Use of Pasolini's Film Theory and Practice* (1993).

Other Films Include: *La rabbia* (1963); *Comizi d'amore, Sopralluoghi in Palestina* (1964); *Le streghe/The Witches* (ep. *La terra vista dalla luna*), *Uccellacci e uccellini/The Hawks and the Sparrows* (1966); *Capriccio all'italiana* (ep. *Che cosa sono le nuvole?*), *Amore e rabbia* (1968, ep. *La sequenza del fiore di carta*); *12 Dicembre* (1972).

PASSER, Ivan   Prague 1933

Czech director. Educated at FAMU*, Passer began his career as an assistant on films by Ladislav Helge, Zbyněk Brynych and Vojtěch Jasný* before collaborating with Miloš Forman* on all four of his principal Czech films. He directed a short film, *Fádní odpoledne/A Boring Afternoon*, in 1964, and a feature, *Intimní osvětlení/Intimate Lightning*, in 1965. Adapted from a story by Bohumil Hrabal, *Fádní odpoledne* is a beautifully observed study of an afternoon in a Prague pub, focusing on the minutiae of life in a way that is both captivating and lyrical. *Intimní osvětlení* is the story of a weekend in the country where two musicians meet and reflect on the meaning of life. Almost without plot, its gentle observation of the mundane seems a logical extension from the style of Forman's early films. Passer left Czechoslovakia in 1968 for a career in the US, where his films have assumed quite differ-

ent forms. Films such as *Law and Disorder* (1974) and *Silver Bears* (1978) are interesting satires on modern corruption, but his best-known works are *Born to Win* (1971), an unusual approach to the drug scene, and *Cutter's Way* (also *Cutter and Bone*, 1981), a classic *film noir* that is also a disturbing portrait of the post-Vietnam experience. PH

Other Films Include: *Crime and Passion* [also *An Ace Up My Sleeve*] (1976); *Creator* (1985); *Haunted Summer* (1988); *Stalin* [TV] (1992).

PASTERNAK, Iosif   Kiev, Ukraine [USSR] 1950

Russian documentary director. After studies at the Kiev Conservatoire, Pasternak worked from 1973 at the Kiev Nauchfilm Studios, before moving to Mosfilm in 1983. His *Chërnyi kvadrat/The Black Square* (1988) surveys the experience of the nonconformist artists of the 1960s–80s, and provides a striking visual record of their work, while its archival footage of the Stalin and Khrushchev periods expands the analysis of the relationship between artists and power to cover the entire Soviet period. *Alexandre Galich: Moscou-Paris/Aleksandr Galich: Izgnanie/Alexander Galich: Exile* (1989) uses the fate of the exiled poet to examine the history of the Soviet emigration. Since 1990 Pasternak has made documentaries for French television, including *De la petite Russie à l'Ukraine/From Little Russia to Ukraine* (1990); *Moscou* (1990), showing the city as imagined by the Russian avant-garde artist Francisco Infante; and *Moscou: Trois jours en août/Moscow: Three Days in August* (1991), which contains remarkable footage shot inside the Moscow White House during the abortive 1991 coup. His most recent film, *Le Fantôme Efremov/The Phantom of Efremov* (1992), visits a typical central Russian town to discover how little it was affected by the events of 1991. JGf

PASTRONE, Giovanni   Piero Fosco; Asti 1883 – Turin 1959

Italian director and producer. Starting his career in 1905 on the administrative and technical side of the film industry in Turin, Pastrone was one of the moving spirits of the Itala film company. In 1908 he went to Paris and enticed the successful Pathé* comedian André Deed* to join Itala, under the name Cretinetti. Graduating to production and direction, he scored a hit with the early spectacular *La caduta di Troia/The Fall of Troy* (1912) and an even greater one with *Cabiria* (1914), the film in which the character of Maciste* made his first appearance in Italian cinema. He went on to direct a number of other films, including *Tigre reale* (1916), adapted from the story by Giovanni Verga, and a sonorised version of *Cabiria* (1931). But it was as producer and studio organiser that he made his greatest impact. From 1910 onwards he rationalised production at Itala, kept its finances in order by balancing safe successes such as *Cretinetti* comedies with more ambitious productions, experimented with colour, and hired Segundo de Chomón* from Pathé to develop the company's special effects department. Even Pastrone's gift for management, however, could not save Itala from the crisis which ensued in the early 1920s, and the company went into liquidation until resurrected by Stefano Pittaluga* at the end of the decade. GNS

PATHÉ, Charles   Chevry-Cossigny 1863 – Monaco 1957

French pioneer, arguably the world's first 'movie mogul', who became the head of the most powerful film company in France. The son of modest parents, Charles Pathé was a brilliant entrepreneur who exploited Edison's phonograph and Kinetoscope by selling counterfeit copies of the latter made in Britain by R. W. Paul*. With his associate Henri Joly, Pathé produced a film in October 1895. He then switched to marketing the Lumière* Cinematograph and founded Pathé Frères with his brother Emile in September 1896. The company prospered as Pathé applied modern business principles to the emerging entertainment form. It expanded vertically – into equipment, film stock manufacture and processing, exhibition and film-making, with factories, laboratories and studios near Paris – and internationally, from 1902 taking its Gallic cockerel logo to the far corners of the earth. In 1907 it switched from sale to rental, inaugurating modern film distribution.

Charles Pathé's reputation is that of a businessman with little interest in films. However, like his rival Léon Gaumont*, he shaped French and world cinema. Through his team of film-makers (Ferdinand Zecca, Alfred Machin, Louis Gasnier, René Leprince, Albert Capellani, Segundo de Chomón* and many others) Pathé codified early film genres: burlesque chase films – precursors of Mack Sennett – and comic series with Prince-Rigadin* and André Deed*, and created the first major international star of French cinema, Max Linder*. He commissioned scientific films, produced newsreels, serials and melodramas, trick films and *féeries* (fantasies), and the literary adaptations of the Film d'Art*. Pathé produced newsreels (Pathé-News) and shot serials in America during World War I, but the war damaged the Pathé empire. Branches closed down from 1920, and French operations were reduced to film stock and equipment. The diminished company was taken over by Bernard Natan in 1929, a year before Pathé retired. Natan, a Romanian émigré involved in pornographic film, created Pathé-Natan, which until 1935 was a relatively successful mainstream production outfit. Recession and fraud brought the company down, however. (Natan was tried for fraud and later died in a concentration camp; it has recently been suggested that he may have been a scapegoat for politicians who had covertly enjoyed his pornographic movies). Pathé-Cinéma was bailed out during the war, and the name Pathé survives to this day in production, newsreels and exhibition, though with only distant links to the original company.

Charles Pathé said, 'I did not invent the cinema, I industrialised it'; his genius was precisely to understand the industrial dimension without which it could not have become the art or educational form he also predicted: 'Cinema will be the theatre, the newspaper and the school of tomorrow.' GV

Bib: Jacques Kermabon (ed.), *Pathé, premier empire du cinéma* (1995).

PATZAK, Peter   Vienna 1945

Austrian director, who has worked in film and television since the 1970s. His attempts to establish a political cinema in Austria connect him with the 'New Austrian Cinema' of Franz Novotny*, Wolfgang Glück and Wolfram Paulus*. With writer Helmut Zenker, Patzak created the popular television detective series *Kottan ermittelt* (1976–84), built round a fictional Viennese police officer, Kottan, and his eccentric team. *Kottan* contains a great deal of slapstick, references to popular culture and anarchic parodies of Austrian clichés and genre conventions. Patzak has also made literary adaptations (*Die Försterbuben*, 1984), social dramas such as *Kassbach* (1979), the portrait of a petit-bourgeois and his latent fascism, and action thrillers (*Killing Blue*, 1988). He has worked with international stars such as Elliott Gould (*Strawanzer*, 1983, Aust./Ger.) and Eddie Constantine* (*Tiger – Frühling in Wien*, 1984, Aust./Ger.). Fascist attitudes in everyday life, hatred of foreigners and political corruption are Patzak's subjects, while his use of dialect and lower-class heroes, as well as borrowings from classic cinematic genres, have attracted a wide audience. He is one of the few recent Austrian directors to have produced films with regularity. IR/AL

Bib: AG Film (eds.), *Peter Patzak, Filme* (1983).

Other Films Include: *Situation* (1973); *Phönix an der Ecke* (1982); *Der Joker* (1987); *Im Kreis der Iris* (1992).

PAUL, R. W.   London 1869–1943

British pioneer inventor and producer, who may be responsible for the first British 'made-up film', *The Soldier's Courtship*, a comic narrative scene made in March 1896, and for the first covered studio, which he built at Sydney Road, New Southgate, London in 1899. Paul was an instrument maker, whose camera design, according to Barry Salt, was the one used by Georges Méliès* for superimpositions and who invented the first panning head to allow him to film the processions at Queen Victoria's Diamond Jubilee in 1897. His interest in film was scientific rather than artistic, and he retired from film in 1910, returning to instrument making and other scientific interests. JC

Bib: Barry Salt, *Film Style and Technology: History and Analysis* (1983).

PAULUS, Wolfram   Grossarl, Salzburg 1957

Austrian director, scriptwriter and editor. An exponent of 'New Austrian Cinema', Paulus started by making short films. His first feature, the black-and-white *Heidenlöcher* (1985), based on a true story from the Nazi period, was set in a mountain village in the Salzburg province. It uses local dialect and mainly amateur actors and was described as a 'New *Heimatfilm*' [> HEIMATFILM], winning many prizes. Paulus' work aims at a deromanticised (though poetic), culturally and sociologically based image of life in the countryside, with its routines and conflicts, in contrast to the glossy representations of the 1950s and 1960s. It deals with the devastating impact of tourism on rural communities and with conflicts related to Catholicism, as well as with neglected parts of Austrian history of the 1930s and 1940s, with its 'everyday' fascism. Paulus' second and third features, *Nachsaison/Off Season* (1987) and *Ministranten/The Altar Boys* (1990, the story of schoolboys in the 1960s who form a gang in a rural valley), continued in the same vein but in a less radical form. *Du bringst mich noch um/You're Driving Me Crazy* (1994) represents his attempt at a new orientation: it is a comedy with urban surroundings and professional actors, and more literary dialogue. SS

PAVLENKO, Pyotr A.
St Petersburg 1899 – Moscow 1951

Russian writer and scriptwriter. Pavlenko co-scripted Sergei Eisenstein's* *Aleksandr Nevskii/Alexander Nevsky* (1938), Mikhail Chiaureli's* *Klyatva/The Vow* (1946) and *Padenie Berlina/The Fall of Berlin* (1949), and Grigori Alexandrov's* *Kompozitor Glinka/The Composer Glinka* (1952). He was elected to the USSR Supreme Soviet and awarded a Stalin Prize in 1948. RT

PAVLOVIĆ, Živojin
Šabac, Serbia 1933

Serbian director and writer. A leading figure of the Yugoslav 'Black Wave'*, Pavlović discovered movie treasures in the Belgrade film archive during his studies of decorative painting in the late 1950s. He soon began to give lectures, travelling around Serbia and talking about films. He never lost his intimate contact with the realities of provincial life, but he was at the same time capable of transforming them into cinematographic moments of truth. His existentialism is evident in two of the most interesting Yugoslav films of the 1960s: *Budjenje pacova/Awakening of the Rats* and *Kad budem mrtav i beo/When I am Dead and White* (both 1967). Both films are tragic and depressive – so depressive that Pavlović was subsequently deprived of work by the communist authorities for more than fifteen years. He 'escaped' to Slovenia, where he directed two rural dramas (*Rdeče klasje/Red Wheat*, 1971; *Let mrtve ptice/Dead Bird's Flight*, 1973) and a controversial evocation of war, *Nasvidenje v naslednji vojni/Farewell Until the Next War* (1980), based on a best-selling Slovene novel by Vitomil Zupan [> YUGOSLAV 'PARTISAN FILMS']. The prophetic title of this film became true ten years later, when the rest of what used to be Yugoslavia was plunged into bloodshed. Pavlović did not hesitate to choose Vukovar, a Croatian town razed to the ground by Serb forces, as a location for *Dezerter/Deserter* (1992). SP

Other Films: *Neprijatelj/The Enemy* (1965); *Povratak/Homecoming* (1966); *Zaseda/Ambush* (1969); *Hajka/Pursuit*

(1977); *Zadah tela/Body Scent* (1983); *Na putu za Katangu/On the Road to Katanga* (1987).

PAXINOU, Katina
Katina Konstandopoulou; Piraeus 1900 – Athens 1973

Greek actress. Katina Paxinou was an exceptional actress, the leading performer of Greek classical tragedy. She began her career as an opera singer but turned to the theatre in 1929, soon joining the Greek National Theatre. At the start of World War II she was performing in London. Unable to return to Greece, she moved to the US, where she gained international fame (and an Oscar for best supporting actress) for her powerful portrayal of Pilar in *For Whom the Bell Tolls* (1943). She featured in several Hollywood productions before returning to Greece, where she and her husband Alexis Minotis established the Royal Theatre of Athens, which became one of the most celebrated theatre companies in Europe. She continued to appear sporadically in films, notably Luchino Visconti's* *Rocco e i suoi Fratelli/Rocco and His Brothers* (1960), but her main concern was the theatre. TNe

Other Films Include: in the US: *Hostages* (1943); *Confidential Agent* (1945); *Mourning Becomes Electra* (1947); *Mr Arkadin* (1955); *The Miracle* (1959); **in France**: *Tante Zita/Zita* (1968); *Un été sauvage* (1970).

PEARSON, George
London 1875 – Malvern 1973

British director, who entered the film industry from school-teaching in 1912. During the early years of World War I, he made 'topicals' such as *Incidents of the Great European War* (1914), and directed the six-reel *A Study in Scarlet* (1914). He created the 'Ultus' thriller series, encouraged by Léon Gaumont* to duplicate the success of Louis Feuillade's* *Fantômas* series in France. In 1918, Pearson formed the Welsh-Pearson Company with his partner, Thomas Welsh. His popularity was ensured when he discovered Betty Balfour*, the most successful female star of the 1920s, and launched her into the 'Squibs' series. Pearson, however, aspired to an artistic cinema in films like *Love, Life and Laughter* (1923) and, particularly, *Reveille* (1924), claimed by one critic as 'the greatest achievement of the British silent cinema'. *The Little People* (1926) was made in France with Thorold Dickinson* as assistant and Alberto Cavalcanti* as designer, and his adaptation of John Buchan's *Huntingtower* (1927) had Sir Harry Lauder as the retired Glasgow grocer, Dickson McCunn. Pearson was relegated to 'quota quickies' during the 1930s, but joined the Colonial Film Unit in 1940 and used his experience to train a new generation of film-makers. JC

Bib: George Pearson, *Flashback: An Autobiography of a British Film Maker* (1957).

PEPLUM

Italian genre. The peplum was a cycle of internationally successful Italian adventure films running from *Le fatiche di Ercole/The Labours of Hercules/Hercules* in 1958 to c. 1965. There had been a comparable cycle from *Quo Vadis?* (1912) to c. 1926, and Italian cinema has produced historical spectaculars throughout its history. The term refers to the short skirt worn by the heroes. These heroes are drawn from the ancient world: Hercules, Spartacus, Samson and, most popular of all, Maciste*, invented for *Cabiria* (1914). Peplum heroes range freely, and without explanation, from classical antiquity to prehistoric times (for example *Maciste l'uomo più forte del mondo/Maciste the Strongest Man in the World/The Mole Men Battle the Son of Hercules*, 1961), through non-Western ancient worlds (Aztec civilisation in *Ercole contro i figli del sole/Hercules versus the Sons of the Sun*, 1964) to more recent history (such as seventeenth-century Scotland in *Maciste all'inferno/Maciste in Hell/The Witch's Curse*, 1962). They are played by body-builders, who either were from the US (notably Steve Reeves) or appeared to be so (Adriano da Venezia, for instance, became Kirk Morris). The peplum affirmed the worth of male physical strength in a rapidly industrialising society and addressed the fascist imagery of the superhero, often condemning totalitarian societies while asserting the need for strong, white male leadership. The cycle's comic-book qualities (one-dimensional imagery, freedom to range in time and space), its energy and fun, continue to give it a cult status. RD

Bib: Domenico Cammarota, *Il cinema peplum* (1987).

PERESTIANI, Ivan N.   Taganrog, Ukraine [Russian Empire] 1870 – Moscow 1959

Georgian Soviet director, scriptwriter and actor. A stage actor from 1886 and in cinema from 1916, he played about twenty roles before the 1917 Revolution. Perestiani made agit-films* during the Civil War and taught at VGIK*. He directed the first Soviet Georgian feature *Arsen Dzhordzhiashvili* (1921) but is best remembered for *Krasnye d'yavolyata/The Little Red Devils* (1923), in which he used the techniques of the American adventure film to tell a revolutionary tale, thus appealing to a broad and youthful audience. After working in Odessa and Armenia, Perestiani returned to Tbilisi in 1933 and subsequently concentrated on acting and scriptwriting for the Georgian studios. RT

PETERSEN, Wolfgang   Emden 1941

German director. A graduate of the Deutsche Film und Fernsehakademie Berlin, Petersen directed numerous television productions, notably thrillers for the popular crime series *Tatort*, before making his first feature film, *Einer von uns beiden* (1973), a solid, professionally crafted piece of story-telling. Hired by producer Günther Rohrbach, he turned the big-budget WDR/Bavaria production *Das Boot/The Boat* (1981) into one of the German cinema's rare

international box-office hits. Petersen's follow-up, the most expensive film ever made in Germany (*Die unendliche Geschichte/The Never-Ending Story*, 1984), was shot in English, becoming his passport to Hollywood, where Petersen seems set to remain a successful director of thrillers (*Shattered*, 1991; *In the Line of Fire*, 1993, *Outbreak*, 1994). MW

PETRI, Elio   Rome 1929–82

Italian director. After a stint as a junior official in the Italian Communist Party, Petri worked for the Communist daily *L'Unità*, where his functions included that of assistant film critic. He found his way into cinema thanks to Giuseppe De Santis*, for whom he carried out the investigation that was to serve as a basis for *Roma ore 11* (1952), and with whom he worked as scriptwriter. He also co-wrote scripts with Carlo Lizzani*, Puccini and Dino Risi* (*I mostri/The Monsters*, 1963). In 1961 he directed his first film, *L'assassino*, an anti-realist thriller with an acid – even Kafkaesque – vein. The same taste for mixing genres (in particular realism and Antonioni*-style symbolism) can be found in his following film, *I giorni contati* (1962), starring the excellent stage actor Salvo Randone. Petri was less successful with 'fantastic' plots (*La decima vittima/The 10th Victim*, 1965) or manifestly metaphysical ones (*Un tranquillo posto di campagna/A Quiet Place in the Country*, 1968). With scriptwriter Ugo Pirro*, however, he found the perfect blend of allegory and politics. Together they made *A ciascuno il suo/To Each His Own* (1967), a story of the Sicilian mafia adapted from a Leonardo Sciascia novel, and *Indagine su un cittadino al di sopra di ogni sospetto/Investigation of a Citizen Above Suspicion* (1969, Oscar for best foreign film), about a petit-bourgeois character (skilfully played by Gian Maria Volonté*) who gives authoritarian vent to his sexual inhibitions and bureaucratic conformism. But after *La classe operaia va in paradiso/Lulu the Tool* (1971, Palme d'or at Cannes) and *La proprietà non è più un furto* (1973), Petri's work degenerated into a compendium of all the vices of Italian 'leftist cinema', whether in their tendency towards increasingly stylised and mannered characters, or in their unnecessarily virulent pessimism, as can be seen in his last films, *Todo modo* (1976, again from Sciascia) and *Buone notizie* (1979, also known as *La stanza delle buone notizie*). PM

Other Films Include: *Il maestro di Vigevano* (1963); *Alta infedeltà* (ep. *Peccato nel pomeriggio*, 1964).

PETROV, Valeri   Sofia 1920

Bulgarian writer, who contributed significantly to the artistic development of postwar Bulgarian cinema. Valeri Petrov took up freelance writing in 1956 and became famous a few years later through his collaboration with director Rangel Vălčanov* on the breakthrough film *Na malkija ostrov/On a Small Island* (1958). He collaborated with Vălčanov on two more films, *Părvi urok/First Lesson* (1960) and *Slănceto i sjankata/Sun and Shadow* (1962); and these three films were hailed internationally as evidence of a poetic awakening in Bulgarian cinema.

When the Bulgarian 'new wave' ground to a halt shortly after the downfall of Khrushchev, Petrov turned to writing poems, essays and plays, while also translating Shakespeare into modern Bulgarian for the stage. His penchant for writing stories and plays for children eventually brought him back to the Boyana* Studios in the mid-1960s: his scripts for Borislav Šaraliev's *Ricar bez bronja/Knight without Honour* (1966) proved to be such a commercial success among both young and adult audiences that children's films thereafter became a production factor at Boyana. More than a decade after he first worked with Vălčanov, Petrov collaborated with him again on *S ljubov i nežnost/With Love and Tenderness* (1978), in which an aging sculptor and a young girl confront bureaucrats, hangers-on and a cross-section of ordinary citizens enjoying the 'Black Sea Riviera'. But, attractive as the film was on the aesthetic level, its theme appeared outmoded at the time, a throwback to the 1950s when Bulgarian poetic realism* was in style.

Critics have speculated on how Bulgarian cinema might have developed, and been recognised abroad, had Petrov been able to devote more of his considerable talents to writing for the cinema. RH

PETROV, Vladimir M.   St Petersburg 1896 – Moscow 1966

Soviet director and scriptwriter, who studied acting at the Alexandrinsky Theatre in Petrograd and made his stage debut in 1917. Petrov worked with Gordon Craig in England in 1918 and went into film-making in 1925. He made a series of films for children and young people, beginning with *Zolotoi mëd/Golden Honey* (1928) and ending with *Fritz Bauer* (1930). His first great success was a film adaptation of Ostrovsky's play *Groza/The Storm* (1934). Petrov is principally remembered for his two-part historical epic *Pëtr I/Peter the Great* (1937–39), with Nikolai Cherkasov* as the tsarevich, which won the Grand Prix at the Paris International Exhibition in 1937 and the Stalin Prize in 1941. In 1944 he turned to the Napoleonic Wars with *Kutuzov* and in 1950 contributed to the Stalin cult with *Stalingradskaya bitva/The Battle of Stalingrad*. In his last films he concentrated on adaptations of the Russian classics from Gogol to Kuprin. RT

PETROVIĆ, Aleksandar   Paris, France 1929–94

Serbian director and scriptwriter. One of the most prominent film-makers of the former Yugoslavia, with Dušan Makavejev* and Emir Kusturica*. After film criticism and several documentaries, Petrović made two feature films – *Dvoje/Couple/When Love is Gone*, 1961, and *Dani/Days*, 1963 – clearly influenced by the French New Wave* tendency of deconstructing conventional narration into fragments of everyday life and love, and heralding a Yugoslav 'new wave' known as the 'Black Wave'*. His real breakthrough came in 1965 with *Tri/Three*, a complex interweaving of three stories reflecting on death. With his next film, *Skupljači perja/I Even Met Some Happy Gypsies* (1967), which shared the Special

Jury Prize at Cannes, Petrović achieved international recognition. He later needed this accolade, since his domestic career was in trouble: his adaptation of Bulgakov's novel *Majstor i Margarita/The Master and Margarita* (1972) was perceived as a direct offence to the communist regime, and Petrović was out of work for some time. Another scandal involving his student Lazar Stojanović's graduate film, *Plastic Jesus*, was used as an excuse to remove Petrović from the Belgrade Film Academy in 1973. His comeback should have been the European epic adaptation of Serbian writer Miloš Crnjanski's 'roman fleuve' *Seobe/Migrations* (1985, released 1994), but Petrović became embroiled in endless judicial procedures, financial problems and bad timing. SP

Other Films: *Jedini izlaz/The Only Way Out* (1958); *Biče skoro propast sveta/It Rains in My Village* (1968); *Gruppenbild mit Dame/Group Portrait with Lady* (1977, Ger./Fr.).

PHILIPE, Gérard   Cannes 1922 – Paris 1959

French actor. Philipe's wonderful looks, his elevated status as one of the great classical stage actors of his time, and his untimely death all contributed to his mythic position in French cinema. His film portrayal of the deranged Prince Myshkin in *L'Idiot* (1946) and the fragile, boyish hero of *Le Diable au corps/Devil in the Flesh* (1947) set his early persona as the tortured young romantic, in evidence also in Yves Allégret's* *noir* drama *Une si jolie petite plage/Riptide* (1949). Rising quickly to the top of the box-office rankings, Philipe became the sophisticated male star of the 'tradition of quality'* costume film, in comedies such as the successful *Fanfan la Tulipe* and *Les Belles de nuit* (both 1952), and, more frequently, in prestigious literary adaptations such as Stendhal's *La Chartreuse de Parme/La certosa di Parma* (1948) and *Le Rouge et le noir/Scarlet and Black* (1954), and Zola's *Pot-bouille/The House of Lovers* (1957). By contrast with the rugged Jean Gabin* and action man Eddie Constantine*, his equally famous rivals, Philipe was very much a star of 'women's films'. French critic Claude Beylie sees his image as split between the 'smooth fashion plate' of many films, and the 'perverse dandy' of others, notably René Clair's* *Les Grandes manoeuvres/Summer Manoeuvres* (1955), in which he is caught in his own love games, and in the contemporary settings of Roger Vadim's* *Les Liaisons dangereuses* (1959), where he is a brilliant Valmont. In fact, the power of Philipe's on-screen masculinity was that he incorporated elements of both aspects of his image, subtly commenting on the cynical and predatory nature of the male hero of romance while at the same time giving a beguiling portrait of just such a man. GV

Other Films Include: *La Beauté du diable/Beauty and the Devil* (1949); *La Ronde* (1950); *Juliette ou la clé des songes* (1951); *Les Orgueilleux/The Proud Ones, Monsieur Ripois/Knave of Hearts* (1953); *Les Aventures de Till L'Espiègle/The Adventures of Till Eulenspiegel* (1956; co-dir); *Montparnasse 19/Modigliani of Montparnasse* (1958); *La Fièvre monte à El Pao/Republic of Sin* (1960).

PIALAT, Maurice
Cunlhat 1925

French director, one of the most important *auteurs* to emerge since the New Wave*. Originally a painter, Pialat worked for the stage and television, acted, and shot documentaries. He made his first cinema feature, *L'Enfance nue*, in 1968. This examination of deprived childhood heralded Pialat's most original period in which, in such films as *La Gueule ouverte* (1974), *Loulou* (1979) and *A nos amours/To Our Loves* (1983), he revealed an ethnographic concern with unglamorous aspects of French society. Pialat's potent, bleak realism combines a demanding, quasi-*cinéma-vérité** approach – some non-professional actors, very long takes, improvisation, colloquial language – with the reworking of personal issues such as marital breakdown. *Police* (1985), like *Loulou* starring Gérard Depardieu*, was a departure towards genre, here the thriller, though sociological interest was in evidence in the (problematic) portrayal of the immigrant milieu. Subsequently, Pialat moved to literary adaptation (*Sous le soleil de Satan/Under Satan's Sun*, 1987) and period drama (*Van Gogh*, 1991). Both films, though, are consistent with his focus on tortured individuals, *Van Gogh* especially a reflection on the 'difficult' artist, a description comprehensively earned by Pialat himself. But it is in his earlier work that Pialat's cinematic power is most in evidence. GV

Other Films Include: *L'Amour existe* (1960, short); *Janine* (1961, TV); *La Maison des bois* (1971, TV); *Nous ne vieillirons pas ensemble* (1972); *Passe ton bac d'abord...* (1979).

PICAZO, Miguel
Miguel Picazo Dios; Cazorla 1927

Spanish director, who taught at the Escuela Oficial de Cinematografía* and launched his career with one of the finest films of the New Spanish Cinema*, *La tía Tula/Aunt Tula* (1964), based on a novella by Miguel de Unamuno. Cut by the censors, the film explores solitude and anxieties about sex with rare understatement and feeling. None of his other films managed to recapture its gentle pathos. Picazo continued to work in cinema – for instance with *Oscuros sueños de agosto/Obscure August Dreams* (1960) and *Extramuros/Beyond the Walls* (1985) – and television, where he has made interesting literary adaptations. PWE

PICCOLI, Michel
Jean Daniel Michel Piccoli; Paris 1925

French actor of Italian origins. A classically trained stage actor, Piccoli moved from dependable character actor, with small parts in such classics as Jean Renoir's* *French Cancan* (1955) and Jean-Pierre Melville's* *Le Doulos* (1963), to major figure of European art cinema*. In his immense filmography, titles such as *Le Mépris/Contempt* (1963), *Belle de jour* (1967), *Themroc* (1973), *Le Charme discret de la bourgeoisie/The Discreet Charm of the Bourgeoisie* (1972) and *La Grande bouffe/Blow Out* (1973) stand out, as well as his work with Claude Sautet*. A consummate and subtle actor, Piccoli emerged as the sexually opportunistic middle-class intellectual with a hint of the perverse libertine (he starred in a French television version of *Don Juan* in 1965), a character usually mobilised to serve 'progressive' themes. Piccoli unusually combined *auteur* credibility with box-office success throughout the 1970s. Since then his career has fluctuated, though he has continued to support French *auteur* films, appearing memorably in Leos Carax's* *Mauvais Sang/The Night is Young* (1986) and Jacques Rivette's* *La Belle Noiseuse* (1991). He has also returned successfully to the stage. GV

PICHUL, Vasili
Moscow 1961

Russian director. After studying at VGIK* from 1977 to 1983, Pichul worked in television. In 1986 he joined the Gorky Film Studios in Moscow, where in 1987 he made *Malen'kaya Vera/Little Vera*, a film which came to epitomise the *perestroika* period [> GLASNOST AND THE CINEMA]. Set in Pichul's home town of Maryupol (Zhdanov) in southern Ukraine, and scripted by his wife, Maria Khmelik, *Malen'kaya Vera* amazed Soviet audiences by its sexual frankness, and made something of an international celebrity of its star, Natalia Negoda. Several years on, the film's importance can be seen to lie more in its bleak evocation of Soviet working-class life. Holed up in a cramped high-rise flat with her drunken father and overworked mother, ill-educated Vera is destined for a dead-end job as a telephonist until she meets work-shy student Sergei... The film was seen by over 50 million people in Russia and variously interpreted, in the acres of press coverage devoted to it, as exposing or condoning all that was wrong in late-Soviet society. Pichul's independently made *V gorode Sochi tëmnye nochi/Dark Nights in Sochi* (1989) was, by contrast, a commercial flop. After that he directed *Mechty idiota/Dreams of an Idiot*, an eclectic and challenging version of *The Golden Calf*, a classic work by the Soviet satirists Ilf and Petrov. JGf

PICK, Lupu
Jassy, Romania 1886 – Berlin 1931

Romanian-born director and actor, who as an actor played in Richard Oswald* fantasy films, Henny Porten* comedies and the Joe Jenkins and Stuart Webb detective series. His last and best-known role was as the Japanese diplomat Massimoto in Lang's* *Spione/The Spy* (1928).

Pick's first directorial assignments were popular star vehicles, including a futuristic anticipation of television (*Der Weltspiegel/The Mirror of the World*, 1918). In the early 1920s he collaborated closely with writer Carl Mayer* on *Kammerspielfilme**, which they inaugurated with *Scherben/Shattered* (1921) and *Sylvester* (1923). The films' critical success and aesthetic influence on Weimar* cinema are traditionally attributed to Mayer, but it was as much due to Pick's distinctive use of camera movement, sparse decors, and the natural flow of *mise-en-scène* (with only one intertitle in *Scherben*) that the genre generated an atmospheric intensity around its sociological representation of the everyday. A trilogy was conceived that would have included *Der letzte Mann/The Last Laugh* (1924), but a disagreement between

Pick and Mayer led Pick to leave the project and the assignment went to F. W. Murnau*. Thereafter, Pick made only a few films, some unjustly forgotten, like the intriguingly off-beat *Gassenhauer* (1931). MW/TE

Other Films Include: *Mr. Wu* (1918); *Herr über Leben und Tod* (1919); *Zum Paradies der Damen* (1922); *Eine Nacht in London/A Night in London* (1928); *Napoleon auf St. Helena* (1929).

PIEL, Harry   Düsseldorf 1892 – Munich 1963

German actor and director. At first employed by Gaumont* and working for Léonce Perret, Piel wrote and directed a number of increasingly successful action films and detective series, which not only earned him the label of 'dynamite director' but also allowed him to establish his own production company in 1915. With *Der große Unbekannte* (1919), he created the adventure hero 'Harry Piel', played by himself, making him one of the most famous screen actors in Germany.

Benefiting from hyper-inflation, he produced big-budget films in Germany largely with hard currency: *Rivalen* (1923) for the British Apex Film, *Schneller als der Tod* (1925) for Gaumont. In the late 1920s he completed several films for German companies, among them *Sein größter Bluff* (1927), starring Marlene Dietrich*, and was able to re-establish his place within the industry through a number of box-office hits (*Menschen, Tiere, Sensationen*, 1938). During the war years he completed only one film, *Panik* (1943), which was banned because its war sequences were deemed too realistic. Piel re-established his Ariel-Film company in 1950, producing his own film, *Der Tiger Akbar* (1951). MW

Bib: Matias Bleckmann, *Harry Piel: Ein Kino-Mythos und seine Zeit* (1993).

PIETRANGELI, Antonio   Rome 1919 – Gaeta 1968

Italian director. After studying medicine, Pietrangeli wrote for the film journals *Bianco e nero* and *Cinema*, becoming an important theorist and advocate of neo-realism*. As a scriptwriter, he contributed to some of the most significant films of the period: Luchino Visconti's* *Ossessione* (1942) and *La terra trema* (1948), Alberto Lattuada's* *Senza pietà/Without Pity* (1948), and Roberto Rossellini's* *Europa '51* (1952) and *Viaggio in Italia/Voyage to Italy* (1953). Although still within the external framework of neo-realism, his debut film, *Il sole negli occhi/Celestina* (1953), was remarkable for its ideological acuteness and sensitive psychological analysis and for the almost unprecedented significance attached to women, a recurrent theme in almost all his later works. This theme was touched upon in varying degrees by *Nata di marzo* (1958), a somewhat bitter middle-class marital comedy; *Adua e le compagne/Love à la Carte* (1960); and *Lo scapolo/Alberto il conquistatore* (1955) and *Souvenir d'Italie* (1957), all reflecting a shift towards comedy. It was, however,

in the magnificent trilogy made up of *La parmigiana* (1963), *La visita* (1964) and *Io la conoscevo bene/I Knew Her Well* (1965) that the director portrayed three unforgettable female figures while at the same time refining a distinctly personal film language. An original but always somewhat marginal figure, Pietrangeli created through the tender, provocative and highly intelligent *Fantasmi a Roma/Phantom Lovers* (1961) a new fusion of the imaginary and comedy, a combination generally regarded with suspicion in Italian culture. Pietrangeli died in an accident on the set of *Come, quando, perchè* (1968), which was completed by Valerio Zurlini*. PV

Other Films Include: *Amori di mezzo secolo* (1954, ep. *Girolanda 1910*); *Il magnifico cornuto* (1964); *Le fate* (1966, ep. *Fata Marta*).

PINSCHEWER, Julius   Hohensalza-Posen 1883 – Berne 1961

German-Swiss producer and director, who started in film in Berlin in 1910 and during the same year began producing short advertising films (for his company Pinschewer Film), convinced that promotional film-making should attain the same standards as narrative film. Diversifying into short commercial scenes, trick-movies (some photographed by Guido Seeber*) and slapstick comedies – with popular stars such as Otto Gebühr*, Curt Bois*, Alfred Braun and Asta Nielsen* – Pinschewer soon became one of Germany's leading producers. Making political propaganda on the same principles as commercial advertising, Pinschewer also gained an influential position in German propaganda during World War I, as head of his own distribution company, Vaterländischer Filmvertrieb. Increasingly specialising in industrial films and animated shorts after 1920, Pinschewer's studios collaborated with prominent artists such as Lotte Reiniger* and Walter Ruttmann* and animators such as Harry Jaeger, Hermann Abeking and Fischerkoesen. In 1925, the year in which his *Kipho* (co-dir. Guido Seeber*) was presented at the Kino- und Photoausstellung Berlin, Pinschewer held the monopoly for exhibiting advertising films in all German Ufa* cinemas as well as in other cinemas, variety halls, and operetta houses in over 450 cities

Increasingly ousted from the German market in the late 1920s by the newly founded Echo Reklame Gesellschaft, Pinschewer still pioneered the first sound commercial, the nine-minute *Die chinesische Nachtigall* (1929), before he took refuge from the Nazis in Berne in 1934. Back to square one, he soon managed to establish a new studio and produced animated advertising films for the Swiss and sometimes the British market until the mid-1950s, in the process becoming the founder of the Swiss animation film tradition. Among the small number of his non-commercial productions are *Chad Gadjo* (1930), *Hatikwah* (1949), *Ein Schweizer Bauernkünstler. Jean-Jacques Hauswirth 1808–1871* (1952). MW

Bib: Roland Cosandey, *Julius Pinschewer: Cinquante ans de cinéma d'animation* (1989).

PINTER, Harold
London 1930

British playwright and scriptwriter (and originally actor) best known in the cinema for his collaboration with Joseph Losey* on *The Servant* (1963), *Accident* (1967) and *The Go-Between* (1970). His play *The Caretaker*, staged in 1960 and filmed in 1963, was inspired more by Samuel Beckett than by the social realism of the British (theatrical or cinematic) New Wave*. Pinter's plays, like his scripts for Losey, are allusive and elliptical, with an unstated menace hiding in the cracks. He adapted *The Birthday Party* (1968) and *The Homecoming* (1973, US/UK) for the screen. His interest in complex temporal structures is evident in his treatment of *The French Lieutenant's Woman* (1981), but most developed in *The Proust Screenplay* (1977), a project begun with Losey but which has not been produced. For Volker Schlöndorff* he wrote the screenplay of *The Handmaid's Tale* (1990, US/Ger.), based on Margaret Atwood's novel, and for Paul Schrader he adapted Ian McEwan's *The Comfort of Strangers/Cortesie per gli ospiti*, 1990, It./UK). Pinter won a New York Film Critics award for *The Servant*, and British Academy awards for *The Pumpkin Eater* (1964) and *The Go-Between*. He directed *Butley* (1973, US/UK/Canada), adapted from Simon Gray's stage play, in 1976. JC

PINTILIE, Lucian
Tarutyne [then Romania, now Ukraine] 1933

Romanian director, who helped achieve international credibility for Romanian cinema with *Reconstituirea/The Reconstruction* (1969), went into exile and returned after twenty years, in 1990, as Director of Film at the Ministry of Culture. After attending theatre and film school Pintilie made his reputation as a stage director, and first worked in film as assistant director to Victor Iliu*. *Duminică la ora 6/Sunday at Six* (1965), his directorial debut, was a skilfully shot war film devoid of cliché – highly original for Romania. *Reconstituirea*, about two students forced to reconstruct a fight in a bar, is a complex allegorical tragi-comedy of collective irresponsibility, with striking use of camera and crowd scenes. Despite official criticism and delays in domestic release, it was hailed in Europe as a breakthrough for Romanian cinema. Following criticism of his stage work at home Pintilie worked in Yugoslavia, France and America as a stage and opera director, returning to film with *Paviljon 6* (1978), a stylish Chekhov adaptation made in Yugoslavia; and briefly to Romania for *De ce bat clopotole Mitică?/Carnival Stories* (planned for a 1981 release but shelved until the 1989 revolution). Adapted from I. L. Caragiale's grotesque and satirical play, it echoes Gogol's *Inspector-General*. Pintilie's 1990 return to Romania resulted in *Le Chêne/Steiarul/The Oak* (1992), a French-Romanian co-production and the major depiction to date of the degradation of the late Ceauşescu years. MM

Bib: Anca Visdei, 'Entretien avec Lucian Pintilie', *L'Avant-Scène du cinéma* (October 1992).

PINTO, Joaquim
Oporto 1957

Portuguese sound engineer, cinematographer, director and producer. A remarkably versatile film-maker, Pinto graduated in sound from the Lisbon film school and began working in 1980. His debut coincided with Paulo Branco's* return to Portugal from France, and Pinto was sound engineer or assistant on some of Branco's early productions, including João Botelho's* *Conversa Acabada/The Other One* (1981), Raul Ruiz's* *Território/Le Territoire/The Territory* (1981) and Wim Wenders'* *The State of Things* (1982). Pinto rapidly became one of Portugal's leading sound engineers (often working with Vasco Pimentel), with international connections. He worked on several films directed by Ruiz and Botelho, and with Werner Schroeter* and Manoel de Oliveira*, among others. The late 1970s marked a turning point in Pinto's career. He became a producer, director and cinematographer in order to make *Uma Pedra no Bolso/Tall Stories* (1988) and *Onde Bate o Sol/Where the Sun Beats Down* (1989), the first made with a crew of four, the second with a crew of five. As director, Pinto's only subsequent credits were for *Das Tripas Coração* (1992), part of the anthology *The Four Elements*, and a short, *Para Cá dos Montes* (1993). He took up producing, his titles including *Recordações da Casa Amarela/Recollections of the Yellow House* (1989), directed by João César Monteiro*; *A Idade Maior/Alex* (1991) and *Três Irmãos/Two Brothers, One Sister* (1994) by Teresa Villaverde; and *Pax* by Eduardo Guedes (1994). As a producer Pinto was almost as low-key as he was as a director. His directing style is both sensitive – even shy – and disturbing, as befits his subject matter: the secrets and emotions (friendship, sexuality) of growing up, the rites of passage from childhood to adolescence and the delicate relations with adults. AMS

PIRRO, Ugo
Salerno 1920

Italian scriptwriter. Starting his career as a journalist, Pirro first worked in the cinema with Carlo Lizzani* (*Achtung banditi!*, 1951), sharing his idea of a cinema midway between commitment and entertainment. For twenty years he was one of the most significant scriptwriters of an Italian cinema centred on political, historical and social themes [> ITALIAN POLITICAL CINEMA]. Lizzani's *Il processo di Verona/The Verona Trial* (1962) and *Svegliati e uccidi/Wake Up and Kill* (1966), Gianfranco Mingozzi's powerful Sardinian picture *Sequestro di persona/Kidnap* (1968), Pasquale Squitieri's colourful *I guappi* (1974), Elio Petri's* *A ciascuno il suo/To Each His Own* (1967), Damiano Damiani's *Il giorno della civetta/Mafia* (1968), Mario Bolognini's *Metello* (1970) and *L'eredità Ferramonti/The Inheritance* (1976) and Gillo Pontecorvo's* *Ogro* (1979) are the most important stages in Pirro's artistic career. He adapted his own novels to provide scripts for Martin Ritt's *Jovanka e le altre/Five Branded Women* (1960) and Valerio Zurlini's* *Le soldatesse/The Girl Soldiers* (1965), and transposed Giorgio Bassani for Vittorio De Sica's* *Il giardino dei Finzi-Contini/The Garden of the Finzi-Continis* (1970). In his own words, 'half hunter, half voyeur', Pirro elaborated the notion that cinematic ideas 'act and advance within the movie like an underground river'. His relationship with Elio Petri* is precisely the expression of such a complexity, especially in *Indagine su un cittadino al di sopra di ogni sospetto/Investigation of a Citizen Above Suspicion* (1969), with its description of the interior mechanisms of power, and *La classe operaia va in paradiso/Lulu the Tool* (1971), where reality becomes expression, metaphor, hyper-reality, but is never merely 'repeated'. GVo

PIŢA, Dan
Dorohei 1938

Romanian director and scriptwriter, who with *Nuntă de pia-tră/Stone Wedding* (1972, co-directed and scripted with Mircea Veroiu*) achieved a breakthrough in the inter-national recognition of Romanian film. A medical assistant for ten years before studying under Victor Iliu*, his silent stu-dent film about a driver and cyclist, *Viaţa in roz/'La Vie en rose'* (1969), was shown worldwide. In *Nuntă de piatră*, Piţa's quiet observation of social subversion at a traditional wed-ding subtly understates the conflict between conformism and individuality. The film is complemented by its sequel, *Duhul aurului/Lust for Gold* (1973). The contemporary drama *Filip cel bun/Philip the Good* (1975) is comparable to Lucian Pintilie's* *Reconstituirea* in its attention to social realism. Piţa directed some films in a popular series parodying the Western, starting with *Profetul, aurel şi Ardelenii/The Prophet, the Gold and the Transylvanians* (1977), which played on the incongruousness of Transylvanian peasants transplanted to Texas. *Concurs/The Contest* (1982) is a grip-ping commentary on leadership and psychology. *Dreptate în lanturi/Chained Justice* (1983) deploys elegant black-and-white photography in a Robin Hood-style adventure. *Pas în doi/Paso Doble* (1986), also co-scripted by Piţa, breaks Romanian social taboos in its handling of a *ménage-à-trois*. Piţa's claims to magic realism are extended in *Noiembrie, ul-timul bal/November, the Last Ball* (1989), with its mirage-like tragic relationships in a nineteenth-century provincial town. *Hôtel de lux* (1991) was well received at Venice shortly after Piţa's new administrative powers had embroiled him in an in-dustry-wide strike. MM

PITTALUGA, Stefano
Campomorone 1887 – Rome 1931

Italian entrepreneur. Originally an exhibitor, Pittaluga played a crucial role in the revival of the Italian film industry after its collapse in the aftermath of World War I. In order to acquire product to supply his rapidly expanding chain of theatres (concentrated in northern Italy), he moved into film distri-bution in the mid-1920s. Then, faced with a continuing lack of suitable Italian films and with the stranglehold exercised by the American majors, he took the next logical step and be-came a producer. He resurrected Itala Film and Cines*, and constructed Italy's first sound stages; he was also responsible for the production of two of Italy's most famous early sound films, Alessandro Blasetti's* *Sole/Sun* (1929) and Mario Camerini's* *Rotaie/Rails* (1929–31). He successfully lobbied a previously indifferent government for help for film produc-tion and distribution. After his early death in 1931, Cines be-came Italy's most important and innovative production

company, while his theatre chain served to structure the gov-ernment's ENIC – a state-sponsored system of film distri-bution. GNS/JHa

PLATEAU, Joseph
Brussels 1801 – Ghent 1883

Belgian inventor of the Phenakisti(s)cope, the principles of which, when applied to photography, contributed to the invention of cinema. Perfected around 1832, the Phenakisti(s)cope was the result of five years work on the persistence of light impressions in the retina, or 'persistence of vision'. It consisted of a disc with slots cut around its cir-cumference. On the reverse side of the disc were a series of pictures, each representing a different phase of motion. When observed in a mirror through its own rotating slots, the opti-cal illusion of motion was achieved. Ironically, studying reti-nal perception affected Plateau's own eyes; ten years after his discovery he lost his sight, though he continued his research in other areas. CF

PLEASENCE, Donald
Worksop 1919 – St. Paul de Vence, France 1995

British actor, whose general appearance seems to fit him for bank manager roles, but whose lizard eyes, steely gaze and tightly constricted voice were increasingly exploited in horror movies. A station manager in Yorkshire in the mid-1930s, he began acting in theatre in 1939, but did not make his film debut until 1954. Mainly a character actor in supporting roles in the 1950s and 1960s, he was given a lead role in the screen adaptation of Harold Pinter's* *The Caretaker* (1963) and ap-peared in Roman Polanski's* *Cul-de-Sac* (1966). During the 1970s and 1980s he was increasingly associated with the more eccentric and bizarre elements of crime and horror, culminat-ing in an association with John Carpenter in *Halloween* (1978, US) and its sequels. JC

PODNIEKS, Jūris
Riga, Latvia [USSR] 1950 – Alsunga, Latvia 1992

Latvian documentary director, who graduated from the cine-matography faculty of VGIK* and gained a reputation as a cinematographer. He directed his first film, *Sozvezdie strelkov/Constellation of Riflemen*, in 1982, but international success came with the pioneering and timely *Legko li byt' molodym?/Is it Easy to be Young?* (1987), a series of inter-views with young people in his native Riga. Podnieks's secret was to let the young people speak in their own words, and the unprecedented authenticity of what they had to say led to extraordinarily high audiences for a documentary. The suc-cess and originality of Podnieks's film led the British company Central Television to commission from him a series of five hour-long documentaries, broadcast in Britain in 1990 as *Hello, Do You Hear Us?* (Russian title, *My/We*), which will remain a key document for understanding the last years of the Soviet Union. Here, too, though Podnieks includes all the major events of the period, it is the testimonies of individuals,

335

from the Baltic to Central Asia, that are most effective. From 1991 Podnieks became increasingly involved in documenting the struggle of the Baltic peoples to regain their independence, the subject of his film *Homeland* (Russian title, *Krestnyi put'/Calvary*, 1991). In January 1991, an attempt to repress this movement led to violence in Vilnius and Riga. While Podnieks and his team were filming in Riga, his cameramen, Andris Slapiņš and Gvido Zvaigzne, were shot dead by troops, events captured in the short *Postscript* (*Posleslovie*, 1991) to *Homeland*. Podnieks's final completed film for Central, *End of Empire* (Russian title, *Krushenie imperii*, 1991), combined footage of Moscow during the August 1991 putsch and sequences from his earlier films. Podnieks, who said he never made films but filmed life, was shooting another film, *Unfinished Business*, set in several parts of the former Soviet Union, and thinking of moving into features, when he died in a freak diving accident. JGf

POETIC REALISM

French stylistic trend of the 1930s. The term 'Poetic Realism' was originally applied to literature; in the cinema it was first used in relation to Pierre Chenal's* *La Rue sans nom* (1933). It is a critical construction with blurred edges – terms such as 'populist melodrama', 'the social fantastic', '*noir* realism' and 'magic realism' can also apply. However, 'Poetic Realism' designates pessimistic urban dramas, usually set in Paris (though there were colonial examples) in working-class settings, with doomed romantic narratives often tinged with criminality. The supreme examples are the films of Marcel Carné* and Jacques Prévert* – *Quai des brumes* (1938), *Le Jour se lève* (1939) – but the canon also includes Jean Vigo's* *L'Atalante* (1934), Jean Renoir's* *La Bête humaine* (1938), Jacques Feyder's* *Le Grand jeu* (1933), Julien Duvivier's* *La Belle équipe* (1936) and Jean Grémillon's* *Gueule d'amour* (1937); to which could be added Marie Epstein's* *La Maternelle* (1933), Raymond Bernard's* *Faubourg-Montmartre* (1931) and several films by Chenal. As its name indicates, Poetic Realism proposes a duality between the everyday and the lyrical/emotional, the poetry arising precisely *from* the everyday, from a world created – beyond individual directors – by an exceptional ensemble of craftsmen and artists: the decors of Alexandre Trauner*, the dialogues of Prévert, Charles Spaak and Henri Jeanson*, the photography of Jules Kruger, Eugen Schüfftan*, Curt Courant*, the music of Maurice Jaubert* and Joseph Kosma*; and of course the stars: Jean Gabin*, but also Arletty*, Jules Berry*, Charles Vanel* and others. It was a highly stylised world, both in its *mise-en-scène* and in its 'mythical' characters, yet the box-office success of the films shows that they 'spoke' to their popular audience.

Often – superficially – seen as a reflection of the collapse of the Popular Front* and of the gloomy prewar years, Poetic Realism was rather the product of a long French cultural tradition, which went back to nineteenth-century classic (Balzac, Eugène Sue, Zola) and crime literature (including Georges Simenon*), to the populist novels of the 1920s and 1930s (Eugène Dabit and Pierre MacOrlan), and to popular songs, magazines and photography. Cinematically, antecedents can be found in both French and German cinema, especially the *Kammerspielfilm** and the *Straßenfilme**. Although only one important trend among many in French 1930s cinema, Poetic Realism caught historians' attention not only for its formal beauty and cultural prestige, but also because it formed such a strong contrast to Hollywood. While Carné and Prévert's *Les Enfants du paradis* (1943–45) and *Les Portes de la nuit* (1946) are considered respectively the culmination and the swan-song of Poetic Realism, by the mid-1940s it had become, as Dudley Andrew put it, 'codified and citable'. GV

Bib: Dudley Andrew, *Mists of Regret: Culture and Sensibility in Classic French Film* (1995).

POIRÉ, Jean-Marie   Paris 1945

French director. A successful director of comedies since 1977, Poiré is the film-maker of the *café-théâtre* generation [> COMEDY (FRANCE)] which includes Christian Clavier, Gérard Jugnot, Thierry Lhermitte and Josiane Balasko*, producing irreverently funny comedies whose titles are an art form in themselves – *Les Hommes préfèrent les grosses/Men Prefer Fat Girls* (1981), *Le Père Noël est une ordure/Santa Claus is a Louse* (1982, recently remade in Hollywood as *Mixed Nuts*, 1994), *Opération Corned Beef* (1991). But none of this could have suggested the extraordinary success of *Les Visiteurs* (1993), starring Clavier, Valérie Lemercier and Jean Reno, in which present-day middle-class characters meet their medieval equivalent. As in Poiré's previous films, linguistic puns and social ridicule are the key, but clearly the film hit a nerve in France, where it has become the most popular film ever at the box office, an astonishing achievement considering that the audience is considerably smaller than in the mid-1960s, when Louis de Funès* and Bourvil* were the box-office champions. GV

POLAND

At the birth of cinema Poland was 'officially' non-existent. Since 1795 the country had been partitioned between Austria, Prussia and Russia, and Polish artistic and cultural life had mostly relocated to Paris. However, a strong sense of national identity survived. In the late 1890s several Poles made attempts to develop 'moving pictures', but only Kazimierz Proszynski's 'Pleograf' enjoyed any success; in 1902 and 1903 he shot around fifteen documentary and comedy shorts, which were very popular. The success of the Pleograf was short-lived and, after its first screening in Cracow on 14 November 1896, the Lumière* Cinematograph soon led the field. Poland's first cinema was established in Łódź in 1899, and by 1902 the first film studio was making and distributing short films. It was not until 1908, however, that the first Polish feature was produced: *Antoś po raz Pierwszy w Warszawie/Anthony's First Trip to Warsaw*, made by Pathé cameraman Josef Meyer.

In the years that followed, film production grew slowly but steadily. Antoni Fertner, a comic inspired by Max Linder*, became a celebrity in Poland and Eastern Europe. Alexander Hertz established the Sfinks studio in 1909 and was soon the most important figure in the development of a Polish national cinema. Hertz produced films of excellent technical quality – if rather theatrical style – and was responsible for discovering and fostering Poland's first stars. Pola Negri's* debut in *Niewolnica Zmysłów/Slave of Sin* (1914, dir. Jan Pawłowski) was a major hit and Hertz also introduced Jadwiga Smosarska in Danny Kaden and Władysław Lenczewski's *Strzał/The Shot* (1922); Smosarska subsequently became a major Polish screen actress of the 1930s. Hertz was joined by directors Richard Ordyński and Edward Puchalski as cinema blossomed during the war. By 1919 there were 400 cinemas in the newly independent Poland and, with state support, the industry produced 21 features and 61 shorts. This boom was short-lived, and by 1922 American films dominated the market. Three main Polish film companies functioned in the 1920s and 1930s: Sfinks, Falanga and Leofilm. Apart from popular comedies, farces and melodramas, historical films like Ryszard Bolesławski's *Cud nad Wisłą/Miracle on the Vistula* (1921) and adaptations of classic literary texts were popular genres. There was also a growing Yiddish cinema*, developed by Joseph Green and catering for the large Polish-Jewish community.

A strong critical tradition was established in Poland as early as 1898 with Bolesław Matuszewski's recognition of film as an art form. Karol Irzykowski, an eminent philosopher and literary critic, published many articles on cinema, culminating in his book *Dziesiąta Musa* ('The Tenth Muse', 1921). This lively atmosphere of debate surrounded the success of popular film-makers like Wiktor Biegański, whose *Wampiry Warszawy/Vampires of Warsaw* (1925) was widely acclaimed for its use of a truly cinematic language. In 1928 Poland had its first international success with *Huragan/Hurricane*, Joseph Lejtes' debut feature, and in the following year Michal Waszyński won a prize for the erotic *Kult Ciała/Cult of the Flesh*, Poland's first sound film.

Despite these critical and box-office successes, Polish film production declined in quality and quantity during the late 1920s. The arrival of sound in the midst of an economic depression stretched the young industry to its limit. An attempt to create an alternative cinema was made by START (Stowarzyszenie Miłośników Filmu Artystycznego/Society of Devotees of Artistic Film), an organisation which prefigured the French New Wave* and British 'Free Cinema'*. Established in 1930 by such directors as Aleksander Ford*, Wanda Jakubowska*, Stanisław Wohl, Jerzy Bossak and Eugeniusz Cekalski, START called for a cinema based in social reality, higher artistic and technical standards and support from the state (Ford, Jakubowska and others, with Franciszka and Stefan Themerson*, also founded the world's first film-makers' cooperative, SAF, in 1935). The films made by START's members were artistically ambitious, influenced by German expressionism* and Soviet montage*, and many won prizes abroad, notably Cekalski and Wohl's *Trzy Etudy Chopina/Three Chopin Studies* at Venice in 1937. The government responded in the mid-1930s by improving tax conditions and in 1937 a record number of 27 features and 102 shorts were produced. Although START was short-lived, its ideas and personnel provided a base for the postwar Polish film industry. Following the German occupation of Poland in 1939, film production was suspended and German films dominated the screens. The war, in which about one in five of the Polish population were killed, also devastated the film industry: equipment, facilities and prints were destroyed in the bombing.

The new communist Poland regarded film as an important asset, and in 1945 the 'industry' was nationalised. Based on the Czołówka Filmowa (a war film unit which operated on the Soviet front in June 1943), Film Polski*, with Ford at its head, was established as the leading production house. Technical equipment was 'acquired' from the Soviet-held part of Germany and the precursor of the famous Łódź* film school was established in Cracow. By 1947 production was again under way. The first international success was Jakubowska's *Ostatni Etap/The Last Stage* (1948), about the horror of the concentration camps. Indeed, the war – occupation, resistance, the disintegration of Polish society – provided the subject matter for many films of this period: Leonard Buczkowski's *Zakazane Piosenki/Forbidden Songs* (1948), Ford's *Ulica Granicowa/Border Street* (1949), Andrzej Wajda's* *Pokolenie/A Generation* (1955). But under the impact of the official ideology, these themes soon fell prey to rigid formulae: the communist underground was portrayed as the singular embodiment of the resistance in relation to the suspect Home Army, the collective hero was celebrated at the expense of the individual, and general adherence to Socialist Realism* was required.

By the mid-1950s film production had risen to an average of eight features annually, with cinemas numbering 2,672. The political thaw following Stalin's death (1953) allowed a significant restructuring of film production, giving film-makers greater artistic control. A new 'zespół', or production unit system, was established at Film Polski, lasting until 1990. The eight (state-funded) units, headed by eminent film-makers, had nominal artistic and financial autonomy. However, decisions still had to be verified by the Central Office of Cinematography, so that censorship occurred at script stage, and political content rather than economic or artistic considerations determined the distribution and exhibition fate of any title.

Under these conditions of limited autonomy and ideological constraint, a new era in Polish film-making was launched. Between 1954 and 1963 a group of films known as the 'Polish School' emerged, characterised by romantic pessimism, a preoccupation with the subjection of the individual to the forces of history, and a re-examination of Poland's tragic war years. Films like Wajda's *Kanał/Canal* (1956) and *Popiół i Diament/Ashes and Diamonds* (1958), Andrzej Munk's* *Eroica* (1958) and Wojciech Has'* *Pożegnania/Farewells* (1958) turned the constraints of the censor to their advantage, using striking visual symbols, allusion and tone to create a rich subtext. International audiences and critics were fascinated, though at times symbols and allusions were so nationally specific as to be lost on non-Polish audiences.

The 1960s, as in Hungary and Czechoslovakia, produced a new generation or 'second wave' of film-makers. Directors like Roman Polanski*, with *Nóz w Wodzie/Knife in the Water* (1962), and Jerzy Skolimowski*, with *Walkower/Walkover* (1965), dealt with individual morality in contemporary Poland, in a style influenced by the French New Wave*. Historical themes were also explored in epic films, including adaptations of Polish literature like Has' *Rękopis Znaleziony w Saragossie/The Saragossa Manuscript* (1965) and *Lalka/The Doll* (1968), and Ford's *Krzyżacy/Knights of the Teutonic

Order (1960). The political disruptions of the late 1960s and early 1970s prompted some reorganisation of the industry with the number of film units reduced from eight to six; Ford, Jerzy Toeplitz (head of the Łódź Film School) and Jerzy Bossak (head of the Kamera film unit) lost their administrative positions. The student demonstrations and workers' protests of this period gave impetus to a reappraisal of documentary by a group of young film-makers. Krzysztof Kieślowski*, Marcel Łozinski, Antoni Krauze* and others explored the form to its limits, making a series of exciting, incisive, engaging and often political films. While many of these films were banned or shelved for several years, audience interest was strong and it was not uncommon to go to the cinema just to see the short film.

Wajda's *Człowiek z Marmuru/Man of Marble* (1976) signalled a new mood of social consciousness, witnessed in the rise of the trade union 'Solidarity' and the intense political battles of the period. It also paved the way for the so-called 'cinema of moral unrest'. These films, by Kieślowski, Agnieszka Holland*, Janusz Zaorski*, Filip Bajon, Wojciec Marczewski*, Ryszard Bugajski* and others, eschewed symbolism and allusion in order to comment more directly on the Polish malaise. Thus Kieślowski's *Bez Końca/No End* (1984), Holland's *Kobieta Samotna/A Woman Alone* (1981) and Marczewski's *Dreszcze/Shivers* (1981) evoked a deep unease about the bankruptcy of Polish society. Drawing on their documentary roots, these film-makers focused on everyday realities and moral quandaries with which their audiences could identify. With the growing strength of Solidarity and the popular Lech Wałęsa's vocal criticism of the government, films also became more direct in their approach, examining contemporary society and recent history. Felix Falk's* *Wodzirej/Top Dog* (1979) deals with the corruption of small town politics. Wajda's *Człowiek z Żelaza/Man of Iron* (1981, Palme d'Or at Cannes) mixes documentary footage with fiction, showing tanks descending on protesting crowds in the 1970s and the resulting casualties. And Krauze's *Prognoza Pogody/Weather Forecast* (1983) provided a comic treatment of contemporary issues. (Many of these films, however, were not seen by audiences until martial law was lifted in 1989.)

When General Jaruzelski imposed martial law in 1981, the subsequent imprisonments and retaliations forced many of the film-makers most closely associated with Solidarity to leave Poland or stop working. Others survived by conforming to censorship, which, while stringent politically, became tolerant towards sex and violence. The public responded by largely avoiding cinemas and turning instead to a thriving underground culture. A network of film clubs and cultural activities flourished, using churches as venues. Foreign films were borrowed from embassies, and pirate videos and 16mm copies of shelved titles were screened. A few films continued to be made, like Janusz Zaorski's* *Matka Królów/Mother of Kings* (1982; rel. 1987). Meanwhile established directors such as Wajda and Zanussi* turned to foreign financing. As the economic depression grew worse, young film-makers concentrated on documentaries and shorts. The largest commercial successes proved to be a new strand of 'science-fiction' comedies, notably Juliusz Machulski's* *Seksmisja/Sex Mission* (1983). By 1986 the industry, like the country, was in severe financial crisis.

The dawn of Poland as a new democracy in 1989 brought hopes for a cinematic revival. Dozens of shelved films were shown domestically and internationally; Bugajski's *Przesłuchanie/The Interrogation* (1981) was particularly applauded. Polish cinema and television productions were concerned once more with setting the historical record straight, this time of the most recent past. Documentaries by Marcel Łoziński, Maria Zmarz-Koczanowicz and Andrzej Titkow had audiences queuing round the block. However, the euphoria soon vanished when the gravity of Poland's financial crisis became apparent. Those who could, turned to foreign co-productions, 'the today and tomorrow of Polish cinema' as *Kino* put it: Kieślowski to France for *Podwójne Życie Weroniki/The Double Life of Véronique* (1991) and the *Three Colours* trilogy (1993–94), Zanussi to Britain and Denmark for *Dotknięcie/The Touch* (1990). As elsewhere in Eastern Europe, the Polish government opted for privatisation of the film industry, backed by a strong industry lobby, and the hitherto predominantly *auteur*-based cinema turned towards commercialism. Interest in 'serious' film magazines like *Film* and *Kino* has also diminished, while new, more gossipy publications are popular. Censorship has been abolished. Some film units survive as private companies, raising money on a project-by-project basis. A new Ministry of Film offers production monies for projects selected by a panel of experts, on a matching fund basis. Many film-makers, working independently, often have to raise finance through advertising and television. Further problems occur in the distribution and exhibition areas, for Hollywood has been quick to exploit the 'free' Polish market, establishing links with new distribution and exhibition chains and investing heavily in advertising and promotion. Against a background of rising ticket prices and falling wages, and a steady decline in the number of cinemas (from 2,500 in the 1970s to 900 in 1992), America has taken over the screens. Whereas in the 1980s there had been an opening towards Western European film, by 1991 all top 20 box-office successes were US productions. Despite some subsidies to art-house cinemas and distribution companies via the Film Ministry, it is hard to see a Polish film on a Saturday night. Paradoxically Hollywood has boosted the international reputation of Polish production. With art director Allan Starski and director of photography Janusz Kamiński winning Oscars for their contribution to Spielberg's *Schindler's List* (1993), which was shot in Poland, Polish film professionalism has never been held in higher regard. AW

POLANSKI, Roman — Raymond Polanski; Paris, France 1933

Polish director. Perhaps the most famous expatriate Polish film-maker. Polanski's international success, as well as his tragic and infamous private life, have been well documented. Polanski first made shorts, including the much noticed *Dwaj Ludzie z Szafą/Two Men and a Wardrobe* (1958). He shot to fame with his feature debut *Nóż w Wodzie/Knife in the Water* (1962), making the cover of *Time* magazine as the face of new foreign cinema. Subsequently moving to the West, he consolidated his promise with *Repulsion* (1965) and *Cul-de-Sac* (1966), both made in Britain, before moving on to Hollywood. Polanski nonetheless maintained his connection to Poland; his association with composer Krzysztof Komeda continued up to his first Hollywood success, *Rosemary's Baby* (1968), and he often uses Polish cinematographers. Versatile and idiosyncratic, his best work is characterised by his ability to look at the dark side of human nature with a sharp irony and a sense of the absurd. His Hollywood success continued with *Chinatown* (1974), starring Jack Nicholson and Faye Dunaway, but was then cut short when Polanski's private life was brought under legal scrutiny; he moved to France in 1977 to avoid prosecution by US courts. Polanski's European films have ranged from a successful adaptation of Thomas Hardy's classic novel *Tess of the d'Urbervilles* (*Tess*, 1979), through the Hitchcockian overtones of *Frantic* (1988), to the commercial failure of his comedy romp on the high seas, *Pirates* (1986). *Lunes de fiel/Bitter Moon* (1992) refers back to Polanski's earlier work, with echoes of *Nóz w Wodzie* in a tale of sexual obsession. In 1994, he directed *Death and the Maiden*, starring Sigourney Weaver and Ben Kingsley. Polanski continues to make acting contributions in his own films and others, including, recently, *Grosse fatigue* and *Une pure formalité*, the latter co-starring Gérard Depardieu* (both 1994, Fr.). AW

POLICIER

French genre, embracing any crime film (whether the police appear or not). France is the only country outside the US to have built up a large and consistent body of thrillers. Although considered a 'bread-and-butter' genre (virtually all French directors have made at least one such film), unlike comedy* the *policier* often combines critical status with popular appeal. This has undoubtedly to do with its literary origins in the nineteenth-century *noir* novels of Eugène Sue and the realism of Balzac, Victor Hugo and Zola; and later, crime literature proper – Marcel Allain and Pierre Souvestre (*Fantômas*), Maurice Leblanc (*Arsène Lupin*), Georges Simenon*. After the war, interest was renewed by Marcel Duhamel's famous *Série noire* imprint which translated US and British writers and published French ones; English-language crime literature always enjoyed great popularity and intellectual credence in France, from Edgar Allan Poe to Jim Thompson.

In films, the popularity of the *policier* sprang instantly from silent crime series and the serials of Louis Feuillade* – *Fantômas* (1913–14) and *Les Vampires* (1915–16). It continued through the 1930s with Simenon adaptations (*La Nuit du carrefour/Night at the Crossroads*, *La Tête d'un homme*, both 1932), with Duvivier's* *Pépé le Moko* (1936), Pierre Chenal's* *Le Dernier tournant* (1939, the earliest film version of James M. Cain's *The Postman Always Rings Twice*), and the work of émigré directors such as Kurt Bernhardt* and Robert Siodmak*. Simenon adaptations were popular during the war and after, and directors such as Henri-Georges Clouzot* bent the *policier* to the extreme *noir* trend in France at the time. But the greatest burst of energy was triggered by Jacques Becker's* immensely popular *Touchez pas au gris-bi/Honour Among Thieves* (1954), which relaunched Jean-Gabin's* postwar career, followed by Jean-Pierre Melville's* *Bob le flambeur* (1956) and Jules Dassin's* *Du Rififi chez les hommes/Rififi* (1955). These films gave rise to countless de-rivations and established the genre as a kind of professional test paper for directors and male stars (some critics argue that the 1950s *policier* obliquely evokes the trauma of the German occupation). The 1960s saw the *policier* evolve either along comic lines (the films of Georges Lautner) or towards abstraction (those of Melville), and in the 1970s it moved in the direction of political critique (directors Yves Boisset*, Alain Corneau*, Costa-Gavras*). It also served as a regular format for the star vehicles of Alain Delon* and Jean-Paul Belmondo*. In the 1980s and 1990s the genre was revisited by *auteurs* as disparate as Maurice Pialat*, Bertrand Tavernier* and Claude Chabrol*, by the post-modern films of the *cinéma du look** (*Subway*, 1985, *Nikita*, 1990), and again by comedy (Claude Zidi's* *Les Ripoux/Le Cop*, 1984), taking stock of social changes (the presence of immigrant communities, the breakdown of families).

Through this huge corpus common motifs recur, helping to define a specifically French thriller, quite different from the Hollywood version: the centrality of Paris (*qua* Paris, not just 'the city'), the consistent weight placed on social observation, and the blurring of law and lawlessness within more ambiguous moral codes (the French *policier* never showed much interest in the social origins of crime). GV

Bib: François Guérif, *Le Cinéma policier français* (1981).

POLITIQUE DES AUTEURS

French critical concept, evolved by critics at *Cahiers du cinéma** in the 1950s, especially François Truffaut*, Jean-Luc Godard*, Jacques Rivette* and Eric Rohmer*. Building on the work of André Bazin* and Alexandre Astruc's notion of *caméra-stylo* ('camera pen'), but also distantly on the debates of the 1920s [> FRENCH AVANT-GARDE], the *politique des auteurs* was both a romantic notion and a polemic designed to promote personal film-making and establish the director-*auteur* as artist in charge. The professionally organised, polished cinema of the French 'tradition of quality'* was the *politique's* main target (Truffaut said: 'I do not believe in the peaceful co-existence of the Tradition of Quality and an *auteur's* cinema'), but it also championed American directors such as Howard Hawks and Alfred Hitchcock* as true *auteurs* (as opposed to mere *metteurs-en-scène*) struggling against the Hollywood studio system and therefore responding *personally* to constraints. This was possible through the assertion of *mise-en-scène* as the primary indicator of a director's personality, although thematic continuity was also valued. As John Hess put it, this concentration on the personal could be read at the time as 'a justification, couched in aesthetic terms, of a culturally conservative, politically reactionary attempt to remove film from the realm of social and political concern'. The *politique* has been enormously influential on film criticism, from Andrew Sarris in the US to film journals such as *Movie** and *Sight and Sound** and even the mainstream press, and continues to shape film history – sometimes beneficially, as in the defence of independent small-scale films, especially in Europe, sometimes less so (the ignorance of or contempt for popular genres outside Hollywood). GV

POLYGOON

Dutch production company set up in 1920, consisting of the non-fiction department of Maurits Binger's* Hollandia studio in Haarlem. The company is best known for its weekly newsreels screened in Dutch cinemas between 1922 and 1985, initially entitled *Hollands Nieuws* and after 1945 *Neerlands Nieuws*. Polygoon's newsreels paid much attention to royalty, sports, fashion and the occasional disaster, and avoided social and political tensions. During the company's golden era Polygoon newsreels were produced and distributed independently. Marginalised by television and subsidised by the state after 1964, they turned into a vehicle for Dutch promotion. From the start, Polygoon also made documentaries for education and industry. The first managers, the brothers B. D. and I. A. Ochse, succeeded in outstripping their main competitor, Willy Mullens'* Haghe Film, by hiring talented cameramen and directors such as Cor Aafjes, Jan Jansen and Jo de Haas. They created quality films – *De Nederlandsche Noordzee-visscherij/The Dutch North Sea Fishery* (1923), *Handelsbladfilm* (1928, on making a newspaper), *Groei: de schepping van een warenhuis/Growth: the Creation of a Department Store* (1930), *Stalen knuisten/Steel Fists* (1930, for the steel workers' union), and *Triomf/Triumph* (1931, for the trade union federation). Though Polygoon was unable to maintain its originality and exceptional standards into the 1930s, its outstanding output of the 1920s set an example to future generations. In 1984 Polygoon's rich film archive was sold to the national broadcasting centre, NOB, in Hilversum. KD

Bib: Bert Hogenkamp, *De Nederlandse documentaire film, 1920–1940* (1988).

POMMER, Erich
Hildesheim 1889 – Los Angeles, California 1966

German producer, both driving force and *éminence grise* of fifty years of German cinema history. A former employee of Gaumont* and Eclair, Pommer founded Decla (Deutsche Eclair) in 1915, which later merged with Bioskop (Decla-Bioskop) and in 1923 was absorbed by Ufa*, where he became a key member of the directorial board. A European by temperament and conviction [> FILM EUROPE], Pommer produced many of the most artistically and commercially successful German films of the Weimar* cinema. After a brief stint in Hollywood (1926–27), he returned to Germany, on loan from his American employers. The Nazi takeover forced Pommer to resume his globe-trotting, which took him to Paris (1933), Hollywood (1934), London – where he founded Mayflower Pictures with Charles Laughton* in 1937 – and again Hollywood (1940). He returned to Germany as an officer in the US Army in 1946, supervising the first licensing of production companies in the post-Nazi film industry. He returned to Hollywood in 1956. TE/MW

Bib: Wolfgang Jacobsen, *Erich Pommer: Ein Produzent macht Filmgeschichte* (1989).

PONCELA, Eusebio
Eusebio Poncela Aprea; Madrid 1947

Spanish actor, identified early in his career with the underground and experimental scene with such cult films as Iván Zulueta's *Arrebato/Rapture* (1979). Poncela's soft-spoken, sensitive performances, especially in films by Pedro Almodóvar* – *Matador* (1986) and, above all, *La ley del deseo/The Law of Desire* (1987, as Antonio Banderas's* lover) – have made him one of Spain's most prominent leading men. He has also appeared in Pilar Miró's* *Werther* (1986), Carlos Saura's* *El Dorado* (1988) and Imanol Uribe's* *El rey pasmado/The Stupefied King* (1991). PWE

PONTE, María Luisa
María Luisa Ponte Mancini; Molina de Rioseco, Valladolid 1918

Spanish actress of both popular and *auteur* films. She typically plays the strong but rather ill-humoured, 'spinsterish' background figure whose cynicism adds further black humour to often dark comedies, for instance Marco Ferreri's* *El pisito/The Little Flat* (1958) and *El cochecito/The Little Car* (1960), and Luis García Berlanga's* *El verdugo/The Executioner* (1963). Her more recent films, variations on her trademark shrewish malcontent, include Pilar Miró's* *La petición/The Engagement Party* (1976) and Mario Camús'* *La colmena/The Beehive* (1982). PWE

PONTECORVO, Gillo
Gilberto Pontecorvo; Pisa 1919

Italian director. Pontecorvo started his career as an unwilling student of chemistry. However, a change of residence to Paris as a result of racial discrimination enabled him to continue his music studies (he wrote the music for all his films), to sign up for a journalism course and later to find his way into the world of cinema. During the war he joined the Italian Communist Party and played an important part in the Resistance. He was an assistant to Yves Allégret* and Joris Ivens* after the war and made some short films. His first feature, *La grande strada azzurra/The Wide Blue Road* (1957), is a condensed version of a 'social' novel by Franco Solinas*, his favourite scriptwriter. *Kapò* (1960) was an uneasy amalgam of crude description of the Nazi death camps with a melodrama of love and redemption (and as such was fiercely criticised by Jacques Rivette* in *Cahiers du cinéma*). *La battaglia di Algeri/Battle of Algiers* (1966), his most famous film, awarded a Golden Lion at the Venice Festival, revealed his mastery of a political cinema capable of explaining rather than judging. Produced almost entirely with Algerian government money, the film adopts a quasi-documentary style to describe the struggle and suffering of a whole country rather than identifying individual heroes. The success of this film (except in France, where it was banned for a long time and is even now rarely shown) paved the way for his Hollywood debut, directing Marlon Brando in *Queimada!/Burn!* (1969), a somewhat schematic treatise on capitalism and colonialism. Ten years later, *Ogro* (1979), about Basque terrorism, proved too unfocused to be of genuine interest. In 1992 Pontecorvo was appointed Director of the Venice* Film Festival, where he used his international prestige to organise the 'Assise degli Autori' (an annual meeting held in defence of artistic liberty) and to entice Hollywood productions to Italian film festivals away from the hegemony of Cannes*. PM

PONTI, Carlo
Magenta 1910

Italian producer. A lawyer, Ponti entered cinema in the early 1940s, working for Lux*. In 1950 he left Lux to found Ponti-De Laurentiis with Dino De Laurentiis*, setting in motion an industry combine characterised by high investment and cultural profile. Their productions spanned the range from art films – Roberto Rosselllini's* *Europa '51* (1952) and Federico Fellini's* *La strada* (1954) – to popular comedies: Mario Monicelli's* *Guardie e ladri/Cops and Robbers* (1951), Totò* films, and many others. After breaking with De Laurentiis, Ponti migrated to the US with Sophia Loren*, whom he married in 1957 and whose stardom provided him with many successful productions. An expert player of the international market, and a shrewd businessman, he worked in the US as an independent producer, masterminding complex operations which culminated with *Doctor Zhivago* (1965). At the European end, in between Italy (where he encountered some legal and tax-related problems) and France (whose citizenship he acquired in 1964), Ponti's company Champion produced some high-quality movies like Vittorio De Sica's* *La ciociara/Two Women* (1960) starring Loren, Jean-Luc Godard's* *Une Femme est une femme/A Woman is a Woman* (1961, Fr.), Elio Petri's* *La decima vittima/The 10th Victim* (1965), Michelangelo Antonioni's* *Blowup* (1967, UK/It.), *Zabriskie Point* (1969, US), and *Professione: Reporter/The Passenger* (1975), Ettore Scola's* *Una giornata particolare/A Special Day* (1977), as well as films by Roman Polanski*, Claude Chabrol* and Agnès Varda* among others. Although he never attended the set during the shooting of a film, he claimed the last word on it, sometimes asking for substantial changes, as he did for Godard's *Le Mépris/Contempt* (1963, Fr./It.) and Marco Ferreri's* *Break-up* (1965), reduced to a single episode (an uncensored version was released in 1969). Before retiring, Ponti produced Maurizio Ponzi's *Qualcosa di biondo/My Three Loves* (1984), built entirely around Sophia Loren. GVo

PONTOPPIDAN, Clara
Clara Wieth; Copenhagen 1883–1975

Danish actress. Clara Pontoppidan studied ballet and, later, acting at the Royal Theatre in Copenhagen. She made her theatre debut in 1901 and her film debut in 1910. A brilliant stage actress, she adapted quickly to film (and later television). Her earliest screen success was in *Ved Fængslets Port/Temptations of a Great City* (1911), produced by Nordisk Films* and directed by August Blom*, which was followed by many films for Nordisk. From 1913 she worked in Sweden, returning to Denmark in 1915 to continue her dual career on stage and screen. She appeared in *Häxan/Witchcraft*

Through the Ages (1922), among other films, but from 1935 worked mainly on stage for the Royal Theatre in Copenhagen, with forays into radio and television. She played in the television drama *En kvinde er overflødig/A Woman is Superfluous* (1956), and its film version (1957), both directed by Gabriel Axel*. Her best-known film part is probably that of the Finnish Siri in Carl Theodor Dreyer's* *Blade af Satans Bog/Leaves from Satan's Book* (1921). A graceful actress, Pontoppidan owed much of her screen elegance to her early ballet training. She was particularly popular in Italy during the silent period. ME

POPESCU-GOPO, Ion
Bucharest 1923–89

Romanian animator and director, who was largely responsible for modern Romanian animation's success with a worldwide audience. A graduate of the Bucharest Fine Arts Institute and a former sculptor, cartoonist, journalist and book illustrator, Gopo founded the first Romanian animation department in 1950 (which became AnimaFilm* in 1964). After following the Disney line prevalent in eastern Europe, he created in *Scurtă istorie/A Short History* (1956) the 'little man with the flower' – a character both grotesque and funny, cruel and opportunist, determined to survive, travelling through time and human culture always grasping his flower. It won the Palme d'Or at Cannes, and formed the first of a trilogy. The series inspired UNESCO to sponsor a sequel, *Allo, allo* (1961). In the 1960s Gopo abandoned pure animation. After *S-a furat o bombă/A Bomb was Stolen* (1962), a parody thriller against nuclear war, he concentrated on children's films, science fiction and live-action animation, even combining all three. *Maria, Mirabella* (1981) is a magical children's musical. In the 1970s Gopo revived the 'little man with the flower': in *Ecce homo* (1978), faced by hunger, pollution and war, he departs the planet leaving his flower behind. *Quo vadis homo sapiens* (1982) is an anthology of Gopo's shorts, and a new film in its own right, in which the 'little man' looks at the history of inventions, philosophy and the failings of humanity. Gopo was chairman of the Romanian Film-makers' Association and maintained a prolific output of features and animation almost until his death. MM

POPULAR FRONT CINEMA

French film movement of the late 1930s, embracing a body of films made at the time of, and engaging with, the Popular Front, the historic left political alliance which ruled from May 1936 to October 1938. As well as introducing significant social changes (paid holidays, trade union rights, a health service), the Popular Front unleashed a ferment of cultural experiment as intellectuals and artists poured into the political arena. Newsreels, documentaries and propaganda films were made in an extraordinary burst of activity and enthusiasm, especially at the cooperative Ciné-Liberté, of which Jean Renoir* was a member. With others, including Jacques Becker* and Jean-Paul Dreyfus (Le Chanois), Renoir directed the Communist propaganda film *La Vie est à nous* (1936) and then (on his own) the epic *La Marseillaise* (1937), financed by public subscription. Renoir's marvellous *Le*

Crime de Monsieur Lange (1935, script by Jacques Prévert*) is the story of a workers' cooperative, symptomatic in its exuberant celebration of the power of popular culture and imagination. Julien Duvivier's* *La Belle équipe* (1936) is also about a cooperative, although its use of star Jean Gabin* and particularly its original bleakly pessimistic ending inflect it towards Poetic Realism*. Other films directly dealing with Popular Front themes include Le Chanois' *Le Temps des cerises* (1937), Georges Monca's *Choc en retour* (1937) and the documentary *Les Bâtisseurs* (1938, dir. Jean Epstein*). Some films outside this canon dealt with contemporary social trends, such as *Club de femmes*, *Avec le sourire/With a Smile* (1936), *L'Entraîneuse/Night Club Hostess*, *Eusèbe député/ Eusèbe MP*, *Altitude 3200* (1938); many others, in their avoidance of the subject, may be just as characteristic of the period. GV

Bib: Ginette Vincendeau and Keith Reader (eds.), *La Vie est à nous, French Cinema of the Popular Front 1935–1938* (1986).

PORTEN, Henny
Frida Ulricke Porten;
Magdeburg 1890 – Berlin 1960

German actress. Daughter of the cameraman and director Franz Porten, Henny Porten began assisting her father at an early age and soon became the star attraction of the Messter* Projektion company, having her own series by 1913. During her career of almost fifty years, Porten played under the direction of reliable entertainment directors such as Adolf Gärtner, Curt A. Stark, Rudolf Biebach and Carl Froelich* (*Mutter und Kind*, 1924), as well as with more ambitious directors like Ernst Lubitsch* (*Kohlhiesels Töchter, Anna Boleyn*, both 1920), Robert Wiene* (*I.N.R.I. Ein Film der Menschlichkeit*, 1923), E. A. Dupont* (*Die Geier-Wally*, 1921), Paul Leni* (*Hintertreppe/Backstairs*, 1921, co-dir. Leopold Jessner) and G. W. Pabst* (*Skandal um Eva*, 1930, her first sound movie). Also a producer, she was the star embodiment of the typical German 'wife and mother'. In the 1930s, her career was uneven, despite remakes of her silent successes. The target of accusations from the political left as well as the right, after World War II Porten found it difficult to continue, opting for minor roles in two DEFA* films (*Carola Lamberti – Eine vom Zirkus*, 1954; *Das Fräulein von Scuderi*, 1955), before retiring from filming. TE/KU

Bib: Helga Belach, *Henny Porten: Der erste deutsche Filmstar 1890–1960* (1986).

Other Films Include: *Schatten des Meeres* (1912); *Die blaue Laterne* (1918); *Das alte Gesetz* (1923); *Violantha/Die Königin der Berge* (1927); *Alle machen mit* (1933); *Wenn der junge Wein blüht* (1943).

PORTUGAL

R. W. Paul's* Animatograph was first presented in Lisbon by a 'Hungarian electrician', one Edwin Rousby, in June 1896.

On 12 November 1896, the first Portuguese films were shown in Oporto by Aurélio da Paz dos Reis. *A Saída dos Operários da Fábrica Confiança/Workers Leaving the Confiança Factory* and *Chegada de um Comboio Americano a Cadouços* must have been very similar to the Lumière* films *La Sortie des usines Lumière* and *L'Arrivée d'un train en gare de La Ciotat* (1895). In 1899 the first Portuguese production company, Portugal-Film, was founded in Lisbon by Manuel da Costa Veiga, and a second, Portugália Film, in 1908 by João Freire Correia. Reis, Veiga and Correia were all photographers for whom *prises de vue* with the Lumière Cinematograph were an extension of their previous work. Meanwhile, the first film theatres opened in Lisbon in 1904 and in Oporto two years later. In 1911, *Os Crimes de Diogo Alves/The Crimes of Diogo Alves* became the first Portuguese fiction film, based on 'a true story'.

Portuguese film production proper began in 1917 with the building of the Invicta-Film studios in Oporto. In the absence of trained Portuguese, technicians were imported from France with the support of Pathé*, the most important being the director Georges Pallu. Invicta productions were mainly based on adaptations of well-known novels by nineteenth-century Portuguese authors. 1921 saw the first adaptation of Portugal's mythic romantic novel, *Amor de Perdição/Ill-fated Love*. But two years later the company was already in crisis, and it finally died in 1931. The new centre of film activity was Lisbon, where young 'modernists' formed the first real generation of Portuguese film-makers: men such as Leitão de Barros*, Brum do Canto and António Lopes Ribeiro*. Meanwhile another 'modernist', Manoel de Oliveira*, was beginning to work in Oporto. The first Portuguese sound film, *A Severa* (1931), was shot by Barros in the Epinay studios near Paris. Adapted from a conventional play, the film had as its two main characters a 'fado' singer (the 'fado' is the traditional Lisbon song, obsessed with destiny) and her aristocratic macho lover, both central to Portuguese mythology. Its success helped persuade Tobis-Klangfilm to build a sound stage in Lisbon. *A Canção de Lisboa/Song of Lisbon*, in 1933, was the first sound film made in Portugal; it was also the first Portuguese comedy [> COMEDY (PORTUGAL)] and the only film directed by Cottinelli Telmo, a leading modernist architect.

In 1926 the military dictatorship took power, and six years later Salazar's grip was absolute. Some of the 'modernists' backed the regime, for which António Ferro was appointed propaganda chief. Ferro scripted *A Revolução de Maio/The May Revolution* (1937) under a pseudonym; directed by Lopes Ribeiro (another 'convert'), it was the regime's most ambitious attempt at cinema propaganda. Otherwise production was desultory and confined to comedies, biopics and adaptations of nineteenth-century novels. A noteworthy exception is *A Canção da Terra/The Song of the Earth*, shot on the island of Porto Santo by Brum do Canto in 1938.

A new period began in 1941 as Portugal profited from its non-participation in the war. Lopes Ribeiro was its key figure as both director and producer. This was the great era of comedy and co-productions with Spain; one of these co-productions, *Três Espelhos/Three Mirrors* (1946), was directed by the Hungarian émigré Ladislao Vajda*. However, the domestic market was too small for financial viability, and there were no significant exports: cinema was 'that terribly expensive industry', as Salazar told Lopes Ribeiro. From 1948, state support was forthcoming from the National Cinematographic Fund, but films seemed to become less and less interesting and production remained difficult. In 1955, the year television began broadcasting, Portugal produced no films at all.

As in other European countries, a Portuguese counter-movement began with the development of film societies. Rejecting the existing national cinema (with the exception of Oliveira, who ironically was unable to work at the time), they tried to recreate a cinema based on Italian neo-realism*. Eventually Ernesto de Sousa made one film, *Dom Roberto* (1962), but the most significant events were elsewhere: the return of Oliveira with *Acto da Primavera/Rite of Spring/ Passion of Jesus* (1963) and the advent of a 'second generation' of film-makers who formed the New Portuguese Cinema* around the producer António da Cunha Telles*. The public, however, failed to respond; while star-vehicles for singers continued to generate an audience, the New Portuguese Cinema all but vanished, to be resurrected in 1971 with the cooperative CPC and a new law setting up the Portuguese Institute of Cinema. The Institute's first production subsidies were announced just weeks before the restoration of democracy on 25 April 1974 (and the complete abolition of censorship). Militant cinema – 'free at last!' – and political antagonism, with the majority of film-makers opposing attempts to make production exclusively dependent on the state, were the salient developments of the following years. Titles include the collectively made *As Armas e o Povo/The Guns and the People* (1974–75, with the participation of Glauber Rocha), Rui Simões' *Deus, Patria, Autoridade/God, Fatherland, Authority* (1975) and *Bom Povo Portugues/Good Portuguese People* (1980), João César Monteiro's* *Que Farei Eu Com Esta Espada?/What Shall I Do With This Sword?* (1975) and Luís Rocha's *Barronhos, Quem Teve Medo do Poder Popular?/Barronhos, Who Was Afraid of the People's Power?* (1976).

The 1980s brought significant changes, however. Two of the most important factors were the increasing productivity of Manoel de Oliveira and the activities of Paulo Branco* in production. Being dependent on state subsidies rather than the market, film-makers felt free to concentrate on art cinema, full of literary references and obsessive reflections on Portugal. Portuguese cinema became an art-house ghetto. Several films were not released, and there was growing public suspicion of the success of Portuguese art films at international festivals. In the two years after the revolution audiences grew, but cinemas soon began to close under the combined squeeze of recession on the one hand and the extreme popularity of Brazilian soap operas on the other. The most successful Portuguese film of all time – *O Lugar do Morto/Deadman's Shoes* (1984) by António-Pedro Vasconcelos (284,533 viewers) – failed to recoup its costs on the home market; the Portuguese profits of even a blockbuster like *ET* fall short of financing the average Portuguese film. State support thus became imperative and every Portuguese film (with very few exceptions) over the last twenty years has been made with official support from the IPACA (Portuguese Institute for Cinema and Audio-visual Art). But although the state supports film production it ignores distribution, which is why Portugal has among the

highest rates of American film penetration in Europe. In the late 1970s, a 'third generation' of film-makers began to appear, less concerned with historical reflection and more with personal relationships. Among this group Teresa Villaverde and Pedro Costa are the most important new directorial talents, Joaquim Pinto* eventually becoming more involved in production.

Since the end of World War II, the number of Portuguese films has averaged eight a year. Given that some of these are not actually released, Portuguese audiences are little used to hearing their own language on screen, and even avoid Portuguese-speaking films. All foreign films on the Portuguese market are released with subtitles, with the exception of Disney animation films, and even those are spoken with a Brazilian accent (*The Lion King*, 1994, was the first dubbed film to be released in Portugal).

After the first private television networks began broadcasting in 1993, the already limited support for cinema of RTP, the beleaguered state television channel, shrank still further. Figures of ten films produced in 1991, ten in 1992 and fourteen in 1993 may seem high for a country the size of Portugal. But in 1994 the situation became extreme in its contradictions: while six films were made (three of them parts of anthologies), no less than twelve (four as parts of anthologies) were released. A mystery? Some films had waited years for release – a brief release on a tiny scale at that. AMS

POSITIF

French film journal. Founded in 1952 in Lyons by Bernard Chardère (and based in Paris since 1954), *Positif* has long been the rival of *Cahiers du cinéma**, although sharing with it fundamental values such as the promotion of *auteur* cinema (albeit different *auteurs*). *Positif* was initially the more politicised journal, taking up virulent anti-New Wave* positions and showing concern for political events (such as the Algerian war). Its libertarian attitude, inherited from Surrealism, made it champion, for instance, Jerry Lewis and Italian comedy. In the early 1980s it took part in debates on 'American imperialism'. The fact that *Positif* writers did not become film-makers, and that it did not specifically champion any theory, explains the absence of translations of its texts in English. Nearly fifty years on, *Positif* and *Cahiers* remain the two quality French magazines of film criticism. GV

POTTER, Sally   London 1947

British director, whose background in avant-garde music, dance and performance art plays an important part in the construction of her films. Her short film *Thriller* (1979) became one of the classics of British feminist independent cinema. Replete with references to *film noir*, and using a music track which combines Bernard Herrmann's score from *Psycho* with Puccini's *La Bohème*, the film is an investigation into why Mimi had to die. Her first feature, *The Gold Diggers* (1983), again investigates the conventions of narrative cinema to expose their construction of women, and was made with an all-woman crew on which everyone – including Julie Christie* – received the same daily rate. With *Orlando* (1992, UK/

USSR/Fr./It./Neth.), adapted from Virginia Woolf, starring Tilda Swinton*, co-produced between St Petersburg, Rome, Paris and Maarsen, gloriously shot on location in England and Russia, with a compelling score co-written by Potter and David Motion, she addresses a wider art cinema audience while retaining the integrity of her exploration of gender and identity. JC

POWELL, Dilys
Bournemouth 1902 – London 1995

British film critic, who, with C. A. Lejeune* at the *Observer*, dominated British film reviewing during and after World War II. She was film critic of the *Sunday Times* from 1939 until 1976, a regular broadcaster long after that, and her influential book, *Films Since 1939*, published in 1947, established many of the values of 'quality cinema'. These values were rooted in the documentary movement, and the cinema which she advocated was one which brought 'documentary truth' to the fiction film. Sharing many of Lejeune's tastes and prejudices, she was dismissive of triviality, and contemptuous of, for example, the excess of the Gainsborough* melodramas. At the same time, many of her critical judgments ran against the grain of contemporary opinion: she admired Michael Powell* and Emeric Pressburger before it was fashionable to do so; she supported Alfred Hitchcock* when *Sight and Sound** still wrote him off as a mere 'master of suspense'; and she wrote approvingly of Diana Dors* when she was treated as a joke by the rest of the press. Dilys Powell was awarded a BFI* Fellowship in 1986, and received the Critics' Circle Film Section award in 1988. JC

Bib: Christopher Cook (ed.), *The Dilys Powell Film Reader* (1991).

POWELL, Michael
Canterbury 1905 – Avening 1990
and
PRESSBURGER, Emeric
Miskolc, Hungary 1902 – Aspall 1988

British director, producer and writer team (Pressburger of Hungarian origin). Opinion has fluctuated on Powell and Pressburger. At the popular level, *A Matter of Life and Death* (1946) was chosen for the first Royal Command Performance, but Powell fell from grace after the 'scandal' of *Peeping Tom* (1960), whose disturbed, sadistic serial killer outraged critical and public opinion. Critically, the editors of *Movie**, in their 1962 chart of British *auteurs*, placed Powell in the 'Competent or ambitious' category along with Michael Anderson and Robert Day. More recently, however, as critical taste has moved away from realism, Powell and Pressburger have been reclaimed as the jewels in the crown of British cinema.

Powell began as an assistant in Rex Ingram's studio in Nice in 1925, and his own 'un-British' style carries traces of Ingram's stylish expressionism. He learned his craft in 'quota quickies', directing twenty-three films between 1931 and 1936. In 1937, he went to the remote island of Foula in the Shetland archipelago to direct *The Edge of the World*, and in 1940 he was one of the directors on Alexander Korda's* *The Thief of Bagdad*. Pressburger, born in Hungary, had been a scriptwriter in Germany, Austria and France before arriving in England as a contract writer for Korda in 1936. Korda put Powell and Pressburger together for *The Spy in Black* in 1939, and the two worked together for the next seventeen years, forming 'The Archers' company in 1942 and sharing writing, directing and producing credits on all their films between *The Life and Death of Colonel Blimp* (1943) and *Ill Met by Moonlight* (1957). After they split up, Powell continued to direct, including such distinctive films as *Peeping Tom* and *Age of Consent* (1969, Aust.), and Pressburger directed *Twice Upon a Time* (1953), but it is The Archers period which forms the core of their work, cutting a bright dash in the utility realism of postwar British cinema.

Together, Powell and Pressburger received a Special Award from the BFI* in 1978, and a Golden Lion award at Venice in 1982. In 1981, Powell became Senior Director in Residence at Coppola's Zoetrope Studios. In his autobiography, *A Life in the Movies* (1986), he wrote:

'I love England. I have mirrored England to the English in my films. They have not understood the image in the mirror. I am writing these lines in a foreign country [...] because for the last ten years I have been made to feel an outcast by my own people. I was "too big a risk". I was "too independent". I wanted my own way. I was all the things that have made my films different from my contemporaries' films. I have grown up. Audiences have grown up. Films have stayed in the nursery.' JC

Bib: Ian Christie, *Arrows of Desire: The Films of Michael Powell and Emeric Pressburger* (1985).

Other Films: **Powell As Director, Pressburger As Writer –** *Contraband* (1940); *49th Parallel* (1941); *...One of Our Aircraft is Missing* (1942). **As 'The Archers' –** *The Volunteer* [short] (1943); *A Canterbury Tale* (1944); *I Know Where I'm Going!* (1945); *Black Narcissus* (1947); *The Red Shoes* (1948); *The Small Back Room* (1949); *Gone to Earth, The Elusive Pimpernel* (1950); *The Tales of Hoffmann* (1951); *Oh ... Rosalinda!!* (1955); *The Battle of the River Plate* (1956); *They're a Weird Mob* (1966, Aust./UK); *The Boy Who Turned Yellow* (1972). **Films Directed By Michael Powell Include –** *Two Crowded Hours* [first feature] (1931); *The Fire Raisers* (1933); *Red Ensign* (1934); *Luna de Miel/Honeymoon* (1956, Sp./UK); *The Queen's Guards* (1961); *Herzog, Blaubarts Burg/Bluebeard's Castle* (1964, Ger.); *Return to the Edge of the World* [for BBC] (1978).

PRAUNHEIM, Rosa von
Holger Mischwitzky; Riga, Latvia 1942

German director and radical militant gay activist. He started out in the underground cinema and then made hilarious genre parodies – many for television – such as *Die Bettwurst/The Bedroll* (1970). Praunheim became internationally famous with the provocative *Nicht der Homosexuelle ist pervers, sondern die Situation, in der er lebt*

(1971). This television film was highly controversial because it used negative stereotyping of gay men in order to politicise them, and indeed the film helped bring about the gay liberation struggle in West Germany. Praunheim made a musical about AIDS, *Ein Virus kennt keine Moral/A Virus Knows no Morality* (1986), and an AIDS trilogy: *Positiv/Positive* (1989), *Schweigen = Tod/Silence = Death* (1989), *Feuer unterm Arsch/Asses on Fire* (1990). Many of his films, whether fiction or documentary, are about social outsiders: *Tally Brown in New York* (1979) is about an ageing female performer; *Stadt der verlorenen Seelen – Berlin Blues/City of Lost Souls* (1983) brings together black transexuals and transvestites, a Jewish trapeze artist and other performers; and *Ich bin meine eigene Frau/I Am My Own Woman* (1992) is not only a funny and compassionate biopic of the witty transvestite Charlotte von Mahlsdorf but also a political reflection on life in the former East Germany. Praunheim's aim is to change attitudes towards minorities, not just gays. His work is usually humorous, though always confrontational in its attacks on dominant notions of good taste and decency. US

Bib: Richard Dyer, *Now You See It: Studies on Lesbian and Gay Film* (1990).

PRÉJEAN, Albert   Paris 1893–1979

French actor and singer. Préjean emerged internationally as the singing hero of René Clair's* *Sous les toits de Paris* (1930), one of the most important early French sound films, and in the French version of G. W. Pabst's* *L'Opéra de quat' sous/Die Dreigroschenoper/The Threepenny Opera* (1930). He was already well established in French silent films, including Clair's *Paris qui dort* (1924) and *Un chapeau de paille d'Italie/An Italian Straw Hat* (1928); he directed a short, *L'Aventure de Luna Park*, in 1929. Sound cinema suited his Parisian accent and brand of popular *chanson*. A substantial career followed, embracing over forty films in the 1930s, among them Robert Siodmak's* *La Crise est finie* (1934, co-starring Danielle Darrieux*) and *Mollenard* (1937), Edmond T. Gréville's *Princesse Tam-Tam* (1935, co-starring Josephine Baker*), Marcel Carné's* *Jenny* (1936), and Pierre Chenal's* *L'Alibi* (1937). Préjean played a theatrical and optimistic version of Jean Gabin's* tragic proletarian hero. He was very active during the war, notably incarnating Inspector Maigret in a series of adaptations of Simenon's* novels. As a prominent personality during the war, he attended social occasions with Germans and visited Germany for film premieres; he was briefly arrested at the Liberation. His postwar career was lacklustre, but thanks to his 1930s films and his song recordings, his place as one of the best-liked actors of the *'cinéma du sam'di soir'* is secure. GV

PREOBRAZHENSKAYA, Olga I.   Moscow 1881–1971

Soviet director, actress and scriptwriter. Preobrazhenskaya studied acting at the Moscow Art Theatre Studio and first appeared on screen in the popular *Klyuchi schast'ya/The Keys to Happiness* (1913); she was a leading actress of the pre-

Revolutionary cinema. In 1916 she co-directed *Baryshnia-krestianka/The Lady Peasant* with Vladimir Gardin*. Her first film as solo director was *Viktoriia/Victoria* (1917). Though she continued directing until 1941, she is best known for her film about the oppression of women in the pre-Revolutionary Russian countryside, *Baby ryazanskie/Peasant Women of Ryazan* (1927). Preobrazhenskaya taught at VGIK* from 1927 to 1941. RT

PRESLE, Micheline   Micheline Chassagne; Paris 1922

French actress. Although less famous internationally than her contemporaries Michèle Morgan* and Danielle Darrieux*, the beautiful Presle was a top box-office star from the late 1930s to the early 1950s. Her first important roles were in G. W. Pabst's* *Jeunes filles en détresse/Young Ladies in Distress*, and the dual lead – as mother and daughter – in Abel Gance's melodrama *Paradis perdu* (both 1939). She emerged as a major star during the German occupation, in comedies and costume dramas like *Félicie Nanteuil* (1942–45), and contemporary dramas such as Jacques Becker's* *Falbalas* (1945). At the Liberation she starred in Christian-Jaque's* *Boule de suif/Angel and Sinner* (1945). Her star persona combined elegance, effervescence, energy and modernity and she acquired a reputation for sophisticated comedy. Her best-known film, Claude Autant-Lara's* *Le Diable au corps/Devil in the Flesh* (1947, co-starring Gérard Philipe*), was a return to melodrama. A first trip to Hollywood in 1948 produced disappointing films and a brief marriage to Morgan's ex-husband, William Marshall (Marshall and Presle's daughter, Tonie Marshall, is an actress and successful director; her second film, *Pas très catholique*, 1994, starring Anémone, is an excellent comedy).

Presle's subsequent French career in costume dramas (Sacha Guitry's* *Napoléon*, 1955) and comedies (*La Mariée est trop belle/The Bride is Too Beautiful*, 1956, with Brigitte Bardot*) was mixed, though she starred in Jean Grémillon's* remarkable *L'Amour d'une femme* (1954), one of the few 'feminist' films of the time. Presle has since alternated mainstream films, *auteur* work (Jacques Rivette's* *La Religieuse*, 1965, rel. 1967), television series and theatre. She generously supports young *auteur* cinema, notably by women – for instance Marie-Claude Treilhou's *Le Jour des rois* (1991), co-starring Darrieux and Paulette Dubost. GV

PRESSBURGER, Emeric – see POWELL, Michael

PRÉVERT, Jacques   Neuilly-sur-Seine 1900 – Omonville-la-Rogue 1977
and
PRÉVERT, Pierre   Neuilly-sur-Seine 1906 – Paris 1988

French scriptwriters and directors. The Prévert brothers were at the centre of the Surrealist group in Paris in the early 1920s.

Pierre became assistant to Alberto Cavalcanti* and later Jean Renoir*, while Jacques worked for an advertising agency and began writing poetry. Both appeared in minor film parts (including Jean Vigo's* *L'Atalante*, 1934). In 1932, Jacques joined the agit-prop 'Groupe Octobre', many of whose members appeared in Pierre's medium-length film *L'Affaire est dans le sac* (1932), a witty Surrealist fantasy but a commercial flop. Pierre's career as a director was sketchy (two features – *Adieu Léonard*, 1943, *Voyage-surprise*, 1947 – and some shorts, including *Paris La Belle*, 1959, with scenes shot in 1928 with Jacques, and several unrealised projects). His work for television included a film about his brother (1961).

Jacques meanwhile was for almost thirty years one of the most important script and dialogue writers in French cinema, beginning with the 1933 *Ciboulette*; his last film was *Les Amours célèbres* (1961). He worked with Renoir on *Le Crime de Monsieur Lange* (1935) [> POPULAR FRONT CINEMA] and Jean Grémillon* on *Remorques/Stormy Waters* (1939–41) and *Lumière d'été* (1943), among others, but is best known for his collaboration with Marcel Carné, with whom he formed the central team of Poetic Realism* on films such as *Jenny* (1936), *Drôle de drame* (1937), *Quai des brumes* (1938), *Le Jour se lève* (1939) and *Les Enfants du paradis* (1943–45). The publication of *Paroles* in 1946 made him the best-selling French poet ever, and Joseph Kosma's* music turned some of his poems into songs that became international hits; one such was 'Les Feuilles mortes', sung by Yves Montand* in *Les Portes de la nuit* (1946). The latter film neatly encapsulates the dominant Prévertian theme of 'pure' young love struggling against a corrupt and cynical world. Although Prévert's texts for Carné were sometimes overladen with doom, the abiding characteristic of his work is wit; his dialogues, poems and songs sparkle with humour, erudition, romanticism and genuinely popular language. GV

PRINCE-RIGADIN
Charles Petit-Demange; Maisons-Laffitte 1872 – Paris 1933

French actor. With Max Linder*, one of the two first comic stars of French cinema. Both were dubbed 'the kings of the cinematograph' and reaped unprecedented benefits of stardom, fame and large salaries. 'Prince', as he was known on stage, became 'Rigadin' in a series of successful and influential early French comedies, many directed by Georges Monca for Pathé*, although he himself helped develop the stories. Raymond Chirat describes the Rigadin persona as 'lumpish and bewildered, with a clowning routine inherited from vaudeville'. Before World War I, Prince-Rigadin (like Linder) was, in his own words, 'the international ambassador of Gallic humour in all the countries where cinema penetrated. I had a different surname in each country: *Whiffles* in England and the Commonwealth, *Moritz* in Germany, *Maurice* in Romania, *Salustiano* in Spain, *Tartufini* in Italy, *Prenz* in Scandinavian and Slav countries, *Rigadin* everywhere else. In the Orient, if you please, I was *the prince Rigadin*!' Though he appeared in a couple of sound films, his career belongs to the early, exuberant phase of French silent cinema. GV

PROKOFIEV, Sergei S.
Sontsovka, Russia 1891 – Moscow 1953

Russian composer. Prokofiev wrote his first film score for Alexander Fainzimmer's* *Poruchik Kizhe/Lieutenant Kijé* (1934), but is better known for his work for Sergei Eisenstein* on *Aleksandr Nevskii/Alexander Nevsky* (1938) and *Ivan Groznyi/Ivan the Terrible* (1943–46), which explore Eisenstein's ideas on 'orchestral counterpoint' where the music not merely supports the image but also clashes with and comments on it. The most famous instance of these techniques is the 'Battle on the Ice' sequence in *Aleksandr Nevskii*. RT

PROTAZANOV, Yakov A.
Moscow 1881–1945

Russian director. Protazanov studied at the Moscow Commercial Academy. After a trip to Paris, where he visited the Pathé* factory, he joined the Gloria company in Moscow, working first as a translator. His first screenplay was for a 1909 version of Pushkin's *Bakhchisaraiskii fontan/The Fountain of Bakhchisarai*, and the first film he directed was *Pesn' katorzhanina/The Convict's Song* (1911). Of the seventy-three films he made before the Revolution, only seven are extant, but they include such remarkable work as *Ukhod velikogo startsa/The Departure of a Grand Old Man* (1912), about the last days of Tolstoy, and, after his move to the Yermolev company, a masterly version of Pushkin's *Pikovaya dama/The Queen of Spades* (1916), with a mesmeric performance by Ivan Mosjoukine* as Herman. Mosjoukine worked for him again in the proto-Expressionist *Satana likuyushchii/Satan Triumphant* (1917), in the bleak northern tale of repression *Malyutka Elli/Little Ellie* (1917), and in a version of Tolstoy's *Otets Sergii/Father Sergius* (1918). After the Revolution, Protazanov moved with Yermolev first to Yalta, and then into emigration, to Paris in 1920, where he gave René Clair* his first chance as an actor in *Le Sens de la mort/The Meaning of Death* (1921), and then to Berlin. There he was persuaded by Moisei Aleinikov to return to Soviet Russia to work in the new Mezhrapom*-Rus studio.

His first film on his return was *Aelita* (1924), famous as the first Soviet science-fiction film, as well as for its Constructivist sets and the costumes designed by Alexandra Exter, but also remarkable for its acute vision of Russia under the New Economic Policy. Though a popular success, it aroused criticism from both the Party and younger film-makers, and Protazanov followed it with the conventional *Ego prizyv/His Call* (1925), a melodrama which ends with its 'fallen' heroine responding to Lenin's call to join the Party. Throughout the 1920s, Protazanov produced a steady stream of melodramas and comedies. *Sorok pervyi/The Forty-First* (1926), from Boris Lavrenev's story, is about a Red Army girl, Maryutka, marooned on a desert island with a White officer who is her prisoner. Despite falling in love with him, she eventually remembers her duty and makes him her forty-first victim. *Chelovek iz restorana/The Man from the Restaurant* (1927) is set in 1916 and chronicles the social awakening of its little man hero. Among Protazanov's successful comedies of the period are *Zakroishchik iz Torzhka/The Tailor from Torzhok* (1926), with Igor Ilyinsky* as the eponymous hero who eventually finds love and wealth when he wins the state lottery; *Protsess o trëkh millionakh/The Three Millions Trial* (1926), a satire, set in Italy, about the world of banking; and *Don Diego i Pelageya/Don Diego and Pelageia* (1927), which mocks provincial bureaucrats. Protazanov's first sound film was *Tommi/Tommy* (1931), in which an English soldier serving in the Intervention forces during the Russian Civil War is brought to political awareness. During the 1930s Protazanov's projects encountered increasing difficulties and he was less prolific, but among his most important films of this decade was a powerful version of Ostrovsky's play *Bespridannitsa/Without a Dowry* in 1937. His final film, *Nasreddin v Bukhare/Nasreddin in Bukhara* (1943), is a kind of Uzbek *Thief of Baghdad*. With the sheer scope and variety of his work, Protazanov is increasingly recognised as one of the leading Russian directors. JGf

Bib: Ian Christie and Julian Graffy (eds.), *Protazanov and the Continuity of Russian Cinema* (1993).

PSILANDER, Valdemar   Copenhagen 1884 – Tårbak 1917

Danish actor, the most popular male star of the silent Danish cinema. Psilander began as a theatre actor in 1903 in Copenhagen and rose to stardom with *Ved Fængslets Port/Temptations of a Great City* (1911), directed by August Blom* for Nordisk Films*. His success rested in part on his relaxed, naturalistic performance, in contrast to the exaggerated gestures of most actors of the period, Danish or otherwise. This modern style, together with a handsomely virile appearance and a natural charm, turned Psilander into a matinée idol, especially with female audiences. Fan letters poured in from all over the world; he was particularly popular in Russia, where he was known as 'Mr Harrison' and was imitated by many Russian actors. Psilander was the leading male actor in many of the Danish erotic melodramas*, notably *Balletdanserinden/The Ballet Dancer* (1911), co-starring Asta Nielsen*, and *Den Stærkeste/The Strongest/Conquered* (1912). One of his last films was *Klovnen/The Clown* (1916), a sentimental story of a circus clown whose marriage is shattered when he sees his wife with another man. This was possibly his most popular film. He left Nordisk in 1916 to set up his own company, but died in 1917 after only one day's shooting. ME

Other Films Include: *Den sorte Drøm/The Black Dream* (1911); *Dødsprind til Hest fra Cirkuskuplen/The Great Circus Catastrophe, Vor Tids Dame/A Modern Girl* (1912); *Evangeliemandens liv/The Evangelist, Et Revolutionsbryllup/A Revolutionary Marriage* (1915); *Manden uden Fremtid/The Man Without a Future* (1916).

PUDOVKIN, Vsevolod I.   Penza, Russia 1893 – Riga, Latvia [USSR] 1953

Soviet director, actor and theorist. Pudovkin originally studied chemistry and physics at Moscow University but was called up in 1914 and later captured and imprisoned by the Germans. After the Revolution he became a founder member of Lev Kuleshov's* workshop at the State Film School (later VGIK*) and acted in his *Neobychainye priklyucheniya Mistera Vesta v strane bol'shevikov/The Extraordinary Adventures of Mr West in the Land of the Bolsheviks* (1924), *Luch smerti/Death Ray* (1925) and *Vesëlaya kanareika/The Happy Canary* (1929). Pudovkin's own first film as director was a short comedy, *Shakhmatnaya goryachka/Chess Fever* (1925), and this was followed by a short, *Mekhanika golovnogo mozga/The Mechanics of the Brain* (1926). His three major silent films were *Mat'/The Mother* (1926), based loosely on Gorky's account of the 1905 Revolution; *Konets Sankt-Peterburga/The End of St Petersburg* (1927), made to celebrate the tenth anniversary of the October Revolution; and *Potomok Chingis-khana/The Heir to Genghis Khan* (1928, released in the West as *Storm over Asia*), his treatment of British involvement in Mongolia.

Influenced by Kuleshov, Pudovkin laid greater emphasis on the role of the actor than did Sergei Eisenstein* but he was nevertheless co-signatory with Eisenstein and Grigori Alexandrov* of the 1928 'Statement on Sound', which warned of the dangers of the abandonment of montage and the re-theatricalisation of cinema through the use of purely illustrative sound. But, unlike Eisenstein, Pudovkin did not pursue these ideas thoroughly in practice, apart from his first experimentation with sound in *Prostoi sluchai/A Simple Chance* (1932) and *Dezertir/The Deserter* (1933). He used professional actors and his films all had individual heroes. Pudovkin's writings developed these ideas and he was the first Soviet film director to have his works published in English, in *Film Technique* (1929) and *Film Acting* (1935), not published fully in Russian until after his death. Pudovkin also proved more pliable than some other film-makers during the Great Terror and was not always averse to protecting his own interests at the expense of others. His later work deteriorated for reasons that were not entirely within his control, as can be seen from *Pobeda/Victory* (1938), *Admiral Nakhimov* (1946) and *Vozvrashchenie Vasiliya Bortnikova/The Return of Vasili Bortnikov* (1953). Nevertheless he remains one of the great names from the formative period of Soviet cinema. RT

PULA

National film festival of the former Yugoslavia. This annual presentation of Yugoslav feature films was first held in 1954 in the Croatian town of Pula on the northern Adriatic coast. The films were shown in a Roman arena dating from the first century, transformed into a huge open-air film theatre (with a capacity for 13,000 people). In 1955 the festival began to award prizes, for direction, acting, photography, art direction and music. The award for the best film of the year was the 'Golden Arena'. For the next thirty-five years Pula was the main Yugoslav film event. With the collapse of Yugoslavia, the festival experienced organisational problems, and in 1993 it was remodelled as the National Croatian film festival. SP

PULVER, Liselotte   Berne 1929

Swiss-born actress, who worked originally on the stage, and became much loved for her blonde vivaciousness, pert personality and high-spirited laughter. She first appeared in Leopold Lindtberg's* *Swiss Tour* (1949), and Kurt Hoffmann* first directed her in a detective comedy (*Klettermaxe*, 1952), one of ten films they made together. Her breakthrough came with *Ich denke oft an Piroschka/Piroschka* (1955), after which she received international offers from, among others, Jacques Becker* in France (*Les Aventures d'Arsène Lupin*, 1956) and Douglas Sirk (Detlef Sierck*) in the US (*A Time to Love and a Time to Die*, 1958). In her German productions she cultivated a comic, often capricious and obstinate persona and she became one of the most popular young actresses of German film, performing in numerous box-office hits such as *Das Wirtshaus im Spessart* (1957), *Kohlhiesels Töchter* (1962), *Die Bekenntnisse des Hochstaplers Felix Krull/The Confessions of Felix Krull* (1957) and *Buddenbrooks* (1959). She became one of the 'European' stars of the 1950s and 1960s; apart from Becker and Sirk, Billy Wilder directed her as James Cagney's provocative secretary in *One, Two, Three* (1961), and she worked in Spain, the US and France, where she appeared both in popular cinema, with stars such as Jean Gabin* (*Monsieur*, 1964), and in *auteur* films, notably Jacques Rivette's* *Suzanne Simonin, la religieuse de Diderot/La Religieuse/The Nun* (1965–67). MW/GV

PUTTI, Lya de   Vesce 1897 – New York 1931

Hungarian-born actress, best remembered as the seductive Bertha-Marie in E. A. Dupont's* *Varieté /Variety* (1925). She began her career in a string of supporting roles, as in Richard Oswald's* *Die Liebschaften des Hektor Dalmore* (1921) and *Othello* (1922) with Emil Jannings*. In 1922 she appeared in two films by F. W. Murnau*, *Der brennende Acker* and *Phantom*. By the mid-1920s, de Putti starred in Lothar Mendes' *S.O.S. Die Insel der Tränen* (1923, opposite Paul Wegener*) and in Karl Grune's* *Eifersucht* (1925, opposite Werner Krauß*). After the success of *Varieté*, Adolph Zukor invited her to Hollywood in 1926, where she was typecast as the exotic, European *femme fatale* in five films, including D. W. Griffith's *Sorrows of Satan* (1926) and as a Russian revolutionary in *The Scarlet Lady* (1928). MW

Bib: Johannes Zeilinger, *Lya de Putti: Ein vergessenes Leben* (1991).

PUTTNAM, (Sir) David   London 1941

British producer, who was hailed as the saviour of the commercial British film industry in the early 1980s, when it seemed, for a brief moment, that it would be saved. Coming to film from advertising, he brought to the cinema a number of other first-time directors from the world of advertising: Alan Parker*, Ridley Scott*, Hugh Hudson. His first production, *S.W.A.L.K./Melody* (1971), was written by Parker, with whom he went on to produce *Bugsy Malone* (1976) and *Midnight Express* (1978). He engaged Scott to direct *The Duellists* (1977), the first production of Puttnam's own production company, Enigma; and hired Hudson to direct *Chariots of Fire* (1981). The Best Picture Oscar for *Chariots*

348

of Fire, followed by the success and cultural prestige of *Local Hero* (1983) and *The Killing Fields* (1984), both of which he produced for Goldcrest*, seemed to herald a renaissance in the British commercial feature film, which in the event proved to be short-lived. They did, however, establish him as a major force in the British film industry. Puttnam has been compared to Michael Balcon*, with his productions in the 1980s reflecting his own liberal morality and mildly suburban sentimentality: an Ealing for the Thatcher years most apparent in the 'First Love' films which Enigma produced for Channel 4*. He is, however, unambiguously commercial, targeting and tailoring his films as entertainment for an international market. In the late 1980s he had a brief, and unhappy, flirtation with Hollywood as head of production for Columbia Pictures, before returning to Britain as a producer and campaigner (with Richard Attenborough*) for the revitalisation of Britain as a centre of European film production. He was knighted in 1995. JC

PUUPÄÄ FILMS

Finnish genre of the 1950s. Pekka Puupää was a cartoon character who appeared in thirteen films between 1953 and 1960. The character was created by the advertising designer Ola Fogelberg (1894–1952) in the 1920s, probably drawing on a famous contemporary comic couple in Danish films, *Fyrtaarnet og Bivognen**. Puupää ('Blockhead') was a tall, skinny simpleton whose adventures with his buddy Pätkä ('Runt') and angry wife Justiina amused readers of the social democratic press for years. The first (live-action) film based on the character, *Pekka Puupää/Pete Blockhead*, was made in 1953, to huge success. Puupää's role was played by the comedian and musician Esa Pakarinen, and many of the scripts were written by Reino Helismaa*. Pakarinen and Helismaa were central figures in the '*rillumarei*' films of the 1950s, popular entertainments featuring comic plots with musical numbers. The films' milieu was often proletarian, although not overtly political. Puupää films contain large amounts of the verbal humour typical of Finnish cinema, as well as sitcom elements, gags and visual tricks. Except for the first and the last, Armand Lohikoski directed the dozen or so Puupää films. *Pekka ja Pätkä pahassa pulassa/Pete and Runt in Hot Water* (1955) offers a typical Puupää storyline: Pekka and Pätkä are afraid to go home because Justiina is cross with them, so they hide on a boat supposedly on its way to Argentina. After nine days they find they have been sailing on a Helsinki ferry commuting between the market square and the zoo. The harmless humour of Puupää films was dressed in simple plot lines and caricatures to appeal to children and child-minded audiences. In the 1980s Visa Mäkinen directed a series of Puupää remakes for television and the cinema, but they never attained the box-office success of the originals. AH-H

PYRIEV, Ivan A.   Kamen, Russia 1901 – Moscow 1968

Soviet director and scriptwriter. After a brief career as an actor in the Proletkult and Meyerhold Theatres, Pyriev began scriptwriting in 1925. His first film as director was *Postoronnaya zhenshchina/A Woman on the Side* (1929), a satirical attack on bourgeois morality. This was followed by a similar approach to bureaucracy in *Gosudarstvennyi chinovnik/A State Official* (1931). *Konveier smerti/The Assembly Line of Death* (1933) depicted the life of three women against the background of the rise of fascism in contemporary Germany. *Partiinyi bilet/Party Card* (1936) and *Sekretar' raikoma/District Committee Secretary* (1942) carried a more overtly propagandist message, but Pyriev is best remembered for his musical comedies like *Bogataya nevesta/The Rich Bride* (1938), *Traktoristy/Tractor Drivers* (1939), *Svinarka i pastukh/The Swineherd and the Shepherd* (1941) and *Kubanskie kazaki/The Kuban Cossacks* (1950), all awarded the Stalin Prize. Towards the end of his career he devoted himself to adaptations of the works of Dostoyevsky, such as *Brat'ya Karamazovy/The Brothers Karamazov* (1968). He was head of the Mosfilm studio for many years. RT

Q

QUALTINGER, Helmut   Vienna 1928–86

Austrian actor, who became famous in the 1950s, primarily as a cabaret artist. Qualtinger created the characters of Travnicek and Herr Karl, malicious representations of 'true Viennese' figures whose easy-going nature and charm cover up stupidity, xenophobia and ignorance. In his first films, the oversize actor appeared in supporting roles based mainly on his corpulence. Later, in movies such as *Kurzer Prozess* (1967, dir. Michael Kehlmann), he was able to display his dramatic talent as the cranky police superintendent Pokorny. His parts became increasingly challenging in the 1970s, for example in *Das Schloß/The Castle* (1971, based on Kafka), in *Das falsche ewicht* (1971), and in *Grandison* (1979), where he impersonates a judge who 'crushes' the wife of a thief both physically and psychologically. One of his internationally famous films is Jean-Jacques Annaud's* film version of Umberto Eco's *Le Nom de la Rose/Der Name der Rose/The Name of the Rose* (1986). FM

Bib: Michael Horowitz, *Helmut Qualtinger* (1987).

QUEREJETA, Elías   Elías Querejeta Gárate; Hernani 1935

Spanish producer, whose name on the credits signifies 'quality' and is often as important as those of the distinguished *auteurs* whose films he produces. Querejeta attended the Escuela Oficial de Cinematografía* and gained production experience at the Unión Industrial de la Cinematografía, the company that produced Luis Buñuel's* *Viridiana* (1961) and which was for a time run by Juan Antonio Bardem*. Querejeta's first credits were as co-director, along with Anton Eceiza, of *A través de San Sebastián/Through San Sebastian* (1961) and *A través del fútbol/Through Football* (1962). He was also co-screenwriter of such distinguished films as *Pascual Duarte* (1975) and *A un Dios desconocido/To an Unknown God* (1977). But it is as a producer of art cinema that he is most celebrated. Querejeta's collaboration with Carlos Saura* from *La caza/The Hunt* (1965) to *Dulces horas/Sweet Moments* (1981) is legendary, and resulted in many award-winning films. JA

QUINN, Bob   Dublin 1939

Irish director and writer. The most prolific Irish film-maker, who worked in Radio Telefis Eireann* (RTE) in the 1960s before establishing an independent production company, Cinegael, in an Irish-speaking area of the West of Ireland, because it is 'isolated by its language from the English-American world'. He made the first Irish-language fiction film, *Caoineadh Airt Ui Laoire/Lament for Art O'Leary* (1975), which explored the relationship between the eighteenth century and the present in a formally innovative manner, casting the English playwright John Arden and his wife Margaretta D'Arcy in the unfamiliar roles of colonialist oppressors. His *Poitin* (1978) inserted a realist aesthetic into a West of Ireland previously populated by 'Quiet Man' quaintness and 'Man of Aran' celebration of land and sea. Continuing to work in often quirky contrast to other Irish film-makers, Quinn made a three-part television series, *Atlantean* (1984), which sought to overturn the Celtic myth of Irish origins and argued that the Irish came via the Atlantic from North Africa. Quinn's largely silent feature, *Budawanny* (1987), unconventionally explored the publicly unacknowledged reality of a supposedly celibate priest having a relationship with a woman. In one of the film's wittiest sequences the priest announces from the pulpit to his bewildered parishioners that 'soon you'll have another reason to call me Father'. Continuing with this theme, *The Bishop's Story* (1994) is a version of the controversy surrounding the real-life Bishop Casey, forced to resign as Bishop of Galway in 1992 after it became known that he had had a child in the 1970s. The film confirms Quinn's continuing challenge to established views and institutions. KR

R

RABAL, Francisco
Francisco Rabal Valera; Aguilas 1926

Spanish actor. His dark, brooding good looks and deep voice have made him one of the most popular male stars of the Spanish cinema. His career took off in the 1950s through a string of leading roles in films often directed by Rafael Gil*. These brought him to the attention of Luis Buñuel*, who cast him in *Nazarín* (1958), *Viridiana* (1961) and *Belle de Jour* (1967), to which he brought sensitivity and humour in roles identified with asceticism, business acumen and gangsterism respectively. His moving portrayal of the crisis-torn priest in *Nazarín* led to a long and varied international career, in films by Michelangelo Antonioni*, Claude Chabrol* and Jacques Rivette*, among others. At the same time, Rabal continued to make major films in Spain, including Carlos Saura's* *Llanto por un bandido/Lament for a Bandit* (1963), where his dashing looks served him well in a narrative exploring questions of masculinity and political responsibility, set back in history but clearly referring to political engagement in difficult times. Other important films in which Rabal has appeared include Mario Camús'* *La colmena/The Beehive* (1982) and Pedro Almodóvar's* *¡Atame!/Tie Me Up! Tie Me Down!* (1989), where he plays the wheelchair-bound director of pornographic films, obsessed by his star, Victoria Abril*. PWE

RABENALT, Arthur Maria
Vienna 1905

Austrian director, who stage-managed his first opera at the age of sixteen and for the next twelve years worked at several opera houses and theatres as a director, but was banned from stage management in 1933 because of his avant-gardist style. He trained with G. W. Pabst* and Alexander Korda* and turned to writing and directing entertainment films such as *Was bin ich ohne Dich* (1934). From 1935 to 1938 he worked in Austria, Italy and France (working on the dialogue of *Die klugen Frauen*, the German-language version of Jacques Feyder's* *La Kermesse héroique/Carnival in Flanders*, 1935). After 1938 he directed a series of light-hearted musical (for instance *Leichte Muse*, 1941) and circus (*Zirkus Renz*, 1943) films in Germany, but he is equally known for his propagandist film *... reitet für Deutschland* (1941). After the war he continued stage work (founding the cabaret group 'Schaubude', directing musicals and dramas, managing theatres), published on theatre and film history, and stayed active as a film and, since 1959, television director. KU

Bib: Arthur Maria Rabenalt, *Der Film im Zwielicht* (1958).

Other Films Include: *Weißer Flieder* (1940); *Das Mädchen Christine* (1948); *Glücksritter* (1957); *Ein Haus voll Musik* (1965).

RADDATZ, Carl
Werner Fritz; Mannheim 1912

German actor, specialising in 'officer and gentleman' roles, whose debut was in *Urlaub auf Ehrenwort* (1937, dir. Karl Ritter*), a nationalist army drama. Typecast as the aloof but acceptable face of the military in air force films about World War I (such as *Stukas*, 1941), Raddatz managed to infuse his performances in melodramas and women's films with an ambivalent sex appeal, lending credibility to roles as either hero or villain (*Verklungene Melodie*, 1938; *Immensee*, 1943). He worked for directors as different as Veit Harlan* (*Opfergang*, 1944) and Helmut Käutner* (*Unter den Brücken*, 1945), and his charm remained in demand after the war. In the early 1960s Raddatz retired from cinema, concentrating instead on theatre and television work. TE/KU

Other Films Include: *Wunschkonzert* (1940); *In jenen Tagen* (1947); *Das Mädchen Rosemarie* (1958); *Jons und Erdme* (1959).

RADEMAKERS, Fons
Alphonse Marie Rademakers; Roosendaal 1920

Dutch director, producer and actor. Rademakers began his career as a stage actor and director. After working as an assistant to Vittorio De Sica* and Jean Renoir* he made his directorial debut with *Dorp aan de rivier/Doctor in the Village* (1958), scenes from a country doctor's life; the picture was well received internationally, culminating in an Oscar nomination. His second film, *Makkers staakt uw wild geraas/That Joyous Eve* (1960, Silver Bear in Berlin), is a tragi-comic study of three families trying to suppress their marital problems in order not to spoil their children's Christmas. After finishing *Het mes/The Knife* (1961), about a boy's disturbing experience of sexual awakening, a film fraught with Freudian imagery, Rademakers turned away from intimate family themes. *Als twee druppels water/The Spitting Image* (1963) uses a complex doppelgänger motif to present a daring evocation of the grey area between resistance and collaboration during World War II, a paranoid world of moral ambiguities and dubious assumptions. *Mira* (1971), a box-office hit, dramatised the opposition of a local community to the building of a new bridge; it stars Willeke van Ammelrooy* (in her first major role) as Mira, the woman who confuses all contending parties with her sensual good looks. *Max Havelaar* (1976), based on a classic Dutch novel, tackled the issue of Dutch colonial rule in the nineteenth century. Rademakers is a master of adaptation; almost all his films are well-crafted versions of highly regarded novels from modern Dutch and Flemish authors, even if his ambition is unmistakably international. *De aanslag/The Assault* (1986) is another adaptation, this time from a novel by Harry Mulisch. Here the director returned to the issue of traumatic war experiences and failing memories, for which Hollywood awarded him an Oscar. Rademakers produced two interesting films directed by his wife Lili Rademakers, *Menuet/Minuet* (1982) and *Diary of a Mad Old Man* (1987). KD

Other Films as Director: *De dans van de reiger/The Dance of the Heron* (1966); *Because of the Cats* (1973); *Mijn vriend of het verborgen leven van Jules Depraeter/My Friend* (1979); *The Rose Garden* (1989).

RADEV, Vălo   Lesidren 1923

Bulgarian cinematographer, director and writer. One of the key figures in the school of Bulgarian poetic realism*. After graduating from the Moscow Film Theatre (VGIK*) in 1953 as a cameraman, Radev worked on various projects, notably Nikola Korabov's historical epic *Tjutjun/Tobacco* (1962). His first film as director was *Kradecăt na praskovi/The Peach Thief* (1964), for which he also wrote the script (adapted from a story by Emilian Stanev). The international success of *Kradecăt na praskovi* was due in large part to the performance of Nevena Kokanova*, who was to become Bulgaria's most popular screen star. Together with Rangel Vălčanov* and Binka Željazkova*, Radev spearheaded a Bulgarian 'new wave' with a pronounced trend towards 'poetic realism'.

Radev was often entrusted with major innovative productions designed to enhance the professional reputation of Bulgarian cinema. His *Tsar i general/Tsar and General* (1966), depicting the conflict between Tsar Boris and General Zaimov on the eve of World War II on both psychological and philosophical levels, was Bulgaria's first widescreen production. And *Čerhite angeli/Black Angels* (1970), an 'Eastern' about teenage partisans fighting fascists in the mountains, was Boyana* Studios' first commercially successful colour spectacle. RH

RADIČKOV, Jordan   Kalimanitsa 1929

Bulgarian writer. Jordan Radičkov is sometimes referred to as the 'Bulgarian Gogol' for his mixture of the grotesque and the folkloric, while his surrealist vision, ironic sensibility and black humour lead others to compare him to Beckett and Ionesco.

Radičkov's prolific output of stories and plays during the 1960s and 1970s proved to be a rich source of inspiration for film directors seeking an alternative to the schematic formula of Socialist Realism*. Zako Heskija was the first to collaborate with him, adapting one of his stories to the screen: *Gorešto pladne/Torrid Noon* (1966), about a sleepy village on a hot summer's day that is stirred to life when a boy playing in a river suffers an accident. Then Binka Željazkova* adapted another of Radičkov's stories into the most controversial production in Bulgarian film history: *Privărzanijat balon/The Attached Balloon* (1967), withdrawn from circulation shortly after its release and banned until 1988. This modern fairy tale about village peasants faced with the opportunity to fly off in a big balloon appeared on the screen just when neo-Stalinism was being reintroduced in Warsaw Pact countries. Another controversial Radičkov adaptation was Hristo Hristov's* award-winning *Posledno ljato/The Last*

Summer (1972–74), banned for two years and released only after being severely cut and re-edited. The protagonist – a stubborn peasant who refuses to leave an abandoned village that is soon to be flooded owing to the construction of a dam – was played by eminent stage and screen actor Grigor Vačkov*, making it all the more difficult for the authorities to ban the film altogether.

Other Radičkov adaptations proved less successful artistically and commercially. However, animation director Stojan Dukov paid Radičkov the ultimate compliment by satirising his highly successful, Beckett-like, one-man stage production of *Januari/January* in his cartoon *Fevruari/February* (1977). RH

RADIO TELEFIS EIREANN (RTE)

Irish television service. The public broadcasting television service, originally founded as a radio station in 1926, began television transmission in 1961. Historically, it has been the most important employer in the Irish audio-visual sector, and, with the absence of formal film training until recent years, the training ground for many film-makers, including Bob Quinn* and Pat O'Connor*. Its support for independent film and television production has been sporadic, but following a ministerial directive its IR£3.5 million contribution to the sector in 1993 increased to £5 million in 1994 and it will invest IR£12.5 million by 1999, about 10 per cent of its current budget. Its own soaps, dramas, documentaries and other programmes are consistently more popular than imported programmes, indicating, as with Irish-theme theatrical films, that Irish audiences in general engage with Irish material when given the chance.

During the 1960s RTE provided an important forum for hitherto publicly unarticulated views and as a result aided the process of modernisation and internationalisation of Irish culture and society. Its strengths during the 1960s and 1970s lay in such areas as successfully combining light entertainment with controversial discussion, most especially in the long-running *The Late Late Show*; current affairs, where numerous challenges were made to governments and other interest groups through investigative reporting; and in both rural and urban soap operas such as *The Riordans, Glenroe* and *Fair City*. By the 1980s RTE seemed to have lost its programming direction, especially its commitment to drama, which was a result in part of an engineer-dominated management structure. Its weak challenges to increased demands for the privatisation of its service, and its unenthusiastic engagement with independent film-makers, also lost it residual public and critical support as an institution. KR

Bib: Martin McLoone and John MacMahon (eds.), *Television and Irish Society: 21 Years of Irish Television* (1984).

RAI (Radio [subsequently Radiotelevisione] Italiana)

Italian broadcaster and production house. RAI, Italy's public broadcasting service, held a monopoly in radio and (from

1955) television broadcasting until the mid-1970s. In terms of film production, for many years it supported both famous and unknown *auteurs*. With a series including *L'età del ferro/The Iron Age* (1964) and *Atti degli apostoli/Acts of the Apostles* (1969), Roberto Rossellini* was the first to be given the chance to work free of commercial constraints. Whereas this first phase was characterised by low-cost, independent made-for-television productions, a second phase aimed at more ambitious projects. In the 1970s, despite a climate of ideological intolerance and political censorship, RAI played a fundamental role in Italian cinema, both culturally and economically. It achieved great success with the Taviani* brothers' *Padre padrone/Father Master* (1977) and Ermanno Olmi's* *L'albero degli zoccoli/The Tree of Wooden Clogs* (1978); it offered Fellini the opportunity to shoot *I clowns* (1970) and *Prova d'orchestra/Orchestra Rehearsal* (1978); it allowed Antonioni to experiment with documentary (*Chung-Kuo*, 1973) and electronics (*Il mistero di Oberwald/The Oberwald Mystery*, 1980) and produced some of the finest work by Liliana Cavani*, Nelo Risi, Bernardo Bertolucci*, the Taviani brothers, Olmi, Marco Bellocchio* and many others, including Vittorio Cottafavi*, Pier Paolo Pasolini* and Pupi Avati*. With Francesco Rosi's* *Cristo si è fermato a Eboli/Christ Stopped at Eboli* (1979), RAI started making two versions of each title: a feature-length one for theatrical release and a longer one for television. More recently, RAI has played, albeit decreasingly, an important role in promoting experimental film, in association both with Olmi's school in Bassano and with Nanni Moretti's* company Sacher, and has financed the work of young *auteurs* such as Gianni Amelio*. Since the early 1980s film production in Italy would have ground to a halt without the intervention of television, although RAI's proportion has been largely eclipsed in the last few years by the massive investment by companies associated with Berlusconi's Fininvest*. GVo

RAIMU
Jules Muraire; Toulon 1883 – Neuilly-sur-Seine 1946

French actor. Originally a comic actor, Raimu also imposed a magisterially humane presence in some key French films of the 1930s and 1940s, for which Orson Welles called him 'the greatest actor in the world'. Raimu, then 'Rallum', started as a *comique troupier** in the music halls of his native town before moving on to Paris in 1910, where he quickly became one of the most popular *boulevard* stage actors. Although he made two silent films, it was sound cinema's ability to exploit his formidable voice and picturesque Midi accent which made him a star (after which, except for a brief spell at the Comédie Française, he abandoned the stage). After two comedies, *Le Blanc et le noir* (1930, based on Sacha Guitry*), and *Mam'zelle Nitouche* (1931, directed by Marc Allégret*), the adaptation of Marcel Pagnol's* *Marius* (1931), for which he had already played the lead on stage, shot him to fame. *Marius* was followed by *Fanny* (1932) and *César* (1936), consolidating Raimu's image as the authoritarian yet vulnerable patriarch, deeply believable despite the obvious theatricality of the films. He played similar roles in two other Pagnol films, *La Femme du boulanger/The Baker's Wife* (1938) and *La Fille*

du puisatier/The Well-Digger's Daughter (1940), and, in a darker register, in films such as Marc Allégret's* *Gribouille* (1937) and Jeff Musso's *Dernière jeunesse* (1939). But while such films, as well as Jean Grémillon's* *L'Etrange Monsieur Victor* (1937) and Henri Decoin's* *Les Inconnus dans la maison/Strangers in the House* (1942), confirmed him as the formidable dramatic actor admired by Welles, Raimu continued to act in many comedies based on vaudeville or *boulevard* plays, such as the hilarious *Ces Messieurs de la Santé* (1933) and *Le Roi* (1936), which were equally responsible for his popularity at the time. Pagnol's work, however, gave Raimu the scope to combine both comic and dramatic registers, making *Marius* one of the best-loved French films, now officially declared an inalienable part of the French cultural patrimony. GV

RAIZMAN, Yuli Ya.
Moscow 1903–94

Soviet director and scriptwriter, who began his career as literary adviser to Mezhrabpomfilm* studio and assistant director to Yakov Protazanov*. His first major film was *Katorga/Penal Servitude* (1928). He next used sound experimentally in *Zemlya zhazhdet/The Earth is Thirsty* (1930). In a long career as director and teacher his most important films were *Lëtchiki/Pilots* (1935), *Poslednyaya noch'/The Last Night* (1937, Grand Prix at the 1937 Paris Exhibition and Stalin Prize in 1941), *Mashenka* (1942), *Kavaler zolotoi zvezdy/The Cavalier of the Gold Star* (1951), *Kommunist/The Communist* (1957), *A esli eto lyubov'?/But What If This is Love?* (1962), *Tvoi sovremennik/Your Contemporary* (1968), *Strannaya zhenshchina/A Strange Woman* (1978), *Chastnaya zhizn'/Private Life* (1982, USSR State Prize in 1983) and *Vremya zhelanii/A Time of Desires* (1984). Although Raizman worked throughout the darkest period of Soviet history, his constant attempts to expand the thematic frontiers of Soviet cinema and his conscientious example made him one of the most respected of the older generation of Soviet filmmakers, many of whom worked as his assistants at the Mosfilm studio. RT

RANK, J. Arthur
Hull 1888–1972

British film financier, and founder of the Rank Organisation, which, from the beginning of World War II, became the dominant force in British cinema, exercising near monopolistic control over production, distribution and exhibition. His biographer, Alan Wood, says that Rank's 'greatest virtue of all was undoubtedly the fact that he knew nothing whatever about making films.' A millionaire flour miller from Yorkshire and a devout Methodist, Rank first became involved in film through a desire to promote Christian values. In 1934 he and his business partner Lady Yule formed British National and built Pinewood Studios. Infuriated by the lack of distribution for their critically acclaimed first feature, *Turn of the Tide* (1935), he acquired a controlling interest in General Film Distributors. When his partnership with Lady Yule dissolved, she retained her interest in British National and he kept Pinewood. In 1938, Rank relieved the financially embarrassed Alexander Korda* of Denham Studios, and acquired the new studios at Elstree. When the war started, the industry anticipated a downturn and Rank was able to gain control, at knockdown prices, of two of the three largest cinema circuits, Odeon and Gaumont-British (which also brought him control of Gainsborough Pictures). In fact, cinema attendance spiralled upwards, and Rank's profits soared, forcing him to expand his investments in production to avoid tax, and fuelling what now looks like a golden age. By the end of the war, through his subsidiary, Independent Producers Ltd., Rank was financing independent production companies such as The Archers (Michael Powell* and Emeric Pressburger), Cineguild, Two Cities, Individual and Ealing. At the same time, seeking outlets for the films in which he was investing, Rank had acquired holdings in cinema chains in Australia, New Zealand, Canada and South Africa, and had become the largest single shareholder in Universal, offering him a platform from which to challenge Hollywood itself. Unfortunately, Labour government policy intervened in 1947 with import taxes and other restrictions, causing an Atlantic war of attrition with boycotts on both sides. It was a war which Rank could not win, and though, when the dust settled, select films like *Hamlet* (1948) and *The Red Shoes* (1948) continued to do well in select cinemas, J. Arthur Rank posed no future threat to American market dominance. The Rank Organisation became a finance house, exerting its main influence through the duopoly in exhibition which it shared with ABC, and subseqently EMI, and making its real profits from its acquisition of Xerox. In 1980, eight years after the death of its founder, Rank announced it was pulling out of film production altogether. JC

Bib: Geoffrey Macnab, *J. Arthur Rank and the British Film Industry* (1993).

RAPPENEAU, Jean-Paul   Auxerre 1932

French director and scriptwriter. After serving as an assistant to Raymond Bernard* among others, Rappeneau worked as a scriptwriter, collaborating with such directors as Jacques Becker* and Louis Malle*. Two strands emerge in this early career – comedy and costume film – which also inform Rappeneau's later directorial work. His first feature, *La Vie de château* (1966), was a light comedy set during the German occupation, starring Catherine Deneuve* and Philippe Noiret*, and a critical and popular success. Other successful comedies followed, including *Les Mariés de l'an II* (1971) and *Le Sauvage* (1975). These were nothing, however, compared with the worldwide triumph of *Cyrano de Bergerac* in 1990, winner of ten Césars* and one of the most popular French films ever outside France. *Cyrano* reclaimed both a popular-classic literary heritage – Edmond Rostand's play, with English subtitles in verse by Anthony Burgess [> HERITAGE CINEMA IN EUROPE] – and the epic tradition, with swirling camerawork, dynamic editing and sumptuous sets and costumes. As a character, Cyrano also perfectly fitted Gérard Depardieu's* dual star persona, both larger than life national hero and vulnerable romantic. Rappeneau subsequently made the costume epic *Le Hussard sur le toit* (1995). GV

RASP, Fritz   Bayreuth 1891 – Gäfelfing 1976

German actor, who played chillingly impressive villains for more than five decades. After supporting roles in Fritz Lang's* films, Rasp took leads in G. W. Pabst's* *Die Liebe der Jeanne Ney/The Loves of Jeanne Ney* (1927), *Tagebuch einer Verlorenen/The Diary of a Lost Girl* (1929) and *Die Dreigroschenoper/The Threepenny Opera* (1931). His refusal to feature in Ufa* propaganda films obliged him to work with smaller companies in the 1930s and 1940s, where one of his most memorable parts was as the visionary scholar in Pabst's *Paracelsus* (1943). Rasp's comeback in the late 1950s centred on the renewed popularity of the Edgar Wallace crime series, with his acting in *Froen med Masken* (1959, Den.), *Die Bande des Schreckens* (1960) and *Der Zinker* (1963) a mock-ironic version of the evil malevolence Rasp himself had so decisively fashioned in the 1920s. MW

Other Films Include: *Schuhpalast Pinkus* (1916); *Schatten/Warning Shadows* (1923); *Das Haus der Lüge* (1926); *Dreyfus* (1930); *Emil und die Detektive/Emil and the Detectives* (1931); *Nanu, Sie kennen Korff noch nicht!* (1938); *Es war eine rauschende Ballnacht* (1939); *Irgendwo in Berlin* (1946); *Magic Fire* (1955, US); *Dr. med. Hiob Praetorius* (1964); *Lina Braake – oder: Die Interessen der Bank können nicht die Interessen sein, die Lina Braake hat* (1975).

REA, Stephen   Belfast 1946

Irish actor. When Rea came to international prominence with his performance in Neil Jordan's* *The Crying Game* (1992), for which he was nominated for an Oscar, he was already an experienced stage, television and film actor. He played in Jordan's *Angel* (1982) in a role not dissimilar to that in *The Crying Game*. As a director of the Field Day Theatre Company, based in Derry, he has helped to rejuvenate Irish theatre. His television work includes the role of a local council employee in *Bad Behaviour* (1993). KR

Other Films Include: *The House* (TV), *The Company of Wolves* (1984); *Life is Sweet* (1990); *Angie* (1994, US).

REBENGIUC, Victor   Born 1933

Romanian actor and occasional director, who gained European recognition in Liviu Ciulei's Cannes award-winning *Pădurea spînzuraţilor/Forest of the Hanged* (1964). After graduating in Bucharest he became one of Romania's leading actors, helped by a striking stage presence and piercing eyes. Film roles – beginning with *Furtuna/The Storm* (1960) – tested his elegant and powerful presence in stories based on Romanian classics. In *Pădurea spînzuraţilor* he played a tragic hero refusing to fight fellow citizens in World War I, co-starring with his wife Mariana Mihut. In 1967 he played a British World War II officer in the Bulgarian *Noatta cea mai lungă/The Longest Night*, and has since regularly appeared in war films. A range of more realistic contemporary roles in the 1960s, such as *Poveste sentimentala/Sentimental Story* (1963), won Rebengiuc popular and critical acclaim. Through the

1970s and 1980s he balanced stage and screen careers, and in 1976 he co-directed with Dan Piţa* the powerful period drama *Tănase scatiu/A Summer Tale*. Rebengiuc has maintained his popularity by playing complex and heroic individuals who reject authority when necessary, as in the contemporary drama *Doctorul Poenaru* (1978), co-starring Stefan Iordache. He won the Best Male Performance award at San Remo for his role in the poignant peasant saga *Morometii* (1986). Following the 1989 revolution he played the mayor in Lucian Pintilie's* profound study of late Ceauşescu Romania, *Le Chêne/Steiarul/The Oak* (1992). MM

REDGRAVE, (Sir) Michael

Bristol 1908 –
Denham 1985

British actor. Co-founder (with Rachel Kempson) of the Redgrave 'dynasty' (which includes daughters Vanessa* and Lynn and son Corin), educated at Cambridge where he wrote film reviews, and a member of John Gielgud's* famous Old Vic theatre company from 1937, Redgrave claimed an ambivalence about his success in the cinema, insisting that he only ever took his debut lead role in Alfred Hitchcock's* *The Lady Vanishes* (1938) because he had a family to support. Ambivalence may be the key to his persona. Never an aggressively romantic hero, nor quite one of the league of postwar chaps, the character which Redgrave projected simply seemed unsure of himself and looking for something else – either out of idealism or discomfort. This might express itself through a frustrated passion, as in the socially idealistic but domestically inept mine-worker's son of *The Stars Look Down* (1939), the excruciating distraction of Barnes Wallis in *The Dam Busters* (1955), or the eccentric dithering of his lighter roles, *The Lady Vanishes* for example. Though he may have been doubtful about cinema, apparently finding it suspiciously easy, Redgrave's later filmography does not reveal quite so many embarrassments as those of some of the other theatrical knights.

Redgrave was nominated for an Oscar for his performance as Orin in *Mourning Becomes Electra* (1947, US). He was knighted in 1959. JC

Bib: Michael Redgrave, *In My Mind's I: An Actor's Autobiography* (1983).

Other Films Include: *Climbing High* [with Jessie Matthews] (1938); *Kipps* (1941); *The Big Blockade, Thunder Rock* (1942); *Dead of Night, The Way to the Stars, A Diary for Timothy* [narrator] (1945); *The Captive Heart* (1946); *Fame is the Spur* (1947); *Secret Beyond the Door* (1947, US); *The Browning Version* (1951); *The Importance of Being Earnest* (1952); *Oh ... Rosalinda!!, The Dam Busters, Confidential Report/Mr Arkadin* [Sp./Switz.] (1955); *1984* (1956); *Time Without Pity* (1957); *The Quiet American* [US], *Law and Disorder, The Immortal Land* [narrator] (1958); *The Wreck of the Mary Deare* [US], *Shake Hands with the Devil* (1959); *The Innocents* (1961); *The Loneliness of the Long Distance Runner* (1962); *Young Cassidy, The Hill* (1965); *Oh! What a Lovely War, Goodbye, Mr Chips* (1969); *The Go-Between* (1970).

REDGRAVE, Vanessa

London 1937

British actress, who made her London stage debut in 1958 and had a distinguished career in London and Stratford (including a famous Rosalind in *Much Ado About Nothing*) before making an impact in cinema in 1966, first with Karel Reisz's* *Morgan a Suitable Case for Treatment* and then in Michelangelo Antonioni's* *Blowup* (1967). As with Redgrave* *père*, there is a tentativeness in her acting, an edge of self-conscious awkwardness, which gives a fragile complexity to the independent and forthright women she plays. Andy Medhurst refers to 'a lingering sense of something great' which is never quite realised, and it is true that her screen performances give off a sense of energy with not enough to work on. Some of the energy is diverted into left-wing political activity, much of it funded from her earnings, and into her commitment to the Palestinian cause which has frequently lost her a sympathetic audience in the US. She won Best Actress awards at Cannes for *Morgan* and for *Isadora* (1969), an Oscar for Best Supporting Actress for *Julia* (1977, US), and a New York Film Critics' Best Supporting Actress award for her role as Peggy Ramsay in *Prick Up Your Ears* (1987). She was given a BFI* Fellowship in 1988. JC

Bib: *Vanessa Redgrave: An autobiography* (1991).

Other Films Include: *A Man for All Seasons* (1966); *Camelot* [US], *The Sailor from Gibraltar* (1967); *The Charge of the Light Brigade, Un Tranquillo posto di campagna/A Quiet Place in the Country* [It./Fr.] (1968); *The Sea Gull* (1969); *Oh! What a Lovely War* [as Sylvia Pankhurst] (1969); *La vacanza/Vacation* [It.], *The Devils* (1971); *The Trojan Women, Mary Queen of Scots* (1972); *Murder on the Orient Express* (1974); *The Palestinian* [prod.] (1977); *Agatha* [US], *Yanks* (1979); *The Bostonians* (1984); *Wetherby, Steaming* (1985); *Comrades* (1986); *The Ballad of the Sad Café* (1991, US/UK).

REED, (Sir) Carol

London 1906–76

British director. The son of the famous theatrical actor-manager Herbert Beerbohm Tree, Carol Reed was a stage actor and director before directing his first feature, *Midshipman Easy*, in 1935. During the 1930s he directed Jessie Matthews* and Michael Redgrave* in the musical comedy *Climbing High* (1938), but he was principally identified with the realism of ordinary lives and everyday settings: *Laburnum Grove* (1936), *Bank Holiday* (1938) and *Penny Paradise* (1938). *The Stars Look Down* (1939), a remarkably committed account of working-class life and trade union activity adapted from A. J. Cronin, won well-deserved critical praise, and *Night Train to Munich* (1940) and *The Young Mr Pitt* (1942) gave him an international audience. During the war, Reed worked on propaganda documentaries. In 1945, with Garson Kanin, he co-directed *The True Glory*, a feature-length compilation charting the progress of the war from D Day to VE Day. In the postwar cinema, Reed, like David Lean*, comes close to being a 'classic' British film-maker, his acknowledged classics being *The Way Ahead* (1944), *Odd Man Out* (1947), *The Fallen Idol* (1948) and his best-known film, *The Third Man*

(1949), the last two scripted by Graham Greene*, with whom he also made *Our Man in Havana* (1960). These films confirmed his critical reputation as a leading director of British quality cinema, a reputation which was enhanced by *Outcast of the Islands* (1951) and *The Man Between* (1953). He received the Academy Award as Best Director for *Oliver!* in 1968. He was knighted in 1952. JC

Bib: Nicholas Wapshott, *The Man Between: A Biography of Carol Reed* (1990).

REED, Oliver   Wimbledon 1938

British actor, whose first starring role was as the werewolf in Terence Fisher's* *The Curse of the Werewolf* (1961). If there is a tradition of decency and restraint in British postwar cinema, Reed belongs to that of excess, which would also contain Hammer horror* and Ken Russell*, for whom Reed starred in *Women in Love* (1969), *The Devils* (1971) and *Tommy* (1975). Reed was one of Richard Lester's* musketeers in *The Three Musketeers* (1974, Panama) and *The Four Musketeers* (1975, Panama/Sp.). He is the nephew of Carol Reed*, for whom he played a notable Bill Sykes in *Oliver!* (1968). He appeared in *The Brood* (1978, Canada) for David Cronenberg and in *Castaway* (1986) for Nicolas Roeg*. Much loved by the popular press as a source of scandal, he is given to displays of boozy masculinity on television chat shows. JC

REINECKER, Herbert   Hagen 1914

German scriptwriter, notable for the length of his career in both film and television. Reinecker's first treatment for a feature film was *Der Fall Rainer* (1942), after which he co-scripted with A. Weidemann the propaganda film *Junge Adler* (1944). Because of his association with ideologically dubious projects, his postwar return to cinema was slow, but after his screenplay for *Canaris* (1954) won the Deutscher Filmpreis he was once more much in demand. In the 1960s, Reinecker specialised in adventure and crime stories. With television producer Helmut Ringelmann he pioneered the first, long-running German television detective series at ZDF, *Der Kommissar*, scripting ninety-seven episodes. Since 1973 Reinecker has been chief writer on the nationally and internationally successful German television crime series, *Derrick*. JG

Bib: Ricarda Strobel, *Herbert Reinecker* (1992).

Other Films Include: *Kinder, Mütter und ein General* (1955); *Spion für Deutschland, Der Stern von Afrika* (1956); *Der Fuchs von Paris* (1957); *Taiga, Die Trapp-Familie in Amerika* (1958); *Bumerang* (1959); *Schachnovelle* (1960); *Der Hexer, Die Goldsucher von Arkansas* (1964); *Rheinsberg* (1967); *Der Tod im roten Jaguar, Winnetou und Shatterhand im Tal der Toten* (1968).

REINERT, Charles   Basle 1899 – Fribourg 1963

Swiss film publicist. A Jesuit priest, Reinert founded the Zurich Filmbüro des schweizerischen katholischen Volksvereins and its periodical *Der Filmberater* in 1941, thereby establishing the long and still continuing history of denominational involvement in the Swiss film scene. Through the institution and the periodical he tried to exert moral influence on the Swiss film industry, during and after World War II. In addition, Reinert edited probably the first comprehensive encyclopedia of all aspects of world cinema (*Kleines Filmlexikon*, 1946, Italian version by Pasinetti, 1948), which, supplemented by a handbook in 1960 (*Wir vom Film*), was to remain for some three decades one of the primary sources of information on film for the German-speaking public. MW

REINHARDT, Max   Maximilian Goldmann; Baden, near Vienna 1873 – New York 1943

Austrian-born director, who, through his theatre work, was the single most important stylistic influence on Expressionist film* and *Kammerspielfilm**. As the director and later owner of the Deutsche Theater Berlin (1905–20 and 1924–33), Reinhardt redefined stagecraft in Germany and dominated the bourgeois theatre. Between 1909 and 1914 he directed four films, including *Sumurun* (1909), *Insel der Seligen* (1913), based on motifs from Shakespeare, and *Eine venezianische Nacht* (1914), but he was particularly crucial in training the elite of German actors who were to move between the theatre and the cinema during the 1910s and 1920s. His staging of crowds found echoes in the films of Fritz Lang* and F. W. Murnau*, and he decisively shaped the atmospheric lighting style and *mise-en-scène* of German art cinema up to 1924, in contrast to Erwin Piscator's constructivist theatre, which influenced Brecht and proletarian cinema [> ARBEITERFILME]. As the Nazis expropriated his theatres, Reinhardt toured Europe. In 1934 he emigrated to the US, where he directed *A Midsummer Night's Dream* (1935, co-dir. Wilhelm Dieterle*), for Warner Bros, before concentrating on his acting school in New York. One of his sons, Gottfried Reinhardt, became a Hollywood producer. TE/KU

Bib: Lotte Eisner, *The Haunted Screen: Expressionism in the German Cinema and the Influence of Max Reinhardt* (1969).

REINIGER, Lotte   Berlin 1899 – Dettenhausen 1981

German film animator, famous for her silhouette films, created from back-lit paper cut-outs. After designing film titles, Reiniger made her first animation film in 1919 and between 1920 and 1924 perfected her style in advertising films for Julius Pinschewer*. Reiniger animated a dream sequence (the famous falcon dream) for Fritz Lang's* *Die Nibelungen* (1924), which, although removed from the finished film, was widely screened. The banker Louis Hagen funded Reiniger's masterpiece, a feature-length silhouette film (*Die Abenteuer des Prinzen Achmed/The Adventures of Prince Achmed*, 1926;

credited by some as the first feature-length animation film) for which she created 250,000 single images and had a 'multi-plane' camera specially designed and built.

From the late 1920s to the mid-1930s, Reiniger worked within the Berlin avant-garde milieu, making experimental shorts while continuing with silhouette films, for instance *Doktor Dolittle und seine Tiere* (1928). She also contributed silhouette sequences to live-action films, notably G. W. Pabst's* *Don Quichotte/Don Quixote* (1933) and Jean Renoir's *La Marseillaise* (1937). From 1936 she lived in Britain and worked for the Crown Film Unit and the General Post Office Film Unit, making some short films [> BRITISH DOCUMENTARY MOVEMENT]. In 1953–55 she received commissions from British and Canadian television, and in the 1960s shifted her work to the theatre, opera and book illustrations. MW

Bib: Christel Strobel and Hans Strobel, *Lotte Reiniger* (1993).

REINL, Harald
Bad Ischl, Austria 1908 – Puerto de la Cruz, Tenerife 1986

Austrian-born director. Reinl was Leni Riefenstahl*'s stunt double in *Stürme über dem Montblanc* (1930), and her assistant director on *Tiefland/Lowlands* (1940–44, released 1954), and in 1948–49 directed his first feature film, *Bergkristall* (1949). Reinl's service to German popular cinema was his re-crafting of traditional genres for postwar consumption. His knack of adapting popular Edgar Wallace crime novels (*Der Frosch mit der Maske*, 1959) and Karl May adventure stories (*Der Schatz im Silbersee/The Treasure of Silver Lake*, 1962; *Winnetou I, II, III*, 1963–65; *Winnetou und Shatterhand im Tal der Toten*, 1968) made him one of the most bankable but also most critically scorned directors of the 1960s. TE/KU

REIS, António
António Ferreira Gonçalves dos Reis; Valadares 1927 – Lisbon 1991
and
CORDEIRO, Margarida
Margarida Martins Cordeiro; Mogadouro 1939

Portuguese directors. Reis began his film career in the late 1950s in Oporto (his earlier films are lost). An assistant to Manoel de Oliveira* on *O Acto da Primavera/Rite of Spring/ Passion of Jesus* (1963), he wrote the dialogue for Paulo Rocha's* *Mudar de Vida/Change of Life* in the same year (1966) that he published his most important book, *Poemas do Quotidiano/Everyday Poems*. Margarida Cordeiro is a psychiatrist. The painter Jaime Fernandes, one of her patients then interned in an asylum, is the subject of their joint medium-length film *Jaime* (1973), on which Cordeiro is credited as sound engineer and assistant editor. In this film, Reis and Cordeiro were searching for alternative 'reason' in the work and person of a man apparently insane. They then made the outstanding *Trás-Os-Montes* (1976) on Cordeiro's home ground, an isolated province in north-east Portugal. From then on their films would be co-directed. Going beyond the ethnographic approach of the Portuguese cinema of the 1970s, *Trás-Os-Montes* searches for the inner life of human beings and nature and explores the boundaries between documentary and fiction in a non-linear narrative. The film shifts in time from the present to the Middle Ages in a labyrinth of underground connections, for instance between a text by Kafka and the Great Wall of China. Their next two films – *Ana* (1982) and *Rosa de Areia/Desert Rose* (1989) – were increasingly experimental, concerned with the 'reality' of dreams (in *Ana*, one of Rilke's *Sonnets to Orpheus* is read in voice-over while a child sleeps) and the primary senses, in a chaotic cosmology outside conventional knowledge. Reis was the most influential teacher at the Lisbon cinema school. He also played cameos in films by João Botelho* and Fernando Lopes. AMS

REISZ, Karel
Ostrava, Czechoslovakia 1926

British director of Czech origins who came to England as a refugee at the age of twelve. He worked with Lindsay Anderson* on the Oxford journal *Sequence**, and was involved in Free Cinema*. The short documentary which he co-directed with Tony Richardson*, *Momma Don't Allow* (1956) and *We are the Lambeth Boys* (1959), were shown in the Free Cinema season at the National Film Theatre, London. Reisz published the influential *The Technique of Film Editing* in 1953. His first feature, *Saturday Night and Sunday Morning* (1960), was both a critical and a commercial success, and a landmark in the British New Wave*. Reisz was to have directed *This Sporting Life* (1963), but elected to produce, with Anderson directing. *Morgan a Suitable Case for Treatment* (1966) has a certain cult status for those who still believe in the mythology of the 1960s. Outside the context of British social realism, Reisz's work has been consistently interesting – *The Dog Soldiers/Who'll Stop the Rain* (1978, US), *The French Lieutenant's Woman* (1981) – but never overwhelming. Like many other British directors, he was forced to turn to Hollywood in the 1970s and 1980s. JC

Bib: Karel Reisz, *The Technique of Film Editing* (1953).

Other Films: *Night Must Fall* (1964); *Isadora* (1968); *The Gambler* (1974, US); *Sweet Dreams* (1985, US); *Everybody Wins* (1990, US).

REITZ, Edgar
Morbach 1932

German director. Reitz shared directing and scripting credits for a number of films with Alexander Kluge*, for whom he was cameraman on *Abschied von gestern/Yesterday Girl* (1966). A co-signatory of the 'Oberhausen Manifesto' (1962), Reitz co-founded the Ulm Film Academy (Institut für Filmgestaltung Ulm), where he taught until 1968.

Reitz's early feature films, from *Mahlzeiten/Mealtimes* (1967) to *Stunde Null/Zero Hour* (1977), and including *Geschichten vom Kübelkind* (1963–70) and *Das goldene Ding* (1971), both co-directed by Ula Stöckl, established his place in the New German Cinema*, a fact only fully appreciated when *Heimat* (1984) became a worldwide success, both with audiences and critics, and Reitz's previous work was reassessed. By homing in on an ideologically loaded term, Reitz prompted much public soul-searching in Germany, while ostensibly responding to the controversy caused by the US television series *Holocaust*. *Heimat* examined German history from 1919 to 1982 as seen by the inhabitants of a small village. Its sequel, *Die zweite Heimat. Chronik einer Jugend* (1993), which concentrated on a shorter period (the late 1960s) and a different social environment (students in Munich), did not evoke the same public response. *Heimat* and its sequel were made for both theatrical and television release. MW/TE

Bib: Reinhold Rauh, *Edgar Reitz: Film als Heimat* (1993).

RELPH, Michael – see DEARDEN, Basil

RENAUD, Madeleine   Paris 1903–94

French actress. Like Jean-Louis Barrault* (whom she met in 1936 and married in 1940), Renaud, one of the most important French theatrical personalities, worked primarily on stage. However, she also made her mark on French cinema of the 1930s and 1940s in play adaptations and in dramas, especially Marie Epstein* and Jean Benoît-Lévy's remarkable *La Maternelle* (1933) and *Hélène* (1936), and four films directed by Jean Grémillon*: *L'Etrange Monsieur Victor* (1937), *Remorques/Stormy Waters* (1939–41), *Lumière d'été* (1943) and *Le Ciel est à vous* (1943–44). A brilliant actress, her performances were always devoid of theatricality. She often played unusually modern heroines. Her postwar career was mostly devoted to the theatre, with a few exceptions such as Max Ophuls'* *Le Plaisir* (1951) and Marguerite Duras'* *Des journées entières dans les arbres/Whole Days in the Trees* (1976). GV

RENOIR, Jean   Paris 1894 – Beverly Hills, California 1979

French director, also actor, scriptwriter and producer. François Truffaut* and Orson Welles described Renoir as 'the greatest film-maker in the world'. There is no doubt that Renoir has dominated both the French cinema of the classical period and the international pantheon of great *auteurs*.

The second son of Impressionist painter Auguste Renoir, Jean grew up in the artistic milieu of turn-of-the-century Paris. Much – too much – has been made of this legacy, though it was of consequence for Renoir's realist aesthetics and financial independence. Following World War I, in which he was wounded, and an attempt at ceramics, Renoir's film career began when he scripted *Catherine* (or *Une Vie sans joie*, 1924, directed by Albert Dieudonné), prompted by his admiration for Stroheim and Chaplin and the desire to promote his wife Catherine Hessling, a former model of his father. Renoir then directed his first film, *La Fille de l'eau* (1925), followed by several more, notably *Nana* (1926) and *La Petite marchande d'allumettes/The Little Match Girl* (1928, with Jean Tedesco), all displaying Hessling's expressionist performances, in contrast to Renoir's naturalistic use of actors in his later films. The coming of sound propelled him

on to a higher plane – commercially with *On purge Bébé* (1931), and artistically with the remarkable *La Chienne* (1931). This story of a petit-bourgeois' obsession with a prostitute (remade as *Scarlet Street* by Fritz Lang* in 1945) introduced cardinal Renoir features. He not only directed, but helped script, produce and edit. Thematically, it signalled his fascination with popular milieux (shared by other French film-makers) and his disregard of conventional morality: 'respectable' Legrand (Michel Simon*) kills Lulu (Janie Marèse) and ends up unpunished as a tramp (a very Renoirian figure, reprised in *Boudu sauvé des eaux/Boudu Saved from Drowning*, 1932), although the price of male anarchic freedom is female punishment or repression. *La Chienne* also exemplifies Renoir's *mise-en-scène*. An exceptional sense of space is created by complex, though unobtrusive, staging in depth, long takes (even by French standards), and the use of sound counterpoint. The overall effect is a dynamic linking of characters to their environment. Casual acting, sometimes by non-professionals (here Georges Flamant, later Renoir and his friends), is also a hallmark. Yet Renoir's realism goes hand in hand with the theatrical, most of his films alluding to, or staging, spectacles.

Renoir's 1930s films offer a Zolaesque panorama of French society: petit-bourgeois shop-keepers (*Boudu*, *Partie de campagne*, 1936, rel. 1946), Provençal farm and immigrant workers (*Toni*, 1935, hailed as a precursor of neo-realism*), railway workers (*La Bête humaine*, 1938), the aristocracy (*La Règle du jeu/Rules of the Game*, 1939). Across this diversity, however, a benevolent Renoirian humanism has been identified ('Everyone has their reasons', says Octave/Renoir in *La Règle du jeu*), made up of easy-going sensuality and a feeling that human beings transcend national or class divisions, as in the pacifist *La Grande illusion* (1937). But some important Renoir films of the 1930s were not only aware of class divisions, they analysed them. Sympathy for the anti-fascist Popular Front* informs the working-class solidarity of *Le Crime de Monsieur Lange* (1935), as well as *La Vie est à nous* (1936, a collectively directed Communist manifesto) and *La Marseillaise* (1937), a chronicle of the French Revolution. Renoir's populism, later increasingly backward-looking, was (in the 1930s) sharpened by left politics; it produced a sensual and generous yet ideologically incisive universe, epitomised by *Le Crime de Monsieur Lange* (scripted by Jacques Prévert*). Because several Renoir films found little commercial success and *La Règle du jeu*, considered his masterpiece, was a resounding failure, he is often regarded as a misunderstood genius. But Renoir was also supremely capable of addressing popular tastes: *Les Bas-fonds/The Lower Depths* (1936), *La Grande illusion* and *La Bête humaine*, with melodramatic plots and major stars like Jean Gabin*, were box-office triumphs.

The war was a decisive break in Renoir's life and career. He left France for Italy to work on *La Tosca* (1940, completed by Carl Koch), and then went to Hollywood, accompanied by Dido Freire, who became his second wife. A classic European in Hollywood, Renoir made six American films with limited success, including, for the war effort, *This Land is Mine* (1943) and *Salute to France* (1944). Renoir became a US citizen in 1944 (keeping French nationality) and lived on and off in California, travelling to India to make *The River* (1951), Italy for *Le Carrosse d'or/The Golden Coach* (1953),

357

and France where he shot five more films. With the exception of *French Cancan* (1955), a dazzling tribute to the music hall, these never matched his 1930s successes. Nor, despite the backing of *Cahiers du cinéma**, did these films benefit from the critical standing of his prewar work. As his film career stalled, he turned to writing (novels and autobiographies), to the theatre, and to television. Renoir liked to say that an artist must keep his cultural roots. He was right, not only because his great works were made when his virtuosity and emotions were engaged with French subjects, but less obviously because he was nourished by the French prewar industrial context, when it was possible to combine a craft-based, informal way of filming with reaching a popular audience. This is no doubt why he became such a role model for the directors of the New Wave*. Renoir was awarded an Oscar for life achievement in 1975 and the French *légion d'honneur* in 1977.

Jean Renoir's brother Pierre Renoir (Paris 1885–1952) was a distinguished stage and film actor, who played in several of Jean's films, notably *La Nuit du carrefour/Night at the Crossroads* (1932, as Inspector Maigret) and *La Marseillaise* (1937, as Louis XVI). Pierre's son Claude Renoir (born Paris 1914) became a prominent cinematographer, starting with some of his uncle's 1930s films and working on numerous postwar French films. Jean's great-niece Sophie Renoir (Claude's daughter) has appeared in some of Eric Rohmer's* films. Special mention should be made of Marguerite Houllé (sometimes Houllé-Renoir, sometimes Renoir), Jean Renoir's editor and partner in the 1930s. Though they never married, she took his name and pursued a brilliant career as an editor in France after Renoir left for the US. GV

Bib: André Bazin, *Jean Renoir* (1971); Alexander Sesonske, *Jean Renoir, The French Films 1924–1939* (1980).

Other Films: *Charleston/Sur un air de Charleston* (1926); *Marquitta* (1927); *Tire-au-flanc* (1928); *Le Tournoi dans la cité/Le Tournoi, Le Bled* (1929); *La Nuit du carrefour/Night at the Crossroads, Chotard et Cie* (1932); *Madame Bovary* (1933); *Swamp Water* (1941, US); *The Southerner* (1945, US); *The Diary of a Chambermaid* (1946, US); *The Woman on the Beach* (1947, US); *Eléna et les hommes/Elena and Men/Paris Does Strange Things* (1956); *Le Déjeuner sur l'herbe* (1959); *Le Testament du Dr Cordelier* (1961); *Le Caporal épinglé/The Elusive Corporal* (1962); *La Direction d'acteurs par Jean Renoir/Jean Renoir Directing Actors* (1969, short); *Le Petit Théâtre de Jean Renoir/Jean Renoir's Little Theatre* (1970).

RESINES, Antonio
Antonio Fernández Resines; Santander 1954

Spanish actor, who came to film via film studies and the 'Escuela de Madrid' (Madrid School) comic group [> COMEDY (SPAIN)]. His performances, almost exclusively in comedy, began to gain popular acclaim in the late 1970s. His first success was *Opera prima* (1980), followed by the even more popular *Sé infiel y no mires con quién/Be Wanton and Tread No Shame* (1985), both directed by Fernando Trueba*, and Fernando Colomo's* *La vida alegre/A Happy Life* (1986). A peanut-shaped head, bristly moustache and irascible delivery

make him ideal for comedy, although he has, with some success, moved towards more dramatic roles in Mario Camús'* *La colmena/The Beehive* (1982) and in *Todo por la pasta/Anything for Bread* (1991). PWE

RESNAIS, Alain
Vannes 1922

French director. One of the most consistently interesting *auteurs* of French cinema, Resnais was making short silent films as early as 1936. A graduate of IDHEC*, he started shooting documentaries on art in 1948 with *Van Gogh*. Many other documentaries followed, including *Gauguin* and *Guernica* (both 1950), *Toute la mémoire du monde* (1956) and the celebrated *Nuit et brouillard/Night and Fog* (1955), a testimony to the Holocaust alternating archive documents with long tracking shots (in colour) of the empty concentration camps. Resnais' interest in social and political issues, his modernist concerns and drawing on serious literature (rather than pulp fiction) set him apart from other New Wave* directors right from his first feature, *Hiroshima mon amour* (1959, with a script by Marguerite Duras*), in which the catastrophe of the atomic bomb is juxtaposed with the personal tragedy of a French woman. Resnais' modernism came to the fore in his stunning though controversial collaboration with Alain Robbe-Grillet, *L'Année dernière à Marienbad/Last Year at Marienbad* (1961), in which the camera glides along the corridors of a baroque palace, revealing seemingly frozen characters who may or may not remember 'last year at Marienbad' – the greatest art film for some, pretentious nonsense for others. What unites both the social and the formal strands of Resnais' work is the theme of time and memory, of how to retrieve traces of the past, as well as complex work on narrative structure, especially evident in *Muriel ou le temps d'un retour/Muriel* (1963), *La Guerre est finie/The War is Over* (1966), *Mon oncle d'Amérique/My American Uncle* (1980) and *La Vie est un roman/Life is a Bed of Roses* (1982). He has also experimented with the theatrical style, with *Mélo* (1986) and the two-part *Smoking/No Smoking* (1993). GV

Other Feature Films: *Loin du Viêt-Nam/Far from Vietnam* (1967, ep.); *Je t'aime, je t'aime* (1968); *L'An 01* (1973, ep. 'Wall Street'); *Stavisky...* (1974); *Providence* (1977); *L'Amour à mort* (1984); *I Want to Go Home* (1989).

REY, Fernando
Fernando Casado Arambillet Vega; La Coruña 1917 – Madrid 1994

Spanish actor. The son of a Republican soldier, Rey enjoyed initial success if not star status in 1940s Cifesa* productions like *La princesa de los Ursinos/The Princess of the Ursinos* (1947), *Don Quijote de la Mancha* (1948), *Locura de amor/Love Crazy* (1948) and *Agustina de Aragón/Agustina of Aragon* (1950). All these triumphalist roles were later ironised in the 1960s and 1970s films by Luis Buñuel* which launched him as a major international star. By now in early middle age, in *Viridiana* (1961) Rey brought a mixture of menace and pathos to the role of Don Jaime, the down-at-heel landowner obsessed with transforming his young ward into the living picture of his dead wife. *Tristana* (1970) is another film where his elderly, aristocratic qualities suited a part characterised simultaneously by an old man's passion for a virginal waif and the triumph of conservative values over liberalism. Rey's projection of nobility, easy charm and *savoir-faire* masking diabolical urges, are brilliantly in evidence in his last two Buñuel films, *Le Charme discret de la bourgeoisie/The Discreet Charm of the Bourgeoisie* (1972) and *Cet obscur objet du désir/That Obscure Object of Desire* (1977). In the 1980s he was Spain's most internationally known star, appearing in films like *The French Connection* (1971, US), where his charmingly corrupt patrician style was again at its best. His most significant later work in Spain, drawing on his more benign patriarchal qualities, includes Carlos Saura's* *Elisa, vida mía/Elisa, My Love* (1977) and Francisco Regueiro's *Padre nuestro/Our Father* (1985). PWE

REY, Florián
Antonio Martínez del Castillo; La Almunia de Doña Godina, Zaragoza 1894 – Alicante 1962

Spanish director. After working as a journalist in Zaragoza, Rey went into films, initially as an actor, before directing his first feature, *La revoltosa/The Mischief-maker* (1924), a popular *zarzuela* (operetta). He married Imperio Argentina*, and directed her in fifteen films. Rey tried to offset the success of Hollywood movies by drawing on the native traditions of *sainete* (one-act farces), *zarzuela* and *costumbrista* (regional) narratives reflecting local or national customs. His most notable films, perhaps, are his folksy celebrations of rural life in Aragon: *Nobleza baturra/Aragonese Virtue* (1935), *La aldea maldita/The Cursed Village* (1929 silent, 1942 sound) – a patriarchal, honour-obsessed narrative – and *La hermana San Sulpicio/Sister San Sulpicio* (1927 silent, 1934 sound). PWE

RIBEIRO, António Lopes
Lisbon 1908–95

Portuguese director and producer. Active from 1926 as a film critic for a daily newspaper and for film magazines, Ribeiro travelled in Europe to learn film-making, a practice then almost non-existent in Lisbon. In Moscow he met Sergei Eisenstein*. Assisting some of the first refugees from Germany did not stop him following the example of the propaganda secretary António Ferro and becoming a strong supporter of Salazar. His first film, *Gado Bravo/Brave Bulls* (1934), was a curious mixture of Portuguese tradition and German influence, also to be seen in the official propaganda film of the regime, *A Revolução de Maio/The May Revolution* (1936), written by Ferro under a pseudonym, and the colonial exhortation *O Feitiço do Império/The Spell of the Empire* (1940). Returning to a kind of 'home front' (though Portugal was not at war), Ribeiro directed *O Pai Tirano/The Tyrannical Father* (1941), his most famous film and one of the best examples of Portuguese comedy [> COMEDY (PORTUGAL)]; he also produced *O Pátio das Cantigas/Song of the Courtyards* (1942) directed by his brother 'Ribeirinho', Manoel de Oliveira's* *Aniki-Bóbó* (1942), and later Leitão de Barros'* *Camões* (1946). After 1938 he supervised the newsreel *Jornal Português/Portuguese Journal*, and made countless propaganda films both short and full-length, an actitivy that would last until the end of the regime in 1974.

In 1944, with his brother, he founded a theatrical company, and after *Amor de Perdição/Ill-fated Love* (1943), the second screen adaptation of Camilo Castello Branco's classic novel, he directed only films based on well-known plays and novels: *A Vizinha do Lado/The Girl Next Door* (1945), *Frei Luís de Sousa/Friar Luis de Sousa* (1950) and *O Primo Basílio/Cousin Basílio* (1959). In the early days of Portuguese television he was responsible for a programme called 'Museu do Cinema', a televised film archive which made him known to thousands of viewers. Having always been against dubbing, in his eighties Ribeiro was still active in subtitling. AMS

RICHARD, (Sir) Cliff
Lucknow, India 1940

British singer and actor, and idol of the pre-Beatles pop scene in the early 1960s. He made four successful films between 1959 and 1962, *Expresso Bongo* (1959), *The Young Ones* (1961), *Wonderful Life* (1964) and *Summer Holiday* (1963). Modelled on Elvis Presley's movies in the US, Cliff's films were a wonderfully British variant: like a pop version of Ealing*, they placed civic-spirited youth against weary bureaucrats and businessmen of The Older Generation. The music was good, the direction was lively, and there was just enough teenage rebellion to make parents anxious and thus ensure Cliff the enthusiastic approval of their kids. He went on to make two further films, *Finders Keepers* (1966) and *Take Me High* (1973), but the times they had a-changed and the youth audience had moved on, leaving Cliff stranded at home with the grown-ups. JC

RICHARD-WILLM, Pierre
Pierre Richard; Bayonne 1895 – Paris 1983

French actor. With a few exceptions such as Jacques Feyder's* *Le Grand jeu* (1933) and Julien Duvivier's* *Un carnet de bal* (1937), Richard-Willm was not a star of classic films, which explains his present obscurity. Yet in the 1930s and 1940s he was extremely popular, presenting a romantic alternative to the proletarian heroes embodied by the likes of Jean Gabin*. His blond good looks made him ideal for costume dramas such as *Le Roman de Werther/Werther* (1938) and *Le Comte de Monte-Cristo* (1943). Very much a 'women's star', he anticipated the Gérard Philipe* of the 1950s. GV

RICHARDSON, (Sir) Ralph
Cheltenham 1902 – London 1983

British actor, who made his stage debut in *Les Misérables* in 1921, and with John Gielgud* and Laurence Olivier* formed the leading triumvirate of theatrical knights for five decades. Despite turning up to rehearsals on his motorbike in his seventies, Richardson seems never to have been completely young, and his 1930s persona already contains the seeds of his dotage. In his second film, Victor Saville's* *Friday the Thirteenth* (1933), Richardson partnered Jessie Matthews* as the proper schoolmaster to her exuberant showgirl, and in *The Divorce of Lady X* (1938) he was already the dotty aristocrat who reappears forty-six years later in *Greystoke The Legend of Tarzan Lord of the Apes* (1984). Karol Kulik, in her biography of Alexander Korda*, compares Richardson's swaggering Chief in *Things to Come* (1936) to a mixture of Charles Laughton* and W. C. Fields, a mixture which reputedly did not please Mussolini on whom the characterisation was based. But the eccentric dottiness and apparent befuddledness did not undermine the strength of his characters. His performance as the Tory squire in Saville's *South Riding* (1938), caught between conscience and straitened circumstances, is richly drawn. However recognisable and consistent Richardson's characterisations were, they were never dull or predictable, and each performance was precisely measured. In 1952 he directed himself in *Home at Seven* (1952), an unpretentious murder mystery, and in 1962 he played James Tyrone in the screen adaptation of *A Long Day's Journey into Night* [US]; but for the most part his postwar film career was in distinctive supporting roles and character parts. JC

Bib: Garry O'Connor, *Ralph Richardson: An Actor's Life* (1982).

Other Films Include: *The Man Who Could Work Miracles* (1936); *The Citadel* (1938); *The Four Feathers, The Lion Has Wings* (1939); *The Silver Fleet* (1943); *School for Secrets* (1946); *Anna Karenina, The Fallen Idol* (1948); *The Heiress* (1949, US); *Outcast of the Islands* (1951); *The Sound Barrier* (1952); *Richard III* (1955); *Our Man in Havana, Exodus* [US] (1960); *Doctor Zhivago* (1965); *Campanadas a medianoche/ Chimes at Midnight* [narrator] (1966, Sp./Switz.); *Oh! What a Lovely War* (1969); *Tales from the Crypt* (1972); *O Lucky Man!, A Doll's House* (1973); *Time Bandits* (1981).

RICHARDSON, Tony
Cecil Antonio Richardson; Shipley 1928 – Los Angeles, California 1991

British director, who was a leading figure in the British New Wave* in both cinema and theatre. After Oxford, Richardson worked in BBC television drama, and in 1955 formed the English Stage Company with George Devine at the Royal Court Theatre. It was his production of John Osborne's *Look Back in Anger* (1956) – or at least Kenneth Tynan's review of it – which set the theatre 'new wave' in motion and gave birth to the 'angry young men'. Simultaneously, the documentary which he co-directed with Karel Reisz*, *Momma Don't Allow* (1955), was appearing in the Free Cinema* season. In 1958, Richardson formed Woodfall Productions with Osborne, to translate the new wave to cinema, and in 1959 his film directing debut, *Look Back in Anger,* began a series of adaptations: *The Entertainer* (1960) from Osborne's play, *A Taste of Honey* (1961) from Shelagh Delaney's play, and *The Loneliness of the Long Distance Runner* (1962) from a short story by Alan Sillitoe. Richardson's career with Woodfall ended exuberantly with *Tom Jones* (1963), which won the Oscar for Best Director. Much of the rest of Richardson's career was in Hollywood, but it failed to build on the verve of *Tom Jones*. In *The Charge of the Light Brigade* (1968), how-

ever, he almost produced a national epic of triumphant defeat. JC

Other Films Include: *The Loved One* (1965, US); *The Sailor from Gibraltar* (1967); *Hamlet* (1969); *Ned Kelly* (1970); *A Delicate Balance* (1974, US); *Joseph Andrews* (1977); *The Border* (1982, US); *Hotel New Hampshire* (1984, US).

RICO, Paquita
Francisca Rico Martínez; Seville 1929

Spanish actress, singer and dancer, discovered by Florián Rey*. Her debut film, *Debla, la virgen gitana/Debla, the Gypsy Virgin* (1950), was a success at Cannes. She was the archetypal witty star of the *folklóricas**, appearing in many comedies and bringing a comic edge to melodramatic roles in *Malvaloca/Hollyhock* (1954) and *Suspiros de Triana/Sighs of Triana* (1955). In the late 1950s she took on more dramatic parts in *La Tirana/The Cruel Lady* (1958), *¿Dónde vas Alfonso XII?/Where Are You Going, Alfonso XII?* (1958) and *Ventolera/Whirlwind* (1961). Her film career came to an end with the *destape* (nudity) era of the late 1970s and her refusal to accept nude roles. PWE

RIEFENSTAHL, Leni
Berlin 1902

German director. Trained as a dancer, Riefenstahl started her film career as an actress in Arnold Fanck's* 'mountain films' (*Der heilige Berg/The Holy Mountain*, 1926, among others). With her first film as a director, *Das blaue Licht/The Blue Light* (1932), Riefenstahl not only gained critical and commercial success, but also won Hitler's personal approval, leading to a commission to film the Nuremberg Party Convention in 1934. *Triumph des Willens/Triumph of the Will* (1935), with its careful orchestration of narrative structure and spectacle, remains the best-known film of Nazi cinema, retaining its ambivalent power of propaganda and visual pleasure. Riefenstahl thought of herself as an independent film artist but claimed that it was her close personal relationship with the Führer which led to her second feature-length documentary, the two-part *Olympia* (1938), a record of the 1936 Olympic Games. Detained in Allied prison camps for almost four years on charges of pro-Nazi activity, she found herself economically as well as socially isolated after the war. After numerous attempts to restart a career in film, she turned successfully to photography, attracting fiercely loyal admirers but also implacable and unforgiving critics. MW

Bib: Leni Riefenstahl, *The Sieve of Time* (1992).

Other Films as Director: *Der Sieg des Glaubens/Victory of Faith* (1933, short); *Tag der Freiheit: Unsere Wehrmacht/Day of Freedom: Our Armed Forces* (1935); *Tiefland/Lowlands* (1940–54).

RISI, Dino

Italian director, who graduated in medicine (specialising in psychiatry), before working as an assistant to Alberto Lattuada* and Mario Soldati*. After the war and emigration to Switzerland, he returned to the cinema, shooting documentaries, writing on film and working as a scriptwriter, an enthusiastic participant in the creative climate of the northern Italian cities of the time. Before finding his vocation as the sceptic and ironic castigator of contemporary mores, Risi, like many others, went through 'social' neo-realism* (he took part in the collective film inspired by Cesare Zavattini*, *Amore in città/Love in the City*, 1953) and then 'rose-tinted' neo-realism (*neo-realismo rosa*), of which he was one of the creators with his enormously successful *Poveri ma belli/Poor But Beautiful* (1956). Risi became the perfect screen interpreter of the greed and arrogance of the 1950s and 1960s, and a master of the caustic comedy of manners [> COMMEDIA ALL'ITALIANA], helped by the producer Mario Cecchi Gori* and a brilliant team of comedy scriptwriters and actors, including his favourite star, Vittorio Gassman*. He directed Gassman in *Il mattatore/Love and Larceny* (1959) and in the masterly *Il sorpasso/The Easy Life* (1962), a skilful description of Italy's and his own transition from youthful euphoria to utilitarian cynicism; Gassman with Ugo Tognazzi* in *La marcia su Roma/The March to Rome* (1962) and *I mostri/The Monsters* (1963); and Gassman again in *Il tigre/The Tiger and the Pussycat* (1967), *In nome del popolo italiano/In the Name of the Italian People* (1972) and *Profumo di donna/Scent of a Woman* (1974). One of his most successful films was *Una vita difficile/A Difficult Life* (1961), which gave Alberto Sordi* the chance to prove his capability as a dramatic actor. Risi's later work became increasingly melancholy (with a few notable exceptions such as *Straziami ma di baci saziami/Hurt Me, But Cover Me with Your Kisses*, 1968), to the detriment of the more trenchant side of his talent, which had made him an undisputed master of Italian caustic comedy. PDA

Other Films Include: *Pane, amore e .../Scandal in Sorrento* (1955); *Belle ma povere/Beautiful But Poor* (1957); *Venezia, la luna e tu/Venice, the Moon and You* (1958); *Poveri milionari/Poor Millionaires, Il vedovo/The Widower* (1959); *A porte chiuse/Behind Closed Doors* (1961); *Il gaucho/The Gaucho* (1964); *L'ombrellone/The Parasol/Weekend, Italian Style, Operazione San Gennaro/Treasure of San Gennaro* (1966); *Vedo nudo/I See Everybody Naked* (1969); *La moglie del prete/The Priest's Wife* (1970); *Noi donne siamo fatte così/Women: So We Are Made* (1971); *Mordi e fuggi/Bite and Run, Sessomatto/How Funny Can Sex Be?* (1973); *Telefoni bianchi/White Telephones/The Career of a Chambermaid, Anima persa/Lost Soul* (1976); *La stanza del vescovo/The Bishop's Room, I nuovi mostri/Viva Italia* [co-dir.] (1977); *Primo amore* (1978); *Caro papà* (1979); *Sono fotogenico* (1980); *Fantasma d'amore/Ghost of Love* (1981); *Sesso e volentieri/Sex and Violence* (1982); *Scemo di guerra* (1985); *Il commissario Lo Gatto/Inspector Lo Gatto* (1986); *Teresa* (1987); *Tolgo il disturbo* (1990).

RISI, Marco

Italian director. The son of Dino Risi* and nephew of the poet and director Nelo Risi, he started his apprenticeship within the family circle as assistant and scriptwriter for his father's film *Caro papà* (1979), and worked with Alberto Sordi*, Duccio Tessari and Carlo Vanzina. Marco Risi directed his first film in 1983, *Vado da vivere da solo*, followed by *Un ragazzo e una ragazza* (1984) and *Colpo di fulmine* (1985), all starring comic actor Jerry Calà. From the start his work met with popularity. With *Soldati, 365 all'alba* (1987), about military life, he tried a new theme and a new genre, together with a more personal style. Similarly, *Mery per sempre* (1989) and *Ragazzi fuori* (1990), both depicting events from the lives of young Sicilian delinquents, seemed to initiate a new current of 'neo-neorealism'. More journalistic was *Il muro di gomma* (1991), the reconstruction of the 'Ustica case' (an unexplained air crash) in which he denounced the serious military and political responsibilities for this tragic event. In *Nel continente nero* (1992), Risi tried to resurrect the satiric vein of the *commedia all'italiana* of the 1960s, of which his father's masterpiece *Il sorpasso/The Easy Life* (1962) was an archetype. PDA

RIVELLES, Amparo

Spanish actress. Oval-faced, aquiline-featured, dark-eyed leading lady who came from an acting family and made her film debut at thirteen. She became enormously popular as an ingénue, before taking on stronger roles at Cifesa* in the 1940s, where she soon became a top star. Here, in films like *Malvaloca/Hollyhock* (1942), *Eloisa está debajo de un almendro/Eloísa is Underneath an Almond Tree* (1943), *Fuenteovejuna* (1947) and, later, in *La Leona de Castilla/The Lioness of Castile* (1950) and *Alba de América/The Dawn of America* (1951), she developed a more powerful aura, combined with a self-conscious, detached humour. She left for Mexico in 1957, where she stayed for twenty years making film, stage and television appearances. Returning to Spain, she appeared in supporting roles in major films such as Josefina Molina's* *Esquilache* (1989). PWE

RIVETTE, Jacques

French director. With his first feature, *Paris nous appartient/Paris Belongs to Us* (1958–60), and his critical work, Rivette was a central figure in the New Wave*. Along with Jean-Luc Godard* he was also its most experimental member (because of their unconventional narratives and length – some exceed four hours – Rivette's films are rarely shown). The dual motif of plot (as conspiracy and narrative) and performance (often improvised) provides a complex reflection on narrative, fiction and imagination in, for instance, *L'Amour fou*, 1967–69, and *L'Amour par terre/Love on the Ground*, 1984.

Rivette frequently focuses on women. The celebrated *Céline et Julie vont en bateau/Céline and Julie Go Boating*

(1974) remains a brilliant challenge to narrative and patriarchal structures: Céline and Julie control their destiny (actresses Juliet Berto and Dominique Labourier contributed to the script), live by their wits and reject men and marriage. *Le Pont du Nord* (1981) and *L'Amour par terre* also centred on two women and involved the actresses in the writing process. On the other hand, *La Belle Noiseuse* (1991, based on a Balzac short story), while a profound reflection on the nature of artistic creation and the relationship between painting and the cinema, endorsed a conventional patriarchal vision of a male painter and his female model. It has been Rivette's most successful film. GV

Other Films: *Le Coup du Berger* (short, 1956); *La Religieuse/The Nun* (1965, rel. 1967); *Jean Renoir, le Patron* (1966, TV); *Out 1: Noli Me Tangere* (1971, TV); *Out 1: spectre* (1973); *Duelle/Twilight, Noroît/Nor'west* (1976); *Merry-go-round* (1978–83); *Hurlevent/Wuthering Heights* (1985).

RIZZOLI, Angelo   Milan 1889–1970

Italian producer. A publishing tycoon, Rizzoli first ventured into the cinema in the early 1930s with the publication of popular weekly magazines such as *Novella Cinema*, followed by the creation of a company which produced Max Ophuls'* *La signora di tutti* (1934) and Mario Camerini's* *Darò un milione* (1935). His next involvement came in the 1950s with the creation of Cineriz and other joint-stock companies (Dear, Riama, Rizzoli Film). Rizzoli was an unusual producer, the cinema representing only one of his many activities. He possessed a strong sense of the 'popular', leading to huge success with the Don Camillo comedy series, starring Fernandel* and Gino Cervi*, 'film operas' (Carmine Gallone's* *Puccini*, 1953), melodramas and sensationalist documentaries (Gualtiero Jacopetti's *Mondo cane*, 1962). The producer of a very large range of titles (more than forty films between 1952 and 1955 alone), he was a pioneer of international co-productions, including René Clair's* *Les Belles de nuit* (1952, Fr./It.) and *Porte des Lilas* (1957, Fr./It.), Joseph Mankiewicz's *The Barefoot Contessa* (1954, US/It.), Fritz Lang's* *Der Tiger von Eschnapur/The Tiger of Bengal* and *Das indische Grabmal/The Hindu Tomb* (1959, both Ger./It./Fr.). He gave *carte blanche* to his *auteurs*, relying on his ability to choose the right director in the first place, with some justification since he produced, among other films, Roberto Rossellini's* *Francesco giullare di Dio/The Flower of St Francis/Francis, God's Jester* (1950), Vittorio De Sica's* *Umberto D.* (1952), Michelangelo Antonioni's* *L'eclisse/The Eclipse* (1962), and Federico Fellini's* *La dolce vita* (1960), *8½* (1963) and *Giulietta degli spiriti/Juliet of the Spirits* (1965). After Rizzoli's death, Cineriz still found some success with Nino Manfredi's *Per grazia ricevuta* (1970) and popular films starring Paolo Villaggio and former rock star Adriano Celentano. Cineriz came to an end in the early 1980s when it was involved in the intricate financial, political and legal vicissitudes of Angelo Rizzoli Jr's RCS and of the daily *Corriere della Sera*; it was eventually sold to emerging television tycoon Silvio Berlusconi. GVo

ROBERTS, Rachel   Llanelli, Wales 1927 – California 1980

British actress. Though primarily a stage actress, Rachel Roberts gave two of the most memorable female performances in the British New Wave* cinema. In *Saturday Night and Sunday Morning* (1960) she played a mature, defeated woman trapped in an empty marriage and an affectionless and humiliating relationship with a younger lover (Albert Finney*). In *This Sporting Life* (1963), her Mrs Hammond is unremitting in her refusal of life, affection or sexual pleasure, or of Frank Machin (Richard Harris*), whose response is rape. The Roberts character is, in fact, the most painful of the sacrificial victims of the misogynist current in the British New Wave. Her performances in *Saturday Night and Sunday Morning* and *This Sporting Life* received Best Actress awards from the British Academy, from whom she also won a Best Supporting Actress award for *Yanks* (1979).

She had a troubled relationship with Rex Harrison*, moved to California, suffered from alcoholism, and died of an overdose in 1980. JC

Bib: Alexander Walker (ed.), *The Rachel Roberts Journals* (1984).

Other Films Include: *The Good Companions* (1957); *The Reckoning* (1970); *O Lucky Man!, The Belstone Fox* (1973); *Murder on the Orient Express* (1974); *Picnic at Hanging Rock* (1975, Australia); *Charlie Chan and the Curse of the Dragon Queen* (1980, US).

ROBESON, PAUL   Princeton, NJ, USA 1898 – Philadelphia 1976

American singer/actor. Robeson was based in Britain during much of the 1930s while he developed his European singing and acting career (appearing with Peggy Ashcroft* in a 1930 production of *Othello*), and he appeared in a number of films which exploited his colour and his singing voice to mixed effects. He had already appeared in Oscar Micheaux's *Body and Soul* (1925, US). His appearance, with his wife Eslanda, in Kenneth Macpherson's *Borderline* (1930, Switz.) placed him in contact with the British avant-garde group around the magazine *Close Up**. He was tempted into Zoltan Korda's *Sanders of the River* (1935) by the promise of authentic African music and tribal life, but the result was a vindication of paternalistic colonialism, and Robeson attempted to prevent the film's release. Stevenson's *King Solomon's Mines* (1937) had more adventure but little more enlightenment. *Song of Freedom* (1936) and *The Big Fella* (1937), both directed by J. Edgar Wills and featuring Elizabeth Welch, were low-budget features, but *Song of Freedom*, at least, was welcomed by the Harlem press (and Langston Hughes) for its representation of the black man. Most successful, but no less compromised in its representation of race, was *The Proud Valley* (1940), directed by Pen Tennyson, which integrates Robeson effortlessly into a Welsh mining community through his singing voice, but still leaves him in the anteroom when the miners negotiate with the bosses. JC

Bib: Martin Bauml Doberman, *Paul Robeson* (1989).

ROBSON, (Dame) Flora
South Shields 1902 – Sussex 1984

British actress, renowned as one of the great character players of the British theatre and cinema. At the age of 32, Robson played the old Empress Elizabeth in Alexander Korda's* *Catherine the Great* (1934); she played Queen Elizabeth I in *The Sea Hawk* (1940, US); but most famously she played the same role in *Fire Over England* (1937), uttering the lines which have become part of Elizabethan mythology: 'I know I have the body of a weak and feeble woman, but I have the heart and valour of a King. Aye, and of a King of England too.' After the war, demonstrating her range, she appeared in *Holiday Camp* (1947), the first of a series of films which featured the very ordinary Huggett family; as the Mother Superior in Michael Powell* and Emeric Pressburger's *Black Narcissus* (1947); as a magistrate in *Good-time Girl* (1948); as a prospective Labour MP in Basil Dearden's* excellent *Frieda* (1947); and in Dearden's costume melodrama, *Saraband for Dead Lovers* (1948). For the rest of her career she remained in the theatre, though she gave a memorable performance in John Ford's *7 Women* (1966, US). She was made a Dame in 1960. JC

ROCHA, Paulo
Oporto 1935

Portuguese director, who studied at IDHEC* in Paris and trained as an assistant to Jean Renoir* on *Le Caporal épinglé/The Vanishing Corporal* (1962). Back in Portugal he made the first film of the New Portuguese Cinema*, *Os Verdes Anos/The Green Years* (1963) and *Mudar de Vida/Change of Life* (1966). Fascinated by Japan, he began working on the life of the Portuguese poet Wenceslau de Moraes, who lived and died there. Conceived after *Mudar de Vida*, and given official production support in 1974, *A Ilha dos Amores/The Island of Loves* was only finished in 1983 and not released until 1991. There was a sequel, *A Ilha de Moraes/The Island of Moraes* (1984; Moraes is an anagram of 'amores', loves), a documentary that was as much about Moraes as it was about Rocha, himself a Portuguese émigré in Japan and cultural attaché in Tokyo from 1975 to 1983. More recently, Rocha treated the same character again in a video based on a theatrical production, *Portugaru-san ou o Senhor Wenceslau de Moraes em Tokushima/Portugaru-san or Mr Wenceslau de Moraes in Tokushima* (1993).

Rocha marked his return to Portugal by making *O Desejado ou As Montanhas da Lua/The Desired One or The Mountains of the Moon* (1987). Based on a classical Japanese story transposed to present-day Portugal and featuring Luís Miguel Cintra* as a former political exile who becomes prime minister, it was unreleased at the time. When both *A Ilha dos Amores* and *O Desejado* were finally released in 1991 to coincide with the re-release of Rocha's previous films, it was the first time that Portuguese audiences had seen his films for a quarter of a century. This bizarre situation, a telling commentary on Portuguese cinema in general and the weakness of commercial distribution in particular, is mirrored in Rocha's films, all of which have to do with distance, arrival, to stay or to return. In *Os Verdes Anos* a young man moves from the country to Lisbon; in *Mudar de Vida*, the hero returns from Africa, finds his ex-fiancée married to his brother and meets a young woman with whom he emigrates to France; in *A Ilha dos Amores* Moraes travels to Macao and then Japan; *O Desejado* is about a man returning from exile. Maybe in no other *auteur* of the New Portuguese Cinema is the relationship with Portugal so problematic. 'We are the sons of an anonymous fatherland,' says the poet Pessanha in *A Ilha dos Amores*. This, Rocha's most important film, is a mourning ceremony combining the Japanese element (Mizoguchi in particular) already present in *Mudar de Vida* with the theatrical and operatic tendencies of *A Pousada das Chagas/The Stigmata Inn* (1971, short). These are the two quintessential aspects of his films. Rocha played small parts for Manoel de Oliveira* and Fernando Lopes. AMS

Other Films: *Sever de Vouga, Uma Experiência/Sever de Vouga, an Experience* (1970, doc. supervised by Oliveira); *Máscara de Ferro contra o Abismo Azul/Steel Mask vs. Blue Deep* [TV] (1988); *Cinéastes de notre temps: Oliveira, l'architecte* [TV] (1993, Fr.).

ROEG, Nicolas
London 1928

British director. Roeg seems like a product of the 1960s art schools, but is in fact a product of the Marylebone dubbing studios from 1947, camera operator from 1958 on, for example, Roger Corman's *The Masque of the Red Death* (1964), second unit camera on *Lawrence of Arabia* (1962), and cinematographer on such films as the screen adaptation of Harold Pinter's* *The Caretaker* (1963), François Truffaut's* *Fahrenheit 451* (1966) and John Schlesinger's* *Far from the Madding Crowd* (1967). His directing debut, *Performance* (1970), co-directed with Donald Cammell and starring Mick Jagger and James Fox, became a cult movie of the 1970s. Roeg's films are characterised by intricately edited time warps in which opposing worlds clash. With *Walkabout* (1971), set in the Australian outback, the cultural clash and the temporal ellipses were still connected, in *Don't Look Now* (1973) the gap between this world and the other was chilling, and in *The Man Who Fell to Earth* (1976) there was a sense of ideas just beyond the edge of the screen. But the later films often seem, in Chuck Kleinhans' phrase, 'permutations without profundity'. Roeg seems to inhabit a peculiarly British territory, an art cinema (like Peter Greenaway's*) whose cleverness leaves it stranded between pretentiousness and seriousness. JC

Bib: Jonathan Hacker and David Price, *Take 10: Contemporary British Film Directors* (1991).

Other Films Include: *Bad Timing* (1980); *Eureka* (1983); *Insignificance* (1985); *Castaway* (1986); *Track 29* (1987).

ROHMER, Eric
Jean-Marie Maurice Schérer; Nancy 1920

French director, former academic and film critic. Like other French New Wave* directors, Rohmer began working in the

1950s, but it was not until *Ma nuit chez Maud/My Night with Maud* (1969) that he became internationally recognised. His films, most of them divided into 'moral tales' (1962–72) and 'comedies and proverbs' (1980–87), are chamber pieces, focusing on the moral, intellectual and romantic dilemmas of highly articulate characters. This has led to Rohmer's characterisation as a 'literary' film-maker. But while in the tradition of psychological French literature, Rohmer's work is eminently cinematic – in its mastery of a classical economical style, and in its recourse to *cinéma-vérité** techniques.

Even when focusing on the dilemmas of male protagonists, Rohmer's films give women a prominent place. The title character in *Maud* is the prototypical 'moral tales' heroine: sensually and intellectually superior to the prim and rather dull hero. With the 'comedies and proverbs' Rohmer increasingly became a 'woman's director', and his semi-artisanal methods often closely involve his actresses, for instance Marie Rivière for *Le Rayon vert/The Green Ray* (1986). In these later films, it is the women's desire which drives the narrative, even if often thwarted, as in the powerful *Les Nuits de la pleine lune/Full Moon in Paris*, 1984. Still made with small budgets and crews, and shot on location, Rohmer's latest films, *L'Arbre, le maire et la médiathèque* (1993, a brilliant combination of *vérité* documentary and frivolous *marivaudage*), and the new series, 'Tales of the Four Seasons', show his continuing commitment to the aesthetics as well as the methods of the New Wave. GV

Bib: Pascal Bonitzer, *Eric Rohmer* (1992).

Other Films Include: *La Collectionneuse* (1967); *Le Genou de Claire/Claire's Knee* (1970); *L'Amour l'après-midi/Love in the Afternoon* (1972); *Die Marquise von O.../La Marquise d'O* (1976, Ger./Fr.); *La Femme de l'aviateur/The Aviator's Wife* (1980); *Le Beau mariage/A Good Marriage, Pauline à la plage* (1982); *Quatre aventures de Reinette et Mirabelle/Four Adventures of Reinette and Mirabelle, L'Ami de mon amie/My Best Friend's Boyfriend* (1987); *Conte de printemps/A Tale of Springtime* (1989); *Conte d'hiver/A Winter's Tale* (1992); *Les Rendez-vous de Paris* (1995).

RÖKK, Marika   Cairo 1913

German actress and leading revue-film star. Her film debut was in two British comedies (*Kiss Me, Sergeant, Why Sailors Leave Home*, both 1930), followed by two Hungarian films, before an Ufa* contract led to *Leichte Kavallerie* (dir. Werner Hochbaum*, 1935). But it was Georg Jacoby* (married to Rökk since 1940) who directed her star vehicles with rare continuity until 1959 (*Der Bettelstudent*, 1936; *Kora Terry*, 1940; *Die Frau meiner Träume*, 1944; *Kind der Donau*, 1950; *Bühne frei für Marika*, 1958). An exceptionally attractive and talented dancer, Rökk could carry off the cliché romance plot-lines, lavish settings and glamour costumes. More than any other film star of the Nazi period, she benefited from Ufa's enormous efforts to copy American musicals with the coming of sound and colour. MW

Bib: Helga Belach (ed.), *Wir tanzen um die Welt: Deutsche Revuefilme 1933–1945* (1979).

Other Films Include: *Hallo Janine!* (1939); *Frauen sind doch bessere Diplomaten* (1941); *Maske in Blau* (1953); *Die Fledermaus* (1962); *Schloß Königswald* (1987, TV).

ROMANCE, Viviane   Pauline Ortmans; Roubaix 1909 [1912?] – Nice 1991

French actress. Viviane Romance came to prominence in the mid-1930s in roles that repeatedly cast her as the 'bitch', notably in Julien Duvivier's* *La Belle équipe* (1936) and Augusto Genina's* *Naples au baiser de feu* (1937). A beautiful and talented actress, she was limited by this typecasting (which was reinforced by her scandalous private life) and the fact that in her populist register the leading parts went to male stars such as Jean Gabin*, Charles Vanel* or Michel Simon*. The war provided an interesting break by offering her leads in melodramas, including the unusual *Vénus aveugle* directed by Abel Gance* in 1941 (rel. 1943). In the conservative climate of Vichy, her 'bitch' persona underwent a dramatic change, too dramatic perhaps for her audience. In 1947, Duvivier's *Panique* again cast her as a malevolent seductress, but such characters do not age well and her subsequent career never regained its prewar momentum; she appeared fleetingly in *Mélodie en sous-sol/The Big Snatch* (1963) and *Nada* (1973). She will remain, however, the memorable 'number one French vamp' of the 1930s, her sensual performances often transcending her limiting roles. GV

Other Films Include: *L'Etrange Monsieur Victor* (1937); *Le Puritain, La Maison du Maltais, Prisons de femmes* (1938); *La Boîte aux rêves, Carmen* (both 1943–45); *L'Affaire du collier de la reine* (1946).

ROMANIA

Though a Lumière* brothers' screening took place in Bucharest in 1896, Romanian cinema development was slow and sporadic. The first feature of note was the epic *Războiul independenței/War of Independence* (1912), directed by the actor Grigore Brezeanu. More artistically noteworthy was Jean Mihail's *Manasse* (1925). Lack of opportunity led Romanians with serious film ambitions, like Lupu-Pick* and Jean Negulescu (later Negulesco), to emigrate, respectively to Germany and Hollywood. However, a network of cinemas developed in the 1920s, and films based on Romanian folk myths, which also drew on the American Western, were popular, such as *Haiducii* (1929). In 1934 a fund was set up to encourage production, and 1936 saw Romania's first regular film production, of newsreels and documentaries, under the auspices of the National Tourist Office. Romanian cinema won its first international accolade (first prize at Venice) with *Tara Moților/Land of the Motzi* (1938) by Paul Călinescu. Comedies and musicals also began to appear shortly before World War II.

Postwar production (the film industry was nationalised in 1948) was at first undistinguished, with limited range, technique and quantity. The decimated artistic community was alienated from the Soviet-imposed regime. Film strictly followed the Moscow line of popular instruction, though apart from Dinu Negreanu directors were locally trained. Calinescu's *Răsuna valea/The Valley Resounds* (1949) set the Socialist Realist* style, concentrating on triumphs of progress and social justice in rural areas. Victor Iliu* dominated the genre with skill, beginning to pose artistic as well as political questions, but Jean Georgescu's attempts at socialist comedy showed its limitations. The regime's vulnerability made the 'thaw' slower than elsewhere, though in the late 1950s approved cultural links with other 'Romance' nations allowed the first of many co-productions, for example with France for *Ciulinii Baraganului/Baragan Thistles* (1957, dir. Louis Daquin). The wave of new film-makers from the I. L. Caragiale Institute of Theatre and Film Art (IATC) in Bucharest, founded in 1950, still had to conform, and their skills were needed at the Buftea* studios, which produced fifteen features a year from 1958. The Alexandru Sahia documentary and short film studio (founded in 1950 and named after the Marxist writer) also grew at this time under Ion Bostan. The animation skills of Ion Popescu-Gopo* led to the creation of another studio, AnimaFilm*. The making of children's films was pioneered by Elisabeta Bostan*.

Iulian Mihu and Manole Marcus' *Viaţa nu iartă/Life Will Not Forgive* (1958), based on Sahia's war stories, is a classic of the new generation. Liviu Ciulei, coming from the theatre, made three films, culminating in *Pădurea spînzuraţilor/Forest of the Hanged* (1964), a morality tale from World War I scripted by the skilled and prolific Titus Popovici, shot by Ovidiu Gologan and starring Victor Rebengiuc* and Silvia Popovici. It won the Best Director prize for Ciulei at Cannes. Mircea Dragan, the most versatile IATC graduate, promulgated the official line at IATC and in film criticism. His *Lupeni 29* (1962), based on a miners' strike, and Lucian Bratu's massive *Tudor* (1963), about a revolt against the Turks, paved the way for Dragan's and Sergiu Nicolaescu's* 'patriotic' film epics, glorifying Romanian history and spawning a whole series of historically based adventure yarns. They reflect the new nationalism – and its apotheosis under Ceauşescu's regime (1965–89) – of controlled cultural emancipation from Moscow, creating an ideological orthodoxy more acceptable to the people and the intelligentsia.

In the late 1960s a less schematic representation of society was seen in more contemporary, realistic and challenging films. Andrei Bleier's *Diminețele unui băiat cuminte/The Mornings of a Sensible Youth* (1966) features young people unsure of their future. Gheorghe Vitandis' *O femeie pentru un anotimp/A Woman for One Season* (1969), scripted by Nicolae Breban, shows sensuality and emotional crisis. Theatre director Lucian Pintilie* broke through barriers of form and political acceptability in the subtle political subversion of *Reconstituirea/Reconstruction* (1969). These signs of a 'new wave' were hit by Ceauşescu's consolidation of power, and by delayed reaction to events in Czechoslovakia. Ceauşescu's Stalinism, anti-intellectualism and puritanism imposed a harder line on content, though allowing some experimentation in form. Adaptation to circumstance is evident in Dan Piţa* and Mircea Veroiu's* overpowering and widely acclaimed *Nuntă de piatră/Stone Wedding* (1972); and in Manole Marcus' *Canarul şi viscolul/The Canary and the Storm* (1970), though here the striking visual effects tend to obscure the story. Radu Gabrea's biography of an anarchist hero, *Dincolo de nisipuri/Beyond the Sands* (1973), breached the limits on content, and the released version was rewritten and given a new slant.

Gabrea, Pintilie and Ciulei left Romania in the 1970s to find artistic freedom, and joined Romania's exiled communities in America and France. Piţa and Veroiu led, if not a new wave, perhaps a 'renaissance' into the 1980s, encouraged by praise for their work abroad. Alexandru Tatos* explored relations between individuals and authority in *Mere roşii/Red Apples* (1976) and other films. Iosef Demian's *O lacrima de fata/A Girl's Tear* (1981) showed the militia making a film 'for internal use' about a mysterious death. From the late 1970s Mircea Daneliuc* achieved a measure of subversion with psychology and magic realism, especially in *Probă de microfon/Microphone Test* (1979) and *Glissando* (1984), starring Stefan Iordache. Ada Pistiner's *Stop cadru la masă/Freeze-Frame at Table* (1980) played ironically with personal frustration; and veteran director Malvina Ursianu's *O lumină la etajul 10/A Light on the Tenth Floor* (1985) also confronted contemporary issues in its story of a released female political prisoner (Irina Petrescu). Meanwhile box-office favourite Nicolaescu, together with Dragan, Marcus, Blaier and others, made competent and popular adaptations of literary classics, historical epics, war films, thrillers, comedies, and some contemporary dramas; while Transylvania* provided the backdrop to a series of Romanian 'Westerns' by various leading directors, starring Ilarion Ciobanu, Ovidiu Iuliu Moldovan and Mircea Diaconu.

The 1989 revolution brought in its wake political and economic paralysis in the film industry. While formal censorship ended, so did guaranteed state support, and film-makers went on strike to break free from the tainted Ministry of Culture. New financial and legal frameworks, and the powers of the new central budget authority – the National Cinematography Centre (CNC) – have been slow to emerge; a strike in 1991 challenged Dan Piţa's alleged mismanagement of the CNC. Pintilie's appointment at the Ministry of Culture, and commissioning of Stere Gulea's documentary *Piata Universităţii – Romania/University Square – Romania* (1990), with its criticism of the new president Ion Iliescu, generated conflict with the ruling party. Pintilie's *Le Chêne/Stejarul/The Oak* (1992) is a powerful account of the last years of the Ceauşescu regime in Romania. A Romanian-French co-production which won international recognition, it represents some hope for a renewed Romanian cinema.

Buftea production peaked in the early 1980s at thirty-two features annually, while the Sahia documentary studio made 300 shorts, eighty of them on scientific subjects. Both studios have suffered a steep decline recently, with only fourteen features completed in 1992. AnimaFilm significantly increased output through the 1980s, making sixty shorts and four long features in 1989. Its dominance (over 75 per cent) of film export earnings, and a Spanish link-up in 1991, indicate a more secure future.

Cinema has traditionally been a mass medium in Romania; typically half the population would see major releases, overwhelmingly domestic productions until the 1970s when the regime selectively imported the 'escapism' of American movies and Western television (non-Romanian films are subtitled). Audiences peaked in 1984 at 217 million (for a population of 23 million), boosted by the reduction in television output as part of the regime's economy drive. However, the boom in video, and since 1989 the transformation of television (with commercial channels in development), have cut cinema audiences by over 50 per cent. The number of cinemas has declined from a peak of 6,500 in 1965, and a first batch was offered for sale in 1992. Compared to other (former) Eastern bloc countries, American film penetration of Romania remains low (though it is currently rising) because of limited availability. In 1991 only four of the top ten films were American, the biggest hit being the Romanian *Adolescenţi/High School Rock* (1991). There are signs that, as the industry shows that it can be self-financing, the downturn may be at an end.

Romania has one specialist film magazine, *Cinema* (founded 1963). The Film Archive in Bucharest, established in 1957, contains 22,500 shorts. The national film festival has taken place at Costineşti since 1976, though its future is in doubt.

Film in Romania, first harnessed as a tool of ideology and economic development, became in the 1960s a central element in a new ideology based on Romanian national identity. It has remained partly in the shadow of theatre, sharing a directing and acting talent which considers theatre its first home. Its influence is currently small compared to television, which dominated the 1989 revolution and remains the central political arena. An east European-style 'new wave' or 'school' ultimately proved politically impossible, but the alternative paths taken have inspired in a few directors some of the subtlest and strongest imagery in world cinema – reflecting Romania's unique political and cultural experience. MM [> TRANSYLVANIA]

ROMM, Mikhail I.
Zaigraevo, Siberia [Russian Empire] 1901 – Moscow 1971

Soviet director and scriptwriter. Romm fought in the Red Army during the Civil War, studied sculpture, translated Flaubert and Zola, and wrote scripts before directing his first film, the Maupassant adaptation *Pyshka/Boule de Suif* (1934). Best known in the 1930s for his two revolutionary anniversary films, *Lenin v oktyabre/Lenin in October* (1938) and *Lenin v 1918 godu/Lenin in 1918* (1939, Stalin Prize in 1941), he then tended to toe the Party line with films such as *Mechta/The Dream* (1943), *Russkii vopros/The Russian Question* and *Vladimir Ilyich Lenin* (both 1948), *Sekretnaya missiya/Secret Mission* (1950) and *Ubiistvo na ulitse Dante/Murder on Dante Street* (1956), but much of his subsequent work was devoted to an exploration of sensitive moral dilemmas, as in *Devyat' dnei odnogo goda/Nine Days of One Year* (1962) and, above all, *Obyknovennyi fashizm/Ordinary Fascism* (1966). His last film, *I vse-taki ya veryu/Nonetheless I Believe* (1976), was completed by Marlen Khutsiev*, Elem Klimov* and German Lavrov. Romm taught at VGIK* from 1949 and his pupils included Tengiz Abuladze*, Grigori Chukhrai*, Vasili Shukshin*, Georgi Danelia* and Gleb Panfilov*. He was known in film circles for his outrageous anecdotes and imitations of his colleagues, which have since been issued on record and published in book form. RT

ROMMER, Claire
Berlin 1904

German actress, whose brief but phenomenal success lasted from 1922 to 1926 and is indicative of a largely forgotten popular film culture. Unlike many other German films stars, Rommer's fame was based less on the films she appeared in than on her fans' perception of her star image, cultivated via publicity material in fashion magazines and photographs on postcards and cigarette cards. Her first screen hit was *Wem nie durch Liebe Leid geschah!* in 1922, but she was equally known as a stage actress in light comedies (*Foppke, der Egoist* [Berliner Residenztheater, 1926]) and in soubrette roles from operettas and variety theatres (such as the Berlin Scala). Rommer emigrated when the Nazis came to power and was quickly forgotten in Germany. Because she is not associated with any of the 'classics' of Weimar* cinema, she has continued to be ignored by film historians. JG

ROOM, Abram M.
Vilna, Lithuania [Russian Empire] 1894 – Moscow 1976

Soviet director and scriptwriter. After studying psychology, Room joined Meyerhold's theatre in 1923. He began teaching at VGIK* and made his first short comedy films in 1924. His first features were *Bukhta smerti/Bay of Death* and *Predatel'/The Traitor* (both 1926), but he achieved notoriety with his study of an eternal triangle in the social context of the New Economic Policy, *Tret'ya Meshchanskaya/Bed and Sofa/Third Meshchanskaya Street* (1927), from a script written with Viktor Shklovsky* and starring Nikolai Batalov*. *Prividenie, kotoroe ne vozvrashchaetsya/The Ghost That Never Returns*, set largely in a penal colony in Mexico, and *Plan velikikh rabot/Plan for Great Works*, the first Soviet sound feature film, followed in 1930. His next project, *Odnazhdy letom/Once One Summer*, was stopped during filming in 1932 and his next completed film, *Strogii yunosha/A Strict Young Man*, made in 1934, was banned because it dealt with the sensitive question of equality in Soviet society. After this, although he went on making films, his career as teacher ceased and as a film-maker he went into decline: he ended up making a series of literary adaptations of no great interest. RT

ROOS, Jørgen
Copenhagen 1922

Danish director, specialising in documentaries. Roos began as a cameraman in 1939, ran a film club, and together with painter Albert Mertz made the first Danish experimental film, *Flugten/The Escape* (a short) in 1942. He assisted Carl Theodor Dreyer*, notably on the documentary *De nåede færgen/They Caught the Ferry*. In 1950, Roos directed his first film about Greenland, a subject to which he repeatedly returned, especially in the 1960s, as in *Knud* (1966, Silver Bear at Berlin), about the Danish Arctic explorer Knud Rasmussen, and *Ultima Thule/Thule – Furthest Outpost* (1968). He made a film about Hans Christian Andersen, *Mit Livs Eventyr/The Story of My Life* (released 1955). His attempt at fiction, *Seksdagesløbet/The Six-Day Bicycle Race* (1958), was not entirely successful, though the tense atmosphere of the race was excellently recreated. Particularly interesting is his later *De unge, gamle/The Young, Old* (1984), a very personal film in which he discusses old age with a group of friends. Roos is the most talented and versatile documentary film-maker currently working in Denmark. The Greenland films are especially remarkable, his passion for the Greenlanders clearly expressed in his portrayal of that country's difficult path to modernisation. ME

Other Films Include: *Det definitive afslag på anmodningen om et kys/The Definite Refusal to a Kiss Requested* (1949); *En by ved navn København/A City Called Copenhagen* (1960).

ROSAY, Françoise
Françoise Bandy de Nalèche; Paris 1891–1974

French actress. Françoise Rosay's long career is closely linked to that of her husband, the director Jacques Feyder*, with whom she started her film career proper (after parts on stage and a few in films) in *Gribiche* (1926). While in Hollywood with Feyder, she appeared in French versions of multi-language films. Back in France, she co-starred with Fernandel* in the scandalous *Le Rosier de Madame Husson/ The Virtuous Isidore* (1931), based on Maupassant. Her greatest performances were still to come: in Feyder's *Le Grand jeu* (1933), *Pension Mimosas* (1934), and *La Kermesse héroïque/ Carnival in Flanders* (1935), and in Marcel Carné's* *Jenny* (1936) and the surrealist *Drôle de drame* (1937). During and after World War II she pursued a prolific European career, her films including the British resistance drama *Johnny Frenchman* (1945) and Claude Autant-Lara's* comedy *L'Auberge rouge/The Red Inn* (1951). As shown by her classic 1930s parts, Rosay had the talent to impose herself as a humorous and seductive presence while already in her forties, like Arletty*, with whom she shared the ability to be both world-weary and touching. GV

ROSI, Francesco
Naples 1922

Italian director. Rosi's apprenticeship began in 1948, when he was assistant director to Luchino Visconti* on *La terra trema* – a film whose uncompromising neo-realism* and dedication to the Sicilian proletariat were to influence Rosi's own investigative approach to film-making and his perennial return to the 'Southern Question'. Rosi was Visconti's assistant again on *Bellissima* (1951) and *Senso* (1954), while working with other postwar directors, including Michelangelo Antonioni*, Goffredo Alessandrini*, Luigi Zampa* and Mario Monicelli*. His directorial debut was *La sfida/The Challenge* (1958), a film about the *camorra* (the Neapolitan Mafia), which won a prize at the Venice* festival. By 1962, the year of *Salvatore Giuliano*, Rosi had perfected his technique of *cine-inchiesta*, or investigative cinema, about cases involving power relationships between charismatic individuals, corporations, criminal organisations, and the state. Refusing to sensationalise his subject matter and adopting a dispassionate view that was nonetheless partisan, Rosi labelled his approach 'a second phase of neo-realism', characterised by a

new 'critical realism of overt ideological intentions' and anticipating the cinema of Costa-Gavras* and Elio Petri* in the late 1960s and the 1970s [> ITALIAN POLITICAL CINEMA]. *Salvatore Giuliano* best exemplifies Rosi's investigative film-making, with its inquiry into the death of the Sicilian bandit turned political hero turned right-wing terrorist. The prize-winning *Le mani sulla città/Hands Over the City* (1963), starring Rod Steiger, concerned a scandal in the Neapolitan construction industry, while *Il caso Mattei/The Mattei Affair* (1972, starring Gian Maria Volonté*, like several other Rosi films) probed the mysterious death of an oil magnate. *Lucky Luciano* (1973), like *Salvatore Giuliano*, applied Rosi's anti-spectacular approach to a flamboyant criminal character; Rosi was more interested in how American and Italian authorities used Luciano to further their own agendas.

The year 1975 signalled Rosi's turn to literary (and in the case of *Carmen*, operatic) sources, though this did not imply a withdrawal from committed film-making. Leonardo Sciascia's all too topical novel *Il contesto* provided the model for *Cadaveri eccellenti/Illustrious Corpses* (1976), about the serial assassinations of magistrates presiding over politically and criminally sensitive trials in Sicily, while Edmonde Charles Roux's text inspired Rosi's exposé of Mafia links between Sicily and New York in *Dimenticare Palermo/To Forget Palermo* (1990). Even the adaptation of Carlo Levi's *Cristo si è fermato a Eboli/Christ Stopped at Eboli* (1979), set in 1935–36, was topical in its treatment of the seemingly irresolvable Southern Question. Andrei Platonov's short story *The Third Son* was transformed into an allegory of the internal Italian diaspora in *Tre fratelli/Three Brothers* (1981), in which a mother's funeral brings together the three sons who had strayed, both geographically and ideologically, from their southern roots. As well as being a leading exponent of political cinema, Rosi is an emblematic figure in his attempt to negotiate powerful realist experiences within an exploration of the medium's own spectacular properties. MMa

Other Films Include: *I magliari* (1959); *Il momento della verità/The Moment of Truth* (1965); *C'era una volta/More Than a Miracle* (1967); *Uomini contro* (1970); *Cronaca di una morte annunciata/Chronicle of a Death Foretold* (1987).

ROSSELLINI, Roberto
Rome 1906–77

Italian director. Roberto Rossellini is generally regarded, alongside Vittorio De Sica* and Luchino Visconti*, as one of the great masters of postwar Italian neo-realism*. Yet his neo-realist work was only a small part, and in some ways an anomalous one, of a long and varied career that included many types of artistic experiment both in cinema and television.

Rossellini began his film career in the late 1930s as a maker of short films and as scriptwriter and assistant director on Goffredo Alessandrini's* *Luciano Serra pilota/The Pilot Luciano Serra* (1938), a film conceived and supervised by Mussolini's son Vittorio. His first feature as director was *La nave bianca* (1941), a narrativised documentary about a hospital ship, which was followed by two more conventionally fictional war films, *Un pilota ritorna* (1942) and *L'uomo dalla croce* (1943). Rossellini's next film, *Roma città aperta/Rome,*

Open City, is generally considered a founding work of neo-realism and, along with his following two films, comprises his 'neo-realist trilogy'. Although the documentary look of some sequences of *Roma città aperta*, filmed in part during the nine-month Nazi occupation of Rome, conveys the sense of happening 'on location', the film's narrative is firmly rooted in the conventions of Italian family and religious melodrama. *Paisà*, his next film, explores the ironies pervading the Allied 'liberation' of Italy. It intercuts newsreel footage of the Allied advance with staged vignettes occurring across Italy, with many of these scenes shot on location amid the recently transformed landscape of postwar Italy. The third of the trilogy, *Germania anno zero/Germany Year Zero* (1947), through a studio-set narrative and location shots of war-devastated Berlin, examines the plight of defeated Germany. Thereafter Rossellini increasingly separated himself from the neo-realist mainstream. By the late 1940s, with *Una voce umana* (based on Jean Cocteau's* play *La Voix humaine*), *Il miracolo* (based on a story by Federico Fellini*) [the two films released as *L'amore/Love*, 1948] and *La macchina ammazzacattivi/The Machine that Kills Bad People* (made in 1948, released in 1952), about a man who turns a camera into a killing machine, the projection and construction of reality became central concerns to Rossellini. The first two films, with central performances by Anna Magnani*, also explored a woman's social alienation and consequent psychic unravelling. These are themes that Rossellini developed further in his films with Ingrid Bergman*, with whom he was by then identified in the public mind, and who was to star in *Stromboli, terra di Dio/Stromboli* (1950). Their much publicised off-screen romance and the fact that in the film the Bergman character leaves her husband led to public scandal and the film's release by RKO (who had commissioned it) in a cut and modified version. Rossellini's subsequent films with Bergman – now his wife – were commercial failures though critically praised; *Viaggio in Italia/Journey to Italy* (1954) in particular was much admired in France by André Bazin* and the future New Wave* directors.

To revive his career Rossellini made a number of more mainstream films, notably *Il generale Della Rovere* (1959, starring Vittorio De Sica*). But after *Anima nera* (1962) he abruptly abandoned the cinema, to return to it only in 1974 with *Anno uno/Italy Year One* (a biopic of Christian Democrat leader Alcide De Gaspari). Instead he turned to television, for which he directed a long series of dramatised historical documentaries tracing the development of Western civilisation from Ancient Greece to the present day. Of these the (deservedly) most famous is *La Prise de pouvoir par Louis XIV/The Rise to Power of Louis XIV*, made for French television in 1966. Most, however, were made by Rossellini's own company in association with RAI*, with a view to worldwide sales which were rarely forthcoming. In spite of the limited impact of his television work, Rossellini was not discouraged and at the time of his death he was working on a television biography of Karl Marx. JHa

Bib: Peter Brunette, *Roberto Rossellini* (1987).

Other Films: **Shorts**: *Daphne* (1936); *Prélude à l'après-midi d'un faune* (1938); *Fantasia sottomarina, Il tacchino prepotente, La vispa teresa* (1939); *Il ruscello di ripasottile* (1941).

Features: *Desiderio* (1943, completed by Marcello Pagliero in 1946); *Francesco giullare di Dio/The Flowers of St Francis/Francis, God's Jester* (1950); *I sette peccati capitali/The Seven Deadly Sins* (1951, ep. *L'invidia*); *Europa '51* (1952); *Siamo donne/We, the Women* [ep. *Ingrid Bergman*]; *Dov'è la libertà?* (1953); *Amori di mezzo secolo/Mid-Century Loves* [ep. *Napoli '43*], *Giovanna d'Arco al rogo/Joan of Arc at the Stake, La paura/Fear* (1954); *India* (1958); *Era notte a Roma/Escape By Night, Viva l'Italia/Garibaldi* (1960); *Vanina Vanini* (1961); *RoGoPaG/Laviamoci il cervello* (1963, ep. *Illibatezza*). **Television**: *Torino nei cento anni* (1961); *L'età del ferro/The Iron Age* (1964); *La lotta dell'uomo per la sua sopravvivenza, Idea d'un isola* (1967); *Atti degli apostoli/Acts of the Apostles* (1969); *Socrate* (1970); *Intervista con Salvador Allende* (1971); *Blaise Pascal, Agostino d'Ippona, L'età di Cosimo de' Medici* (1972); *Cartesius/Descartes* (1974); *The World Population, Il messia* (1975); *Concerto per Michelangelo, Beaubourg, Centre d'art et de culture Georges Pompidou* (1977).

ROTA, Nino   Nini Rinaldi; Milan 1911 – Rome 1979

Italian composer. Although he composed nearly 150 scores for film and television, Nino Rota is mostly remembered for his close collaboration with Federico Fellini*, director and composer having worked together from *Lo sceicco bianco/The White Sheik* (1952) to *Prova d'orchestra/Orchestra Rehearsal* (1978). Rota's music has been described as a 'consistently sympathetic musical alter ego for Fellini in his quixotic leaps in style', and it is undoubtedly an essential constituent of the film-maker's best work, whether this be the haunting theme from *La strada* (1954), the circus band from $8\frac{1}{2}$ (1963) or the hypnotic synthesised score which structures much of *Casanova* (1976). Because of this celebrated partnership, there is a danger of overlooking Rota's work with other major directors both in and outside Europe. Rota scored important films for, among others, Luchino Visconti* – notably *Rocco e i suoi fratelli/Rocco and His Brothers* (1960) and *Il gattopardo/The Leopard* (1963) – and Francis Ford Coppola. The lush melodic score which Rota composed for Coppola's *The Godfather* (1972, US) received a BAFTA Award and an Oscar nomination, and his work for *The Godfather, Part II* was awarded an Oscar in 1974.

A child musical prodigy (composing his first oratorio aged eleven), Rota leaves an impressive body of concert music which spans the range of classical genres from chamber music to opera. Rota was also director of the Bari Conservatory from 1950 until 1978. SH

ROTHA, Paul   Paul Thompson; London 1907 – Wallingford 1984

British director, critic and author, who had already written the first edition of his influential *The Film Till Now: A Survey of World Cinema* (1930) when he joined John Grierson* at the Empire Marketing Board (EMB) in 1932. The book, which was updated in 1948 and 1958, was the first of several, including *Documentary Film* (1935), an influential expression of what Michael Balcon* later characterised as 'the documentary attitude' in British cinema, the ethos of a cinema of moral and social responsibility. Rotha sought to maintain independence from government and the 'official' British Documentary Movement*, and only remained at the EMB for a few months. He established Strand Films in 1935, producing sponsored documentaries such as *Today We Live* (1937), on unemployment in the mining industry; and founded the *Documentary News Letter* in 1939. During the war he made documentaries for the Ministry of Information. After the war, as well as documentaries, he made three feature films. From 1953 until 1955 he was Head of the Documentary Film Department at the BBC, and oversaw the production of a number of early dramatised documentaries. He received British Film Academy awards for *The World is Rich* (1947) and *World Without End* (1953), the latter co-directed with Basil Wright*. JC

Bib: Paul Morris (ed.), *Paul Rotha* (1982).

Other Films Include: **Documentaries** – *Contact* (1932); *Shipyard* (1933); *The Future's in the Air* (1936); *New Worlds for Old* (1939); *World of Plenty* (1943). **Features** – *No Resting Place* (1951); *Cat and Mouse* (1958); *De Overval/The Silent Raid* (1962, Neth.).

ROTUNNO, Giuseppe   Rome 1923

Italian cinematographer. After a lengthy period of activity as a camera operator, Rotunno made his debut as director of photography in the final part of *Senso* (1954), taking over the work of the great G. R. Aldo*, who had died in a road accident. Other important stages in his career, in the US and Italy, were: Mario Monicelli's* *La grande guerra/The Great War* (1959), where he reproduced old-fashioned colours, as he did for the newsreels in Federico Fellini's* *E la nave va/And the Ship Sails On* (1983); *On the Beach* (1959, US), about post-atomic desolation, with extensive use of filters and backlighting; *All That Jazz* (1980, US), and *The Adventures of Baron Munchausen* (1989, US/Ger.). Although such films as Huston's *La Bibbia/The Bible in the Beginning ...* (1966), Fred Zinnemann's *Five Days One Summer* (1982, US), and *Regarding Henry* (1991, US) are – among others – indicative of his high standards of professionalism, it was with Fellini and Luchino Visconti* that he was most creative. For Visconti he was eminently successful in heightening the poetic effects of *Le notti bianche/White Nights* (1957) through widespread use of gauzes and the mixing of two different types of film stock. He continued in the same vein in *Rocco e i suoi fratelli/Rocco and His Brothers* (1960) and *Il gattopardo/The Leopard* (1963). For Fellini, he orchestrated the brilliant colours of *Fellini-Satyricon* (1969) and the funereal setting of *Casanova* (1976), especially the scene of the empty theatre, regarded by many as a masterpiece, and went through a whole range of approaches for *Roma/Fellini's Roma* (1972), *Amarcord* (1973) and *La città delle donne/City of Women* (1980), sincerely convinced, like Fellini, that 'truth can be recreated'. GVo

ROUCH, Jean   Paris 1917

French ethnographer and director. Rouch studied ethnography in Paris and became interested in Africa in the early 1940s, making his first documentaries there in 1947. He transformed the practice of ethnographic film-making by using light, portable cameras and direct sound, heavily influencing the New Wave*, but also – more controversially – by increasingly implicating himself and the subjects of his films in the film-making process. His best-known documentaries are *Initiation à la danse des possédés/Initiation to Possession Dancing* (1949), *Les Maîtres fous/The Manic Priests* (1955) and *Moi, un Noir* (1958). He later turned his camera on Parisians, producing (with Edgar Morin) *Chronique d'un été/Chronicle of a Summer* (1961), a key work of *cinéma-vérité*. The marriage of *cinéma-vérité* and the New Wave is best seen in Rouch's 'Gare du Nord' episode for *Paris vu par...* (1965), a virtuoso twenty-minute sequence shot entirely in two takes, where the camera follows two characters in a flat, and then one of them in the street. Rouch has made over ninety films; he was president of the Cinémathèque Française* from 1987 to 1991. GV

RTE – see RADIO TELEFIS EIREANN

RÜHMANN, Heinz   Essen 1902 – Berlin 1994

German actor, director and producer. For over fifty years Rühmann typified the 'good German': an apolitical, reliable, shy Everyman who, while recognising official authorities, maintained his independence which he expressed through impudence and wiliness. Rühmann made nearly a hundred films, in practically all of which the plot revolves around the conflict between the hero's middle-class ideals and the real-life circumstances which thwart him (*Wenn wir alle Engel wären*, 1936; *Der Mustergatte*, 1937).

In 1948, Rühmann attempted to change his image by co-founding the film company Comedia, which went bankrupt in 1952, proof that its star's image was fixed in the German audience's imagination and could not be changed at will. From the 1920s Rühmann also acted on stage, and he appeared frequently on television after 1968. As one of the most enduring of the nation's idealised self-images, he received many film awards for his contribution to the German entertainment industry. He also directed: *Lauter Lügen* (1938); *Lauter Liebe* (1940); *Sophienlund* (1943); *Der Engel mit dem Saitenspiel* (1944); *Die kupferne Hochzeit* (1948); *Briefträger Müller* (1953). JG

Bib: Hans Hellmut Kirst and Mathias Forster, *Das große Heinz Rühmann Buch* (1990).

RUIZ, Raúl   Puerto Montt, Chile 1941

Chilean director working in Europe, based in France since 1973. Ruiz briefly studied theology and tried playwriting before composing scripts for Mexican and Chilean television. His first feature, *Los tres tristes tigres/Three Sad Tigers* (1968), won the Grand Prix at the Locarno* film festival, immediately establishing his reputation. His European work, ranging from Portugal to Sicily and the Netherlands, has promoted him to the status of a cult art-film director. His eclectic, ironic films display great imagination, combining realism with fantasy and narratives of exile with popular entertainment; they have elicited from critics terms such as 'baroque', 'surrealist' and 'postmodern', their *mise-en-scène* drawing on non-naturalistic techniques, with frequent use of filters, mirrors and disorienting camera angles. Among his prolific output, better-known titles include *L'Hypothèse du tableau volé/The Hypothesis of the Stolen Painting* (1978), *Território/Le Territoire/The Territory* (1981), *Le Tôit de la baleine/On Top of the Whale* (1982), *La Ville des pirates/City of Pirates* (1983), *L'Île au trésor/Treasure Island* (1986–90), *L'Oeil qui ment/Dark at Noon* (1992), and *Fado Majeur et Mineur* (1994). Ruiz also made a five-minute film in defence of Salman Rushdie, *The Dark Night of the Inquisitor* (1994). Confusingly but typically, he defines himself as 'a monomaniac with several manias'. GV

RUSSELL, Ken   Southampton 1927

British director. The excess and 'bad taste' of Russell's later work is in sharp contrast to the 'good taste' of his work in the early 1960s for the television arts series *Monitor*, where he directed lyrical documentaries on romantic composers. His critical reputation in cinema was established by *Women in Love* (1969). He hit problems with the censors on *The Devils* (1971), and outraged music lovers everywhere with the Tchaikovsky biopic, *The Music Lovers* (1970), and with subsequent 'outrageous' film biographies of the sexual and political deviances of romantic composers: *Mahler* (1974) and *Lisztomania* (1975). His obsession with the romantics turned to gothic horror in the 1980s with *Gothic* (1986) and *The Lair of the White Worm* (1988). Russell is a self-confessed cultural conservative. While there may be subtleties and contradictions in his attitude to sexuality, his very unsubtle presentation of it looks like misogyny. Though his visual imagination is often striking, it leaves little room for the imagination of the spectator, and his erotic imagery ends up being curiously and unsensuously intellectual. His bad taste ought to be a relief from the proprieties of a cinema of restraint, but ends up being rather wearying. JC

Bib: Barry Keith Grant, 'The Body Politic', in Lester Friedman (ed.), *British Cinema and Thatcherism* (1993).

Other Films Include: *Amelia and the Angel* [short] (1957); *French Dressing* (1964); *Billion Dollar Brain* (1967); *The Boy Friend* (1971); *Savage Messiah* (1972); *Tommy* (1975); *Valentino* (1977); *Altered States* (1980, US); *Crimes of Passion* (1984, US); *Salome's Last Dance* (1987); *The Rainbow* (1988); *Whore* (1991, US).

RUTHERFORD, (Dame) Margaret   London 1892 – Chalfont St Peter 1972

British actress, who became one of the best-loved eccentric character actresses in the postwar cinema. As Sylvia Paskin has suggested, 'character actress' is 'a term applied to women not considered attractive enough to be the love interest in films', but Rutherford seemed to accept the role with particular gusto and considerable craft, sporting her tweediness with pride. While her ample frame lacked the conventional appearance of the female star, her performances never lacked sparkle, though her gung-ho ebullience was often laced with something quite touching. Some of her finest parts came from theatre – she had already played Madame Arcati and Miss Prism on the stage before she repeated the roles in the screen adaptations of *Blithe Spirit* (1945) and *The Importance of Being Earnest* (1952). She was mystically dotty in *Blithe Spirit*, academically dotty in *Passport to Pimlico* (1949), domestically dotty in *I'm All Right Jack* (1959), classically dotty as Mistress Quickly in Welles' *Campanadas a medianoche/Chimes at Midnight* (1966, Sp./Switz.), and inquisitively dotty as Agatha Christie's Miss Marple in the series of films she made for MGM in the early 1960s – *Murder She Said* (1961), *Murder at the Gallop* (1963), *Murder Most Foul* (1964), *Murder Ahoy* (1964) and *The Alphabet Murders* (1965). She received an Oscar as Best Supporting Actress for *The V.I.P.s* (1963). JC

Bib: Dawn Langley Simmons, *Margaret Rutherford: A Blithe Spirit* (1983).

RUTTMANN, Walther   Frankfurt 1887 – Berlin 1941

German director. After studying painting and architecture, Ruttmann began working on a series of non-figurative shorts (*Lichtspiel Opus I–IV*, 1921) which brought him a considerable reputation in film circles and finally the assignment of the falcon dream sequence in Fritz Lang's* *Die Nibelungen* (1924) on which Lotte Reiniger* also worked, along with a commission to do commercials for Julius Pinschewer*. With *Berlin die Sinfonie der Großstadt/Berlin – Symphony of a City* (1927), Ruttmann turned a quota production for Fox Europe into the one film that assures his place in film history. Applying graphic principles of his abstract geometrics to realistic photographs from the city of Berlin, Ruttmann achieved a perfection of rhythmic montage, enhanced by Edmund Meisel's* score and cinematography by Karl Freund*, which not only impressed S. M. Eisenstein*, but has affected generations of avant-garde and documentary filmmakers since [> DOCUMENTARY (GERMANY); AVANT-GARDE CINEMA IN EUROPE]. His most radical project, *Wochenende/Weekend* (1931), was a film without images, recorded with a sound-on-film camera. Ruttmann became a Nazi, wrote an anti-semitic prologue (which was not used) to Leni Riefenstahl's* 1935 *Triumph des Willens/Triumph of the Will* and did supervisory editing on Riefenstahl's *Olympia* (1938). He was fatally wounded on the Eastern front while shooting newsreel footage in 1941. MW

Bib: Jeanpaul Georgen (ed.), *Walter Ruttmann: Eine Dokumentation* (1989).

Other Films Include: *Melodie der Welt/World Melody* (1929); *Feind im Blut* (1931); *Metall des Himmels* (1935); *Mannesmann* (1937); *Aberglaube* (1940).

RUVEN, Paul J. H.   Den Helder 1958

Dutch director, who studied stage direction in Amsterdam and scriptwriting in the US before entering the Netherlands Film Academy. His first films were produced very quickly as 'minimal movies', with a minute budget, minimal scripts and a maximum of improvisation. Over a period of six years, he directed twelve such films in various genres, beginning with a screwball comedy, *Max & Laura & Henk & Willie* (1989), and two *noir* thrillers, *How to Survive a Broken Heart* (1991) and *Sahara Sandwich* (1991). Following the example of R. W. Fassbinder*, Ruven makes creative use of generic formulae to provide structures for artistic experiment and critical expression. Next came a musical film inspired by Jacques Demy*, *De tranen van Maria Machita/The Tears of Maria Machita* (1991); a historical epic/comedy, *Ivanhood*; and a morbid science-fiction picture, *The Best Thing in Life* (1992). His innovative talents have been hailed at home and abroad, and this creative hurricane may be expected to lead Dutch film-making into the twenty-first century. KD/FW

Other Films: *Testament* (1991); *Shocking Blue, Méliès in Color* (1992); *En route* (1993); *Paradise Framed, Zap* (1995).

RYAZANOV, Eldar A.   Samara, Russia [USSR] 1927

Russian director, scriptwriter and playwright. Ryazanov graduated from VGIK*, where he had studied with Kozintsev*, in 1950. After work as a documentarist, he made the musical comedy *Karnaval'naya noch'/Carnival Night* (1956), in which the humourless arts bureaucrat Ogurtsov is played by Igor Ilyinsky*. *Chelovek niotkuda/The Man from Nowhere* (1961) is a satirical comedy involving an anthropologist discovering a wild man and bringing him to Moscow. The hugely successful *Beregis' avtomobilya/Mind That Car!* (1966), the story of an eccentric thief who steals cars from crooks, sells them and gives the money to kindergartens, marked the beginning of a long and productive partnership with the playwright Emil Braginsky. Ryazanov and Braginsky were responsible for some of the most popular comedies of the next two decades, including *Zigzag udachi/The Zigzag of Luck* (1968), *Ironiya sud'by, ili s lëgkim parom!/The Irony of Fate, or Have a Good Sauna!* (1975), *Sluzhebnyi roman/An Office Romance* (1977) and *Garazh/The Garage* (1980). In *Vokzal dlya dvoikh/Station for Two* (1983), the popular star Lyudmila Gurchenko, who made her debut for Ryazanov in *Karnaval'naya noch'*, plays a middle-aged waitress who falls in love with a travelling musician. *Zhestokii romans/A Cruel Romance* (1984), starring Nikita Mikhalkov*, is a new version of the Ostrovsky play *Without a Dowry* earlier filmed by Yakov Protazanov*. *Zabytaya melodiya dlya fleity/Forgotten Melody for Flute* (1987) returns to satirising bureaucracy in the figure of Filimonov, head of the 'Central Leisure Directorate', a (fictitious) state institution devoted to deciding how Soviet citizens should spend their free time. *Dorogaya Yelena Sergeevna/Dear Yelena Sergeyevna* (1988), based on a play by Lyudmila Razumovskaya, is an altogether darker piece about the terrorising of a lonely teacher by her teenage students. After a long but ultimately unsuccessful attempt to film Vladimir Voinovich's *Chonkin* novels, Ryazanov made *Nebesa obetovannye/Promised Heavens* (1992), which he describes as a cry of both hope and despair at the present state of Russia, followed, in 1993, by *Predskazanie/The Prophecy*. JGf

RYBCZYŃSKI, Zbigniew   Born 1950

Polish director. Rybczyński studied Fine Art in Warsaw and graduated as a cameraman from Łódź* in 1973. He made several experimental shorts for various animation studios in Poland, including *Tango* (1980), which won an Academy Award and first prize at Annecy. On the strength of his international reputation, he emigrated to America in the early 1980s and established his own studio, Zbig Vision. Rybczyński is at the forefront of video production, using high-definition technology and exploring film form in videos like *Steps* (1987, US) and *Orchestra* (1990, US). His experiments and achievements with the new possibilities offered by video have led to comparisons with film pioneer Georges Méliès*. AW

Other Films Include: *The Day Before* (1984); *Imagine* (1987); *Mistrz i Małgorzata/The Master and Margarita* (1993).

RYE, Stellan   Rånders 1880 – Western Front 1914

Danish director. Rye began his career as an officer in the Danish army and made his debut as a playwright at the Dagmar Theatre in Copenhagen in 1906, writing several plays over the next few years. He worked as a stage director from 1910 and in 1911 wrote his first film script. The same year he was arrested and sentenced for homosexuality. He left for Berlin in 1912, where he worked again in theatre and film. In 1913 he directed *Der Student von Prag/The Student of Prague*, a macabre fantastic film, generally considered a key early example of German Expressionism*. This was followed by half a dozen films, including *Evinrude, die Geschichte eines Abenteurers/Evinrude, Die Augen des Ole Brandis/The Eyes of Ole Brandis*, and *Das Haus ohne Tür/The House Without a Door* (all 1914). Rye joined the German army in 1914 and died on the Western front later the same year. ME

S

SABU   Sabu Dastagin; Karapur, Mysore, India
1924 – Hollywood 1963

Indian/British actor, who was 'discovered' by Robert
Flaherty* for the title role of *Elephant Boy* (1937), and
brought to Britain to play Prince Azim in Zoltan Korda's *The
Drum* (1938) and Abu in *The Thief of Bagdad* (1940). He
went to Hollywood to play similar exotic roles, and was
brought back to Britain to play the young Indian prince in
Michael Powell* and Emeric Pressburger's *Black Narcissus*
(1947). By the time he was 25, however, there was no longer
a call for young Indian princes. He tried unsuccessfully to establish himself in Italian exotica in *Buongiorno, Elefante!*
(1953, It.), returned to Hollywood for *Jungle Rampage* (1962)
and *A Tiger Walks* (1963), but died of a heart attack at the age
of 39. JC

SACRISTÁN, José   José Sacristán Turiégano;
Madrid 1937

Spanish actor and director, who made his first screen appearance in *La familia y uno más/The Family Plus One* (1965). His
career took two directions: in the late 1960s and early 1970s,
as the young, light leading man of popular comedy, in films
mostly directed by Pedro Lazaga* and Mariano Ozores*,
such as *No desearás la mujer del vecino/Thou Shalt Not Covet
Thy Neighbour's Wife* (1971) or *La graduada/The Graduate*
(1971); then as the more troubled liberal, struggling with his
conscience, saddened by frustrated ambitions in films like
El diputado/The Congressman (Eloy de la Iglesia*, 1978), *Las
largas vacaciones del 36/The Long Holidays of 1936*
(Camino*, 1976). In these later roles he seems to embody the
uncertainties of a society coming to terms with a new freedom. He also directed and starred in *Soldados de plomo/Lead
Soldiers* (1983), *Cara de acelga/Silver-Beet Face* (1987), *Yo me
bajo en la próxima ¿y usted?/I Get Off at the Next Stop, What
About You?* (1993). PWE

SADOUL, Georges   Nancy 1904 – Paris 1967

French film historian. A Surrealist, then a Communist and a
member of the Resistance during World War II, Sadoul was
a journalist, lecturer (including at IDHEC*) and passionate
cinéphile who in 1936 conceived his ambitious *Histoire
générale du cinéma*. Volume I was published in 1945, volume
II in 1947, volume III in 1951 and volume IV in 1952 – and
they still only reached 1920. An isolated volume on the
1939–45 period was published in 1954, but Sadoul never finished his project, although he published numerous articles
and other books, including two dictionaries (of films and of
directors, both 1965), a history of French cinema (1962) and
many monographs on film-makers. Sadoul's political convictions (like those of his ideological opposites Maurice
Bardèche* and Robert Brasillach*) structured his work; his

general history, building on Marxist principles, attempts to
place the cinema within an industrial and social context; he
championed Soviet cinema and criticised Hollywood entertainment; at the same time he shared some of the aesthetic
values of his time, for instance for *auteur* cinema over popular genres. Although they can be criticised for factual errors
and obvious *parti pris*, Sadoul's works were central to the development and popularisation of film culture in France. GV

SÁENZ DE HEREDIA, José Luis   José Luis
Sáenz de Heredia y Osio; Madrid 1911–92

Spanish director. After subtitling foreign films, Sáenz de
Heredia directed his first film, *La hija de Juan Simón/Juan
Simon's Daughter* (1935), produced by Luis Buñuel* during
his spell at Filmófono. A conservative (cousin of Primo de
Rivera), he contributed to the Spanish religious films* genre
with *La mies es mucha/The Harvest is Rich* (1949), a story
about missionaries. His other films, especially the Alarcón-
based *El escándalo/Scandal* (1943), and *Mariona Rebull*
(1947), inspired by Ignacio Agustí, show a sure touch and are
rarely without humanism and warmth. For a time (1961–63),
he was director of the Escuela Oficial de Cinematografía*.
But Sáenz de Heredia's reputation will always be largely defined through *Raza/Race* (1941), the *caudillo*-scripted melodrama on the triumph of Francoism. PWE

SAGAN, Leontine   Leontine Schlesinger; Vienna
1899 – Pretoria, South Africa 1974

Austrian director. Sagan's main career was as a theatre director and stage actress (she studied with Max Reinhardt*), but
she became famous with her first feature film, *Mädchen in
Uniform/Maidens in Uniform* (1931), set in a girls' boarding
school. On release it created a scandal, more for its criticism
of the Prussian authoritarian education system than for its depiction of homoerotic desire. Feminist and gay film scholars
reclaimed Sagan in the 1970s as one of the few female directors of the Weimar* period, and hailed her film as a milestone
in lesbian film-making. She emigrated to Britain, where she
made one more film, *Men of Tomorrow* (1932) for Alexander
Korda*, and later went to South Africa. US

SANDBERG, Anders Wilhelm   Viborg 1887 –
Bad Nauheim, Germany 1938

Danish director. After a career as a journalist and press photographer, Sandberg began working as a cameraman in 1913.
He joined Nordisk Films* as a director in 1914 and quickly established his reputation, first for the crime series *Manden med
de ni Fingre/The Man with the Missing Finger* (1915), and then
for melodramas such as *Klovnen/The Clown* (1917, starring
Valdemar Psilander*), which he remade in 1926. After World

War I, as part of Nordisk's attempt to regain foreign markets (especially the English-speaking ones), Sandberg, now artistic director of the company, filmed a number of Dickens adaptations such as *David Copperfield* (1922) and *Lille Dorrit/ Little Dorrit* (1924). The project was less than successful, the films tending to be static and sentimental. Sandberg left for Germany in 1926, where he directed a couple of films, returning to Denmark at the coming of sound. In the 1930s he directed three films for Palladium*, including *Fem raske Piger/Five Fine Girls* (1933). ME

SANDER, Helke   Berlin 1937

German director, and activist in the German women's movement. After working for television in Finland, Sanders attended the Berlin Deutsche Film- und Fernsehakademie (DFFB) and was the founder of *Frauen und Film**, which she edited from 1974 to 1983. Her semi-autobiographical fiction films (*Die allseitig reduzierte Persönlichkeit REDUPERS/The All-round Reduced Personality*, 1977; *Der subjective Faktor/ The Subjective Factor*, 1981; *Der Beginn aller Schrecken ist Liebe/Love is the Beginning of all Terrors*, 1984, in two of which she played the lead), comprised a sort of trilogy of different stages of women's self-realisation. Since 1980 she has held a post as professor of film at the Hochschule für Bildene Künste Hamburg, and has published short stories and novels. TE/KU

Other Films Include: *Viimeinen yö* (1964, TV, Fin.); *Brecht die Macht der Manipulateure* (1968, doc.); *Kindergärtnerin, was nun?/What Now, Nursery Workers?*, *Kinder sind keine Rinder/Children are not Cattle* (1969); *Eine Prämie für Irene/A Bonus for Irene* (1971); *Macht die Pille frei?* (1972, TV doc.); *Die Erfahrungsschere* (1985, TV); *Felix* (1987, codir.); *Die Deutschen und ihre Männer/The Germans and Their Men* (1990); *Befreier und Befreite/Liberators Take Liberties* (1992, two parts).

SANDERS-BRAHMS, Helma   Emden 1940

German director. A television presenter before making documentary portraits and a number of features dealing with working-class issues in didactic political film essays, Sanders-Brahms turned to the then much discussed 'foreign worker problem' for her first international success, *Shirins Hochzeit/ Shirin's Wedding* (1976). Although she won the main federal prize for her next project, a Kleist adaptation (*Heinrich*, 1977), she was singled out by critics as the main offender in the general uproar about the abuse of literary adaptations.

From 1974 onwards she produced or co-produced most of her own films and altered their style, discarding political didacticism for radical subjectivism. These films visualised German history as female '*Trauerarbeit*' (mourning work), usually by trying to exorcise Oedipal mother-daughter relationships, a subject that had emerged with force in German women's cinema [> FRAUENFILM]. Her best-known film in this genre is *Deutschland, bleiche Mutter/Germany, Pale Mother* (1980), though her (generally ignored) follow-up, *Die*

Berührte/No Mercy No Future (1981), is in many ways a cinematically tighter, visually more harrowing and emotionally more impressive achievement. Her work has since evolved in the direction of the 'European' art cinema*, as in *Flügel und Fesseln/The Future of Emily* (1984, Ger./Fr.) and *Laputa* (1986). She was one of the co-directors of the women's portmanteau film *Felix* (1987). Despite her manifold efforts in the early 1990s to preserve the DEFA* studios as a site of film production, Sanders-Brahms is one of the least-loved directors in Germany, a fact she has commented upon in numerous articles and polemics since the 1980s. TE/MW

Bib: Brigitte Tast (ed.), *Helma Sanders-Brahms* (1980).

SÁNDOR, Pál   Budapest 1939

Hungarian director, one of the most distinctive and controversial talents of contemporary Hungarian cinema. Sándor graduated from the Academy of Theatre and Film Arts in 1964 and made a few shorts at the Balázs Béla Stúdió*. From his first feature, *Bohóc a falon/Clown on the Wall* (1967), Sándor's films have been concerned with the relationship between the individual and history, expressed with incisive humour but also a compassion rare in Hungarian film. The novelty of his approach lies in his ability to create microcosms which reflect history and society through a handful of characters, abolishing in the process the boundaries between the everyday and the historical. The necessity to belong is a primary goal for many of his characters, presented as stumbling through a hostile world which they fail to understand while stubbornly clinging to their ideals. This is best seen in *Régi idők focija/Football of the Good Old Days* (1973). Minarik, the protagonist, is a direct descendant of Chaplin, and Sándor's irony and humanism merge in a burlesque tone which conceals the biting seriousness of his subject matter. Minarik (Dezső Garas) evolved into the more mature and solitary figure of Svéd in *Szabadíts meg a gonosztól/Deliver Us From Evil* (1978) and appeared as a cabaret clown in *Ripacsok/The Salamon and Stock Show* (1981), always struggling with the same problem: how to keep a group together, whether it be a ragged suburban football team, a disintegrating family in the midst of a nightmarish war, or two ageing clowns grotesquely sewn together in one pair of trousers.

Since *Ripacsok*, Sándor's idealism has gradually crumbled away, together with the tight narrative structure and abundant though disciplined imagery of his earlier films. Lately he has been working as a film and television producer. FC

Other Feature Films: *Szeressétek Ódor Emíliát!/Love Emilia!* (1969); *Sárika, drágám/Sarah, My Dear* (1971); *Herkulesfürdői emlék/Improperly Dressed* (1976); *Szerencsés Dániel/ Daniel Takes a Train* (1983); *Csak egy mozi/Just a Movie* (1985); *Miss Arizona* (1988, Hung./It.).

SANDRELLI, Stefania   Viareggio 1946

Italian actress. The winner of a beauty contest, Stefania Sandrelli was noticed by Pietro Germi*, who gave her the role of the adolescent who drives the Baron (Marcello Mastroianni*) to uxoricide in *Divorzio all'italiana/Divorce – Italian Style* (1961). Characterised by an androgynous beauty, graceful gestures and a vivacious expression, she stood out immediately for her charming self-confidence before the camera. After this dazzling debut, Sandrelli's artistic success reached its height in Antonio Pietrangeli's* masterpiece *Io la conoscevo bene/I Knew Her Well* (1965). She plays the unforgettable Adriana, a frail, alienated woman of the boom years, uprooted and adrift in the greedy and hostile city, a character that was to fix her 'type' for a while. In her rich but discontinuous career certain roles stand out, such as the narrow-minded wife in Bernardo Bertolucci's* *Il conformista/The Conformist* (1970), the southern worker in Luigi Comencini's* *Delitto d'amore* (1974) and the washer of dishes who finds liberation in marriage and militancy in Ettore Scola's* *C'eravamo tanto amati/We All Loved Each Other So Much* (1974). After the success of Tinto Brass' *La chiave/The Key* (1984) she entered a phase dominated by sexually explicit films, although this was soon followed by some impressive characterisations, particularly in 'choral' films such as Mario Monicelli's* *Speriamo che sia femmina/Let's Hope It's a Girl* (1986) and Scola's *La famiglia/The Family* (1987). PV

Other Films Include: *La bella di Lodi* (1962); *Sedotta e abbandonata/Seduced and Abandoned* (1963); *L'immorale/The Climax* (1966); *Partner, L'amante di Gramigna* (1968); *Brancaleone alle Crociate* (1970); *Alfredo Alfredo* (1972); *Novecento/1900* (1976); *L'ingorgo/Bottleneck, La terrazza* (1979); *Segreti segreti* (1984); *Mignon è partita* (1984).

SANDREWS

Swedish company, founded by Anders Sandrew (1885–1957), the owner of a successful and expanding chain of cinemas in the 1930s. Towards the end of that decade, together with Shamyl Bauman, Sandrew established an independent film production unit. The new company, Sandrews, produced some of Ingmar Bergman's* films but generally relied on mainstream films for the bulk of its production. Sandrews, which is still the most important integrated film company in Sweden along with Svensk Filmindustri*, also maintains some comedy theatres in Stockholm. LGA

SANDROCK, Adele   Rotterdam 1863 – Berlin 1937

Dutch-born actress, who had her breakthrough in 1919 when, playing an old matron, she created a persona that she was to repeat with slight variations in most of the hundred-odd films she appeared in up to 1936. Sandrock often achieved comedy effect by exaggerating and parodying her own persona, especially when underscoring it with imperious gestures or when dressed in lavish, heavy costumes. Perfectly suited to represent old-fashioned battle-axes, she often played noblewomen, as in *Der Kongreß tanzt* (1931), although her best-remembered role is as the goddess Juno in Reinhold Schünzel's* *Amphitryon* (1935). Some of her other notable films include *Marissa, genannt die Schmugglermadonna*

(1921), *Das Mädchen mit der Protektion* (1925), *Die Durchgängerin* (1928), *Die Förstelchristel* (1931), *Alles hört auf mein Kommando* (1934), and *Die Puppenfee* (1936). KU

Bib: Adele Sandrock, *Mein Leben* (1940).

SANZ, Jorge   Jorge Sanz Miranda; Madrid 1969

Spanish actor, who began as a child star [> SPANISH CHILD STARS], making his first film, *La miel/Honey* (1979), when he was nine. Graduating from adolescent roles – such as the obsessively masturbating patient in love with Maribel Verdú* in *El año de las luces/The Year of Enlightenment* (1986, dir. Fernando Trueba*) – he has been mostly identified with films by Vicente Aranda* (who also directed him in the television series *Los jinetes del alba/Riders of the Dawn*): *El lute II* (1988), *Si te dicen que caí/If They Tell You I've Fallen* (1989) and *Amantes/Lovers* (1990). His pretty-boy looks have become more virile, without losing their adolescent moodiness, but his almost incomprehensible rapid-fire delivery may be an ill-judged gesture of homage to the New York Actors' Studio. PWE

SÁRA, Sándor   Tura 1933

Hungarian cinematographer and director, one of the most important representatives of the traditionalist trend in Hungarian cinema. Sára graduated from the Academy of Theatre and Film Arts in 1957 and was among the founders of the Balázs Béla Stúdió*. As well as making some remarkable documentaries, he was cinematographer for a number of important Hungarian films by the young generation of the 1960s, like *Sodrásban/Current* by István Gaál (1963), *Tízezer nap/Ten Thousand Suns* by Ferenc Kósa (1965), *Apa/Father* by István Szabó* (1966), and *Szindbád* by Zoltán Huszárik* (1970). His distinctive cinematographic style is characterised by rather static but expressive compositions and his 1960s work, based on geometrically organised long shots, was a unique stylistic choice at the time. He made his first feature film as a director, *Feldobott kő/Upthrown Stone*, in 1969. This is a powerful story about the conflicts between different cultural traditions and ways of life in a political situation which turned cultural and ethnic minorities against each other. Sára continued to make feature films in the 1970s and 1980s, though they never matched the quality of his earlier work. Nevertheless, Sára was the initiator of a series of 'historical documentaries' – adopting an oral history-based reportage approach that was to dominate Hungarian documentary film-making in the 1980s and which occasionally provoked political controversy because of its critical stance towards official history. In the late 1980s and early 1990s, Sára continued to make documentaries dealing with the historical tragedies of the Hungarian people. Lately, he has been nominated as the President of Duna TV, the Hungarian satellite programme aimed at the Hungarian minorities living in neighbouring countries. KAB

SÄRKKÄ, T. J. Toivo Jalmari Särkkä; Mikkeli 1890 – Helsinki 1975

Finnish director, producer and scriptwriter. T. J. Särkkä was the head of Suomen Filmiteollisuus (SF) for three decades during which it was the largest film production company in Finland. Särkkä was also a prolific director and scriptwriter, making over fifty films.

Särkkä came to film late, having worked previously in commerce and banking. He had a university degree in Russian but no experience of film-making when he arrived at SF in 1934 as a stock-owner and member of the board. He took up film-making on the untimely death in 1935 of SF's founder Erkki Karu*. Särkkä ran SF on a tight rein, choosing film subjects and closely monitoring production. By 1936 he had already released two films. Co-director on these early works was Yrjö Norta, a specialist in audio technology. Under Särkkä's guidance SF expanded rapidly: in 1937 the company had two separate crews, the following year three, and at the end of the decade, four, outdoing rival Suomi-Filmi. Unlike Risto Orko's* Suomi-Filmi, in which documentaries, the import of foreign films and exhibition were also important, SF under Särkkä concentrated on feature films. The two companies consciously differentiated their images, Särkkä preferring to address country audiences with agrarian themes, reflecting the expansion of the cinema in rural areas. In terms of genre, the distinction is clearest in comedies: as a counterpoint to Suomi-Filmi's urban and sophisticated screwball comedies, SF made farces and melodramas based on folk literature. The melodramas were often historical; the most spectacular were directed by Särkkä himself. A good example is Norta's and Särkkä's *Helmikuun manifesti/The February Manifesto* (1939), which chronicled the struggle for Finland's independence from the perspective of the 'White' bourgeoisie. Other films, such as *Runon kuningas ja muuttolintu/The King of Poems and the Migrating Bird* (1940) and *Ballaadi* (1944), were historical romances about the 'forbidden' loves of national heroes, or purely fictional love stories with history functioning only as decor; for instance *Kaivopuiston kaunis Regina/The Beautiful Regina from Kaivopuisto*, and the most popular Finnish film of the war years, *Kulkurin valssi/The Vagabond's Waltz* (both 1941). In addition to these historical spectacles, Särkkä produced and directed the first Finnish colour feature, *Juha* (1956). After World War II, SF's output shrank along with its audiences. Särkkä ushered in the new era of the 1950s by turning his attention to cheap and cheerful comedies, turning out on average fourteen films a year. SF productions in general and popular farces such as the Puupää* films in particular were greatly disparaged by critics who admired Italian neo-realism*. The culminating point of SF's 1950s output was Edvin Laine's* *Tuntematon sotilas/The Unknown Soldier* (1954), the biggest Finnish box-office hit. SF invested the income in other films, but the coming of television as well as socio-cultural changes such as the move to the cities continued to undermine cinema audiences. The industry faced its biggest crisis in the early 1960s. Hit harder than its rivals Suomi-Filmi and Fennada-Filmi, SF went bankrupt and sold its film catalogue to the Finnish broadcasting company YLE in 1962–63. KL

SASS-DORT, Barbara Łódź 1936

Polish director. Sass-Dort is popularly regarded in Poland as a feminist director. Her first feature, *Bez Miłości/Without Love* (1980), featured well-known actress Dorota Stalińska as a new type of heroine, intent on making a career rather than fulfilling her 'woman's role'. Sass-Dort's films follow a classical narrative structure, and characteristically look at women in Polish society, often featuring strong female protagonists who manipulate men and the system in order to get what they want. Sass-Dort directed television films for Andrzej Wajda's* 'X' production unit and features for the 'Kadr' unit headed by Jerzy Kawalerowicz*. Her 1993 feature *Pajęczarki/Web-spinners* looks at post-communist Poland, telling the story of two sisters who turn to crime in order to fund a trip to America. AW

Other Films Include: *Debiutantka/The Outsider* (1982); *Krzyk/The Scream* (1983); *Dziewczęta z Nowolipek i Rajska Jabłon/The Girls from Nowolipek and the Apple Tree of Paradise* (1985); *W Klatce/Caged* (1987).

SAURA, Carlos Carlos Saura Atares; Huesca 1932

Spanish director and scriptwriter of international stature, initially associated with the New Spanish Cinema* of the 1960s, who has produced some of the most varied and original work in modern Spanish cinema. The recipient of many festival prizes, Saura has directed twenty-four features, four short films and a television adaptation of Borges' story *El sur*. Working as a photographer in the early 1950s, Saura studied engineering at Madrid University before moving to the IIEC* as student and later teacher. His blistering first feature, *Los golfos/The Hooligans* (1959), a study of juvenile delinquents inspired by neo-realism*, established him as a provocative film-maker working beyond the boundaries of classical cinema. In the 1960s and 1970s, working with a first-rate team of producer Elías Querejeta*, actors (including his companion Geraldine Chaplin*), co-scriptwriters (Angelino Fons and Rafael Azcona*), and technicians (especially Luis Cuadrado*), Saura consolidated his position as Spain's premier director in a series of films which, beginning with *La caza/The Hunt* (1965), explored the legacy of bitterness and despair left by the Civil War and its aftermath for a generation of Spaniards. Constrained by Francoist censorship, Saura was forced to look for more oblique and elliptical ways of dealing with social themes, in such films as *Peppermint frappé* (1967), *Ana y los lobos/Ana and the Wolves* (1972) and *Cría cuervos/Raise Ravens* (1975), his greatest international critical successes. Nevertheless, the fact that his use of allegory and theatricality, and reliance on non-linear narratives, have been as much a feature of his post-Franco work as the films produced between 1955 and 1975 indicates that his style was determined as much by a desire to interrogate the possibilities of the medium as by censorship. Since the late 1970s Saura's work has entered another phase, characterised by diversity and experiment with popular genres, especially the musical and period drama. With the very successful flamenco trilogy made with dancer and choreographer Antonio Gades*,

375

Bodas de sangre/Blood Wedding (1981), *Carmen* (1983) and *El amor brujo/Love the Magician* (1985), Saura produced an original, culturally specific variant on the European Heritage* 'genre'. *¡Ay, Carmela!* (1990), starring Carmen Maura*, is a musical which revisits the Franco period through a troup of performers. Although his films of the 1980s and 1990s have met with varying success, Saura remains a key figure of contemporary Spanish cinema. MD

Bib: Marvin D'Lugo, *The Films of Carlos Saura: the Practice of Seeing* (1991).

Other Films Include: *Elisa, vida mía/Elisa, My Love* (1977); *Mamá cumple cien años/Mum's a Hundred Years Old* (1979); *Deprisa, deprisa/Hurry, Hurry* (1980); *Los zancos/Stilts* (1984); *La noche oscura/The Dark Night* (1989).

SAUTET, Claude — Montrouge 1924

French director. A graduate of IDHEC*, Sautet worked as a scriptwriter and assistant to, among others, Jacques Becker*; his own films can indeed be seen in the Becker tradition of 'French-style' intimate realism and classic *mise-en-scène*, although his early features were thrillers – the excellent *Classe tous risques/The Big Risk* (1960) and *L'Arme à gauche/Guns for the Dictator* (1965). His major work came in the 1970s, with an impressive body of intimist romantic stories in a carefully depicted middle-class setting: *Les Choses de la vie/The Things of Life* (1970) was a critical and popular success, as were *César et Rosalie* (1972), *Vincent, François, Paul … et les autres* (1974), *Mado* (1976) and *Garçon!* (1983). Sautet's work has been little known outside France, until his *Un coeur en hiver/A Heart in Winter* (1993), with Emmanuelle Béart and Daniel Auteuil, a major international art-house hit. GV

SAVCHENKO, Igor A. — Vinnitsa, Ukraine [Russian Empire] 1906 – Moscow 1950

Ukrainian Soviet director, scriptwriter and teacher. After training as an actor, Savchenko began directing agit-films* in 1931. He played a leading role in *Dvadsat' shest' komissarov/Twenty-Six Commissars* (1933) and directed his first major film, the musical comedy *Garmon'/The Accordion*, in 1934. The film provided a rather sanitised view of collectivisation in the Ukraine. During World War II he made several patriotic films but is probably best remembered for two epic depictions of Ukrainian history, *Bogdan Khmelnitsky* (1941) and *Taras Shevchenko* (1951). From 1946 he headed the Directors' Workshop at VGIK*, where he taught, among others, Marlen Khutsiev*, Alexander Alov and Vladimir Naumov. RT

SAVILLE, Victor — Victor Salberg; Birmingham 1897 – London 1979

British director, who was prominent as both director and producer in the 1930s. Saville entered the film industry in 1917 as the manager of a cinema in Coventry, and in 1920 he formed a small renting firm in Birmingham in partnership with Michael Balcon*. In the late 1920s he was a producer and writer, directing his first feature, *The Arcadians*, an adaptation of the stage success, in 1927. His major successes came in the 1930s, beginning with *The Good Companions* (1933), the first of five highly popular films he directed with Jessie Matthews*: the others were *Friday the Thirteenth* (1933), *Evergreen* (1934), *First a Girl* (1935) and *It's Love Again* (1936). Saville was at home with the Hollywood-style sophisticated musical, but his range extended to the thriller with *I Was a Spy* (1933), which made Madeleine Carroll* an international star; to political comedy with the fascinating *Storm in a Teacup* (1937), addressing fascism in the guise of Scottish nationalism; and to social drama with the excellent *South Riding* (1938), described by Jeffrey Richards as the supreme example of the 1930s 'consensus film'. Saville moved to Hollywood as a producer and director for MGM in 1939. JC

Bib: Jeffrey Richards, *The Age of the Dream Palace: Cinema and Society in Britain, 1930–1939* (1984).

SCHEIN, Harry — Vienna 1924

Austrian-born Swedish film critic and official. Initially an engineer, Schein came to Sweden in 1939. During the 1950s he was one of the most distinguished film critics in Sweden. He was also responsible for outlining the important reform of film policy in Sweden which led to the creation of the Swedish Film Institute in 1963, of which he was made managing director. Throughout the 1960s Schein was an advocate of the Social Democrat government and its cultural policy. Together with his powerful position, this made him a controversial head of the Institute; however, he worked there until 1978, when he came into conflict with the new conservative government. He has since worked as chairman of the Swedish broadcasting corporation (Sveriges Radio) and the national investment bank. He is also a novelist and columnist. LGA/BF

SCHELL, Maria — Margarethe Schell; Vienna 1926

Austrian-born actress, who made her debut at sixteen in the Swiss films *Steinbruch* and *Maturareise* (both 1942). Her first German film after World War II, *Der Engel mit der Posaune/The Angel with the Trumpet* (1948), brought her international fame and offers from the German film industry. Postwar German audiences warmed to Schell's overtly emotional acting as a vulnerable young woman, though critics were derisive. In the early 1950s she appeared with Dieter Borsche (*Dr Holl*, 1951) and O. W. Fischer (*Solange Du da bist*, 1953) in melodramas and love stories. Her subsequent success in artistically more ambitious films like *Die letzte Brücke/The Last Bridge* (1954), René Clément's* *Gervaise* (1956, Fr.) and Alexandre Astruc's *Une Vie* (1958, Fr.) gave her an international career. She played in Luchino Visconti's* *Le notti bianche/Nuits blanches/White Nights* (1957, It./Fr.) and in *The Brothers Karamazov* (1958, US) by Richard

Brooks. Unlike German critics, Americans valued Schell's acting for its European sophistication. She continues to work in German-speaking film, theatre and television. TE/KU

Other Films Include: *The Magic Box* (1951, UK); *Die Ratten* (1955); *Rose Berndt* (1956); *Ich bin auch nur eine Frau/Only a Woman* (1961); *Folies bourgeoises/Die verrückten Reichen* (1976); *Der Besuch der alten Dame* (1982, TV, Switz.).

SCHLESINGER, John   London 1926

British director. Schlesinger graduated to film after acting (his credits include *The Battle of the River Plate* [1956] and *Brothers in Law* [1957]), and directing television documentaries in the late 1950s for *Tonight* and *Monitor*. In 1961 his documentary on the daily life of Waterloo Station, *Terminus*, made for Edgar Anstey* at British Transport Films, won an award at Venice. His first features, *A Kind of Loving* (1962) and *Billy Liar* (1963), inhabit the territory of the British New Wave*, but Schlesinger seemed less committed to it than the other 'angry young men'. In *Darling* (1965), he turns to the new, consumerist middle class, with Julie Christie* representing both the destructiveness of 'Swinging Sixties' values and the desire for something else, and in *Sunday Bloody Sunday* (1971) he returns to the same concerns at a more intimate and enclosed level. Since the 1960s, and following the success of *Midnight Cowboy* (1969), which won Oscars for Best Director, Best Screenplay and Best Film, Schlesinger has found it easier to make films in the US than in Britain, and even *Yanks* (1979), though set in the North of England, had to raise its finance in America and Germany. He has directed a number of films for television, including the award-winning *An Englishman Abroad* (1983). JC

Other Films Include: *Far from the Madding Crowd* (1967); *The Day of the Locust* (1975, US); *Marathon Man* (1976, US); *Honky Tonk Freeway* (1981, US); *The Falcon and the Snowman* (1985, US); *The Believers* (1987, US); *Madame Sousatzka* (1988); *Pacific Heights* (1990, US).

SCHLÖNDORFF, Volker   Wiesbaden 1939

German director, whose debut film was *Der junge Törless/ Young Törless* (1966), the first international success of the Young German Cinema [> NEW GERMAN CINEMA]. In 1969 he founded (with Peter Fleischmann) the Munich-based production company Bioskop-Film, which since 1974 has produced all his films. Schlöndorff's speciality became literary adaptations, and his film based on a novella by Heinrich Böll, *Die verlorene Ehre der Katharina Blum/The Lost Honour of Katharina Blum* (1975, co-directed by Schlöndorff's wife Margarethe von Trotta*), caught well the mood of latent hysteria in the years of left extremism and conservative witch-hunts. Schlöndorff also participated in topical collaborative projects, such as *Deutschland im Herbst/Germany in Autumn* (1978). Since winning an Oscar for the Günter Grass adaptation *Die Blechtrommel/The Tin Drum* (1979), Schlöndorff has preferred to work with large budgets and international stars in Europe and the US, directing films such as *Swann in*

Love/Un amour de Swann (1984, Fr./UK) with Jeremy Irons*, Ornella Muti and Alain Delon*, *Death of a Salesman* (1985, US) with Dustin Hoffman and John Malkovich, and *Homo Faber/The Voyager* (1991) with Sam Shepard. TE/SG

Bib: Rainer Lewandowski, *Die Filme von Volker Schlöndorff* (1981).

Other Films Include: *Mord und Totschlag/A Degree of Murder* (1967); *Michael Kohlhaas Der Rebell* (1969); *Der plötzliche Reichtum der armen Leute von Kombach* (1971); *Strohfeuer/Summer Lightning* (1972); *Der Fangschuß* (1976); *Die Fälschung* (1981); *A Gathering of Old Men* (1987); *The Handmaid's Tale* (1990).

SCHMID, Daniel   Flims 1941

Swiss director, who studied history, political science, advertising and art history in Berlin, Mexico and Berkeley before enrolling at the Film Academy in Berlin and assisting Peter Lilienthal between 1966 and 1970. Schmid's own films, beginning with his fictional documentary about the last servants' school in Europe (*Thut alles im Finstern, Eurem Herrn das Licht zu ersparen*, 1971), and an account of an annual banqueting ritual during which traditional master and servant roles are reversed (*Heute nacht oder nie*, 1972), are part of a baroque, romantic and theatrical tradition. This situates him closer to the work of German directors such as R. W. Fassbinder*, Hans Jürgen Syberberg* and Werner Schroeter* (on whose films Schmid repeatedly collaborated as actor or assistant director) than to the more realistic aesthetics of the 'new Swiss cinema' developed in French-speaking Switzerland at the time. Equally 'German' preoccupations are in evidence in the morbid melodrama *La Paloma* (1974) and in his first international production *Violanta* (1977, starring Lucia Bosé*, Anne-Marie Blanc* and Gérard Depardieu*), as well as in *Hécate* (1982), but above all in the controversial *Schatten der Engel/Shadows of Angels* (1975), an adaptation of R. W. Fassbinder's* provocative play *Die Stadt, der Müll und der Tod*, co-written by and co-starring Fassbinder himself. A bewildering amalgam of occultism, psychiatry, drugs and politics in *Der Tee der drei alten Damen* (1990), and the visual conjuring of memories in *Hors saison* (1992), are also more on the margins of Swiss national cinema. Schmid's dreamlike reflections on excess, artifice and cinematic representation have nevertheless secured him a place as the 'magician' among the directors of his generation. MW

Bib: Patrizia Landgraf (ed.), *Daniel Schmid* (1988).

Other Films Include: *Notre Dame de la Croisette* (1981); *Mirage de la vie* (1983, a portrait of Douglas Sirk); *Il bacio di Tosca* (1984); *Jenatsch* (1987).

SCHNÉEVOIGT, George
Copenhagen 1893–1961

Danish director and cinematographer. Schnéevoigt trained in Berlin as a photographer and actor. He returned to Denmark in 1913 and directed films for a short-lived company before joining Nordisk Films* as a cameraman and director in 1915. His claim to fame during the silent period is his cinematography on Carl Theodor Dreyer's* Danish and Swedish films. In 1929 he directed his last silent film, *Lajla*, in Lapland, and in 1930 made the first Nordic sound film, *Eskimo*, a Danish/Norwegian co-production, shot in Greenland from a script by the Danish polar explorer Einar Mikkelsen. The film was made in four versions: silent, Norwegian, German and French. This prompted Nordisk to hire Schnéevoigt as the director of its first sound film, *Præsten i Vejlby/The Vicar of Vejlby* (1931), a great success which led Schnéevoigt to direct nine more films for Nordisk, including *Hotel Paradis/Hotel Paradise* (1931) and *Champagne galoppen/The Champagne Gallop* (1938). He directed a Finnish remake of *Lajla* in 1937 and made his last film in 1942. ME

SCHNEIDER, Romy
Rosemarie Albach-Retty; Vienna 1938 – Paris 1982

Austrian-born actress. The daughter of actors Wolf Albach-Retty and Magda Schneider, the beautiful Romy Schneider played her first role as her real mother's daughter in *Wenn der weiße Flieder wieder blüht* (1953, Ger.), the duo becoming the most popular film couple of 1950s German-speaking cinema. Schneider also enjoyed popular success as Queen Victoria in *Mädchenjahre einer Königin* (1954), but Ernst Marischka's* 'Sissi' trilogy – *Sissi* (1955), *Sissi – die junge Kaiserin* (1956) and *Sissi –Schicksalsjahre einer Kaiserin* (1957) – in which she played the romanticised Empress Elizabeth of Austria, turned her into a mass icon. Disparaged by critics, the movies enjoyed huge popular acclaim throughout Europe, and helped consolidate a particular Austrian image by quoting the country's myths (the scenery, the Habsburg dynasty, Viennese waltzes …). After appearing in two successful remakes – *Mädchen in Uniform* and *Christine* – in 1958, she moved to France. Against the wishes of producers and audiences, she distanced herself from the Sissi image and embarked on a career as a serious character actress (successfully, except in Germany). In the 1960s and 1970s she worked in international art cinema, with Luchino Visconti*, Orson Welles (*Le Procès/The Trial*, 1962), Joseph Losey* (*L'Assassinat de Trotsky/The Assassination of Trotsky*, 1972), but especially in France, mostly with Claude Sautet*. In Sautet's *Les Choses de la vie/The Things of Life* (1970), *César et Rosalie* (1972) and *Mado* (1976) among other films, she portrayed, alongside actors like Michel Piccoli* and Yves Montand*, 'modern' women, though her characters' emancipation was limited to sexuality and usually ended in compromise. She reached the height of her international career in Visconti's *Ludwig* (1972), portraying a mature, hard Elizabeth who had nothing in common with the Sissi of the earlier films. Her relationship with her native country and its history was ambivalent and she appeared in several films critical of fascism, including *La Passante du Sans-Souci/Die*

Spaziergängerin von Sans-Souci (1982, Fr./Ger.), her last film. Schneider was for long an object of gossip press speculation, especially at the time of her liaison with Alain Delon* (with whom she appeared in, among other films, *La Piscine/The Swimming Pool*, 1968), but she became a much-liked actress in France, eliciting popular sympathy especially for the tragic death of her son. SG/AL/GV

Bib: Michael Jürgs, *Der Fall Romy Schneider: Eine Biographie* (1991).

Other Films Include: *Robinson soll nicht sterben* (1957); *Katia* (1959); *The Cardinal* (1963, US); *What's New Pussycat* (1965); *Le Train* (1973, Fr./It.); *Le Trio infernal* [Fr./It./Ger.], *L'Important c'est d'aimer* (1974, Fr.); *Le Vieux fusil* (1975. Fr.); *Gruppenbild mit Dame* (1977, Ger.); *La Mort en direct/Deathwatch* (1979, Fr.); *La Banquière* (1980, Fr.).

SCHNYDER, Franz
Burgdorf 1910–1993

Swiss director, who began as actor and director in Swiss and German theatre before making his film debut in 1941 with a contribution to the nationalistic cinema of the 'spiritual defence of the nation', *Gilberte de Courgenay*, the sentimental portait (set during during World War I) of an inn-keeper's daughter (Anne-Marie Blanc*) who becomes the guardian angel of a group of mobilised Swiss soldiers. More ambitious in form and content, *Wilder Urlaub* (1943), a critical, class-conscious account of contemporary Swiss democracy, was such a box-office failure for Lazar Wechsler's* Praesens-Film that Schnyder had to make short industrial and documentary films for eleven years before he could return to feature films. He then made a number of dialect films (*Heidi und Peter*, 1955, *Zwischen uns die Berge*, 1956) and literary adaptations of works by Jeremias Gotthelf (*Uli der Knecht*, 1954, *Uli der Pächter*, 1955, *Die Käserei in der Vehfreude*, 1958, *Anne Bäbi Jowäger*, 2 parts, 1960–61, *Geld und Geist*, 1964), which established him as one of the most prolific Swiss directors of the 1950s and early 1960s. To the younger generation of the 'new Swiss cinema' film-makers Schnyder was the exemplary representative of 'daddy's cinema'. The reality was less simple and Schnyder remained a highly contradictory and temperamental personality. No sooner had he taken over Neue Film (Zurich) in 1957 than he denounced the heroic-idealistic clichés about Swiss national identity prevailing in films about World War II, a tradition to which he had himself significantly contributed, for instance with his reconstruction of the conflicting national reactions to the 1940 invasion of Belgium and the Netherlands by Nazi Germany (*Der 10. Mai*, 1957). MW

Other Films Include: *Der Souverän* (1947); *Der Sittlichkeitsverbrecher* (1963); *Die sechs Kummerbuben* (1968).

SCHORM, Evald
Prague 1931–88

Czech director. Regarded as the 'philosopher' of the Czech New Wave*, Evald Schorm graduated from FAMU* in 1962.

Noted for an impressive range of documentaries made between 1959 and 1964, he directed his first feature, *Každý den odvahu/Everyday Courage*, in 1964. A controversial analysis of the crisis of a party worker alienated from those he claims to represent, it was followed in 1966 by *Návrat ztraceného syna/Return of the Prodigal Son*, a study of suicide linked to an analysis of a society in crisis. Schorm's films can be characterised as intense moral reflections framed in a fairly conventional narrative form. After refusing to sign the obligatory acknowledgment of the correctness of the 1968 invasion, Schorm was unable to make films, and turned his attention to the stage, where he worked extensively on productions ranging from Janáček and Mozart to Shakespeare and Brecht. Schorm returned to the studios for *Vlastně se nic nestalo/Killing with Kindness* (1988), in which the stars of *Každý den odvahu* and *Návrat ztraceného syna*, Jana Brejchová* and Jan Kačer, were reunited, but he died before the editing was completed. PH

Other Films Include: *Proč?/Why?* [short] (1964); *Zrcadlení/Reflections* [short], *Perličky na dně/Pearls of the Deep* [episode, *Dům radosti/House of Joy*] (1965); *Pět holek na krku/Saddled with Five Girls* (1967); *Pražské noci/Prague Nights* [episode, *Chlebove střevíčky/The Bread Slippers*], *Farářův konec/End of a Priest* (1968); *Zmatek/Confusion* [short] (1968, released 1990); *Den sedmý, osmá noc/Seventh Day, Eighth Night* (1969, released 1990); *Psi a lidé/Dogs and People* (1971).

SCHOUKENS, Gaston   Brussels 1901–61

Belgian director. On purchasing his first camera in 1918, Schoukens began his career shooting newsreels. Versatile and enthusiastic, when money was lacking he produced comic sketches (under a pseudonym). When denied a licence for features during World War II, he made cultural documentaries, and when talkies were developed he added sound (in French and Dutch) to his second film, *La Famille Klepkens* (1929), which therefore merits the title of Belgium's first sound film.

Schoukens was often referred to as 'a Belgian Marcel Pagnol'* and his popular comedies were frequently adapted from Walloon literature or folklore. He used a recognised team of theatre actors and actresses (in particular Gustave Libeau and Suzanne Christy) who spoke with the Bruxellois accent. His specific style of local humour, known as '*zwanze*' (a blend of irony and slapstick), is perhaps most evident in his box-office hit *Un soir de joie/A 'Soir' of Joy* (1954). Set during the Occupation, when the Germans had taken over the publication of *Le Soir*, the film relates the attempt by the Belgian resistance to publish and circulate a false edition of the newspaper, crammed with satirical articles against the Nazi occupiers.

Schoukens' films appealed to their audience by telling familiar stories in local accents. Despite the inexportability of his work, he remains the only director of his generation to achieve box-office success without subsidies or international distribution. CF

Other Films Include: *Monsieur mon chauffeur/My Chauffeur*

(1926); *Les Croix de l'Yser* (1928); *Les Quatre mousquetaires/The Four Musketeers* (1934); *C'était le bon temps/Those Were the Days* (1936); *Ceux qui veillent/Those Who Kept Awake* (1939); *Les Invités de huit heures/Our 8 o'clock Guests* (1946); *Zig-zag* (1956).

SCHROETER, Werner   Georgenthal, Thuringia 1945

German director. A seminal figure of the New German Cinema* who has gained an international cult following for his cinema of camp excess and artifice. Schroeter's films occupy a transitional space between avant-garde and art cinema, neither quite narrative nor quite abstract. His emotionally charged, performance-inspired cinema draws on, and radically reinterprets, opera, oscillating between parody and celebration. For Schroeter, a gay director, the central figure is always the outsider, and his major theme is the yearning for self-realisation, through passionate love and artistic creativity.

Eika Katappa (1969), a camp appropriation of nineteenth-century opera, provided Schroeter with an international breakthrough. As a consequence he was taken up by television. *Der Tod der Maria Malibran/The Death of Maria Malibran* (1972), sublime and bizarre, and considered by many (including Michel Foucault and Schroeter himself) as one of his best films, is also his most difficult. With *Regno di Napoli/Kingdom of Naples* (1978), Schroeter shifted towards art cinema; it became his first commercial release. *Der Rosenkönig/The Rose King* (1986), dedicated to the singer Magdalena Montezuma, is an excessive and entrancing hallucinatory fable of Oedipal and homosexual passion, and his most explicitly gay film. Schroeter continues to break with received aesthetics by aestheticising the model of the 'social problem film'. Many who regard him as a film-maker of fantastic fables were surprised at his politically hard-hitting documentaries: *Der lachende Stern/The Laughing Star* (1983) and *De l'Argentine/To the Example of Argentine* (1985). Working since the 1980s mainly as a theatre and opera director, Schroeter had a brief comeback as a film-maker with a big-budget production, *Malina* (1991), starring Isabelle Huppert*. US

Bib: Peter W. Jansen and Wolfram Schütte (eds.), *Werner Schroeter* (1980).

SCHÜFFTAN, Eugen   Breslau 1893 – New York 1977

German cinematographer of genius who developed a complex optical matte, the 'Schüfftan process', which combined miniature sets and full-size action in a single shot with the aid of mirrors. Schüfftan used his technique most memorably in Fritz Lang's* *Metropolis* (1927), on which he supervised all the special effects. A brief sojourn in Hollywood followed. Back in Germany by the early 1930s, Schüfftan photographed Robert Siodmak's* *Abschied* (1930) and G. W. Pabst's* *Die Herrin von Atlantis* (1932). In the wake of the Nazi takeover he emigrated to France, where he was cinematographer on

Marcel Carné* and Jacques Prévert's* *Drôle de drame* (1937) and *Quai des brumes* (1938), as well as several Max Ophuls* films. The German invasion in 1939 forced him into a second exile in the US. He was initially barred from working, but fellow émigrés such as Douglas Sirk (Sierck*), Edgar G. Ulmer and Siodmak made it possible for him to earn a living, and he left his mark on the *film noir* lighting style of the 1940s. A US citizen since 1947, he moved back and forth between Europe and Hollywood, his career culminating in an Academy Award for the photography of *The Hustler* (1961, US). TE/MW

Other Films Include: *Eifersucht* (1925); *Madame Pompadour, Love Me and the World is Mine* (1927); *Menschen am Sonntag/People on Sunday* (1930); *Das Ekel* (1931, also directed); *Der Läufer von Marathon* (1933); *La Tendre Ennemie* (1936, Fr.); *Yoshiwara* (1937, Fr.); *Le Roman de Werther/Werther* (1938, Fr.); *Sans lendemain* (1940, Fr.); *Hitler's Madman* (1943, US); *Summer Storm* (1944, US); *The Dark Mirror* (1946, US); *Ulisse/Ulysses* (1954, It.); *La Tête contre les murs* (1959, Fr.); *Lilith* (1964, US).

SCHÜNZEL, Reinhold   Hamburg 1888 – Munich 1954

German director, producer and actor. Schünzel started his career as a director in 1918 with short comedy films, and soon became one of the most prolific directors of the Weimar* popular cinema, equally at home with proletarian subjects (*Das Mädchen aus der Ackerstrasse*, 1920), big-budget historical drama (*Katharina die Große*, 1920) and comedy (*Hallo Caesar*, 1927). He was extremely popular as an actor (often starring in his own films); his comic persona ranged from foppish aristocrats to street-wise Berlin good-for-nothings, combining both in the character of Tiger Brown in G. W. Pabst's* *Die Dreigroschenoper/The Threepenny Opera* (1931).

Outside Germany, Schünzel the director did not become known until the sound era, when he directed, with *Viktor und Viktoria* (1933), *Die englische Heirat/The English Marriage* (1934) and *Amphitryon* (1935), three of the most popular sophisticated comedies of the time. Though he was Jewish on his mother's side, his films were such big box-office that the Nazis were anxious to keep him on. In 1937, however, Schünzel left Germany for the US, but his directorial career foundered. As actor, Schünzel played Germans in anti-Nazi films such as Fritz Lang's* *Hangmen Also Die!* (1943), Dorothy Arzner's *First Comes Courage* (1943) and Alfred Hitchcock's* *Notorious* (1946). Schünzel went back to Germany in 1949 to return to the stage and only occasionally appeared on screen. TE/MW

Bib: Jörg Schöning (ed.), *Reinhold Schünzel: Schauspieler und Regisseur* (1989).

SCHWARZ, Hanns   Ignatz Schwartz; Vienna 1890[2?] – USA 1945

Austrian director. A student of interior design and painting, Schwarz was asked to make a documentary film for the Bulgarian government. He then worked as an independent director in Berlin from 1923. After 1925 he was, along with Joe May*, the most successful director of Erich Pommer's* production group at Ufa*, where, with a first-class team at his disposal, his comedies and silent operetta films combined popular entertainment formulas with high technical and artistic quality (for instance *Das Fräulein vom Amt*, 1925). The exceptional success of *Ungarische Rhapsodie* (1928) and *Die wunderbare Lüge der Nina Petrowna* (1929) led Pommer to commission Schwarz to make Ufa's first feature-length sound film, *Melodie des Herzens* (1929), which was followed by many internationally popular Pommer/Schwarz sound operettas in the early 1930s (*Einbrecher*, 1930; *Bomben auf Monte Carlo*, 1931, among others) that are said to have considerably influenced the development of the genre in Germany and the US. In 1933 Schwarz emigrated first to Britain, where he directed *The Return of the Scarlet Pimpernel* (1937), and later to the US, though he did not work in film there. KU

Other Films Include: *Liebling der Götter* (1930); *Zigeuner der Nacht* (1932).

SCHWARZENBERGER, Xaver   Vienna 1946

Austrian cinematographer and director. After apprenticeship in Britain, Schwarzenberger worked primarily in television, including five films for Axel Corti* and four episodes of *Alpensaga* (1976–80) [> HEIMATFILM]. His work in Germany with R. W. Fassbinder* began in 1978 and lasted until the latter's death in 1982. In their collaborations, they succeeded in finding a visual concept to suit each story. Their thirteen-part television film, *Berlin Alexanderplatz* (1980), was inspired by Josef von Sternberg's lighting; in *Lili Marleen* (1980), Schwarzenberger quoted the extreme lighting of the old Ufa* films; the symbolic colours in *Lola* (1981) recalled the Hollywood melodramas of the 1950s. Schwarzenberger's debut as a director in 1984 (*Donauwalzer*, which he saw as a tribute to Willi Forst*) received much attention. His subsequent work, however, appears more conventional. AL

SCHWIZGEBEL, Georges   Born 1944

Swiss director, a rare figure among Swiss animation film-makers in his combining of stylistic distinctiveness with artistic vision. Apart from Ernest Ansorge*, only Schwizgebel has left his mark in the field, though he has only managed to make films at the rate of one every three years. This slow pace can be explained both by Schwizgebel's desire to pursue a parallel career as graphic artist, poster-maker and more recently set designer for the theatre, and by the intricacies of funding from both public and private sources. His films are impeccable in their formal rigour and orchestrated according to seriality, variations and correspondences along musical lines. He has tried to find a delicate equilibrium between 'structural' film-making and emotion, based on dynamic situations rather than narrative. Schwizgebel's latest films, dealing with such subjects as an obsessional latter-day Frankenstein monster (*Le Ravissement de Frank N. Stein*, 1981), and a quest for the female form as glimpsed from one painting to another (*Le Sujet du tableau*, 1989), offer some of the most interesting work among contemporary European animation. Schwizgebel is associated with the graphics studio GDS in Geneva, which includes animators such as Claude Luyet and Daniel Suter, bringing together diverse talents and styles and earning them the somewhat hastily applied title of the 'Geneva school' of animation. RC

Other Films Include: *Patchwork* (1970, co-dir.); *Le Vol d'Icare* (1974); *Perspectives* (1975); *Hors-Jeu* (1977); *78 Tours* (1986); *La Course à l'abîme* (1992).

SCHYGULLA, Hanna   Katowice, Poland 1943

Polish-born German actress, closely associated with the work of R. W. Fassbinder*, who created her early star image. She copied gestures and appearance from Hollywood screen goddesses and gave them a self-mocking inflection. Until 1972 she had parts in nearly all of Fassbinder's films, enjoying her greatest public success in Germany as the eponymous heroine of *Fontane Effi Briest/Effi Briest* (1974). However, it was her lead in *Die Ehe der Maria Braun/The Marriage of Maria Braun* (1979) which brought her international fame, while the big-budget production *Lili Marleen* (1981) confirmed her reputation as Europe's most vulnerable *femme fatale*. After Fassbinder's death, Schygulla successfully continued her work with leading European directors such as Jean-Luc Godard*, Carlos Saura*, Marco Ferreri*, Andrzej Wajda*, Volker Schlöndorff* and Margarethe von Trotta*. Critics abroad acclaimed her, but in Germany she failed to retain a following. TE/SG

Other Films Include: *Jagdszenen in Niederbayern/Hunting Scenes from Lower Bavaria* (1969); *Liebe ist kälter als der Tod/Love is Colder than Death, Katzelmacher* (1969); *Götter der Pest/Gods of the Plague* (1970); *Warnung vor einer heiligen Nutte/Beware of a Holy Whore* (1971); *Der Händler der vier Jahreszeiten/The Merchant of Four Seasons* (1972); *Wildwechsel/Jailbait* (1972); *Falsche Bewegung/Wrong Movement* (1975); *Ansichten eines Clowns* (1976); *Die dritte Generation/The Third Generation* (1979); *Die Fälschung* (1981); *Il mondo nuovo* (1982); *Passion* [Fr.], *Antonieta, Heller Wahn* (1983); *Storia di Piera, Eine Liebe in Deutschland* (1983).

SCOLA, Ettore   Trevico 1931

Italian director and scriptwriter. After a period as a comic journalist, the young Scola was instrumental, as a scriptwriter, in the emergence of *commedia all'italiana**, working on Stefano Steno's *Un americano a Roma* (1954) and Dino Risi's* *Il sorpasso/The Easy Life* (1962) and *I mostri/The Monsters* (1963), the last two co-written by Ruggero Maccari. With Maccari again he co-scripted a number of films directed by Antonio Pietrangeli*, including *Nata di marzo* (1958), *Fantasmi a Roma/Phantom Lovers* (1961), *La parmigiana*

(1963) and, best of all, *Io la conoscevo bene/I Knew Her Well* (1965). Scola quickly rose to prominence as a director of comedies of manners informed by social criticism, with *Se permettete parliamo di donne/Let's Talk About Women* (1964), *La congiuntura* (1965, starring Vittorio Gassman*), *Il commissario Pepe* (1969, with Ugo Tognazzi*), *Dramma della gelosia: tutti i particolari in cronaca/The Pizza Triangle* (1970) and *Permette? Rocco Papaleo* (1972, starring Marcello Mastroianni*). A complete change of direction came with *Trevico-Torino, viaggio nel Fiat-Nam* (1973), depicting, in *cinéma-vérité** style, the migration of southern workers to the Fiat factories of the north. From this point onwards, he alternated different styles and sensitivities. On the one hand, he took on the legacy of *commedia all'italiana*, in particular with *C'eravamo tanto amati/We All Loved Each Other So Much* (1974), *Brutti, sporchi e cattivi* (1976), *La terrazza/The Terrace* (1979), *Maccheroni* (1985) and the ambitious *La famiglia/The Family* (1987). On the other hand, he looked abroad with *La nuit de Varennes* (1982, Fr.) and *Le Bal* (1983, Fr.), which brought him international recognition. Scola reached his peak with *Una giornata particolare/A Special Day* (1977), a close confrontation between a man and a woman (Mastroianni and Sophia Loren*, both cast against type) marginalised by Fascism yet capable of relating to each other; the film represents a particular aspect of Italian cinema at its best, with its combination of clearly defined milieu and humanism. Scola was an active member of the former Communist Party (PCI) and in charge of its cultural activities. He dedicated *Mario, Maria e Mario* (1992) to the PCI's recent crisis (which led to a change of name, from PCI to PDS – Partito Democratico della Sinistra). PDA

Other Films Include: *Thrilling* (1965, ep. *Il vittimista*); *L'arcidiavolo/The Devil in Love* (1966); *Riusciranno i nostri eroi a ritrovare l'amico misteriosamente scomparso in Africa?* (1968); *Signore e signori, buonanotte* (1976, co-dir.); *I nuovi mostri/The New Monsters/Viva Italia* (1977, co-dir.); *Passione d'amore/Passions of Love* (1981); *Splendor* (1988); *Che ora è?/What Time is It?* (1989); *Il viaggio del capitan Fracassa* (1990).

SCOTT, Ridley   South Shields 1939

British director. Scott is representative of a group of British directors who emerged from advertising in the 1970s and gravitated towards Hollywood in the 1980s. A graduate of the Royal College of Art (and described by David Puttnam* as 'a painter who happens to use film'), Scott made his first short film, *Boy and Bicycle*, funded by the BFI* Experimental Film Fund, in 1966: 'An ambitious first film that combines adventurous camerawork with a voice-over monologue by Tony Scott [his brother], exploring the sensibility of a schoolboy.' He started in television as a set designer turned director. He left television in 1967 to direct commercials, winning awards for, among others, the Hovis Bread series, and, incidentally, employing Hugh Hudson, later director of *Chariots of Fire* (1981). In 1977, he was engaged by Puttnam, also a former advertising man, to direct *The Duellists*, to which he brought the period style of the Hovis ads, toughened up by strong performances from Harvey Keitel and Keith Carradine into an intriguing male melodrama. In Hollywood, he has managed to make at least one very good film per decade: *Alien* (1979), *Blade Runner* (1982), and *Thelma & Louise* (1991), each marked by the visual style and narrative shocks of the art school and the television commercial. There is always the danger, however, that his pictures will swamp his stories, as in the Christopher Columbus extravaganza, *1492 Conquest of Paradise* (1992, UK/Fr./Sp.). JC

SCREEN

British journal. Started in 1960 by the Society for Education in Film and Television (SEFT), *Screen* in the early 1970s became the leading international journal of film theory in the English language. 'Screen theory' combined the semiotics of Metz, Kristeva and Barthes, the psychoanalysis of Freud and Lacan, and the marxism of Althusser, to which were added, sometimes uneasily, the advances of feminist theory and of independent and avant-garde film practice. The journal imported the excitement of post-'68 French theory not only to film studies, to which it gave the academic respectability necessary to establish it in higher education, but to a wider sphere of critical studies, and it exported theory to North America and Australia. SEFT, a grant-in-aid body of the British Film Institute*, also published *Screen Education*, which extended debates to education and cultural studies. *Screen* was frequently accused of jargon, intellectual terrorism and political naivety, but its success in the 1970s was in creating a constituency, through weekend schools as well as through the journals, and in defining debates. The constituency and the debates became more multiple in the 1980s, and the agenda more inclusive. In 1989 the BFI withdrew funding from SEFT, and *Screen* moved to an academic base in the John Logie Baird Centre in Glasgow. JC

SEEBER, Guido   Chemnitz 1879 – Berlin 1940

German cameraman. The leading pioneer of lighting and trick photography during the first three decades of German cinema, Seeber was in charge of the construction of the first large film studios in Babelsberg in 1911–12. Subsequently he gained his reputation as 'the grand master of trick film' (S. M. Eisenstein*) with his work on films such as *Der Student von Prag/The Student of Prague* (Stellan Rye*, 1913), Paul Wegener* and Henrik Galeen's *Der Golem* (1914) and Lupu Pick's* *Sylvester* (1924). In 1925 he created his own 'absolute' film in the form of the intriguingly titled *Kipho-films*, which were at one and the same time promotion films (for the installation of a permanent museum of the cinema's beginnings), avant-garde films and films about film. He remained active as head of the special effects department at Ufa* until his death. MW

Bib: Norbert Jochum (ed.), *Das wandernde Bild: Der Filmpionier Guido Seeber* (1979).

Other Films Include: *Weihnachtsglück* (1909); *Die geheimnisvolle Streichholzdose* (1910); *Der fremde Vogel* (1911); *Das wandernde Bild* (1920); *Lebende Buddhas* (1925);

Geheimnisse einer Seele/Secrets of a Soul (1926); *Die Zirkusprinzessin* (1929); *Ein Mädchen mit Prokura* (1934); *Ewiger Wald* (1936).

SELLERS, Peter   Richard Henry Sellers; Southsea 1925 – London 1980

British actor, who first rose to fame on radio as the source of several idiotic voices in *The Goon Show*, a national cult in the mid-1950s. It was as an impersonator that he was most skilled, and it was sometimes difficult to dissociate his skills as a mimic from his dramatic performance. Even in *I'm All Right Jack* (1959), where his satiric role as the Stalinist Fred Kite brought him a British Academy Best Actor award, there is the sense of Peter Sellers, the Goon, putting on a funny voice to 'do' a trade unionist, just as he 'did' Asians in *The Millionairess* (1960) and *The Party* (1968, US). In the context of Stanley Kubrick's* *Dr Strangelove* (1963), Sellers' mimicry in multiple roles works brilliantly, but in the same director's *Lolita* (1962) it simply pulls the film out of focus. His performance in the dramatic role of Chance in *Being There* (1979) was well received critically, but his lasting achievement may be the creation of Inspector Clouseau in Blake Edwards' *Pink Panther* series, a legendary comic creation whose disastrously misplaced aplomb (pronounced 'aplöm') has entered popular memory and whose misplaced 'French' vowels have entered the vocabulary. JC

Bib: Alexander Walker, *Peter Sellers: The Authorised Biography* (1981).

Other Films Include: *The Ladykillers, The Case of the Mukkinese Battle-horn* [short] (1955); *The Naked Truth* (1957); *Carlton-Browne of the F.O., The Mouse That Roared* (1959); *The Battle of the Sexes* (1960); *Mr Topaze* [+ dir.] (1961); *The Wrong Arm of the Law* (1962); *The Pink Panther* (1963, US); *A Shot in the Dark* (1964, US); *What's New Pussycat* (1965, US/UK/Fr.); *The Wrong Box* (1966); *Casino Royale* (1967); *I Love You, Alice B. Toklas* (1968, US); *There's a Girl in My Soup* (1970); *The Optimists of Nine Elms* (1973); *The Return of the Pink Panther* (1975); *The Pink Panther Strikes Again* (1976); *Revenge of the Pink Panther* (1978); *Trail of the Pink Panther* (1982).

SEQUENCE

British journal (1947–52), published initially at Oxford University, and subsequently in London. Edited by Gavin Lambert, Lindsay Anderson* and Penelope Houston, with contributions from Karel Reisz*, *Sequence* formed the breeding ground of Free Cinema* and the British New Wave*. It was also, like *Close Up** before it and *Movie** after, a reaction against the dominant traditions of British film criticism and the postwar quality cinema which it supported. The journal set itself against the 'sociology' of the British Documentary Movement* and British realist cinema, seeking out the 'living poetry' which came from 'creative direction', a poetry which it was as likely to find in John Ford's Westerns as in the cinema of important themes favoured by *Sight and Sound**. It anticipated *Movie* in its careful analyses, though not in the breadth of its tastes. Gavin Lambert became editor of *Sight and Sound* in 1950, and the poachers became the game-keepers for the next generation. JC

SERATO, Massimo   Oderzo 1916 – Rome 1989

Italian actor. After leaving the Centro Sperimentale* in Rome, Serato walked straight into cinema as Alida Valli's* co-star in *Piccolo mondo antico/Old-Fashioned World* (1941). His handsome profile made him the favourite young actor of the 'calligraphic' directors of the period, including Alberto Lattuada* (*Giacomo l'idealista*, 1942), Ferdinando Poggioli (*Le sorelle Materassi*, 1943) and Mario Soldati* (*Quartieri alti*, 1944). During the war he also worked in variety shows alongside Anna Magnani* (with whom he had a son). In the postwar period, he specialised in charming scoundrels, and won a Silver Ribbon for his Nazi officer in *Il sole sorge ancora* (1946). He attracted attention for his ironic Don Juan in *Una domenica d'agosto/Sunday in August* (1950), for the cynical protagonist of *Febbre di vivere* (1953), and for *Il magistrato* (1959). Like Rossano Brazzi* a durable 'eternal masculine' type, he starred in all popular genres: melodrama, swash-buckler, peplum* and Italian Westerns*, historical film and science-fiction, co-starring with Hedy Lamarr and Martine Carol*. Until the early 1970s he appeared as 'guest star' in American super-productions filmed in Europe, although he also contributed some good characterisations in films by Elio Petri*, Carlo Lizzani*, Nicholas Ray and Nicolas Roeg. In De Crescenzo's *32 dicembre* (1987) he embodied a character who, though no longer young, was still full of vitality. MMo

SERBIA – see YUGOSLAVIA (former)

SERNA, Assumpta   Assumpta Rodés Serna; Barcelona 1957

Spanish actress, who began her career with the independent Catalan theatre group 'Dagoll Dagom'. Her first film was *L'orgia/The Orgy* (1978). Her career took off in the early 1980s, with roles in international films and, in Spain, in the work of major directors like Carlos Saura* (*Dulces horas/Sweet Hours*, 1981), Pedro Almodóvar* (*Matador*, 1986) and Juan José Bigas Luna* (*Lola*, 1985). Her graceful beauty, aura of mystery and slinky sensuality are given vibrant expression by Almodóvar in *Matador*, where she is the modern, assertive 'New Woman' giving as much as she takes in the arena of sexual desire. PWE

SERREAU, Coline   Paris 1947

French director, who trained as a stage actress and trapeze artist before acting in films from 1970. Her coming of age in the 1968/early feminist era determined the first direction of her career. In 1975 she made an acclaimed feminist documentary, *Mais qu'est-ce qu'elles veulent?/What Do They Want?* (rel. 1977), a series of interviews with women from all backgrounds. This was followed by a fiction film, *Pourquoi pas!*, a libertarian vision of a *ménage à trois*, which demonstrated Serreau's utopian streak, strong in all her subsequent films. With *Qu'est-ce qu'on attend pour être heureux?/Why Wait to Be Happy?* (1982), and more spectacularly *Trois hommes et un couffin/Three Men and a Cradle*, she moved into mainstream comedy. The box-office triumph of the latter (1985 César for best film, remade in Hollywood as *Three Men and a Baby*) derived from Serreau's meticulous social observation, the excellent performances she elicited, and her knack for choosing topical issues, here the 'new fathers'. *Romuald et Juliette* (1989, about a white company executive and his black cleaning lady) and *La Crise* (1992, on the tribulations of an executive who loses wife and job) have done well without being quite so successful. Serreau's comic universe is bourgeois, affectionate and soft-centred; her essentialist view of femininity makes her a controversial figure for feminists. Nevertheless, she has importantly changed French comedy, making possible a woman-oriented exploration of masculinity and other issues unimaginable before feminism. GV

SERVAIS, Raoul   Ostend 1928

Belgian animator, whose worldwide status is reflected in his position as president of ASIFA (the Association of Professional Cartoonists). Servais has had a profound influence on Belgian animation, teaching at the Akademie voor Schone Kunsten/Académie des Beaux-Arts, Ghent (where he himself was taught), and founding the Centre Belge du Film d'Animation in Ghent in 1976. His films have received international acclaim, starting with *Havenlichten/Lumières de port/Harbour Light*, which won a prize at Antwerp in 1960.

Servais' hallmark is versatility. While *Sirène* (1968) uses mythical imagery to tell the story of a sailor and a mermaid, *Pegasus* (1972–73) is visually akin to the style of Flemish expressionist painters. In *Harpya* (1978) Servais used actors for the first time, combining human action with fantastical images. In 1994 he completed his first feature-length animation film, *Taxandria* (ten years in the making). This story of a bewitched village combines myth and real action with a more substantial story. CF

SEVILLA, Carmen   María del Carmen García Galisteo; Seville 1930

Spanish actress, singer and dancer. During the 1950s, Sevilla was the *folklóricas** star who best captured the 'girl next-door' quality, presenting an on-and-off screen image of the 'good' Catholic girl. She starred with actor-singer Luis Mariano* in 1950s Spanish/French co-productions like the very popular *Violetas Imperiales/Violettes impériales/Imperial Violets* (1952, dir. Richard Pottier). She appeared in remakes of *sainetes* (traditional comedies) such as Luis Lucia's* *La hermana San Sulpicio/Sister San Sulpicio* (1952), and despite an excursion into *auteur* cinema with Juan Antonio Bardem's* *La venganza/Revenge* (1957), she was mostly confined to stereotypical parts in melodramas and epic productions, both at home and abroad, including Hollywood. NTT

SEXUALITY, EROTICISM AND PORNOGRAPHY IN EUROPEAN CINEMA

Representations of sexuality and eroticism are as old as the cinema in Europe. While 'actualities' and little comic scenes entertained audiences in fairgrounds, short pornographic movies drew a few of them into brothels. A wide underground network of porn or 'stag' films flourished, usually unknown to mainstream audiences and film history alike, except when they surfaced in 'scandalous' manifestations, as with the Romanian-born French entrepreneur Bernard Natan [> PATHÉ] who directed, and starred in, a large number of them. In the 'legitimate' cinema, eroticism quickly became a feature too, in early French movies for instance and, notoriously, in the pre-World War I Danish erotic melodrama*, credited with the 'invention' of the on-screen passionate kiss.

In 1935, the American authorities burned a print of the Czech film *Extase/Ecstasy* (1932, dir. Gustav Machatý*), in which Hedy Lamarr appeared naked. This took place five years after the introduction of the notoriously censorious Hays Code in the US and, for a good thirty years afterwards, the cinema of Europe was regarded as comparatively free in its depiction of sexuality. Of course, such 'freedom' was, as it would be later, within the confines of dominant (and often misogynistic) representations of women as sexual icons. It was also subject to censorship laws in the European countries themselves. Germany, for example, banned *Extase*, but that was on the grounds of Lamarr being Jewish. And if, in Arletty*, the French cinema of the 1930s and 1940s had an icon of 'independent' female sexuality, her brief 'nude' shower scene in *Le Jour se lève* (1939) was nevertheless excised.

The national cinemas of postwar Europe, particularly those of France and Italy, began to redefine the permissible limits of cinema's depiction of on-screen sexuality. The Italian neorealist* cinema achieved an immense international visibility based on the perceived 'realism' of its depiction of specific social milieux. Such success might equally be said to have been achieved by its depiction of female sexuality. The 'earthiness' of Silvana Mangano* in *Riso amaro/Bitter Rice* (1949) and the revealing filming of Anna Magnani*, not to mention the barely concealed lesbian subplot in *Roma città aperta/Rome Open City* (Roberto Rossellini*, 1945), prepared international audiences for the appearances in the 1950s and 1960s of Italian stars such as Gina Lollobrigida*, Sophia Loren* and Claudia Cardinale*.

In France, in a string of films starting with *Caroline Chérie* (1950), Martine Carol* continued the line of French female stars whose presence guaranteed that their vehicles would be, as Claude Beylie wrote, 'lightly spiced with a pleasant eroticism'. If Carol and others, such as Françoise Arnoul, gave international currency to certain ideas of French cinema and French femininity, the advent of Brigitte Bardot* in *Et Dieu ... créa la femme/And God Created Woman* (1956) promoted different, modern versions both of this femininity and this cinema. The same might be said, forty years on, of Béatrice Dalle*, whose explosive performance in *37°2 le Matin/Betty Blue* (1985) can be read as a reprise of the Bardot sex-kitten persona, treated with *Emmanuelle*-like explicitness.

In François Truffaut's *Les Quatre cents coups* (1959), Jean-Pierre Léaud* steals a publicity still of an Ingmar Bergman* film showing Harriet Andersson* in a revealingly off-the-shoulder outfit. It is a moment in which one European art cinema*, the French New Wave*, addresses the important figure of Bergman, the most celebrated European *auteur* of the period, via the concern common to both: the 'realistic', 'adult' and hence 'explicit' treatment of sexual themes. These three terms, often interchangeable, became associated with the European art cinemas of the 1960s. It was equally the case that the 'adult' treatment of sexuality by these cinemas was accompanied by the *frisson* of the well-publicised relationships between male *auteurs* and their leading actresses, Roberto Rossellini and Ingrid Bergman*, Jean-Luc Godard* and Anna Karina*, Michelangelo Antonioni* and Monica Vitti*, Ingmar Bergman and Liv Ullmann*. Interestingly, the postwar rise in European art cinema was also paralleled by the burgeoning genre of pornography.

If the difference between pornography and eroticism is that between display and suggestion, the late 1960s and the 1970s saw a short-lived convergence of the two. While the sex industry in Europe had formerly restricted itself in the 1950s to low-tech 'stag films' and 'loop movies' for peep shows, and with cinema encroaching progressively upon its territory either in pseudo-documentaries on naturism, so-called 'nudie cuties' and American B-movie exploitation, the late 1960s saw a major increase in the profile of films normally associated with the sex industry.

Two moments are worth isolating in the growing explicitness of sexually oriented material – the first production of hardcore pornography in colour magazines in Scandinavia in 1967, and the international *succès de scandale* of the Swedish film *Jag är nyfiken – gul/I am Curious – Yellow* (1967), which dispensed with any documentary alibis in its straightforwardly explicit depiction of (simulated) sexual action. These two events presaged the increasing commercial importance of explicit sexual content in European cinema of the 1970s. The first half of the decade saw the great commercial success of Bernardo Bertolucci's* *Ultimo Tango a Parigi/Last Tango in Paris* (1972), whose superbly performed confection of stellar cast, hack psychoanalysis and chic sodomy set a model that many *auteurs* would follow throughout the decade. Most notable among examples of this increasing hybridisation of art cinema and pornography were Dušan Makavejev's* Brechtian disquisition on sexual theorist Wilhelm Reich, *W. R. Misterije organizma/W. R. Mysteries of the Organism* (1971), Bertrand Blier's* anarchic, misogynistic *Les Valseuses/Going Places* (1973); Alain Robbe-Grillet's* vacuous exercise in softcore imagery and narrative origami, *Le Jeu avec le feu/Giochi di fuoco* (1975, Fr./It.); Pier Paolo Pasolini's* punishing Sadian parable of Italian fascism, *Salò o le 120 giornate di Sodoma/Salò* (1975); Nagisa Oshima's brilliant, French co-produced excursion into hardcore, *Ai no corrida* (1976); and Jean-Luc Godard's highly mediated take on sexuality and domesticity, *Numéro deux* (1975).

The 'sexual revolution' of the 1960s created a climate in which the explicit depiction of sex was more acceptable to a mainstream audience. For a while, softcore and hardcore pornography flourished on European screens, especially in France where censorship began to be phased out from 1967. The most spectacular example of mainstream softcore success was *Emmanuelle* (1974), the top-grossing film of its year, making an international star of its lead actress, Sylvia Kristel.

A year later, French hardcore took to similarly mainstream screens with *Exhibition* (1975). The response of the French government was not so much one of outright censorship as a fiscal and institutional one that created, in the law of 31 October 1975, the 'X' certificate to designate pornographic films, the creation of a specialised distribution circuit and the imposition of taxes on domestic pornography and a heavier tax on imported porn. While this approach kept the domestic pornography industry marginalised but financially healthy for a short period, it equally serviced the conventional film industry through the siphoning off of porn-tax income into the 'avances sur recette' funding of art cinema. However, the bubble soon burst and by the 1980s the porn cinema accounted for only 5 per cent of the national audience.

The brief foray into mainstream public consciousness that the 1970s bought to the genre of pornography, particularly in France, also saw, towards the end of that decade, the beginnings of the video boom. The European porn industries latched onto video as a means of bypassing cinematic censorship but also as a way of producing low-budget porn. While the genre of 'amateur porn' began inauspiciously in Germany in the 1970s with the so-called *Hausfrauenporn* (housewife porn), by the 1990s video had become hugely lucrative and the standard means of distribution, so that in France an organisation such as 'Nanou Contact' can organise casual sexual encounters, tape them and market them as product. Equally, the European porn industry has its own stars, many of them celebrities beyond their particular fan-base: Brigitte Lahaie and Tabatha Cash in France, Teresa Orlovski in Germany and La Cicciolina (Ilona Staller) in Italy.

If censorious worries with on-screen sexual explicitness have recently been replaced with a concern over levels of violence, it is clear that, as screens themselves have multiplied, the concern is now as much over access to such images as over their contents. The French pay-channel Canal Plus, for example, programmes soft and hardcore pornography regularly. The extension and multiplication of the audiovisual media throughout Europe with cable and satellite will doubtless revivefy the old debates. CDa

Bib: Nick Anning and David Hebditch, *Porn Gold: Inside the Pornography Business* (1988).

SEYRIG, Delphine   Beirut, Lebanon 1932 – Paris 1990

French actress. Two films – Alain Resnais'* *L'Année dernière à Marienbad/Last Year at Marienbad* (1961) and *Muriel ou le temps d'un retour/Muriel* (1963, Best Actress at Venice) – made Seyrig an icon of European art cinema (she also appeared in American underground films). Seyrig's blonde, ethereal beauty and upper-class yet seductive voice graced other art film classics: *Accident* (1967, UK), *Baisers volés/Stolen Kisses* (1968), *Le Charme discret de la bourgeoisie/The Discreet Charm of the Bourgeoisie* (1972), as well as the cult vampire film *Le Rouge aux lèvres/Les Lèvres rouges/Daughters of Darkness* (Harry Kümel*, 1971). A committed feminist, Seyrig also supported women's cinema – Marguerite Duras'* *India Song* (1975), Chantal Akerman's* *Jeanne Dielman, 23 Quai du Commerce 1080 Bruxelles* (1975)

and *Golden Eighties* (1985), and Ulrike Ottinger's* *Freak Orlando* (1981), among others. She co-founded the audiovisual Centre Simone de Beauvoir in Paris in 1982, and directed two videos. GV

SHAKHNAZAROV, Karen G.   Moscow 1952

Russian director and screenwriter. Studied at VGIK* in the studio of Igor Talankin, graduating in 1975. His film *My iz dzhaza/Jazzmen* (1983) follows the rise to fame of an Odessa jazz quartet in the 1920s, and was a great hit. It was followed by *Zimnii vecher v Gagrakh/A Winter Evening in Gagra* (1985) and *Kur'er/Messenger Boy* (1986), a coming-of-age comedy. *Gorod zero/Zero City* (1989) is an absurd comedy in which an engineer's visit to a provincial Russian town turns into a nightmarish existential journey through Soviet experience. *Tsareubiitsa/Assassin of the Tsar* (1991), a British-Russian co-production, starring Malcolm McDowell* and the leading Russian actor Oleg Yankovsky, begins as psychological drama but lapses into a dull period piece about the last days of the Russian imperial family. In 1993 Shakhnazarov and his regular scriptwriter Alexander Borodyansky co-directed *Sny/Dreams*. JGf

SHENGELAYA, Eldar N.   Tbilisi, Georgia [USSR] 1933

Georgian director, the son of the director Nikolai Shengelaya, a key figure in the development of Georgian cinema, and the brother of Georgi Shengelaya*. He graduated from Sergei Yutkevich's* workshop at VGIK* in 1958. Among his early successes was *Neobyknovennaya vystavka/An Unusual Exhibition* (1969), a tragi-comedy about the compromises in the life of a provincial sculptor. *Golubye gory/Blue Mountains* (1984), a whimsical comedy set in a Tbilisi publishing house, brought him international success. JGf

SHENGELAYA, Georgi N.   Tbilisi, Georgia [USSR] 1937

Georgian director and actor, son of the director Nikolai Shengelaya and brother of Eldar Shengelaya*. He graduated from Alexander Dovzhenko* and Mikhail Romm's* workshop at VGIK* in 1963. Shengelaya achieved early renown with his visually compelling 1971 film *Pirosmani*, a portrait of the brilliant Georgian primitive painter Niko Pirosmanashvili (1862–1918). *Melodii Veriiskogo kvartala/Melodies of the Veriisky Quarter* (1973) is a musical set in pre-Revolutionary Tbilisi, and shows the influence of *Seven Brides for Seven Brothers*. *Pridi v dolinu vinograda/Come to Grape Valley* (1977) concerns the effect of construction work on a beautiful Georgian valley. *Puteshestvie molodogo kompozitora/The Journey of a Young Composer* (1985) is set in 1907; while repression continues in the wake of the failure of the 1905 revolution, the young composer wanders eastern Georgia in search of folk songs. JGf

SHEPITKO, Larisa E.　Artemivsk, Ukraine [USSR] 1938–79

Russian director. Shepitko graduated from VGIK*, where she had studied in the workshop of Alexander Dovzhenko* (whom she always referred to as her mentor) and Mikhail Romm* in 1963. Her diploma work was *Znoi/Heat* (1963), made for Kirgizfilm from 'The Camel's Eye', a story by the Kirgiz writer Chingiz Aitmatov, about a clash of generations on a collective farm. It was followed by *Kryl'ya/Wings* (1966), in which a middle-aged woman, director of a civil engineering school, yearns for her days as a pilot during World War II and struggles to understand her daughter's generation. Shepitko's next project was the short film *Rodina elektrichestva/ Homeland of Electricity* (1967), from the story by Andrei Platonov about the coming of electricity to a Russian village after the Revolution. Frequently compared to the work of her master Dovzhenko, this film, like Andrei Smirnov's* *Angel*, was shot as part of a portmanteau film, *Nachalo nevedomogo veka/The Beginning of an Unknown Century*, made to mark the fiftieth anniversary of the Revolution. But the films were banned for twenty years, and *Rodina elektrichestva* surfaced only in 1987, long after Shepitko's death. In *Ty i ya/You and I* (1971) a brain surgeon suddenly experiences an identity crisis and goes to Siberia to sort out his life. Shepitko's greatest achievement is *Voskhozhdenie/The Ascent* (1976), taken from Vasil Bykau's story 'Sotnikov' and set in German-occupied Belorussia in 1942. This story of the tragic fate of a group of partisans is replete with spiritual strength and religious symbolism. It won the Golden Bear at Berlin in 1977. Shepitko died in a car crash in 1979, after beginning work on a version of Valentin Rasputin's lament for a Siberian village, 'Farewell to Matyora'. The film was completed by her husband, Elem Klimov*, as *Proshchanie/Farewell* (1983). He also directed a short film made in her memory, *Larisa* (1980). JGf

SHERIDAN, Jim　Dublin 1949

Irish director and writer. Sheridan's career began in the 1970s as a theatre director and playwright. Eight of his own plays have been produced, especially when he was a director at the Project Arts Centre, the main alternative venue for theatre, visual arts and film at the time. He moved to New York where he was Artistic Director of the Irish Arts Centre and studied film at New York University. He spent many years attempting with producer Noel Pearson to gain backing for his adaptation of the autobiography of writer Christy Brown, which became eventually *My Left Foot* (1989). It was the first Irish-produced film to be nominated for five Oscars (only to be exceeded by Neil Jordan's* *The Crying Game*, 1992) and it won two: for actors Daniel Day-Lewis* and Brenda Fricker*.

The Browns are depicted in *My Left Foot* as a Dublin working-class family struggling to overcome adversity, with the mother binding the family together despite hints of violence from the father. The film avoids the more uncomfortable realities of a large family in a society where contraception was illegal. Sheridan's second film, *The Field* (1990), was also nominated for an Oscar: for Richard Harris'* performance as Bull McCabe, a farmer who is seeking to purchase a field he has long tilled. The film radically altered the play by John B.

Keane from which it was derived, by shifting the story from the late 1950s/early 1960s to the 1930s, and changing the Bull's rival from English to Irish-American (Tom Berenger) – changes dictated by the foreign funding of the film. The need to retain audience recognition for a character and the reinforcement of a pre-modern, pastoral view of Ireland, as historically constructed in the international cinema, requires a film-maker such as Sheridan, despite his earlier success, to compromise in a manner that largely neutralises its cultural impact in Ireland. Sheridan's third feature, *In the Name of the Father* (1993), explores the Guildford Four miscarriage of justice case when Irish people were wrongly convicted of terrorist offences and as a result spent fifteen years in jail. KR

SHKLOVSKY, Viktor B.　St Petersburg 1893 – Moscow 1984

Soviet writer, critic and theorist. In the course of a long career Shklovsky scripted a number of films, including Lev Kuleshov's* *Po zakonu/By the Law* (1926) and *Gorizont* (1932); Abram Room's* *Bukhta smerti/Bay of Death*, *Predatel'/The Traitor* (both 1926) and *Tret'ya Meshchanskaya/Bed and Sofa/Third Meshchanskaya Street* (1927); Boris Barnet's* *Dom na Trubnoi/The House on Trubnaya* (1928); and Vsevolod Pudovkin's* *Minin i Pozharskii/Minin and Pozharsky* (1939). A leading Formalist, he also wrote a number of theoretical works on cinema and literature, including *Literatura i kinematograf* ('Literature and Cinema', 1923), *Gamburgskii schët* ('The Hamburg Reckoning', 1926), *Tret'ya fabrika* ('The Third Factory', 1926, translated into English in 1977), *Ikh nastoyashchee* ('Their Present-Day', 1927), *Kak pisat' stsenarii* ('How to Write a Script', 1931), a study of Sergei Eisenstein* (1978), a volume of memoirs (1966) and countless articles of film criticism and theory. RT

Bib: Viktor Shklovsky, *Third Factory* (1977).

SHOSTAKOVICH, Dmitri D.　St Petersburg 1906 – Moscow 1975

Russian composer. While studying at the Leningrad Conservatoire, Shostakovich earned money by playing piano accompaniment to films. His first film score was for Grigori Kozintsev* and Leonid Trauberg's* *Novyi Vavilon/New Babylon* (1929) and he also scored their *Odna/Alone* (1931) and 'Maxim trilogy' (1935–39), and Kozintsev's two Shakespearean films, *Gamlet/Hamlet* (1964) and *Korol' Lir/King Lear* (1971). Shostakovich also wrote music for Fridrikh Ermler* and Sergei Yutkevich's* *Vstrechnyi/Counterplan* (1932), Grigori Alexandrov's* *Vstrecha na El'be/Meeting on the Elbe* and Mikhail Chiaureli's* *Padenie Berlina/The Fall of Berlin* (both 1949). RT

SHUB, Esfir I.　Chernigov district, Ukraine [Russian Empire] 1894 – Moscow 1959

Soviet director. From 1922 to 1942 Shub worked as an editor of fiction films, rendering foreign films 'suitable' for Soviet audiences by excising politically incorrect aspects. She worked with Sergei Eisenstein* and they influenced one another considerably, a debt which both acknowledged. Shub was also involved in archival work on pre-Revolutionary newsreel and documentary footage, from which she made the compilation films for which she is most famous: *Padenie dinastii Romanovykh/The Fall of the Romanov Dynasty* (1927) and *Rossiya Nikolaya II i Lev Tolstoi/Lev Tolstoy and the Russia of Nicholas II* (1928). She went on to make compilations of contemporary Soviet footage, such as *Velikii put'/The Great Path* (1927); *Segodnya/Today* (1930); *KShE/Komsomol – Patron of Electrification*, with its highly experimental use of sound (1932); *Moskva stroit metro/Moscow Builds the Metro* (1934); and *Strana sovetov/The Land of the Soviets* (1937). In 1939 she made a compilation of footage shot by Soviet cameramen in the Spanish Civil War, *Ispaniya/Spain*. Although less interesting aesthetically than the work of Dziga Vertov*, Shub's films did reach larger audiences. Her memoirs, *Krupnym planom* ('In Close-Up', 1959), are an important historical source, while her films preserve much footage that might otherwise have been destroyed. RT

SHUKSHIN, Vasili M.
Srostki, Siberia [USSR] 1929 – Kletskaya, Russia [USSR] 1974

Siberian-born Russian writer, director and actor. Shukshin worked on his local collective farm in the Altai region from the age of sixteen, and was then employed in a factory in Central Russia. He served as a sailor from 1949 to 1952 before returning to his village. In 1954 he began to study direction at VGIK* with Mikhail Romm*, graduating in 1960. In 1957 Shukshin began to act in films, starring in Marlen Khutsiev's* *Dva Fëdora/Two Fyodors* in 1959. His first short story was published in 1958, followed by his first collection, *Sel'skie zhiteli/Villagers*, in 1963. His first film as a director, *Zhivët takoi paren'/There is a Lad* (1964), is based, like all his subsequent films, on his own stories, and finds humour both in village innocence and urban pseudo-sophistication. In *Vash syn i brat/Your Son and Brother* (1966) a young man returns to his village between prison sentences. *Strannye lyudi/Strange People* (1971) combines the tales of three eccentrics; while in *Pechki-lavochki/Happy Go Lucky* (1973) Shukshin himself stars, with his wife, Lydia Fedoseyeva-Shukshina, as a peasant couple leaving their Altai village for the first time on a long train journey to a southern resort. In his last completed film, *Kalina krasnaya/The Red Snowball Tree/Snowball Cherry Red* (1974), Shukshin again plays the hero, Yegor Prokudin, an ex-convict who makes an ultimately tragic attempt to start a new life in a remote village with a simple peasant woman (again played by his wife). After Shukshin's death, his screenplay *Pozovi menya v dal' svetluyu* ('Call Me From Afar', 1978) was directed by the actor Stanislav Lyubshin and the cinematographer German Lavrov. As well as acting in his own films, Shukshin appeared in such films as Gleb Panfilov's* *Proshu slova/I Wish to Speak* and Sergei Bondarchuk's* *Oni srazhalis' za rodinu/They Fought for Their Country* (1975), his last acting role. But Shukshin's major film project, about the seventeenth-century Cossack rebel Stenka Razin, which he fought to make for several years, was never allowed by Soviet censors. The screenplay,

Ya prishel dat' vam volyu ('I Have Come to Give You Freedom'), was published as a novel in 1971. JGf

SHUMYATSKY, Boris Z.
Near Lake Baikal 1886 – [?]1938

Soviet politician. Shumyatsky was an Old Bolshevik who had joined the Party in 1903 and played a leading part in the revolutionary movement in Siberia. He was Soviet plenipotentiary in Persia in the mid-1920s and it was there that he realised the propaganda potential of film, attracting large and enthusiastic audiences by showing Soviet films depicting unveiled women. This was his only experience of cinema when he was appointed head of the centralised state Soyuzkino organisation in late 1930. He followed Lenin's* and Lunacharsky's* dictum that cinema must both entertain *and* propagandise and set about establishing what he called a 'cinema for the millions' that would do just that. Thus he sponsored Grigori Alexandrov's* musical comedies and encouraged other directors to make films that were 'intelligible to the millions', like the 'Maxim trilogy' by Grigori Kozintsev* and Leonid Trauberg*. He mistrusted intellectuals and the avant-garde and stopped Sergei Eisenstein* completing *Bezhin lug/Bezhin Meadow* (1935–37). As head of a delegation to Hollywood in 1935, he returned to propose a 'Soviet Hollywood', also known as 'Cine-City', in the Crimea, where the climate would allow filming throughout the year. But the decline in production, resulting from increased political controls and from the shadow cast by the purges, and his own growing power, made him appear to threaten Stalin* and in 1938 he was arrested, denounced and executed. RT

SIERCK, Detlef [US: SIRK, Douglas]
Hans Detlef Sierck; Hamburg 1900 – Lugano, Switzerland 1987

German director. Sierck was a successful stage producer and director in the years before 1933. Of the political left, he transferred to the cinema, less strictly censored in the mid-1930s than the theatre because of its international market. He turned to features in 1935, soon gaining a reputation for the visual quality of his films and his talent for directing women. He was employed by Ufa*, and his first international success was the musical melodrama *Schlußakkord/Final Accord* (1936). The peak of his German career, however, were two Zarah Leander* melodramas, *Zu neuen Ufern/To New Shores* (1937) and *La Habanera* (1937). In autumn 1937, Sierck emigrated to the US, where he changed his name to Douglas Sirk and had to rebuild his reputation. After several false starts, he succeeded with a number of Technicolor melodramas, characterised by baroque *mise-en-scène* and powerful emotional appeal, most notably *All That Heaven Allows* (1956), *Written on the Wind* (1957) and *Interlude* (1957, partly shot in Europe). After a production completed in West Germany (*A Time to Love and a Time to Die*, 1958), Sirk made his last American film for Universal with *Imitation of Life* (1959), before retiring to Switzerland.

Once thought of as mere soap opera tear-jerkers, Sirk's American melodramas were rediscovered in the 1970s by critics who appreciated their 'distancing' excess (and feminists who noted their powerful female characters). Sirk was emulated by Rainer Werner Fassbinder*, who saw in him not only a kindred spirit but living proof of a continuity with German film culture which could encompass popular genres as well as intelligent art cinema. TE/MW

Bib: Michael Stern, *Douglas Sirk* (1979).

Other Films Include: *April, April* (1935); *Das Mädchen vom Moorhof* (1935); *Stützen der Gesellschaft* (1935); *Das Hofkonzert* (1936; also Fr. version, *La Chanson du souvenir*, 1936). **In the US**: *Hitler's Madman* (1943); *Lured* (1947); *All I Desire* (1953); *Magnificent Obsession* (1954); *There's Always Tomorrow* (1955); *Battle Hymn* (1956); *The Tarnished Angels* (1958).

SIGHT AND SOUND

British journal, established in 1932, and taken under the wing of the British Film Institute* when it was established in 1933. Both came out of an Institute of Adult Education commission set up in 1929 to 'consider suggestions for improving and extending the use of films for educational and cultural purposes and to consider methods for raising the standard of public appreciation of films'. In the 1930s and 1940s, *Sight and Sound*'s main constituencies were education and the film societies, and its influence on the national cinema was limited. Since the late 1940s, however, *Sight and Sound*, has been the rock of official film culture against which succeeding waves and new waves have crashed. Under the editorship of Gavin Lambert (1949–56) and Penelope Houston (1956–90), it spoke with some authority in the debates of the 1950s and early 1960s, but it seemed out of touch with the radical, oppositional and multicultural currents which emerged in the 1970s and 1980s. In 1991, a new series was launched which has sought an eclectic mix of international popularity, domestic influence, critical diversity, and financial viability. The jury is still out. JC

SIGNORET, Simone
Simone Kaminker; Wiesbaden, Germany 1921 – Autheuil 1985

French actress and novelist. The glowing sensual beauty of the young Signoret, as seen in her most famous film, Jacques Becker's* *Casque d'or/Golden Marie* (1952), is a familiar icon of French cinema. But Signoret signified more for her French audience. One of the rare female stars (a term she rejected) who aged on screen as 'an act of defiance', she also made a mark through her strong left-wing views, as well as her tumultuous marriage to Yves Montand*. Signoret's 'prostitute with a heart of gold' in Yves Allégret's* *Dédée d'Anvers* (1948) set the tone for a number of similar roles in the popular French cinema of the late 1940s and early 1950s. A more misogynistic variant was the schemer, as in Allégret's *Manèges/The Cheat* (1950) and Henri-Georges Clouzot's* *Les Diaboliques* (1955). *Casque d'or* stands as an exception in both her career and in French cinema, in allowing her char-

acter (a prostitute again) to assert her desire and independence. Despite an Oscar for *Room at the Top* (1958, UK), Signoret's acting was perhaps not fully recognised, and in the early 1960s her notoriety came more from the fracas around Montand's affair with Marilyn Monroe. The maturing Signoret embodied strong heroines in thrillers and psychological dramas such as Jean-Pierre Melville's* *L'Armée des ombres/The Army in the Shadows* (1969), which while (again) not devoid of misogyny, projected her powerful personality. Her role opposite Jean Gabin* in *Le Chat* (1971) is emblematic of such parts. Later in her life, Signoret took up writing and produced a successful autobiography and two novels. Her daughter Catherine Allégret is a film and television actress. GV

Bib: Catherine David, *Simone Signoret* (1990, trans. 1992).

Other Films Include: *La Ronde* (1950); *Thérèse Raquin* (1953); *Compartiment Tueurs/The Sleeping Car Murders* (1965); *La Veuve Couderc* (1971); *Police Python 357* (1975); *L'Adolescente* (1979); *L'Etoile du Nord* (1983).

ŠIJAN, Slobodan
Belgrade, Serbia 1946

Serbian director. After graduating in painting and film at the Belgrade Academy, Šijan shot several films for television which clearly expressed his fascination with the classical American tradition of Ford and Hawks. His critically acclaimed feature debut, *Ko to tamo peva/Who's Singing Over There?* (1980), was one of the box-office hits of the 1980s in Yugoslavia. The story of a group of people journeying by bus to Belgrade on the eve of the World War II bombardments was more than grotesque comedy: it was a clever and authentic tribute to John Ford's *Stagecoach* (1939). Šijan repeated this strategy in later films, with references to Ealing comedy* and classical horror, but his first direct encounter with American cinema, the 1988 co-production *The Secret Ingredient*, was a failure. SP

Other Films: *Maratonci trče počasni krug/Marathon Lap of Honour* (1982); *Kako sam sistematski uništen od idiota/How I Was Systematically Destroyed by an Idiot* (1983); *Davitelj protiv davitelja/Strangler vs. Strangler* (1984).

SIM, Alastair
Edinburgh 1900 – London 1976

British actor, who spiced British comedy with a gallery of Dickensian eccentrics. In the late 1930s, he was inclined towards the sinister with films like *The Terror* (1938), but he also appeared with George Formby* in *Keep Your Seats Please* (1936), with the Crazy Gang in *Alf's Button Afloat* (1938), and with Jessie Matthews* in *Climbing High* (1938). During the war, he gained recognition as Sergeant Bingham in the Inspector Hornleigh films, but it was after the war that he developed his true eccentric genius. Though he could be the benign doctor of *Waterloo Road* (1945), and is probably best remembered for his doubling and cross-dressing in *The Belles of St. Trinian's* (1954), a sinister element remained in many of his best parts. His charm could be of the leering sort, and his eyes could flicker in a moment from sunny geniality to languid malignity. His Henry Squales in *London Belongs to Me* (1948) is one of the classic creations of dark comedy. Only one of his Frank Launder and Sidney Gilliat* films, *Geordie* (1955), is actually set in Scotland, but he seldom disguises his Scottish accent: it is simply another feature which he draws on to colour, and perhaps explain, his eccentricity. JC

Other Films Include: *Green for Danger* (1946); *Captain Boycott, Hue and Cry* (1947); *The Happiest Days of Your Life, Stage Fright* (1950); *Laughter in Paradise, Scrooge, Lady Godiva Rides Again* (1951); *Folly to be Wise* (1952); *Innocents in Paris* (1953); *An Inspector Calls* (1954); *Blue Murder at St Trinian's* (1957); *The Doctor's Dilemma, Left, Right and Centre* (1959); *School for Scoundrels, The Millionairess* (1960); *The Ruling Class* (1972); *Royal Flash* (1975).

SIMENON, Georges   Liège 1903 – Lausanne, Switzerland 1989

Belgian novelist, who worked in France, the US and Switzerland. The phenomenally successful and prolific Simenon wrote pulp novels, essays, memoirs and hundreds of crime stories, many featuring the character of Inspector Maigret. Simenon's brand of crime fiction was based on social observation and atmosphere rather than conventional detection, which perhaps explains why he has been one of the most adapted writers in French cinema.

The first Simenon adaptation was *La Nuit du carrefour/Night at the Crossroads* (1932), directed by Jean Renoir*. Over fifty, mostly French, films followed, and many great European actors have embodied the gruff, pipe-smoking Maigret: Pierre Renoir [> JEAN RENOIR], Harry Baur*, Gino Cervi*, Charles Laughton*, Albert Préjean* in the 1940s and Jean Gabin* in the 1950s and 1960s. Prominent French directors have successfully translated Simenon's misanthropic view of the world: from Renoir to Julien Duvivier* (*Panique*, 1946 – remade as *Monsieur Hire* by Patrice Leconte, 1989), Marcel Carné* (*La Marie du port*, 1950), Claude Autant-Lara* (*En cas de malheur/Love is My Profession*, 1958), Bertrand Tavernier* (*L'Horloger de Saint-Paul/The Watchmaker of Saint-Paul*, 1974) and Claude Chabrol* (*Les Fantômes du chapelier/The Hatter's Ghosts*, 1982; *Betty*, 1992). Though he professed to dislike most film adaptations of his novels, Simenon inspired some of France's best *noir* works, for instance *Panique* and *Les Inconnus dans la maison* (1942, scripted by Henri-Georges Clouzot* and directed by Henri Decoin*). GV

SIMMONS, Jean   London 1929

British actress, who became a major star in Hollywood after moving there in the early 1950s. In Britain, she made her debut at the age of 14 as Margaret Lockwood's* sister in *Give Us the Moon* (1944). Following a brief but effective appearance as a singer in *The Way to the Stars* (1945), she made a considerable impact as the young Estella in David Lean's* *Great Expectations* (1946) before Estella grew up and became Valerie Hobson. Michael Powell* put her into slightly em-

barrassing make-up to play an Indian seductress in *Black Narcissus* (1947), but at least he recognised the power of her sexuality, just as Laurence Olivier* recognised the power of her vulnerability when he cast her as Ophelia in his *Hamlet* (1948), a role for which she won an Oscar nomination and a Best Actress award at Venice. She starred in *The Blue Lagoon* (1949), one of J. Arthur Rank's* many attempts to break into the American market, and appeared with Dirk Bogarde* in *So Long at the Fair* (1950), but Hollywood beckoned – and with seriously starring roles in big pictures: *Angel Face* (1953), *The Robe* (1953), *Guys and Dolls* (1955), *The Big Country* (1958), *Spartacus* (1960) and *Elmer Gantry* (1960). She returned to Britain to play Susan Lampton in the not very distinguished *Life at the Top* (1965). JC

SIMON, Michel   Geneva, Switzerland 1895 – Bry-sur-Marne 1975

Swiss-born French actor. After stage roles in Geneva and Paris and a few bit parts in silent films, the screen adaptation of his stage success *Jean de la lune* (1931) launched Michel Simon on a career of some hundred films, establishing his reputation as one of the most gifted and versatile stars of French cinema. Like many actors of the 1930s, Simon appeared in numerous adapted plays, usually comedies (like *Fric-Frac*, 1939), in which he was gloriously funny. Film history, however, has preferred to concentrate on his roles in two films by Jean Renoir* – Legrand, the repressed petit-bourgeois of *La Chienne* (1931), and the anarchic tramp Boudu in *Boudu sauvé des eaux/Boudu Saved from Drowning* (1932) – and one by Jean Vigo* (*L'Atalante*, 1934). Simon's prematurely aged looks even in youth and his quaky, grating voice led to many parts trading on ambivalence, sexual or otherwise – for example as Molyneux in Marcel Carné's* *Drôle de drame* (1937), the repulsive father-figure in *Quai des brumes* (1938), the hero of Julien Duvivier's* *Panique* (1947), both threatening and pathetic, and the dual protagonist of René Clair's* *La Beauté du diable/Beauty and the Devil* (1950).

Simon's presence in Swiss films is confined to an important role in *La Vocation d'André Carel* (1925) and appearances in *Es geschah am hellichten Tag/It Happened in Broad Daylight* (1958; dir. Ladislao Vajda*) and the short *Nicolas mon ami* (1961). MW/GV

Bib: André Klopmann, *Michel Simon* (1993).

SIMON, Simone   Béthune 1911

French actress. Though rarely given lead parts, the delicate, cat-like Simone Simon made a memorable mark on two classics: Jean Renoir's* *La Bête humaine* (1938) and Jacques Tourneur's cult horror movie *Cat People* (1942, US). A singer and model, she began her film career in 1931. Her role in Marc Allégret's* *Lac aux dames* (1934, scripted by Colette*) brought her fame in France and a contract in Hollywood. For a while she was a top French actress, and relatively successful in Hollywood. Her sex-kitten sensuality found an expression in *Cat People* but, to her dismay, was considerably toned

389

down by US censorship in several other films, including the Maupassant adaptation *Mademoiselle Fifi* (1944, dir. Robert Wise). Back in France, however, it glowed in a more mature form in Jacqueline Audry's* *Olivia/The Pit of Loneliness* (1951, co-starring Edwige Feuillère*), and in two Max Ophuls* films, *La Ronde* (1950) and *Le Plaisir* (1951). GV

SIODMAK, Robert   Dresden 1900 – Locarno, Switzerland 1973

German director, who first made his mark as co-director of the feature documentary *Menschen am Sonntag/People on Sunday* (1930) with Edgar G. Ulmer. Siodmak went on to direct feature films at Ufa*, among them one of the earliest German sound films, *Abschied* (1930). After the completion of *Brennendes Geheimnis/The Burning Secret* (1933), adapted from a novella by Stefan Zweig, Siodmak was forced into exile, first to France, where he had the most prolific career of all the German émigrés, making a number of seminal *noir* movies, especially *Le Chemin de Rio* (1937), *Mollenard* (1938) and *Pièges* (1939), as well as outstanding musicals like *La Crise est finie* (1934) and *La Vie parisienne* (1935).

Late in 1938, Siodmak moved to Hollywood, and directed a succession of B-pictures and atmospherically charged psychological thrillers for Universal, which count among the key examples of American *film noir*: *Phantom Lady* (1944), *The Spiral Staircase* (1945), *The Killers* (1946). Siodmak returned to Europe, directing various and variable films in France, Britain and, from 1954, Germany, but in 1957 he once more conjured up, with *Nachts, wenn der Teufel kam/The Devil Strikes at Night*, about a mentally disturbed mass-murderer, his skill as the 'master of *film noir*'. TE/MW

Bib: Hervé Dumont, *Robert Siodmak: Le Maître du film noir* (1981).

Other Films Include: *Der Kampf mit dem Drachen oder: Die Tragödie des Untermieters* (1930); *Der Mann, der seinen Mörder sucht* (1931); *Voruntersuchung* (1931); *Stürme der Leidenschaft/The Tempest* (1932); *Quick, König der Clowns* (1932); *West Point Widow* (1941, US); *Son of Dracula* (1943, US); *The Suspect* (1944, US); *The Dark Mirror* (1946, US); *Time out of Mind* (1947, US); *Cry of the City* (1948, US); *Criss Cross, The Great Sinner* (1949, both US); *Die Ratten* (1955).

SJÖBERG, Alf   Stockholm 1903–80

Swedish director. A talented stage actor and especially director, Sjöberg was from 1927 director of the Royal Dramatic Theatre, Stockholm, where he introduced modern drama. He became one of Sweden's most important film-makers, bridging the gap between the great silent directors (Mauritz Stiller* and Victor Sjöström*) and Ingmar Bergman*, to whom he acted as a mentor ('like a father', according to Bergman). His thematic and stylistic versatility mean, however, that he has been less readily given the status of an *auteur* than his illustrious colleagues. His film debut was the successful adventure epic *Den starkaste/The Strongest* (1929), a tale of seal hunting in the Arctic, which has been compared by

many historians to the work of Robert Flaherty*. After ten years back in the theatre, Sjöberg returned to the cinema in the 1940s, directing dramas such as *Med livet som insats/They Staked Their Lives* (1940) and *Kungajakt/Royal Hunt* (1944), often regarded as oblique comments on Nazism. His most prominent work was still to come: the spiritual drama *Himlaspelet/The Road to Heaven* (1942), *Hets/Frenzy/Torment* (1944, about a sadistic schoolteacher, based on a script by Bergman), the socially conscious *Bara en mor/Only a Mother* (1949), and especially his beautiful version of Strindberg's *Fröken Julie/Miss Julie* (1951), co-awarded the Golden Palm at Cannes that year, and which Bergman called 'a masterpiece ... it's Sjöberg's *Miss Julie*, not Strindberg's'. Sjöberg continued to work until the late 1960s (his last film was *Fadern/The Father*, 1969) but his later style, reminiscent of German expressionism*, was the object of harsh criticism. LGA/BF

Other Films Include: *Den blomstertid.../This Blossom Time...* (1940); *Hem från Babylon/Home from Babylon* (1941); *Resan bort/Journey Out* (1945); *Iris och löjtnantshjärta/Iris and the Lieutenant* (1942); *Barabbas* (1953); *Karin Månsdotter* (1954); *Vildfåglar/Wild Birds* (1955); *Sista paret ut/Last Pair Out* (1956); *Domaren/The Judge* (1960); *Ön/The Island* (1966).

SJÖMAN, Vilgot   Stockholm 1924

Swedish director and novelist. After writing plays, novels and scripts (including Gustaf Molander's* *Trots/Defiance*, 1952) and attending a film course in the US, Sjöman collaborated with Ingmar Bergman*, notably on *Nattvardsgästerna/Winter Light* (1963), an influential apprenticeship. His first film, *Älskarinnan/The Mistress* (1962), stars Bergman actors Bibi Andersson* and Max von Sydow*. His next films, *491* and *Klänningen/The Dress* (both 1964), and *Syskonbädd 1782/My Sister, My Love* (1966), combine a trenchant view of contemporary Sweden with an interest in sexual relations (taking in, respectively, juvenile delinquents, mother/daughter rivalry, brother/sister incest). Sjöman has, however, gone down in film history as the director of *Jag är nyfiken – gul/I Am Curious – Yellow* (1967) and its sequel *Jag är nyfiken – blå/I Am Curious – Blue* (1968), unusual combinations of sociopolitical commitment and graphic sexual representation. The films were extremely successful outside Sweden, especially in the US and Britain (benefiting from the *succès de scandale* of court cases and censors' cuts), promoting the image of 'liberated' Sweden and anticipating the sexually explicit and pornographic cinema of the 1970s [> SEXUALITY, EROTICISM AND PORNOGRAPHY IN EUROPEAN CINEMA]. Sjöman's subsequent films have continued to oscillate between social and existential themes and sexuality, but without the same success. He is also a distinguished novelist and has written literary criticism as well as on film and film production. LGA/BF

Bib: Stig Björkman, *Film in Sweden: The New Directors* (1977).

Other Films Include: *Stimulantia* (1967, ep. *Negressen i skåpet/The Black Woman in the Closet*); *Ni ljuger/You're*

Lying! (1969); *Lyckliga skitar/Blushing Charlie* (1970); *Troll/ Trolls/Till Sex Do Us Part* (1971); *En handfull kärlek/A Handful of Love* (1974); *Garaget/The Garage* (1975); *Tabu/ Taboo* (1977); *Linus eller Tegelhusets hemlighet/Linus* (1979); *Jag rödnar/I Am Blushing* (1980); *Malacca* (1987); *Fall- gropen/The Trap* (1989).

SJÖSTRÖM [SEASTROM], Victor
Silbodal 1879 – Stockholm 1960

Swedish director and actor, one of the two great directors of early Swedish cinema (the other being Mauritz Stiller*), Sjöström was also a distinguished actor throughout his career, often appearing in his own films. He was partly raised in America. On his return to Scandinavia, he trained and worked as an actor, first in Finland and then in provincial Swedish theatres, before being hired by Charles Magnusson* (shortly after Stiller) at Svenska Bio*, the leading Swedish company. His first film as director was *Trädgårdsmästaren/ The Head Gardener* (1912), in which he also acted. His first mature work, the social melodrama *Ingeborg Holm* (1913), proved ground-breaking. This tale of forced labour for children was an international success which in Sweden also aroused considerable debate about the welfare system and led to new social legislation in 1918. It was also the film on which Sjöström's reputation as an 'earnest' realist film-maker first rested. With *Terje Vigen/A Man There Was* and *Tösen från Stormyrtorpet/The Lass from Stormyrtorpet* (both 1917), Sjöström initiated the 'Swedish school' and opened the Golden Age of Swedish silent film – prestige productions characterised by adaptations of canonical Swedish literature and a lyrical use of landscape, and which for a while propelled Swedish cinema to the forefront of the international scene. *Terje Vigen* was based on Ibsen, and *Körkarlen/The Phantom Carriage/Thy Soul Shall Bear Witness* (1920), as well as *Tösen från Stormyrtorpet*, on Selma Lagerlöf, a particularly important writer for Sjöström. Films such as *Tösen från Stormyrtorpet* and *Berg-Ejvind och hans hustru/The Outlaw and his Wife* (1918), in which, as Louis Delluc* put it in 1919, 'The visual beauty of the images is doubled by their psychological harmony', also crystallise Sjöström's treatment of the Swedish landscape, as expressive of the psychological states of characters (an early cinematic use of landscape as pathetic fallacy) as well as having a dramatic presence and aesthetic function in its own right. As C. A. Lejeune* wrote in 1931, 'With the Scandinavians, as with no other people in the world, we get a vivid sense of inborn life in every stick and stone.' Location shooting was key to the Swedish school, and Sjöström often used the great cinematographer Julius Jaenzon* to develop a style marked by lyrical intimacy, expressed through the handling of space and light (particularly remarkable in *Körkarlen*, both in the realist scenes and in the 'fantastic' ones, where he makes imaginative use of super- impositions).

Sjöström went to Hollywood in the 1920s, where – under the name of Seastrom – he directed a number of films, of which *He Who Gets Slapped* (1924) but especially *The Scarlet Letter* (1926) and *The Wind* (1928), both starring Lillian Gish and Lars Hanson*, are the most remarkable. He returned to Sweden at the time of the coming of sound, which virtually marked the end of his directing career, though he continued to act, both on screen and on stage. In the 1940s he worked as a producer at Svensk Filmindustri (the former Svenska Bio) and supported the young Ingmar Bergman*, for whom, in 1957, he played the part of the ageing Professor Isak Borg on a journey of self-discovery in *Smultronstället/Wild Straw- berries*, one of the most impressive performances in Swedish cinema. LGA/BF

Other Films: In Sweden: *Ett hemligt giftermål/A Secret Marriage, En sommarsaga/A Summer Tale* (1912); *Äkten- skapsbyrån/The Marriage Bureau, Löjen och tårar/Ridicule and Tears, Lady Marions sommarflirt/Lady Marion's Summer Flirtation, Blodets röst/The Voice of Blood, Livets konflik- ter/Life's Conflicts, Miraklet/The Miracle, Prästen/The Priest* (1913); *Kärlek starkare än hat/Love Stronger than Hate, Halvblod/Half-Breed, Strejken/The Strike, Högfjällets dot- ter/Daughter of the Highlands, Dömen icke/Do Not Judge, Bra flicka reder sig själv/A Good Girl Fends for Herself, Gatans barn/Children of the Street, Hjärtan som mötas/Hearts that Meet, Sonad skuld/Debt Redeemed* (1914); *En av de många/One out of Many, Det var i maj/It Was in May, Landshövdingens döttrar/The Governor's Daughters, Skomakare bliv vid din läst/Keep to Your Trade, Judaspengar/Judas Money, I prövningens stund/In the Hour of Trial* (1915); *Skepp som mötas/Ships that Meet, Havsgamar/Sea Vultures, Hon segrade/She Won, Thérèse, Dödskyssen/The Kiss of Death* (1916); *Ingmarssönerna (del I och II)/The Sons of Ingmar (pts I and II)/Dawn of Love, Hans nåds testamente/His Grace's Will* (1919); *Klostret i Sendomir/The Monastery of Sendomir, Karin Ingmarsdotter/ Karin, Daughter of Ingmar, Mästerman/A Lover in Pawn/ Masterman* (1920); *Vem dömer?/Love's Crucible, Det om- ringade huset/The Surrounded House* (1922); *Eld ombord/Fire on Board/The Hell Ship/Jealousy* (1923); *Markurells i Wadköping/The Markurells of Wadköping, Väter und Söhne* [Ger. version of *Markurells i Wadköping*] (1931). **In the US**: *Name the Man* (1923); *Confessions of a Queen* (1924); *The Tower of Lies* (1925); *The Divine Woman* (1927); *A Lady to Love, Die Sehnsucht jeder Frau* [Ger. version of *A Lady to Love*] (1929). **In the UK**: *Under the Red Robe* (1937).

SKLADANOWSKY, Max
Berlin 1863–1939

German film pioneer. From 1892, in collaboration with his brother Emil (Berlin 1859–1945), Skladanowsky constructed a double projection apparatus which was patented in 1895 under the name of the 'Bioskop' (Bioscope). The Bioskop made possible the first public presentation of moving pictures in Germany at the Berlin Wintergarten on 1 November of the same year, six weeks ahead of the Lumière brothers' first screening. Apart from this opening programme, which con- sisted of nine short sketches, Skladanowsky put together a second series of Berlin city views for touring through Germany in 1896–97 (*Berlin Alexanderplatz*). However, the Bioskop proved uncompetitive against both domestic (Messter*) and French (Lumière*) machines. Skladanowsky attempted to find other ways of commercially exploiting his invention and had a modest success with photograph flip books. MW

Bib: Barbara Cantow (ed.), *Max Skladanowsky und die Erfindung des Kinos* (1993).

SKOLIMOWSKI, Jerzy   Łódź 1938

Polish director. A poet, actor, athlete and ex-boxer, Skolimowski co-scripted Andrzej Wajda's* *Niewinni Czarodzieje/Innocent Sorcerers* (1960) and Roman Polanski's* *Nóż w Wodzie/Knife in the Water* (1962). His first feature, *Rysopis/Identification Marks: None* (1965) was made while studying at Łódź* and revealed an ironic and cynical attitude to the political optimism of the times. A distinctive film talent, Skolimowski has garnered international awards for his subsequent films. His 1967 anti-Stalinist allegory, *Ręce do Góry/Hands Up*, was banned (and not shown until 1985) and Skolimowski settled in Britain. His imaginative and original exploration of sexual awakening in *Deep End* (1970, UK) quickly established his international reputation. However, his subsequent career has fared better when he has dealt with a Polish theme: both in *Moonlighting* (1982, UK), his response to the imposition of martial law, and in *Success is the Best Revenge* (1984, UK), he deftly intertwines his experience as a Polish artist abroad with astute insights into the eccentricities of the British. Skolimowski returned to Poland to film *Ferdydurke/30 Door Key* (1991), an adaptation of a novel by Gombrowicz, one of Poland's most distinguished modern writers. AW

Other Films Include: *Walkower/Walkover* (1965); *Bariera/Barrier* (1966); *Le Départ* (1967, Belg.); *The Shout* (1977, UK); *The Lightship* (1985, US).

SKOUEN, Arne   Oslo 1913

Norwegian director, formerly a journalist and writer, who spent the World War II years in exile. Skouen is considered the first genuine *auteur* and most assured director of Norwegian cinema. He wrote the screenplays for all his films except one, and towards the end of his career established his own production company to ensure greater independence. His first film, *Gategutter/Street Urchins* (1949) – inspired by Italian neo-realism* – starred the future director Pål Bang-Hansen. Thematically, Skouen was attracted to the lives of outsiders, whether they were so by choice or oppression. In his numerous films set during the German occupation [> NORWEGIAN OCCUPATION DRAMAS], he used the theme of treason to explore this theme, while some of his later films look at handicapped children. Skouen also made a few popular comedies, characterised by warmth and humanism. A realist filmmaker, Skouen shot most of his films on location, imbuing nature and landscapes with symbolism, as evident in his most famous film, *Ni liv/Nine Lives* (1957).

Ni liv was the first Norwegian film to be nominated for an Oscar (for Best Foreign Picture). The film is based on the true exploits of war hero Jan Baalsrud, as described in David Howarth's book *We Die Alone*. In it Baalsrud and a group of comrades fall into German hands when landing in occupied Norway in March 1943, betrayed by a local shoemaker loyal to the Quisling regime. Baalsrud escapes the Germans, but then has to overcome the hostility of nature to survive. Before finally crossing into Sweden (from where his story is told in a long flashback from his hospital bed), he falls victim to snow blindness, gangrene and hallucinations; he takes refuge in a 'grave' hollowed out of the snow on a mountain slope. The film's reputation rests mainly on Skouen's brilliant representation of landscape. A 1992 poll among Norwegian cinemagoers chose *Ni liv* as the best Norwegian film ever. KS

Films: *Gategutter/Street Urchins* (1949); *Nødlanding/Emergency Landing* (1952); *Circus Fandango* (1954); *Det brenner i natt!/Burning Nigh, Barn av solen/Children of the Sun* (1955); *Ni liv/Nine Lives* (1957); *Pastor Jarman kommer hjem/The Return of Pastor Jarmann* (1958); *Herren og hans tjenere/The Master and his Servants* (1959); *Omringet/Surrounded* (1960); *Bussen/The Bus* (1961); *Kalde spor/Cold Tracks* (1962); *Om Tilla/About Tilla* (1963); *Pappa tar gull/Daddy's Success* (1964); *Vaktpostene/The Guards* (1965); *Reisen til havet/A Journey to the Sea* (1966); *Musikanter/Musicians* (1967); *An-Magritt* (1969).

SLOCOMBE, Douglas   London 1913

British cinematographer, who began his career as a photojournalist for *Life* and *Paris-Match*, becoming a newsreel camera operator during World War II before making his debut as a lighting cameraman at Ealing on *Dead of Night* (1945). Slocombe deserves much of the credit for the distinctive, unpretentious look of Ealing, his work being seen at its best perhaps in *It Always Rains on Sunday* (1947) and, in particular, in the luminous Romney Marsh locations of *The Loves of Joanna Godden* (1947). After Ealing, his career developed as a freelance cinematographer on both sides of the Atlantic, with British Academy awards for *The Servant* (1963), *The Great Gatsby* (1974, US) and *Julia* (1977, US). Since the late 1970s he has shot a number of films for Spielberg, most notably *Close Encounters of the Third Kind* (1977, US), *Raiders of the Lost Ark* (1981, US) and *Indiana Jones and the Temple of Doom* (1984, US). JC

Other Films Include: *The Captive Heart* (1946); *Hue and Cry* (1947); *Saraband for Dead Lovers* (1948); *Kind Hearts and Coronets* (1949); *The Lavender Hill Mob, The Man in the White Suit* (1951); *Mandy* (1952); *The Titfield Thunderbolt* (1953); *The Young Ones* (1961); *Freud* [US], *The L-Shaped Room* (1962); *Guns at Batasi, A High Wind in Jamaica* (1965); *Dance of the Vampires* (1967); *The Music Lovers* (1970); *Travels with My Aunt* (1972, US); *Jesus Christ Superstar* (1973, US); *Rollerball* (1975, US); *Never Say Never Again* (1983).

SLOVENIA – see YUGOSLAVIA (former)

SLUIZER, George   Paris, France 1932

Dutch director and producer. Bilingual, Sluizer studied film at IDHEC* in Paris, graduating in 1956. He became an assistant to leading Dutch documentary film-maker Bert

Haanstra* and travelled extensively, shooting films for the Royal Dutch/Shell oil company such as *De lage landen/Hold Back the Sea* (1961) and *The World of Chemistry* (1964). After making documentaries in Ireland and Brazil (among other countries), and various shorts, Sluizer returned to Brazil to make his debut feature, the Dutch-financed *João en het mes/João*, in 1972. There followed a large number of documentaries and the English-language, Amsterdam-based adaptation of the Dutch novel *Twee vrouwen/Twice a Woman* (1979), starring Bibi Andersson* and Anthony Perkins. He produced another Dutch literary adaptation, *Het jaar van de kreeft/Year of the Cancer* (1975), for director Herbert Curiël. After the Mexican documentary *Tepito Si!* (1982) and an experimental American feature, *Red Desert Penitentiary* (1985), Sluizer directed a Franco-Dutch psychological thriller about a kidnapping, entitled *Spoorloos/L'Homme qui voulait savoir/The Vanishing* (1988), and based on a novel by Dutch author Tim Krabbé. The international success of the film, which launched the career of Dutch actress Johanna ter Steege, led to a watered-down Hollywood remake, also directed by Sluizer for 20th Century-Fox and called *The Vanishing* (1993, starring Jeff Bridges and Kiefer Sutherland). Previously, Sluizer had adapted Bruce Chatwin's novel *Utz* (1992), starring Armin Mueller-Stahl. In 1995 he directed *The Tenants*. HB

(1969), her mutation into the perpetual 'neurotic spinster' may be a disappointment. The success of her best known screen role in *The Prime of Miss Jean Brodie* (1969) locked her into the stereotype, demonstrating her ability to draw a triumphant pathos out of comic mannerisms and a slightly ludicrous sensitivity. The role has been repeated with varying blends of triumph, pathos and comedy, and always with consummate skill. In Jack Clayton's low-key *The Lonely Passion of Judith Hearne* (1987) she animates the type with real feeling, but rather too often, as in her playing of the lonely Charlotte Bartlett in *A Room with a View* (1985), there is a sense of watching Maggie Smith doing her thing, and her later career in the cinema seems to strain a little less than it might against the leash. *Hook* (1992, US), *Sister Act* (1991, US) and *Sister Act 2* (1993, US) do little to extend her. She is, however, a highly respected actress, winning Oscars as Best Actress for her Miss Jean Brodie, and as Best Supporting Actress for *California Suite* (1978), and receiving a BAFTA Lifetime Achievement award in 1993. JC

Other Films Include: *Go to Blazes* (1962); *The V.I.P.s* (1963); *The Pumpkin Eater* (1964); *Travels with My Aunt* (1973, US); *Death on the Nile* (1978); *Clash of the Titans, Quartet* (1981, UK/Fr.); *Evil Under the Sun, The Missionary* (1982); *A Private Function* (1984).

SMIRNOV, Andrei S.   Born 1941

Russian director and scriptwriter, who studied in Mikhail Romm's* workshop at VGIK*, graduating in 1962. His 1967 short film, *Angel*, from the story by Yuri Olesha, was made as part of a planned portmanteau film to mark the fiftieth anniversary of the Russian Revolution, *Nachalo nevedomogo veka/The Beginning of an Unknown Century*. However, the films' bleak vision, and in particular *Angel*'s shocking account of the savagery of the Civil War, caused them to be shelved for twenty years, until *Angel*, and Larisa Shepitko's* *Rodina elektrichestva/Homeland of Electricity*, were released in 1987. In *Belorusskii vokzal/The Belorussian Station* (1971), Smirnov uses an encounter between four war veterans to contrast the idealism of their life at the front with the compromises of the postwar period. His next film, *Osen'/Autumn* (1975), an intimate story of a passionate love affair, had restrictions placed on its release, and his 1979 *Veroi i pravdoi/By Faith and Truth* was so radically altered by censorship that Smirnov abandoned direction in disgust and turned to writing plays and scripts. In May 1986, at the Fifth Congress of the Union of Cinematographers*, Smirnov was elected to the board, and from 1988 to 1990 he served as acting First Secretary of the Union. In the late 1980s Smirnov played a leading part in getting hitherto banned films to Soviet viewers and in encouraging new talents. JGf

SMITH, G. A.   George Albert Smith; Brighton 1864 – Hove 1959

British pioneer inventor and producer, who was one of the leading figures, with James Williamson* and Esme Collings, of the 'Brighton School'. A portrait photographer, he developed his own camera in 1896, and went on to anticipate Georges Méliès* in many of the advances in trick photography. The catalogue description of Smith's *The Corsican Brothers* (July 1898) leads Barry Salt to credit him with using superimposition, or 'spirit photography', before Méliès and Smith are believed to have corresponded with each other. Salt also credits Smith with the first 'true temporal and action continuity' in *The Kiss in the Tunnel* (1899) and the first scene dissection in *Grandma's Reading Glass* (1900), in which a boy looks at various objects through a magnifying glass. In association with Charles Urban, Smith patented Kinemacolor, the only commercially viable two-colour process before Technicolor, and he spent much of the rest of his career developing it, with Urban, in the Natural Colour Kinematograph Company, using colour most effectively in the feature-length *The Durbar at Delhi* (1911). JC

Bib: Barry Salt, *Film Style and Technology: History and Analysis* (1983)

SMITH, (Dame) Maggie   Ilford 1934

British actress. To anyone who recalls Maggie Smith's highly charged Shakespearean roles in the theatre of the 1960s, her tragic Desdemona repeated on film (*Othello*, 1965), or even the vivacity of her cameo trouper in *Oh! What a Lovely War*

SMOKTUNOVSKY, Innokenti M.   Tatyanovka, Siberia [USSR] 1925 – Moscow 1994

Russian actor. Smoktunovsky trained in Krasnoyarsk and began acting on stage in 1946 and on screen in 1957. He first came to prominence with one of the leading roles in Mikhail

Romm's* *Devyat' dnei odnogo goda/Nine Days of One Year* (1962) and achieved international recognition in the title role of Grigori Kozintsev's* Shakespeare adaptation, *Gamlet/Hamlet* (1964), which won him the Lenin Prize in 1965. He played a wide range of roles from the comic to the composer *Chaikovskii/Tchaikovsky* (Igor Talankin, 1970), a prizewinner at San Sebastian. He was Mozart in *Motsart i Sal'eri/Mozart and Salieri* (1962) and Salieri in *Malen'kie tragedii/The Little Tragedies* (1980), and after 1976 regularly appeared with the Moscow Art Theatre. RT

SMOLJAK, Ladislav

Prague 1931

and

SVĔRÁK, Zdenĕk

Prague 1936

Czech writers, actors and directors. Smoljak and Svĕrák made their reputations as the principal playwrights and producers of the Jára Cimrman Theatre. Their success in the 'normalised' cinema of the 1970s and 1980s was all the more remarkable given their reputation for black and absurdist humour. After an initial success as actors/writers on *Marečku, podejte mi pero!/Mareček, Pass Me a Pen* (1976) and *Jáchyme, hod' ho do stroje!/Joachim, Put it in the Machine!* (1974), directed by the veteran comedy film-maker Oldřich Lipský, they moved to the production of their own scripts with Smoljak as director. These ranged from the absurdist *Rozpuštěný a vypuštěný/Dissolved and Let Out* (1983), a detective story in which the main character is twinned with a clockwork replica, to perhaps their best film, *Kulový blesk/Ball Lightning* (1978), a brilliant ensemble film about how to move apartments in Prague. Familiar for their cameo roles in other people's films, they also worked with Jiří Menzel* (*Na samotě u lesa/Seclusion Near a Forest*, 1976), while Svĕrák wrote the scripts for two Oscar-nominated films: Menzel's *Vesničko má, středisková/My Sweet Little Village* (1985), and his son Jan Svĕrák's *Obecná škola/The Elementary School* (1991). In 1993, Svĕrák scripted Menzel's *Život a neobyčejná dobrodružství vojáka Ivana Čonkina/The Life and Extraordinary Adventures of Private Ivan Chonkin*, and collaborated on Jan Svĕrák's *Akumulátor 1*. PH

Other Films as Writers: *At' žijí duchové!/Long Live Ghosts!* [Svĕrák only] (1977); *Vrchní, prchni!/Run, Waiter, Run!* [dir. Smoljak], *Trhák/Smash Hit* (1980); *Jára Cimrman, ležící, spící/Jára Cimrman, Lying, Asleep* (dir. Smoljak, 1983); *Nejistá sezóna/Uncertain Season* (d. Smoljak, 1987).

SNEZHKIN, Sergei

Born 1954

Russian director, who studied at VGIK*. His first major success was *ChP raionnogo masshtaba/Emergency on a Regional Scale* (1988), from the story by Yuri Polyakov, which exposed corruption and cynicism in the Young Communist League, a subject sensitive enough to cause the film to be widely banned. He followed it with *Nevozvrashchenets/Non-returnee* (1990), from the popular story by Alexander Kabakov, a dystopian vision of the imminent Russian future. JGf

SOCIALIST REALISM

Socialist Realism was the official doctrine supposedly governing all artistic practices in the Soviet Union and its dependent states (it was imposed as a constituent part of the Soviet hegemony over Central and Eastern Europe after 1945) from its proclamation at the First Congress of Soviet Writers in August 1934 until the collapse of the Soviet system in 1991. Socialist Realist art had, above all, to be easily accessible and 'intelligible to the millions'. It therefore eschewed experimentation in both form and content. It consisted of two fundamental elements. The first was 'Realism', in the tradition of nineteenth-century critical realism, depicting a reality that audiences would recognise and feel familiar with. This realism could be critical, but only if the criticism furthered the revolutionary cause, as defined by the authorities of the moment. The second element was 'Revolutionary Romanticism', a romanticism that looked forward to the future communist utopia and explained and justified whatever sacrifices or difficulties were currently required. This meant in practice that Socialist Realism could mean different things to different people in different situations at different times. As Stalin's cultural henchman Zhdanov noted in 1934, the artist had to depict life 'not simply as "objective reality", but to depict reality in its revolutionary development'. Probably the most succinct definition of Socialist Realism was given in 1933 by a somewhat cynical Anatoli Lunacharsky*: 'Socialist Realism depicts not reality as it is, but as it *ought* to be.' RT

SÖDERBAUM, Kristina

Stockholm 1909

Swedish-born actress. On account of her marriage to Veit Harlan* and her Nordic, child-like features, Söderbaum became famous for leading parts in Nazi melodramas and propaganda films: *Jud Süss* (1940), *Immensee* (1943), *Die goldene Stadt* (1942), in which Harlan's *mise-en-scène* made her into the foremost symbol of the fascist obsession with racial purity ('Reinheitsfanatismus'), riding, virtually naked and on a white stallion, into the sea to sacrifice herself in *Opfergang* (1944). From 1951 (*Unsterbliche Geliebte*) to 1958 (*Ich werde Dich auf Händen tragen*) she starred in seven more films, showing a hitherto unplumbed depth in her acting, which, together with her historic associations, made her an impressive apparition when in Hans Jürgen Syberberg's* *Karl May* (1974) she once more stepped in front of the camera. KU

Bib: Kristina Söderbaum, *Nichts bleibt immer so: Rückblenden auf ein Leben vor und hinter der Kamera* (1983).

SOKUROV, Alexander N.

Podorvikha, Russia [USSR] 1951

Russian director. After a career in television from 1969 to 1975 in Gorky (Nizhny Novgorod), where he attended university, Sokurov studied at VGIK* (1975–78), though he would later state categorically: 'I got nothing out of VGIK.' Though now recognised as among the most important

Russian directors of the last two decades, Sokurov's work remained invisible until the intervention of the Conflict Commission of the Union of Cinematographers*, set up in 1986. This released from the notorious 'shelf' the feature films *Odinokii golos cheloveka/The Solitary Voice of Man* (1978), a poetic version of the Platonov story filmed so differently by Andron Mikhalkov-Konchalovsky* as *Maria's Lovers*, and his free adaptation of Shaw's *Heartbreak House* known as *Skorbnoe beschuvstvie/Mournful Indifference/ Anaesthesia Dolorosa* (1983), as well as a number of documentaries. *Maria* (1975–88) began as a study of a typical collective-farm worker, but when Sokurov returned in 1988 Maria was dead and her husband and daughter parted by feuding. Among other shelved documentaries eventually released were *Sonata dlya Gitlera/Sonata for Hitler* (1979); *Al'tovaya sonata. Dmitrii Shostakovich/Sonata for Viola. Dmitri Shostakovich* (1981); *Zhertva vechernaya/Evening Sacrifice* (1984), a montage of people returning from a demonstration in Leningrad; and *Elegiya/Elegy* (1985), a vision of Russia's fate based on the career of the great bass Chaliapin. Since then Sokurov has continued a prolific career in documentaries and features. His documentaries include *Moskovskaya elegiya/Moscow Elegy* (1987), made in memory of Andrey Tarkovsky*, as well as *Sovetskaya elegiya/Soviet Elegy* (1989) and *Primer intonatsii/An Example of Intonation* (1991), both about Boris Yeltsin. The feature *Dni zatmeniya/Days of Eclipse* (1988) casts a young Russian doctor adrift in a remote Central Asian town, and deploys a continually dynamic camera and inventive soundtrack to create a haunting picture of alienation. *Spasi i sokhrani/Save and Protect* (1989) is a challenging version of *Madame Bovary* set in the Caucasus. In *Krug vtoroi/The Second Circle* (1990), a young man returns to the flat of his deceased father, and Sokurov provides a relentlessly austere vision of the Soviet way of death, an examination he deepens in *Kamen'/Stone* (1992). Sokurov's concern with death and the significance of human life continues in two films made in 1993, the documentary *Elegiya iz Rossii/Russian Elegy*, which incorporates late nineteenth-century photographs and early twentieth-century war footage, and the feature *Tikhie stranitsy/ Whispering Pages*, set in a St Petersburg of the mind and steeped in the dark world of the 'insulted and the injured' of nineteenth-century Russian literature. JGf

SOLDATI, Mario   Turin 1906

Italian director and writer. A well-known writer of both fiction and non-fiction (*America primo amore/America – First Love*, 1935), Soldati studied for a while at Columbia University in New York. Unable to obtain US citizenship, he returned to Italy and joined Cines* in 1931, soon becoming an assistant director and a leading scriptwriter. He scripted films for Alessandro Blasetti* (*La tavola dei poveri/The Poor Men's Table*, 1932), for Walther Ruttmann* (*Acciaio/Arbeit macht Frei/Steel*, 1934), and for Augusto Genina* (*Castelli in aria/Ins blau leben/Castles in the Air*, 1939, Ger./It.). But his most famous collaboration was with Mario Camerini*, for whom he worked as assistant director and scriptwriter. His first full feature as director was *Dora Nelson* (1939), a comedy of mistaken identity starring Camerini's wife Assia Noris*.

He then went on to direct a number of successful adventure films and light comedies throughout the 1940s and 1950s. Sceptical of the cinema's potential as an art, he claimed that he only made films because they brought in more money than writing. Nevertheless he achieved distinction with his adaptations of nineteenth-century novels, notably Antonio Fogazzaro's *Piccolo mondo antico/Old-Fashioned World* (1941) and *Malombra* (1942), which aligned him with the so-called 'calligraphic' school of film-makers who concentrated on visual refinement and elegance as a deliberate withdrawal from Fascist culture. Unlike others in the calligraphic school, however, Soldati did not wholeheartedly embrace neorealism* after the war, preferring to make popular genre films for producers such as Carlo Ponti* and Dino De Laurentiis*, for instance *La donna del fiume/Woman of the River* (1954), which gave Sophia Loren* one of her early starring roles. JHa

Other Films as Director Include: *Tutto per la donna/Anything for the Lady* (1940); *Quartieri alti* (1943, released 1945); *Le miserie del signor Travet/His Young Wife* (1945); *Eugenia Grandet* (1947); *Her Favourite Husband* (1950, UK); *O.K. Nerone/OK Nero* (1951); *I tre corsari/Three Pirates* (1952); *Jolanda – la figlia del Corsaro Nero* (1953); *Policarpo, ufficiale di scrittura/Policarpo, Master Writer* (1959).

SOLER LEAL, Amparo   Madrid 1933

Spanish actress, who grew up in a theatrical family and made her screen debut in 1952. She made a considerable number of mainstream popular films, in roles that alternated between comedy (for instance Luis García Berlanga's* 'National' trilogy) and melodrama. In the latter she was often a tormented soul, her almond-shaped, lazy, secretive eyes mixing mystery or forcefulness with pathos. Her role in Fernando Fernán Gómez's* *Mi hija Hildegart/My Daughter Hildegart* (1977) as the monstrous matriarch, whose prohibition of her daughter's relations with men leads to disastrous consequences, brings out her steely qualities, while her comic talents are more in evidence in films like Pedro Almodóvar's* *¿Qué he hecho yo para merecer esto?/What Have I Done to Deserve This?* (1984). PWE

SOLINAS, Franco   Cagliari 1927 – Fregene 1982

Italian scriptwriter, possibly the most important and most coherent Marxist writer in European cinema during the 1960s and 1970s. After apprenticeship with Stefano Steno and Mario Monicelli*, he turned his novel *Squarciò*, about Sardinian poachers, into the script for *La grande strada azzurra/The Wide Blue Road* (1957), directed by Gillo Pontecorvo*, with whom he had already worked on *Giovanna* (1957, an episode of *Die Windrose*, Ger.). His association with Pontecorvo continued for *Kapò* (1960), *La battaglia di Algeri/The Battle of Algiers* (1966) and *Queimada!/Burn!* (1969), all of which present civilian suffering with documentary rigour in their uncompromising rejection of totalitarianism. Solinas showed a particular interest in ambiguous anti-heroes animated by some sort of historical awareness. It was in this spirit that he wrote *Salvatore*

Giuliano (1962, dir. Francesco Rosi*), *Etat de siège/State of Siege* (1973, Fr./It./Ger., dir. Costa-Gavras*) and *Il sospetto* (1975, dir. Francesco Maselli*) [> ITALIAN POLITICAL CINEMA], as well as *Mr. Klein* (1977, Fr./It., dir. Joseph Losey*). Solinas also made a significant contribution to the Italian Western* with *Quién sabe?/A Bullet for the General* (1966), *La resa dei conti/The Big Gundown* (1967), *Il mercenario/A Professional Gun* (1968) and *Tepepa/Blood and Guns* (1969). Before his death Solinas wrote a splendid script for Losey on *Ibn Saud* (1969), the unifier and first king of Saudi Arabia. It was never made into a film but was published posthumously as *La battaglia* (1984). MMo

Other Films Include: *Persiane chiuse/Behind Closed Shutters* (1950); *Ombre bianche/The Savage Innocents* (1960, It./Fr./US); *Vanina Vanini* (1961); *Una vita violenta* (1962); *Le soldatesse* (1965); *Hanna K.* (1983).

SOLOVYOV, Sergei A. Kem, Russia [USSR] 1944

Russian director and scriptwriter. After working in television (1960–62), Solovyov studied at VGIK*, graduating in 1968 from the workshop of Mikhail Romm* and Alexander Stolper. His first work as a director was literary adaptations: two episodes from Chekhov stories in *Semeinoe schast'e/Family Happiness* (1970), a version of Gorky's *Egor Bulychev i drugie/Yegor Bulychev and Others* (1971), and the television film *Stantsionnyi smotritel'/The Stationmaster* (1972), from Pushkin. But Solovyov's main concern has been the lives of modern young people. *Sto dnei posle detstva/One Hundred Days After Childhood* (1975), *Spasatel'/Lifeguard* (1980) and *Naslednitsa po pryamoi/Direct Descendant* (1982) are all about the growing pains of young adults. In *Chuzhaya belaya i ryaboi/The Wild Pigeon* (1986) the cosmonaut hero recalls his postwar childhood and his craze for pigeons. During the 1980s Solovyov taught at VGIK*. In the late 1980s he ran the Krug (Circle) production division for new projects, and made two eclectic films with the artists and aesthetics of the new rock culture. *ASSA* (1988) is a tale of the Soviet mafia and the new youth set in wintry Yalta, with music by Boris Grebenshchikov and a central role for Viktor Tsoi, singer with the famous group 'Kino'. It was followed by the eccentric farce of *Chërnaya roza – emblema pechali, krasnaya roza – emblema lyubvi/Black Rose Stands for Sadness, Red Rose Stands for Love* (1989). Eccentricity also features prominently in Solovyov's next film, *Dom pod zvëzdnym nebom/A House Below the Starry Sky* (1992). JGf

SONEGO, Rodolfo Florence 1921

Italian scriptwriter, an important contributor to neo-realism* with scripts for *Achtung banditi!* (1951, dir. Carlo Lizzani*), *Roma ora 11* (1952, dir. Giuseppe De Santis*), and two films by Alberto Lattuada*, *Anna* (1952) and *La spiaggia/The Beach* (1954). His own comic vein emerged in the mid-1950s. He was one of the scriptwriters on *Totò e Carolina* (1953), one of the best of the many (often mediocre) films starring Neapolitan comedian Totò*. But what finally brought Sonego into the world of *commedia all'italiana**, and marked a turn-

ing point in his career, was his encounter with Alberto Sordi*, for whom he wrote scripts for many years. *Il seduttore* (1954) is a landmark of the genre, both a mature version of earlier dialect farces and the introduction of new themes, social milieux (the emerging middle classes) and modes of thinking. Further films included *Il marito* (1958), *Il moralista* (1959), *Il vedovo/The Widower* (1959), *Il vigile/The Cop* (1960) and *Il diavolo* (1963), all depicting the hypothetical 'average' Italian on which Sordi successfully built his image. Sonego's masterpiece – and the best of Sordi's many roles – was undoubtedly *Una vita difficile/A Difficult Life* (1961), an exemplary parable of an ex-partisan who refuses the 'liberal' yet conformist new moral thinking of Italy's economic miracle. The success of this film was also due to skilful direction by Dino Risi*, for whom Sonego also provided the story for *Il sorpasso/The Easy Life* (1962). The collaboration with Sordi continued through the 1970s, producing two more films of note: *Detenuto in attesa di giudizio* (1971) and *Lo scopone scientifico* (1972). PDA

SORDI, Alberto Rome 1920

Italian actor and director. Though less well-known internationally than some of his compatriots, such as Marcello Mastroianni* and Vittorio Gassman*, Sordi is one of the funniest and most successful postwar Italian actors. His career began in the early 1940s in variety. For the cinema he dubbed Oliver Hardy's voice and on the radio (in the late 1940s) he developed a pair of successful characters – Mario Pio and Conte Claro – who became the basis of his screen persona. After he appeared in Federico Fellini's* *Lo sceicco bianco/The White Sheik* (1952) and *I vitelloni/The Spivs* (1953), a character was created for him in Stefano Steno's episode film *Un giorno in pretura* (1953). This character, based on the new lifestyle imported into Italy by the 'liberators', and further elaborated in Steno's *Un americano a Roma*, initiated a long and prosperous career. Sordi was the new young suburban Roman, voluble and uninhibited in his way of dressing. This exhilarating character ran through more than twenty years of Italian cinema and society, maturing as he went along, and generating a counter-history 'from the bottom' of Italy's profound changes from Fascism to the '*anni di piombo*' (literally 'leaden years', of terrorism) and up to the 1980s. In the late 1980s and early 1990s, Sordi's prime concern has been a series of television programmes significantly entitled *Storia di un italiano*, 'The story of an Italian'. But the best of his work, under the guidance of talented scriptwriters (Age* and Scarpelli*, Sonego*) and directors, was in the 1950s and 1960s. With Mario Monicelli's* *La grande guerra/The Great War* (1959), Luigi Comencini's* *Tutti a casa/Everybody Go Home!* (1960) and Dino Risi's* *Una vita difficile/A Difficult Life* (1961), Sordi added dramatic weight and stature to his comic acting without sacrificing the 'anti-hero' image which has become, for better or worse, a model of Italianness. Beginning with *Fumo di Londra/London Smoke* (1966), Sordi also directed himself in a number of films. Although he rarely found again the balance of his golden years, he has continued to enjoy success with some excellent roles, such as the tragic father figure in Monicelli's *Un borghese piccolo piccolo/An Average Man* (1977). PDA

Other Films as Actor Include: *Mamma mia, che impressione!* (1951); *Il seduttore* (1954); *Un eroe dei nostri tempi* (1955); *Il conte Max* (1957); *Fortunella, ladro lui, ladro lei* (1958); *Il moralista* (1959); *I magliari* (1959); *Il giudizio universale/The Last Judgment* (1961); *Il commissario, Il mafioso* (1962); *Il boom* (1963); *Il medico della mutua* (1968); *Nell'anno del signore/In the Name of the Lord* (1969); *Lo scopone scientifico* (1972); *L'ingorgo/Bottleneck* (1979); *Il marchese del Grillo* (1981). **As Director**: *Amore mio aiutami* (1969); *Polvere di stelle/Stardust* (1973); *Finchè c'è guerra c'è esperanza* (1974); *Il comune senso del pudore* (1976); *Le vacanze intelligenti* (1978); *Io e Caterina* (1980); *Io so che tu sai che io so* (1982); *In viaggio con papà* (1982); *Il tassinaro* (1983); *Tutti dentro* (1984); *Un tassinaro a New York* (1987); *Assolto per avere commesso il fatto* (1992).

SOUTENDIJK, Renée P.   The Hague 1957

Dutch actress. Soutendijk gave up her training as an Olympic gymnast for an acting career. Stage, film and television parts followed graduation from the Dutch Academy of Performing Arts. Her appearance in Wim Verstappen's* *Pastorale 1943* (1978) was already a revelation, but the real breakthrough came when Paul Verhoeven* offered her a leading role in *Spetters/Hunks* (1980), in which she plays the ambitious beauty of the fish and chip stall who works her way up the social ladder. Soutendijk endows her characters with a winning combination of phlegm and passion, ambition and compassion – witness the resistance fighter Hannie Schaft in *Het meisje met het rode haar/The Girl with the Red Hair* (1981) or the emotionally complex Hedwig in Nouchka van Brakel's* *Van de koele meren des doods/Hedwig/The Cool Lakes of Death* (1982). Verhoeven and Ben Verbong cast her in other lead parts, for instance in *De vierde man/The Fourth Man* (1983) and *De flat/House Call* (1994), but here they appealed less to her intelligent acting than to the controlled splendour of her physical presence. She also starred in several international productions of the fantastical genre, such as *Eve of Destruction* (1990). KD

Bib: Hans Beerekamp, 'Renée Soutendijk', *Nederlands Jaarboek Film 1985* (1985).

SOUTTER, Michel   Geneva 1932–91

Swiss director, part of the group of film-makers, including Claude Goretta*, Alain Tanner*, Yves Yersin* and Jean-Louis Roy, who were at the core of the loosely termed 'new Swiss cinema' of the 1960s and 1970s. Soutter worked as assistant to Goretta and Jean-Jacques Lagrange and for French Swiss television from 1964, directing dramas, films and documentaries on artists. His early black and white features – *La Lune avec les dents* (1966), *Haschisch* (1967), *La Pomme* (1968) and especially *James ou pas* (1970) and *Les Arpenteurs* (1972) – are ironic and subtle comedies about the paralysing narrowness and ponderousness of Swiss society. He pursued these themes while moving on to colour and French co-productions, attaining international recognition with

L'Escapade (1973) and *Repérages* (1977). The appeal of Soutter's films, which include *L'Amour des femmes* (1982), *Adam et Eve* (1983) and *Signé Renart* (1985), derives from his way of representing Swiss society with incisiveness, humour and tenderness. MW/GV

Bib: Michel Boujut, *L'Escapade ou le cinéma selon Soutter* (1973).

SOVIET (AND RUSSIAN) FILM PRESS

The film press has played a particularly important part in the history of the Russian and Soviet cinema. Before the Revolution the established press tended to regard cinema as something like a toy and virtually ignored it. The rapid growth in cinema, and the cut-throat competition, led to different studios producing their own promotional magazines. In the 1920s a variety of regional and interest groups continued this tradition, but with the centralisation of the industry in the 1930s the situation changed. Since 1936 the principal theoretical and historical journal, which also reviews current films, has been *Iskusstvo kino* ('The Art of Cinema'), published monthly. Many leading film-makers, from Sergei Eisenstein* and Dziga Vertov* onwards, have published articles even when their film-making activities were officially out of favour. On the other hand, it was often through this journal that official disapproval was first made explicit as, for example, with the denunciation of Boris Shumyatsky* in January 1938. In the late Soviet period a mass-circulation popular illustrated magazine was also produced and translated into several languages, including English, under the title *Sovetskii ekran* ('Soviet Screen'). In recent years, as *Iskusstvo kino* has moved towards a discussion of more popular and imported films, such as *Crocodile Dundee* or the work of Sylvester Stallone, scholarly research and historical documentation have been increasingly focused elsewhere, since 1988 particularly in *Kinovedcheskie zapiski* ('Scholarly Film Notes'), produced by a group associated with the Cinema Research Institute of the Russian Cinema Committee in Moscow. RT

SOVIET MONTAGE

Early Russian film critics homed in on movement and space as the distinctive characteristics of cinema as opposed to theatre, and it fell to Lev Kuleshov* to define the manner in which film images were cut together as the key element in marking the specificity of cinema. In 1917 he wrote: 'The essence of cinema art lies in the creativity of the director and the artist: everything is based on composition. To make a picture the director must compose the separate filmed fragments, disordered and disjointed, into a single whole and juxtapose these separate fragments into a more advantageous, integral and rhythmical sequence, just as a child constructs a whole word or phrase from separate scattered blocks of letters.' He termed this process 'montage', and it formed the basis of the so-called 'Kuleshov effect' when, with his pupils, Kuleshov demonstrated the different meanings an audience would attribute to the same shot when it was placed in different sequences.

Sergei Eisenstein* went further, proclaiming montage to be the basis of cinema art. But his idea of a 'montage of attractions' was not one of building bricks but of objects in collision, producing an explosion that would arouse the viewer. In its more sophisticated form this became known as 'intellectual montage', the foundation for the 'intellectual cinema' exemplified by his film *Oktyabr'/October* (1927). Eisenstein went on to examine ways of incorporating sound, and later also colour, into his montage system, investigating the possibility of establishing common denominators for audio-visual montage. Dziga Vertov* also believed that montage represented the essence of cinema and he too experimented with sound, although his principal concerns were to create a new sense of cinematic space and time through the use of montage. It was in Soviet cinema that the notion of montage was most extensively examined and promoted, yet the early practitioners of the Soviet montage school of film-making would have been the first to acknowledge their debt to what they termed 'Americanism', acclaiming D. W. Griffith as the pioneering exponent of montage and *The Birth of a Nation* (1915) and *Intolerance* (1916) as paradigms of the techniques involved. RT

SOVIET STATE CINEMA ORGANISATIONS

Russian cinema became the first nationalised cinema in the world by decree on 27 August 1919, but it was not until 1922 that the first state production and distribution organisation, Goskino, was established. Starved of funds, it did not produce the goods and in January 1925 it was replaced by Sovkino. This was also short of funds and made commercially oriented films in order to compete with the imports that dominated the market and make money for further production. At a Party conference in 1928, Sovkino was severely criticised for putting 'cash before class', and it was in turn replaced in 1930 by a more centralised body, Soyuzkino, shortly afterwards headed by Boris Shumyatsky* with his vision of a 'cinema for the millions'. The increasing importance of cinema as a propaganda weapon at a time of great economic, social and political upheaval – the period of forced collectivisation and rapid industrialisation and urbanisation – led to a further reorganisation in 1934 when Soyuzkino gave way to GUKF, which was directly under the control of the Council of People's Commissars. It was at this time that the studio system which survived until the 1980s was established, with Mosfilm in Moscow, Lenfilm in Leningrad, and so on, and central studios for documentaries (TsSDF) and children's films (Soyuzdetfilm). GUKF itself survived the Great Terror, even if the individuals who peopled it did not, and in 1946 it was replaced by a Ministry of Cinematography, which in turn survived until 1954, when it was subsumed into the Ministry of Culture. In 1963 responsibility for cinema was again devolved, to Goskino, the State Cinema Committee, which, like GUKF, was directly responsible to what was now the Council of Ministers. Goskino was dissolved after the collapse of the Soviet Union in 1991 and post-Soviet cinema is now facing the shock of privatisation. RT

SOVIET UNION (FORMER)

Cinema first came to Russia in May 1896 as a music-hall turn when the Lumière* brothers' Cinematograph was demonstrated between two acts of an operetta performance in St Petersburg and gained immediate popular success. In the early years itinerant tradesmen travelled from town to town with a selection of short films imported from France. Cinema's novelty attracted audiences. The writer Maxim Gorky saw the new invention at the Nizhny Novgorod annual fair in 1896 and was one of the first to realise its potential, describing it as 'the kingdom of the shadows ... so unusual, so original and so complex'. In the same year the first newsreel filming in Russia took place – of the coronation of Tsar Nicholas II. The itinerant tradespeople gradually built up an audience for the new medium, so that by 1903 the first permanent cinemas were being opened in Moscow and St Petersburg, while Pathé* and Gaumont* opened offices in Moscow to cope with the increased demand.

Initially cinemas were installed in what had previously been shops or private apartments, and it was only gradually that Russian cinemas acquired the later conventional shape of the long auditorium. The early films depended very much on the novelty value of the moving picture, but as audiences slowly became more sophisticated the films became longer and more complex. By 1907–08 the filmgoing public was large enough, and sufficiently demanding, to warrant the production of the first Russian feature films, based on events from Russia's turbulent history, Drankov's (uncompleted) *Boris Godunov* and *Sten'ka Razin*. These were followed by a series of adaptations from the Russian classics: Pushkin's *Pikovaya dama/The Queen of Spades* (1910) and *Yevgeni Onegin/ Eugene Onegin* (1911), Tolstoy's *Zhivoi trup/The Living Corpse* and *Kreitserova sonata/The Kreutzer Sonata* (both 1911) and works by Chekhov, Gogol and Dostoyevsky. In 1912, two years after Tolstoy's death, Yakov Protazanov* made a film, using both newsreel footage and staged action, entitled *Ukhod velikogo startsa/The Departure of a Grand Old Man*. Its ending showed Tolstoy being led into heaven hand-in-hand with an angel. The Orthodox Church regarded this as blasphemous and the film was not released in Russia. Indeed the Church exercised considerable censorship over cinema, of which it generally disapproved as morally reprehensible and even degenerate, at least in part because the foyers of some cinemas in the larger cities were frequented by prostitutes. The tsar also viewed cinema with some disdain. In 1913, despite allowing his family to be filmed with some frequency, he was to describe cinema as 'an empty, totally useless, and even harmful form of entertainment ... It is complete rubbish and no importance whatsoever should be attached to such stupidities.' Because of its demotic appeal and its concentration in the towns and cities of the Empire, cinema appeared to threaten the old order – spiritual, political and aesthetic – and that is why it first appealed to artistic iconoclasts such as the Futurists, above all the poet Vladimir Mayakovsky, who was later to script and act in a number of films.

Despite – or perhaps to some extent because of – the prevailing climate of disapproval, audiences for the 'forbidden fruit' of film grew rapidly until, on the eve of World War I, the audience for cinema outstripped that for all other forms of urban entertainment put together. The war increased the desire for escapism and boosted audiences even further, but it also hindered the import of films and caused an explosion in Russian film production, dominated by Alexander Khanzhonkov*, Pavel Thiemann and Reinhardt, and Iosif Yermolev, and bringing the names of Protazanov and Yevgeni Bauer* in particular to the fore. Bauer's films were heavily influenced by the tenets of Russian literary Symbolism, exploring themes at the margins of society and of life and death. Indeed it was almost *de rigueur* for pre-Revolutionary films to have an unhappy ending, following the tradition of Russian melodrama. The *kheppi end*, as it became known, was added purely for export. The war years also produced the first home-grown stars of the Russian cinema – Vera Kholodnaya*, who was to die in the influenza epidemic in 1918, and Ivan Mosjoukine*, who emigrated after the Revolution.

The tsarist government was slow to realise the propaganda potential of film. At first, as elsewhere in Europe, all filming at the front was banned; later it was placed in the hands of a veterans' charity, the Skobelev Committee. Some propaganda shorts were made, but on the whole the potential of Russian cinema for war propaganda remained unrealised. After the February Revolution of 1917 the Provisional government set up the first government newsreel, *Svobodnaya Rossiya* ('Free Russia'), but very few newsreels were released and they were not widely distributed.

When the Bolsheviks seized power in October 1917, cinema was not an urgent priority for them: survival was. Their coup did, however, frighten a significant number of film producers, artists and entrepreneurs into leaving the cities of northern Russia and fleeing to the Crimea, still held by White forces in the ensuing Civil War, and many later emigrated altogether, to France, Germany or Hollywood [> EMIGRATION AND EUROPEAN CINEMA, EUROPEAN CINEMA AND HOLLYWOOD]. The Civil War itself helped the Bolsheviks to realise that, if they were to survive, they needed an effective propaganda weapon to win over the hearts and minds of a hostile population and to maintain morale in the ranks of the Red Army. They chose cinema: as Lenin* remarked, in contrast to Nicholas II, 'Of all the arts, for us cinema is the most important.' As a silent visual medium it could appeal to the more than three-quarters of the population who were illiterate and to an audience who spoke more than a hundred different languages and had different cultural standards; as a portable medium it could be transported to wherever it was most useful. Moving pictures had a dynamism and simplicity lacking in the other media available at the time and therefore appealed to everybody, especially the all-important population of the rural areas (including regions populated by ethnic minorities) who had mostly never seen a film before. For them cinema was to be the technological wonder that presaged mechanisation and industrialisation and demonstrated the progressive nature of the new government. That was the theory, but the reality at first was somewhat different. During the Civil War agit-films* were used in a network of agit-trains and ships to maintain morale and propagandise the population of areas newly captured from White forces. At the same time, in August 1919, the government issued a decree nationalising all cinema property. This was more a gesture than a reality: many of those active in pre-Revolutionary cinema had fled

the country, taking their expertise, and in some cases their portable property, with them. After years of wartime neglect the cinema network was in poor repair and lines of production and distribution had broken down. Above all, there was a chronic shortage of materials and equipment, and an attempt at importation from the USA proved abortive.

The end of the Civil War in March 1921 led to the introduction of the relatively liberal New Economic Policy, designed to release enterprise to bring Russian production up to 1913 levels. A variety of mainly regionally based official organisations began to compete for business against the first centralised state cinema organisation, Goskino, established in 1922 but never adequately funded. At the end of 1924, against a barrage of complaints about its failings, Goskino was replaced by Sovkino, which subsumed some of the other organisations and was granted an all-important monopoly over import and export. The middle to late 1920s are associated in the Western mind with the 'golden age' of Soviet silent cinema and with such giant figures of the avant-garde as Sergei Eisenstein*, Lev Kuleshov*, Vsevolod Pudovkin* and Dziga Vertov*. But their works, especially the documentaries of Vertov and his Cine-Eye group, were neither widely distributed nor widely seen. These film-makers were determined to create a new perception of reality through identifying the essence of cinema specificity in the theory and practice of montage*. But montage, at least as they practised it, tested popular audiences who preferred to be entertained, so that the diet of the average Soviet cinemagoer in this period differed little from that of audiences in most advanced countries in Europe or North America. Chaplin, Keaton and, above all, Mary Pickford and Douglas Fairbanks were as popular in the USSR as elsewhere in Europe. Even films by lesser directors that attempted to highlight contemporary social problems, such as Abram Room's* *Tret'ya Meshchanskaya/Bed and Sofa/Third Meshchanskaya Street* (1927), failed to stimulate widespread audience interest even when they provoked a critical scandal. The most popular Soviet films were those that imitated Hollywood melodrama, made by men like Protazanov, one of the few survivors from the pre-Revolutionary era.

The tenth anniversary of the Revolution in 1927 was a time for taking stock. Cinema's production levels, like those of other branches of industry, had risen to match 1913 levels but film had still scarcely penetrated beyond the urbanised areas of the Soviet Union. The anniversary produced a range of celebratory avant-garde films (such as Eisenstein's *Oktyabr'/October*, Vertov's *Odinnadtsatyi/The Eleventh Year*, Esfir Shub's* *Padenie dinastii Romanovykh/The Fall of the Romanov Dynasty* or Pudovkin's *Konets Sankt-Peterburga/The End of St Petersburg*) that failed to strike a popular chord. In January 1928 Anatoli Lunacharsky*, who, as People's Commissar for Enlightenment, had overall political responsibility for cinema, remarked on the need to bring 'cinema closer to the masses, especially the rural masses' and observed that 'boring agitation is counter-agitation'. In March 1928 the Party held its first conference on cinema and demanded a complete reorganisation, criticising Sovkino for emphasising 'cash rather than class', and calling for 'a cinema that is intelligible to the millions'. The task of creating this cinema was eventually entrusted to an Old Bolshevik, Boris Shumyatsky*, who became head of the recently formed

Soyuzkino in October 1930. He called it a 'cinema for the millions', a cinema that would be both ideologically effective and entertaining.

The 'cultural revolution' that accompanied the rapid industrialisation and forced collectivisation of the first Five Year Plan period from 1928 to 1932 was characterised by a brutal cultural iconoclasm in the name of 'proletarian culture'. In a desperate attempt to forge the new Soviet citizen, all perceived forms of bourgeois influence were ruthlessly attacked and rooted out. This campaign in cinema coincided with the advent of sound, for which the Soviet Union was ill equipped and poorly prepared, being unable to choose at first between optical and mechanical sound systems. Striving to achieve self-sufficiency in the production of the necessary film stock and equipment, to expand the cinema network through the new collective farms into the countryside, to establish cinema studios in the national republics, and to provide that extended network with suitable films, proved more than the protagonists of proletarian cultural hegemony had bargained for, and in April 1932 the Party decided to call a halt to partisan campaigning and abolished all proletarian cultural organisations in cinema and elsewhere.

This was but a prelude to the proclamation of the official cultural doctrine of Socialist Realism* at the First Congress of Soviet Writers in August 1934: its tenets were adopted by the Congress of Workers in Soviet Cinema in January 1935, a month after the assassination of the Leningrad Party chief, Sergei Kirov, had unleashed the first purges of the Great Terror. But the brave proclamations 'for a great cinema art' were belied by increasing difficulties. The transition to sound was more prolonged and wasteful than had been anticipated and the advent of sound had complicated the spread of cinema to the national republics. Film production was still grossly old-fashioned and inefficient compared to that of the West, and the rapid political changes associated with the Great Terror were making it more difficult for film-makers to complete politically acceptable films, and more hazardous to embark on the film-making process in the first instance. Soviet cinema had been bedevilled since its inception by recurrent 'screenplay crises' since, despite official exhortations, writers continued to regard scriptwriting as an inferior activity to 'real' writing. Their disdain was reinforced by the insecurity engendered by the purges.

In an effort to overcome this crisis, Shumyatsky led a delegation to the West in the summer of 1935: they visited Paris, New York, Hollywood and London (and the rest of the delegation also went to Babelsberg [> NATIONAL SOCIALISM AND GERMAN CINEMA], by then the powerhouse of the Nazi film industry) and returned to produce a draft proposal for a studio complex in the Crimea to be known as 'Cine-City' or, more popularly, 'the Soviet Hollywood'. The project was, however, too grandiose and proved to be a fatal albatross around Shumyatsky's neck: he fell victim to the purges in January 1938, when he was arrested, denounced as a 'fascist cur' and subsequently shot. Many lesser-known colleagues – directors, scriptwriters and actors – were banished to the Gulag or perished in the purges too. But Shumyatsky's legacy – the notion of a cinema that was both entertaining and ideologically effective – shaped Soviet sound cinema, and his ghost was to haunt it until its demise.

In 1936 what had hitherto been referred to as 'film fac-tories' became 'film studios', as part of Shumyatsky's 'Hollywoodisation' process, and film directors were increasingly obliged to involve themselves in the training of new generations of film-makers. At the height of his troubles over *Bezhin lug/Bezhin Meadow*, for instance, Eisenstein was made a Professor at VGIK*. A workshop system was introduced which ensured that old and young worked in tandem and a continuity of ideas and practices was assured. This led initially to a higher technical and artistic quality in Soviet films, but in the longer term to timidity and stagnation. But it did ensure a familiar style with which audiences felt increasingly comfortable, as for instance in Grigori Alexandrov's* series of superficially escapist musical comedies, which also represented one of the few examples of films in which the heroic role model was played by a woman. Greater contact with reality was, however, also maintained through a series of overtly anti-fascist films, of which Eisenstein's *Aleksandr Nevskii/Alexander Nevsky* (1938) is probably the most widely known example.

When Nazi Germany attacked the USSR in June 1941, cinema was again mobilised to maintain and boost morale, at first through newsreel footage and a series of short 'fighting film albums', and later through a number of costume pictures recalling significant episodes from Russian history, such as the war against Napoleon. The greatest of these historical epics, Eisenstein's *Ivan Groznyi/Ivan the Terrible* (1943–46), was also from the official point of view the most disturbing, and the second part was banned until 1958. The war created a sense of solidarity against a common enemy and the peace that eventually followed built upon this foundation to create the period of high Stalinist culture [> STALIN] that marked the apotheosis of the personality cult, in which the heroicised depiction of the war itself played a central role, as in Mikhail Chiaureli's* *Klyatva/The Vow* (1946) and *Padenie Berlina/The Fall of Berlin* (1949). The centrality of cinema to the creation of this culture was underlined by the establishment of a separate Ministry of Cinematography in 1946 and by a further wave of purges unleashed by Zhdanov, who by this time was effectively Stalin's cultural commissar. Ironically, severe 'screenplay crises' in these years necessitated the release of around fifty 'war booty' films retrieved from Babelsberg by the invading Red Army in 1945. At the height of the Cold War, Nazi propaganda films such as *Ohm Krüger/Uncle Krüger* (released as *Tranzvaal' v ogne/The Transvaal in Flames*), *Mein Leben für Irland/My Life for Ireland* (released as *Shkola nenavisti/School for Hatred*) or *Titanic* (released as *Gibel' Titanika/The Loss of the Titanic*) filled a significant gap in the film schedules and fed Soviet audiences with the anti-British propaganda that their own cinema industry was unable to provide in sufficient quantity.

After Stalin's death in 1953 and Khrushchev's 'secret speech' in 1956 denouncing the excesses of the personality cult, Soviet cinema turned to less heroic themes and began to examine the downside even of heroism, in war films such as *Letyat zhuravli/The Cranes Are Flying* (1957) and *Ballada o soldate/The Ballad of a Soldier* (1959), for example. This tendency may well have been in part encouraged by greater familiarity with more downbeat, smaller-scale films regularly produced by other socialist countries in Eastern Europe. In 1957 the Union of Cinematographers* of the USSR was established, ostensibly to protect the interests of film-makers but actually to help the authorities control both them and their output. It collaborated in this process with Goskino, the State Committee for Cinematography, set up in 1963.

Although the Brezhnev 'period of stagnation' produced its own more laughable versions of the Stalinist cult films, exaggerating the new leader's historical role in the war and the development of Soviet socialism, the filmgoer's diet moved increasingly towards 'chamber' films dealing with everyday problems (while not, of course, explicitly criticising the system that had created or exacerbated those problems), and mass entertainment pictures. Throughout this period a complex system of censorship and differentiated categories of release meant that experimental films (such as those of Andrey Tarkovsky* or Sergo Paradzhanov*) continued to be made in state studios, but were usually given only limited release. In peripheral republics film-makers achieved a more substantial degree of freedom, albeit still limited: in Georgia and Latvia, in particular, this was reflected, for example, in the work of film-makers such as Tengiz Abuladze*, Irakli Kvirikadze* or Jūris Podnieks*. Nevertheless, many films, such as Alexander Askoldov's* Komissar/The Commissar, Alexei German's* Moi drug Ivan Lapshin/My Friend Ivan Lapshin, or the works of Kira Muratova* were shelved for years because of their theme, content or treatment, or all three. The leading foreign films were often available for viewing by film-makers, but not at this stage by audiences, although from the late 1970s onwards popular international films were increasingly imported for mass consumption, among them My Fair Lady and Crocodile Dundee.

With the advent of glasnost* and perestroika, following the appointment of Mikhail Gorbachev as Communist Party General Secretary in 1985, Soviet cinema entered its death throes. In 1986, in an act unprecedented in Soviet history, the Fifth Congress of the Union voted in a new and radical board headed by Elem Klimov*, which really did aim to protect the interests of film-makers against political and other forms of interference. The Conflict Commission that the Union then established unshelved many banned films from the Brezhnev period and, when released, a number of them attracted vast audiences, the best example being Abuladze's Monanieba/Repentance, which was also widely distributed in the West. Film-makers were now able to address hitherto taboo subjects such as the Stalinist labour camps (Marina Goldovskaya's Vlast' solovetskaya/Solovki Power, 1988), sex and social problems (Vasili Pichul's* Malen'kaya Vera/Little Vera, 1987), ecological disaster, drugs, prostitution or AIDS.

The disintegration of the USSR after the abortive coup of August 1991 and the increasingly hectic pace of the transition to a market economy undermined the unique position that Soviet cinema had held in the Soviet state: the two institutions disappeared together. Audiences feverishly demanding the hitherto largely forbidden earthly delights of consumerist societies further West, and above all America, undermined the market even for domestic popular films. Specialist films continue to be made, increasingly with money invested by Western companies or the nouveaux riches of the new Russian mafias, but in mainstream production 'Soviet Hollywood' – as in the 1920s – has failed to keep pace with its American mentor, quite simply because the real Hollywood does Hollywood films better. If Soviet cinema has by now disappeared, Russian cinema is in danger of following in its foot-

steps in the looming chaos of transition to shadowy notions of capitalism and democracy. A seminal chapter in the history of European and world cinema has come to an end. RT
[> MEZHRABPOM, SOVIET (AND RUSSIAN) FILM PRESS, SOVIET STATE CINEMA ORGANISATIONS]

SPAGHETTI WESTERNS – see ITALIAN WESTERNS

SPAIN

The exhibition and production of films in Spain date from 1896, with the screening of the Lumière* brothers' shorts L'Arrivée d'un train en gare de la Ciotat and La Sortie des usines Lumière, and the making of the Jimeno brothers' Salida de misa de doce del Pilar de Zaragoza/Leaving High Mass at the Pilar Cathedral, Zaragoza. The first fiction film made in Spain was Riña en un café/Fight in a café (1897), by Fructuoso Gelabert*, whose early efforts were matched by Segundo de Chomón's* experiments, using techniques paralleling those developed by Georges Méliès* in France.

After the initial faltering steps of the pioneer period, the early years of sustained film production were characterised by a series of zarzuelas (operettas) and literary adaptations. Early adaptations of Spanish classics include Don Juan Tenorio (1909, dir. Ricardo de Baños), the dramatist Benavente's version of his own play Los intereses creados/Vested Interests (1918), and El Lazarillo de Tormes (1925, dir. Florián Rey*). Spanish intellectuals and artists soon developed an interest in the cinema – Benavente, for example, founded Madrid Cine in 1919 – but this was a trend given its most sustained expression in the 1920s through the enthusiasm of the so-called 'Generation of 27'. During that period La Gaceta Literaria began to publish film reviews, film clubs sprang up in Madrid and Barcelona, and writers began to acknowledge or refer to the cinema in their work. But the initial emphasis on material originating in stage or literary sources meant that in the work of early directors, like Julio Buchs, Spanish cinema failed at first to engage directly with everyday life. Buchs's contemporaries Florián Rey and Benito Perojo went on to make even more impact on the history of Spanish cinema. These two directors made some of the most successful musicals (folklóricas*) and melodramas of the 1920s and 1930s, both genres emphasising regional and local customs. Among the more significant of Rey's films were those based on literary texts by Palacio Valdés: La hermana San Sulpicio/Sister San Sulpicio (1927 [silent] and 1934 [sound]) and La aldea maldita/The Cursed Village (1929, considered by most the masterpiece of Spanish silent cinema; sound version, 1942), an ultra-conservative narrative about a woman's transgression and eventual embrace of traditional notions of family honour. Covering the same sort of thematic territory as Rey's, Perojo's work is perhaps best represented by the female sinner turned saint narrative, Malvaloca/Hollyhock (1927), and the folksy musical La verbena de la Paloma/Paloma Fair (1935).

Even though by 1914 there were more than 900 cinemas in Spain, with a turnover of more than 20 million pesetas, the native market was soon to a large extent colonised by

Hollywood, mainly because of the failure of Spanish industrialists to recognise the economic potential of the new medium. Poor investment led to the rapid closure of the considerable number of film companies that had mushroomed (in 1916 all seventeen companies set up in Barcelona two years previously folded), as well as to unavoidable reliance on foreign films, technology and hardware. Eventually, in 1919, the government did respond to mild pressure from the Unión Cinematográfica Española (Spanish Film Society), who were asking for subsidies and protectionist policies – above all to curb the number of foreign film screenings – but too little too late was achieved at a time of economic hardship in a country that could not afford the realistically competitive heavy expenditure demanded by the industry. National economic instability was soon compounded by the consequences of worldwide Depression. Eventually, too, the coming of sound, and the necessary investment in replacing equipment for production and exhibition, made even more burdensome the industry's already crippling expenses.

The socio-political changes that took place in Spain following the collapse of the dictatorship of Primo de Rivera (1924–29) eventually led, after an interregnum heralding the formation of the Second Republic in 1931, to a healthier economic and political climate for film-making. While the new Republican government was slow both in realising the industry's potential and in providing it with the necessary financial support and protectionist policies, the changed atmosphere in the country generated the industry's own various initiatives. Spanish film production rose from six films in 1932 to twenty-eight in 1936. Sound stages were built in Barcelona and Madrid, major studios were formed – such as Cifesa* (in Valencia, 1932) – documentary as well as feature film production began to flourish, and a film-going culture, already well established, saw the number of cinemas reach the very respectable figure of 3,000 nationwide.

Most films made in the 1930s avoided overtly political issues. At the same time, films on serious themes, though often not welcome even in Republican times, were now being made – Luis Buñuel's* Las Hurdes/Land Without Bread (1932) on regional poverty, Fernando Roldán's Fermín Galán (1932) on political dissent, Perojo's erotically permissive social satire, El hombre que se reía del amor/The Man Who Laughed at Love (1933). This was the period, too – with feminism making significant advances in Europe and America – which marked the appearance of Spain's first woman film-maker, Rosario Pi. Setting up her own film company, and writing screenplays, she also directed El gato montés/The Wild Cat (1936) and Molinos de viento/Windmills (1939).

In the immediate pre-Civil War period the Spanish film industry boomed, reflecting the left-right split that would eventually lead to the outbreak of war in 1936. The period of hostilities (1936–39) saw, at both ends of the political spectrum, a substantial reduction of feature film production. But, since they played a crucial part in the propaganda war also being waged on both sides, documentaries and newsreels flourished. Notable films on the Right included Romancero marroquí/Moroccan Ballad (1939), eulogising the contribution to the Nationalist effort by Moorish forces, while on the Left, films like Nuestros enemigos/Our Enemies (1937) denounced the failure of Western democracies to defend the Republic.

In the cinema, Franco's triumph led to what has been described as 'the hour of silence'. From this point onwards, only film-makers embracing Francoist ideology could expect to achieve any measure of success. In the new climate directors either adapted themselves, often reluctantly, to prevailing realities, or else – like Sáenz de Heredia*, for instance – welcomed them with undisguised enthusiasm. Nevertheless, regardless of wartime sympathies, some directors (José López Rubio, Luis Marquina, Edgar Neville*) retained their liberal convictions, making films which, while not actually criticising the new state of affairs, managed to avoid the apolitical banalities or triumphalist endorsements favoured by the regime and happily provided by numerous other directors. This was the period of Spain's strictest laws of censorship*, the obligatory dubbing of all foreign films, and the rise of Cifesa. It was also a period of renewed popularity for literary adaptations, partly because the censors showed a greater tolerance for prestigious literary authors. Rafael Gil*, for instance, made Don Quijote de la Mancha (1947), and Eloísa está debajo de un almendro/Eloisa is Underneath an Almond Tree (1943), from the play by Jardiel Poncela. Two of the best adaptations of the period are Sáenz de Heredia's Mariona Rebull (1947), from a novel by Ignacio Agustí, and Neville's Nada/Nothing (1947), from Carmen Laforet's novel. A new version of Rey's El Lazarillo de Tormes (1959, dir. Fernández Ardavín) received the Golden Bear in Berlin.

Yet, despite these extremely adverse conditions for film-making, dissenting voices began to be heard. The faltering steps taken by Neville and others perhaps encouraged Juan Antonio Bardem* and Luis García Berlanga* to take more confident strides towards the creation of a cinema engaging with everyday life. Their collaboration Esa pareja feliz/That Happy Couple (1951) recalled in some ways the populist comic melodramas of Frank Capra, but it also drew heavily on the native dramatic tradition of the sainete, or one-act farce. The film was, like El último caballo/The Last Horse (Neville, 1950) or Surcos/Furrows (José Antonio Nieves Conde*, 1951), characterised by its adoption of Italian neo-realist* techniques [> SPANISH NEO-REALISM]. Subsequent films, made independently by Bardem and García Berlanga, continued to tackle issues disapproved of by the government, a policy that inevitably led to confrontations with the censors.

Both men were key figures in the famous 'Conversaciones de Salamanca' conference (14–19 May 1955), which encouraged film-makers to take greater risks, while earning the contempt of the government. As an increasing number of film-makers (Marco Ferreri*, Carlos Saura*, José Luis Borau*, Jaime Camino*, Vicente Aranda* and many others) were now prepared to question the orthodoxies of the day, a 'New Spanish Cinema'* forced itself into existence, a difficult parturition partly made possible by the appointment of another Salamanca 'congresista', José María García Escudero, as Director General of Film. The presence, too, of the mildly liberal Manuel Fraga Iribarne at the Ministry of Information and Tourism, as well as policies designed to help improve the government's image abroad, ensured that this generation of film-makers, individual directors as well as group-identified figures like those belonging to the Barcelona School*, could work in an atmosphere of relative apertura (openness) and posibilitismo (greater opportunity), making films in sharp opposition to mainstream popular genres: religious films*, films with child stars*, historical films*, melodrama, comedy* or musicals (directed by, among others, Ladislao Vajda*, Rafael Gil* or Sáenz de Heredia, and starring Joselito, Marisol, Sara Montiel* or Paquita Rico*). Literary adaptations also continued to be made. One of the most successful in the 1960s was Miguel de Unamuno's *La tía Tula/Aunt Tula* (1964, dir. Miguel Picazo*). Pérez Galdós was also adapted several times in this period, in *Fortunata y Jacinta* (1969) and *Marianela* (1972), Pedro Olea's* *Tormento/Torment* (1974) and, most famously, Luis Buñuel's* *Tristana* (1970). This was the period, too, of increased co-productions, a trend epitomised above all by the making of Italian Westerns* in Almería or Samuel Bronston-produced epics in studios set up just outside Madrid.

Towards the end of the 1960s, the Spanish film industry entered another period of crisis. Although the government seemed to relax its attitudes by setting up in 1967 art-house cinemas for the screening of foreign art movies, films made by dissidents continued to be handicapped by censorship, and film production in general fell in 1968 to forty-eight exclusively Spanish productions. In a period, too, of the peseta's devaluation and a government debt in subsidies to the film industry that stood, by 1970, at 300 million pesetas, the climate of *apertura* was beginning to vanish, and the regime's death rattle was now sounding its last discordant notes. In 1975 Franco died and film-makers could begin at last to speak the hitherto unspeakable, without needing metaphor and allegory. At this point the *Tercera Vía** (third way) genre of film-making of the early 1970s – a type of film combining popular appeal with social criticism, and steering a course between dissent and endorsement of official ideology – also lost its *raison d'être*. While memories of the Civil War and its legacy have continued to haunt some film-makers, the past has at last begun to fade and the majority of film-makers now address contemporary issues.

The most immediate effect on film-makers of the abolition of censorship in 1977 was the *destape* phenomenon, the mania for nudity both in popular and *auteur* films. Less frivolously, Spanish films, exemplified above all by Pedro Almodóvar's*, began to recapture the heterogeneity, colour, irreverence and sensuality of Spanish life. The voices of gay (such as Eloy de la Iglesia*) and women directors (such as Pilar Miró* and Josefina Molina*) began to be heard, in a film industry now sufficiently revitalised to produce outstanding work. In the period of UCD (Conservative Party) government that followed the end of Francoism, free market policies had proved disastrous for an industry ill-equipped to survive without subsidies and foreign imports control. Yet the protectionist policies of the *Decretos* Miró (1983), Semprún (1989), and more recently the GATT agreement of 1993, have failed to give the Spanish film industry a proper basis for development. Increasing financial difficulties have made producers rely heavily on the cultural prestige of literary adaptations. Most acclaimed among them were two films by Mario Camús*: *La colmena/The Beehive* (1982), from the novel by Nobel Prize-winner Camilo José Cela, and *Los santos inocentes/The Holy Innocents* (1984), from a novel by Delibes. Another important literary adaptation was Victor Erice's* *El Sur/The South* (1983), based on a short story by Adelaida García Morales, though maybe the most interesting recent group of adaptations are those directed by Aranda. Despite these successes,

the failures of government policy have compounded the adverse effects of the video boom and the continuing unassailable popularity of Hollywood films and their publicity machines. Three hundred cinemas closed down in 1983; by 1984 only 3,354 cinemas were left in the whole of Spain. Even so, with films like *Belle Epoque* (1992, dir. Fernando Trueba*), stars like Antonio Banderas* and others making their mark internationally, and with young directors like Almodóvar, Juanma Bajo Ulloa*, and Julio Medem*, or older ones like Saura, Borau, Miró, García Berlanga, Fernando Colomo*, Manuel Gutiérrez Aragón*, Aranda and others working in cinema or television, Spanish film-making continues to be distinguished by some of the liveliest talents of European or world cinema. PWE

CENSORSHIP IN SPAIN – see p. 75

SPANISH CHILD STARS

The child star was a characteristic phenomenon of the family-centred Francoist ideology. The first child star in Spanish cinema was Pablito Calvo (born 1946), 'discovered' by Hungarian-born director Ladislao Vajda* for *Marcelino pan y vino/Marcelino, Bread and Wine* (1955), about a boy who talks to Jesus. Vajda also directed him in *Mi tío Jacinto/Uncle Hyacinth* (1955) and *Un ángel pasó por Brooklyn/An Angel Passed Through Brooklyn* (1957). Joselito (José Jiménez, born 1947), nicknamed 'the little nightingale', inaugurated the fashion for child singers in Spanish cinema, with the immensely popular *El pequeño ruiseñor/The Little Nightingale* (1956), followed by *Saeta del ruiseñor/Nightingale Song* (1957) and *El ruiseñor de las cumbres/Nightingale of the Heights* (1958), directed by Antonio del Amo. Del Amo directed Joselito in another five films, but the inevitable disappearance of the 'nightingale' pitch in his voice brought about his rapid decline. Marisol (Josefa Flores, born 1948), first appearing as Joselito's female counterpart, became one of the greatest stars of the Spanish cinema, directed by Luis Lucia* in her first three films – *Un rayo de luz/Ray of Light* (1960), *Ha llegado un ángel/An Angel Has Appeared* (1961) and *Tómbola* (1962) – all lachrymose melodramas in which the young protagonist saves her family from social or economic disaster. She also starred in a series of adolescent comedies – *Búsqueme a esa chica/Find That Girl* (Fernando Palacios, 1964), *Cabriola/Caper* (Mel Ferrer, 1965), *Sólo los dos/Together Alone* (Lucia, 1968) and others – memorable for their optimistic view of 1960s Spanish society; she vainly tried, in the 1970s, to adopt a more sexualised image. Other child and adolescent singing stars of the 1960s were Rocío Durcal (born 1945) and Ana Belén* (born 1950).

In the 1970s, Ana Torrent (born 1966) became the child star of Spanish art cinema thanks to Victor Erice's* *El espíritu de la colmena/The Spirit of the Beehive* (1973) and Carlos Saura's* *Cría cuervos/Raise Ravens* (1975). CDe

SPANISH HISTORICAL FILMS

Spanish film genre of the immediate postwar years, characterised by Falangist ideology. Typical films include *Raza/Race*

(1941), *¡Harka!* (1941) and *¡A mí la legión!/Follow Me, Legion!* (1942). The chauvinistic obsession of these films, made by Cifesa*, remained intact while projection of this ideal shifted from male to female heroics. Films like *La princesa de los Ursinos/The Princess of the Ursinos* (1947), *Locura de amor/Love Crazy* (1948) and *Agustina de Aragón/Agustina of Aragon* (1950) achieved huge box-office success.

Franco's death signalled a re-examination of the Civil War, in films such as *Canciones para después de una guerra/Songs for After a War* (1971), *Caudillo/Leader* (1974–77), *Las largas vacaciones del 36/The Long Holidays of 1936* (1976), *Raza, el espíritu de Franco/Race, the Spirit of Franco* (1977). Although set during the conflict, *La vaquilla/The Heifer* (1985) deals with historical complexities equally relevant to the contemporary period and is, as such, representative of a didactic tendency in recent examples of the genre, which also strive to emphasise the presence of the past: *La ciutat cremada/The Burnt City* (1976), *La verdad sobre el caso Savolta/The Truth about the Savolta Case* (1978), *El crimen de Cuenca/The Cuenca Crime* (1979), *¡Ay Carmela!* (1989), *El Dorado* (1988). DK

SPANISH NEO-REALISM

Spanish film style influenced by Italian neo-realism*. Vittorio De Sica's* *Ladri di biciclette/Bicycle Thieves* (1948), first screened in Madrid and Barcelona in October 1950, had an enormous impact on Spanish film-makers, writers and opposition intellectuals. It was followed by two important Italian Film Weeks in 1951 and 1953, whose programmes showcased Italian neo-realist films and were supported by guest appearances from leading Italian figures. Spanish colleagues (many linked to the Communist Party) responded with the creation of the new film magazine *Objetivo* (1953–55) and, in 1955 (14–19 May), with the now legendary 'Conversaciones de Salamanca' conference. From the early 1950s to the early 1960s elements of neo-realism appeared in Spanish films, for instance in *Surcos/Furrows* (1951), and in Juan Antonio Bardem* and Luis García Berlanga's* co-directed first feature *Esa pareja feliz/That Happy Couple* (1951), a chronicle of the frustrations of working-class aspirations. Bardem was highly influential in developing a realist film style in Spain in the 1950s and in bringing lower-class characters and their problems to the screen. He was joined in 1955 by Marco Ferreri*, who blended the neo-realist 'look', social issues and mordant black humour. This combination was further developed by García Berlanga in *El verdugo/The Executioner* (1963), while the socially problematic side of adolescent behaviour was realistically portrayed in Carlos Saura's* *Los golfos/The Hooligans* (1959).

Spanish neo-realism had been largely promoted by Communist Party fellow travellers and sympathisers. By the early 1960s, with the Party in disarray over repeated policy failures, opposition intellectuals gradually abandoned the neo-realist aesthetic. BJ

SPANISH REGIONAL CINEMA

The uneven development of regional cinema in Spain is related to issues of political self-determination. The centralised policies of Franco's regime hindered the development of regional traditions. Spain's transition from dictatorship to a parliamentary democracy was immediately followed by a process of decentralisation of the political system. In May 1983, the reorganisation of the Spanish state into seventeen autonomous communities was established and the regional governments set out to elaborate their respective cultural programmes, including the promotion of indigenous cinema. Two of the so-called historical regions, the Basque country and Catalonia, took the lead. Catalonia's cosmopolitanism, which had informed a rich tradition of documentary and amateur cinema, thwarted after the Civil War, was kept alive in film clubs, whose existence was instrumental in the development of the Barcelona School* in the 1960s. The autonomous government initially instituted a much criticised nationalistic policy intended primarily to promote and disseminate the Catalan language, subsidising large-scale historical productions and comedies which failed to break through into a wider market. The most acclaimed productions of the 1980s, Francisco Betriu's *La Plaça del Diamant/Diamond Square* (1982) and Juan José Bigas Luna's* *Angustia/Anguish* (1987), owe more to state and television funding than to Catalan policies. The Basque administration, more pragmatically, directed its efforts towards building up a tradition of Basque film-makers with a distinctive quality, incorporating both veteran film-makers such as Imanol Uribe*, Alfonso Ungría and Pedro Olea* and new talents such as Julio Medem* and Juanma Bajo Ulloa*. The lack of an industrial infrastructure has hindered the development of other cinemas such as the Galician, whose government has only recently started subsidising films. In Castilian-speaking regions only the Community of Madrid, with an established film industry, enjoys a large market. In other regions, official funding has been sporadic and the results generally ephemeral. XR

SPANISH RELIGIOUS FILMS

Religion is a constant of Spanish cinema, present from the first truly national film, *Salida de misa de doce del Pilar de Zaragoza/Leaving High Mass at the Pilar Cathedral, Zaragoza* (1896). The 1940s and 1950s saw a plethora of '*cine de sacerdotes*' (priest films, or religious dramas), a stock genre under Franco, satisfying the censor and often attracting government subsidies for so-called 'national interest' films. Historical dramas of the recent Civil War or set in the distant past highlighted religious faith and dedication, and folkloric musicals and comedies were seldom without a clear moral or religious subtext. Such films often achieved considerable popular success, as was the case of *Balarrasa* (1950), in which a reformed reveller and would-be priest has to prove his religious commitment and resistance to worldly temptation. Other successes of the genre include folkloric or 'historical' hybrids such as the various versions of *La hermana San Sulpicio/Sister San Sulpicio* and *Alba de América/American Dawn* (1951). One of the most popular films of the Spanish child star* genre of the 1950s and 1960s, Ladislao Vajda's*

Marcelino, pan y vino/Marcelino, Bread and Wine (1954), recounts the miraculous appearance of a reincarnated Christ to a small orphan boy adopted by a community of monks.

Religious dogma and ritual also became the critical focus of many oppositional films of the 1960s and 1970s, such as Luis Buñuel's* *Viridiana* (1961), banned in Spain (after winning the 1962 Palme d'Or at Cannes) for its 'blasphemous' sequences of the burning of a crown of thorns and the Beggars' Banquet parody of Leonardo da Vinci's *Last Supper*. Films of the New Spanish Cinema* frequently linked their protagonists' emotional trauma to childhood moral/religious indoctrination. The legacy of a repressive Catholicism is clearly present in the work of contemporary film-makers like Pedro Almodóvar*, whose postmodern comedies parody the excesses of religious dogma. RM

SPIO (Spitzenorganisation der deutschen Filmindustrie/-wirtschaft)

German motion picture association. The 'Chief Organisation of the German Film Industry' was founded in 1923 as an umbrella for the film business' largest professional organisations, to act as a pressure group and crafts guild in relations with the government. It had two weaknesses: it tried to bring together too many incompatible constituents (for instance, distributors and exhibitors), and it was from the very beginning strongly dominated by Ufa* interests. The highly influential 'SPIO Plan' of Autumn 1932 featured the centralisation of the industry and its demands were met by the Propaganda Ministry and the big financial institutions when they established the Filmkreditbank in May 1933. In June 1933, SPIO was integrated in the Reichsfilmkammer, which was answerable only to Goebbels [> NATIONAL SOCIALISM AND GERMAN CINEMA]. In 1959, SPIO was revived and given added responsibilities for copyrights, patents and the commercial exploitation of films on television. SPIO is also in charge of selecting the German entries at national and international film festivals, and publishes a statistical yearbook. TE/MW

STÅHLBERG, Karl Emil   Kuhmo 1862 – Helsinki 1919

Finnish film pioneer and engineer Karl Emil Ståhlberg was the most important figure in early Finnish cinema. A businessman, producer and cinema owner, he practically launched cinema in Finland. In 1889 he founded a photographic studio, Atelier Apollo, in Helsinki. The studio expanded rapidly, and in 1892 Ståhlberg hired Frans Engström from Sweden and I. K. Inha from Finland to photograph the Finnish landscape. In terms of national identity, this project was of capital importance since Finland was then still part of Russia. In 1896 Ståhlberg went to Paris, where he bought a projector and some films. His first screening took place in the musical salon of the Students' Union at the University of Helsinki in January 1897, six months after the showing of the Lumière* Cinematograph. Ståhlberg promptly announced his aim to 'represent Finnish landscapes and natural beauty' with moving pictures. In 1904 Ståhlberg founded the first permanent cinema in Helsinki, the Maailman Ympäri ('Around

the World'), showing films imported from London and Paris, but also his own productions. The first documentary produced by Atelier Apollo was *Kuvia Eugen Schaumannin hautajaisista Porvoossa/Images from Eugen Schaumann's Funeral in Porvoo*, released in September 1906. The subject was nationally sensitive, since Schaumann had assassinated the Russian governor-general, Nikolai Bobrikoff. This film initiated a series of important national themes which became Atelier Apollo's trademark.

Atelier Apollo is also notable for producing the first Finnish fiction film, *Salaviinanpolttajat/The Moonshiners* (1907), from an idea by Teuvo Puro, an actor at the Helsinki National Theatre who also appeared in this short film. The subject was chosen by open competition, with more than 650 scripts submitted. *Salaviinanpolttajat*, like most early films produced by Ståhlberg and others, has disappeared; of the thirty-two fiction films made in Finland before 1920 only a short extract from Teuvo Puro's *Sylvi* (1913) has been recovered. Atelier Apollo was crucial to early Finnish cinema. Until its demise in 1913, the company produced around 110 films, roughly half the entire Finnish production of these early years, mostly newsreels and documentaries. HS

STAIKOV, Ljudmil   Sofia 1937

Bulgarian director and writer. Upon graduating in 1962 from the Sofia Academy of Dramatic Art (VITIS), Staikov worked as an actor and stage director in Burgas before joining Bulgarian television in 1965 as a director of short films and televised stage plays. His modern style and prolific output paved the way for the success of his first feature film at the Boyana* Studios: *Obič/Affection* (1972). A youth theme dealing with the painful side of the generation gap, it shared First Prize at the 1973 Moscow film festival. Appointed artistic manager of the Mladost (Youth) film unit at the Boyana Studios, where he specialised in historical chronicles in a thriller context – *Dopălnenie kăm zakona za zaštita na dăržavata/Amendment to the Defence of State Act* (1976) and *Iljuzija/Illusion* (1980) – Staikov crowned these state-supported achievements with the three-part epic *Han Asparuh/Khan Asparukh* (1981), the cornerstone production for the 1,300th anniversary of the founding of the Bulgarian state and the most expensive production in Bulgarian film history. It was re-edited later into an abridged English-synchronised version for world distribution, titled *681 – Veličieto na hana/681 AD – The Glory of Khan* (1983). In 1987, Staikov was appointed head of the Bulgarian Cinematography Corporation, a position he held until 1991. Despite official duties in the Ministry of Culture, he still found time to direct his heavily nationalistic *Vreme na nasilie/Time of Violence* (1988), about a clash in a village between Turks and Bulgars during Ottoman rule. RH

STALIN, Joseph V.   Gori, Georgia [Russian Empire] 1879 – Moscow 1953

Soviet dictator. Like many political leaders of his epoch, Stalin enjoyed watching films. Initially he saw cinema as a substitute for vodka, in terms of both leisure time and state revenue, but, like Lenin* (whom he succeeded in 1924), he soon realised the importance of cinema for Soviet propaganda and this led him to intervene increasingly in the production process, influencing the final release versions of, for instance, Sergei Eisenstein's* *Staroe i novoe/The Old and the New* (1929), *Aleksandr Nevskii/Alexander Nevsky* (1938) and *Ivan Groznyi/Ivan the Terrible* (1943–46), and suggesting projects like Alexander Dovzhenko's* *Shchors* (1939). The terror he unleashed on the population at large made film-makers adhere to 'Socialist Realism'* rather than actual realism and Khrushchev argued that Stalin's view of the Soviet countryside after collectivisation was entirely shaped by propaganda films, showing him what film-makers thought he wanted to see. Soviet film in this period had to be 'intelligible to the millions' and experimental notions like montage* were excoriated. Under the guidance of Boris Shumyatsky*, Soviet film-makers were encouraged to make films with a simple plot construction and a straightforward notion of good and evil, hero(ine) and villain(ess). The musical comedy genre, pioneered in the USSR by Grigori Alexandrov*, was particularly popular both with officialdom and with audiences. These films entertained the masses in the new collectivised farms and the rapidly industrialising towns and cities, while propagating the ideology of common sacrifice for the common future. Film played a central part in the propagation of the personality cult, ordinary heroes being paralleled by glorified icons from a heroicised past. The process of deification of the leader figure can be seen, for instance, in Eisenstein's *Aleksandr Nevskii* and in numerous films based on the events of the Revolution and the ensuing Civil War, but it reached its cinematic apotheosis with Mikhail Chiaureli's* *Padenie Berlina/The Fall of Berlin* (1949), presented by the Mosfilm studio to Stalin on his seventieth birthday in 1949. RT

STAMP, Terence   London 1938

British actor, who became one of the icons of 'swinging London' in the 1960s in both his screen appearances and his public life. Stamp won an Oscar nomination for Best Supporting Actor for his first film, *Billy Budd* (1962), and a Best Actor award from Cannes for *The Collector* (1965). He chose his films and his directors carefully, working with William Wyler, Joseph Losey*, Ken Loach*, John Schlesinger*, Pier Paolo Pasolini* and Federico Fellini* in the space of three years. For Pasolini, he was particularly striking in *Teorema/Theorem* (1968, It.), and much of his best work in the early 1970s was done in France or Italy. In his 1960s roles, Stamp's ethereal beauty and striking blue eyes were used to create a dangerous innocence, an almost sinister naivety. In his more commercial roles in Hollywood since General Zod in *Superman* (1978), the eyes have become harder but no less striking. His performance as Sir Larry Wildman in Oliver Stone's *Wall Street* (1987, US) threatened to steal the movie, but he has had a shortage of movies worth stealing. He gives, however, an excellent performance as a transsexual in the Australian cross-dressing comedy *The Adventures of Priscilla, Queen of the Desert* (1994). JC

Bib: Terence Stamp, *Stamp Album* (1987); *Coming Attractions* (1988); *Double Feature* (1989).

Other Films Include: *Modesty Blaise* (1966); *Far from the Madding Crowd, Poor Cow* (1967); *Blue* [US], *Histoires extraordinaires/Spirits of the Dead* ['Toby Dammit' episode; dir. Fellini] (1968, Fr./It.); *The Mind of Mr Soames* (1969); *Hu-nan* (1975, Fr.); *Divina Creatura* (1976, It.); *Meetings with Remarkable Men* (1979, US); *Superman II* (1981, US); *The Hit* (1984); *Legal Eagles* (1986, US); *The Sicilian* (1987, US); *Alien Nation, Young Guns* (1988, both US).

STAUDTE, Wolfgang   Saarbrücken 1906 – Zigarski, Slovenia 1984

German director, who emerged as a talent during the war (*Akrobat schööön*, 1943; *Ich hab' von Dir geträumt*, 1944). Working at DEFA* after 1945, he became widely known with the very first German postwar feature film, *Die Mörder sind unter uns/The Murderers are Amongst Us* (1946) and subsequently continued, first with *Rotation* (1949) and then with the Heinrich Mann adaptation *Der Untertan/The Underdog* (1951), to lead East German cinema's own dissection of the country's recent history. Staudte's decision in 1955 to continue his work in the West forced him to compromise with commercial demands. In *Rosen für den Staatsanwalt/Roses for the Prosecutor* (1959) and *Herrenpartie/Stag Party* (1964) Staudte returned to his critical stance, connecting the fascist past with West Germany's present. The public outcry that ensued virtually silenced one of Germany's most gifted and intelligent directors. TE/KU

Bib: Eva Orbanz and Hans Helmut Prinzler (eds.), *Staudte* (1991).

Other Films Include: *Die Geschichte vom kleinen Muck* (1953); *Madeleine und der Legionär* (1958); *Der Maulkorb* (1958); *Die Herren mit der weißen Weste* (1970); *Zwischengleis* (1978).

STEELE, Barbara   Liverpool 1938

British actress, who became a cult icon of Italian horror films* in the 1960s. After seeing her in a small role in one of her British films, Mario Bava* hired her for the lead in his directorial debut, *La maschera del demonio/Mask of the Demon/Black Sunday* (1960). Steele has always maintained that anyone could have played the role, but the film is structured around her physical presence, as were the horror films she subsequently made in Italy. Her operatic, gestural style of performance brought back the figure of the silent film *diva* [> DIVISMO], but it was her face in close-up that inspired a unique fetishistic fascination. With her chalky skin, high cheekbones and flowing black hair, she became the paradoxical image of a living-death mask, a head of the Medusa which the camera could never fix or penetrate as completely as the mask of the title does when its spikes are hammered into her. This snuff-movie aesthetic (similar to that of Michael Powell's* *Peeping Tom*, released the same year) is crucial to Steele's films, whose narratives perpetually suspend her as a figure of life-in-death. Steele made a few films in Hollywood and appeared in such art films such as Federico Fellini's* 8½ (1963) and, later, Louis Malle's* *Pretty Baby* (1978, US), but her career slowed down considerably after the mid-1960s and she remains indelibly associated with a short but intense phase of the Italian horror film. CJ

Other Films Include: *L'orribile segreto del Dottor Hichcock/ The Terror of Doctor Hichcock* (1962); *Danza macabra/ Castle of Blood, I lunghi capelli della morte/The Long Hair of Death* (1964).

STEINHOFF, Hans
Marienberg 1882 – Luckenwalde 1945

German director, who made his name with one of his first films, *Kleider machen Leute* (1922). During the following twelve years he became an experienced director and screenplay writer of witty entertainment movies shown all over Europe. An early Nazi sympathiser, Steinhoff was an exemplary director for promoting cleverly packaged Nazi ideology. Together with producer Karl Ritter he served the regime with powerful films of unambiguously propagandistic intent, backed by enormous budgets and top crews: *Hitlerjunge Quex* (1933), *Ohm Krüger* (1941), *Der alte und der junge König* (1935), *Rembrandt* (1942). He died in a plane crash while attempting to escape from the Red Army advancing on Prague in 1945. TE/KU

Bib: Pierre Cadars and Francis Courtade, 'Hans Steinhoff', *L'Avant-scène du cinéma*, no. 87 (March 1976).

Other Films Include: *Der Mann, der sich verkaufte, Gräfin Mariza* (1925); *Angst* (1928); *Nachtgestalten/The Alley Cat* (1929); *Die Pranke/L'Uomo dall'artiglio* (1931); *Kopfüber ins Glück* (1931; also Fr. version, *Chacun sa chance*); *Robert Koch, der Bekämpfer des Todes* (1939); *Die Geierwally* (1940); *Gabriele Dambrone* (1943).

STEINWENDNER, Kurt
Curt Stenvert; Vienna 1920

Austrian director. Steinwendner studied painting and sculpture at the Vienna Art Academy. In the 1950s he started working in Austrian cinema as a set decorator, later writing scripts and becoming a director of experimental shorts, documentaries and feature films. His films, in particular *Wienerinnen – Schrei nach Liebe* (1952) and *Flucht ins Schilf* (1953), belong on the margins of Austrian film history. They differ notably from the nostalgic 'Viennese films' of their time, and the harsh image of Vienna they give has been compared to that of Carol Reed's* *The Third Man* (1949) and to Italian neo-realism*. Steinwendner later continued to make documentaries. IR

STELLING, Jos
Utrecht 1945

Dutch director. The self-taught Stelling, who makes his living running a cinema and a bar, directed his first feature in 1974 using a non-professional cast and crew, whom he cajoled into working during weekends and holidays for less than a pittance. The medieval fresco *Mariken van Nieumeghen*, based on a classic morality play and employing very little dialogue, had to be re-edited by a professional editor. A surprise entry at Cannes, the film impressed viewers with its harsh pictorial qualities. Stelling repeated the formula in *Elckerlijc/ Everyman* (1975) and the less favourably received non-narrative portrait of the painter Rembrandt, *Rembrandt fecit 1669* (1977). He finally became something of a story-teller – though still not very keen on dialogue – with *De pretenders/ The Pretenders* (1981), about a gathering of working-class misfits in a snack bar in the wake of Marilyn Monroe's death. His next two films attracted an international following, especially in Italy where Stelling is regarded as a leading European film-maker by some critics. *De illusionist/The Illusionist* (1983) is a wordless, offbeat fable of Dutch windmill-dwellers, centred around Dutch comedian Freek de Jonge. *De wisselwachter/The Pointsman* (1986) follows the tribulations of an isolated railwayman through four seasons. In 1995, Stelling, the founding father of the Netherlands Film Festival in Utrecht, completed another large-scale period fantasy, *De Vliegende Hollander/The Flying Dutchman*, with Nino Manfredi in the starring role. HB

Bib: Bob Bertina, 'Jos Stelling', *Nederlands Jaarboek Film 1987* (1987).

STENO
Stefano Vanzina; Rome 1915–88

Italian director and screenwriter. Stefano Vanzina, who signed almost all his films simply as Steno, was one of the most prolific Italian directors of the postwar period, often functioning as co-screenwriter. At first in collaboration with Mario Monicelli* and then on his own, he directed a stream of starring vehicles for the great comedian Totò* in the 1950s, including the brilliant *Totò a colori* (1952). Although he also directed films in other genres, it was as a writer and director of comedy that he was most successful. GNS

ŠTIGLIC, France
Kranj, Slovenia 1919 – Ljubljana 1993

Slovene director. When Slovenia was looking for someone to direct its first feature film after World War II, Štiglic – a former law student, Tito partisan, cultural promoter and war correspondent turned film critic – was a perfect choice. *Na svoji zemlji/On Our Own Land* (1948) combines the spirit of resistance with a surprisingly accomplished narration [>YUGOSLAV 'PARTISAN FILMS']. Štiglic always knew how to tell stories, whether it was a search for paradise by two children in the company of a black American soldier (*Dolina miru/The Valley of Peace*, 1956; Best Actor award for John Kitzmiller at the 1957 Cannes festival), or the journey through hell of a young Jewish girl (*Deveti krug/The Ninth Circle*, 1960; Oscar nomination for Best Foreign Film). Evoking the eternal battle between good and evil in human nature, Štiglic's films create sublime moments that transcend their historical context. Such was the case with *Balada o trobenti in oblaku/Ballad of a Trumpet and a Cloud* (1961), based on a short story by Slovene writer Ciril Kosmač, in which an episode from the war was transformed into a timeless tragedy filmed with a light modernist touch. In the 1970s Štiglic 'discovered' the north-eastern region of Slovenia called Prekmurje, where he shot three films. As the title of one of them, *Povest o dobrih ljudeh/The Story of Good People* (1975), suggests, he seemed to have discovered a place where the forces of good had won out. SP

Bib: Vladimir Koch, Rapa Šuklje *et al.*, *France Štiglic* (1983).

Other Films: *Trst/Trieste* (1950), *Svet na Kajžarju/Life in Kajžar* (1952); *Volčja nok/The Night of the Wolf/One Dreadful Night* (1955); *Viza na zloto/The Visa of Evil* (1959); *Tistega lepega dne/That Fine Day* (1962); *Ne joči, Peter/Peter, Don't Cry* (1964); *Amandus* (1966); *Pastirci/Shepherds* (1973); *Praznovanje pomladi/Return of Spring/Call of Spring* (1978); *Veselo gostüvanje/Happy Marriage* (1984).

STILLER, Mauritz
Mosche Stiller; Helsinki, Finland [then Russia] 1883 – Stockholm 1928

Swedish director and actor (of Russian-Polish origin). Stiller began his career as a stage actor, first in Helsinki, then in Stockholm, where he worked at Lilla Teatern ('The Little Theatre'). In 1912 he was hired by Charles Magnusson* at Svenska Bio*, where, together with Victor Sjöström*, he became a key film-maker of Swedish silent cinema. While Sjöström was more of a realist, Stiller belonged to the tradition of international melodrama and comedy; one important strand of his work was comprised of comedies of sexual and social mores. From *Kärlek och journalistik/Love and Journalism* (1916) to *Thomas Graals bästa film/Wanted, a Film Actress/Thomas Graal's Best Film* (1917) and *Thomas Graals bästa barn/Marriage à la Mode/Thomas Graal's First Child* (1918) – the last two starring Sjöström – Stiller's comic world was one of couples involved in schemes of amorous deception, replete with visual gags. The remarkable *Thomas Graals bästa film*, which involves the melodramatic fantasies of a scriptwriter infatuated with a studio secretary, is as self-reflexive and as concerned with cinematic artifice and its comic possibilities as Buster Keaton's *Sherlock Jr.*, made seven years later. Stiller's best-known comedy of sexual manners, *Erotikon/The Bonds That Chafe* (1920), a sensation at the time for its risqué connotations, was regarded as slightly stilted compared to the playful lightness of touch of the earlier films. Nevertheless, such sophisticated comedies have been seen as anticipating those of Ernst Lubitsch*.

Stiller – like Sjöström – made literary adaptations, such as the first version of *Sången om den eldröda blomman/The Song of the Scarlet Flower* (1919) from a classic Finnish novel. Like Sjöström too he adapted the novels of Selma Lagerlöf. His *Herr Arnes pengar/Snows of Destiny/Sir Arne's Treasure* (1919) is an imaginative, powerful version of the original story, as are *Gunnar Hedes saga/Gunnar Hede's Saga* (1923)

and *Gösta Berlings saga (del I och II)/The Story of Gosta Berling (pts I and II)* (1924), although none was quite as popular as Sjöström's Lagerlöf adaptations. The first two films, however, display Stiller's own mastery of epic and allegorical representations of the Nordic landscape. *Gösta Berlings Saga*, Stiller's last Swedish film, featured future star Greta Garbo*, with whom he later left first for Berlin, then Hollywood, acting as her mentor. But while Garbo flourished in Hollywood, Stiller experienced difficulties with the studio system. He made two films, *Hotel Imperial* (1926) and *The Woman on Trial* (1927), both with Pola Negri* (and worked on three others, all completed by different directors: *The Temptress*, 1926, *Barbed Wire*, 1927, *The Street of Sin*, 1928); he returned to Sweden and died shortly after. LGA/BF

Other Swedish Films: *Mor och dotter/Mother and Daughter, De svarta maskerna/The Black Masks, Den tyranniske fästmannen/The Tyrannical Fiancé* (1912); *Barnet/The Child, Vampyren/The Vampire, När kärleken dödar/When Love Kills, När larmklockan ljuder/When the Alarm Bell Rings, Den okända/The Unknown, På livets ödesvägar/On Life's Roads of Destiny/The Smuggler, Den moderna suffragetten/The Modern Suffragette, Gränsfolken/Brother Against Brother/People of the Border, En pojke i livets strid/A Boy in the Battle of Life, Mannekängen/The Mannequin* (1913); *Bröderna/The Brothers, När svärmor regerar/When Mother-in-law Reigns, För sin kärleks skull/For One's Love's Sake, Stormfågeln/The Stormbird/A Daughter of Russia, Skottet/The Shot, Det röda tornet/The Red Tower* (1914); *När konstnärer älskar/When Artists Love, Lekkamraterna/The Playmates, Madame de Thèbes/The Son of Destiny, Hans hustrus förflutna/His Wife's Past, Hans bröllopsnatt/His Wedding Night, Mästertjuven/The Son of Fate/The Master Thief, Hämnaren/The Avenger, Minlotsen/The Mine-Pilot, Dolken/The Dagger* (1915); *Lyckonålen/The Lucky Pin, Kampen om hans hjärta/The Struggle for His Heart, Vingarne/The Wings, Balettprimadonnan/The Ballet Prima Donna/Anjuta, the Dancer* (1916); *Alexander den Store/Alexander the Great* (1917); *Fiskebyn/The Fishing Village* (1920); *Johan, De landsflyktige/The Exiles* (1921).

STORARO, Vittorio
Rome 1940

Italian cinematographer. A graduate of the Centro Sperimentale* (1960) and of Camillo and Luigi Bazzoni's school, Storaro made his debut as director of photography with Franco Rossi's *Giovinezza, giovinezza* (1969), his only black-and-white film. This creative *'metteur en lumière'* is linked first and foremost with Bernardo Bertolucci*, having been in charge of photography on all but one of his films from *Strategia del ragno/The Spider's Stratagem* (1970) to *Little Buddha* (1993). For Bertolucci, Storaro is 'the hand of the painter which I am not and never will be', the artist who miraculously manages to 'give physical form to an idea of light or colour'. A theorist of 'photographic ideology', he produced two very different versions of Paris in *Il conformista/The Conformist* (1970) and *Ultimo tango a Parigi/Last Tango in Paris* (1972), worked with natural light in *Novecento/1900* (1976) and with symbolic and tonal effects in *La luna* (1979), followed by the inventiveness of *The Last Emperor* (1987) and *The Sheltering Sky* (1990), in which he fully demonstrated his ability to 'write' with light. The only European cinematographer to win three Oscars, Storaro found new critical and professional recognition in America for his work with Francis Ford Coppola on *Apocalypse Now* (1979), especially in the extensive night scenes; *One from the Heart* (1982), in which he experimented with electronics and used different colours to portray different characters; *Tucker: The Man and His Dream* (1988); and the Coppola episode of *New York Stories* (1989). Also notable were his contributions to Warren Beatty's *Reds* (1981) and *Dick Tracy* (1990). Among other directors for whom he produced innovative work were: Salvatore Samperi (*Malizia*, 1973, and *Scandalo*, 1976); Dario Argento* (*L'uccello dalle piume di cristallo/The Gallery Murders*, 1970); and Giuseppe Patroni Griffi (*Addio fratello crudele/Tis a Pity She's a Whore*, 1971, and *Identikit*, 1973). Mention should also be made of Storaro's television work, from Rossi's serial *Eneide* (1970) to *Orlando Furioso* (1972), a complex adaptation by the great theatre director Luca Ronconi, and from the high-definition experiments of Giuliano Montaldo's *Arlecchino a Venezia* to Marvin J. Chomsky's *Peter the Great* (1985, for NBC). MMo

STORCK, Henri   Ostend 1907

Belgian director. Next to Charles Dekeukeleire*, one of Belgium's pioneering documentary film-makers, whose work is as impressive and prolific as it is diverse. An early influence was a group of artists in Ostend, among them painters such as James Ensor. After working in photography, Storck read Léon Moussinac's *Naissance du cinéma* and decided to make films. He was Jean Vigo's* assistant on *Zéro de conduite* (1933).

Storck's first documentaries – *Trains de plaisir/Pleasure Trains* (1930), *Images d'Ostende* (1920-30) – are refined lyrical poems, with strong impressions of nature, justifying the label of 'innocent cinema' given to his work. *Une idylle à la plage/Idyll on the Beach* (1931) contains fictional elements. *Histoire du soldat inconnu/Story of the Unknown Soldier* (1932) combined avant-garde techniques with a strong anti-militarist ideology. Storck saw his role as a social and moral one, as is shown by his most famous film, *Misère au Borinage/Borinage* (1933, with Joris Ivens*) as well as *Les Maisons de la misère/Houses of Poverty* (1937*).* *Borinage*, one of the most important European documentaries, showed the intolerable living conditions in this mining region (where a protest had been violently put down), using direct cinema methods as well as reconstruction. Made in the most difficult conditions (vividly described in Ivens' memoirs), it is a cry of indignation, with clear leftist sympathies. For a long time it could only be shown in private clubs; it was, however, shown early in Britain and thus had an impact on the work of John Grierson* and the GPO film unit. Storck also made an important anthropological series on Belgian rural life, *Symphonie paysanne/Peasant Symphony* (1942–44), and another series on the country's traditional carnivals, *Feesten in België/Folklore en Belgique/Festivities in Belgium* (1969–72). Alongside this socially committed cinema, Storck is well known for his *films sur l'art**, including *Le Monde de Paul Delvaux* (1944–46) and *Rubens* (1947–48, with Paul

Haesaerts). In 1951 he made a fiction feature, *Le Banquet des fraudeurs*.

Storck was one of the founder members of the Cinémathèque Royale de Belgique* in the 1930s, and was instrumental in the creation of the CBA* in 1978, and of the CFA (Centre du Film sur l'Art) in 1980. A Henri Storck professorship was established at the Brussels Free University in 1987, and his films are now preserved by the Henri Storck Foundation (Brussels). Chantal Akerman* paid tribute to Storck by casting him as one of the 'clients' in *Jeanne Dielman 23 Quai du Commerce 1080 Bruxelles* (1975). SS

STRASSENFILME

German film genre (the term, meaning 'street film', was coined by film critic Siegfried Kracauer*) describing a particular form of German (Weimar*) urban melodrama made between 1923 and 1930, in which a middle-class (generally male) protagonist strays onto 'the street' seeking relief from both the *ennui* and the moral confinement of bourgeois existence, while a lower-class (generally female) protagonist tries to escape the underworld milieu.

Typically, the protagonists are chastised or destroyed by the experience of the city's darker or licentious side (personified in the figure of the prostitute). While testifying to the iniquities of modern urban life and the repressions of the Wilhelmine past, the classic *Straßenfilme* – Karl Grune's *Die Straße/The Street* (1923), G. W. Pabst's* *Die freudlose Gasse/The Joyless Street* (1925), Bruno Rahn's *Dirnentragödie/Tragedy of the Street* (1927), and Josef von Sternberg's *Der blaue Engel/The Blue Angel* (1930) – tended to end up deterministically reaffirming existing class divisions and the primacy of middle-class values. Films which attempted a less melodramatic, quasi-documentary treatment of city life, like *Menschen am Sonntag/People on Sunday* (1930), were rare. Even *Mutter Krausens Fahrt ins Glück/Mother Krause's Journey to Happiness* (1929), the most famous 'alternative' street film made by the Marxist film collective Prometheus, deployed the melodramatic devices of its rivals. Directed by Piel Jutzi, it purported to be the first real 'Zille-film' (the *Straßenfilme* being influenced by the proletarian milieu depictions of Berlin artist Heinrich Zille) and was hailed as the 'first German Proletarian-Revolutionary film' by the Communist press. As in many other *Straßenfilme*, the main female protagonist perishes as a victim of her milieu. This film rejects, however, the typical determinism of its mainstream kin, ending instead with the next 'class-conscious' generation taking to the street in protest as part of an organised Communist demonstration [> ARBEITERFILME].

Beyond its role in the debate about Weimar cinema's ideological responsibilities, the *Straßenfilm* genre was significant in terms of gender politics. As a vehicle in which actresses such as Greta Garbo*, Asta Nielsen* and Marlene Dietrich* starred as prototypical *femmes fatales*, it offered audiences models of 'new women' capable of threatening the patriarchal order. JM

Bib: Patrice Petro, *Joyless Streets: Women and Melodromatic Representation in Weimar Germany* (1989).

STRAUB, Jean-Marie – see HUILLET, Danièle

STRAUCH [SHTRAUKH], Maxim M.   Moscow 1900–74

Soviet actor. Strauch's early career is closely associated with that of Sergei Eisenstein*, who was a childhood friend. They worked together in the Proletkult Theatre and Strauch played the police spy in *Stachka/The Strike* (1925) and acted as Eisenstein's assistant on his next three films, including *Staroe i novoe/The Old and the New* (1929). Strauch later became one of the first to play the role of Lenin on stage and screen, in such films as Sergei Yutkevich's* *Chelovek s ruzh'ëm/The Man with a Gun* (1938), where he appeared alongside Mikhail Gelovani*; *Rasskazy o Lenine/Tales of Lenin* (1958); and *Lenin v Pol'she/Lenin in Poland* (1966). He also appeared in Mikhail Kalatozov's* *Zagovor obrechën-nykh/Conspiracy of the Damned* (1950) and Mikhail Romm's *Ubiistvo na ulitse Dante/Murder on Dante Street* (1956). He was twice awarded a State Prize for his stage work with the Mayakovsky Theatre. RT

STUHR, Jerzy   Cracow 1947

Polish actor. The 'discovery' of the 1970s, Stuhr had established a successful theatre career before achieving acclaim for his comic roles in Felix Falk's* *Wodzirej/Top Dog* (1978) and Krzysztof Kieślowski's* *Amator/Camera Buff* (1979). Stuhr's portrayal of small-time hustlers and amoral careerists who make up the small cogs in the great Communist Party wheel, established him as one of the leading actors of the 'cinema of moral unrest'. AW

SUÁREZ, Gonzalo   José Suárez Sánchez; Oviedo 1934

Spanish director and writer. Formerly a newspaper sports correspondent and amateur actor, Suárez developed his literary career parallel to his films, often writing his own scripts. His first films of the late 1960s, in which he appeared in the leading role (for instance *Ditirambo/Dithyramb*, 1967), display the iconoclastic style of the Barcelona School*. Less radical in his formal experimentation than most of his counterparts, Suárez joined the mainstream Spanish cinema of the mid-1970s, directing a series of adaptations, such as *Parranda/Party* (1977). After a spell of three years in advertising, and having established his own production company, Ditirambo Films, in Madrid in 1981, he returned to film in 1984, collaborating with Spanish television. He made a large-budget television series co-financed by RAI, *Los Pazos de Ulloa/The Country Houses of Ulloa* (1984), while his films – for example *Epílogo/Epilogue* (1984) – adopted an art cinema style designed to make headway in the European market. Self-reflexivity has always been a prominent feature of Suárez's films. His later ones – *Remando al viento/Rowing with the Wind* (1988), *El detective y la muerte/Death and the Detective* (1994) – are also characterised by visual lavishness, pictorial allusiveness and literary subject matter. XR

SUCKSDORFF, Arne   Stockholm 1917

Swedish director and producer (also scriptwriter and cinematographer, on his own films), who studied art and photography. Sucksdorff is Sweden's leading documentary film-maker, and has been enormously influential in Swedish documentary, especially nature and wildlife films (although some of his films encompass everyday-life subjects). His films have widely documented the Swedish landscape, but he has also covered other countries (India, Brazil). His short films *En sommarsaga/A Summer's Tale* (1941) and *Människor i stad/People of the City/Rhythm of a City* (1947) are typical of his early period, in their lyricism as well as in their great precision of detail. His features include *Det stora äventyret/The Great Adventure* (1953), *Pojken i trädet/The Boy in the Tree* (1961), and a remarkable picture of the poverty and desperate vitality of the boys of Rio de Janeiro, *Mitt hem är Copacabana/My Home is Copacabana* (1965). LGA/BF

SUKOWA, Barbara   Bremen 1950

German actress, remarkable for her strong facial features and her ability to put across fiercely independent personalities. Working for theatre and television since 1971, she was 'discovered' by Rainer Werner Fassbinder*, who cast her in his television productions *Frauen in New York* (1977) and *Berlin Alexanderplatz* (1980), where she played the child-whore Mietze, brutally murdered in the woods. In 1981, Sukowa rose to wider recognition in Fassbinder's *Lola* and as the 'terrorist' Marianne in Margarethe von Trotta's* *Die bleierne Zeit/The German Sisters* (1981). In subsequent women's films [> FRAUENFILM], such as von Trotta's *Rosa Luxemburg* (1986) and Jeanine Meerapfel's *Die Verliebten/The Lovers* (1987), Sukowa played the intellectual consumed by an inner fire. On the strength of her roles in Fassbinder and von Trotta films, she had her 'international' debut in Lars von Trier's* postwar, postmodern thriller *Europa/Zentropa* (1991). TE/MW

SUMMERS, Manuel   Manuel Summers Rivero; Seville 1935

Spanish director, graduate of the IIEC*. His earliest film, *Del rosa al amarillo/From Pink to Yellow* (1963), the first major success of the New Spanish Cinema*, has a dual structure, tracing the pre-pubertal romance between two schoolchildren and a relationship between two senior citizens in an old folks' home. Summers developed here a delicate sensibility for comedy and pathos, something not always maintained in subsequent films. Other prominent films include *La niña de luto/The Girl in Mourning* (1963), satirising bereavement rituals in Andalusia, *El juego de la oca/Snakes and Ladders* (1964), a narrative of desire, and *Juguetes rotos/Broken Toys* (1966), a fascinating docu-drama on famous personalities falling on hard times. The box-office failure of this film probably led Summers to surrender to the 'sexy Spanish comedy' genre [> COMEDY (SPAIN)], whose features he adopted in much of his later work, for instance *Ya soy mujer/Now I'm a*

Woman (1975) and *La primera experiencia/The First Time* (1976). PWE

ŠVANKMAJER, Jan   Prague 1934

Czech director of animated films, visual and ceramic artist. Educated at the School of Applied Art and the Academy of Performing Arts (Puppetry Department), Švankmajer worked with the Black Theatre of Prague and the Laterna Magika theatre before making his first puppet film, (*Poslední trik pana Schwarcewalldea a pana Edgara/The Last Trick of Mr Schwarzwalld and Mr Edgar*, 1964). While he made a number of important films in the 1960s, including the live-action and Kafkaesque *Byt/The Flat* and *Zahrada/The Garden* (both 1968), it was not until the retrospective of his work at the 1983 Annecy Animation Festival in France that he made an international impact. A committed surrealist (he joined the Prague group in 1970), his aggressive, even sadistic, work with its emphasis on texture, juxtaposition and montage is best characterised by *Možnosti dialogu/Dimensions of Dialogue* (1982), in which opposing heads confront and devour each other in destructive interplay. In 1987 he made his first feature, *Něco z Alenky/Alice*, adapted from Lewis Carroll, following this with *Lekce Faust/Faust* (1994), based on an unproduced play written for the Laterna Magika. PH

Bib: Peter Hames (ed.), *Dark Alchemy: The Films of Jan Švankmajer* (1995).

Other Films: *J. S. Bach: Fantasia g-moll/J. S. Bach: Fantasy in G-minor, Spiel mit Steinen/Play With Stones* (1965, Aust.); *Rakvičkárna/Punch and Judy, Et cetera* (1966); *Historia naturae (suita)* (1967); *Picknick mit Weissmann/Picnic with Weissmann* (1968, Austr.); *Tichý týden v domě/A Quiet Week in a House* (1969); *Kostnice/The Ossuary, Don Šajn/Don Juan* (1970); *Žvahlav/Jabberwocky* (1971); *Leonardův deník/Leonardo's Diary* (1972); *Otrantský zámek/The Castle of Otranto* (1973–79); *Zánik domu Usherů/The Fall of the House of Usher* (1980); *Do pivnice/Do sklepa/Down to the Cellar, Kyvadlo, jáma a naděje/The Pendulum, the Pit and Hope* (1983); *Mužné hry/Virile Games* (1988); *Tma–Světlo–Tma/Darkness–Light–Darkness* (1989); *Konec stalinismu v Čechách/The Death of Stalinism in Bohemia* (1990, UK); *Jídlo/Food* (1992).

SVENSKA BIO (from 1919, SVENSK FILMINDUSTRI, or SF)

Swedish film company. Svenska Bio – short for AB Svenska Biografteatern – was founded in 1907 in Kristianstad in southern Sweden. Initially a cinema chain, under Charles Magnusson* the company hired a photographer and began making documentaries and short fiction films. In 1908, it added laboratories and a studio in Kristianstad. In 1911 the company moved to Lidingö, near Stockholm, and Magnusson hired Victor Sjöström* and Mauritz Stiller* as directors. Together with cinematographer Julius Jaenzon*, they created a distinctive body of work in a period often referred to as the

Golden Age of Swedish silent cinema, which lasted until the early 1920s, characterised by quality literary adaptations from classic (often Swedish) literature and a predominantly realist style with great attention paid to landscape (as opposed to the policy of rival company Hasselblads* Fotografiska Aktiebolag, which favoured popular literature). Svenska Bio's artistic and creative success was matched on the financial side, allowing the company to expand into the largest and most diversified film enterprise in Sweden. In 1919 it merged with Skandia (itself incorporating former rival Hasselblads) and changed its name to Svensk Filmindustri, usually abbreviated to SF. Alongside the Swedish Film Institute*, SF is still the most important force in Swedish film production. The company was bought by the daily newspaper *Dagens Nyheter* (owned by the powerful Bonnier family) in 1973. In 1984 SF took over Europafilm and during the 1980s it continued to work in its traditional fields, while expanding into video and the new media. LGA

SVENSKA FILMINSTITUTET (SWEDISH FILM INSTITUTE)

Swedish institution, founded in 1963 with the twin aims of promoting Swedish cinema and film culture and providing a financial base for film production. The Institute indeed became a powerful economic force, channelling funds raised by an entertainment tax back into the film industry and boosting Swedish film production. The high state subsidies in Sweden (as elsewhere) have generally been applied to promote 'quality films' and defend national film production against the pressure of American imports. Without the SFI, art cinema and non-commercial film in general might not have survived.

Through its many cultural and educational activities – library, archive, screenings, the film magazine *Chaplin** – Svenska Filminstitutet has functioned as the centre of Swedish film life for the last three decades. It was instrumental in developing film studies in Sweden, by financing a Professorship in Cinema Studies at Stockholm University in 1969. The first appointment was Rune Waldekranz*, film scholar and former producer at Sandrews*. The Department of Cinema Studies now admits 400 students a year. The Institute is also associated with the National Swedish Filmography, a gigantic research project instituted by Jörn Donner* and the cultural bureau of the Institute in the early 1970s. As of 1995 seven volumes have appeared, detailing all Swedish films from 1897 to 1979. The eighth volume, dealing with the 1980s, is forthcoming. A separate institution, the Arkivet för Ljud och Bild (Swedish National Archive of Recorded Sound and Moving Images), was founded in 1978 to collect copies of all films released in Sweden as well as all television programmes and radio transmissions. LGA/BF

SVENSK TALFILM

Swedish production company. Svensk Talfilm was founded in 1933 by Gösta Sandin. The company concentrated mostly on indigenous 'folk comedies', becoming famous in the 1950s for the exceptional success of the – critically disparaged – *Åsa-*

Nisse films (based on a series of magazine short stories), about the adventures of a comic middle-aged farmer with a domineering wife. The typically 'unexportable' low-budget *Åsa-Nisse* films were all variations on this basic formula, with roughly the same cast and a few topical elements thrown in, such as Swedish rock'n'roll singer Little Gerhard in *Åsa-nisse i kronans kläder/Åssa-Nisse in Military Uniform* (1958). Most were directed by Ragnar Frisk, with a few directed by Arne Stivell. Svensk Talfilm made fifteen *Åsa-Nisse* films between 1948 and 1963, when the company closed down and *Åsa-Nisse* productions transferred to a small company, Filmcenter, which continued the series until the late 1960s. BF

SVĚRÁK, Zdeněk – see SMOLJAK, Ladislav

SWEDEN

The first official film screening in Sweden took place in Malmö on 28 June 1896. The new entertainment was soon introduced in Göteborg and Stockholm. The Skladanowsky* brothers visited Stockholm in August 1896 and recorded the first film ever made on Swedish territory, a slapstick reel called *Komische Begegnung im Tiergarten zu Stockholm* (never released in Sweden). The breakthrough for the new medium took place at an exhibition of art and industry in Stockholm during the summer of 1897, when photographer Numa Peterson screened the films of the Lumière* brothers. Court photographer Ernest Florman has been called the first Swedish cinematographer and film director. His short documentary on the visit of the Siamese king Choulalongkorn to Stockholm in 1897, *Konungens af Siam landstigning vid Logårdstrappan,* was the earliest Swedish film proper.

Cinema's first decade saw the setting up of many small film companies and cinemas all over the country, especially in Stockholm, Göteborg and Malmö. Film production consisted mainly of documentaries, the Lumière tradition exercising a strong hold over the work of Peterson and his associates. There were, however, other independent directors and producers such as Frans Lundberg, who made melodramas in Malmö and Copenhagen, and Anna Hoffman-Uddgren, the first Swedish woman director, who shot adaptations of Strindberg's plays. Peterson and Lundberg also made early experiments with sound. As in many other countries the new medium soon produced a 'moral backlash' among Sweden's *bien pensants*, as a result of which the Swedish Board of Film Censors, Statens Biografbyrå, was set up in 1911. Perhaps paradoxically, it became an important promoter of film culture. The board, one of the oldest of its kind in the world, still retains the power to ban films. Over the years, however, it has been increasingly lenient towards sexuality, especially since the late 1950s, while still being concerned with violence and, especially, the protection of the young. Its archive is one of the most important existing sources of knowledge about early Swedish cinema.

Critical to the development of early Swedish film was the founding in 1905 of a small company in Kristianstad which two years later took on its definitive incarnation as Svenska Biografteatern, or Svenska Bio*; in 1909, the charismatic and ingenious Charles Magnusson* took over as managing direc-

tor and launched the firm into immediate full-scale feature production. Svenska Bio's earliest features were adaptations of literary works such as *Värmlänningarne/The People of Värmland* (1910). Technically and artistically they were mediocre, often mere recordings of stage plays, but the company's move to Stockholm in 1911 presaged a notable change. Magnusson hired two theatre directors/actors, Mauritz Stiller* and Victor Sjöström*, and these three, together with cinematographer Julius Jaenzon*, formed the creative nucleus which shaped the Swedish silent film in the period of its greatest glory. Their films drew on the national literary heritage and celebrated the Swedish landscape in both its pictorial and symbolic dimensions, and their technical sophistication was admired throughout the world. This phenomenon must be seen in the perspective of contemporary film production and especially of a strong Swedish reaction to a flood of melodramas and Danish (and Danish-style) sensationalist pictures – often attracting the attention of the censors [> DANISH EROTIC MELODRAMA]. The 'Golden Age' was thus in part the result of a conscious attempt by the film companies to safeguard the new medium by emphasising quality and a distinctively 'national' approach.

Sjöström's first major success was the social melodrama *Ingeborg Holm* (1913). With its direct impact on the Swedish welfare system, this film coloured the subsequent relationship between film and society in Sweden where, ever since, cinema has been considered a potent agent for social change. Sjöström's great artistic career, however – and for many the Swedish Golden Age itself – began with *Terje Vigen/A Man There Was* (1916), an adaptation of Henrik Ibsen's epic poem. His adaptation from the work of novelist Selma Lagerlöf, *Körkarlen/The Phantom Carriage/Thy Soul Shall Bear Witness* (1921), is perhaps the most beautiful film of the period, and its technical perfection and complexity influenced film-makers worldwide for decades to come (including, later, Ingmar Bergman*). Sjöström's stablemate Mauritz Stiller was more attracted to comedy and continental melodrama. *Thomas Graals bästa film/Wanted, a Film Actress/Thomas Graal's Best Film* (1917) and *Erotikon/The Bonds That Chafe* (1920) are typical examples of his light touch, prefiguring Ernst Lubitsch*. Stiller also made adaptations from Lagerlöf, but he was never as successful in this 'sub-genre' as Sjöström, who, as David A. Cook has put it, 'managed to integrate the rugged Swedish landscape into the texture of his films with an almost mystical force'. On the other hand, *Gösta Berlings saga (del I och II)/The Story of Gosta Berling (pts I and II)* (1923–24) is notable for the first role it offered to a young actress called Greta Garbo*. It is significant that Garbo participated in the last great film of the Golden Age. Soon afterwards she, Sjöström and Stiller left for Hollywood, and Svenska Bio, which in 1919 had become Svensk Filmindustri, lost its position as the major creative force in Swedish film production (Stiller's disappointing US career came to an abrupt end and he died in 1928, while Sjöström, more successful in Hollywood, came back to Sweden mainly to work as an actor). Sjöström and Stiller were not, however, the only important film-makers of this formative period; significant contributions were also made by Gustaf Molander*, Georg af Klercker*, John W. Brunius and Gustaf Edgren. Together they explored film as an art form in its own right, separate from the early stage productions of the *film d'art*. With self-confidence derived from the national literary heritage, they endowed Swedish film with cultural prestige.

The 1920s and early 1930s were scarred by economic depression. Artistic achievements were fewer. A new, popular film culture was growing up, characterised by film magazines, ornate cinemas and new genres, especially comedies derived from the Swedish vaudeville tradition, as well as melodrama. One of the most prolific and successful directors was Molander, who showed himself a master of melodrama with *Intermezzo* (1936) and *En kvinnas ansikte/A Woman's Face* (1938), both with Ingrid Bergman* (and both remade in Hollywood). Other important directors were Gustaf Edgren, Schamyl Bauman and Ivar Johansson, but, as Swedish film historian Leif Furhammar has noted, the 1930s were not primarily an age of directors but of actors. These actors, mainly male and mainly comedians, became extremely popular: Thor Modéen, Adolf Jahr, Åke Söderblom, Fridolf Rhudin and (especially) Edvard Persson (1888–1957), who enjoyed enormous success with burlesque films such as *Larsson i Andra Giftet/Larsson's Second Marriage* (1935) and *Livet på landet/ Life in the Country* (1943). Actresses like Dagmar Ebbesen, Sickan Carlsson, Tutta Rolf and Rut Holm also came to the fore. Together these performers painted a picture of Swedish society which was a mixture of social democracy and old hierarchical structures. Although Sweden never developed a full genre system, comedies were the most popular films over the years, and here at least specifically Nordic sub-genres evolved, such as the burlesque 'folk comedy' of which the Persson films are a good example, and the military farce as in Finland and France [> COMIQUE TROUPIER, FINNISH MILITARY FARCE].

Although Sweden was not a combatant in World War II, the film industry was affected by the international turmoil. Production burgeoned to fill the gap left by dwindling foreign imports. Cinema became an important factor both as an escape from the mood of war and as part of the psychological defence of the realm. Sweden's relationship with Germany was ambivalent, and the film industry handled this with care. Although many films were 'about' the war, initially the enemy was diffuse, almost metaphysical. Some war dramas were, however, serious and artistically satisfying, for instance Molander's *Rid i natt!/Ride Tonight!* (1942) and *Det brinner en eld/There Burned a Flame* (1943). The 1940s were also the launch-pad for several talented new film-makers. Alf Sjöberg*, one of the few internationally oriented Swedish *auteurs*, made films such as *Hets/Frenzy* (1944) and *Bara en mor/Only a Mother* (1949). His most important film was an adaptation of a Strindberg play, *Fröken Julie/Miss Julie* (1951). Other significant directors of the period are Arne Sucksdorff*, Hasse Ekman*, Arne Mattsson and Hampe Faustman, as well as Molander. Sucksdorff's *Det stora äventyret/The Great Adventure* (1953), Ekman's *Flicka och hyacinter/The Girl with Hyacinths/Suicide* (1950), Mattsson's *Hon dansade en sommar/One Summer of Happiness* (1951), Faustman's *När ängarna blommar/When Meadows Bloom* (1946) and Molander's *Eva* (1948) are all high points of the period. *Hon dansade en sommar* became an international success, despite suffering at the hands of censors on account of its scenes of nudity and sex.

The 1940s also saw the emergence of Ingmar Bergman*, whose *oeuvre* is undoubtedly the greatest Swedish contri-

bution to film art since the silent age. Throughout the postwar period Bergman was the dominant *auteur* and presence in Swedish cinema and one of the few to bulk large internationally. Bergman's was no overnight success, though. As a young director he laboured to find a personal style, attracted opprobrium from critics and frequently clashed with producers. His early films were melodramatic accounts of unhappy love and youth in conflict with established society, influenced by *film noir* and reflecting the downbeat mood of the mid-1940s. Bergman's chequered production career continued until he set up his own company, Cinematograph, at the end of the 1960s. By that time, however, he had secured his international reputation with a string of films (*Sommaren med Monika/Summer with Monika*, 1952; *Gycklarnas afton/ Sawdust and Tinsel/The Naked Night*, 1953; *Sommarnattens leende/Smiles of a Summer Night*, 1955; *Det sjunde inseglet/ The Seventh Seal*, 1957; and *Smultronstället/Wild Strawberries*, 1957, starring Victor Sjöström) which did much to define European art cinema*, even if their reception at home was mixed. While Bergman dominated foreign perceptions of Swedish cinema, indigenous popular films continued to be made, again mostly comedy. Typical of the period is the extremely popular *Åsa-Nisse* series built round the adventures of a middle-aged farmer [> SVENSK TALFILM]. A thriving production of children's films also began.

A turning point for Swedish film history came with the foundation of the Swedish Film Institute in 1963. As well as fulfilling the traditional function of film archive and cultural institution, the Institute initiated academic film studies in Sweden and set up Sweden's first film school in 1964 (replaced by the Dramatic Institute – Dramatiska Institutet – in 1969, headed by Kjell Grede, it has since been the official training institution for television, film, theatre and radio). But it also, importantly, became a powerful economic force in its own right, channelling funds raised by an entertainment tax back into film production. It was one of the most important factors in the increased output of Swedish films, and without it art (and non-commercial) film might not have survived in Sweden. Other changes to the institutional structure of Swedish cinema included the foundation of Filmcentrum in 1968 by a group of radical independent film-makers, as an alternative to commercial cinema distribution. Suddenly there was money and a context for experiments, and a new generation of film-makers emerged from the shadow of Ingmar Bergman: Bo Widerberg*, Vilgot Sjöman*, Jan Troell* are the most prominent names, followed by Mai Zetterling*, Jonas Cornell, Jörn Donner*, Jan Halldoff and Kjell Grede. Widerberg countered Bergman's 'aestheticism' with a series of films influenced by the French New Wave*. Sjöman, a novelist and the director of several complex psychological dramas, achieved notoriety with his sexually explicit *Jag är nyfiken – gul/I am Curious – Yellow* (1967) and *Jag är nyfiken – blå /I am Curious – Blue* (1968), which triggered long-running debates on politics and censorship at home but were international hits, especially in the US. Troell made the epic *Utvandrarna/The Emigrants* (1971) and *Nybyggarna/The Settlers* (1972), based on the Swedish novelist Vilhelm Moberg's works on Swedish emigration to America at the end of the nineteenth century. The late 1960s and early 1970s saw the emergence of new talents such as Johan Bergenstråhle, Lars Magnus Lindgren, Lasse Forsberg,

Stellan Olsson and Roy Andersson*, while an older generation of directors such as Arne Sucksdorff and Arne Mattsson was still active. One of Sucksdorff's pupils was Stefan Jarl, who, together with Jan Lindqvist, made an important documentary *Dom kallar oss mods/They Call Us Misfits* (1968). During the 1970s and 1980s Jarl became the most influential Swedish documentarist, with films on ecological as well as social problems.

From the 1970s on, as political commitment and the sexual curiosity of the 1960s faded, directions in Swedish cinema become more confused. It is hard to find consistent lines or themes in the last two decades. Lasse Åberg has tried to return to the popular comedy of the 1930s, and actors such as Gösta Ekman Jr.* have made their mark in cabaret-type comedies. The continued popularity of children's films should be noted; these include some animated features, and also the important *Pippi Långstrump/Pippi Longstocking* series, based on Astrid Lindgren's novel about an eight-year-old tomboy's wild adventures. In *auteur* cinema, Suzanne Osten* and Marie-Louise Ekman have delved into the nation's political soul and the responsibility of the artist respectively, both with some originality. Hans Alfredson, Tage Danielsson, Mats Arehn, Gunnel Lindblom and Marianne Ahrne have all made interesting contributions, and Lasse Hallström's *Mitt liv som hund/My Life as a Dog* (1985) was an international art-house success. It should be noted, however, that many of the most intriguing recent films made in Sweden are the work of foreigners – Anja Breien*, Colin Nutley, Bille August*, Larus Oskarsson and Andrey Tarkovsky*. These foreign interventions are an important step in the evolution of Swedish cinema. For while at the beginning of the century there were many Swedish–Danish co-productions, and *auteurs* like Stiller, Sjöström and Bergman (and a few others) made Swedish film international, for many decades Swedish film culture has been insular and isolated. Since the 1970s film production has been in constant crisis, the result of competition from television, video and satellite channels, but also because of the lack of a consistent tradition. This isolation may not be permanent, though. The Golden Age of Swedish silent film can never be recreated, Bergman cannot be replaced and it is probably impossible ever again to achieve the prolific production of the vibrant 1960s – but together these form a heritage which film-makers can mine while they unavoidably embrace a more international dimension. LGA/BF

SWEDISH FILM INSTITUTE – see SVENSKA FILMINSTITUTET

SWINTON, Tilda   Scotland 1961

British actress. Swinton, who appeared in a number of Derek Jarman* films in the 1980s, established herself as one of the most interesting actresses in current British cinema as Queen Isabella in his *Edward II* (1991), and confirmed her strength in the title role of Sally Potter's* *Orlando* (1992). An actress of great economy and concentration, in *Edward II* she suffers the indignities of Galveston and the rejection of Edward with moving dignity, then transforms herself into a chilling parody of Margaret Thatcher with no apparent change of gear. In *Orlando*, as Virginia Woolf's androgynous hero/heroine, she gives a lighter performance with knowing winks to the audience, but maintains a strong screen presence. The blankness of her expression and stillness of her concentration give her a fluidity perfectly suited to a cinema which is exploring sexual difference and identity. JC

SWITZERLAND

Any attempt to give a precise account of Swiss film production runs up against the problem that there is very little reliable quantitative data for any period or any type of production. The only figures released with regularity are those relating to federal subsidies since 1963 and the number of ticket sales per film (a figure which had long remained confidential, if not unobtainable).

In economic terms, the Swiss market is dominated by imported films, most of which, since the end of World War I, have been American and French products. True, the overwhelming predominance of the service sector (distribution and exhibition) has not prevented films from being made. But it has relegated production to a minor place on the domestic market, which caters for a population that is not only numerically small but spread over three linguistic areas of unequal size (in decreasing order: German, French and Italian, to which should be added a fourth, tiny, area speaking Romansch). What is more, care needs to be taken when defining what we mean by Swiss film production. From the 1910s onwards, a handful of companies of local dimension were in operation. From time to time, one or other of them would emerge to occupy a strong leading position (Eos-Film, Praesens-Film, Central-Film, Gloria-Film). Such companies mostly did commissioned work – short and medium-length films for which there was such demand that laboratories like Eos, AAP, Cinégram and Schwarz came into existence though they also occasionally produced features.

Taking the period as a whole, the commissioned film market has undoubtedly been the only permanent basis of what might be called the Swiss film production economy. Even so, it would be difficult to describe the precise activity of the 144 companies listed under the heading 'Feature and documentary film production companies' in the 1992 edition of *Cinémemo*. As regards the last thirty years, the problem of defining Swiss film production along the same lines as that of countries possessing a properly established film industry is compounded by the diversity of visual media and designations, and by the inadequacy of the notion of *auteur*, or of using the 35mm feature film as sole criterion. Two figures, for what they are worth, illustrate the complexity of the situation, as well as giving some idea of production volume. Between 1908 and 1964, the total number of feature-length standard-format 35mm films produced in Switzerland was probably about 230, most of them fiction, a quarter of which were made during the years 1938–45. (At least 30,000 features were imported over the same period.) Between 1972 and 1990, the Centre Suisse du Cinéma registered nearly 500 feature-length films (of sixty minutes or more), mostly shot on 16mm, of which 65 per cent were fiction films and 35 per cent documentaries.

1896–1937: In Switzerland as elsewhere, the earliest film-making was bound up with the advent of film screenings (Casimir Sivan in 1896, Lavanchy-Clarke and the Lumière* Cinematograph in 1896–98). It later catered for fairground showings (Hipleh-Walt and others), and eventually for a number of permanent cinemas that opened from 1907 and 1908 (Rosenthal in Basle, Roth de Markus in Lausanne, Speck in Zurich, etc.). Local subject matter – official ceremonies, military manoeuvres and picturesque locations – had some points of resemblance with the 'open air' films that major European companies came to shoot in Switzerland's 'natural studio' of railway tracks, mountains and holiday resorts from 1900 onwards. This asset was exploited by films made for the export market (travelogues by Burlingham in Montreux), as well as by a great many of the feature films shot sporadically during the period, whether wholly Swiss-produced (Eduard Bienz's *Der Bergführer*, 1917; Jean Hervé's *Le Pauvre village*, 1921; Jacques Béranger's *La Croix du Cervin*, 1922; Jean Choux's *La Vocation d'André Carel*, 1925) or co-productions (Jacques Feyder's* *Visages d'enfants/Faces of Children*, 1923–25; Emil Harder's *Die Entstehung der Eidgenossenschaft*, 1924; Hanns Schwarz's* *Petronella*, 1927; Dimitri Kirsanoff's *Rapt/The Mystic Mountain*, 1934; Max Haufler's *L'Or dans la montagne/Farinet*, 1938, based on a novel by Charles Ferdinand Ramuz). The most original contributions were certainly those of Choux, Feyder, Kirsanoff and Haufler during a period when the largest single cinematic oeuvre was that of Jean Brocher, who made, as an amateur, twelve 35mm films with a moral message that were distributed outside the normal commercial circuit. The coming of sound did not help Swiss production to flourish, though it did encourage comedies with local appeal shot in dialect, which remained lastingly popular thanks to actors like Heinrich Gretler*, Elsie Attenhofer, Schaggi Streuli, Zarli Carigiet, Fredy Scheim, Alfred Rasser and Walter Roderer – for example *Wie d'Wahrheit würkt/The Effects of Truth* (1933) and *Jä-soo!* (1935).

Perhaps the most remarkable productions of the 1930s were more directly bound up with the 'war of images' which took place then, and which attracted the attention of the government and the political community – propaganda films like *Ein Werktag* (Richard Schweizer, 1931), a silent electoral film commissioned by the Socialist Party, Charles-Georges Duvanel's* *Pionniers* (1936), an evocation of the cooperative movement, and Jean-Marie Musy's anti-communist *Die rote Pest* (1938). This same battle of ideas is also evident in Terra Film's German-Swiss co-productions (1931–35) and in the 'film essays' made in Switzerland by Hans Richter (*Die neue Wohnung*, 1930; *Die Börse als Markt*, 1939).

1938–1964: The veritable boom in domestic production which resulted from Switzerland's isolation during the war was, however, fragile because it was conditional on the temporary closing of the nation's borders. It was driven by a powerful sense of national identity, heightened both by the country's position of non-involvement and by its conviction that it represented a model of humanity in a world of barbarity.

The most prominent role was played by Lazar Wechsler's* company, Praesens-Film (1924–80), and its resident director, the Austrian-born Leopold Lindtberg*, one of the few people then working in Switzerland who regularly turned out solidly professional and varied works (cinematographer: Emil Berna*). While some of his films display a patriotic zeal whose form and content may seem ponderous today (*Füsilier Wipf*, 1938; *Landammann Stauffacher*, 1941, scriptwriter: Richard Schweizer; leading actor: Heinrich Gretler), others strive for a form of psychological realism (*Wachtmeister Studer*, 1939; *Die Mißbrauchten Liebesbriefe*, 1940). At least two other films from the war period are worth mentioning, Valerian Schmidely and Hans Trommer's *Romeo und Julia auf dem Dorfe* (1941), and Franz Schnyder's* *Wilder Urlaub* (1943), which, because they seem out of tune with the heroic mood of the times, are perhaps all the more deserving of a place in an ideal anthology of Swiss cinema.

Wechsler went on to exploit the international success of Lindtberg's *Die letzte Chance/The Last Chance* (1944–45), a key work of the immediate postwar period, by mounting international productions such as Fred Zinnemann's *The Search/Die Gezeichneten* (which won an Oscar in 1948) in very much the same humanitarian vein as Praesens' earlier productions. The postwar years were marked by two other trends, exploited by Schnyder and Kurt Früh* respectively. Schnyder's briskly directed adaptations of J. Gotthelf's novels are basically Westerns set in the Bernese Oberland (*Uli der Knecht*, 1954; *Uli der Pächter*, 1955, with Liselotte Pulver* and Hannes Schmidhauser, produced by Gloria-Film); his *Der 10. Mai* (1957) was the only film that attempted to look critically at Swiss attitudes during World War II. Früh opted for an easy-going realism whose greatest originality was the featuring of an urban family milieu in what had otherwise been a very rural cinema (*Polizist Wäckerli*, 1955; *Oberstadtgass*, 1956; *Bäckerei Zürrer*, 1957, Gloria-Film).

Since 1964: On 28 December 1962, the cinema was included in the Federal Constitution in an article (27c) that authorised the state to pass legislation aimed at 'encouraging Swiss film production and cultural activities in the field of the cinema'. Its implementation did not have an immediate effect on the production system, which was changed solely by the determination of a new generation of directors and technicians who had decided to work outside the traditional production framework and opt for the more precarious conditions of shoestring budgets and uncommercial subjects. Although earlier Swiss film-makers had been aware of the social role played by their medium, an ideological and stylistic change took place in the 1960s: the cinema was now seized upon as a critical tool and a means of personal expression. The lack of any corporation or film industry in the true sense of the word, and the ever more intensive use of 16mm film and lighter sound equipment, were factors that led to an almost total renewal of the small Swiss cinema milieu and revolutionised the sort of subject matter covered by both features and documentaries (which now had equal ranking in the hierarchy of genres). Immigrant labour, the working conditions of apprentices, 'Swiss happiness', national myths and economic imperialism were all subjects focused on by 'militant' film-makers motivated at best by a critical and almost ethnographical stance and a genuine urge to express themselves, and at worst by ideological cliché. This was the decade when documentary film-makers Henry Brandt, Reni Mertens* and Walter Marti*, and Alexander Seiler came to the fore, and when the work of directors like Jean-Louis Roy, Michel

Soutter*, Alain Tanner*, Claude Goretta*, Rolf Lyssy, Fredi Murer*, Yves Yersin* and Francis Reusser was seen as part of the 'young' or 'new' European cinema, and has even been labelled 'new Swiss cinema'.

Production conditions became less precarious from 1970, when changes in legislation at last enabled feature films to be subsidised and introduced the so-called 'independent' production system still in operation today. It hinges on a two-pronged mechanism which creates a relationship of simultaneous interdependence between two distinct financial sources, one of them strictly 'cultural', funded by federal subsidies and complemented by cantonal and private contributions, and the other 'commercial', to which the exhibition sector contributes very little. In 1983 an outline agreement with Swiss television (which is franchised by the state within national interest guidelines) reinforced television's decisive contribution as a third financial source. This system has enabled an artistic and committed approach to film-making to survive and thrive, yet has not produced a situation where public money, whose contribution may seem small in absolute terms but is in fact crucial, encourages a cinema of consensus. On the contrary, much cinematic output has uncompromisingly tackled cultural and creative issues, whether it be the work of Geneva-based film-makers who, in the intellectual climate before and after May 1968, brought international recognition to the 'new Swiss cinema', or films like Richard Dindo's* *Die Erschiessung des Landesverräters Ernst S.* (1976), Yersin's *Les Petites Fugues/Little Escapes* (1978), Markus Imhoof's *Das Boot ist voll/The Boat is Full* (1980) and Murer's *Höhenfeuer/Alpine Fire* (1985).

Two phenomena in particular are worth noting: the films just mentioned, which were largely inspired by a political determination to ensure the survival of a specifically Swiss cinema, espouse a 'civic' tradition that has resurfaced in the films of Imhoof, Kurt Gloor, Goretta, Lyssy, Thomas Koerfer* and Xavier Koller, not unconnected to the producer playing an increasingly important role; other directors, such as Tanner, Reusser and B. Kuert, have continued to work in their distinctive original 'auteurist' vein. The most notable themes remain concern for other peoples, as reflected in films about the handicapped, Brazilian peasants, Turkish workers and second-generation immigrants, and, conversely, a constant self-questioning about what it means to be Swiss. This output, however heterogeneous it may be (and that is something the 'Solothurner Filmtage' or Solothurn festival accurately reflects [> FESTIVALS (SWITZERLAND)]), shows a certain unity, a consistency that may from time to time lapse into routine, and above all a legitimacy that earlier Swiss film-makers never enjoyed. The most evident sign of this is the fact that many directors – Daniel Schmid*, Hans-Ulrich Schlumpf, Peter von Gunten, Villi Hermann and Jacqueline Veuve, in addition to those already mentioned – have succeeded in building up a genuine oeuvre, even if it has been a slow process (over two decades) and required considerable persistence: many make an average of only one film every three years or so.

Members of the subsequent generation, such as Kuert, Jean-François Amiguet, Marcel Schupbach, Matthias von Gunten, Bernhardt Giger and Samir, have run into greater difficulties in the last few years as a result of the increasingly important role of television, rising production costs, the inevitable freezing of the value of state subsidies in real terms,

the problems of co-production, and the blurred definition created by the abstract notion of a 'Euro-film'. This situation has aroused particularly strong feelings in Switzerland because in the last twenty years the industry has become much more professional – a vital precondition for any continuity. RC/CK

Swiss film periodicals. If Switzerland never enjoyed a numerically substantial film production, the vitality of its film culture can be measured by its range of film periodicals. *Close Up** is the most famous, a unique international experiment (with connections especially in Britain) which took place during the first wave of serious film culture in the 1920s and 1930s (see separate entry). Other important Swiss publications include: *Zoom*. Originally a bulletin produced by the Swiss Catholic Film Commission (1938), *Zoom–Zeitschrift für Film* is the oldest of the current Swiss film journals. The original bulletin aimed to provide moral criteria for the appreciation of films distributed on the Swiss market, while promoting film education, hence its first title *Der Filmberater* ('The Film Counsellor'). In 1973 it absorbed another journal, *Zoom*, and took over its title. This signalled an important evolution, away from the religious point of view and towards world cinema, Swiss production, and cinema as a social and cultural phenomenon. *Zoom* also runs *Zoom–Dokumentation*, an important documentation centre. *Ciné-Bulletin*. Since 1975, *Ciné-Bulletin* has regularly provided information on Swiss cinema, including valuable statistics. Neither trade publication nor critical journal, this bilingual (German/French) publication has become indispensable to anyone interested in the political and cultural debates relating to cinema in Switzerland. *Filmbulletin*. Originally a modest journal published by a Catholic youth organisation from 1959, *Filmbulletin* developed into a journal inspired by the cult of cinema. Lavishly illustrated, it offers the most *cinéphile* version of Swiss criticism, in the tradition of the glorious years of *Cahiers du cinéma.* Cinema*. In 1961, *Cinema* took over *Filmklub-Cineclub* (1955–59/60), a periodical linked to the cine-club movement, and retained connections with the Swiss federation of cine-clubs until 1973. With *auteur* or thematically based issues, the journal single-handedly ensured the permanence of a film culture intellectually inspired by France and fed by the programmes of the Cinémathèque Suisse*. From 1974 to 1982, a new editorial team centred the debates on the 'new Swiss cinema'. In 1983, *Cinema* entered its third phase: it is now published yearly, with a thematic formula offering scope for in-depth essays. RC

SYBERBERG, Hans Jürgen   Nossendorf, Pomerania 1935

German director. Syberberg began in German television, producing hundreds of current affairs and documentary shorts and programming features between 1963 and 1966, before turning to longer documentaries on theatrical subjects. His first fiction film was the Tolstoy adaptation *Scarabea – Wieviel Erde braucht der Mensch?* (1969), followed by the Kleist-based *San Domingo* (1970). His most famous films, the so-called 'German trilogy', began with *Ludwig – Ein Requiem für einen jungfräulichen König/Ludwig – Requiem for a*

Virgin King in 1972, followed by *Karl May* (1974), and *Hitler – Ein Film aus Deutschland/Our Hitler/Hitler – A Film from Germany* (1977), to which must be added two 'by-products', *Theodor Hirneis oder: Wie man ehem. Hofkoch wird* (1973) and *Winifred Wagner und die Geschichte des Hauses Wahnfried 1914–1975* (1975). Syberberg uses intricate stylistic strategies of distanciation, thematic clashes and intertextual echoes in order to give body to complex but also often confused thoughts on history, culture and politics. Regarded in France and the US as a serious spokesman for the New Germany, he found himself at home an outcast, variously accused of incompetence, plagiarism, arrogance and protofascism, charges to which he has responded pedantically in numerous books, essays and newspaper articles. MW

Bib: Thomas Elsaesser, 'Myth as the Phantasmagoria of History: H. J. Syberberg, Cinema and Representation', *New German Critique*, no. 24–25 (1981–82).

Other Films Include: *Parsifal* (1982); *Die Nacht* (1985); *Edith Clever liest James Joyce* (1985); *Fräulein Else, Penthesilea* (1987); *Die Marquise von O* (1989).

SYDOW, Max von
Carl Adolf von Sydow; Lund 1929

Swedish actor, best known for his part as the angular Knight who plays chess with Death in Ingmar Bergman's* *Det sjunde inseglet/The Seventh Seal* (1957). Max von Sydow then had a long association with Bergman, which includes *Smultronstället/Wild Strawberries* (1957), *Jungfrukällan/The Virgin Spring* (1960), *Såsom i en spegel/Through a Glass Darkly* (1961), *Vargtimmen/Hour of the Wolf* and *Skammen/Shame* (both 1968). Like most of his Swedish colleagues he was trained in the theatre and he has continued an active career on stage, in Sweden and abroad, including Britain and the US. His post-Bergman film career has been prolific and international, encompassing Hollywood genre films such as *Three Days of the Condor* (1975) and *Conan the Barbarian* (1982), a Woody Allen film (*Hannah and Her Sisters*, 1986) and European art films (Bertrand Tavernier's* *La Mort en direct/Death Watch*, 1980). As well as these predominantly character parts he has had leading roles in Jan Troell's* two-part epic *Utvandrarna/The Emigrants* (1971) and *Nybyggarna/The Settlers* (1972), and in Bille August's* *Pelle Erobreren/Pelle the Conqueror* (1987), for which von Sydow won a best actor Felix* award in 1988. He has directed a film, *Ved vejen/Vid vägen/Katinka* (1988, Den./Swed./UK). GV

SYNCHRONOS KINIMATOGRAFOS

Greek film magazine, 1969–85. *Synchronos Kinimatografos* ('Contemporary Cinema'), founded in September 1969, was the first film magazine in Greece to deal seriously with cinema in aesthetic and artistic terms, all previous publications being trade journals or fan magazines. In effect, *Synchronos Kinimatografos* introduced Greek readers to the spectrum of theoretical debate, from early Soviet writings to semiology and the role of cinematic genres. *Synchronos Kinimatografos* was the nearest Greek equivalent of the seminal French magazine *Cahiers du cinéma**. As the sole Greek journal of its type for many years, its influence was substantial. In particular, during the repressive years of the dictatorship (1967–74) it kept alive the desire for a different kind of cinema which burgeoned into the New Greek Cinema* after the junta's collapse. It also blazed a trail for other film magazines to follow, notably *Othoni**. Several of its contributors went on to become directors, among them Thodoros Angelopoulos*, Pandelis Voulgaris*, Kostas Sfikas and Frida Liappa, or to work in film in other capacities. Internal divisions among the editorial board, together with external political and financial considerations made the magazine's passage a difficult one. There were often long intervals between issues, and once publication was suspended. *Synchronos Kinimatografos* published sixty-three issues. TNe

SZABÓ, István
Budapest 1938

Hungarian director. The best-known and most successful of the second postwar generation of Hungarian film-makers, Szabó graduated from the Academy of Theatre and Film Art in 1961. He was one of the founders of the Balázs Béla Stúdió*, where he made several remarkable short films. His first feature, *Álmodozások kora/The Age of Daydreaming* (1964), showed the influence of the French New Wave*, and especially of François Truffaut*. In his second film, *Apa/Father* (1966), he created a distinctive subjective style, successfully adapting the lyricism of the New Wave to the interest in historical analysis which prevailed in Hungarian cinema at the time. In the 1970s his style became highly abstract and often symbolic, while the city of Budapest was a thematic source for both his feature and short films. In the 1980s Szabó made an important career shift, leaving behind his lyrical-abstract style, anchored in melancholic reminiscences of a near-obsolete Hungarian middle-class mentality. Instead, he embarked on a series of films focusing on issues of personal identity in Eastern Europe, couched in a form accessible to an international audience. The first film of the series, *Mephisto* (1981), was a major international success – winning the 1982 Academy Award for Best Foreign Film – though subsequent films of the decade were less successful in both critical and box-office terms. In his most recent film, *Édes Emma, drága Böbe/Sweet Emma, Dear Böbe* (1992), Szabó returned to Hungarian social reality, with a story about the struggle of two elementary school teachers for material and moral survival after the collapse of a (communist) social system that had provided them with basic security. KAB

Other Films Include: *Szerelmesfilm/Love Film* (1970); *Tüzoltó utca 25/25 Fireman's Street* (1973); *Budapesti mesék/Budapest Tales* (1976); *Bizalom/Confidence, Der Grüne Vogel/The Green Birds* (1979, Ger); *Redl Ezredes/Colonel Redl* (1985, Hung./Ger./Aust.); *Hanussen* (1988, Hung./Ger.); *Meeting Venus* (1991, UK).

SZŐTS, István   Vályaszentgyőrgy 1912

Hungarian director, the first important representative of *auteur* cinema in Hungary. Szőts started his film-making career in 1940 and two years later directed *Emberek a havason/Men on the Mountains*, which won first prize at the Venice Biennale and was Hungarian cinema's first international success. Szőts' film was very different from the mainstream popular comedies and melodramas that had dominated Hungarian film production since the early 1930s. Deploying a narrative style resembling the Hungarian folk tale, *Emberek a havason* depicted with ethnographic authenticity the arduous life of the people living on the high mountains of Transylvania*. Not only was this a unique stylistic initiative in Hungarian cinema, it was also a revelation for Italian cinema since it dovetailed with the neo-realism* that was soon to emerge in Italy. Immediately after the war, in 1945, Szőts published a manifesto setting out how Hungarian film production should be reorganised. This is a fervent defence of art cinema and of the cultural-educative function of film. Szőts directed one more feature film in the 1940s, *Ének a búzamezőkről/Song of the Cornfields* (1947), which, unlike his first film, was made in an expressionist style. Though approved by the censors, the film was banned just before its planned release because of the religious nature of the story. Szőts made short films during the 1950s. He emigrated to Austria during the 1956 revolution, where he has made several shorts on art and other cultural topics. KAB

T

TADIĆ, Zoran   Zagreb, Croatia 1941

Croatian director, scriptwriter and critic. The title of Tadić's film debut, *Hitch..., Hitch..., Hitchcock* (1969), is indicative of his film taste. In his film journalism Tadić promoted the cause of thrillers, B-movies and *auteur* cinema. In a national cinema with no tradition of this kind, he was obliged to shoot documentaries before he could make his feature film debut, at the age of forty. But in the 1980s he directed almost a film per year, most of them with the same team: writer Pavao Pavličić, cinematographer Goran Trbuljak, actor Fabijan Šovagović. Like Polish director Krzysztof Kieślowski*, Tadić proved that the dark suburbs of communist capitals can make perfect surroundings for modern *films noirs*. SP

Other Films: *Ritam zločina/The Rhythm of Crime* (1981); *Treči ključ/The Third Key* (1983); *San o ruži/Dream of a Rose* (1986); *Osudjeni/The Condemned* (1987); *Čovjek koji je volio sprovode/The Man who Loved Funerals* (1989); *Orao/Eagle* (1990).

TANNER, Alain   Geneva 1929

Swiss director, the dominant figure of the 'new Swiss cinema' of the 1960s and 1970s. After graduating in economics, Tanner worked for a Geneva shipping company before moving to London, where he worked at the BBC and at the British Film Institute*. In the context of the 'Free Cinema'* movement, he directed (with Claude Goretta*) his first short, the experimental documentary *Nice Time* (1957), about night life in London's Piccadilly Circus. Returning to Switzerland in 1960, Tanner made many documentaries for French-Swiss television, including the feature *Les Apprentis/The Apprentices* (1964), about a group of teenagers, and *Une ville à Chandigarh* (1966), on Le Corbusier's architecture. *Les Apprentis* in particular has gained canonical status as prefiguring the 'new Swiss cinema', a movement Tanner was central to, especially with the founding of the 'Groupe des Cinq' with Goretta, Michel Soutter*, Jean-Louis Roy and Yves Yersin*. *Charles, mort ou vif/Charles, Dead or Alive* (1969), about a successful industrialist who rejects 'the system' (played by François Simon, Michel Simon's* son), was a revelation. Even more so were *La Salamandre/The Salamander* (1971) and *Jonas qui aura vingt-cinq ans en l'an 2000/Jonah Who Will Be 25 in the Year 2000* (1976), both scripted by the British Marxist novelist and art critic John Berger and both epitomising Tanner's style, a blend of ethnographic documentary and fiction typical of the European New Wave* movements, as well as a merging of specific Swiss concerns with international, post-1968 issues such as alienation and, especially, sexual and political utopias. *La Salamandre* and *Jonas* also revealed, along with French stars Bulle Ogier and Miou-Miou*, the excellent Jean-Luc Bideau and Jacques Denis to world audiences. The 1970s utopias run sour in *Messidor* (1978), a tale of two female drop-outs who encounter hostility towards their 'alternative' lifestyle and turn into criminals rampaging through the Swiss countryside. Apart from *Dans la ville blanche/In the White City* (1983), shot in Portugal, Tanner's later work has had less international resonance. *Une Flamme dans mon coeur/A Flame in My Heart* (1987) and *Le Journal de Lady M.* (1993) especially disappointed critics. It seems that the sexual energy of *La Salamandre* has fizzled out into soft porn. MW/GV

Bib: Jim Leach, *A Possible Cinema: The Films of Alain Tanner* (1984).

Other Films: *Ramuz, passage d'un poète* (1961, short); *L'Ecole* (1962, short); *Le Retour d'Afrique/Return from Africa* (1973); *Le Milieu du monde/Middle of the World* (1974); *Temps mort* (1977); *Les Années lumière/Light Years Away* (1981); *No Man's Land* (1985); *La Vallée fantôme*

(1987); *La Femme de Rose Hill* (1989); *L'Homme qui a perdu son ombre* (1991).

TAPIOVAARA, Nyrki
Hämeenlinna 1911 – Tohmajärvi 1940

Finnish director. Nyrki Tapiovaara made only a few films in the late 1930s before he was killed in the war. Nevertheless, he is widely considered the most talented director Finland has produced. In the mid-1930s he was a journalist writing for left-wing publications on cultural issues, especially cinema. His perceptiveness won him the commission to adapt Juhani Aho's novel *Juha* for the screen. This became Tapiovaara's first film in 1937. In his next film, *Varastettu kuolema/Stolen Death* (1938), Tapiovaara and his cinematographer Erik Blomberg* told the story of young anti-Russian activists in Helsinki at the beginning of the century; lighting, camerawork and editing reflect trends in European art cinema*, blending Soviet, French and German influences. More avant-garde was Tapiovaara's next film, a socially critical comedy, *Herra Lahtinen lähtee lipettiin/Mr Lahtinen Slouches off* (1939). Tapiovaara made two more films: *Kaksi Vihtoria/Two Victors* (1939), a satire about the petty bourgeoisie, and the drama *Miehen tie/Man's Way* (1940). AH-H

TARKAS, Aarne
Pori 1923 – Spain 1976

Finnish director and scriptwriter. Aarne Tarkas came to film in the early 1950s and became one of the most productive directors of the period when Finnish film output was at its highest. His first film, *Yö on pitkä/The Night is Long* (1952), a story about rootless young people and delinquency, was made outside the major studios. *Olemme kaikki syyllisiä/We are All Guilty* (1954), made for Mauno Mäkelä's* Fennada-Filmi, was another ambitious project based on events that took place in Helsinki in 1948: a corrupted milieu is shown to be the cause of murder and jealousy. Later Tarkas directed dramas: *Jokin ihmisessä/Something in People* (1956), *Naiset jotka minulle annoit/Women You Gave to Me* (1962) and *Hän varasti elämän/She Robbed My Life* (1962). From the mid-1950s Tarkas attained prominence as one of the most prolific Finnish directors of comedies and action movies. Between 1956 and 1963 – the last years of the 'classical' studio era – he directed twenty-six movies, a fifth of the entire national production. His colourful career embraced smooth comedies (*Paksunahka*, 1958), military farce (*Herra sotaministeri/Mr Minister of War*, 1957) [> FINNISH MILITARY FARCE], romances (*Kulkurin masurkka/The Vagabond's Mazurka* (1958), and adventure (*Ei ruumiita makuuhuoneeseen/No Bodies in the Bedroom*, 1959). Also worthy of mention is the eccentric trilogy of 'Westerns' Tarkas shot during this period – *Villi Pohjola/The Wild North* (1955), *Villin Pohjolan kulta/Gold from the Wild North* (1962) and *Villin Pohjolan salattu laakso/The Secret Valley of the Wild North* (1963) – in which the mythical Wild West has become a 'wild north' where male heroes in cowboy garb ride around the tundra dealing with the native Saami people. After studio-based film production collapsed in the early 1960s, Tarkas moved on to direct and produce for television. HS

TARKOVSKY, Andrey A.
Zavrazhye, Russia [USSR] 1932 – Paris, France 1986

Russian Soviet director and theorist. Son of the poet Arseni Tarkovsky, Andrey first studied Arabic, then worked as a geologist, and finally graduated from VGIK*, where he had been a pupil of Mikhail Romm*, in 1961. At VGIK he made a short television film, *Segodnya uvol'neniya ne budet/There Will Be No Leave Today* (1959), and for his graduation diploma a children's film entitled *Katok i skripka/The Steamroller and the Violin* (1961). His first feature, *Ivanovo detstvo/Ivan's Childhood* (1962), dealt with the relationship between the generations in World War II, mixing footage of the grim realities of war with dream sequences of a more tranquil past; it won the Grand Prix at the Venice film festival. But it was his next film, the epic *Andrei Rublëv* (1966; released 1971), which won the FIPRESCI Prize at Cannes, that brought him international fame, partly because it was suppressed in its complete form. The film, about the fifteenth-century icon painter, dealt with the problem of the artist's relationship with his environment and confronted the issue of artistic freedom, a dangerous notion in the USSR at that time. *Andrei Rublëv* was given only a limited home release and cut for distribution abroad. Tarkovsky's next film was the science-fiction epic *Solyaris/Solaris* (1972), which marked a significant shift towards the more metaphysical obsessions of his later work. He then shot two deeply personal and somewhat obscure films, which were partly autobiographical, *Zerkalo/The Mirror* (1974) and *Stalker* (1979), both characterised by a sense of longing and a search for meaning. Subsequently he worked abroad, making *Vremya puteshestviya/Tempo di viaggio/A Time for Voyaging* (1982) and *Nostalghia* (1983) in Italy. When *Nostalghia* was shown at Cannes the Soviet representatives, led by Sergei Bondarchuk*, successfully prevented it winning the Palme d'or and instead it was joint winner of a Special Jury Prize. Tarkovsky's treatment by his compatriots was one factor impelling him to the exile he dreaded, and his last film, *Offret/Zhertvoprinoshenie/The Sacrifice* (1986), was shot in Sweden. During his final illness from cancer there were moves towards a reconciliation, but he died in Paris, still an exile. Tarkovsky was very much a film-maker's film-maker, rejecting Eisensteinian notions of montage and believing instead that cinema represented what he called 'sculpted time'. Some of his writings have been published in English as *Sculpting in Time: Reflections on the Cinema* (1986) and *Time within Time: the Diaries* (1991). RT

Bib: Maya Turovskaya, *Tarkovsky: Cinema as Poetry* (1989).

TARR, Béla
Pécs 1955

Hungarian director. Tarr was only 22 when he made one of the most successful of the documentary-fiction [> DOCUMENTARY (HUNGARY)] films with his *Családi tűzfészek/Family Nest* (1979). It was only after completing this film that he started his studies at the Hungarian Academy of Theatre and Film Art. Since then he has made four feature films, moving steadily away from his generic starting point. His third film, *Panelkapcsolat/Prefabricated People* (1982), used professional actors whose style, as in many examples of Italian neo-realism*, was intended to look non-professional, although the storyboard still followed the conventions of the documentary-fiction genre. In his next film he adopted a highly stylised setting and improvised dialogue (though by professional actors). In *Kárhozat/Damnation* (1988) Tarr used black-and-white film stock and highly literary dialogue to achieve a mode of sophisticated abstraction. His most recent film (in production in 1993) is based on the novel *Sátántangó* (*Satan-Tango*) by László Krasznahorkai and reputedly runs for more than six hours. KAB

Other Films Include: *Szabadgyalog/The Outsider* (1980); *Őszi Almanach/Autumn Almanac* (1985).

TATI, Jacques
Jacques Tatischeff; Le Pecq 1908 – Paris 1982

French director. For filmgoers throughout the world, Jacques Tati *is* French comedy. In France, his critical reputation is high, but after the immense popularity of his 1950s films his career was chequered. While acting in a few films and in music hall as a mime, he directed six shorts, drawing on silent comics Max Linder*, Chaplin and Keaton. Like them, he was an actor-*auteur*, and like them his comic style, based on sight gags, was universally exportable. His Monsieur Hulot, first seen in *Les Vacances de Monsieur Hulot/Monsieur Hulot's Holiday* (1953), derived from François the postman in *Jour de fête* (1947, rel. 1949) and resurfaced in *Mon Oncle* (1958), *Playtime* (1964, rel. 1967), *Trafic/Traffic* (1971) and *Parade* (1974). With his tall, ungainly figure, and his signature raincoat, hat and pipe, Tati made Hulot the universal childlike innocent who creates chaos by ignoring adult rules – breaking implements in his sister's kitchen in *Mon Oncle*, wrecking an entire restaurant in *Playtime*. But Tati's novelty was to combine slapstick with a modernist sensibility. Formally, his films are extremely complex (and increasingly so, explaining his loss of popularity after *Mon Oncle*), exploiting to the full the possibilities of the frame and of sound. His soundtracks, mixing noises, grunts, expletives, advertisements, snatches of songs and different languages, are the aural equivalent of Jean-Luc Godard's* visual *bricolage*. From the start, too, Tati's films were a running commentary on the struggle between modernisation (or 'Americanisation') and tradition in France. An independent figure in the industry, he always had great difficulties raising finance (as well as satisfying the taxman); hence his small number of films. GV

Bib: Lucy Fischer, *Jacques Tati: A Guide to References and Resources* (1983).

TATOS, Alexandru
Bucharest 1937–[?] 1990

Romanian director and occasional scriptwriter whose subtle films show individuals as cogs in history. Tatos began as a playwright, then graduated as a stage director at the Bucharest Theatre and Film School and worked in theatre, often in collaboration with television. Following the major

television series *Un August în flăcări/August in Flames* (1973), co-directed with Dan Pița*, Tatos' first feature *Mere roșii/Red Apples* (1976) was a drama about a solitary young surgeon's conflict with authority in a provincial town, told with wit and sarcasm. The engineer Radu in *Casa dintre cîmpuri/The House Among the Fields* (1979) also isolates himself through his professional commitment. Tatos regarded *Secvențe/Sequences* (1982), which he also wrote, as his best film and a personal statement: 'reality' is the film crew, and fiction the film-within-the-film concerning torturer and victim. Tatos found that his own scripts were often unfilmable, and he was forced to adapt others' work. In *Întunecare/Gathering Clouds* (1985), influenced by Billy Wilder's *Sunset Boulevard*, a man is victim of his egotism, surrounded by complex and powerful women. The distinctive strands are all visible in his last film, *Cine are dreptate?/Who is Right?* (1990), about the solitude and loves of a district lawyer. Always a frail man, Tatos died at the height of his career a few weeks after the December 1989 revolution. MM

Bib: Cristina Corciovescu, 'Alexandru Tatos', *Moveast* (1992).

TAVERNIER, Bertrand
Lyons 1941

French director, former press attaché (notably for Georges de Beauregard*) and *Positif* critic. From his *Positif* days, Tavernier inherited a distrust of New Wave* auteurism, but a love of cinema (American as well as French). While his work is indeed eclectic, his first feature, *L'Horloger de Saint-Paul/The Watchmaker of Saint-Paul* (1973), contains several characteristic motifs, combining thriller elements (from a Simenon* novel) with a naturalistic view of a popular milieu in old Lyons, his home town. Intimist realism also marks *Une semaine de vacances* (1980) and *Daddy nostalgie/These Foolish Things* (1990), while *L.627* (1992) further elaborates the thriller-naturalism combination. Written by ex-policeman Michel Alexandre, this bleak film follows a drugs squad ineffectually tracking down immigrant dealers in rundown areas of Paris. Though Tavernier has also ventured into the futuristic (*La Mort en direct/Deathwatch*, 1980), most of his other work is historical. Influenced by the 'new history' of the 1970s, *Que la fête commence* (1974) and *La Passion Béatrice* (1987) attempt a non-glamorous look at history, while *Coup de Torchon/Clean Slate* (1981, in which a Jim Thompson thriller is transposed to colonial Africa) started a more traditional type of period reconstruction: 1950s Paris (*Round Midnight/Autour de minuit*, 1986, US/Fr.) and pre-World War I France (*Un dimanche à la campagne/Sunday in the Country*, 1984), in the Heritage cinema* genre. *La Fille de d'Artagnan/D'Artagnan's Daughter* (1994), a light swashbuckler, marks yet another departure. Tavernier has also made shorts and documentaries, including *Mississippi Blues* (1983, co-dir. Robert Parrish), and worked as a scriptwriter and producer. Tavernier's name has become synonymous with quality popular French cinema (solid scripts, classic performances, social issues, evoking the 'tradition of quality'*). During the 1993 GATT negotiations he was an ardent campaigner on behalf of European cinema. *L'Appât* (1995) won the Silver Bear at the Berlin film festival. His son Nils Tavernier is an actor. GV

Other Films: *Le Juge et l'assassin* (1975); *Des enfants gâtés* (1977); *La Vie et rien d'autre/Life and Nothing But* (1988).

TAVIANI, Paolo   San Miniato 1931
and
TAVIANI, Vittorio   San Miniato 1929

Italian directors. The first films of the Taviani brothers were made with their long-standing friend, Valentino Orsini. Together they experimented in a documentary mode in an attempt to go beyond neo-realism* while preserving certain realist imperatives. They succeeded with the intelligently constructed *Un uomo da bruciare/A Man for Burning* (1962), which retraces the life and death of a Sicilian trade unionist murdered by the Mafia, but rather less well with the incoherent *I fuorilegge del matrimonio/Outlaws of Marriage* (1963). The two brothers on their own then directed *I sovversivi* (1967), an ambitious attempt to combine several stories of personal or political crisis against the background of the funeral of Communist leader Palmiro Togliatti, and the cryptic *Sotto il segno dello Scorpione/Under the Sign of Scorpio* (1969), which initiated their characteristic cinema of utopia, eclectic in style but held together by a consistent Marxism. A sense of stylistic maturity emerged in *San Michele aveva un gallo/St Michael Had a Rooster* (1971), an apologia for a latter-day anarchist. Then, after the grotesque *Allonsanfan* (1974), they made the harsh and sober *Padre padrone/Father Master* (1977), the story of an ultimately victorious struggle against oppressive patriarchal power, and the film which brought them to international attention. Another breaking point was the 'peasant fresco' *La notte di San Lorenzo/The Night of San Lorenzo* (1982), which used a combination of reportage and fantasy, epic and elegy to depict the struggle against Fascism. Since then the Tavianis have distanced themselves somewhat from the political-existentialist tension of their earlier films, concentrating on the pleasures of storytelling and elegant *mise-en-scène*. *Kaos* (1984), a retelling of some Sicilian stories by Luigi Pirandello, is their most successful film in this vein. GVo

Other Films Include: *Il prato/The Meadow* (1980); *Good Morning Babilonia/Good Morning Babylon* (1987); *Il sole sorge anche di notte* (1990); *Fiorile* (1993).

TÉCHINÉ, André   Valence d'Agen 1943

French director. A former film critic, Téchiné is one of the important post-New Wave* French directors. His *Souvenirs d'en France* (1975) explored the relation between history and personal 'histories' (the title contains a pun on 'en France' and 'enfance', childhood), focusing on a family from the 1930s to the 1970s. His subsequent work concentrated on the personal, couched in a spectacular, elegant though rather cold *mise-en-scène*: *Barocco* (1976), *Les Soeurs Brontë/The Brontë Sisters* (1979, with a distinguished cast including Isabelle Huppert*, Isabelle Adjani*, Marie-France Pisier and the writer Roland Barthes in a cameo part), *Hôtel des Amériques* (1981) with Catherine Deneuve*, and *Rendez-vous* (1985).

Later films have narrowed the canvas to smaller-scale, intense family dramas such as *Le Lieu du crime* (1986), *Ma saison préférée* (1993) – both with Deneuve – and *Les Roseaux sauvages* (1994). One unusual characteristic of Téchiné's work is his unsensational evocation of homosexuality (*Les Innocents*, 1988, *J'embrasse pas*, 1991, *Les Roseaux sauvages*, 1994). Another is his use of his native south-west, acknowledging the beauty of the landscape while avoiding touristic cliché. GV

Bib: Jill Forbes, *The Cinema in France After the New Wave* (1992).

TELLES, António da Cunha   Funchal 1935

Portuguese producer and director. After graduating from IDHEC* in Paris, Telles returned to Lisbon and founded a production company which signalled the birth of the New Portuguese Cinema*, its first film being Paulo Rocha's* *Os Verdes Anos/The Green Years* (1963). As part of an international strand to his strategy, Telles also co-produced Pierre Kast's *Vacances portugaises* (1963) and François Truffaut's* *La Peau douce* (1964) in France. In 1967 the company was bankrupt. Believing it was still possible to make successful 'new cinema', Telles turned director with *O Cerco/The Roundup*, a title that sums up the feelings of his generation. Providing the actress Maria Cabral with her first screen opportunity, *O Cerco* was indeed a success. In 1972 Telles founded Animatógrafo, an extremely important distribution and later exhibition company, which introduced films by *auteurs* such as Bernardo Bertolucci*, Alain Tanner* and Glauber Rocha to Portuguese audiences; its most glorious exploit, however, was perhaps to secure the first Portuguese release of Sergei Eisenstein's* *Bronenosets Potëmkin/The Battleship Potemkin* just days after the revolution of 25 April 1974. In the late 1970s and early 1980s, Telles was manager of the Portuguese Institute of Cinema and of the Tobis studio in Lisbon. Returning to production in 1983 with Animatógrafo (now minus its distribution branch), Telles attempted to turn Portugal into an international film-making centre. Though he produced some Portuguese films and co-produced foreign ones, he basically became a line producer. In 1994 he launched a third effort to support Portuguese production with the Companhia de Filmes Príncipe Real. His films as director are *Meus Amigos/My Friends* (1973), *Continuar a Viver ou Os Índios da Meia-Praia/Carry on Living or the Natives of Meia-Praia* (documentary, 1975), *Vidas/Lives* (1984) and *La Dérive/Drifting* (1994). It is no accident that 'living' or 'lives' figure in two of these titles. Telles' films are closely based on the observation of people. In the final shot of *Meus Amigos*, his best film, a couple is still arguing as the woman asks, 'Is this still part of the film?' The couple was real, and the situation is characteristically and ambiguously suspended between reality and fiction. His characters are often drifting, as suggested by the title of his latest work, *La Dérive*. Shot in French, it continues an international strategy whose merits, thirty years on, are still controversial. AMS

Other Films as Producer: *Belarmino* (1964; dir. Fernando Lopes); *Mudar de Vida/Change of Life* (1967; dir. Paulo

Rocha*); *Balada da Praia dos Cães* (1986; dir. José Fonseca e Costa); *O Bobo* (1987; dir. José Àlvaro Moraes); *Paraíso Perdido/Lost Paradise* (1985–90; dir. Seixas Santos); *O Fio do Horizonte/On the Edge of the Horizon* (1993; dir. Fernando Lopes); *Aqui na Terra/Here on Earth* (1993; dir. João Botelho*). **As co-producer**: *Street of No Return* (1989; dir. Samuel Fuller); *1871* (1990; dir. Ken McMullen); *Belle Epoque* (1992; dir. Fernando Trueba*).

TEPTSOV, Oleg   Born 1954

Russian director, who trained in the Higher Courses for Directors organised by Goskino, the State Cinema Committee. His first film, *Gospodin oformitel'/Mr Designer* (1987), is scripted by the poet Yuri Arabov, from the Soviet writer Alexander Grin's story 'The Grey Car', and contains music by the avant-garde composer Sergei Kurekhin. Set in St Petersburg at the beginning of the twentieth century, it tells the story of a mannequin which comes to life and destroys its artist creator. Teptsov's artistic boldness is also apparent in his second film, *Posvyashchënnyi/The Initiate* (1989), also from an Arabov script and with Kurekhin's music, in which the angel of destruction gives the hero the frightening power to judge and execute people at will. JGf

TERCERA VÍA

Spanish film genre. The term refers to Spanish film-makers steering a course between dissidence and endorsement of Francoism in the later stages of the regime. Spanish *tercera vía* (third way) cinema became prominent in the early 1970s, promoted in particular by producer José Luis Dibildos. It drew on both Hollywood farce and domestic comic genres [> COMEDY (SPAIN)], depended heavily on sexual innuendo and capitalised on the cosmetic relaxation of censorship in respect of such issues as on-screen nudity. The attempt to combine popular appeal with social criticism achieved some box-office success but provoked accusations of frivolity and opportunism. Although failing to attract the foreign audiences to which they also aspired, *tercera vía* films nevertheless succeeded in introducing hitherto taboo subjects such as extramarital sex, contraception and abortion, highlighting an anachronistic and hypocritical morality in Spanish society. Early precursors include such films as Manuel Summers'* *No somos de piedra/We're Not Made of Stone* (1968), which ridicules social attitudes towards contraception, but it was with Roberto Bodegas's *Españolas en París/Spaniards in Paris* (1970), about a group of women émigrées in France, that the genre came into its own. A plethora of *tercera vía* films followed, such as Bodegas's *Vida conyugal sana/Healthy Married Life* (1974), concerning the advertisement-induced obsessions of a middle-class business executive, and Vicente Escrivá's *Lo verde comienza en los Pirineos/Smut Starts in the Pyrenees* (1973), which focused on a group of young men on a porn-movie jaunt to Biarritz. Jaime de Armiñán's* *El amor del Capitán Brando/The Love of Captain Brando* (1974), in which a young teacher is sacked for attempting to introduce sex education in a village school, marks the apex of the *tercera*

vía. Franco's death in 1975, which allowed film-makers freedom of expression, marked the decline of the genre. RM

TERRY-THOMAS   Thomas Terry Hoar-Stevens;
London 1911 – Godalming 1990

British actor, of the comic rotter school, particularly associated with the Boulting Brothers* comedies in the 1950s. Postwar British film comedy, with its links back to radio and music hall, produced a stable of actors who became comic types (Wilfrid Hyde-White, Arthur Mullard, Irene Handl). Terry-Thomas' type was a combination of the raffish World War II pilot and the upper-class cad who spent too much time at the racecourse, a type which exported well when he played the RAF pilot, alongside Bourvil* and Louis de Funès*, in *La Grande vadrouille/Don't Look Now ... We're Being Shot At* (1963, Fr./UK), one of the most popular French films ever. His flamboyant moustache, his gap-tooth, his cigarette holder, his sports cars and his tendency to dress on the loud side were the familiar emblems of 'class' trying too hard to be 'classy'. His popularity as a comic cad was ensured by his ultimate ineptitude and underlying innocence. JC

Other Films Include: *Private's Progress, The Green Man* (1956); *Brothers in Law, Lucky Jim, Blue Murder at St Trinian's, The Naked Truth* (1957); *Too Many Crooks, Carlton-Browne of the F.O., I'm All Right Jack* (1959); *School for Scoundrels* (1960); *How to Murder Your Wife, Strange Bedfellows* [US], *Those Magnificent Men in their Flying Machines* (1965); *Diabolik* (1967, It.); *Monte Carlo or Bust!* (1969); *The Abominable Dr Phibes* (1971); *Le braghe del padrone/The Master's Pants* (1978, It.); *The Hound of the Baskervilles* (1978).

THEMERSON, Franciszka   Warsaw 1907 –
London 1988
and
THEMERSON, Stefan   Płock 1910 – London
1988

Polish film-makers and artists who lived in Paris from 1938 and London from 1942. The Themersons' masterpiece, *Europa* (1932), which gave a dramatic, lyrical and abstract form to the social protest of Anatol Stern's futurist poem, was hailed as the first Polish avant-garde film. They were founder-members in 1935 of SAF, the world's first film-makers' co-operative (others were Aleksander Ford* and Wanda Jakubowska*), created its journal *f.a.* ('Artistic Film') and forged links with France and Britain (including with John Grierson*).

Constructivist abstraction rubs shoulders with Dadaist humour in the Themersons' work. They invented an apparatus for making 'photograms in motion', scratched and painted on film, and fused animation and photomontage with live action. Apart from stills and photograms, *Przygoda Człowieka Poczciwego/The Adventure of a Good Citizen* (1937) was the only one of their five Polish films to survive the war. It uses free narrative to subvert conventional notions of culture/

nature, abstraction/realism and content/form, and was influential on Polish postwar film, not least Roman Polanski's* *Dwaj Ludzie z Szafą/Two Men and a Wardrobe* (1958). *The Eye & the Ear* (1944–45, UK), their culminating 'music to picture essay', typifies their lifelong interest in unexpected meaning arising from translation. *Calling Mr Smith* (1943, UK) was a propaganda film for the exiled Polish government, which, like their early commissioned films, transcended its brief and became a poetic technical experiment. The Themersons scripted, directed, shot and edited their films in partnership. Subsequently they followed independent careers, Franciszka as artist, Stefan as writer, but co-founded a publishing house, Gaberbocchus Press (1948). Their last illustrated book, *The Urge to Create Visions* (1983), which includes Stefan's prophetic 1928 piece on 'radio with images', is a manifesto of their vision of cinema as an open medium. IH
[> AVANT-GARDE CINEMA IN EUROPE]

Bib: *Pix*, vol. 1 (1993–94).

THEODORAKIS, Mikis   Chios 1925

Greek composer; also politician. Theodorakis' career spans music and politics, often combining the two. Since his youth he has been active in both fields, his activities in radical politics resulting in long periods of imprisonment and exile. He was first imprisoned during the German occupation when he was still a student at the Athens Conservatory. Since his return to Greece after the fall of the dictatorship in 1974, he has changed party allegiance several times, recently serving as a minister in the Conservative government. His musical activities have been as varied. He has written orchestral music, oratorios, ballets, song cycles, theatre and film music. His music is often inspired by political and historical events. He rose to international prominence with the music for *Zorba the Greek* (1964), and has worked regularly with Michael Cacoyannis* and Costa-Gavras*, notably for *Z* (1969). TN

Bib: Gail Holst, *Theodorakis, Myth and Politics in Modern Greek Music* (1980).

Other Films Include: *To xipolito tagma/Barefoot Battalion* (1954); *Electra, Phaedra* (1962); *The Trojan Women* (1971, US); *Etat de siège/State of Siege* [Fr.], *Serpico* [US] (1973); *Actas de Marusia/Letters from Marusia* (1976, Mex.); *Iphigenia* (1977); *O anthropos me to garifalo/The Man with the Carnation* (1980).

THESSALONIKI (SALONIKA) FILM FESTIVAL

Greek film festival, the major annual cinematic event in the country. The first Greek Cinema Week took place in September 1960. Despite the misgivings of Greek producers, it was soon firmly established, renamed the Greek Film Festival seven years later and given new rules and a more democratic structure. A separate international section was established in 1966, coinciding with the emergence of a new generation of film-makers prefiguring the arrival of the New Greek Cinema*. The conflict between 'new' and 'old' cinematic approaches stirred the emotions of the public. At the heart of the conflict was the audience of the Second Balcony (the cheapest seats) of the Salonika State Theatre, the traditional venue of the festival. Students, young people and cinephiles expressed their points of view, sometimes violently, often interrupting screenings.

In 1974 the fall of the junta gave new impetus to the festival, which turned into a showcase for the New Greek Cinema, with screenings, discussions, arguments and manifestos. The Second Balcony became a separate institution, giving its own awards and pressing for reforms. Subsequent festivals took place against a background of continuous conflict between the Ministry for Industry (responsible for the cinema and the festival), film-makers' unions and the public, which reached a peak in 1977 when a parallel anti-festival was held. In 1981 the Ministry of Culture took over responsibility for the festival. The international section was cancelled, and by the end of the decade declining Greek production was too meagre to sustain the event. In 1992, in an attempt at rejuvenation, the festival decided to go for an international profile, with a Greek section. The 1993 International Film Festival made a promising start, with a competitive section for directors presenting their first or second feature film. NF

THIELE, Rolf   Redlice, Czechoslovakia 1918

German producer, scriptwriter and director, co-founder of one of the many small companies the Allies licensed after World War II, in order to decentralise the post-Ufa* German film industry. Filmaufbau Göttingen, set up in 1946, did better than most, with Thiele the producer responsible for some of the biggest box-office hits of the 1950s, such as *Nachtwache* (1949), *Königliche Hoheit* (1953) and *Die Buddenbrooks* (1959, two parts). The company had its first major success with a *Trümmerfilm* ('ruin film'), *Liebe 47* (1949).

As a director, Thiele seemed to have two passions. One was Thomas Mann adaptations (including *Tonio Kröger*, 1964); the other, double standards in matters of sexuality (*Primanerinnen*, 1951; *Sie*, 1954). The film for which he is remembered is *Das Mädchen Rosemarie* (1958), with Nadja Tiller* as the high-class prostitute in a satirical account of an infamous Frankfurt society scandal involving patricians, new money and politicians: just the sort of tale of hypocrisy and lust to fire Thiele's imagination. In the late 1960s, when hypocrisy was no longer an issue, Thiele concentrated on lust and made sex films. TE

Bib: Hans-Michael Bock, Wolfgang Jacobsen (eds.), *Filmaufbau GmbH Göttingen* (1993).

THIELE, Wilhelm   Wilhelm Isersohn; Vienna 1890 – Los Angeles, California 1975

Austrian director and scriptwriter, who studied music and worked as a stage actor and director in Austria. Influenced by Erik Charell's stage operettas, he went to Germany as a stage director, was hired as a film actor (1920–22; his first film was *Orchideen*), then as a scriptwriter (for instance *Die kleine* vom Varieté, 1926; dir. Hanns Schwarz*) and director (from 1922). Although relatively successful as writer and director of silent film operettas (his first film as director was Carl Michael Ziehrer, der letzte Walzerkönig, 1922) and comedies (Adieu Mascotte, 1929), Thiele became famous for his innovative use of sound in Liebeswalzer/The Love Waltz (1929, Ger./UK) and Die Drei von der Tankstelle/Le Chemin du paradis (1930, Ger./Fr.), which made him the father of the German Tonfilmoperette (sound film operetta). He made French and English versions of his German-speaking films. His use of sound and image for comic effects and integration of singing and dancing in the plot foreshadowed the 'integrated' Hollywood musical. Thiele emigrated in 1933 and found work in Britain, Austria and New York before going to Hollywood, where he made his first film in 1935 (Lottery Lover), followed by more or less successful B-movies (such as Tarzan Triumphs, 1943) and series (such as The Cavalcade of America, 1952–56), but no musicals. He also made documentaries and promotional films and worked in television from 1951. In 1960 Thiele directed two comedies in Germany – Der letzte Fußgänger and Sabine und die 100 Männer – before going back to Hollywood. KU

THULIN, Ingrid   Solleftea 1929

Swedish actress. Like Bibi Andersson*, Harriet Andersson* and Liv Ullmann*, the stage-trained Thulin has been closely associated with the films of Ingmar Bergman*, starting with Smultronstället/Wild Strawberries (1957) and including Tystnaden/The Silence (1963), Vargtimmen/Hour of the Wolf (1968) and Viskningar och rop/Cries and Whispers (1973). Her portrayal of Professor Borg's (Victor Sjöström*) daughter-in-law in Smultronstället, contrasted to the bubbly (and younger) Bibi Andersson, encapsulates her screen image as the cool and distinguished blonde beauty who suffers with dignity. Alain Resnais* used this image astutely in La Guerre est finie/The War is Over (1966, Fr.) to signify the temptation of embourgeoisement for the Spanish anti-fascist militant hero Yves Montand*. Thulin has had a substantial international career, especially in Italy, where her most prominent film was Luchino Visconti's* La caduta degli dei/The Damned (1969). She has worked as a scriptwriter and directed a film, Brusten Himmel/Broken Sky (1982). GV

TILLER, Nadja   Maria Tiller; Vienna 1929

Austrian actress. Though she trained as an actress and dancer at Max Reinhardt's* school, Tiller initially mainly played characters of little depth, and after being elected 'Miss Austria' she mostly embodied beautiful young women in such films as Märchen vom Glück/Traum vom Glück (1949) until her mentor, Rolf Thiele*, provided a new departure for her. In Thiele's Die Barrings (1955) and Harald Braun's Die Botschafterin (1960), and in Gilles Grangier's Le Désordre et la nuit (1958, with Jean Gabin*), she embodied sexy but stronger women; in Thiele's scandalous and very successful Das Mädchen Rosemarie/The Girl Rosemarie (1958) she was a high-class prostitute, and she finally 'became' the ultimate femme fatale in Lulu (1962). Tiller subsequently mainly

worked in French and Italian film, and for German television and theatre. KU

TISSE, Eduard K.   Liban, Latvia [Russian Empire] 1897 – Moscow 1961

Latvian-born Soviet cameraman. Tisse worked at the front in both World War I and the Russian Civil War, during which he made a number of agit-films*. He is best known for his association with Sergei Eisenstein*, working on all his films, including the abortive Mexican project. After Eisenstein's death Tisse collaborated with Grigori Alexandrov* on Vstrecha na El'be/Meeting on the Elbe (1949) and Kompozitor Glinka/The Composer Glinka (1952). Regarded as one of the leading Soviet cameramen, Tisse taught at the state film school in Moscow, later VGIK*, from 1921. RT

TITANUS

Italian production company. The history of Titanus is closely identified with the Lombardo family. The father, Gustavo, moved from Naples to Rome and in 1928 founded Titanus, initially a distribution company with just a few in-house productions: between 1932 and 1935 it produced thirteen run-of-the-mill films. When Gustavo's son Goffredo (born Naples, 1920) joined the company, Titanus went more systematically into production: it enlarged its Farnesina studios, bought the Scalera theatre chain, and created an integrated distribution and exhibition circuit. It developed a balanced strategy for the production of popular films – by such directors as Raffaello Matarazzo* and Dino Risi* – and auteur cinema, with film-makers like Giuseppe De Santis* (Roma ore 11, 1952), Alberto Lattuada* (La Spiaggia/The Beach, 1954) and Federico Fellini* (Il bidone/The Swindlers, 1955). Goffredo Lombardo put a personal stamp on his films and influenced the course of Italian cinema as much as the auteurs he produced. In the late 1950s he stood out as a remarkable pioneer of a technically and culturally 'European' cinema, producing Luchino Visconti's* Rocco e i suoi fratelli/Rocco and His Brothers (1960) as well as films by Vittorio De Sica*, Mario Monicelli*, Valerio Zurlini*, Elio Petri*, and many others. Titanus experienced a severe crisis in the early to 1960s, mostly because of two super-productions in which it invested enormous funds: Visconti's Il Gattopardo/The Leopard (1963) and the disastrous Sodoma e Gomorra/Sodom and Gomorrah (1961, dir. Robert Aldrich). But it survived and managed more successful productions, including the 'discovery' of Giuseppe Tornatore* (Il camorrista/The Camorra Member, 1986). However, the company's main assets were acquired by the Romagnoli construction group, and ten years later Titanus disappeared. Only a small production house survived, controlled by Goffredo Lombardo and mainly devoted to occasional television productions. GVo

TODD, Ann   Hartford 1909 – London 1993

British actress, probably best known for her role in two Sydney and Muriel Box* productions, both directed by

Compton Bennett: *The Seventh Veil* (1945) and *Daybreak* (1946). If Margaret Lockwood* claimed the high ground of wicked lady in the women's films of the 1940s, Todd inhabited the realms of neurosis, sensitivity and instability familiar from American *film noir*. She had already played Ralph Richardson's* 'mad wife in the attic' in *South Riding* (1938), and in *The Seventh Veil* she plays the tyrannical James Mason's* victim/protégée: a pianist pursued by young men, dominated by the Mason father figure, and finally restored to health and romantic love by the intervention of psychoanalysis. *Daybreak* also has *film noir's* predilection for figures caught in the past, with Todd escaping through suicide. Todd married David Lean* in 1949, and made three films with him: *The Passionate Friends* (1949), *Madeleine* (1950) and *The Sound Barrier* (1952). In the 1960s and 1970s she wrote, produced and directed a number of travel documentaries. JC

Other Films Include: *The Ghost Train* (1931); *The Return of Bulldog Drummond* (1934); *Things to Come* (1936); *Perfect Strangers* (1945); *Gaiety George* (1946); *The Paradine Case* (US, 1947); *Time Without Pity* (1957); *Il figlio del Capitano Blood/The Son of Captain Blood* (1962, It./Sp.).

TOGNAZZI, Ugo   Cremona 1922 – Rome 1990

Italian actor. Unlike Vittorio Gassman* or Marcello Mastroianni*, Tognazzi had to wait until his mature years before his talent was fully recognised. He served a long apprenticeship in variety shows and cheap comic television programmes (together with Raimondo Vianello) before finding his way to the cinema. In film, he worked with directors such as Luciano Salce (*Il federale/The Fascist*, 1961), Dino Risi* (*La marcia su Roma/The March to Rome*, 1962) and especially Marco Ferreri*, who made repeated use of him from *L'ape regina/The Conjugal Bed* (1963) onwards. Ferreri was the first to recognise Tognazzi's special talent, particularly his covert sense of humour, which made him more flexible than, for example, the standard Alberto Sordi* character. Tognazzi was one of the key figures in *commedia all'italiana**, whose remarkable flexibility inspired a range of *auteurs* to create non-comic roles for him: Bernardo Bertolucci* (*La tragedia di un uomo ridicolo/The Tragedy of a Ridiculous Man*, 1981, which won Tognazzi an award for best actor at the Cannes film festival), Pier Paolo Pasolini* (*Porcile/Pigsty*, 1969), Alberto Bevilacqua (*La califfa*, 1970). The films for which he will be best remembered include Antonio Pietrangeli's* *Io la conoscevo bene/I Knew Her Well* (1965), Ettore Scola's* *Il commissario Pepe* (1969) and Risi's *In nome del popolo italiano/In the Name of the Italian People* (1972). In all these he specialised in the predicaments of masculinity in the context of provincial or metropolitan despair. A very skilled actor, he gained the esteem of his directors, was encouraged by the critics and adored by the public (yet he bitterly criticised the cinema shortly before he died). His considerable range overlapped with that of other great comic actors of his generation: he could be Sordi's mean 'average' Italian, Gassman's ostentatious braggart, Nino Manfredi's well-behaved 'everyman', and Mastroianni's tormented bourgeois, but he always succeeded in adding some qualities of his own. PDA

Other Films Include: *I cadetti di Guascogna* (1950); *Una bruna indiavolate* (1951); *Noi siamo due evasi* (1959); *La voglia matta* (1962); *Le ore dell'amore/The Hours of Love, I mostri/The Monsters* (1963); *La donna scimmia/The Ape Woman* (1964); *Marcia nuziale* (1966); *Barbarella* (1967, Fr.); *La bambolona, Straziami ma di baci saziami/Hurt Me, But Cover Me with Your Kisses* (1968); *Venga a prendere il caffè da noi/Come Have Coffee With Us* (1970); *L'udienza* (1971); *La Grande Bouffe/La grande abbuffata* [Fr./It.], *Vogliamo i colonnelli* (1973); *Touche pas la femme blanche/Non toccare la donna bianca* [Fr./It.], *Amici miei/My Friends* (1975); *La Cage aux folles/Il vizietto* (1978, Fr./It.); *La terrazza/The Terrace* (1979); *Dagobert* (1984); *Bertoldo, Bertoldino e Cacasenno* (1984).

TORNATORE, Giuseppe   Born 1956

Italian director. On the strength of a promising first film, *Il camorrista/The Camorra Member* (1986), starring Ben Gazzara and produced for Silvio Berlusconi's Fininvest* group, Giuseppe Tornatore went on in 1988 to write and direct *Nuovo Cinema Paradiso/Cinema Paradiso*, the story of a young boy who takes over as projectionist in a cinema in Sicily in the 1930s (the film co-stars Philippe Noiret*). After an unsuccessful first release, *Nuovo Cinema Paradiso* was cut and radically reshaped under the supervision of its producer, Franco Cristaldi*, and went on to win the Palme d'or at Cannes and international art-house success in Europe and the United States. He was unable to repeat this success with his next film, *Stanno tutti bene/Everybody's Fine*, about an aged Sicilian patriarch (played by Marcello Mastroianni*) who goes to see his five children who have emigrated to mainland Italy and finds that, contrary to the film's title, they are not doing fine at all. GNS

TORNES, Stavros   Athens 1932–88

Greek director, scriptwriter and actor. Tornes worked both as an actor and as an assistant director in Greece from 1958 and in Italy between 1967 and 1981. As a performer he appeared in films by Francesco Rosi*, the Taviani* brothers and Roberto Rossellini*. As assistant director he worked with Elia Kazan (*America, America*, 1963) and Michael Cacoyannis* (*Zorba the Greek*, 1964). He made his first feature, *Coatti* (1977), in Italy. Tornes is a uniquely individual film-maker, dedicated to his own personal vision [> NEW GREEK CINEMA]. His films are poetic and magical journeys, often into virtually unknown communities or areas of Greece, such as gypsy bands or the central Peloponnese, through which he investigates universal themes such as the relationship of time and space (*Balamos*, 1982) or fear of dying (*Karkalou*, 1984). TN

Other Films Include: *Thiraikos orthros/Thira Matins* (1968, short, co-dir. Kostas Sfikas); *Danilo Treles* (1986); *Enas erodios ya tin Germania/Heron for Germany* (1987).

TOTÒ
Antonio de Curtis; Naples 1898 – Rome 1967

Italian actor. Although the quality of the films in which he appeared is sometimes debatable, there is no questioning Totò's status as one of the greatest European comics. He made his name as a variety artist, and entered films at the end of the 1930s. His first films were in the gently absurdist tradition of late 1930s Italian humour. After *Fermo con le mani* (1937, dir. Gero Zambuto), roles were scripted for him by Achille Campanile (*Animali pazzi*, 1939, dir. Carlo Ludovico Bragaglia) and Cesare Zavattini* (*San Giovanni Decollato*, 1940, dir. Amleto Palermi). But that whimsical mode was unsuited to Totò's aggressive character – perpetually hungry for food, for sex, for a place in the sun – which he had created for himself on stage and was to establish in his postwar films. This character had its roots in popular tradition, going as far back as Pulcinella in the *commedia dell'arte* and indeed beyond.

Throughout the postwar period, Totò dominated Italian film production, churning out film after film, most of them written and directed as vehicles for his distinctive talent and persona. The films directed for him by Mario Mattoli, which include *I due orfanelli* (1947), *Totò al giro d'Italia* (1948), the involuntary masterpiece *I pompieri di Viggiù* (1949), *Totò Tarzan* (1950), *Un Turco napoletano* (1953), and *Miseria e nobiltà/Poverty and Nobility* (1954), are probably the most typical. But the first films directed by Stefano Steno* and Mario Monicelli* (*Totò cerca casa/Totò Wants a Home*, 1949; *Totò e i re di Roma*, 1951), or Carlo Ludovico Bragaglia (*Totò cerca moglie*, 1950), Luigi Comencini* (*L'imperatore di Capri*, 1949), Camillo Mastrocinque (*Siamo uomini o caporali?*, 1955 – the film Totò most thought of as his own), Sergio Corbucci, Lucio Fulci and Mario Amendola follow much the same path. Heir to the acrobatic '*buffi*' of variety, Totò carried over to the screen his most famous sketches (an anthology of which can be found in Steno's *Totò a colori*, 1952, a minor classic). Totò typically would burst out in a set of frenzied variations, helped by a limitless capacity for improvisation and a disjointed physique which he used like a surreal puppet. The Totò persona, ultimately larger and more 'human' than his characters, was located between the sub-proletariat and the lower middle class; it was resentful, vulgar, aggressive, intolerant of convention and in constant struggle for survival – an ambivalent breath of freedom in the suffocating Italy of the 1950s. The encounter with neo-realism* gave rise to a compromise which humanised the character but fortunately without losing any of its craziness or vitality, as shown by his performances in Eduardo De Filippo's* *Napoli milionaria/Side Street Story* (1950), Steno and Monicelli's *Guardie e ladri/Cops and Robbers* (1951) and the (censored) *Totò e Carolina* (1953), and above all as the madcap hero of Vittorio De Sica's* *L'oro di Napoli/The Gold of Naples* (1954). The Totò persona was exploited by other prestigious directors, including Roberto Rossellini* (*Dov'è la libertà?*, 1953), Alberto Lattuada* (as the villainous priest in *La mandragola*, 1965) and Pier Paolo Pasolini*, who constructed around it the figure of the itinerant sub-proletarian of *Uccellacci e uccellini/The Hawks and the Sparrows* (1966) and the extraordinary Iago of *Che cosa sono le nuvole?* (1967, an episode of *Capriccio all'italiana*).

Right until the end of his long career (and even when his eyesight began to fail) Totò remained the consummate professional, true to his roots in Neapolitan popular comedy. Impervious to high-art influence (except perhaps Pirandello) or to that of other screen comics, he was prized by the Italian public for his timelessness, a film personality to add to the great stage ones of Harlequin and Pulcinella. GF

TOURNEUR, Maurice
Maurice Thomas; Paris 1876–1961

French director. An actor and then director at the Eclair studio, Tourneur had a successful career in Hollywood, where he was considered a great 'pictorialist', and came back to France in 1926. His thirty (mostly sound) French films show his skill with popular genres. *Les Gaietés de l'escadron/The Joys of the Squadron* (1932) is a classic *comique troupier** with a remarkable cast (Raimu*, Fernandel*, Jean Gabin*); *Justin de Marseille* (1934) a thriller set in Pagnol* territory; *Avec le sourire/With a Smile* (1936) a cynical comedy with – and to some extent about – Maurice Chevalier*. *Koenigsmark* (1935) and *Katia* (1938) are two melodramas of great visual beauty in the 'Slav' sub-genre; *Cécile est morte/Cécile is Dead* (1944) a Simenon* adaptation with Albert Préjean* as Inspector Maigret; and *Impasse des deux anges* (1948) a *noir* drama with Paul Meurisse and Simone Signoret*. Tourneur's son, Jacques Tourneur (Paris 1904 – Bergerac 1978), learnt his trade in Hollywood with his father and worked with him on some of his French films. In the US, he made the cult horror film *Cat People* (1942) and the *noir* thriller *Out of the Past/Build My Gallows High* (1947). GV

TOYE, Wendy
London 1917

British director. One of very few women directors in British cinema, Toye began as a dancer at the age of seven, staging a performance at the London Palladium when she was ten. She appeared as a dancer in *Invitation to the Waltz* (1935), and toured Europe with her own ballet company, Ballet-Hoo, in the late 1940s. She directed a widely acclaimed short fantasy, *The Stranger Left No Card* (1953), and on the strength of its success was given a contract by Alexander Korda* at London Films, where she made *The Teckman Mystery* (1954). Her films include such comedies as *Raising a Riot* (1955) and *All for Mary* (1955), but she mostly worked in theatre and opera. She has directed occasionally for television since 1955, including a remake of *The Stranger Left No Card* (called *Stranger in Town*, 1982) for the Anglia television series 'Tales of the Unexpected'. JC

Other Films Include: *Three Cases of Murder* [ep.] (1955); *True as a Turtle* (1957); *We Joined the Navy* (1962); *The King's Breakfast* (1963).

TRADITION OF QUALITY

French stylistic trend within mainstream French films made in the 1940s and 1950s. On the one hand, the term refers to a loose industry category, actively promoted (by financial aid and prizes) to project a 'quality' image of French film: expertly crafted pictures with high production values and often derived from literary sources. Psychological and/or costume dramas such as Jean Delannoy's* *La Symphonie pastorale* (1946), Claude Autant-Lara's* *Douce* (1943), René Clément's* *Jeux interdits/Forbidden Games* (1952), Max Ophuls'* *La Ronde* (1950), Jacqueline Audry's * *Minne, L'ingénue libertine/Minne* (1950), Jean Renoir's* *French Cancan* (1955), René Clair's* *Les Grandes manoeuvres* (1955), all projected an image of Frenchness tied to good taste and high culture. Many were co-productions, often with Italy, on account of cost, and most were box-office hits. On the other hand, the term was turned by François Truffaut* into one of abuse against what he labelled 'A certain tendency of French cinema' (*Cahiers du cinéma**, January 1954). Truffaut's dislike of the 'quality' films rested on four notions antithetical to the future *auteur* cinema of the New Wave*. First, it was a 'cinema of scriptwriters' [> AURENCHE, JEAN AND BOST, PIERRE], as opposed to being made by 'men of the cinema'; second, its focus was on psychological realism– often pessimistic, anti-clerical and 'anti-bourgeois' rather than 'existential' romantic self-expression; third, the *mise-en-scène* was too polished (studio sets, scholarly framings, complicated lighting, classical editing), as against a more casual, improvised cinema of the 'open air'; fourth, it was mass-appeal cinema, relying on genres and especially stars, as opposed to the personality of the *auteur*. Truffaut's contempt was polemic and excessive (but has had a massive influence on the dominant historiography of French cinema ever since). If some of the 'quality' films are mannered and 'academic', others are sumptuous, lively or ironically distant. The costume dramas also presented to a mass audience subjects marginalised in other genres, such as women's desires – for instance Audry's *Olivia/The Pit of Loneliness* (1951) and Jacques Becker's* *Casque d'Or/Golden Marie* (1952). GV

TRANSYLVANIA

Central European province now part of modern Romania (but historically disputed territory with Hungary), given mythical status in film as the homeland of the hero of Bram Stoker's novel *Dracula* (1897), much adapted in European – as well as American – cinema: over 160 versions are recorded, among which the most famous are: F. W. Murnau's* *Nosferatu, eine Symphonie des Grauens/Nosferatu the Vampire* (1922, Ger.), Terence Fisher's* *Dracula* (1958, UK) and *Dracula, Prince of Darkness* (1965, UK), and Werner Herzog's* *Nosferatu – Phantom der Nacht/Nosferatu the Vampyre* (1979, Ger.). Transylvanian Romanians, however, view Dracula, based on the medieval Romanian prince Vlad Tepeş, as a national hero and resent his bloodthirsty image in European film culture. *Vlad Tepeş/Vlad the Impaler* or *The True Life of Dracula* (1980, dir. Dimitru Fernoagă) presents the Romanian version. Transylvania is a semi-mythic cultural heartland for both the Hungarian and the Romanian nations, and is regularly used as the backdrop for nationalist Romanian historical epics such as *Dacii/The Dacians* (1966). The earliest Romanian and Hungarian documentaries recorded Transylvanian peasant life and scenery, notably Paul Călinescu's *Tara Moţilor/Land of the Motzi* (1938)

and *Emberek a havason/Men on the Mountains* (1942, by the Hungarian director István Szőts*); and the first Romanian Western mildly parodied hardy peasant virtues in *Profetul, aurel şi ardelenii/The Prophet, the Gold and the Transylvanians* (1977). Until recently, Romanian and Hungarian film-makers have been unable to examine seriously the complex interweaving of diverse national cultures in the region, since the political passions are too strong (in Hungary the subject was taboo during the communist period), and the large Hungarian, Romany and other Transylvanian minorities are poorly represented in Romanian film. A brief postwar balance of power in the region, however, allowed a Romanian-Hungarian co-production to be made – the romantic comedy *Doua lumi şi o dragoste/Two Worlds and One Love* (1947). MM

TRAUBERG, Leonid Z.
Odessa, Ukraine [Russian Empire] 1902 – Moscow 1990

Soviet director and writer, who began his career by organising a theatre studio in Odessa in 1919 and in 1921 co-founded FEKS with Grigori Kozintsev*, with whom he worked closely until 1945. Their joint works were always suffused with a strong degree of experimentalism, from the early parodies like *Pokhozhdeniya Oktyabriny/The Adventures of Oktyabrina* (1924) and *Mishka protiv Yudenicha/Mishka versus Yudenich* (1925), through *Chërtovo koleso/The Devil's Wheel*, in which the action is played out against a fairground setting, and their version of Gogol's *Shinel'/The Overcoat* (both 1926), to their films depicting the history of the international revolutionary movement. These began with *S. V. D.* (1927), which dealt with the Decembrist uprising of 1825, and *Novyi Vavilon/New Babylon* (1929), centring on a department store during the Paris Commune of 1870. These silent films (*Novyi Vavilon* had a score by Dmitri Shostakovich*) and their first sound film, *Odna/Alone* (1931), prepared the ground for their most famous achievement, the so-called 'Maxim trilogy' which portrayed the revolutionary awakening of its eponymous hero in *Yunost' Maksima/The Youth of Maxim* (1935), *Vozvrashchenie Maksima/The Return of Maxim* (1937) and *Vyborgskaya storona/The Vyborg Side* (1939). Their last collaborative effort was *Prostye lyudi/Simple People*, made in 1945 but not released until 1956. After this Trauberg's film-making career went into a severe decline but he enjoyed an Indian summer as director of the Higher Courses in Direction in the 1960s and as an author of many books about cinema, operetta and popular culture in the 1970s and 1980s. RT

TRAUNER, Alexandre
Sandor Trauner; Budapest, Hungary 1906 – Omonville-la-Petite 1993

Hungarian-born French set designer. Trauner studied painting in Budapest and moved to France in 1929, becoming assistant to Lazare Meerson*, then the greatest set designer in France. Trauner's name is closely connected with Poetic Realism*, a style of French film of the 1930s to which he contributed the most immediately recognisable element: a stylised yet minutely observed reconstruction of urban decors. Trauner's concern for accurate detail is well illustrated by his fight with the producer of *Le Jour se lève* (1939), who wanted to shorten the central building of the set by one storey to save money; understanding the close relationship between character and set in Poetic Realist films, Trauner insisted that the height of the building was crucial. He designed the sets of so many French films that one can pick almost at random: *Drôle de drame* (1936), *Quai des brumes* (1938), *Les Enfants du paradis* (1943–45), *Les Portes de la nuit* (1956), *Du rififi chez les hommes/Rififi* (1955), *Mr Klein* (1977), *Subway* (1985), *Round Midnight/Autour de minuit* (1986, US/Fr.). Trauner was also much in demand internationally, designing, among other films, Billy Wilder's *The Apartment* (1960), for which he won an Oscar, and Joseph Losey's* *Don Giovanni* (1979). GV

TRENKER, Luis   St. Ulrich, Italy 1892 – Bozen 1990

Italian-born Austrian actor and director, who was working as a mountain guide in the Alps when he was hired in 1921 to guide Arnold Fanck's* production unit for *Das Wunder des Schneeschuhs*. A robust, handsome athlete, he found himself playing the lead part in several Fanck 'Mountain films'*, usually as the partner of Leni Riefenstahl* (*Der Berg des Schicksals/Peak of Fate*, 1924; *Der heilige Berg/Peaks of Destiny*, 1927; *Der Kampf ums Matterhorn/The Fight for the Matterhorn*, 1928). From the early 1930s he himself also wrote and (co-)directed mountain films (*Der Berg ruft/The Challenge*, 1937), often with elements of the war film (*Berge in Flammen/The Doomed Battalion*, co-dir. Karl Hartl*, 1931; *Der Rebell/The Rebel*, co-dir. Kurt Bernhardt*, 1932), historical films (*Condottieri/Giovanni di Medici*, 1937), and comedies (*Liebesbriefe aus dem Engadin*, 1938). Living in Venice and Rome after the war, Trenker continued to make features and, increasingly, documentaries about mountains for Italian, Austrian and German companies, but without achieving the visual power and authenticity of his earlier features. However, he sustained his popularity in Austria and Germany as the author of successful books and narrator of multi-part series for German and Austrian television on mountains and mountaineering. MW

Bib: Piero Zanotto (ed.), *Luis Trenker: Lo schermo verticale* (1982).

Other Films as Director Include: *Der verlorene Sohn* (1934, also actor); *Der König der Berge* (1938, short); *Der Feuerteufel* (1940, also actor); *Im Banne des Monte Miracolo* (1943–48, also actor); *Il prigioniero della montagna/Flucht in die Dolomiten* (1955, also actor); *Von der Liebe besiegt* (1956, also actor); *Wetterleuchten um Maria* (1957); *Sein bester Freund* (1962).

TRESSLER, Georg   Vienna 1917

Austrian-born director, who began as a caricaturist before working as an actor and assistant director to Geza von

Bolvary* and Arthur Maria Rabenalt* in Austria between 1935 and 1939. Tressler made his directorial debut with a short fiction film, *Urlaub im Schnee* (1947). Unable to direct a full-length feature film in Austria, he moved to Germany, where he rose to prominence with two films modelled on Hollywood juvenile delinquency dramas, *Die Halbstarken* (1956) and *Endstation Liebe* (1957). A result of his collaboration with scriptwriter Will Tremper, the detailed observation of urban teenagers in both films prepared the way for the 'Young German cinema' [> NEW GERMAN CINEMA] and brought Horst Buchholz*, the leading man in both films as well as in Tressler's subsequent *Das Totenschiff* (1959), to international attention. After directing Liechtenstein's first feature film in 1958 (*Ein wunderbarer Sommer*), Tressler was assigned to Walt Disney's biopic of Beethoven, *The Magnificent Rebel* (1961), a financial and critical failure which ended his international career as soon as it had begun. Tressler was, however, one of German television's most prolific directors. MW

Other Films Include: *Spielereien* (1949); *Unter achtzehn* (1957); *Geständnis einer Sechzehnjährigen* (1961).

TREUT, Monika   Mönchen-Gladbach 1954

German film-maker, whose controversial films feature porn star Annie Sprinkle, safe-sex educator Susie Bright and gender-bending performance artist Shelly Mars. *Bondage* (1983) explored S & M before it was fashionable, and Treut's first feature film, directed with Elfi Mikesch, *Verführung: Die grausame Frau/Seduction: The Cruel Woman* (1985), had its government grant withdrawn. *Jungfrauenmashine/Virgin Machine* (1988), a lesbian coming-out story, is refreshingly anti-moralistic, provocative and formally inventive. Although Treut won The Jack Babuscio Award for her contribution to Lesbian and Gay Cinema in 1993, her films have frequently angered the lesbian community. Rejecting the exclusiveness of lesbian politics, its political correctness and its promotion of 'positive images', she prefers to make films that through humour are accessible and pleasurable to all. *Female Misbehaviour* (1992), a collection of documentaries, includes a portrait of Camille Paglia. She also directed *Erotique* in 1994. US

Bib: Julia Knight, 'The Meaning of Treut?', in Pam Cook and Philip Dodd (eds.), *Women and Film* (1993).

TRIER, Lars von   Lars Trier; Copenhagen 1956

Danish director, who studied film at the University of Copenhagen. His student film *Orkide gartneren/The Orchid Gardener* (1977) opened the door to Den Danske Filmskole (the Danish Film School), where he studied from 1979 to 1982. His debut feature, *Forbrydelsens element/The Element of Crime* (1984), a post-modernist film inspired by German Expressionism*, American *film noir* and Andrey Tarkovsky*, established him as the most talented new Danish film-maker in years, particularly in terms of mood setting, use of location and art direction. After two short films, he directed *Medea

(1987) for Danish television, based on the script that Carl Theodor Dreyer*, another of von Trier's heroes, had worked on but never made. The same year saw the release of his next feature, *Epidemic*, followed by *Europa/Zentropa* in 1991. Undoubtedly an original talent, von Trier gives hope for the future of Danish cinema. ME

TRINTIGNANT, Jean-Louis   Pont Saint-Esprit 1930

French actor. An imposing presence rather than a 'star', the stage-trained Trintignant has acted in over 120 films since the mid-1950s, pursuing his prolific career in popular and art cinema in France and Italy (notably in Bernardo Bertolucci's* *Il Conformista/The Conformist*, 1970). He came to public attention as Brigitte Bardot's* timid husband (and off-screen lover) in *Et Dieu ... créa la femme/And God Created Woman* (1956) and was the romantic hero of Claude Lelouch's* *Un homme et une femme/A Man and a Woman* (1966), racing from the Côte d'Azur to meet Anouk Aimée on the beach at Deauville. Trintignant has played variations on the shy seducer, as in Eric Rohmer's* *Ma nuit chez Maud/My Night at Maud's* (1969), and repressed, sinister characters, for instance in Costa-Gavras'* *Compartiment Tueurs/The Sleeping Car Murders* (1965) and Alain Robbe-Grillet's* *Trans-Europ-Express* (1966), evolving into an increasingly complex figure. A former student at IDHEC*, he has directed two films. He was married to director Nadine Trintignant (and starred in several of her films) and is the father of actress Marie Trintignant. GV

TRNKA, Jiří   Plzen [then Austria-Hungary] 1912 – Prague 1969

Czech director of animated and puppet films, painter and designer. After working as a designer in Josef Skupa's puppet theatre, Jiří Trnka studied at the Arts and Crafts School in Prague from 1929 to 1935. Active as a graphic artist, cartoonist, painter and book illustrator, he founded his own puppet theatre in 1936. Together with Hermina Týrlova and Břetislav Pojar, he was one of the pioneers of the puppet film and began making his own films in 1946. He established his reputation with the feature-length *Špalíček/The Czech Year* (1947) and *Staré pověsti české/Old Czech Legends* (1953), based on the book by Alois Jirásek, devoting the late 1950s to his adaptation of Shakespeare's *A Midsummer Night's Dream* (*Sen noci svatojánské*, 1959). At a time of conformity, his invention served to keep artistic traditions alive and, in his later films, he moved to a more visionary level with works such as *Kybernetická babička/Cybernetic Grandmother* (1963) and *Ruka/The Hand* (1965), a striking parable about the role of the artist under totalitarianism. PH

Other Films Include: *Zasadil dědek řepu/Grandfather Planted a Beet* (1945); *Zvířátka a petrovští/The Animals and the Brigands*, *Perák a SS/The Springer and the SS Man* (1946); *Císařův slavik/The Emperor's Nightingale*, *Román s basou/Novel with a Contrebass*, *Arie prérie/Song of the Prairie* (1949); *Čertův mlýn/The Devil's Mill* (1950); *Osudy dobrého*

vojáka Švejka/The Good Soldier Švejk (1954); *Vášeň/Passion* (1961); *Archanděl Gabriel a paní Husa/Archangel Gabriel and Mother Goose* (1964).

TROELL, Jan   Malmö 1931

Swedish director. Alongside Bo Widerberg* and Vilgot Sjöman*, Troell is one of the few Swedish directors who has been able to step out of the dominating shadow of Ingmar Bergman*. After a series of shorts in the early 1960s, Troell made his feature-film debut with *Här har du ditt liv/Here is Your Life* (1966), a faithful and vivid adaptation of a novel by the Swedish writer Eyvind Johnson. He won international acclaim with two films based on the work of another writer, Vilhelm Moberg; *Utvandrarna/The Emigrants* (1971) and *Nybyggarna/The Settlers* (1972) adapt Moberg's account of the massive Swedish emigration to the US in the nineteenth century. Starring Liv Ullmann* and Max von Sydow*, the two-part epic was one of the most expensive Swedish productions and a huge popular success. Since then Troell's career has been erratic, but *Ingenjör Andrées luftfärd/The Flight of the Eagle* (1982) has been acknowledged as a masterpiece of cinematography. *Sagolandet/The Fairy Land* (1987) is a critical documentary about Sweden, *Il Capitano/A Swedish Requiem* (1991) a controversial investigation based on a real murder story. Troell is a master of the epic, the wide sweep of nature and human enterprise: he has some claims to be regarded as an inheritor of the Swedish Golden Age. LGA

Bib: Stig Björkman, *Film in Sweden: The New Directors* (1977).

Other Films Include: *4 × 4* (1965, ep. *Uppehåll i myrlandet/Stopover in Marshland*); *Ole Dole Doff/Who Saw Him Die?* (1968); *Zandy's Bride* (1974, US); *Bang!* (1977); *Hurricane* (1979, US).

TROISI, Massimo   Naples 1953 – Rome 1994

Italian actor and director. Troisi is the most southern of the young actors/*auteurs* known as the 'new Italian comics'* who entered Italian cinema in the 1970s and 1980s. Coming out of cabaret and television, Troisi broke box-office records with his first film, *Ricomincio da tre/Beginning with Three* (1981). Although still within the framework of classic stage comedy, Troisi's shy and clumsy Gaetano was the first male character in Italian cinema who showed the extent of the revolution brought about by feminism. Using monologue, gestures, frequent pauses and interruptions, Troisi established himself with *Scusate il ritardo/Sorry I'm Late* (1983) as a worthy exponent of the Neapolitan theatre of which Eduardo De Filippo* was both master and model. *Non ci resta che piangere* (1984), co-directed and co-acted with Roberto Benigni*, is a disconnected journey to a past Tuscany, in the year 'almost 1500'. In *Le vie del signore sono finite* (1987) Troisi moved once again to the past (Fascist Italy of the 1920s and 1930s), and tackled the theme of illness. *Pensavo fosse amore ... invece era un calesse* (1991), like earlier films written with Anna Pavignano, is a reflection on the impossibility of marriage and relationships; the interest of their work lies in its roots in both a generation and a city (Naples). In addition to acting in all his own films, Troisi distinguished himself as an actor in Gasparini's *No, grazie, il caffè mi rende nervoso* (1982) alongside Lello Arena, with whom, together with Enzo Decaro, Troisi formed the theatre group 'La Smorfia'. Troisi also made his mark in Ettore Scola's* *Splendor* (1988) and *Che ora è?/What Time is It?* (1989) alongside Marcello Mastroianni*, and in *Il viaggio del capitan Fracassa* (1990). He is a very fine mailman in Radford's *Il postino*, whose final scene was shot just a few days before his death from heart disease. MMo

TROTTA, Margarethe von   Berlin 1942

German director. Starting with *Das zweite Erwachen der Christa Klages/The Second Awakening of Christa Klages* (1978), von Trotta's films stand out from the semi-documentary and autobiographical works of German woman filmmakers such as Jutta Brückner* and Helke Sander* through their storytelling gusto and closely scripted narratives. Nonetheless, her theme is a feminist one: the impossible quest for female identity, both barred by and founded on the emotional interdependence of two women. Sisters either by blood (*Schwestern oder die Balance des Glücks/Sisters or the Balance of Happiness*, 1979, *Die bleierne Zeit/The German Sisters*, 1981) or by affinity (*Christa Klages*, *Heller Wahn*, 1983), her heroines are always political creatures, most apparent in her overtly political psycho-thriller *Die bleierne Zeit*, based on the life of the terrorist Gudrun Ensslin, and *Rosa Luxemburg* (1986), both starring Barbara Sukowa*. Von Trotta has not always pleased her critics: feminists object to her conventional (melo)dramatic narration, and men find her male characters pale and perfunctory. Yet her early films especially – including the underrated *Der Fangschuß/Coup de Grâce* (1976), co-scripted and co-directed by her – are enduring landmarks of the New German Cinema*. TE

Other Films Include: *Eva* (1988); *Felix* (1987, co-dir.); *Paura e amore/Fürchten und Lieben/Three Sisters* (1988); *L'Africana/Die Rückkehr* (1990); *Zeit des Zorns* (1994).

TRUEBA, Fernando   Fernando Rodríguez Trueba; Madrid 1955

Spanish director, main exponent of the '*Escuela de Madrid*' (Madrid School) [> COMEDY (SPAIN)], which sought to escape the more transcendental style of pre-democracy Spanish cinema while retaining sociological awareness. Freshness of *mise-en-scène* and dialogue made *Opera prima/First Work* (1980) a commercial and critical success, not repeated by *Sal gorda/Coarse Salt* (1984) but surpassed by *Sé infiel y no mires con quién/Be Wanton and Tread No Shame* (1986), a masterful comedy of intrigue performed by some of the most popular Spanish actors of the time (Ana Belén*, Antonio Resines*, Carmen Maura*, Verónica Forqué*, Guillermo Montesinos*). Trueba's refusal to be classified as a director of city comedy led him to experiment with the thriller genre in the internationally cast *El sueño del mono loco/The Dream of*

the Crazy Monkey (1989). The Oscar-winning *Belle Epoque* (1992), described by Trueba as a story of 'incestuous friendships', displays a delightful collection of Spanish archetypes, treated – as is his practice – with humour and affection. IS

TRUFFAUT, François   Paris 1932–84

French director, with Jean-Luc Godard* the most famous director of the New Wave*. His first feature, *Les Quatre cents coups/The 400 Blows* (1959), was effectively one of the manifestos of the movement – the other was Godard's *A Bout de souffle/Breathless* (1960) – with its autobiographical focus, its independent production and its location shooting in the streets of Paris.

Truffaut had already made a name for himself as a critic at *Cahiers du cinéma**, where in 1954 he published 'A Certain Tendency of the French Cinema', a famously ferocious critique of the mainstream French cinema of the late 1940s and early 1950s [> TRADITION OF QUALITY]. Truffaut prized American cinema, especially Hitchcock, and Jean Renoir*. A Renoiresque realism informed *Les Quatre cents coups* and, after his pastiche of US *film noir*, *Tirez sur le pianiste/Shoot the Pianist* (1960), and his adaptation of Henri-Pierre Roché's novel *Jules et Jim* (1962), Truffaut moved increasingly in the direction of a classic-realist *mise-en-scène*. Notable in this respect is the Antoine Doinel saga, which follows the main character of *Les Quatre cents coups*, still played by Jean-Pierre Léaud*, through late adolescence and adult life, in *Baisers volés/Stolen Kisses* (1968), *Domicile conjugal/Bed and Board* (1970) and *L'Amour en fuite/Love on the Run* (1979). Even if the sentimentality can be irritating ('Are women magic?'), the Doinel series is charming, funny and both accurate and evocative in its picture of middle-class Parisian life. Truffaut's other major strand was his love for popular entertainment, evidenced by his unfinished trilogy of films on filmmaking (*La Nuit américaine/Day for Night*, 1973) and the theatre (*Le Dernier métro/The Last Metro*, 1980, a major success); the third would have been on the music hall. Uniting all Truffaut's work, as Anne Gillain shows, is a deeply personal 'matrix' of Freudian motifs related to his childhood relationship to his mother, displayed by the emphasis on immature male characters (archetypally Léaud, but also Charles Denner in *L'Homme qui aimait les femmes/The Man Who Loved Women*, 1977) and cool mature women (Delphine Seyrig* in *Baisers volés*, Catherine Deneuve* in *Le Dernier métro*).

Truffaut wrote abundantly, including a book on *Hitchcock* (first published 1967), film reviews collected in *The Films in My Life* (1978) and *The Early Film Criticism of François Truffaut* (1993), and letters (1990) [all dates English translations]. He also acted, in his own *L'Enfant sauvage/The Wild Child* (1970) and *La Chambre verte/The Green Room* (1978) and in Steven Spielberg's *Close Encounters of the Third Kind* (1977, US). GV

Bib: Anne Gillain, *François Truffaut, Le Secret perdu* (1992).

Other Films: *Une visite* (1955, short); *Les Mistons* (1957, short); *Une histoire d'eau* (1958, short, co-dir. Godard); *L'Amour à vingt ans/Love at Twenty* (1962, ep. 'Antoine et

Colette'); *La Peau douce/Silken Skin* (1964); *Fahrenheit 451* (1966, UK); *La Mariée était en noir/The Bride Wore Black* (1968); *La Sirène du Mississippi/The Mississipi Mermaid* (1969); *Les Deux Anglaises et le continent/Anne and Marie* (1971); *Une belle fille comme moi/A Gorgeous Bird Like Me* (1972); *L'Histoire d'Adèle H/The Story of Adèle H* (1975); *L'Argent de poche/Small Change/Pocket Money* (1976); *La Femme d'à côté/The Woman Next Door* (1981); *Vivement Dimanche!/Finally Sunday* (1983).

TSCHECHOWA, Olga
Alexandropol, Russia 1897 – Obermenzing 1980

Russian-born German actress and director, whose first film role as the sensual Countess in F. W. Murnau's* *Schloß Vogelöd* (1921) set the pattern for her subsequent career. Appearing in over forty films in less than ten years, often as a highly strung or erotically overcharged aristocrat, she was also much in demand elsewhere, filming in Paris, London and Hollywood. In 1929 she directed *Der Narr seiner Liebe*. The coming of sound proved no obstacle. Her Slav vowels made her the perfect Austrian sophisticate, and for just such a role Max Ophuls* cast her in his Schnitzler adaptation *Liebelei* (1933). A top star thereafter, vying with Zarah Leander* for the title of the National Socialist cinema's leading lady, Tschechowa – no differently from her frequent partner Willi Forst* – benefited in 1945 from the 'Austria bonus' and preserved her political innocence. *Mit meinen Augen*, for instance, shot in the last weeks of the war, was released in 1948, smoothing the transition to such aptly named comedies as *Kein Engel so rein/No Angel so Pure* (1950). In the 1970s, she came out of retirement to play the grandmother in *Die Zwillinge vom Immenhof* (1973) and *Frühling auf Immenhof* (1974). TE

Bib: Hans-Michael Bock and Wolfgang Jacobsen (eds.), *Olga Tschechowa* (1992).

Other Films Include: *Nora* (1923); *Mädels von heute, Die Stadt der Versuchung* (1925); *Brennende Grenze* (1927); *Moulin Rouge* (1928), *Der Choral von Leuthen* (1933); *Peer Gynt* (1934); *Burgtheater* (1935); *Liebe geht seltsame Wege, Unter Ausschluß der Öffentlichkeit, Gewitterflug zu Claudia* (1937); *Rote Orchideen, Verliebtes Abenteuer* (1938); *Bel Ami, Befreite Hände* (1939); *Angelika* (1940); *Menschen im Sturm/Men in the Storm* (1941); *Gefährlicher Frühling* (1943).

TSYMBAL, Yevgeni V.
Yeisk, Russia [USSR] 1949

Russian director and screenwriter. Tsymbal worked at Mosfilm as assistant to such directors as Andrey Tarkovsky*, Larisa Shepitko*, Nikita Mikhalkov* and Eldar Ryazanov*, before making the short film *Zashchitnik Sedov/Defence Counsel Sedov* in 1988. Shot in black and white, and seamlessly incorporating archival footage, the film offers an astonishingly acute picture of the Stalinist 1930s in its tale of the vicissitudes of a lawyer hired to defend four men unjustly condemned to death for sabotage. It achieved great success at international festivals, and won a British BAFTA Best Short

Film award in 1989. Tsymbal returned to the Stalinist period with his next film, *Povest' nepogashennoy luny/The Tale of the Unextinguished Moon* (1990), adapted from the short story by Boris Pilnyak about the death of the Soviet Commissar for War, Mikhail Frunze, after an operation in 1925, a fate widely interpreted as Stalin's* surgical murder of a potential rival. JGf

TULIO, Teuvo
Theodor Tugai; St Petersburg, Russia 1912

Finnish director, actor and producer. Teuvo Tulio is one of the oddest but also most interesting figures in Finnish cinema. During the Finnish studio era he stayed outside the main studios and directed delirious, angst-ridden melodramas rarely understood by contemporary critics. Born to a Lithuanian family, Tulio developed an interest in film as a schoolboy in Helsinki. Together with Valentin Ivanov (later Valentin Vaala*) he directed a love story, *Mustat silmät/Black Eyes* (1928), in which he played the leading role and gained the title of 'the Finnish Valentino'. Vaala and Tulio made another silent movie, *Mustalaishurmaaja/The Gypsy Charmer* (1929), and an early sound film, *Laveata tietä/On the Broad Road* (1931). Tulio's solo career as a director began with three literary adaptations: *Taistelu Heikkilän talosta/Struggle for the House of Heikkilä* (1936), *Silja, nuorena nukkunut/ Silja, Fallen Asleep When Young* (1937) and *Kiusaus/ Temptation* (1938), all of which alas are lost. Tulio's fourth film, *Laulu tulipunaisesta kukasta/Song of the Scarlet Flower* (1938), still in 'classical' style, was based on Johannes Linnankoski's novel previously adapted in Sweden by Mauritz Stiller* (1918) and Per-Axel Branner (1934). Another rural melodrama was *Unelma karjamajalla/Dream in the Cowshed* (1940), about an innocent country maid. Tulio also made a screwball comedy, *Vihtori ja Klaara* (1939). But when he went back to work at the end of World War II, his style had changed radically.

The seven films Tulio made between 1944 and 1955 are dark, anxious, urban melodramas, mostly featuring Regina Linnanheimo*. Whereas in his rural melodramas innocence and corruption are typically divided between two characters, in the urban cycle they are united in the same (female) figure. In *Sellaisena kuin sinä minut halusit/The Way You Wanted Me* (1944), *Rakkauden risti/The Cross of Love* (1946), *Levoton veri/Restless Blood* and *Intohimon vallassa/In the Grip of Passion* (both 1947), *Rikollinen nainen/The Crooked Woman* (1952), *Mustasukkaisuus/Jealousy* (1953) and *Olet mennyt minun vereeni/You Have Got into My Blood* (1955), Tulio created a northern, 'Lutheran' melodrama in which pagan sensuality confronts Christian renunciation, a contradiction which drives the characters to the edge of madness. The strongest of these films is *Levoton veri*, which mixes elements from German expressionism, horror movies and American *film noir*. After the mid-1950s, Tulio directed only two films, *Se alkoi omenasta/It Started from an Apple* (1961) and *Sensuela* (1973). Tulio also produced most of his films. Contemporary criticism praised his visual talent but treated him very harshly otherwise. It was not until the 1980s that he began to be re-evaluated as an independent *auteur* who consistently returned to his own obsessions. HS

U

UCICKY, Gustav
Vienna 1899 – Hamburg, Germany 1961

Austrian director. Ucicky's ability, as cameraman and director, to create pictures of intense atmosphere and appealing beauty put him at the core of German entertainment film-making at Ufa* from 1929 to 1936, successfully exploiting every popular genre from the musical (*Der unsterbliche Lump*, 1929) and comedy (*Hokuspokus*, 1930) to historical film (*Yorck*, 1931, *Mensch ohne Namen*, 1932, and *Morgenrot*, 1933). The unveiled nationalism of his early films, including his best-known 'Fridericus Rex' film *Das Flötenkonzert von Sanssouci* (1930), made him a welcome collaborator on propaganda films after 1933. His successful treatment of a Gerhard Menzel script in *Morgenrot* founded his cooperation with the fascist author for the next few years (*Flüchtlinge/ Refugees*, 1933; *Das Mädchen Johanna*, 1935; *Savoy Hotel 217*, 1936; *Heimkehr*, 1941). Having 'fulfilled his duty', Ucicky was released from the Ufa headquarters to Vienna and to less offensive melodramas in 1942 (*Späte Liebe*, 1943; *Am Ende der Welt*, 1943; banned, released 1947). Regularly employed by the German and Austrian film industries after 1945, he specialised in literary adaptations of Carl Zuckmayer (*Nach dem Sturm*, 1948), Ludwig Ganghofer (*Der Jäger von Fall*, 1957), Selma Lagerlöf (*Das Mädchen vom Moorhof*, 1958) and Trygve Gulbranssen (*Das Erbe von Björndal*, 1960), before he died during the preparation of *Das letzte Kapitel* in 1961. KU/MW

Other Films Include: *Der zerbrochene Krug/The Broken Jug* (1937); *Der Postmeister* (1940); *Das Herz muß schweigen* (1944).

UFA

German film company. Eventually becoming the most vertically and horizontally integrated German film conglomerate, Ufa was created in 1917 as a result of a government-sponsored merger of Nordisk's*, Messter's* and Union's German branches. While Ufa took the leading position among German film companies, it did not hold a monopoly. Unlike the American majors, Ufa had to face competition – in 1922 there were 380 distributors and 360 production firms in Germany. In contrast to the American film industry, where distribution policies usually determined production plans, at Ufa the production team was in charge of output. The result was a permanent overproduction of films and often poor exploitation in the cinemas. Between February 1923 and January 1926, Erich Pommer* acted as central producer, introducing a novel policy: directors were encouraged to work as creative teams, paying less attention to budgets or shooting schedules. Free to experiment, directors created films informed by established art forms (expressionism*, romanticism, lighting styles inspired by Rembrandt and Max Reinhardt*) as well as stylistic-technical innovations such as the 'Schüfftan* process' – for example in *Die Nibelungen*

(1924) and *Metropolis* (1927), and Karl Freund's* 'unchained camera' in *Der letzte Mann/The Last Laugh* (1924).

In 1924, Ufa experienced an economic crisis because of its organisational structure and, under the managerial iron fist of Ludwig Klitzsch, the restructuring of the company proceeded apace. Independent production and distribution firms were integrated into Ufa to neutralise competition, while finances and production were strictly separated. Changing Ufa's structure according to principles of market economy also affected film style. Experimentation was relegated to the margins (documentary, animation), and innovations such as sound no longer belonged to the artists' domain but were implemented according to industry standards and demands. The Nazi Party took over Ufa's shares on 18 March 1937, and in January 1942 Ufa was subsumed under the conglomerate into which the entire industry had been organised [> NATIONAL SOCIALISM AND GERMAN CINEMA]. At the end of World War II, Ufa expired as a legal entity, but its various businesses were to keep both the government and the courts busy for decades. DEFA*, the GDR's nationalised film company, took over the Ufa studios in Babelsberg. JG/TE

Bib: Hans-Michael Bock and Michael Töteberg (eds.), *Das Ufa-Buch* (1992); Klaus Kreimeier, *Die Ufa Story* (1992).

UHER, Štefan
Prievidza 1930 – Bratislava [now Slovakia] 1993

Slovak director. Štefan Uher graduated from FAMU* in 1955, becoming the leading figure in the first generation of Slovak directors. His early film, *Slnko v sieti/Sunshine in a Net* (1962), was one of the key Slovak films of the 1960s and paved the way for the more open cultural approaches that developed in both Czech and Slovak cinema during the remainder of the decade. Its intricate and associative structure challenged classical narrative, and its use of introspection and metaphor earned an initial ban. It was also the beginning of Uher's collaboration with the leading novelist Alfonz Bednar, which was to extend for a further eight features. In 1966, Uher made his most unusual film when he adapted *Panna zázračnica/The Miraculous Virgin* from the novel by the surrealist writer Dominik Tatarka. His post-1969 films, many made in association with Bednar, avoided the bland entertainments of some of his Czech colleagues but, like most Slovak films, went unnoticed by international critics. *Správca skanzenu/Down to Earth* (1988), again unrecognised, was a profound attack on the distortions of 'normalisation'. PH

Other Films Include: *Organ* (1964); *Tri dcéry/Three Daughters* (1967); *Génius* (1969); *Keby som mal pušku/If I Had a Gun* (1971); *Javor a Juliana/The Maple and Juliana* (1972); *Dolina/The Valley* (1973); *Vel'ká noc a vel'ky deň/Great Night and Great Day* (1974); *Keby som mal dievča/If I Had a Girl* (1976); *Penelopa* (1977); *Zlaté časy/Great Times* (1978); *Kamarátky/Friends* (1979); *Kosenie jastrabej lúky/Mowing Crane Meadow* (1981); *Pásla kone na* *betóne/She Grazed Horses on Concrete/Concrete Pastures* (1982); *Šiesta veta/The Sixth Sentence* (1986).

ULLMANN, Liv   Tokyo, Japan 1938

Norwegian actress, internationally known for her work in Swedish films, especially those of Ingmar Bergman*. Ullmann started on stage in *Anne Frank* (1957), and has since pursued a long and distinguished career in the theatre, both in Norway and internationally. Her first Norwegian film role was a minor part in Edith Carlmar's *Fjols til fjells/Fools in the Mountains* (1957) and her first lead in *Ung flukt/Young Escape* (1959), by the same director.

Ullmann's close (professional and personal) relationship with Bergman started with *Persona* (1966), and she played the lead in *Vargtimmen/Hour of the Wolf* (1968), *Skammen/ Shame* (1968) and *En passion/Passion/The Passion of Anna* (1969), among other films. Bergman's intense use of facial close-ups brought Ullmann's sensitivity and understated performance style to the world, and made her one of the stars of the European art cinema*. Her beauty is characterised by classically pure Nordic features, with blue eyes and long blonde hair and an aura of the 'natural'. Her persona is that of the troubled, suffering 'modern' woman, combining intellect with elemental wisdom. She continued to work with Bergman in the 1970s, notably in the acclaimed *Viskningar och rop/Cries and Whispers* (1973), and played leads in his international television series *Scener ur ett äktenskap/Scenes from a Marriage* (1974) and *Ansikte mot ansikte/Face to Face* (1975). She was also celebrated for her part as Ingrid Bergman's* daughter in *Höstsonat/Autumn Sonata* (1978). Ullmann has worked with other Swedish film-makers, playing the lead in Jan Troell's* epics on the Swedes' contribution to the American West, *Utvandrarna/The Emigrants* (1971) and *Nybyggarna/The Settlers* (1972). She has for many years been engaged in humanitarian work for UNICEF, and has written two volumes of autobiography: *Forandringen* (*Changing*, 1977) and *Tidevann* (*Choices*, 1984). In 1992, *Sofie*, her first film as a director, was released (she had co-directed *Love* in 1982). The story of a Jewish girl growing up in Denmark towards the end of the nineteenth century, *Sofie* is a beautiful and thought-provoking film, and was a critical success. KS

Other Films Include: *Tonny* (1962); *An-Magritt* (1969, Nor./Swe.); *Pope Joan* (1972, UK); *Lost Horizons* (1973, US); *Zandy's Bride* (1974, US); *A Bridge Too Far* [UK], *Das Schlangenei/The Serpent's Egg* [US/Ger.] (1977); *The Wild Duck* (1983, Australia); *Speriamo che sia femmina/Let's Hope It's a Girl* (1985, It.); *The Rose Garden* (1989, US).

ULLRICH, Luise   Vienna 1911 – Munich, Germany 1985

Austrian-born actress. Her very first screen appearance in Luis Trenker's* *Der Rebell/The Rebel* (1932, co-dir. Kurt Bernhardt*) typecast her as the domestic and sacrificing woman, a role she played throughout the next forty years. Especially during the Nazi regime, Ullrich was ideally suited for the brave wife and mother (for instance in Josef von Baky's* *Annelie: Geschichte eines Lebens*, 1941). One of the few films to provide a challenge for her was the early Mizzi Schlager part in Max Ophuls'* *Liebelei* (1933), which remained her best-known role, along with her portrayal of an impudent grandmother in R. W. Fassbinder's* five-part television series, *Acht Stunden sind kein Tag/Eight Hours Are Not a Day* (1973). KU.

Bib: Luise Ullrich, *Komm auf die Schaukel, Luise: Balance eines Lebens* (1973).

Other Films Include: *Regine* (1934); *Versprich mir nichts!* (1937); *Nora* (1944).

UNION OF CINEMATOGRAPHERS OF THE USSR

Soviet institution. The Union, which combined directors, scriptwriters, actors, camera operators, designers, composers, sound engineers, critics and film writers, editors and technicians, was inaugurated at its First Congress in November 1965, though the Organisational Committee of the Union had been set up in 1957. Its explicit aims included promoting the creation of works which 'affirm the principles of Communist ideology and help in the formation of good taste'; 'participating in the elaboration of a Marxist-Leninist theory of cinema art'; and 'helping in the ideological and aesthetic education of young people'. The Union was to have a congress every five years, and to be administered between congresses by a board, elected at the congress. The board would elect a secretariat and set up creative and practical commissions. The director Lev Kulidzhanov* was elected First Secretary in 1965. Each republic of the Soviet Union had its own Union of Cinematographers. The Union set up a complex system of creative commissions and sub-sections covering such areas as theory and criticism; scriptwriting; feature, documentary, scientific, animated and children's films; acting; television; technical questions; foreign links; work with young people; dubbing foreign films; and distribution. It organised conferences, discussions, film screenings, and seminars to discuss future production. It created cinematic centres known as 'Houses of Cinema' in major cities. It organised the publication of film journals such as *Iskusstvo kino* ('The Art of Cinema') and the more popular *Sovetskii ekran* ('Soviet Screen'). In 1971 the Union was awarded the Order of Lenin.

But if this 'official' description of the Union's activities suggests an efficiently run industry, the Union's main purpose was to collaborate with Goskino, the State Committee for Cinematography, set up in 1963, in the strict ideological control of all aspects of cinema production and distribution. Just how far its secretariat, still headed by Kulidzhanov, failed to defend the true interests of film-makers during the Brezhnev period is evident not only from the number of important films shelved during that period, but also from the proceedings of the revolutionary Fifth Congress of May 1986, one of the first major cultural breakthroughs of the Gorbachev years, which removed most of the Union's board, including Kulidzhanov, and at which a new generation of film-makers at last assumed positions of power. The new First Secretary was Elem Klimov*, most of whose earlier films, like those of his new deputy Andrei Smirnov*, had been subject to banning and delay. Other new board members included the directors Vadim Abdrashitov* and Eldar Shengelaya*. The old board and secretariat were accused of failing to influence the creative process in a positive way, and the nineteen decisions taken at the congress revealed the extent of the industry's crisis, whether in its lamentable technical level, in its failure to support young people in making careers in cinema, or in the conformist unprofessionalism of the cinema press. The crucial decision of the congress was the establishment of a Conflict Commission headed by the *Pravda* film critic Andrei Plakhov, charged with viewing all banned films and deciding whether they should be released. The Commission reviewed scores of films, and the subsequent release of work by directors such as Tengiz Abuladze*, Alexander Askoldov*, Andron Mikhalkov-Konchalovsky*, Kira Muratova* and Alexander Sokurov* altered the picture of Soviet cinema of the Brezhnev years.

At its Sixth Congress, held early, in June 1990, the Union elected the Tadzhik director Davlat Khudonazarov as its new First Secretary, and reorganised itself into a 'Federation of Sovereign National and Territorial Organisations of Cinematographers'. It also introduced a system of 'guilds' for directors, actors, camera operators and other groups, and expressed concern about authors' and artists' rights, and about production and distribution. But by now the rapid changes introduced by marketisation of the industry were making the Union an anachronism, and by the time of the demise of the Soviet Union in 1991, the Union of Cinematographers had been reduced to a number of squabbling groups. JGf

UNSWORTH, Geoffrey   London 1914 – France 1978

British cinematographer, who began as camera operator on *The Drum* (1938) and continued with such films as *The Thief of Bagdad* (1940), *The Life and Death of Colonel Blimp* (1943) and *A Matter of Life and Death* (1946). He became a cinematographer for Gainsborough in the mid-1940s, with *Jassy* (1947) as one of his early credits. He is possibly best known as a technical innovator for his collaboration with Douglas Trumbull on *2001: A Space Odyssey* (1968), for which he invented a special front-projection system. His craftsmanship as a colour cinematographer was widely respected, winning him Academy Awards for his work on *Cabaret* (1972, US) and *Tess* (1981). JC

Other Films Include: *The Blue Lagoon, Scott of the Antarctic* (1948); *The Spider and the Fly* (1949); *Simba* (1955); *A Town Like Alice* (1956); *A Night to Remember* (1958); *Becket* (1964); *Half a Sixpence* (1967); *Cromwell* (1970); *Love and Pain and the Whole Damn Thing* (1973, US); *Zardoz, Murder on the Orient Express* (1974); *The Return of the Pink Panther, Royal Flash* (1975); *A Bridge Too Far* (1977); *Superman* (1978).

URBANUS   Urbain Servranckx; Schepdaal 1949

Belgian actor. Urbanus has become the biggest star of the Dutch-language Belgian box office after only two films, both directed by Stijn Conninx. He began as a television and stage comedian, making his reputation in music hall. Both films are constructed around his melancholy comic personality. *Hector* (1988), which won the main prize at Chameroisse, a festival specialising in comedies, is Belgium's biggest box-office success of all time. *Koko Flanel* (1990) cashes in on the success of *Hector*, yet is less funny, trying to appeal to an even wider audience. Both films play on Urbanus' large, ungainly physique, casting him, respectively, as semi-retarded orphan and simpleton, but his performance redeems him as an appealing underdog. This simple moral frame explains the general appeal of the films, though Urbanus' strain of farce also has a particularly 'Flemish' appeal. Its nostalgic evocation of the popular comedies of Jan Vanderheyden* managed to overcome the anti-national snobbism which frequently accompanies home-grown products in Belgium. He also appeared in *Le Septième ciel/Seventh Heaven* (1993, dir. Jean-Paul Lilienfeld). CF

URIBE, Imanol   Imanol Uribe Bilbao; San Salvador, El Salvador 1950

Salvadorian director working in Spain (also scriptwriter and producer), a pivotal figure in the Basque film industry. Uribe first went into film production, founding Zeppo films with Fernando Colomo* and Angel Díaz in 1975. The critical success of *El proceso de Burgos/The Burgos Trial* (1979), a dramatisation of the infamous 1970 trial of ETA activists, established him as a committed political director prepared to dissect Francoism's repression of Basque dissent. *La fuga de Segovia/The Segovia Escape* (1981) was equally concerned with the reappropriation of recent Basque history. Able to make use of the Basque government's generous subsidies to film-makers willing to shoot their work in Euskera, Uribe has over the past twelve years interrogated the lasting impact of Francoism on regional identity and the more controversial realities of democracy in Euskadi. *La muerte de Mikel/Mikel's Death* (1984) is an astute observation of the limitations of the democratic process, focusing on the conflicts experienced by the homosexual Mikel within Basque society. More recently Uribe has turned his attention to horror and to period comedy. He has also lectured in media studies at the Universidad del Pais Vasco. MD

USTINOV, (Sir) Peter   London 1921

British actor, director and scriptwriter – and broadcaster, raconteur, playwright, theatre director, opera director and novelist. Ustinov seems to be the inspired amateur of British cinema, hard to categorise under the usual professional labels. Of Russian and French parentage, he is one of the more European figures of British cinema, appearing in a number of French, Italian and Spanish films, including two with Max Ophuls* in France: as the narrator in *Le*

Plaisir/House of Pleasure (1952), and as the ringmaster in *Lola Montès* (1955). As he never seems to take himself too seriously, the seriousness of his career is always surprising. He co-scripted *The Way Ahead* (1944), won Best Supporting Actor Academy Awards for *Topkapi* (1964, US) and for *Spartacus* (1960, US), scripted, directed and starred in *Romanoff and Juliet* (1961), adapted from his own stage play, and co-scripted *Billy Budd* (1962), adapted from Herman Melville. JC

Bib: Peter Ustinov, *Dear Me: An Autobiography* (1977).

Other Films Include (As Actor Unless Indicated): *Let My People Sing, The Goose Steps Out, ... One of Our Aircraft is Missing* (1942); *The True Glory* (1945); *School for Secrets* [+ dir., sc., prod.] (1946); *Private Angelo* [+ co-dir.] (1949); *Odette* (1950); *Quo Vadis* [US], *The Magic Box* (1951); *I Girovaghi/The Wanderers* (1956, It.); *Un angel paso sobre Brooklyn/An Angel over Brooklyn* [Sp./It.], *Les Espions/The Spies* [Fr.] (1957); *The Sundowners* (1961, UK/Aust.); *Lady L* [+ dir., sc.] (1965); *Hammersmith is Out* [+ dir.] (1972); *Death on the Nile, Doppio delitto* [It.] (1978); *Charlie Chan and the Curse of the Dragon Queen* [US], *Evil Under the Sun* (1982); *Memed My Hawk* [+ dir., sc.] (1984); *Appointment with Death* (1988).

UUNO FILMS

Finnish comic film series, based on a protagonist called Uuno Turhapuro ('Numbskull Emptybrook'). The character of Uuno, played by actor Vesa-Matti Loiri, was created by the producer Pertti 'Spede' Pasanen for his television show in the early 1970s. 'Spede' is an institution in popular Finnish entertainment, at once film producer, director, actor, writer, comedian and television host. The first film in the Uuno series, *Uuno Turhapuro*, was made in 1973; sixteen others have followed, the latest, *Uuno Turhapuron poika/The Son of Uuno Turhapuro*, in 1993. For the past two decades Uuno films have been financially, though not critically, Finland's most successful films. Uuno's grotesque appearance and wildly irresponsible behaviour are often condemned as insults to good taste; similarly ridiculed are repetitive and formulaic plots, stereotypical characters, episodic constructions, and the simple-mindedness of the gags. Nevertheless, audiences love Uuno's unchanging formula: the ill-dressed, unkempt, unshaven country boy who at the drop of a hat reveals the hidden talents of disco king, golf champion or immortal matador. Uuno is at once an incurable hedonist and a rigid rationalist. His appeal to children and – mostly – male audiences derives from his representation of a regressive utopian masculinity: in the end, Uuno joyfully denies, and withdraws from, the norms and values of a Finnish culture so forcefully established by denial and prohibition. JS

UUSITALO, Kari   Pyhäjärvi 1933

Finnish film historian and critic, the author of numerous books and articles on Finnish cinema over the past three decades. In the 1960s and 1970s, with critical and historical interest in Finnish cinema practically non-existent, he was alone in the field. Today, the material he collected forms an indispensable basis for all research in this area. Uusitalo's interest in the cinema dates from his student years in the early 1950s. Thereafter he worked in various jobs for SF and Suomi-Filmi, while collecting material on Finnish studio-based production. His first major book was *Suomalaisen elokuvan vuosikymmenet* ('The Decades of Finnish Cinema', 1965), still the basic history of 'classical' Finnish film. Later he published a chronological series of books dealing with Finnish film production from the silent era to the 1970s. In addition, Uusitalo has written monographs on SF and Suomi-Filmi, and biographies of Risto Orko*, T. J. Särkkä*, Väinö Mäkelä and Erkki Karu*. Uusitalo's most recent project is the ten-volume *Suomen Kansallisfilmografia* ('Finnish National Filmography'), which includes all essential material concerning the production and reception of every fiction film made in Finland since 1907 and of which he is editor-in-chief. He has also directed short films and documentaries. KL

V

VAALA, Valentin   Valentin Ivanov; St Petersburg, Russia 1909 – Helsinki 1976

Finnish director, who started his career with Teuvo Tulio*. While still very young, Vaala and Tulio founded a production company called Fennica for which they produced five features between 1929 and 1934. *Mustat silmät/Black Eyes* and *Mustalaishurmaaja/Gypsy Charmer* (both 1929) launched Tulio as 'the Finnish Valentino'. The duo's early films belong to the Finnish modernist movement of the 1920s known as 'Tulenkantajat' (the 'Torch Carriers'), with which they shared an urge towards European metropolitan life and a desire for anything exotic and dangerous. These feelings are well represented by *Laveata tietä/On the Broadwalk* (1931).

In 1935 Vaala moved to Suomi-Filmi, Risto Orko's* company, where he directed thirty-seven features in twenty-eight years. As a studio director he became famous for modern comedies and adaptations of Hella Wuolijoki's dramas based on the Niskavuori* tales. Vaala's comedies found subjects in contemporary urban life and differed significantly from the tradition of Finnish folk farce. Typically the female protagonist is a young 'flapper', and the narrative negotiates gender tensions. Vaala initiated the genre with films such as *Vaimoke/Substitute Wife* and *Mieheke/Substitute Husband* (both 1936, and both based on novels by one of Finland's most popular female writers, Hilja Valtonen). In the 1940s Vaala collaborated with another popular female author, Kersti Bergroth, and with his favourite actress, Lea Joutseno*. Vaala's first Wuolijoki adaptation was *Juurakon Hulda/Hulda from Juurakko* (1937), the emancipatory tale of a poor settler's daughter who becomes a member of parliament and spokesperson for the poor. A mixture of comedy and social consciousness, *Juurakon Hulda* became one of the most popular Finnish films of the 1930s. AK

VAČKOV, Grigor   Sofia 1931–80

Bulgarian actor. An eminent stage and screen actor, Grigor Vačkov first appeared in films in a minor role in Peter Donev's *Bednata ulica/Poor Man's Street* (1960). He is best known as an interpreter of dramatist-screenwriter Jordan Radičkov's* tragic heroes: the recalcitrant peasant in Hristo Hristov's* *Posledno ljato/The Last Summer* (1972–74) and the defiant tree-dweller in the monologue play *Januari/January*. RH

VADIM, Roger   Roger Vadim Plemiannikov; Paris 1928

French director. A former photographer, journalist and assistant to Marc Allégret*, Vadim is famous for directing his then wife Brigitte Bardot* in *Et Dieu ... créa la femme/And God Created Woman* (1956), a film often credited as a precursor of the New Wave* because of its small production team and location shooting in Saint-Tropez. Vadim's subsequent career blows this myth apart – instead he anticipated the erotic explosion of the late 1960s and 1970s – with films such as *Le Repos du guerrier/Warrior's Rest* (1962), *Le Vice et la vertu/Vice and Virtue* (1963) and *Barbarella* (1968). However, *Les Liaisons dangereuses* (1959), with Gérard Philipe* and Jeanne Moreau*, cleverly caught the fashionable edge of 'modern' life in France at the dawn of the Fifth Republic, with seductive black-and-white photography and a jazz score by Thelonius Monk and others, with a number of musicians playing, including Art Blakey's Jazz Messengers. He has been a prolific director and has also acted. In 1987 he directed a lacklustre remake of his early triumph, *And God Created Woman* (US), with Rebecca De Mornay in the lead. GV

VAJDA, Ladislao   Laszlo Vajda Weisz; Budapest, Hungary 1906 – Barcelona, Spain 1965

Spanish director of Hungarian origins. After making films in Hungary, Britain, France and Italy, Vajda moved to Spain in 1942, and directed *Se vende un palacio/A Palace for Sale* (1943), the first of many comedies, including *Doce lunas de miel/Twelve Honeymoons* (1943), *Te quiero para mí/I Want You for Myself* (1944, starring Sara Montiel*) and *El testamento del virrey/The Viceroy's Will* (1944). But Vajda is best

remembered for *Marcelino, pan y vino/Marcelino, Bread and Wine* (1954), a classic of the Spanish religious film* genre, so crucial an element of Francoism's mission to atrophy the intellect of the nation. At the same time, *Marcelino* is a splendid melodrama, a narrative of pious charm in which Christ befriends an orphan boy taken in by a community of friars. Pablito Calvo's playing of the boy set a trend for films using child stars*. PWE

VĂLČANOV, Rangel   Krivina 1928

Bulgarian director. Bulgaria's best known director abroad, and the individual most responsible for the rapid postwar development of a new national cinema in Eastern Europe. The poetic, philosophical tone of Vălčanov's first feature film, *Na malkija ostrov/On a Small Island* (1958) heralded a promising awakening in Bulgarian cinema; the film's success was the result of a close collaboration with writer Valeri Petrov*, cameraman Dimo Kolarov, composer Simeon Pironkov, and several of the country's finest actors. The same team then collaborated on *Părvi urok/First Lesson* (1960) and *Slănceto i sjankata/Sun and Shadow* (1962), save that Vălčanov now preferred to work with non-professional as well as professional actors (a method he has employed with astonishing success to the present day).

Despite the international success of the trilogy, Vălčanov and Petrov's style of personal poetic cinema was officially frowned on during the post-'thaw' period, and Vălčanov was thereafter forced to accept scripts approved by the government. Nevertheless, he was able to experiment in various genres and to inject into each film he made from the early 1960s to the late 1970s a challenging moral question. When the domestic release of his Bulgarian-Czechoslovakian co-production *Ezop/Aesop* (1970) was cancelled without explanation, the director decided to stay on in Prague to enjoy the more liberal atmosphere of the 'Czech New Wave'* and make *Tvar pod maskou/Face behind the Mask* (1970) and *Šance/Chance* (1970). He also went to North Africa to shoot the lyrical documentary *Meždu dva brjaga/Journey between Two Shores* (1967), before settling in Sofia again to make the folkloric documentary *Bulgarski ritmi/Bulgarian Rhythms* (1973), along with two commissioned documentary portraits of state artists: *Tvorčeski portret na Konstantin Kocev/Portrait of Artist Konstantin Kotsev* (1973) and *Tvorčeski portret na Ljubomir Pipkov/Portrait of Composer Ljubomir Pipkov* (1974).

After winning the Golden Peacock at the New Delhi film festival for *Lačenite obuvki na neznajnijat voin/The Unknown Soldier's Patent Leather Shoes* (1979), directed from his own screenplay (which had been shelved for fifteen years), Vălčanov was instrumental in launching a Bulgarian film revival. His later feature films – *Posledni želania/Last Wishes* (1983), *Za kăde pătuvate?/Where Are You Going?* (1985), *A sega nakăde?/Where Do We Go From Here?* (1987) – all underscore his continuing search for truth and integrity within a prescribed social structure. After editing a compilation film of short features titled *Razvodi, razvodi/Divorces, Divorces* (1989) – composed of episodes by directors and scriptwriters on marriage, infidelity and divorce in contemporary Bulgarian society – he was prompted to contribute his own personal statement on the matter in a separate feature film: *Nemirnata ptica ljubov/Love is a Wilful Bird* (1990). His latest project is *Mečtata na alkimika/The Dream of the Alchemist*, a Bulgarian-French co-production. RH

VALENTIN, Albert
La Louvière, Belgium 1908 – Paris 1968

French director and scriptwriter. An underrated director of French classic cinema, Valentin was assistant to René Clair* and worked in German studios making French versions of German musicals such as Reinhold Schünzel's* *Amphitryon* (1935; French version: *Les Dieux s'amusent*). Despite the hit comedy *L'Héritier des Mondésir* (1939) with Fernandel*, Valentin's two most interesting films are sombre women's melodramas. *L'Entraîneuse* (1938) stars Michèle Morgan* as a young nightclub hostess who tries unsuccessfully to pass for a respectable woman, and *Marie-Martine* (1943) features Renée Saint-Cyr and Jules Berry* in another tale of a woman who tries and fails to escape her past. Valentin's emphasis on women and on clearly pointing the finger at oppressive patriarchal figures was unusual; he co-wrote another great woman's film of the Occupation period, *Le Ciel est à vous* (1943–44), directed by Jean Grémillon*. GV

VALENTIN, Karl
Valentin Ludwig Fey; Au, Bavaria 1882 – Planegg 1948

German actor and writer, the most popular stage comedian in Germany from the 1910s to the 1940s. A Munich folk-hero, with a background in variety theatre and music hall, Valentin was encouraged by the success of his visual gags and verbal routines to record, from 1912 onwards, some of his stage acts on film. His part in the surrealist goings-on of *Die Mysterien eines Frisiersalons* (Erich Engel*/Bertolt Brecht, 1923) makes one wish for more, and in Max Ophuls'* *Die verkaufte Braut/The Bartered Bride* (1932) he almost runs away with the film: brief highlights in a film career that never quite did justice to Valentin's unique talent. His distinctive face and impossibly gaunt body were important props for his comic gags (*Der neue Schreibtisch*, 1914), but the grotesque verbal exchanges (often with his partner Lisl Karlstadt, and documented in more than 400 written sketches) did not come across on the silent screen and later suffered from (self?) censorship in, for instance, *Die Erbschaft/The Heritage* (1936). His films lay forgotten until the interest in early cinema, and the efforts of the Munich Filmmuseum, restored his reputation as one of the German cinema's great comic geniuses. TE/MW

Bib: Wolfgang Till (ed.), *Karl Valentin: Volkssänger? Dadaist?* (1982).

Other Films Include: *Der 'entflohene' Hauptdarsteller* (1921); *Der Sonderling* (1929); *Im Photoatelier* (1932); *Der Theaterbesuch, Der Firmling* (1934); *Der Antennendraht* (1938); *Der Tobis-Trichter. Volkshumor aus deutschen Gauen* (1941).

VALLI, Alida
Alida Maria Altenburger; Pola [now Croatia] 1921

Italian actress. One of the most famous actresses of Italian cinema in the 1940s, Valli later appeared in many international productions. Her striking beauty, with her extraordinary, slanted eyes, has been put to many different uses during her long career: from youth idol in the 1940s, to seductress in the 1950s and horror film heroine in the 1970s.

A teenage student at the newly formed Centro Sperimentale* in Rome, Valli appeared as a supporting actress in several films in 1936–38 before being cast as the female lead in five films directed by Max Neufeld: *La casa del peccato/The House of Shame* (1938), *Assenze ingiustificata/ Absent Without Leave* (1939), *Manon Lescaut* (1939), *Mille lire al mese/A Thousand Lire a Month* (1939), and *Ballo al castello/The Castle Ball* (1938). By the early 1940s, having barely turned twenty, she had become one of the Italy's most famous stars, receiving laudatory reviews as the lead in such critically acclaimed literary adaptations as Carmine Gallone's* *Oltre l'amore/Beyond Love* (1940), Mario Soldati's* *Piccolo mondo antico/Old-Fashioned World* (1941), Goffredi Alessandrini's* *Noi vivi/We the Living* (1942), and in Mario Camerini's* remake of his 1930s success, *T'amerò sempre/I'll Always Love You* (1943). Her image was closely tied, in part because of her youth and the success of school films such as *Ore 9 – lezione di chimica* (1941), with that of a serious student.

Both because of her fame and because of the neo-realist* cinema's tendency to eschew prewar stars, Valli signed a contract with David Selznick to make films in Hollywood, where she was billed simply as 'Valli'. Her most noteworthy films for Selznick include Alfred Hitchcock's* *The Paradine Case* (1948, US) and Carol Reed's* *The Third Man* (1949, UK). In the 1950s, after her contract with Selznick expired, she returned to Europe and appeared in Italian and international co-productions, notably Luchino Visconti's* sumptuous *Senso* (1954) and Michelangelo Antonioni's* *Il grido/The Cry* (1957). Her career suffered a temporary setback in 1954 when she was involved in a drugs, sex and murder scandal. She later founded a theatrical company and kept working in film co-productions, especially in France. The mature Valli was cast by Bernardo Bertolucci* in *Strategia del ragno/The Spider's Stratagem* (1970) and *Novecento/1900* (1976) as, respectively, the former mistress of an anti-Fascist hero who holds the key to his past and a matriarch landowner whose world is transformed with the onset of Fascism. After appearing in several French horror films, she was cast as the leader of a coven of witches in Dario Argento's* *Suspiria* (1977). JHa

VANČURA, Vladislav
Háj u Opavy [then Austria-Hungary] 1891 – Prague 1942

Czech novelist and director. Originally a doctor, and a life-long communist, Vančura was one of the leading novelists of the inter-war years. Unlike that of Jaroslav Hašek and Karel Čapek, his work is not known in translation and his inventive and experimental use of language is culturally specific. Although successful in traditional literary fields, he wrote many unrealised film scripts. His first film, *Před maturitou/Before the Finals* (1932), co-directed by Svatopluk Innemann, impressed through its delicate and lyrical observation of life at a boys' school. He was very much at the centre of Czech intellectual life, his collaborators on *Na sluneční straně/On the Sunnyside* (1933) including the surrealist poet Vitězslav Nezval, the linguist Roman Jakobson and the architect Bedřich Feuerstein, while *Marijka nevěrnice/Faithless Marijka* (1934) bought together novelists Karel Nový and Ivan Olbracht and composer Bohuslav Martinů. Vančura was dedicated to the notion of a film art independent of commercial demands, and his use of anti-psychological acting, symbolism and unconventional camera effects marked out ambitions that could never be fully realised. In 1942, he was one of the intellectuals executed by the Nazis in response to the assassination of the Reichsprotektor, Reinhard Heydrich. A number of his novels have subsequently been filmed, including *Marketa Lazarová* (František Vláčil*, 1965–67), *Rozmarné léto/Capricious Summer* (Jiří Menzel*, 1967), *Luk královny Dorotky/The Bow of Queen Dorothy* (Jan Schmidt, 1970), *Konec starých časů/The End of Old Times* (Menzel, 1989), and *Útěk do Budína/The Flight into Budin* (Ivan Balada, 1992). PH

Other Films as Director: *Burza práce/Labour Exchange* [short] (1933); *Láska a lidé/Love and People, Naši furianti/Our Defiant Ones* [both co-dir. Václav Kubásek] (1937).

VAN DER KEUKEN, Johan, see – KEUKEN, Johan van der

VAN DORMAEL, Jaco   Ixelles 1957

Belgian director. Van Dormael's first feature, *Toto le héros* (1991), which won the Caméra d'or prize at Cannes in 1991, granted him a place among the list of talented European newcomers. Yet before *Toto* Van Dormael had been making short films for some ten years, of which *E pericoloso sporgersi* (1984) won prizes at both the Clermont-Ferrand and Brussels festivals of fantasy film.

Raised in Germany until he was seven, when his parents moved back to Belgium, Van Dormael studied film in Paris and Brussels, while also working as a clown. For Van Dormael the style of the film must follow the story; thus *Toto*'s tale of mistaken identity is matched by a *mise-en-scène* of short sequences which together form an ambiguous tapestry of mystery and suspense. CF

VANDERHEYDEN, Jan   Antwerp 1890–1962

Belgian exhibitor, distributor, producer and director. Vanderheyden started as a distributor in London in 1915; he moved back to Antwerp and set up his own company (1925), specialising in German films. With his companion, Edith Kiel (the first Belgian woman film director), he turned producer in 1931, releasing German films dubbed into Dutch. *De Witte/Towhead* (1934), scripted by Kiel from a novel by

Ernest Claes and produced and directed by Vanderheyden, marked the beginning of a partnership which would dominate Dutch-language/Belgian cinema for twenty-five years. Vanderheyden's dominance is partly explained by his position of power during World War II. From 1940 to 1943, as head of Belgian distribution, he monopolised feature film production by denying a licence to other directors. In addition, his role as liaison officer between the Belgian and German authorities later earned him a prison sentence.

The prewar films of Vanderheyden and Kiel are the Dutch-language equivalent, but made on a shoestring, of Gaston Schoukens'* Walloon films and of the German popular musical comedies of the period, mixing rural settings, sentimental songs, a love story and gross jokes, enacted by popular cabaret comedians often speaking in slightly cleaned-up Antwerp dialect. *Alleen voor U/Only for You* (1935), *Uilenspiegel leeft nog/Uylenspiegel Still Lives* (1936) and *Wit is Troef/White is Trumps* (1939) are typical of the genre. After his release from prison in 1952, Vanderheyden continued to work with Kiel, now head of the AFO (Antwerp Film Onderneming), collaborating secretly on some sixteen provincial comedies, mostly with popular Antwerp cabaret performers drawing on their theatrical and radio routines. None managed to repeat the success of *De Witte* (which was remade in 1980 as *De Witte van Sichem/Towhead of Sichem* by Robbe De Hert). Vanderheyden's films can best be seen as forerunners of the cheaper end of contemporary television sitcoms. CF/PW

VANEL, Charles   Charles-Marie Vanel; Rennes 1892 – Cannes 1989

French actor. Vanel's career was extremely long: born before the cinema, he allegedly made over 160 films, the last in 1987. Rugged and solid, Vanel embodied a variety of tough, taciturn and sometimes tragic male heroes, epitomised by the lorry driver of Henri-Georges Clouzot's* *Le Salaire de la peur/The Wages of Fear* (1953, which won him a prize at Cannes). Highlights of his lengthy filmography, which mixes mainstream and *auteur* films, include: Germaine Dulac's* *Ame d'artiste* (1923), Raymond Bernard's* *Les Misérables* (1933, as Javert), Marcel Carné's* *Jenny* (1936), Curt Bernhardt's* *Carrefour* (1938), Jean Grémillon's* *Le Ciel est à vous* (1943–44), and Clouzot's *Les Diaboliques* (1955) and *La Vérité* (1960). He also appeared in Italian films, among them Francesco Rosi's* *Cadaveri eccellenti/Illustrious Corpses* (1976) and *Tre fratelli/Three Brothers* (1981). In his own words, Vanel 'never was, nor claimed to be, a star', yet he was much more than a character actor and he retained a consistent image throughout his extremely varied roles. GV

VANGELIS   Vangelis Papathanassiou; Volos 1943

Greek composer and rock musician. Since the mid-1970s Vangelis has followed a successful international career as rock musician and film composer. His career began in the 1960s with membership of local rock groups, including the legendary Forminx. During this period he also composed music for Greek films. He rose to international fame as a member of another rock band, Aphrodite's Child, which also included Demis Roussos. After the group's dissolution Vangelis embarked on a solo career, collaborating initially with the French documentary film-maker Frédéric Rossif. His first major success as a film composer came with *Chariots of Fire* (1981, UK, dir. Hugh Hudson) for which he won an Academy Award. He wrote the music for Ridley Scott's* *Blade Runner* (1981, US), perhaps his best score, and Costa-Gavras'* *Missing* (1982, US). Vangelis specialises in the creation of atmospheric music, using synthesizers and electronic keyboard instruments. His most recent work was for Ridley Scott's *1492 Conquest of Paradise* (1992, UK/Fr./Sp.). TN

VARDA, Agnès   Brussels, Belgium 1928

French director (of features and shorts) trained in art and photography. Her first feature, *La Pointe courte* (1956), anticipated the New Wave* in production methods and aesthetics. World recognition came with *Cléo de 5 à 7/Cleo from 5 to 7* (1962). *Sans toit ni loi/Vagabonde* (1985) was a universal success. Both films are powerful portraits of a female protagonist.

Varda's work manifests a central belief in film as personal expression, though she carefully places the inner world of her characters in a social context (her left-wing politics are explicit in *Black Panthers*, 1970 [US], and in her participation in *Loin du Viêt-Nam/Far from Vietnam*, 1967). She places equal emphasis on realism and symbolism, as in *Sans toit ni loi*, a statement on the disillusioned post-1968 generation combined with Christian and pagan myths. Varda's relationship to feminism is complex. Some of her work is avowedly feminist, for instance *L'Une chante, l'autre pas/One Sings, the Other Doesn't* (1977), a fictional rendering of the early French women's movement. However, in its celebration of biological femininity, it comes close to what feminist critic Claire Johnston saw, in the earlier *Le Bonheur* (1965), as endorsing patriarchal myths of women. On the other hand, in her search for a specific '*cinécriture*', Varda is seen by others as radical. *Jane B. par Agnès V.* and *Kung-Fu Master* (both 1988) – both starring Jane Birkin – continue her in-depth reflection on the representation of femininity and female desire. Varda has directed a documentary on her late husband Jacques Demy, *Jacquot de Nantes* (1991), and a feature on the centenary of the cinema, *Les Cent et une nuits du cinéma* (1995). GV

Bib: Agnès Varda, *Varda par Agnès* (1994).

Other Films: Shorts: *Ô saisons ô châteaux* (1958); *L'Opéra-Mouffe, Du côté de la côte* (1959); *Salut les Cubains, Les Enfants du musée* (1964); *Elsa la rose* (1966, TV); *Oncle Yanco* (1968, TV); *Réponse de femmes* (1975); *Plaisir d'amour en Iran* (1977); *Quelques femmes bulles* (1978); *Ulysse, Les Dites cariatides* (1984); *7 P., cuis., s. de b... (à saisir), T'as de beaux escaliers... tu sais* (1986); *Une minute pour une image* (1990, TV, series of two-minute episodes). **Features**: *Les Créatures* (1966); *Lions Love* (1969, US); *Nausicaa* (1970, TV); *Daguerréotypes* (1975); *Mur murs, Documenteur* (1982); *Les Demoiselles ont eu 25 ans* (1993, TV); *L'Univers de Jacques Demy* (1994).

VASILIEV 'BROTHERS': Georgi N.   Vologda, Russia 1899 – Moscow 1946
and
Sergei D.   Moscow 1900–59

Soviet directors and scriptwriters. Georgi and Sergei Vasiliev shared the same surname but were not actually brothers. Georgi worked from 1924 as an editor for the Goskino studio, cutting foreign films for Soviet distribution. Sergei held a similar job in the Moscow office of Sevzapkino. After the two studios merged the 'brothers' began to work together and became pupils of Sergei Eisenstein*. Their first film was the documentary *Podvig vo l'dakh/Exploit on the Ice* (1928), a film about the Polar expedition of the Italian explorer Nobile (a subject taken up again in Mikhail Kalatozov's* *Krasnaya palatka/The Red Tent*, 1970). The Vasilievs' first feature was *Spyashchaya krasavitsa/The Sleeping Beauty* (1930), from a script by Grigori Alexandrov*. Their most famous film, however, was *Chapayev* (1934), set in the Civil War in which they both participated: it was one of the most popular Soviet films of the 1930s, a seminal contribution to the Civil War genre, and it was held up by the authorities as the model Socialist Realist* film. They made two more films about the Civil War – *Volochaevskie dni/Volochayev Days* (1938) and *Oborona Tsaritsyna/The Defence of Tsaritsyn* (1942) – and their last collaborative work was *Front/The Front* (1943). RT

VÁVRA, Otakar   Hradec Králové [then Austria-Hungary] 1911

Czech director. Vávra originally studied architecture and made his way into the film industry via publicity work. After a number of experimental films, he moved to features in the late 1930s. His 1938 film, *Cech panén kutnohorských/The Guild of the Kutna Hora Maidens*, won the Golden Lion at Venice but was banned by the Nazis during the occupation. For reasons of both conviction and strategy, Vávra found himself drawn to literary subjects and a conventional academic style that allowed him to survive the vicissitudes of different regimes. He was active in the preparation of plans for the nationalisation of the film industry, and a key figure in the creation of FAMU*, the Prague Film School. In 1970, Vávra was dismissed from FAMU when one of the students, Vlastimil Venclík, made the film *Nezvaný host/The Uninvited Guest*, seen as having a rather obvious political reference. Vávra soon reinstated himself with an expensive wartime trilogy, *Dny zrady/Days of Treason* (1973), *Sokolovo* (1974) and *Osvobození Prahy/The Liberation of Prague* (1976). The first was a responsible drama-documentary about Munich, the last about the Soviet liberation of 1945. As he later put it, it didn't tell lies but neither did it tell all of the truth. His subsequent films drew directly on his interest in Czech literature and history. PH

Other Films Include: *Světlo proniká tmou/The Light Penetrates the Dark* [short] (1931); *Listopad/November* [short] (1935); *Filosofská historie/A Philosophical Story, Panenství/Virginity* (1937); *Humoreska/Humoresque* (1939); *Dívka v modrém/The Girl in Blue* (1940); *Turbína/The*

Turbine (1941); *Rozina sebranec/Rosina the Foundling* (1945); *Cesta k barikádám/The Way to the Barricades* (1946); *Krakatit* (1948); *Němá barikáda/The Silent Barricade* (1949); *Jan Hus* (1955); *Jan Žižka* (1956); *Proti všem/Against All* (1957); *Občan Brych/Citizen Brych* (1958); *První parta/First Rescue Party* (1959); *Zlatá reneta/The Golden Rennet* (1965); *Romance pro křídlovku/Romance for Trumpet* (1966); *Kladivo na čarodějnice/Witchhammer* (1969); *Příběh lásky a cti/A Meeting With Love and Honour* (1977); *Putování Jana Amose/The Wanderings of Jan Amos* (1983); *Oldřich a Božena/Oldřich and Božena* (1984); *Veronika* (1985); *Evropa tančila valčík/Europe Danced the Waltz* (1989).

VEIDT, Conrad
Berlin 1893 – Hollywood, California 1943

German actor. After he had appeared in a number of sex education films, Veidt's pale face and deep-set eyes predestined him for phantasmagoric parts in films of the uncanny, starting with his best-known role as the somnambulist Cesare in *Das Cabinet des Dr Caligari/The Cabinet of Dr Caligari* (1920). By the time he played the lead in *Der Student von Prag/The Student of Prague* (1926), Veidt had become the quintessential icon of Expressionist* film, having embodied Ivan the Terrible, Cagliostro, Jekyll and Hyde, Richard III and scores of similar monsters. Enticed to Hollywood, Veidt starred in historical costume dramas (*The Beloved Rogue*, 1927) and Victor Hugo *grand guignol* (*The Man Who Laughs*, 1928, dir. Paul Leni*), but he returned to Germany with the coming of sound in 1929. For E. A. Dupont's* multi-language productions he went to Britain, then to Germany (*Der Kongreß tanzt*, 1931), and back to Britain. During a visit to Berlin he was briefly put under house arrest by the Nazis for acting in the English adaptation of Feuchtwanger's *Jew Süss* (dir. Lothar Mendes, 1934; not to be confused with Veit Harlan's* antisemitic 1940 version), and left Germany for good. Although he was never out of work (he also made films in France), his roles tended to be in underfunded émigré projects, until necessity became a virtue and Veidt lent his features to a number of memorable screen Nazis, most famously in Michael Powell* and Emeric Pressburger's* U-boat drama *The Spy in Black* (1939), and as Major Strasser in Michael Curtiz's classic *Casablanca* (1942). TE/MW

Bib: Jerry C. Allen, *Conrad Veidt: From Caligari to Casablanca* (1987, 2nd ed. 1993).

Other Films Include: *Der Weg des Todes* (1917); *Das Tagebuch einer Verlorenen/The Diary of a Lost Girl* (1918); *Anders als die Anderen/Different from the Others, Wahnsinn Unheimliche Geschichten, Satanas* (1919); *Das indische Grabmal* (1921); *Lucrezia Borgia* (1922); *Das Wachsfigurenkabinett/Waxworks* (1924); *Der Kongreß tanzt* (1931); *Der schwarze Husar* (1932); *Wilhelm Tell* (1934); *The Passing of the Third Floor Back* (1935, UK); *King of the Damned* (1935, UK); *A Woman's Face* (1941, US); *Nazi Agent* (1942, US); *Above Suspicion* (1943, US).

VELASCO, Concha
Concepción Velasco Verona; Valladolid 1939

Spanish actress. She began as a dancer and was launched as a film actress by her role in the comedy *Las chicas de la Cruz Roja/The Red Cross Girls* (1958). Initially she appeared in comedies, and later as the morally upstanding heroine of melodramas like *El indulto/The Reprieve* (1960) and *La paz empieza nunca/Peace Begins Never* (1960). She starred in many popular comedies directed by Mariano Ozores* during the late 1960s and early 1970s. More recently, her career has concentrated on maturer dramatic roles, as in Mario Camús'* *La colmena/The Beehive* (1982) and the television series *Teresa de Jesús* (1984). NTT

VENGOS, Thanassis
Piraeus 1927

Greek actor; also director and producer. Having appeared in over 110 films – sixty of them as star – with a parallel career on stage, Vengos is perhaps the most popular contemporary Greek comedian. Self-taught, he entered cinema through a chance meeting with director Nikos Koundouros* in the Makronissos concentration camp. He made his debut in Koundouros' first film *Mayiki poli/Magic City* (1954). His first lead role was in *Periplanomeni Ioudei/Wandering Jews* (1959, dir. Vassilis Georgiadis). Between 1964 and 1969 he ran his own production company, producing and directing his own films. Artistically, this was his most interesting period, as he more or less single-handedly renewed Greek film comedy with elements from slapstick and the comedy of the absurd [> COMEDY (GREECE)]; financially, it left him bankrupt. Vengos then starred in a series of comedies with a message (1971–80) and, more recently, in video films of little artistic interest. He received Best Actor Awards at the Thessaloniki* festival for *Ti ekanes ston polemo Thanassi?/What Did You Do in the War, Thanassi?* (1971) and *Thanassi pare t' oplo sou/Thanassi, Get Your Gun* (1972). AM

Other Films Include: *O drakos/The Ogre of Athens* (1956); *Pote tin Kiriaki/Never on Sunday* (1959); *Psila ta heria Hitler/Hands Up, Hitler, O vassilias tis gafas/King of Blunder* (1962); *Politehnitis ke erimospitis/Jack of Many Trades and Master of None* (1963); *Trellos, palavos ke Vengos/Mad, Crazy and Vengos* (1967); *Thou-Vou: falakros praktor, epihirissis 'Gis Madiam'/The Baldheaded Agent and the Land of Destruction Mission* (1969); *Diktator kali Thanassi/Thanassi and the Dictator* (1973).

VENICE

Italian film festival. The 'Mostra Internazionale d'Arte Cinematografica' in Venice is the world's oldest film festival. It was first held at the Lido in Venice in 1932 as a touristic and cultural promotional event by the hotel industry and the Biennale degli Arti. It was declared an annual event (with prizes) in 1934. The Palazzo del Cinema was completed in 1937 (and is still in use today), while the introduction of major retrospectives in 1938 signalled the recognition of cinema as an art. Embraced by the Fascist government as a social event and political status symbol, and directed until 1942 with those objectives by Ottavio Croze, Venice was throughout the 1930s a showcase for the best of world cinema, irrespective of ideology. In 1939, however, American films were withdrawn, and in 1940 and 1941 the Festival became an Italo-German Film Week. Suspended for the rest of the war, it was revived in 1946 under the direction of Elio Zorzi, and soon recovered its international prestige, despite new competition from Cannes*. However, after the 1948 election it came under political pressure from the Christian Democrat government, which appointed a series of placemen directors, badly compromising its cultural role and interfering with the prize-giving process (though not so much with the selection of films, which remained of quality). Increasing pressure in support of the Festival's independence led to the appointment of the prestigious film-maker and critic Luigi Chiarini* as director. From 1963 to 1968 under Chiarini's direction the Festival pursued a rigorous policy in favour of artistic quality and a 'politique des auteurs'*. But the student protests of 1968, and those of the film-makers in 1972–73, created a new turmoil which lasted throughout the 1970s. Between 1979 and 1983, under the direction of Carlo Lizzani*, and in a context radically altered by the emergence of new and competing festivals, Venice pursued a more flexible and lively policy, open to the tastes of younger cinéphiles and to a mingling of European and American, art and popular cinema, an approach which remained in place throughout the 1980s. Gillo Pontecorvo* was nominated director in 1992. GVo

VENNERØD, Petter: see WAM, Svend

VENTURA, Lino   Angelo Borrini Ventura; Parma, Italy 1919 – Saint-Cloud 1987

French actor. As the gangster Angelo in Jacques Becker's* *Touchez pas au grisbi/Honour Among Thieves* (1954), newcomer Ventura impressed both the film's star Jean Gabin* (a determining influence) and the public with his muscular presence and laconic delivery. A former wrestler and salesman from a poor immigrant background, Ventura was catapulted overnight into the cinema limelight. *Grisbi* inaugurated a long series of *policiers** in which he excelled both as gangster and policeman: Claude Sautet's* *Classe tous risques/The Big Risk* (1960), Jean-Pierre Melville's* *Le Deuxième souffle/The Second Breath* (1966), Henri Verneuil's* *Le Clan des Siciliens/The Sicilian Clan* (1969) and many more, including comic pastiches of the genre. Parallel to this popular and commercially fruitful career, Ventura appeared in art films such as Melville's *L'Armée des ombres/The Army in the Shadows* (1969), Francesco Rosi's* *Cadaveri eccellenti/ Illustrious Corpses* (1976) and Claude Miller's *Garde à vue* (1981); prestige productions like the 1982 version of *Les Misérables* (1982); and comedies such as *L'Emmerdeur* (1973). His minimalist acting in the thrillers evolved into a self-contained masculinity, which his lived-in face endowed with a combination of world-weariness, toughness and sensitivity. Popular in France for both his films and his charity work for handicapped children, Ventura, despite his Italian origins, came to represent a version of French masculinity in the Gabin and Yves Montand* lineage, deeply felt as 'authentic'. GV

VERDÚ, Maribel   María Isabel Verdú Rollán; Madrid 1970

Spanish actress, who made her film debut at fourteen in Vicente Aranda's* *El crimen del Capitán Sánchez/Captain Sanchez's Crime* (1987) and has since shot to stardom in a number of major films. Her blend of unselfconscious sensuality and adolescent vulnerability is well used in films like *El aire de un crimen/Scent of a Crime* (1989) and Aranda's *Amantes/Lovers* (1991), both of which exploit her graceful, full-figured beauty, though at the same time restricting her to roles of eroticised passive victim, a trend continued in Juan José Bigas Luna's* *Huevos de oro/Golden Balls* (1993). PWE

VERHAVERT, Roland   Melsele-Waas 1927

Belgian director and producer, an important figure in postwar Flemish cinema. From 1953 to the late 1960s, Verhavert worked for BRT (Flemish public television), where he produced shorts, features and documentaries, for instance *De vijanden/The Enemies* (Hugo Claus*, 1967) and *Zaman* (Patrick Le Bon, 1983), and presented *Première*, a cinema programme. As a director Verhavert has shown a preference for (Flemish) literary adaptations. *De Loteling/Le Conscrit/ The Conscript* (1973) was based on Hendrick Conscience's novel and *Pallieter* (1975) on Felix Timmerman. His first feature, *Rolande met de bles/Rolande with the Blaze* (1972), is probably his most interesting, using beautiful costumes to evoke a recent past where rural residents confront the challenges of a new age. He also directed *Brugge die stille/ Bruges-la-Morte/Bruges the Silent One* (1981). Verhavert has taught at RITCS, the main Dutch-language film school, and heads the Dutch-language Association of Film and Television artists. SS

VERHOEFF, Pieter   Lemmer 1938

Dutch director, who worked for television after graduating from the Dutch Film Academy. Verhoeff made many documentaries before turning to fiction film. From the start he has been a critical observer of social relations and cultural change. In several television docu-dramas of the 1970s he painted a chilling portrait of city life threatened by real estate development and security services, in a style similar to that of Ken Loach* and Tony Garnett. In his feature films, however, he seems more interested in rural working-class life torn between modernisation and provincialism. The drama of emancipation is filmed with a mixture of compassion and distance enhanced by irony and the use of the vernacular. Verhoeff's heroes are provincial outcasts struggling with the temptations of modern life and revolutionary ideas. *Het teken van het beest/The Mark of the Beast* (1981) and *The Dream* (1985)

441

both deal with a tragic *cause célèbre* in the early history of the radical socialist movement in rural Holland. Though Verhoeff changed the setting and the tone in his subsequent films, the results were further variations on the theme of ambivalent identity – for example *Van geluk gesproken/Count Your Blessings* (1987), a comedy of modern city life, and *De zondagsjongen/The Sunday Child* (1992), a psychological study of bi-cultural (Dutch–German) education. *De vuurtoren/The Lighthouse* (1994) is a period film with autobiographical scenes of provincial childhood reminiscent of Federico Fellini*. KD/RdK

VERHOEVEN, Paul Amsterdam 1938

Dutch director. When he left for Hollywood in 1986, Verhoeven was the most successful Dutch director of the century. A maths graduate, he made shorts before being commissioned to direct an adventure series for television: *Floris* (1968–69), a Dutch counterpart to *Ivanhoe*. The series marked the beginning of a long-standing partnership with scriptwriter Gerard Soeteman. In *Floris*, under the supervision of producer Rob Houwer*, they created the most popular series ever made in the Netherlands. Their star Rutger Hauer* would appear in five other films by Verhoeven. Verhoeven's passion for spectacle and provocation was evident from the start. *Wat zien ik/Business is Business* (1971), his first film hit, featured droll scenes from the Amsterdam red light district. It was followed by *Turks fruit/Turkish Delight* (1973), an unconventional love story, and *Keetje Tippel/Cathy Tippel* (1975), a play on sexual exploitation and social mobility in a nineteenth-century setting. These films already show Verhoeven's taste for the gross effects, scatological details, exaggerated contrasts and schematic characters that feature in his later work. They also have in common a high-speed, elliptical style and an episodic structure, giving them a frantic and fragmented look. The popular appeal comes with a price, however: most of Verhoeven's films are of misanthropic and pessimistic cast, their sexual obsessions joyless and shot through with a fascination with death. These qualities are particularly marked in *Soldaat van Oranje/Soldier of Orange/Survival Run* (1977), a film about the Dutch armed resistance in World War II, and in his portrayal of working-class youngsters in *Spetters/Hunks* (1980). *De vierde man/The Fourth Man* (1983), a 'magic-realist' thriller about a male homosexual caught in the web of a predatory widow, is more complex, adding an imaginative evocation of subjectivity and a touch of *film noir* to the habitual themes. The film paved the way for the international career of its lead actor, Jeroen Krabbé*. It also marked the end of Verhoeven's Dutch period. He made *Flesh and Blood* (1985) in Spain, a historical spectacle derived from the *Floris* series. The huge success of *Robocop* (1987) marked Verhoeven's effortless absorption into the Hollywood big time. *Total Recall* (1990), a science-fiction tale starring Arnold Schwarzenegger, and the thriller *Basic Instinct* (1992), which propelled Sharon Stone to notoriety, were also international box-office hits. KD

Bib: *Postscript*, special issue, 12–13 (1993).

VERNEUIL, Henri Achod Malakian; Rodosto, Turkey 1920

French director. Verneuil's refugee Armenian family arrived in France in 1924. He studied engineering and came to the cinema through journalism at the Liberation, adopting his pseudonym then. After a spell as an assistant director, Verneuil was lucky to have Fernandel* – then one of the biggest French stars – appear (free) in his first short film, *Escale au soleil* (1949), which was selected for Cannes. This resulted in about thirty more shorts, and Fernandel also starred in Verneuil's first six features – including *Le Boulanger de Valorgue* (1953), *L'Ennemi public nº 1* (1954) and *Le Mouton à cinq pattes/The Sheep Has Five Legs* (1954) – with immense box-office success. Well established as a comedy director (*La Vache et le prisonnier/The Cow and I*, 1959, again with Fernandel, was one of the comic triumphs of the decade), Verneuil moved on to thrillers and psychological dramas, producing a number of hits, including *Mélodie en sous-sol/The Big Snatch* (1963) and *Le Clan des Siciliens/The Sicilian Clan* (1969, both co-starring Jean Gabin* and Alain Delon*) and a number of solid star vehicles for the likes of Yves Montand* and Jean-Paul Belmondo*. Ironically (and surprisingly), Verneuil was unsuccessful at the box office with his most personal projects, the melodramatic but moving *Mayrig* (1991) and *588, rue Paradis* (1992), based on his autobiography and starring Claudia Cardinale*, Omar Sharif and Richard Berry. GV

VEROIU, Mircea Tirgu Jiu 1941

Romanian director and occasional scriptwriter and actor, who places visual imagery above narrative development. Initially a sports teacher, Veroiu attended film school in Bucharest under Victor Iliu*, and achieved immediate fame co-directing and scripting, with Dan Piţa*, *Nuntă de piatră/Stone Wedding* (1972) and *Duhul aurului/Lust for Gold* (1973), taken from classic short stories. *Fefeleaga* – Veroiu's section of *Stone Wedding* – has an austere style reminiscent of Bresson* in its ritualistic treatment of characters and landscape. His first solo feature, the thriller *Şapte zile/Seven Days* (1973), as well as the science-fiction film *Hyperion* (1975), can be seen as pretexts for a display of visual imagery. Since then Veroiu has generally worked with cameraman Calin Ghibu. The elegant historical drama *Dincolo de Pod/Beyond the Bridge* (1975) shows the consummation of his style, though it is perhaps weighed down by its literary theme and precise period reconstruction. *Între oglinzi paralele/Between Opposite Mirrors* (1978) uses glass and mirrors as exquisite metaphors within a politically orthodox storyline. *Să mori rănit din dragoste de viață/To Die from Love of Life* (1983) is almost pure *film noir*. As in the Chekhovian and sensual *Adela* (1984), the story is tied to male friendship – one of Veroiu's preferred themes. *Adela* won the main award at a San Remo retrospective in 1985. MM

Bib: Manuela Cernat, 'Romania – Focus on Mircea Veroiu', *International Film Guide* (1987).

VERSTAPPEN, Wim   Gemert 1938

Dutch director and producer. Verstappen spent his youth in Curaçao, returning to the Netherlands to study chemistry briefly before entering the Netherlands Film Academy in 1961. There he met Surinam-born Pim de la Parra. 'Pim & Wim' co-founded the monthly film journal *Skoop* in 1963 and set up the production company Scorpio two years later. Scorpio produced twenty-eight films between 1965 and 1976. Of these, eleven were directed by Verstappen, making him one of the most prolific postwar Dutch directors of feature films. His debut, *De minder gelukkige terugkeer van Joszef Katús naar het land van Rembrandt/Joszef Katús's Not Too Fortunate Return to the Land of Rembrandt/Joszef Katús* (1966), attracted attention for its candid depiction of Amsterdam's hectic street life. *Blue Movie* (1971), with explicit scenes of male nudity, was a box-office hit. Scorpio's aim was more to bolster the Dutch film industry than to create a national school. However, despite the international flavour of their films – something like a mix of French New Wave*, Don Siegel, Martin Scorsese and Dušan Makavejev* – their zest, anarchy and humour reveal more about Dutch life and mores than most Dutch movies. After he split with De la Parra, Verstappen directed *Pastorale 1943* (1978), a tragi-comedy about the Dutch resistance during World War II, and *Het verboden Bacchanaal/The Forbidden Bacchanal* (1981), analysing the Dutch middle classes' hypocrisy in sexual matters. Both films, screen versions of Simon Vestdijk's novels, demonstrate Verstappen's strengths: a sharp and ironic view of Dutch society, intense involvement with the characters and a knack for extracting fine performances from his actors. Verstappen was an outspoken champion of Dutch film-makers' (copy)rights in the 1980s. SL

Bib: Oscar van der Kroon, 'Pim en Wim', *Nederlands Jaarboek Film 1985* (1985).

VERTOV, Dziga   Denis A. Kaufman; Białystok, Poland [Russian Empire] 1896 – Moscow 1954

Soviet director and theorist. Vertov studied psychoneurology in Petrograd in 1917 but, after the Revolution, was offered a film job by an old friend. He soon became head of the Moscow Cinema Committee's newsreel section and started to experiment with the camera, using his scientific knowledge to gain experience of the effects on audiences of different cinematic techniques. In 1918 he began producing his *Kinonedelya* ('Cine-Week') newsreel series and in 1919 formed the Cine-Eye (*Kino-Glaz*) group, whose guiding spirit he was to remain. During the Civil War Vertov continued to shoot newsreel footage while working on the agit-trains and this was subsequently used in his first full-length films, *Godovshchina revolyutsii/The Anniversary of the Revolution* (1918) and *Istoriya Grazhdanskoi voiny/The History of the Civil War* (1922). The Cine-Eye theory of documentary film-making was first publicly proclaimed in the August 1922 manifesto 'We: A Version of a Manifesto', and developed the following year in 'The Cine-Eyes: A Revolution'. These manifestos announced that 'the future of cinema lies in the re-jection of its present' and argued that 'the cinema eye is more perfect than the human eye' and therefore that cinema was capable of creating a more perfect reality than reality itself, partly through imaginative camerawork but mainly through montage. Yet at the same time Vertov also set out to portray 'life caught unawares'. Fiction film, in the Cine-Eyes' view, evaded the responsibilities of documentary film and was therefore denounced as unreal, dishonest and fundamentally counter-revolutionary. Vertov set out to realise this new reality in his next newsreel series, called *Kinopravda/Cine-Truth*, in a play on the title of the Party newspaper. Working with his brother Mikhail Kaufman* (a third brother, Boris, emigrated to France, where he worked with Jean Vigo*, and then went to Hollywood [> EMIGRATION AND EUROPEAN CINEMA, EUROPEAN CINEMA AND HOLLYWOOD]) and his wife Yelizaveta Svilova, Vertov also produced a number of stunning full-length documentaries intended to portray Soviet 'life caught unawares' – *Shagai, Sovet!/Forward, Soviet!* and *Shestaya chast' mira/A Sixth Part of the World* (both 1926), *Odinnadtsatyi/The Eleventh Year* (1928), and the best known of them, *Chelovek s kinoapparatom/The Man with the Movie Camera* (1929) – as well as a series of innovative films extending the use of montage to sound: *Entuziazm/Enthusiasm*, also known as *Simfoniya Donbassa/The Donbass Symphony* (1930), *Tri pesni o Lenine/Three Songs about Lenin* (1934), which won a prize at the Venice film festival, and *Kolybel'naya/The Lullaby* (1937), which was re-edited without his permission to enhance the role of Stalin. He found it increasingly difficult to get work as official interest moved towards popular fiction films and he ended his career working on the regular Soviet newsreel *Novosti dnya* ('News of the Day').

Vertov's theory of documentary film suffered from a fundamental contradiction that he never resolved between the desire to show 'life caught unawares' and the urge to reformulate that life through the mechanical 'Cine-Eye' of the camera. The virulence of his attacks on fiction film-makers, notably Sergei Eisenstein*, made him enemies and he never adequately responded to their critiques of his own positions. His films challenged conventional narrative patterns and demanded considerable effort on the part of audiences unfamiliar with his methods. They were not widely shown and therefore never became conventionally acceptable. Vertov's attempts to create a new cinematic non-linear narrative form led him to experiments that were vulnerable, in the increasingly rigid artistic climate of the 1930s, to accusations of Formalism, and a brilliant career was thus prematurely eclipsed. RT

Bib: Annette Michelson (ed.), *Kino-Eye: The Writings of Dziga Vertov* (1984).

VGIK (Vsesoyuznyi gosudarstvennyi institut kinematografii/All-Union State Cinema Institute)

Soviet film school, the most important school of film-making, cinema history and criticism in the USSR. Founded in 1919 by Vladimir Gardin*, Lev Kuleshov* and others as the State

Film School, it was reorganised in 1925 as the State *Technicum* for Cinema (GTK). In 1930, as part of the general centralisation of cinema institutions, it became the State Institute for Cinema (GIK) and, in 1934, VGIK. Almost all the leading figures in Soviet cinema have taught at VGIK, including the following who all have entries in this encyclopedia: Nikolai Batalov, Sergei Bondarchuk, Alexander Dovzhenko, Sergei Eisenstein, Sergei Gerasimov, Marlen Khutsiev, Grigori Kozintsev, Lev Kuleshov, Vsevolod Pudovkin, Mikhail Romm and Sergei Yutkevich. The majority of those staffing Soviet film studios also passed through the institution. In the 1960s, VGIK came to be seen as a bastion of the old order and of the 'period of stagnation', and rival 'Higher Directors' Workshops' were established, although they never threatened VGIK's hegemony. Institutes for the study of cinema history and theory were, however, more effectively decentralised, and research in these areas benefited from these changes from the 1970s onwards. RT

VIGO, Jean Paris 1905–34

French director, one of the most talented romantic and tragic figures in French cinema. Vigo's father, an anarchist who died in jail in mysterious circumstances in 1917, came from an Andorran family. Jean Vigo was attracted to the avant-garde of the late 1920s [> FRENCH AVANT-GARDE; AVANT-GARDE CINEMA IN EUROPE]. After a brief spell in the Nice studios as an assistant cameraman, he made the iconoclastic short *A propos de Nice* (1930) with Boris Kaufman (one of Dziga Vertov's* brothers) and a documentary on a swimmer, *Taris* (1931). He directed only two features before his untimely death from tuberculosis, but they remain two of the most beautiful French films ever made. The forty-five minute *Zéro de conduite* (1934), set in a boy's boarding school, is a powerful indictment of authoritarianism (partly based on Vigo's own school experience). The schoolmasters are portrayed as puppets and the children give the film a raw authenticity and energy, while some scenes, such as the pillow fight, are dreamily poetic. In *L'Atalante* (1934), an erotic romance set on a barge (starring Michel Simon*, Jean Dasté and Dita Parlo), Vigo made one of the key films of the 1930s, his own version of 'Poetic Realism'* *avant la lettre*; in the words of John Grierson*, 'At the base of it is a sense of documentary realism which makes the barge a real barge ... but on top of the realism is a crazy Vigo world of symbols and magic.' Vigo's films have a peculiar historical standing. *Zéro de conduite* was immediately banned and *L'Atalante* was briefly shown in various cut or altered versions, largely to indifferent audiences. But though they had little impact on contemporary audiences, his films were enormously influential on other film-makers, both in terms of his aesthetics and of Vigo's model of an *auteur* struggling against adversity; they now indelibly colour our vision of 1930s French cinema. GV

Bib: Marina Warner, *L'Atalante* (1993).

VISCONTI, Luchino Milan 1906 – Rome 1976

Italian director. Born into a distinguished patrician family, Visconti developed an early interest in music which would resurface later in his films and operatic work. At the age of thirty he moved to Paris, immersed himself in international film culture, and assisted Jean Renoir* on *Une Partie de campagne* (1936). After a brief visit to Hollywood, he returned to Rome, where he became part of the goup around the journal *Cinema* which was beginning to lay the theoretical groundwork for a new realism based on the literature of nineteenth-century *verismo*, typified by the novels and stories of Giovanni Verga. When his proposal for an adaptation of Verga's story *L'amante di Gramigna* was rejected by the Fascist censors, Visconti turned instead to an adaptation of James Cain's thriller *The Postman Always Rings Twice*. The resulting film, *Ossessione* (1942), shot on location in the Po valley, was subsequently hailed as a precursor of neo-realism* in its location shooting and naturalistic treatment of ordinary men and women. In 1944, his anti-Fascism earned Visconti a short spell in a Gestapo prison. After the war he went to work in the theatre before accepting funding from the Italian Communist Party to make what was planned to be a series of three films about the fishermen, miners and peasantry in Sicily. In the event, only the 'Episode of the Sea' was made under the title *La terra trema* (1948). Based on Verga's novel *I Malavoglia*, *La terra trema* was a paragon of neo-realist purity in its location shooting and use of non-professional actors speaking a local dialect so incomprehensible that it had to be supplemented by a voice-over narration in standard Italian. The film's disappointing performance at the box office forced Visconti to accept a less than congenial script by Cesare Zavattini* for the film *Bellissima* (1951). The opportunity of working with Anna Magnani*, however, overrode his distaste for the screenplay and the film emerged as both a fine satire of Cinecittà* and a convincing portrait of a working-class woman.

Visconti's first colour film, *Senso* (1954), triggered a storm of controversy in its exploitation of the star system (Farley Granger and Alida Valli*), its recourse to historical reconstruction (the Risorgimento), and its lush, aristocratic milieu. Against those who called *Senso* a betrayal of neo-realist populism, the influential Guido Aristarco defended the film as the logical progression of neo-realism towards a critical realism based on a rethinking of the nineteenth-century origins of the Italian state. Visconti's 1963 adaptation of Giuseppe Tomasi di Lampedusa's *Il Gattopardo/The Leopard* deepens his critique of the Risorgimento by filtering events through the consciousness of a Sicilian prince who is aware that his class is doomed and is resigned to accept change. It is this character, played with great subtlety by Burt Lancaster, who best expresses Visconti's own plight as a man temperamentally bound to the old order but ideologically committed to its demise. Visconti's command of spectacle – his power to reconstruct in glorious detail a lost aristocratic world and to direct hundreds of extras with naturalness and grace – is admirably displayed in the film's hour-long ball sequence, mutilated by US distributors but fortunately restored to its full splendour in the film's 1983 re-release. In *La caduta degli dei/The Damned* (1969) – a chronicle of the Krupp family whose steel empire supported Hitler's rise to power –

Visconti takes to decadent extremes his fondness for recreating privileged worlds on the verge of extinction. Class demise is also the theme of his adaptation of the Thomas Mann novella *Morte a Venezia/Death in Venice* (1972), where Gustav von Aschenbach's (masterfully played by Dirk Bogarde*) fatal bondage to aesthetic purity and homoerotic desire allegorises the aristocracy's inertia in the face of historical obliteration. The protagonist of *Ludwig* joins Gustav as an autobiographical projection of Visconti's own tormented aestheticism. The badly cut (from 246 to 150 minutes) 1972 version of the film regained its integrity on its re-release in 1980 as an epic account of the Bavarian king more given to art than politics. *Gruppo di famiglia in un interno/Conversation Piece* (1974), made during Visconti's last illness, stars Burt Lancaster again as an intellectual confronted with a revolution (this time, the sexual and political revolution of 1968) into which he is unwillingly drawn. The aristocratic protagonist of Visconti's last film, *L'innocente/The Innocent* (1976), an adaptation of Gabriele D'Annunzio's novel, chooses withdrawal through suicide as a commentary both on his own interpersonal failure and that of the *belle époque* whose end is both merited and mourned.

Forerunner and practitioner of neo-realism, Visconti was instrumental in transcending its limitations by incorporating influences from the other arts (primarily literature, but also opera and theatre) as well as legitimising forays into historical subject matter. He had an enormous impact on successive generations of film-makers, including Bernardo Bertolucci*, Franco Zeffirelli*, Francesco Rosi*, Liliana Cavani*, and Stanley Kubrick*. MMa

Bib: Elaine Mancini, *Luchino Visconti: A Guide to References and Resources* (1986); Geoffrey Nowell-Smith, *Visconti* (1973).

Other Films Include: *Siamo donne/We the Women* [ep. *Anna Magnani*], *Le notti bianche/White Nights* (1957); *Rocco e i suoi fratelli/Rocco and His Brothers* (1960); *Boccaccio '70* (1962, ep. *Il lavoro*); *Vaghe stelle dell'orsa/Sandra* (1965); *Le streghe/The Witches* [ep. *La strega bruciata viva*], *Lo straniero/The Stranger* (1967).

VITTI, Monica   Maria Luisa Ceciarelli; Rome 1931

Italian actress, remarkable in her ability to incarnate such antithetical film-making modes as *auteur* cinema and *commedia all'italiana**, and in her power, as a woman, to penetrate cinematic terrain previously restricted to men. As the privileged vehicle for Michelangelo Antonioni's* exploration of modernist consciousness in the 1960s, Vitti became intimately associated with the auteurist movement in Italy. Later, as the 'queen' of *commedia all'italiana*, she helped break the all-male hold on the genre through the creation of her own, enormously successful comic-grotesque persona.

Vitti attended the Accademia Nazionale d'Arte Drammatica and enjoyed early success in the theatre. She made her cinematic debut in Mario Amendola's *Le dritte* (1958), but it was Antonioni's tetralogy *L'avventura* (1960), *La notte/The Night* (1961), *L'eclisse/The Eclipse* (1962) and *Deserto rosso/The Red Desert* (1964) that won her international acclaim and established her reputation as an actress of considerable talent. In her portrayal of deeply troubled middle-class women, unable to establish satisfying relationships and incapable of connecting with their environment, the glamorous blonde Vitti came to embody the modernist dilemma in all its complexity and angst. 'The female consciousness', claimed Antonioni, 'is the best filter of reality I know', and Vitti, with her intensely cerebral performance style, provided the perfect vehicle for the film-maker's own alienated, highly abstract vision of the real. Vitti's image underwent a sea-change in the late 1960s with her award-winning performance in Mario Monicelli's* comedy *La ragazza con la pistola/The Girl with a Pistol* (1968). In Ettore Scola's* proletarian tragi-comedy *Dramma della gelosia: tutti i particolari in cronaca* (1970), ingeniously entitled *The Pizza Triangle* in English, Vitti played the common love object of Marcello Mastroianni* and Giancarlo Giannini and established her international reputation as comedienne. Just as Vitti came to feel constrained by her role as alienated woman in the 1960s, however, so she began to chafe at the limitations imposed by her type-casting in *commedia all'italiana*. The late 1970s were a time of reassessment and experimentation – she accepted Michael Ritchie's invitation to perform a different type of role in *An Almost Perfect Affair* (1979, US), then rejoined Antonioni in the critically disappointing *Il mistero di Oberwald/The Oberwald Mystery* (1980), and reappeared on screen, after a hiatus of two years, in the first directorial effort of photographer Roberto Russo, *Flirt*. 1986 marked her return to the theatre, both as teacher and actress. In recent years, Vitti has performed and directed for television, and has sponsored the careers of such young directors as Francesca Archibugi and Massimo Guglielmi. Vitti's debut as a film director came in 1990 with *Scandalo segreto/Secret Scandal* (starring Elliott Gould and Catherine Spaak), which was well received critically but met with limited box-office success. MMa

VLÁČIL, František   Český Těšín 1924

Czech director. Vláčil, who originally studied philosophy and art history, began his film career in documentary, moving to features with his poetic parable *Holubice/The White Dove* (1960), which won several international awards. He is best known for his remarkable trilogy of historical films, *Ďáblova past/The Devil's Trap* (1961), *Marketa Lazarová* (1965–67) and *Údolí včel/Valley of the Bees* (1967). All are deliberate attempts to resurrect the psychology of a past age and deal with the tragic outcomes of cultural and ideological conflict. His post-1969 work continued to show his dramatic and poetic talents and his frequently bleak vision, while retaining a commitment to historical themes. The visionary and barbaric qualities of *Marketa Lazarová* now mark it as one of the key Czech films of the 1960s, and it was singled out for revival at the 1992 Karlovy Vary* Festival. PH

Other Films Include: *Adelheid* (1969); *Dým bramborové natě/Smoke on the Potato Fields* (1976); *Stíny horkého léta/Shadows of a Hot Summer* (1977); *Koncert na konci léta/Concert at the End of Summer* (1979); *Hadí jed/Serpent's Poison* (1981); *Pasáček z doliny/The Little Shepherd Boy*

(1983); *Stín kapradiny/The Shadow of the Fern* (1984); *Mág/The Magus* (1987).

VOLONTÉ, Gian Maria
Milan 1933 – Florina, Greece 1994

Italian actor. After studying at the Accademia Nazionale d'Arte Drammatica, Volonté embarked on a theatrical career, including appearances in radical theatre. It was in the cinema, however, that he gained remarkable popularity. His first success was in Italian Westerns*, displaying his histrionic talent and ability to express cold 'post-expressionist violence' as the bad guy in Sergio Leone's* *Per un pugno di dollari/A Fistful of Dollars* (1964) and *Per qualche dollaro in più/For a Few Dollars More* (1965) and in Damiano Damiani's 'political' Western *Quién sabe?/A Bullet for the General* (1966). Before that he had played a trade union representative murdered by the Mafia in the Taviani* brothers' *Un uomo da bruciare/A Man to Burn* (1962) and a terrorist in Gianfranco De Bosio's *Il terrorista* (1963), and over the years it is this 'political' image which he became associated with. Nationally and internationally, he became the star of the 'Italian political cinema'* of the 1960s and 1970s. Landmarks in this 'genre' include his power-hungry police inspector in Elio Petri's* *Indagine su un cittadino al di sopra di ogni sospetto/Investigation of a Citizen Above Suspicion* (1969), and the tragic Lulu, the working-class protagonist of *La classe operaia va in paradiso/Lulu the Tool* (1971). He became especially associated with a series of films directed by Francesco Rosi*: he was the anti-militarist official of *Uomini contro* (1970), the government official of *Il caso Mattei/The Mattei Affair* (1972), the emigrant gangster of *Lucky Luciano* (1973), and later the novelist Carlo Levi discovering the South in *Cristo si è fermato a Eboli/Christ Stopped at Eboli* (1979). He twice played the role of the Christian Democrat prime minister Aldo Moro, in Petri's *Todo modo* (1976) and in Giuseppe Ferrara's *Il caso Moro/The Moro Affair* (1986), the latter made after Moro's death at the hands of the Red Brigades.

A modern follower of the naturalist tradition, Volonté had extraordinary presence and expressiveness. He increasingly developed an interiorised and melancholic mode (particularly after a long period of illness) as can be seen in his portrayal of the embittered and laconic protagonist of Claude Goretta's* *La mort de Mario Ricci/The Death of Mario Ricci* (1983) and his stoic and thoughtful judge in Gianni Amelio's* *Porte aperte/Open Doors* (1990). He died of a heart attack a few days before the end of the shooting of Thodoros Angelopoulos'* *To vlemma tou Odissea/Ulysses' Gaze* (released 1995), the story of a film-maker from Belgrade in search of the archives of early Greek cinema. GVo

Other Films Include: *Vent d'Est, Le Cercle rouge/The Red Circle* (1970, Fr.); *Sacco e Vanzetti* (1971); *Giordano Bruno* (1973); *Svegliati e uccidi/Wake Up and Kill* (1966); *Banditi a Milano/The Violent Four* (1968); *Il sospetto* (1975).

VORKAPICH, Slavko
Dobrinjci, Serbia 1894 – Mijas 1976

Serbian-American editor and theoretician; also director. After studying painting in Belgrade, Budapest and Paris, Vorkapich moved to Hollywood in 1921. He began collaborating with different art directors, and co-directed one of the earliest American avant-garde experiments, *The Life and Death of 9413 – a Hollywood Extra* (1927, with Robert Florey). His speciality soon became creative editing and special effects, in such films as W. S. Van Dyke's *Manhattan Melodrama* (1934), George Cukor's *David Copperfield* (1935), Frank Capra's *Mr Smith Goes to Washington* (1939) and many others. His courses at the University of Southern California, New York's MOMA and the Belgrade Film Academy were based on a specific view of *gestalt* perception theory. He considered film as an autonomous medium, a visual composition in time, capable of liberating fragments of visible dynamic energy from reality and of producing new meanings through the process of creative editing. He published articles but his theory was never systematically developed in book form, so his work is mostly available from the transcription of his lectures. SP

VOSKOVEC, Jiří
Sázava Budy [then Austria-Hungary] 1905 – Pear Blisson, USA 1981
and
WERICH, Jan
Prague [then Austria-Hungary] 1905 – Prague 1980

Czech actors, writers and producers. Voskovec and Werich were one of the major Czech comic influences of the twentieth century, extending beyond their origins in theatre to influence the whole arena of Czech culture. Principally associated with Osvobozené divadlo (The Liberated Theatre), they worked on no less than twenty-five original productions between 1927 and 1938. Musical satires and parodies, the plays featured Voskovec and Werich made up as clowns, whatever their costume, with key improvised interludes. Their 'pure humour and semantic clowning' (Roman Jakobson) was combined with a similar talent for physical comedy.

A year after their 1930 appearance in Paramount's all-star revue, *Paramount on Parade*, they made their first feature film, *Pudr a benzin/Greasepaint and Gasoline* (1931), which is an invaluable record of their theatrical work. In *Pudr a benzin* and *Peníze nebo život/Your Money or Your Life* (1932), both directed by their stage director, Jindřich Honzl, the influence of American crazy comedy is most in evidence. *Peníze nebo život* has some notable sequences, including an elaborate routine on a sinking raft and a climactic battle with criminals in a museum that looks forward to the Marx Brothers. Their later films, *Hej rup!/Heave Ho!* (1934) and *Svět patří nám/The World Belongs to Us* (1937), both directed by Martin Frič*, have more orthodox and tightly constructed scripts and parallel the increasing political commitment of their theatrical work. *Hej rup!* deals with the destruction of a corrupt capitalist at the hands of a workers' collective, while in *Svět patří nám* Voskovec and Werich defeat a Hitler-like demagogue and his big business supporters with the help of the workers. Voskovec and Werich spent the war years in the US and briefly continued their partnership in Czechoslovakia in 1946–47. Voskovec subsequently settled in the US where, as George Voskovec, he became a successful stage and screen actor, while Werich remained in Prague. At the height of Stalinism, Werich appeared in Frič's film adaptation of a Voskovec and Werich play, *Císařův pekař – Pekařův císař/ The Emperor's Baker – The Baker's Emperor* (1951), and in 1963 he played a key role in Vojtěch Jasný's* 'new wave' film *Až přijde kocour/That Cat*. Their work was a major influence on other directors of the Czech New Wave* such as Miloš Forman* and Jiří Menzel*. PH

VOULGARIS, Pandelis   Athens 1940

Greek director. A one-time contributor to *Synchronos Kinimatografos**, Voulgaris studied film-making in Greece. From 1961 to 1965 he worked as assistant director on more than thirty Greek films. His first full-length feature, *To proxenio tis Annas/The Engagement of Anna* (1972), helped inaugurate the New Greek Cinema*. Voulgaris has made a series of films dealing with events in recent Greek history (*Happy Day, Eleftherios Venizelos, Petrina hronia/Stone Years*). Arguably more successful, however, are his sensitive, small-scale stories *To proxenio tis Annas* and *Issihes meres tou Avgoustou/Quiet August Days*, personal evocations of contemporary exploitation, alienation and loneliness against the background of the social conditions which give rise to them. TN

Other Films Include: *Tzimis o tigris/Jimmy the Tiger* (1966); *O megalos erotikos/The Great Love Songs* (1973); *I fanela me to 9/The Striker with the No. 9* (1988).

VOUYOUKLAKI, Aliki   Athens 1937

Greek actress. Vouyouklaki made her stage debut in 1953 with the National Theatre. As well as sustaining a successful stage career (she has managed her own company since 1961), she became thanks to cinema the most famous figure in the history of Greek entertainment. She made her film debut in 1954 (*To pontikaki/The Little Mouse*, dir. Nikos Tsiforos). Her first major role came in one of the three 1955 versions of *O agapitikos tis voskopoulas/The Shepherdess' Lover*. By 1957 she was starring in three films a year. Since then she has been undisputed leading star of the Greek cinema, a pivotal figure in the entertainment business. Her film persona plays variations on the theme of a Snow White-like girl of modest means who uses her wit and fundamental generosity to charm her way into the higher classes. Vouyouklaki was the Greek film industry's most valuable asset. Most of her films topped the box-office lists, and she was the star of the three top-grossing Greek films ever, all produced by Finos Film*. Some of her films were also moderately successful abroad. TN

Bib: Marinos Kousoumidis, *Aliki* (1979).

Other Films Include: *Astero, To xilo vgike ap' ton Paradisso/Spare the Rod and Spoil the Child* (1959); *To klotsoskoufi/The Plaything* (1960); *Mandalena, I Aliki sto naftiko/ Alice in the Navy* (1961); *I kori mou i sossialistria/My Daughter, the Socialist* (1966); *I arhontissa ke o alitis/The Lady and the Pauper* (1968); *I daskala me ta hrissa mallia/The Teacher with the Blonde Hair* (1969); *Ipolohagos Natassa/ Lieutenant Natassa* (1970).

W

WAGENSTEIN, Angel   Plovdiv 1922

Bulgarian scriptwriter.The author of more than thirty internationally recognised screenplays for feature films, television films, documentaries, and animated cartoons. Upon graduating in 1950 from Moscow's VGIK*, Angel Wagenstein collaborated with Socialist Realist* dramatist Orlin Vassilev on the screen version of the latter's play, *Trevoga/Alarm* (1951), directed by documentarist Zahari Žandov*; it marked the beginning of modern Bulgarian cinema. Žandov then collaborated with Wagenstein again on the young scriptwriter's diploma work, *Septemvrici/Septembrists* (1954), on a revolutionary theme. While studying in Moscow, Wagenstein had made the acquaintance of director Konrad Wolf, and they collaborated on *Zvezdi/Sterne/Stars* (1959), a Bulgarian-East German co-production that ranks as a milestone in both national cinemas. *Zvezdi*, a love story praised as an example of Bulgarian Poetic Realism*, dealt with the tragic fate of a Jewish girl about to be transported to Auschwitz and her relationship with a young German soldier torn by his conscience.

Wagenstein's major talent as an award-winning film-writer is his ability to sketch vulnerable and warmly human characters. One example is his script for Ivan Ničev's *Zvezdi v kossite, sălzi v očite/Stars in Her Hair, Tears in Her Eyes* (1977), a nostalgic story about a wandering troupe of actors set at the turn of the century during the period of the Bulgarian National Revival. His feel for the significance of the historical moment also singled him out from other scriptwriters in the treatment of revolutionary and anti-fascist themes. His *Dopălnenie kăm zakona za zaštita na dăržavata/Amendment to the Defence of State Act* (1976), directed by Ljudmil

Staikov*, found room for flesh-and-blood portraits of well-known political personalities during the troubled 1920s. And his script for Rangel Vălčanov's* *Ezop/Aesop* (1970), a Bulgarian-Czechoslovak co-production, was a profound political allegory about the possibility of 'socialism with a human face' as propagated by Alexander Dubček; the film was banned in both Czechoslovakia and Bulgaria.

In addition, Wagenstein wrote the script for Konrad Wolf's *Goya* (1971), an East German production shot in 70mm. And he collaborated with Wolf again on a new interpretation of Saint-Exupéry's adult fairy tale *Le Petit prince* in *Der kleine Prinz/The Little Prince* (1966), produced for East German television. RH

WAJDA, Andrzej   Suwalki 1927

Polish director. A world-class director, Wajda has dominated Polish cinema for over forty years. He was a resistance fighter in World War II and a Fine Art student before studying film at Łódź*. His debut feature, *Pokolenie/A Generation* (1954), is the first of a trilogy which includes *Kanał/Canal* (1956) and *Popiół i Diament/Ashes and Diamonds* (1958), and looks at the Polish experience of war in a bleak, unromantic light. The trilogy launched the 'Polish School' and introduced Wajda to international audiences. His subsequent films varied in theme: contemporary and social issues in *Niewinni Czarodzieje/Innocent Sorcerers* (1960), about the disillusionment and cynicism of modern youth; an examination of the death of actor Zbyszek Cybulski* and of the nature of illusion and reality in the film world in *Wszystko na Sprzedaz/Everything for Sale* (1968). He also made several adaptations of Polish literature, including Żeromski's *Popioły/Ashes* (1965) and Wyspiański's *Wesele/The Wedding* (1972).

In the early 1970s Wajda formed his own film unit, the 'X' unit. There he gathered a group of young film-makers, including Agnieszka Holland* and Ryszard Bugajski*, and used his international status to push through politically 'difficult' projects. In 1976 he finally gained permission to film a project dating from 1961, *Człowiek z Marmuru/Man of Marble*. This daring exposé of the Stalinist propaganda machine of Poland's recent past paved the way for the 'cinema of moral unrest'. Powerful and uncompromising, both *Człowiek z Marmuru* and its sequel, *Człowiek z Żelaza/Man of Iron* (1981), played an important role in documenting and supporting the changing public consciousness of the Solidarity years. Somewhat protected from political retribution by his international standing, Wajda worked partly outside Poland during the martial law period. Although he remained resident in Warsaw, he shot *Danton* (1982) in France with Gérard Depardieu* as Danton and the great Wojtek Pszoniak as Robespierre, and *Eine Liebe in Deutschland/A Love in Germany* (1983), starring Hanna Schygulla*, in Germany.

With the changes of the late 1980s Wajda became a parliamentary senator. He continued film-making, however, returning to war themes in *Korczak/Dr Korczak* (1990) and *Pierścionek z Orłem w Koronie/The Ring with a Crowned Eagle* (1993). In 1991 Wajda was awarded a Felix* for his achievements as a film-maker and his contribution to the creation of a new cultural and political climate in Poland. AW

Bib: Andrzej Wajda, *Double Vision: My Life in Film* (1990).

Other Features Include: *Lotna* (1959); *Samson, Sibirska Ledi Magbet/Siberian Lady Macbeth/Fury is a Woman* (1961, Yug.); *L'Amour à vingt ans/Love at Twenty* [ep] (1962, Fr.); *The Gates to Paradise/Vrata Raja* (1967); *Polowanie na Muchy/Hunting Flies* (1969); *Krajobraz Po Bitwie/Landscape After Battle* (1970); *Ziemia Obiecana/Promised Land* (1974); *Bez Znieczulenia/Rough Treatment* (1978); *Panny z Wilka/Les Demoiselles de Wilko/The Young Ladies of Wilko, Dyrygent/The Conductor* (1979); *Kronika Wypadków Miłosnych/A Chronicle of Amorous Incidents* (1985); *Les Possédés/The Possessed* (1987, Fr.).

WALDEKRANZ, Rune   Turinge 1911

Swedish producer and scholar. Between 1942 and 1963 former film critic Rune Waldekranz worked as chief of production at Sandrews*, also writing a number of books on film history. He was appointed founding director of Sweden's first film school in 1964, and from 1970 held the first professorship in cinema studies at Stockholm University. Waldekranz has recently completed an extensive history of narrative film. BF

WALTARI, Mika   Helsinki 1908–79

Finnish novelist and scriptwriter. Mika Waltari is the most filmed Finnish writer and the author of a number of original scripts. He wrote short stories, poetry, rural stories, historical novels, modern city stories, fairytales and detective novels. Most of Waltari's scripts were filmed during the 1930s and 1940s. For T. J. Särkkä's* SF, he wrote historical spectacles like *Helmikuun manifesti/The February Manifesto* (1939), and light dramas using music, dance and comedy, such as *Kulkurin valssi/The Vagabond's Waltz* (1941), the most popular Finnish film of the 1940s. His range is vast, encompassing realist stories based on contemporary social problems (*Jokin ihmisessä/Something in People*, 1956, dir. Aarne Tarkas*), light but perceptive stage comedies (*Kuriton sukupolvi/Fearless Generation*, 1957, dir. Matti Kassila*), historical epics (*Tanssi yli hautojen/Dancing on Graves*, 1950, dir. Särkkä), and detective stories (*Komisario Palmun erehdys/Police Inspector Palmu's Mistake*, 1960, dir. Kassila). As a writer of both popular literature and more considered historical works, Waltari's reputation in Finnish culture has fluctuated, and he is often considered melodramatic and sentimental by the cultural elite. KL

WAM, Svend   Son 1946
and
VENNERØD, Petter   Oslo 1948

Norwegian directors and producers, the most productive of their generation. Wam and Vennerød founded their production company Mefistofilm in 1976 and directed their first film, *Det tause flertall/Silent Majority*, in 1977. They write their own scripts and use a regular troupe of actors. Wam and Vennerød's films deal with contemporary society and life, and their anti-bourgeois stance has given them a reputation as 'rebels'. This, together with their recourse to comedy as well as melodrama, and their skilful marketing techniques, explains their success in attracting a large and devoted audience. KS

Other Films as a Team Include: *Hvem har betsemt...?/Who Decided?* (1978); *Liv & død/Life & Death* (1980); *Julia Julia* (1981); *Leve sitt liv/Living One's Life* (1982); *Adjø solidaritet/Goodbye Solidarity* (1985); *Drømmeslottet/The Castle of Dreams* (1986); *Hotel st. Pauli* (1988); *Bryllupsfesten/The Wedding Party* (1989); *Lakki, gutten som kunne fly/Lakki, the Boy Who Knew How to Fly* (1992). **Wam only**: *Åpen framtid/Open Future* (1983).

WARM, Hermann   Berlin 1889 – 1976

German art director, responsible, together with Walter Reimann and Walter Röhrig, for the painted decor of *Das Cabinet des Dr Caligari/The Cabinet of Dr Caligari* (1920; dir. Robert Wiene*). No overnight wonder, Warm had been a 'film architect' since 1912, working for PAGU* and Greenbaum before transferring to Erich Pommer's* Decla, where he also did the sets for Fritz Lang's* *Die Spinnen* (two parts: 1919 and 1920) and supervised art direction on *Der müde Tod/Destiny* (1921). At Ufa* he was in charge of F. W. Murnau's* *Schloß Vogelöd* (1921) and *Phantom* (1922), but also of *Der Student von Prag/The Student of Prague* (Henrik Galeen, 1926) and G. W. Pabst's* *Die Liebe der Jeanne Ney/The Loves of Jeanne Ney* (1927). In the late 1920s he worked in France for Carl Theodor Dreyer*, designing an entire walled city for *La Passion de Jeanne d'Arc/The Passion of Joan of Arc* (1927) and creating the eerie mill in *Vampyr/The Vampire* (1932). After spending World War II in Switzerland, he continued in the German cinema until 1960 and his last film, Harald Braun's* *Die Botschafterin*. TE/MW

WARNER, Jack   London 1896–1981

British actor, whose career on both film and television made him an icon of responsible postwar ordinariness. His role as the paterfamilias of the Huggetts in the series of Gainsborough films which grew out of *Holiday Camp* (1947) represented the values of working-class decency and community inspired by the Attlee Labour government. As Robert Murphy suggests, the Huggetts anticipated such television families as the Appleyards and the Groves of the 1950s, and the community values of the early *Coronation Street*. Despite his role as an embittered and heartless killer in *My Brother's Keeper* (1948), Warner's role as PC George Dixon in *The Blue Lamp* (1950) established him as the image of benevolent community policing. Translated to television in 1955 as *Dixon of Dock Green*, his Saturday night homilies on order, justice and the British way of life ran until 1976, by which time both Jack Warner (who played the part until he was 80) and the image of the police which he represented were ready for retirement. JC

Bib: Jack Warner, *Jack of All Trades: The Autobiography of Jack Warner* (1975).

Other Films Include: *The Captive Heart, Dear Murderer, Hue and Cry* (1947); *Here Come the Huggetts* (1948); *Vote for Huggett* (1949); *The Huggetts Abroad* (1949); *The Square Ring, Albert RN, The Final Test* (1953); *The Quatermass Experiment, The Ladykillers* (1955); *Carve Her Name with Pride* (1958).

WATT, Harry   Edinburgh 1906 – Amersham 1987

British director, who was a prominent member of the British Documentary Movement* throughout the 1930s. He assisted Robert Flaherty* on *Man of Aran* (1934), directed *North Sea* (1938), and co-directed *Night Mail* (1936) with Basil Wright*, and *London Can Take It!* (1940) with Humphrey Jennings*. During the early years of the war he was associate producer of the Crown Film Unit, scripting and directing the hugely successful *Target for To-night* (1941), described by Watt as 'an understated and unemotional account of an average air raid'. He joined Ealing Studios in 1942, directing all his feature films in either Australia or Africa, including *The Overlanders* (1946), which he wrote and directed in Australia. He joined Granada Television as a producer in 1955. JC

Bib: Harry Watt, *Don't Look at the Camera* (1974).

Other Films Include: *BBC: Droitwich* [co-d.] (1934); *The Saving of Bill Blewitt* (1936); *The First Days* [co-d.] (1939); *Squadron 992* (1940); *Christmas Under Fire* (1941); *Nine Men* (1943); *Fiddlers Three* (1944); *Eureka Stockade* (1949); *Where No Vultures Fly* (1951); *West of Zanzibar* (1954); *The Siege of Pinchgut* (1959).

WECHSLER, Lazar   Petrikau, Poland 1896 – Zurich 1981

Polish-born Swiss producer, who moved to Switzerland in 1914 as an engineering student, and ten years later founded the country's first major production company, Praesens-Film in Zurich, which was to remain Switzerland's most profitable film company well into the 1950s.

Wechsler began producing documentaries in collaboration with aviator, camera operator and later shareholder Werner Mittelholzer (1894–1937); his interest in current affairs and his idealistic commitment persuaded S. M. Eisenstein* to shoot the material for a documentary about abortion during a short visit to Switzerland in 1930 (*Frauennot – Frauenglück*). During World War II, Wechsler's exceptional acumen led him to spearhead the 'spiritual defence of the nation' [> LINDTBERG] at Praesens-Film, with a number of feature films distilling a strong sense of Swiss national identity, mediated through the representation of the Army, the literary heritage and the regions. These films were made in close collaboration with his personnel, including directors Leopold Lindtberg*, Hermann Haller and Franz Schnyder*, cine-

449

matographer Emil Berna*, scriptwriter Richard Schweizer, composer Robert Blum, and actors Heinrich Gretler* and Anne-Marie Blanc*. Notable titles include *Füsilier Wipf* (1938), *Wachtmeister Studer* (1939), *Die mißbrauchten Liebesbriefe* (1940), *Der Schuß von der Kanzel* (1942), *Marie-Louise* (1944) and *Die letzte Chance/The Last Chance* (1944–45), all hugely successful at home and abroad, putting Switzerland for the first time on the world cinema map. Encouraged by this outcome, Wechsler turned to a more expensive though ultimately less successful (co-)production policy, aiming at the international market, the most memorable results being Fred Zinnemann's *The Search/Die Gezeichneten* (1947) and Lindtberg's *Die Vier im Jeep/Four in a Jeep* (1950). Despite occasional popular success at home (*Heidi*, 1952; *Heidi und Peter*, 1954) or cultural prestige (*Es geschah am hellichten Tag*, 1958), Wechsler's star waned perceptibly through the 1950s and 1960s, and with it Praesens' national pre-eminence. MW

Bib: Walter Boveri *et al.*, *Morgarten kann nicht stattfinden: Lazar Wechsler und der Schweizer Film* (1966).

WEGENER, Paul Jerrentowitz/Arnoldsdorf 1874 – Berlin 1948

German director and actor. Already one of the leading character actors from the Max Reinhardt* theatre, Wegener gained wider fame with his screen debut as the student Balduin in the first *Der Student von Prag/The Student of Prague* (1913). As producer, co-director and leading actor in *Der Golem* (1915), Wegener clearly felt close to this theme, since he made two other versions, *Der Golem und die Tänzerin* (1917) and *Der Golem, wie er in die Welt kam/The Golem* (1920). But Wegener the producer-director, in contrast to the actor, has been underrated as a key intellectual force behind the stylistic and thematic development of Wilhelmine cinema. His 1916 lecture, 'The Artistic Possibilities of Film', is one index of his interest in the cinema as an autonomous medium, but his selection of fantastic, gothic and fairy-tale motifs for his films, along with his choice of Guido Seeber* as cinematographer and technical adviser, is proof that Wegener sought to shape a 'national' cinema by combining German romanticism with technological excellence. It is thus not altogether surprising that this far-sighted artist, with his distinctive broad face and massive body, often described as 'Asian', should – after star parts in the films of Ernst Lubitsch*, Richard Oswald* and Joe May* – not hesitate in 1933 to continue acting in nationalist productions such as *Ein Mann will nach Deutschland* (1934) and *August der Starke* (1936), and even support outright propaganda efforts such as Veit Harlan's* *Der große König* (1942) and *Kolberg* (1945). TE/MW

Bib: Kai Möller (ed.), *Paul Wegener: Sein Leben und seine Rollen* (1954).

Other Films Include: *Der Verführte* (1913); *Sumurun* (1920); *Das Weib des Pharao/The Loves of Pharaoh* (1921); *Lukrezia Borgia* (1922); *The Magician* (1926, US); *Die Weber* (1927);

Alraune/Unholy Love (1928); *Das unsterbliche Herz* (1939); *Hochzeit auf Bärenhof* (1942); *Der große Mandarin* (1948).

WEIMAR CINEMA

Historical period of German cinema. The first German republic, known as the Weimar Republic, lasted from 1918 to 1933. The economic might of Ufa* ensured that the Weimar cinema created the first mass audience for film. The number of movie theatres in Germany grew from roughly 2,000 in 1918 to 5,000 at the beginning of the 1930s; 300 films were produced annually at the beginning of the 1920s as inflation hit Germany, and even at the end of the Weimar period more than a hundred films were still being produced every year. A growing number of (small) film companies ensured diversity of production, and a proliferation of trade journals indicates how highly developed the commercial film industry was at this time. Although German films were popular in countries outside Germany, Weimar cinema remained primarily a national cinema built on domestic genres and stars. Some of the most popular Weimar genres included sex films, costume films, 'Prussian' films, comedies and musicals, and most of the popular stars were German: Henny Porten*, Claire Rommer* and Conrad Veidt*, among others.

The image of Weimar cinema has largely been formed by two film historians, themselves film critics during the Weimar period in Germany. Their books, both written in exile, explained Weimar cinema retrospectively in the light of their experience of the Holocaust. In *From Caligari to Hitler* (1947), Siegfried Kracauer* demonstrates how collective psychic dispositions led to acquiescence in the Third Reich, while Lotte Eisner*, in *L'Ecran démoniaque* (1952, published in English as *The Haunted Screen* in 1973), often basing herself on the same films as Kracauer, tries to show how the Weimar cinema reanimated German romanticism, later perverted by the Nazis. Many Weimar films were considered art cinema at the time, since some directors deliberately tried to create a stylistic link between their films and more traditional, prestigious areas of high culture. The celebrated expressionist* films were aimed at an elite section of the middle class whose approval helped establish the films', but also the cinema's, general cultural value. Accordingly, the Weimar cinema was a cinema of directors whose development and dynamics were determined by cineastes and not by mass audiences. In fact, though, many of the films of directors such as Fritz Lang*, Friedrich Wilhelm Murnau* and G. W. Pabst*, who received their first training in fine arts, were also extremely popular, especially when they followed or reshaped genre conventions. Lang's most popular films were thrillers (*Dr. Mabuse, der Spieler/Dr. Mabuse, the Gambler*, 1922; two parts), *Spione/The Spy*, 1928), historical spectaculars (*Die Nibelungen*, 1924), and science-fiction films (*Metropolis*, 1927, *Die Frau im Mond/Woman in the Moon*, 1929). It is true, on the other hand, that the production system of the 1920s allowed those with creative talent a larger measure of freedom to experiment with techniques specific to film than in the American film industry [> ERICH POMMER; UFA]. Films made under these conditions received international critical acclaim – *Der letzte Mann/The Last Laugh* (1924), *Varieté/Variety* (1925), *Faust* (1926) – and the American film industry wooed German film personalities (Murnau, E. A. Dupont*, Karl Freund* and Emil Jannings*, for example) in order to produce European-type films in America which would be more popular in Germany than pure American-style films. After the reorganisation of Ufa in 1927, the possibility for personal innovation within the German film industry also changed.

Because the Weimar cinema is tied to the Weimar Republic in name, 1933 traditionally marks a sharp break in the history of German film, with the coming to power of the Nazis and the systematic persecution of Jews in the German film industry. However, the types of film produced at this time did not undergo any fundamental change. Traditional German genres, such as operetta films and mountain films*, continued to be produced after 1933 and stars such as Jannings, Paul Wegener*, Olga Tschechowa*, Lilian Harvey* and Heinz Rühmann* continued to have successful careers, illustrating the problem of using the political history of Germany for the periodisation of its film history. JG/TE

Bib: Lotte Eisner, *The Haunted Screen: Expressionism in the German Cinema and the Influence of Max Reinhardt* (1973); Siegfried Kracauer, *From Caligari to Hitler: A Psychological History of German Film* (1947)

WEISS, Jiří   Prague [then Austria-Hungary] 1913

Czech director. Jiří Weiss originally studied law, then worked as a journalist before making his first film *Lidé na slunci/People in the Sun* (1935), which won an award at Venice. He worked consistently in documentary until World War II, moving to Britain to work for the Crown Film Unit [> BRITISH DOCUMENTARY MOVEMENT], where his films included *Before the Raid* (1943). Besides writing a novel in English, *The Lost Revolution*, he made his fiction film debut with the medium-length *Who Killed Jack Robins?* and *John Smith Wakes Up* (both 1940). Weiss became one of Czechoslovakia's leading postwar directors with films such as *Uloupená hranice/The Stolen Frontier* (1947), about the Munich crisis, achieving international recognition with *Vlčí jáma/The Wolf Trap* (1957) and *Romeo, Julie a tma/Romeo, Juliet and Darkness* (1960), both noted for their psychological depth and dramatic visual style. Weiss left Czechoslovakia after the Soviet invasion, but returned to film his own script, *Martha und Ich/Martha and I* (1990), starring Marianne Sägebracht and Michel Piccoli*, a deeply felt portrait of pre-war Czechoslovakia and one of his best films. PH

Other Films Include: *Dejte nám křídla/Give Us Wings* [short] (1936); *Píseň o smutné zemi/Song of a Sad Country* [short] (1937); *Cesta ze stínu/Journey from the Shadows* [short] (1938); *The Rape of Czechoslovakia* [short] (1939, UK); *Vstanou noví bojovníci/New Heroes Will Arise* (1950); *Můj přítel Fabián/My Friend the Gypsy* (1953, released 1955); *Taková láska/Appassionata/That Kind of Love* (1959); *Zbabělec/The Coward* (1961); *Zlaté kapradí/The Golden Fern* (1963); *Třicet jedna ve stínu/90° in the Shade* (1965); *Vražda po našem/Murder, Czech Style* (1966); *Spravedlnost pro Selvina/Justice for Selwyn* [TV] (1968).

WEISZ, Frans   Berlin, Germany 1938

Dutch director. The son of a Hungarian-Jewish actor, Weisz moved to the Netherlands as a child, became one of the first students of the Amsterdam Film School in 1960 and learnt his craft at the Centro Sperimentale* in Rome. A leading figure in the so-called 'first wave' of young Dutch directors in the 1960s, Weisz won a Silver Bear in Berlin for his imaginative short *Een zondag op het eiland van de Grande Jatte/A Sunday on the Island of Grande Jatte* (1965). Literary and theatrical subjects are his forte, and he has acquired a fine reputation for working with actors, for his imaginative, intimate style and warm lighting. After the commercial flop of his critically acclaimed *Het gangstermeisje/Illusion is a Gangster Girl* (1967), and short-lived box-office success with two crime pictures, *De inbreker/The Burglar* (1972) and *Naakt over de schutting/Same Player Shoots Again* (1973), Weisz maintained his independence by becoming a leading director of commercials. His best work includes play adaptations such as *Rooie Sien/Red-Headed Sien* (1975), *Een zwoele zomeravond/A Hot Summer Night* (1982) and *Leedvermaak/Polonaise* (1989). A poll of Dutch critics and viewers placed his international co-production *Charlotte* (1980), based on the art work of Holocaust victim Charlotte Salomon, among their all-time favourites. Weisz's screen version of the best-selling novel *Havinck* (1987) garnered several national awards. In the 1990s Weisz has won regard as the director of *Hoogste Tijd/Last Call* (1995) and the creator of several ground-breaking television mini-series which had limited theatrical distribution, all of them adapted by Jan Blokker* from influential literary works, such as *Bij nader inzien* (1991) and *Op afbetaling/The Betrayed* (1993). HB

WENDERS, Wim   Düsseldorf 1945

German director, one of the few internationally known directors of the German cinema to graduate from a film school where, still a student, he made his first full-length feature film, *Summer in the City* (1971). Also active as a critic, producer and co-founder of the Filmverlag der Autoren*, he possesses an extensive film culture and is highly aware of the many threads that link him to German film history, both the 1920s and the Paris–Hollywood axis of the 1930s.

Falsche Bewegung/Wrong Movement (1975) and *Im Lauf der Zeit/Kings of the Road* (1976) brought Wenders critical, commercial and popular success, and with it bigger budgets: *Der amerikanische Freund/The American Friend* (1977) led to a US contract with Francis Ford Coppola to direct *Hammett* (1982). A sobering experience, it was reflected in a number of subsequent Wenders films: *Lightning Over Water* (1980), on and with his friend the director Nicholas Ray; *The State of Things* (1982) featuring another Hollywood director, Sam Fuller; and *Paris, Texas* (1984), shot in the US, though a Franco-German production. Refocused on Germany since his *Der Himmel über Berlin/Wings of Desire* (1987), a poetic meditation on the impossibility of coming home, Wenders has made the German past (*Alice in den Städten/Alice in the Cities*, 1974) a continuing theme in both *Bis ans Ende der Welt/Until the End of the World* (1991) and *In weiter Ferne, so nah!/Far Away, So Close* (1993). The latter film looks at a post-unification Berlin, caught between a still murky past and ever more nomadic existences. Perhaps too readily seen as the reinventor of the American road movie, Wenders shares his detached observational stance (which covers deep narcissistic wounds) with the Austrian writer Peter Handke, who has written three scripts for him. A director with an unmistakable visual style and rhythm, and winner of many prizes at festivals, he often works with the same team, including cameraman Robby Müller*, editor Peter Przygodda and the actors Rüdiger Vogler, Bruno Ganz* and Hanns Zischler. TE

Bib: Robert Philipp Kolker and Peter Beik, *The Films of Wim Wenders: Cinema as Vision and Desire* (1993).

Other Films Include: *Schauplätze* (1967); *Same Player Shoots Again* (1968); *Silver City* (1969); *Alabama: 2000 Light Years* (1969); *Die Angst des Tormanns beim Elfmeter/The Goalkeeper's Fear of the Penalty* (1972); *Chambre 666* (1982); *Tokyo-Ga* (1985); *Notebook of Cities and Clothes* (1989).

WERICH, Jan – see VOSKOVEC, Jiří

WERNER, Oskar   Oskar Josef Bschließmayer; Vienna 1922 – Marburg an der Lahn 1984

Austrian-born actor. Originally a stage actor, Werner played the Nazi Hermann Alt in Karl Hartl's* *Der Engel mit der Posaune* (1948), which initiated his international film career. Werner's sensitive acting and the fine, melodic beauty of his speech were the foundation of his success. His characters were intellectual, often overly sensitive heroes, many of whom 'failed' as a result of their resistance to conformism. His film work includes barely twenty-five films, among them François Truffaut's* *Jules et Jim* (1962, Fr.) and *Fahrenheit 451* (1966, UK), and Max Ophuls'* *Lola Montès* (1955, Fr./Ger.), and, in the US, Stanley Kramer's *Ship of Fools* (1965); in the UK he appeared notably in *The Spy Who Came in from the Cold* (1965) and *Voyage of the Damned* (1976). FM

WERTMÜLLER, Lina   Arcangela Felice Assunta Wertmüller von Elgg Spanol von Braueich; Rome 1928

Italian writer and director. A disciple of Federico Fellini*, Wertmüller soon developed her own original blend of carnivalesque style and scathing social satire which took the critical establishment by storm and enjoyed tremendous box-office success in many countries in the 1970s.

Wertmüller graduated in 1957 from the Accademia Teatrale directed by Pietro Sharoff and worked intensively as assistant director and scriptwriter for vaudeville as well as legitimate theatre. She entered the film world as Fellini's assistant director on *8½* (1963) and shot a documentary of the film's making. At the completion of *8½* Wertmüller wooed away most of Fellini's crew to Sicily, where she filmed her own first feature, *I basilischi/The Lizards* (1963), a critique of middle-class life in a small Italian town. Her next three films were blatantly commercial ventures: *Questa volta parliamo di uomini/Let's Talk About Men* (1965), a film in four episodes, *Rita la zanzara/Rita the Mosquito* (1966), and *Non stuzzicate la zanzara/Don't Tease the Mosquito* (1967). These last two works, made under the pseudonym of George Brown, were musical comedies starring the popular singer Rita Pavone, along with Giancarlo Giannini, who became Wertmüller's leading man through the 1970s. Upon returning to theatre, she met and married Enrico Job, her future art director and the person responsible for the set and costume design so integral to her filmic universe.

The year 1972 marked the beginning of Wertmüller's golden age: for a while she made at least one hit annually, most of them starring the remarkably versatile and expressive Giannini, teamed up three times with the equally powerful Mariangela Melato. In this couple, Wertmüller found the perfect vehicle for exploring her preferred theme: the tangle of political and sexual passions that link personal stories to public history during moments of revolutionary social change. Thus the Sicilian Mimi (Giannini), politically enlightened and sexually liberated by his mistress Fiore (Melato), turns into a Mafioso caveman when confronted with his wife's infidelity in *Mimì metallurgico ferito nell' onore/The Seduction of Mimi* (1972); the anarchist Tunin (Giannini), pledged to assassinate Mussolini, abdicates his free will to prostitutes, one of them his comrade, Salome (Melato), in *Film d'amore e d'anarchia ovvero: 'Stamattina alle 10 in Via dei Fiori nella nota casa di tolleranza …'/Love and Anarchy* (1973); and the proletarian male supremacist Gennarino (Giannini) capitulates to his bourgeois love-slave, Raffaela (Melato), in *Travolti da un insolito destino/Swept Away* (1974). With *Pasqualino Settebellezze/Seven Beauties* (1975), based on the true experiences of a concentration camp inmate who abdicated his humanity for survival, Wertmüller launched Giannini to international stardom. The actor performed in two more Wertmüller films, playing a brooding intellectual opposite Candice Bergen in *La fine del mondo nel nostro solito letto in una notte piena di pioggia/Night Full of Rain* (1978) and a sleazy Mafioso in *Fatto di sangue fra due uomini per causa di una vedova, si sospettano moventi politici …/Blood Feud* (1978), but the intensity of the early 1970s collaborations had dissipated by then. Wertmüller's 1980s films have all been topical in focus: high-tech security goes awry in *Scherzo del destino in agguato dietro l'angolo come un brigante da strada/Joke of Destiny* (1983), lesbian desire complicates marital relations in *Sotto … sotto … strapazzato da anomala passione* (1984), drugs and organised crime are attacked in *Un complicato intrigo di donne, vicoli e delitti/Camorra* (1985), environmentalism and kidnapping converge in *Notte d'estate con profilo greco, occhi a mandorla e odore di basilico/Summer Night* (1986), and the fear of AIDS takes over *In una notte di chiaro di luna/Crystal or Ash, Fire or Wind, as Long as It's Love* (1989). Wertmüller also made sporadic returns to the theatre, including the writing and directing of *Amore e magia nella cucina di mamma*, performed in Spoleto in 1979 and New York in 1980. She added opera to her repertory in 1987 with a production of *Carmen* at the prestigious San Carlo theatre in Naples. In 1988 she was appointed Commissario Straordinario at the Centro Sperimentale*.

Wertmüller's powerful 1970s films combined the intense

energy and physicality of the *commedia dell'arte* tradition with the high emotionalism of her theatrical training, and applied them to the post-1968 political consciousness. Her achievement was not met without controversy, however – critical discomfort ran high, especially in feminist circles. Wertmüller's resolve to communicate her political messages to mass audiences through hyperbolic and grotesque comic techniques raised serious questions about whether or not the regional, gender and class stereotypes which sustain her cinema do not reinforce the public's most regressive prejudices. If such polemics are an index of success, then Wertmüller's 1970s production fully achieved its goals. MMa

Other Films Include: *Tutto a posto e niente in ordine/All Screwed Up* (1974); *Sabato, domenica e lunedì* (1990).

WESSELY, Paula   Vienna 1908

Austrian actress, who mainly performed on stage but in 1934 accepted an offer from Willy Forst* to play the female lead in *Maskerade/Masquerade in Vienna*, a role that suited her Viennese temperament and dialect. The film brought her to the attention of Joseph Goebbels, who subsequently built her up as the star who represented his ideal of the 'wholesome' German woman, conceived as an alternative to the unbridled eroticism of emigrant Marlene Dietrich*. Wessely reliably delivered this image in a string of propaganda melodramas directed by some of Ufa's* most experienced hands, such as Geza von Bolvary* (*Spiegel des Lebens*, 1938) and Gustav Ucicky* (*Heimkehr*, 1941). In the postwar period, despite appearing in few films, Wessely not only successfully resumed her stage career, but transformed her past film successes into an enduring myth, making her the *grande dame* of Austrian film culture and popular entertainment. KU

Bib: Cinzia Romani, *Tainted Goddesses: Female Film Stars of the Third Reich* (1992).

Other Films Include: *Episode* (1935); *Die ganz großen Torheiten* (1937); *Maria Illona* (1939); *Das Herz muß schweigen* (1944).

WHITELAW, Billy   Coventry 1932

British actress. Whitelaw is well respected for her work on television and theatre, where she is renowned both in working-class realism and as the leading female interpreter of Samuel Beckett, with whom she collaborated. She has made surprisingly few films, often in supporting character roles. She received a British Film Academy award for her part in Albert Finney's* *Charlie Bubbles* (1967), played opposite Finney in Stephen Frears'* *Gumshoe* (1971), and, more recently, gave an utterly convincing performance as the matriarch in Peter Medak's *The Krays* (1990). JC

Other Films Include: *Miracle in Soho* (1957); *Make Mine Mink* (1960); *Twisted Nerve* (1968); *Leo the Last* (1970); *Frenzy* (1972); *The Omen* (1976, US); *An Unsuitable Job for a Woman* (1982).

WICKI, Bernhard   St. Pölten 1919

Austrian actor and director. Wicki's first success as an actor was in the war film *Die letzte Brücke/The Last Bridge* (1953), and, as director, six years later in another war film, *Die Brücke/The Bridge* (1959), considered among the best German productions of the 1950s. Awarded best director prize at the Berlin film festival for his next picture, *Das Wunder des Malachias* (1961), Wicki was assigned to prestigious international projects (*Der Besuch/The Visit*, 1964; *Morituri/The Saboteur Code Name – 'Morituri'*, 1965, US), which formed the basis of his reputation outside Germany. From the 1970s, he specialised in literary adaptations commissioned by West German television (*Das falsche Gewicht*, 1970; *Die Eroberung der Zitadelle*, 1977), some of which were co-produced by the East German DEFA*: *Die Grünstein – Variante* (1984), *Sansibar oder der letzte Grund* (1987). From 1977 he worked on *Das Spinnennetz* (based on Joseph Roth), which grew to be his late *magnum opus*, and premiered at Cannes in 1989, though to a reserved critical reception. MW.

Bib: Robert Fischer, *Sanftmut und Gewalt: Der Regisseur und Schauspieler Bernhard Wicki* (1991).

WIDERBERG, Bo   Malmö 1930

Swedish director. Originally a novelist, Widerberg wrote a polemical book on Swedish film, *Visionen i svensk film*, in 1962, championing a Swedish New Wave* and criticising the dominant influence of Ingmar Bergman*. Realistic and socially committed, *Kvarteret Korpen/Raven's End* (1963) and *Barnvagnen/The Pram* (1963) are Widerberg's contributions to this 'new wave'. Filmed in black and white with small budgets, they bear a strong visual resemblance to their counterparts in France and elsewhere. Widerberg had great success with the romantic *Elvira Madigan* (1967). In *Ådalen 31* (1969) and *Joe Hill/The Ballad of Joe Hill* (1971, US) he tackled moments in the history of the Swedish and American labour movements, again with international success. In Sweden, Widerberg reached new audiences with his thrillers *Mannen på taket/The Man on the Roof* (1976) and *Mannen från Mallorca/The Man from Majorca* (1984). *Ormens väg på Hälleberget/The Serpent's Way* (1986) is an adaptation of a novel by Torgny Lindgren. Widerberg has also directed some important television dramas. LGA/BF

Bib: Stig Björkman, *Film in Sweden: The New Directors* (1977).

Other Films Include: *Kärlek 65/Love 65* (1965); *Heja Roland/Thirty Times Your Money* (1966); *Fimpen/Stubby* (1974); *Victoria* (1979, released in Sweden 1987).

WIENE, Robert   Breslau 1881 – Paris 1938

German director. Wiene is mostly remembered as the director of the legendary *Das Cabinet des Dr Caligari/The Cabinet of Dr Caligari* (1920), but had by then already directed dozens of films. A rather conventional director, he tried to re-peat the success of *Caligari*, using similarly abstract settings and fantastic subjects in *Genuine* (1920) and *Raskolnikov* (1923). Having moved to Vienna in 1924, Wiene once more picked a fantastic subject in *Orlacs Hände/The Hands of Orlac* (1924), about a pianist (Conrad Veidt*) who, after a train accident, is given the hands of an executed murderer. Wiene also turned a script by Hugo von Hofmannsthal into the filmed opera *Der Rosenkavalier* (1926). In exile in Paris, he directed *Ultimatum* (1938, starring Erich von Stroheim), but died only days before the shooting was completed (by Robert Siodmak*). MW

Bib: Uli Jung and Walter Schatzberg, *Robert Wiene* (1992)

Other Films Include: *Die Königin vom Moulin Rouge* (1926); *Die Geliebte* (1927); *Die berühmte Frau* (1927), *Die Frau auf der Folter, Die große Abenteuerin* (1928); *Der Andere* (1930); *Taifun* (1933).

WILCOX, Herbert   Cork, Ireland 1891 – London 1977

British producer/director. 'The guiding principle of my company,' Wilcox said in 1935, 'will be productions based on outstanding star personalities with music, romance and com-edy as the basic ingredients.' In the 1920s he had already tested the formula, adapting proven stage successes such as *Chu Chin Chow* (1923) and engaging Dorothy Gish to star in four films, including the highly successful *Nell Gwyn* (1926). *Dawn* (1928), with Sybil Thorndike as Nurse Edith Cavell, was the subject of a censorship case initiated by the German embassy, but was highly praised in *Close Up**. In the 1930s Wilcox discovered his star and future wife in Anna Neagle*, casting her first in *Goodnight Vienna* (1932) and remaking *Nell Gwyn* with her in 1934. He unashamedly cashed in on public patriotism with *Victoria the Great* (1937) and *Sixty Glorious Years* (1938). Wilcox and Neagle spent the early years of the war in Hollywood, returning to Britain in 1942 and marrying in 1943. Wilcox maintained his success after the war with the 'Mayfair' cycle – *I Live in Grosvenor Square* (1945), *Piccadilly Incident* (1946), *The Courtneys of Curzon Street* (1947) and *Maytime in Mayfair* (1949) – but in the 1950s he began to lose his feel for what the audience wanted. He co-produced Peter Brook's *The Beggar's Opera* (1953) with Laurence Olivier*, but his long and successful career ended in bankruptcy in 1964. JC

Bib: Herbert Wilcox, *Twenty-Five Thousand Sunsets: The Autobiography of Herbert Wilcox* (1967).

Other Films Include: *Madame Pompadour* (1927); *The Triumph of the Scarlet Pimpernel* (1928); *The Woman in White* (1929); *The King's Cup, Bitter Sweet, The Little Damozel* (1933); *The Queen's Affair* (1934); *Peg of Old Drury* (1935); *London Melody* (1937); *No, No, Nanette, Irene* (1940, both US); *They Flew Alone* (1942); *Odette* (1950); *The Lady with a Lamp* (1951); *Trouble in the Glen* (1954); *King's Rhapsody* (1955); *These Dangerous Years* (1957); *The Lady is a Square* (1958).

WILLIAMSON, James   Scotland 1855 – [?] 1933

British pioneer inventor and producer. A chemist with an interest in photography, Williamson became one of the mem-bers of the 'Brighton School' along with G. A. Smith* and others. He is credited by Barry Salt with the first action con-tinuity sequence in *Stop Thief!* (1901), in which a thief is chased out of one frame and into the next in a different lo-cation, and is finally caught in the third frame. This became the basic grammar of the chase sequence. After 1904, Williamson concentrated on the manufacturing of equipment. JC

Bib: Barry Salt, *Film Style and Technology: History and Analysis* (1983).

WINTER, Leon de   Den Bosch 1954

Dutch director, scriptwriter and novelist. De Winter's debut film, *De verwording van Herman Dürer/The Demise of Herman Dürer* (1979), was an adaptation of his first novel, the tragic story of a day-dreamer who identifies with a character in a nineteenth-century novel. *De grens/Frontiers* (1983), a European co-production using Dutch, German and French actors, was an attempt to combine European left political pre-occupations, particularly terrorism, with American-style film-making. In the 1980s De Winter introduced another theme into his work: the struggle for a post-Holocaust Jewish ident-ity. He wrote the script for *Place de la Bastille* (1984, dir. Rudolf van den Berg) from one of his novels, and in 1987 again turned one of his novels into a script directed by van den Berg, *Zoeken naar Eileen/Looking for Eileen*, a melo-dramatic love story. In 1993 De Winter wrote and directed his most ambitious production, *Hoffman's Hunger*, an inter-national mini-series starring Elliott Gould and Jacqueline Bisset. It is a characteristic work, dealing with Jewish identity problems and shot in a manner that mixes commercial and art-house styles. He directed *Supertex* in 1995. HK

WISDOM, Norman   London 1920

British actor. A late, postwar addition to the music-hall tra-dition, Wisdom did not make his music-hall debut until 1946, and it was through success on television from 1948 that he en-tered films. Like that of George Formby* or Will Hay*, his comedy is based on a stable character – 'the Gump' – sub-jected to disaster-laden situations which get in the way of his romantic intentions. His performance, however, is much more physical and slapstick (to the point of masochism), and Wisdom may have more in common with the Hollywood tra-dition of Chaplin, particularly as reworked by Jerry Lewis. Associated with two directors, John Paddy Carstairs and Robert Asher, he was at his best when Carstairs set tight limits to the sentimentality inherent in the character. JC

Films Include: *Trouble in Store* (1953); *One Good Turn* (1954); *Man of the Moment* (1955); *Up in the World* (1956); *Just My Luck* (1957); *The Square Peg* (1958); *Follow a Star*

(1959); *There Was a Crooked Man, The Bulldog Breed* (1960); *On the Beat* (1962); *The Early Bird* (1965); *Press for Time* (1966); *The Night They Raided Minsky's* (1968, US); *Going Gently* [TV] (1981).

WITHERS, Googie   Georgette Withers; Karachi, India 1917

British actress, who learned her craft in 'quota quickies' during the 1930s and found her strongest roles with Ealing, and in particular with Robert Hamer*, in the 1940s. She made over thirty films between 1934 and 1941, including *Trouble Brewing* (1939) with George Formby*, a brief, giggly appearance for Alfred Hitchcock* in *The Lady Vanishes* (1938), and three 'quota quickies' directed by Michael Powell*: *The Girl in the Crowd* (1934), *The Love Test* (1935) and *Her Last Affaire* (1935). Powell rewarded her by giving her her first leading dramatic part in ...*One of Our Aircraft is Missing* (1942). At Ealing, she played a series of determined women struggling against the constraints of a conservative, respectable male society, her boldly drawn, assertive sexuality sitting uneasily with the image of Ealing's gentle revolution. For Hamer, she appeared in the 'Haunted Mirror' episode of *Dead of Night* (1945), *Pink String and Sealing Wax* (1945), and, probably her best film, *It Always Rains on Sunday* (1947). Hamer was also closely involved in Charles Frend's *The Loves of Joanna Godden* (1947) – her other best role as a Mildred Pierce of the Romney Marshes. Married to John McCallum, her leading man in her two best films, Googie Withers moved to Australia in the 1950s. She returned to Britain in the 1980s and gave two fine television performances in *Hotel du Lac* (1986) and *Northanger Abbey* (1987). JC

Other Films Include: *The Silver Fleet* (1943); *On Approval, They Came to a City* (1944); *Miranda, Once Upon a Dream, Traveller's Joy* (1949); *Night and the City* (1950); *White Corridors, The Magic Box* (1951); *Derby Day* (1952); *The Nickel Queen* (1970, Australia).

WOHLBRÜCK, Adolf [WALBROOK, Anton]   Vienna 1896 – Garatshausen 1967

Austrian-born actor. After occasional roles in silent films, Wohlbrück embarked on a regular film career in 1931, playing in, among other films, *Viktor und Viktoria* (1933). In 1934, he succeeded in consolidating his image in Willi Forst's* *Maskerade/Masquerade in Vienna* as the painter Heideneck. Wohlbrück's elegant men-of-the-world were rooted in an acting style typical of the 'Viennese films' of the 1920s and 1930s. Restrained speech and abbreviated gestures seem to elevate this elegant *bon vivant* above the mediocrity surrounding him. Wohlbrück emigrated to Britain in 1936. He continued his career under the name Anton Walbrook, starring in *Gaslight* (1940) and working with such directors as Michael Powell* and Emeric Pressburger* in Britain (*The Life and Death of Colonel Blimp*, 1943; *The Red Shoes*, 1948; *Oh ... Rosalinda!!*, 1955) and with Max Ophuls* in France in *La Ronde* (1950) and *Lola Montès* (1955). FM

WOLLEN, Peter – see MULVEY, Laura

WORKSHOP MOVEMENT

British movement, which became institutionalised with the arrival of Channel 4*, but had its roots in the politics of collective practice associated with 1968 and feminism. Early collectives, which included Cinema Action, Amber Films, the Berwick Street Collective, the London Women's Film Group and Four Corners, saw their work as politically oppositional rather than alternative. Film was conceived as a social practice, with Cinema Action using *Song of the Clyde* (1971) in support of the Upper Clyde Shipyards occupation, the Berwick Street Collective making *Nightcleaners* (1975) in support of a cleaners' strike, and the London Women's Film Group campaigning for equal pay with *The Amazing Equal Pay Show* (1974). Though distinct from the formal preoccupations of the London Film-makers Co-op, many of the groups became increasingly concerned with the politics of form, engaging particularly with the debates about Brecht and cinema which *Screen** was promoting. The films were distributed by The Other Cinema, formed in 1970 and opening its own cinema in 1976, and in 1974 the Independent Film-makers Association was formed to coordinate and promote the interests of the grant-aided sector.

The arrival of Channel 4 gave an institutional form to the Movement. An agreement between the ACTT (Association of Cinematograph, Television and Allied Technicians – the main trade union), the British Film Institute*, and Channel 4 known as the 'Workshop Declaration' accredited a number of 'franchised workshops', recognising them for the production of commissioned work for Channel 4 at lower than normal rates and crewing levels. The Declaration encouraged the formation of workshops within communities of region, race and gender. Some existing collectives were franchised, and new regional workshops were established in, for example, Cardiff, Birmingham and the East Midlands. Women's workshops were franchised in Leeds (the Leeds Animation Workshop) and Sheffield, and black workshops such as Sankofa, Ceddo and Black Audio Film Collective were formed in the mid-1980s. Material was shown on the Channel 4 series, 'The Eleventh Hour', but the revenue funding was also intended to support educational and cultural work within the workshops' own communities. The system gave financial security to the participants, and brought new forms of film-making to a wider audience than could be reached through commercial cinema distribution.

There were, however, contradictions. A concern with the politics of form was a difficult training ground for television, and many programmes were criticised for being more concerned with form than with audiences. More insidiously, the institutionalisation of workshops had the effect of localising them within their communities, coherent as a unit but not as a movement. Nevertheless, at the local level the workshop system represented an astonishing form of social and cultural patronage from a commercial television channel.

By 1990 the climate and the economy had changed, and both the BFI and Channel 4 withdrew their guarantees of revenue funding, leaving the workshops to operate like any other small business seeking clients where it could find them. While many groups continue to produce interesting and even oppositional work, and while there is a sense of a greater access to production than at any time since the 1930s, the history of the Workshop Movement charts quite sharply a particular trajectory of British political culture and cultural politics since 1968. JC

Bib: Alan Lovell, 'That was the Workshops that was', *Screen* 31/1 (Spring 1990), and Rod Stoneman, 'Sins of Commission', *Screen*, 33/2 (Summer 1992).

WRIGHT, Basil   London 1907–87

British director and producer, and the first of John Grierson's* recruits to the Documentary Movement, joining him at the Empire Marketing Board in 1931. In 1934, with *Song of Ceylon*, Wright established the distinctive poetic quality which he brought to the British Documentary Movement*, and in 1936 he co-directed *Night Mail* with Harry Watt*. 'It is conceivable,' suggests Elizabeth Sussex, 'that [Wright] brought the one distinctive quality that actually put British documentary on the map.' He formed the Realist Film Unit with John Taylor and Alberto Cavalcanti* in 1937, and during the war worked at the Crown Film Unit, producing, for example, Humphrey Jennings'* *A Diary for Timothy* (1945). In 1953 he co-directed *World Without End* with Paul Rotha*. He taught at the University of California from 1960, and wrote *The Use of Film* (1948) and *The Long View* (1974). JC

Other Films Include: *O'er Hill and Dale* (1932); *Windmill in Barbados, Cargo from Jamaica, Liner Cruising South* (1933); *Children at School* (1937); *The Face of Scotland* (1938); *This Was Japan* (1945); *Waters of Time* (1950); *Stained Glass at Fairford* (1955); *The Immortal Land* (1958).

X

XANTHOPOULOS, Nikos   Athens 1936

Greek film actor; also singer. One of the two superstars of Greek cinema (the other is Aliki Vouyouklaki*), Xanthopoulos reached the peak of his popularity in the 1960s. He rose to stardom with roles in melodramas, usually directed by Apostolos Tegopoulos and co-starring Martha Vourtsi [> GREEK MELODRAMA]. His star persona is that of the impoverished young Greek who is obliged to fight all kinds of social oppression to survive. Dubbed the 'child of the people', he embodied the aspirations and values of immigrant, lower-middle and working-class audiences. His stature, like that of the films he starred in, was long denigrated by the critical establishment, but the enduring popularity of his films on television has enforced a recent reappraisal. TN

Films Include: *Missos/Hate* (1963); *Kardia mou papse na ponas/My Heart, Stop the Pain, Apokliroi tis kinonias/Society's Outcasts* (1965); *Eho dikeoma na s' agapo/I Have the Right to Love You* (1966); *Xerizomeni genia/Uprooted Family* (1968); *I odissia enos xerizomenou/Odyssey of the Uprooted* (1969).

Y

YERSIN, Yves   Lausanne 1942

Swiss director, educated at the Vevey School of Photography (1959–61), who began as a camera operator and assistant director. A member of the 'Groupe des Cinq' in 1969, he was associated with the 'new Swiss cinema' of the late 1960s and the 1970s. He started his own film-making career as a director with documentaries that combine precise documentary observation with a profound poetic imagination. *Die letzten Heimposamenter/The Last Home Lace-makers* (1973) is one of the most important Swiss documentaries* of the 1970s. Yersin's dialectic between ethnography and emotion also informs his first fiction film, the successful *Les Petites Fugues/Little Escapes* (1978), considered to be an early reworking of the Swiss 'Heimatfilm' [> HEIMATFILM]. Apart from his involvement in the film side of the celebrations for the Swiss Confederation's 700th anniversary in 1991, Yersin played a central role in the development of film education in Switzerland and in 1988 founded the audiovisual department at the Lausanne Ecole Cantonale d'Art. MW

Other Films Include: *Valvieja* (1967); *Celui qui dit non* (ep. 'Swiss Made', 1968); *Inventaire lausannois* (1981).

YIDDISH CINEMA IN POLAND

At the beginning of the twentieth century Poland was home to over three and a half million Jews. There was a thriving Yiddish and Hebrew cultural tradition, particularly in the theatre. The first forays into film were made as early as 1908 by the Sila Company, which filmed Yiddish plays. It was not until the 1930s, however, and the arrival of Polish-born Joseph Green from America, that Yiddish cinema really established itself in Poland.

Green saw an opportunity to make films cheaply in Poland for the American-Jewish market. He founded Green-Film, the Polish arm of his company, in 1936. His first production introduced American-Jewish comedienne Molly Picon in the musical comedy *Yidl Mit Fidl/Yiddle with a Fiddle* (1937), an international success. Green operated in true movie-mogul fashion, with publicity splashes and American 'stars'. Under his guidance, Yiddish cinema began to play a prominent role on the Polish film scene, and his films were distributed throughout Europe. It was not unusual for mainstream directors to make Yiddish films. Aleksander Ford* shot *Chalutzim/Sabra* in 1934 with actors from the famous Habimah theatre in Palestine, and it was popular comedy director Michal Waszyński who made the true Yiddish classic, *The Dybbuk* (1937). Most of Joseph Green's productions survived the war because he took the negatives to America in 1939. When comedians Shimon Dzigan and Israel Schumacher made a semi-documentary in 1949 – *Unzere Kinder/Our Children* – the new Polish government banned the film and the film-makers emigrated to Israel. More recently, with the demise of communism, Yiddish cinema is being re-explored in Poland, and a selection of titles was screened at the 1990 Festival of Culture in Cracow. AW

Bib: Judith Goldberg, *Laughter Through Tears* (1983).

YOUNG, Freddie   London 1902

British cinematographer, with a long and distinguished career stretching over half a century in British and Anglo-American films. His first film as co-cinematographer was *The Flag Lieutenant* (1926), and through the 1930s he was Herbert Wilcox's* principal lighting cameraman, shooting such films as *Goodnight Vienna* (1932), *Bitter Sweet* (1933), *Nell Gwyn* (1934), *Victoria the Great* (1937) and *Sixty Glorious Years* (1938). He continued to be associated with distinguished films during and after the war, working with such British directors as Michael Powell*, Carol Reed* and Anthony Asquith*, and Hollywood directors such as George Cukor, John Ford and Vincente Minnelli. In 1962, at the age of 60, he began an association with David Lean* which brought him Academy Awards for *Lawrence of Arabia* (1962), *Doctor Zhivago* (1965) and *Ryan's Daughter* (1970). He was the first recipient of the American Society of Cinematographers' International Achievement Award. JC

Other Films Include: *Goodbye, Mr Chips* (1939); *Contraband* (1940); *49th Parallel* (1941); *The Young Mr Pitt* (1942); *Caesar and Cleopatra* (1946); *The Winslow Boy* (1948); *Edward, My Son* (1949); *Treasure Island* (1950); *Lust for Life, Bhowani Junction* (1956, both US); *The Barretts of Wimpole Street, Gideon's Day, The Inn of the Sixth Happiness, Indiscreet* (1958); *Lord Jim* (1965); *You Only Live Twice* (1967); *Battle of Britain* (1969); *Nicholas and Alexandra* (1971, US); *Luther* (1973, US/UK/Can.); *The Tamarind Seed* (1974); *The Blue Bird* (1976, US/USSR). JC

YUGOSLAV 'BLACK WAVE'

Radical Yugoslav films of the late 1960s/early 1970s. The 1960s saw the first great political and economic liberalisation in postwar Yugoslavia. At the same time, film-makers used their newly acquired knowledge of neo-realism* and the French New Wave* in order to reject the unwritten rules of 'real socialism' (Socialist realism*) – imitation of life, combined with patriotic education. They turned 'naughty', and suddenly the dark side of the new society emerged on the screen: corruption and hypocrisy, and the narrow-mindedness and boorishness of the ruling class. Two 1967 Živojin Pavlović* films (*Budjenje pacova/Awakening of the Rats* and *Kad budem mrtav i beo/When I am Dead and White*) are representative of this movement. No more heroes: the lack of any individual perspective can be seen as a kind of desperate cry. Together with those of Dušan Makavejev*, Aleksandar Petrović*, Želimir Žilnik and Bata Čengić, they form a core of twenty to thirty films which were labelled 'Black Wave' (or 'Black Film'). The term was first used pejoratively by the communist authorities in order to censor and even ban some of the films. Much later, 'Black Wave' became a positive critical notion embraced by oppositional film culture. SP

YUGOSLAV 'PARTISAN FILMS'

Yugoslav genre, designating World War II action films. The appeal of the first postwar films in Yugoslavia derived from the fact that they knew how to combine the triumphalism of the official postwar posture with a certain naivety of narration. Examples include Nikola Popović's *Živjeće ovaj narod/This Nation Will Live!* (1947) and France Štiglic's* *Na svoji zemlji/On Our Own Land* (1948). Emphasis was put on psychology and emotions. As the films evolved, much of this dimension was lost and replaced with pure, Western-like action, and the 'partisan' genre was born. The schema was simple: every big battle from the rich history of Yugoslavia's World War II experience deserved a monument – and a movie. Veljko Bulajić's* *Kozara* (1962) and *Bitka na Neretvi/Battle on the River Neretva* (1969) are two examples of such historic battles used as a pretext to stage a confrontation between bad Nazi soldiers and good partisans in action. As the good guys usually won, the genre was extremely popular with the audience, and some actors – such as Ljubiša Samardžić and Bata Živojinović – achieved stardom through it. The 1970s were the golden age of these commercially successful but aesthetically simple films that were often turned into even more successful television series. Such was the case with two Aleksandar Djordjević films about the resistance movement in Belgrade, *Otpisani/Written Off* (1974) and *Povratak otpisanih/The Return of the Written Off* (1976).

457

Two factors made 1980 the final year for this genre: Tito died, and Živojin Pavlović* shot *Na svidenje v naslednji vojni/Farewell Until the Next War*. If the death of Tito symbolically closed the period of partisan triumphs, Pavlović's film was a clinical diagnosis of the death of the genre itself. SP

YUGOSLAVIA (former)

A film tradition in Yugoslavia existed before the actual birth of the state (the kingdom of Serbs, Croats and Slovenes was named 'Yugoslavia' in 1929) and will certainly outlast it: the death of the Socialist Federal Republic of Yugoslavia came in 1991 with the proclaimed independence of several states, including Slovenia, Croatia, Bosnia–Herzegovina, and Macedonia. However, since Yugoslavia was a country in the time-span covered by most of the following material, it will be referred to here as such.

The first film screenings on the territory of the future Yugoslavia took place only six months after the Lumière* brothers' first screening in Paris: the films of the Lumière Cinematograph were shown in Belgrade on 6 June 1896. Most of the early travelling operators were foreign – and it was they who filmed the first footage shot in these regions. Some sixty metres of views of the port of Šibenik (Croatia), shot in 1903 by the Polish operator Stanislaw Noworyta, are considered to be the first known film ever shot in Yugoslavia. National pioneers also emerged in the first two decades of the century: Karol Grosmann* in Slovenia and Milton Manaki* in Macedonia. Svetozar Botorić, the owner of several Belgrade hotels and the film theatre Paris, started to produce short documentaries in collaboration with the French company Pathé*. This collaboration also produced the first feature-length film shot in Serbia (and Yugoslavia): *Život i dela besmrtnog vožda Karadjordja/The Life and Work of the Immortal Leader Karadjordje*. This biographical portrait of the Serbian leader who fought against the Turks and founded the dynasty of Karadjordjević was shot in 1910 and distributed in 1911 under the title *Karadjordje*. Čiča Ilija Stanojević, the leading actor, was credited as a director. Several film companies were established in the 1920s and 1930s whose main field of interest was documentary, but we can hardly speak of regular film production before 1945. Al Popović's *S verom u boga/In God We Trust* (1934), a fresco about the sufferings of the Serbian people in World War I, Janko Ravnik's *V kraljestvu zlatoroga/In the Kingdom of the Goldhorn* (1931), a *Heimat*-like glorification of the Slovene Alps, and some 'fantastic' parodies by Croat Oktavijan Miletić (*Faust*, 1931, *Nocturno*, 1938) are the most noteworthy films of the prewar period.

All organised film production ceased with the onset of World War II, with the exception of the company Hrvatski Slikopis ('Croatian Image-writing') in the pro-Nazi independent state of Croatia. At the same time, Tito's partisans began to document their battles on film. In 1943, his military headquarters (then in Bosnia) issued a 'decree for documenting partisan battles' and formed the first official team of film cameramen, but most of their footage was destroyed. On 13 December 1944, Tito signed the first official act of the new state administration, establishing a film section. This act is considered the formal beginning of cinematography in socialist Yugoslavia. The Yugoslav communist authorities took seriously Lenin's* dictum about film as 'the most important art'. Film became elevated to a cultural and national resource and was consequently allocated significant financing. The National Film Company (DFJ) was created in 1945 and the government's Committee for Cinematography formed in 1946. By 1947 the process of nationalisation was complete, and film became a state art. Film companies were then founded in every republic: Triglav Film in Ljubljana, Jadran* Film in Zagreb, Avala Film and Zvezda Film in Belgrade. Belgrade also opened a Kinoteka (film archive) in 1949 and a Film Academy in 1950.

The first postwar Yugoslav feature was Vjekoslav Afrić's *Slavica* (1947). Like most early postwar films, it was a barely disguised eulogy of the Resistance and the triumphalist spirit. National reconstruction became an overriding theme – even obsession – as titles like *Živjeće ovaj narod/This Nation Will Live!* (Nikola Popović, 1947) or *Na svoji zemlji/On Our Own Land* (France Štiglic*, 1948) suggest. However, it is possible that the popular appeal of these films derived less from their historical relevance than from the authenticity of their characters and a certain naivety of narration. It would be unfair to label all films from this period as state propaganda. On the one hand, the centralised administration of film ended in 1951, following the introduction of the concept of 'self-management' into most economic, social and political structures, including film production and distribution. The founding of the famous 'workers' councils' also had its cinematic equivalent in the creation of associations of producers enjoying creative and financial autonomy. On the other hand, some directors were quite successful in carving out their own niches even in the 1950s. At least two figures stand out in this regard: Branko Bauer* and France Štiglic. Both were capable of directing nuanced emotional scenes, usually with a strong children's presence, as in Bauer's *Ne okreći se, sine/Don't Turn Back, Son* (1956) and Štiglic's *Dolina miru/The Valley of Peace* (1956). Their careers flourished, and were crowned by the 1956 Cannes festival Best Actor award for John Kitzmiller in *Dolina miru* and a 1960 Oscar nomination for Bauer's *Deveti krug/The Ninth Circle*.

The first (and only) Oscar for Yugoslav film came much later from a completely different genre: animation. The Zagreb School of Animation* was founded in the 1950s by Dušan Vukotić, who later won an Oscar for *Surogat/The Substitute* in 1962. Although there was never really a scholarly institution, this movement of animators (including Nedeljko Dragić, Borivoj Dovniković, Joško Marušić and many others) set new standards, both in animation experiment and socially critical content, proving that Disney-like cartoons were not exhaustive of the genre's possibilities.

In the late 1950s and early 1960s, Yugoslavia was producing around fifteen films per year and the first signs of different themes began to appear. The films of Bauer and Štiglic revealed a significant shift towards the problems of modern life. Adaptations of famous literary titles were also adopted as a way to circumvent the proclaimed values of Socialist Realism*. Forms of 'poetic licence' allowed some film-makers to develop more complex stories with less transparent messages (Štiglic's existentialist drama *Balada o trobenti in oblaku/Ballad of a Trumpet and a Cloud* from 1961 is one example). Serbian director Puriša Djordjević also introduced his lyrical and oneiric style into films about the partisan war, with his trilogy *Devojka/Girl* (1965), *San/Dream* (1966) and *Jutro/Morning* (1967). Slowly, films became more critical, while subjects were chosen from hitherto untouched territory, such as the failures of the social welfare system or corruption within the communist leadership (Bauer's *Samo ljudi/Traces*, 1957, and *Licem u lice/Face to Face*, 1963).

This trend led directly to a strong movement of socially conscious directors, who formed a kind of Yugoslav new wave known as the 'Black Wave'*, which flourished in the late 1960s. Živojin Pavlović* was the leading figure of this movement (*Budjenje pacova/Awakening of the Rats, Kad budem mrtav i beo/When I am Dead and White*, both 1967), which also included Dušan Makavejev*, Aleksandar Petrović*, Želimir Žilnik and others. The movement was closely linked to the liberalisation of the country in the 1960s; one can detect evidence of a less rigid Marxist ideology in Žilnik's *Rani radovi/Early Works* and of a more permissive regime in Makavejev's *Misterije organizma/W. R. – Mysteries of the Organism*. At the same time, the 'freedom' of the movement was limited. Most of the works were censored in one way or another; they were either officially banned or their distribution was impeded, while some of the film-makers were forced to work abroad. The 1960s were also the years of powerful individual cinematic stylistics. Slovene directors Boštjan Hladnik and Matjaž Klopčič* were strongly influenced by the French New Wave*, and Croat Zvonimir Berković 'composed' his first film, *Rondo*, in 1966. These films were not as strongly attached to themes of everyday life as the 'Black Wave' films, but they shared a common atmosphere of despair.

The 1970s in Yugoslavia were marked by both an expansion of social welfare (financed by foreign loans) and increased repression, as the regime became dominated by hard-line communists. One of the ways to escape the tensions created by these contradictory forces was to produce popular mainstream films. Two main popular genres emerged. The first is the so-called 'newly composed Serbian comedy', named by analogy with a popular Serbian musical genre called 'newly composed music', an amalgam of folk songs and pop. This genre is based on simple situations and character comedy, and includes work by directors such as Zoran Čalić, Milan Jelić and Miča Milošević. The second genre is that of the 'partisan films'*, Western-like movies using World War II battles as a pretext for action (Hajrudin Krvavac, Aleksandar Djordjević). Such was the popularity of these genres that more than thirty films were produced annually during this period. The 'newly composed Serbian comedy' succeeded in combining a traditional comedy of errors with the 'new primitivism' of vulgar jokes and ambiguous sexual messages, based on clichés of betrayed husbands, lusty girls-next-door and voyeuristic grandfathers. The comedies of the 1950s – those of František Čap*, for example – used teenagers to address adults, and therefore possessed a certain innocence. The 1970s took away all the charm and turned the genre into adult cinema for teenagers, on the edge of soft-core pornography.

A breakthrough in Yugoslav cinema came at the end of the 1970s, when the first generation of Yugoslav students returned from Prague's film school FAMU*; they were henceforth referred to as the 'Prague School'. Most famous among them is Emir Kusturica*, whose films have won accolades at almost every international festival in the last decade: *Sjećaš li se Dolly Bell?/Do You Remember Dolly Bell?* (Venice 1981), *Otac na službenom putu/When Father Was Away on Business* (Cannes 1985), *Dom za vešanje/Time of the Gypsies* (Cannes 1989), *Arizona Dream* (Berlin 1993). Other 'Prague School' directors made their mark: Goran Paskaljević combined popular comedy with a human touch (*Čuvar plaže u zimskom periodu/The Beach Guard in Winter*, 1976; *Pas, koji je voleo vozove/The Dog That Loved Trains*, 1977); Goran Marković has moved with great elegance over the whole generic range (from social melodrama in *Specijalno vaspitanje/Special Education*, 1977, to the disaster movie *Variola Vera*, 1982, and the psycho-thriller *Déjà vu*, 1987); Srdjan Karanović chose a more melancholic point of view, whether depicting the elderly (*Zemaljski dani teku/The Fleeing of Earthly Days*, 1979) or the difficulties of rural life (*Petrijin venac/Petrija's Wreath*, 1980); Rajko Grlić revisited the territory of World War II partisans in a brilliant melodrama, *Samo jednom se ljubi/You Only Love Once/The Melody Haunts My Reverie*, 1981; Lordan Zafranović also returned to this topic in order to examine different wartime positions, from partisans and Uštaše traitors to the broken aristocracy of Dubrovnik (*Okupacija u 26 slika/Occupation in 26 Images*, 1979). Beyond their differences, the 'Prague school' generation can be seen to share a belief in simple, everyday stories (as opposed to epics and historical dramas), pinpointing the same problems as the 'Black Wave' films of the 1970s but with more humour and a gentler sarcasm.

Another generation of independent film-makers with recognisable individual styles and a respect for the classical film tradition emerged in the 1980s: the Slovene Karpo Godina*, the Croat Zoran Tadič*, the Serbs Miloš Radivojević and Slodoban Šijan* and the Macedonian Stole Popov. These film-makers have been supported by a young generation of film critics gathered around magazines such as *Ekran** in Ljubljana, *Filmska kultura* in Zagreb, *Sineast* in Sarajevo and *Filmograf* in Belgrade.

Although the directors of the 1980s have not been as commercially successful at home as some of their 'partisan' predecessors, they can be credited with making Yugoslav cinema known throughout the world. Kusturica, Godina, Šijan, Marković and Paskaljević have been regular guests at international festivals. A huge retrospective of Yugoslav cinema at the Pompidou Centre in Paris in 1985 represented a culmination of their achievement. From today's point of view, this retrospective can be seen as a requiem for Yugoslav film. The economic difficulties of the 1980s drastically reduced the number of films produced, and the increasingly intractable political problems began to be reflected in the politics of national cinema too. Acrimonious debates at the national film festival in Pula* were perhaps symptomatic of the imminent collapse of the country as a whole.

The 1990s have seen not only the breakdown of Yugoslavia as a political unit, but also a radical change in the economic system of each of the new states. Conditions for film financing have drastically changed: once fully subsidised by the ministries of culture, film production is now subject to the laws of the market. The number of films produced per year has dangerously fallen – and each new film is greeted almost as a miracle. SP

YUTKEVICH, Sergei I.

St Petersburg 1904 – Moscow 1985

Soviet director and writer, who graduated from Meyerhold's theatre workshop and, with Sergei Eisenstein*, produced a number of stage shows for Foregger's studio, before joining the 'Blue Blouse' travelling theatre troupe. He was co-founder, with Leonid Trauberg* and Grigori Kozintsev*, of FEKS in 1922. His first involvement in cinema was with the Eccentric comedy *Daësh' radio!/Give Us Radio!* (1924). His first features attempted to combine FEKS circus techniques with a degree of social comment, as in *Kruzheva/Lace* (1928) and *Chërnyi parus/The Black Sail* (1929), while *Zlatye gory/The Golden Hills* (1931) developed individual characters and marked a transition culminating in Yutkevich's first sound film, *Vstrechnyi/Counterplan* (1932), made with Fridrikh Ermler*. He went on to direct a number of historical biographical films, such as *Yakov Sverdlov* (1940), *Przewalski* (1952) and *Skanderbeg* (1954), but he is probably most remembered for a series of films about Lenin, from *Chelovek s ruzh'ëm/The Man with a Gun* (1938) – starring Maxim Strauch* and Mikhail Gelovani* as Lenin and Stalin respectively – through *Rasskazy o Lenine/Tales of Lenin* (1958) and *Lenin v Pol'she/Lenin in Poland* (1966), to *Lenin v Parizhe/Lenin in Paris* (1981). At the same time Yutkevich continued to stage plays, including the works of Mayakovsky and Blok. In 1962 he directed an animated film version of Mayakovsky's *Banya/The Bathhouse*. He chaired the commission that oversaw the publication of Eisenstein's writings, wrote a number of articles and books on cinema, including the main Soviet cinema encyclopedias, and taught at VGIK* from 1929. RT

Z

ZAGREB SCHOOL OF ANIMATION

Yugoslav animation movement attached to the 'Studio for animation' of the Croatian film production company Zagreb Film. The name was suggested in the late 1950s by French critics Georges Sadoul* and André Martin to describe a coherent movement that began to attract festival audiences around the world. Although they did not constitute an institution as such, the animators shared a certain philosophy: experiment and abstract animation were combined with themes of alienation and dehumanisation. The films of Nedeljko Dragić – such as *Idu dani/The Days Are Passing* (1969), *Tuptup* (1972) and *Dnevnik/Diary* (1974) – show most clearly the harmony between the simplicity of the drawings and the complexity of the message. Another film-maker of great expressive power is Vladimir Kristl (*Don Kihot/Don Quixote*, 1961), who left Croatia in 1962 to work in Germany (*Prometheus*, 1966). The achievements of the Zagreb school were reflected in an Oscar for Dušan Vukotić's *Surogat/The Substitute* in 1962 and the organisation of the first World Festival of Animation in Zagreb in 1970 (one of four major international animation festivals). Among other animators of the school are Vatroslav Mimica, Borivoj Dovniković, Nedeljko Dragić, Pavao Štalter, Zdenko Gašparović and Joško Marušić. SP

Bib: Ron Holloway, *Z is for Zagreb* (1972).

ZAHARIEV, Eduard

Moscow, Russia 1938

Bulgarian director. Better known for his satirical comedies, although equally respected as a director of perceptive documentaries. Upon graduating in 1961 from the Budapest Academy of Theatre and Film Art, Zahariev returned to Bulgaria to work in the Documentary Newsreel Film Studio in Sofia. His style of dramatising labour and industry themes won him immediate recognition in the documentary field for *Relsi v nebeto/Rails in the Sky* (1962), *Skok/Leap* (1965), *Sol/Salt* (1965), *Stomana/Steel* (1971), and *BDŽ/Bulgarian State Railways* (1972). But when two of his provocative fiction-documentaries – *Ako ne ide vlak/If the Train Doesn't Arrive* (1967), made in collaboration with satirist scriptwriter Georgi Mišev*, and *Nebeto na Veleka/The Sky over the Veleka* (1968) – irritated the authorities at the Documentary Studio (*Nebeto na Veleka* was banned shortly after release), he transferred his allegiance to the feature film department at the Boyana* Studios. Collaborating again with Mišev, he made two of the most successful comedies in Bulgarian film history: *Prebrojavane na divite zajci/The Hare Census* (1973) and *Vilna zona/Villa Zone* (1974), both starring popular deadpan comic actor Icak Finci as a socialist petit bourgeois and both the recipients of major festival awards at, respectively, Locarno and Karlovy Vary*. Zahariev's *Măžki vremena/Manly Times* (1977), a stolen-bride mountain tale made in collaboration with writer Nikolai Haitov*, established him as one of Bulgaria's most popular film directors. His subsequent films, however, were not as successful, in large part because of the restoration of government restrictions on thematic content towards the end of the 1970s. RH

ZAMPA, Luigi

Rome 1905–91

Italian director. A typically exuberant and cultured Roman, Zampa emerged as a scriptwriter and director from the Fascist cinema of the 'white telephones'. Also a writer of comic plays and novels, he left his mark above all in the field of film comedy. He achieved success with *Vivere in pace/To Live in Peace* (1946), a rural variation on the Allied Occupation theme, mixing pathos and farce. Highly regarded abroad as a masterpiece of neo-realism*, the film was voted Best Foreign Feature of 1947 by New York film critics. Zampa continued in a similar vein in *L'onorevole Angelina/Angelina* (1947), with Anna Magnani* as a popular village leader. He shifted focus somewhat with a trilogy of satirical films written by the Sicilian novelist Vitaliano Brancati: *Anni difficili/Difficult Years* (1948), *Anni facili/Easy Years* (1953) and *L'arte di arrangiarsi* (1954). The last of these, the portrait of a man whose opinions change to fit different regimes, remains one the best performances of Alberto Sordi*, with whom Zampa made a dozen or so films. These include very successful films like *Il vigile/The Cop* (1960) and *Il medico della mutua* (1968), whose indictment of the Italian health system is continued in a more melodramatic mode in *Bisturi, la mafia bianca* (1973). This vein of denunciatory films, in a direct and pithy style, sometimes tending towards demagogy, includes *Il magistrato/The Magistrate* (1959), *Una questione d'onore/A Question of Honour* (1965), *Gente di rispetto* (1975) and *Il mostro* (1977). In the course of his career Zampa made some three dozen films of uneven quality, but none of them entirely without merit. His best is probably *Processo alla città/The City Stands Trial* (1952), in which the inquiry by the judge played by Amedeo Nazzari* reveals a tough network of power and racketeering in Naples at the turn of the century. MMo

Other Films Include: *L'attore scomparso, Fra Diavolo* (1941); *Signorinette, C'è sempre un ma ...* (1942); *L'abito nero da sposa* (1943); *Un americano in vacanza/A Yank in Rome* (1945); *Campane a martello/Children of Change* (1949); *È più facile che un cammello ..., Guerra o pace/Cuori senza frontiere* (1950); *Signori, in carrozza!* (1951); *Siamo donne/We the Women* (1953, fourth episode); *Questa è la vita* [ep. *La patente*], *La romana* (1954); *Ragazze d'oggi* (1955); *Tempo di villeggiatura* (1956); *La ragazza del palio/The Love Specialist* (1957); *Ladro lui, ladra lei* (1958); *Anni ruggenti/Roaring Years* (1962); *Frenesia dell'estate* (1963); *I nostri mariti* (1966, ep. *Il marito di Olga*); *Le dolci signore* (1967); *Contestazione generale* (1970); *Bello, onesto, emigrato Australia sposerebbe compaesana illibata* (1971); *Letti selvaggi* (1979).

ŽANDOV, Zahari   Ruse 1911

Bulgarian director. The father of the postwar Bulgarian documentary and the director of the breakthrough feature film in Bulgarian cinema. Although over fifty feature films had already been made in Bulgaria before the then documentary film-maker Žandov was assigned to direct *Trevoga/Alarm* (1951), this adaptation of a play by Socialist Realist* dramatist Orlin Vasiliev is generally recognised as the birth of a new national cinematography. One of the older generation of Bulgarian film-makers who learnt their trade before World War II, Žandov first made his mark abroad at international film festivals with humanistic documentaries and short films, for instance *Edin den v Sofia/A Day in Sofia* (1946) and *Hora sred oblacite/Men amid the Clouds* (1947), the latter about weather stations and winner of the First Prize at the Venice festival. Žandov also collaborated with documentarist Joris Ivens* as his cameraman on the Bulgarian episode of

Pierwsze Lata/The First Years (1949), a co-production with several Eastern European countries including the USSR.

Although restricted in its artistic expression by the schematic formula of the personality cult, *Trevoga* possessed a documentary freshness in its portrayal of the anti-fascist struggle in 1944. Žandov had the good fortune to collaborate with talented screenwriter Angel Wagenstein* on both *Trevoga* and *Septemvrici/Septembrists* (1954), but he was not as fortunate thereafter – until he made *Bojanskijat majstor/Master of Boyana* (1981), the first of a series of historical epics celebrating the 1,300th anniversary of the founding of the Bulgarian state. The film drew its visual strength from the renowned frescoes painted by an unknown artist in the Boyana church near Sofia in 1259. RH

ZANUSSI, Krzysztof   Warsaw 1939

Polish director and producer. Zanussi studied physics and philosophy and was active in the amateur film movement before graduating from Łódź* in 1966. His feature debut, *Struktura Kryształu/The Structure of Crystals* (1969), looked at the problems and complexes facing the Polish intelligentsia, and their social marginalisation. It also prefigured themes that would soon typify the 'cinema of moral unrest': decline in moral and cultural values, breakdown of relationships, and the compromises of everyday life. Both *Struktura Kryształu* and *Iluminacja/Illumination* (1973) were important landmarks in Polish cultural life of the period. In offering a bleak and depressing picture of the individual's prospects in 1970s Poland, Zanussi was speaking to a generation who felt constrained and cut off from the rest of the world. His filmic exploration of philosophical and moral questions proved popular in European and American art-house circles and he established co-production links with Germany, France, America and Britain. This allowed him to continue working throughout the difficult climate of the 1980s, although he remained based in Poland. Using international casts and locations, in films like *Rok Spokojnego Słonca/The Year of the Quiet Sun* (1985), Zanussi looked at the difficult choices faced by individuals in times of war and social crisis.

A strong participant in the restructuring of the cinema industry since 1989, Zanussi heads the successful Tor film unit, acting as producer as well as director. His 1990 feature, *Dotknięcie/The Silent Touch*, stars Max von Sydow* as a classical composer and alcoholic Holocaust victim who is coaxed back to creativity by a mysterious young man. AW

Other Films Include: *Barwy Ochronne/Camouflage* (1977); *Constans/The Constant Factor* (1980); *Der Unerreichbare/The Inaccessible* (1982, Ger.); *Stan Posiadania/The State of Possession* (1989).

ZAORSKI, Janusz   Warsaw 1947

Polish director. Zaorski graduated from Łódź* in 1969 and worked in television. He made his first feature, *Uciec Jak Najbliżej/Run Away Nearby* (1972), at the age of twenty-five. The same year, he submitted a script to the Central Office of Cinematography for *Matka Królów/Mother of Kings* but had to wait until 1980, and the help of Andrzej Wajda's* 'X' unit, to film it. *Matka Królów*, released in 1982, is the epic tale of the life of a Polish woman and her four sons between 1933 and 1956. It is based on a book by Kazimierz Brandys, who was unpopular with the authorities, and perhaps for this reason, as well as the frank portrayal of life under communism, the film was shelved. Zaorski continued to work, however, and in 1986 initiated a ninth Polish film unit, Dom, headed by himself. Dom has made a reasonable transition to privatisation, producing documentaries and features for cinema and the expanding television market. AW

Other Films Include: *Awans/Advance* (1975); *Pokój z Widokiem na Morze/Room with a Sea View* (1978); *Baryton/Baritone* (1985); *Jezioro Bodeńskie/Boden Lake* (1986); *Piłkarski Poker/Football Poker* (1988).

ZAVATTINI, Cesare   Luzzara 1902 – Rome 1989

Italian scriptwriter and novelist. One of the most prolific scriptwriters of Italian cinema (with over a hundred scripts), Zavattini is particularly well-known as the theoretician of neo-realism*, an advocate of a realist, anti-illusionist cinema steeped in the quotidian, best exemplified by *Umberto D.* (1952), directed by Vittorio De Sica*.

A law graduate, Zavattini went straight into journalism, working first for a minor provincial paper and then for some of the most important magazines of the period. He moved to Milan, where he worked for the publishers Rizzoli, Mondadori and Bompiani and published his first two great novels, the extraordinary *Parliamo tanto di me* (1931) and *I poveri sono matti* (1937). He collaborated with the humorist Giaci Mondaini on a script called *Buoni per un giorno*, which was directed by Mario Camerini* in 1935 under the title *Darò un milione*. The film was so successful that it was remade in Hollywood as *I'll Give a Million* (1938). As a result of this activity Zavattini moved to Rome, where he made an essential contribution to Alessandro Blasetti's* important film *Quattro passi fra le nuvole/Four Steps in the Clouds* (1942). His fruitful collaboration with Vittorio De Sica* led to a first film of considerable interest, *I bambini ci guardano* (1943), after which Zavattini spent the postwar years working on what are now considered to be the milestones of neo-realism*: *Sciuscià/Shoeshine* (1946), *Ladri di biciclette/Bicycle Thieves* (1948), *Miracolo a Milano/Miracle in Milan* (1951) and *Umberto D.* Of great significance also are his contributions to Luchino Visconti's* *Bellissima* (1951), Blasetti's *Prima comunione/Father's Dilemma* (1950), Giuseppe De Santis'* *Roma ore 11* (1952), and the works of an impressive number of other directors (of both art and popular films), from Alberto Lattuada* to Domenico Paolella, Renato Castellani* and Mario Mattoli*. The 1950s saw a puzzling decline in his scriptwriting activities as he became involved in increasingly routine projects. Nonetheless, in other respects he continued to row against the tide, as was his custom, with a series of ingeniously utopian – and partially abortive – projects: popular episode films – *L'amore in città* (1953), *Siamo donne/We the Women* (1953), *Le italiane e l'amore* (1961) and *I misteri di Roma* (1963) – the committed 'Newsreels for peace' and 'Freedom Newsreels', protests at the Venice* film festival in

1968, cultural animation, impromptu live broadcasts in the 1980s. In 1982, at over eighty years of age, he directed his first and only film, *La veritàaaa*, a distinguished though outlandish digest of his deeply felt pacifism.

To mention only Zavattini's (albeit crucial) scriptwriting and theoretical contributions to neo-realism, as is often the case, would be to paint an incomplete picture. He was also one of the best Italian novelists of the twentieth century, a very fine poet, a humorist, the author of comic-strip texts, a painter of recognised talent, a publishing and general media mandarin. He inhabited half a century of Italian culture and marked it profoundly. PV

Other Films as Scriptwriter Include: *I nostri sogni* (1943); *La porta del cielo* (1944); *Caccia tragica/Tragic Hunt* (1946); *Una domenica d'agosto/Sunday in August* (1950); *È primavera/It's Forever Springtime* (1949); *Il cappotto/The Overcoat* (1952); *Un marito per Anna Zaccheo* (1953); *L'oro di Napoli/The Gold of Naples* (1954); *Il segno di Venere* (1955); *Il tetto* (1956); *La ciociara/Two Women* (1960); *Cuba baila* (1961, Cuba); *Historias de la revolucion* (1961, Cuba); *Il giudizio universale/The Last Judgment* (1961); *Boccaccio '70* (1962); *Un mondo nuovo/A Young World* (1966); *Una breve vacanza/A Brief Vacation* (1977).

ŽELJAZKOVA, Binka   Slivengrad 1923

Bulgarian director. A prominent member of the Bulgarian 'new wave' of the late 1950s and early 1960s. After graduating in 1953 from the Sofia Academy of Dramatic Art (VITIS), Binka Željazkova worked as assistant director on Anton Marinovič's *Rebro Adamovo/Adam's Rib* (1956). With the coming of the 'thaw', she co-directed, with her scriptwriter husband Hristo Ganev, *Partizani (Životăt si teče tiho)/ Partisans (Life Flows Quietly By)* (1958, banned for thirty years, released 1988). The pair then 'redeemed' themselves with the authorities with the poetic *A byahme mladi/We Were Young* (1961), directed by Željazkova from a script by Ganev and based on autobiographical experiences in the resistance movement. Her next film, *Privărzanijat balon/The Attached Balloon* (1967), shelved shortly after release and also banned until 1988, was the last high-water mark in Bulgarian cinema before Socialist Realism* was restored at the Boyana* Studios. A political fairy tale adapted for the screen by writer Jordan Radičkov* from his own story, it deals with a group of villagers who dream of climbing into a giant balloon and thus, in an allegorical sense, escaping from the bonds of Stalinist ideology. Although her subsequent films were all politically oriented, none was to attain the same political immediacy and stylistic standards set by *Privărzanijat balon*. Nevertheless, her commitment to film at personal risk to her career won her praise and respect as one of the most important film-makers in Eastern Europe. RH

ZEMAN, Karel   Ostroměř [then Austria-Hungary] 1910 – Prague 1989

Czech director of animated films. In the 1930s, Zeman worked as a poster designer and artist with various advertising agencies in Paris. In 1943 he joined the Baťa Film Studios and, after becoming assistant to Hermína Týrlová, began directing in 1946. He is noted for making perhaps the largest number of feature-length animated films anywhere, including *Cesta do pravěku/A Journey to Primeval Times* (1955), *Vynález zkázy/An Invention for Destruction* (1958), *Baron Prášil/Baron Münchhausen* (1961), and *Bláznova kronika/A Jester's Tale* (1964). With its blend of graphic illustration, special effects and live action, his work recalls the conjuror's world of Georges Méliès*. In *Vynález zkázy*, adapted from Jules Verne, and *Baron Prášil*, from Bürger, he based his graphic design on illustrations from the original novels. PH

Other Films Include: *Ukradená vzducholoď/The Stolen Airship* (1966); *Na kometě/On a Comet* (1970); *Pohádky tisíce a jedné noci/Tales of a Thousand and One Nights* (1974); *Čarodějův učeň/The Magician's Apprentice* (1977); *Pohádka o Honzíkovi a Mařence/The Tale of Honzík and Mařenka* (1980).

ZETTERLING, Mai
Västerås 1925 – London 1994

Swedish actress and director, who made much of her career in the UK. Mai Zetterling secured her first part at the age of sixteen and won international attention for her role (which she always considered her best) as the prostitute in *Hets/Frenzy/ Torment* (1944), directed by Alf Sjöberg*. In the late 1940s the film company Rank brought her to the UK, where she did most of her work as an actress in film, television and theatre for the next decade (an exception was her casting in Ingmar Bergman's* *Musik i mörker/Night is My Future*, 1948). Disillusioned with acting, in the 1960s Zetterling made documentaries for the BBC and an allegorical short called *The War Game* (1962), which won a prize at Venice. Her first feature as director was *Älskande par/Loving Couples* (1964), based on the work of Swedish author Agnes von Krusenstjerna. Two years later she filmed her own novel *Nattlek/Night Games*, with some success and much controversy – the film was banned in Venice for some of its more extreme scenes, just as *Älskande par* had created a stir at Cannes. In 1986 she returned to von Krusenstjerna and made a film about the author's 'scandalous' life and destructive artistic drive, *Amorosa* (1986), again a controversial work. Her last (British) film, *Scrubbers* (1982), was a disturbing (though to some overly melodramatic) look at the grim life of young women in a borstal. Zetterling the actress, with her blonde hair and clear blue eyes, had a graceful femininity, both frail and lively. As a director, she was sharp, tough and socially uncompromising, creating psychologically complex characters often from an overtly feminist point of view. BF

Other Films Include: *Flickorna/The Girls* (1968); *Doktor Glas/Doctor Glas* (1968, Den.).

ZIDI, Claude
Paris 1934

French director. A former assistant and cameraman, Zidi made his first films in what critics consider the *bas de gamme* (bottom drawer) of French comedy: the *comique troupier**, a genre which he updated with a then popular group of comic singers, Les Charlots – *Les Bidasses en folie* (1971), *Les Bidasses s'en vont en guerre* (1974) – and two Louis de Funès* vehicles, *L'Aile ou la cuisse* (1976) and *La Zizanie* (1978). He moved on to take in the *café-théâtre* generation [> COMEDY (FRANCE)] with *Inspecteur la bavure/Inspector Blunder* (1980, starring Coluche and Gérard Depardieu*), *Les Sous-doués/ The Dimwits* (1979) and *Les Sous-doués en vacances/The Dimwits on Holiday* (1982). In 1984, *Les Ripoux/Le Cop* – starring Thierry Lhermitte and Philippe Noiret* – was a major hit, abroad as well as domestically, attracting a more favourable critical reception. The film scathingly sends up corruption in the police, always a favourite subject in France; its slang title ('ripoux' is the reverse of 'pourri', rotten) is now part of the French language. There was a sequel, *Les Ripoux II/Le Cop II*, in 1989. Zidi's talent for inventive comic narratives received a dubious tribute when *La Totale* (1991, with Lhermitte and Miou-Miou*) was remade as *True Lies* (1994, US) with Arnold Schwarzenegger and rather more special effects. GV

ZIEGLER, Regina
Quedlinburg 1944

German producer, who, together with Clara Burckner's Basis Verlag, reflects the presence of women in all aspects of the New German Cinema*. Ziegler produced her first film in 1973 (*Ich dachte, ich wäre tot*), the debut film of director Wolf Gremm, with whom she has worked regularly since. Within a few years she became one of the most active producers, working with Ulrich Schamoni (*Chapeau Claque* 1974), Marianne Lüdcke and Ingo Kratisch (*Familienglück*, 1975), Helma Sanders-Brahms* (*Heinrich*, 1977) and Peter Stein (*Klassen-Feind*, 1983). Her biggest commercial success was an adaptation of the novel by Erich Kästner, *Fabian* (1980). Also involved in international productions and co-productions, she has completed projects in Poland (Andrzej Wajda*'s *Korczak/Dr Korczak*, 1990), France and Italy. TE/KU

ZURLINI, Valerio
Bologna 1926 – Verona 1982

Italian director. Trained as a lawyer with a deep and abiding interest in art, Zurlini made his feature debut with a screen adaptation of Vasco Pratolini's novel *Le ragazze di San Frediano* (1954). His sense of the fragility of human life and emotion was further explored in *Estate violenta/Violent Summer* (1959), *La ragazza con la valigia/Girl With a Suitcase* (1961) and especially in *Cronaca familliare/Family Diary* (1962), again adapted from Pratolini, and widely considered his masterpiece. His subsequent films were all honourable but on the whole unsuccessful. *Le soldatesse* (1965) examined the guilt of Italians in wartime Greece; *Seduto alla sua destra/Out of Darkness* (1968) combined a meditation on divine grace with a reflection on the assassination of Patrice Lumumba, while a deep philosophical pessimism informs *La prima notte di quiete* (1972). His last production was *Il deserto dei tartari*, an international co-production based on Dino Buzzati's novel, which allowed him the resources to develop his filmmaking in a manner inspired by the classics of science-fiction and by surrealist painting. PV

FILM PRODUCTION FIGURES

Dates

Countries	1945	1946	1947	1948	1949	1950	1951	1952	1953	1954	1955	1956	1957	1958	1959	1960	1961	1962	1963	1964	1965	1966	1967	1968	1969
Albania	-	-	-	-	-	-	-	-	-	-	-	-	-	-	1	1	1	-	-	1	1	-	-	-	1+2
Austria	1	3	13	25	25	15+2	23+5	16+3	18+10	16+6	22+6	28+9	24+2	19+4	17+2	18+2	21+2	16+4	13+2	11+8	11+5	7+11	7+5	2+5	10/0
Belgium	9	3	1	2	1	0	1	1/0	0	0	0/5	8	3	4+1	3+2	2/0	6+0	5+0	0/1	1+1	1/1	1/1	3/1	5/1	13+2
Bulgaria	2	3	4	-	1	1	3	3	1	2	4	6+1	6+4	7+2	12	11	7	9	11	13	11+1	12+2	12+2	13+2	42+8
Czechoslovakia	3	12	22	20	-	20	8	17	18	15	17	21+1	24+3	29	33+2	35+1	44+1	35+4	39	41	42+3	40	49	44+1	20
Denmark	10	13	8	8	8	14	15	16	13	14	13	17	17	14	16	17	24	19	21	17	18	21	20	20	11
Finland	21	12	14	16	16	12	18	26	23	29	29	17	20	18	17	15	20	19	11	9	9	6	3	12	-
France	72	94	72	91	99+8	99+18	94+18	88+21	64+47	52+46	76+34	90+39	81+61	75+51	68+65	79+79	69+98	43+82	36+105	45+103	34+108	45+85	47+73	49+68	70+84
Germany (East)	-	-	-	-	-	10	-	-	-	-	13	18	21	25	28	29	27	27	20	15	15	-	-	-	-
Germany (West)	-	1	9	23	61+1	73+9	57+3	78+4	89+15	94+15	120+8	115+8	96+11	98+17	85+21	85+10	69+11	43+18	44+22	35+42	25+47	27+33	56+40	61+46	82+39
Greece	5	4	5	8	13	13	15	22	21	14	24	30	31	51	52	58	68	82	92	93	101	117	99	108	98
Hungary	3	-	-	6+0	-	4	8	5	8	7	11+0	9	16	13	18	15	19	16	18+1	19+1	23	21	21+1	36+1	22+1
Iceland	0	-	-	-	-	-	-	-	-	-	-	-	-	-	-	-	-	-	-	-	-	-	-	-	-
Ireland	-	-	-	-	-	0	0	2	-	-	1	-	4	3	3	2	2	3	1	3	1	3	1	1	0
Italy	-	62	60	54	76	92+0	104+0	119+13	125+21	144+46	74+52	68+23	66+71	76+65	83+81	94+66	117+88	139+106	135+95	135+155	94+109	89+143	130+117	130+116	146+103
Luxemburg	-	-	-	-	-	-	0	-	-	0	-	0	0	0	0	0	0	0	0	0	0	0	0	0	0
Netherlands	2	0	1	2	2	1	0	1	1	-	3	2	2	4	2	5	1	6	5	3	1	5	-	-	-
Norway	4	6	2	5	5	4	11	10	7	10	11	9	10	12	8	8	8	6	6	7	9	6+1	4	7	5+1
Poland	0	1	2	4	4	4	4	1	9	6	9	13	10	23	15	19+2	24	23	27	23	20+0	25	-	-	-
Portugal	4	9	10	4	7	2	4	8	4	-	0	4	1	4	5	2	2	4+1	7+1	5+3	6	5	5+2	4	4
Romania	1	-	-	-	1	1	2	2	2	3	5	3	4	4	5	8	10	12	14	14	14+1	11+4	16	6+2	12+2
ex-Soviet Union	19	23	23	17	18	13	9	24	45	51	81+3	104	108	121	137	119	133	121	133	-	167	159	175	161+2	194+2
Spain	33	38	49	45	36	47+2	37+5	33+7	37+7	56+13	49+7	53+22	50+22	51+24	50+17	55+18	72+19	64+24	59+55	67+63	53+98	67+97	55+70	49+68	55+70
Sweden	44	42	45	32	38	36	32	33	32	37	37	34	32	29	21	24	18	17	21	19	25	29	23	36	28
Switzerland	1	0	1	1	1	0	1	2	-	-	3	3	4	3	5	4	7	4	2	4	10	5	3	3	5
UK	51	66	73	120	125	99	102	132	142	148	115	130	164	135	140	157	151	171	150	126	97	99	140	107	112
ex-Yugoslavia	0	-	2	4	3	4	6	5	9	4+3	12+2	11+1	14+2	14+2	13+2	15+1	32+0	22+0	14+4	17+1	18+2	17+3	33+3	32+1	27+4

Figures are for feature film production by country. 47+2 indicates films + co-productions. 5/1 indicates division of French language/Dutch and Flemish language films produced. A dash (-) indicates no figure available. Zero (0) indicates no films produced.

FILM PRODUCTION FIGURES

Dates

Countries	1970	1971	1972	1973	1974	1975	1976	1977	1978	1979	1980	1981	1982	1983	1984	1985	1986	1987	1988	1989	1990	1991	1992	1993
Albania	-	3	-	-	6	10	14	4	10	12	5	3	12	7	14	12	-	-	-	11	5	0	1	-
Austria	3+4	2+3	4+5	3+3	4+4	2+4	3+2	4+4	1+2	5+1	5+2	3+2	12+1	8+3	16+1	9+3	11+2	8+2	8+1	10+1	10+5	11	10+0	-
Belgium	3/1	3/4	11/3	9/4	4/2	-	8/0	3/2	3/3	8/2	4+2	1/2	4/1	4/3	3/2	6+1	4+1	7+5	4+11	10+0	9+11	3+3	3+9	4+4
Bulgaria	14+2	17+1	22	19+1	19	22+3	26+2	19+2	30	29	31	42	-	32	-	40	23	35	15	20	19	22	3	5+3
Czechoslovakia	52+2	57+2	45+4	65+3	63+3	54+8	65+3	61+2	48	47	52	48	-	66	-	50	63	55	58	70	62	17	15	20
Denmark	20	28	18	20+0	22+0	16+2	20+0	16+0	17+0	9+0	13+0	12+0	7+0	11+0	10+1	7+2	10+0	9+2	14+2	16+2	12+1	9+2	10+5	11+3
Finland	9	8	8	7	2	2	9	7	10	9	7+3	12	17	16	17	13	23+1	12	10	7+3	14	11	20	20
France	66+72	67+60	71+98	97+103	137+97	160+62	170+44	190+32	116+44	126+48	144+45	186+45	134+31	101+30	120+41	106+45	97+37	96+37	93+44	66+70	81+65	73+83	72+83	67+85
Germany (East)	-	-	10+7	14+2	14+1	15+1	17+1	16	10	9	17	12	17	16	-	16	16	5	10	-	-	-	-	-
Germany (West)	86+27	68+31	57+28	80+18	58+22	47+26	42+18	38+14	50+7	53+12	37+12	60+16	57+13	69+8	62+13	46+18	45+15	47+18	49+8	53+15	38+10	53+19	53+10	50+17
Greece	87	90	64	44	42	38	17	17	15	27	25	46	48	37	40	30	27	26	13	14	10	15+0	6+4	15+3
Hungary	21+2	15+4	21	21	19+1	19	19	24+1	28	21+5	26	25	-	25	11+6	21	27	26	14+6	37	23	15+4	17+5	9+7
Iceland	-	-	-	-	-	0	-	0	1	-	1	3	3	4	5	4	2+0	1+0	2+0	2+0	2+0	4	1+2	0+2
Ireland	5	2	6	4	2	2	0	0	1	1	5	2	1	3	5	2+0	3+1	1+3	2+3	2+1	3	1	3+1	3+3
Italy	132+99	128+88	169+111	171+81	176+55	177+53	203+34	142+23	119+24	122+24	128+32	79+24	99+15	101+9	86+17	81+8	94+15	106+10	103+21	102+15	98+21	111+18	114+13	86+20
Luxembourg	1	1	0	0	0	0	0	0	1	0	0	3	0	0	1	2+0	1	1	1	3	1	1+1	1+2	0+4
Netherlands	4	4+1	6+1	8+3	8	16	8+2	7+2	-	0	7	11	10	10	12	10+1	13+0	15+3	8+2	1	13	14	13+0	16+0
Norway	11	7+1	8	9+2	12	13+1	14	9	7	13	10	10	10	8	6	10	13	7+2	10	11	9	10	8	9
Poland	24+0	27	19	19	27	20+1	-	27	31	32	33+6	17+2	23+3	31+5	35	37	34	35	34	22	27	-	8+13	11+10
Portugal	4	7	6	3	-	6	10	9	21	6	9	6	8	4	8	8	6	9+2	16	4+3	2+7	6+3	2+6	10+6
Romania	9+2	15	19	22	22	24	19+3	23	24	28	32	31	32	32	-	26	30	26	23	23	4+5	15+4	12+6	10+5
ex-Soviet Union	215+3	208+6	230+4	166	162+7	176+8	150+6	146+2	-	-	156	-	-	-	-	158	142	158	153	160	300	400	65	137
Spain	42+63	48+43	52+51	73+45	71+41	89+21	90+18	83+19	77+30	56+33	82+36	92+45	118+28	81+18	63+12	65+12	49+11	62+7	54+9	43+5	37+10	46+18	38+14	41+15
Sweden	23	17	19	15	21	25	18	26	15	20	23+3	22+3	14+4	17+6	16+2	12	17+3	26+1	13+8	15+6	20+5	10+17	9+11	13+14
Switzerland	5	6	6+2	17+3	13+4	28+2	19+1	16+4	-	-	13	11	-	19	20	15	3+19	6+15	6+12	8+8	8+11	5+12	3+6	0+16
UK	122	67	131	98	89	91	92	73	77	77	61	66	46	56	51	53	29+6	42+6	38+2	22+5	39+8	24+22	29+13	31+29
ex-Yugoslavia	23+0	21+3	20+2	20+3	14+1	17+2	14+0	20+0	20+1	27+1	24+2	23+3	32+2	23+2	30+3	30+2	21+4	23+4	28+7	26+7	21+4	-	3	-

Figures are for feature film production by country. 47+2 indicates films + co-productions. 5/1 indicates division of French language/Dutch and Flemish language films produced. Zero (0) indicates no films produced. A dash (-) indicates no figure available.

AUDIENCE FIGURES (Millions)

Countries	1945	1946	1947	1948	1949	1950	1951	1952	1953	1954	1955	1956	1957	1958	1959	1960	1961	1962	1963	1964	1965	1966	1967	1968	1969
Albania	-	-	-	-	-	-	-	-	4.6	-	5.9	-	5.9	6.6	8.0	-	7.6	-	-	-	7.8	-	-	-	8.4
Austria	-	-	-	-	-	92.5	93.9	94.1	107.9	110.0	114.0	116.1	119.9	122.0	114.9	106.5	100.5	90.8	84.9	76.0	72.1	65.8	57.7	50.6	39.5
Belgium	-	-	-	-	-	116.4	114.1	110.4	112.2	111.4	106.0	109.7	106.7	99.9	88.7	80.0	71.7	63.9	52.7	46.6	40.9	39.5	36.7	33.9	31.5
Bulgaria	-	-	-	-	-	-	37.0	39.0	42.0	55.2	60.0	69.0	77.9	89.4	101.2	112.1	118.0	122.8	124.0	125.0	126.4	124.1	119.9	114.0	110.2
Czechoslovakia	-	-	-	-	-	-	128.0	135.0	144.0	152.0	162.6	185.5	186.2	183.3	174.0	176.5	166.0	152.0	140.7	134.2	128.4	127.0	118.8	118.7	120.6
Denmark	47.0	53.8	54.4	-	-	52.2	56.6	57.3	59.0	58.7	55.0	52.1	51.3	50.0	46.7	44.0	42.0	39.3	34.5	33.2	33.9	33.5	29.7	26.8	25.6
Finland	36.3	30.0	29.6	29.1	26.2	25.7	26.8	26.8	29.4	30.3	33.5	31.2	31.3	28.8	25.5	24.6	23.8	17.8	13.2	10.6	14.0	15.1	14.5	10.1	10.5
France	402.0	419.0	424.0	-	-	370.7	372.8	359.6	370.6	382.8	394.9	398.9	411.7	371.0	353.7	354.7	328.4	311.7	292.1	275.8	257.2	234.7	211.4	203.2	182.1
Germany (East)	-	-	-	-	-	184.0	-	-	-	-	310.0	-	-	273.1	258.6	237.9	-	191.2	-	140.6	119.0	-	99.2	100.6	93.3
Germany (West)	-	-	-	-	-	487.4	554.8	614.5	680.2	735.6	766.1	817.5	801.0	749.7	670.8	604.8	516.5	442.9	366.0	320.4	294.0	257.1	215.6	180.4	180.6
Greece	-	-	-	10.0	-	37.5	38.8	41.3	42.6	45.3	49.5	56.9	62.2	66.8	74.8	84.2	86.3	96.1	100.5	109.5	121.1	131.8	137.1	137.4	135.3
Hungary	-	-	-	-	35.6	47.1	63.0	69.0	73.0	98.0	115.8	113.6	133.4	131.0	135.0	140.1	135.4	122.0	115.7	111.1	106.0	104.6	96.8	84.5	82.2
Iceland	-	-	-	-	-	-	-	-	-	-	-	-	-	-	-	-	-	-	-	-	-	2.3	-	-	-
Ireland	-	-	-	-	-	46.1	47.8	49.1	50.7	54.1	50.9	52.1	49.8	45.6	43.8	41.2	38.0	35.0	-	-	30.0	-	-	-	-
Italy	-	411.0	525.0	580.0	600.0	661.5	705.7	748.1	777.9	800.7	819.4	790.2	758.4	730.4	747.9	744.8	741.0	728.6	697.5	683.0	663.1	632.0	568.9	559.9	550.9
Luxemburg	-	-	-	-	-	-	-	-	-	-	4.0	5.0	5.0	5.0	5.0	4.5	5.0	4.0	4.0	3.5	3.0	-	2.1	1.9	1.5
Netherlands	-	-	-	-	-	63.9	63.5	63.1	63.7	65.1	66.0	69.9	65.6	64.2	55.5	55.4	51.0	47.9	43.1	38.7	36.4	34.3	31.6	27.4	24.8
Norway	-	30.1	-	-	-	30.0	32.0	34.0	33.0	34.0	33.0	35.0	35.0	35.0	35.0	35.0	33.9	32.8	26.5	24.5	23.0	21.8	21.0	19.2	19.2
Poland	-	-	-	-	-	-	121.0	136.0	152.0	166.0	208.3	198.0	231.4	205.3	195.5	196.0	186.0	194.0	164.8	177.0	168.0	164.7	163.1	-	141.3
Portugal	-	17.7	20.9	20.7	19.9	20.6	20.9	23.0	22.1	24.1	25.9	27.0	27.9	26.5	26.6	26.6	26.1	25.6	24.8	24.5	25.7	26.1	27.7	26.6	26.4
Romania	-	-	-	-	-	52.4	66.0	67.0	83.0	84.0	85.4	113.0	119.0	113.5	134.1	150.3	164.3	181.0	191.0	181.7	204.7	216.1	209.2	203.7	200.4
ex-Soviet Union	-	-	-	-	-	-	315.0	310.0	314.0	320.0	2506.0	324.0	3063.0	3392.0	3519.9	3610.0	3849.0	3900.0	3900.0	-	4280.0	4200.0	4502.8	4715.0	4655.9
Spain	-	-	-	-	-	-	315.0	310.0	314.0	320.0	310.0	324.0	360.0	362.0	365.0	370.0	370.0	-	320.0	-	435.2	403.1	393.1	376.6	364.6
Sweden	-	-	-	-	-	55.0	60.0	67.0	70.0	65.0	60.0	67.0	65.0	70.0	60.0	55.0	54.0	50.0	39.5	40.0	38.2	37.3	35.4	32.6	30.4
Switzerland	-	-	-	-	-	-	60.0	33.0	-	34.0	34.0	37.0	40.0	42.0	44.0	40.0	40.0	40.0	39.0	37.0	45.0	34.0	32.0	35.0	33.0
UK	1585.0	1635.0	1462.0	1514.0	1430.0	1395.8	1365.0	1312.0	1284.5	1275.8	1181.8	1100.8	915.2	754.7	581.0	515.0	449.1	395.0	357.2	342.8	326.6	288.8	264.8	237.3	214.9
ex-Yugoslavia	-	-	-	-	-	-	64.0	60.0	68.0	85.0	97.0	101.4	108.0	114.3	125.0	130.1	129.0	121.8	117.0	123.0	121.2	114.6	104.9	100.2	90.3

AUDIENCE FIGURES (Millions)

Countries	1970	1971	1972	1973	1974	1975	1976	1977	1978	1979	1980	1981	1982	1983	1984	1985	1986	1987	1988	1989	1990	1991	1992	1993
Albania	-	8.4	-	8.4	-	-	-	-	-	-	-	-	-	-	-	-	-	-	-	3.8	-	-	-	-
Austria	32.9	28.5	26.7	23.9	23.4	20.8	17.5	17.9	17.4	17.5	17.5	18.2	16.6	17.9	16.1	17.0	12.6	11.5	10.0	11.8	10.2	10.5	9.3	12.0
Belgium	30.5	29.8	29.4	26.3	26.5	24.9	23.2	22.3	21.7	19.8	21.6	20.1	20.5	21.3	19.0	17.9	17.7	15.7	15.2	15.0	16.2	16.9	16.6	18.3
Bulgaria	109.6	111.1	112.3	114.0	112.3	114.3	114.7	113.4	111.3	109.4	100.0	91.4	92.5	93.5	-	95.5	93.2	84.2	81.0	79.0	65.0	25.7	30.0	11.0
Czechoslovakia	114.8	110.7	98.4	89.3	87.7	85.9	85.3	86.4	84.7	82.5	82.3	81.0	78.6	-	-	76.7	76.6	73.8	73.8	70.6	65.0	40.6	43.0	31.0
Denmark	24.3	22.1	20.7	18.9	19.2	18.9	18.6	16.7	17.4	17.2	15.9	16.2	14.3	13.7	12.0	11.3	11.3	11.4	10.0	10.3	9.6	9.2	8.6	10.2
Finland	11.7	13.0	10.1	10.9	9.6	9.6	8.9	9.0	9.8	10.1	9.9	9.4	9.1	9.1	7.6	6.7	6.3	6.5	6.7	7.2	6.2	6.0	5.4	5.8
France	184.4	177.0	184.4	176.0	179.4	180.7	177.3	170.3	178.5	178.1	174.8	189.2	201.9	198.8	190.8	172.2	163.4	136.7	124.7	120.9	121.8	117.0	115.9	133.3
Germany (East)	91.4	83.4	81.5	84.5	79.5	76.9	79.7	84.1	-	-	79.5	-	72.4	-	73.4	70.0	70.2	69.2	69.3	64.0	30.0	13.0	11.2	-
Germany (West)	160.1	152.1	149.8	144.3	136.2	128.1	115.1	124.2	135.5	142.0	143.8	141.3	124.5	125.2	112.1	104.2	105.2	108.1	108.9	101.6	102.5	106.9	94.7	57.7
Greece	128.6	118.0	92.6	62.2	57.1	47.9	39.9	39.0	39.2	34.1	43.0	40.5	35.3	35.0	22.0	23.0	22.0	22.5	17.0	17.5	16.5	6.2	6.7	7.0
Hungary	79.6	79.7	74.7	74.4	77.9	74.4	73.6	76.0	71.7	69.0	60.7	67.1	70.0	68.9	71.0	70.2	68.0	55.9	50.7	45.8	36.2	22.3	15.6	15.2
Iceland	1.7	1.8	2.0	2.0	2.3	2.6	2.5	-	-	-	2.6	-	2.2	-	-	1.4	1.2	1.3	-	1.2	1.2	1.2	1.2	1.2
Ireland	20.0	-	-	18.0	18.0	15.0	-	-	-	-	9.5	-	11.4	12.7	14.0	11.6	11.0	5.2	6.0	7.0	7.4	8.1	8.2	9.3
Italy	525.0	535.7	553.7	544.8	544.4	513.7	454.5	373.8	318.6	276.3	241.9	215.2	195.4	162.0	131.6	123.1	124.8	112.5	93.0	95.2	90.5	88.6	83.6	92.2
Luxemburg	1.3	1.1	1.1	1.0	1.0	1.1	0.8	0.7	-	-	0.8	-	0.7	0.7	0.7	0.7	0.7	0.7	0.5	0.5	0.5	0.6	0.6	0.7
Netherlands	24.1	25.7	25.0	26.5	28.1	28.3	26.5	26.2	28.4	25.8	27.9	24.7	20.5	20.2	17.4	15.3	14.9	15.5	14.8	15.6	14.6	14.9	13.7	15.9
Norway	18.6	18.9	18.3	17.5	17.9	18.5	16.8	16.8	16.8	17.8	17.5	16.4	15.1	14.8	12.8	12.9	11.1	12.4	11.5	12.6	11.4	10.8	9.6	10.9
Poland	137.8	130.4	136.2	140.6	142.8	143.4	144.2	131.6	116.0	96.2	96.9	91.1	89.4	99.7	127.6	107.0	100.0	94.0	95.3	86.4	38.0	18.0	12.0	13.7
Portugal	28.0	27.2	28.1	28.9	35.7	41.6	42.8	39.1	34.0	32.6	30.8	28.8	26.0	22.9	21.0	19.0	18.4	16.9	13.0	13.8	11.0	11.8	12.0	12.7
Romania	198.8	189.2	179.7	177.4	182.3	185.7	191.2	183.5	187.9	185.7	193.6	198.3	143.7	209.4	217.0	191.5	204.7	208.3	-	170.0	130.0	76.0	41.0	30.0
ex-Soviet Union	4651.8	4656.3	4569.0	4583.3	4566.9	4497.3	4211.0	4080.0	-	-	4260.0	-	4220.0	-	-	4100.0	-	3775.0	3920.2	3640.0	3500.0	2000.0	1000.0	-
Spain	330.9	295.3	295.2	278.3	262.9	255.8	249.0	211.0	220.0	200.0	176.0	173.7	156.0	141.0	118.6	101.1	87.3	85.7	69.6	78.1	78.5	79.1	83.3	87.7
Sweden	28.2	26.0	26.7	22.9	22.1	23.7	23.7	22.5	23.5	25.1	24.9	23.2	21.3	19.0	17.1	17.9	16.4	17.4	17.5	19.2	15.3	15.1	15.7	16.0
Switzerland	32.0	30.0	28.0	27.0	25.5	23.7	20.4	21.2	20.0	21.3	20.9	20.4	20.1	19.7	17.9	16.4	16.3	16.2	14.9	15.2	14.3	15.4	15.0	15.9
UK	193.0	176.0	156.6	134.2	138.5	116.3	103.9	103.5	126.1	111.9	101.0	83.0	64.0	65.7	58.4	70.2	72.6	74.8	84.0	96.0	98.2	101.6	103.6	114.4
ex-Yugoslavia	86.3	81.5	84.2	86.3	83.3	81.7	79.7	75.8	75.4	-	80.0	76.5	80.0	85.0	87.0	81.0	80.8	78.1	70.8	65.0	58.0	25.7	20.9	-

MAIN SOURCES FOR STATISTICS

Europe: *European Cinema Yearbook. A Statistical Analysis, 1989–1992* (Milan: Cinema D'Europa Media Salles, 1993). *European Market and MediaFact, 1993* (London: Zenith Media Worldwide, 1993). *The Film Industry in Six European Countries: Denmark, Norway, Sweden, Italy, France, UK* (Paris: UNESCO, 1950). Michel Gyory and Gabriele Glas, *Statistics of the Film Industry in Europe* (Brussels: The European Centre for Research and Information on Film and Television [CERICA], 1992). David Hancock, André Lange and Jean Dacie, *The World Film and Television Market, vol. 2* (Montpellier: IDATE Industrial Analyses, 1992). *International statistics relating to education, culture and mass communications* (Paris: UNESCO, 1961). *Screen Digest* (London: 1971). *Statistics on Film and Cinema 1955–1977* [Statistical reports and studies, no. 25] (Paris: UNESCO, Division of statistics on culture and communication, 1981). *World Communications: A 200 country survey of press, radio, television, film* (Epping & Paris: Gower Press & The UNESCO Press, 1975).

Albania: *The Albanian Film* (Tirana: 8 Notori Publishing House, 1978, 1987).

Czechoslovakia: Myrtil, Frída and Kolár, *Československý nemy film, 1898–1930* (Prague: Ceskoslovensky film, 1962). Bartošková, Frída and Kolár, *Československý zvukovy film, 1930–1945* (Prague: Film Institute, 1965). Boček, *Modern Czechoslovak Film, 1945–1965* (Artia, 1965). Škvorecký, *All the Bright Young Men and Women* (Peter Martin, 1971). Frühauf and Svobodová, *Československé filmy, 1972–1976* (Prague: Czechoslovak Film Institute, 1983). Bartošková and Bartošek, *Československé filmy, 1977–1980* (Czechoslovak Film Institute, 1983). Bartošek, *Československé filmy, 1981–1985* (Czechoslovak Film Institute, 1989). Jiří Havelka, *Kronika našeho filmu* (Prague Film Institute, 1967).

Denmark: *Danish Films, 1994–5* (Copenhagen: Danish Film Institute, 1995). Figures supplied by Marguerite Engberg.

Finland: Figures supplied by Jukka Sihvonen.

France: Centre National de la Cinématographie, Paris.

Greece: Y. Soldatos, *Istoria tou ellinikou kinimatografou* (Egokeros, 1988–92). C. Sotiropoulou, *Elliniki kinimatografia* (Themelio, 1989). C. Sotiropoulou, 'I diaspora ston elliniko kinimatografo' (Ph.D thesis, 1994). *Statistical Annuals* (National Greek Statistical Service, ESIE, 1956–1986). *Theamata* (Greece: issues from 1960–1985). Figures supplied by Thodoros Natsinas.

Hungary: Figures supplied by András Bálint Kovács. *Utközben a magyar filmterjesztés rendszere* (Budapest: 1993).

Iceland: *Icelandic Films 1992* (Icelandic Film Fund, Reykjavik, 1992).

Ireland: John Hill, Martin McLoone and Paul Hainsworth (eds.), *Border Crossing: Film in Ireland, Britain and Europe* (Belfast: Institute of Irish Studies, Queen's University of Belfast, the University of Ulster and the BFI, 1994).

Netherlands: Centraal Bureau Statistiek. *Dutch Film, 1991–1994* (The Hague: Government Publishing Office). *Filmkeuring, 1929–1940. Jaarverslagen Nederlandse Bioscoopbond, 1921–1990* (Amsterdam). J. van Taalingen, *NBB 60 jaar* (1978). Figures supplied by Karel Dibbets.

Norway: Figures supplied by Jukka Sihvonen.

Poland: Oscar Sobariski, *Polish Feature Films: A Reference Guide. 1945–1985* (West Cornwall, CT: Locust Hill Press, 1987). State Committee of Polish Cinematography, 1994.

Portugal: Manuel de Azevedo, *Projecção (Cadernos de cinema), 3: Perspectiva do cinema português* (Portugal [Matosinhos]: Clube Portugués de cinematografía, 1951). Augusto M. Seabra, *Cinema novo portoghese e oltre...* (Pesaro: Mostra Internazionale del Nuovo Cinema, 1988). Nelson Traquina, 'Portuguese Cinema: In the doldrums of neglect', *European Journal of Communication* (London: Sage Publications, 1994), vol. 9, no. 3, Sept. 1994.

Romania: Manuela Cernat, *A Concise History of the Romanian Film* (Bucharest: Editura Ştiintifiča şi enciclopedică, 1982). *Ecran National* (Bucharest: National Centre of Cinematography, 1993). *The Romanian Film* (Bucharest: Foreign Press & Publicity Department of Romania Film, 1966–1990).

(Former) Soviet Union: *Sovetskie khudozhestvennye fil'my. Annotirovannyi katalog* [Soviet Feature Films. An annotated catalogue] vol. 3: Supplements, & vol. 4: (1958–1963) (Moscow: Iskusstvo, 1961 & 1968).

Spain: Ministerio de Cultura, Instituto de la Cinematografía y de las Artes Audiovisuales, Spain, 1994.

Sweden: Brian McIlroy, *World Cinema 2: Sweden* (London: Flicks Books, 1986), pp. 166–9.

United Kingdom: *British Film and Television Handbook* (London: BFI, 1991 & 1993). James Curran and Vincent Porter (eds), *British Cinema History* (London: Weidenfeld and Nicolson, 1983). Dennis Gifford, *The British Film Catalogue, 1895–1985: a reference guide*, 2nd edition (Newton Abbot, Devon & London: David and Charles, 1986). Rachael Low, *The History of the British Film* [7 vols.] (London: Allen & Unwin, 1949–1979). *Screen Digest Dossier* 'British Cinema and Film Statistics' (London: October 1990).

(Former) Yugoslavia: *Filmografija jugoslovenskog dokumetraznog filma; vol. 1 (1945–1980), vol. 2 (1981–1985), vol. 3 (1986–1990)* [The filmography of Yugoslav Feature Film] (Belgrade: Institut za film, 1981, 1987, 1991). Figures supplied by Stojan Pelko.

BIBLIOGRAPHY

Europe

Roy Armes, *The Ambiguous Image: Narrative Style in Modern European Cinema* (London: Secker and Warburg, 1976).

Grzegorz Balski, *Directory of Eastern European Film-makers and Films, 1945–1991* (Trowbridge, Wilts: Flicks Books, 1992).

Peter Cowie, *International Film Guide* (now *Variety International Film Guide*) (London: Andre Deutsch, annual from 1964).

Peter Cowie, *Scandinavian Cinema: a survey of film and film-makers in Denmark, Finland, Iceland, Norway and Sweden* (London: Tantivy Press, 1992).

Richard Dyer and Ginette Vincendeau (eds.), *Popular European Cinema* (London and New York: Routledge, 1992).

The European Film in the World Market (Vienna: The Austrian Film Commission, 1988).

Daniel J. Goulding (ed.), *Five Filmmakers: Tarkovsky, Forman, Polanski, Szabó, Makavejev* (Bloomington: Indiana University Press, 1994).

Daniel J. Goulding (ed.), *Post New Wave Cinema in the Soviet Union and Eastern Europe* (Bloomington: Indiana University Press, 1989).

Thomas H. Guback, *The International Film Industry: Western Europe and America since 1945* (Bloomington: Indiana University Press, 1969).

Thomas H. Guback, 'Cultural Identity and Film in the European Economic Community', in *Cinema Journal*, vol. 14, no. 1, 1974.

Nicholas Hewitt (ed.), *The Culture of Reconstruction. European Literature, Thought and Film, 1945–1950* (Basingstoke and London: Macmillan, 1989).

Andrew S. Horton and Joan Magretta (eds.), *Modern European Film-makers and the Art of Adaptation* (New York: Frederick Ungar, 1981).

Mira and Antonín J. Liehm, *The Most Important Art: East European Film After 1945* (Berkeley and London: University of California Press, 1977).

David W. Paul (ed.), *Politics, Art, and Commitment in the East European Cinema* (New York: St. Martin's Press, 1983).

Duncan Petrie (ed.), *Screening Europe: Image and Identity in Contemporary European Cinema* (London: BFI, 1992).

James Quinn, *The Film and Television as an Aspect of European Culture* (Leyden: A. W. Sijthoff, 1968).

Pierre Sorlin, *European Cinemas, European Societies 1939–1990* (London and New York: Routledge, 1991).

Albania

The Albanian Film (Tirana: 8 Nötori Publishing House, 1978, 1987).

Guy Gauthier, 'Le Cinéma Albanais' in *La Revue du cinéma – Image et Son*, November 1977.

Belgium

Annuaire du Film Belge/Jaarboek van de Belgische film (Brussels: Koninklijk Belgisch Filmarchief/Cinémathèque Royale de Belgique, yearly).

Francis Bolen, *Histoire authentique, anecdotique, folklorique et critique du cinéma belge depuis ses plus lointaines origines* (Brussels: Memo & Codec, 1978).

Guy Jungblut, Patrick Leboutte, Dominique Païni (eds.), *Une Encyclopédie des Cinémas de Belgique* (Paris: Musée d'Art Moderne de la Ville de Paris, Editions Yellow Now, 1990).

Jean-Claude Burgelman, Daniël Biltereyst, Caroline Pauwels, *Audiovisuele media in Vlaanderen Analyse en beleid* (Brussels: Vubpress, 1994).

Marc Vanhellemont, 'Le cinéma en Belgique, une histoire morcelée', *Guide Des Medias*, vidéo, film, photo et moyens audiovisuels Suppl. 1 (1989).

Bulgaria

Jean-Pierre Brossard, *Aspects nouveaux du cinéma bulgare* (La Chaux-de-Fonds: Cinédiff, 1986).

Albert Cervoni, *Les écrans de Sofia, Voyage français dans le cinéma bulgare* (Paris: Pierre L'Herminier, 1976).

Ronald Holloway, *The Bulgarian Cinema* (Rutherford-Madison-Teaneck: Fairleigh Dickinson University Press. London and Toronto: Associated University Presses, 1986).

Sergio Micheli, *Il Cinema bulgaro* (Padua: Marsilio Editori, 1971).

Maria Ratschewa and Klaus Eder, *Der bulgarische Film: Geschichte und Gegenwart einer Kinomatografie* (Frankfurt: Kommunales Kino, 1977).

Czechoslovakia

Šárka Bartošková and Luboš Bartošek, *Filmové profily: Československí scenáristé reziséri, kameramani, hudebrú skladatelé a architekti hraných filmů* (Prague: Československý filmový ústav, 1986).

Šárka Bartošková and Luboš Bartošek, *Filmove profily 2: Českovenští filmoví herci* (2 vols.).

Jaroslav Brož and Myrtil Frída, *Historie Československého filmu v obrazech, 1898–1930* (Prague: Orbis, 1959).

Jaroslav Brož and Myrtil Frída, *Historie Československého filmu v obrazech, 1930–1945* (Prague: Orbis, 1966).

Langdon Dewey, *An Outline of Czechoslovakian Cinema* (Informatics, 1971).

Peter Hames, *The Czechoslovak New Wave* (Berkeley, California: University of California Press, 1985).

Antonín J. Liehm, *Closely Watched Films: the Czechoslovak*

experience (White Plains, New York: International Arts & Sciences Press, 1974).

Josef Škvorecký, *All the Bright Young Men and Women: a personal history of the Czech Cinema* (Toronto: Peter Martin Associates with *Take One* magazine, 1971).

Denmark

Niels Jörgen Dinnesen and Edvin Kau, *Filmen i Danmark* (Copenhagen: Akademisk forlag, 1983).

Marguerite Engberg, *Dansk Stumfilm – de store år* (Copenhagen: Rhodos, 1977).

Marguerite Engberg, *Dansk filmhistorie 1896–1985* (Reitzel, 1987).

Marguerite Engberg, *Danish Films Through the Years* (1990, English edition).

Helge Krarup and Carl Nörrested, *Eksperimentalfilm i Danmark* (Akademisk forlag, 1983).

Ron Mottram, *The Danish Cinema before Dreyer* (Metuchen, NJ & London: Scarecrow Press, 1988).

Ebbe Neergaard, *Historien om dansk film* (Copenhagen: Gyldendal, 1960) [English edition, 1963].

Erik Nörgaard, *Levende billeder i Danmark* (Copenhagen: Lademann, 1971).

Gunnar Sandfeld, *Den stumme Scene: Dansk biografteater in-dtil lydfilmens gennembrud* (Copenhagen: Arnold Busck, 1966).

See also: Peter Cowie, *Scandinavian Cinema* (under **'Europe'**)

Finland

Francesco Bono, *Cinema Finlandia* (Rome: A.I.A.C.E., 1989).

Roger Connah, *K/K: A Couple of Finns and Some Donald Ducks. Cinema in Society* (Helsinki: VAPK Publishing, 1991).

Peter Cowie, *Finnish Cinema* (Helsinki: VAPK Publishing, 1990).

Jim Hillier (ed.), *Cinema in Finland. An Introduction* (London: BFI, 1975).

Juha Partanen (ed.), *Finnish Intoxication on the Screen* (Helsinki: State Alcohol Monopoly Social Research Institute of Alcohol Studies, 1993).

Jukka Sihvonen, 'Cinema', in Päivi Molarius (ed.), *From Folklore to Applied Arts. Aspects of Finnish Culture* (Helsinki: University of Helsinki, 1993).

Suomen Kansallisfilmografia/Finnish National Filmography (in Finnish), parts 3–6. (Helsinki: VAPK, 1989, 1991, 1992, 1993).

See also: Peter Cowie, *Scandinavian Cinema* (under **'Europe'**)

France

Richard Abel, *The Ciné Goes to Town. French Cinema 1896–1914* (Berkeley, Los Angeles, London: University of California Press, 1994).

Richard Abel, *French Cinema: The First Wave, 1915–1929* (Princeton: Princeton University Press, 1984).

Roy Armes, *French Cinema* (London: Secker and Warburg, 1985).

Françoise Audé, *Ciné-modèles, Cinéma d'elles: situation des femmes dans le cinéma français 1956–1979* (Lausanne: L'Age d'Homme, 1981).

Mary Lea Bandy (ed.), *Rediscovering French Film* (New York: Museum of Modern Art, 1983).

André Bazin, *Le Cinéma français de la libération à la Nouvelle Vague (1945–1958)* (Paris: Cahiers du Cinéma, Editions de l'Etoile, 1983).

Stéphane Brisset, *Le Cinéma des années 80* (Paris: M.A. Editions, 1990).

Freddy Buache, *Le Cinéma français des années 60* (Paris: Hatier, 1987).

Freddy Buache, *Le Cinéma français des années 70* (Renens: 5 Continents/Hatier, 1990).

Raymond Chirat, *Le Cinéma français des années 30* (Renens: 5 Continents, Hatier, 1983).

Raymond Chirat, *Le Cinéma français des années de guerre* (Renens: 5 Continents, Hatier, 1983).

Raymond Chirat, *La IVe République et ses films* (Paris: Hatier, 1985).

Raymond Chirat and Olivier Barrot, *Les Excentriques du cinéma français (1929–1958)* (Paris: Henri Veyrier, 1983).

Francis Courtade, *Les Malédictions du cinéma français* (Paris: Alain Moreau, 1978).

Colin Crisp, *The Classic French Cinema, 1930–1960* (Bloomington and Indianapolis: Indiana University Press, 1993).

Jacques Deslandes and Jacques Richard, *Histoire comparée du cinéma, I: 1826–1896* (Paris: Casterman, 1966); *Histoire comparée du cinéma, II: 1896–1906* (Paris: Casterman, 1968).

Evelyn Ehrlich, *Cinema of Paradox, French Filmmaking Under the German Occupation* (New York, Columbia University Press, 1985).

Sandy Flitterman-Lewis, *To Desire Differently: Feminism and the French Cinema* (Urbana and Chicago: University of Illinois Press, 1990).

Jill Forbes, *The Cinema in France After the New Wave* (London: BFI/Macmillan, 1992).

Peter Graham (ed.), *The New Wave* (London: Secker and Warburg, 1968).

Susan Hayward, *French National Cinema* (London and New York: Routledge, 1993).

Susan Hayward and Ginette Vincendeau (eds.), *French Film, Texts and Contexts* (London and New York: Routledge, 1990).

Jean-Pierre Jeancolas, *Le Cinéma des Français – La Ve République, 1958–78* (Paris: Stock, 1979).

Jean-Pierre Jeancolas, *15 ans d'années trente, le cinéma des Français 1929–44* (Paris: Stock, 1983).

Jean Mitry, *Histoire du cinéma, art et industrie* [5 vols] (Paris: Editions Universitaires, 1967–80).

René Prédal, *Le Cinéma français depuis 1945* (Paris: Nathan, 1991).

Georges Sadoul, *French Film* (London: Falcon Press, 1953).

Jacques Siclier, *Le Cinéma français 1: de la Bataille du rail à La Chinoise 1945–1968* (Paris: Ramsay, 1990).

Jacques Siclier, *Le Cinéma français 2: de Baisers volés à Cyrano de Bergerac 1968–1990* (Paris: Ramsay, 1991).

Alan Thiher, *The Cinematic Muse: Critical Studies in the History of French Cinema* (Columbia and London: University of Missouri Press, 1979).

Alan Williams, *Republic of Images. A History of French Filmmaking* (Cambridge, Mass. and London: Harvard University Press, 1992).

Germany

Hans-Michael Bock (ed.), *CineGraph: Lexikon zum deutschsprachigen Film* (Munich: Edition Text and Kritik, 1984ff.).

Hans-Michael Bock and Michael Töteberg (eds.), *Das Ufa-Buch* (Frankfurt am Main: Zweitausendeins, 1992).

Paolo Cherchi Usai and Lorenzo Codelli (eds.), *Prima di Caligari: Cinema tedesco, 1895–1920/Before Caligari: German Cinema, 1895–1920* (Pordenone: Edizioni Biblioteca dell'Immagine, 1990).

Lotte H. Eisner, *The Haunted Screen: Expressionism in the German Cinema and the Influence of Max Reinhardt* (London: Thames and Hudson, 1969).

Thomas Elsaesser, *New German Cinema: A History* (London: BFI/Macmillan, 1989).

Wolfgang Jacobsen, Anton Kaes and Hans Helmut Prinzler (eds.), *Geschichte des deutschen Films* (Stuttgart/Weimar: Metzler, 1993).

Uli Jung (ed.), *Der deutsche Film: Aspekte seiner Geschichte von den Anfängen bis zur Gegenwart* (Trier: Wissenschaftlicher Verlag, 1993).

Siegfried Kracauer, *From Caligari to Hitler: A Psychological History of the German Film* (Princeton: Princeton University Press, 1947).

Klaus Kreimeier, *Die Ufa-Story. Geschichte eines Filmkonzerns* (Munich: Hanser, 1992).

Stephen Lowry, *Pathos und Politik: Ideologie in Spielfilmen des Nationalsozialismus* (Tübingen: Niemeyer Verlag, 1991).

Paul Monaco, *Cinema and Society: France and Germany during the twenties* (New York: Elsevier, 1976).

Corinna Muller, *Frühe deutsche Kinematographie: Formale, wirtschaftliche und kulturelle Entwicklungen* (Stuttgart/Weimar: Metzler, 1994).

Bruce Murray and Christopher Wickham (eds.), *Framing the Past: The Historiography of German Cinema and Television* (Carbondale/Edwardsville: Southern Illinois University Press, 1992).

Julian Petley, *Capital and Culture: German Cinema 1933–1945* (London: BFI Publishing, 1979).

Patrice Petro, *Joyless Streets: Women and melodramatic representation in Weimar Germany* (Princeton, NJ: Princeton University Press, 1989).

Hans Günther Pflaum and Hans Helmut Prinzler, *Film in der Bundesrepublik Deutschland* (Munich: Carl Hanser Verlag, 1979. Revised and enlarged edition, 1994).

Thomas G. Plummer, et al. (eds.), *Film and Politics in the Weimar Republic* (Minneapolis, Minn.: University of Minnesota, Dept. of German, 1982).

Eric Rentschler (ed.), *German Film and Literature: adaptations and transformations* (New York and London: Methuen, 1986).

Eric Rentschler, *West German Film in the Course of Time: Reflections on the twenty years since Oberhausen* (Bedford Hills, NY: Redgrave Publishing, 1984).

Ralf Schenk (ed.), *Das Zweite Leben der Filmstadt Babelsberg: DEFA-Spielfilme 1946–1992* (Potsdam: Fimmuseum, 1994).

Heide Schlüpmann, *Unheimlichkeit des Blicks: Das Drama des frühen deutschen Kinos* (Frankfurt am Main: Stroemfeld/Roter Stern, 1990).

Greece

Cine Griego (Madrid: Filmoteca Nacional de España, 1979). Pamphlet.

Incontro con il cinema greco (Venice: La Biennale di Venezia, 1975).

Marinos Koussoumidis, *Istoria tou ellinikou kinimatografou* (Athens: Kastaniotis, 1981).

Aglaia Mitropoulou, *Ellinikos kinimatografos* (Athens: 1980).

Aglae Mitropoulos, *Découverte du cinéma grec* (Cinema Club Seghers, 1968).

1981–1986 New Greek Cinema/Nouveau Cinéma Grec (Athens: Greek Film Centre, 1987).

1987–1990 New Greek Cinema/Nouveau Cinéma Grec (Athens: Greek Film Centre, 1990).

Mel Schuster, *The Contemporary Greek Cinema* (Metuchen, NJ and London: Scarecrow Press, 1979).

Yannis Soldatos, *Istoria tou ellinikou kinimatografou*, 6 vols. (Athens: Nefeli and Egokeros, 1979–90).

25 Years of Greek Movies (Athens: Ministry of Culture, Film Department, 1985).

Hungary

Jean-Pierre Jeancolas, *Le Cinéma hongrois 1963–1988* (Paris: Editions du centre national de la recherche scientifique, 1989).

Károly Nemes, *A magyar filmmüvészet története 1957 és 1967 kózött* (Filmtudományi Intézet, 1978).

István Nemeskürty, *Magyar Film 1939–1944* (Filmtudományi Intézet, 1980).

Graham Petrie, *History Must Answer to Man: the contemporary Hungarian cinema* (Budapest: Corvina Kiado, 1978).

Gábor Szilágyi, *Tűzkeresztség* [The Hungarian Film from 1945 to 1953] (Magyar Filmintézet, 1992).

Iceland

'Iceland', in Peter Cowie (ed.), *International Film Guide* (now *Variety International Film Guide*) (London: Andre Deutsch, annual from 1964).

Icelandic Films, 1980–1983 (Reykjavik: Icelandic Film Fund, 1983).

Icelandic Films, 1979–1988 (Reykjavik: Icelandic Film Fund, 1988).

Icelandic Films, 1992 (Reykjavik: Icelandic Film Fund, 1992).

See also: Peter Cowie, *Scandinavian Cinema* (under '**Europe**')

Ireland

John Hill, Martin McLoone and Paul Hainsworth (eds.), *Border Crossing: Film in Ireland, Britain and Europe* (Belfast: Institute of Irish Studies in association with the University of Ulster and the BFI, 1994).

Brian McIlroy, *World Cinema 4: Ireland* (Trowbridge: Flicks Books, 1989).

Kevin Rockett, John Hill and Luke Gibbons, *Cinema and Ireland* (London: Routledge, 1988).

Italy

Adriano Aprà and Patrizia Pistagnesi (eds.), *The Fabulous Thirties* (Milan: Electa, 1979).

Roy Armes, *Patterns of Realism* (New York: A. S. Barnes, and London: Tantivy Press, 1971).

Aldo Bernardini (ed.), *Archivio del cinema italiano. Vol. 1: Il cinema muto, 1905–1931* (Rome: Edizioni Anica, 1991).

Aldo Bernardini (ed.), *Archivio del cinema italiano. Vol. 2: Il Cinema sonoro, 1930–1969* (Rome: Edizioni Anica, 1992).

Aldo Bernadini and Jean A. Gili (eds.), *Le cinéma italien de La Prise de Rome (1905) à Rome ville ouverte (1945)* (Paris: Centre Georges Pompidou, 1986).

Aldo Bernardini and Vittorio Martinelli, *Il cinema italiano degli anni Venti* (Rome: Cineteca Nazionale del Centro Sperimentale di Cinematografia, 1979).

Peter Bondanella, *Italian Cinema: From Neorealism to the present* (New York: Continuum, 1990).

Gian Piero Brunetta, *Cent'anni di cinema italiano* (Rome/Bari: Editori Laterza, 1991).

Gian Piero Brunetta, *Storia del cinema italiano. Vol. i: 1895–1945* (Rome: Editori Riuniti, 1980).

Gian Piero Brunetta, *Storia del cinema italiano. Vol. ii: Dal 1945 agli anni ottanta* (Rome: Editori Riuniti, 1982).

Giuliana Bruno, *Streetwalking on a Ruined Map: Cultural theory and the city films of Elvira Notari* (Princeton NJ: Princeton University Press, 1993).

Monica Dall'Asta, *Un cinéma musclé: le surhomme dans le cinéma muet italien (1913–1926)* (Crisnée: Editions Yellow Now, 1992).

Angela Dalle Vacche, *The Body in the Mirror: Shapes of history in Italian Cinema* (Princeton NJ: Princeton University Press, 1992).

Franca Faldini and Goffredo Fofi, *L'avventurosa storia del cinema italiano: raccontato dai suoi protagonisti, 1935–1959* (Milan: Feltrinelli, 1979).

Franca Faldini and Goffredo Fofi, *L'avventurosa storia del cinema italiano: raccontato dai suoi protagonisti, 1960–1969* (Milan: Feltrinelli, 1981).

Franca Faldini and Goffredo Fofi, *Il cinema italiano d'oggi, 1970–1984: raccontato dai suoi protagonisti* (Milan: Arnoldo Mondadori, 1984).

David Forgacs (ed.), *Rethinking Italian Fascism: Capitalism, Populism and Culture* (London: Lawrence and Wishart, 1986).

Vernon Jarratt, *The Italian Cinema* (London: Falcon Press, 1951).

Pierre Leprohon, *The Italian Cinema* (London: Secker and Warburg, and New York: Praeger, 1972).

Mira Liehm, *Passion and Defiance: Film in Italy from 1942 to the Present* (Berkeley, Ca.: University of California Press, 1984).

Millicent Marcus, *Italian Film in the Light of Neorealism* (Princeton, NJ: Princeton University Press, 1986).

Lorenzo Quaglietti, *Storia economico-politica del Cinema italiano, 1945–1980* (Rome: Editori Riuniti, 1980).

Francesco Savio, *Ma l'amore no: realismo, formalismo, propaganda e telefoni bianchi nel cinema italiano di regime (1930–1943)* (Milan: Sonzogno, 1975).

Luxemburg

'Luxembourg', in Peter Cowie (ed.), *International Film Guide* (now *Variety International Film Guide*) (London: Andre Deutsch, annual from 1964).

Hollywood Reporter, vol. 304, no. 15, 18/9/90, pp. S1–S9.

Anthony Slide, *The International Film Industry: A Historical Dictionary* (New York, Westport, CT., London: Greenwood Press, 1989), pp. 239–40.

The Netherlands

Hans Beerekamp (ed.), *Occupation, collaboration and resistance in Dutch film* (Amsterdam, 1986).

Ruud Bishoff, *Hollywood in Holland: de geschiedenis van de Filmfabriek Hollandia, 1912–1923* (Amsterdam: Uitgeverij, 1988).

Francesco Bono, *Nuovo cinema olandese, 1966–1987* (Rome: A.I.A.C.E., 1988).

Peter Cowie, *Dutch Cinema: An Illustrated History* (South Brunswick and New York: A. S. Barnes. London: Tantivy Press, 1979).

Karel Dibbets and Frank van der Maden (eds.), *Geschiedenis van de Nederlandse film en bioscoop tot 1940* (Weesp: Het Wereldvenster, 1986).

Karel Dibbets, *Sprekende films: de komst van de geluidsfilm in Nederland, 1928–1933* [Contains summary in English] (Amsterdam: Cramwinckel, 1993).

Kathinka Dittrich van Weringh, *Der Niederländische Spielfilm der dreissiger Jahre und die deutsche Filmemigration* (Amsterdam: Rodopi, 1987).

Bert Hogenkamp, *De Nederlandse documentaire film, 1920–1940* (Amsterdam: Van Gennep, 1988).

Jaarboek Mediaeschiedenis (Amsterdam, 1989).

Rob de Kam and Hans Kroon, *World Cinema: Holland* (Trowbridge: Flicks Books, 1995).

Thomas Leeflang, *De bioscoop in de oorlog* (Amsterdam, 1990).

Nederlands Jaarboek Film (Houten: Het Wereldvenster, 1981–1990).

J.Th. van Taalingen, *Nederlandse Bioscoopbond 60 jaar* (Amsterdam, 1978).

Dorothee Verdaasdonk, *Beroep filmregisseur: het verkrijgen van continu teit in een artistiek beroep* (Zeist, 1990).

Norway

Pal Bang-Hansen, *Norske filmplakatar, 1917–88* (Oslo: Det Norske Samlaget, 1989).

Film in Norway (Oslo: Norwegian Film Institute, 1979). Pamphlet.

See also: Peter Cowie, *Scandinavian Cinema* (under '**Europe**')

Poland

Frank Bren, *World Cinema 1: Poland* (Trowbridge: Flicks Books, 1986).

Małgorzata Hendrykowska, *Śladami Tamtych Cìeni, Film w Kulturze Polskiej Przetomu Stuleci 1895–1914* (Poznań: Oficyna Wydawnicza Book Service, 1993).

Stanislaw Janicki, *The Polish Film: Yesterday and today* (Warsaw: Interpress, 1985).

Stanislaw Janicki, *Polskie Filmy Fabularne 1902–1988* (Warsaw: Wydawnictwa Artystyczne i Filmowe, 1990).

Maria Kornatowska, *Wodzireje i Amatorzy* (Warsaw: Wydawnictwa Artystyczne i Filmowe, 1990).

Boleslaw Michalek and Frank Tura, *The Modern Cinema of Poland* (Bloomington: Indiana University Press, 1988).

Donald Pirie, Jekaterina Young and Christopher Carrel (eds.), *Polish Realities (The Arts in Poland 1980–1989)* (Glasgow: Third Eye Centre, 1990).

Portugal

Alves Costa, *Breve história do cinema português, 1896–1962* (Instituto do Cultura Portuguesa, 1978).

Fernando Duarte, *Primitivos do cinema português,* 2nd rev. ed. (Santarem: 8th Festival Internacional de cinema, 1978).

Jean-Loup Passek, *Le Cinéma portugais* (Paris: Centre Georges Pompidou/L'Equerre, 1982).

Luis de Pina, *História do cinema português* (Lisbon: Publiçaçòes Europa-América, 1986).

Augusto M. Seabra (ed.), *Cinema novo portoghese e oltre...* (Pesaro: Mostra Internazionale del Nuovo Cinema, 1988).

Nelson Traquina, 'Portuguese Cinema: In the Doldrums of Neglect', *European Journal of Communication*, vol. 9, no. 3 (Sept. 1993).

A. Videira Santos, *Para a história do cinema em Portugal (1). Do diafanorama a os cinematógrafos de Lumière e Joly-Normandin* (Portugal: Cinemateca Portuguesa, 1990).

Romania

Ion Cantacuzino and B. T. Rîpeanu, *Productia cinematografică din România (1897–1970): filmografie adnotata* (Bucharest: Arhiva Nationala de Filme, 1970).

Manuela Cernat, *A Concise History of the Romanian Film* (Bucharest: Editura Ştiintifică şi enciclopedică, 1982).

Manuela Cernat, 'Romania' in Peter Cowie (ed.), *International Film Guide* (now *Variety International Film Guide*) (London: Andre Deutsch, annual from 1964).

Moritz de Hadeln (ed.), *Romania: the documentary films (1898–1990)* (Nyon: Festival International du film documentaire, 1990).

Judith Roof, 'Romania', in Thomas J. Slater (ed.), *Handbook of Soviet and East European Films and Filmmakers* (New York and London: Greenwood Press, 1992).

(Former) Soviet Union

Lynne Attwood (ed.), *Red Women on the Silver Screen. Soviet Women and Cinema from the Beginning to the End of the Communist Era* (London: Pandora, 1993).

Andrew Horton (ed.), *Inside Soviet Film Satire: Laughter with a Lash* (Cambridge and New York: Cambridge University Press, 1993).

Andrew Horton and Michael Brashinsky, *The Zero Hour: Glasnost and Soviet Cinema in Transition* (Princeton, NJ: Princeton University Press, 1992).

Peter Kenez, *Cinema and Soviet Society, 1917–1953* (Cambridge: Cambridge University Press, 1992).

Peter Kenez, *The Birth of the Propaganda State: Soviet Methods of Mass Mobilization, 1917–1929* (Cambridge: Cambridge University Press, 1985).

Kino: Entsiklopedicheskii slovar' (Moscow: Sovetskaya entsiklopediya, 1986).

Kinoslavar' (2 vols.) (Moscow: Sovetskaya entsiklopediya, 1966 & 1970).

Anna Lawton, *Kinoglasnost: Soviet Cinema in Our Time* (Cambridge and New York: Cambridge University Press, 1992).

Anna Lawton (ed.), *The Red Screen: Politics, Society, Art in the Soviet Cinema* (London: Routledge, 1992).

Jay Leyda, *Kino. A History of the Russian and Soviet Film* (London: Allen and Unwin, 1960).

Judith Mayne, *Kino and the Woman Question: Feminism and Soviet Silent Film* (Columbia: Ohio State University Press, 1989).

Jean-Loup Passek et al., *Le Cinéma russe et soviétique* (Paris: Centre Georges Pompidou/l'Equerre, 1981).

Luda and Jean Schnitzer, *Histoire du cinéma soviétique 1919–1940* (Paris: Editions Pygmalion/Gérard Watelet, 1979).

Richard Stites, *Russian Popular Culture: Entertainment and Society in Russia since 1900* (Cambridge: Cambridge University Press, 1992).

Richard Taylor, *The Politics of the Soviet Cinema 1917–1929* (Cambridge: Cambridge University Press, 1979).

Richard Taylor, *Film Propaganda: Soviet Russia and Nazi Germany* (London and New York: Croom Helm & Barnes and Noble, 1979).

Richard Taylor and Ian Christie (eds.), *The Film Factory: Russian and Soviet Cinema in Documents, 1896–1939* (London and New York: Routledge and Kegan Paul, 1988).

Richard Taylor and Ian Christie (eds.), *Inside the Film Factory. New Approaches to Russian and Soviet Cinema* (London: Routledge, 1991).

Richard Taylor and Derek Spring (eds.), *Stalinism and Soviet Cinema* (London: Routledge, 1993).

Yuri Tsivian, *Early Cinema in Russia and Its Cultural Reception* (London: Routledge, 1994).

Yuri Tsivian, et al. (eds.), *Silent Witnesses: Russian Films 1908–19/Testimoni silenziosi: Film russi 1908–19* (London and Pordenone: British Film Institute and Edizioni Biblioteca dell'Immagine, 1989) [English-Italian edition].

Maya Turovskaya, et al., *Kino totalitarnoi epokhi (1933–1945)* (Moscow: Moscow Film Festival, 1989).

Denise J. Youngblood, *Movies for the Masses. Popular Cinema and Soviet Society in the 1920s* (Cambridge: Cambridge University Press, 1992).

Denise J. Youngblood, *Soviet Cinema in the Silent Era, 1918–1935* (Ann Arbor, Michigan: UMI Research Press, 1985, reprinted Austin, Texas: University of Texas Press, 1991).

Neya Zorkaya, *The Illustrated History of the Soviet Cinema* (New York: Hippocrene Books, 1989).

Spain

Carlos Aguilar and Jaume Genover, *El cine español en sus intérpretes* (Madrid: Verdoux, 1992).

Peter Besas, *Behind the Spanish Lens: Spanish cinema under Fascism and democracy* (Denver, Colorado: Arden Press, 1985).

Enrique Brasó, *Carlos Saura* (Madrid: Taller de Ediciones – Josefina Betancor, 1974).

José María Caparros Lera, *El cine español de la democracia* (Barcelona: Anthropos, 1992).

Thomas G. Deveny, *Cain on Screen: Contemporary Spanish Cinema* (Metuchen, NJ, and London: Scarecrow Press, 1993).

Marvin D'Lugo, *The Films of Carlos Saura; the Practice of Seeing* (Princeton: Princeton University Press, 1991).

Gwynne Edwards, *The Discreet Art of Luis Buñuel: a reading of his films* (London: Marion Boyars, 1982).

Peter William Evans, *The Films of Luis Buñuel; Subjectivity and Desire* (Oxford: Clarendon Press, 1994).

Félix Fanés, *Cifesa: la antorcha de los éxitos* (Valencia: Institución Alfonso el Magnánimo, 1982).

Robin W. Fiddian and Peter Besas, *Challenges to Authority: fiction and film in contemporary Spain* (London: Tamesis Books, 1988).

María Antonia García de León and Teresa Maldonado, *Pedro Almodóvar: la otra España cañí (sociologíca y crítica cinematográficas)* (Ciudad Real: Biblioteca de Autores y temas Manchegos, 1989).

Ramiro Gómez B. de Castro, *La producción cinematográfica española de la transición a la democracia (1976–1986)* (Bilbao: Mensajero, 1989).

José Luis Guarner and Peter Besas, *El inquietante cine de Vicente Aranda* (Madrid: Imagfic 85, 1985).

Román Gubern, *La censura: función política y ordenamiento juridico bajo el franquismo (1936–75)* (Barcelona: Ediciones Península, 1981).

Virginia Higginbotham, *Luis Buñuel* (Boston: Twayne Publishers, 1979).

John Hopewell, *Out of the Past: Spanish Cinema after Franco* (London: British Film Institute, 1986).

Marsha Kinder, *Blood Cinema: the Reconstruction of National Identity in Spain* (Berkeley, California and London: University of California Press, 1993).

Fernando Lara (ed.), *Siete trabajos de base sobre el cine español* (Valencia: Fernando Torres, 1975).

Fernando Méndez-Leite, *Historia del cine español*, 2 vols (Madrid: Ediciones Rialpe, 1965).

Vicente Molina-Foix, *New Cinema in Spain* (London: British Film Institute, 1977).

José Enrique Monterde, *Veinte años de cine español; un cine bajo la paradoja, 1973–1992* (Barcelona: Paidós Ibérica, 1993).

Miguel Juan Payán, *El cine español de los 90* (Madrid: Editiones J.C., 1993).

Agustín Sánchez Vidal, *El cine de Carlos Saura* (Zaragoza: Caja de Ahorros de la Inmaculada de Aragon, 1988).

Agustín Sánchez Vidal, *José Luis Borau* (Zaragoza: Caja de Ahorros de la Inmaculada de Aragon, 1990).

Agustín Sánchez Vidal, *Luis Buñuel: obra cinematográfica* (Madrid: Ediciones J.C., 1984).

Agustín Sánchez Vidal, *El mundo de Bruñuel* (Zaragoza: Caja de Ahorros de la Inmaculada de Aragon, 1993).

Vicente Sánchez-Biosca and Rafael R. Tranche, *No-Do: el tiempo y la memoria* (Madrid: Ministerio de Cultura, 1993).

Paul Julian Smith, *Desire Unlimited: the Cinema of Pedro Almodóvar* (London and New York: Verso, 1994).

Paul Julian Smith, *Laws of Desire: Questions of Homosexuality in Spanish Writing and Film 1960–1990* (Oxford: Clarendon Press, 1992).

Augusto M. Torres (ed.), *Spanish Cinema 1896–1983* (Madrid: Ministerio de Cultura, 1984).

Nuria Vidal, *The Films of Pedro Almodóvar* (Madrid: Ministerio de Cultura, 1988).

Sweden

Maria Bergom-Larsson, *Film in Sweden: Ingmar Bergman and Society* (London: Tantivy Press, South Brunswick and New York: A. S. Barnes, 1978).

Stig Björkman, Torsten Manns and Jonas Sima, *Bergman on Bergman: Interviews with Ingmar Bergman* (London: Secker and Warburg, 1973).

Peter Cowie, *Ingmar Bergman: A Critical Biography* (London: Secker and Warburg, 1982).

Peter Cowie, *Swedish Cinema from Ingeborg Holm to Fanny and Alexander* (Stockholm: Swedish Film Institute, 1985).

Jörn Donner, *The Personal Vision of Ingmar Bergman* (Bloomington: Indiana University Press, 1964).

Stuart M. Kaminsky and Joseph F. Hill (eds.), *Ingmar Bergman: Essays in Criticism* (New York: Oxford University Press, 1975).

Einar Lauritzen, *Swedish Films* (New York: Museum of Modern Art Film Library, 1962).

Brian McIlroy, *World Cinema 2: Sweden* (London: Flicks Books, 1986).

Vlada Petric (ed.), *Film and Dreams: An Approach to Bergman* (New York: Redgrave, 1981).

Vilgot Sjöman, *L 136: Diary with Ingmar Bergman* (Ann Arbor, Karoma: University of Michigan Press, 1978).

Svensk filmografi 1–7: 1897–1919; 1920–29; 1930–39; 1940–49, 1950–59; 1960–69; 1970–79 (Stockholm: Svenska Filminsitutet, 1986, 82, 79, 80, 83, 77 & 88).

Vernon Young, *Cinema Borealis: Ingmar Bergman and the Swedish Ethos* (New York: David Lewis, 1971).

See also: Peter Cowie, *Scandinavian Cinema* (under '**Europe**')

Switzerland

Giovanni Barblan and Giovanni M. Rossi (eds.), *Il volo della chimera: Profilo del Cinema svizzero 1905–1981* (Florence: La Casa Usher, 1981).

Freddy Buache, *Le cinéma suisse* (Lausanne: Editions L'Age d'Homme, 1978).

Freddy Buache, *Le cinéma suisse francophone, 1976–1985* (Brussels: APEC, 1985).

André Chaperon, Roland Cosandey and François Langer (eds.), *Histoire(s) des cinéma(s)* (Lausanne: Equinoxe no. 7, 1992).

Hervé Dumont, *Histoire du cinéma suisse: films de fiction 1896–1965* (Lausanne: Cinémathèque suisse, 1987).

Michael Günther, *Filmschaffende, Film produktion und Filmwirtschaft in der Schweiz* (Zurich: Philosophischen Fakultät 1 der Universität Zurich, 1987).

Elaine Mancini, 'Switzerland', in William Luhr (ed.), *World Cinema since 1945* (New York: Ungar, 1987), pp. 542–9.

Rémy Pithon, 'Essai d'historiographie du cinéma suisse (1945–1991)', *Revue suisse d'histoire* (Basle), vol. 41 (1991).

Stephan Portmann, *Der Neue Schweizerfilm 1965–1985: Ein Studienbericht zur Analyse ausgewählter Spiel- und Dokumentarfilme* (Freiburg: Universitätsverlag, 1992).

Martin Schaub, *The New Swiss Cinema*, 1963–1974 (Zurich: Pro Helvetia, 1975).

Martin Schlappner and Martin Schaub, *Vergangenheit und Gegenwart des Schweizer Films 1896–1987: Eine kritische Wertung* (Zurich: Schweizerisches Filmzentrum, 1987).

United Kingdom

Anthony Aldgate and Jeffrey Richards, *Britain Can Take It: The British cinema in the Second World War* (Oxford: Basil Blackwell, 1986).

Roy Armes, *A Critical History of British Cinema* (London: Secker & Warburg, 1978).

Martyn Auty and Nick Roddick, *British Cinema Now* (London: BFI Publishing, 1985).

Charles Barr (ed.), *All Our Yesterdays*: *Ninety years of British cinema* (London: BFI Publishing, 1986).

David Berry, *Wales and Cinema: The First Hundred Years* (Cardiff: University of Wales Press, in co-operation with the Wales Film Council and the BFI, 1994).

James Curran and Vincent Porter (eds.), *British Cinema History* (London: Weidenfeld and Nicolson, 1983).

Eddie Dick (ed.), *From Limelight to Satellite: A Scottish film book* (Glasgow: Scottish Film Council, and London: BFI, 1990).

Margaret Dickinson and Sarah Street, *Cinema and State*: *The film industry and the British government, 1927–1984* (London: BFI Publishing, 1985).

Raymond Durgnat, *A Mirror for England, British movies from austerity to affluence* (London: Faber, 1970).

Lester Friedman (ed.), *Fires Were Started: British Cinema and Thatcherism* (Minneapolis: University of Minnesota Press, and London: UCL Press, 1993).

Jonathan Hacker and David Price (eds.), *Take Ten*: *Contemporary British film directors* (Oxford: Clarendon Press, 1991).

Bert Hogenkamp, *Deadly Parallels: Film and the Left in Britain, 1929–1939* (London: Lawrence & Wishart, 1986).

Marcia Landy, *British Genres: Cinema and society, 1930–1960* (Princeton, NJ: Princeton University Press, 1991).

Antonia Lant, *Blackout*: *Reinventing women for wartime British cinema* (Princeton, NJ: Princeton University Press, 1991).

Alan Lovell and Jim Hillier, *Studies in Documentary* (London: Secker & Warburg/BFI, 1972).

Rachael Low and Roger Manvell, *The History of British Film, 1896–1906* (London: Allen & Unwin, 1948).

Rachael Low, *The History of the British Film, 1906–1914; 1914–1918; 1918–1929; 1929–1939: documentary and educational films of the 1930s; 1929–1939: film making in 1930s Britain; 1929–1939: films of comment and persuasion of the 1930s* (London: Allen & Unwin, 1949, 1950, 1971, 1979, 1985, 1979).

Geoffrey Macnab, *J. Arthur Rank and the British Film Industry* (London: Routledge, 1992).

Don Macpherson (ed.), *Traditions of Independence: British cinema in the Thirties* (London: BFI Publishing, 1980).

Colin McArthur (ed.), *Scotch Reels*: *Scotland in cinema and television* (London: BFI Publishing, 1982).

Brian McFarlane (ed.), *Sixty Voices: Celebrities recall the Golden Age of British Cinema* (London: BFI Publishing, 1992).

Kobena Mercer (ed.), *Black Film, British Cinema: ICA document no. 7* (London: Institute of Contemporary Arts, 1988).

Robert Murphy, *Realism and Tinsel: Cinema and society in Britain, 1939–1948* (London and New York: Routledge, 1989).

Robert Murphy, *Sixties British Cinema* (London: BFI Publishing, 1992).

Duncan Petrie (ed.), *New Questions of British Cinema* (London: BFI Publishing, 1992).

John Pym, *Film on Four, 1982–1991*: *A Survey* (London: BFI Publishing, 1992).

Jeffrey Richards, *The Age of the Dream Palace: Cinema and Society in Britain, 1930–1939* (London: Routledge & Kegan Paul, 1984).

(Former) Yugoslavia

'Jugoslavia' in *Filmska enciklopedija 1. (A-K)* (Zagreb: 1986).

Daniel J. Goulding, *Liberated Cinema: the Yugoslav experience* (Bloomington: Indiana University Press, 1985).

Zoran Tasić and Jean-Loup Passek, *Le Cinéma yougoslave* (Paris: Centre Georges Pompidou, 1986).

Petar Volk, *Istorija jugoslovenskog filma 1896–1982* (Belgrade: Institut za Film/Partizanska knjiga, 1986).

FILM INDEX

This film index is designed to be used in conjunction with the A-to-Z encyclopedia entries. The English language title, when available, always appears under the key word and preceeding the foreign language title. All foreign language titles are indexed as written.

486

493

494

500

505

507

508

SUBJECT INDEX

This subject index is designed to be used in conjunction with the A-to-Z entries. The main A-to-Z entries are indicated by **bold-face** page references.

511

512

519